MACMILLAN

INFORMATION NOW ENCYCLOPEDIA

The Ethics of Sex and Genetics

The Encyclopedia of Bioethics

Warren Thomas Reich, Editor in Chief
Emeritus, Georgetown University

Stephen G. Post, Associate Editor
Case Western Reserve University

AREA EDITORS

Dan E. Beauchamp
University at Albany, State University of New York

Arthur L. Caplan
University of Pennsylvania School of Medicine

Christine K. Cassel
University of Chicago

James F. Childress
University of Virginia

Allen R. Dyer
East Tennessee State University

John C. Fletcher
University of Virginia Health Services Center

Stanley M. Hauerwas
Duke University

Albert R. Jonsen
University of Washington

Patricia A. King
Georgetown University Law Center

Loretta M. Kopelman
East Carolina University School of Medicine

Ruth B. Purtilo
Creighton University

Holmes Rolston III
Colorado State University

Robert M. Veatch
Georgetown University

Donald P. Warwick
Harvard University

M A C M I L L A N

INFORMATION NOW ENCYCLOPEDIA

The Ethics of Sex and Genetics

SELECTIONS FROM THE FIVE-VOLUME

Macmillan *Encyclopedia of Bioethics*

Revised Edition

Warren Thomas Reich

Editor in Chief

MACMILLAN REFERENCE USA

Simon & Schuster Macmillan

New York

Prentice Hall International

London Mexico City New Delhi Singapore Sydney Toronto

Macmillan Reference USA
Simon & Schuster Macmillan
1633 Broadway
New York, NY 10019

Designed by Kevin Hanek. Composition by G & H Soho, Inc.

Manufactured in the United States of America.

printing number
1 2 3 4 5 6 7 8 9 10

ISBN: 0-02-864917-6
LC #: 97-25526

Library of Congress Cataloging-in-Publication Data

The Library of Congress has cataloged another edition of this work as follows:
Bioethics: sex, genetics, & human reproduction
p. cm. - (Macmillan compendium)
Includes index.
1. Sexual ethics-Dictionaries. 2. Human reproduction-Moral and ethical aspects-Dictionaries. 3. Marriage-Moral and ethical aspects-Dictionaries. I. Series.
HQ32.E86 1997
176-dc21 97-25526
CIP

This paper meets the requirements of ANSI/NISO Z39.48-1992 (Permanence of Paper).

Table of Contents

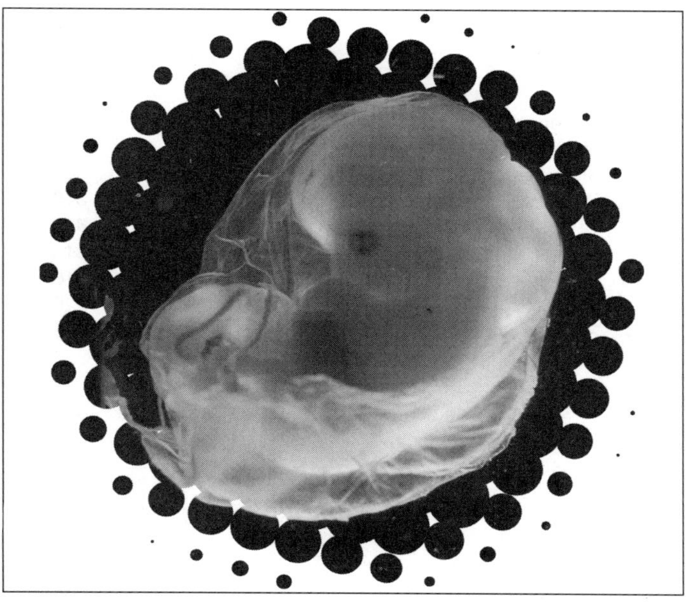

Cover Image: This photo of a human fetus in early stages of development illustrates the moral and ethical challenges addressed in this volume. Science Pictures Limited/Corbis

Preface

CRITERIA FOR SELECTION AND ORGANIZATION

Broad in scope, *The Ethics of Sex and Genetics* is organized in an A-to-Z format. In preparing this one-volume version of the *Encyclopedia of Bioethics,* it was agreed that articles and/or article subsections would be excerpted in their entirety to retain the integrity of the source. Warren Thomas Reich, Editor in Chief of this volume as well as the original encyclopedia, chose articles to present a coherent introduction to bioethics as well as an overview of the complex subject of the ethics of sexuality, human reproduction, and genetics. Entries have been titled and organized in a manner we hope readers will be most likely to consult first. A comprehensive index appears at the end of the volume to provide additional aid for the reader.

FEATURES

To add visual appeal and enhance the usefulness of the volume, the page format was designed to include the following helpful features.

- **Cross-Reference Quotations:** These quotations, extracted from related articles in the volume, will lead to further exploration of the subject. Page numbers are provided for easy reference.
- **Notable Quotations:** Found throughout the text in the margin, these thought-provoking quotations will complement the topic under discussion.
- **Definitions and Glossary:** Brief definitions of important terms in the main text can also be found the margin and in the glossary at the end of the book.
- **Cross References:** Use of the encyclopedia is facilitated by a system of cross-references that lead the reader to other entries in the Encyclopedia. These cross references can be found in the margin column toward the bottom of the page.
- **Sidebars:** Appearing in a gray box, these provocative asides relate to the text and amplify topics.
- **Index:** A thorough index provides thousands of additional points of entry into the work.
- **Appendixes:** We have included in the appendixes complete texts of several codes, oaths, and directives related to bioethics.

ACKNOWLEDGMENTS

We are grateful to our colleagues who publish the *Merriam Webster's Collegiate® Dictionary.* Definitions used in the margins and most of the glossary terms come from the distinguished *Webster's Collegiate® Dictionary,* Tenth Edition, 1996.

The articles herein were written for the *Encyclopedia of Bioethics* by leading authorities in the field. Warren Thomas Reich served as Editor in Chief of the original set. Dr. Reich has recently retired as Professor of Bioethics and Director of the Division of Health and Humanities, Center for Clinical Bioethics, Kennedy Institute of Ethics at Georgetown University in Washington, D.C.

This book would not have been possible without the hard work and creativity of our staff. We offer our deepest thanks to all who helped create this marvelous work.

Macmillan Reference USA

Foreword

When the editors of Macmillan Reference USA informed me they wanted to publish a one-volume reference work on bioethics that would contain the range of titles you find in this book, I was delighted at the opportunity it offered, for several reasons. First, I am convinced that the revised edition of the *Encyclopedia of Bioethics,* from which these articles are taken, is a unique treasure of well-organized and superbly crafted writings unequalled anywhere in the world. The opportunity of disseminating a select set of materials from that intellectual legacy for the benefit of a new group of readers brings joy to the heart of the scholars who worked so hard preparing the full, five-volume 1995 edition. Second, the dual focus of this one-volume reference work offers some of the most important, even urgent, material from the full edition.

By "dual focus," I mean that the reader will find here a generous collection of articles in two areas of bioethics. First, it includes a significant collection of extremely well written articles on bioethics in general—its origins, its methods, its influence, and its implications for the burning issues of today. Second, the reader will find here an unparalleled collection of articles on a cluster of topics dealing with sexuality, genetics, and human reproduction. Human reproductive technologies have raised the most complex ethical questions in modern times; genetics is altering medical services while redefining some of the most basic human assumptions that are ingredient in bioethics; and developments in our understanding of sexuality and gender are raising questions that affect much of our society and its social conduct.

The *Encyclopedia of Bioethics,* the parent of this book, has been unmatched in publishing history. It was the first encyclopedia in the history of book publishing that was developed concomitantly with, and contributed to the development of, the field on which it reported. The first honor it received (in its first edition) was the 1979 Dartmouth Medal for "outstanding quality and significance." In spite of the fact that the revised edition did not qualify for a Dartmouth Award (no revised editions do), officials of the American Library Association felt that the revised edition was so thoroughly original (and excellent) that they gave it the highest available award in 1995.

In its review of the edition of the *Encyclopedia of Bioethics,* from which this work is drawn, the Hastings Center Report made this comment: "If you have never contemplated sitting down and reading any encyclopedia through, we would encourage you seriously to consider doing so with this one. Newcomers to the field will find it a remarkably comprehensive survey of topics, authors, and positions; veterans will find it a stimulating overview of the last decade of discussion and debate."

If you are a student, teacher, researcher, or scholar in any of the fields touched on in this book, or if you are simply an "intelligent, interested person," I hope you experience in this compact reference work the delight of discovery and the discovery of the useful.

—Warren Thomas Reich
Editor in Chief

The Ethics of Sex and Genetics

ABORTION

MEDICAL PERSPECTIVES

Medical information and perspectives on abortion are not just data untinged by values. Throughout history medical facts and moral values regarding abortion have been inextricably intertwined, and the current era is no exception.

People interested in the ethics of abortion turn to medicine and medical practitioners for the following sort of information and perspectives, which will be considered in this article: (1) whether medical knowledge clarifies the moral status of the fetus as a human being; (2) whether medical information on abortion confirms it to be safe for the woman; (3) what the medical perspectives are on performing early versus late abortions (and the attendant question of the fetus that survives an abortion); and (4) what the public health and international perspectives are on abortion.

Medical knowledge regarding status of the fetus

However much information biomedical investigation may provide regarding pregnancy, fetal development, and abortion, it cannot provide a determination as to when human life begins. The answer to that question—which deals with the moral status of the fetus—is arrived at by a process that entwines medical facts with experiences, values, religious and philosophical beliefs and attitudes, perceptions of meaning, and moral argument. Such a process extends beyond the special competency of medicine. For example, medicine has never had the ability to establish when ensoulment—an ancient criterion involving the "infusion" of the soul into the body of the fetus, thus conferring moral status on the fetus—occurs. Similarly, today there is disagreement among some physicians over the moral status of the fetus and the permissibility of abortion.

There is some confusion about the definition of abortion. Spontaneous abortion, or what is commonly termed a miscarriage, refers to a spontaneous loss of a pregnancy before viability (at about 25 or 26 weeks of gestation). Losses after that point in a pregnancy are termed "preterm deliveries," or, in the case of the delivery of a fetus who has already died, "stillbirths." The terminology commonly used in relation to induced abortion is different. Here, viability is not the key point. Rather, any termination of a pregnancy by med-

Governments around the world legislate whether, when, why, and how the estimated 40 million abortions that occur each year may or must occur.

PAGE 16

WHAT DO WE DO?

The medical, legal, and moral aspects of abortion can pose extreme dilemmas—particularly for young couples facing their first sexual relationships.

The surgical removal of an ectopic pregnancy could provide a still-living embryo or fetus.

PAGE 243

ical or surgical means is termed an abortion, regardless of the stage of the pregnancy.

Safety and harm for the woman

POSSIBLE PHYSICAL HARM. There is a close tie between medical information on the safety of abortion practices and ethical positions on abortion. For example, at a time when abortions were frequently harmful to women—such as when legal restrictions increased recourse to untrained practitioners—opponents of abortion appealed to information on the likelihood of medical harm to the woman and risks of future pregnancies as arguments against abortion (Kunins and Rosenfield, 1991).

At the present time, induced abortions performed within the first twelve weeks of pregnancy are among the safest and simplest forms of surgery and, based on maternal mortality ratios (number of deaths per 100,000 live births), both first- and second-trimester abortion, when performed by properly trained personnel, in general are safer than carrying a pregnancy to term (Cates and Grimes, 1981). As a result, ethical arguments against abortion now tend to be restricted to areas other than maternal safety. Nonetheless, some aspects of medical safety and harm—including possible complications and psychological sequelae—continue to be important for ethical discourse, especially since a basic tenet of medical ethics is to avoid harm.

The major immediate complications of induced abortion, listed in order of frequency, are infection, hemorrhage, uterine perforation, and anesthesia-related complications. Overall complication rates for legal first-trimester abortions are less than 0.5 deaths per 100,000 abortions performed (as compared to more than four per 100,000 in the early 1970s, before the U.S. Supreme Court decision *Roe* v. *Wade* [1973] permitted medically supervised abortions).

Medical complications associated with induced abortion are directly related to gestational age and the type of procedure used to terminate the pregnancy. Most abortions (over 90 percent) done in the United States are performed within the first twelve weeks of pregnancy, when abortion is safest. More serious complications may occur in procedures done later in pregnancy.

ABORTION PROCEDURES. Information on abortion procedures often sheds light on questions of safety as well as on other aspects of abortion that are relevant to ethics. The most common early-trimester abortion procedure (done between seven and twelve weeks gestation) is suction curettage, in which a thin plastic tube (canula) is inserted through the cervix and, by negative pressure vacuum, the contents of the uterus are aspirated. Usually, following the aspiration procedure, a curettage (using a sharp, spoon-shaped surgical instrument, a curette) is performed to ensure that all fetal tissue has been removed.

Complications of suction curettage procedures are rare, and even when they occur, are usually not serious. General anesthesia is considered by many to be an unnecessary additional risk, since local anesthesia, injected into the cervix, often is quite effective (Grimes et al., 1979). A short course of prophylactic antibiotics is sometimes prescribed, although postabortion infection is uncommon with suction curettage. Because of its safety, suction curettage is performed most often in free-standing clinics or outpatient centers in hospitals.

COMMON ABORTION PROCEDURES

- suction curettage (between 7–12 weeks' gestation)
- dilation and evacuation (12–20 weeks' gestation)
- instillation abortion (12–20 weeks' gestation)

At twelve to twenty weeks' gestation, the most common method used for abortion is dilation and evacuation (D&E), which uses specially designed forceps in conjunction with vacuum aspiration to facilitate the removal of the uterine contents. Prior to initiating the procedure, the cervix is dilated gradually over a number of hours using spongelike materials that expand as they absorb local cervical fluids. Though still considered a minor surgical procedure, D&E is clearly more involved and invasive than suction curettage, and a trained and skilled clinician is essential. Although it is possible to use only local anesthesia for D&E, the procedure is considerably more uncomfortable than suction curettage, and general anesthesia is often used, making the procedure more risky. The D&E procedure can be performed in free-standing clinics, but often ambulatory surgical services in a hospital setting are chosen for the procedures performed later in pregnancy (after the fourteenth week) because emergency care can be quickly provided in case of a complication. Informed-consent procedures require that the various methods of abortion be discussed as well as the possible anesthesia alternatives.

The other abortion procedure used fairly commonly in the second trimester is instillation abortion, in which a solution instilled into the amniotic cavity through the abdomen via amniocentesis results in the death of the fetus and termination of the pregnancy. Uterine contractions signaling labor begin twelve to twenty-four hours later and culminate with the expulsion of the fetus. Anesthesia is not commonly used for instillation procedures. Discomfort varies widely among patients, usually in relation to the length of labor and the time before complete expulsion of the fetus and placenta. More serious complications can occur during instillation procedures, including inadvertent introduction of the solution into the mother's bloodstream, excessive bleeding at the time of expulsion of the fetus, or retention of placenta, and for this reason hospital admission is usually advised. Instillation procedures are now used mainly for procedures beyond the twentieth week of gestation. All late-pregnancy abortion procedures carry significant risk if carried out by physicians not specially trained in the technique.

A promising alternative to surgical abortion for early first-trimester terminations of pregnancy is chemical abortion. For example, the antiprogestin drug RU-486 works by blocking progesterone production by the ovaries, an essential hormone in the early stages of pregnancy and in the implantation of the embryo. The drug is given within the first forty-nine days of a confirmed pregnancy and is used in conjunction with a prostaglandin, which produces uterine contractions and subsequent expulsion of the uterine contents. A follow-up visit is necessary eight to twelve days later to ensure that complete termination of the pregnancy has occurred. Thus, in the United States—assuming that the drug will be approved by the USFDA as expected—three visits will be necessary for this medical means of pregnancy termination: the first to make the diagnosis and to give the RU-486, the second, two days later, for the prostaglandin, and the third for the final follow-up. In France, a fourth visit is required by law since a one-week delay between the diagnosis of pregnancy and the initiation of an abortion procedure is mandated.

As a result of the requirement for three visits (or four in France) and because there may be a few days before the abortion occurs and as many as ten or more days of vaginal bleeding thereafter, many women in France still prefer suction curettage as their method of choice, and this may well prove to be the case in the United States when the drug becomes available. However, there is anticipation that many women will still prefer a medical means of abortion, not wishing to undergo surgery (albeit a minor procedure) or to be subjected to the harassment that may occur outside some clinic facilities.

Successful termination has been shown to occur in 96 percent of patients, with the remaining patients requiring suction curettage for complete removal of the products of conception. For surgical procedures, less than 1 percent require a second curettage because the procedure was incomplete. In France, RU-486 is provided only through clinic facilities. One of the questions that needs to be answered in the new clinical investigation trials being undertaken in the United States is whether or not it is safe and efficient to provide RU-486 plus prostaglandin in a private doctor's office. Most women develop strong cramping after taking the prostaglandin (because the drug induces uterine contractions) and usually have the abortion within a few hours after receiving prostaglandin. In a clinic setting, this often occurs during the same four hours women remain in the clinic after taking the prostaglandin. However, some French physicians believe that a clinic setting is not essential.

Although RU-486 has been used primarily to interrupt a pregnancy after the missed period, there are also studies assessing its effectiveness as a "morning after" pill, for use after unexpected midcycle intercourse.

POSSIBLY HARMFUL EFFECTS ON SUBSEQUENT PREGNANCIES. Questions have been raised about possible long-term harmful effects of induced abortion, especially for women who have had multiple

"If men could get pregnant, abortion would be a sacrament."

FLORYNCE KENNEDY
IN THE PORTABLE CURMUDGEON, 1987

ABORTION
Availability of Providers

The majority of abortion procedures in the United States are provided by obstetrician-gynecologists, with a small percentage performed by other providers such as family practice physicians, midwives, or nurse practitioners. There are serious concerns about the provision of abortion procedures in the future for several reasons. Although most obstetrician-gynecologists believe that women should have the right to choose to terminate a pregnancy, at the same time, most do not wish to perform them. As a result, approximately 80 percent of counties in the United States do not have an abortion facility. A majority of ob/gyn residency training programs do not offer abortion training routinely; rather, most provide it on an optional basis, making abortion the only gynecological surgical procedure that is considered an elective part of training. As a result, a majority of graduating residents have little or no training in this area.

Finally, even where training has taken place, the increasing incidence of harassment and even violence (including the 1993 and 1994 murders of abortion providers in Florida) has resulted in more reluctance on the part of physicians to be involved in the provision of this service. This raises serious ethical questions as to the social responsibility of professionals in this field to make certain that this procedure is available to all patients.

— ALLAN ROSENFIELD
SARA IDEN

It is generally recognized that laws that decriminalize and deregulate abortion do not guarantee that every woman who desires an abortion will get one.

PAGE 25

abortions. Much of the concern centers on subsequent pregnancies, following one or more induced abortions. Medical evidence has consistently shown that a woman who has one properly performed induced abortion in the first trimester of pregnancy has the same chance of a normal outcome of a subsequent pregnancy as a woman who has never had an abortion. The evidence is less definitive for women who have had more than one induced abortion or an abortion with complications, although there is no reason to believe that additional abortion procedures, carried out by well-trained professionals, will have a long-term adverse effect. Overall, in terms of medical risk, abortion procedures, particularly those carried out in the first trimester of pregnancy, are among the safest of all surgical procedures.

Early versus late abortions: Controversies in medicine

Medical practitioners often have more difficulty with late abortions as compared to earlier ones, both because the procedures are more difficult to perform in late abortions and because of the more advanced state of fetal development. A particularly difficult issue relates to the survival of a fetus in which instillation procedure has been the method of termination. Although this is rare, when it does occur, most physicians would take all steps to treat the surviving premature newborn. With the D&E procedure, no fetus survives, due to the destructive nature of the technique.

Medical attitudes toward abortion have constantly been shaped by the medical profession's knowledge of and attitude toward the stage of development of the fetus, interacting with local cultural, religious, and legal ideas and beliefs. Together, these factors have had a significant impact on medical practice.

Prior to the latter half of the nineteenth century, abortion was available in the United States under the doctrines of British common law that permitted termination of a pregnancy until the time of "quickening" (detection of fetal movement). However, medical knowledge available at that time made it difficult to confirm a pregnancy with certainty prior to "quicken-

MEDICAL PERSPECTIVES
Psychological Effects of Abortion

No grayer area exists than that of the psychological consequences of induced abortion. It is difficult to generalize about the emotional responses of patients to pregnancy termination but, like physical complications, psychological complications may be related to the type of procedure and the gestational age at the time of termination, with earlier suction curettage theoretically leading to fewer psychological complications than later procedures.

However, most studies in this area suffer from methodological problems, including a lack of consensus about symptoms, inadequate study design, and lack of adequate follow-up. Furthermore, the so-called postabortion syndrome does not meet the American Psychiatric Association's definition of trauma (Gold, 1990).

Despite the many problems with most investigations, "the studies are consistent in their findings of relatively rare instance of negative responses after abortion and of decreases in psychological distress after abortion compared to before abortion" (Adler et al., 1990). Former U.S. Surgeon General C. Everett Koop, at the request of the White House, undertook a major assessment of the literature on this topic and concluded in a 1989 congressional hearing that "the data were insufficient . . . to support the premise that abortion does or does not produce a postabortion syndrome and that emotional problems resulting from abortion are minuscule from a public health perspective" (Koop, 1989a). Given Koop's personal opposition to abortion, the conclusions of his assessment are of particular importance.

Approximately 10 percent of induced abortions in the United States take place between twelve and twenty weeks of gestation, and less than 1 percent take place between twenty and twenty-four weeks. This means that more than 150,000 second-trimester procedures occur each year, a much larger number than in other developed nations where abortion is legal. Most would agree that decreases in the total numbers of abortions would be highly desirable, particularly decreases in second-trimester procedures.

The most common reasons for these later procedures, particularly among younger teens, are indecision about termination and failure to recognize (or denial of) pregnancy. A much smaller percentage of these later abortions occur because of medical or genetic reasons, which theoretically may correlate with greater psychological distress.

Choosing to terminate a pregnancy is a serious decision that is rarely made lightly. In addition to complete information about abortion procedure options, counseling should be made available to women faced with a decision about an unplanned pregnancy.

— ALLAN ROSENFIELD
SARA IDEN

ing," for it was only this detection of fetal movement that confirmed the existence of a living human fetus. There is little in the historical literature that describes how physicians in that era actually felt about abortions, although based on the information discussed below, one can assume that there were concerns about abortion.

By the second half of the nineteenth century, as scientific knowledge grew, so did the realization that fetal development occurs on a continuum, suggesting that the fetus is a living entity before fetal movement is felt. Prompted by this new medical knowledge, physicians, particularly those who were members of the newly formed American Medical Association (AMA), began openly to oppose abortion and urged its criminalization as an immoral practice. As a basis for this change, the Hippocratic Oath was used to oppose abortion at any time during pregnancy.

The concept of the fetus as a human entity separate from the mother has long been the subject of ethical concern within the medical profession. The AMA's Principles of Medical Ethics permit physicians to perform abortions, provided they are done in accordance both with the law and with "good medical practice" (Council on Ethical and Judicial Affairs, 1994, Opinion 2.01). In general, for the last 100 years or more, and especially since the 1973 U.S. Supreme Court decision in *Roe* v. *Wade* greatly liberalized the legal permissibility of abortion, medical practitioners have tended to place the value of the life of the mother above that of the fetus and there has been general agreement that abortion is permissible in those cases where the health of the mother is seriously compromised by a pregnancy.

However, just as *Roe* v. *Wade* allowed for some restrictions on abortions in the second trimester, so the medical profession has shown a reluctance to perform abortions later in pregnancy. In addition to new ethical dilemmas over fetal and maternal rights, many medical professionals remain ambivalent about the morality of abortion, a conflict that is heightened by increased technological sophistication in the field of perinatology and genetics.

Depending on the technology available to a physician and the condition of the individual fetus (gestational age and any developmental deformity), it is now routinely possible to save the lives of premature babies born at thirty weeks gestation. Babies born at twenty-six to twenty-seven weeks and earlier have survived with intensive neonatal intervention and support, though often with some degree of functional impairment. With abortions occasionally performed up to twenty-five or twenty-six weeks' gestation, one can see the conflict within medicine: Fetuses that might be aborted by one group of physicians are aggressively supported as patients by another group.

Physicians who provide abortion services prefer to do early abortions, that is, up to twelve weeks, for several reasons. First, it is generally agreed that, though a fetus may exhibit primitive reflexes before twenty weeks' gestation, there is no evidence that the brain and neurological system are developed enough even at twenty-four weeks for the fetus to experience pain. Second, as discussed earlier, second-trimester techniques that might appear to be more humane or to show more respect for the fetus, generally entail more danger for the woman. Third, the physicians who are committed to offering abortion procedures are intent on offering the safest procedures for the woman and regard the benefit to the woman as superseding the goal of minimalization of harm to the fetus.

Most abortion practitioners do not perform abortions past twenty-four weeks, and even then, usually only when the fetus has a condition incompatible with life outside the uterus. Extremely few U.S. practitioners will perform elective late abortions (beyond twenty-four weeks). Antiabortion activists often single out these atypical practitioners for their demonstrations.

With early abortion methods, such as dilation and curettage (D&C) or suction curettage, the fetus is destroyed. In instillation abortion procedures, where the viability of the fetus may be an issue, the fetus occasionally survives an abortion; and the further question sometimes arises in bioethics of whether the abortion technique chosen should be that which maximizes the possibility of fetal survival. Again, techniques that could possibly terminate a pregnancy without causing fetal death are more risky for the woman; in fact, in very late abortions the appropriate procedure for the woman may require inducing fetal death prior to delivery. Because of the medical commitment to benefit the mother, and since most physicians who have a high level of respect for the life and survival of the fetus do not engage in the practice of abortion, very few fetuses are aborted alive. It is assumed that abortion will always entail the death of the fetus: The goal of that medical practice is deliberately to accomplish the death of the fetus while terminating the pregnancy. However, most institutions require that fetuses surviving the procedure be provided with immediate neonatal care.

Public-health and international perspectives

Abortion is widely available with varying restrictions throughout the industrialized world. In recent years, there also has been a trend toward liberalization of abortion laws in many developing countries, such as in India, where abortion has been legalized; and in Bangladesh, where an early first-trimester procedure called menstrual regulation (which is really an early suction curettage) has been officially sanctioned by the

Fetuses are generally defined as the unborn young of a vivaparous [live-bearing] animal.

PAGE 232

Once removed or delivered from the body of a pregnant woman, it is no longer a fetus but an abortus or a newborn.

PAGE 238

A

ABORTION

Contemporary Ethical and Legal Aspects

It is sometimes argued that certain moral positions ought not to be enforced legally because the laws that codify them will be violated anyway, and their surreptitious violation will lead to many tragic results.

PAGE 436

government even though abortion per se has not been legalized. Abortion laws are most restrictive in Latin America, sub-Saharan Africa, and Central Asia.

Many of these countries have high rates of maternal mortality, and complications of illegal abortions are one of its leading causes. According to the World Health Organization, as many as 100,000 or more maternal deaths occur each year as a result of complications of an unsafe, usually illegal abortion attempt. Even in the United States, some illegal abortions continue to be performed in cases where women are without the resources to obtain a legal abortion. Although reliable incidence data are lacking as to the number of illegal abortions performed worldwide, there clearly is a strong demand for abortion, a demand that will probably always exist. As evidenced by the estimated number of women who undergo illegal abortion attempts, most women who are so determined to terminate a pregnancy will attempt to do so either by themselves or with assistance.

Consequently, the public-health concerns about the complications of unsafe abortion attempts, coupled with the complex issues relating to the reproductive and autonomy rights of women versus the rights of the fetus, suggest the continuing importance that must be given by the field of bioethics to abortion, particularly to the question of whether abortion should be made available equally to all persons requesting it regardless of national citizenship, ethnic or racial identity, or economic status.

— ALLAN ROSENFIELD
SARA IDEN

CONTEMPORARY ETHICAL AND LEGAL ASPECTS

Contemporary ethical perspectives

There is probably no issue in bioethics more controversial and more difficult to resolve than that of abortion. There are several reasons for this, reasons that are more political than they are matters of ethical principle. The first is that unlike many ethical issues in biology and medicine, the abortion debate is not limited to scholars and practitioners but has engulfed the entire society in the United States. Candidates for public office feel compelled to take a stand on abortion. In the legal and regulatory sphere, there is constant activity in state and federal courts, in bills introduced into legislatures, and in regulations promulgated by the Department of Health and Human Services and other government agencies.

CENTER STAGE

With its 1973 Roe *v.* Wade *decision, the U.S. Supreme Court set the legal parameters for abortion in America.*

A second reason for the intractability of the abortion issue is that at the extremes, both proponents and opponents of the right to abortion hold views more akin to ideologies than to rationally held positions. Opponents at one extreme defend an absolute prohibition of abortion, while proponents at the opposite extreme support the absolute right of women to procure an abortion on demand. The rhetoric used by both sides reveals the ideological character of the debate. Spokespersons for opponents of abortion adopted for their side the label "pro-life," thereby implying that anyone willing to allow abortion is "anti-life." Supporters of the right of women to have an abortion, for their part, selected a label that reflects the cherished American value of freedom to choose, calling themselves "pro-choice."

Although opponents of abortion do not always identify the religious underpinnings of their views, a demographic analysis links the antiabortion movement with particular religions and denominations, chiefly Roman Catholicism and fundamentalist Protestantism. It is also true, however, that many people on the pro-choice side are deeply religious, believing in the sacredness of life and humanity created in the image of God, for example. If it is impossible to argue about the rightness or wrongness of fundamental religious convictions, so too will it be impossible to mount a rational argument about an ethical position that is deeply rooted in a religious worldview. Dogmatic adherence to an ideology, whether religious or secular, tends to make people unwilling to argue rationally in defense of their positions.

Between these extremes, however, is a range of moderate positions on the morality of abortion. These positions acknowledge that abortion is ethically problematic yet can be justified. Scientific advances in prenatal diagnosis now make it possible to detect numerous abnormalities in utero. All but the extreme pro-life faction agree that abortion is ethically justifiable in cases of serious, uncorrectable disorders detected by amniocentesis, chorionic villus sampling, sonography, and other diagnostic techniques. Less agreement exists regarding minor abnormalities or cases in which the genetic disease is eventually lethal but the affected individual could live for many years. However, profound disagreement surrounds the practice of prenatal diagnosis followed by abortion for the purpose of selecting the sex of the child. Advances in knowledge of human genetics continue to increase the number and kinds of different genetic abnormalities that can be detected in utero, giving rise to worries that the sheer number of abortions will multiply as more and more information becomes available.

The contemporary controversy surrounding abortion focuses on three central ethical issues: the moral standing of embryonic and fetal life, the conflict of "rights" between the pregnant woman and her fetus, and whether the harmful consequences for women likely to result from restricting their right to an abortion outweigh the negative consequences of terminating fetal life.

Somewhat less prominent in the overall debate, but related to those major issues, is a question of social justice. Ample evidence exists to show that restrictive policies on abortion adversely affect more minority-group and poor women than white middle-class or wealthy women. The most prominent disagreements in the abortion controversy focus on the rights of the individual woman and the permissible role of government in restricting those rights. Nevertheless, questions of social justice are also ethical concerns, whether they involve women's access to information about abortion services, access to the services themselves, or government funding for abortions for poor women.

Personhood and the abortion debate

The question of the "personhood" of the fetus is one of the central questions in the abortion controversy (Garfield and Hennessy, 1984). However, one feminist line of thought contends that too much emphasis has been placed on that question, to the detriment of concerns about women, including their physical and mental health and their prospects for social equality and independence (Sherwin, 1992). The latter approach affirms the capacity of women for moral agency and thus places little emphasis on the search for objective criteria for defining when personhood begins.

At the most fundamental level, the personhood question is whether an entity resulting from fertilization of a human egg by human sperm can properly be said to have rights—in particular, a right to life—at any point during the nine-month gestational period. This question gives rise to the related yet different question: "What is a person?" or "When does personhood begin?" The two questions are joined because of the underlying premise that persons are legitimate bearers of rights. Therefore, it is argued, if an embryo or fetus can be termed a person, it can be said to have rights. However, the problem of arriving at a consensus on criteria for personhood has proved as difficult as resolving the abortion issue itself.

That difficulty was acknowledged by the U.S. Supreme Court in its landmark decision in 1973 in the case of *Roe* v. *Wade*. The Court decided that a fetus is not a person for the purposes of the Fourteenth Amendment to the Constitution, but declined to embark on the task of defining "personhood": "We need not resolve the difficult question of when life begins. When those trained in the respective disciplines of medicine, philosophy, and theology are unable to arrive at any consensus, the judiciary, at this point in the development of man's knowledge, is not in a position to speculate as to the answer." The fundamental disagreement on which the abortion controversy rests concerns the point at which human life acquires moral standing, a point typically characterized as the beginning of personhood.

The answers offered at opposite poles of this debate are that personhood begins at conception, and so a very early embryo has rights, and that personhood begins at the moment of birth or later, thus disqualifying all prenatal life from the category of personhood. Philosophers, theologians, and others who contribute to the literature on this topic hold as many different views about when personhood begins as they do on the topics of fetal rights and the right of women to have an abortion. Even if everyone agrees that rights can properly be ascribed only to persons, that agreement would not settle the abortion debate because of sharp disagreements over the proper criteria for personhood.

The difficulty of reaching agreement on a set of defining criteria for personhood stems from the value-laden quality of the concept of personhood, no matter which definition is adopted. For example, one position holds that at no stage of development does the fetus meet criteria of personhood. The philosopher Mary Anne Warren proposes a set of criteria for personhood so rigorous that even a newborn infant might not fulfill them. For ease of reference, we may call this a "strict" standard of personhood. The following traits, Warren argues, are those "most central to the concept of personhood, or humanity in the moral sense" (Warren, 1978, p. 224):

PERSONHOOD

Central Traits

1. consciousness (of objects and events external or internal to the being) and in particular the capacity to feel pain
2. reasoning (the developed capacity to solve new and relatively complex problems)
3. self-motivated activity (activity that is relatively independent of either genetic or direct external control)

Opponents of abortion argue that life begins at conception and that the deliberate termination of a pregnancy is the taking of a human life, which is seen to be immoral or even comparable to murder.

PAGE 441

Physicians and hospitals may refuse to perform abortions on the grounds of moral convictions and limitation of funds.

PAGE 703

4. the capacity to communicate, by whatever means, messages of an indefinite variety of types—that is, not just with an indefinite number of possible contents but on many indefinite, possible topics
5. the presence of self-concepts and self-awareness, individual or racial or both

At the opposite end of the spectrum are criteria for personhood that are easy to fulfill. Again, for ease of reference, let us term this a "lenient" standard of personhood. This position is also value-laden, resting on a traditional set of religious values. John T. Noonan, arguing that personhood begins at conception, identifies this as "the Christian position as it originated" (Noonan, 1983, p. 304). Noonan contends that this position does not depend on a narrow theological or philosophical concept, although many Christian theologians and historians disagree with his contention. Noonan's criterion for personhood is "simple and all-embracing: if you are conceived by human parents, you are human" (Noonan, 1983, p. 304). Although Noonan refers to "humanity" rather than to "personhood," it is clear that he takes these two concepts to be equivalent, since the moral question related to when a being is human is "When is it lawful to kill?" Noonan and others, such as the Protestant theologian Paul Ramsey (1975), have thus adopted a very lenient standard of personhood, which they further buttress with modern scientific findings. Conception is the "decisive moment of humanization" because that is when the new being receives the genetic code; "a being with a human genetic code is man" (Noonan, 1983, p. 307).

The state of Connecticut passed the first American legislation against abortion in 1821.

PAGE 22

Between these two extremes lies a range of other criteria for personhood, some of which are matters of traditional belief while others have been introduced more recently as a result of scientific developments. An example of the former is "quickening," the time at which a pregnant woman first feels fetal movement. Another example is "animation"; Thomas Aquinas and early Christian authors talked about "ensoulment," the time at which the embryo or fetus becomes infused with a soul.

According to Aristotle, life is defined by the possession of a soul, or vital force, through which an entity is rendered animate and given shape.

PAGE 438

An example of a criterion that relies on modern scientific knowledge is the presence of electroencephalographic (brainwave) activity. This criterion, defended by the philosopher Baruch Brody (1978), has the feature of symmetry, as it can be used to determine the beginning as well as the end of "human life." One interpretation of this criterion holds that the onset of encephalographic activity is the time when the fetus becomes a person (about six weeks' gestational age), just as the cessation of brainwave activity serves as a determination of death, even if other vital functions are sustained by artificial life supports. However, this interpretation has been contested in another account of the significance of brainwave activity. Nancy Felipe Russo asks, "Why can't we agree on access to abortion before the developing human becomes 'brain alive'?" Yet she contends that "being able to produce a squiggle is not [the same as] having a human brain wave. Cortical functioning that is comparable to human brain waves doesn't happen until much later. There is debate on when—connections to the cortex are established certainly before thirty weeks, but also certainly after twenty weeks" (Russo, 1992, p. 21).

Viability—the capability of surviving outside the womb with or without artificial support—is one other point between conception and birth that many people hold to be the time at which the fetus acquires moral standing. Although the U.S. Supreme Court declined to define "personhood," the importance accorded to "viability" in *Roe* v. *Wade* (1973) appears to have underwritten the position that the fetus becomes a person at the point of viability. Yet it is important to recall that the Supreme Court's decision did not prohibit abortion, the termination of fetal life, after viability. Instead, the Court used viability as a place to draw a line beyond which the state may interfere with a woman's "right to privacy":

> *With respect to the State's important and legitimate interest in potential life, the "compelling" point is at viability. This is so because the fetus then presumably has the capability of meaningful life outside the mother's womb. . . . If the State is interested in protecting fetal life after viability, it may go so far as to proscribe abortion during that period, except when it is necessary to preserve the life or health of the mother.*

The tendency to confuse ethics and law is found in the abortion controversy, as in other bioethical debates. The ethics of abortion, including attempts to specify when a fetus acquires personhood, must be kept distinct from Supreme Court rulings and other legal developments. After a period of increasing liberalization of abortion laws in the United States, the 1980s and early 1990s saw a tightening of restrictions. Nevertheless, despite wide variations in state laws regulating abortion, fetal viability remains the point where many people draw a moral line. Beyond that point, the fetus is thought to be a person or—what amounts to the same thing in these ethical arguments—acquires rights. Even outside the abortion context, arguments that pit maternal rights against fetal rights invoke viability: for example, the issue of whether a pregnant woman has the right to refuse a medical procedure. Medical professionals frequently argue that before viability, they are obligated to accept a pregnant woman's refusal of treatment but that once the fetus becomes viable, their obligation shifts to the second "patient" and requires them to act to preserve fetal life or health. Thus the concept of fetal viability, used in a 1973 Supreme Court decision to mark the point at which the state acquires an interest in potential life, has been elevated to a criterion for according moral standing to the fetus.

One approach to the personhood of prenatal life has been termed the "developmental" view. This approach denies that there is a single point or a sharp line that distinguishes personhood from an intrauterine existence that lacks moral standing. Lisa Sowle Cahill contends that "an individual member of the species does not self-evidently have exactly the same status morally and therefore in terms of 'rights' that other members at other stages may have." Cahill finds a developmental view of fetal status most convincing and states that "even at conception the fetus has very considerable value, simply because of its human identity and immense potentiality." The difficulty for Cahill is "how to assign an amount or degree of value, whether at the beginning or at a later point" (Cahill, 1992, p. 24). Although the developmental view is likely to be appealing to many people, its shortcoming lies in the difficulty, if not impossibility, of translating it into public policy.

A final strategy for defining "personhood" makes use of the potentiality principle. It is simply the *potential* for developing into an adult human being that confers on a fertilized ovum the moral status of a full-fledged adult. This strategy thus takes the moment of conception as marking the beginning of personhood. John T. Noonan (1983) embraces this argument explicitly, while Michael Tooley, Baruch Brody, and Mary Anne Warren argue directly against it. Judith Jarvis Thomson does not offer an argument against using the potentiality principle but observes that similar things might be said about the development of an acorn into an oak tree: ". . . it does not follow that acorns are oak trees, or that we had better say they are. . . . A newly fertilized ovum, a newly implanted clump of cells, is no more a person than an acorn is an oak tree" (Thomson, 1978, p. 199).

"PERSONHOOD" Central yet Irresolvable

The wide range of criteria proposed for defining "personhood" should serve to demonstrate the impossibility of using this strategy to resolve the abortion controversy. Proponents of choice advocate freedom and equality for women and propose a strict definition of "personhood," thereby giving women a wide moral latitude for terminating pregnancy. Opponents of abortion tend to favor sex-appropriate social roles and an idealized, traditional family, and adopt a lenient definition that identifies a woman as a "mother" immediately after fertilization. The futility of trying to resolve the abortion controversy by appealing to the concept of a person can best be shown by noting that proponents of both extreme standards believe that agreement about personhood is crucial for settling the abortion issue. Warren and Tooley propose criteria for personhood that a newborn infant cannot meet, while Noonan adopts a criterion that a newly fertilized ovum can meet. The questionable utility of defining "personhood" is further demonstrated by Thomson's argument that abortion may be morally justified even if it is acknowledged that the fetus is a person from the moment of conception. The reason the task of trying to arrive at objective criteria for personhood is bound to fail is that the values people already hold about abortion are imported into the debate over when personhood begins.

Nor is any progress made toward a resolution when analogies are used to buttress a right-to-life argument. Arguments from analogy are often flawed, and the following example is a case in point. Some foes of abortion argue that refusal to recognize the rights of embryos or fetuses has historical analogues in refusal to recognize the rights of blacks who were enslaved or Jews who were killed in the Holocaust. One Roman Catholic theologian, Richard John Neuhaus, uses this analogy when he asks: "*If* one believes that 20 million abortions are equivalent to 20 million instances of the taking of innocent human life, does not the analogy with the Holocaust become more appropriate? Perhaps even inevitable?" (Neuhaus, 1992, p. 222).

Neuhaus does believe that abortion is the taking of innocent human life, so for him the analogy is apt. As he notes, however, supporters of the right to abortion are "understandably outraged" when those abortions are compared with the Holocaust. No one who does not already subscribe to the view that embryos and fetuses have rights will be convinced by an argument from analogy citing the doctrine of the Third Reich that Jews, gypsies, homosexuals, Slavs, and others were not human beings in the full meaning of the term. By using this analogy, Neuhaus attempts to show that like those people then, fetuses today are not included in the community of legal rights, protections, and entitlements.

In spite of all the difficulties with these arguments and analogies, appeals to the personhood of the fetus are unlikely to disappear from the abortion debate. This is because the contention that the fetus is a person is the basis for ascribing rights, including the right to life.

— RUTH MACKLIN

Fourty-four percent of respondents said they thought the anti-abortion advocates in their states were extremists, the same level as in 1989.

THE NEW YORK TIMES/CBS NEWS POLL, JANUARY 16, 1998

In 1989, fifty-seven percent said they thought most abortion rights advocates in their state were reasonable; that rose to sixty-six percent in 1998.

THE NEW YORK TIMES/CBS NEWS POLL, JANUARY 16, 1998

Rights and the abortion controversy

Ascribing rights to the fetus poses two profound problems: first, whether the fetus is a type of entity to which rights can properly be assigned and, second, how to resolve conflicts of rights assigned to the fetus with those ascribed to the pregnant woman.

The initially promising path of trying to ascertain whether a fetus is a person and therefore possesses rights is evidently of little use. It is no less controversial to bypass the intermediate step of defining "personhood" and go directly to ascribing rights to an embryo or fetus. The position that human life acquires moral standing from the moment of conception is an article of religious faith for some people and an absurd proposition for others. The latter group finds it impossible to construct a rational defense of the assertion that a cluster of cells attached to the lining of the womb should be granted the rights normally accorded living children and adult human beings. Yet despite the lack of any similarity between the properties of a conceptus and those of a woman, man, or child, opponents of abortion contend that human life deserves protection from the moment of conception.

In the abortion debate, the rights of the fetus are typically pitted against the rights of the pregnant woman. In the political debate carried on first in the United States and later in other countries, feminists adopted the phrase "a woman's right to control her own body," identifying a right that could presumably override the right to life of the fetus. "The right to control one's own body" is a way of specifying the right to self-determination.

In the international sphere, the basic right to control reproduction has been ascribed both to couples and to individuals. In 1974 in Bucharest, a fundamental right was agreed upon as part of the World Population Plan of Action. Representatives of 136 governments stated that "all couples and individuals have the basic right to decide freely and responsibly the number and spacing of their children and to have the information, education, and means to do so" (United Nations, 1975). In order for this potential right to become an actual right, individuals, groups, and governments would have to refrain from interfering with the freedom of women or couples to make and carry out family-planning decisions, including the decision to have an abortion. Despite the efforts of some religious and political groups in various countries to curtail this basic right, it has been reaffirmed by statements such as the Convention on the Elimination of All Forms of Discrimination Against Women (U.N. General Assembly, 1980).

The underlying basis for this reproductive right is the right to liberty. The principle of liberty dictates that individuals have a right to freedom of decision and action, to the extent that their actions do not interfere with the rights of others. Opponents in the abortion controversy do not disagree on the soundness of that fundamental ethical principle itself, yet they disagree profoundly over its application: Foes of abortion claim that the act of terminating a pregnancy does interfere with the rights of another (the fetus), while advocates of a woman's right to procure an abortion deny that killing a fetus is a violation of rights.

As is true of any conflict of rights, this one might be resolved in favor of either party—the woman or the fetus. If a right to life is ascribed to fetuses and a right to terminate a pregnancy is assigned to women, a higher priority could be given to the rights of the woman. However, as important as the value of liberty is in Western philosophical and political thought, only rarely is it held to outweigh the value of human life when the two values conflict. Therefore, the most reasonable way to resolve this apparent conflict of rights in favor of the woman is to deny that the fetus can properly be considered an entity having rights.

Still, an argument in support of assigning the right to choice a higher priority than the right to life has been put forward. Thomson constructs an argument using a fanciful analogy that has become well known among readers of the abortion literature. She posits that you awake one morning to find yourself hooked up to the body of a famous violinist, who needs the help of your kidneys to sustain his own life for a period of nine months. After that, the violinist will have recovered. The violinist is a person, and so he has a right to life. Your life is not endangered, but your freedom to move about for nine months is drastically inhibited. The analogy invites us to consider the violinist as an analogue to a fetus, and you and your kidneys as analogous to a pregnant woman and her life supports for the fetus. If your right to liberty—that is, to disconnect yourself from the violinist—overrides his right to life, the argument goes, should it not follow that a woman's right to terminate her pregnancy overrides the fetus's right to life? That conclusion rests on an appeal to the intuition that no one should have to remain involuntarily hooked up to another person, even to sustain that person's life (Thomson, 1978).

Thomson's philosophical imagination notwithstanding, the soundness of her analogy has been rejected by both opponents and proponents of the right to abortion. Arguing in general against the use of artificial cases in the abortion debate, Noonan decries this one in particular, claiming that "the similitude to pregnancy is grotesque" (Noonan, 1978, p. 210). Taking the opposite side from Noonan in the abortion debate, Warren criticizes Thomson's analogy on the grounds that it is too weak to do the work required for defending women's right to abortion: "The Thomson analogy can provide a clear and persuasive defense of an abortion only with respect to those cases in which the woman is in no way responsible for her pregnancy, e.g., where it is due to rape" (Warren, 1978, p. 221). The trouble with philosophical arguments that rely on the use of analogies is that they stand or fall with the strength of the analogy.

Liberal feminists like Warren rest their defense of a right to abortion on the premise that the fetus is not a person and therefore lacks a right to life. In contrast, a more radical line of feminist thought defends the moral rightness of abortion itself. Catharine MacKinnon contends that "the abortion choice should be available and must be *women's*, but not because the fetus is not a form of life. In the usual argument, the abortion decision is made contingent on whether the fetus is a form of life. I cannot follow that. Why should not women make life or death decisions?" (MacKinnon, 1984, p. 46). The matter of women's moral agency is the central issue in this defense of women's right to choose.

This line of feminist analysis emphasizes the interests and experiences of women. Susan Sherwin identifies as the central moral feature of pregnancy the fact that it takes place in women's bodies and has profound effects on women's lives: "Unlike nonfeminist accounts, feminist ethics demands that the effects of abortion policies on the oppression of women be of principal consideration in our ethical evaluation" (Sherwin, 1992, pp. 104-105). This feminist approach seeks to avoid an exclusive focus on rights and other "masculinist conceptions of freedom (such as privacy, individual choice, and individuals' property rights with respect to their own bodies)" (Sherwin, 1992, p. 100).

There is another, quite different problem underlying the abortion debate framed as a conflict of rights between the pregnant woman and the fetus. This is a moral inconsistency, which only a few pro-life advocates acknowledge to be a problem. Many opponents of abortion, holding that a right to life outweighs a right to choose, are nonetheless prepared to grant exceptions in the case of pregnancies resulting from rape and incest. Why should such exceptions be permitted? If the fetus has a genuine right to life in virtue of the type of entity it is, why should the circumstances that led to its existence alter that right? A thoroughly consistent opposition to abortion that rests on the right to life of the fetus would not grant the priority of the right of the woman to choose simply because the pregnancy occurred as the result of rape or incest.

This conclusion becomes evident when we reflect on what is ethically permissible in the case of individuals whose right to life is unquestioned and undisputed. If it were discovered that the mother of a five-year-old child, or even a one-year-old infant, had borne the child as the result of rape or incest, that would not grant the woman (or anyone else) moral license to kill the child. The fact that in such cases the child is no longer in the womb should make no moral difference if a fetal right to life is the basic premise of the antiabortion position. Right-to-life advocates Jack and Barbara Willke state their disagreement with those who "would return the violence of killing an innocent baby for the violence of rape" (Willke and Willke, 1988, p. 151) and ask, regarding the case of incest: "Isn't it a Twisted Logic that would Kill an Innocent Unborn Baby for the Crime of his Father?" (Willke and Willke, 155).

Opponents of abortion who are prepared to grant exceptions to the priority of the right to life of fetuses in the case of rape and incest must account for an apparent moral inconsistency. Either they must explain why a fetus that results from rape or incest has a lower moral status or less of a right to life than other fetuses or they must adopt the more restrictive but consistent position that all fetuses have a right to life, regardless of the way they came into being. Those who ascribe an absolute value to fetal life cannot consistently allow exceptions in the case of rape or incest. More moderate opponents of abortion are not inconsistent in allowing such exceptions, but they must then provide a cogent account of their basis for holding that abortion is morally wrong.

Consequentialist arguments

Both in the bioethics literature and in the political arena, the abortion debate in the United States has been carried out almost exclusively in the language of rights. Yet consequentialist ethical arguments, those that appeal to the good and bad results of actions or social practices, provide an alternative mode of ethical analysis. The long history of women's deaths and diseases from self-induced abortions, along with data

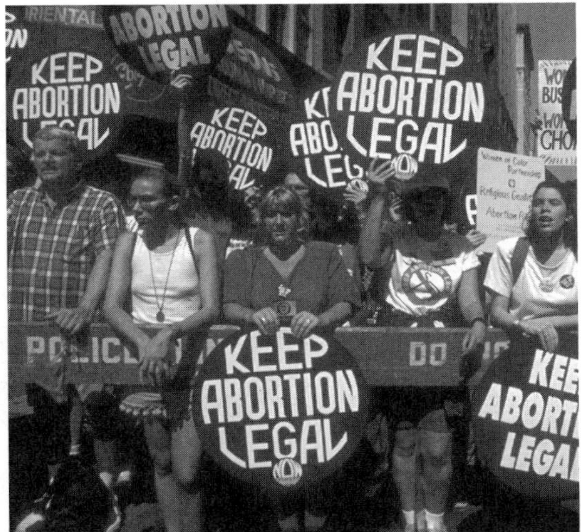

NOT BUDGING

Both pro- and antiabortion factions in the U.S. strongly proclaim the righteousness of their positions.

Eighty-eight percent said they did not believe the disagreements between supporters and opponents of legal abortion would ever be resolved.

THE NEW YORK TIMES/CBS NEWS POLL, JANUARY 16, 1998

Historically and economically, women have not been in a position to set or achieve their own reproductive goals.

PAGE 699

about the persistence of morbidity and mortality resulting from clandestine abortions, documents the harmful consequences of antiabortion policies. These consequences affect not only women but also the children they bear and the entire society in countries where population growth strains monetary and natural resources. Thus the negative consequences of restricting access to safe abortions are a compelling factor to consider in an ethical assessment.

Since safe, legal abortions have been available to most women in the United States at least since 1973, and in some states even before *Roe* v. *Wade* (1973), the consequences of a prohibitionist or highly restrictive policy on abortion as a contemporary issue can best be evaluated by looking at less developed countries. An estimated 200,000 or more Third World women die every year as a result of botched abortions (Germain, 1989). In Bangladesh alone, reports indicate that at least 7,800 women die each year due to abortion complications (Kabir, 1989). In most African countries, where safe abortion either is not available or is legally restricted, illegal abortion is the only solution for women with unwanted pregnancies. Complications of these abortions include hemorrhage, infection, abdominal perforations, and secondary infertility (Mashalaba, 1989). Infertility itself produces catastrophic consequences in Africa, and is almost always blamed on the woman, especially in rural areas (Mashalaba, 1989). Similar reports from Latin American countries document that most abortions are performed in sordid and clandestine conditions and that physicians use medicines such as hormone shots to induce menses, or unsafe curettage that can be harmful to women's health (Toro, 1989).

The negative consequences of enforcing restrictive policies on abortion are not limited to risks to the lives and health of women but extend also to the children they bear. Close spacing of children produces more high-risk pregnancies, premature births, and low-birth-weight infants. The very large number of "street children" (millions in Brazil alone) is a clear testimony to another dramatic consequence of unwanted pregnancies (Pinotti and Faúndes, 1989). Reports from developed as well as less developed countries and assessments by experts in the field of reproductive health throughout the world leave no room for doubt that women will continue to seek to end unwanted pregnancies regardless of legal or religious prohibitions.

It is instructive to compare the consequences for women's lives and health in countries that have changed their abortion laws in the past few decades. Legalization of abortion has tended to reduce maternal mortality, while making laws more restrictive has had the opposite effect. For example, in Czechoslovakia abortion laws were made less restrictive during the 1950s, and abortion-related mortality fell by 56 percent and 38 percent in the periods 1953-1957 and 1958-1962, respectively. In contrast, in Romania a restrictive abortion law was enacted in 1966, resulting in a sevenfold increase in deaths from abortion. The abortion mortality per million women aged 15 to 44 rose from 14.3 in 1965 to 97.5 in 1978 (Hagenfeldt, 1989).

Compared with the rights-based framework in which the debate is typically cast in the United States, the discussion in many nations is carried on in terms of the consequences of permitting or prohibiting abortion. This point was emphasized by Fred T. Sai, an African scholar who is one of the leading world authorities on reproductive health, and Karen Newman, working at International Planned Parenthood Federation in London:

> *The ethical arguments about abortion are complex, although often presented simplistically. Often debated is a woman's "right" to control over her body and to refuse to carry to term a pregnancy she does not want. However, not often considered is the ethics of withholding the benefits of a technology which is less hazardous than carrying a pregnancy to term. Nineteenth-century anti-abortion laws were generally designed to save women from the dangerous, and often experimental, surgical procedures of the time. However, this reason is no longer valid, and today the effect of applying anti-abortion laws is to increase rather than reduce risk to women's lives and health.* (Sai and Newman, 1989, p. 162)

Even in places where abortion is a legally available option, antiabortion feelings and behavior can violate the rights and harm the interests of women. Both within and outside the United States, some women who seek abortions are denied information about their options, while others who succeed in procuring abortions are treated punitively by physicians or other health-care workers. Whether the punitive behavior consists of failure to give adequate pain medication, delaying treatment, or simply being rude, women still suffer indignities despite the availability of safe, legal abortions.

CONSEQUENCES OF THE MEDICAL METHOD OF ABORTION. Until the late 1980s, the only available methods for performing abortions were surgical, requiring instruments to remove the products of conception from the uterus. The development of a medical abortifacient, antiprogestin drugs (for example, the French "abortion pill," RU-486), accompanied by the hormone prostaglandin, has stimulated some new features in the debate. Although a careful analysis reveals that, for the most part, the ethical issues are not new or different, the politics of abortion has led to suggestions that antiprogestins bear ethical hazards of a novel sort.

A central ethical issue regarding the introduction of any new technology is the assessment of its risks and benefits. It is important not to overstate the comparative benefits of this medical method over the traditional surgical alternatives. On the one hand, unlike vacuum aspiration or curettage, RU-486 does not involve insertion of instruments into the uterus and thus poses no risk of accidental perforation and infection from unclean instruments. It does not require the same degree of technical skill as the surgical techniques used to terminate pregnancy, so in this respect a medical method of abortion poses less risk to women than existing alternatives. On the other hand, RU-486 requires a follow-up visit to the clinic forty-eight hours later for administration of prostaglandin. Failure to follow the antiprogestin with prostaglandin could lead to greater risks than surgical methods; women may suffer the complications of incomplete abortion and lack proper medical supervision.

In making comparative risk-benefit assessments, it is important to use appropriate data for the locale in which the technology is to be used, since data about risks and benefits gathered about women in developed countries may not be strictly applicable to women in less developed countries. Other local or regional differences can also affect the risk-benefit ratios. Consider two examples.

First, in a society that has an adequate number of properly trained health-care workers, the risks of septic abortion and other complications of termination of pregnancy are much lower than they are in countries with too few or inadequately trained workers. Second, in regions where adequate follow-up is difficult to attain, a method like RU-486, which requires a second visit to the clinic at a prescribed interval, may well have lower safety and efficacy than elsewhere.

Risk-benefit assessments have a built-in relativity. Depending on the characteristics of the providers, the nature of the service delivery systems, and the demographic and cultural features of a country or region, the benefit-risk ratio of a particular method of abortion may vary. The risks include not only the medical and psychological risks of the method itself but also the risk of not having safe, effective, or otherwise acceptable methods available, including backup services to offer surgical abortion in case the medical method fails.

One feature of antiprogestins does raise a novel ethical issue. Antiprogestins work by preventing implantation of the fertilized ovum. Étienne-Émile Baulieu, the French scientist responsible for the research leading to development of RU-486, has proposed the term "contragestion" (a contraction of "contra-gestation") to emphasize that it falls somewhere between contraception and abortion (Baulieu, 1989). Construed as a "contragestive," RU-486 might thus be acceptable to some opponents of abortion who object to termination of pregnancy.

Women who have religious reasons for avoiding or restricting termination of pregnancy can use RU-486 after fertilization has occurred but before implantation of the embryo. At that point, the woman is arguably not yet pregnant. Once the embryo is implanted in a woman's uterus, she is pregnant and removal of the embryo terminates that pregnancy. However, there is debate over whether a woman whose egg has been fertilized should be considered pregnant in the brief time before implantation. Based on current medical knowledge, it is widely held that conception is a process that properly includes both fertilization and implantation (Baulieu, 1989).

The plausibility of this view is heightened by experience following the introduction of in vitro fertilization (IVF). A woman's egg can be fertilized in a dish, but she is not pregnant until the "preembryo" (before implantation) becomes attached to her uterus. Evidence that it is pregnancy, not fertilization, that matters to some from a moral point of view comes from Mexico and other Latin American countries, where physicians are opposed to abortion but not to disposing of ova fertilized by means of IVF.

CONSEQUENCES OF NONSURGICAL ABORTION METHODS. The prospect that this method could become widely available has influenced the political debate surrounding abortion. Opponents of abortion have expressed two worries: that a medical method will make abortion too easy to procure (Cook, 1991; Grimes, 1991) and psychologically easier for women to choose to have them (Callahan, 1991). Both worries stem from the concern that introduction of antiprogestins will lead to the performance of more abortions. Like any argument that rests on probable consequences, this one must be subjected to empirical scrutiny.

One question is whether nonsurgical abortions are "easier" for women to undergo than surgical ones; a second, quite different question is whether less discomfort from the procedure is likely to induce more women to procure abortions. With regard to the empirical likelihood that introduction of medical methods will lead to an increase in the number of abortions, there seems to be no factual basis. As one international authority on abortion observes:

> *There is no evidence that access to non-surgical abortion encourages abortions that would not otherwise occur, or leads to an increase in abortions. . . . Indeed,*

Since the ovum survives about 48 hours after ovulation and sperm can survive in the fallopian tubes for up to five days, the length of the fertile period is about seven days in most women.

PAGE 209

A woman's ability to limit and control her fertility may be a necessary precondition for equality and personal economic status.

PAGE 221

the Netherlands, with publicly funded abortion services widely available, has the lowest abortion rate in the industrialized world. That's because the Dutch also have access to sex education and information as well as contraceptive and voluntary sterilization services. (Cook, 1991, p. B7)

Evidence from one set of clinical trials indicates that women who used RU-486 found it "far less violent" than surgical methods they had previously undergone (Grimes, 1991). Although this psychological evidence clearly counts as a benefit of RU-486 over other methods, opponents of abortion have argued that pain and suffering are just deserts for women who choose to have abortions. Underlying this view is the moral judgment that women are guilty because it is their sexual behavior that results in unwanted pregnancies. Those who argue that it is a good thing when a method of abortion has punishing consequences object to RU-486, among other reasons, on grounds that the consequences are less punitive for women than those of other methods.

This argument against RU-486 distorts the well established means of calculating the risks and benefits of medical procedures. That there are fewer side effects, normally judged to be advantageous in the usual assessment of risks versus benefits, is taken here to be a *disadvantage*. There is no reasonable reply to an argument that construes increased pain and suffering resulting from a medical intervention as a benefit to the patient rather than a harm. In making risk-benefit calculations, taking pain and suffering to be a benefit rather than a harm is a perverse weighing of consequences.

In addition to "more readily procurable," "easier" can also mean "psychologically more acceptable." One opponent of abortion refers to the "moral ambiguity" of RU-486, arguing that this medical method makes it psychologically easier for women to choose abortion. "This ambiguity is present if the woman taking a 'morning-after pill' or a pill like RU-486 that produces an 'overdue period' is not sure whether she is aborting a fertilized embryo" (Callahan, 1991, p. B7). The possibility that this "ambiguity" may make it emotionally easier for some women to choose abortion does not count as a moral advantage of RU-486 for foes of abortion, despite the evident benefits to women of decreased psychological stress. This is because they believe that "taking a human life that has already begun" is morally unacceptable (Callahan, 1991, p.

ETHICAL PERSPECTIVES

Is Abortion an Insoluble Moral Problem?

It is reasonable to wonder whether abortion poses an insoluble moral problem. As a political issue in a pluralistic society, abortion does appear to be unresolvable. Political compromise, the usual mode of settling disagreements in a pluralistic society, is not a satisfactory method for resolving deep moral controversy. Those who believe that a fetus is truly a person, with a right to life equivalent to that of a child or an adult, cannot permit some abortions, under some circumstances, without compromising their moral integrity. Similarly, those who argue that a woman has moral standing at least equal to that of a fetus, and who affirm that women's full moral agency grants them the right to terminate an unwanted pregnancy, see no reason to compromise that principle.

As a matter of individual moral choice, however, the question of whether to have an abortion is taken seriously and has been decided by millions of women. Some women choose to abort only fetuses discovered by prenatal diagnosis to be abnormal. Other women decide to seek an abortion following failed contraception, after determining that they cannot, for financial or emotional reasons, have more children. Within marriage, that choice is typically made by the couple, not by the woman alone. Couples who choose abortion for the purpose of selecting the sex of their child are reflective about their decision but are nonetheless criticized by those who find their reason frivolous or otherwise morally unacceptable.

Few people have argued that abortion poses no moral issues whatsoever. However, even if it is acknowledged that a morally preferable alternative would be to prevent a large number of abortions from taking place, there will always be unwanted pregnancies, and women in those circumstances will risk their lives and their health, if necessary, to have an abortion. It is evident that neither the U.S. Supreme Court's 1973 abortion ruling that granted women constitutional protection nor subsequent laws and judicial decisions that have increasingly eroded that protection have silenced the ethical and political debate surrounding abortion. According to one contemporary line of thought, as long as the moral status of the embryo and fetus cannot be resolved, the abortion debate will not be laid to rest. And according to a feminist critique, as long as oppression of women is ignored or tolerated, abortion will remain one among many social problems whose resolution can be achieved only by increasing the power of women and freeing them from domination based on their sex.

— RUTH MACKLIN

B7). Inability to agree on that fundamental premise—the moral status of a fertilized ovum—is what prevents any compromise in the intractable abortion debate, regardless of the method of pregnancy termination. It also leads to a perverse transformation of what are normally counted as risks into benefits, and to the reverse.

A similar twist has occurred with respect to the value of privacy, a key ingredient in the abortion debate. As a drug that can be prescribed by physicians and taken by women in the doctor's office or even in their own homes, RU-486 clearly offers the opportunity for greater privacy and more control by women than methods that require a visit to a clinic. It has been surmised that if abortions with RU-486 become widely available in physicians' offices, "opponents of abortion might lose their targets for picketing, harassment, and violence. For example, since 1977, 110 abortion clinics have been burned or bombed in this country" (Grimes, 1991, p. B5). If the resulting decreased incidence of disruption and violence is viewed as a *disadvantage* of a medical method of abortion, that is another irrational weighing of harms and benefits. In any rational calculation of harms and benefits, lowering the potential loss of lives, dignity, or property can only reasonably be viewed as a benefit.

Abortion and the issue of justice

A principle of social justice holds that all persons within a given society deserve equal access to goods and services that fulfill basic human needs. A country might have liberal laws pertaining to abortion services, such as those in developed countries that permit women to procure an abortion up to the time of fetal viability. But if a government does not provide financial assistance to poor women who seek abortions, those women are denied equal access to a procedure that is available to financially better-off women. In that situation, a legally guaranteed right to abortion services will be a right in name only. Many rights presuppose the existence of corresponding obligations on the part of persons, agencies, or governments to act in ways that enable those rights to be realized. In the delivery of health care generally, the principle of justice is violated when health services are available only to those with the ability to pay. Feminists emphasize the broader issues of the accessibility and delivery of abortion services in their ethical analysis of abortion (Sherwin, 1992).

Equally problematic from the standpoint of justice are proposals that would deny government-sponsored assistance to family-planning clinics providing information to clients about abortion. If some women are denied access to information about the availability of abortions and the means to procure them, they will lack access to services that are available to women who are better educated or financially better off. The same conclusion holds for population assistance programs that cross national boundaries. For wealthier donor nations to restrict or deny funds to recipient countries that provide abortion services as a component of their family-planning programs is to violate this principle of justice.

The principle of justice mandates that all individuals who need them should have equitable access to health services, including the means to procure an abortion. "Equitable access" means that use of these services should not be based on an ability to pay for them. And a precondition for access is information about the existence and nature of the services. To fulfill the requirements of justice, it is necessary to have the widest possible distribution of reproductive health services, ensuring equitable access for everyone.

Social response to women's reproductive abilities typically has made their bodies part of the public domain in a way that men's are not.

PAGE 699

These conclusions apply both to developed and to less developed countries. Poor women disproportionately bear the burden of restrictive abortion laws and inadequate or nonexistent public services. Describing the situation in Africa, Sai and Newman identify a form of injustice that exists worldwide: "Wealthy women, who can afford private doctors or travel to countries where abortion is legal and safe, can get abortions almost free of risk; but poor women often pay for abortions with their health, their future fertility and possibly their lives" (Sai and Newman, 1989, p. 162).

Whether motivated by political or religious concerns, opponents of abortion erect obstacles that are difficult for providers of abortion services, as well as for women seeking those services, to surmount. An example is the problem women may face in obtaining abortions even in countries with liberal abortion laws. In the United States, a strong, vocal minority not only maintains an opposition to abortion for members of its own religious communities but also seeks to change existing laws to prohibit abortions altogether. These groups disrupt political speeches and heckle candidates for elected office. In the extreme, some antiabortion groups resort to violence, bombing abortion clinics and using physical force to prevent women from entering physicians' offices.

Islamic discussion of abortion is always related to the question of the rights and responsibilities of both the husband and the wife.

PAGE 38

In developed as well as in less developed countries, the tactics used by extreme opponents of abortion have a disproportionate impact on poor women, compounding the existing injustice of the gap between rich and poor. In some countries with liberal abortion laws, lack of medical personnel and facilities or the behavior of physicians and hospital administrators have the effect of curtailing access to abortion services, especially for economically or socially deprived women. Examples include parts of Austria, France, India, Italy, and the

United States (Tietze and Henshaw, 1986). This serves as a reminder that the mere existence of laws on the books is not sufficient to ensure ethically just practices.

— RUTH MACKLIN

The model of prohibition

The model of prohibition governs official abortion policy in many African, Latin American, and Islamic countries, including Bangladesh, Indonesia, and Nigeria (Sachdev, 1988). Chile, in South America, and Sri Lanka, in southern Asia, permit abortion only to save the life of the woman. Most jurisdictions in Europe and North America reject the model of prohibition; they permit abortion, if only where pregnancy results from rape or incest or where the continuation of pregnancy threatens the health of the woman (Petersen, 1993; Glendon, 1987).

REGULATORY ISSUES

Should Abortion Be Legal?

Most contemporary legal systems regulate the practice of abortion (Petersen, 1993; Sachdev, 1988; Glendon, 1987). Governments around the world legislate whether, when, why, and how the estimated 40 million abortions that occur each year may or must occur. In some countries, such as Belgium and Denmark, abortion is governed primarily by national laws; in others, such as Australia, abortion is governed mainly by state or regional laws. The belief that abortion is unsafe, irreligious, immoral, unjust, or genocidal has tended to push regulation in the direction of laws that expressly prohibit some or all abortions. The conviction that abortion can alleviate overpopulation, avert economic hardship, protect women's health, promote sex equality, or eliminate undesirable progeny has tended to produce laws that permit, guarantee, or even compel abortion.

ABORTION REGULATION

Four Models

- Prohibition: The laws of a jurisdiction punish most abortions as criminal offenses, as in Ireland.
- Permission: Laws permit abortions that meet more or less stringent criteria established by government and designated third-party decision makers, as in Germany.
- Prescription: Laws specifically require or encourage the termination of pregnancies falling into certain specific categories, as in China.
- Privacy: Laws restrain government from enactments that criminalize or severely restrict medically safe abortions, as in the United States under *Roe* v. *Wade* (1973). The model of privacy treats abortion decisions as substantially a matter of private choices rather than public law.

An international survey of existing law reveals four basic patterns or "models" of express abortion regulation: (1) a model of prohibition; (2) a model of permission; (3) a model of prescription; and (4) a model of privacy. Under the model of prohibition, the laws of a jurisdiction punish most abortions as criminal offenses, as in Ireland. Under the model of permission, laws permit abortions that meet more or less stringent criteria established by government and designated third-party decision makers, as in Germany. Under the model of prescription, laws specifically require or encourage the termination of pregnancies falling into certain specific categories, as in China. Finally, under the model of privacy, laws restrain government from enactments that criminalize or severely restrict medically safe abortions, as in the United States under *Roe* v. *Wade* (1973). The model of privacy treats abortion decisions as substantially a matter of private choices rather than public law.

Yet, beginning in 1989, a number of Supreme Court rulings critical of *Roe* v. *Wade* moved the United States away from the model of privacy toward a model of permission. Public-opinion surveys conducted between 1987 and 1991 show that a "majority of Americans . . . approved limited legal access to abortion" (Cook et al., 1992). Some polls indicate an overwhelming approval rate for abortion privacy among highly educated and affluent women (Sachdev, 1988), and among African-American, Asian-American, and Native American women (National Council of Negro Women, 1991). A national poll conducted in 1994 by Barna Research Groups showed that 78 percent of the adults surveyed approved the legalization of some (49%) or all (29%) abortions. An even higher approval rate was obtained in a 1994 survey conducted by Yankelovich Partners, Inc. In this survey 85 percent said a woman should be able to obtain an abortion no matter what the reason (46%) or in certain circumstances (39%). A CBS News/New York Times poll conducted in 1994 found that 77 percent of those surveyed favored "generally available" abortion (40%) or abortion with "stricter limits" (37%); only 21 percent said abortion "should not be permitted." Despite widespread public support for keeping some abortions legal, organized opponents of abortion rights continue to pressure lawmakers to reinstate blanket prohibitions.

— ANITA L. ALLEN

Ireland, a largely Roman Catholic nation, is one of the few Western countries—Belgium and Malta are two others—whose laws continued beyond the 1970s to criminalize abortions either absolutely or subject to a strictly limited number of exceptions (Solomons, 1992). Under a 1983 amendment to the Irish constitution, Irish law permits abortion only to save the life of the woman. Overturning a ruling that a teenage rape victim who credibly threatened suicide could not travel to England for an abortion, the Irish Supreme Court found in 1992 that abortion would be permissible "if it is established as a matter of probability that there is a real and substantial risk to the life as distinct from the health of the mother, which can only be avoided by the termination of her pregnancy."

Jurisdictions whose laws reflect the model of prohibition often assert a strong religious or humanitarian policy interest in protecting what are thought to be the rights and interests of unborn children. However, other objectives have also prompted strict abortion prohibition. For example, during the nineteenth and twentieth centuries, abortion opponents in the United States have cited the need to protect pregnant women from medical and psychological risks of abortion. There can be no doubt that unskilled, unsanitary abortion procedures are a health risk, and that some women who obtain abortion experience medical complications and emotional anguish. However, some lawyers and judges doubt that medical abortion performed during the first three months of pregnancy is less safe than pregnancy and childbirth (Tribe, 1990; Rhode, 1989). They similarly doubt that elective medical abortion poses a serious risk of psychological harm. Although one writer has concluded that "psychological problems occur in the lives of almost all aborted women" (Reardon, 1987), a report of the American Psychological Association concludes that "severe emotional reactions" rarely follow abortion, even in the case of minors (Melton and Pliner, 1986).

Countries whose populations have been ravaged by war and genocide have sometimes proscribed abortion in an effort to increase the birth rate. Strict abortion prohibition has had the additional, if only implicit, goal of reinforcing social roles. The cultural assumption that motherhood is the appropriate social role for women buttressed Joseph Stalin's 1936 abortion prohibitions enacted to furnish the former Soviet Union with "a new group of heros" (Sachdev, 1988). The belief that bearing children is women's natural destiny may lead some to assume that birth control and abortion are both immoral and unhealthful. After 1933, Adolf Hitler prohibited contraception and declared abortion a capital offense on the belief that birth control was unhealthful. On the other hand, abortion prohibitions adopted in Germany in 1943 aimed at the

SELF-INDUCED ABORTION
Difficulties of Enforcing Prohibition

Criminalizing self-induced abortion poses special problems of detection and law enforcement. Self-induced abortion has often involved risky procedures, such as inserting knitting needles, wire coat hangers, or other foreign objects through the cervix. Many self-induced abortions are detected because they end tragically in medical and police emergencies. In 1989, a health-care group in California promulgated a videotape demonstrating "menstrual extraction," a nonmedical abortion technique trainers say women can learn to perform safely at home with the help of a friend. To the extent that they are workable, abortion procedures that can be performed without medical assistance fall beyond the practical reach of law.

Prohibitive abortion law requires lawmakers to define what counts as abortion, and therefore what is subject to criminal penalties. The surgical and medical procedures generally in use by physicians in licensed hospitals and clinics in Europe and the United States plainly qualify as abortion. However, certain forms of birth control not viewed as abortion could conceivably fall under the scope of strict abortion prohibitions. Popularly viewed as a form of contraception, the intrauterine device (IUD) may function as a kind of abortifacient, blocking implantation of a fertilized egg, rather than preventing ovulation or fertilization. Étienne-Émile Baulieu's drug, RU-486, named for its French manufacturer, Roussel Uclaf, poses a related difficulty of definition. Described by French Minister of Health Claude Levin as "the moral property of women, not just the property of the drug company," RU-486 arrived on the European scene in the 1980s. Unlike pharmaceutical contraceptives that prevent fertilization or ovulation, RU-486 acts to block the successful implantation of a fertilized egg. Rejecting the popular "abortion pill" label, Baulieu has suggested that RU-486 is neither contraception nor abortion but something new—"contragestation." Still, it seems unlikely that a jurisdiction that strictly prohibits abortion would view "contragestation" as anything other than early abortion.

— ANITA L. ALLEN

Sixty-five percent of respondents said they would be likely to consider ["morning-after" pills] a form of birth control rather than abortion. Less than one-fifth said they would consider use of the morning-after pills to be a form of abortion.

THE NEW YORK TIMES/CBS NEWS POLL, JANUARY 16, 1998

◆ **RU 486**
a drug taken orally to induce abortion esp. early in pregnancy by blocking the body's use of progesterone.

The Comstock Act (1873) equated contraception with obscenity and made it a federal offense to use the postal service for transporting obscene materials, defined to include contraceptive and abortion information and equipment.

PAGE 223

"vitality of the German people" and excluded from criminality abortions performed on "racially" undesirable women (Sachdev, 1988).

The reach of laws prohibiting abortion can be broad. Obtaining an abortion has been subject to criminal penalty in some instances, and so too has distributing abortion information. Provisions of the famous Comstock Law enacted by the Congress of the United States in 1873 and later rescinded, outlawed abortion-related implements and information as "obscene" and "immoral" (Garrow, 1994; Rhode, 1989). Offenders of the Comstock Law faced imprisonment with hard labor and monetary fines. Jurisdictions prohibiting abortion generally aim at the conduct of third-party abortion providers. However, some abortion statutes also criminalize pregnant women's own conduct, making it a punishable offense to obtain or seek abortions from third parties. Legal systems rarely punish medical abortion as the full equivalent of felonious unjustified murder.

In South Africa, Latin America, the Caribbean, and Korea, abortion flourishes under regimes of prohibitive abortion law because the laws are not aggressively enforced (Sachdev, 1988). The criminal code of Bangladesh strictly prohibits most abortions; but physicians commonly induce abortion by performing a uterine evacuation procedure known as "menstrual regulation" on women who are many weeks pregnant. Prohibitive abortion laws commonly fall short of their stated goals and public expectations because governments are unwilling or unable to enforce the letter of the law. The prohibitive laws that governed abortion in the United States prior to *Roe* v. *Wade* were enacted to preserve unborn life and women's physical and mental health (Garrow, 1994). It has been argued that the aim of fetal preservation was at least partly undermined by the large number of clandestine abortions performed notwithstanding prohibitive laws (Tribe, 1990). Although most abortions were illegal in much of the United States prior to 1973, American women obtained an estimated 200,000 to 1,200,000 abortions each year in the 1960s and early 1970s (Tietze et al., 1988), compared to about 1,500,000 each year throughout the 1980s and early 1990s. David Reardon (1987) puts the number of abortions pre-*Roe* at merely 100,000 to 200,000 per year. The aim of preserving women's health may have been frustrated under the regime of prohibition because clandestine abortions were commonplace but were not always performed by skilled practitioners in hygienic settings. This was especially true of the illegal abortions obtained by African-American women, who accounted for a disproportionate number of the victims of illegal procedures. (Twenty percent of the deaths related to pregnancy and childbirth in the United States in 1965 were attributed to illegal abortions.) Legalization of abortion probably resulted in a small-to-moderate increase in the number of abortions, but it appears to have greatly decreased the incidence of abortion-related infertility and death.

Model of permission

The model of permission became the pervasive one around the world in the final quarter of the twentieth century. Under the model of permission, abortion is legally available, but only with the approval of government officials or officially designated decision makers, such as administrative boards, committees, physicians, or judges. In some permission-model jurisdictions, officials grant permission pro forma in nearly every case. In Norway, prior to 1975 reforms that liberalized abortion, as many as 94 percent of the requests for abortions made to Abortion Boards were routinely granted (Olsnes, 1993). Official decision makers in permissive jurisdictions rely upon a handful of factors to determine which abortions to permit and which abortions to prohibit (Petersen, 1993; Sachdev, 1988; Glendon, 1987).

The stage of pregnancy is very frequently a factor. Officials called upon to implement legal norms or exercise discretion often permit "early" abortions and prohibit "late" ones. This no doubt helps to explain the statistic that 90 percent of reported abortions take place within the first three months of pregnancy. Another factor decision makers commonly consider is the woman's medical or social status. Restrictive laws require that officials deny permission to abort for reasons other than medical hardship. Liberal laws often require that officials allow abortions because pregnancy or childbirth would involve social or economic hardship for the woman. In many jurisdictions grounds for social hardship include rape, incest, or the age and marital status of the woman. The health or condition of the fetus can be a third factor in permitting or prohibiting abortion. The law may premise access to abortion on evidence that a child would be born with serious physical or mental abnormalities. With advances in prenatal testing that enable detection of the sex of a fetus, it is now possible for a pregnant woman to abort selectively unwanted male or female offspring. In some instances, abortion for sex selection may be tied to a desire to avoid giving birth to a child with a gender-related genetic disease. However, abortion for sex selection per se is presumably, if not explicitly, illegal in all models of permission jurisdictions. In principle, model of privacy jurisdictions permit early abortion for any reason, including sex selection. The U.S. Supreme Court has not specifically determined whether states must permit abortion for purposes of sex selection.

For some portion of the twentieth century, a number of countries have governed abortion under highly bureaucratic versions of the model of permission (Sachdev, 1988). For a time in the eastern European countries of Hungary, Romania, Poland, and Bulgaria, abortion was lawful only if approved by a state board or committee. These countries reportedly permitted abortion in almost every case through the fourth month of pregnancy. Romania reverted to a prohibitive policy in 1966 in response to concerns about underpopulation and the health effects of multiple abortions. It prohibited most contraception and abortion for women who did not have at least four, and eventually five, children. Abortion prohibition was accompanied by a significant incidence of mortality related to illegal abortion. In the mid-1980s, 86 percent of the women in Romania who died as a consequence of pregnancy or childbirth died as a result of illegal abortions, compared with, for example, 29 percent in the former Soviet Union and 13 percent in Sri Lanka.

Other historical instances of the bureaucratic model of permission are the laws and administrative regulations in force in Denmark from 1939 to 1973, and in Sweden from 1939 to 1974. In Denmark, local and national committees consisting of teams of social workers, physicians, and psychiatrists evaluated the applications of women seeking legal abortions. Scandinavian officials on boards or committees charged with decision making typically assessed the impact of childbirth and child care on the mental or physical health of the woman, and the woman's living conditions. Israeli Ministry of Health regulations enacted in 1978 permitted hospitals and clinics to form committees consisting of two physicians and a social worker for deciding whether to grant women's abortion requests. Although living conditions, such as other children and economic hardship, were initially an authorized basis for granting abortion requests, Israel amended the law in 1980 under pressure from religious groups and in response to concerns about a declining population rate.

Today, a number of countries in Asia, South America, Europe, and North America make a woman's obtaining an abortion dependent upon the approval of one or more physicians, a judge, or one or both parents. Great Britain and countries whose abortion law was modeled on Great Britain's—Hong Kong, Zambia, and Australia—are examples of countries whose laws place decision making in the hands of physicians. The law of Great Britain was transformed over a great many centuries from a law of prohibition, to a law of permission, and even privacy. Early English common law embodied the model of prohibition, at least for abortions taking place after the first few months of pregnancy. The common law proscribed abortion after "quickening," about the fourth month of pregnancy, when fetal "animation" or "ensoulment" was deemed to have taken place. In 1861 the statutory abortion law of Great Britain defined as a felony any act intended to cause abortion, whether induced by the woman herself, if she were pregnant, or by others, whether or not she was in fact pregnant. The Abortion Act of 1967 abolished the nineteenth-century felony. The act's liberal provisions permit an abortion where any two medical practitioners certify in good faith that pregnancy "would involve risk to the life of the pregnant woman, or of injury to the physical or mental health of the pregnant woman or any existing children of her family, greater than if the pregnancy were terminated." Under this rule, qualifying for abortion poses no practical difficulty for women with the money to pay private physicians. As English law illustrates, the model of permission can have the distinct effect of empowering the medical and psychiatric professions to govern reproduction in accordance with their profession's internal standards of judgment.

In the Australian states (Petersen, 1993), abortions are permitted under common law or criminal codes if one or two physicians believe in good faith that it is necessary to save the life of the woman or to protect her mental or physical health. In New South Wales, social and economic conditions are deemed relevant to the assessment of impact on a woman's health. In South Australia and the Northern Territory, abortion is also lawful where there is a risk of a seriously disabled child. In India, the Medical Termination Pregnancy law enacted in 1971 permits abortions that one or, if the woman is more than twelve weeks pregnant, two physicians certify. Grounds for certification are liberal. Abortion may be obtained to preclude a risk to the pregnant woman's mental or physical health, or a risk of the birth of a child with serious mental or physical abnormalities. No abortions after twenty weeks are legal under the law. A woman's mental health is considered at risk in cases of economic hardship and where pregnancy resulted from failed contraception. The 1975 Abortion and Sterilization Act made many abortions lawful in the Republic of South Africa, on the certification of two physicians that statutory requirements are met. The law requires that where abortion is sought on grounds of risk to mental health, one of two certifying physicians be a psychiatrist willing to attest to danger of permanent mental harm.

The model of privacy may best describe the overall aspiration of *Roe* v. *Wade*. However, the model of permission is arguably more descriptive of United States abortion law pertaining to unemancipated minors. The Supreme Court has taken the position that minors have

In 1918, Margaret Sanger was convicted and sentenced to thirty days in the workhouse under New York State's Comstock law.

PAGE 223

See Also

Minorities and Birth Controllers: A History of Skepticism

Nonvoluntary Sterilization

In many societies and in virtually all historical periods, very young infants, female infants, bastards, and infants and older children believed to be "defective" in some way were frequently killed.

PAGE 376

THE FRENCH MODEL
Permission in Case of Hardship

In contrast to South African, Indian, Australian, English, and most western European law, French law permits women to make their own judgments (early in pregnancy) about whether they are entitled to abortion on grounds of hardship. In this respect, French law resembles the federal law of the United States under *Roe* v. *Wade.* French regulations enacted in 1975 are representative of international responses to the judicial transformation of United States law with *Roe* v. *Wade* in 1973. Reflecting the aspirations of both the model of permission and the model of privacy, the French enactment begins with a declaration that the law guarantees respect for every human being from the beginning of life, and that this principle is to be sacrificed only in case of necessity and according to specific conditions. But the law authorizes any woman who is ten weeks pregnant or less to request a physician for an abortion if she believes pregnancy or childbirth will create hardship. Moreover, at any stage of pregnancy, right up to the moment of birth, abortion is lawful if two physicians, one of them from an official list, certify that continuation of pregnancy would put the woman's health gravely in peril, or that there is a strong possibility that the child would suffer from an incurable condition.

The French abortion law imposes numerous conditions on all abortions. Attending physicians must inform women of the medical risks of abortion and give them an official guide to the forms of assistance available to families, mothers, and children, and to relevant social service organizations. Women must then consult one of the listed social services. Women wishing to proceed with abortion must confirm their request in writing, after a one-week waiting period. Abortions must be performed by physicians in a public or recognized private hospital and must be reported to the regional health authorities. Hospitals must provide women who have obtained abortions with birth control information.

— ANITA L. ALLEN

a constitutional right to privacy and may terminate their pregnancies without parental consent, but that minors may not object on constitutional grounds to parental notification requirements and waiting periods. Individual justices on the Court have argued that requiring pregnant minors to notify family members of pregnancy and abortion, in effect, gives veto powers to third parties in a way that is inconsistent with the spirit of *Roe* v. *Wade.* Yet, a majority held in *Hodgson* v. *Minnesota* (1990) that states providing a "judicial bypass procedure" may attempt to involve one or both parents in minors' abortion decision making by requiring minors or their physicians to contact parents in advance of abortion. In judicial bypass procedures, minors must be permitted to ask a judge to waive parental notification requirements. The judge is expected to waive the requirement if he or she determines that the minor is mature or that notification is not in the minor's best interests. Justices in the minority have objected that bypass procedures are unwarranted, since most minors notify parents or other responsible adults of pregnancy and abortion, and most minors seeking judicial waiver obtain it. In addition, the practical effect of mandatory notification is that some teens will delay abortion, increasing costs and medical risks. Some justices have argued that laws requiring parental involvement place minors with abusive parents or broken homes at a disadvantage and even at mortal risk.

Model of prescription

Under the models of permission and privacy, government permits some or all of the abortions women want. Under the model of prescription, government compels or virtually compels women to obtain abortions the government wants. Far-reaching compulsory abortion laws have been rare in the modern world. In the West, policymakers frown upon official and unofficial policies of mandatory abortion for poor and mentally incompetent women. Although health-care providers reportedly recommend abortion in some instances—for example, when a pregnant woman is addicted to cocaine or infected with the AIDS virus—the United States government does not officially recommend or mandate abortion for any class of pregnancy. Under a penal code adopted in 1979, Cuban law proscribes abortion performed without the permission of the woman.

In an effort to control overpopulation and protect its economy, China began adopting "planned birth" family-planning measures in 1953. These measures aggressively encourage abortion through a system of penalties and rewards. Under the Chinese constitution, both the government and individuals are responsible for the planned-birth policy. In 1974, couples were limited to two children. Since 1979 couples wishing to bear children have been authorized to have only one child, and then only after securing a government permit. To encourage compliance, abortion is offered at no cost and may entitle the woman to a two-week paid leave of absence; women who have an IUD inserted or

See Also
Coercive Policies: China's Missing Girls

a tubal ligation along with abortion may receive additional paid leave. The effect of the planned-birth policy on the abortion rate in China is not known in the West. However, female infanticide and abortion for sex selection are reported. Chinese families have reportedly resorted to infanticide and selective abortion to ensure that their one-child quota is filled by a child of the culturally preferred male sex.

Model of privacy

Under the model of privacy, the law rarely compels abortion and permits all or virtually all abortions, as long as they are performed by medically qualified persons in clinics, hospitals, or other qualified facilities. Safety is a frequent goal of legal systems characterized by the model of privacy, although safety is not necessarily suggested by "privacy" nomenclature. The former Soviet Union adopted the model of privacy on safety and privacy grounds in 1920, more than a half century before the model came to dominate understandings of U.S. law. The goal of the Soviet decree legalizing any abortion performed by a physician in a state hospital was both to keep women safe from unskilled abortionists and to secure women's freedom and equality in work, education, and marriage. In 1936, the decree was rescinded in favor of a law prohibiting abortion other than to spare the life or health of the woman or prevent transmission of an inheritable disease. The shift back to the models of prohibition and permission seems to have been motivated by concern about declining birthrates, health effects of medical abortions, and diminished regard for marriage and childbearing. But in 1955, the Soviet law moved back toward the model of privacy, again to protect women from unskilled abortionists and to give women themselves an opportunity to decide whether to become mothers (Sachdev, 1988).

In Japan, abortion has been legal since the government passed Eugenic Protection Laws in 1948 to protect women's health and deter the birth of what were considered undesirable offspring. The lack of trust by government and the medical profession in oral contraceptives has led to abortion becoming a major form of birth control in Japan. In practice, abortion is available to women upon request. The law does limit abortion, but the limitations are extremely liberal. Abortion is permitted when performed by designated physicians to avert mental and physical disease or abnormalities; when pregnancy results from violence; or when the woman's health would be impaired for physical or economic reasons. Functionally, one can view Japan as a model of privacy jurisdiction; yet women's autonomy and equality are not the express policy objectives of its liberal abortion law. Japan follows the model of permissions insofar as laws restrict abortion and have not been designed specifically to promote autonomous, private decision making.

In the United States, abortion policy since the early 1970s has been directed to women's rights. During the early 1970s, the United States and a number of other countries adopted laws approximating the model of privacy. The theory that during the first trimester abortion ought to be available without any restrictions gained popularity. In effect, it was adopted in the former East Germany in 1972, Denmark in 1973, Sweden in 1974, France in 1975, and Norway in 1978 (Sachdev, 1988; Olsnes, 1993). "Fetal viability," the point at which, in some of these countries, the interests of the woman cease to be accorded overriding weight, is variously fixed between twenty weeks and twenty-eight weeks. In Norway, under 1978 amendments to a 1975 law, a woman "shall herself make the final decision concerning termination of pregnancy provided that it is possible to perform the operation before the twelfth week of pregnancy has elapsed." After the twelfth week, abortion sought for a number of medical or social indications is available upon successful application to an "Abortion Board" (Olsnes, 1993).

In *Morgentaler et al.* v. *The Queen* (1988), the Supreme Court of Canada found by a margin of five to two that provisions of the Criminal Code infringed Section 7 of the Canadian Charter of Rights and Freedoms promising "life, liberty and security of the person." The Canadian justices argued that personal security, and with it bodily integrity, human dignity, and self-respect, were threatened by interference with reproductive choices (Morton, 1993). The Canadian legislature remains free to regulate abortion consistent with the *Morgentaler* decision. However, in 1990 a bill to restrict abortion access to women whose physicians certified a health-related need for the procedure failed. The government thereafter announced that it would not seek new abortion legislation (Morton, 1993).

In Canada, the United States, and other model-of-privacy jurisdictions, liberal abortion law permits autonomous choices about matters that profoundly affect women's bodies, lifestyles, and equality. However, it is now generally recognized that laws that decriminalize and deregulate abortion do not guarantee that every woman who desires an abortion will get one. Abortion is costly, and may or may not be covered by the health insurance of women who have insurance. The U.S. Supreme Court has repeatedly held that state and federal governments may encourage childbirth over abortion by refusing to include abortion among Medicaid and other entitlements awarded the poor. As a consequence, public funding for abortion is not available as a matter of right; publicly funded civilian and military hospitals are not required to perform abortion

"If the right of privacy means anything, it is the right of the individual, married or single, to be free from unwarranted governmental intrusion into matters so fundamentally affecting a person as the decision whether to bear or beget a child."

WILLIAM J. BRENNAN, JR.
EISENSTADT V. BAIRD, 1972

See Also

Information Disclosure

Research Studies: Why Tell a Lie?

ABORTION

Contemporary Ethical and Legal Aspects

"The right of privacy . . . is broad enough to encompass a woman's decision whether or not to terminate her pregnancy."

HARRY A. BLACKMUN
ROE V. WADE, 1973

services; and states may prohibit physicians employed by public hospitals from performing abortions.

Focus: The United States

The Constitution of the United States does not mention "abortion" by name. However, the Supreme Court has consistently held since *Roe* v. *Wade* (1973) and *Doe* v. *Bolton* (1973) that the due process clause of the Fourteenth Amendment guarantees American women a fundamental right to obtain medically safe abortions. States may not categorically ban abortion or unduly burden women's fundamental constitutional right to terminate pregnancy.

The state of Connecticut passed the first American legislation against abortion in 1821 (Garrow, 1994). At first, American law did not penalize early (pre-quickening) abortion. However, between 1827 and 1860, twenty states or territories passed statutes against abortion at all stages of pregnancy. By 1868, thirty-six states or territories had antiabortion statutes in place, enforcement of which was often lax. In 1965, all fifty states treated abortion and attempted abortion at all stages of pregnancy as felonies, subject to certain exceptions. In forty-six states and the District of Columbia, the relevant statutes explicitly permitted abortion to save the mother's life, while in two of the other four states a similar exception was recognized by the courts.

Between 1967 and early 1973, a dozen jurisdictions in the United States adopted somewhat permissive abortion laws patterned on the model legislation suggested in 1962 by the influential American Law Institute. These laws permitted abortion when performed by a licensed physician who determined that there was a substantial risk that pregnancy would seriously injure the physical or mental health of the mother; that the child would be born with grave physical or mental defect; or that the pregnancy resulted from rape or incest. Almost all of the other reforming jurisdictions nevertheless sought to strengthen the institutionalization of abortion practice by stipulating that an abortion would be lawful only if performed in an accredited hospital after approval by a committee established in the hospital for that purpose.

The decriminalization of abortion on the national level lagged behind the decriminalization of contraception. In 1965 the Supreme Court decided *Griswold* v. *Connecticut*, holding that states may not outlaw a married woman's use of birth control. The Court based its ruling on an unenumerated constitutional "right to privacy" implicit in the Bill of Rights and the Fourteenth Amendment. This same right to privacy was invoked in 1973 in *Roe* v. *Wade* to limit government interference with abortion. The right to privacy was, and is, controversial among lawyers and judges reluctant to recognize novel unenumerated rights. However, both the American Medical Association and the American College of Obstetricians and Gynecologists favored legalization of abortion. The immediate effect of *Roe* v. *Wade* and *Doe* v. *Bolton*, its simultaneously decided, lesser-known companion case, was to invalidate the laws regulating abortion in every state, except perhaps the already very permissive laws adopted in 1969 and 1970 in New York, Alaska, Hawaii, and Washington.

THE *ROE* AND *DOE* DECISIONS

Four Consequences

1. No law can restrict the right of a woman to have a physician abort her pregnancy during the first three months, or first trimester, of her pregnancy.
2. During the second trimester the abortion procedure may be regulated by law only to the extent that the regulation reasonably relates to the preservation and protection of maternal health.
3. At the point at which the fetus becomes "viable," a law may prohibit abortion, but only subject to an exception permitting abortion whenever necessary to protect the woman's life or health (including any aspects of her physical or mental health).
4. No law may require that all abortions be performed in a hospital, or that abortions be approved by a hospital committee or by a second medical opinion, or that abortions be performed only on women resident in the state concerned.

The Court in *Roe* and *Doe* concluded that the Constitution does not accord legal personhood status to the fetus. Critics of this conclusion point out that the unborn are implicitly treated as legal persons in several other areas of the law. The unborn are taken into account in the allocation of property rights and the attribution of criminal and civil responsibility. For example, the unborn can inherit property. Negligently killing or injuring a fetus can give rise to civil liability for wrongful death, wrongful birth, battery, and other torts.

Roe made clear that women were not to be ascribed a right to exclusive control over their bodies during pregnancy. Yet the case signaled that the Constitution limits the role government may play in abortion decisions. In the first decade and a half after *Roe*, the Court struck down numerous state abortion restrictions. States attempted to control abortion through advertising restrictions; zoning restrictions; record-keeping and reporting requirements; elaborate "informed consent" and physician-counseling requirements; mandatory waiting periods; bans on abortions for sex selection; the requirement of the presence of a second physician during the abortion procedure; the requirement that physicians employ methods of abortion calculated to save the lives of viable fetuses; the oversight requirement that physicians send all tissue removed during an abortion to a laboratory for analysis by a certified pathologist; the requirement that insurance companies offer at a lower cost insurance that does not cover most elective abortion; legislating a statewide information campaign to communicate an official state policy against abortion; legislating criminal sanctions for physicians who knowingly abort viable fetuses; and requirements that some or all abortions after the first trimester be performed in a hospital. However, the Supreme Court has repeatedly validated state and federal government policies that prefer childbirth to abortion by declining to pay for the abortions of poor women entitled to welfare benefits for prenatal care and childbirth.

A major reaffirmation of *Roe, Thornburgh* v. *American College of Obstetricians and Gynecologists* (1986), held that states were not permitted to indirectly prohibit abortion by encumbering the decision to seek abortion with unnecessary regulations. A series of highly publicized Court decisions handed down since 1989 appear to permit more extensive regulation of first- and second-trimester abortions than *Roe* and *Doe* seemed to contemplate. *Webster* v. *Reproductive Services* (1989) permitted legislation requiring viability testing and limits on publicly funded physician care. The Court declined in *Webster* to decide the constitutionality of the declaration in the preamble of a Missouri statute that "[the] life of each human being begins at conception," and that "unborn children have protectable interests in life, health and well being" because the state had not yet sought to limit abortion by appeal to it. Encouraged by the *Webster* decision, several states and the territory of Guam sought between 1989 and 1992 to ban or discourage abortion through aggressive new regulation and enforcement. Anticipating that the Supreme Court would welcome an opportunity to overrule *Roe* in the 1990s, Guam enacted legislation prohibiting most abortion and its advocacy. A federal judge quickly declared Guam's law unenforceable under *Roe*.

In two 1990 cases critical of *Roe, Hodgson* v. *Minnesota* and *Ohio* v. *Akron Center for Reproductive Health*, the Court upheld parental notification requirements for minors. *Rust* v. *Sullivan* (1991) upheld a federal "gag rule" statute, subsequently eliminated by Congress, prohibiting abortion counseling by physicians in federally supported facilities. *Planned Parenthood* v. *Casey* (1992) affirmed *Roe* v. *Wade* as the law of the land and invalidated spousal notification. However, the case upheld a twenty-four-hour waiting period as part of a state's "informed consent" procedures. *Casey* shed the trimester framework of *Roe*, opening the door to regulation at any stage of pregnancy. *Casey* also announced a weaker standard of review in abortion cases that promised to permit more state regulation. Under *Roe*, abortion statutes were to be struck down if they did not further a "compelling" state interest. Under *Casey*, statutes "rationally related" to a "legitimate" state interest are to be upheld, assuming they do not "unduly burden" the abortion right.

This weakening of the standard of review in abortion cases underscores that constitutional abortion law in the United States hovers uneasily between the models of permission and privacy. For this reason, it seems likely that the Supreme Court will be asked again and again to clarify the extent to which the state and federal government may restrict abortion rights.

As long as it stands, *Roe* v. *Wade* will serve to provide a national abortion law standard for the United States. Since *Roe* in 1973, several attempts have been made in both houses of the national Congress to undercut the judicial decision through legislation. One attempt, premised on the idea of "states' rights," involved legislation which, if adopted, would have established that no right to an abortion is secured by the Constitution and, therefore, that the fifty states are free to adopt restrictions on abortions. A second attempt, premised on "fetal personhood," would have expanded the definition of "person" under the due process and equal protection clauses of the Fifth and Fourteenth Amendments. The fetal personhood legislation would have declared that the right to personhood attaches from the moment of conception.

Supporters of *Roe* in Congress have attempted to legislate the holding of *Roe* through a federal statute. The Freedom of Choice Act was introduced into Congress several times after *Webster*, beginning in November 1989. Its passage by Congress would prohibit states from enacting restrictions on the right to abortion before fetal viability. A 1994 survey conducted by the Hickman-Brown Research Company found that 56 percent of those polled "strongly" or "somewhat" favored passage of a Freedom of Choice Act, while 38 percent somewhat or strongly opposed such a law. Initiatives to amend the federal constitution to include pro-life or pro-choice strictures have not advanced far beyond the drafting table.

State statutes and state constitutions are an increasingly significant source of protection for abortion rights. With *in re T.W.*, the Florida Supreme Court invalidated that state's parental consent requirement, relying upon the state constitution (T.W., 1989). As a result of this decision, Florida recognized a fundamental abortion right independent of *Roe* v. *Wade*. A Maryland referendum endorsed by voters in 1992 sim-

The country remains irreconcilably riven over what many consider the most divisive American issue since slavery.

THE NEW YORK TIMES/CBS NEWS POLL, JANUARY 16, 1998

Public opinion has shifted notably away from general acceptance of legal abortion and toward . . . a more nuanced, conditional acceptance that some call a "permit but discourage" model.

THE NEW YORK TIMES/CBS NEWS POLL, JANUARY 16, 1998

ilarly established state abortion rights not tied to the fate of *Roe* v. *Wade* in the Supreme Court.

The implications of abortion law

The liberalization of abortion law establishes rights for women who wish to terminate their pregnancies. The full implications of those rights for (1) the disposal of fetal remains and eggs fertilized in vitro; (2) the enforceability of surrogate contract; (3) the criminalization of pregnant women's conduct; and (4) organized protest at abortion sites are unclear. An important set of issues spawned by liberal regulation surrounds the disposition of fetal remains. Do women who elect to abort have a familial, proprietary, or other interest in fetal tissue remains? State statutes typically require that abortion providers dispose of fetal remains in the way physicians dispose of other excised tissues. Yet some effort has been made to treat abortion tissues and fetuses differently, either because of their possible commercial value for research into the treatment of diabetes, leukemia, Alzheimer's disease, and Parkinson's disease; or because of their possible value as lost "children." In 1984, a federal judge in Louisiana held that a statute requiring abortion providers to present patients with the option of burial or cremation was an unconstitutional burden on freedom of choice. Over 90 percent of all abortions performed in the United States, and other countries, are performed during the first trimester. The court implied that women might be discouraged from first-trimester abortions on the mistaken belief that extracted tissue would resemble a baby. American courts and legislators are unlikely to permit outright sales of abortion tissues for research purposes. Indeed, federal agency policies adopted in the 1980s declared a moratorium on the use of abortion tissues derived from elective abortions partly out of concern that women might be encouraged to abort for gain. Signaling a change in policy, in 1993, very early in his administration, Democratic President Bill Clinton issued an executive order lifting the moratorium on fetal tissue research.

Technology has spawned perplexing questions about the need to regulate the disposal of unwanted fertilized eggs and "frozen" embryos. Should abortion strictures apply? The liberal tenor of *Roe* may imply that neither pregnant women nor laboratory technicians do wrong to destroy potential life in its early stages of development. In jurisdictions where early abortion is strictly prohibited or restricted, some decision must be made about whether to regard fertilized eggs and frozen embryos as human beings or as merely potential human beings comparable to gametes. For some, extending abortion prohibitions to, for example, a frozen embryo suggests an exaggerated respect for human life. For others, failure to dignify laboratory-based potential human life with ethical and legal concern suggests an egregious want of humanity.

Hundreds of men and women have been parties to commercial surrogate motherhood contracts in recent decades. Commercial surrogacy agreements commonly obtain provisions in which the would-be surrogate undertakes that she will not obtain an abortion should she become pregnant as a result of the surrogacy transactions. In the celebrated *Baby M* case, Mary Beth Whitehead agreed in writing that she would "not abort the child once conceived" unless a physician determined it necessary to protect her health or "the child has been determined . . . to be physiologically abnormal." Although the Supreme Court of New Jersey refused to enforce the surrogacy contract in *Baby M*, other jurisdictions have not done so and face questions about the commercial alienability of constitutional abortion rights.

Another set of issues relates to the extent to which abortion rights may prevent government from intervening to enjoin or punish risky behavior by pregnant women who, for example, smoke cigarettes, consume alcohol, abuse drugs, and fail to heed medical advice. In a number of isolated cases in the United States, judges have jailed pregnant women they feared would abuse or neglect their fetuses. A somewhat different concern is the legal implications of government intervention in the event that a pregnant woman refuses a blood transfusion needed to save her life, or a cesarean delivery physicians believe to be in the best medical interest of the unborn. Some view *Roe* v. *Wade* as holding by implication that women have a broad right to control—and even abuse—their own bodies without regard to fetal well-being. Yet a plausible counterview is that *Roe* does nothing more than immunize women from prosecution for early abortions, if they choose to have them.

Abortion is controversial in many countries, and the controversy is highly politicized. Violence aimed at abortion providers has occurred both in Canada and the United States. In May 1992, a bomb blast blamed on antiabortion radicals destroyed the Morgentaler abortion clinic in Toronto. Rare in Canada, dozens of abortion clinic bombings and fires have occurred in the United States. Pro-life antiabortion activists throughout the United States have demonstrated at abortion sites to focus attention on their concerns. Generally peaceful, these demonstrations have sometimes become blockades that interfere with the ability of patients and staff to utilize facilities where abortions are believed to take place. Demonstrators have sometimes resorted to harassment, noise nuisance, property damage and violence. The shooting deaths of two Florida physicians outside abortion facilities in 1993 and again in 1994 dramatized the conflict between protesters and clinics. The United States Congress passed the Freedom of Access to Clinic Entrances Act of 1994 in an effort to assure freedom of access to reproduction services. The act makes acts of obstruction and interference at places providing reproductive services a federal offense punishable by fines and imprisonment.

Abortion rights and free-speech rights clash in the context of conflicts over abortion clinic protests. Women have a legal right to seek abortion and to protection from physical assault and harassment. But antiabortion protesters have a First Amendment right to freedom of speech and expression. In 1990, a Maryland court applying the First Amendment upheld a state law proscribing a religious protestor's "loud and unseemly" antiabortion litany. In light of First Amendment values, some federal courts have been reluctant to enjoin abortion protestors accused of actual or threatened violence on the basis of state or federal statutes, such as the Ku Klux Klan Act, not clearly enacted for that purpose. In *National Organization for Women* v. *Scheidler*, however, the Supreme Court determined that the federal Racketeer Influences and Corrupt Organizations (RICO) statute could apply to a coalition of antiabortion groups alleged to be members of a nationwide conspiracy to close abortion clinics. The alleged conspirators unsuccessfully argued that RICO applies only to conspiracies in which the alleged racketeers act for the sake of economic gain rather than out of religious, moral, or political conviction. The Court found that acts that did not generate income for alleged racketeers but that adversely affected businesses such as abortion clinics were potentially conspiratorial under the RICO statute. In sum, the practice of abortion raises numerous legal issues in the jurisdictions that permit it. Because so many oppose abortion on religious and moral grounds, abortion-related questions of legal policy will remain especially complex in the United States and other pluralistic societies. In addition, should reproductive technologies for creating, preserving, and terminating gametes and fetuses continue to proliferate, the number of legal concerns about reproductive rights and responsiblilties is as likely to expand as to contract.

— ANITA L. ALLEN

JEWISH PERSPECTIVES

The abortion question in Talmudic law begins, but does not remain, with an examination of the legal status of the fetus. For this the Talmud has a phrase, *ubar yerekh immo*; the fetus, that is, is "part of the mother," rather than an independent entity. This designation says nothing about the right of abortion; the term is found only in theoretical contexts. It defines, for example, ownership in the case of an embryo found in a purchased animal; as intrinsic to its mother's body, the embryo belongs to the buyer. On the human level, in religious conversion of a pregnant woman to Judaism, her unborn child is automatically included and requires no added ceremony.

Nor does the fetus have power of acquisition; gifts or transactions made on its behalf, except by its parents, are not binding, and it inherits from its father naturally, without transaction or legal transfer. Germane as such technical information might seem to the question of abortion, it tells us only that the fetus, in Jewish as in Roman law, has no "juridical personality" of its own.

Palestinian and Alexandrian thought

In Judaism, the morality of abortion is a function of the legal attitude to feticide, as distinguished from homicide or infanticide. The law of homicide in the Torah, in one of its several formulations (Exod. 21:12), reads: "*Makkeh ish . . .*" (One who slays a man . . .). Does "man" here include any human, say, a day-old child? Yes, says the Talmud, pairing it with another text (Lev. 24:17): *ki yakkeh kol nefesh adam* (If one slays any *nefesh adam*, any human person). The "any" is understood to include the day-old child, but the *nefesh adam* is taken to exclude the fetus in the womb, for the fetus in the womb is *lav nefesh hu*, not a person, until born. In the words of Rashi, the classic commentator (with authority of legal pronouncement) on Bible and Talmud, only when the fetus "comes into the world" is it a "person" (Sanhedrin 72b).

The basis, then, for denying capital-crime status to feticide in Jewish law is scriptural. Alongside the *nefesh adam* source-text is another basic one, in Exod. 21:22, 23: "If men strive together, and wound a pregnant woman, expelling her progeny, with no harm befalling [her], then [the offender] shall surely be punished [by fine]. But if harm befall [her], then shalt thou give life for life." The Talmud makes explicit the teaching of this passage: Only monetary compensation is exacted of him who causes a woman to miscarry. And though the abortion spoken of here is accidental, the passage is still a source for the teaching that feticide is not a capital crime. Neither murder nor accidental homicide can be expiated by monetary fine.

This fundamental passage has an alternative rendering in the Septuagint, the Greek translation of the Bible produced in the third century B.C.E. One word change there yields an entirely different statute on miscarriage. Viktor Aptowitzer's essays analyze the difference; the school of thought represented by the Septuagint he calls the Alexandrian view, as opposed to the Palestinian—that is, the Talmudic—view set forth

Whoever destroys a single life is as guilty as though he had destroyed the entire world; and whoever rescues a single life earns as much merit as though he had rescued the entire world.

THE TALMUD, MISHNA, SANHEDRIN COMPILED 6TH C. A.D.

See Also

Jewish "Pronatalism": Historical Imperatives

ABORTION

Jewish Perspectives

It was about timing that Americans expressed their clearest sense of a hierarchy of sin. 61% said abortions should be permitted during the first three months of pregnancy, up from 50% in 1982; but that support dwindled to 15% in the second three months and just 7% in the third.

THE NEW YORK TIMES/CBS NEWS POLL, JANUARY 16, 1998

See Also

Family Planning: How Influential Is Religion?

above. The word in question is *ason*, rendered above as "harm"; hence, "if no harm [i.e., death] befall [her, the mother], then shall [he] be fined. . . ." The Greek sees the word ason as "form," yielding instead something like: "If no form [to the fetus], then punishment by fine; if form, then life for a life." The "life for life" clause is thus applied to the fetus, not just the mother, and a distinction is made—as Augustine later formulated it—between *embryo informatus* and *embryo formatus*. For the latter, though not yet born, the text so rendered prescribes the death penalty (Aptowitzer, 1924).

Among the Christian church fathers, the consequent doctrine of feticide as murder was preached by Tertullian, who accepted the Septuagint, and by Jerome, whose classic Bible translation nonetheless renders this passage according to the Hebrew text official within the Church. Closer to the main body of the Jewish community, we find the Samaritans and Karaites reflecting the Alexandrian view, and more important, so does Philo, the popular first-century philosopher of Alexandria. On the other hand, Philo's younger contemporary, Josephus, bears witness to the Palestinian (*halakhic*) tradition. Aside from its textual warrant, the Palestinian is the more authentic reading, Aptowitzer declares, while the other is a later tendency, "which, in addition, is not genuinely Jewish but must have originated in Alexandria under Egyptian-Greek influence" (Aptowitzer, 1924, p. 88).

Noahide restrictions

In the rabbinic tradition, then, abortion remains a noncapital crime at worst. But a curious factor further complicates the question of the criminality of the act. One more biblical text, this one in Genesis and hence "before Sinai" and part of the Commandments of the "Descendants of Noah," served as the source for the teaching that feticide is indeed a capital crime—for non-Jews. Gen. 9:6 reads, "One who sheds the blood of man, through man [i.e., through the human court of law] shall his blood be shed." The Hebrew (*shofekh dam ha-adam ba-adam . . .*) allows for a translation of "man, in man" as well as "man, through man" (or "person, in person"). The Talmud records the exposition of Rabbi Ishmael: "What is this 'man, in man'? It must refer to a fetus in its mother's womb" (Sanhedrin 57b). The locus of this text in Genesis, standing as it does without the qualifying balance of the Exodus (Sinaitic) passage, made feticide a capital crime for the rest of the world (i.e., those not heir to the Sinaitic covenant) in Jewish law. Some modern scholars hold this exposition to be more sociological than textually inherent, representing a reaction to abuse. In view of rampant abortion and infanticide, they claim, Rabbi Ishmael expounded the above exegesis of the Genesis text in order to render judgment against the Romans.

Regardless of its rationale, this teaching associated with Rabbi Ishmael remains part of codified Jewish law, as Moses Maimonides (1135-1204), for example, formulates it: "A 'Descendant of Noah' who killed a person, even a fetus in its mother's womb, is capitally liable." His Legal Code goes on to describe the court, whose members are to be Israelites or the resident aliens themselves. The stricture, however, does not extend to lifesaving ("therapeutic") abortion nor, according to some, to abortion during the first forty days of pregnancy. Implications of this anomaly—a different law for the "Descendants of Noah"—were dealt with in a Responsum (a unit in a series of Responsa, formal answers to questions of Jewish law submitted to rabbinic authority) of the eighteenth century. "It is not to be supposed," writes Rabbi Isaac Schorr, "that the Torah would consider the embryo as a person [*nefesh*] for them [Noahides] but not a person for us. The fetus is not a person for them either; the Torah was just more severe in its practical ruling in their regard. Hence, therapeutic abortion would be permissible to them, too" (Responsa *Koach Shor*, No. 20).

In the rabbinic system, then, abortion is not murder. Nor is it more than murder, as would be the case if "ensoulment" were at issue. Talmudic discussions raise the possibility of the moment—conception, birth, postbirth—at which the soul joins the body. However, this is seen to be irrelevant to the abortion question, because the soul is immortal no matter when it enters or leaves the body. And, more important than being immortal, it is a pure soul, free of the taint of "original sin." In the words of the Talmud, cited verbatim in the Daily Prayer Book, "My God, the soul with which Thou has endowed me is pure."

Broader legal discussion

Murder (killing of the innocent) is always forbidden in Jewish law, even to save life. The three cardinal sins that call for martyrdom instead of transgression are idolatry, adultery-incest, and murder. "For all sins in the Torah, *ya-avor v'al ye-hareg* (let one transgress rather than endanger one's life). But, for idolatry, adultery, and murder—*ye-hareg v'al ya-avor* (let him surrender his life rather than transgress)." Abortion, then, would require martyrdom if it were deemed murder, and, having been removed from that category, it becomes permissible and, where indicated, even mandated. The Mishnah sets forth the basic Talmudic law in this regard:

> *If a woman has [life-threatening] difficulty in childbearing, the embryo within her should [even] be dismembered limb by limb. For, her life takes precedence over its life. Once its head (or its greater part) has emerged, it may not be touched.*

For, we may not set aside one life [nefesh] for another life. *(Mishnah, Oholot, 7:6)*

In its analysis of such provisions, the Talmud had suggested that the reason for ever permitting abortion is that the fetus may be in the category of an "aggressor," that is, its life would be forfeited under the law that permits killing a "pursuer" in order to save the intended victim. An attacker, not being innocent, forfeits protection under "Thou shalt not murder." The Talmud proceeds to dismiss this reasoning, since the fetus is quite innocent, with no malice aforethought. Also, since we cannot know "who is pursuing whom," the predicament must be deemed an "act of God"—she is "being pursued from Heaven"—and the pursuer provision cannot apply. Yet, in his great Law Code, Maimonides reintroduced the possibility, which became, incidentally, the source for Aquinas of the "aggressor" idea in the Christian tradition. Maimonides formulates the Mishnaic rule as follows:

This, too, is a (Negative) Commandment—not to "take pity" on the life of a pursuer. Therefore, the Sages ruled that when a woman has [life-threatening] difficulty in childbearing, the fetus in her womb is to be removed—either with drugs or by surgery—because it is like a pursuer seeking to kill her.

Once its head has emerged, it may not be touched, for we do not set aside one life for another; this is the natural course of the world. (Mishnah Torah, Laws of Murder and Preservation of Life, 1:9)

Commentators to Maimonides' Code suggest, in view of the obvious difference between his conclusion and that of the Talmud, that his point is the gravity of abortion. Though technically not murder, the deed is so grave that it is comparable; hence, he writes, "the fetus is *like* a pursuer."

Maternal welfare

The subsequent rabbinic tradition seems to align itself either to the right, in the direction of Maimonides, or to the left, toward Rashi, above. The first approach can be identified especially with the late Chief Rabbi of Israel, Issar Unterman, who sees any abortion as "akin to homicide" and therefore allowable only in cases of corresponding gravity, such as saving the life of the mother. This approach then builds *down* from that strict position to embrace a broader interpretation of lifesaving situations, which include a threat to her health, for example, as well as a threat to her life.

The second approach, associated with another former Chief Rabbi of Israel, Ben Zion Uziel, and oth-

PRONATALISM
Be Fruitful and Multiply

Procreation ("Be fruitful") is an affirmative commandment in the Jewish legal system, and even the neglect to father or conceive is termed "bloodshed," very much in the figurative sense. The pronatalist attitude of Judaism helps account for its abhorrence of casual abortion, not to mention the self-brutalizing effect. There may be legal sanction for recourse to abortion where necessary, but the position remains one of hesitation before the sanctity of even potential life and a pronatalist reverence for the gift of life.

Accordingly, abortion for "population control" is repugnant to the Jewish mind, as is abortion for reasons other than deeply serious ones, parallel to the gravity of the deed. Orthodox, Conservative, and Reform Jews, though different in the degree of their respective adherence to ritual law, share this attitude to the moral question. Termination of pregnancy for economic reasons is not admissible, either. Whereas taking precaution by birth control or abortion against physical threat remains a mitzvah, this is not the case when the fear is financial hardship. In the state of Israel, abortion is illegal according to its secular statutes, unless approved by a hospital committee for any of the following circumstances: age of mother, her single status, rape/incest, danger to her health, or fetal deformity, which exclude financial or other considerations. But "Just One Life"—from the Talmudic teaching that "If one saves just one life, it is as if he saved an entire world"—is an agency in the voluntary sector that provides an alternative: economic assistance and counseling for childbirth and child care.

In the Jewish community today, with a conscious or unconscious impulse to replenish ranks decimated by the European Holocaust, contemporary rabbis invoke not the more lenient but the more stringent Responsa of the earlier and later authorities. Even the permissive decisions, they point out, presupposed a natural hesitation to resort to abortion. Against a contemporary background of rights claimed for their own sake, consulted rabbis tend to move away from Rashi's position and its followers, closer to that of Maimonides and those who uphold it, allowing abortion only for the gravest of reasons.

— DAVID M. FELDMAN

Historical circumstances of . . . decimation of Jewish communities added the impulse to compensate for losses to an existing instinct to procreate.

PAGE 517

ers, assumes that no explicit prohibition against abortion exists—other than an antiprocreational one—and builds *up* from that permissive position to safeguard against indiscriminate abortion. This includes the example of Rabbi Yair Bacharach in the late seventeenth century, whose classic Responsum saw no legal bar to abortion in the case before him, but disallowed it on other grounds. The case was one of a pregnancy conceived in adultery; the woman, "in deep remorse," wanted to destroy the fruit of her sin. The author refuses to allow it, not on legal but social grounds, as a safeguard or deterrent against immorality. Other authorities in the "lenient" line disagreed on this point, reaffirming the legal sanction of abortion for the woman's welfare, whether life or health or mental health, or even avoidance of "great pain." Rabbi Jacob Emden (d. 1776) suggested the latter justification would even include the case of unmarried pregnancy, since there is no greater pain than shame.

The counsel of one rabbinic authority invoked the notion of "lifeboat ethics," whereby the lifeboat in which we all find ourselves, like Noah's Ark according to a Talmudic observation, must be kept from sinking as a result of overpopulation.

PAGE 517

The criterion in both approaches remains maternal rather than fetal welfare. A principle in these matters is *tza'ara d'gufah kadim*, that is, avoidance or prevention of "her pain should be the first consideration." The mother's welfare is primary, and hence maternal indications rather than fetal ones—or, remarkably, rather than the husband's wishes—are determinative. Rabbinic rulings on abortion are thus amenable to the following generalization: If a possibility or probability exists that a child may be born with abnormalities, and the mother seeks abortion on grounds of pity for the life of such a child, the consulted rabbi would decline permission. If, however, an abortion for that same potentially deformed child were sought on grounds of severe anguish suffered now by the mother, permission would be granted. The fate of the fetus is unknown, future, potential, part of "the secrets of God"; the mother's condition is known, she is present and asking for compassion.

In the matter of genetic diseases such as Tay-Sachs disease, rabbinic authorities recommend screening before rather than during pregnancy. (A computerized registry, called *Dor Yesharim*, allows for determination before marriage of carrier status.) This is to avoid amniocentesis after the first trimester, with possible abortion on the basis of its findings. Such abortion, for fetal rather than maternal reasons, would not ordinarily be sanctioned by Jewish law. Yet the one can blend into the other: Fetal risk can mean mental anguish for the mother; the fetal indication becomes a maternal one. The woman's welfare is thus the key to warrant for abortion. A recent rabbinic opinion on terminating a pregnancy caused by rape or incest reflects this position. Unlike "Mother Earth," which receives and fructifies seed planted by the farmer, writes Rabbi Yehudah Perilman of nineteenth-century Minsk, the woman's humanity dictates that she "not be asked to nurture seed implanted within her against her will" (Responsa *Or Gadol,* No. 31).

Implicit in the Mishnah cited above is the teaching that the rights of the fetus are secondary to the rights of the mother until the moment of birth. This principle is obscured by the contemporary phrase "right to life." In the abortion context, the issue is not right to life but right to be born. The right to be born is relative—to the welfare of the mother, for example—while the right to life, of existing persons, is absolute. "Life" may begin before birth, but prehuman life, like animal life or plant life, has a status different from human life. Rabbinic law has determined that human life begins with birth; or, to put it more aptly, life begins to be called human only at birth. This is neither a medical nor a legal judgment, but a metaphysical one, and it serves only to give the mother, who is actual, priority over the fetus, which is potential, in any mortal clash.

According to the same Mishnah, this disparity ends at the moment of birth. "Once the fetus has emerged . . . we may not set aside one life for another." Now the "sanctity of life" principle means that the infant is inviolable, regardless of supposed "quality of life" differences. A mortal clash of rights is no longer resolved in her favor; mother and newborn baby are equal from the moment of birth, and the right to continued life even of a defective child is absolute.

— DAVID M. FELDMAN

ROMAN CATHOLIC PERSPECTIVES

The following is a revision and update of the first edition article "Abortion: Roman Catholic Perspectives" by John R. Connery. The Roman Catholic tradition has always treated abortion as a serious sin. Yet Catholic teaching on abortion has not always centered on the "right to life" of the individual fetus, nor has it always viewed all abortion as homicide. For several centuries, early abortion in particular was characterized more as a sexual sin than as killing, and was condemned as an interference in the natural outcome of the reproductive process, often assuming as its context an illicit sexual liaison.

The fact that Catholic views of the precise status of the fetus as human life have changed over time, and that the church's position has a philosophical rather than a religious basis, are key to late-twentieth-century church teaching on abortion. That teaching is that the fetus must be given the benefit of the doubt, and be treated as if it were a person from conception onward. This teaching is not stated as a sectarian religious proposition, but as a humanistic and philosophical truth to be recognized in civil laws guaranteeing appropriate protection to fetal life. Although exhortations to protect life in the womb have often been supported

See Also

Population Ethics: Religious Traditions

with religious allusions (for instance, to the will of the Creator or to the image of God in humanity), the duties to continue pregnancy and to sustain infants have been grounded primarily in the "natural law," understood as a shared human morality innate to all persons and knowable by reason.

In examining the foundations and development of the Catholic position, it is important to place modern teaching in the context of changing views of women's roles in family and society. Other factors influencing debates about Roman Catholicism and abortion are the relation of scientific knowledge about the beginnings of human life to the moral status of life; the relation among civil law, morality, and the church as an institutional factor; and contraception and population, especially in international perspective.

Historical development

Although Catholic claims about abortion are not narrowly religious, certain biblical and early Christian characterizations of life in the womb no doubt have contributed to an ethos in which abortion is viewed negatively. The Hebrew Scriptures (Old Testament) did not treat the killing of a fetus as the killing of an infant (Exod. 21:22), although the Greek Septuagint translation of the Hebrew (early third century B.C.E.) adds a distinction between the formed and the unformed fetus, and presents abortion of the former as homicide. This distinction reflects the ancient Greek view (Aristotle) that the matter and form of any being must be mutually appropriate (the "hylomorphic theory"), and that the embryo or fetus could not have a human soul ("form") until the body ("matter") was sufficiently developed. Often quoting the Septuagint, patristic and medieval theologians maintained this distinction, which remained a key component of Roman Catholic discussion of abortion until at least the eighteenth century.

Contraceptive and abortifacient drugs, as well as infanticide, were certainly used widely in the ancient world, not only to conceal sexual crimes but also to limit family size and conserve property. Early Christian authors such as Tertullian, Jerome, and Augustine in the Western church, and Clement of Alexandria, John Chrysostom, and Basil in the Eastern church, repudiated these practices. They did not, however, challenge their patriarchal social context, with its requirement that female sexuality serve the good of the family and its assumption that women seeking to avoid pregnancy were usually guilty of sexual infidelity. Local councils tended to support this stand. In 303 C.E., on the Iberian Peninsula, the Council of Elvira excluded from the church for the rest of her life any woman who had obtained an abortion after adultery. In 314, the Eastern church, at the Council of Ancyra (Ankara), reduced the period of penance to ten years, although it retained the lifetime ban for voluntary homicide. Such church laws made no distinction between the formed and the unformed fetus, but Tertullian, Jerome, and Augustine considered that the sin of abortion might not be homicide until after ensoulment. (The fetus was considered by many ancient writers to receive a soul only after the body had "formed," or reached an appropriate level of development, at about three months.)

Formation of the fetus became a consideration in assigning penance in private confession during the seventh century, but it was not universally recognized in church law until the decree *Sicut ex* of Innocent III in 1211. The decree dealt with irregularity, which could be incurred for homicide. An irregularity is a canonical impediment that bars a man from receiving or exercising holy orders. Irregularities are based on defects (such as mental or physical illness) or crimes (including attempted suicide, murder, and abortion). According to the decree, irregularity would not be incurred for abortion unless the fetus was animated. Since the time of animation was identified with formation, the decree implied that only abortion of the formed fetus was considered homicide. Following Aristotle, forty and ninety days were accepted as the time of animation for the male and the female fetus, respectively. Confusion

ABORTION
What the Gospels (Don't) Say

The Gospels do not address abortion explicitly, though the infancy narratives manifest interest in the importance of the individual before birth, at least in respect of God's will for him or her in the future (Matt. 1:18-25; Luke 1:5-45). In Paul's Letter to the Galatians (5:20) and in Revelation (9:21), condemnations of magical drugs (*pharmakeia*) associated with various forms of immorality, including promiscuity and lechery, may very likely extend to abortifacients. The connection is made clear in two early Christian texts, the *Didache* and the *Epistle to Barnabas*. "'You shall not kill. You shall not commit adultery. You shall not corrupt boys. You shall not fornicate. You shall not steal. You shall not make magic. You shall not practice medicine (*pharmakeia*). You shall not slay the child by abortions (*phthora*). You shall not kill what is generated. You shall not desire your neighbor's wife' (*Didache* 2.2)" (Noonan, 1970, p. 9).

— LISA SOWLE CAHILL

Based on data provided to the Centers for Disease Control and Prevention (CDC), the abortion rate–the number of abortions per 1,000 women age 15 to 44–declined to 21 in 1994, the smallest number since 1976.

THE NEW YORK TIMES ALMANAC, 1998

See Also

Catholic Tradition: The Teaching on Contraception

arose, however, from a parallel tradition that extended the notion of homicide not only to the abortion of the unformed fetus but also to sterilization. Both traditions claimed a factual base, the one in the premise that the "man" is contained in miniature in the male seed, and the other in Aristotle's reported observation of aborted fetuses. During the Middle Ages, the distinction between formed and unformed was generally accepted, notably by Thomas Aquinas, and only the abortion of the formed fetus was classified as homicide, even in reference to sacramental penances. Earlier abortions were not murder, but they were still forbidden as serious sins because they interfered with the procreative outcome of sexual acts.

In the early fourteenth century, the Dominican John of Naples introduced an exception, subsequently accepted by several others: It would be permissible to abort the unformed fetus in order to save the life of the mother. Later theologians, particularly Thomas Sánchez (sixteenth century), used the argument of self-defense against an unjust aggressor (so characterizing the fetus) or the principle of totality (looking on the fetus as part of the mother). In 1588, Sixtus V reaffirmed a more rigid position, classifying even sterilization as homicide, and (in the decree *Effraenatam*) making excommunication a penalty of the universal church for the sin of abortion. A modification in 1591 again limited the provision to the case of the animated fetus, at either forty or ninety days. This legislation remained in effect until 1869, when Pius IX extended it to all direct abortion. Twenty years later, the Holy Office of the Vatican declared that neither craniotomy nor any other action to destroy the fetus directly would be permitted, even if without it both mother and child would die. Until that point, the exception to save maternal life had been debated by the theologians without receiving official condemnation. While theologians sought a balance of the value of the fetus with other values, especially the life of the mother, papal legislation moved toward a reinforcement of the abortion prohibition.

> *"To me the nations with legalized abortion are the poorest nations."*
>
> MOTHER TERESA
> NOBEL PEACE PRIZE ACCEPTANCE SPEECH, 1979

A moderating influence that continues today was exerted via the "principle of double effect." This principle, pertaining to acts that have both good and evil effects, permits a moral distinction between direct and indirect abortion. Only direct abortions are absolutely prohibited in official Roman Catholic teaching. Indirect (permitted) abortions are those operations that have as their primary effect the saving of the mother's life, with the death of the fetus a foreseen but not directly intended secondary effect. The classic example is the removal of the cancerous uterus of a woman who is pregnant. In this case, the death of the fetus is neither in itself the desired outcome of the intervention, nor even willed and caused as the means by which the woman's life is saved. The removal of the cancer, not the fetus, heals. Double effect may also be applied to the removal of a fallopian tube in the case of an ectopic pregnancy. The premise behind the justification of indirect abortion is that while the direct killing of an innocent human being is immoral, the woman's life is at least equal in value to that of her unborn offspring, so that she has no duty to assume serious risk to her own life in order to sustain the child.

Contemporary teaching

In his 1930 encyclical on marriage, *Casti connubii*, Pius XI affirmed the equal sacredness of mother and fetus, but condemned the destruction of the "innocent child" in the womb, who can in no way be considered an "unjust assailant." (The sticking point here, of continuing interest to moralists, is whether it is necessary to have an unjust intention to qualify as an unjust aggressor, or whether unintentionally posing an unjust danger to another is sufficient. Soldiers in war, for instance, may have noble personal intentions, yet validly be viewed by their opponents as unjust attackers.) The Second Vatican Council *(Gaudium et spes,* no. 51) referred to abortion and infanticide as "unspeakable crimes." The complex agenda of and challenges to current church teaching are well focused by the 1974 Vatican "Declaration on Abortion."

This document is a response to changed Western abortion laws, as well as to population measures in developing nations. Even as it resists these pressures, it adapts its message on abortion to cultural and legal contexts characterized by the emancipation of women and the need to control births. The document responds to the Western political value of free choice by asserting that "freedom of opinion" does not extend further than the rights of others, especially the right to life. It observes that while ensoulment has been debated historically, abortion has always been condemned. Most important, the document insists that human reason can and should recognize respect for human life as the most fundamental of all goods, and the condition of their realization. It sees modern science as confirming that human life begins with fertilization, though allowing that science can never definitively settle what is properly a philosophical question. Still, "it is objectively a grave sin to dare to risk murder" if there is doubt as to whether the fetus is fully a human person.

The "Declaration on Abortion" recognizes that pregnancy can pose serious burdens for the health and welfare of women, families, and children themselves. It advocates that individuals and nations exercise "responsible parenthood" by natural means of avoiding conception. It also exhorts "all those who are able to do so to lighten the burdens still crushing so many men and women, families and children, who are placed in situations to which in human terms there is no solu-

See Also
Teaching of John Paul II

tion" (no. 23). It excludes abortion as an answer but also concludes that what is necessary "above all" is to "combat its causes" through "political action" (no. 26). The "Declaration" anticipates later efforts, notably by the U.S. episcopacy, to advocate moral consistency on killing, in that it contrasts growing protests against war and the death penalty with the social vindication of abortion. From the standpoint of both the Vatican and the U.S. bishops, the unborn should be included within a greater respect for life in general, and be protected by more stringent social limits on killing of all kinds.

Critical debates

A major point of debate within Roman Catholicism is the level of legal compromise acceptable to those who would accord the fetus more value than does the current consensus. Following the principle that law and morality are not coterminous, some argue that a policy that encourages early abortion and restricts it to "hard cases" (e.g., threat to life or health, rape, incest, serious birth defects) could command enough broad support to justify it as a practical advance in the limitation of abortion. Advocates of a more stringent position insist that the full weight of the church's moral authority be marshaled behind a policy that would outlaw abortion altogether.

Also, can the church credibly defend its antiabortion position while disallowing the most effective forms of birth control? It is relevant to this question that many nations' aspirations to economic and cultural prosperity are plagued by limited freedom for women in marriage and family, and by increasing overpopulation. In the industrialized countries, the abortion controversy tends to focus on individual rights, either of the fetus or of the mother, with Roman Catholic proponents framing the issue in terms of a legally protectable right to life. In such nations, the church tends to address itself to the absolutization of private choice over what it sees as human life, and the trivialization of the abortion decision as it becomes a substitute for sexual responsibility and contraception.

However, the Roman Catholic church is an international organization, with a substantial or growing

QUESTIONING THE CHURCH

Three Central Issues

Among the debated questions regarding the Roman Catholic tradition on abortion are certainly the following. First, is it reasonable and scientifically sound to urge that the fetus be treated as a "person" from conception onward, especially if to do so will have dire consequences for the woman who bears it? While most Roman Catholic theologians assume a conservative attitude toward the value of prenatal life, not all accept that full value is present at the outset; rather, it increases in some developmental fashion, at least through the earlier stages. Several authors (Carol Tauer, 1984; Richard McCormick, 1984; Thomas Shannon and Allan Wolter, 1990) have pointed to the time of implantation, at about fourteen days, as a "line" after which individuality appears more settled (the possibility of "twinning" being past) and the chance of survival greatly magnified (for a discussion, see Cahill, 1993).

Second, is the equality of women, and the substantive legal, social, and material support for women and families enjoined by the "Declaration," really as high on the practical pro-life agenda of Roman Catholicism as is the enactment of punitive sanctions for abortion? A deep skepticism about whether this is so gives the "abortion rights" cry of many feminists its immense symbolic value in the struggle for gender and sexual equality. While some Catholic feminists believe that sexual self-determination and effective birth control is a better way to ensure women's liberation than recourse to a form of killing, other Catholic feminists insist that the choice to terminate pregnancy must be available to women as long as a patriarchal church and society identify women's roles as reproductive and domestic in order to constrain women's moral agency and to exclude women from the range of social participation available to men.

Third, even granted that the fetus has significant value, can and should restrictive abortion laws be kept in place—or reenacted in nations that have moved toward liberalization? John Courtney Murray (1960, ch. 7) distinguishes between law and morality. Morality in principle governs all human conduct, while law pertains to the "public order," the minimum moral requirements of healthy social functioning. Modern nations vary in the degree of restraint on abortion choice they see public order as requiring (see Glendon, 1987). Abortion policy debates, especially in more lenient systems like that of the United States, challenge Roman Catholicism to reshape the social consensus about the value of the unborn. Any legislation not backed by a consensus favoring enforcement will lead both to disrespect for the law and to the proliferation of unregulated extralegal alternatives. A precondition for a less permissive abortion consensus is the creation both of avenues other than "abortion rights" for the exercise of women's social and personal freedoms, and of social supports encouraging women and families to raise children.

— LISA SOWLE CAHILL

The rate of abortion among American women is greater than among women in many other industrialized nations.

THE NEW YORK TIMES ALMANAC, 1998

membership in, for example, Latin America, the Philippines, and Africa. In many nations, the question of women's freedom to combine family with public vocation as the context for the abortion debate is overshadowed by dire poverty; the inaccessibility of education, adequate employment, and health care; the ambiguous economic implications of a large family in rural, agricultural settings; and the radically disadvantaged position of girls and women within the family in some traditional cultures. Especially in the absence of ready access to contraception, abortion may appear to such women, to families, and even to government agencies to be a desperate but necessary means of controlling fertility. As the 1974 "Declaration on Abortion" indicates, the global Roman Catholic position on abortion must go beyond the condemnation of abortion as murder to address personal and social situations in which abortion appears as the only viable answer to deprivation or oppression.

— LISA SOWLE CAHILL

PROTESTANT PERSPECTIVES

Reviews of the history of Protestant teaching on abortion focus most often upon specific comments regarding abortion in the writings of leaders of the various church reform movements in European Christianity beginning in the sixteenth century. Several of the most effectual Reformation leaders, including Martin Luther (1483-1546) and John Calvin (1509-1564), were powerful both in reconceiving church practice and in articulating reformulations of Christian theological and ethical teaching. Consequently, for many of their followers and spiritual heirs, their teaching has remained uniquely authoritative in discerning Protestant truth claims. The formal criteria for discerning Christian truth proposed by these reformers, however, is best characterized as privileging the role of Christian scripture (usually referred to by Protestants as the Old and New Testaments) in adjudicating doctrinal and moral disputes. This primacy of scripture as theological and moral norm also characterized the teaching of most other sixteenth-century reformers, including the theological leaders of the many Anabaptist movements.

Since the sixteenth century, all dissent from authoritative Roman Catholic teaching and practice, including newly emergent Christian movements, receives the label "Protestant." The rapidly growing Pentecostal movements in Latin America, indigenous Christian movements in Asia, and the African indigenous churches that are now numerically preponderant among Christians on that continent all fall under this rubric. As a result, extreme caution needs to be exercised in characterizing "Protestant" moral teaching in any contemporary moral dilemma. Even when interpreters are familiar with very diverse Protestant cultural traditions, those who identify themselves as Protestants interpret the meaning of conformity to scriptural norms in a wide variety of ways, and reveal wide differences in biblical "hermeneutics," or principles of interpretation, of sacred texts. The diversity of hermeneutical options available accounts in part for the complexity of Protestant voices on abortion today.

Before identifying contemporary Protestant hermeneutical diversity and therefore the range of existing contemporary Protestant viewpoints on abortion, it is important to clarify the cultural roots of Protestantism that shape them.

Early Protestant views of abortion

Martin Luther's and John Calvin's theological and moral reforms were shaped by their reconceptions of both the meaning of Christian life and Christian ritual practice. Neither could be said to have proposed shifts in the foundational notions of human nature embedded in late medieval Christianity. Traditional notions of human nature, including gender and human species reproduction, were not in dispute and did not shift at the time of the Reformation. What is notable among Protestant reformers is the paucity of comment on any questions about human sexuality and reproduction, including abortion. Martin Luther, a prolific preacher and writer, did not mention abortion at all. Had he done so, he likely would have presumed its moral wrongness because he was educated as an Augustinian monk and was learned in the available theological texts of the period, including especially Sentences by the twelfth-century theologian Peter Lombard, which contained collations of opinions on abortion by earlier theologians. The lists included the judgments of many who associated abortion with sexual immorality, especially with adultery, and condemned the practice.

John Calvin also knew this authoritative tradition that explicitly condemned abortion, as his commentaries on Gen. 38:10 make clear. His remarks on Exod. 21:22 further attest that he believed abortion to be wrong morally. Modern critical biblical exegetes agree that Exod. 21:22 is the only text in Christian scripture that explicitly refers to abortion, albeit to abortion that occurs because of injury to a pregnant woman. The issue in this passage was not elective abortion. Even so, Calvin used the occasion of comment on this text to make known his view that the fetus is already a person, a matter the text does not address.

On gender, sexuality, and reproduction, these reformers maintained continuity with earlier traditions. Both Luther and Calvin also followed what they took to be early Christian theological consensus, that divine ensoulment (i.e., the point of spiritual anima-

See Also

Celibacy and the Value of Christian Marriage

tion of human beings by God) of human life occurs at conception, though not all the Protestant theologians who followed them agreed. Modern conservative historical interpreters construe Calvin and Luther's views on this point as confirming their own current belief that Protestant teaching agrees with modern papal teaching, namely, that full human life occurs at conception. Caution needs to be exercised here, however. Although the majority of Protestant theologians followed the view that ensoulment occurred when the "seed" was planted in utero, their perspectives were not developed in relation to questions about human gestation. To argue that these views speak to the value of fetal life is misleading, since their opinions were developed as aspects of the theological debate about sin and salvation, and not in relation to modern embryological understanding. In any case, Protestant ritual practice suggests that commonsense norms were in fact applied to actual fetuses. Protestants, like Roman Catholics, did not practice baptism in relation to miscarriages or aborted fetuses.

Modern Protestant views on abortion

Specific comment on abortion is rare in most Reformation traditions until the twentieth century. Perhaps in deference to the lack of biblical discussion, most reformers considered matters regarding the morality of abortion, like matters governing all sexual and reproductive behavior, to be ordered by human rational discernment. They were issues of "natural morality" rather than of revealed truth. Despite emphasis on recovering the meaning of Christian biblical tradition, Lutherans, Calvinists, and Anglicans (post-Roman Church of England adherents) maintained the view, long-standing in Western Christianity, that much moral knowledge, including the order of human sexuality and reproduction, falls within the purview of "natural" human knowledge, that is, they are matters for rational deliberation and discernment. Contrary to the trend of modern Protestant fundamentalist biblicism in discussions of abortion, most Protestant traditions tended to embrace a type of reasoning that accepted human rational (and therefore "scientific") data as relevant to these moral judgments on these issues. The Anabaptists were often exceptions methodologically, however. They sought guidance on moral issues exclusively from scripture without reference to other sources. However, Anabaptists also stressed freedom of conscience in deliberating moral dilemmas, and often resisted fixed ecclesiastical standards on questions such as abortion. Not surprisingly, contemporary Anabaptist heirs often oppose with great adamance state-prescribed policies making abortion illegal.

PROTESTANT VIEWS

Effects of the Reformation

The major impact of the Reformation in shaping Protestant attitudes on abortion is rarely mentioned in traditional historiography. The most important influence of Protestantism in the abortion debate arose from the changes in spiritual practice initiated by Reformation Christianity; these changes in turn led to a powerful shift in how socialization into Christian faith took place. Initiation into Christianity moved from a locus in the church-based penitential system to the Christian family, which gradually became the basic social unit of Christian piety. Protestant spirituality was pervasively formed by this embrace of the family as the proper site for transmission of both faith and morals. The change engendered by the Reformation overturned celibacy not only as the proper norm for clerical life but also as the norm of optimal Christian piety. The Reformation movements made the sexually monogamous, procreation-centered family both the center of their basic community and their strongest metaphor for divine blessing. For Calvinists, explicitly from the outset, and for Lutherans, Anglicans, and Anabaptists more slowly, adherence to this form of social practice came to be taught as a Christian duty. Parents were to oversee their children's successful entrance into procreative-centered marriage literally as a mandate of faith.

This shift in the structure of Christian sociology, more than any change in explicit moral teaching, shaped subsequent moral sensibilities toward abortion among Protestants. This new emphasis on the sacerdotal character of the family reinforced the appeal of Protestant Christianity in traditionalist non-European cultures as well. Both ancient Hebraic and Jewish and pre-Protestant Christian sources had at times equated procreation and biological fertility or fruitfulness as signs of divine blessing, and such pronatalist sentiments had had some influence in earlier Christian attitudes toward abortion. However, the rise of Protestantism made such sensibilities powerful in European cultures and central to modern Christian moral sensibility about reproduction. This portended a deep suspicion regarding elective abortion when the practice became widespread and safe.

— BEVERLY WILDUNG HARRISON

Among the mainline Protestant denominations, the United Methodist Church [in 1972] developed what may be the most systematic position on population ethics.

PAGE 529

Protestant denominational statements do not generally enjoy the authoritative status of Roman Catholic papal encyclicals.

PAGE 530

It is not too much to say that Protestantism possessed neither an explicitly developed tradition of moral reasoning about abortion nor any elaborated body of teaching on the ethics of so-called medical practice until well into the nineteenth century. Reproduction in Protestant communities, as in all premodern communities, was shaped by female cultural practice and midwifery until at least the very late nineteenth century. Contemporary cultural historians agree that nearly all female subcultures encouraged some means of fertility control, and that most took recourse to abortifacients (substances that induce abortions) in extreme cases. Such methods were primitive and dangerous, however, and documentation regarding the range and scope of their use is all but nonexistent. The fact that women, and not men, both comprised and knew the culture of reproduction probably limited public awareness in prevailing practices. Knowledge about available interventions in pregnancies may not have been widely shared, and such knowledge may have been quite rare among male theologians until the "medicalizing" of pregnancy and reproduction in the twentieth century. In the nineteenth century, male medical practitioners increasingly attempted to discredit midwifery, frequently on the grounds that midwives practiced abortion, but Protestant clergy in the United States showed great reluctance to support such efforts.

Many modern Protestants arrive at their judgments about the morality of abortion from a deep-seated sense that any pregnancy is intrinsically a sign of divine blessing and that to deny this is impious. So deep does the equation of fertility and divine blessing run in Protestant cultures that Western Christianity itself has strongly reinforced traditional patriarchal norms that female "nature" is centered in and fulfilled only through maternity. Today, traditional Protestant cultures (those untouched by religious pluralism) tend to experience any weighing of questions about the status of fetal life as expressing a "secular" or "antireligious" mindset.

Despite the strong pronatalist disposition of traditional Protestant spirituality, however, critical historians have also noted a certain tension between Protestant teaching on abortion and Protestant pastoral practice. Even in traditionalist Protestant cultures, where moral and theological discourse is unequivocal in condemning abortion, pastoral practice is frequently far less censorious. Scattered evidence exists that Protestant priests, pastors, and elders often treated those who had abortions or administered them with a surprising degree of compassion or even leniency. There is no evidence that the practice of abortion was deemed "an unforgivable sin," as some ancient church canons insisted, or that abortion was equated with "murder" or "unjustified killing." Even among contemporary Protestant fundamentalists, historians have observed this tension between formal moral condemnation and more permissive ecclesiastical practice. Theological and moral condemnation notwithstanding, noncelibate clergy may be in touch with many of the concrete conditions and dilemmas of pregnancy and reproduction that shape women's lives. In any case, the general stance of Protestant traditionalism and of the newer, postmodernist biblical hermeneutics is toward a degree of pastoral compassion, even if abortion is starkly condemned at the formal level.

All current available data suggest that the rate of recourse to abortion among women who are part of Christian communities that formally condemn abortion—Protestant traditionalist, Protestant fundamentalist, or Roman Catholic—is at least as great as it is among women who come from liberal Protestant and Jewish communities or who are nonpracticing with regard to religion.

The most typical contemporary Protestant attitude toward abortion remains a traditionalist, pronatalist negativity toward the practice, with a reluctant recognition that abortions do occur frequently, even within the Protestant communities of faith. Such cautious negativity is maintained without strong, elaborated moral justification, chiefly because the strong cultural ethos of the existing family-centered sociology of the Protestant churches gives this view such plausibility. Traditionalist consensus tends to break down, however, whenever Protestant communities are confronted with debates shaped by conflicts within the wider culture or from newly articulate dissent within these Protestant communities themselves. Such debate is now ongoing in all churches rooted in the continental Reformation. For the most part the debate reflects the divisions in biblical hermeneutics already mentioned.

Three newer hermeneutical positions appear in the abortion debate. First, there is a quite unprecedented biblical fundamentalist hermeneutic asserting itself in many Protestant cultural contexts. This new fundamentalism is developed particularly to resist change in issues involving gender, sexuality, family, and reproduction. On all of these issues, restoration of a premodern interpretation of sex/gender and the reproductive system is the primary goal. Human gender and sexual identity, this approach insists, are rooted in "nature" and in "divine decree" central to the presumed "biblical" message. Using both the language of natural law and tradition of the mandate of divine revelation as synonymous and as equally legitimated by scripture, the new fundamentalists contend that the essence of the biblical witness is the

See Also

Family Planning: How Influential Is Religion?

Pronatalism: Be Fruitful and Multiply

Jewish "Pronatalism": Historical Imperatives

biological-religious "givenness" of male/female nature and the revealing of the proper "telos," or end, of human sexuality. Abortion is unthinkable, a violation of all of the norms of faith and morals. This hermeneutic aims to make even the discussion of abortion taboo in Protestant theological and moral discourses, to make it literally unthinkable. This approach tends to drive from the field several generations of historical-critical study by Protestant theological liberals. Previously, liberal biblical scholarship had successfully persuaded interpreters of the Bible within mainline Protestantism that interpretation of scriptural texts had to be guided by awareness of different historical times and variations among cultures. Liberals recognized that biblical worldviews do not presuppose modern ideas about the origin and nature of the universe and its inhabitants. Such considerations undergirding previous Protestant biblical interpretation, once widely accepted, are often forgotten in the wake of the force of the new fundamentalist hermeneutic.

Second, although the new fundamentalism gains force in Protestant communities, most "oldline" Protestant denominations (rooted in Europe) remain informed by historical-critical methods of scriptural interpretation and continue to speak in a voice consistent with conclusions of the earlier liberal biblical hermeneutic. Broadly speaking, these churches acknowledge that biogenetic and other scientific knowledge must be given its due in deliberating the morality of abortion. Most concede that decisions to have abortions are justified in some cases and can be consistent with biblical faithfulness. This casts several major Protestant denominations on the side of the public policy debate that supports limited legality of abortions. Although several of the "old line" denominations have been strongly pressed by fundamentalists and traditionalists in their ranks to shift to antiabortion public-policy positions, Lutherans, Anglicans, Methodists, Presbyterians, and United Church of Christ denominations, among others, have maintained their public positions. Discussion of what may constitute "justifiable reasons" for choosing abortion is decidedly underdeveloped in such Protestant communions. A strong consensus prevails that supports abortions in cases of pregnancies due to sexual violence (rape and incest); in cases where the life or physical health of the mother is at stake; and, perhaps, in cases where prospective parents lack the spiritual and physical resources to rear an additional child. There are also important historical reasons why old-line liberal Protestant communities place a strong emphasis on "responsible parenthood," but that story is outside the scope of this article. This too is an important and largely unexamined chapter in understanding Protestant views on both family planning and abortion.

Finally, in nearly all contemporary Protestant communities/cultures, another hermeneutic for interpreting the Christian abortion tradition is emerging. It may be called a "liberationist" or even a "profeminist liberationist" principle of interpretation. Although it is still a decided minority position within formalized Protestant theological-moral discourse, this hermeneutic is influencing many, especially women. It calls upon Protestant theology and ethics to reformulate moral and religious judgments with special attention to concerns for women's well-being and in recognition that Christian teaching on gender, sexuality, and reproduction is embedded in a wider system of social control of women's lives. Acknowledging internal contradictions within scripture, a liberation hermeneutic refuses authority to culturally repressive male-supremacist readings of biblical texts and postscriptural theological interpretations. Like liberals, proponents of the emerging liberation hermeneutic represent a spectrum of convictions about what reasons might justify specific acts of abortion, but strongly concur that the Protestant Christian moral voice must actively advocate broad-based social change to enable women to shape their reproductive capacity. They contend that the moral evaluation of abortion must not be predicated on discourse that obscures women's full standing as moral agents or that fails to include realism about the historical pressures surrounding biological reproduction in women's lives. Among Protestants, only Unitarian/Universalists have adopted such a hermeneutic officially.

The contesting voices characterized here are most visible and most intense within Protestant Christian communities in the United States. However, analogous dynamics are at work in Protestant communities in other areas of the globe, as they are within Roman Catholic, Orthodox, and other religious communities. The struggle over which hermeneutical voice shall prevail in Protestant teaching on abortion remains unresolved.

— BEVERLY WILDUNG HARRISON

ISLAMIC PERSPECTIVES

Since ancient times every human society has dealt with the issue of abortion. The way each treats the issue has depended on the way each views fundamental questions of individual and societal life, such as the meaning and sanctity of human life, sexuality and gender relations, the role of marriage and family, the meaning of human freedom, and the related issues of rights and responsibilities of the individual.

The Presbyterian Church in the U.S.A. advocated voluntary planned parenthood and population limitation as early as 1965.

PAGE 529

In June 1997, the rank and file of the American Medical Association ratified their board's endorsement of the ban [against intact dilation and extraction, or "partial birth" abortion], marking the first time the AMA had taken sides on an abortion matter.

THE NEW YORK TIMES ALMANAC, 1998

ABORTION

Islamic Perspectives

RECONCILER

Trained as a physician, Ibn Rushd (or Averroës, d. 1198) was an influential Islamic philosopher whose writings reconciled Islamic and Greek thought.

The roles of medicine and law in the Islamic debate on abortion

Islam's response to abortion during the fourteen centuries of its existence has been documented mostly in the jurisprudential works of its doctors of law and the medical writings of its physicians. Islamic perspectives on abortion have been shaped directly by both its theology and its revealed law (Shari`a). Because of the centrality of the latter as a practical guide in the religious and spiritual life of Muslims, however, they depend heavily on the deliberations and ethico-legal decrees (*fatwas*) of experts whenever practical problems arise in society. The main practical role of theology is to provide the necessary spiritual and intellectual framework within which ethico-legal debates are pursued.

"Knowledge is the conformity of the object and the intellect."

AVERROËS
DESTRUCTIO DESTRUCTIONUM

Since the Divine Law of Islam refuses to make a separation between law and ethics, the traditional Muslim jurist (*faqih*) is at once an ethicist and a legal expert. The physician's duty in matters concerning abortion is to provide medical advice and recommendations befitting each individual case, as Islamic law generally permits abortion on medical and health grounds up to a certain stage of pregnancy. Close collaboration between medicine and law in Islam has generated a well-developed branch of Islamic jurisprudence that deals with many biomedical issues, including contraception and abortion.

In all cases of abortion, the physician is an important witness. The idea of the testimony of a trustworthy physician is well known in Islam, since Islamic law puts great emphasis on the idea of a trustworthy witness, whom it always defines in terms of believing in God and having a good moral character. The close rapport between medicine and law in Islam is further strengthened by the fact that this religion has produced a sizeable number of jurists who either practiced medicine or at least possessed a sound general knowledge of the subject. Ibn Rushd (known by the Latin name Averröes, d. 1198), Ibn al-Nafis (d. 1288), the discoverer of the minor circulation of the blood, Ibn Hazm (d. 1064), Fakhr al-Din Razi (d. 1209), and in more recent times, Hasan al-`Attar al-Khalwati (d. 1835), a rector of the prestigious al-Azhar University in Cairo, were some of the most famous jurists-medical practitioners. Al-Shafi`i (d. 820), the founder of one of the four Sunni schools of law, is credited in traditional sources with knowledge of medicine.

Conversely, there have been many Muslim physicians who were well versed with the philosophy of the Shari`a and the ethical teachings of the Qur'an and hadiths (i.e., recorded sayings, behavior, and actions attributed to the Prophet, and in the case of the Shi'ite branch of Islam, also to the Imams, their foremost spiritual leaders), but who were never recognized as jurists in the technical sense of the term. The most famous of these was Ibn Sina (d. 1037). These physicians were generally knowledgeable in embryology. As scholars of natural philosophy, of which psychology is a part, many of these physicians also developed a comprehensive theory of the soul that includes a treatment of the problem of identifying the stage of pregnancy when the ensoulment of the body takes place in the womb. The connection between embryology and psychology is therefore of great practical interest to Islamic law.

At ensoulment a fetus attains the legal status of a human being, with all the rights accorded by the Shari`a. Although Muslim jurists rely substantially on the Qur'an and prophetic medicine for their knowledge of embryology, they also demonstrate a positive attitude toward the scientific embryology of the philosopher-physicians, since they do not see any basic contradiction between the two sources.

The Qur'an refers more than once to the ensoulment of the human body, almost always in the context both of describing God's creation of Adam, the first ancestor of the human race, and of affirming the superiority of humans over the rest of creation, including the angels (for example, at 15:28-30). There is also a more specific reference to the ensoulment of the human fetus that is made as part of its description of the process of pregnancy and birth. The Qur'anic passage quoted perhaps most often in the abortion debate is, "We [i.e., God and his cosmic agents] have created man out of an extraction of clay [the origin of semen]; then we turn it into semen and settle it in a firm receptacle. We then turn semen into

ISLAMIC VIEWS
The Theological Context

The abortion debate in Islam takes place in a particular religious environment created by the divinely revealed teachings of the religion. These teachings are accepted by Muslims as sacred and immutable and have remained unquestioned in the debate over the centuries. The most important of these teachings concerns the meaning and purpose of human life.

Islam teaches that human life is sacred because its origin is none other than God, who is the Sacred and the ultimate source of all that is sacred. Human beings are God's noblest creatures by virtue of the fact that he has breathed his spirit into every human body, male and female, at a certain stage of its embryological development. This breathing of the divine spirit into the human fetus is called its ensoulment; it confers on the human species the status of theomorphic beings. Islam shares with Judaism and Christianity the teaching that God has created humans in his own image.

Islam teaches that a human is not just a mind-body or soul-body entity that has come into existence through an entirely physical, historical, or evolutionary process. He or she is also a spirit whose reality transcends the physical space-time complex and even the realm of the mind. This spiritual substance present in each human individual, to which Muslim philosophers and scientists refer as the most excellent part of the rational soul and which has cognitive powers to the extent of being able to know itself, God, and the spiritual realm in general, is what distinguishes humans from the rest of earthly creatures.

— OSMAN BAKAR

a clot [literally, something which clings] which we then fashion into a lump of chewed flesh. Then we fashion the chewed flesh into bones and we clothe the bones with intact flesh. Then we develop out of it another creature. So blessed be God, the best of creators" (23:12-14).

Both ancient and modern commentators on the Qur'an generally agree that the last stage in the formation of the human fetus as indicated by the phrase "develop out of it another creature" mentioned in this Qur'anic passage refers to the ensoulment of the fetus, resulting in its transformation from animal into human life. As to exactly when the ensoulment of the fetus takes place, the Qur'an does not provide any information. The prophetic hadiths contain a detailed periodization of each of the different stages of fetal growth mentioned in the Qur'an. In theology as in law, matters on which the Qur'an is either silent or held to be less explicit than the hadith, the latter takes a decisive role. Thus it is the testimony of the hadith concerning the ensoulment of the fetus that has proved decisive in the formulation of Islamic theological doctrine concerning abortion.

According to one hadith, organ differentiation in the fetus does not begin to take place until six weeks after the time of fertilization. According to another, an angel who is a divine agent of ensoulment of the fetus is sent to breathe a distinctively human soul into it after 120 days of conception have passed. In his commentary on the Qur'anic verse on human reproduction cited above, basing his views on hadiths as well as on the findings of physicians, Jalal al-Din al-Suyuti (d. 1505), an encyclopedist and author of a popular work on prophetic medicine, declared, "All wise men are agreed that no soul is breathed in until after the fourth month" (Elgood, 1962, p. 240).

If God has given a theomorphic nature to human persons and has created them in the best of molds (Qur'an, 95:4), having unique faculties not enjoyed by creatures of other species, it is not without a noble purpose. According to the Qur'an, human beings have been created to know God and to be God's servants and representatives on Earth in accordance with his own wishes as revealed to all branches of the human family through his prophets and messengers. One of the six fundamental articles of the Islamic creed is belief in a future life—not in this world of sensual experience and mental images, but in another world whose space-time complex is entirely different from the one we presently experience.

In the Qur'anic view, human life does not end with death. In reality, death is only a passage between two parts of a continuous life, namely the present and the posthumous. How we fare in that future life depends on how we conduct ourselves in this present life. By leading a spiritually, ethically, and morally healthy life in this world, we will attain salvation and prosperity in the after-death life. The previously cited verse on human conception and birth is immediately preceded by a reference to life in paradise and immediately followed by a statement on the certainty of death and resurrection. Muslims understand from this and other verses that there is a grand divine scheme for humans that they have no right to disturb. On the contrary, they are to participate fully in this cosmic scheme as helpers of God in both their capacities as his servants and representatives.

The application of Islam to population issues has been conditioned by local circumstances and customs as well as personal piety.

PAGE 510

See Also

Islamic Perspectives: Sterilization and Abortion

In contrast to the Christian and Jewish traditions, from earliest times the Islamic tradition showed acceptance of family planning and contraception.

PAGE 511

ISLAM
On Reproduction

The general implication of the Islamic teachings on the meaning and purpose of life for reproduction and abortion is clear. Although reproduction is not explicitly commanded in the Qur'an, it does appear to be encouraged. A few hadiths are explicit in their encouragement of procreation. The most popular is the hadith that says that, on the Day of Resurrection, the Prophet would be proud of the numbers of his community compared with other communities and that he admonishes his followers to reproduce and increase in number.

One can say with certainty that the general religious climate that prevailed in Muslim societies throughout the ages even until modern times is one in which procreation is encouraged and abortion very much discouraged. Cyril Elgood observes that "in Islamic countries moral approval of the practice of abortion was not readily given" (Elgood, 1970) although procurement of abortion, of which there were many cases, was not necessarily considered a criminal act. When he further says that "it is almost universally recognized by civilized nations that abortion is to be practiced only on the rarest of occasions" (Elgood, 1970, p. 240), the majority of Muslims would make the spontaneous response that this is precisely the Islamic view of abortion.

— OSMAN BAKAR

ISLAM
On Marriage and Sexuality

The Islamic view of marriage and sexuality also casts a long shadow on the abortion debate. Human reproduction should take place within the framework of the sacred institution of marriage. Islam describes marriage as "half of religion" and strongly condemns sexual relations outside of marriage. The main purpose of the institution of marriage is the preservation of the human species, although Islam also recognizes the spiritual, psychological, and socioeconomic functions of marriage. That there is indeed much more to marriage than just procreation or sexual fulfillment has been amply clarified by many classical Muslim thinkers.

One of the best treatises on the wisdom of marriage in all its dimensions was composed by the prominent jurist, theologian, and Sufi, al-Ghazzali (d. 1111). This highly influential religious scholar and critic of Aristotelian philosophy defends the permissibility of married couples' practicing contraception on the ground of their need to secure a happy marriage. He goes so far as to hold that a man who fears that his wife's bearing children might affect her health or good looks and that he might therefore begin to dislike her, should refrain from having children (Rahman, 1987). Al-Ghazzali's view clearly suggests that procreation is not the sole purpose of marriage.

— OSMAN BAKAR

Islamic teachings on methods of fertility control depend on the method used.

PAGE 511

Human reproduction, birth, and death are part of this grand divine scheme. Indeed, the Qur'anic view is that there is even a preconception phase of human existence. The Qur'an refers to a covenant between God and all the human souls in the spiritual world before the creation of this world. God addressed the souls collectively, asking them "Am I not your Lord?" Without hesitation they all bore witness to his Lordship, thus implying that God-consciousness is in the very nature of the human soul.

If Islam encourages the propagation of the human species, then it also insists that every human life be given due protection. (Abortion, however, is not considered the ending of a human life unless ensoulment of the fetus has occurred.) One of the fundamental goals of Islamic law is the protection of human life. Islam takes a serious view of the taking of human lives (except in cases that have been legitimized by the Divine Law itself) and of all acts injurious to life. One of the five basic human rights enshrined in the Shari`a is the protection by the state of every human life. The Qur'an asserts that "whosoever kills a [single] human for other than murder or other than the corruption of the earth [i.e., war], it is as though he has killed all humankind and whosoever has saved one human, it is as though he has saved all humankind" (5:35). The phrase "other than murder" in this verse refers to justifiable homicide, like self-defense and capital punishment as prescribed under the Islamic law of equality (qisas).

Islamic discussion of abortion is always related to the question of the rights and responsibilities of both the husband and the wife. One of the major issues in contemporary debate on abortion in the West concerns the rights of women to procure abortion. Islam answers the question not only by appealing to its theological doctrines on the meaning and scope of human rights and responsibilities, but also to its religious theory of conception based on revealed data and hadith teachings. The Qur'an stresses the idea that everything in the heavens and on earth belongs to God. Metaphysically speaking, humans do not own anything, not even their own bodies. It is God who has apportioned rights and responsibilities to males and females, husbands and wives, fathers and mothers. Men and women in Islam obtain their mutual rights through the arbitration of the Divine Law.

In general, Muslim jurists pay great attention to women's rights in the practice of contraception and the procurement of abortion. In the words of Basim F. Musallam, "One can speak of a classical Islamic opinion on contraception generally and consistently adopted in Islamic jurisprudence, regardless of school. This classical opinion was the sanction of coitus interruptus with a free woman provided she gave her permission" (Musallam, 1983). A "free woman" is a nonslave and married. Islamic jurisprudence treats coitus interruptus under three categories, namely (1) with a wife who is a free woman; (2) with a wife who is a slave of another party; and (3) with a man's own slave or concubine. All schools of Islamic law consider coitus interruptus permissible. The majority of them insist on the woman's consent only if she belongs to the first category, since Islamic law recognizes her basic rights to children and sexual fulfillment. No permission is needed from a slave woman. In the case of abortion, the Hanafis granted the pregnant woman the right to abort even without her husband's permission provided she has a valid reason in the eyes of the Shari`a. (The Hanafis are followers of the Islamic school of law founded by the prominent jurist Abu Hanifah and are mainly found in Turkey and the Indian subcontinent.) The Qur'anic teaching that children are not created of the man's semen alone, but of both parents together, has a bearing also on Muslim discussion of the mutual rights of husband and wife in the permissibility of abortion.

Islamic law and abortion

The Islamic view of fetal development based on the Qur'an and hadith is central to the Muslim arguments on abortion. All Muslim jurists believe that the fetus becomes a human being after the fourth month of pregnancy. Consequently, abortion is prohibited after that stage (Musallam, 1983). However, the jurists differ in their views concerning the permissibility of abortion during the first four months of pregnancy, that is, the period prior to the ensoulment of the fetus.

Jurists of the Hanafi school of law allowed abortion to be performed at any time during the four-month period. A special document compiled by 500 Hanafi

THE PROPHET

Mohammed (or Muhammad, 570?–632) spread prophetic teachings, recorded in the Koran, that became the basis of Islamic civilization.

`ulama' (religious scholars), decrees that "the woman has the right to adopt some method of obtaining abortion if quickening of the fetus has not occurred, which happens after 120 days of conception" (Abedin, 1977, p. 121).

Most Maliki jurists, by contrast, prohibit abortion absolutely. Their main argument is that although the fetus does not become a human until after its ensoulment, one should not tamper with the natural process of conception once the semen has settled in the womb, since the semen is destined for ensoulment. A minority of Maliki jurists, however, allow abortion of a fetus up to forty days old. Other schools of Islamic jurisprudence, among both Sunnis and Shi'ites, agree with the Hanafis in their tolerance of abortion, although again they differ on the specifics.

It is important to emphasize the fact that there is a specific theological and ethico-legal context in which abortion has been permitted in Islam. Abortion, at the most liberal level, has been placed by jurists in the third category, that of the allowable. Jurists have deliberated on the special conditions under which abortion is permitted, apart from the biological factor of ensoulment. They have also discussed cases of criminal abortion and types of penalties to be imposed on convicted wrongdoers.

FIVE CATEGORIES OF HUMAN ACTION

1. *wajib,* the obligatory
2. *mandub,* the recommended
3. *mubah,* the allowable
4. *makr,* the blameworthy
5. *haram,* the forbidden

Muslim jurists permit abortion mostly on medical and health grounds. One of the valid reasons often mentioned is the presence of a nursing infant. It is feared that a new pregnancy would put an upper limit on lactation. The jurists believe that if the mother could not be replaced by a wet nurse, the infant would suffer, if not die.

Contemporary Muslim society is faced with the reality that the practice of abortion is on the rise. In a number of Muslim countries, many unwanted pregnancies result from illicit sexual relations as well as from rapes. There are also related issues of birth control or family planning as a national policy, easy access to modern contraceptives, and the challenge to traditional Islamic doctrines on abortion and contraception arising from advances in genetics and biomedical technology. A well-defined Islamic response to these contemporary challenges has not yet emerged, but interest in these subjects is gaining momentum. As contemporary Muslim intellectuals and religious scholars debate these problems, traditional sources on contraception and abortion will be of immense value.

— OSMAN BAKAR

"God changes not what is in a people, until they change what is in themselves."

KORAN, 13:11

ADOLESCENTS

Adolescents in the United States, defined as persons between thirteen and eighteen, today have much greater rights to make health-care decisions than they did a generation ago.

General consent to medical procedures

Under British common law—the system by which cases decided by judges and then used as precedents were far more important than statutes enacted by Parliament, a system that the United States retained when it declared its independence—a minor was effectively a chattel of his or her parents. (A "minor" meant someone under twenty-one until the Twenty-sixth Amendment in 1971 gave voting rights to eighteen-year-olds, to whom the states then granted majority.) Child abuse was not against the law anywhere in the United States until 1903 because it interfered with parental rights of discipline. A physician who treated a minor without parental consent except in a life-threatening emergency could be liable, even in cases of a satisfactory medical outcome, to the child's father for interference with his control of his child. (Married women, until about the time of World War I, could not bring lawsuits, for themselves or for their children.)

Beginning in the early 1960s, however, physicians urged state legislators to recognize that adolescents were contributing to an epidemic of venereal disease in this country. Because adolescents knew that physicians were reluctant to treat them without parental consent, these young people were not seeking medical care. They were afraid, with cause, that parents would be

TREATING ADOLESCENTS Exceptions to Parental Consent

Children of any age (including infants) can be treated without parental consent in an emergency—"emergency" being broadly defined to include anything requiring immediate care, even if not life-threatening. Thus a two-year-old with a fracture or laceration who is brought to the emergency room by a twelve-year-old baby-sitter would be treated even if parents could not be located.

The other exception at common law—and today an exception to requirements for parental consent to treatment—is the "emancipated minor," a concept since the early days of English law. Its modern definition covers minors who are married, who are in military service, or who are not living at home and are not financially dependent on their parents. In some states minors living at home but self-supporting are considered emancipated. In almost all states unmarried minor mothers, as young as eleven or twelve, are emancipated even if they are living with their parents; and in some states pregnant minors of any age are emancipated.

Adolescents who meet the definition of emancipation in the states where they are living may consent to or refuse any medical care, buy and sell real estate, and sue or be sued without appointment of a guardian. The parent is not financially responsible for supporting the emancipated minor and is not obliged to provide any further parental care to him or her.

— ANGELA RODDEY HOLDER

See Also

Contraceptive Prevalence Rates in Islamic Countries

ADOLESCENTS

General Consent to Medical Procedures

notified of the diagnosis even if no treatment was provided, so they refused to enter the health-care system. By the end of the 1960s, all states had enacted statutes permitting treatment of minors for venereal disease without parental notification. In the early 1970s, legislatures provided the same protection for physicians who dealt with adolescents' problems involving drug and alcohol abuse. Also beginning in the 1960s, many states enacted statutes providing that minors of a given age (from fourteen to sixteen) might consent generally to medical or surgical care.

Regardless of statutory authority, however, it has been at least forty years since any court in the United States has allowed parents of a child of fifteen or older to recover damages from a physician for treating their adolescent without their consent, when consent was given by the child. Courts in these cases now uphold treatment given when the patient is mature enough to understand the medical information and to give the same sort of informed consent that would be accepted from an adult patient. This has become known as the "mature minor" rule. The decision to treat an adolescent without parental involvement, of course, depends as much on the nature of the illness and the risks of the treatment as it does on the age of the patient. Although most physicians would treat an adolescent on his or her own for a sore throat or earache, it is not likely that an oncologist would accept as a patient an adolescent with leukemia who refused to involve his or her parents.

In any case, these decisions rarely involve critical illness because hospitals, for financial reasons, refuse to admit minors without parental consent except in emergencies. Since adolescents, if they are insured, are insured as dependents on their parents' health insurance policies, the consent of the policyholders is required for nonemergency admission. Thus issues about treatment of adolescents without parental involvement almost always are confined to outpatient care given in clinics and physicians' offices where the health-care provider will accept whatever payment the young person can make on his or her own.

REFUSAL OF TREATMENT. Another issue arises when minors wish to refuse treatment that their parents wish to be provided. In the context of "necessary" medical care, when an adolescent's life is not at stake, most courts will permit the young person to decide.

Only one case has reached the appellate level in which an adolescent, a Jehovah's Witness, wished to refuse life-saving treatment. She had leukemia and needed blood transfusions, which are forbidden by her religious beliefs. The trial judge decided that the patient understood her situation, understood that she would die without treatment, and that her refusal was based on her religious convictions and not on parental

EARLY AUTONOMY

In recent decades, adolescents have had—and exercised—much greater rights to make their own health-care decisions.

coercion or fear of abuse if she consented. He therefore allowed her to refuse on the same basis that an adult would be allowed to refuse. The decision was upheld on appeal (*In the Interests of E.G.*, 1987/1989).

The limits of an adolescent's right to refuse life-saving treatment are ill-defined in law. At least one court has held that a young adolescent and her parents had no right on religious grounds to refuse treatment for her bone cancer, and ordered it provided (*Hamilton*, 1983). This situation is so rarely presented to courts—although it obviously must occur at least occasionally within the health-care system—that no one knows whether oncologists and other physicians caring for adolescents with life-threatening conditions are adept at dealing with the psychosocial issues, such as appearance, that arise with these patients, and at resolving the issue with the adolescent. How much weight should be given to a fourteen-year-old's conviction that he would rather die than lose his leg as part of the treatment of his bone cancer? Perhaps the oncologists who deal with these young people are able to resolve the issues through decisions that respect the patients' autonomy while preserving their lives. Are these adolescents treated over their objections but with parental consent, no outsider such as a judge ever knowing about it? Or are these adolescents being allowed to refuse treatment? Since no studies exist of such cases, there is no information on which to base conclusions.

"Nothing is more difficult, and therefore more precious, than to be able to decide."

NAPOLEON
MAXIMS, 1804–1815

CONFIDENTIALITY Adolescents and HIV Infection

The urgent question today about confidentiality of adolescent patients in terms of disclosures to parents concerns HIV infection. On one hand, not only is the HIV-infected young person confronted with a life-threatening problem for which he or she should receive loving support, but the cost of medications (such as AZT) to delay the onset of full-blown AIDS is usually far beyond the reach of a teenager without parental assistance and insurance coverage from the parent. On the other hand, AIDS clinics serving adolescent patients have ample evidence that, as was true about venereal disease in the 1960s, adolescents will not come for testing or for care unless they trust clinic personnel not to involve their parents. Long-term follow-up studies from New York City indicate that teenagers whose parents do not know they are HIV-positive fare as well as those whose parents are involved (Kipke and Hein, 1990). In order to get adolescents into testing and treatment, if discussions over time do not result in the adolescent's agreement to let his or her family be involved, some hospital clinics are providing these young people with free medications.

— ANGELA RODDEY HOLDER

CONFIDENTIALITY. If an adolescent is accepted for treatment without the knowledge of his or her parents, the next question is what information, if any, the parents are entitled to have. Once the young person is accepted for treatment, presumably because the physician feels confident that the patient can give informed consent, it appears that a promise of confidentiality has been given. If the physician is not comfortable dealing with the adolescent alone, then he or she should not agree to provide the treatment without parental involvement.

The statutes of most states providing for treatment of minors for venereal diseases, drug abuse, or alcohol problems without parental consent forbid disclosure to parents, without the patient's consent, that the treatment has been provided or the condition exists. Some of these statutes forbid sending a bill to the parents for the care, lest they question the adolescent about the reason for the visit to the physician or clinic.

It is likely that in any serious medical situation, from a positive pregnancy test to a diagnosis of HIV-positivity, physicians and nurses urge adolescents to tell their parents and agree to help them do it. It is also likely that, confronted with a crisis, most adolescents eventually agree to involve a family member. Physicians and nurses who care for adolescents, however, know that for the remainder, "My father will kill me" may not be hyperbole. Moreover, adolescents in problematic, unsupportive families will not seek care unless they know that their confidences will be protected.

◆ **contraception**
Devices that prevent conception, including sterilization.

◆ **abortion**
Any termination of a pregnancy by medical, surgical, or natural means.

CONTRACEPTION. In 1965 the U.S. Supreme Court held that state statutes forbidding the prescription of contraceptives to a married woman violated her and her husband's constitutional right of privacy. In 1972 the Court applied the same rule to unmarried adults. In 1977 the Supreme Court held that minors have the same constitutional right of privacy and that state statutes making it a criminal offense to provide contraceptives to minors were unconstitutional.

Title X of the U.S. Public Health Service Act of 1970 requires that family-planning services be available at federally funded clinics without regard to age, as well as religion, race, or other attribute. In 1978 Title X was amended specifically to include adolescents, but in 1981 it was again amended to read, "To the extent practical, entities which receive grants or contracts under Title X shall encourage family participation in projects assisted under this subsection." Federal regulations were then enacted that required any entity receiving federal funds for family-planning services to notify parents within ten days that their minor daughter had received contraceptive services, but these regulations were immediately declared unconstitutional on the grounds that they violated congressional intent as expressed in the act. Thus a minor has the right to obtain contraceptive services from an entity receiving federal funds. This statute does not apply to a physician in private practice, who thus—when asked to provide contraceptives to an adolescent—is legally able to refuse on the basis of ethical objections.

ABORTION. Although recent decisions give state legislatures more power to regulate abortions than they had after *Roe* v. *Wade*, the Supreme Court has preserved the basic principles of its initial decision. The rationale of the Supreme Court in the 1973 decision was that a woman's right to privacy and her right to control her own body give her the right to decide whether to bear a child. All the women bringing the 1973 cases were adults, and the rights of minors to have abortions have been the subject of many appellate decisions since then.

Beginning in 1979 (*Bellotti* v. *Baird*) and continuing in a line of cases that has not yet resolved the issue, the Supreme Court has held that if a state wishes to enact legislation requiring parental consent to a minor's abortion, it must provide an alternative forum to per-

See Also

Trust

Communication: Shared Decision-Making

Bioethics and the Ethics of Virtue

mit the young woman to bypass the requirement by seeking approval of her choice from a judge. The judge's view of abortion is to be irrelevant—his or her role is to determine whether the young woman is sufficiently mature to make an informed decision. If she is sufficiently mature, she has a right to a court order permitting an abortion.

To put this issue in its social and ethical context, the Children's Defense Fund notes that in the United States every day twenty-seven thirteen- and fourteen-year-olds have their first baby, and thirteen sixteen-year-olds have their second child.

In discussion of a minor's right to decide about contraception or abortion, it should be remembered that an adolescent mother, no matter how immature, has always been considered emancipated for the purpose of releasing her baby for adoption, even over the objections of her parents, and parents have never been able to force a daughter to surrender the baby for adoption. In the context of discussions about minors' rights to choose to have abortions, it should also be noted that no matter how young the adolescent mother, she assumes the same responsibilities and decision-making authority for her child as a woman of twenty-five. Her parents have no obligation whatever to support or care for her baby, except in Wisconsin, where a statute imposes this obligation until the minor mother is eighteen. In many states, since she becomes emancipated by virtue of having a baby, her parents have no further obligations to support or care for her. And if they have prevented her abortion, they are legally free to expel an eleven-year-old and her infant from the family home. The compelling ethical issue in this area, which is almost never mentioned in the literature, is this dichotomy between decision making and responsibility for the long-term effects of that decision.

SEXUAL ABUSE. Most child-abuse statutes requiring mandatory reporting by health-care providers of abuse or well-founded suspicion of abuse apply to all minors. Sexual activity may, of course, constitute child abuse. If a young child "consents" to sexual activity of any sort, it is legally reportable abuse; but in the teen years, whether sexual activity—heterosexual or homosexual—constitutes abuse may be much more problematic.

In 1984 the California attorney general issued an opinion that all sexual activity by children under fourteen had to be reported as child abuse, regardless of whether the minor was the victim of abuse or was engaged in voluntary sexual contact. Anyone under fourteen who was "treated for venereal disease, birth control, for pregnancy or for abortion" was to be reported as "abused." Planned Parenthood and several physicians brought suit to challenge that ruling, on the grounds that it invaded the minors' privacy rights. The Court of Appeals of California declared the ruling unconstitutional and held that child-abuse reporting laws do not require professionals who have no knowledge or suspicion that actual abuse has occurred to report such activities solely because the minor is under fourteen, if he or she indicates that the activity was voluntary, consensual, and with another minor of "similar age" *(Planned Parenthood Affiliates of California* v. *Van de Kamp, 1986).*

It should be remembered that if an adolescent is reported as abused, child-welfare agencies begin investigations with home visits. There is then no possibility that pregnancy or venereal disease (in spite of specific statutory provisions of confidentiality) will not be revealed to parents. This being the case, young teens in need of treatment for sexually related problems will usually not present themselves for medical care.

MINORS AND ABORTION

What Age Is "Too Immature"?

The rationale for state legislatures' enaction of statutes requiring parental consent or judicial bypass for abortion is the belief that young women are "too immature" to make this decision for themselves. If a girl requires parental consent to choose abortion, does she have the right to refuse an abortion her parents wish her to have? If she is "too immature" to decide for herself, and her parent or parents must agree with her decision to have an abortion in order "to protect her interests," is she also too immature to decide to have her baby and to refuse abortion if the parental assessment is that she is too young to be a mother and should abort? In the few cases where parents have tried to obtain court orders to force an adolescent daughter to have an abortion, courts have held that the girl had the right to make the decision. None of these decisions, however, have come from states with parental consent statutes.

— ANGELA RODDEY HOLDER

◆ **mature**
based on slow careful consideration; having completed natural growth and development; characteristic of or suitable to a mature individual.

Mental-health issues

CONSENT TO TREATMENT. The issue of the young person's right to seek mental-health treatment is unlikely to involve private psychotherapy, since the parent can refuse to pay the bill and in most cases a young person cannot afford it. A more practical question involves an adolescent's right of access to a com-

See Also
Sexual Development: Adolescence

> *"Children have never been very good at listening to their elders, but they have never failed to imitate them. They must, they have no other models."*
>
> JAMES BALDWIN
> NOBODY KNOWS MY NAME
> 1961

ADOLESCENT MENTAL HEALTH
Refusal of Treatment

Many forms of behavior that may seem perfectly rational to an adolescent can be interpreted by a parent as sufficiently abnormal to warrant psychiatric intervention, at least on an outpatient basis. By definition, this discussion involves those minors who would generally be considered "normal neurotics" in adult psychiatry. Such adolescents are functional and are not engaging in criminal or dangerous antisocial behavior. They have not engaged in definitive delinquent behavior and are not dangerous to themselves or others.

As discussed above, if minors have the right to consent to treatment, a court would probably hold that they have the right to refuse it. More to the point, however, as a fact of psychiatric practice, although it might be possible to subdue a teenager physically in order to remove his or her appendix, it is absolutely impossible to carry out any form of effective psychotherapy on an unwilling patient. The patient will simply refuse to discuss anything. At least one court has held that a school system violates the minor's right of privacy if it sets up a system of routine psychological evaluations in the absence of any behavior that indicates serious emotional disturbance that may require treatment.

— ANGELA RODDEY HOLDER

munity mental-health facility, a drug treatment center, or a counseling center for troubled adolescents. Community mental-health centers are probably covered by the normal rules of minor consent that apply to other medical treatment, since those institutions, most of which receive federal funds, must be careful to comply with requirements of proper licenses and credentials for all staff.

In some cases, however, treatment may be offered by caregivers without formal medical credentials. In drug rehabilitation centers, for example, many of the personnel may be former drug addicts without formal mental-health training. Although this may be a viable method of treating addiction, it complicates the issue of the legal right of the adolescent to seek care. All statutes granting adolescents specific authority to consent to medical treatment, and all cases in which these issues have been decided, have dealt with the rights of young people to receive treatment from physicians, nurses, and other heath-care providers who fall within the boundaries of "mainstream medicine." Minor treatment statutes quite specifically refer to treatment given by physicians. Although there are no cases on the point, it is unlikely that courts would extend these rights of consent to encompass an unemancipated minor's right to seek treatment from a chiropractor; it is even more unlikely that a court would hold that an adolescent's right to consent to care would apply to situations where the minor would choose to consult an alternative healer such as a naturopath. Parents in many cases have been found guilty of child neglect if they refused treatment from physicians and took their children to alternative healers, so it is most improbable that the young person has the right to go to the same practitioners on his or her own. Drug-rehabilitation clinics not directed by physicians and nurses and places where therapy is provided by persons outside the credentialed health-care system, undoubtedly would be held to fall into the same category.

CONFIDENTIALITY AND PSYCHIATRIC TREATMENT. What is the psychiatrist's obligation of confidentiality to a minor patient? There are only a few state court decisions on confidentiality in regard to any right a minor may have to keep statements to physicians protected from invasion by parental curiosity.

Since young children are almost never treated outside a family-centered therapeutic situation, this conflict probably arises infrequently with them, but it does arise often with adolescent patients. In a parent-adolescent conflict, the parent and child may be genuinely adversarial parties because of the nature of their relationship, and the psychiatrist must frequently assume that anything told to the parent will be used against the child.

Some authorities seem to take the position that a psychiatrist is perfectly free to, and probably should, discuss anything she or he chooses with the parents of minor patients—from young children through adolescents—and, moreover, to discuss the situation with patients' teachers. This is a violation of any child's right of privacy and may also be questionable therapeutically. Particularly where an outside person such as a teacher is involved, merely telling the teacher that the student is in psychiatric treatment may elicit a negative attitude toward the student and may cause the fact of treatment to be entered on the permanent school record for anyone to see. Except in cases where the psychiatrist is or should be convinced that the college student, adolescent, or younger child will do harm to himself or herself or to others, the minor should have the same right of confidentiality that exists in any psychotherapeutic relationship. Thus, as would be true of any adult patient, information should be given to parents or others only with permission of the patient.

What constitutes an emergency for justified revelation to a parent or other person is, in the last analysis,

See Also

Protective Privilege and Public Peril: The *Tarasoff* Case

a matter of professional judgment; but in the past few years courts have begun to hold psychiatrists to a duty to warn potential victims if a patient communicates plans to harm them. The problem, of course, is to establish whether the patient really intends harm to others. If it is decided that a psychiatrist had reasonable cause to have thought that danger actually existed but neither committed the patient nor warned the victims and harm then occurred, the psychiatrist may be found liable in an action brought by the victims or their survivors.

A parent's right to know is less restricted than any right to know of anyone else. And the level of suspicion that something is wrong necessary for disclosure to the parent of a child should probably be far lower than in the case of a psychiatrist trying to assess a duty to warn or to divulge information involving an adult patient. If the young person is threatening suicide or injury to another person, the psychiatrist's decision to report the information to the parents should be based on a far less stringent prediction of probability than would be necessary to divulge the information to the police, the threatened victim, or anyone other than a parent.

Conclusion

The U.S. political system ignores the rights of those who cannot vote. Instead of adequate drug treatment facilities, teenagers are told, "Just say no" (even if they have already said yes and are in desperate need of help). While politicians make speeches about adolescent girls' inability to decide for themselves about abortion, many girls are on their own with their babies as two generations of throwaway children. Many political figures apparently would prefer to see adolescents die of AIDS than to have them educated about safe sex and condom use. Even with ample evidence that some mental hospitals have paid employees of high schools to bring them patients, legislators have made no change in the commitment laws for minors. While most parents attempt to love and be responsible for their children at any age, some do not. Health-care providers who treat adolescents try to respect their dignity, their autonomy, and their privacy, but the care they receive is administered within the boundaries of a society that seems to be growing increasingly hostile to their interests.

— ANGELA RODDEY HOLDER

AIDS

PUBLIC-HEALTH ISSUES

At the conclusion of *Plagues and People*, a magisterial account of epidemics and their impact on history, William McNeill asserts, "Infectious disease, which antedates the emergence of humankind, will last as long as humanity itself and will surely remain, as it has been hitherto, one of the fundamental parameters and determinants of human history" (McNeill, 1976, p. 291). In the mid-1970s, this observation seemed overdrawn, especially in relation to economically advanced societies, where chronic diseases had displaced infectious threats to communal well-being. Yet just five years later, McNeill's comment seemed prescient.

In June 1981, the first cases of what would ultimately be called acquired immunodeficiency syndrome (AIDS) were reported by the U.S. Centers for Disease Control (CDC). Within three years of the first CDC report, human immunodeficiency virus (HIV), the viral agent responsible for AIDS, was identified. Although those who were infected could experience a long disease-free state—50 percent remained symptom-free for up to ten years—in the end the virus attacked the immune system, resulting in a series of ultimately fatal opportunistic disorders. By the beginning of the 1990s, it was estimated that approximately one million Americans and ten million people worldwide were infected. Found on every continent, AIDS had made its most stunning impact on Africa. Projections by the World Health Organization forecast an even grimmer picture. By the year 2000, forty million would be infected worldwide, and the level of infection in Asia would surpass that in Africa.

Although in the first years of the epidemic there was considerable uncertainty about how AIDS was transmitted, the epidemiological picture that emerged indicated that the new disease was transmitted in a limited number of ways: during sexual intercourse—both homosexual and heterosexual; by blood-to-blood contact, for example, transfusions; by the sharing of drug injection equipment; and by pregnant women to their fetuses. Both the distribution of AIDS cases in the population (its epidemiology) and the understanding of how the virus behaved soon made it clear that AIDS was not an airborne disease. HIV could not be transmitted by casual contact.

The epidemiology of AIDS not only gave those concerned with public health an understanding of the nature of the risks posed by the new disease, it also shaped the public response to the epidemic during its formative period. Because gay and bisexual men and intravenous drug users were among those first diagnosed with AIDS in the United States and western Europe, and because they accounted for the vast majority of the cases—in Africa, however, AIDS was in most instances heterosexually acquired—the disease was quickly identified as an affliction of the socially marginal and despised. The stigma associated with all sexually transmitted diseases was thus amplified.

"I remember my youth and the feeling that will never come back any more—the feeling that I could last forever . . . "

JOSEPH CONRAD
YOUTH, 1902

◆ **AIDS**
A disease, at least moderately predictive of a defect in cell-mediated immunity, occurring in a person with no known cause for diminished resistance to that disease.

AIDS

Public-Health Issues

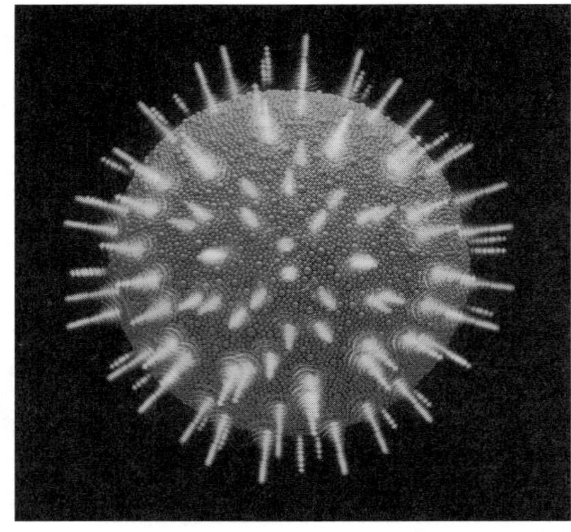

AIDS VIRUS

The human immunodeficiency virus responsible for AIDS was first identified in 1984. By 1990, the infected numbered 10 million worldwide.

Indeed, AIDS became known in the popular culture as the "gay plague" (Sontag, 1990). That stigma extended to those who became infected through blood transfusions or as a result of treatment with clotting factor, and as a result of maternal infection, even though such individuals were viewed as "innocent victims."

Stigma, reinforced by popular fears about casual transmission, was responsible for a pattern of discrimination that soon developed. Parents sought to bar children with AIDS from the classroom; employers attempted to exclude the infected, whether symptomatic or not, from the workplace; landlords sought to evict the sick from their homes. And even within the health-care system, nurses, doctors, hospitals, and nursing homes sought to avoid contact with the "new lepers." Repeated here was a pattern of social response that was no less awful because it was predictable on the basis of the history of epidemic disease.

The emergence of AIDS represented an immediate challenge to public-health officials in the advanced industrial nations, which had begun to focus their attention on chronic diseases. When the term "epidemic" was used in industrial nations, it was typically applied in a figurative manner to describe the pattern of morbidity and mortality associated with poor diet and behaviors such as smoking. Against unhealthy eating habits and smoking, the conventional public-health strategies developed to confront viral and bacteriological conditions—case finding, public-health reporting, and control—seemed inappropriate. For both pragmatic and political reasons, public-health officials instead developed campaigns of mass education designed to encourage changes of behavior.

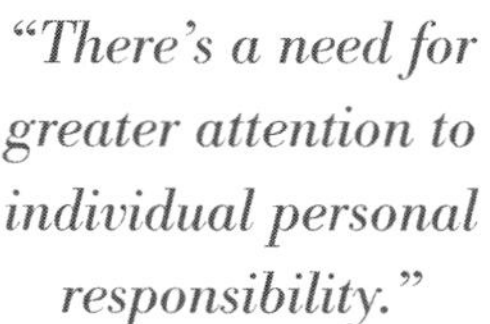

"There's a need for greater attention to individual personal responsibility."

DANIEL ZINGALE
EXECUTIVE DIRECTOR, AIDS ACTION
NEW YORK TIMES, FEBRUARY 9, 1998

Confronted with AIDS, a disease at once viral and behavioral, those responsible for the public health had to determine whether the strategies historically used in the face of epidemic disease, or those interventions associated with the control of chronic conditions, would be more effective against the epidemic of HIV infection. Would the strategy of control, with its reliance on the police powers of the state, or the voluntaristic approach of mass persuasion prevail (Bayer, 1991a)?

In the United States, as well as in virtually all other liberal democracies, a determination was made to reject the traditional public-health approach to epidemic control—Sweden, with its strong paternalistic welfare state, was a striking exception (Kirp and Bayer, 1992). AIDS was typically transmitted in intimate settings between consenting adults. An incurable disease, it affected marginalized populations with deeply rooted fears of the state and its agencies. Traditional public-health strategies of control would entail intrusions on privacy and create antagonism among those whose cooperation was required to halt the spread of HIV infection. Since radical modifications in sexual and drug-using behaviors—behaviors that were the source of pleasure—were essential, it would be necessary to create a social context conducive to change. Persuasion rather than coercion was deemed the most effective approach to this daunting challenge. Respect for privacy and the pragmatics of mass behavioral change required a voluntarist approach to AIDS. The determination to reject traditional public-health measures, to embrace a posture of "HIV exceptionalism," was endorsed by public-health officials, gay leaders, proponents of civil liberties, and their generally liberal political allies (Bayer, 1991b).

AIDS education

The controversial centerpiece of the voluntarist approach to AIDS was education. What was to be the content of the education campaign? Those committed to "traditional" moral values believed that the AIDS epidemic was the result of sexual license and a social climate that tolerated drug use. The antidote was a message of conventional sexual morality: abstinence among the unmarried, fidelity within heterosexual marriage, refraining from drug use. Against this perspective, which had strong support among some political conservatives and in the highest councils of the Reagan administration, public-health officials urged a strategy of pragmatism (Shilts, 1987). It was not sexual behavior per se that increased the risk of HIV transmission, they argued, but unprotected sexual behavior. Thus they sought to promote the use of condoms among all sexually active persons. Recognizing the difficulty of discouraging drug use among the addicted, they urged drug injectors not to share syringes and needles.

With homosexual behavior illegal in half the American states—a situation that did not prevail in other liberal democracies—and drug use illicit in all the states, public-health officials were challenged repeatedly by those who interpreted this pragmatic strategy as an endorsement of illegal and immoral behaviors. Messages characterized by great timidity were often the result. Nevertheless, the virulence of the AIDS epidemic and effective leadership by public-health officials, including Surgeon General C. Everett Koop, made possible campaigns for condom use hardly imaginable in the period before the epidemic. The bluntest and most imaginative educational campaigns were undertaken by community-based gay organizations, often with public funding.

One of the most complex ethical questions posed by the educational effort to prevent the spread of HIV infection centered on what to tell infected women of childbearing age. Should they be discouraged from becoming pregnant? If pregnant, should they be encouraged to seek abortion (Arras, 1991)? HIV is transmitted from mother to fetus in 20 to 30 percent of pregnancies. From the perspective of the infected woman, the chance of having a healthy child is thus 70 to 80 percent. From the perspective of those concerned with preventing the transmission of HIV, however, the collective consequence of infected women choosing to become mothers could be many thousands of infected babies (Bayer, 1990).

When the CDC as well as many state health departments adopted a position urging infected women to postpone pregnancy, it provoked a storm of controversy. Critics charged that the recommendation to postpone pregnancy represented a radical departure from the norm of nondirective counseling that had been the ethical standard in reproductive counseling more generally. That the vast majority of infected women were poor and African-American or Hispanic only fueled the sense of outrage on the part of those who viewed the effort to discourage pregnancy as a reflection of the legacy of racism and eugenics in America.

HIV TESTING
Efforts to Protect Confidentiality

To encourage individuals to come forward for HIV testing, public-health officials placed great stress on the importance of protecting the confidentiality of the results. Immediately after the test became available, public-health officials in locales with large numbers of AIDS cases sought to encourage testing through the creation of testing sites where individuals could be screened anonymously—they did not provide their names and were identified only by a number.

While the principle of voluntary testing was endorsed by public-health officials, federal authorities responsive to conservative political pressure moved quickly to require HIV tests of all military recruits, Job Corps applicants, and those seeking to enter the foreign service. Those who were infected were to be excluded. Mandatory testing was also initiated in federal prisons. Finally, HIV testing became a condition for immigration into the United States.

— RONALD BAYER

Testing and screening for HIV infection

From 1985, when the HIV antibody test was first developed, it became the focus of controversy. The test was first intended to screen the blood supply in order to prevent the transmission of infection to transfusion recipients and those dependent upon clotting factor. It immediately became apparent that it could be used to identify those who were asymptomatic but could nevertheless transmit HIV during sexual relations, childbearing, or intravenous drug use. To those who believed such identification could play a crucial role in the strategy of prevention, the test represented an opportunity. To those who believed that identification would be used as a basis for discrimination in employment, insurance, housing, access to health care, and the right to travel, the test was viewed as a threat. Furthermore, since counseling and education about the importance of the modification of sexual and drug-use behavior were crucial regardless of one's HIV status, the test was characterized by opponents as unnecessary from the perspective of public health.

These controversies pitted gay rights advocates, proponents of civil liberties and privacy, and their political allies against public-health officials who wanted to foster widespread voluntary testing and some archconservatives who proposed extensive mandatory testing on a traditional public-health model. From among these disparate viewpoints, a consensus emerged (Bayer et al., 1986). Testing was to be undertaken only after individuals gave their specific informed consent. As part of the consent process, individuals were to be informed of the risks and benefits of testing. After testing, extensive counseling was to be given to all who were tested. The extraordinary array of protections built into this process and codified in a number of states as a matter of law was one of the hallmarks of the extent to which HIV was to be treated differently from other sexually transmitted and communicable diseases. Indeed, the requirement of specific

◆ **human immunodeficiency virus (HIV)**
A viral agent that infects the patient with a chronic illness that progresses from asymptomatic infection to AIDS.

See Also
Confidentiality
AIDS and Confidentiality
HIV/AIDS and Information Disclosure

"When a person has sex, they're not just having it with that partner, they're having it with everybody that partner has had it with for the past ten years."

OTIS RAY BOWEN
STATEMENT ON AIDS
1987

informed consent set the HIV test apart from other blood tests performed as part of diagnostic work in clinical practice.

For many clinicians, requiring specific informed consent intruded on sound diagnostic practice by creating barriers to the routine testing of those deemed by the physician to be at risk. It also represented a barrier to detecting infection in patients who could be a source of danger in case of accidents involving needle sticks or surgical mishaps. Surreptitious testing—without consent—was reported in a number of hospitals. Physicians pressed for a looser definition of consent, one that would permit routine testing on the presumption of consent. Such pressure intensified as the prospects improved for clinical intervention during the asymptomatic phase of HIV infection.

Nowhere was the pressure for unconsented testing more obvious than in the context of pediatrics (Institute of Medicine, 1991). Newborn testing had long been proposed by some pediatricians, who argued that routine testing of neonates for a host of conditions—for example, PKU—was widely viewed as good public-health practice and ethically acceptable. But until the end of the 1980s, it was possible to resist such proposals for two reasons. First, antibody testing was a poor diagnostic strategy in newborns, since all babies born to infected mothers carried maternal antibodies for up to eighteen months, regardless of whether they were truly infected. Thus, the false-positive rate was 70-80 percent. Second, there was no clinical advantage to identifying asymptomatic newborns, since there was then no therapeutic intervention that could be prescribed to all children who tested positive. Under these circumstances mandatory newborn testing would achieve little for the child. It would, on the other hand, represent mandatory surrogate screening of their mothers. As the importance of early presymptomatic treatment of infants became clear in the early 1990s, and as the capacity to identify infection improved, the case for treating HIV more like PKU became stronger.

In the proposals both for newborn testing and for more routine screening of adults, a move away from the HIV exceptionalism of the epidemic's formative decade could be seen.

Reporting

The shift toward a more traditional public-health practice also became apparent in terms of reporting the names of those with HIV infection to public-health registries. Early in the epidemic AIDS became reportable to all state health departments. Despite concern about confidentiality, this move, which required physicians and hospitals to report the names and addresses of AIDS patients—as they were required to report the names of those diagnosed with a host of other infectious conditions—provoked little controversy. Support for AIDS case reporting reflected the widespread recognition that the public-health authorities needed such information to assist in the characterization of the epidemic's course. The picture was very different with regard to asymptomatic HIV infection. Soon after the initiation of antibody testing, some public-health officials, typically those from states with few AIDS cases, called for the extension of reporting to HIV positives. These proposals provoked a storm of controversy. It was argued that such reporting would represent a profound violation of privacy and discourage individuals from coming forward for voluntary testing. The latter argument persuaded public-health officials in states with large AIDS caseloads to resist the extension of AIDS reporting to HIV. HIV became reportable in only a handful of states with few cases.

By the beginning of the 1990s, the alliance that had resisted HIV reporting had been fractured. The American Medical Association (AMA), the CDC, and increasing numbers of public-health officials had begun to press for HIV reporting. Three arguments for such a move were made. First, whatever foundation for distinguishing between HIV and AIDS had existed early in the epidemic no longer existed. Early clinical intervention in the asymptomatic state had shifted the focus of attention from full-blown AIDS to the spectrum of HIV disease. Second, it was claimed that public-health officials needed to know who had HIV infection in order to assure adequate clinical follow-up, more important in the early 1990s, when large numbers of poor African-American and Hispanic men and women were being diagnosed with HIV. Third, only with HIV reporting would it be possible to develop aggressive partner notification programs designed to reach individuals exposed to those with HIV infection. By the early 1990s, about half the states had adopted some form of HIV reporting.

Partner notification

In programs designed to treat and control sexually transmitted diseases (STDs), contact tracing has played a central role for more than five decades. Patients diagnosed with STD are urged to reveal the names of their sexual partners so that they may be examined and, if infected, treated. Contact tracing thus serves two functions: case finding and interrupting the chain of transmission. To encourage individuals to provide the names of their partners, a guarantee of absolute anonymity is provided: those who are notified are never informed of the identity of the person who provided their name. In this way, contact tracing has

See Also
Protective Privilege and Public Peril: The *Tarasoff* Case

always been voluntary and has always rested on the foundation of confidentiality.

In the early years of the AIDS epidemic, contact tracing programs designed to reach sexual partners who unknowingly may have been placed at risk were greeted with protest. Despite the long history of such programs for STDs, proposals to initiate them were deemed coercive. They were viewed as an intrusion on the privacy of the notified partner. In the absence of a therapy for HIV infection, the information provided by the public-health official was considered an unwelcome burden (Bayer and Toomey, 1992).

By the end of the first decade of the AIDS epidemic, most of the principled opposition to contact tracing had vanished, and public-health departments began to devote greater resources to such programs.

The issues raised by contact tracing are fundamentally different from those posed to the physician faced with an infected patient who makes clear the intention not to inform sexual partners of that fact. Does the duty to protect confidentiality take precedence over the obligation to protect unsuspecting partners? (Dickens, 1990). If a duty to protect exists, it requires that the clinician act despite the preferences of the patient. It may require that the identity of the threatening patient be revealed to the endangered party. Thus, the duty to warn is in all fundamental respects different from voluntary contact tracing.

As clinicians and public-health officials confronted this issue, they were faced with a dilemma that was starkly presented in the landmark *Tarasoff* case, in which the California Supreme Court held that a psychotherapist had a duty to protect or warn the potential victims of a violent patient. If it became known that under some circumstances clinicians would breach confidentiality, would this inhibit patient candor? Would such a reduction in candor, if it occurred, deprive clinicians of the capacity to affect patients' behavior? In short, might the duty to warn ultimately subvert the very good it was designed to achieve—enhanced public safety?

Faced with this complex situation in the context of the AIDS epidemic, many state legislatures opted to grant physicians a "privilege to disclose," thus freeing them from Tarasoff-like liability if they did not warn, as well as from liability for breaching confidentiality if they did warn. In a striking reflection of the concerns about privacy provoked by the AIDS epidemic, a number of states have prohibited physicians who do warn third parties from revealing the patient's identity to those being notified.

Criminal law and public health law

In the long history of epidemic control, quarantines have played a significant role, though the efficacy of such measures has remained a matter of some controversy (Musto, 1988). With the changing pattern of morbidity in advanced industrial nations and the availability of effective therapies, the use of quarantine all but vanished in the pre-AIDS era. Because AIDS was not casually transmitted, and because HIV transmission typically involved activities between consenting adults, only those utterly without concern for individual rights have even suggested that all HIV-infected persons be quarantined. Only Cuba has taken such a drastic measure. There, public-health officials argue that since it is impossible to know which individuals will behave responsibly, the communal health requires that all HIV-infected persons be treated as potentially dangerous (Bayer and Healton, 1989). Quarantine in the context of AIDS is thus equivalent to preventive detention.

The question of how to respond to those individuals who know themselves to be infected but who continue to place unsuspecting partners at risk is more complex (Gostin, 1989). In many ways, this was an issue that took on greater salience in the context of heterosexual transmission of HIV, when infected persons

PUBLIC-HEALTH ISSUES
From Privacy to Equity

In the epidemic's first years the central debates focused on questions of the right to privacy and its limits. As the decade progressed, increasing attention was given to assuring access to care for those in need, both the symptomatic and those infected but symptom-free. Not only was the number of individuals large, but the proportion of those who were poor, African-American, and Latino was increasing. Who would pay for such care? Would the poor be deprived of potentially life-prolonging but expensive treatments? Before these issues, early concern about the refusal of some health-care workers to treat AIDS patients (Zuger, 1991) and the discriminatory practices of many private insurers paled (Daniels, 1990). At stake was the fundamental issue of whether America's inequitable health-care system could or would help those with AIDS. As AIDS activists demanded that individuals with HIV be cared for regardless of cost, it was inevitable that questions would be raised about the equity and viability of disease-specific solutions to the crisis in American health care.

— RONALD BAYER

Sex Partners Often Silent About H.I.V.; New Survey Reveals High-Risk Behavior

NEW YORK TIMES,
FEBRUARY 9, 1998

See Also
Privacy: It's a Cultural Thing

failed to inform their unsuspecting partners of their status, or when men refused to use condoms when asked to do so.

Two approaches to this matter have been considered; one based on the use of public-health law, the other on the use of the criminal law (Field and Sullivan, 1987). From the perspective of the former, an individual who has demonstrated by past acts an unwillingness to behave in a sexually responsible way could be subject to public-health control in order to prevent future harm. As an alternative, some have proposed that individuals who have willfully or recklessly exposed their unsuspecting partners to the risk of HIV infection be subject to criminal sanctions.

Forty-one percent of those surveyed said they had become infected through the use of injected drugs.

NEW YORK TIMES, FEBRUARY 9, 1998 STUDY PUBLISHED IN ARCHIVES OF INTERNAL MEDICINE

As the first decade of the AIDS epidemic drew to a close, there had been only a few instances in the United States of efforts to control the behavior of HIV-infected individuals through the use of the public-health law, most commonly by the issuance of cease-and-desist orders to those defined as "recalcitrants." More common, although relatively rare, has been the use of the criminal law to punish individuals for such behavior. But in either case, such interventions have been widely viewed as at best marginal to the overall strategy of AIDS prevention focused on mass behavioral change through mass persuasion and individual counseling.

AIDS and the Third World

This article has focused on issues that have been of central concern to economically advanced democratic nations and, more specifically, to the United States. Yet as the next decade of the AIDS epidemic commences, it is clear that the trauma will be most severe in the Third World. There the incidence of infection remains high, but therapeutic agents now under development in the economically advanced countries move further and further out of reach. The solidarity born of a common viral threat in the early 1980s, when little could be done for the sick, whether in the United States or Africa, has been shattered. Increasingly we will witness the phenomenon of one virus but many epidemic patterns of AIDS. The fundamental moral question posed by this challenge centers on the nature and the extent of the obligations of the rich nations to those that are poor, not only to provide therapies and a vaccine, if one were to become available, but also to make available the resources to assist in the efforts to prevent the further spread of infection.

— RONALD BAYER

See Also
Blood Transfusion
AIDS and the Blood Supply

HEALTH-CARE AND RESEARCH ISSUES

This article discusses the duty of health-care workers to treat persons with human immunodeficiency virus (HIV) infection, the risk to patients from health-care workers infected with HIV, insurance coverage for HIV infection, and clinical research regarding HIV infection. HIV infection is a chronic illness that progresses from asymptomatic infection to acquired immunodeficiency syndrome (AIDS), which is defined by opportunistic infections and cancers and end-stage debilitating conditions, such as dementia and a wasting syndrome characterized by severe weight loss.

Duty to treat persons with HIV infection

Health-care workers are most likely to contract HIV infection if they injure themselves with a needle or other sharp instrument contaminated with the blood of a patient who is HIV-positive. Needle sticks are frequent and, fearing for their own safety, many physicians are reluctant to care for HIV-infected patients. The self-interest of health-care workers to avoid occupational HIV infection, however, may conflict with their professional duty and the need such patients have for medical care.

THE RISK OF OCCUPATIONAL HIV INFECTION. The risk of occupational HIV infection is small but not zero (Lo and Steinbrook, 1992). The risk of contracting HIV after a single needle-stick exposure to the blood of a seropositive patient is estimated to be 0.3 percent. The cumulative risk of occupational HIV infection depends on the health-care worker's specialty. Surgeons and operating room staff are at highest risk for occupational HIV infection; they sustain skin injuries in 1.7 percent to 6.9 percent of operations (Gerberding et al., 1990).

The magnitude of risk is only one component of a person's perception of risk. People regard familiar and voluntary risks as more acceptable than unfamiliar, involuntary, and uncertain risks, even if the latter are statistically far less likely. The risk of occupational HIV infection seems especially ominous since the progression of HIV is fatal and the virus can be transmitted to loved ones. Physicians do not have complete control over the risk because percutaneous exposure can occur despite precautions.

STRATEGIES FOR MINIMIZING OCCUPATIONAL HIV INFECTION. Threatened by a currently incurable and fatal illness, health-care workers may respond in several ways. Some advocate testing all hospitalized or surgical patients for HIV infection because it would allow health-care workers to take precautions with patients identified as seropositive. This strategy, however, has several drawbacks: results are not available in emergencies, and HIV antibody tests may be falsely negative, particularly during the early stages of the infection. In addition, mandatory testing of hospitalized or surgical patients is problematic for ethical and political reasons discussed below.

The Centers for Disease Control and Prevention (CDC) recommends universal precautions such as gloves, masks, goggles, and gowns whenever there is a risk that a health-care worker will be exposed to a patient's body fluids (CDC, 1988). Health-care workers should always use infection control procedures. However, universal precautions have some drawbacks. In areas with a low prevalence of HIV and hepatitis, the cost of supplies may be prohibitive compared with the number of cases of HIV their use would prevent. Caregivers find it difficult to be equally vigilant with all patients. Most important, universal precautions do not eliminate the risk of occupational HIV infection: gowns and gloves, even double gloves, do not protect against needlesticks and scalpel cuts.

Professional societies such as the American College of Physicians have condemned refusals to care for HIV-positive patients (Health and Public Policy Committee, 1988). One physician-philosopher has written, "To refuse to care for AIDS patients, even if the danger were much greater than it actually is, is to abnegate what is essential to being a physician. The physician is no more free to flee from danger in the performance of his or her duties than the fireman, the policeman, or the soldier" (Pellegrino, 1987, p. 1939). Some writers argue that there is a binding precedent for the profession. Throughout history many physicians have provided care to patients during epidemics, even at great personal risk.

Most clinical care does not involve invasive procedures and therefore presents little risk of occupational HIV infection. Physicians should be willing to provide such care as needed. With respect to invasive procedures, how can the patient's need for medical care and the risk to health-care workers be balanced? Health-care workers should be willing to perform invasive procedures in spite of the risk of contracting HIV infection, if the medical benefit to the patient is clearly established, highly probable, and substantial. For example, obstetricians should care for seropositive women, including performing emergency cesarean sections. However, there are some justified exceptions to the physician's moral obligation to treat. If the benefits of intervention for the patient are unproved, uncertain, or marginal, physician safety should be given more weight in management decisions.

DOCTORS REFUSING THE RISK
A Neglect of Duty?

The most effective way for physicians to reduce their risk of occupational HIV infection is not to care for persons who are infected with or at risk for HIV. Physicians commonly offer several reasons to justify their refusal to care for HIV-infected persons. First, in the absence of an established doctor-patient relationship or contractual obligations, physicians have no legal obligation to care for particular patients (Annas, 1988). The legal right to decline to care for individuals, however, is limited in many important ways, for example, in emergency situations. Employment contracts with hospitals or health maintenance organizations may oblige physicians to care for all qualified persons who seek treatment. Antidiscrimination laws may also limit the physician's right to decline care for individuals on the basis of disability or illness.

Second, some physicians claim that they should not care for HIV-infected individuals because they lack the necessary expertise. However, caring for patients who are asymptomatic or who have common opportunistic infections are within the scope of expertise of primary-care physicians. In addition, physicians who completed their training before the HIV epidemic began cannot legitimately claim their lack of knowledge as justification for not treating persons with HIV infection. After completing formal training, physicians have a professional obligation to update their knowledge and skills.

Third, some physicians argue that the risks outweigh their duty to treat patients. Being a health-care professional is an inescapable mixture of self-interest and altruism. Financial remuneration, lifestyle, prestige, and personal satisfaction are all factors in career decisions. Virtually all health-care workers also regard personal safety as a pertinent consideration.

— BERNARD LO

People with only one sexual partner were three times more likely to have told their partners than people with multiple partners.

NEW YORK TIMES, FEBRUARY 9, 1998 STUDY PUBLISHED IN ARCHIVES OF INTERNAL MEDICINE

HIV-infected health-care professionals

In 1990, publicity concerning Kimberly Bergalis, a twenty-three-year-old woman who contracted HIV infection during dental care, caused public alarm about the risk of HIV infection from health-care workers. The patient asserted that she should have been told about the dentist's HIV status: "I'm not asking that we be able to live in a risk-free world. I want people to be able to choose their risks. I didn't have a choice to walk out of the office and seek another dentist" (Lo and Steinbrook, 1992, p. 1100). The Bergalis case posed several questions: What risk do HIV-positive health-care workers present to patients? Do patients have a right to know if their health-care workers are HIV infected? Should the practice of HIV-infected health-care workers be restricted?

THE RISK OF TRANSMITTING HIV TO PATIENTS. The CDC has estimated the risk that a patient will contract HIV from a seropositive surgeon during an operation to be between 1 in 42,000 and 1 in 420,000 (Lo and Steinbrook, 1992). This risk is comparable with the risk of HIV infection after the transfusion of screened blood and less than the risk of mortality due to general anesthesia. As of early 1994, such transmission of HIV to patients has been documented only in the six cases traced to the same dentist who infected Kimberly Bergalis.

Twenty-one percent were men who said they had become infected through contact with same-sex partners; 39% said they had become infected through heterosexual contact.

NEW YORK TIMES
FEBRUARY 9, 1998
STUDY PUBLISHED IN ARCHIVES OF INTERNAL MEDICINE

The public perceives the risk of contracting HIV infection from health-care workers as much greater than the data would suggest. This risk seems especially ominous, for the reasons previously discussed. In addition, patients have no control over the risk if they do not know that a health-care worker is infected. In contrast, if informed that a surgeon is seropositive, patients can completely avoid the risk by switching care to a seronegative physician. Patients feel betrayed if a physician or dentist places them at any risk beyond that caused by their illness. Furthermore, recalling the Bergalis case, the public distrusts reassurances that patients are unlikely to contract HIV in health-care settings. Dramatic cases, however, may distort policy-making. In general, such cases lead people to overestimate the frequency of unusual events, and to downplay the long-term and indirect consequences of policies.

Strong arguments can be made for restricting the clinical activities of certain HIV-infected health-care workers (Lo and Steinbrook, 1992). The ethical principle of nonmaleficence requires that physicians avoid harming their patients. Physicians also have a duty to act in the best interests of their patients, even if they harm their own interests in the process.

The principle of respect for patient autonomy requires physicians to obtain informed consent for procedures. Physicians must generally disclose to patients information that a reasonable person would find material to the decision at hand. Even a very small risk may need to be disclosed if it is serious or if patients would find it material. Most patients would want to know that their surgeon is infected with HIV. While some patients might proceed with surgery, many would seek another surgeon or decline surgery.

Cogent arguments can also be made against broad restrictions on the clinical activities of HIV-infected health-care workers (Lo and Steinbrook, 1992). Health-care workers, like other individuals, have a right to privacy, and seropositive health-care workers should be protected from discrimination. Several HIV-infected health-care workers have been excluded from practice, even though they did not perform invasive procedures and were qualified to work.

Physicians and public health officials contend that the risk that patients will contract HIV infection is too low to justify restrictions on the work and the livelihood of seropositive health-care workers who follow infection-control precautions. Furthermore, a policy of testing health-care workers for HIV and restricting the clinical work of those who are seropositive would be counterproductive. Thus, to reduce their own risk and protect their livelihood, health-care workers might decide to avoid patients who are seropositive or who are suspected of being so. Public hospitals, which care for large numbers of HIV-infected patients, might find it impossible to recruit workers.

Justice also requires that the resources devoted to reducing the risk of nosocomial infection (an infection acquired during hospitalization) be proportionate to the expected benefits. The cost of testing all health-care workers in the United States once for HIV infection is projected to be $250 million. It would cost an estimated $50 million to prevent a single case of HIV infection (U.S. National Commission, 1992). Opponents of testing health-care workers for HIV contend that it would only divert attention and finances from combating the predominant modes of transmission: unprotected sexual intercourse and injection drug use.

Some argue that it is unfair to require health-care workers to know and disclose their HIV-antibody status to patients without allowing such workers the protection of identifying their seropositive patients. For example, the American Medical Association (AMA) advocated relaxing the requirements for informed consent for HIV-antibody testing, making HIV testing part of a routine lab workup. But such testing is not just a "routine" laboratory test because patients identified as seropositive may face subtle or overt discrimination.

Federal responses to HIV-infected health-care workers have struggled to accommodate sharply divergent interests. In July 1991, the CDC recommended restrictions on HIV-infected health-care workers who perform certain types of "exposure-prone" invasive procedures on patients (CDC, 1991). The CDC recommended voluntary HIV testing of such health-care workers, but rejected mandatory HIV testing. HIV-infected health-care workers should perform exposure-prone invasive procedures only if an expert review panel so advises and if they inform patients that they are seropositive. The CDC posed no restrictions on the clinical activities of seropositive health-care workers who do not perform exposure-prone invasive procedures, provided they comply with infection-control precautions.

The CDC guidelines provoked strong and conflicting responses (Lo and Steinbrook, 1992). Congress required states to adopt the CDC recommendations or their equivalent as a condition of receiving federal Medicare and Medicaid funds. Professional groups strongly opposed the CDC guidelines and none was willing to draw up a list of exposure-prone invasive procedures. According to the American College of Surgeons, such a list would be "irrelevant and counterproductive" because such procedures "cannot be defined in any scientific or rational way" (Lo and Steinbrook, 1992, p. 1102).

In December 1991, faced with strong opposition from health-care professionals, the CDC withdrew its plan to compile a list of exposure-prone invasive procedures. Instead, the CDC recommended that health-care workers who perform "invasive surgical, dental, or obstetric procedures" know their HIV-antibody status (Lo and Steinbrook, 1992). An expert review panel should decide on an individual basis which invasive procedures a seropositive health-care worker may or may not perform and when patients must be told that a health-care worker is infected. The focus shifted from the nature of the procedure to "the skill and technique of the individual infected health care worker and the health care worker's physical condition" (Lo and Steinbrook, 1992, p. 1102). Policies for assessing HIV-positive health-care workers on a case-by-case basis, taking into account their technique, skill, and possible impairment, are considered in compliance with CDC recommendations.

Financial barriers to health care

Financial barriers prevent many persons with HIV infection from receiving optimal medical care. The lifetime cost of care for a person with HIV infection is $119,000, based on 1991 data on charges (Hellinger, 1993).

COVERAGE OF HIV INFECTION BY SELF-INSURED EMPLOYERS. Employers and insurers may seek to control the soaring cost of health insurance by limiting coverage for HIV infection. John McGann, an employee of a small company, was diagnosed with AIDS and filed a claim under the company's group medical plan. The policy provided lifetime medical benefits of $1 million. Several months later, the company became self-insured and limited benefits for HIV-related illnesses to $5,000, while maintaining coverage for other illnesses. McGann sued, alleging discrimination. In rejecting his suit, an appeals court declared that employers have the "freedom to amend or eliminate employee benefits" in health insurance (*McGann* v. *H & H Music Company*, 1990). The court allowed self-insured employers to reduce or eliminate benefits for any particular illness, even if all other medical conditions are covered.

For employees and patients, the *McGann* ruling, while legally unimpeachable, is deeply disturbing. When people purchase health insurance their purpose is to gain access to medically needed health care. This goal is negated if self-insured employers can restrict benefits after illness strikes and a claim is filed. To some critics, the *McGann* case suggests that the current system of U.S. health insurance is untenable.

COVERAGE OF HIV INFECTION BY THIRD-PARTY INSURERS. Virtually all commercial insurers either deny coverage to individual applicants with HIV infection, or offer more expensive or more limited coverage. Under the U.S. system for health insurance, people who know that they are at high risk for illness try to purchase more coverage, while those who know they are at low risk purchase less coverage. Furthermore, those who know they are at high risk for illness try to take advantage of insurance companies that offer the most favorable rates and coverage. To ensure actuarial accuracy, insurers insist on setting higher rates for those with serious illness. Furthermore, to avoid expensive claims, insurers seek to exclude persons with high-cost conditions such as HIV infection. In a competitive market, companies that do not exclude high-risk persons will be at a disadvantage because they will enroll a disproportionately large number of high-risk applicants.

Critics of such underwriting policies, however, assert that actuarial accuracy must not be confused with moral fairness (Daniels, 1990). In order to avoid violating important social values, society in fact prohibits insurers from using certain factors in setting rates. For example, overt racial discrimination is considered so objectionable that race is not a morally acceptable variable in underwriting, even though it helps to estimate future expenditures on claims.

SHIFTING TO PUBLIC FUNDS. Ultimately, employers' and insurers' reluctance to insure persons with HIV infection increases the burden on the public sector to provide care through the Medicaid program and at public hospitals. Over one half of hospitalizations for persons with AIDS are financed by Medicaid. The proportion of costs covered by private insurance has decreased during the course of the epidemic (Green and Arno, 1990). Several factors explain this trend. The diagnosis of AIDS makes most persons presumptively eligible for Medicaid. As their disease progresses, previously employed persons cease working and lose their health insurance.

This shift to Medicaid funding causes several problems. Because of low reimbursement levels, many physicians do not accept Medicaid patients. Thus, patients who lose private insurance may also lose access to care. As a result, emergency departments and public hospitals bear a greater burden of care. In addition, because of large budget deficits, many states and counties are finding it increasingly difficult to pay for such indigent care.

Not until 1985 was a test for the presence of antibodies to the AIDS virus introduced.

PAGE 81

Self-deferral involves asking individuals who are members of high-risk groups . . . not to donate blood.

PAGE 81

THE DEFINITION OF AIDS. Earlier definitions of AIDS were criticized because the list of indicator diseases, such as opportunistic infections and cancers, did not include some major clinical syndromes, particularly in women. In January 1993, the CDC expanded the list of indicator diseases. During that year, the number of persons classified as having AIDS more than doubled under the new definition, with women, blacks, and injection drug users especially likely to be newly classified as persons with AIDS (CDC, 1994a).

The definition of AIDS has great impact on access to health care and social services. Public funds may be allocated according to the number of AIDS cases in a region. Under the older definition, persons with AIDS were eligible for extended benefits, such as Medicaid, disability, and community-based social services. It is not clear whether such benefits will be extended to persons who are labeled as having AIDS under the new CDC definition.

Exclusion of high-risk groups raises substantial problems of confidentiality and informed consent.

PAGE 82

Clinical research in HIV infection

Compound Q, a drug extracted from Chinese cucumber roots, was found in 1989 to have a strong activity against HIV in the laboratory and was touted as a therapeutic breakthrough. Frustrated by the slow pace of research conducted by the medical establishment, Project Inform, an HIV-activist group, organized its own clinical trials to evaluate Compound Q. Supplies of the drug were smuggled into the United States from China. Several participants in this underground study developed serious side effects, including seizures, coma, and death. As of May 1994, Compound Q had not been shown to be clinically effective, but its story dramatized how the hope for a cure may conflict with the need to evaluate new drugs rigorously (Lo, 1992).

Two types of errors can be made regarding unproven new therapies. On the one hand, delaying the approval of an effective new drug harms patients. On the other hand, releasing a drug that is later shown to be ineffective or unsafe is also harmful. Persons with HIV infection and their advocates may weigh these errors differently than do scientists or governmental officials. Activists and the scope of the HIV epidemic have forced society in general, and scientists in particular, to reconsider fundamental questions about clinical trials of promising new therapies (Lo, 1992).

ETHICAL QUESTIONS ABOUT CLINICAL TRIALS AND THE HIV EPIDEMIC

- Should HIV-infected participants be required to adhere to clinical protocol even if clinical group is denied access to promising new drugs and treatments?
- Is it unethical to place HIV-infected participants into a placebo group?
- Who should be excluded from clinical trials? Children? Women of childbearing age?
- What are the appropriate end points for HIV-related clinical trials? Death? Laboratory indicators?

First, what is the goal of the clinical trial? To most scientists and to the U.S. Food and Drug Administration (FDA), the goal is to determine the safety and effectiveness of new drugs. Historically, clinical research has been considered dangerous for subjects. Currently, however, many patients consider clinical trials beneficial rather than risky, because they offer promising new treatments, closer medical follow-up, and more sophisticated laboratory monitoring than does standard care (Levine et al., 1991). Participants motivated by the goal of obtaining promising new drugs may feel no obligation to follow the protocol. If they do not receive the active drug, they may drop out of the study or obtain the drug outside the clinical trial. Similarly, subjects may take other drugs not on the protocol. Such deviations from protocol undermine the clinical trial's power to determine if the drug under study is actually effective.

Second, should participants be randomly assigned to treatment and control groups? Randomized clinical trials (RCTs) are more convincing than other research designs, because randomization minimizes baseline differences between the treatment and control groups. Thus if the treatment group fares better than the control group, randomization strengthens the inference that the difference is due to the treatment and not to some confounding factor, chance, or bias. RCTs convincingly showed that HIV infection could be effectively treated with antiviral agents and prophylactic antibiotics (Lo, 1992). These new therapies were adopted as standard practice months before the results of clinical trials were published in peer-reviewed journals and scrutinized by the scientific community. In addition, these RCTs convinced physicians, federal agencies, and advocacy groups to urge that persons at risk be tested for HIV infection. Insurers have provided coverage for these therapies, and drug manufacturers have been pressured to reduce their prices. It is highly unlikely that nonrandomized trials would have been considered so conclusive.

RCTs in HIV infection, however, have been criticized because the disease is considered fatal. Some people consider it unethical to conduct any clinical trials in which some participants receive placebos rather than the promising new drugs. Moreover, they point out that in general most medical interventions have not been subjected to RCTs. In one instance,

See Also

Transfusions: The Right to Refuse

nonrandomized trials provided sufficient evidence of a drug's effectiveness in HIV infection. A randomized, placebo-controlled trial was originally planned to evaluate the antiviral drug gancyclovir in cytomegalovirus retinitis, an opportunistic infection that usually causes blindness (Lo, 1992). Advocates for persons with HIV infection complained that the natural history of the infection was so grim it was unnecessary and unethical to give patients RCTs, especially since historical controls had already demonstrated the drug's effectiveness. Furthermore, the proposed protocol would exclude patients taking other drugs. Critics protested that the proposed RCT would be unethical not only because it was unnecessary, but also because it would harm participants by denying them other therapies known to be beneficial. Ultimately, such thinking prevailed and gancyclovir was approved by the FDA without randomized trials.

Third, who should participate in clinical trials? Critics contend that access to clinical trials is inequitable. Many persons are excluded from clinical trials because there are no study sites in their geographic area. In addition, women, children, and people of color are underrepresented in clinical trials. Usually, children are restricted from clinical trials to protect them from the risks of unproven therapies. Unlike adults, children cannot give informed consent to take on such risks. The rationale for excluding women of childbearing age, particularly women who are pregnant, is to protect their developing and future children from possible long-term side effects of unproven drugs. But restricting women and children from clinical trials also harms them. They lack access to potentially beneficial therapies. In the long run, there is no rigorous information about the effectiveness of interventions in women and children.

Finally, what are the appropriate end points of clinical trials? Traditionally, clinical trials employ "hard" end points such as patient death or the development of opportunistic infections. Critics, however, object and say that using such end points needlessly prolongs research and delays the release of beneficial new therapies. Alternatively, using laboratory tests such as CD4 lymphocyte counts as surrogate end points, clinical trials can be conducted more quickly. The development of opportunistic infections is associated with a drop in CD4 counts. Drugs that increase CD4 levels may also prevent opportunistic infections. In July 1991, an FDA expert panel relied on surrogate end points in recommending that the drug didanosine be approved for marketing. Clinical trials showed increases in CD4 lymphocytes, compared with zidovudine. Data regarding the impact of the drug on hard end points were not yet available. While surrogate end points can lead to quicker approval of new drugs, they can be misleading. For example, while zidovudine causes a sustained improvement in CD4 counts, it offers no long-term clinical benefits (Concorde Coordinating Committee, 1994).

TREATMENT QUESTIONS
Access to Unproven Drugs

Persons with HIV infection and their advocates complain that the testing and release of new drugs have been delayed needlessly. Stirred by compassion for persons with HIV infection, some have urged greater access to unproven drugs. These advocates claim that informed persons with a rapidly fatal illness have a right to choose their treatments, including those of unknown safety and effectiveness. These advocates argue that it makes no sense to talk about protecting such patients from harm because they will die without treatment. Compared with ineffective standard treatment, unproven treatments at least offer patients hope and a sense of control over their illness.

Patients who are denied access to unproven therapies through the medical system may still obtain them through underground channels. In the gay community, newsletters disseminate detailed information about unproven therapies for HIV infection, and buyers' clubs import drugs from other countries. But this underground market has potential risks. The dosage and purity of drugs may be uncertain. Desperate patients may be financially exploited, and self-medication without individualized physician monitoring or advice may be dangerous.

In response to demands for greater access, the National Institutes of Health (NIH) and the FDA have established a "parallel track" to provide unproven therapies to certain persons with HIV infection outside of clinical trials. Eligible persons include those who cannot tolerate standard treatments, who have not responded to them, or who are otherwise not eligible for clinical trials of the therapy. The goal of this approach is to provide earlier access to promising but unproven drugs, while researchers conduct clinical trials. The parallel track, however, has been criticized because it facilitates the use of unproven and possibly dangerous drugs and may hinder recruitment of participants into clinical trials.

— BERNARD LO

Some lawsuits resulting from transfusion-related AIDS have led to court decisions to permit identification of donors.

PAGE 82

See Also
Rights of Patients/Clients

"It could be said that the AIDS pandemic is a classic own-goal scored by the human race against itself."

PRINCESS ANNE
IN THE DAILY TELEGRAPH U.K.
1988

HIV infection in women and children

The epidemiology and clinical picture of HIV infection in women may differ from that in men. Among women in the United States, the HIV epidemic is concentrated among women of color in inner cities along the East Coast. As of 1994, AIDS is the leading cause of death among women of reproductive age in New York and New Jersey. Women acquire HIV infection through heterosexual contact and injection drug use (CDC, 1993). The two modes of transmission are linked because heterosexual transmission occurs most commonly in women who are sexual partners of injection drug users. Worldwide, most women contract HIV infection through heterosexual sex. In parts of Africa, 30 percent of women of childbearing age are infected with HIV.

The clinical presentation of AIDS in women differs from that in men. Responding to criticisms that AIDS was being underdiagnosed in women, the CDC modified its case definitions for AIDS in 1993 to include invasive cervical cancer, which commonly occurs in women with HIV infection (CDC, 1992). Many women with HIV infection are poor and lack health insurance. As a result, they find access to care problematic and often present for medical care later in the course of their illness.

In pediatrics, the vast majority of pediatric cases of HIV infection are transmitted vertically, from mother to infant. All infants whose mothers are HIV-infected also have HIV antibodies because of passive transfer of maternal antibodies through the placenta. These maternal antibodies, which persist from fifteen to eighteen months, are detected by HIV testing at birth. However, only a minority of such infants, about 30 percent but perhaps as low as 13 percent, are themselves infected with HIV. Currently there are no additional tests that accurately determine which infants are actually infected with HIV infection and which test positive for HIV infection because antibodies from their mothers have crossed the placenta.

Conclusion

In summary, the HIV epidemic has raised new ethical and policy dilemmas and forced reconsideration of established guidelines and policies that apply to a much broader range of issues. In the future, controversies will likely occur regarding insurance coverage, the approval of promising new therapies, and mandatory HIV testing for pregnant women. In turn, these debates will have important implications for the larger issues of health-care reform, the role of the FDA in regulating new drugs, and compulsory treatment of pregnant women.

— BERNARD LO

VEXING ISSUES
Pregnancy and HIV Testing

The most difficult issues regarding the care of women with HIV infection occur when pregnant women make choices about their health care that conflict with the well-being of the fetus. Treatment of pregnant women and their newborn children with antiviral agents has been shown to lower the rate of HIV infection in the children, in addition to any medical benefits to the women (CDC, 1994b). Thus it would be desirable to identify pregnant women who are seropositive. However, HIV testing of pregnant women may harm them. Poor pregnant women, once identified as HIV-positive, often find services, such as drug addiction programs, pregnancy care, or abortion services, difficult or impossible to obtain because of discrimination. Most women consent to HIV testing when it is recommended for their own sake or for the sake of their child or fetus. Controversy occurs when they do not consent.

Screening of infants and pregnant women for HIV infection raises several difficult questions (Faden et al., 1991; Hardy, 1991). First, who should be targeted for testing? Most women with HIV infection are black and Latina/Hispanic. While epidemiologically sound, targeting women of color or their infants for HIV testing has been criticized as racist and discriminatory (Faden et al., 1991; Hardy, 1991). Screening programs for sickle-cell anemia in the 1970s illustrate problems with targeting persons according to ethnicity. Mandatory screening programs were criticized as "racist eugenic measures" (U.S. Congress, 1992, p. 259). In addition, these sickle-cell anemia screening programs were flawed because they confused sickle-cell disease with the benign carrier condition, failed to protect confidentiality, and led to job and insurance discrimination.

On the other hand, testing of women or infants at very low risk for HIV infection would not be cost-effective. Currently it is reasonable to recommend voluntary HIV testing to women with risk factors for HIV infection and to all pregnant women in high-risk geographic areas. Second, do women and children identified as seropositive have adequate access to services? Some contend that more widespread testing programs are unwarranted unless better access to services is assured. Third, is mandatory HIV testing ethically acceptable under some circumstances? To the extent that discrimination is eliminated, access to care is improved, and the benefits of treatment are demonstrated to be substantial, the arguments for mandatory HIV testing of pregnant women would be more compelling.

— BERNARD LO

B

BEHAVIOR CONTROL

Behavior control and health care

The term "behavior control" may elicit images of neurosurgical techniques that transform a person into a robot subject to the whim of the controller. In ordinary usage, however, to control is "to exercise restraining or directing influence over." "Behavior control" refers broadly to systematic attempts by an agent or institution to influence behavior. Although health-care providers and institutions routinely influence the decisions and conduct of their patients, important ethical concerns arise when they do so through methods that endanger the morally acceptable relationships between them and their patients. Thus, moral evaluation of various methods of influence requires a theory of acceptable relationships.

Advocates of various moral theories might differ regarding the defensible purposes and parameters of health-care relationships. Utilitarians, for example, endorse relationships and decision making expected to maximize happiness. Communitarians identify a community standard of the common good and promote health-care relationships expected to conform to and promote that common good. Virtue theorists advance an account of the virtuous person, endorsing health-care relationships that exemplify and promote the identified virtues.

THREE BASIC MORAL PERSPECTIVES

- utilitarian
- communitarian
- virtue theory

This article adopts the patient-centered approach to health care in order to illustrate the manner in which one mainstream theory generates standards of acceptable influence. Competing theories might produce different conclusions about certain forms of influence, but they share a common structure of analysis. Each theory provides an account of acceptable relationships between patients and providers or institutions and evaluates various modes of influence for consistency with these relationships. The patient-centered approach contemplates a process of shared decision making in which competent patients retain authority over their treatment. Providers diagnose disorders and recommend treatment, explaining the advantages and disadvantages of the available alternatives. Patients exercise a right to informed consent and the concomitant right to refuse treatment by selecting from among the options (Buchanan and Brock, 1989; *Cruzan* v. *Director, Missouri Department of Health*, 1990; Prosser and Keeton, 1984).

Patient-centered health care ordinarily promotes respect for autonomy as a right to self-determination within a sphere of personal sovereignty and conforms to the principle of beneficence, requiring that the provider actively promote the patient's well-being (Beauchamp and Childress, 1989; Feinberg, 1986). It supports autonomy because under the appropriate conditions, either informed consent or treatment refusal constitutes an exercise of personal sovereignty. It promotes well-being because fully informed patients are usually in the best position to make treatment decisions that are likely to promote their interests (Buchanan and Brock, 1989). This approach encounters a variety of difficult issues including the relative priority and weight of autonomy and well-being, the appropriate conception and criteria of informed consent, and the theory and implementation of surrogate decision making (Buchanan and Brock, 1989).

◆ **communitarian theorist**
Identifies a community standard of the common good and promotes relationships expected to conform to and promote that common good.

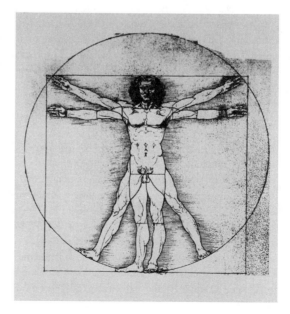

VITRUVIAN MAN
Leonardo da Vinci's famous sketch is based on the Roman architect Vitruvius's writings on human proportion in De Architectura.

B

BEHAVIOR CONTROL

Persuasion, Coercion, and Manipulation in Health Care

Important moral questions regarding behavior control also arise outside of the health-care system. The criminal and juvenile justice systems, advertising, and research in the life and social sciences, for example, raise important concerns about morally acceptable methods of social influence on human behavior. This discussion directly addresses only behavior control in health care, while acknowledging that the underlying principles apply to the broader contexts of behavior control.

Some attempts by health-care providers to influence the decisions or behavior of their patients threaten the underlying value of autonomy, raising apparent conflicts between the duties to respect autonomy and to promote well-being. Ethical assessment of these practices requires examination of their significance for the two values underlying patient-centered health care.

Persuasion, coercion, and manipulation in health care

Some methods by which providers influence their patients' behavior are clearly ethical. For example, providers routinely influence their patients' decisions and conduct regarding diet, exercise, and treatment through rational persuasion by explaining the probable benefits and costs of the available alternatives. Rational persuasion facilitates patients' exercise of informed consent, enhancing their ability to exercise autonomy and pursue well-being in most circumstances.

The morally troubling instances of behavior control in health care include those in which patients are coercively confined and subjected to intrusive forms of treatment such as surgery or medication despite their express objection. Recent legal cases have addressed the control of psychotic or severely retarded residents of state institutions who engaged in violent behavior, thus endangering themselves and others. These residents challenged various aspects of their treatment, including physical restraint, medication, and training programs, methods intended to alter their dangerous behavior. The courts were called upon to evaluate the legality of administering these methods of behavior control in these circumstances without voluntary consent (*Washington* v. *Harper*, 1990; *Youngberg* v. *Romeo*, 1982).

According to one view, subjective irresistibility is central to the relevant conceptions of coercion and control. Coercion completely undercuts individual sovereignty, as the will of the coercing agent controls that of the subjugated patient through a subjectively irresistible threat. Persuasive influences, in contrast, never control the patient because persuasion does not involve subjectively irresistible threats (Faden et al., 1986). The involuntarily committed patient who accepts treatment in response to threats of restraint and unwanted medication, for example, cannot effectively resist this mode of influence.

Emphasis on subjective irresistibility encounters at least three types of difficulty. First, no one has identified a practical criterion of subjective irresistibility (Faden et al., 1986). Second, and perhaps more important, no one has provided any clear interpretation of this notion of "subjective irresistibility." Notions such as "irresistible influence," "unable to resist," "overborne will," or "unable to do otherwise" have proven notoriously difficult to explain in a manner that supports the moral significance often attributed to them (Frankfurt, 1988; Schopp, 1991). Third, irresistibility does not capture the moral quality of some interventions.

Consider, for example, patient Anderson. Mr. Anderson rejects provider Cook's recommendation of outpatient therapy for chronic depression. Ms. Cook threatens to initiate legal proceedings in order to have Anderson involuntarily committed and medicated. Both Ms. Cook and Mr. Anderson doubt Ms. Cook's ability to carry out this threat because Mr. Anderson represents a borderline case under the state's civil commitment law as interpreted and applied by the courts. He suffers chronic depression with episodic exacerbation and remission and has been subject to several previous petitions for commitment with variable results depending on the circumstances. In addition, during one previous commitment, Mr. Anderson refused medication, and the court refused to order it administered involuntarily.

In a second case, provider Davis knows that patient Baker is deeply committed to a set of moral and religious principles vesting fundamental value in protecting human life and maintaining traditional families. Mr. Davis recommends a course of treatment that Mr. Baker rejects due to certain aversive side effects. Mr. Davis confronts Mr. Baker with irrefutable logic and overwhelming empirical evidence demonstrating that Mr. Baker's commitments to maintaining his family as an intact unit and to protecting human life, including his own, mandate his participation in this treatment.

It seems clear that the first case, but not the second, involves coercive pressure. Yet, in an important sense, the influence exerted in the first case is resistible while the influence brought to bear in the second is not. Mr. Anderson has resisted such pressure previously, sometimes prevailing at the commitment hearings. If he decides to accept the prescribed treatment, there is no apparent reason to think that he is unable to resist rather than that he simply decides not to. If he resists the threat, Ms. Cook does not successfully control Mr. Anderson. It seems more accurate to say that Mr. Anderson resists coercive pressure than to say that this particular threat is not coercive. That is, Ms. Cook exerts coercive pressure but does not successfully coerce Mr. Anderson (Feinberg, 1986). Although Mr. Davis's persuasive influence toward Mr. Baker would not usu-

See Also
Trust
Freedom and Coercion

ally be considered coercive, Mr. Baker may explain his decision to accept the treatment by stating that in the face of Mr. Davis's reasoning, he "has no choice" or "can do nothing else," suggesting that Mr. Baker finds Mr. Davis's argument subjectively irresistible.

Coercive influence qualifies as coercive and morally troubling, although not necessarily wrong, due to the manner in which it affects the choices and behavior of the subject. The coercive influence brought to bear on Mr. Anderson differs from the persuasive influence exerted on Mr. Baker in that a qualitatively different type of influence is used. The former involves the threat of force, the latter appeals to reason and the patient's values.

Some theorists explain coercion as a psychological concept, while others interpret it as inherently normative, classifying only wrongful interventions as coercive. On the psychological conception, a coercing agent exerts coercive pressure against an individual when the agent threatens the individual with some unwanted state of affairs unless he or she complies with the agent's demand. The coercive pressure constitutes coercion proper when the agent successfully elicits compliance by rendering it less aversive than resistance. Any particular case of coercion may or may not be morally objectionable. The normative conception, in contrast, classifies influence as coercive only when the coercing agent limits the subject's alternatives in a manner that wrongs him or her (compare Feinberg, 1986, with Wertheimer, 1987). In either interpretation, however, coercive influence raises at least prima facie moral concerns under the patient-centered theory that requires informed consent, because the coercive influence raises doubts about the voluntariness of that consent.

Although manipulation does not rely on coercive threats, it also raises a prima facie moral reservation under the patient-centered approach. Manipulative influences appeal to psychological processes in a manner not limited to rational persuasion. Perhaps deception provides the most widely cited example of manipulation. Others include exploitation of vulnerability and appeal to desires the individual experiences but does not endorse, does not want to be motivated by, or does not accept as part of the person he or she wants to be (Faden et al., 1986; Feinberg, 1978; Rudinow, 1978).

Providers can manipulate patients by deceiving them about the likely costs, benefits, or side effects of particular options, particularly when that deception is calculated to circumvent the values or priorities of the patient. Suppose, for example, that Mr. Davis persuades Mr. Baker to accept the treatment by concealing a potential side effect rather than by providing relevant information and rational argument. Mr. Davis would undermine Mr. Baker's values rather than respect them.

Providers can manipulate without deception through arguments, evidence, or appeals to authority that are calculated to overwhelm, confuse, or intimidate the patient rather than to explain to and rationally convince the patient. Providing accurate information in circumstances that prevent careful reflection due to inadequate time or, for example, to the presence of family members who are likely to exhort the patient to accept the treatment, can undermine independent judgment.

Providers who are familiar with a patient can exploit the patient's vulnerability by appealing to motives such as vanity or jealousy, or to ideas that the individual considers foreign or immoral, or of which he or she is ashamed. A plastic surgeon might secure consent for cosmetic surgery, for example, by exploiting the patient's fear that his wife is losing interest in him. Some forms of behavior control combine coercive and manipulative elements. When the patient is physically restrained and involuntarily administered psychotropic medication, for example, the provider coercively overrides the patient's decision not to accept the drugs. The chemical effect on the patient constitutes a manipulative influence in that it alters the psychological processes in a manner other than through rational persuasion.

Though different theorists may define the parameters of rational persuasion, manipulation, and coercion somewhat differently, each constitutes a method of influencing behavior. Each might prove more or less effective in some circumstances. They differ primarily by virtue of the mechanisms through which they influence an individual's decisions and conduct. Under a patient-centered approach to health care that grants primary authority to the patient's informed consent and the concomitant right to refuse treatment, coercion and manipulation raise prima facie moral concerns, but

ON COERCION AND MANIPULATION

Although many people ordinarily think of coercion as a more severe infringement than manipulation, manipulative influence can inflict injury that is in one sense deeper than that inflicted by coercion. Coercion relies in some manner on force or threats, but manipulation sometimes harnesses one's own vulnerabilities in order to turn one against oneself, often striking at an intimate level of one's psychology.

— ROBERT F. SCHOPP

Many ethicists believe that freedom of will is an essential part of positive internal freedom.

PAGE 245

See Also

Population Policies : Strong Persuasion

Compulsion

BEHAVIOR CONTROL

Autonomy, Well-being, and Behavior Control in Health Care

rational persuasion does not. These concerns arise due to the relationship between these methods of influence and the underlying values of autonomy and well-being.

Autonomy, well-being, and behavior control in health care

AUTONOMY, LIBERTY, AND FREEDOM. Although autonomy is widely accepted as a core value in contemporary health-care ethics, the precise conception of autonomy at issue often remains vague. Joel Feinberg distinguishes four senses of autonomy as a right, a condition, an ideal, and a set of capacities. Autonomy as a right takes the form of a right to self-determination within a sphere of personal sovereignty. Theorists differ as to the proper boundaries of this sphere, but it generally encompasses central self-regarding life decisions regarding one's body, work, family, privacy, and property (Feinberg, 1986).

Positive internal freedom is perhaps the most plausible candidate for the status of an intrinsic good.

PAGE 247

FOUR ASPECTS OF AUTONOMY

1. right
2. condition
3. ideal
4. set of capacities

Autonomy as a condition is a set of virtues derived from the conception of a person as self-governing. These include self-reflection, direction, reliance, and control; moral authenticity and independence; and responsibility for self (Feinberg, 1986). Feinberg's set of autonomous virtues corresponds roughly to Gerald Dworkin's conception of autonomous persons as those who critically reflect upon and endorse or alter their own motives and values. Dworkin's autonomous persons develop integrated lives by reviewing and shaping projects, motives, and conduct according to higher-order values. They define their lives and make them their own through this process of self-evaluation and development (Dworkin, 1988a, 1988b). Individuals approach autonomy as an ideal to the extent that they develop autonomous virtues and exercise self-determination in defining and pursuing a life in a manner compatible with their membership in communities (Feinberg, 1986).

In order to exercise sovereign self-determination and develop the autonomous virtues, individuals need autonomous capacities. These are the psychological capacities such as consciousness, understanding, and reasoning used in critical self-reflection, deliberation, and decision making (Feinberg, 1986; Dworkin, 1988a, 1988b). For the sake of clarity, the term "autonomy" is reserved for the comprehensive value embracing all four senses in which the term is used. "Autonomous virtues" is used for the virtues that comprise autonomy as a condition, the optimal development of which constitutes autonomy as an ideal. Autonomy as a right is referred to as "sovereignty." Autonomy as capacity is referred to as "autonomous capacities." Autonomous capacities serve as necessary conditions for sovereignty and autonomous virtues. As sovereignty is a threshold concept that applies dichotomously rather than by degree, the autonomous capacities necessary to support personal sovereignty also serve as a threshold concept. Capacities beyond the minimal level required for sovereignty cannot increase the degree to which one is sovereign, although they might improve one's ability to exercise the right. Individuals manifest autonomous virtues in various degrees, however, and the extent to which they develop these virtues depends in part on the degree of autonomous capacities they possess (Feinberg, 1986).

Liberty and freedom are closely related to sovereignty, although not identical to it. Liberty is the absence of rule-imposed limitations on action within a political system, and freedom is the presence of open options. One has an open option if one lacks external personal constraints, so that one can either perform an action or refrain from performing it. The more options one has open, the more freedom one has. Some people might be at liberty to move into a particular neighborhood, for example, because no law forbids such a move. Yet they might not be free to do so if owners refuse to rent available housing to them. Sovereignty is a moral right that constitutes part of autonomy. A political system that respects autonomy must protect individual liberty of action within the domain of sovereignty. A corresponding degree of freedom is necessary to give this sphere of sovereignty and liberty practical effect.

Social and economic conditions can also limit a patient's effective exercise of autonomy. If poverty precludes access to the health-care system, for example, the individual's right to informed consent has little practical value. Similarly, those who lack the education needed to enable them to ask pertinent questions, understand the answers, or negotiate the unfamiliar structure and procedures of health-care institutions suffer disadvantage in their ability to exercise sovereignty. Legal or social discrimination leading to secondary status in the eyes of health-care providers or institutions can generate patterns of interaction that burden participation in a system ostensibly grounded in the patient-centered ethic. Thus, the practical implementation of the patient-centered ethic requires social commitment to effect the opportunity and ability to exercise sovereignty.

One can exercise one's sovereignty in such a manner as to decrease one's freedom. Some people voluntarily decide, for example, to participate in Antabuse therapy that effectively closes their option to drink alcohol dur-

See Also

Freedom and Coercion: The Value of Freedom

ing the period of participation. Others voluntarily undergo surgical sterilization, closing the option of having children. By taking action that decreases freedom, people limit the range within which they can exercise their sovereignty, but they do not become "less sovereign." They retain discretionary control within their sphere of sovereignty.

BEHAVIOR CONTROL, AUTONOMY, AND WELL-BEING. The patient-centered model of health care protects individual sovereignty by requiring informed consent. Autonomous acts must involve the exercise of autonomous capacities; that is, the actor must act intentionally, voluntarily, and with understanding of important relevant information. By granting informed consent for health care, patients exercise their sovereignty through an autonomous act, authorizing the treatment and accepting responsibility for the decision (Buchanan and Brock, 1989; Faden et al., 1986).

In ordinary circumstances, the requirement of informed consent promotes well-being. Some theorists identify individual well-being with some form of preference satisfaction, while others endorse an objective criterion of well-being such as happiness or self-fulfillment. According to either type of theory, people have welfare interests in certain states of affairs that allow them to pursue their ultimate good. These welfare interests include some minimal level of tangible goods, health, psychological functioning, and freedom to act as they see fit. Attainment of most plausible conceptions of individual well-being will be very difficult or impossible unless these welfare interests are met (Buchanan and Brock, 1989; Feinberg, 1984). The right to informed consent ordinarily allows patients the opportunity to select health care that is expected to promote their welfare interests and their ultimate good.

The significance of informed consent for autonomy and well-being explains the prima facie moral objections to coercive and manipulative methods of behavior control. Under ordinary conditions, rational persuasion facilitates informed consent, influencing behavior in a manner consistent with both values, but coercion and manipulation distort informed consent, undermining both values. Rational persuasion appeals to the autonomous capacities that serve as a necessary condition for sovereignty and autonomous virtues. Thus, those who respond to persuasion in a manner appropriate to that mode of influence exercise their autonomous capacities within their sphere of sovereignty. By appealing to autonomous capacities in order to elicit an exercise of sovereignty, rational persuasion respects sovereignty and, insofar as exercising these capacities promotes their development and that of autonomous virtues, it encourages that development.

AUTONOMY
When Dysfunction Limits Sovereignty

In some circumstances, particularly those in which the individual lacks autonomous capacities, individual decision making neither constitutes an exercise of sovereignty nor promotes well-being. Incompetent patients suffer impairment of autonomous capacities. A thorough discussion of incompetence would require careful examination of traditionally difficult psychological, legal, and philosophic issues including competing theories of responsibility, moral agency, and free will (Buchanan and Brock, 1989). It is sufficient to say here that certain types of psychological dysfunction undermine the autonomous capacities required to meet the threshold for sovereignty, although most individuals who suffer these disorders possess autonomous capacities and virtues to some degree. Also, most have the potential to develop further these traits.

— ROBERT F. SCHOPP

Manipulation and coercion, in contrast, distort or override the exercise of autonomous capacities. These processes undermine sovereignty, depriving patients of the opportunity to exercise their autonomous capacities and develop autonomous virtues. To the extent that the individual is in the best position to make accurate decisions regarding his or her own well-being, these methods interfere with the ability to pursue it.

Respect for the comprehensive value of autonomy demands both deontological and consequentialist components (Beauchamp and Childress, 1989). The deontological value of autonomy requires respect for competent self-regarding choice as an exercise of sovereignty, although it allows temporary intervention to ascertain whether the choice is competent, informed, and voluntary (Feinberg, 1986). It vests significance in the intrinsic nature of the choice as an exercise of sovereignty by a competent moral agent. The consequentialist aspect of autonomy, in contrast, emphasizes the expected consequences of any decision or action on the development of autonomous capacities and virtues. Those who recognize the consequentialist value of autonomy evaluate an act positively insofar as it promotes development of these traits and negatively insofar as the act undermines them. Encouraging development of autonomous capacities increases the probability that certain individuals will qualify for sovereignty.

◆ **autonomy**
the quality or state of being self-governing; self-directing freedom and esp. moral independence

See Also

Natural Law: Is there a "Right to Autonomy?"

B

BEHAVIOR CONTROL

Competence and Behavior Control in Health Care

Competence and behavior control in health care

INCOMPETENCE AND WELL-BEING. Ordinarily, coercive and manipulative but not persuasive methods of influence raise moral concerns from the perspective of the patient-centered approach because the former but not the latter infringe on sovereignty and circumvent autonomous capacities. In certain circumstances, however, these three modes of influence interact with the underlying values of well-being and the deontological and consequentialist aspects of autonomy in a different manner. Incompetent individuals lack the capacities needed to qualify for sovereignty, reducing the importance of autonomy and thus, increasing the relative significance of well-being for them. Some severely impaired patients lack the potential to develop further their autonomous capacities and virtues. In such circumstances, providers adhering to the patient-centered approach can only maximize other aspects of well-being. The severely retarded resident in *Youngberg* v. *Romeo* (1982), for example, lacked the capacity to significantly improve his cognitive functions. Thus, providers were limited to promoting other aspects of his well-being by training him in a manner intended to reduce his violent behavior, decreasing the probability of injury and increasing freedom from restraint.

Autonomy remains a fundamental value, however, for those patients who possess some degree of autonomous capacities or virtues or the potential to develop these traits. The consequentialist aspect of autonomy commands weight both in itself and as a component of the patient's well-being. It commands independent weight because autonomous capacities and virtues constitute part of the comprehensive value for autonomy. Concern for patients' well-being demands concern for their autonomous capacities because they retain a welfare interest in maintaining these psychological capacities that enable them to pursue their ultimate interests effectively. Finally, self-fulfillment as development of the autonomous virtues constitutes at least part of a person's well-being in a moral system vesting fundamental value in autonomy.

◆ **incompetent**
Lacking the capacities to develop autonomy or to pursue one's interests effectively; also inadequate or unsuitable for a particular purpose.

In some cases, autonomy and well-being converge in that promoting the consequentialist aspect of autonomy also promotes well-being without violating sovereignty because the patient in question lacks the capacities necessary to qualify for sovereignty. Medicating grossly psychotic and assaultive patients without their consent, for example, may improve their cognitive functioning and reduce assaultive behavior, allowing more freedom from restraint, decreasing risk of injury, and improving autonomous capacities. The *Harper* Court, for example, allowed the involuntary administration of antipsychotic drugs to seriously mentally ill prisoners who are dangerous to themselves or to others when the treatment is in their medical interests as determined by the clinical review procedure provided by statute (*Harper*, 1990). If "serious mental illness" is sufficient to undermine the capacities necessary for sovereignty, *Harper* allows manipulative influence of prisoners' behavior in a manner that improves well-being by promoting safety from injury, freedom of motion, and autonomous capacities without violating sovereignty.

In different circumstances, however, it may be possible to influence incompetent patients through several different methods, each of which will address different aspects of well-being, requiring a choice regarding the most important component to pursue. For example, medication might reduce a severely disturbed patient's injurious behavior by sedating him or her in a manner that further reduces an already impaired alertness, comprehension, and capacity to make conscious choices, thus undermining already impoverished autonomous capacities. A strictly applied behavioral program involving both positive and aversive consequences for the patient's behavior, in contrast, might avoid reducing autonomous capacities at the cost of inflicting the aversive consequences.

Ms. Jones, for example, is a severely disturbed patient who engages in repetitive self-injurious behavior such as severely biting her hands and wrists as well as banging her head against the walls and floor. Psychotropic medication might reduce her injurious behavior, but it would do so at the expense of sedating her and slowing her already impaired mental processes. A behavioral treatment program including contingent electric shock might reduce her injurious behavior without sedating her, but she would experience the aversive shock.

Priorities among values

Decision makers who encounter these cases must establish priorities between autonomy and well-being as well as among various components of these basic values. Some writers advocate a categorical priority for sovereignty over well-being, rejecting any paternalistic intervention concerning voluntary self-regarding decisions. Others balance sovereignty against well-being in each case (Buchanan and Brock, 1989; Feinberg, 1986). Certain aspects of contemporary U.S. law appear consistent with each school of thought. The common law right of competent individuals to control their body is often interpreted to include the right to refuse all treatment, including life-sustaining procedures. In constitutional analysis, however, courts balance the liberty interest in being free from unwanted treatment against countervailing state interests, includ-

See Also
Value and Valuation
Genetics and Human Behavior
Genes and Crime: What We Don't Study *Can* Hurt Us

ing the protection of human life and well-being (Conroy, 1985; *Cruzan* v. *Director, Missouri Department of Health*, 1990).

Theorists from both schools can accept intervention in the case of an incompetent patient in order to promote well-being, but they may differ regarding which aspect of well-being to emphasize. Those who endorse a comprehensive priority for autonomy opt to maximize autonomous virtues and capacities at the expense of other components of well-being. Those who balance autonomy and well-being as well as some who advocate a priority for sovereignty balance the consequentialist value for autonomous virtues and capacities against other aspects of well-being. Some theorists might endorse the priority of sovereignty over well-being but balance the consequentialist aspects of autonomy against other components of well-being.

Consider, for example, the following cases. Mr. Johnson is an elderly widower with serious coronary disease. He knows smoking and drinking markedly increase his probability of suffering a fatal heart attack. He continues to smoke regularly and meets with three old friends to share a bottle of bourbon twice a week, explaining that these activities provide the only real enjoyment in his life.

Ms. Bell is a moderately retarded adult who suffers a painful form of cancer. The only effective treatment for the pain is medication that significantly sedates her, decreasing her alertness and mental acuity, reducing her already impaired autonomous capacities and virtues. Due to Ms. Bell's incompetence, a surrogate must decide either to administer the medication, reducing the pain and her already impoverished autonomous capacities and virtues or to withhold the treatment, maximizing her autonomous capacities and virtues but leaving the pain unabated. In short, the surrogate must choose between the physical comfort that constitutes one aspect of Ms. Bell's well-being and the autonomous capacities and virtues that constitute the consequentialist aspect of autonomy and another component of her well-being.

Ordinary practice and contemporary law would respect Mr. Johnson's sovereign choice but call upon a surrogate to decide for Ms. Bell. Some might accept the intuitive judgments that Mr. Johnson's sovereignty ought to prevail over his well-being as evaluated from an external perspective and that the surrogate ought to opt for the medication, weighing Ms. Bell's physical comfort more heavily than the marginal cost to her autonomous capacities and virtues. Can one consistently advocate a priority for the deontic aspect of the value of autonomy over well-being by endorsing respect for Mr. Johnson's sovereignty, yet sacrifice the consequentialist aspect of the value for autonomy to other aspects of Ms. Bell's well-being? What justifies a priority for the deontic aspect of the value for autonomy but allows balancing of the consequentialist aspect?

Two arguments support a priority for sovereignty over well-being. The first is conceptual. State authority to monitor and intervene in the individual's domain of "sovereignty" undermines the claim of discretionary control, even if the state never exercises this power. The mere fact that some external source retains the authority to review and reverse decisions renders the person less than sovereign regarding these choices. Thus, one cannot consistently endorse individual sovereignty and state authority to intervene in that domain in order to promote well-being.

The second argument develops from the ramifications of the first. Individuals merit praise or blame and define their lives and the principles they live by through the exercise of sovereign discretion. Each individual creates his or her own life as an extended project uniquely his or her own by exercising sovereign choice regarding the central self-defining decisions. Certain interests, including food, shelter, and safety, form part of virtually everyone's well-being. Only by exercising sovereignty, however, can one define one's life and embrace one's own well-being (Dworkin, 1988b; Feinberg, 1986; Rachels and Ruddick, 1988). Thus, others can act to promote various states of affairs that would be good for Mr. Johnson, but only by exercising sovereignty can he render them part of his good. Sovereignty takes priority because it enables Mr. Johnson to define his own life and embrace various aspects of well-being as his well-being.

Increases in autonomous capacities that qualify an individual for sovereignty take priority over other aspects of well-being for similar reasons. Such increases provide persons with the opportunity to exercise sovereignty and define their lives. Merely incremental increases in autonomous capacities below the threshold that qualifies one for sovereignty do not have this effect. Thus, one can advocate a priority for sovereignty but balance these consequentialist aspects of the value for autonomy because the latter lack the special significance of the former in enabling the individual to define his or her life.

Values are concepts we use to explain how and why various realities matter.

PAGE 679

Conclusion

Behavior control in health care raises ethical concern when it threatens the morally acceptable relationship between the provider and the patient. Ordinarily, coercive and manipulative but not rationally persuasive influences undermine this relationship. Ethical evaluation of any specific application of behavior control requires examination of the method used in light of the circumstances and the underlying values of health care. The search for the most defensible account of the values underlying health care and the patient-provider

See Also

Values in Society and Culture

To be viable, a society requires a shared set of reasonably cohesive values.

PAGE 681

WHEN VALUES CONFLICT
Autonomy vs. Well-Being

Some cases require choices between the deontological and consequentialist aspects of autonomy. Mr. Michaels is chronically moderately depressed, but he suffers no major cognitive dysfunction. He remains civilly competent and understands his condition, its pattern of periodic exacerbation and partial remission, and the proposed treatments. Mr. Michaels endangers neither his own life nor others' well-being, but he fails to develop his talents, pursue any interests or projects, or enrich his life. Mr. Michaels refuses offers of voluntary treatment. His history of responsiveness to structured treatment and his fear of civil commitment suggest that threats to initiate commitment proceedings would probably motivate his participation in an outpatient program and that doing so would likely improve his well-being, including his autonomous capacities and virtues. When a competent patient refuses treatment that is likely to improve well-being by promoting autonomous capacities or virtues, the deontological value for autonomy conflicts with the consequentialist aspect of the same value.

The reasoning that supports the priority for sovereignty over well-being but allows balancing of the consequentialist aspect of autonomy against other components of well-being also supports the priority for the deontological value of autonomy over the consequentialist aspect. To promote Mr. Michaels's good is to promote the human good that he chooses, pursues, and endorses as his own (Frankfurt, 1988). To violate sovereignty, and thus the deontological value of autonomy, in favor of the consequentialist aspect of autonomy that constitutes part of his well-being, is to alienate that good from this person, undermining both the values for autonomy and for well-being. Doing so severs the well-being from Mr. Michaels, rendering its attainment no longer attributable to him.

— ROBERT F. SCHOPP

relationship continues. The patient-centered theory is one viable candidate that converges reasonably well with current practice and law.

The debate between those who would grant priority to autonomy over well-being and those who would balance the two values remains active. The patient-centered approach to health care and the legal right to informed consent suggest that some legal and ethical institutions favor the priority for sovereignty. The moral reasoning that supports the priority for sovereignty rejects coercive and manipulative forms of influence intended to promote the competent patient's well-being, including those components of well-being that also constitute the consequentialist aspects of autonomy. When incompetence justifies the use of coercive influence in order to protect the incompetent patient's well-being, however, this reasoning does not demand a priority for promoting autonomous capacities and virtues over other components of well-being unless the improved autonomous capacities would be sufficient to qualify the individual for sovereignty. Many plausible circumstances that justify resorting to modes of influence other than persuasive ones apparently justify coercion rather than manipulation.

— ROBERT F. SCHOPP

See Also
Ethics

BIOETHICS

"There is," says the biblical book of Ecclesiastes, "no new thing under the sun." Those words are worth pondering in light of the emergence of the field of bioethics since the 1950s and 1960s. From one perspective it is a wholly modern field, a child of the remarkable advances in the biomedical, environmental, and social sciences. Those advances have brought a new world of expanded scientific understanding and technological innovation, seeming to alter forever what can be done about the vulnerabilities of nature and of the human body and mind, and about saving, improving, and extending human lives. Yet from another perspective, the kinds of questions raised by these advances are among the oldest that human beings have asked themselves.

They turn on the meaning of life and death, the bearing of pain and suffering, the right and power to control one's life, and our common duties to each other and to nature in the face of grave threats to our health and well-being. Bioethics represents a radical transformation of the older, more traditional domain of medical ethics; yet it is also true that, since the dawn of history, healers have been forced to wrestle with the human fear of illness and death, and with the limits imposed by human finitude.

It is wholly fitting that an encyclopedia of the ethics of sex and genetics devote some of its space to defining and understanding the field that it would examine in both breadth and depth. Yet that is not an easy task with a field that is still evolving and whose borders are hazy. The word "bioethics," of recent vintage, has come to denote not just a particular field of human inquiry—the intersection of ethics and the life sciences—but also an academic discipline; a political force in medicine, biology, and environmental studies; and a cultural perspective of some consequence. Understood narrowly, bioethics is simply one more new field that has emerged in the face of great scientific and technological changes. Understood more broadly, however, it is a field that has spread into, and in many places has changed, other far older fields. It has reached into law and public policy; into literary, cultural, and historical studies; into the popular media; into the disciplines of philosophy, religion, and literature; and into the scientific fields of medicine, biology, ecology and environment, demography, and the social sciences.

The focus here will be on the broader meaning, place, and significance of bioethics. The aim will be to determine not only what the field means for specific ethical problems in the life sciences, but also what it has to say about the interaction of ethics and human life, and of science and human values. Bioethics is a field that ranges from the anguished private and individual dilemmas faced by physicians or other health-care workers at the bedside of a dying patient, to the terrible public and societal choices faced by citizens and legislators as they try to devise equitable health or environmental policies. Its problems can be highly individual and personal— what should I do here and now?—and highly communal and political—what should we together do as citizens and fellow human beings?

While the primary focus of this entry will be on medicine and health care, the scope of bioethics has come to encompass a number of fields and disciplines broadly grouped under the rubric "the life sciences." They encompass all those perspectives that seek to understand human nature and behavior, characteristically the domain of the social sciences, and the natural world that provides the habitat of human and animal life, primarily the population and environmental sciences. Yet it is the medical and biological sciences in which bioethics found its initial impetus, and in which it has seen the most intense activity. It thus seems appropriate to make that activity the center of attention here.

Historical background

An understanding of the emergence of bioethics will help to capture the panoramic breadth and complexity of the field. The 1960s is a pertinent point of departure, even though there were portents of the new field and issues in earlier decades. That decade brought into confluence two important developments, one scientific and the other cultural. In biomedicine, the 1960s was an era of extraordinary technological progress. It saw the advent of kidney dialysis, organ transplantation, medically safe abortions, the contraceptive pill, prenatal diagnosis, the widespread use of intensive-care units and artificial respirators, a dramatic shift from death at home to death in hospitals or other institutions, and the first glimmerings of genetic engineering. Here was a truly remarkable array of technological developments, the palpable outcome of the great surge in basic biomedical research and application that followed World War II. At the same time, stimulated by Rachel Carson's book *Silent Spring*, there was a gradual awakening to the environmental hazards posed by the human appetite for economic progress and the domination of nature (Carson, 1962). Taken together, these developments posed a staggering range of difficult, and seemingly new, moral problems.

Bioethics as a field might not have emerged so strongly or insistently had it not been for parallel cultural developments. The decade was the spawning ground for a dazzling array of social and cultural reform efforts. It saw a rebirth, within the discipline of moral philosophy, of an interest in normative and applied ethics, both out of a dissatisfaction with the prevailing academic emphasis on theoretical issues and in response to cultural upheavals. It was the era of the civil-rights movement, which gave African-Americans and other people of color new rights and possibilities. It was the era that saw the rebirth of feminism as a potent social movement, and the extension to women of rights often previously denied them. It was the era that saw a fresh surge of individualism—a by-product in many ways of postwar affluence and mobility—and the transformation of many traditional institutions, including the family, the churches, and the schools. It was an era that came to see the enormous possibilities the life sciences offer to combat disease, illness, and death—and no less to see science's possibilities for changing the way human beings could live their lives.

Some of these possibilities had been foreseen in the important book *Medicine and Morals*, written by Joseph Fletcher, an Episcopal theologian who eventually came to reject religious beliefs (Fletcher, 1954). He celebrated the power of modern medicine to liberate human beings from the iron grip of nature, putting instead in their hands the power to shape lives of their own choosing. This vision began to be lived out in the 1960s. That decade brought together the medical advances that seemed to foreshadow the eventual conquest of nature and the cultural changes that would empower newly liberated individuals to assume full control of their own destinies. There was in this development both great hope and ambition, and perhaps great hubris, the prideful belief that humans could radically transcend their natural condition.

Since its origins in classical times, ethics has sought to understand how human beings should act and what kind of life is best.

PAGE 151

See Also

Religious Concepts: The Ancient Greek View of the Body

B

BIOETHICS

Facts and Values

The advances of the biomedical sciences and their technological application had three great outcomes that came clearly into full view by the 1960s. They transformed first many traditional ideas about the nature and domain of medicine, then the scope and meaning of human health, and, finally, cultural and societal views of what it means to live a human life. Medicine was transformed from a diagnostic and palliative discipline into a potent agent able to cure disease and effectively forestall death. Human "health" more and more encompassed the 1947 World Health Organization definition with its broad emphasis on health as "a state of complete physical, mental, and social well-being and not merely the absence of disease or infirmity." Traditional notions of the living of a life were changed by longer life expectancies, the control of procreation, and powerful pharmacological agents able to modify mood and thought. The advent of bioethics can be seen as the principal social response to these great changes.

FUNDAMENTAL QUESTIONS OF BIOETHICS

- How are we to confront the moral perplexities posed by the unprecedented medical, technological and cultural changes?
- Who should have control over new technology?
- How can the benefits of medical advances be most fairly distributed?
- What kind of character or human virtue would be most conducive to a wise use of new technologies?
- What institutions, laws or regulations are needed to manage the coming changes in a moral fashion?

◆ **bioethics**
A field of human inquiry into the broad terrain of moral problems in life sciences, encompassing medicine, biology, and important aspects of environmental, population, and social sciences, and is devoted to human survival and an improved quality of life.

Facts and values

It soon became evident that such questions required more than a casual response. Two important tasks emerged. One of them, logically the first, was to distinguish the domain of science from that of ethics and values. As a consequence of the triumphalist positivism that during the late nineteenth and the first half of the twentieth century had come to dominate the general understanding of science, matters of ethics and values had been all but banished from serious intellectual discussion. A sharp line could be drawn, it was widely believed, between scientific facts and moral values (MacIntyre, 1981b). The former were solid, authoritative, impersonally true, while the latter were understood to be "soft," relativistic, and highly, even idiosyncratically, personal. Moreover, doctors should make the moral decisions no less than the medical decisions; indeed, a good medical decision was tantamount to a good moral decision. The first task of bioethics, then, was to erase the supposedly clear line that could be drawn between facts and values, and then to challenge the belief that those well trained in science and medicine were as capable of making the moral decisions as the medical decisions.

The second important task was to find or develop the methodologies necessary to come to grips with the new moral problems. If there is no sharp line between facts and values, how should their relationship be understood? If there is a significant difference between making a medical (or scientific) decision and making a moral decision, how are those decisions different and what kinds of skills are needed to make the one or the other? Who has a right to make the different kinds of decisions? If it is neither sensible nor fair to think of moral and value matters as soft and capriciously personal, hardly more than a matter of taste, then how can rigor and objectivity be brought to bear on them?

TASKS OF BIOETHICS

- The first task of bioethics was to challenge the belief that those trained in science and medicine were as capable of making the moral decisions as the medical decisions.
- The second task was to develop ways to deal with the new moral problems.

As the scope and complexity of these two large tasks became more obvious, the field of bioethics began to emerge. From the first, there was a widespread recognition that the moral problems would have to be approached in an interdisciplinary way (Callahan, 1973). Philosophy and religion, long the characteristic arenas for moral insight, analysis, and traditions, should have an important place, as should the historical moral traditions and practices of medicine and biology. Ample room would also have to be made for the law and for the social and policy sciences. Moral problems have important legal, social, political, and policy implications; and moral choices would often be expressed through court decisions, legislative mandates, and assorted regulatory devices. Hardly less important was the problem of which moral decisions should be left to private choice and which required some public standards. While there was a strong trend to remove procreational choices from public scrutiny, and thus to move toward the legal use of contraception and abortion, environmental choices were being moved from private choice to governmental regulation. Debates of this kind require the participation of many disciplines.

While the importance of an interdisciplinary approach was early recognized, three other matters were more troublesome. First, what should be the scope of the field? The term "bioethics," as it was first

See Also

Virtue Ethics: Ego and the Common Good

Natural Law in Law and Bioethics

used by the biologist Van Rensselaer Potter, referred to a new field devoted to human survival and an improved quality of life, not necessarily or particularly medical in character (Potter, 1971). The term soon was used differently, however, particularly to distinguish it from the much older field of medical ethics. The latter had traditionally been marked by a heavy, almost exclusive emphasis on the moral obligations of physicians and on the doctor-patient relationship. Yet that emphasis, while still important, was not capacious enough to embrace the huge range of emerging issues and perspectives. "Bioethics" came to refer to the broad terrain of the moral problems of the life sciences, ordinarily taken to encompass medicine, biology, and some important aspects of the environmental, population, and social sciences. The traditional domain of medical ethics would be included within this array, accompanied now by many other topics and problems.

Second, if the new bioethics was to be interdisciplinary, how would it relate to the long-standing disciplines of moral theology and moral philosophy? While those disciplines are able to encompass some interdisciplinary perspectives, they also have their own methodologies, developed over the years to be tight and rigorous. For the most part, moreover, their methodologies are broad, aimed at moral problems in general, not just at biomedical issues. Can they, in their broad, abstract generality, do justice to the particularities of medical or environmental issues?

Another problem becomes apparent. An interdisciplinary field is not necessarily well served by a tight, narrow methodology. Its very purpose is to be open to different perspectives and the different methodologies of different disciplines. Does this mean, then, that although parts of bioethics might be rigorous—the philosophical parts taken by themselves or the legal parts—the field as a whole may be doomed to a pervasive vagueness, never as strong as a whole as its individual parts? This is a charge sometimes leveled against the field, and it has not been easy for its practitioners to find the right balance of breadth, complexity, and analytical rigor.

THREE INHERENT PROBLEMS IN BIOETHICS

1. What should be the scope of bioethics?
2. How would the new bioethics relate to traditional moral philosophy and theology?
3. How would bioethics balance complexity and analytical rigor?

Varieties of bioethics

As the field has developed, it has become clear that because of the range of diversity of bioethics issues, more than one methodology is needed; by the same token, no single discipline can claim a commanding role. At least four general areas of inquiry can be distinguished, even though in practice they often overlap and cannot clearly be separated.

THEORETICAL BIOETHICS. Theoretical bioethics deals with the intellectual foundations of the field. What are its moral roots and what ethical warrant can be found for the moral judgments made in the name of bioethics? Part of the debate turns on whether its foundations should be looked for within the practices and traditions of the life sciences, or whether they have philosophical or theological starting points. Philosophers and theologians have a central place in this enterprise, but draw strongly upon the history and practices of the life sciences to grasp the aims and developments of these fields.

CLINICAL ETHICS. Clinical ethics refers to the day-to-day moral decision making of those caring for patients. Because of that context, it typically focuses on the individual case, seeking to determine what is to be done here and now with a patient. Should a respirator be turned off? Is this patient competent to make a decision? Should the full truth be disclosed to a fearful cancer patient? Individual cases often give rise to great medical and moral uncertainty, and they evoke powerful emotions among those with a role in the decisions. Decision-making procedures, as well as the melding of theory and practice—what Aristotle called "practical reason"—come sharply into play. It is the concreteness of the judgment that is central here: What is to be done for *this* patient at *this* time? The experience of practicing physicians, other health-care workers, and patients themselves takes a prominent place, yet on occasion can require a collaborative interplay with those trained more specifically in ethics.

VARIETIES OF BIOETHICS

1. theoretical
2. clinical
3. regulatory and policy
4. cultural

REGULATORY AND POLICY BIOETHICS. The aim of regulatory and policy bioethics is to fashion legal or clinical rules and procedures designed to apply to types of cases or general practices; this area of bioethics does not focus on individual cases. The effort in the early 1970s to fashion a new legal definition of clinical death (from a heart-lung to a brain-death definition), the development of guidelines for the use of human subjects in medical research, and hospital rules for do-not-resuscitate (DNR) orders are examples of regulatory ethics. It can also encompass policies

Eudaimonia is the ancient Greek word for being fortunate or doing well in life, and eudaimonism is the view that our first concern in ethics is with the nature and conditions of human happiness and well-being.

PAGE 154

See Also
Law and Bioethics: Famous Cases

designed to allocate scarce health-care resources or to protect the environment. Regulatory ethics ordinarily seeks laws, rules, policies, and regulations that will command a wide consensus, and its aim is practical rather than theoretical. The law and the policy sciences are highly important in this kind of bioethics work; but it also requires a rich, ongoing dialogue among those concerned with theoretical bioethics, on the one hand, and clinical ethics and political realities, on the other. Regulatory bioethics seeks legal and policy solutions to pressing societal problems that are ethically defensible and clinically sensible and feasible.

CULTURAL BIOETHICS. Cultural bioethics refers to the effort systematically to relate bioethics to the historical, ideological, cultural, and social context in which it is expressed. How do the trends within bioethics reflect the larger culture of which they are a part? What ideological leanings do the moral theories undergirding bioethics openly or implicitly manifest? A heavy emphasis on the moral principle of autonomy or self-determination can, for example, be said to display the political and ideological bias of culturally individualistic societies, notably the United States. Other nations—those in central and eastern Europe, for instance—give societal rather than individual concerns a more pronounced priority (Fox, 1990). Solidarity rather than autonomy would be their highest value.

The social sciences, as well as history and the humanities, have a central place in this interpretive effort (Marshall, 1992). If done well, the insights and analysis they provide can help everyone to a better understanding of the larger cultural and social dynamic that underlies the ethical problems. Those problems will usually have a social history that reflects the influence of the culture of which they are a part. Even the definition of what constitutes an ethical "problem" will show the force of cultural differences. Countries with strong paternalistic traditions may not consider it nec-

BIOETHICS
The General Questions

While bioethics as a field may be understood in different ways and be enriched by different perspectives, at its heart lie some basic human questions. Three of them are paramount. What kind of a person ought I to be in order to live a moral life and to make good ethical decisions? What are my duties and obligations to other individuals whose life and well-being may be affected by my actions? What do I owe to the common good, or the public interest, in my life as a member of society? The first question bears on what is often called an ethic of virtue, whose focus is that of personal character and the shaping of those values and goals necessary to be a good and decent person. The second question recognizes that what we do can affect, for good or ill, the lives of others, and tries to understand how we should see our individual human relationships—what we ought to do for others and what we have a right to expect from them. The third question takes our social relationships a step further, recognizing that we are citizens of a nation and members of larger social and political communities. We are citizens and neighbors, sometimes acquaintances, and often people who will and must live together in relatively impersonal, but mutually interdependent, ways.

These are general questions of ethics that can be posed independently of the making of biomedical decisions. They can be asked of people in almost any moral situation or context. Here we encounter an important debate within bioethics. If one asks the general question "What kind of person ought I to be in order to make good moral decisions?" is this different from asking the same question with one change—that of making "good moral decisions in medicine"? One common view holds that a moral decision in medicine ought to be understood as the application of good moral thinking in general to the specific domain of medicine (Clouser, 1978). The fact that the decision has a medical component, it is argued, does not make it a different kind of moral problem altogether, but an application of more general moral values or principles. A dutiful doctor is simply a dutiful person who has refined his or her personal character to respond to and care for the sick. He or she is empathic to suffering, steadfast in devotion to patients, and zealous in seeking their welfare.

Another, somewhat older, more traditional view within medicine is that an ethical decision in medicine is different, precisely because the domain of medicine is different from other areas of human life and because medicine has its own, historically developed, moral approaches and traditions. At the least, it is argued, making a decision within medicine requires a detailed and sensitive appreciation of the characteristic practices of medicine and of the art of medicine, and of the unique features of sick and dying persons. Even more, it requires a recognition of some moral principles, such as primum non nocere (first, do no harm) and beneficence, that have a special salience in the doctor-patient relationship (Pellegrino and Thomasma, 1981). The argument is not that the ethical principles and virtues of medical practice find no counterpart elsewhere, or do not draw upon more general principles; it is their combination and context that give them their special bite.

— DANIEL CALLAHAN

essary to consult with patients about some kinds of decisions; they will not see the issue of patient choice or informed consent as a moral issue at all—yet they may have a far livelier dedication to equality of access to health care.

The foundations of bioethics

There may not be a definitive resolution to the puzzle of whether bioethics should find its animating moral foundations within or outside medicine and biology. In any case, with time these two sources become mixed, and it seems clear that both can make valuable contributions (Brody, 1987). Perhaps more important is the problem of which moral theories or perspectives offer the most help in responding to moral issues and dilemmas.

Does an ethic of virtue or an ethic of duty offer the best point of departure? In approaching moral decisions, is it more important to have a certain kind of character, disposed to act in certain virtuous ways, or to have at hand moral principles that facilitate making wise or correct choices? The traditions of medicine, emphasizing the complexity and individuality of particular moral decisions at the bedside, have been prone to emphasize those virtues thought to be most important in physicians. They include dedication to the welfare of the patient and empathy for those in pain. Some philosophical traditions, by contrast, have placed the emphasis on principlism—the value of particular moral principles that help in the actual making of decisions (Childress, 1989; Beauchamp and Childress, 1989). These include the principle of respect for persons, and most notably respect for the autonomy of patients; the principle of beneficence, which emphasizes the pursuit of the good and the welfare of the patient; the principle of nonmaleficence, which looks to the avoidance of harm to the patient; and the principle of justice, which stresses treating persons fairly and equitably.

The advantage of principles of this kind is that, in varying ways and to different degrees, they can be used to protect patients against being harmed by medical practitioners and to identify the good of patients that decent medical and health care should serve. Yet how are such principles to be grounded, and how are we to determine which of the principles is more or less important when they conflict? Moral principles have typically been grounded in broad theories of ethics—utilitarianism, for example, which justifies acts as moral on the basis of the consequences of those acts (sometimes called consequentialism). Utilitarian approaches ask which consequences of a choice or an action or a policy would promote the best possible outcome. That outcome might be understood as maximizing the widest range of individual preferences, or promoting the greatest predominance of good over evil, or the greatest good of the greatest number. Just what one should judge as a "good" outcome is a source of debate within utilitarian theory, and a source of criticism of that theory. Such an approach to health-care rationing, for instance, would look for the collective social benefit rather than advantages to individuals.

A competing theory, deontology, focuses on determining which choices most respect the worth and value of the individual, and particularly the fundamental rights of individuals. The question of our basic obligations to other individuals is central. From a deontological perspective, good consequences may on occasion have to be set aside to respect inalienable human rights. It would be wrong, for instance, to subject a human being to dangerous medical research without the person's consent even if the consequences of doing so might be to save the lives of many others. Our transcendent obligation is toward the potential research subject.

Not all debates about moral theory come down to struggles between utilitarianism and deontology, though that struggle has been central to much of the moral philosophy that influenced bioethics in its first decades. Other moral theories, such as that of Aristotle, stress neither principles nor consequences but see a combination of virtuous character and seasoned practical reason as the most likely source of good moral judgment. For that matter, a morality centering on principles raises the problems of the kind of theory necessary to ground those principles, and of how a determination of priorities is to be made when the principles conflict (Clouser and Gert, 1990). A respect for patient autonomy, stressing the right of competent patients to make their own choices, can conflict with the principle of beneficence if the choice to be made by the patient may actually be harmful. And autonomy can also conflict with the principle of nonmaleficence if the patient's choice would seem to require that the physician be the person who directly brings harm to the patient.

Another classical struggle turns on the dilemma that arises when respect for individual freedom of choice poses a threat to justice, particularly when an equitable distribution of resources requires limiting individual choice. Autonomy and justice are brought into direct conflict. Recent debates on health-care rationing, or setting priorities, have made that tension prominent.

Even if principles—like autonomy and justice—are themselves helpful, their value declines sharply when they are pitted against each other. What are we supposed to do when one important moral principle conflicts with another? The approach to ethics through moral principles—often called "applied ethics"—has emphasized drawing those principles from still broader ethical theory, whose role it is to ground the principles. Moral analysis, then, works from the top down, from theory to principles to case application. An alternative way to understand the relationship between principles

See Also

Ethical Issues: Informed Consent in Genetic Counseling

Rights in Bioethics

The issues in bioethics are some of the most sensitive and most divisive confronted by our society, not least because of the rapid development of the life sciences.

PAGE 430

and their application, far more dialectical in its approach, is the method of "wide reflective equilibrium." It espouses a constant movement back and forth between principles and human experience, letting each correct and tutor the other (Daniels, 1979).

Still another approach is that of casuistry, drawn from methods commonly used in the Middle Ages. In contrast with principlism, it works from the bottom up, focusing on the practical solving of moral problems by a careful analysis of individual cases (Jonsen and Toulmin, 1988). A casuistical strategy does not reject the use of principles but sees them as emerging over time, much like the common law that has emerged in the Anglo-American legal tradition. Moral principles derive from actual practices, refined by reflection and experience. Those principles are always open to further revision and reinterpretation in light of new cases. At the same time, a casuistical analysis makes prominent use of analogies, employing older cases to help solve newer ones. If, for instance, general agreement has been reached that it is morally acceptable to turn off the respirator of a dying patient, does this provide a good precedent for withdrawing artificially provided hydration and nutrition? Is the latter form of care morally equivalent to the former, so that the precedent of the former can serve to legitimate the latter? Those are the kinds of questions that a casuistical analysis would ask. At the same time, a casuistical analysis runs the risk of being too bound to past cases and precedents. It can seem to lack the capacity to signal the need for a change of moral direction (Arras, 1991).

Still another principle-oriented approach proposes a new social contract between medicine and society (Veatch, 1981). Such a contract would be threefold. It comprises basic ethical principles for society as a whole, a contract between society and the medical profession about the latter's social role, and a contract between professionals and laypersons that spells out the rights and prerogatives of each. This strategy is designed both to place the ethics of medicine squarely within the ethical values of the larger society and to make sure that laypeople have sufficient choice and power to determine the kind of care they, and not paternalistic physicians, choose. Still another approach, more skeptical about finding any strong consensus on ethical foundations, stresses an ethic of secular pluralism and social peace, devising a minimal ethic for the community as a whole but allowing great play to the values and choices of different religious and value subcommunities (Engelhardt, 1986).

How important is moral theory?

There can be little doubt that the quest for the foundations of bioethics can be difficult and frustrating, no less so than the broader quest for the foundations of ethics in general (MacIntyre, 1981a). Yet how important for bioethics are moral theory and the quest for a grounding and comprehensive theory? Even the answers to that question are disputed. At one extreme are those who believe that bioethics as a discipline cannot expect intellectual respect, much less legitimately affect moral behavior, unless it can show itself to be grounded in solid theory justifying its proposed virtues, principles, and rules. At the other extreme are those who contend that even if there is no consensus on theory, social, political, and legal agreement of a kind sufficient to allow reasonable moral decisions to be made and policy to be set can be achieved. The President's Commission for the Study of Ethical Problems in Medicine and Biomedical and Behavioral Research of the early 1980s, and the National Commission for the Protection of Human Subjects in the mid-1970s, were able to achieve considerable agreement and gain general public and professional respect

BIOETHICS
Feminist Perspectives

Contemporary feminist approaches to bioethics, like casuistry, reject the top-down rationalistic and deductivist model of an ethic of principles (Baier, 1992; Sherwin, 1992). They reject even more adamantly what is seen as the tendency of an ethic of principles to universalize and rationalize. Feminist ethics lays a far heavier emphasis on the context of moral decisions, on the human relationships of those caught in the web of moral problems, and on the importance of feeling and emotion in the making of moral decisions. Feminist approaches, rooted in ways of thinking about morality that long predate the feminist movement of recent decades, also reflect a communitarian bias, reacting against the individualism that has been associated with a principle-oriented approach. Feminist thinkers commonly argue that those who lack power and status in society are often well placed to see the biases even of those societies that pride themselves on equality. While feminism has gained considerable prominence in recent years, it is only one of a number of efforts to find fresh methods and strategies for ethical analysis and understanding. These include phenomenological analyses, narrative-based strategies, and hermeneutical, interpretive perspectives (Zaner, 1988; Brody, 1987).

— DANIEL CALLAHAN

See Also

Bioethics and the Ethics of Virtue

even though individual members disagreed profoundly on the underlying principles of the consensus. There is of course nothing new in that experience. The American tradition of freedom of religion, for instance, has been justified for very different reasons, both theological and secular—reasons that in principle are in fundamental conflict with each other, yet are serviceable for making policy acceptable to believers and nonbelievers alike.

What kind of authority can a field so full of theoretical and practical disputes have? Why should anyone take it seriously? All important fields, whether scientific or humanistic, argue about their foundations and their findings. Bioethics is hardly unique in that respect. In all fields, moreover, agreement can be achieved on many important practical points and principles even without theoretical consensus. Bridges can be built well even if theoretical physicists disagree about the ultimate nature of matter. But perhaps most important, one way or another, moral decisions will have to be made, and they will have to made whether they are well grounded in theory or not. People must do the best they can with the material at hand. Even in the absence of a full theory, better and worse choices can be made, and more or less adequate justification can be offered. As the field progresses, even the debates on theory can be refined, offering greater insight and guidance even if the theories are still disputable.

Where, then, lies the expertise and authority of bioethics (Noble, 1982)? It lies, in the end, in the plausible insight and persuasive rationality of those who can reflect thoughtfully and carefully on moral problems. The first task of bioethics—whether the issues are clinical, touching on the decisions that must be made by individuals, or policy-oriented, touching on the collective decisions of citizens, legislators, or administrators—is to help clarify *what* should be argued about. A closely related task will be to suggest *how* these issues should be argued so that sensible, moral decisions can be made. Finally, there will be the more advanced, difficult business of finding and justifying the deepest theories and principles. There can, and will, be contention and argument at each of these stages, and it well may appear at first that no resolution or agreement can be found. Endless, unresolved disagreement in fact rarely occurs in practice, and that is why, if one looks at bioethics over a period of decades, achieved agreement and greater depth can be found, signs of progress in the field. The almost complete acceptance of such concepts as "patient rights," "informed consent," and "brain death," for instance—all at one time heatedly disputed concepts—shows clearly enough how progress in bioethics is and can be made.

THREE ELEMENTS OF MORAL DECISIONS

1. self-knowledge
2. knowledge of moral theories and traditions
3. cultural perception

Making good moral decisions

Good individual decision making encompasses three elements: self-knowledge, knowledge of moral theories and traditions, and cultural perception. Self-knowledge is fundamental because feelings, motives, inclinations, and interests both enlighten and obscure moral understanding. In the end, individual selves, alone with their thoughts and private lives, must wrestle with moral problems. This sort of struggle often forces one to confront the kind of person one is, to face one's character and integrity and one's ability to transcend narrow self-interest to make good moral decisions. And once a decision is made, it must be acted upon. A decision of conscience blends moral judgment and the will to act upon that judgment (Callahan, 1991). A complementary kind of knowledge, not easy to achieve, is also needed. Even as individuals we are social creatures, reflecting the times in which we live, embodied in a particular society at a particular time. Our social embeddedness will shape the way we understand ourselves, the moral problems we encounter, and what we take to be plausible and feasible responses to them. Moral theory by itself is hardly likely to be able to give us all the ingredients needed for an informed, thoughtful moral judgment. Only if it is complemented by self-understanding and reflectiveness about the societal and cultural context of our decisions, can moral theory be fleshed out sufficiently to be helpful and illuminating. Good moral judgment requires us to move back and forth among the necessary elements: the reflective self, the interpreted culture, and the contributions of moral theory. No one element is privileged; each has an indispensable part to play.

Yet something else is needed as well: a vision of the human good, both individual and collective. The biomedical, social, and environmental sciences produce apparently endless volumes of new knowledge about human nature and its social and natural setting. However, for that knowledge to be useful or meaningful, it must be seen in light of some notions of what constitutes the good of human life. What should human beings seek in their lives? What constitute good and worthy human ends? Proponents of the technological advances that emerge from the life sciences claim they can enhance human happiness and welfare. But that is likely to be possible only to the extent we have some decent idea of just what we need to bring us happiness and an enhanced welfare.

See Also

Law and Morality

Bioethics must pay sustained attention to such issues. It cannot long and successfully attend only to questions of procedure, or legal rules and regulations, without asking as well about the ends and goals of human life and activity. Ethical principles, rules, and virtues are in part a function of different notions of what enhances human life. Implicitly or explicitly, a picture of human life provides the frame for different theories and moral strategies of bioethics. This picture should animate living a life of our own, in which we develop our own understanding of how we want to live our individual lives, given the vast array of medical and biological possibilities; living our life with other human beings, which calls up ideas of rights and obligations, bonds of interdependency, and the creation of a life in common; and living our life with the rest of nature, which has its own dynamics and ends but provides us with the nurturing and natural context of our human lives.

Is there such a thing as *the* human good, either individually or collectively? Is there something we can, in an environmental context, call *the* good of nature? There is no agreement on *the* answer to those questions; on the contrary, there is fundamental disagreement. Some would argue that ethics can proceed with a relatively thin notion of the human good, placing the emphasis on developing those moral perspectives that would make it most possible to live with our differences about the meaning and ends of life. Others stress the importance of the substantive issues and reflect some basic doubt about whether ethics can proceed very far, or have sufficient substance, without trying to gain some insight into, and agreement upon, those basic matters (Kass, 1985; Callahan, 1993). Those debates must continue.

The greatest power of the biomedical, social, and environmental sciences is their capacity to shape the way we as human beings understand ourselves and the world in which we live. At one level—the most apparent—they give us new choices and thus new moral dilemmas. At another level, however, they force us to confront established views of our human nature, and thus to ask what we should be seeking: What kind of people do we want to be? A choice about artificial reproduction, say surrogate motherhood, is surely a moral choice. But it is also a way into the question of

BIOETHICS
Do the Ends Justify the Means?

In its early days, contemporary bioethics was generally seen as an activity on the fringes of research and practice in the life sciences; it had no place within environmental analysis. The dominant view was that the life sciences were a strictly scientific endeavor, with questions of morality and values arising only now and then in the interstices. That view has gradually changed. The life sciences are increasingly understood as, at their core, no less a moral endeavor than a scientific one. Ethics lies at the very heart of the enterprise, if only because facts and values can no longer be clearly separated—any more than the ends of the life sciences can be separated from the means chosen to pursue them.

No less important, questions of the moral means and ends of the life sciences cannot be long distinguished from the moral means and ends of the cultures and societies that pursue and deploy them. Here, fundamental questions must be asked. First, what kind of medicine and health care, what kind of stance toward nature and our environment, do we need for the kind of society we want? Such a question presupposes that we have some end in view for our society, though that may not be all that clear. What *is* clear, however, is that it is almost impossible to think for long about bioethics without being forced to think even more broadly about the society in which it will exist and whose ends—for better or worse—it will serve.

The second question reverses the first: What kind of a society ought we to want in order that the life sciences will be encouraged and helped to make their best contribution to human welfare? The contribution bioethics makes will in great part be a function of the goals sought by the life sciences, and those in turn will be stimulated or formed by society's goals. The life sciences shape the way we think about our lives, and thus they increasingly provide some key ingredients in society's vision of itself and in the lives of the citizens who comprise society.

Understood in terms of these two broad questions, bioethics takes its place at the heart of the enterprise of the life sciences. Only a part of its work will bear on dealing with the daily moral dilemmas and ethical puzzles that are part of contemporary health care and environmental protection. A no less substantial part will be to help shape the social context in which those dilemmas and puzzles play themselves out. At its best, bioethics will move back and forth between the concreteness of necessary individual and policy decisions and the broad notions and dynamic of the human situation. It is still a new field, seeking to better define itself and to refine its methods. It has made a start in shaping its direction and possible contribution, but only a start.

— DANIEL CALLAHAN

how we should understand the place of procreation in our private lives and in society. To see that is to appreciate profound challenges to our understanding of sexual and familial roles and purposes. The boundaries of bioethics cannot readily be constrained. The expanding boundaries force us to take up larger and deeper problems, much as a small stone tossed into the water creates larger and larger ripples.

— DANIEL CALLAHAN

BIOLOGY, PHILOSOPHY OF

Biology is the science of organisms. Some areas, like ecology, deal only with living organisms, looking especially at their behaviors in natural surroundings. Some areas, like physiology, move organisms into the laboratory, often dividing them in an attempt to understand how the parts work. Yet other areas, like paleontology, delve into the past. Looking at the fossil record, paleontologists try to reconstruct and explain life's history.

THREE AREAS OF THE PHILOSOPHY OF BIOLOGY

1. The science of biology itself: Is there something about life itself that demands a special kind of understanding beyond the reach of such "hard" sciences as physics and chemistry?
2. Questions about biology's broader moral, political, and social implications in the practical issues of human life.
3. Questions about biology and the societies and cultures in which its practitioners work, e.g., the effects of new discoveries on religious customs or sensibilities.

Philosophers are not scientists. They do not cut up animals or search rocks for traces of pollen. They look at the work and the results of science, considering problems that grow out of such efforts. Philosophers of biology therefore look at the work and claims of biologists, and they find three major areas of interest. First, there is a cluster of questions about the science of biology itself. Second, there are questions about the broader implications of biology for the practical problems of human living. Third, there are questions about biology and the societies or cultures in which it is produced. From the viewpoint of bioethics, the second set of questions is most pressing. But all three areas say things of interest. (A comprehensive review can be found in Ruse, 1988a; and a collection of articles in Ruse, 1988b.)

L'ÉLAN VITAL

Henri Bergson (1859–1941), a French philosopher whose influential writings explored intuition as a way of apprehending knowledge and the élan vital *present in all living things.*

Vitalism

The first group of questions opens with the most basic of all: Is there something about life itself that demands a special kind of understanding beyond the grasp of sciences like physics and chemistry? Philosophers and biologists, as far back as the Greek philosopher Aristotle, have thought that there is. They have claimed that there is some kind of life force (the early twentieth-century French philosopher Henri Bergson [1913] called it the *élan vital*) that makes living things living, as it were. A plant or an animal is by its very nature more than a collection of molecules, and as such cannot be understood by the laws and concepts of the physical sciences.

The technical term for the issue around which this controversy swirls is "reduction." Those who defend the special nature of organisms claim that biology cannot be "reduced" to physics and chemistry. The precise meaning of this claim has been a matter of much debate. At one level, the claim might be—and often has been—that the life force is some kind of event or thing. It is visualized as rather like a gas or a liquid, although clearly it has to be a peculiar kind of gas or liquid. This view, which is known as vitalism, is not easy to refute. Many suspect that the difficulty for the critic indicates a weakness in the position itself. Whatever properties the life force may have, it is not visible or tangible. It cannot be located in the same way that normal physical substances are located. Cut open a cabbage, and the life force cannot be seen oozing out of

"For a conscious being, to exist is to change, to change is to mature, to mature is to go on creating oneself endlessly."

HENRI BERGSON
CREATIVE EVOLUTION, 1907

it. Nor would a microscope help to make the life force visible.

On close examination, the life force proves to be elusive. Perhaps it is so difficult to locate because it is nonexistent. Might it be that, incredible though it may seem at first, organisms—even humans—are no more than fantastically complicated pieces of machinery?

Life's organization

At this point, the antireductionists often fall back on a second level of argument: that no one thinks there is an actual force. It is more of a metaphor, acknowledging that the structure and the mechanisms of organisms are different from those of inanimate objects. It is less a matter of substance and more a question of organization. The average plant or animal is put together in a way that defies physicochemical understanding.

It is not so easy to counter this antireductionist position; philosophers warn that the argument must be approached with caution. Indeed, there are obvious apparent counterexamples. The greatest triumph of modern biology came in 1953, when James Watson and Francis Crick discovered the "double helix," the structure of DNA, the ultimate threads of heredity. It thus became possible to decipher the "genetic code," which showed how the information needed for building each new generation of organisms was simply a matter of putting together relatively simple molecules in a special order.

The body of research and findings on DNA is thoroughly molecular and physicochemical. The DNA molecule, though very complex, is not mysterious. And it reveals the most basic information about organisms. Through DNA research the essence of biological organization is being captured more successfully by the physical sciences than it ever was by the biological sciences. This seems to be a very neat case of "reduction." (For more on this point, see Schaffner, 1980.)

Teleology

The case against the distinctive nature of biology is closing fast. Yet there is still something about biology as a science, a result of the distinctive nature of organisms, that marks it off from the physical sciences. Consider one of the most numerous of the dinosaurs, the stegosaurus. It had a double row of diagonal plates or fins along its back. Why did it have these? This is the pressing question for the paleontologist. What purpose or function did the plates serve? What was their "end"? Why was the beast as it was?

A good and satisfactory answer is that the plates or fins served to cool the animal on hot days, just as similar plates cool the water in hydroelectric plants. By contrast, in physics, no one would dream of asking what purpose the moon serves. Such forward-looking questions and explanations, thinking in terms of ends or final causes, rather than of prior causes, are not appropriate in the physical sciences. Apparently, however, they have their place in the biological sciences.

This kind of thinking is called teleological (Wright, 1976). Most modern philosophers are very wary of it, especially if it is linked either with life forces striving to achieve goals or with causes somehow acting from the future to affect the present. Consider an exercise in imagination. Suppose the stegosaurus is still living. It is a cold day at the end of winter. Obviously the stegosaurus does not have fins so that it can be cool today. Rather, it has them in anticipation of hot days next summer, when it will need cooling. But suppose that before next June, a comet hits the earth and wipes out all of the dinosaurs. It can hardly be that the stegosaurus has its plates today for next summer's heat wave, for that heat wave never comes. Or, if it does come, the stegosaurus is dead. Thus the cause was not only in the future but also nonexistent.

Nevertheless, even granting the truth of the teleological argument, perhaps the antireductionist critic does have a point. There may not be anything peculiar about organisms in respect to their composition or even their underlying organization (although this latter is very complex). Nor is there anything distinctive about the causal workings of organisms. Yet they are different from inanimate objects, like rocks and moons. They do seem "as if" designed—the stegosaurus's plates seem "as if" they were made (by a conscious being) for cooling.

This is why teleological language is appropriate. When human-made artifacts are considered, it is in terms of purposes or ends. "What is the purpose of this strange-looking knife?" "What end does this part play in the engine's functioning?" And so it is in biology. (See Kass, 1985, for more on this point.)

Darwinism

A consideration of teleology leads to the most-debated issue in the philosophy of biology. There is no puzzle today about why organisms seem as if designed. It is known why the stegosaurus, for instance, had plates. These characters are called adaptations. They are the end result of evolution, the long, slow process of development that produced all organisms from the original primitive beginnings. (Biologists today think that the earth is 4.5 billion years old, and that life arose naturally over 3.5 billion years ago.)

What drives evolution? In 1859, in *On the Origin of Species*, Charles Darwin revealed the major mechanism: natural selection. More organisms are born than can possibly survive. This leads to a "struggle for existence." Only a few live to maturity and—more important—to reproduce. Those that are successful will, on

See Also

Life and Life, Quality of

average, be different from those that are not. There will thus be a kind of differential breeding, akin to the artificial selection practiced by farmers and plant and animal fanciers. This is natural selection and, as Darwin stressed, it leads to the production of ever better adaptations.

There is nothing conceptually or causally odd about natural selection. It needs no life forces or causes working out of the future. The stegosaurus had its fins because those of its ancestors that had finlike protuberances survived and reproduced. And those that did not, did not. Yet evolutionary theory—especially natural selection—has been philosophically controversial from its first days. The best-known criticism was made by the distinguished Austrian-British philosopher Karl Popper (1974). He complains that "Darwinism" fails the acid test of genuine science. It cannot, even in principle, be shown wrong by empirical evidence. It is "unfalsifiable" (Popper, 1959, 1963).

According to Popper, the trouble with evolution is that its predictions—the things one would use to test a theory—tend to be very long-range, and thus beyond our scope. Who knows how the elephant's trunk will evolve a million years hence? And if it is not long-range, things are still too slippery for Darwinism to count as genuine science. Suppose someone shows that the stegosaurus's fins could not possibly be used for cooling. Will the Darwinian be abashed? Not one whit! Another pseudo explanation will be invented: that the stegosaurus needed the fins to attract the opposite sex, or some such thing. Hence, Popper concludes that Darwinism is best considered a "metaphysical research programme"—a kind of world philosophy—rather than hard science.

This is not a conclusion that biologists much like, nor do many philosophers of biology. They argue that Popper is ignorant of much of modern evolutionary biology, and that when it is properly understood, it can be seen as fully testable or falsifiable. Most Darwinian studies, far from being long-range, center on immediate effects and are fully testable. For instance, today there is (as there was by Darwin himself) much interest in mimicry (one animal or plant camouflages itself by pretending to be another organism or thing). Butterflies pretend to be other butterflies, and insects pretend to be leaves. In testing a claim here, a claim that will be based on the power of natural selection, Darwinism opens itself to check and refutation no less than does any theory of physics or chemistry. That a theory is not in fact refuted does not mean that it is unfalsifiable. It may indeed be true. (Gould, 1977, contains many articles dealing with criticisms of natural selection. Some of his more pertinent discussions are reprinted in Ruse, 1986. The best technical treatment of natural selection by a philosopher is Sober, 1984.)

ORIGIN OF CONTROVERSY

British naturalist Charles Darwin (1809–1882) rocked Western science with his theory of evolution by natural selection in On the Origin of Species *(1859).*

Even if Popper's basic criticism is not well founded, he is hinting at something important. Theories of biology, evolutionary biology in particular, do seem to have a looseness of logical argument—critics would say "flabbiness"—alien to the products of the physical sciences. Whatever the soundness of the overall framework, the biologist working on a particular problem frequently fails to achieve the tight logical control evidenced by the best of physics and chemistry. One mark of this is that much biology stays at the level of description. People working in biology are often unable to bring to bear the formal tools of logic and mathematics, so powerful and so pervasive in the physical sciences.

There are reasons why the biological sciences are as they are in these respects. The most obvious is that such sciences have lagged behind the physical sciences. Their problems are bigger and more challenging, and hence their finished products are incomplete. But perhaps there are other reasons—reasons that bring us toward problems of concern to the bioethicist. Science is made up of laws bound together into theories. For these laws to exist, the world must be analyzable into reasonably uniform sets or groups of entities. Johannes Kepler's laws about planets presuppose that there are readily identifiable groups of things properly called planets. Likewise, the biology of the DNA molecule presupposes that the components will be more or less like another. The completed molecules may be unique, but the parts are as alike as are the blocks in a child's Lego set.

"Man with all his noble qualities . . . still bears in his bodily frame the indelible stamp of his lowly origin."

CHARLES DARWIN
ON THE ORIGIN OF SPECIES
1859

As the net of biology spreads out to organisms, identifiability and uniformity become highly problematic. It is true that biologists divide the living world into groups. The basic class is the species, the group within which organisms breed with and only with themselves. Thus there is a set of fruit flies called *Drosophila melanogaster*, and a set of mammals called *Homo sapiens*. But even in these most basic groups, there is massive variation from one member to another. There must be, if Darwinism be true, for natural selection can work only if there is difference, with one type or form being successful over another.

How, then, can there possibly be generally applicable laws and theories? If the essence of the biological world is variation and difference, then it seems that the tight generality and rigor of the physical sciences (where one can readily pick out repeated instances) is unobtainable. Perhaps this is so. There are indeed genuine laws and theories of biology, but they come at a higher level of generality than particular species. There can be a law about genes, where there is repeatability. There cannot be a law about organisms in a species, for there is no such repeatability. Therefore, there are biological laws about genes—Mendel's law, for instance. However, for all that philosophers like to use such examples, in biology there are never laws like "All swans are white." All swans are never white.

All of this seems to mean that a species is not really like the set or class of the mathematician, for which there are precise membership criteria. Perhaps, especially since species members are bound by blood ties, species are more like supraorganisms. They are biological individuals in their own right. To use the language of the mathematicians, therefore, a particular organism like Michael Ruse or Julius Caesar is a part of the whole, the species *Homo sapiens*, just as a hand is part of a person. Humans are not members of the set *Homo sapiens*, analogous to the way in which a square is a

HUMAN SOCIOBIOLOGY

Hot Topic, Controversial Ideas

This is the attempt to look at animal social behavior from an evolutionary perspective, seeing it as something caused and maintained by natural selection. What has made sociobiology such a "hot" topic is the fact that today's evolutionists have been able to give convincing reasons for the evolution of the most famous case of social behavior: those sterile worker insects who spend their whole lives working for the good of their nests, apparently without any thought for themselves.

What makes sociobiology controversial is that its practitioners, led by Harvard biologist Edward O. Wilson (the Wilson of the ecological equilibrium theory), have applied their science to the human species (Lumsden and Wilson, 1981). But humans are not ants—although some people have suggested that perhaps homosexuals are analogous to sterile workers, and they have looked for evidence that such people do aid their close relatives. The human sociobiologists argue that perhaps humans are controlled in much that they do by their biology, because natural selection favors such control. Perhaps, for instance, the Victorian anthropologist Edward Westermarck was right in suggesting that people do not generally want to have sex with close relatives because biology has provided contrary emotions. It is an established fact that such close interbreeding leads to biologically handicapped offspring. (See Wilson, 1978.)

Wilson certainly has no hidden motives in pushing his science. Yet the history of the twentieth century shows only too well how, in the hands of fanatics, biological determinism can lead to dreadful consequences. Philosophers have therefore been at the front of those who have looked long and skeptically at human sociobiology and its claims. As in the ecology case, they are keenly aware of how easy it is to slide from supposed science to social prescriptions. Even the most moderate of sociobiologists are liable to harbor beliefs about teaching, for instance, and about the degrees to which children are biologically capable of learning. More controversially, they may hold views about the variations between learning capacities, and the futility of expecting some people ever to achieve the heights of others.

For a start, philosophers realize that although analogies and metaphors are invaluable, they should be approached with extreme caution. Take the claim that human homosexuals are akin to sterile worker ants. Humans are not ants, even of a peculiar mammalian variety. Nor is there any evidence whatsoever that gay men and lesbians have reduced fertility. Indeed, even though it is probable that homosexuals have fewer offspring than do heterosexuals, at best this is a matter of averages and by no means a universal truth. In many societies, including those of North America, there is strong social pressure on people (especially females) to marry and have families—no matter who their desired sex partners may be.

This does not mean that the science of human sociobiology necessarily collapses. Some of the greatest moves in science have come through innovative metaphors. Perhaps it is ultimately fruitful to compare people to worker ants. However, when people want to draw social conclusions from science, they should carefully scrutinize the science itself and its links to the conclusions. (For very different assessments of human sociobiology, see Ruse, 1979a, 1986, 1989 [pro]; and Kitcher, 1985 [contra].)

— MICHAEL RUSE

member of the set of quadrilaterals. (Hull, 1989, discusses these questions authoritatively.)

If species really are biological individuals, that seems to be another factor separating biology from physics. There are bioethical implications also. Minorities have often been judged inadequate because they do not measure up to the supposed criteria for inclusion in the set *Homo sapiens*. Those with Down syndrome are judged inadequate because they do not have the standard number of chromosomes. Homosexuals are judged immoral because they do not have a typical sexual orientation, or because they are not part of the breeding pool. However, if species themselves are thought of as individuals, then such judgments are not simply unkind but conceptually flawed. Diversity is part of life, and in itself being heterosexual or homosexual is no more a species matter than being blue-eyed or brown-eyed. (This is not to swing to another extreme and deny the existence of genetic disease. The point is that one judges a genetic disease as one judges all disease, in terms of quality of life, and not by biological class membership.)

There is another point at which highlighting the variation within species has major repercussions. A major biotechnological enterprise is the Human Genome Project (HGP), which involves trying to map (that is, decipher) the total molecular underpinning of human heredity. If variation is the rule rather than the exception, then crude, one-and-for-all readings are doomed to failure or inadequacy. Human nature at the molecular level is far too varied to hope for one archive, wherein all pertinent information must be sorted. To be really useful, there must be a range of readings, telling all of the possible variants. (For more on some of the technical issues of evolutionary theory, see Rosenberg, 1985; and Sober, 1993. For more on the HGP, see Kevles and Hood, 1992.)

Recombinant DNA

The second set of questions of interest to the philosopher of biology comprises the questions that deal with the implications of biology for matters of moral, political, and social concern. What happens, for example,

ECOLOGY
The Fragility of Our Planet

A concern of ongoing interest is the threat posed to the environment by population growth, by the profligate use of limited natural resources, by the indifference to the effects of the use of synthetic substances, and by many other factors. Here the science of ecology has a major role to play, as life scientists try to understand the fragile and volatile relations between the living components of this planet. And here, philosophers of biology have a major role to play as they try to discover and assess the moral and social implications of the ecologists' findings.

This becomes clearest through consideration of one of the major theoretical branches of modern ecology, the MacArthur/Wilson theory of "island biogeography." With elegant simplicity, this theory relates two groups of factors. The size of an island and its distance from the mainland are linked with the carrying capacity of the island, which means not just the number of inhabitants the island can hold but also the overall number of species on the island. Essentially, the claim is that a kind of equilibrium is achieved, with the number of species leaving the island or becoming extinct being balanced by the number of new arrivals.

The broader implications of this theory are obvious. Given sufficient time, accidental or intentional cases of island denudation will be righted naturally. It is true that the theory talks only of numbers of species on or off an island, without specifying actual kinds of organisms. It might involve replacement of indigenous flora and fauna by the Norwegian rat. But the bottom line is that nature has a way of righting itself.

Unfortunately, as critics have been able to show, if ever a theory came close to failing Popper's falsifiability criterion, it is the MacArthur/Wilson theory. The direct evidence is slight (and, incidentally, raises questions of its own, for it entails the poisoning of entire populations of small islets). It is not clear what types of evidence actually support the MacArthur/Wilson theory and what types only appear to provide such support. One of the first things that philosophy teaches is to question the use of words—their meaning and their application. Never was such wisdom more needed than at this point, for ecologists are deeply divided over their terms. When is an island an island, and when is an island not an island? Does it have to be surrounded by water? If so, does it matter if there is a connection to the mainland at low tide? Can there be substitutes for water—desert? jungle? Or simply something inhospitable to a certain species, as savanna might be to a tree-dwelling monkey?

Decisions on questions such as these can influence profoundly the conclusions drawn about whether nature can restock itself naturally, or whether, once disturbed, nature can ever truly regain equilibrium. The trouble is that evidence becomes almost irrelevant as words are expanded and contracted to give the right answers. What appeared to be solid science is exposed as environmental expediency masquerading as genuine knowledge.

— MICHAEL RUSE

when biologists devise new techniques of inquiry that promise powerful insights into the nature of living beings, yet pose possible threats to the well-being of society?

The obvious example of a tension of this kind came in the 1970s, with the advent of recombinant DNA (r-DNA) techniques for investigating the nature and composition of the basic molecular building blocks of organisms. Here was a powerful new tool—more precisely, a range of tools—that promised ready insights into the functioning of the inner parts of the cell, as well as ways of fabricating new organic forms. Many of these forms could have direct value to humans in medicine, in agriculture, and the like. Yet this set of tools held the threat of potentially dangerous new forms of life that could wreak havoc on humankind and the environment.

Philosophers played a significant role in this debate and in its resolution, drawing up guidelines for the sensible prosecution of r-DNA research. They were able to disentangle some of the moral issues that arise in a conflict between individual rights and interests and the common good and welfare. A simple but important point was showing that many moral conflicts arise not because people differ about the ultimate principles of right and wrong but because the empirical facts of the case are unclear or disputed. In the r-DNA case, it soon became clear that the real problem was that those who devised the new technology were abysmally ignorant of the basic facts of epidemiology, the branch of medicine that treats organisms dangerous to humankind. As soon as some essential empirical information about the spread of disease was brought forward, many of the fears about the dangers of r-DNA research were seen to be ill-founded. (See Jackson, 1979.)

See Also
Sexism

Creationism

The third set of issues that has engaged today's philosophers of biology has to do with a broad spectrum of matters about biology and the culture(s) within which biologists think and work. The most visible is religion. Darwin's *Origin* upset religious sensibilities, and into the twentieth century in America there were strenuous moves to keep the teaching of evolution out of schools. Nor has such opposition subsided, although most Christians and Jews today accept evolution fully. The Fundamentalists, who take the early chapters of the Bible (six days of creation, six-thousand-year earth span, a universal flood) literally,

IS BIOLOGY SEXIST?

The cries of the creationists may be misguided, but they are heartfelt. Evolution may not be atheistic secular humanism, as they claim, but their fears should lead to consideration of science in its own right and as a reflection of the culture from which it emerges. There is no sharp distinction between a science and its society. Darwinism, for instance, reveals its beginnings both in the central role given to struggle—an idea taken from the influential socioeconomic writings of Thomas Robert Malthus—and in the key place accorded to adaptation—which highlights the designlike nature of organisms, and was taken by Darwin from the natural theology of his day. (See Ruse, 1979b.)

Feminist critics of science are very sensitive to the links between science and society, and they have had some very severe things to say about biology (Harding, 1986; Birke, 1986; Hubbard, 1983; Keller, 1984; but also see Hrdy, 1981). They claim that the biological sciences are tainted by the inherently sexist values of Western society. Darwin is highlighted as a persistent offender, for (particularly in the *Descent of Man*) he was much given to portraying women as men's intellectual and physical inferiors. At present, Wilson is the feminists' favorite bête noire, for he supposedly tends to see women as having a natural (that is, biological) propensity for second-class status.

Some of these criticisms are unfair—or at least unbalanced. Alfred Russel Wallace, the codiscoverer with Darwin of natural selection, was an ardent feminist, arguing that the future of the human race lies in the hands of young women, who can be trusted to breed only with the best young men. (He derived this somewhat optimistic idea from Edward Bellamy's novel *Looking Backward*.) Nor does one often hear that Wilson's student, the primatologist Sarah Hrdy, has argued that because human females have concealed ovulation (they do not come into heat), biology has ensured that females are the major driving force in the species today. Males have to be present in the home and be involved in child care; otherwise, in their absence, females could cheat on them and they would never know that their supposed children are their real children.

Nevertheless, sexist and other offensive ideologies do seep into biology. Ongoing caution is demanded, and here philosophers can, and do, have a significant part to play. This is not to say that the philosopher has to smooth everything to a uniformly gray surface, satisfying only to the politically correct. Rather, as always, the philosopher has to play the gadfly, making people examine their most cherished beliefs. If and when a science makes unwarranted judgments about people, it is the philosopher who must blow the whistle. (Haraway, 1989, is a good place to start with the feminist critique of biology.)

— MICHAEL RUSE

have had considerable success in recent years in influencing educators and others. They have even been able to influence legislative bodies, most notoriously in 1981, when the state of Arkansas mandated the teaching of "creation science" alongside evolution in publicly funded schools.

Philosophers have long been at the forefront of showing why it is reasonable to accept evolution as a fact. Indeed, it was a philosopher who showed Darwin the way. How do you persuade someone of the plausibility of a position when (as in the case of evolution) there is no direct evidence, no eyewitness? The answer, identical to that used by lawyers attempting to determine guilt without such testimony, is to work through circumstantial evidence, showing how many pieces of information point unambiguously to one cause that validates the separate pieces. The English philosopher of science William Whewell (1840) called this procedure a "consilience of inductions," and he taught it to Darwin, who strove (successfully) to show how all the areas of biology—ecology, physiology, paleontology, and more—are unified and explained by evolution through selection. Things like the fossil record are the clues of evolution.

Thus, it is misleading to say "Evolution is just a theory and not a fact." It is both. It is a scientific theory about natural selection. It is an established fact that evolution occurs. It shows also how disastrous it would be if religious enthusiasts dislodged evolution's place in biology teaching. As the geneticist Theodosius Dobzhansky once said, "Nothing in biology makes sense except in the light of evolution." Or, to modify another remark, teaching biology while questioning evolution would be like teaching French while querying the significance of the irregular verbs.

The Arkansas law on teaching "creation science" was overturned. In this case, and in the subsequent and ongoing fight against the pressure of the biblical literalists, philosophy of biology played a crucial role. At the heart of the issue are the relative statuses of evolution and of "creation science." Are they genuine science, or are they religion masquerading as science? No one is denying the right of creationists to believe as they do. The question is whether creationism is truly religion. If it is, then it cannot legally be taught in public schools. The Arkansas court (and other legal bodies, up to the U.S. Supreme Court) have agreed that "creation science" is truly not genuine science. Most crucially, it fails the test of being falsifiable. And no matter what evidence arises, its proponents simply refuse to allow that it could impinge negatively on their central beliefs. (Ruse, 1988c, collects articles dealing with philosophical aspects of the creationism controversy.)

Biological education

That science tends to reflect culture is not a cause for concern. It is a cause for caution. Consider, for example, an aspect of evolutionary thought that has repeatedly been highlighted by the well-known biologist Stephen Jay Gould (1989). From its beginnings in the eighteenth century, evolutionary thought has been infected with "progressionism." The history of life has been portrayed as a more or less uniform succession from the simplest forms to the sophisticated end point, *Homo sapiens*. But, as Gould insists, this interpretation has been a vehicle not just for speciesism but also for racism. What more natural than to assume that there is biological progress among humans, with blacks at the bottom and Anglo-Saxons at the top?

Philosophers of biology have thought about and worked extensively on this very point. They have tried to document the extent to which every evolutionist has espoused progressionism; what senses of progressionism have been favored; whether a progress-free evolutionism is attainable; and whether one can separate the scientific from the social. Nor is this inquiry merely some academic exercise. Survey after survey shows that when evolution is taught, it is taught in a progressionist manner. The myth is being perpetuated.

It might be countered that Gould's fears are exaggerated, and that no one today would use biology in the way of the imperialists of old. Perhaps this is true, although if the threat has diminished, it is certainly a break with history. Or it might be countered that it is better that evolution of some sort be taught than none at all. Again, perhaps this is true, although it is hard to see why things should not be put right at once. It is enough to conclude by saying that if science is a glorious product of the human imagination, and perhaps the salvation of the future, it must be taught and taught well. This being so, the philosophy of biology has its role to play here, as it has a role to play in so many other areas. (See Nitecki, 1988, for more on evolutionary biology and progress.)

— MICHAEL RUSE

"Evolution is not a force but a process; not a cause but a law."

JOHN, VISCOUNT MORLEY OF BLACKBURN
ON COMPROMISE, 1874

BLOOD TRANSFUSION

Blood transfusion is one of the essentials of preserving life and maintaining health. Transfusion is required to replace red cell or whole blood loss as a result of chronic illnesses such as hemophilia or thalassemia, or blood loss through acute trauma or surgery. The process of transfusion involves removing blood from one individual (the donor) and giving it to another (the recipient). Defined in such simple terms, it would seem to pose

A policy of testing health-care workers for HIV would be counterproductive.

PAGE 52

B

BLOOD TRANSFUSION

The Collection and Distribution of Blood

few problems. Yet the collection and distribution of blood require a complex medical technology and raise a set of ethical and legal issues pitting confidentiality and the privacy rights of individuals against the equally compelling public-health demands for a safe blood supply. The onset of acquired immunodeficiency syndrome (AIDS) has exacerbated these concerns.

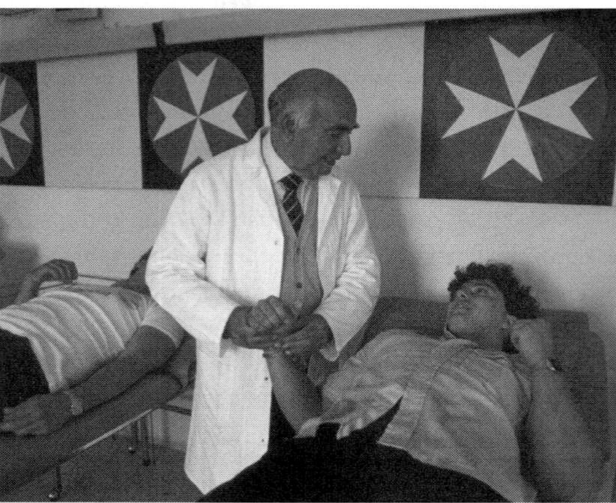

YOU'LL FEEL BETTER

Virtually painless, donating blood is widely seen as a selfless act of giving for the common good.

The symbolic, historical, and religious meaning of blood makes its exchange a metaphor for community. Blood relatives are family; blood feuds indicate disagreement between rival families or clans. The central act of Christian observance, as defined by the New Testament, is the real or symbolic changing of wine into the blood of Christ, thus delineating the community of Christians from outsiders (Murray, 1991). Blood donation has been similarly used to delineate community boundaries. As late as 1968 in Louisiana and Alabama, blood was labeled by the race of the donor and transfusions limited to recipients of the donor's race (Titmuss, 1971). In contemporary society, where the link between blood and the human immunodeficiency virus (HIV) has been documented, exclusion from the ability to participate in this gift-giving relationship results not from external characteristics of individuals but from characteristics of the individuals' blood, unseen but potentially fatal.

The collection and distribution of blood

One significant ethical question with respect to the blood supply relates to the method of collection and distribution of blood. The essential issue is whether blood is to be considered a commodity or a social resource (Titmuss, 1971). Both cash payments, in which individuals are compensated for giving blood, and insurance (credit) systems, in which blood is donated in exchange for the recipient's agreement to supply blood when needed, treat the collection and distribution of blood as commercial transactions. In contrast, voluntary systems are based on the implicit assumption that blood is a social resource. From the late 1940s until the early 1980s, all three systems existed simultaneously in the United States, with some regions utilizing one of the systems exclusively and others relying on a mixture of all three systems.

Because blood is such a vital commodity, commercial approaches to its supply raise questions of social justice. For example, under systems of cash payment, the poor and low-income segments of the population (and thus racial and ethnic minorities, because of their high correlation with poverty) are most likely to participate in the selling of blood yet do not always have the means to pay for blood when it is needed.

The seminal work of the British sociologist Richard Titmuss (1971) characterized the donation of blood as a measure of social connectedness, fulfilling an essential need in persons to act for the benefit of community. He strongly criticized the commercial approach to the blood supply in the United States. Comparing the United States with England and Wales, Titmuss argued that the all-voluntary system in the latter countries assisted in maintaining the sense of community, while the predominantly commercial donor recruitment efforts in the United States threatened the fragile fabric of society. He stated that the use of payment and "blood insurance" as incentives for donation in the United States produced a traffic in blood that reflected this nation's dominant commitment to capitalism. It was Titmuss's view that the commercialization of blood in the United States denied its inhabitants the opportunity to see themselves as participating in a voluntary act of giving and resulted in an inadequate and unsafe supply.

In contrast to Titmuss, Alvin Drake, Stan Finkelstein, and Harvey Sapolsky (1982) found that regardless of the presence of credit systems, the American donors were in fact similar to British donors in that they came if the message was clear and collection agencies made donating simple in an easily accessible place. So, they argued, despite the underlying economic system that might be attached to the collection agency, the American donor approached the act of giving with a desire to participate in providing something needed by another.

The formation of a national blood policy was influenced by Titmuss's argument that however small the percentage of commercial donors, their participation led to a greater risk to the blood supply because of the relationship between a paid donor and infection, particularly with hepatitis B. Thus the adoption of the national blood policy in 1974 began a shift toward a volunteer model for the collection of whole blood, and by the late 1980s nearly all whole blood was collected from voluntary donors.

Whole blood includes red cells, plasma, platelets, and other components. It is increasingly common today for patients to receive only the particular blood component most desirable for their required therapy. This practice, known as component therapy, allows for more efficient utilization of the whole-blood supply and minimizes the risk to recipients that comes from exposure to unneeded substances in the blood (Drake et al., 1982).

Although commercial whole-blood collection has been effectively eliminated in the United States, the plasma fractionation industry, which is the domain of the private pharmaceutical firms, continues to obtain most of its products from paid donors. In addition to plasma, albumin for the treatment of shock and trauma and Factor VIII for treatment of hemophilia are important products of this industry. A major reason for the continued involvement of the United States in for-profit plasma production is the role that the country plays in the supply of plasma to world markets; in recent years, the United States has produced approximately one-third of the world supply of albumin and one-half the Factor VIII (U.S. Congress, Office of Technology Assessment, 1985). In contrast, many western European countries collect more blood than they require for whole-blood transfusions through purely voluntary donations, and use the overage to produce sufficient plasma. This overbleeding to produce a sufficient supply of plasma results in an oversupply of red blood cells, some of which are exported to the United States. Overbleeding in western Europe introduces commercialism into what is commonly thought of as a purely voluntary system and raises a set of issues for treatment of donors.

AIDS and the blood supply

INFECTION RISK IN BLOOD TRANSFUSION

Infection Type	Risk per Unit
HIV	1 in 225,000
Hepatitis B	1 in 50,000
Hepatitis C	1 in 3,300

Concerns about the safety of the blood supply took on new significance in 1982 when the possibility of contracting AIDS from blood transfusion became clear. Although the actual risk of contracting AIDS through transfusion is less than the risk of contracting hepatitis B or C, AIDS, unlike other diseases transmitted through the blood, is inevitably fatal. Thus it has radically altered the relationship between donors and recipients of blood. AIDS has raised profound questions about the potential conflict between protection of the rights of donors and the right of society to a safe blood supply. AIDS is also an example of a situation where public perception, rather than actual data based on relative risks, guides what we tell a patient. Physicians tend to have patients sign special consents for transfusion that clarify the AIDS-related risks but do not always include information about other risks. Provision of more complete information might, however, result in too much complexity for the patient to deal with.

Not until 1985 was a test for the presence of antibodies to the AIDS virus introduced. This test, however, allows some blood with the AIDS virus to remain undetected because there is a forty-five-day window of vulnerability (Dodd, 1992), in which an infected individual may not have developed sufficient antibodies to be detected. Only the development of a test for the virus itself will further reduce the danger of contracting AIDS through use of blood or blood products.

Prior to the introduction of the test, donor deferral guidelines were the basis for protecting the safety of the blood supply. Self-deferral involves asking individuals who are members of high-risk groups, such as homosexual men and intravenous drug users of both sexes, not to donate blood (U.S. Congress, Office of Technology Assessment, 1985). Adoption of such guidelines, however, was resisted at first by many of the involved groups. The homosexual community, particularly in San Francisco, was concerned about the consequences of self-deferral to the progress they were making through the increasingly successful homosexual rights movement. In addition there were some general concerns about the violation of the civil rights of individuals excluded from donating through self-deferral. The fact that the groups first seen as potential carriers of AIDS were drug abusers and male homosexuals led some to suggest that, because these groups were personally responsible for having contracted the disease, they had forfeited their civil rights and should be banned from giving blood.

Gradually, however, a sophisticated system for self-deferral was developed. The health history now taken when an individual comes to give blood contains questions about high-risk behaviors including homosexual or bisexual behavior, intravenous drug use, and travel to sub-Sahara Africa. Potential donors may choose to defer after reading the reasons why they should not donate. Testing and self-deferral have substantially reduced the risk factor of contracting AIDS.

The group approach to a safer blood supply involves exclusion of certain categories of individuals from the donor population because they are deemed high-risk groups. Selection of groups to be excluded may reflect societal prejudices rather than scientific judgment. For example, Haitians were first an excluded

See Also

AIDS: Health-Care and Research Issues

TRANSFUSIONS
The Right to Refuse

Both the right to receive transfusions and the right to refuse them have become increasingly significant issues. In the years since the development of transfusions as a treatment technique, the supply of blood has been increased, and today an inadequate supply is not a barrier to treatment. Therefore, as is the case with other issues in medical decision making, the physician determines the need for transfusion without regard to the economic status of the patient. In U.S. society, however, there are many ways in which the economic status of the patient affects the type of treatment he or she receives, and these factors also affect decisions about transfusions.

General questions of the right to refuse treatment have been raised in recent years, particularly with regard to the terminally ill. Related issues apply, specifically in connection with transfusion, because of the view of Jehovah's Witnesses that the transfusion of whole blood and most of its components is prohibited. This refusal raises dilemmas including the right to informed consent, the ability to help versus the respect for autonomy, and the potential liability for treating versus the potential liability for failing to treat. In the case of adults, court decisions have generally upheld the right to informed consent. Where a child's life is in danger, however, the decisions have favored the transfusion of blood (Lentz, 1990).

The operation of the blood-supply system demonstrates how what initially appears to be a technical or scientific advance frequently gives rise to fundamental ethical and political issues. As explained above, transfusion involves a technology that enables blood to be taken from one individual and given to another, frequently to sustain the life of the recipient. This technical definition, however, is too simplistic. In the collection and distribution of blood, we encounter significant issues of community, social justice, privacy, and the equitable distribution of the gift of life that extend far beyond the promise of the technology.

— LOUANNE KENNEDY

group, but the exclusion has since been removed as a result of political pressure by Haitians in the United States and of evidence that their infection rate, though higher than the general rate in the United States, is considerably lower than that of persons from countries in sub-Sahara Africa. With the exception of homosexual men, those excluded in the United States are predominantly racial minorities.

Exclusion of high-risk groups raises substantial problems of confidentiality and informed consent. The names of individuals who test positive for HIV antibodies or hepatitis B or C, or who carry other viral agents, are placed on registries maintained by agencies within the blood supply system (e.g., the American Red Cross, the American Association of Blood Banks). Individuals are not always informed, in advance of volunteering, of the possibility of being listed on a registry.

In addition, individuals placed on a registry in one system may or may not be identified as at risk in another, which has led to recent efforts to try to coordinate this information. Since all blood is tested and registries are not checked until after the blood is taken, it is not clear that registries significantly increase safety. Moreover, some tests, including the test for hepatitis C, have produced high false-positive rates. The test for hepatitis C is so new that many who have given blood for decades suddenly find themselves deferred from future donations, resulting in their alienation from the system of collection. In this case, weighing the consequences of this alienation of individuals who have been long-term donors against the potential for life-threatening disease for the recipient has led to a decision to protect the recipient.

Problems of confidentiality also arise because potential donors are asked intimate questions about their sexual life and drug usage. While asking these questions may be justified on public-health grounds, past cases in which government agencies have obtained confidential information raise justifiable belief that the information should not be recorded. There is no federal statute that prohibits disclosure of the information except to blood banks, and there is no assurance under most state law that a court might not order disclosure in unexpected circumstances. In fact, some lawsuits resulting from transfusion-related AIDS have led to court decisions to permit identification of donors (Willett, 1986). Although the issues are similar in some respects to those arising in current debates regarding the testing of alleged rapists to determine HIV status, in the latter case the courts have taken the position that the primary concern is protecting the rights of the accused.

Alternatives to the system of transfusion

Although the gift relationship is founded on altruistic motivation, anthropologists have long recognized that giving gifts creates bonding and an expectation of

See Also

AIDS and Confidentiality

receipt of gifts (Titmuss, 1971). In the context of the blood supply, voluntary donors expect the availability of blood when they need it and that the blood will be safe. Because of the fatal nature of AIDS, many have begun to fear that the exchange feature of donating has been taken away and have sought alternative ways to assure themselves of a safe, adequate blood supply. These techniques wholly or partially sever the broad community relationship.

For example, autologous transfusion, in which individuals store their own blood for future use, has increased substantially and is safe. A technique has also been developed to recycle the patient's own blood during surgery (interoperative blood salvage). Another alternative is directed donation, in which the patient receives blood from family and friends who are asked to donate. While directed donation may seem a safe alternative to patients, there is no evidence that the blood of directed donors is safer than that of the general donor pool; and if directed donors are unwilling to identify high-risk behavior, the risk may actually be greater because many directed donors are first-time donors. To reduce this risk, donors are given an opportunity to have their blood taken but to indicate through a choice of bar codes that their blood should not be used for transfusion (Shulman, 1991).

Considerable work is being done on the development of artificial blood substitutes. Research has continued for more than twenty-five years on the development of red-cell substitutes but has not yet resulted in an alternative approved for human use (Winslow, 1992). Applied researchers are also at work on the manufacture of biological proteins that plasma now supplies, and a biosynthetic version of one such protein, clotting Factor VIII, has been in clinical trials for several years. Success in the development of artificial blood substitutes would increase the safety of the blood supply and resolve a number of the issues discussed here.

— LOUANNE KENNEDY

BODY

SOCIAL THEORIES

Everywhere one looks in medicine, one finds bodies. Not only are bodies ubiquitous, they are essential to the practice of medicine. Whenever something seems to go awry with our bodies, we seek the services of medicine and become "patients." Medical personnel often reduce patients' bodies to the particular problems they present, for example, "the coronary bypass in room 14B" or the "end-stage renal disease case." Bodies are the material upon or through which medicine is practiced: clinicians touch, scan, listen to, cut into, comfort, rehabilitate, alter, and monitor the bodies of patients. Likewise, practitioners bring their bodies with them when they enter the clinic. Clinicians not only interact with patients and families through their bodies (e.g., shaking hands, touching, probing, lifting, bathing patients), they also bring to the clinical setting their own unique embodied experience—gendered, professional, perhaps overtired, young or old, ill or healthy, angry or compassionate, prejudiced, and so on. Thus, the body is an indispensable component of those persons experiencing illness and those giving care, as well as to the dynamics of illness and healing. Without a body, there is no person, no identity, no relationship, no health, no illness, no healing.

Yet despite the fact that bodies are so central to medicine, "the body" is rarely mentioned in the literature of bioethics. Discussions in bioethics generally center on concepts of personhood (Is the patient a person? Is the person competent?), issues related to personhood (such as autonomy, informed consent, rights, confidentiality, choice), and questions of cost/benefit analysis (Do the benefits outweigh the risks? How can we achieve the greatest good for the greatest number at the lowest cost?). A patient's "personhood" is generally understood in terms of rationality or mental capacity (rather than, for example, a beating heart, membership in the species *Homo sapiens*, or one's ability to form emotional bonds to others), personal values and preferences (rather than, for example, obligations based on relationships or social roles), and ability to function autonomously (rather than, alternatively, one's ability to recognize and to function within our essential interdependence and interrelatedness).

Moreover, because "personhood" has been so narrowly defined, and because bioethics has made personhood its central category, many of the significant problems in bioethics center on bodies whose status as "persons" is unclear, bodies that lack or have lost rationality, for example: "defective" neonates, anencephalic newborns, brain-dead potential organ donors, patients in persistent vegetative state, fetuses to be aborted or experimented on, mentally handicapped and incarcerated individuals to be used as research subjects, or elderly individuals suffering from dementia or Alzheimer's disease. When these patients have not left rational and autonomous specifications of what their preferences would be (e.g., living wills, organ donor cards), other individuals possessing rationality, preference, and autonomy (either patient surrogates or the courts) decide what to do with their bodies.

There is a growing consensus that this notion of personhood is too narrow, and that by excluding attention to the body, bioethics does not fully take into

Feminist critics complain that research focusing on genital physiology as the standard of sexual involvement evidences a "phallic fallacy."

PAGE 645

See Also

Social Constructionists: "Phallic Fallacies?"

FOUNDERS OF EMPIRICIST MATERIALISM

Name	Birth/Death	Major Influence on Western Thought
Francis Bacon	1561–1626	credited with development of the modern scientific method
René Descartes	1596–1650	viewed body as a machine, inferior to, and separate from, the mind
John Locke	1632–1704	views on private property have influenced they way the body in bioethics is often treated as property rights

"We have rudiments of reverence for the human body, but we consider as nothing the rape of the human mind."

ERIC HOFFER
THE PASSIONATE STATE OF MIND, 1954
PAGE 84

account all the morally significant dimensions of the practice of medicine. If we cannot be a self or act in the world without our body, then that body must be included into the description of the moral situation. At the same time, there is a concern that, in spite of the rhetoric of freedom, personal fulfillment, and rights, by overlooking the body, medicine and bioethics can become (some would say "have become") avenues through which society restricts the freedom of its members through repression and control.

The body in medicine and bioethics: Empiricist materialism

The fact that the body is overlooked is due in large part to the ways in which the body is understood by medicine, bioethics, and contemporary Western culture. Richard Zaner has provided a helpful outline of the development of the view of the body that dominates contemporary medicine and is shared by bioethics (Zaner, 1994). This view is called "empiricist materialism."

Francis Bacon is credited with the development of the modern scientific experimental method. The development of this method required a new understanding of the meaning of "nature." Bacon demythologized nature, declaring it to be little more than brute, inert, morally neutral, raw material, available to be dissected and manipulated through empirical investigation in order to gain knowledge of its universal laws and regularities. Such knowledge is power, Bacon proposed, for in spite of its status as totally object, nature was also understood as containing within it great power, chaotic power that threatened to undo the orderliness of civilization (take, e.g., the destructive power of tornadoes, earthquakes, and illness). As the human mind gained knowledge of nature, through rational empirical investigation and quantification, this power could be channeled and controlled, thus giving humanity power over nature and making it fulfill human needs.

One aspect of nature affected by this change in understanding was the human body. The body, understood as inert, morally neutral raw material, became likewise amenable to scientific investigation and control. This reconceptualization of the body was accelerated by the work of Descartes. Descartes asserted that the mind (or soul) is both entirely distinct from and morally superior to the body (Descartes, 1968). This view is called "mind/body dualism" and exerted a strong influence on the development of Western philosophy. Allied to this mind/body dualism was Descartes's view of the body as a machine (Descartes, 1968).

This Cartesian metaphor of the body as a machine, in conjunction with Baconian empiricism, has been greatly influential in medical research and contemporary medicine. Medicine has made significant progress by understanding the body as being comprised of separable and identifiable mechanisms. Because the body has been understood as natural and universal, medical science has been able to conduct empirical investigation of the body, yielding statistical standards defining the "normal" human body and methods by which medicine can manipulate and control bodies that diverge from those norms. In fact, some have deemed the body most "human" when it is most completely manipulated, controlled, transformed, or created by human agency (Fletcher, 1971). While medicine has adopted the legacies of empiricism and mechanism, it has been the Cartesian view of mind/body dualism that has most strongly influenced contemporary bioethics, allowing it to focus almost exclusively on the "mind," "self," or "person" when it defines and describes the issues and moral parameters of medicine.

A third influence on contemporary bioethics with respect to the body has been John Locke. In his *Second Treatise on Government*, Locke sought a framework for understanding political society. Locke posited that individuals initially exist in a "state of nature," that is, individual and unconstrained, until they consent to join an ordered society. While Locke's discussion of consent, rights, duties, and so forth are too complex to summarize here (see Copleston, 1964a), these concepts and particularly his notion of private property have notably influenced the worldview of contemporary bioethics. This is especially evident in the way bioethics has become increasingly intertwined with the U.S. legal system and involved in the formation of public policy. While Locke did not discuss the body as such, his views on private property and ownership have

See Also
Bioethics

been incorporated into the subsequent labor theory of value and applied to contemporary understandings of the body. For Locke, in the state of nature, insofar as an individual invests labor in raw material to produce a product, that individual receives ownership and utilization rights over that product. Correlatively, insofar as the body is a natural resource, a raw material, and insofar as one's body and the bodies of one's offspring are the products of one's labor, the body in bioethics is often treated under the paradigm of property rights (Campbell, 1992; Englehardt, 1985).

A contemporary critique: Social theories of the body

If a primary purpose of bioethics is to reflect on the moral and ethical dimensions of practices and to resolve issues that arise in medicine and scientific research, one must take into account all relevant factors. How one perceives the issues and problems depends largely on how one describes the situation.

Dissatisfaction with a bioethics that employs a philosophical framework rendering the body superfluous to ethical and moral reflection has resulted in the recent emergence of a number of alternative approaches that seek fuller descriptions of the moral situation. These approaches employ philosophical frameworks that envision relationships—between self and body, between persons and their experiences, and between persons—differently than the framework that draws on Descartes, Locke, and other forebears of liberal political philosophy. These approaches (specifically phenomenology, feminism, an ethics of care, virtue, narrative, and hermeneutics) are critical of a medicine that treats merely "the body" and not "the whole person." They are also critical of a bioethics that reduces persons to their rationality and choice, severing the connections between persons and their bodies. (See, for example, Zaner, 1988, and Leder, 1990, who take a phenomenological approach; and Sherwin, 1992, who takes a feminist approach. For fuller discussions of virtue ethics, narrative ethics, phenomenology, and hermeneutics, see DuBose et al., 1994.)

An additional alternative framework for describing "what is going on" in medicine and understanding the function of bioethics is an analytical approach called "social theories of the body." Social theories of the body examine the interrelationships between social orders and the bodies within their jurisdiction. To understand their approach to the body, we must first discuss their broader framework. Every society, they suggest, has an "order," that is, integrated structures of power, institutions, codes of behavior, practices, and beliefs. The "order" of a society is also referred to as the "politics" of the society, that is, the formal and informal relations of power and control that govern a society.

BODIES AND SOCIAL ORDER

Thou Shalt/Thou Shalt Not

One objective of every social order is to perpetuate (or reproduce) itself. Social orders perpetuate themselves by incorporating new members who assume the roles, espouse the beliefs, support the institutions, and participate in the practices of the society. The primary way in which social orders incorporate new members is through the social institutions and practices with which they intersect, touch, or agree not to touch human bodies. Social practices comprise a broad range of activities through which a culture regulates the private actions and public interactions of its members: eating customs (e.g., fasting or *kashrut* [kosher laws]), sexual practices (e.g., monogamy or polygamy, prostitution, adultery, homosexuality), economic structures (e.g., capitalism, communism, barter), practices of dress (e.g., Amish "plain and simple," clerical robes), judicial and penal structures (e.g., public hangings, incarceration, excommunication), religious practices (e.g., confession, pilgrimage, ancestor worship), and so on. Clearly, such practices vary significantly both among and within cultures ("subcultures" are groups which adopt unconventional practices—practices that are often meant to counter the dominant culture).

Through these practices, those bodies within the jurisdiction of a particular social order internalize the order's beliefs and become constructed in conformity with the order's structures. In every culture, certain practices are considered the norm or the ideal, although deviations from the norm are generally tolerated as most cultures hold to beliefs that are often contradictory (for example, a culture that idealizes monogamous marriage may also sanction a thriving prosititution industry). By participating in these practices, individuals learn and internalize the beliefs and norms (as well as the contradictions) of the culture. The more a practice impinges upon one's body, especially the bodies of infants and children, the more deeply the norms are internalized or "embodied," the more unconsciously and effortlessly the "politics" of the culture is learned. (For a display of the dynamic between practices, bodies, and social orders, see Douglas, 1966.)

— M. THERESE LYSAUGHT

Some Gnostics' disapproval of marriage (and its consequences, children) led to an opposition to all sexual intercourse and a favoring of celibacy.

PAGE 645

See Also

Sexuality in Society: Social Control of Sexual Behavior

B

BODY

Social Theories

Anyone concerned about power and justice needs to scrutinize so-called scientific claims about human sexuality.

PAGE 662

The interaction between social institutions and human bodies may be potential (government), indirect (media, advertisement), direct but intermittent (medicine, religion), or direct and constant (prisons, asylums). Through these institutions, cultures seek to normalize, discipline, and regulate both the bodies of individuals (in Michel Foucault's term, "anatomo-politics") and the bodies of its total population or subgroups ("biopolitics" or "biopower").

In addition, social theories of the body hold not only that through practices individuals embody the beliefs of their cultures. At the same time, they suggest, cultures require different "kinds" of bodies to maintain their power structures or they find themselves faced with different kinds of bodies that need to be located in the social order, and they subsequently "construct" them to fit the needs of the social order. For example, the economic and social order of antebellum Georgia depended upon the institution of slavery. To maintain this order, a set of practices designed to construct the bodies of blacks as slaves was required to internalize the cultural view that understood them as slaves. These practices included kidnapping and incarceration, physical punishment, rape, total economic dependence upon owners, selling individual family members, marginalized and impoverished dwellings, and so on.

In addition, for whites to participate in these practices in good conscience and for blacks to submit, the practices required conceptual rationalizations that constructed an understanding of blacks as inferior to whites. For example, religious discourse construed blacks as inferior either due to their "heathen" status or due to their descent from Ham, a less privileged son of Noah. Medical discourse, drawing on Darwinian concepts, asserted that blacks were not as advanced as whites on the evolutionary spectrum, or drew normative conclusions from real physiological differences. In short, the order of a given culture requires this interdependence between practices, discourses, and institutions. As will be discussed below, this interdependence is also the location for resistance and change.

While this is a graphic and coercive example of the ways in which the bodies of particular individuals and a particular group were constructed, social theories of the body would maintain that all people's bodies are constructed. Feminist theory has been a major proponent of this view (see Walker, 1991). But because people internalize and generally accept the norms of their culture, they do not generally understand their bodies as constructed. Because of the objective reality of institutions, the official status of discourses, and the embodied dimension of practices, they see the abilities, constraints, limits, perceptions, and experiences of their bodies as "natural," "given," "the way things are," "right," or "true."

The primary analytical and ethical category for social theories of the body is power. Social theories of the body understand bodies as the medium through which social institutions derive power, authority, reality, and meaning as the site upon which power and social control are maintained. Bodies, as Elaine Scarry suggests, are material and real, while political and social configurations are abstractions, precisely lacking material reality. Through the ways in which they intersect human bodies, social orders appropriate the materiality of human bodies and gain the appearance of reality (Scarry, 1985). The most significant analyst of the relationships between power, knowledge, and the body, and therefore the most central figure in the development of social theories of the body, has been Michel Foucault (1973, 1979, 1980).

While not denying that power can and often is exercised in ways that are negative, coercive, or repressive, social theories of the body instead see power as a pervasive and necessary part of every social order. They focus on four other characteristics of power, specifically that it is "productive," "local," "continuous," and "capillary." Power is "productive" insofar as it is that quality that enables individuals and groups to act (generally toward their own advantage) and to effect desired ends and goals. Power is "local" because it is exercised at the level of individual bodies through techniques and technologies of surveillance (quantification, examination, classification, statistical ranking) and discipline. Power operates "continuously" because individuals, by willingly participating in official practices of surveillance, classification, and self-discipline, become self-surveying, internalizing the normative intent of the practices. And finally, power is "capillary" (drawing on the metaphor of arterial and venous capillaries that are the smallest conduits of blood flow, feeding the furthest reaches of the body); power operates through the most common and least formal channels of the social body in everyday practices, such as eating, medicine, and sexuality.

An essential element in establishing systems of power are discourses, as illustrated above by the roles medical and religious discourses played in the institution of slavery. Discourses are verbal and literary constructs through which systems of knowledge are established. Discourses generally belong exclusively to a professional group and are the means by which that profession defines and advances norms for human subjectivity, actions, and bodies. Bioethics would be an example of such a discourse. Bioethics belongs to the professional group of philosophers, theologians, and clinicians who have learned the language. Through this discourse, bioethicists have defined the normative essence of human personhood as rationality, and they have advanced a system of ethical evaluation based on rational autonomous action, and so forth.

When discourses and practices become the exclusive domain of a select group of professionals, domination by that group is almost unavoidable, yet almost imperceivable. Joanne Finkelstein (1990) describes how technology, especially medical technology, is crucial to this dynamic. Through discourse, practices, and technologies, professions cultivate consumer desires and offer the means to satisfy those desires. Yet by exclusively possessing a desired commodity, those providing the service (e.g., in vitro fertilization [IVF]) control access to it. At the same time, since consumers have been cultivated to desire the service (through what Lisa Sowle Cahill has called the "rhetoric of desperation"), they do not perceive the monopoly as dominating or exploitative, even though they (1) are increasing the scope of medical dominance; (2) may bear great burdens and costs in the process (especially women); and (3) may end up with no outcome (for example, there is only a 20 percent success rate with IVF), while the professionals are guaranteed benefits, such as income, professional status, or social power. When power becomes accumulated in an institution or professional group in such a way that the group can define another's interests, influence individuals to act contrary to their own interests, or influence those individuals to act in ways that simply further the power of the professional group, power becomes domination. (For further discussion of the new reproductive technologies from the perspective of social theories of the body, see Corea et al., 1987.)

Application: Social theories of the body and bioethics

With regard to bioethics, social theories of the body will prove more critical than constructive. In the above discussion of IVF, we have already begun to show how bioethics looks different when approached from a social theories perspective. Rather than asking the standard questions of bioethics (Is the patient competent? Who decides? Did the patient give an informed consent? Do the benefits outweigh the costs?), it will ask questions of power (Who benefits most from a particular practice or discourse? Is this a practice of surveillance, and if so, for what end? Who has power in this particular situation?). It will describe how power functions within medical institutions; for instance, power rests mainly with physicians or hospital administrators rather than nurses who provide the hands-on, bodily care (see feminist bioethics, especially Sherwin, 1992; Holmes and Purdy, 1992). It will analyze the dynamics of "choice," suggesting what social factors constrain choices (e.g., in the case of IVF described above), and how individual choices are circumscribed

FOCUS ON THE BODY

In The Birth of the Clinic *(1973), French philosopher Michel Foucault examines relationships between medical technologies, surveillance, and consolidation of professional power.*

so as to further the interests of institutions and professional groups (Corea et al., 1987). It will illuminate how bioethics, with medicine, functions as an agent of social regulation (e.g., bioethics' emphasis on crafting national policies).

For social theories of the body, medicine has emerged as one of the principal agents of social regulation, the crucial actor in contemporary biopower. In his work *The Birth of the Clinic* (1973), Michel Foucault examines the relationships between medical technologies, practices of surveillance, specialization of knowledge, and consolidation of professional power (see also Turner, 1987). Increasingly, medicine offers treatments for aspects of embodied human life—fertility, height, baldness, death (e.g., euthanasia)—thereby defining an expanding number of human conditions as pathological and amenable to treatment and expanding its own influence. Even when treatments are not available, through seemingly benign techniques of surveillance (especially, for example, genetic testing), medicine seeks to bring all individuals, and increasingly all parts of individuals' lives, into its purview in order to "normalize" individuals and populations. The Human Genome Project, the massive research initiative founded by the National Institutes of Health to map "the" human genome, which will be employed as a standard of normality, is just one example. In addition, medicine serves to marginalize and control those who are not considered normal. Through the judgment and practice of medicine, the sick and disabled are removed from the center of public space to the margins—to the home, to the hospital, to the nursingcare facility. Moreover, a movement (advocating euthanasia, assisted suicide, and/or advanced directives) encourages that those "disordered" bodies (bodies that do not fit with the order of the culture) be moved beyond the boundaries of the human community, beyond the boundary of life and death.

It can be likewise argued that this function of medicine as an agent of social regulation is bolstered by bioethics. Generally, bioethics seeks to create arguments and algorithms that justify, rather than challenge or critique, medical "advances." The discourse of bioethics often provides an additional lens by which individuals or groups are rendered more or less "normal," often offering medicine and society moral justifications for practices that further marginalize those deemed nonnormative. Bioethicists increasingly seek to create a professional space for themselves, an area of expertise, from which they can exercise benign dominance in the moral evaluation of medical and biomedical practices; this role is increasingly attested to by the frequency of "bioethicists" in news sound bites.

Bioethics from the perspective of a social theory of the body, however, challenges this trend. How might social theories of the body illuminate the analysis of a typical bioethical issue? Joanne Finkelstein offers a cogent example in her analysis of genetics. She notes how genetic science promises to improve the lives of individuals and populations by monitoring and altering human bodies at the subcellular level through high technology medicine. However, these technologies—for all their apparent neutrality—carry with them significant normative power, that is, "the power of determining which human lives are more valuable, or in utilitarian terms, which individuals are potential welfare burdens to the community in the long term" (Finkelstein, 1990, p. 13). Genetic screening is a technique of surveillance, the penultimate extension of Foucault's "medical gaze." Through a combination of screening, intervention to abort defective fetuses, and interventions to alter human characteristics, genetic technologies undergird cultural efforts to define and institutionalize "normalcy." Genetic science has been granted the ability to define which human characteristics are to be defined as pathological or unacceptable, which are open to genetic remediation, and "which populations will become the experimental subjects used in the future development of the field" (Finkelstein, 1990, p. 14).

One might comment at this point that it seems that even in this approach, one does not hear much about "the body." This illustrates how difficult it is to keep the focus on the body. However, what distinguishes social theories of the body from other approaches is that they consistently begin with bodies—with techniques that are practiced on bodies (e.g., genetic screening), with definitions of bodies or different types of embodiment (e.g., definition of death), with the ways in which the bodies of different groups are treated (e.g., access to health care for the underserved), with the ways in which "political" structures position, appeal to, or ignore the bodies within them (e.g., issues of women's health). For this approach, the point of intersection between institutions, practices, discourses, and human bodies serves as the window through which to analyze political and social structures, relationships of power and dominance, and their moral and ethical effects.

While generally critical and analytical, social theories of the body may also serve a constructive function in the practice of bioethics. For example, analysts may use social theories of the body to identify ideological, oppressive, or coercive power relationships within the practice of medicine; they may then offer alternative "politics" that better embody a preferred set of values. By doing so, they illustrate how bodies, in conjunction with alternative practices, discourses, and institutions, also serve as the context for resistance to domination. Bodies, as the locus for power, are equally the site for control and the site for freedom. However, by illustrating the complexity of embodied social orders, these theories also indicate how difficult resistance can be and how resistance requires community. Those who resist often find themselves de facto members of a subculture. Feminist approaches to bioethics are particularly illustrative in this regard (Corea et al., 1987; Sherwin, 1992; Holmes and Purdy, 1992).

— M. THERESE LYSAUGHT

CULTURAL AND RELIGIOUS PERSPECTIVES

Scholarly and popular thought alike have typically assumed that the human body is a fixed, material entity subject to the empirical rules of biological science. Such a body exists prior to the mutability and flux of cultural change and diversity, and is characterized by unchangeable inner necessities. Beginning with the historical work of Michel Foucault and Norbert Elias, the anthropology of Pierre Bourdieu, and phenomenological philosophers such as Maurice Merleau-Ponty, Hans Jonas, Max Scheler, and Gabriel Marcel, however, scholarship in the social sciences and humanities has begun to challenge this notion. Late twentieth-century commentators argue that the body can no longer be considered as a fact of nature, but is instead "an entirely problematic notion" (Vernant, 1989, p. 20); that "the body has a history" insofar as it behaves in new ways at particular historical moments (Bynum, 1989, p. 171); that the body should be understood not as a constant amidst flux but as an epitome of that flux (Frank, 1991); and that "the universalized natural body is the gold standard of hegemonic social discourse" (Haraway, 1990, p. 146).

See Also

Early Influences on Christian Understandings of Sex

This scholarly perspective—that the body has a history, and is not only a biological entity but also a cultural phenomenon—goes hand in hand with the increasing number and complexity of bioethical issues in contemporary society, many of which have strong religious overtones. Some decades ago the only such issue arose in cases where religious and biomedical priorities conflicted in the treatment of illness. Within the majority population, various groups such as Christian Scientists, some Pentecostal Christians, and members of small fundamentalist sects occasionally have created controversy by refusing medical treatment on the grounds that faith in medicine undermined faith in God, in other words, that since healing should occur only at the will and discretion of the deity, human medicine was presumptuous upon divine prerogative. This was especially problematic when young children suffered and were kept from medical treatment by their parents. In Native American communities it has been, and occasionally remains, the practice for ill people to seek biomedical treatment only after having exhausted the resources of their spiritually based traditional medical systems. This occasionally results in the discovery of serious illness such as cancer or tuberculosis at a very advanced stage, and creates a dilemma for health-care personnel who are supportive of indigenous traditions yet concerned that their patients also receive timely biomedical treatment.

More recently, the number of bioethical issues with religious overtones has multiplied. The legality of and right of access by women to abortion have been defined not only as issues of civil rights and feminist politics, but also as religious and moral issues. Surrogate motherhood and donorship of sperm and eggs raise ethical dilemmas regarding the biological, legal, and spiritual connections between parent and child. There is also concern about the apparently godlike ability of biotechnology to determine the genetic makeup of the human species; some see this approaching with the increasing sophistication of genetic engineering and the massive Human Genome Project, which will catalogue all possible human genetic characteristics. At the other end of the life course, the problems of euthanasia, technological prolongation of vital functions by means of life-support machines, and physician-assisted death raise moral and spiritual questions about the prerogative to end the life of oneself or of another. Legal and ethical acceptance of the definition of death as "brain death" has particular significance in that the brain dead individual's other organs are still viable for transplantation to other persons. In the United States the bioethical dilemma is whether the brain-dead person can morally be considered dead until all other vital functions have ceased, or whether removing those organs constitutes killing the patient. In Japan an added dilemma is that a person's spiritual destiny as a deceased ancestor depends in part on maintaining an intact physical body.

Each of these issues has to do with religion, not only because religions often define them as within their moral purview, but also because at a more profound level, each taps a concern that is at the very core of religious thought and practice: the problem of what it means to be human. More precisely, the problem is the nature of human persons, of what it means to have and be a body, of life and death, and of the spiritual destiny of humankind. In the succeeding sections of this article these issues are placed in the context of recent thought about the cultural and historical nature of the human body, about religious conceptualizations of the body, and about religious practices that focus on the body.

The body as a cultural phenomenon

It has been suggested that in contemporary civilization the human body can no longer be considered a bounded entity, in part because of the destabilizing impact of "consumer culture" and its accompanying barrage of images. These images stimulate needs and desires, as well as the corresponding changes in the way the social space we inhabit is arranged with respect to physical objects and other people (Featherstone et al., 1991). In this process, fixed "life-cycle" categories have become blurred into a more fluid "life course" in which one's look and feel may conflict with one's biological and chronological age; some people may even experience conflict between age-appropriate behavior and subjective experience. In addition, the goals of bodily self-care have changed from spiritual salvation, to enhanced health, and finally to a marketable self (Featherstone et al., 1991; cf. Foucault, 1986; and Bordo, 1990). As Susan Bordo has observed, techniques of body care are not directed primarily toward weight loss, but toward formation of body boundaries to protect against the eruption of the "bulge," and serve the purposes of social mobility more than the affirmation of social position (Bordo, 1990). Bodily discipline is no longer incompatible with hedonism but has become a means toward it, so that one not only exercises to look good, but also wants to look good while exercising (Bordo, 1990). This stands in sharp contrast not only to early historical periods but to other societies such as that of Fiji where the cultivation of bodies is not regarded as an enhancement of a performing self but as a responsibility toward the community (Becker, 1994).

This transformation in the body as a cultural phenomenon has been related by Emily Martin (1992) to a global change in social organization. In her view the "Fordist body" structured by principles of centralized control and factory-based production is on the decline. It is being replaced by a body characteristic of late cap-

The sexual instinct was considered a gift from God, but it could still be called by the rabbis the "evil impluse."

PAGE 644

italism, a socioeconomic regime characterized by technological innovation, specificity, and rapid, flexible change. She sees these changes particularly vividly in the domains of reproductive biology, immunology, and sexuality, all of which are increasingly intense loci of bioethical debate.

With respect to immunology in particular, Donna Haraway (1991) understands the concept of the "immune system" as an icon of symbolic and material systematic "difference" in late capitalism. The concept of the immune system was developed in its present form as recently as the 1970s, and was made possible by a profound theoretical shift from focus on individual organisms to focus on cybernetic systems. The result has been the transformation of the body into a cybernetic body, one that for Haraway requires a "cyborg ethics and politics" that recognizes radical pluralism, the inevitability of multiple meanings and imperfect communication, and physical groundedness in a particular location.

While holy women sometimes experienced being the mother or lover of Christ, their nature often allowed them to mystically become *the flesh of Christ.*

PAGE 92

This groundedness thus extends to biology itself. In addition to immunology, this is evident in recent feminist theory that eliminates "passivity" as an intrinsic characteristic of the female body and reworks the distinctions between sex and gender, female sexual pleasure, and the act of conception (Jacobus et al., 1990; Bordo, 1990; Haraway, 1990). With biology no longer a monolithic objectivity, the body is transformed from object to agent (Haraway, 1991). The bioethical implications of the body as experiencing agent are evident in recent social science work on the experience of illness (Kleinman, 1988; Murphy, 1987), pain (Good et al., 1992), and religious healing (Csordas, 1990, 1994). New disciplinary syntheses grounded in a paradigm of embodiment are emerging in disciplines such as anthropology (Csordas, 1990, 1994), sociology (Turner, 1986), and history (Berman, 1989).

Many of these new syntheses are predicated on a critique of tenacious conceptual dualities such as those between mind and body, subject and object, and sex and gender (Haraway, 1991; Frank, 1991; Ots, 1991; Csordas, 1990; Leder, 1990). Drew Leder (1990), for example, begins his critique of Cartesian mind-body dualism with the observation that in everyday life our experience is characterized by the disappearance of our body from awareness. He contrasts this with a description of *dys*-appearance, the vivid but unwanted consciousness of one's body in disease, distress, or dysfunction. He then argues that it is the very sense of disappearance, itself an essential characteristic of our bodily existence, that leads to the body's self-concealment, and thus to a mistaken notion of the immateriality of mind and thought. That such a notion is cultural is evident in the technological domain if one compares Western navigational techniques, which are based on intellectualist mathematical instruments and calculations, with traditional Polynesian navigation, which in contrast relied on concrete sensory information regarding clouds and light, wave patterns, star movement, and the behavior of birds (Leder, 1990). Leder further suggests that the Western tradition compounds the error by construing the body as a source of epistemological error, moral error, and mortality. In contrast, based on a phenomenological appreciation of unitary embodiment, he suggests the possibility of a new ethics of compassion, absorption, and communion.

The contemporary cultural transformation of the body can be conceived not only in terms of revising biological essentialism and collapsing conceptual dualities, but also in discerning an ambiguity in the boundaries of corporeality itself. Haraway points to the boundaries between animal and human, between animal/human and machine, and between the physical and nonphysical (Haraway, 1991). Michel Feher construes the boundary between human and animal or automaton (machine) at one end of a continuum whose opposite pole is defined by the boundary between human and deity (Feher, 1989). Cultural definitions of the boundary between human and divine can be significant given the circumstances of corporeal flux and bodily transformation sketched above. This is especially the case when the question goes beyond the distinction between natural and supernatural bodies, or between natural corporeality and divine incorporeality, to the question posed by Feher of the kind of body with which members of a culture endow themselves in order to come into relation with the kind of deity they posit to themselves (Feher, 1989). Thus, if the body is a cultural phenomenon in a way that makes its understanding essential to questions of bioethics, religion is an important domain of culture to address in understanding the body.

Religious conceptualizations of the body

Perhaps the most vivid example from the domain of religion that the body is a cultural phenomenon subject to cultural transformations is given in the classic work on New Caledonia by Maurice Leenhardt, the anthropologist and missionary. Leenhardt recounts his discovery of the impact of Christianity on the cosmocentric world of the New Caledonian Canaques via a conversation with an aged indigenous philosopher. Leenhardt suggested that the Europeans had introduced the notion of "spirit" to the indigenous way of thinking. His interlocutor contradicted him, pointed out that his people had "always acted in accord with the spirit. What you've brought us is the body" (Leenhardt, 1979, p. 164). In brief, the indigenous worldview held that the person was not individuated but was diffused with other persons and things in a unitary sociomythic domain:

> *[The body] had no existence of its own, nor specific name to distinguish it. It was only a support. But henceforth the circumscription of the physical being is completed, making possible its objectification. The idea of a human body becomes explicit. This discovery leads forthwith to a discrimination between the body and the mythic world.* (Leenhardt, 1979, p. 164)

There could be no more powerful evidence that the body is a cultural and historical phenomenon. Insofar as the objectification of the body has the consequences of individuation of the psychological self and the instantiation of dualism in the conceptualization of human being, it has implications for defining a very different regime of ethical relationships and responsibilities. This is not only a relative difference, but—as is clear in the missionary example of Leenhardt—one that has consequences for relations between different cultures.

HINDU CONCEPTUALIZATIONS. In the Hindu worldview *atman*, "self," is understood not as soul in distinction to body, but as the center in relation to an existential periphery, or as whole in relation to parts (Malamud, 1989). The ritual act of sacrifice is personified and has a body, or in other words the body is both the model for and origin of sacrifice (Malamud, 1989). The individual bodies are inherently sexual and are portrayed as couples, or *mithuna*. The masculine is invariably singular and the feminine plural, as in the sun of day in relation to the multiple stars of night, or the singularity of act/mind/silence in relation to the multiplicity of speech. In contrast to the mutable but distinctly individual body of the Greek deities, Hindu ritual portrays a rich "combinatory of the sexes" that constitutes a way of mythically thinking with the body. The *mithunas* achieve cosmic engenderment (begetting) through diverse body operations including dismemberment, multiplication of body parts, replication of bodies, birth, coupling/copulation, merging/incorporation, transformation and transgendering, and the emission of body products/fluids (Malamud, 1989).

JEWISH AND CHRISTIAN CONCEPTUALIZATIONS. If, in Hinduism, engenderment is timeless and instantiated in the cosmos by the sacrificial act, in Judaism it is linear and instantiated in history by the act of procreation. Creation and engenderment are two moments of the same process, a "hiero-history" in which human generation does not imitate a divine process, but is that process (Mopsik, 1989). Whereas in the Christian perspective the biblical injunction for man and woman to "become one flesh" is understood to refer to the indissolubility of marriage, in the Jewish perspective it is understood as the production of a child, and the birth of Christ outside the historical chain of engenderments is the basis for the Pauline splitting of the spiritual and carnal individual (Mopsik, 1989). This view is elaborated further in the Jewish kabbalistic tradition's notion of the *sefirot,* the ten-gendered emanations of the Infinite that are represented as combining to form a body (Mopsik, 1989).

In sharp contrast to the Jewish kabbalistic elaboration of engenderment as life, the Christian gnostic tradition elaborates it as death (Mopsik, 1989). Gnosticism sees the corporeal form as the creation of monstrous demiurges or archons, foremost among whom is Ialdabaoth, the equivalent of Jehovah. The human condition is symbolized in the gnostic tale of the archons' rape of Eve, who escapes with her psychic body while her "shadow" or material body is defiled (Williams, 1989). The latter is a prison or garment, beastly because humans are created by beasts. Sexuality is an aspect of this beastliness, and hence cannot be part of an embodied sacred process, while the upright

RELIGIOUS CONCEPTS
The Ancient Greek Human Body

For the ancient Greeks, as described by Jean-Pierre Vernant (1989), the distinction between the bodies of humans and the bodies of deities was not predicated on that between corporeality and incorporeality, but on the notion that the divine bodies were complete and human bodies incomplete. Furthermore, this distinction emphasized not bodily features or morphology, but the being's place on a continuum of value and foulness. Bodies were understood as mutable along these dimensions without losing their identity, and thus deities could be simultaneously very heavy and very light, moving over the earth without quite touching it while leaving exceedingly deep footprints (Vernant, 1989). The deities thus had bodies that were not bodies, but they had characteristics that never ruptured their continuity with human bodies, and which therefore defined human bodies by their very otherness. The existence of the deities guaranteed that in Greek culture qualities such as royalty and beauty were not abstract concepts or categories, since they were concretely embodied in beings like Zeus and Aphrodite (Vernant, 1989).

—THOMAS J. CSORDAS

The idealization of female virginity affects every aspect of the life of the traditional southern Italian village.

PAGE 665

See Also

Sex in Antiquity: Same-Sex Relationships

TWO MOTHERS

Literary scholar Caroline Walker Bynum has written that the image of Christ as mother was widespread in the medieval imagination.

posture that distinguishes us from animals is attributed to a separate spark from the authentically spiritual Human (Williams, 1989).

From a more mainstream Christian perspective, the profound cultural implications of Feher's question of the kind of body people endow themselves with in order to come into relation with the sacred (Feher, 1989) can be seen by considering the Eucharist. That the consumption of bread and wine transubstantiated into the body and blood of Christ is essentially a form of ritual cannibalism is emphasized by the story of a miracle in which a priest who doubted the divine reality of the Eucharist was forced to experience the bloody flesh, so that he could come to appreciate God's graciousness in presenting it in the tamer appearance of bread and wine (Camporesi, 1989; see also Bynum, 1989). In earlier periods of Christianity the spiritual power of the Eucharist extended to the nourishment of the body, and this, not through ingestion but by means of its aroma (Camporesi, 1989). Unlike ordinary food, however, it does not become us, but we become it through its sanctifying power (Camporesi, 1989). Great anxiety was created among priests with regard to the immense responsibility of transforming something dead into something alive by the utterance of a few words, and among communicants because of the inclusion of such a sacred substance in such a profane terrain as the digestive tract—hence the importance of a fast before communion (Camporesi, 1989). Yet because the Eucharist was thought to release its grace only in the stomach, sick people who could not eat were excluded (Camporesi, 1989). When later the substantial bread was replaced by thin wafers, it became common to let the wafer melt in one's mouth. Well into the twentieth century, Catholics were taught that biting or chewing the Eucharist was an insult and injury to the deity that could result in divine retribution.

MEDIEVAL CONCEPTUALIZATIONS. Recent work on medieval Christian spirituality relates to the notion of the body as a cultural phenomenon. Caroline Walker Bynum (1989) has documented the prominence during the years 1200-1500 of a "somatic spirituality" that stands in contrast to gnostic rejection of the body, and that reflects a less dualist mentality than has heretofore been attributed to the thought of this period. In general, a great deal of concern with embodiment was evidenced in speculation about whether the final "resurrection of the body" might be a natural consequence of human nature rather than a discrete divine act to occur at the Last Judgment, and whether we will taste and smell heaven as well as see it (Bynum, 1989).

The medieval body was defined less by its sexuality than by notions of fertility and decay, but the contrast between male and female was as important as that between body and soul (Bynum, 1989). Somatic spirituality was especially evident among female mystics, who—in contrast to their more cerebral male counterparts' experience of stillness and silence—tended to blur the boundaries among the spiritual, psychological, bodily, and sexual by cultivating a sensualized relationship of human body with divine body (Bynum, 1989). Bynum draws on the cultural-historical context to understand why the male-dominated ecclesiastical hierarchy allowed this female spirituality to flourish: evidence was needed against the contemporary dualist heresy of the Cathars; because they were denied education in Latin, they wrote in the less linear and more oral style of the vernacular; they were encouraged to act out maternal roles vis-à-vis Christ (Bynum, 1989).

In this context the relation between the genders took on remarkable properties. Although ideally a woman would die to defend her holy chastity, it was as likely for a holy man to be resurrected in order to complete a virtuous task (Bynum, 1989). In other ways the genders were blurred, since it was thought that all had both genders within, and that men and women had identical organs with only their internal and external arrangements being different (Bynum, 1989). Because of the powerful symbolic association of the female and the fleshly, while holy women sometimes experienced being the mother or lover of Christ, their nature often allowed them to mystically *become* the flesh of Christ (Bynum, 1989). By the same reasoning, since body is

See Also

Sexualtiy in Society: Social Control: Sex as "Powder-Keg"

equivalent to female, the incarnate Christ had a female nature, and the image of Christ as mother became a feature of medieval iconography (Bynum, 1989).

Religious practices and the body

FASTING. The cultural-historical transformation of the body is highlighted by comparison of fasting as a technique of the body in the medieval somatic spirituality with the phenomenon of anorexia nervosa in the late twentieth century. In a study of 261 holy women in Italy since the year 1200, Rudolf Bell (1985) distinguishes between contemporary anorexia nervosa and what he calls "holy anorexia." While the former is regarded as a syndrome of clinical pathology, in the latter, "the suppression of physical urges and basic feelings—fatigue, sexual drive, hunger, pain—frees the body to achieve heroic feats and the soul to commune with God" (Bell, 1985, p. 13). There are parallels between the two conditions and historical epochs. Bell suggests that the observation that the internal locus of evil as a corrupting force for women in the Middle Ages, in distinction to the external locus of sin as a response to external stimulus for men, corresponds to the Freudian model of anorexia nervosa as a food/sex oral fixation (Bell, 1985). In addition, in both, "the main theme is a struggle for control, for a sense of identity, competence, and effectiveness" (Hilde Bruch, quoted in Bell, 1985, p. 17). However, there is a critical difference, and "whether anorexia is holy or nervous depends on the culture in which a young woman strives to gain control of her life" (Bell, 1985, p. 20).

Bynum (1987) warns against the assumption that these are precisely the same phenomenon, given theological meaning in one epoch and psychiatric meaning in another. She points out that even medieval writers had more than one paradigm for explaining fasting—that it could be supernaturally caused, naturally caused, or feigned—and that there was a clear distinction between choosing to renounce food and the inability to eat (Bynum, 1987). In both historical cases, the behavior "is learned from a culture that has complex and long-standing traditions about women, about bodies, and about food," including what kind of behaviors are in need of cure (Bynum, 1987, p. 198). It is a profoundly cultural fact that in the patristic era miraculous fasting was attributed largely to men, while in the medieval period it was characteristic of women; likewise it is cultural that in the medieval period the illnesses of men were more likely thought of as needing to be cured, while those of women were to be endured (Bynum, 1987). Furthermore, in the later Middle Ages fasting was associated with a wider array of miracles and practices of somatic spirituality, including subsistence on the Eucharist, stigmata, espousal rings, sweet-smelling bodies, bodily elongation, and incorruptibility (Bynum, 1987). Some of the behavior of these women fits the pattern of nineteenth-century "hysteria," some is clearly the result of other illnesses, and some follows the thematic of control, altered body concept/perceptions, and euphoria. Yet one cannot be sure whether symptoms are associated with an inability to eat or are the result of freely chosen ascetic fasting. Finally, insofar as psychodynamic explanation can explain only individual cases, Bynum concludes that it is less helpful to know that contemporary labels can in some cases be applied to the medieval phenomenon than to account for cultural symbols that give meaning to the phenomenon, such as body, food, blood, suffering, generativity, or hunger (Bynum, 1987).

FAITH HEALING. Other contemporary religious practices equally require an appreciation of the body as a cultural phenomenon. How, for example, can we understand the imputed efficacy of "faith healing" among contemporary Christians? An understanding of the body as a cultural phenomenon suggests that ritual healing operates on a margin of disability that is present in many conditions. It is well known, for example, that some people who become "legally blind" are able to engage in a wide range of activities, while others retreat to a posture of near total disability and inactivity. Likewise, persons with chronic pain in a limb may be physically able to move that limb, but refrain from doing so for lack of sufficient motivation to make the risk of pain worthwhile. Disability is thus constituted as a habitual mode of engaging the world. The process of healing is an existential process of exploring this margin of disability, motivated by the conviction of divine power and the committed participant's desire to demonstrate it in himself or herself, as well as by the support of the other assembled devotees and their acclamation for a supplicant's testimony of healing. To be convinced of this interpretation one need only consider the hesitant, faltering steps of the supplicant who, at the healer's request, rises from a wheelchair and shuffles slowly up and down a church aisle; or the slowly unclenching fist of the sufferer of chronic arthritis whose hand is curled by affliction into a permanent fist. Ritual healing allows this by challenging the sensory commitment to a habitual posture, by removing inhibitions on the motor tendency toward static postural tone, and by modulating the somatic mode of attention, that is, a person's attention to his or her own bodily processes in relation to others.

Consider also the practice of "resting in the Spirit" or being "slain in the Spirit" among Charismatic and Pentecostal Christians as evidence for the kind of body with which people endow themselves in order to come into relation with the sacred. In this practice, which occurs primarily in healing services, a person is overcome with divine power, and falls into a semi-swoon

Augustine tried to clarify the place of disordered sexual desire in a theology of original sin.

PAGE 645

See Also

The Sexual Ethics of Saint Augustine and Its Legacy

characterized by tranquility and motor dissociation. Despite its popularity, or perhaps because of it, resting in the Spirit is a controversial phenomenon for Charismatics, and the heart of the issue is its authenticity. More specifically, critics challenge its authenticity while apologists argue for its beneficial effects in terms of healing and spiritual development. Both sides invoke the same biblical scenarios, such as Saul on the road to Damascus and the apostles confronted by the transfiguration of Jesus, and the same religious writers, including the ecstatic mystics Theresa of Avila and John of the Cross, and both sides draw opposing conclusions about whether these constitute examples of resting in the Spirit. They likewise draw opposing conclusions about the historical prototypes of healers known for similar practices, extending backward in time from Kathryn Kuhlman to Charles Finney, George Jeffreys, George Fox, John Wesley, and the fourteenth-century Dominican preacher John Tauler. To be sure, such analogies and precedents suggest that it would be possible to examine the varying meanings of religious falling or swooning across historical and cultural contexts. In the contemporary context, however, the ideological/theological/pastoral debate about authenticity is predicated on the recurrent, constitutive North American psychocultural themes of spontaneity and control, and on the Charismatic cultural definition of the tripartite person as a composite of body, mind, and spirit.

SPIRIT POSSESSION. The sacred swoon leads also to the complex issue of dissociation, common to discussions of "spirit possession." Spirits who inhabit people may be regarded either as malevolent, in which case they must be expelled or exorcised, or as benevolent, in which case becoming possessed is an act of worship and devotion. Possession of both types is widely reported in ethnological literature (Bourguignon, 1976), and is increasingly common in contemporary Western society. Not only is the negative, or demonic, variant reported among some varieties of Christian religions, but the positive variant of possession by deities is characteristic of rapidly growing African religions. These include religions based on the Yoruba tradition of Nigeria, such as *santeria*, *candomble*, and the related *vodun*. The Yoruba religion, in which the possessing deities are called *orixas*, is rapidly aspiring to membership in that select group of "world religions" that once included only so-called "civilized" faiths such as Christianity, Judaism, Islam, Hinduism, Buddhism, Taoism, and Confucianism. This cultural

See Also

Abortion

ABORTION HEALING RITUALS

American and Japanese Practices

A final example of the interplay of religion and bioethics with respect to bodily practices pertains to the contemporary cultural debate over abortion. Among participants in the North American Christian religious movement known as the Charismatic Renewal, and in Japan as a facet of what are called the New Religions, healing rituals are conducted both for the removal of guilt presumed to be experienced by the woman, and for the fetus in order to establish its spiritual status. The American practice is largely a private one that takes place within the membership of a discrete religious movement within Christianity, and is a specific instance of the healing system elaborated within that movement. The Japanese practice has a relatively public profile not limited to a particular social group, and is an instance of a type of ritual common to a variety of forms of Buddhism.

In both societies the affective issue addressed by the ritual is guilt, but whereas in American culture this is guilt occurring as a function of sin, in Japan it is guilt as a function of necessity. For the Americans abortion is an un-Christian act, and both perpetrator and victim must be brought back ritually into the Christian moral and emotional universe; for the Japanese both the acceptance of abortion as necessary and the acknowledgment of guilt are circumscribed within the Buddhist moral and emotional universe. Both rites are intended to heal the distress experienced by the woman, but the etiology of the illness is somewhat differently construed in the two cases. For Charismatics any symptoms displayed by the woman are the result of the abortion as psychological trauma compounded by guilt, along with the more or less indirect effects of the restive fetal spirit "crying out" for love and comfort. In Japan such symptoms are attributed to vengeance and resentment on the part of the aborted fetal spirit that is the pained victim of an unnatural, albeit necessary, act. Finally, not only the etiology but the emotional work accomplished by the two rituals is construed differently. For the Charismatics this is a work of forgiveness and of emotional "letting go." For the Japanese, in whose cultural context gratitude and guilt are not sharply differentiated, it is a work of thanks and apology to the fetus. Thus, "[t]here is no great need to determine precisely whether one is addressing a guilt-pre-supposing 'apology' to a fetus or merely expressing 'thanks' to it for having vacated its place in the body of a woman and having moved on, leaving her—and her family—relatively free of its physical presence" (LaFleur, 1992, p. 147).

— THOMAS J. CSORDAS

development requires a more sophisticated understanding of the possession phenomenon not as mental or cognitive dissociation but as physical and existential incarnation; not as a pathological hysterical amnesia to which the devotee becomes abandoned, but as a form of habitual body memory in which the deity's characteristics are enacted in a contemporary form of somatic spirituality.

Conclusion

The contemporary transformation of the human body and scholarly formulations of it, placed alongside the transformative power of religion in its task of defining what it means to be human, offers an important perspective on issues relevant to bioethics. These range from abortion to brain death, from fasting to resting in the Spirit, from consumer culture to dissociation, and bear on the relation between genders, between cultures, and between the poles of dualities such as mind and body. Such phenomena, and new ways of understanding them, will increasingly come to light with continuing elaboration of the body/culture/religion nexus.

—THOMAS J. CSORDAS

CARE

CONTEMPORARY ETHICS OF CARE

A major contemporary impetus to scholarly discussions of caring occurred with the 1982 publication of Carol Gilligan's *In a Different Voice: Psychological Theory and Women's Development* (Gilligan, 1982). Nursing theorists—and, to a lesser extent, physicians—were exploring moral dimensions of caring prior to the publication of Gilligan's work; but her book led, for the first time in the history of the idea of care, to widespread efforts to develop a systematic philosophical ethic of care beyond the world of health-care practitioners.

Contemporary elements of an ethic of care

In a Different Voice begins by contrasting the primary moral orientation of boys and men with the primary orientation of girls and women. Gilligan proposes that females and males tend to employ different reasoning strategies and apply different moral themes and concepts when formulating and resolving moral problems. According to Gilligan's analysis, females are more likely than males to perceive moral dilemmas primarily in terms of personal attachment versus detachment. From this perspective, which she dubs the "care" perspective, central concerns are to avoid deserting, hurting, alienating, isolating, or abandoning persons and to act in a manner that strengthens and protects attachments between persons. In this analysis, the moral universe of girls and women tends to be primarily "a world of relationships and psychological truths where an awareness of the connection between people gives rise to a recognition of responsibility for one another, a perception of the need for response" (Gilligan, 1982, p. 30). For example, Amy, an eleven-year-old girl whom Gilligan interviews in her book, describes herself in terms of her connection with other people: "I think that the world has a lot of problems, and I think that everybody should try to help somebody else in some way . . ." (Gilligan, 1982, p. 34).

By contrast, Gilligan argues that the primary moral orientation of men and boys tends to focus on moral concerns related to inequality versus equality of individuals. Rather than emphasizing the importance of sustaining personal relationships, this approach emphasizes abstract ideals of fairness and rights, and requires abiding by impartial principles of justice, autonomy, reciprocity, and respect for persons. Viewed from this perspective, which Gilligan refers to as the "justice" perspective, moral dilemmas are defined by hierarchical values and impersonal conflicts of claims. The moral agent, like the judge, is called upon to "abstract the moral debate from the interpersonal situation, finding in the logic of fairness an objective way to decide who will win the dispute" (Gilligan, 1982, p. 32). To illustrate justice reasoning, Gilligan describes the moral reasoning of Jake, an eleven-year-old boy interviewed for her book. Asked how he would resolve a conflict between responsibility to himself and other people Jake answers, "You go about one-fourth to the others and three-fourths to yourself," and adds that "the most important thing in your decision should be yourself, don't let yourself be guided totally by other people . . ." (Gilligan, 1982, pp. 35-36). Gilligan concludes that Jake understands this moral dilemma as an abstract mathematical equation and perceives his responsibility for others as potentially interfering with his personal autonomy.

Gilligan refers to the moral orientation that she finds most prevalent among girls and women as an ethic of "care," and she calls the moral orientation that is most common among boys and men an ethic of "jus-

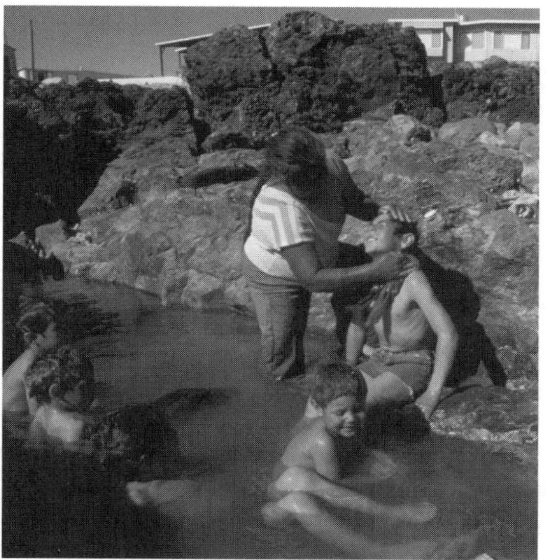

CAREGIVER

Author Carol Gilligan sees moral choices of girls and women as based on personal relationships, while males think in more abstract terms of fairness and justice.

C

CARE

Contemporary Ethics of Care

American families have always been somewhat fragile and subject to rapid reconfigurations.

PAGE 195

tice." Gilligan, a developmental psychologist, argues that an ethic of care has been generally ignored in the past because girls and women have been excluded as subjects in the study of moral development. For example, accounts of moral maturation described by Lawrence Kohlberg (1981, 1984) and Jean Piaget (1965) were based entirely on studies and observations of boys and men. These male-based theories of moral psychology, when applied to girls and women, were interpreted as showing girls and women to be deficient in moral development. Gilligan identifies an ethic of care as a distinctive form of moral reasoning.

Implications for ethics of health care

The implications of Gilligan's analysis for contemporary bioethics are the subject of ongoing discussion. First, an ethic of care may lead to positive changes in bioethical education, including placing greater emphasis on health-care providers' communication skills and emotional sensitivity, and on the effects that ethical issues have on relationships (Carse, 1991). To the extent that bioethicists with formal training in ethics are inclined to emphasize justice over care, it may be desirable to broaden their training to include an ethic of care (Self et al., 1993a).

In addition to producing changes in ethics education, a care orientation within bioethics arguably requires placing greater emphasis on beneficence as the health-care provider's primary responsibility to the patient (Sharpe, 1992). Finally, an ethics emphasizing caring for others may produce substantive changes in the way we resolve moral problems. It may encourage resolutions of moral problems that give greater authority to family members in health-care decision making (Hardwig, 1990, 1991; Jecker, 1990), or it may lead to paying greater attention to how various relationships are affected by moral decisions (Jecker, 1991).

One area within bioethics where an ethic of care has been studied in some detail is abortion. Gilligan found that women who face abortion decisions tend to frame moral issues in terms of a responsibility to care for and avoid hurting others (Gilligan, 1982). These women often base decisions about having an abortion on "a growing comprehension of the dynamics of social interaction . . . and a central insight, that self and others are interdependent" (Gilligan, 1982, p. 74). In other words, rather than conceptualizing abortion in terms of abstract values, such as "life," or in terms of competing claims or rights, these women tend to see abortion as a problem of how best to care for and avoid harming the particular people and relationships affected by their choices. Considered in this light, the resolution of abortion requires taking stock of how any decision might affect not only the pregnant woman and fetus, but also the relationship between the pregnant woman and biological father, and relationships and persons within the wider family circle (Jecker, 1993b). Arguably, an ethic of care illuminates the moral issues abortion raises better than an ethic of justice, because only an ethic of care portrays individuals as uniquely constituted by their connections to others (Gatens-Robinson, 1992).

In addition to these proposed changes, introducing a care orientation within bioethics may shed a negative light on more traditional forms of bioethical analysis (Walker, 1989). For example, Virginia Sharpe claims that a justice orientation has dominated bioethics in the past, and this has encouraged ethicists to treat provider-patient relationships as free exchanges between equals (Sharpe, 1992). She argues that this picture of the provider-patient relationship is seriously distorted. Rather than being equals in relationships with health-care providers, patients typically experience diminished power and authority as a result of being physically and emotionally vulnerable and in need of the provider's help (Sharpe, 1992). Others charge that a justice orientation has traditionally prevailed within bioethics, resulting in too much focus on competition for power, status, and authority and too little focus on the human relationships at stake (Warren, 1989, pp. 73-87). For example, the autonomy-paternalism debate within bioethics concentrates on who has the authority to make treatment decisions. Similarly, when bioethicists emphasize impersonal ethical principles, such as autonomy, nonmaleficence, beneficence, and justice, this can have the effect of making the particular persons and relationships involved in ethical dilemmas incidental, rather than essential, to the crafting of moral responses.

Objections to an ethic of care

Since the publication of *In a Different Voice*, the proposal to develop a feminine ethic of care has met with a variety of concerns and objections. One set of concerns is that a feminine ethic of care may unwittingly undermine feminism. These concerns stem, in part, from a belief that the qualities in girls and women that feminine ethics esteems have developed within the context of a sexist culture. Thus, some suspect that women's competency at caring for and serving others is an outgrowth of their subordinate status within modern societies (Sherwin, 1992; Moody-Adams, 1991), and worry that emphasizing caring as a virtuous feminine quality may simply serve to keep women on the down side of power relationships (Holmes, 1989). Others urge women to aspire to assertiveness, rather than caring, in order to challenge conventional images of women as concerned with serving and pleasing others (Card, 1991). Feminist critics also warn that caring cannot function as an ethic that is complete unto itself. Observing that caring can "be exploited in the service of immoral ends," Card insists on the need to balance caring with justice and other values (Card, 1990,

See Also

Family and Maternal-Fetal Relationship

p. 106). Exclusive attention to caring can also lead to overlooking "the lack of care of women for women" and may preclude "the possibility of our looking at anything but love and friendship in women's emotional responses to one another" (Spellman, 1991, p. 216).

OBJECTIONS TO A FEMININE ETHIC OF CARE

1. Feminine ethic of care undermines feminism.
2. Caring for others leads to neglect of oneself.
3. The concept of care is not helpful at the social and institutional level.
4. Care is a *human* ethic, not exclusively feminine.

A second family of concerns about a feminine ethic of care relates to the belief that caring for others can lead to neglect of self. The phenomenon of "burnout," for example, refers to the situation of parents, nurses, family caregivers, or other individuals who become utterly exhausted by the physical and emotional

FEMININE ETHICS AND FEMINIST ETHICS
Complementary Approaches to Common Goals

Carol Gilligan's ongoing effort (Gilligan et al., 1988; Gilligan et al., 1989; Brown and Gilligan, 1992) to characterize girls' and women's moral reasoning in terms of care has occurred in tandem with important developments in feminist ethics. It is useful, however, to distinguish between the care ethic that Gilligan describes, which has been called a "feminine ethic," and the development of "feminist ethics." According to Susan Sherwin (1992), the primary concern of feminine ethics is to describe the moral experiences and intuitions of women, pointing out how traditional approaches have neglected to include women's perspectives.

In addition to Gilligan, both Nel Noddings (1984) and Sara Ruddick (1989) have made important contributions to feminine ethics. Whereas Gilligan emphasizes the unique form of moral reasoning that caring engenders, Noddings focuses on caring as a practical activity, stressing the interaction that occurs between persons giving and receiving care. From this perspective, she identifies two distinctive features of caring: engrossment and motivational shift. "Engrossment" refers to a receptive state in which the person caring is "receiving what is there as nearly as possible without assessment or evaluation"; "motivational shift" occurs when "my motive energy flows towards the other and perhaps . . . towards his ends" (Noddings, 1984, pp. 33, 34). Critics of Noddings's approach raise the concern that her interpretation of caring may lead to exploitation (Houston, 1990) or complicity in the pursuit of evil ends (Card, 1990).

Unlike Gilligan and Noddings, Ruddick emphasizes "maternal thinking," which she says develops out of the activity of assuming regular and substantial responsibility for small children. Although Ruddick acknowledges that the work of mothering falls under the more general category of "caring labor," she argues that it cannot simply be combined with other forms of caring because each form of caring involves distinctive kinds of thinking arising from different activities (Ruddick, 1989). Ruddick delineates maternal thinking as a response to the small child's demands for preservation, growth, and acceptability. These demands elicit in the mothering person the responses of "preservative love," "fostering growth," "conscientiousness," and "educative control," which Ruddick identifies as the hallmarks of maternal thinking.

In contrast to feminine ethics, the primary concern of feminist ethics is to reject and end oppression against women. Susan Sherwin defines "feminist ethics" as "the name given to the various theories that help reveal the multiple, gender-specific patterns of harm that constitute women's oppression," together with the "diverse political movement to eliminate all such forms of oppression" (Sherwin, 1992, p. 13). By "oppression," Sherwin means "a pattern of hardship that is based on dominance of one group by members of another. The dominance involved . . . is rooted in features that distinguish one group from another" and requires "exaggerating these features to ensure the dominant group's supremacy" (Sherwin, 1992, p. 24). Feminism aims, in this interpretation, to show that the suffering of individual women is related because it springs from common sources of injustice. According to Rosemarie Tong, feminist ethics is typically far more concerned than feminine ethics with making political changes and eliminating oppressive imbalances of power (Tong, 1993).

In many respects, however, feminine and feminist ethics are interrelated. The careful study of women's lives and moral reasoning that feminine ethics undertakes can contribute substantially to dismantling habits of thought and practice that enable women's oppression to continue. Both feminine and feminist ethics share the goal of adding women's voices and perspectives to various fields of scholarly inquiry. Finally, as Ruddick notes, feminist ethics can lend important support to the ideals that feminine ethics upholds. For example, feminist ethics can help to ensure "women's economic and psychological ability to engage in mothering without undue sacrifice of physical health and nonmaternal projects" (Ruddick, 1989, p. 236).

—NANCY S. JECKER
WARREN THOMAS REICH

demands associated with giving care. Especially when care is conceived to be an ethic that is sufficient unto itself, the tendency may be to continue caring at any cost. Attention to other values, such as the rights and dignity of the one caring, may be necessary in order to place reasonable limits on caring. Arguing along these lines, Judith Jarvis Thomson criticizes those who suppose it possible to exclude the language of rights from morality, replacing this language with moral prescriptions to care for others (Thomson, 1990). She cautions that "what has oppressed women in the past is precisely the socially engendered expectation that they will melt into their personal relationships; the women's movement succeeded in bringing home to many that women, like men, have inherently individual interests . . ." (Thomson, 1990, p. 288). Others suggest that in order to care for others—which is an inherently limited ability—one must first be cared for by other individuals, by communities, and by oneself (Reich, 1991).

The existence of sexism raises questions about whether its elimination requires the recognition of multiple oppressions.

626

A third group of objections to developing a feminine ethic of care holds that the concept of care is not helpful at the social and institutional level. This group of objections may acknowledge that an ethic of care serves well within the limited sphere of personal ethics, but finds care unhelpful outside of this sphere. One form this objection takes is to argue that an ethic of care cannot be formulated in terms of the general rights and principles that are necessary for designing public policies. Proponents of a care ethic sometimes acknowledge this limitation. Thus, Noddings states, "to care is to act not by fixed rule but by affection and regard" (Noddings, 1984, p. 24). Similarly, Patricia Benner and Judith Wrubel maintain that caring is always specific and relational; hence, there exist no "context-free lists of advice" on how to care (Benner and Wrubel, 1989, p. 3). They reject the idea of formulating ethical theories or rules about caring on the grounds that general guides cannot "capture the embodied, relational, configurational, skillful, meaningful, and contextual human issues" that are central to an ethic of care (Benner and Wrubel, 1989, p. 6). Despite this view, there exist historically important examples of using the vocabulary of general rights and principles to formulate an ethic of care. For example, the *Universal Declaration of Human Rights* identifies "motherhood and childhood" as "entitled to special care and assistance," and the *Declaration of the Rights of the Child* asserts general principles of caring for children, noting that children need "special safeguards and care" on the basis of their "physical and mental immaturity" (U.N. General Assembly, 1948, 1960).

Another reason why care may be assumed unworkable at a social or institutional level is that historically, public and private spheres have been distinguished as separate moral domains (Elshtain, 1981). During the nineteenth century, for example, the doctrine of separate spheres held that the family constituted a private sphere in which a morality of love and self-sacrifice prevailed; this private domain was distinguished from the public life associated with business and politics, where impersonal norms and self-interested relationships reigned (Nicholson, 1986). To the extent that these historical attitudes continue to shape present thinking, they may lead to the mutual exclusivity of care-oriented and justice-oriented approaches. In response to this structural objection, some ethicists have argued that justice and care are compatible forms of moral reasoning (Jecker, 1993a).

A final set of objections to a feminine ethic of care does not deny the importance of care, but rather argues that care is properly interpreted as a broad human ethic, rather than an ethic that expresses an exclusively feminine form of moral reasoning. Defenders of feminine ethics often meet this objection by claiming that their approach has been misunderstood. Thus advocates of feminine ethics may deny that care is an ethic that only women articulate, or an ethic that is valid only within the moral experience of women. According to Noddings, caring is an important ingredient within all human morality, and moral education should teach all people how and why to care. She concludes that "an ethical orientation that arises in female experience need not be confined to women"; to the contrary, "if only women adopt an ethic of caring the present conditions of women's oppression are indeed likely to be maintained" (Noddings, 1990, p. 171). Gilligan and Jane Attanucci also reject the idea that an ethic of care correlates strictly with gender, and instead report that most men and women can reason in accordance with both care and justice (Gilligan and Attanucci, 1988). Gilligan's research supports the more modest claim that care is gender-related. That is, although women and men can reason in terms of both care and justice, women are generally more likely to emphasize care while men generally emphasize justice. Thus she states that the so-called different voice she identifies is characterized "not by gender, but by theme," and cautions that its association with gender "is not absolute" and is not a generalization about either sex (Gilligan, 1982, p. 2).

Caring and contemporary nursing

Within health care, attention to caring is perhaps most evident within nursing. Emphasizing caring as a central value within nursing often provides a basis for arguing that nursing requires its own description, possesses its own phenomena, and retains its own method for clarification of its own concepts and their meanings, relationships, and context (Jameton, 1984; Fry, 1989a, 1989b; Watson, 1988; Gadow, 1987; Swanson, 1990; Reverby, 1987a, 1987b). For example, Jean

See Also
Sexism
Women

Watson holds that nurses should reject the impersonal, objective models that she says currently dominate ethics and choose instead an ethic that emphasizes caring.

Those who invoke caring in developing a theory of nursing ethics often assign caring a privileged or foundational role. For example, Sarah Fry posits caring as "a foundational, rather than a derivative, value among persons" (Fry, 1989b, pp. 20-21). She argues that other ethical values, such as personhood and human dignity, are an outgrowth of nurses' caring activity. Similarly, Benner and Wrubel argue for the primacy of caring on the grounds that skillful technique and scientific knowledge do not suffice to establish ethical nursing in the absence of a basic level of caring and attachment (Benner and Wrubel, 1989).

Like Fry, Kristen Swanson regards caring as central to nursing ethics. According to her analysis, caring requires acting in a way that preserves human dignity, restores humanity, and avoids reducing persons to the moral status of objects. Specifically, caring requires:

> 1. knowing, or striving to understand an event as it has meaning in the life of the other;
> 2. being with, which means being emotionally present to the other;
> 3. doing for, defined as doing for the other as he or she would do for himself or herself if that were possible;
> 4. enabling, or facilitating the other's passage through life transitions and unfamiliar events; and
> 5. maintaining belief, which refers to sustaining faith in the other's capacity to get through an event or transition and to face a future of fulfillment. (Swanson, 1990)

Susan Reverby finds caring to be a central ethic throughout nursing's history. Tracing the history of nursing to its domestic roots during the colonial era, when nursing took place within the family, Reverby argues that caring for the sick was originally a duty rather than a freely chosen vocation for women. Reverby suggests that nurses today possess "some deep understandings of the limited promise of equality and autonomy in a health care system. In an often implicit way, such nurses recognize that those who claim the autonomy of rights often run the risk of rejecting altruism and caring itself" (Reverby, 1987a).

Some have challenged the proposal to consider care as a concept unique to nursing ethics (Veatch, 1981). Others identify nursing with maternal practice, a specific kind of caring activity (Newton, 1990; O'Brien, 1987). For example, Patricia O'Brien defends the importance of nursing's maternal function by noting that historically the source of nurses' prestige has been the manner in which nurses blend home and hospital. That is, nursing's strength has come from nurses' skill at the traditionally female tasks of feeding, bathing, cleaning, coaching, and cajoling those in one's care. Just as mothers make a home, it is female nurses who have been able to make a home of the hospital, to personalize an increasingly impersonal environment.

Critics of the maternal paradigm for nursing fault this approach as casting women in traditional and stifling roles. Historically, for example, nurses were socialized into the health-care field to know their place and were relegated to the bottom of the pyramid and taught not to ask questions (Murphy, 1984). Casting nursing practice in terms of mothering potentially reverses progress made in the late 1970s when nurses began to see themselves as shared-decision makers rather than handmaidens to physicians (Stein et al., 1990).

A further objection to identifying ethical ideals of nursing with ethical ideals of mothering holds that nurses' proper function is to serve as patients' advocates, rather than as patients' parents. Sally Gadow and Gerald Winslow, for example, argue that advocacy of patients' autonomy, rather than paternalistic promotion of patient benefit, should guide nursing ethics (Gadow, 1980a, 1980b; Winslow, 1984).

Caring and contemporary medicine

Whereas nursing is often associated with a caring function, doctoring has traditionally been associated with a curing function. However, the tendency to associate caring exclusively with nursing is misleading for a variety of reasons (Jecker and Self, 1991). First, both doctors and nurses are engaged in caring for patients. In addition, assigning caring activities to nurses and curing activities to doctors is misleading because certain meanings of "curing" are actually derived from "caring." Thus, the Latin definition of "cure" comes from the word "curare," meaning "care, heed, concern; to do one's busy care, to give one's care or attention to some piece of work; or to apply one's self diligently."

Although there has been less explicit attention to an ethic of care in medicine than in nursing, caring for patients represents a central component of ethics in medicine. Caring is inextricably linked to the physician's obligation to relieve suffering, a goal that stretches back to antiquity (Cassell, 1982).

There are several more specific ways in which an ethic of care becomes manifest in the practice of medicine. First, caring is manifest in the activity of healing the patient. Whereas curing disease typically requires the physician to understand and deal with a physical disease process, healing requires that the physician also respond to the patient's subjective experience of illness (Cassell, 1989). For example, healing a patient who is

From the point of view of the patient, there are no good alternatives to having trustworthy professionals.

PAGE 674

See Also

Trust

CARING IS SHARING

Giving help to those less fortunate is at the center of ethical traditions—and human kindness—worldwide.

"A certain Samaritan . . . had compassion on him. . . . Go and do thou likewise."

LUKE 10:33, 37

suffering from a serious infection requires not only administering antibiotics to kill bacteria but also addressing the patient's feelings, questions, and concerns about his or her medical situation. In cases of serious illness where cure is not possible, caring for the patient may become the primary part of healing. For example, when patients are terminally ill and imminently dying, physicians' primary duty may become providing palliative and comfort care. Under these circumstances, healing emphasizes touch and communication, psychological and emotional support, and responding to the patient's specific feelings and concerns, which may include fear, loss of control, dependency, and acceptance or denial of death and final separation from loved ones.

Caring is also evident in what Albert Jonsen calls the "'Samaritan principle': the duty to care for the needy sick, whether friend or enemy, even at cost to oneself" (Jonsen, 1990, p. 39). The tradition of Samaritanism dates to the early Christian era and the parable of the Good Samaritan described in the Gospel according to Luke; it persists during the modern, secular era as a central ethic for medicine. Jonsen argues that although the original Christian parable of the Samaritan refers to giving aid to a particular individual, the ethical tradition of Samaritanism within medicine bears relevance to entire groups of patients. So understood, Samaritanism underlies the physician's broader social duty to care for indigent persons. In contrast to the past, when physicians provided charity care for indigent persons without financial remuneration, today universal health insurance is the norm in most developed countries. Therefore, in contemporary times physicians are generally compensated for their services through a private or government health insurance mechanism. In the United States, however, large numbers of patients continue to lack health insurance. A principle of Samaritanism continues to be evident in the legal and ethical requirement that U.S. physicians provide emergency treatment to any patient regardless of the patient's ability to pay for care. A stronger Samaritan ethic, mandating access to all forms of basic health care, would require, in the United States, successful implementation of health-care reform.

A third way in which caring is manifest in the ethics of medicine is through the healing relationship of doctor and patient. Edmund Pellegrino and David Thomasma regard this relationship as one of inherent inequality because the patient is vulnerable, ill, and in need of the physician's skill (Pellegrino and Thomasma, 1988). In light of the patient's diminished power, Pellegrino and Thomasma argue that the physician incurs a duty of beneficence, a duty requiring the physician to respond to the patient's needs and promote the patient's good. Other ethical values in medicine can presumably be derived from the physician's primary duty of beneficence. For example, according to Pellegrino and Thomasma, a duty to enhance patients' autonomy is based on the duty to benefit patients.

Some (Sharpe, 1992) have sought to identify the principle of beneficence that Pellegrino and Thomasma delineate with an ethic of care. However, beneficence and care differ in crucial respects. Whereas a principle of beneficence identifies promoting the patient's good as a requirement for right action, an ethic of care is a type of virtue ethic that is basically concerned about the affective orientation and moral commitment—that is, the concern—of the one who cares. For example, a physician may perform actions that promote a patient's good, and thus meet the requirement of beneficence, without caring about or feeling any commitment toward the patient. If this analysis is correct, then actions that fulfill the principle of beneficence do not necessarily fulfill standards associated with an ethic of care. An ethic of care suggests both a feeling response directed to the object of care and a commitment to ensuring that things go well for that person.

Despite the integral role that an ethic of caring plays in medicine, contemporary physicians sometimes neglect to offer adequate palliative and comfort measures to patients (Angell, 1982). This may stem from a failure to teach and nurture empathy in medical education (Spiro et al., 1993), and from financial incentives that discourage spending time at patients' bedsides and getting to know patients as persons. In addition, physicians may overlook caring for patients when conflicts exist about the use of futile treatments (Schneiderman et al., 1994). For example, members of the health-care team may become distracted debating the appropriateness of high-technology interventions and neglect to care for patients' spiritual and emotional needs.

Ethics of care in environmental ethics

Attempts have been made to rethink environmental issues in bioethics—those affecting the health, for example, of nonhuman animals and plant life—on the basis of an ethic of care. Contemporary critics of a rights-based approach to environmental bioethics often criticize it as inadequate to express insights into why we value nonhuman animals and the environment. In an effort to attribute rights to nature, rights-based theorists seek to establish parallels between nature and humans—such as their equality—on the basis of which rights can be granted. But, critics object, it seems that our moral interests may rest on the differences between humans, nonhuman animals, and the environment rather than on their similarities; it seems too that these interests may be better expressed in an ethic of care.

This approach entails reconceiving the grounds on which we understand our relationship to "the world of nature," including a reconsideration of the domination of nonhuman animals according to a patriarchal mindset that has also accounted for the domination of women (Curtin, 1991, p. 60). In addition, the care approach involves a shift from an ethic of rights, rules, and principles to an ethic that "makes a central place for values of care, love, friendship, trust and appropriate reciprocity—values that presuppose that our relationships to others are central to our understanding of who we are" (Curtin, 1991, p. 65). Whether or not animals have rights, we certainly can and do care for them (Curtin, 1991). While a rights-based ethic tries to prevent infringements on individual rights, an ethic of care tries to prevent people from neglecting other people and things. It stresses the importance of recognizing our interconnected web of relationships with elements of the environment, dialoguing with them, and strengthening those bonds. Claims that we ought to protect and respect the environment are made on the grounds that we are in a relationship of interdependence with the environment, a relationship expressed through care. Finally, while animal rights have been argued for on the basis of such criteria as animal sentience, it may be more coherent to argue for the respect and protection of animals on the basis of our caring relationship with them and the responsibilities incurred by that relationship.

Conclusion

Although the development of theories of an ethic of care for health care is new, the idea of care has long presented a moral standard or ideal for health care. Although caring has been an abiding concern within nursing practice, within medicine care has sometimes been overshadowed by other ethical values and goals. The emergence of feminine ethics can play an important role in reemphasizing the value and importance of caring within medicine. However, the close association of care with gender and with the feminine voice may hinder efforts to develop a broader human understanding of care, such as the understanding of care that emerged earlier in human history.

— NANCY S. JECKER
WARREN THOMAS REICH

CHILDREN

RIGHTS OF CHILDREN

Since about 1970, philosophical interest in the rights of children has grown substantially. This growth owes

See Also
Rights of Patients/Clients

CHILDREN

Rights of Children

much to the social upheavals of the 1960s and 1970s, especially the civil rights and women's movements, both of which employed the rhetoric of rights. When the plights of children, homosexuals, and the disabled began to be highlighted, it was natural that advocates for these groups also used the rhetoric of rights.

The invocation of rights in connection with children, however, predated the 1960s. In 1959 the United Nations General Assembly (1960) adopted a ten-principle *Declaration of the Rights of the Child*, itself a descendant of one adopted by the League of Nations in 1924.

Why rights?

Why do activists concerned with the lives of children attempt to protect children's interests by invoking the notion of rights? The key features of the rhetoric of basic rights are (1) that rights are entitlements, and (2) that they impose duties on others. To claim something as a fundamental right is to make the strongest kind of claim one can make; it is to claim that something is an entitlement, not a privilege—something it would be not merely inadvisable or regrettable, but wrong and unjust, to withhold. And, typically, if one person is the bearer of rights, some or all others are the bearers of obligations. In the case of basic rights, the responsibilities fall either on all others as individuals or on the government, which in the case of democracies means on individuals acting as representatives of the citizenry. This is easily seen in the cases of the rights of adults to free speech and to health care.

◆ **fundamental rights**
A claim that something is an entitlement, not a privilege, and that withholding it would be wrong and unjust.

The rights to free speech and health care illustrate two broad classes of rights given a variety of names by theorists. These may be designated "option" rights and "welfare" rights respectively (Golding, 1968). The idea behind option rights is that there is a sphere of sovereignty within which the individual cannot be intruded upon by government, even for the greater good. This idea is at the heart of classical liberal theory. Option rights are rights to choose. For instance, although persons have the right to speak, they may remain silent if they wish. Welfare rights, on the other hand, are rights to direct provision of services, such as medical care, that meet a basic need.

Do both categories apply to children? The notion of option rights motivated children's rights activists who saw children as oppressed by adults. Psychologist Richard Farson stated, "Children, like adults, should have the right to decide the matters which affect them most directly. The issue of self-determination is at the heart of children's liberation" (Farson, 1974, p. 27). The authors of the United Nations *Declaration*, on the other hand, focused almost exclusively on welfare rights. For example:

> *The child, for the full and harmonious development of his* [sic] *personality, needs love and understanding. He shall, wherever possible, grow up in the care and under the responsibility of his parents, and in any case in an atmosphere of affection and of moral and material security; a child of tender years shall not, save in exceptional circumstances, be separated from his mother.*
>
> *(United Nations, 1960, p. 113)*

Although some children's advocates urge recognition of both option and welfare rights, the underlying rationales are quite different. While the rationale for according children option rights conceives of minor status *itself* as a disabling condition that ought to be removed, the rationale for welfare rights urges that various goods and services be provided to minors *as* minors.

Most sensible people would look askance at putting children, especially young children, on a par with adults, insofar as freedom to live as they wish is concerned. The notion of a protected sphere of autonomous decision making is closely linked to the

WHY NOT CHILDREN'S RIGHTS?

Rights discourse does have some limitations in the context of advocacy for children. An initial difficulty lies in identifying universal rights while taking account of the limited resources and diverse values of particular societies. It may not be possible in some countries to fulfill the universal right to grow up in an atmosphere of material security, due to lack of resources. A second difficulty is that alleged welfare rights may be in tension with each other—for example, the right of a child to grow up in material security and the right to love and understanding.

A danger of rights discourse derives from the fact that, taken literally, respect of children's rights may permit substantial intrusion into parents' lives. For example, should government agents monitor parents to make sure they provide their children with the love and understanding they need? A less obvious danger derives from the fact that some of a child's most important needs, such as the need for love, cannot be coerced. If love fails, must the child be taken from the parent and given to another who is known to love the child? It is apparent that the struggle for children's rights may have the potential of making parents and children into adversaries.

— FRANCIS SCHRAG

See Also
Rights
Fetal Rights? The Moral Status of the Unborn

presence of developed capacities for rational choice, capacities that usually are only potential in young children. It may well be that the development of autonomy is impeded when children are not permitted to exercise choices in their lives, but advocating that children be given some options is a far cry from asserting that children have the same rights as adults to live their lives as they please. Paternalism, the coercion of individuals for their own good, is odious only when those coerced are capable of exercising rational choice.

Alternatives to rights

Given children's vulnerability to abuse and neglect by immediate caregivers and by society at large, what ethical bases other than rights might serve to enhance children's welfare? Philosopher Onora O'Neill (1989) suggests that Immanuel Kant's notion of imperfect duty provides such a basis. An "imperfect" duty—the duty to contribute to charity is an illustration—differs from a "perfect" duty in the latitude allowed for fulfillment; toward whom and how much the duty requires is not specified. Thus, although we all have an obligation to help the next generation not only to survive but also to develop its capacities, we may meet this obligation in different ways—some as parents, some as professional caregivers, some as taxpaying citizens. The idea is attractive philosophically, but it admittedly lacks the precision, and hence the force, of the language of rights. Since the precise nature of the duty cannot be specified, it will be difficult to determine when people have or have not done enough to help needy children.

Another stream of ethical reasoning centers on character and virtue. So-called virtue ethics takes the focus away from whether particular acts are obligatory, permitted, or forbidden, and explores the notion of a good or virtuous person, a notion it alleges is fundamental. Proponents of virtue ethics would say, for example, that the idea of a virtuous or good mother cannot be reduced to that of a mother who performs or refrains from performing specific actions viewed as duties. A decided advantage of virtue ethics is that it encourages us to ask a key question: What legal and economic structures are conducive to "good parenting"? Virtuous parents, for example, take time to be with their children, especially when they are ill, but such virtuous actions will be more likely if employed parents enjoy legal protection against punitive actions by employers for their taking family leave.

Unlike the children's rights approach, which may pit parents against children, this approach does not put parents on the defensive. But virtue ethics also has theoretical difficulties, chief of which is defining character traits in ways that do justice to the diverse cultural ideals present in a heterogeneous population like that of the United States. Everyone will agree that virtuous parents, for example, need to teach their children to distinguish right from wrong, but may they use corporal punishment in the process? Here, consensus will break down. Another limitation of the approach is that virtue ethics has little to say about what precisely is owed to, or what ought to be done for, children whose primary caregivers have *already* failed them.

Care ethics, a variant of virtue ethics, is utterly antithetical to the Kantian emphasis on general principles and the development of rational agency. Deriving primarily from the work of feminist psychologists and philosophers, this approach takes close personal relationships, such as that between mother and child, as a model for all moral relations. Emphasis is placed on the need for compassion and empathy in the context of relationships to particular others in concrete settings, rather than on allegiance to abstract principles. Parents, for example, often succeed in meeting the needs of their children because they can empathize with them in particular situations; no abstract duty to care for one's children needs to be evoked. The ethic of care counters a philosophical focus on rationality as the defining essence of humanity.

Is care ethics sufficient to meet the needs of *all* children? For example, should affluent citizens provide funds for intensive professional care of babies born with drug addictions, babies they never will meet? If the answer to such a question is yes, then the notion of duty may provide a more secure basis for persuading people that such contributions are obligatory, since emotional identification with those one does not know is likely to be weak.

If both justice and care are regarded as virtues, then virtue ethics may have the potential to offer moral grounds for the protection and care of all children. Whether such a reconciliation of alternative approaches is possible remains an open question. If it is not possible, then philosophical ethics offers a number of lenses through which to view the status of children. As in the case of actual lenses, however, there may be no single lens that fits all purposes.

— FRANCIS SCHRAG

HEALTH-CARE AND RESEARCH ISSUES

Access to good parenting, food, housing, and sanitation remain the primary aids to enhancing children's well-being and opportunities. The consensus that children should also have basic health-care and social services grew over the twentieth century. Initially, advocates for better health and social care for the many impoverished, neglected, abused, and exploited children included those active in the women's rights movement, the newly recognized specialty of pediatrics, and the visiting home-health nursing programs. As the century progressed, lawyers and social scientists joined the reform move-

Some Gnostics taught that marriage was evil or at least useless because the procreation of children was a vehicle for forces of evil

PAGE 645

See Also

Rights Talk: More Harm Than Good?

ment. They attacked the long-dominant views that children were the property of their parents or guardians and that the state had no authority to intervene even if the children were abused or neglected. Children gained rights to certain medical services and to be protected from abuse, poverty, neglect, or exploitation; adolescents gained liberties such as the right to consent to some kinds of treatments or services without parental approval or notification (Holder, 1985, 1989). Scientists further helped transform children's programs through study of children's growth, development, needs, experiences, illnesses, and perspectives, showing the importance of candor and respect for children's views. A distinctive feature of advocacy for improved health and social care for children remains: Others make most decisions for minors, both in terms of their personal care and in allocation of funds for their programs.

Moral disputes about children's health care generally fall into four areas:

1. Who should make decisions for children?
2. How should decisions be made?
3. When should children be enrolled as research subjects?
4. How much of society's health-care funds should be allocated to children's programs?

Basic moral values

Different solutions to these questions will be evaluated in terms of basic moral values: Solutions are judged superior when they fairly promote children's well-being and opportunities to flourish and help children become empowered, self-fulfilled persons who can develop their potential. The U.N. *Declaration of the Rights of the Child* (U.N. General Assembly, 1960) endorsed these basic values, underscoring their wide acceptance. These values received international support because most adults want to help children and recognize some responsibilities to help them. These values also promote stability by helping to address inequalities of the "natural lottery" (the inequalities caused by nature, such as health status) and of the "social lottery" (inequalities caused by social factors, such as wealth, schooling, or family). Children are not responsible for such inequalities, yet they affect whether children will thrive and flourish. Adequate health-care and social services enhance children's well-being and opportunities by treating diseases, in some cases returning children from the brink of death or permanent disability to full and healthy lives. These services also restore or maintain compromised function, avert or ameliorate suffering, and prevent disease or disabilities through interventions or counseling. Basic prevention, diagnosis, treatment, rehabilitation, and social services not only make children's lives better, they profit society with healthier and more productive citizens. The focus of this article is primarily on preadolescent children, who are clearly not responsible for their quality of life or its inequities and who need help making prudent decisions for themselves.

◆ **mature minor rule**
A physician may treat a child of fifteen or older without the parents' consent when the patient is mature enough to understand the medical information and to give the same sort of informed consent that would be accepted from an adult patient.

Who has authority to decide for children?

Adults are presumed competent and minors incompetent to consent to medical treatment or participation in research. Minors generally lack the capacity, maturity, foresight, and experience to make important choices for themselves, and cannot determine what choices promote their well-being or opportunities. In general, the younger and less experienced the child, the greater the presumption that he or she cannot competently participate in health-care decisions. Some children, especially older adolescents, may overturn this presumption.

SHARED DECISION MAKING. Ideally, important health-care choices should represent a consensus among parents, doctors, nurses, and the child, if he or she is mature enough and willing to participate. Together they find the option best suited to the child and family (U.S. President's Commission, 1982). In the final analysis, however, parents or guardians generally have legal and moral authority to make medical decisions for minor children.

PARENT'S OR GUARDIAN'S AUTHORITY. Parents and guardians have the authority to make decisions for many of the same reasons they have authority to select their children's religion and schooling. Philosophers Allen Buchanan and Dan Brock (1989) discuss several reasons for this policy. First, parents and guardians are generally most knowledgeable and interested in their children, and so are most likely to do the best job for them. Second, the family usually bears the consequences of the choices that are made for the child. Some choices and their resulting consequences suit certain families better than others. Third, children learn values and standards within their families, and different values and standards may lead to different health-care choices. Within limits, it is important to honor the standards and values of families, because it is within the family structure more than anywhere else that people in society learn values. Fourth, families need intimacy with minimal state intrusion. Thus, unless the child is placed at risk, there is reason to tolerate choices that families make for their children and give families wide discretion in selecting health care for their children.

Parents or guardians maintain this authority as long as they promote the well-being and opportunities of those under their care, and prevent, remove, or minimize harms to their minor children. Their authority

See Also
Law and Morality
Family

can be contested, however (Rodham, 1973; Holder, 1985). Moral disputes over when to challenge parental authority to make health-care decisions often center on practical and theoretical issues about when harms or dangers to children warrant interfering with parental authority, and what restrictions on the parental choice are needed to secure the child's well-being.

Parents who abuse, neglect, or exploit their children may lose custody of them temporarily or permanently. Physical, sexual, or emotional abuse inflicted on their children constitutes grounds for loss of parental authority. In addition, parents who make imprudent or neglectful decisions may lose custody temporarily or permanently. For example, parents might temporarily lose custody if they endanger a child by declining standard antibiotic care to treat their child's bacterial meningitis, preferring the use of herbal teas for treatment. Parents might also lose custody temporarily if they endanger a child by acting upon certain beliefs. For example, Christian Scientists object to surgery and Jehovah's Witnesses object to blood transfusions, yet courts can order either intervention if the child is endangered (Holder, 1985; Rodham, 1973). Because children cannot protect themselves, health-care professionals, teachers, neighbors, or other members of the community have a duty to report suspected child abuse, neglect, or exploitation to state agencies for investigation. When parental acts or omissions pose an imminent danger to children, then doctors, nurses, hospital administrators, or social workers have a moral and legal duty to seek a court order for proper care (Holder, 1985).

CHILDREN'S ASSENT AND COMPETENCE. Decisions about when to consult or inform children

FOUR STANDARDS TO GUIDE DECISIONS ABOUT CHILDREN'S HEALTH CARE

1. The first standard, self-determination, applies primarily to competent and informed adults, who should be generally free to make their own choices about their well-being and opportunities as long as they do not harm or violate the rights of others. As minors become more mature and competent, they are accorded more self-determination, but their preferences need not be honored as those of adults (Holder, 1985, 1989). An adolescent with cancer insisting that he or she would rather die than lose a leg needs help in order to understand this reaction. The degree of irreversibility and severity of the consequences often determines whether the minor's preferences should be honored. Minors' choices generally become more morally binding upon adults when minors show that they understand and appreciate the nature of the situation in relation to life goals. Adult guidance is needed when minors cannot demonstrate that their choices enhance their own well-being and opportunities.

2. Second, adults and some older children may prepare advance directives about their health-care choices should they become incompetent. While a minor's choice need not be honored as an adult's decision, it may be an important consideration or even seem morally binding under some circumstances. Dying children may, for example, indicate that they wish to donate organs or plan their funerals. Parents may want to follow such instructions carefully.

3. A third standard, that of substituted judgment, applies to someone who was once competent enough to express preferences. Using this standard, people select the option they believe the person would have chosen were he or she able. Families often know their relatives well enough to make choices their relatives would have made. Children, especially those with serious or chronic illnesses, may also express general preferences that guide parental choices. One child who was very sick insisted that he did not want to be maintained in a persistent vegetative state (PVS), "like a zombie."

4. The best-interest standard applies to those who do not have the ability or authority to make decisions for themselves. This standard maintains that decision makers should try to identify the person's immediate and long-term interests and then determine whether the benefits of an intervention or procedure outweigh the burdens. It does not mean they seek what is absolutely best, since that may be impossible (the best doctor cannot treat everyone), but the best among the available options. The best-interest standard permits complex judgments about what, on balance, is likely to be best for that individual given the available options (Buchanan and Brock, 1989; Kopelman, 1993). For example, the benefit of obtaining a long and healthy life would outweigh the burden of enduring intense pain for a short time. The best-interest standard, however, might be used by parents, doctors, and nurses to consider withholding or withdrawing maximal life-support treatment from children whose lives are filled with intense and chronic pain, with no prospects of improvement or foreseeable pleasures, understanding, or capacities for interaction.

In some cases, objective or intersubjectively confirmable estimates about pain and a well-understood prognosis force parents and doctors to choose between preserving biological life and providing comfort. Some children live in considerable discomfort from the very technologies that keep them alive, such as a gastrostomy (a tube through which food goes directly into the stomach, and which is irritating), intravenous lines, ventilators (breathing machines), long stays in intensive-care units (which can be extremely disorienting), or a tracheotomy (a hole in the throat that aids breathing but often clogs with saliva).

—LORETTA M. KOPELMAN

about their health-care options usually become important for children with serious illnesses where distinct choices result in different outcomes. Some, but not all, children want to understand the decisions about their health care. Older children will often have an opinion about their care (Brock, 1989; Holmes, 1989; Matthews, 1989). Moreover, adolescents do not always need parental consent to gain certain services such as treatment for substance abuse, abortion, or contraception (Holder, 1985, 1989).

This trend to inform or consult children stems from several sources. First, it results from research about what children of different ages and stages of development can understand. Social-science research has found that many children understand a great deal about their diseases and even their imminent death (Bluebond-Langner, 1978). They sense when people are not truthful, and this can cause them to suffer by feeling isolated from discussions, decisions, and support (Bluebond-Langner, 1978; Matthews, 1989). When children are competent and prepared appropriately, truthfulness generally has good consequences by promoting cooperation and enhancing trust in the credibility of their caretakers. Truthfulness can also foster decision-making abilities and maturity. When children have life-threatening or chronic illnesses, it may be especially important to them to gain some control in their lives and some respect for their views. For those facing death, opportunities to become self-fulfilled and self-determining persons may be restricted to choices about how they will live their last months.

Adolescents who meet the definition of emancipation in the states where they are living may consent to or refuse any medical care.

PAGE 40

Second, this trend stems from understanding that competency is task related. In assessing competency, the question needs to be asked: Competence for what? People are competent to do some things and not others, and so may be competent to make some health-care decisions but not others (Brock, 1989; Faden et al., 1986; Matthews, 1989; U.S. President's Commission, 1982). An eleven-year-old child with cancer may understand a great deal about the illness, because he or she has had experiences beyond those of most eleven-year-old children. Consequently, the child may be better able than most children of the same age to understand or participate in health-care decisions.

Children are increasingly competent to participate in health-care decisions as they become better able to understand and reason about their options and life plans. While young children cannot do this, some adolescents may be as competent as most adults in these respects (Holmes, 1989).

One goal of medicine, to be balanced against others, is to preserve and prolong biological life when possible. Since ancient times, this ideal has been understood to mean that one ought to prevent untimely death. However, a question remains regarding the best interests of a person whose life is continued by means of maximal treatment that is a burden to that person (U.S. President's Commission, 1983; Buchanan and Brock, 1989; Kopelman, 1993; Clouser, 1973). In cases where doctors and others disagree about what is best, it is hard to apply the best-interest standard. In such situations, and for the general reasons given above that allow parents wide discretion when doctors disagree about what is best, an established legal and moral consensus using the best-interest standard allows parents to choose from options advanced as best (Buchanan and Brock, 1989; Holder, 1985, 1989; U.S. President's Commission, 1982, 1983).

THE BEST-INTEREST STANDARD AND QUALITY OF LIFE. The best-interest standard was challenged by President Ronald Reagan (1986) and Surgeon General C. Everett Koop (1989), who rejected this standard, believing that quality-of-life considerations were likely to be abused. Under their influence, the federal government in 1984 amended its child-abuse laws and adopted the so-called Baby Doe guidelines ("Child Abuse and Neglect," 1985). These rules forbid withholding or withdrawing lifesaving care from a sick infant unless the child is dying or in an irreversible coma or when treatment is both virtually futile in terms of survival and inhumane. To forgo lifesaving treatments, it is not sufficient that the treatment is inhumane or gravely burdensome, as it would be in Roman Catholic tradition. If the care cannot honestly be deemed virtually futile, then according to these rules, it must be given even if it is inhumane and not very likely to succeed. Suffering cannot be taken into account except where the child cannot survive even with maximal treatment (Kopelman, 1989a, 1993). The Baby Doe rules are controversial because they radically restrict parental discretion and standard medical practice. In a 1988 survey, U.S. neonatologists indicated that the use of this policy for judging when to withdraw or withhold care for infants would result in overtreatment, poor use of resources, and insufficient attention to suffering (Kopelman et al., 1988).

Many commentators disagree with claims that the best-interest standard is open to abuse or that it is excessively vague (Rodham, 1973). For example, the U.S. President's Commission states, "This is a very strict standard in that it excludes considerations of the negative effects of an impaired child's life on other persons, including parents, siblings and society" (U.S. President's Commission, 1983, p. 219). Allen Buchanan and Dan Brock argue that quality-of-life assessments are not especially open to abuse if carefully limited to judgments about what is best for the individual patient. The courts and others who reject quality-of-life judgments made on behalf of incompetent people, they argue, fail to distinguish two kinds

See Also

Treating Adolescents: Exceptions to Parental Consent

of quality-of-life judgments. Quality-of-life judgments based on considerations of social worth try to decide the interests or value of a person's life in relation to the interests or value of other people's lives; they are comparative. In contrast, noncomparative quality-of-life judgments try to consider the value of the life to the person, comparing the value of living the individual's life to having no life at all. While this comparison is difficult to make, it can be guided by choices made by competent adults who decide that there are worse things than death, including certain treatments keeping them alive. Buchanan and Brock hold that in using the best-interest standard, we should use noncomparative estimates, contemplating only the quality of the person's life for that individual; a person's social value should not be a part of this assessment. These noncomparative quality-of-life judgments, then, should be very carefully and strictly circumscribed. We can reflect, for example, upon whether most people would want to live such a life (Buchanan and Brock, 1989).

The debate between those who want to consider the person's quality of life and those who reject such considerations continues. The solution depends, in part, on whether one believes that, in the end, quality-of-life decisions can be avoided. For example, the Baby Doe regulations state that one need not provide maximal treatment to those who are permanently comatose, and this is a quality-of-life judgment. The solution also depends upon whether one believes laws should permit parents, nurses, and doctors to have some discretion in selecting what is the best available option.

Children as research subjects

Children who become sick are not responsible for their illnesses. The natural and social lotteries leave some children with a diminished quality of life due to illness. Good health and social services may be essential to give these children a chance to flourish and develop their potential as self-fulfilled and self-determining persons empowered to develop their talents. In addition, good health care helps children by preventing many illnesses and allows for early diagnosis and treatment. Good health care, however, is the product of study and research, and the problem is how research should be conducted to help children.

FOUR OPTIONS DETERMINING USE OF CHILDREN AS RESEARCH SUBJECTS

1. "surrogate" or "libertarian"
2. "no consent–no research" or "Nuremberg"
3. "no consent–only therapy" or "Helsinki"
4. "risk-benefit" or "U.S. federal regulation"

The ethical basis for research policy with children concerns promoting the same primary values that shape treatment decisions, namely, fairly enhancing well-being and opportunities. Since children, like adults severely impaired with mental illness or retardation, lack the capacity to give informed consent, they are regarded as vulnerable research subjects. Like policy regarding treatment, research policy with children is also shaped by different authority principles (stating who decides) and guidance principles (substantive directions about how decisions should be made). Four important policy options for vulnerable subjects balance these primary values differently.

1. The "surrogate" or "libertarian" solution allows the same sort of research with children as with other subjects, if parents give consent. This solution may not offer adequate protection to children because it permits parents to enroll them in potentially harmful research. Parents' legal and moral authority presupposes the promotion of children's opportunities and well-being, and prevention, removal, or minimization of harms to them. Parents have no authority to enroll their children in potentially harmful research. Volunteering to put another in harm's way is not admirable, and may violate the guardian's protective role.

2. The "no consent-no research" or "Nuremberg" solution excludes children because children are not considered competent to give informed consent to being enrolled as research subjects. This view, expressed in the Nuremberg Code (Germany [Territory Under . . .], 1947), seems too restrictive. It prohibits enrolling a child in a study even if the project could directly benefit the child. Moreover, to test the efficacy of treatments for distinctive groups, some members of the groups must be subjects. Competent, normal adults cannot serve as subjects in projects that test for children's growth or maturity, drugs for premature infants, or treatments for children's life-threatening asthma.

3. The "no consent-only therapy" or "Helsinki" solution holds that persons who lack the capacity to give informed consent may be enrolled only in therapeutic studies. This view, found in the World Medical Association's (1991) Declaration of Helsinki, is controversial because, first, classifying studies as either therapeutic or nontherapeutic may be misleading and arbitrary. Therapeutic studies may have burdensome, nontherapeutic features such as additional tests, hospitalizations, or visits to the doctor. Second, important medical research may hold out benefits other than therapy to subjects, such as gaining special care. Third, nontherapeutic studies that involve little or no risk to children (e.g., identifying at what age children are mature enough to name animals) may be important sources of information about children.

If a girl requires parental consent to choose abortion, does she have the right to refuse an abortion her parents wish her to have?

PAGE 43

See Also

Minors and Abortion: What Age is "Too Immature?"

4. The "risk-benefit" or "U.S. federal regulation" solution allows research with children if it holds out direct benefit to them or does not place them at unwarranted risk of harm, discomfort, or inconvenience. To try to balance the social utility of research with respect for and protection of children, this option stipulates that the greater the risk, the more rigorous and elaborate the procedural protection and consent requirements. Many countries, such as the United States, Canada, the United Kingdom, and Norway, and international organizations, such as the Council for the International Organizations of Medical Science, favor this solution. Research needs approval by local boards known as institutional review boards (IRBs) or research ethics committees (RECs), and in some cases, by federal boards as well. Approval is based on findings that subjects have been selected fairly and that the risks to subjects are minimized and reasonable in relation to anticipated benefits of the study ("Protection of Human Subjects," 1993). Adequate provisions must also be made for the safety and confidentiality of subjects. Investigators must seek parents' informed consent. When possible, they must also obtain the child's assent, where assent means a positive agreement, not merely a failure to refuse. Children's refusals are not binding where their parents and doctors judge it is in the interests of the children to participate, as in studies where children may obtain a scarce resource to treat their deadly disease. This risk-benefit solution tries to determine whether the risks are proportional to the benefits for each individual, and uses risk assessment to try to balance the social utility of encouraging studies that maintain respect for and protection of children's rights and welfare.

DIFFICULTIES. Unfortunately, the risk-benefit solution leaves key terms vaguely defined, allowing different interpretations about when risks of harm are warranted and what constitutes a benefit (Freedman et al., 1993; Kopelman, 1989b). In particular, the pivotal concepts of a "minimal risk" and a "minor increase over minimal risk" are problematic (Kopelman, 1989b). The federal rules state: "*Minimal risk* means that the probability and magnitude of harm or discomfort anticipated in the research are not greater in and of themselves than those ordinarily encountered in daily life or during the performance of routine physical and

FOUR CATEGORIES OF RESEARCH WITH CHILDREN

Using a likely harms-to-benefit calculation, U.S. regulations ("Protection of Human Subjects," 1993), outlined below, specify four categories of research with children. As risks increase, the regulations require increasingly more rigorous documentation of appropriate parental consent, children's assent, direct benefits to each child, and benefits to other children with similar conditions. Local IRBs can approve studies only in the first three categories.

The first category of research permits research with no greater than a minimal risk, provided it makes adequate provisions for parental consent and children's assent. Many important studies are safe, like asking children to perform simple and pleasant tasks. Using this category, investigators might gain approval to study at what ages preschool children can name colors, identify animals, and perform simple tasks like stacking blocks upon request.

The second category of research permits approval of studies with greater than a minimal risk if (1) the risk is justified by the anticipated benefit to each subject; (2) the risks in relation to these benefits are at least as favorable to each subject as available alternatives; and (3) provisions are made for parental consent and the child's assent. This category permits a child to get an investigational drug that is available only in a research study. Moreover, because children have unique diseases and reactions, to study the safety and efficacy of many conventional, innovative, or investigational treatments for children, some children will have to serve as subjects in controlled testing.

The third category of research permits research (1) with a minor increase over minimal risk that holds out no prospect of direct benefit to the individual subject; (2) where the study is like the child's actual or expected medical, dental, psychological, or educational situation; (3) where the study is likely to result in very important information about the child's disorder or condition; and (4) when provisions are made for parental consent and the child's assent. Investigators using this category have been permitted to conduct, for example, additional lumbar punctures on children with leukemia, who get them anyway, to help study leukemia.

Research that cannot be approved under the first three categories might be approved if (1) it presents a reasonable opportunity to understand, prevent, or alleviate a serious problem affecting the health or welfare of children; and (2) the study is approved by the secretary of the Department of Health and Human Services (DHHS) after consulting with a panel of experts about the value and ethics of the study and determining that adequate provisions have been made for the parental consent and the child's assent. Using this category, investigators might gain approval to conduct studies to prevent or treat epidemics affecting children, such as the acquired immunodeficiency syndrome (AIDS) epidemic, or a new infectious disease like the killers of the past (pneumonia, scarlet fever, diphtheria, or polio).

— LORETTA M. KOPELMAN

psychological examinations or tests" ("Protection of Human Subjects," 1993, sec. 102i). The Council for International Organizations of Medical Science (CIOMS) has a similar definition (CIOMS, 1993).

One difficulty with this definition of minimal risk is that it is vague. People's daily risks include dangers such as car accidents or getting mugged. Do we know the nature, probability, and magnitude of these everyday hazards well enough that they could serve as a baseline to estimate research risks for children? It seems easier to determine that a study asking children to stack blocks and name colors is a minimal-risk study than to estimate the nature, probability, and magnitude of whatever risks of harm people normally encounter.

A second problem with the definition of minimal risk is that it offers little guidance about how to assess psychosocial risks, such as breach of confidentiality, stigmatization, labeling, and invasion of privacy. Risks are allegedly minimal if they are either ordinarily encountered in daily life or during routine examinations. Doctors, nurses and psychologists, however, "ordinarily encounter" many psychosocially sensitive discussions in routine examinations and testing, including those about family abuse, substance abuse, sexual preference, and diagnoses, any of which could affect how people are viewed or whether they will be able to gain jobs or buy insurance. Moreover, psychosocial-risk assessment is an increasingly difficult problem. Some genetic and other testing has low physical risks—like taking a drop of blood—but high psychosocial risks. For example, Huntington disease is a genetic condition causing progressive dementia and loss of motor function when the person becomes an adult. A person known to have this condition could be denied a job or insurance or become stigmatized in the community. Thinking of risks of harm as merely physical ignores such profound psychosocial risks.

Third, there is no definition of "a minor increase over minimal risk," the crucial upper limit of what local boards can approve, and it is even unclear what constitutes a minimal risk. The second part of the definition seems to set an upper limit for physical interventions that have a minimal risk: Arterial puncture and gastric and intestinal intubation are not part of routine examinations; they exceed a minimal risk. The difficulty, however, is that there are considerable differences among pediatric experts, in both treatment and research settings, about how to assess the risk of such procedures as venipuncture, arterial puncture, and gastric and intestinal intubation (Janofsky and Starfield, 1981). Investigators and others concluded that better standards of risk assessment in children's research need to be formulated (Janofsky and Starfield, 1981; Lascari, 1981).

Even when it is agreed that the ethical basis for research policies with children is to promote their opportunities, well-being, fair treatment, and self-determination, it is difficult to determine when research involving children can be permitted. On the one hand, if research is not conducted with children as subjects, children may be denied the benefits of advances stemming from research and good information about what procedures or interventions effectively promote health and prevent, treat, or diagnose disease. On the other hand, if children are enrolled as research subjects, then vulnerable individuals who cannot give informed consent are being used.

Resource allocation

Many children throughout the world do not receive basic health-care or social services. In some cases, countries that can afford to do so provide insufficient funds for this purpose. For example, the main health problems of children in the United States arise from a failure to provide such basic care for children's allergies, asthma, dental pathology, hearing loss, vision impairments, and many chronic disorders (Starfield, 1991). Basic health-care and social services promote children's well-being, enhancing their opportunities in fundamental ways and correcting some inequities due to the natural and social lotteries. Children who are sick cannot compete as equals and thus are denied equality of opportunity with other children. The more these conditions are easily correctable, as many of them are, the more unjust it is to leave the children sick or disabled. Failing to provide children with basic health-care and social services, when a society has the means, is unjust based upon any one of four important theories of justice: utilitarianism, egalitarianism, libertarianism, and contractarianism. This point of agreement among widely divergent positions serves as a powerful indictment and proof that as a matter of justice we should redistribute goods, services, and benefits more fairly to children in order to provide them with basic health-care and social services.

Four theories of justice offer different guidance about how to allocate goods, services, and benefits. Proponents have used them to determine children's fair share of health-care funding in relation to adults (intergenerational allocation) and how to set priorities for funding within children's health-care programs (intragenerational allocation). Each theory addresses problems about what kinds of goods and services should be provided to people as a matter of justice and how to choose from among programs when not all can be funded. Although there are many variations of these positions, each seeks a defensible standard to help make choices fairly.

Determining the best interests of a compromised infant can present considerable problems of interpretation.

PAGE 383

See Also

Family; Life, Quality of

C

CHILDREN

Health-Care and Research Issues

Monitoring the quality of care is typically seen as an endeavor of the professions and the private sector in the U.S.

PAGE 335

UTILITARIANISM. Utilitarianism offers one solution to the problem of how to allocate health care justly between generations and among children's programs. In one well-known version, philosopher John Stuart Mill (1863) argued that a just allocation provides the greatest good to the greatest number of people; the utility of following principles of justice was so great, he held, that these were among the most fundamental moral principles. We should not just consider the utility of isolated acts, he maintained, but the rules of conduct that, if adopted and adhered to, maximize utility. Actions are right insofar as they fall under such a rule.

FOUR THEORIES OF JUSTICE USEFUL IN RESOURCE APPLICATION

1. Utilitarianism. In their efforts to maximize utility for the greatest number in accordance with just rules, utilitarians seek to prevent or cure the most common illnesses, adopt programs that help many rather than few persons, and generally use funds where they will have the greatest impact for most people. For example, utilitarians would resist funding expensive organ transplantations that help relatively few persons for a short time if such transplantations sidetrack programs that could help many people.
2. Egalitarianism. What is provided to one person should be available to all. Egalitarians would attempt to provide equal access to benefits, goods, and services for everyone on the same basis. Egalitarians look at outcomes to determine whether distribution is fair.
3. Libertarianism. States should not redistribute people's wealth in accordance with some pattern of distribution that examines outcomes (such as utilitarianism or egalitarianism) or that uses coercive measures to take people's holdings; and adults should be free to fashion social arrangements out of their ideas of compassion, justice, and solidarity (Engelhardt, 1992). People do not have a responsibility to be charitable, say libertarians, but acts of charity are praiseworthy and should be encouraged.
4. Contractarianism. Distributions of social goods are fair when impartial people agree upon the distribution procedures. Equitable procedures are agreed upon by rational and informed people of good will. Each person should have equal right to the most extensive basic liberties compatible with a similar system compatible for all.

Some of the least expensive and most beneficial interventions are education about the benefits of exercise, a good diet, prevention of teenage pregnancy, and avoidance of alcohol, tobacco, and harmful drugs (U.S. DHHS, 1992). Relatively inexpensive interventions can aid in the treatment of many problems common in childhood, including vision impairments, hearing loss, dental pathology, allergies, and asthma as well as the variety of chronic disorders that come in the aggregate and cause considerable functional impairment (Starfield, 1991). Utilitarians favor providing such health care for children because it greatly increases their well-being and opportunities. It is socially useful and cost-effective since it can prevent later costly illnesses and benefit the current generation of adults who, when aged, will need to be supported by a healthy, stable, and productive work force.

Utilitarians might even favor preferential consideration of children. Interventions that benefit both children and adults generally offer children the most years of benefit. These added years of benefit increase the net good and, thus, could justify some preference toward children. For example, in some countries children receive dental care unavailable to adults because it has lifelong benefits and avoids later costly problems. Daniel Callahan (1987, 1990) believes that the young have a stronger claim to health care than the old and that the young should be given priority; the health-care system should see as its first task helping young people become old people, and then helping older people become still older only if money is available. He argues, moreover, that medicine should give its highest priority to the relief of suffering rather than the conquest of death.

In choosing from among children's programs for funding, defenders of utilitarianism assess net benefit for the community of children. A utilitarian would favor funding routine care, mass screening, and prevention programs that help many children rather than the development of costly therapies that help few children. Consequently, utilitarians would probably resist using state funds to give otherwise normal short children growth hormone for many years, at a cost of many thousands of dollars a year, to add several centimeters or inches to their adult height. Utilitarians, however, might permit private insurance or payment (in a multi-tiered health-care system) for these and other services if it increased or did not diminish the net good.

Defenders of utilitarianism presuppose that we can calculate what is best for the greatest number, and critics question this presumption (Brock, 1982). Moreover, the critics continue, whole groups could be excluded from beneficial health care for the sake of the common good; people with expensive or rare conditions, and those with illnesses that are stigmatizing, might be excluded from care. Utilitarians might respond that we would suffer from such exclusions,

See Also
Health Care, Quality of

thus showing that this is not a good option even using utilitarian calculations. This presupposes, however, that enough people would know about the exclusions and be distressed enough to alter the calculation. Sympathy for utilitarianism may depend upon beliefs about whether we can make utility calculations, and whether a theory is acceptable if it permits us to exclude some groups for the common good regardless of the results of the utility calculation (see Brock, 1982). Defenders of rule utilitarianism, a version of utilitarianism clarifying the role of rules in assessing utility, respond that, properly understood, utility prohibits such unfair exclusions of individuals or groups; we adopt rights and justice principles because they are useful, and unjust exclusions undercut the utility of these rights and principles for all (Buchanan, 1991; Mill, 1863). Even if it might be cost-effective or politically expedient to exclude a particular person or group, such an exclusion undercuts something more important: fair rules.

Utilitarians favor basic health-care and social services for all children because of the utility to the children and to society. For example, suppose we could save a great deal of money by excluding certain children from health-care services. Although this might save some money in the short run, defenders of rule utilitarianism might argue that it is unjust because adapting and adhering to the rule that all should receive basic services is more useful in the long run than excluding a few to save money. Accordingly, the rule that all children should receive basic care is vindicated because the rule is useful and making exceptions is less useful.

EGALITARIANISM. Egalitarianism is a theory of justice whose defenders attempt to solve allocation issues and intergenerational disputes by holding that access to the same benefits, goods, and services should be provided to everyone on the same basis. It is a principle of justice that requires us to try to make all people's objective net well-being as equal as possible. Most of us do not want dialysis treatment since we do not have kidney disease, but we want access to it if we should need it. Egalitarians, then, do not want exactly the same treatment for everyone as a condition of justice, but for everyone to have access to the same goods, services, and benefits on the same footing. Egalitarians look at outcomes of distribution schemes to determine whether distributions are fair. Accordingly, defenders of egalitarianism judge it to be unfair, for example, that adults over sixty-five could get their diabetes and asthma treated free of charge in the United States but children could not. Age might be a determinant in deciding who gets benefits, goods, and services, but only as one among other prognosticators of success. For example, people over eighty or under two years of age might be excluded from consideration for a certain type of surgery because they are unlikely to survive the procedure.

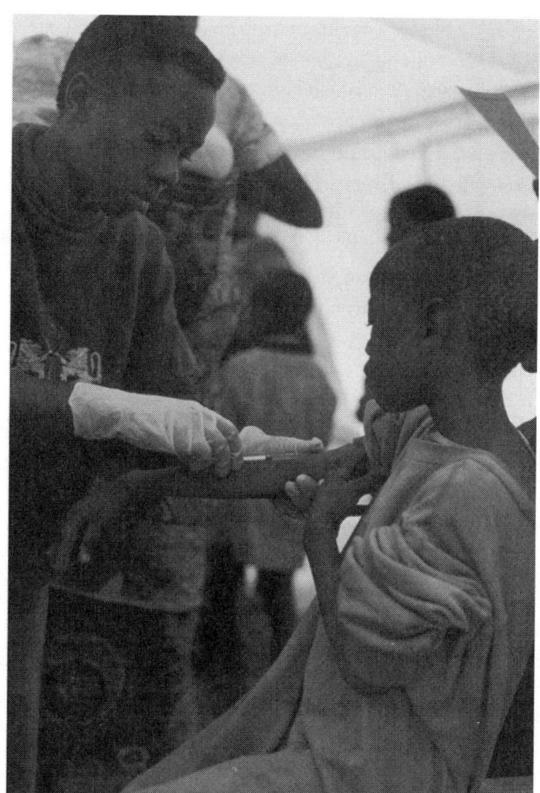

KINDNESS HAS CONSEQUENCES

A child receiving a vaccination is likely more concerned with being well than with the utilitarian considerations that motivate preventive health-care.

Defenders of egalitarianism hold that what is provided to one person should be available to all who are similarly situated. The advantages of good health care are such that, in fairness, they should be distributed on as equal a basis as possible. There should not be a multitiered system with one level of goods and services for the rich and another for the poor. If we are going to allow some normal short children to have growth hormone for many years at a cost of thousands of dollars a year, then all who are similarly situated should have access to similar services. For expensive or scarce resources, many egalitarians favor lotteries so all those similarly situated have an equal opportunity and are recognized as having equal worth (Childress, 1970; Veatch, 1986). Consequently, if organs for transplantation can only be provided to some children, there should be a lottery among those who meet whatever standards are set. In this way, we acknowledge the value of each person and the importance of fair access of each to scarce or costly benefits, goods, or services. One difficulty for egalitarians is that some people's needs are so great they could consume most of the resources of a health-care system. Robert Veatch (1986) tries to defend a commitment to those who are so disadvantaged they could use unlimited resources, while placing limits on their claims upon other members of society.

Because there is no universal entitlement to basic health care, the availability, quality, and utilization of services depend on local conditions.

PAGE 336

In defending egalitarianism, it is difficult to clarify what kind of equality is important. On the one hand, if it is access to the same benefits, goods, and services, age bias and discrimination could be introduced through preference for certain benefits, goods, and services. For example, treatment for prostatic hyperplasia and Alzheimer's disease only helps adults; other care helps adults much more than children, such as treatments for heart disease or lung cancer or treatments at the end of life. Some funding choices discriminate by excluding services equally and for all diseases afflicting people with stigmatizing conditions, such as sexually transmitted diseases. This parallels a problem of utilitarianism, where whole groups could be excluded if society decides, to save money, that none will have treatments for certain conditions.

On the other hand, if equality is understood in terms of outcomes, age bias and discrimination can also be introduced just by the method of collecting and presenting data (Starfield, 1991). In the United States, for example, data collection to determine the health of different populations focuses upon life-threatening illnesses and death. Relatively few children have such morbidity or mortality in comparison to adults, giving the impression that children are generally healthy. This impression, however, is a consequence of how the data are collected. Most children's needs stem from problems that are not life-threatening illnesses, but that have a profound effect on health, such as dental problems, vision impairments, allergies, and asthma. Moreover, although the death rate of children in the United States is low when compared with that of adults, it is the highest in the world when compared with equally affluent countries (Starfield, 1991). Looking at certain outcomes, then, promotes an unfair view of childhood health and morbidity. Programs based upon such data can create unjust age bias against children. Thus, treating everyone as equals is problematic if the measures favor certain groups.

◆ **libertarianism**
Holds that competent adults should not be forced to do anything by the state unless it prevents harm to third parties, that people's right to their fairly obtained property is fundamental, and that people do not have a responsibility to be charitable.

People's willingness to defend egalitarianism depends, in part, on whether they believe it is fair to restrict choices by insisting that no one can have health care that cannot be provided to all on the same basis. If people can squander their assets on frivolous entertainment and flashy clothes, it seems unfair to insist that they cannot spend it on marginally beneficial, exotic, or expensive health care for their families. Some defenders respond that rich people dread single-tiered systems, because it means that they cannot have their usual advantages through money and forces them to live by the same rules as others. They argue that allocation of health care (especially in life and death situations) is too important to be left to unregulated personal choice and market forces. Some defenders of egalitarianism modify their view to permit people to use their discretionary resources as they wish.

LIBERTARIANISM. Libertarians generally agree that competent adults should not be forced to do anything by the state unless it prevents harm to third parties. Their coercion is permissible to prevent theft, murder, physical abuse, and fraud, to enforce contracts, or to punish competent people for harming others (Buchanan, 1981). The best-known defender of this view, Robert Nozick (1974), follows the eighteenth-century philosopher John Locke in maintaining that people's right to their fairly obtained property is fundamental and also determines the proper functions of the state and the moral interactions among individuals. People are entitled to their holdings and may dispose of them as they wish, according to this view.

Libertarians hold that children's health care is the responsibility of their guardians, not the state. Market forces of supply and demand, and choices about how to use their own money, should shape the kind of health care people select for themselves and their children. If parents want to pay for special services, such as growth hormones or repeated organ transplants, they should be permitted to do so. H. Tristram Engelhardt, Jr., argues that societies can decide morally who is entitled to health care of a certain kind, within certain limitations. But a society does not, for example, have "the moral authority to forbid consensual acts among agreeing adults, such as agreement to sell an organ" (Engelhardt, 1992, p. 10).

Sympathy for libertarianism depends upon whether it is believed to offer enough protection for people, especially for children and impoverished or incompetent adults. This view arguably benefits the wealthy and powerful; since most children are neither, it might create an age bias against children. Libertarians argue that competent adults should pay their own way, but when do people really pay their own way? Typically, people's health-care insurance has gained them access to institutions heavily subsidized by public money. People who "pay their own way" may pay just a bit more for a great deal more in the way of services. Those who cannot pay more are unfairly excluded. Libertarians might agree that separate institutions should be set up where people truly pay their full share, even if that would mean few could afford such added care.

Libertarians usually favor special state protection for children, allowing the state to interfere with parents who endanger, neglect, or harm children. This has included providing children with a "safety net" of basic health-care and social services. A system favoring special benefits based upon redistribution of wealth for competent adults, however, is judged unjust. Hence, a system like that in the United States that provides

See Also
Health Policy: Politics and Health Care

many social and health benefits to competent—even wealthy—adults but not to children, such as in the allocation of health-care benefits, goods, and services, would be viewed by libertarians as unjust.

CONTRACTARIANISM. Contractarians hold that distributions of social goods are fair when impartial people agree upon the procedures used for distribution. The best-known defender of this position is John Rawls, who in *A Theory of Justice* (1971) and *Political Liberalism* (1993) contends that the way in which we form stable and just societies is through building consensus that merits endorsement by rational and informed people of good will. This entails commitment to three principles of justice. First, "each person is to have an equal right to the most extensive system of equal basic liberties compatible with a similar system compatible for all." Second, "offices and positions are to be open to all under conditions of equality of fair opportunity—persons with similar abilities and skills are to have equal access to offices and positions." Finally, "social and economic institutions are to be arranged so as to benefit maximally the worst off" (Rawls, 1971, p. 60). These principles are ordered lexically such that the first, or greatest equal-liberty principle, takes precedence over the others when they conflict; and the second, the principle of fair equality of opportunity, takes precedence over the third, the difference principle. Nowhere is health care as a right specifically mentioned in Rawls's attempt to frame the basic structure of a just society. This is understandable, in part, because a society might not have any decent health-care goods, services, or benefits to distribute. In a society that does have such goods, services, and benefits, however, their fair distribution seems central to promoting fair equality of opportunity and benefits to the worst off.

Norman Daniels (1985), building on Rawls's work, argues that we should provide basic care to all, but redistribute health-care goods and services more favorably to children. The moral justification for giving children access to basic health care, argues Daniels, rests on social commitments to what he and Rawls call "fair equality of opportunity" (or affirmative action). Health-care needs are basic insofar as they promote fair equality of opportunity. Health care for children is especially important in relation to other social goods, because diseases and disabilities inhibit children's capacity to use and develop their talents, thereby curtailing their opportunities. For example, children cannot compete as equals among their peers if they are sick or cannot see or hear the teacher. Thus, a society committed to a fair equality of opportunity for children should provide adequate health care. Daniels holds that in order to assess whose needs are greatest, we have to use objective ways of characterizing medical and social needs; the ranking of needs helps determine what is basic and who profits most from certain services. Using the difference principle, free, additional service might be provided to the poorest children so they could compete more effectively with those from more affluent homes. Unlike utilitarians, who would be guided by where money would have the greatest overall impact on the health of the greatest number of children, contractarians try to bring all children of similar talents to the same level of functioning so they can compete as equals.

Contractarianism has its difficulties. Some regard it as a method for arriving at ethical principles, not as an alternative to views like utilitarianism, egalitarianism, or libertarianism (Veatch, 1986). Accordingly, those who think it generates a unique theory need to clarify how it has a distinct content. In addition, it is hard to specify what is meant by people's normal opportunity ranges or how to apply fair equality of opportunity. It seems to suggest (arguably similar to egalitarianism) the unsatisfactory consequence that we should fund treatments, however exotic and costly, offering a chance for the most disadvantaged to improve their normal opportunity range irrespective of the needs of the many; gifted children could be denied opportunities to excel, as a matter of justice, so others can enhance their normal opportunity range or be brought to roughly the same level of well-being and opportunities of average children. Another problem is that contractarianism presupposes, like utilitarianism, that we have a fair and objective system for ranking which medical and social needs are greatest and who benefits most from given services (Brock, 1982). It is unclear if such a comprehensive and objective ranking is possible. Such "objective" choices about appropriate or useful programs might be heavily mixed with social and personal biases about what promotes a fair equality of opportunity for people with similar talents. These problems, however, do not undermine the contractarians' commitment to the justice of equal opportunity for children, including the fairness of providing basic health and social care for children.

A PROPOSED CONSENSUS. Each of these four theories of justice supports the claim that children are entitled to basic health-care and social services to correct inequalities and promote their flourishing as free and self-determining people who can develop their potential. That defenders of such divergent approaches agree on this entitlement reflects a remarkable consensus that children's distress ought to be relieved whether it is related to inadequate health care, poverty, abuse, neglect, malnutrition, or exploitation. A primary duty of a just society is to promote fairly its children's well-being and opportunities to become self-fulfilled persons through access to

It is a widely shared view of obstetricians that the fetus is a patient to whom they owe ethical duties.

PAGE 464

The question of health care as a basic human right has been at the heart of the health-policy debate in the U.S.

PAGE 335

Female circumcision has been wrongly identified as an Islamic rite, though it is not practiced in Saudi Arabia, Algeria, Iran, Iraq, Libya, Morocco, or Tunisia.

PAGES 118-119

basic health-care and social services and to address the inequities resulting from life's natural and social lotteries. Children living in low-income homes in the United States, the richest country in the world, are two to three times as likely as children in high-income homes to be of low birth weight, to get asthma and bacterial meningitis, to have delayed immunizations, and to suffer from lead poisoning. Poor children are also three to four times as likely as rich children to become seriously ill and get multiple illnesses when they get sick (Starfield, 1991). The gap between the rich and the poor is increasing and the rise of poverty is most rapid among children in the world. Health-care costs, driven higher by an aging population and increased demands for expensive technologies, will make it harder for societies to allocate costs justly. Consequently, disputes involving intergenerational and intragenerational allocation are likely to continue as programs compete for funding. Since children depend upon others to advocate on their behalf, adults should continue to set aside their individual interests and consider children's well-being, needs, and opportunities as a matter of justice.

— LORETTA M. KOPELMAN

CIRCUMCISION

FEMALE CIRCUMCISION

"Female circumcision" is the term used to identify the practice of removing healthy normal female genitalia by surgical operation. Because of the severity of the operation and its known harmful effects, the term "female genital mutilation" is now generally used. There are three increasingly severe types of this operation, and each makes orgasm impossible. Clitoridectomy, or sunna (Type 1), is the removal of the prepuce of the clitoris and the clitoris itself. When excited, the clitoris swells and becomes erect, and it is this excitement that causes female orgasms. Excision, or reduction (Type 2), is the removal of the prepuce, the clitoris, and the labia minora, leaving the majora intact. The labia minora produce secretions that lubricate the inner folds of the lips and prevent soreness when these lips rub against each other. Infibulation, or pharaonic circumcision (Type 3), is the removal of the prepuce, the clitoris, the labia minora and majora, and the suturing of the two sides of the vulva, leaving a very small opening for the passage of urine and menstrual blood. This type of circumcision is referred to as pharaonic probably because it is identified with circumcision methods of ancient Egypt under the pharaohs.

TYPES AND FREQUENCY OF FEMALE GENITAL MUTILATION, OR "CIRCUMCISION," IN SIERRA LEONE)

Type	Percentage
1. clitoridectomy, or sunna	39.03
2. excision, or reduction	59.85
3. infibulation,or pharaonic circumcision	1.12

(Koso-Thomas, 1987)

In Somalia, 80 percent of the operations are Type 3 (El Dareer, 1982). The prevalence of circumcision in Africa ranges from 10 percent in Tanzania to 98 percent in Djibouti (Toubia, 1993).

The most common and basic procedure followed during circumcision is the traditional method. In this method, usually employed by circumcisers who have no medical training, the female is firmly held down on dry ground with her legs wide apart to expose the genitalia and the parts to be removed. In some cases, the genital part to be excised is held with a special hemostatic leaf before excision, or the candidates are made to lie near a cold flowing stream so the excised area can be bathed in chilled water to numb the pain. The implements used are often unsterilized razor blades, knives, scissors, broken bottles, or any other sharp implement. Some form of herbal dressing is applied to the raw wound after the operation. The same implement is used for successive operations without sterilization. When the operation is carried out in modern clinics, standard modern surgical practice is followed.

Origin of the practice

We do not know with any precision when, why, and how female circumcision began. There is evidence that female circumcision and female genital surgery have been done in many parts of the world, although currently it is mainly done in different communities in parts of Africa, Asia, the Far East, Europe, and South America.

The early Romans, concerned about the consequences of sexual activity among female slaves, adopted the technique of slipping rings through their labia majora (Figure 1-4) to block access to the vagina. In the twelfth century C.E., Crusaders introduced the chastity belt in Europe for the same purpose; the belt prevented girls and women from engaging in unlawful or unsanctioned sex. This method caused little permanent physical damage to the individual. Genital surgery was permitted in North America and Europe in the late nineteenth century with the intention of curing nymphomania, masturbation, hysteria, depression, epilepsy, and insanity. There is no evidence that such surgery was associated with any ritualistic activity. Elsewhere, the surgery has historical links with either religious or ethnic rituals. It is believed that the ancient Egyptians and ancient Arabs practiced this form of surgery. Genital mutilation seems to have been transplanted to Latin America from Africa during the slave trade and may have taken root first in the central part of Brazil, where groups of West Africans were resettled after the abolition of the slave trade in the middle of the nineteenth century, and to eastern Mexico and Peru through migration. In Asia genital mutilation is found among Islamic religious groups in the Philippines, Malaysia, Pakistan, and Indonesia. Where the mutilation exists in the Middle East and Asia, it is strongly associated with Islam. Female genital mutilation is not practiced in all Islamic countries. Those societies known to practice it, namely, the United Arab Emirates, South Yemen, Oman, and Bahrain in the Middle East, and northern Egypt, Mauritania, Sudan, Somalia, Mali, and Nigeria in Africa, probably inherited it from pre-Islamic cultures.

Alleged benefits of female circumcision

The modern defense of female circumcision allows us to reconstruct the ancient rules that governed moral action or behavior in polygamous communities. The defense enumerates a wide range of health-related and social benefits alleged to result from the practice:

1. maintenance of cleanliness
2. maintenance of good health
3. preservation of virginity
4. enhancement of fertility
5. prevention of stillbirths in women pregnant for the first time
6. prevention of promiscuity
7. increase of matrimonial opportunities
8. pursuance of aesthetics
9. improvement of male sexual performance and pleasure
10. promotion of social and political cohesion

Cleanliness is regarded as a great virtue by women in countries where the practice is common. In some cultures, particularly in Africa, women are required to cleanse their genitalia with soap and water after urinating. Those who justify removing parts of the genitalia that produce secretions cite this preoccupation with the cleanliness of the genital organs. Some traditional circumcision societies claim that circumcised women are generally healthy

MEDICAL ISSUES
Harmful Effects of Female Circumcision

The medical consequences of female genital mutilation are quite grave (El Dareer, 1982; Koso-Thomas, 1987). In Africa an estimated ninety million females are affected (Hosken, 1982). Three levels of health problems are associated with the practice. Immediate problems include pain, shock, hemorrhage, acute urinary retention, urinary infection, septicemia, blood poisoning, fever, tetanus, and death. Occasionally, force is applied to position candidates for the operation, and as a result, fractures of the clavicle, humerus, or femur have occurred. Intermediate complications include pelvic infection, painful menstrual periods, painful and difficult sexual intercourse, formation of cysts and abscesses, excessive growth of scar tissue, and the development of prolapse and fistulae. A fistula is an abnormal passage: a hole (opening) between the posterior urinary bladder wall and the vagina or a hole between the anterior rectal wall and the vagina. Late complications include accumulation of menstrual blood of many months or even years, primary infertility, painful clitoral tumors, recurrent urinary tract infections, and kidney or bladder stone formation. Obstetric complications such as third-degree perineal tear, resulting in anal incontinence and fissure formation, and prolonged and obstructed labor are also known to occur. Psychological problems of anxiety, frigidity, and depression, as a result of the physical inability to have a clitoral orgasm, may also develop.

Women who undergo circumcision suffer various degrees of emotional and mental distress depending on the nature of complications following their operation. Records show that 83 percent of all females undergoing circumcision are likely to be affected by some condition related to that surgical procedure requiring medical attention at some time during their lives. This level of health risk should be of concern to nations with a large proportion of circumcised women, because such women may never make the progress toward the economic and social development required of them.

— OLAYINKA A. KOSO-THOMAS

and that the operation cures women suffering from problems resembling those identified in nontraditional societies as depression, melancholia, nymphomania, hysteria, insanity, epilepsy, and the social disorder of kleptomania. In situations where proof of virginity is essential for concluding a marriage transaction, circumcision is believed to be the guarantee against premarital sex. This guarantee benefits parents who are able to demand a high bridal price for their daughters. Marriage immediately after the transaction ceremony is common, and such marriages, involving pubertal girls, are usually followed by pregnancy within a very short time. Circumcised girls and women are regarded as having an advantage over the uncircumcised in marrying. Where female genital mutilation is an established custom, tradition forbids men to marry uncircumcised girls; hence, circumcision of girls ensures they will be marriageable. Certain traditional communities, such as the Mossi of Burkina Faso and the Ibos of Nigeria, believe that a firstborn child or even subsequent babies will die if their heads touch a mother's clitoris during the birth process. The clitoris is therefore removed at the time of delivery if this has not already been done. Since female genital mutilation reduces or even eliminates sexual pleasure, the practice presumably eliminates the risk of female promiscuity. The justification of the practice to preserve chastity, eliminate promiscuity, foster or improve sexual relations with men, generate greater matrimonial opportunities, protect virginity, and increase fertility reflects the existence in traditional societies of strict controls on social behavior.

◆ **clitoridectomy, or sunna**
The removal of the prepuce of the clitoris and the clitoris itself.

The belief that circumcision enhances beauty stems from the claim that the male prepuce or foreskin is removed mainly for aesthetic reasons, and that the clitoris, the female counterpart to the penis, should be removed for the same reason. If left intact, the clitoris is believed likely to grow to an embarrassing and uncomfortable size. In some patriarchal societies, female genital mutilation is also said to benefit the male by prolonging his sexual pleasure, since the clitoris is thought to increase male excitement during sexual intercourse with a female partner and may rush a man's orgasm. Of great importance to women in such cultures is the status circumcision bestows on the circumcised. It entitles them to positions of religious, political, and social leadership and responsibility.

The argument in favor of circumcision serves narrow social interests and does not achieve the goods desired or guaranteed. Failure to achieve these goods, moreover, is often blamed on the woman rather than the ritual. For example, maintaining cleanliness becomes an agonizing task. The hardened scar and stump that result from circumcision are unsightly, and they halt the flow of urine and menstrual blood through the normal channels. This obstruction causes unnecessary fluid retention and results in odors more disagreeable than those from the natural hormonal secretions that tradition teaches are degrading. Associating the death of babies at childbirth with clitoral contact is clearly refuted by the evidence that millions of healthy babies are born to uncircumcised mothers.

FEMALE GENITAL MUTILATION
Applying Modern Medical Practice

Modern medicine has made impressive strides in investigating, preventing, and treating a wide range of ailments. Through its investigative approaches it has judged that unwarranted surgery is wrong. In the case of female genital mutilation, studies have found that certain of the resulting medical conditions are serious and can lead to complications and permanent health damage requiring both medical treatment and counseling (Koso-Thomas, 1987). Awareness of female genital mutilation's harmful effects has encouraged changes in how the operation is performed, changes that may include sterilization of equipment and dressings and administration of local anesthetic, antibiotics, and antitetanus injections prior to circumcision.

— OLAYINKA A. KOSO-THOMAS

While the desire of organized society to maintain control over people's actions may be understandable, not all such control promotes their well-being or self-determination. Such rituals also cause harm to society by increasing morbidity and mortality levels. In addition, although these rites may promote social and political cohesion, they thwart the individual's freedom to determine what is right and in her best interests. Even women who learn that circumcision is an unsafe and harmful practice may feel pressure from society to agree to it for themselves or their children in order to marry or remain members of the group.

Ethical aspects

Since some followers of Islam in Africa, the Far East, and the Middle East endorse circumcision, it has been widely identified as an Islamic rite. However, female

See Also
Behavior Control

genital mutilation is not practiced in Saudi Arabia, Algeria, Iran, Iraq, Libya, Morocco, or Tunisia. Many Islamic and Christian religious leaders have categorically denied that female circumcision or female genital mutilation is an injunction in the Qur'an or a "commandment" in the Bible. Since the foundations of the practice lie outside Islamic or Christian religious law, the origins of circumcision and its justification must lie in the moral, social, and religious structure and operation of societies practicing it. Individuals practicing it act within a system of rules that strictly regulate sexual behavior in society. Female genital mutilation generally thrives in communities with strictly enforced conventions and social rules. With the knowledge of its harmful effects now common, no social system endorsing this kind of mutilation can be said to promote a favorable climate for a fulfilling life.

The attitudes of women toward circumcision depend on their experiences and level of education. Most women affected by the practice are unaware that circumcision is the cause of their health difficulties (Koso-Thomas, 1987). Once aware of this relationship, however, many women who have some education and training and who are exposed to a modern environment are better able to assess what is involved in circumcision actions and, on that basis, to make a reasoned judgment of its rightness or wrongness. Many such women have come to believe that the practice is unacceptable and have refused to allow their female children to go through the same traumatic experience. Many feminists and health professionals have openly displayed a higher regard for women's health than for tradition.

It has been shown, however, that some women who admit to suffering under the unexpected effects of the operation still feel obliged to support the practice. A study carried out to obtain opinions on circumcision involving 135 men and 120 women showed that 25 percent were shocked at what happened to them on their circumcision day, as it was not what they had expected (Koso-Thomas, 1987). The majority of them, either semi- or nonliterate, believed that they had done the right thing and planned to have their daughters circumcised. Those women who were not shocked by their experiences were also mainly illiterate and did not see why their daughters should not undergo circumcision. The attitude of men in the sample also varied according to their level of education. Illiterate men insisted that all women should be circumcised to keep them in their place, while the literate men argued that women should be given a choice as to whether or not to be circumcised. They felt that to deny women this choice was a violation of their human rights. It has also been found that circumcision is supported in most women's organizations, particularly political and social groups, since these groups reflect the feelings of the majority in the community.

Usually the decision to have a girl circumcised is made by the female elder members of the family/clan who insist on carrying out the procedure. An aura of secrecy, celebration, and pride surrounds the circumcision and encourages voluntarism on the part of recruits by making membership in the group seem more attractive. A few educated women, however, who have had access to modern medical assessment of their health as well as information on the dangers of the practice also support circumcision but advocate changes to reduce its health hazards. A few health-care personnel have felt that medical intervention at the early stages of the operation might prevent the more serious health consequences of circumcision. Since circumcision cannot take place without health consequences, the position of these women and health practitioners is untenable.

Women who live in a traditional environment tend to judge their actions on the basis of traditional rules and principles of their society. There may be some misogynistic attitudes among such women, but the dominant force directing their actions comes from the society that demands, among other things, that this ritual be performed in order for them to qualify for marriage and social acceptance.

There are also attitudes inherent in African sexuality that not only permit circumcision but foster it. In most African cultures, sexuality is regarded as a gift to be used for the procreation of the human species, and any public or even private display of sex-related feeling or enjoyment is seen as debasing this gift. In some communities, only a token expression of the sexual self is permitted. The issue of sexual fulfillment is unimportant. Thus, controls over the sexual behavior of women are designed to curb female sexual desire and response and to encourage disregard for the sexual aspects of their lives. The removal of the organ or organs responsible for sexual stimulation is therefore taken as necessary for the fixation of certain values within the community and for ensuring the acceptance of rigid standards of sexual conduct. Thus, the underlying concern of those who defend the institution of female circumcision is that women's sexuality will be corrupted if women are allowed the freedom to control it or indeed to pursue the personal satisfaction of their sexual desire. Implicit in this argument is the major premise that it is immoral for a woman to act on her sexual desire. Women who still support the practice continue to promote injury with confirmed medical consequences. In this respect the role of the health-care practitioner in the society is crucial and may lead to personal dilemmas that have to be resolved. Many feel anger against the executors and supporters of the ritual and sadness at the futility of

New anthropological studies suggest that women may have enjoyed greater equity with men in prehistorical times.

PAGE 693

See Also

Sexism; Sexuality in Society; Women

the exercise and at the intransigence of traditional circumcising communities. Health-care professionals presented with the choice of treating or not treating women who have chosen to be circumcised are often determined to rescue a life they see as poised on the brink of destruction. On the other hand, traditional circumcisers have no moral dilemmas about the practice. They believe that they have no choice in a matter which concerns the preservation of their cultural heritage. That heritage dictates how women must live, and to them, life should be one of happiness in subservience to the will of the people and in obedience to customary and religious laws.

— OLAYINKA A. KOSO-THOMAS

MALE CIRCUMCISION

Male circumcision entails the surgical removal of the foreskin that covers the glans of the penis. The relative simplicity of the surgical procedure itself belies the complexity of the conflicting values surrounding male circumcision. The primary ethical issue can be simply stated: Are the pain, risks, and costs of routine neonatal circumcision justified by the potential benefits to those who undergo this procedure? Given the strong opposing opinions surrounding circumcision, it is questioned whether children should undergo the procedure prior to an age when they can provide informed consent on their own behalf. Circumcision in adults is less common and will not be the focus of discussion here.

The prevalence of male circumcision

Circumcision is the most common procedure performed on males in the United States; an estimated one million procedures are performed per year. Only about 20 percent of the procedures are performed for religious reasons; the majority are performed in new-

THE HISTORY OF CIRCUMCISION

Tradition with Uncertain Benefits

The walls of Egyptian tombs depict male circumcision, so the practice is known to be at least 5,000 years old. The Jewish and Muslim traditions of circumcision have their origin in the Old Testament. Jews accept the practice as a sign of the covenant between God and Abraham. In Gen. 17:12, God instructs Abraham: "He that is eight days old shall be circumcised among you, every male throughout your generations" (Robson and Leung, 1992). As a Jew, Jesus was circumcised, and the early Christian church debated the need for circumcision as a criterion for joining the Christian fellowship; it decided that circumcision was not necessary for salvation. According to the apostle Paul, "For in Jesus Christ neither circumcision availeth nor uncircumcision; but faith which worketh by love" (Gal. 5:6). These religious traditions remain strong, although the health debate has led to a questioning of the religious practice by a few members of the Jewish community (Milos and Macris, 1992).

The practice of routine neonatal circumcision has been controversial within the U.S. medical profession for over a century. Circumcision was initially advocated in the Victorian era as a measure to reduce masturbation. Medical benefits from the procedure were first widely proposed in 1891 by P. C. Remondino, who claimed that circumcision prevented or cured a host of diseases, including alcoholism, epilepsy, asthma, and renal disease (Wallerstein, 1985). More scientific studies of the potential medical benefits of circumcision began to appear in the professional literature in the 1930s. Urologists observed an association between penile cancer and an intact foreskin (Schoen, 1992). During World War II, American troops stationed in the Pacific and in desert climates had problems with irritation and infection of the penis because of sand and the inability to maintain adequate hygiene. The military response was to circumcise many of the affected soldiers. However, the Japanese did not use circumcision despite their war experience in the same environments (Wallerstein, 1985).

Circumcision became popular, indeed almost universal, after the war. Rates remained high until the 1970s, when both the medical profession and the general public began to question the widespread use of the procedure for newborns. The American Academy of Pediatrics issued two separate statements in 1971 and 1975 declaring there were no valid medical indications for neonatal circumcision (Committee on Fetus and Newborn, 1975). Specific concerns were raised over the pain of the procedure and over potential complications in the face of questionable medical benefits. In 1985, the first in a series of papers was published that documented an increased risk of urinary tract infections in uncircumcised neonates (Wiswell et al., 1985). These reports came in association with an apparent increased risk of sexually transmitted disease, specifically the human immunodeficiency virus (HIV), in uncircumcised males (Schoen, 1993). In 1989 the American Academy of Pediatrics issued a revised statement that concluded that there were both medical advantages and medical disadvantages to the procedure and that full information and informed consent were important for parents who were making this decision (American Academy of Pediatrics, 1989).

— JEFFREY R. BOTKIN

borns for medical, cultural, or aesthetic reasons (Wallerstein, 1985). Estimates suggest that circumcision is performed on 60 percent to 90 percent of boys in the United States. Although observers have noted some variations by region and by cultural group in the use of this procedure, accurate rates for circumcision have not been obtained (Wallerstein, 1985). The best documented rates of newborn circumcision in the United States come from a study of infants delivered in U.S. military hospitals (Wiswell, 1992). The rate of circumcision in 1971 was estimated to be 89 percent, falling to 70 percent in 1984, with a subsequent rise to 80 percent in 1990. These differences show that parents' decisions about circumcision were influenced by debate over the procedure.

MALE CIRCUMCISION RATES AROUND THE ENGLISH-SPEAKING WORLD

Country	Percentage of Male Population Circumcised
Australia	35–40%
Canada	35–40
Great Britain	1
New Zealand	10
United States	60–90

(Wallerstein, 1985)

In Western Europe, the former Soviet Union, China, and Japan, male circumcision is not performed.

Circumcision is performed commonly as a religious ritual by Jews, Muslims, many black Africans, and nonwhite Australians.

Medical and ethical issues

The basic ethical question involved is whether it is justified to perform a surgical procedure on a healthy, unconsenting child to prevent the possibility of future disease. The primary ethical task is to balance the pain and potential complications with the potential benefits. Although the full details of the risks and benefits are beyond the scope of this discussion, key issues will be outlined.

Proponents of circumcision claim several advantages for the procedure: decreased incidence of urinary tract infections in infancy, decreased risk of penile cancer in adults, and decreased risk of sexually transmitted diseases (Wiswell, 1992; Wiswell et al., 1985). In addition, routine circumcision prevents occasional penile problems such as phimosis (a narrowing of the foreskin that prevents its retraction), balanitis (an infection of the head of the penis), and posthitis (an infection of the foreskin). Significant complications of the procedure are quite rare, occurring in less than 1 percent of circumcised neonates (Kaplan, 1983). Until the mid-1980s, circumcision was performed commonly without anesthesia. With the introduction of a variety of simple techniques (Kirya and Werthmann, 1978; Stang et al., 1988), it is claimed that the pain of the procedure can be minimized. In contrast to female circumcision, the procedure has no significant effect on sexual function or pleasure.

Social issues are raised in the debate. Many parents would like their sons to look like the majority of their peers in the locker room, and many parents would like their sons to look like their fathers, the majority of whom are circumcised. Finally, parents who have grown up in a society of circumcised men may find a circumcised penis to be more aesthetically pleasing.

Those who question the value of the procedure counter that the case for reductions in urinary tract infections, cancer rates, and sexually transmitted diseases is not convincing, or that many of the same benefits may be achieved through better personal hygiene (Poland, 1990; Milos and Macris, 1992). While the prodecure is generally safe, there are risks of excessive bleeding, infection, removal of too much tissue, tissue damage and scarring, reactions to anesthetic agents, and retention of urine (Kaplan, 1983). It is argued that the penile problems that may arise in uncircumcised males, such as balanitis, can be treated like any other local skin problems or infections. Further, it is noted that pain-control measures are often ineffective, carry their own risks (Snellman and Stang, 1992), and are associated with some pain as well. It is claimed that the foreskin provides a protective covering for the glans, making the uncircumcised penis more sensitive during sexual activity (Milos and Macris, 1992). Since the 1960s, a cultural shift has placed a higher value on preserving the natural look. Uncircumcised males are now common enough, the argument goes, that the appearance of an uncircumcised penis in the locker room will not be cause for embarrassment. Finally, it is claimed that a simple explanation from father to son will prevent a son's confusion about a different look to his penis.

Of all of the potential medical advantages of circumcision, the reduced risk of urinary tract infection in the infant is the best documented, and this is the benefit most likely to be experienced by the child (Wiswell, 1992; Schoen, 1993). Urinary tract infections in neonates are potentially serious infections that may be lifethreatening and may lead to the later development of renal insufficiency and hypertension. However, the risk of urinary tract infection in uncircumcised infants is still relatively small, occurring in approximately 1 to

◆ **circumcision, male**
The surgical removal of the foreskin that covers the glans of the penis.

4 percent of infants (Wiswell, 1992). Of those infected, only a small minority will suffer long-term kidney damage (Chessare, 1992).

Parents are thus left with a difficult decision. Circumcision might be delayed until the child is old enough to make his own choice, but this alternative obviates the primary medical advantage, that is, decreasing the risk of urinary tract infection in infancy. In addition, performing the procedure beyond the newborn period may be associated with greater risks (Wiswell et al., 1993). Therefore, reliance on surrogate decision making by the parents for the newborn boy remains an ethically appropriate approach. With all of the current data in hand, many physicians and parents find themselves falling between the polar positions in this debate. As the 1989 American Academy of Pediatrics statement concluded, there is no clear answer to the question of whether the benefits of circumcision outweigh the risks. For many parents, the final decision will be made primarily on cultural and social grounds, with less weight placed on the potential health benefits or risks. Fortunately, there is some evidence that most adult men like the way they are, whether circumcised or not (Lee, 1990).

Unless additional medical research documents significantly greater benefits or harms of male circumcision, the social debate over the procedure in the United States is likely to continue. In this context, the responsibilities of both the physician and the parents are to make sure that all are fully informed about the benefits and risks of this procedure, and that the procedure, if elected, is performed in a competent and humane manner.

—JEFFREY R. BOTKIN

CONFIDENTIALITY

◆ **confidentiality**
The communication of, and thus relinquishing personal privacy of, personal and sensitive information to a recipient who is then entrusted not to disclose the information and cause harm.

Confidentiality has its roots in the human practice of sharing and keeping secrets (Bok, 1984). For children, the desire to keep a secret is a manifestation of an emerging sense of self; the desire to share a secret stems from a need to retain or establish intimate relationships with others (Ekstein and Caruth, 1972). The willingness to share secrets presupposes an implicit trust or an explicit promise that they will be dept. Keeping and sharing secrets is a more complex social practice among adults. Some adults keep secrets simply to preserve their personal privacy; others may have something illegal or immoral to hide. Some persons do not reveal private thoughts, feelings, or behavior for fear of embarrassment, exploitation, stigmatization, or discrimination. Still others feel a need to disclose secrets to others to help resolve emotional conflicts or seek solutions to problems arising out of interpersonal relationships. The sharing and keeping of secrets among friends, for instance, creates a context in which ethical issues concerning promises, trust, loyalty, and interests of others may come into conflict. For example, I may promise a friend to keep a secret that she feels an urgent need to tell me. She trusts me not to tell anyone else about her revelation. Out of loyalty to my friend, I promise in advance to keep her secret. But I am thrown into a moral conflict when she unexpectedly discloses her impulse and plan to kill a family member who she believes is plotting against her. I realize that my obligations to keep my promise and preserve loyalty and trust conflict with a desire, if not a responsibility, to prevent my friend's harm to herself as well as serious harm to another. Do I preserve confidentiality or protect others? Similar ethical conflicts arise for health professionals and their clients or patients.

The following discussion clarifies the concept of confidentiality and the related ideas of privacy and privileged communication in health-care settings. The rights of clients/patients and the responsibilities of health professionals to their clients, their professions, and society bring out key ethical issues. Legal regulations both protect and limit confidentiality, sometimes in ways that create ethical conflicts for clients as well as professionals. In health-care contexts neither absolute protection nor total abandonment of confidentiality is plausible. Yet sometimes it is uncertain where boundaries should be drawn because legitimate interests come into conflict. Personal privacy, professional integrity, effective care, economic considerations, and public health and safety influence both general policies and specific practices concerning confidentiality.

PRIVACY, CONFIDENTIALITY, AND PRIVILEGED COMMUNICATION

- *Privacy* refers to limiting access to one's person or limiting disclosure of one's thoughts or feelings.
- *Confidentiality* concerns the communication of private, personal information to a recipient who is entrusted not to disclose the information.
- *Privileged communications* are confidential communications protected by law against disclosure in legal settings.

Conceptual analysis

Confidentiality is closely related to the broad concept of privacy and the narrower concept of privileged communications. All three concepts share the idea of limiting access of others in certain respects (Gavin,

See Also
Genetic Testing and Screening: Ethical Issues

1980; Allen, 1988). Privacy refers to limiting access of others to one's body or mind, such as through physical contact or disclosure of thoughts or feelings. The idea of limited access describes privacy in a neutral way. But privacy is closely linked to normative values. Privacy is usually thought to be good; it is something that individuals typically desire to preserve, protect, and control. Thus privacy and a right to privacy are sometimes not clearly distinguished. In law and ethics "privacy" usually refers to privacy rights as well as limited access. Thus, privacy in law is linked to freedom from intrusion by the state or third persons. It may designate a domain of personal decision, usually about important matters such as personal associations, abortion, or bodily integrity.

Confidentiality concerns the communication of private and personal information from one person to another where it is expected that the recipient of the information, such as a health professional, will not ordinarily disclose the confidential information to third persons. In other words, other persons, unless properly authorized, have limited access to confidential information. Confidentiality, like privacy, is valued because it protects individual preferences and rights.

Privileged communications are those confidential communications that the law protects against disclosure in legal settings. Once again, others have limited access to confidential information. A person who has disclosed private information to a spouse or certain professionals (doctor, lawyer, priest, psychotherapist) may restrict his or her testimony in a legal context, subject to certain exceptions (Smith-Bell and Winslade, 1994; Weiner and Wettstein, 1993).

Privacy and confidentiality are alike in that each stands as a polar opposite to the idea of "public": what is private and confidential is not public. Yet privacy and confidentiality are not the same. Privacy can refer to singular features of persons, such as privacy of thoughts, feelings, or fantasies. Confidentiality always refers to relational contexts involving two or more persons. Privacy can also refer to relational contexts, such as privacy of personal associations or private records. Thus, in this respect the concepts overlap. In many relational contexts the terms "privacy" and "confidentiality" are used interchangeably and sometimes loosely. Professional codes of ethics, for example, often use these terms in this way (Winslade and Ross, 1985).

It should be noted, however, that privacy and confidentiality are significantly different in one important respect. Relinquishing personal privacy is a precondition for establishing confidentiality. Confidentiality requires a relationship of at least two persons, one of whom exposes or discloses private data to the other. An expectation of confidentiality arises out of a special relationship between the parties created by their respective roles (doctor-patient, lawyer-client) or by an explicit promise. Confidentiality, as with its linguistic origins (*con* and *fides*: with fidelity), assumes a relationship based on trust or fidelity. Between strangers there is no expectation of trust. Privacy is given up because confidentiality is assured; unauthorized persons are excluded.

Yet confidentiality does not flow simply from the fact that personal or private information is divulged to another. If persons choose to announce their sexual preferences in street-corner speeches, in books, or on billboards, this information, though private in its origin, is not confidential. Confidentiality depends not only on the information, but also on the context of the disclosure as well as on the relationship between the discloser and the recipient of the information. Confidentiality applies to personal, sensitive, sometimes potentially harmful or embarrassing private information disclosed within the confines of a special relationship. It should be noted, however, that the disclosure of private information from client to professional is one-way, unlike other interpersonal confidentiality contexts (Winslade and Ross, 1985).

Rights of patients/clients

When clients enter into a health-care relationship, they relinquish some personal privacy in permitting physical examinations, taking tests, or giving social and medical histories. Usually this information is documented in a medical record, often stored electronically and held by the health professional or an institution. In exchange for the loss of privacy, clients expect and are promised some degree of confidentiality. In general, all personal medical information is confidential unless the client requests disclosure to third parties or a specific exception permits or requires disclosure. For example, clients may request disclosure to obtain insurance coverage or permit disclosure to a scientific researcher. The law requires health professionals to report certain infectious diseases to public-health departments or to report suspected child abuse to appropriate agencies. Unilateral disclosure of otherwise confidential information to third parties by health professionals or institutions is unethical unless it is authorized by the client or by law.

Traditional ethical theories can be interpreted to provide additional support for the values of privacy and confidentiality. Deontology stresses the rights of persons and the duties of others to respect persons as ends in themselves, to respect especially their personal rights. To the extent that the social practices tied to privacy and confidentiality enhance the welfare of all,

Consent to medical and surgical interventions is an ancient legal requirement.

PAGE 406

See Also
Informed Consent

PRIVACY
It's a Cultural Thing

In the United States and other Western societies, the values of privacy, confidentiality, and privileged communications are closely tied to the values of personal rights and self-determination. These rights include freedom from the intrusion of others into one's private life, thoughts, conduct, or relationships. Interest in protection of personal rights has grown in response to public and private surveillance of individuals through the use of data bases to collect, store, and transmit information about individuals (Flaherty, 1989). In the United States the ideas of privacy and confidentiality have generated much legal and philosophical scholarship, influenced important judicial decisions, and prompted federal and state legislation (Winslade and Ross, 1985). The legal doctrine and ethical ideal of informed consent in health care reinforces the importance of personal autonomy (Beauchamp and Childress, 1989). The right to informed consent, applied specifically to confidentiality, gives patients/clients the right to control disclosure of confidential information. Other countries with less individualistic traditions do not place such high ethical value on privacy or personal rights. Even persons in cultures where privacy is not a prominent value can be harmed, however, by revelations of personal information (Macklin, 1992).

— WILLIAM J. WINSLADE

◆ **privileged communications**
Confidential communications protected by law against disclosure in legal settings.

utilitarianism may also be invoked on behalf of individuals. Virtue theory advocates personal moral aspiration and achievement. Privacy and confidentiality provide a context and an opportunity for cultivation of virtues without outside interference.

Despite the value of privacy and confidentiality to individuals, however, other values—such as collective need for information or public health and safety—limit individual rights. Confidentiality conflicts often arise about information contained in medical records. Clients usually want information to remain confidential. Others—such as employers, insurers, family members, researchers, and litigants—exert pressure to limit confidentiality and to gain access to personal information. Health professionals are often pulled in both directions by their professional loyalty to patients/clients and their broader social responsibilities.

Responsibilities of health professionals

The responsibilities of health professionals, as articulated in codes of professional ethics, reinforce the value of confidentiality. For example, the Hippocratic oath states:

> *What I may see or hear in the course of the treatment or even outside of the treatment in regard to the life of men, which on no account one must spread abroad, I will keep to myself, holding such things shameful to be spoken about.*

Modern codes of professional ethics, like the Principles of Ethics of the American Medical Association, instruct physicians to "safeguard patient confidences within the constraints of the law" (see Appendix). Similarly, ethics codes for psychotherapists, nurses, and other allied health professionals make general, though not always coherent, reference to protection of professional-client confidentiality (Winslade and Ross, 1985). The American Psychiatric Association, however, has also issued detailed official Guidelines on Confidentiality pertaining to special situations, records, special settings, and the legal process (Committee on Confidentiality, 1987). The American Bar Association has offered a handbook, *AIDS/HIV and Confidentiality Model Policy and Procedures*, that addresses the value of confidentiality, consent to disclosures, third-party access to information, and penalties for unauthorized disclosures (Rennert, 1991). The Council on Ethical and Judicial Affairs of the American Medical Association (1992) outlines the scope and value of confidentiality and addresses in detail confidentiality in the context of computerized medical records. These documents stress individual rights and specify professional responsibilities concerning confidentiality.

Professionals are often more aware of confidentiality issues than patients or clients. Professionals realize that privacy and confidentiality may give way to the institutional, governmental, and other third-party pressures for specific information about patients or clients. Health professionals desire to protect the integrity and special value of the professional-client relationship itself. Confidentiality is one basis of professionals' reciprocity with clients who reveal private information. (Other aspects of reciprocity include the clients' payment for the professionals' services in response to the professionals' expertise to meet the clients' needs.)

It should be emphasized that the primary justification for confidentiality is derived from the individual rights of clients and is supplemented by the responsibil-

See Also
Public Health Issues: From Privacy to Equity

AUDIO FUROR
The Sexton Tapes

Despite the explicit attention given to confidentiality in oaths and codes, practical ethical problems arise, occasionally causing heated controversy. For instance, in 1991 an authorized biography of the deceased poet Anne Sexton relied in part upon audiotapes of psychotherapy sessions. One of Sexton's psychiatrists permitted the biographer to listen to some 300 hours of psychotherapy tapes. Prior to the publication of the biography, a front-page story in the *New York Times* about the disclosure of the tapes to the biographer generated a furious ethical debate. On the one hand. some critics believed that release of the tapes violated the deceased patient's privacy. Others pointed out the harm to surviving family members. Still others stressed the duty of the psychiatrist not to reveal anything about the content of therapy. Unless the therapist was required by law to release the information on the tapes, these critics argued, confidentiality should have been preserved. On the other hand, the psychiatrist claimed that his duty was primarily to protect his patient's interests—including her interest in self-revelation, in being understood, and in helping others. The psychiatrist believed that the patient, when competent, had specifically authorized him to use his own best judgment about what to do with the tapes. He also believed that he should cooperate with the request of the patient's literary executor—her daughter—to help make the biography accurate and complete. None of the relevant ethics codes sufficiently clarified or specifically addressed a case of this kind. Although charges were brought that the psychiatrist violated the code of ethics of the American Psychiatric Association, eventually a decision was reached that no ethics violation occurred. But a still-unsettled controversy swirls around these issues.

—WILLIAM J. WINSLADE

ities of professionals and the benefits of the health-care relationship. This is why the client, rather than the health professional, determines what information is to remain confidential. Except where laws or other rules limit clients' rights to confidentiality, the client may not only request but require professionals to disclose otherwise confidential information. It is, after all, the client's private information that has been revealed to the professional.

Some recent critics, including feminist theorists, have questioned the adequacy of rights-based approaches. They argue that an ethics of care or caring must take account of a web of relationships, emotions, and values that include but go beyond individual rights. A care-based ethics stresses the interactive relationships, not only of patients and clinicians, but also families and society. Within the context of caring, humans—especially those who experience special suffering or discrimination—need more than just protection of their legal rights. In the specific context of privacy and confidentiality in medical genetics, for example, an ethics of care rather than rights may better explain the moral reasoning of geneticists (Wertz and Fletcher, 1991). This is discussed further in the later section on genetic and other medical screening.

Other critics think that the preservation of confidentiality should take priority over clients' and professionals' autonomy. This idea is based on the idea that total confidentiality is essential to protect both the integrity and the effectiveness of the professional-client relationship. No third parties should ever be permitted to penetrate the boundaries of a protected professional relationship. Neither the client nor the professional, according to this view, should be required or even permitted to disclose confidential information. Something close to this extreme position was considered but rejected by the California Supreme Court in *Lifshutz* (1970). Neither professional organizations nor their ethics codes endorse this idea, but it does highlight the importance that can be ascribed to confidentiality.

Even if the ideal of complete confidentiality cannot be justified in theory, it can sometimes be achieved in practice. A dyadic, exclusive relationship between client and health professional can sometimes fully preserve confidentiality. For example, a client establishes a relationship with a psychotherapist to explore the meaning of a significant personal loss. The client may not want others to know about the consultation. It is nobody else's business.

◆ **psychotherapy**
Treatment of mental or emotional disorders or of related bodily ills by psychological means.

The therapist's office may have a separate entrance and exit to decrease the likelihood that clients will encounter each other. The therapist may answer personally all phone calls. The therapist may keep no client-specific records and take no notes. The client may pay cash, not file a claim for insurance coverage, explicitly request that all discussions be kept confidential, and take other precautions to prevent others from learning even that the relationship with the therapist exists at all. The client reveals his or her feelings, fantasies, thoughts, or dreams only to the therapist, who seeks to understand and help interpret their meaning only to the client.

See Also
Trust: Communication: Shared Decision-Making

If client confidentiality and professional secrecy were always as unambiguous as the foregoing scenario, there would be little more to say. However, professionals as well as clients have widely divergent attitudes, beliefs, expectations, and values concerning confidentiality (Wettstein, 1994). A few professionals espouse the absolute value of confidentiality in dyadic therapeutic relationships while many others acknowledge only its limited and relative value. Others lament the declining value of confidentiality while accepting the encroachment of legal, economic, public-health and safety, or research interests. A few others view confidentiality as an inflated value that some professionals or clients use as a shield to conceal fraud, malpractice, or even criminal activity.

Rather than a simple dyadic relationship, a more complex, polycentric model is necessary to capture the nuances of confidentiality in health care. Clients, health professionals, and third parties may have varying claims on ethical grounds to protection of or access to confidential information. Clients may waive their rights to confidentiality to obtain other benefits such as insurance coverage or employment. Professionals may discern a conflict between ethical obligations to their clients and legally required reports. Third parties may have a legitimate need to know otherwise confidential information to assess quality of health-care services, uncover fraud, or determine appropriate allocations of health-care resources. Loss of confidentiality may result not only from ethical, legal, or economic factors, but also because of client ignorance or misunderstanding, professional or institutional carelessness, or third-party overreaching. The interplay of those various factors can best be understood by examining in more detail selected problem areas where confidentiality comes into conflict with competing ethical and social interests.

Required reporting

Legal rules that require health professionals to report child or elder abuse, infectious diseases, or gunshot wounds preempt many of the specific ethical conflicts between confidentiality and public health or safety. However, not all ethical issues are resolved by legal rules. For example, some child-abuse-reporting laws are overly broad; health professionals may fail to make mandated reports in part because of the value ascribed to client confidentiality. Other reporting laws are so narrow that protection of threatened victims is undermined by confidentiality rules and practices (Miller and Weinstock, 1987). Some commentators have pointed out, for example, the conflicts created by statutes that require the reporting of not only actual but also suspected child abusers. Some parents alleged to have abused their children have been required to undergo therapy; but to require them to admit abuse before conducting therapy conflicts with the constitutional privilege against self-incrimination.

Professionals, caught between the need for confidentiality in therapy and the legal demand for reporting abuse, sometimes underreport abuse; they protect therapeutic relationships at the risk of legal liability.

See Also

AIDS

HIV Testing: Efforts to Protect Confidentiality

AIDS AND CONFIDENTIALITY

The acquired immunodeficiency syndrome (AIDS) epidemic brings with it a full range of confidentiality issues. Patients who think that they might be HIV-positive are reluctant to be tested for fear that disclosure of such sensitive information may cause them to lose employment or insurance coverage or may make them subject to other types of discrimination. Yet if they are not tested, the benefits of clinical care to diminish the damage of the disease are not available. Patients who know that they are HIV-positive may not want others to know of their status to prevent discrimination. But third parties, such as sexual partners, who are at risk of being infected with a lethal virus, have a legitimate interest in access to otherwise confidential information. If the infected person is unwilling to inform others who may be at risk of getting AIDS, health professionals may be permitted or even required to warn persons who have been or may be put at risk of being infected. Family members may want to know why their relative is sick; they may need to know if they become caretakers. But patients may not be willing to disclose their diagnosis. Health-care workers want to know their patients' HIV status just as patients want to know if their caretakers are infected. Both desire to avoid becoming infected themselves. Those who are at risk of infection may have a justifiable need to know; others may not.

Confidentiality is not the only value at stake, but it does impose substantial burdens on others. For example, in institutional settings, confidentiality of personal information, such as a patient's diagnosis, must be protected by written policies and actual practices. In a recent court case in Maryland, a hospital failed to protect adequately a patient's medical record that included a diagnosis of AIDS. It is not sufficient to state a policy that access to medical records is limited. It is also necessary to have and implement policies that actually restrict physical access to the records (Brannigan, 1992). The hospital was negligent because it did not go far enough to limit physical access of unauthorized persons to the records.

— WILLIAM J. WINSLADE

Other professionals may overreport child abuse because of their concerns about legal liability, strained therapeutic relationships, vulnerability of potential victims, or uncertainty about the value of confidentiality. Some commentators have suggested that child-abuse statutes should be revised to be more specific and limited, requiring professionals to report only when their patients are victims of child abuse, but to give professionals greater discretion about whether to report abusers who are in treatment (Smith-Bell and Winslade, 1994).

Another ethical problem for health professionals that arises in connection with legally required disclosures of otherwise confidential information is what to tell clients prior to or near the outset of therapy. If clients are inadequately apprised about the limits of confidentiality, their trust in health professionals is damaged and their relationship may be ruptured. If clients are fully advised of the legal limits placed on confidentiality, they may withhold essential information, terminate therapy, or not even start it. A further problem is that professionals may not know precisely where legal lines have been drawn. For example, a therapist may know that notification must be made to authorities but may not know how much, if any, of the content of therapy must he disclosed.

Genetic and other medical screening

Genetic and other types of medical screening by epidemiologists, physicians, employers, schools, and other public and private agencies give rise to situations in which confidentiality is threatened by a demand for personal medical information. Individuals who are screened want to control information about themselves to prevent stigma, loss of insurance or employment, or other forms of discrimination. Screeners desire access to such information to promote their interests in knowledge, scientific discovery, publication, or economic considerations as well as therapeutic purposes. Control over the information raises moral issues as well as practical problems. These values must be balanced against individuals' rights to preserve their informational privacy. Blood tests, family medical histories, personal medical histories, DNA assays, and data banking, for instance, all raise questions about confidentiality, access, and control of personal information (De Gorgey, 1990). Lack of consensus about ethical priorities, gaps in legal policies and remedies to individuals, and political uncertainty about jurisdiction and control over medical screening combine to create controversy. Protection of individual rights of privacy and confidentiality requires careful monitoring of the use of data banks to store information obtained by the Human Genome Project (Macklin, 1992).

CONFIDENTIALITY AMONG GENETICISTS
Care-Based and Rights-Based Approaches

Health professionals in genetics differ in their beliefs about the value of privacy and confidentiality. Considerable disagreement has been documented, for example, in an international study in nineteen countries of the attitudes of geneticists toward privacy and disclosure. These health professionals were asked to respond to vignettes concerning disclosure of false paternity; of a patient's genetic makeup to a spouse; to relatives at genetic risk; of ambiguous test results; and to institutional third parties, such as employers and insurers (Wertz and Fletcher, 1991). Some consensus as well as numerous differences were discovered among the geneticists' opinions about what disclosures are appropriate. Dorothy Wertz and James Fletcher also found that geneticists' reasoning was more likely to be based on the complex needs and relationships of the various parties rather than the rights of individuals. A care-based ethics approach poses a theoretical and practical alternative to a rights-based approach.

—WILLIAM J. WINSLADE

Legal protections and limitations

Legal protection of confidentiality in the United States has been sporadic and uneven. The 1974 Federal Privacy Act (P.L. 93-579) included some medical information and records; its passage signaled heightened congressional awareness of threats to privacy and confidentiality. The National Privacy Commission's report (U.S. Domestic Council, 1976) seemed to set the stage for further protective federal legislation. Several subsequent attempts to pass comprehensive federal laws to protect medical information failed; a patchwork of state statutes provides only limited protection of patients' confidentiality. The reason is that patients' interests in confidentiality are balanced against powerful interests of third parties, such as health-care payers, governmental agencies, researchers, and law-enforcement agencies, who wish to have access to otherwise confidential medical information (Hendricks et al., 1990).

Courts have been as hesitant as federal and state legislatures to provide stringent protection of patient confidentiality. The U. S. Supreme Court considered

Disclosure of genetic data to other third parties can seriously harm individuals.

PAGE 317

See Also
Genetic Testing and Screening

but rejected the idea that patients enjoy a constitutional right to "informational privacy" with regard to treatment records (*Whalen* v. *Roe*, 1977). This decision was rendered when the rhetoric of privacy was prominent in Supreme Court opinions; in the 1980s the right to privacy was restricted, and the rhetoric of privacy diminished. State courts, such as those in Florida and California, whose constitutions make explicit reference to a right to privacy, have been more inclined to protect confidentiality of medical information. But state laws provide infrequently enforced bureaucratic protections or opportunities for recovery of damages only after confidentiality has been violated. Even then, litigation is rare because patients are reluctant to further expose confidential matters, damages are difficult to prove, and awards are often limited by statute (Winslade, 1982).

In some settings, such as substance-abuse treatment programs, the federal government has established special rules to protect confidentiality. To encourage persons in need of treatment to enter substance-abuse programs, records are not disclosed to law-enforcement agencies that might otherwise seek to prosecute substance abusers. In sensitive human subject research, special "privacy certificates" can be obtained by researchers from the federal government to give added protection to confidential information. Similarly, coded and locked files, limited access even to authorized personnel, and other precautionary measures against leakage further enhance confidentiality (McCarthy and Porter, 1991).

Public concern about confidentiality surfaces periodically, especially concerning the potential evils of misuses of patient-identifiable information. For example, implications of the Human Genome Project and health-care reform have most recently evoked anxiety about discrimination, violation of personal rights, and commerce in patient information. The potential for a new health-care information infrastructure that relies heavily on computer technology to facilitate the flow of medical information dramatically increases the threat to confidentiality of medical records (Brannigan, 1992). Recent commentaries remind us that current legal policies are inadequate to protect individuals against unwarranted disclosure, to provide security for complex medical-information systems, and to preserve individuals' rights to consent and control the uses of personal medical information (Alpert, 1993; Gostin et al., 1993).

The complexity of particular cases and the variability of judicial interpretations of facts and laws inevitably cause some uncertainty. In this context, as in many others, confidentiality is limited by other important values. For example, suppose a voluntary psychotic in-patient with no history of violence leaves the hospi-

◆ **reasonable protection rule**

In balancing public safety and confidentiality, the law stipulates protective privilege of confidential information "ends where public peril begins," necessitating disclosure to protect threatened victims from harm.

See Also

Adolescent Mental Health: Refusal of Treatment

PROTECTIVE PRIVILEGE AND PUBLIC PERIL

The *Tarasoff* Case

A specific area of law that directly affects confidentiality concerns the obligations of psychotherapists whose potentially violent patients place other individuals at risk of harm. The California Supreme Court, in the case of *Tarasoff* v. *Regents of the University of California* (1974), ruled that psychotherapists of dangerous patients have a duty to use reasonable care to protect threatened victims from harm. To do so may require the disclosure of otherwise confidential patient information. In balancing public safety and confidentiality, the Court observed that "the protective privilege ends where the public peril begins."

In the *Tarasoff* case, a psychotherapist believed that his patient was potentially dangerous to a young woman who had rejected his interest in her. The patient was obsessed with her at the expense of his studies, his work, and his friends. When the patient talked of revenge and was thought to have a gun, the therapist sought to have his patient evaluated for involuntary hospitalization. But the police declined to bring the patient in for an assessment of his mental status. The patient, angry with his therapist, abruptly terminated treatment. A couple of months later the former patient killed the young woman. Her parents sued the therapists and their employer for failing to warn the victim or her family about the dangerous patient. Although this case was settled out of court without a trial, the reasonable-protection rule was articulated by the court for future cases.

Subsequently, a series of judicial decisions have elaborated the duty of psychotherapists to third parties. Some courts have restricted the duty to situations in which there is an imminent threat of serious violence toward an identifiable victim. Others have focused on the broader duty of health professionals to control the conduct of the dangerous patient. Still others have applied the *Tarasoff* standard even when the risk to others is neither serious nor specific. And a few courts have protected confidentiality rather than endorse the *Tarasoff* standard (Felthous, 1989).

—WILLIAM J. WINSLADE

tal against medical advice. He leaves behind some written notes that include violent fantasies about a family member. His therapist discovers the notes (which were left unsealed). Assume the therapist consults the patient, who demands confidentiality; but the therapist is concerned that the patient may be dangerous. The therapist must assess the probability of harm to the patient or the potential victim, consider alternatives to revealing confidential information, and decide what, if anything, to tell the patient, the threatened victim, or others. This delicate balancing inevitably occurs in contexts where information is incomplete, contextual nuances are elusive, and human behavior is notoriously difficult to predict. Nevertheless, decisions must be made and actions taken that will affect the scope of confidentiality as well as bring about other consequences.

Information about limits of confidentiality

When entering into a professional-client relationship, clients have a right to receive explicit information about the scope and limits of confidentiality. Most nonprofessionals assume that disclosures made in the context of health care are confidential (Weiss, 1982). Most clients are uninformed about the limits of confidentiality and pressures to reveal presumably confidential information to third parties. Some clients realize that there are legal and ethical restrictions on confidentiality in health care, but others learn of them only after an undesired disclosure (Siegler, 1982).

Clients for whom confidentiality is especially important may take steps to preserve it. For example, a medical patient who chooses to file an insurance claim may request the right to review all documents released to the insurance carrier. Or the patient may pay privately rather than file an insurance claim. Other clients may be less concerned with confidentiality. Clients have a responsibility to inform themselves about what expectations about confidentiality are reasonable; then they will not be surprised or dismayed because of false assumptions about confidentiality.

Professionals have a responsibility to inform themselves as well as their clients about legal, ethical, and practical aspects of confidentiality. For example, neither patients nor health professionals usually are familiar with the practices of insurance companies concerning redisclosure of confidential information. Patients often sign a blanket waiver of confidentiality in order to obtain insurance benefits. This information may then be sold by the insurer to the Medical Information Bureau, a clearinghouse to protect against insurance fraud. This goal is laudable, but the data-banking process may include erroneous information that is difficult to detect or correct. In addition, many other interests outside health care—such as employers, government agencies, educational institutions, and the media—may gain access to information contained in these data bases (Linowes, 1989; Alpert, 1993).

At the very least, professionals should ask their clients what they want to know about confidentiality. Some professionals prepare a disclosure statement to give each new client, that is, a document that outlines confidentiality practices the particular professional follows. Policies and procedures concerning written medical records might be given to each new client. Further conversation, including clients' questions and professionals' answers, can clarify details that written statements may not address. Because professionals, like their clients, may differ in their attitudes toward confidentiality, it is important that disclosures about confidentiality be particularized. For example, the values of a psychoanalyst in private practice who never publishes patient case reports significantly differs from those of a research-oriented psychoanalyst who tapes and transcribes every session and publishes detailed case reports. Each should fully inform clients about the nature of his or her practice (Stoller, 1988).

Professionals have an obligation to take precautionary measures to protect confidentiality even if their clients have not requested it. Professionals should assume that all client information (including the very existence of the professional-client relationship as well as personal and private information revealed) is strictly confidential unless the client has requested or waived disclosure or unless the law requires it. Professionals should advise their clients of required disclosures, inform them of waivers, explore with them the consequences of disclosing or not disclosing information, and examine the reasons for and against disclosure. But clients retain the authority to decide what voluntary disclosures are to be made to third parties (Winslade and Ross, 1985).

Professionals also have a special responsibility to protect confidential client information from leakage through lax office procedures, professional or personal gossip, or the inappropriate inquiries of unauthorized persons. This is particularly problematic in institutional settings, where many individuals may have routine access to patient information contained in medical records (Siegler, 1982). As computerization of medical records expands further and information storage, retrieval, and distribution technologies become more sophisticated, the need for professionals' vigilance increases.

Many third parties—government officials and agencies, insurance interests, employers, family members, researchers, and others—seek specific information about particular patients. Third parties should not

Discriminaiton from disclosure of genetic status may result from misunderstanding information.

PAGE 321

See Also
Genetic Testing and Screening: Confidentiality

"No one is truly literate who cannot read his own heart."

ERIC HOFFER
THE PASSIONATE STATE OF MIND, 1954

assume, however, that mere interest gives them legitimate authority to have access to confidential information. Third parties have a responsibility to justify to patients and professionals their need for access to confidential information. In some instances, this may require only a routine inquiry and documentation, but in other situations, professionals may find it necessary to confirm that their patients have requested, waived, or forfeited their rights to confidentiality. Too often, professionals, especially in an institutional setting, capitulate to pressure to disclose more information than necessary to third parties. At the very least, third parties as well as professionals should notify patients when access is sought, how it will be used, and whether the information will be redisclosed to anyone else. If appropriate disclosures are made to patients before access to confidential information is granted to third parties, not only will confidentiality be better preserved, but patients will also be better served.

— WILLIAM J. WINSLADE

CONSCIENCE

CONSCIENCE: "The inner voice which warns us that someone may be looking."

H. L. MENCKEN

Matters of conscience arise with some frequency in bioethics. A health professional may cite considerations of conscience in declining to perform or participate in a certain procedure. A patient may refuse a particular treatment on grounds of conscience. And new or unanticipated circumstances may create conflicts of conscience for patients and health professionals alike. What do we mean by "conscience" in these and related contexts? Is conscience an internal moral sense sufficient for distinguishing right from wrong? Is the "voice" of conscience simply the echo of parental and social prohibitions? Or does conscience differ in important ways from either of these? How much weight should be given in ethical reflection to claims of conscience? To what extent and for what reasons should health professionals compromise personal convenience, institutional efficiency, or medical effectiveness in order to respect individual conscience, their own or their patients'?

Three conceptions of conscience

The idea of conscience has a long and complex history (D'Arcy, 1961; Mount, 1969). The word "conscience" derives from the Latin conscientia, introduced by Christian Scholastics. Most generally, it refers to conscious awareness of the moral quality of some past or contemplated action and the disposition to be so aware (conscientiousness). In what follows we consider three main conceptions: (1) conscience as an inner sense that distinguishes right acts from wrong; (2) conscience as the internalization of parental and social norms; and (3) conscience as the exercise and expression of a reflective sense of integrity.

THREE CONCEPTIONS OF CONSCIENCE

1. inner sense of right from wrong
2. internalized parental and social norms
3. reflective sense of integrity

MORAL SENSE. Conscience is sometimes conceived as an internal moral sense sufficient for distinguishing right from wrong. The reliability of this inner sense is usually attributed to its divine origin, its reflection of our true nature, or some combination of the two. There are, however, difficulties with this conception.

Consider, first, a variation of an argument developed by Plato in his *Euthyphro*. Is what makes an act right the fact that it is endorsed by one's conscience? Or does conscience recommend a certain course of conduct because it is right? If the former, the promptings of conscience appear to be arbitrary. Whatever is urged by a person's conscience would, in this view, be right. There would be no way to assess the deliverances of conscience or to compare the consciences of, say, Hitler and Mother Teresa. If, on the other hand, conscience directs us to perform certain acts because they are right, it cannot be the principal source of moral knowledge. We must, in this event, have prior, independent criteria of rightness and wrongness that allow us to distinguish those acts that should be recommended by conscience from those that should not—in which case conscience is not sufficient to guide conduct.

A related difficulty is the prevalence of conflicts of conscience, both within persons and between them. Such conflicts are especially pronounced in bioethics, where advances in knowledge and technology confront us with unprecedented, consequential choices ranging well beyond our ethical traditions. The limitations of conscience, if it is conceived as a sufficient guide to moral decision making, may not be so noticeable in static, homogenous, insular cultures and subcultures. But where new circumstances require members of pluralistic societies to come to some agreement on bioethical questions, appeals to an internal, self-validating sense of right and wrong are apt to generate more heat than light.

INTERNALIZED SOCIAL NORMS. The most plausible explanation for the limitations of conscience in resolving ethical conflicts is that the "voice" of conscience is simply the echo of social and parental admonitions impressed upon the developing psyches of young children (i.e., the Freudian superego). Whatever its psychological and developmental significance, conscience so conceived has little normative import. That we have certain moral compunctions as a result of our socialization does little to establish their validity. We are bound by the voice of conscience only if we can provide independent justification of its dictates. It is the adequacy of the justification, not the persistence of the voice, that carries moral authority. Conceived as internalized social norms, then, conscience plays no direct role in ethical deliberation.

SENSE OF INTEGRITY. "I couldn't live with myself if I were [or were not] to perform the abortion in these circumstances." "I can no longer participate in this treatment plan in good conscience." "How could I continue to think of myself as a Jehovah's Witness if I were to consent to the blood transfusion?" Each of these sentences expresses an appeal to conscience that is neither a deliverance of an internal moral sense nor an internalization of an external social norm. What is expressed in each case is the culmination of *conscientious* reflection about the relationship between a certain course of action and a particular conception of the self. So understood, appeals to conscience are closely connected to reflective concern with one's integrity. The focus is not so much on the objective or universal rightness or wrongness of a particular act as on the consequences for the self of one's performing it.

There is something absurd, Gilbert Ryle has observed, in saying "My conscience says that *you* ought to do this or ought not to have done that" (Ryle, 1940, p. 31). I may be troubled by your wrongdoing, but unless I have advised or assisted you, or culpably failed to prevent you from performing the act in question, my conscience will be clear. The same is not true, however, about those of *my* acts that I have determined, for one reason or another, were or would be morally wrong. Having judged a certain act to be wrong, an appeal to conscience stresses the added wrongness of my performing it. Appeals to conscience therefore presuppose a prior determination of the rightness or wrongness of an act (Childress, 1979). Moreover, one may or may not extend the standards one employs in making this assessment to others in similar situations. If, for example, the standards are universalizable principles of respect for persons, justice, or beneficence, one will maintain that anyone would do wrong in performing the act in question. But if one's standards are grounded in religious convictions, personal ideals, or a particular worldview and way of life, one may not hold everyone else to them. What is at stake in all such appeals is one's wholeness or integrity as a person.

Integrity

"It would be better for me," Socrates says in the *Gorgias*, "that my lyre or a chorus I directed should be out of tune and loud with discord, and that multitudes of men should disagree with me rather than that I, *being one*, should be out of harmony with myself and contradict me" (Arendt, 1971, p. 439). One cannot lead a good and meaningful life, Socrates suggests, unless the self is reasonably unified or integrated—unless, that is, one's words and deeds cohere with one's basic, identity-conferring, moral, religious, and philosophical convictions. Hence the importance of critical reflection on one's life as a whole. The words, deeds, and convictions of an unexamined life are unlikely to be sufficiently integrated to constitute a singular life—let alone one worth living.

Conscience should not, therefore, be conceived as a faculty or component of the self. It is, rather, the voice of one's self as a whole, understood temporally—as having a beginning, a middle, and an end—as well as at a particular moment. Operating retrospectively, what Christian tradition calls "judicial" conscience makes judgments about past conduct. Operating prospectively, what the same tradition calls "legislative" conscience anticipates whether a prospective utterance or course of action is likely to be at odds with one's most basic ethical convictions (D'Arcy, 1961). In each case, the signal that something is wrong—that one's integrity has been, is currently, or would be compromised—is an actual or anticipatory feeling of guilt, shame, or remorse.

Consider, in this connection, the words of Aleksandr N. Chikunov, a veteran of the 1968 Soviet invasion of Czechoslovakia, as he explains sharing his experience with young soldiers called to Moscow to suppress democratic reforms during the abortive coup of August 1991: "I entered Prague in 1968 and I still have an ill conscience about it. I was a soldier then, like these guys. We were also sent like they are now, to defend the achievements of socialism. Twenty-three years have passed, and I still have an ill conscience" (*New York Times*, August 20, 1991, p. A13). Here Chikunov draws upon the lessons of his "ill" judicial conscience to inform and alert the legislative consciences of the young soldiers. His motivation, it seems, is not only to spare them the pangs of an ill conscience but also to help heal his own (and thus to heal himself).

The authority and sanctions of conscience are, Mr. Chikunov suggests, self-imposed. No external source can create or directly relieve a troubled conscience. Nor may we easily rationalize or evade its judgments. "Other judges," as D'Arcy points out, "may be venal or partial or fallible; not so the verdict of conscience" (D'Arcy, 1961, p. 8). The oppressiveness of a guilty conscience is due in part to its identity with the self.

Conscience in bioethics

Three factors contribute to the prevalence of appeals to conscience in bioethics: (1) bioethical decision making

See Also
Bioethics
Bioethics: Do the Ends Justify the Means?

often involves our deepest identity-conferring convictions about the nature and meaning of creating, sustaining, and ending life; (2) health-care professionals and patients and their families will occasionally have radically differing beliefs about such matters; and (3) the complexity of modern health care often requires agreement and cooperation on a single course of action.

CONFLICTS OF CONSCIENCE. Conflicts of conscience arise not only between individuals but also within them. Consider a physician whose patient, suffering greatly from the ravages of the last stages of a terminal illness, is also a longtime friend. The patient requests the physician to provide both the substance and the instruction for taking his own life. The physician finds herself torn. On the one hand, her conception of medicine and professional identity is incompatible with what appears to be physician-assisted suicide. On the other hand, the bonds of friendship and her natural sympathies strongly incline her to accede to her patient's request. The situation has, as a result, precipitated a crisis of conscience, and the physician must engage in what Charles Taylor has called "strong evaluation"—reflection about the self by the self in ways that engage and attempt to restructure one's deepest and most fundamental convictions (Taylor, 1976). Such reflection manifests an admirable concern for wholeness or integrity.

CONSCIENTIOUS REFUSAL. From Socrates to Sir Thomas More to Henry David Thoreau, individuals have appealed to conscience in refusing to comply with a wide range of legal or socially mandated directives. In some cases such noncompliance may be covert and evasive—for example, a physician's providing contraceptive information to married couples in Connecticut before that state's anticontraceptive law was declared unconstitutional (Childress, 1985). In most cases, however, health professionals and patients give reasons of conscience in openly seeking personal exemption from certain standard practices.

◆ **conscience**
The morally self-critical part of the self-encompassing standards of behavior, performance, and value judgments.

Physicians may appeal to conscience in refusing to do procedures that are both legal and performed by their colleagues. Consider an obstetrician's refusal to perform a legal abortion or a pediatrician's refusal to prescribe human growth hormone for short, but normal, children at the behest of their anxious parents. In each case the physician's decision may be based on moral convictions or personal ideals. The obstetrician need not believe that abortion ought to be illegal or that women who request, or physicians who perform, abortions are deeply immoral. The pediatrician may neither urge the legal prohibition of administering human growth hormone to short, but normal, children nor regard parents who request this treatment, or other pediatricians who administer it, as unethical. Both agree, however, that it would be a violation of conscience—a betrayal of their deepest personal convictions about life or the nature of medicine—if they were to perform the act in question.

Similarly, nurses appeal to conscience in seeking exemption from procedures or care plans that threaten their sense of integrity. For example, a nurse may conscientiously refuse to follow a physician's directive to remove medically administered hydration and nutrition from a patient in a persistent vegetative state. Regardless of the act's legality, the family's concurrence, and the physician's directive, given her deepest identity-conferring convictions about the nature and value of life, the nurse may be unable to carry out the action. Her reasoning, she might add, is not strong enough to condemn others who believe differently; but as for herself, she must refrain.

Patients, too, may appeal to conscience in refusing forms of medical treatment. When informed, mentally competent Jehovah's Witnesses refuse blood transfusions on religious grounds, they do not at the same time urge that blood transfusions be legally prohibited, nor do they condemn those who gratefully accept blood transfusions. What they want is not so much respect for the content of their particular convictions as much as respect for their consciences. The same is true of other patients who refuse or request certain forms of treatment on the basis of fundamental moral and religious convictions.

Respect for conscience

Respect for conscience is a corollary of the principle of respect for persons. To respect another as a person is, insofar as possible, to respect the expression and exercise, if not the content, of a person's most fundamental convictions. A society's respect for individual conscience may extend not only to religious toleration but also, for example, to exempting conscripted pacifists from direct participation in war.

In the biomedical context, respect for conscience may be inconvenient, inefficient, or detrimental to medical outcomes. Still, it must always be taken seriously and often should prevail. In some cases, respect for conscience may be balanced with biomedical goals. At a certain level of abstraction, the purpose of health care is strikingly similar to that of protecting individual conscience. Although health care is usually focused on the body, emphasis on informed consent implies that the principal function of medicine is the health or wholeness of the patient as a person. Yet a person's sense of health or wholeness may also be threatened by what the former Soviet soldier, Aleksandr Chikunov, revealingly called an "ill" conscience. The values underlying appeals to conscience within the health-care system are not, therefore, radically at odds with the values underlying medical and nursing care. In each case the aim is to preserve or restore personal

See Also

Virtue and Character: The Role of Virtue in Recent Moral Philosophy

Determining Goodness: Not by Motivation Alone

CONSCIENCE
Conscientious but Wrong

Conscience is not an infallible guide to conduct. Even those who attend carefully to matters of integrity and who critically examine their basic convictions may, at a later date, judge some of their conscientious acts as wrong. Should one, then, always follow one's conscience? If by "conscience" we mean the exercise and expression of good-faith efforts to integrate conduct with reflective ethical conviction, the answer is "yes." Following conscience is obligatory, even if one's act turns out to be wrong, because one is doing what one reflectively believes to be right. Conversely, deliberately acting contrary to conscience is blameworthy, even if one's act turns out to be right, because one is doing what one reflectively believes to be wrong.

We must therefore distinguish the character of an agent from the rightness of a particular act. That an act is required by conscience entails neither that it is right nor that others must endorse the agent's convictions or permit the act to occur. It is difficult, for example, to question the character of Jehovah's Witness parents when they conscientiously refuse to consent to a life-saving blood transfusion for a young child. Yet if we have good reasons for believing that withholding the transfusion would be seriously wrong, we may try to persuade the parents to consent and, if necessary, seek a court order mandating treatment. Distinguishing the conscientiousness of the parents from our judgment of the act, though not eliminating the difficult question of whether, and if so, how, to intervene, enables us to attend more adequately to its complexity.

— MARTIN BENJAMIN

wholeness. Insofar, then, as appeals to conscience and the health-care system share a fundamental commitment to preserving and restoring personal wholeness or integrity, we ought in cases of conflict to seek some sort of balance or accommodation between them.

Health professionals who refuse, withdraw, or dissociate themselves from certain practices or procedures on grounds of conscience may well be among the more thoughtful and effective members of a health-care team. Thus a health-care institution intent on retaining such nurses and physicians has prudential as well as ethical grounds for accommodating their claims of conscience even at the cost of some inconvenience or expense. Respect for conscience requires going to greater lengths for patients, however, than it does for health-care professionals. This is in part because an individual's role as a health-care professional is voluntary in a way that being a patient is not. It is one thing, for example, to respect a Jehovah's Witness patient's conscientious refusal of a blood transfusion; it is quite another to respect the conscientious refusal of a physician who is a Jehovah's Witness to administer blood transfusions. An individual whose moral or religious convictions are incompatible with a common, essential type of health care has no business seeking a position in which such care is a routine expectation.

Problems and limits

At least two important questions remain. First, how do we distinguish genuine claims of conscience from claims serving as smoke screens for laziness, cowardice, distaste for certain procedures, or dislike or prejudice toward certain patients? Second, given that a genuine act of conscience may be morally wrong, should individuals always (or always be permitted to) follow their conscience?

GENUINENESS. Understanding the nature and justification of conscientious refusal allows us to distinguish genuine from spurious or self-deceived appeals to conscience. In assessing the authenticity of such appeals we may, for example, inquire into (1) the underlying values and the extent to which they constitute a core component of the individual's identity; (2) the depth of the individual's reflective consideration of the issue; and (3) the likelihood that he or she will experience guilt, shame, or a loss of self-respect by performing the act in question. Such criteria have been employed with reasonable success by the U.S. Selective Service System in identifying those whose deep and long-standing moral convictions forbid direct participation in war. They can be used with similar success in identifying genuine appeals to conscience in the health-care setting (Benjamin and Curtis, 1992).

— MARTIN BENJAMIN

◆ **conscientious refusal**
To avoid betrayal of deep personal convictions about life or the nature of medicine, a caregiver or patient may seek exemptions from procedures or care plans that threaten their sense of integrity.

DNA TYPING

DNA typing is a technique for identifying people through their genetic constitution. It involves comparing small portions of DNA from different sources—a child and an alleged father; a bloodstain and a criminal suspect—and determining whether those portions match. DNA typing can discriminate among people almost as accurately as fingerprinting, and it can be used in a far wider range of circumstances, since DNA is found in virtually all human cells; can be extracted from blood, semen, saliva, or hair roots; and is highly resistant to decay and contamination.

Since its introduction in the mid-1980s, DNA typing has been employed in thousands of cases of disputed identity, including criminal, paternity, immigration, and other proceedings. It is a versatile technology that can help to implicate or clear a criminal suspect, distinguish serial from copycat crimes, resolve parentage disputes, identify remains, and help parents locate missing children. This article will focus on its use in criminal cases and will address the principal issues that have been raised about its reliability, its impact on the legal system, its threat to privacy, and its regulation.

In theory, we could identify people with absolute certainty by examining their entire genetic sequence, or genome, since each person's genome is unique. But because the genome is spread over forty-six chromosomes, each containing millions of smaller molecules, this is not a practical procedure. DNA identification became feasible with the discovery of small regions of DNA, or loci, that vary from person to person in length and in other respects. Using standard techniques of molecular genetics, investigators can compare these variable loci in DNA taken from different sources. But since the range of possible variants, or alleles, found at any given locus is relatively small, it is necessary to compare several loci to make an accurate identification.

◆ DNA
[deoxyribonucleic acid]
any of various nucleic acids that are usually the molecular basis of heredity and are constructed of a double helix held together by hydrogen bonds.

Consider a case in which a semen stain is found on the clothing of a rape victim. Through DNA typing, investigators can ascertain whether the stain may have come from the suspect by comparing DNA from his blood with DNA extracted from the stain. The failure to obtain a match excludes the suspect as a source of

BAR-CODING DNA

DNA typing involves comparing small portions of DNA—e.g., from a child and an alleged father—and determining whether they match.

the semen; the discovery of a match includes the suspect in a subpopulation of potential sources. The more loci at which matches are obtained, the smaller this subpopulation will be, and thus the smaller the probability that someone besides the suspect contributed the semen.

Admissibility and evidential weight

The controversy over the admissibility of DNA typing has focused in part on the *criteria for declaring a match.* The standard way to measure the length of DNA segments is to measure the extent of their "migration" down an electronically charged gel. But a wide range of field and laboratory conditions may cause fragments of equal length to migrate at different rates—a phenomenon known as band-shifting. And even without band-shifting, there is room for error and bias in comparing DNA segments. These problems have been partially resolved, however, by standardizing match criteria, developing controls for band-shifting, and adopting new typing technologies that do not use electrophoresis.

A second focus of controversy involves the *statistical interpretation of a match.* In calculating the probability that someone other than the suspect was the source of the semen, we need to know the frequency of the matched alleles in the population of potential offenders. At present, geneticists sharply disagree about the extent to which allele frequencies differ among subgroups in the population. If there are significant differences, it becomes a matter of some importance how we define the class of alternative offenders. If a criminal suspect is Dominican, should the statistical interpretation of a match be based on the frequency of the matching alleles among white males, Hispanic males, or Dominican males? If the suspect in a Harlem assault case is white, should the class of alternative offenders be white males, black males, male Harlem residents, or some other subpopulation? Should the resolution of such questions depend on the evidence in the specific case, or should there be a general rule?

In 1992, the National Research Council issued a report that called for using the highest allele frequency for any population subgroup if there were any significant differences among groups. Under this ceiling principle, the probability that someone besides the suspect in the rape case contributed the semen stain would be assessed using the frequency for the subgroup in which the matched alleles were most common, even if there were no reason to think that someone from that subgroup was involved in the incident. This proposal remains controversial—seen by some forensic scientists as excessively conservative, and by some population geneticists as excessively speculative.

Proper testing procedures are no less critical to the accuracy of DNA typing evidence than are valid statistical inferences. Sample-switching and contamination may be at least as significant a source of error as misjudgments about band matches and allele frequency. Blind tests of the laboratories that perform DNA typing have not been totally reassuring; they highlight the need for regular proficiency testing and quality control.

Even if DNA typing is reliably performed and analyzed, some critics are concerned that juries and judges will exaggerate its relevance or misunderstand its significance. For example, a finding that the suspect was the source of semen on the victim's clothing will have only limited inculpatory value if the issue in the case is not identity but consent. Similarly, a finding that the suspect was not the source of the semen will have only limited exculpatory value if the victim had been gang-raped.

Social impact and regulation

Forensic DNA typing may have a significant effect not only in solving crimes, where its impact will be limited to cases where there are bodily residues, but also in fostering a healthy skepticism about other forms of identification evidence. The laboratories performing forensic DNA typing on suspects report exclusion rates of one-third or more; in some of these cases, the suspect had been implicated by an eyewitness or other conventional evidence. While exclusion does not always mean innocence, these findings suggest a high rate of error, and they may increase the sensitivity of law enforcement officials to the risk of mistaken accusations. The attention given to DNA typing may also promote the more frequent and careful utilization of other forensic evidence, which should further enhance the accuracy of criminal adjudication.

The threat to privacy from DNA typing arises from two sources: the ease with which DNA can be obtained and the amount of data it can yield. Usable DNA can be extracted not just from blood and semen (which may be taken only with probable cause and a court order) but also from trace amounts of tissue and saliva. The courts have yet to decide what constraints should govern the "seizure" of such material, or whether people have constitutionally protected privacy interests in such material once it leaves their bodies.

Furthermore, DNA data banks are being developed that will facilitate the broader investigative use of DNA profiles. By 1992, more than a dozen states required DNA samples from all convicted sexual or violent felony offenders. In the future, such data banks may be augmented by other types of information, such as fingerprints, criminal records, and behavioral profiles, and by DNA from other groups, such as military personnel and employees in positions requiring security clearance.

"This [double helix] structure has novel features which are of considerable biological interest. . . . "

JAMES WATSON AND FRANCIS CRICK
MOLECULAR STRUCTURE OF NUCLEIC ACIDS, 1953

"It has not escaped our notice that the specific pairing we have postulated immediately suggests a possible copying mechanism for the genetic material."

JAMES WATSON AND FRANCIS CRICK
MOLECULAR STRUCTURE OF NUCLEIC ACIDS, 1953

It may soon be technically possible to screen a large portion of the population for involvement in any crime where testable body residues are found.

The DNA molecule itself is becoming an increasingly rich source of personal information. Thousands of medical conditions have already been mapped to specific regions of the genome, and genetic markers are likely to be found for many physical traits and psychiatric conditions. While most of the loci used in typing do not appear to have functional significance, the mapping of the human genome may place some of these loci in close proximity to the genes associated with significant traits. Access to personal data could be limited by storing only DNA profiles, but there are reasons for preserving the DNA itself—for example, to allow reanalysis by an independent laboratory or with a new technique. While it is important to develop safeguards to prevent abuse with respect to DNA data banks, it is first necessary to determine what constitutes abuse.

Much of the debate over the acceptance of forensic DNA typing concerns the issue of who should make that determination. Scientists do not want the fate of new technologies to depend on the findings of judges and juries or the vagaries of adversarial justice; lawyers are reluctant to entrust the review of these technologies to scientists, whom they regard as insensitive to values besides accuracy and as inclined to exaggerate the precision of techniques resting on fallible judgment. There has been a promising attempt to bridge the divide between these two cultures in the creation of special panels of scientists and lawyers, most notably the National Research Council's commission on forensic DNA typing. Though these panels have sometimes divided on the very conflicts they were created to resolve, they may serve as prototypes for the cautious reception of other powerful but risky technologies.

— DAVID WASSERMAN

◆ **DNA fingerprinting**
a method of identification (as for forensic purposes) by determining the sequence of base pairs in the DNA, especially of a person

See Also

DNA Banks: Prepare to Register

EMOTIONS

The place of emotions in morality

In bioethics, as in ethics more generally, there is much debate about the significance of emotions in an account of moral character. Intuitively speaking, emotions are important because as moral beings we care not only about how we act but also about how we feel—what our moods are, as well as our attitudes and affects. Within the practice of health care, the emotions of compassion and empathy seem to have a particularly important place in a full description of decent and ethical treatment of a patient. The general point is not that emotion is internal and action external, for both action and emotion have exterior moments that point to deeper interior states, commonly thought of as character. Rather, emotions are important as modes of sensitivity that record what is morally salient and that then communicate those concerns to self and others. Thus, to grieve, pity, show empathy, or love is to focus on an aspect of self or other and to grasp information to which purer cognition or thought may not have access. Additionally, it is to express those concerns in a way that more bland or affectless action fails to do. Thus, emotion is distinct from both thought and action. More specifically, emotions are sensitive to particular kinds of salience. In the case of grief, what is salient is that humans suffer and face loss; in the case of pity, that they sometimes fail through blameless ignorance, duress, sickness, or accident; in the case of empathy, that they need the expressed support and union of others who can understand and identify with them; in the case of love, that they find certain individuals attractive and worthy of their time and attention.

In relations where caring for others is definitive, emotional sensitivity has an important place. In choosing a physician, for example, we tend to value medical skill and ability, but also character and judgment. And part of what we look for in character and judgment is not only reliable and principled action but also a certain range of emotional responsiveness. Medical care ministered without human gesture may not be received in the same way as that conveyed with compassion and empathy. While in some cases emotional tone is neither here nor there—urgency requires other priorities—in other cases, it matters deeply. A physician's sensitivity to a patient's needs, worries, and fears may be relevant to diagnosis and treatment, just as the physician's communication of emotions may be relevant to how a patient confronts illness and recovery. As in any relationship, emotional interaction is part of the exchange. In more intimate friendships, we hope that loved ones will be able to respond to our joy and suffering in more than merely intellectual ways, and will communicate feelings through spontaneous affect and gesture as well as more deliberate action.

"The heart has its reasons which reason does not know."

BLAISE PASCAL
PENSÉES, 1670

The inclusion of emotions as part of what is ethically important faces notorious problems, however. In a familiar series of objections, often embodied in a traditional reading of Immanuel Kant, emotions are viewed as the enemy of both reason and morality. First, there is the problem of partiality: Emotions may respond to what is morally salient, but in a very partial and selective way; for instance, emotions can be unresponsive to more circumspect judgment. In addition, there is the alleged unreliability of emotions; they sometimes emerge on the scene strong and impetuous,

AFTER EARTHQUAKE

Grieving relatives comfort one another, together in sympathy and compassion—emotions that many ethicists find inseparable from moral behavior.

only to peter out into a whimper. They cannot be relied on as motives, and nature and nurture cannot be counted on to distribute emotions evenly in all persons. For these sorts of reasons, emotions are sometimes thought to be an unreliable foundation for virtue. Furthermore, as passions (states that we undergo and suffer; from the Greek *paschein*, to be affected or suffer), emotions come to be construed as involuntary happenings that we endure with little intervention or consent. They come over us like the weather. Unlike action or belief, they appear to be exempt from direct willing. We cannot will to feel in the same way we can will to believe or will to act. Finally, emotions are typically attached to objects and events that are beyond our control. Through emotions, we invest importance in what we cannot control or master or make permanent: loved ones die, friends turn on us, attachment to status and security come undone by sickness and old age. When caregivers experience the death of patients to whom they feel especially attached, fear of loss can generate fear of attachment in future cases. Often emotions are investments in what is impermanent, and thus investments that make us vulnerable to loss.

"The emotions may be endless. The more we express them, the more we may have to express."

E. M. FORSTER
NOTES ON THE ENGLISH CHARACTER, 1936

These are familiar objections well entrenched in the literature. But increasingly they are being countered by philosophers of various stripes (Williams, 1973; Blum, 1980; Sherman, 1989; Nussbaum, 1990), including contemporary expositors of Kant (Herman, 1985). Against the various objections, it can be argued that emotions may sometimes show irrationality, perhaps of a more stubborn sort than beliefs; but even so, as is clear in the Aristotelian tradition, emotions have firm cognitive foundations. That emotions are sometimes irrational is not incompatible with the more basic fact that they seem to rest on appraisals or evaluations of situations that involve cognition. Again, through the emotions, we sometimes attend to situations in a partial and uneven way that does not always befit more universal principle and duty. Where partiality involves inappropriate emotions of bias and parochialism, then, like prejudiced beliefs, these emotions need to be controlled or transformed. But sometimes partiality is permissible and even encouraged. Contemporary Kantian views, for example, emphasize that the positive duty of beneficence must always be carried out by humans who by their nature are finite and subject to limitations of time and resources. Deliberation about the particulars, for example, of whom to help and when and where, must rely materially on emotions and the information they provide us about urgency and moral salience. Here, as suggested above, the report of the emotions may not be final or decisive. But it is an important way to begin to mark a moral occasion. In medical decisions, similar sorts of judgments about the particulars of the case may rely on initial readings of need and urgency conveyed through emotional sensitivity.

Taking up the next objection, certain emotions may be involuntary, being more similar to compulsion and physical disease than to intention. And these may warrant pardon or pity. But emotions are varied and complex phenomena. Passivity need not imply involuntarism. Indeed, many emotions involve their own kind of assent and susceptibility to regulation, even though control and transformation are part of a slow and imperfect process. Though individuals typically cannot will to feel certain emotions at a moment's notice, they can choose to cultivate certain emotional dispositions over time as a significant part of developing moral character.

The vulnerability of the emotional life to contingent events and objects—to the vicissitudes of accident and loss—is a more complex matter. Traditional Kantians do not worry about the contingent aspects of the moral life, viewing them as problems for happiness and not morality. That is, the fulfillments and satisfactions of desire and emotional investment affect one's chances for happiness, not the goodness of one's moral will. More contemporary Kantians, who take emotions to be helpful and important allies to duty, hold that duty must still be on guard as regulator of emotion. Thus, where depression or anger stands in the way of professional or moral requirements to help, duty stands ready to fill the void and in all cases remains the only morally worthy motive.

For the Aristotelian, in contrast, moral motives are partially constituted by emotions, and goodness as well as happiness can be irreversibly affected by the state of one's emotions. There is no separate source of motive, such as Kant's pure practical reason, from which morality issues. Tragic loss can deprive one of happiness, and also of goodness, as in the case of Medea's evil pawning of her own children because of her jealous rage against Jason.

What are emotions?

We have talked in a general way about reasons for including emotions in an account of morality. But what are emotions? What kind of account can we give of them? There are a number of possibilities that it is important to review.

WHAT IS AN EMOTION?

Four Views

1. a sensation we feel when we are in a physical state (David Hume)
2. an awareness of bodily changes in the peripheral nervous system (William James)

3. felt action tendencies (Arnold), or in psychoanalytic terms, discharge impulses
4. thought-dependent and constituted by appraisals (Aristotle)

The first is the commonsense view in which emotion is thought to be an irreducible quality of feeling or sensation. It may be caused by a physical state, but the emotion itself is the sensation we feel when we are in that state. It is a felt affect, a distinctive feeling, but not something dependent upon thought content or appraisal of a situation. This is roughly David Hume's view, 1739. The view quickly falters, however, when we realize that in this view emotions become no more than private states and feel like itches and tickles that have little to do with what the emotions are about and how one construes or represents those states of affairs.

A second view, associated with William James (James and Gurney, 1884) and Carl Lange, is that emotions are an awareness of bodily changes in the peripheral nervous system. We are afraid because we tremble or flee, not the other way around; angry because of the knots in our stomachs. The view, though rather counterintuitive, nonetheless captures the idea that emotions, more than other mental states, seem to have conspicuous physiological and kinesthetic components. These often dominate children's and adults' reports of their emotional experiences. They dominate literary accounts as well. Consider in this vein the lines of the Greek poet Sappho, composed about 600 B.C.E.:

> When I see you, my voice fails,
> my tongue is paralyzed,
> a fiery fever runs through my whole body
> my eyes are swimming,
> and can see nothing
> my ears are filled with a throbbing din
> I am shivering all over . . .

Literary history, social convention, and perhaps evolution conspire to tell us this is love. But even here it is not hard to imagine that what is described could be dread or awe or, perhaps, mystical inspiration. Even well-honed physiological feelings do not easily identify specific emotions. An awareness of our skin tingling or our chest constricting or our readiness to flee or fight does not specify exactly what emotion we are feeling. Many distinct emotions share these features, and without contextual clues and thoughts that focus on those clues, we are in the dark about what we are experiencing (Schacter and Singer, 1962). The chief burden of the work of Walter Cannon (1929) was to show that emotional affects are virtually identical across manifestly different states.

A third view with some kinship to the James-Lange view holds that emotions are felt action tendencies (Arnold, 1960). They are modes of readiness to act or, in the different idiom of psychoanalysis, discharge impulses. Support for this view comes from the fact that we tend to describe emotions in terms of dispositions to concrete behavior: "I felt like hitting him," "I could have exploded," "I wanted to spit," "I wanted to be alone with him, wrapped in his embrace." Yet, the action tendency view seems at best a partial account of emotion. The basic issue here is not that some emotions, such as apathy, inhibition, and depression, seem to lack activation modes while others are more a matter of the rich movement of thought so well depicted, for example, in Henry James's novels. It is, rather, that emotions are about something (internal or external) that we represent in thought. As such they have propositional or cognitive content. They are identified by that content, by what we dwell on, whether fleetingly or with concentrated attention.

This takes us to the fourth and final view of the emotions, which is, in some respects, the most plausible approach. This is the view that emotions are thought-dependent and are constituted by appraisals. (It is the view that Aristotle develops in the *Rhetoric*.) Such an account need not exclude other features of emotion, such as awareness of physiological and behavioral responses or felt sensations. But these, when present, are dependent on the appraisals of circumstances that capture what the emotion is about. Moreover, it is compatible with this view that emotions have neuropsychological structures that can be investigated by science.

More precisely, the appraisal is a belief about or evaluation of the goodness or badness of some perceived or imagined event. Anger requires an evaluation that one has been unjustly slighted by another; fear, that there is present harm or danger; grief, that something valuable has been lost; love, that one values a person as supremely important in one's life. Typically, the evaluation is experienced with pleasure or pain. In some cases the emotion includes a reactive desire not unlike what was referred to earlier as an action tendency. "Anger," Aristotle says, "is a desire (*orexis*) accompanied by pain toward the revenge of what one regards as a slight toward oneself or one's friends that is unwarranted" (*Rhetoric*, 1378a 30-32).

An account of the emotions needs to include evaluations that are weaker than strict belief (Greenspan, 1988). Many of the thoughts that ground emotions are not judgments to which we would give assent but are thoughts, perceptions, imaginings, construals, and fantasies that we nonetheless dwell on in a compelling way without concern about "objective truth." In these cases, there may be a certain laxity in the standards of evidence, or a partiality in what an agent takes to be relevant. There are familiar sorts of examples that illustrate

> *"Seeing's believing, but feeling's the truth."*
>
> THOMAS FULLER, M.D.
> GNOMOLOGIA, 1732

> *"He who cannot give anything away cannot feel anything, either."*
>
> FRIEDRICH NIETZSCHE
> THE WILL TO POWER, 1888

the point. I may fear spiders even though I know that most spiders I am likely to encounter are harmless; or Clarissa may know that Joe is a no-good lover for her but still finds her heart yearning for him. In these cases emotions have thought contents or appraisals, though ones that are at odds with more circumspect judgment. They are mental states that seem to lag behind what we are ready to grasp by belief. The Aristotelian notion of *phantasia*, the capacity by which things appear to us or are seen interpretatively, is helpful here. So, too, is Ludwig Wittgenstein's notion of "seeing as." These notions make clear that emotions are not blind urges but thought-dependent responses that nevertheless can be irrational. Their recalcitrance to reason may reveal, on the one hand, that they are in need of tutoring or at least of the slow healing of time; it may also reveal, on the other hand, a clear view of what we really care about or fear, however irrational that reaction may be and whatever our more public beliefs or postures.

"Perhaps I know best why it is man alone who laughs; he alone suffers so deeply that he had to invent laughter."

FRIEDRICH NIETZSCHE
IN THE PORTABLE CURMUDGEON, 1987

The notion of objectless emotions is sometimes presented as a counterexample to a thought-dependent account, according to which emotions are perceived to have an object. It is true that emotions such as depression seem to be about nothing in particular. The world just goes sour, infecting everything with its bile, without any direct focus. But even here, though the evaluation is indefinite, it still is about something—that something may harm one or in some way disappoint, even if one cannot specify the object. Further specification may simply await reflection, including deep reflection that may unmask what has long been repressed or forgotten.

Another element to review is the pleasant and painful feelings that are a part of emotions. As has been said, pleasure or pain is directed at evaluation. But some emotions have only a slight affective feel. In such cases, there is only a faint stirring in the heart and only mild disquiet of a pleasurable or painful sort. So, for example, a patient reflecting on his or her illness may have fears that all may not turn out well, even though he or she never feels any strong or noticeable tension when focusing on that thought. The thought has a clear negative value. But the person does not feel it with the sort of intensity characteristic of episodes of fear experienced before. Accordingly, a plausible account of the emotions must allow for variations in intensity of felt affect of this sort. There is no one strength that all emotions must have to qualify. Some are more intense, others are more subdued.

"Every person's feelings have a front-door and a side-door by which they may be entered."

OLIVER WENDELL HOLMES, SR.
THE AUTOCRAT OF THE BREAKFAST TABLE, 1858

The felt affect of emotion may be a mixture of both pleasure and pain. According to Aristotle, anger involves felt pain at perceived injury but also the pleasure that comes from focusing on the prospect of revenge or reparation. In its simplest moments love can be bittersweet, infused with the giddy pleasure of vertiginous romance and the pain of vulnerability. A single emotion may thus have different "feels" in subtle mixtures. Even a "flash" of emotion may switch from one affective pole to another. Specific emotions may best be thought of as complex phenomena made up of an array of component emotions with felt affects that vary across them.

It is also important to examine the motivational aspect of emotion. In what sense is an emotion a desire to act? In what sense does emotion involve a reason or motive for action? Again, recognition of the diversity and variety of emotions is crucial here. Some emotions, such as calmness, confidence, and equanimity, do not in an obvious way involve a desire for action. In contrast, anger often involves a desire for revenge, just as envy seems to involve a desire to thwart others from having various goods. These sorts of desires can go on to constitute a motive or reason for full-fledged action, although often we train ourselves not to act and not to take all our impulses and desires as a motive for action. In some cases, we act out our emotions only in our minds, as when, out of anger, we slay the old bugger in our fantasy life. Here there are certainly impulses and urgings, but they are not taken up as reasons for action.

At yet other times we do externally act out our emotions, but in a way that still seems to fall short of that emotion constituting a full-fledged reason or motive for action. In anger, we sometimes act impulsively, slamming the door and storming out of the room. It is a venting, a way of letting out tension, not a strategy for sweet revenge. Defiling a photograph of an ex-lover comes closer to the mark, for here at least there is a symbolic aim. But still, these cases of anger do not really aim at effective revenge. They are more reactive than purposive. And yet, they seem to be voluntary. They are certainly not the involuntary responses of the viscera. In stroking a patient's brow or tousling a child's hair, emotion motivates the action. These two actions are likely done out of compassion and affection. But it seems strained, at least in some of the cases cited, to say that one does these actions in order to show compassion or affection—which is the common pattern a demand for reasons often takes. The gesture just expresses compassion or affection. The explanation stops there. It is not like drinking in order to slake thirst, where drinking strategically promotes that end (Hursthouse, 1991).

Still other cases of emotional motivation might seem more like acting on emotion than acting out of emotion, and in this sense might more fully constitute a case of taking up the emotion as a reason for action. In such cases, there is often control and strategy, as the result of either deliberation or habituation or both. In the case of annoyance or disappointment, the felt desire to respond may be viewed as an opportunity for acting constructively in praiseworthy or socially adaptive ways. One works out ways of dealing with one's emotions—ways, as an agent, of responding to one's more impulsive urgings. Here the idea of a practical syllogism, as a schematizing reason for action, makes good sense. Desires such as those for revenge join with beliefs about how best to act on those desires. The conclusion is a reasoned decision. "Best" may have a moral flavor, but not necessarily; it may simply refer to some notion of what is efficient or effective. One may act on one's anger in ways that deflect it, or in ways that sweeten and deepen it. The point now is that one responds with some deliberateness. One creates an agenda of what to do when in the grip of an emotion. One becomes a practical agent who can exercise a certain amount of choice about how to act on emotions, and how in general to stand toward them. When we stand well toward our emotions, Aristotle would claim, we express virtue.

In this section, we have seen that a thought-dependent account of emotion typically has three components: an appraisal, feelings of pleasure and pain, and a desire for action. We can now turn to further consideration about how we stand well toward our emotions. More specifically, how do we exercise agency in the shaping and cultivation of emotions? In what sense are we agents, not merely with regard to action but also with regard to the experiencing of emotions over a lifetime?

Control and responsibility

One way of posing this question is to ask, To what degree can we be held responsible for our emotions? In what sense are they within our control? Emotions are often sources of excuses for the actions they explain. Remarks such as "I couldn't help it, I was fuming with anger" and "Ignore his actions, he was overcome with passion" focus on emotions as largely involuntary responses. But emotions are a heterogeneous breed. Some occurrences or episodes of emotion, but by no means all, may be involuntary. Setting out to cultivate certain kinds of emotional dispositions is often something within our control, even if a given display falls short because of compulsion or weakness. Aristotle is helpful here. Both action and emotion, he holds, are subject to choice in that we choose to develop a state of character that stabilizes certain dispositions to action and emotion. In this sense, how we feel (and act) may be less a matter of choice at the moment than a product of choice over time. In the case of emotion, especially, there are few shortcuts. For unlike action, emotion does not seem to engage choice (or will) in each episode. At a given moment, we may simply not be able to will to feel a certain way even though we can will to act in a given way. Cultivation of appropriate ways of standing toward our emotions, that is, of dispositions or character states, is our best preparation for those moments.

Both upbringing and genetic inheritance—nurture and nature—have profound effects on how these dispositions are cultivated. But an individual's own contribution, which will vary from one stage to another, is no less important. Also, how a person develops the capacity to respond emotionally will depend in no small measure on the kind and quality of his or her most important relationships and the attachments that are formed.

But more specifically, how do character states involving emotions come to be habituated and controlled? How do we refine emotional states, and make them more discriminating and less impulsive? How do they come to be organized into stable states that can be relied upon for moral motivation?

Common parlance includes many expressions that presume emotions are "up to us" in various ways. We exhort ourselves and others by such phrases as "pull yourself together," "snap out of it," "put on a good face," "lighten up," "be cheerful," "think positive," "keep a stiff upper lip." In many of these cases, we are being implored to assume the semblance of an emotion so that it can "take hold" and rub off on our inner state. Practice as if you believe, and you will believe. As Ronald de Sousa puts it, "Earnest pretense is the royal road to sincere faith" (de Sousa, 1988, p. 324). Sometimes we "pretend" through behavioral changes—changes in facial expressions, body gestures, and vocalizations that evoke in us a changed mood. If we are fuming, relaxing our facial muscles, ungnarling our fingers, breathing deeply and slowly may put us in the frame of mind to see things in a calmer light. We try to inhibit the present emotion by inhibiting the physiognomic or physiological responses that typically accompany it. Conversely, we can fuel the flames of an emotion by allowing it bodily expression. To weep may intensify our grief, or simply bring us to acknowledge its presence. The James-Lange theory may be in the background here, with its notion of proprioceptive feedback from expression. Sometimes it is a matter of shaping an emotional state from outside in—trying on broader smiles as a way of trying to become more loving. By the same token, a newly felt affect may demand a new look, a concrete and stable realization for oneself and others to behold. Here the nudging works from inside out, though it is still the facial or gestural expression that is aimed at coaching the emotion. There are other sorts of actions one might take that are not a matter of body language or putting on a new face. One may try to talk oneself out of love, but discover that only when one changes locales do the old ways begin to lose their grip. Other times, it is more trial by fire: staying

"The old universal truths lacking which any story is ephemeral and doomed—love and honor and pity and pride and compassion and sacrifice."

WILLIAM FAULKNER
NOBEL PRIZE ACCEPTANCE SPEECH, 1950

put and exposing oneself to what is painful in order to become inured. The process involves desensitization.

There are other methods of effecting emotional change that depend upon "depth" psychology. In psychoanalysis, the recapitulation of patterns of emotional response through transference onto an analyst is intended to be a way of seeing at a detached level. The patient relives an emotional experience at the same time he or she watches and interprets it. This is the putative advantage of an empathic, clinical setting: A patient can come to see an emotional pattern in a detached way, free from judgment and accusation, and the crippling emotions that are often involved. In some cases, a patient tries to relieve the pain of present disabling emotions, such as anger, anxiety, or shame, by coming to see their roots in primitive conflicts and frustrations that may have long been repressed. The goal is not to remove the patient from the vulnerabilities of emotion but to make possible a way of experiencing emotions, including shame and anger, that is less crippling and self-destructive.

It is important to grasp the moral dimensions of psychoanalytic therapy, even though these are often not emphasized and are even thought to be at odds with the notion of the clinical hour as a haven from moral judgment. At the most basic level, therapy is a form of deep self-knowledge about emotions and their role in one's life. But it is not merely self-knowledge. On the Socratic model, it is self-knowledge that leads to character change. Depth psychology is meant to be a way of transforming the emotions. To the extent that virtuous character is a way of standing well toward the emotions, psychoanalytic therapy becomes one way of engaging in this process of emotional transformation. Therapy, in general, as a way of taking charge of one's self, including one's emotional self, has an important role in moral development.

WHEN MOOD-RAISING IS MIND OVER MATTER

Sometimes changing one's mood may be more a matter of mental or perceptual strategy than facial or gestural alteration or action. It may be a matter of bringing oneself to focus on different objects and thoughts. One tries to see things under a new gestalt or to recompose the scene. Exhortation and persuasion play an important role here. A patient depressed by the possibility of relapse might be reminded of the favorable statistics and the steady progress he or she has made to date. Seeing things in a new light, with new emphases and stresses, helps to allay the fear. In a different vein, anger at a child may subside when one focuses less on minor annoyances and more on admirable traits. One may work on a more forgiving attitude in general by choosing to downplay others' perceived faults or foibles. In certain cases, experiencing emotions is a matter of giving inner assent—of allowing oneself to feel angry or giving the green light to a new interest or love. It is as if something grabs hold, and then it is one's turn to have some influence.

Mental training can of course follow a more methodical and introspective model. An individual can learn to take more careful note of the onset of certain emotions and the movement of mind from one perceived object of importance to another. He or she can label the kind of mood or emotional experience that is occurring and note how it disposes him or her to others, even when the emotional experience is only a transient flash. He or she can watch how emotions begin to accelerate to clingy attachments or dependencies, and try to disengage from those cravings. What is cultivated is a watchful mindfulness, an intensification of consciousness such that through awareness and knowledge, he or she comes to be more in charge.

— NYANOPONIKA

> *"Not everyone who understands his own mind understands his heart."*
>
> LA ROCHEFOUCAULD
> MAXIMS, 1665

More radical extirpation or removal of emotions

Because emotions are valued as modes of attention, motivation, communication, and knowledge, we tend to put up with their messiness while attempting their reform. But there are venerable traditions in which moderating through transformation and education is viewed as an inadequate therapy and an inadequate way of training moral character and agency. The Stoic view, which influenced later Kantian views and bears rough similarities to certain Eastern traditions, argues that the surges and delusions of emotions warrant their extirpation. Investment in objects and events we cannot control is the source of our suffering, and modification of our beliefs about these values is the source of our cure. In Stoic theory, according to Chrysippus and Zeno, as well as to such later Roman writers as Cicero and Seneca, virtue comes to be rooted in reason alone, for it is reason that is most appropriate to our nature and is under our true dominion. Since this line of argument has had a powerful influence on the history of moral thought, we would do well briefly to review it.

According to Stoic doctrine, emotion is judgment. It is a cognitive assent, an embracing or a commitment to a presentation, typically expressed linguistically,

through a proposition. However, for the Stoics, emotions become by definition defective and in error. They are vicious and faulty states of character in need of extirpation if the equanimity of virtuous living is to prevail. Extirpation works on the assumption that emotions can be treated by radical changes of belief through persuasion and philosophical enlightenment. For if emotions are no more than false beliefs, then they should be treatable by a method that works essentially at the level of belief. Persuasion and argument should be able to grab hold of those beliefs entirely—without remainder. Accordingly, the Stoics propose philosophy as itself a spiritual therapy that cures the diseases or passions of the soul. Its practice involves a thoroughgoing denial of judgments to which voluntary but faulty assent was formerly given. Most fundamentally, what is required is to come to believe that what lies outside the self, and is external to one's true nature or reason, is not a proper object of importance. Attachments to wealth, fame, friends, health, noble birth, beauty, strength, and so on must be severed and these objects recognized as having no intrinsic value in morality or happiness. "The man who would fear losing any of these things cannot be happy. We want the happy man to be safe, impregnable, fenced and fortified, so that he is not just largely unafraid, but completely" (Cicero, 1945, V.40-41).

The attraction of the Stoic view rests in its powerful description of the anguish of the engaged emotional life. Many emotions (though not all) lead to attachment, but objects of attachment are never perfectly stable. Abandonment, separation, failure, and loss are the constant costs of love, effort, and friendship. The more tightly we cling to our investments, the more dependent we become upon what is uncontrolled and outside our own mastery. Self-reproach and self-persecution are often responses to lack of control. In our relations with others, the same clinginess of emotions can lead to overstepping what is appropriate, just as it can lead to exclusionary preferences and partialities. Provincialism can grow out of stubborn preference for what is familiar and comfortable according to class lines or other restrictive values.

This is a reasonable portrait of some moments of the life lived through emotion. Detachment and watchful awareness directed toward the emotions are important therapeutic stances in such a life. In addition, detach-

EMOTIONS IN THE MORAL LIFE

From everyday experience, we can begin to see the importance of emotions in the moral life. Emotions are valued as modes of attention, communication, motivation, and self-knowledge. Each of these modes is a way we express moral character. As modes of attention, they help us discern moral salience in ways that would not be accessible to the cold eye of reason. Such discernment is a crucial preparatory moment for moral judgment and choice. Using them as modes of communication, we interact with others and express our engagement and involvement in ways that go well beyond affectless or bland action. As modes of motivation, emotions involve desires or impulses that can come to constitute more deliberate reasons for action. As modes of self-knowledge, present emotions can be used to relive and awaken past emotions that have been repressed. By looking squarely at such emotions, we begin to relieve the pain involved in repression and self-deception. In all these ways, emotions become a resource for moral agency and an important part of moral character. They help to constitute a notion of moral character in which the capacities for self-knowledge and candid engagement with others become crucial.

We can also begin to see that emotions will play an expanded role within bioethics and within the moral practices of health-care professionals. Emotional sensitivity will be important for discerning the complexity of situations, and for appreciating the competing needs and interests of various parties. A simple matter of noticing a patient's distress or displeasure, perhaps by attending to his or her facial expressions and bodily gestures, could figure importantly in assessing a case. But by the same token, it is important to communicate one's own emotions and not just record those of others. Conveying compassion to a patient can be a significant part of therapeutic treatment, and in general an important part of establishing a relationship in which medical counsel can be trusted and followed. Again, emotions figure in deliberation of choices. Compassion toward a patient can ground a reason for telling a patient the truth of his or her condition in a tone that respects the patient's fragile emotional state. The relevant choice a caretaker faces may not be whether to withhold the truth but how to tell the truth in a way that respects a patient's autonomy and feelings. It is here that a health-care provider's own feelings of compassion and sympathy can importantly ground the specific choices he or she makes. Finally, a health-care provider, as a morally responsible agent, needs to have ready access to his or her own emotions, so that emotions help rather than hinder effective care. Where, for example, fears and prejudice cloud more circumspect judgment, the health-care provider must recognize these as emotional impediments to delivering quality care. In general, a reflective stance toward one's own emotions becomes an important part of caring for others.

— NANCY SHERMAN

"There is a point beyond which good and bad fortune are too much for our emotions."

LA ROCHEFOUCAULD
MAXIMS, 1665

"From winter, plague and pestilence, good Lord deliver us!"

THOMAS NASH
SUMMER'S LAST WILL AND TESTAMENT, 1600

ment and watchful awareness should be directed toward reason itself and its own tendencies toward egoism and imperious control. This is clearly at odds with Stoic practice and more in line with Eastern practices such as Buddhism. But it is difficult to see how a thoroughgoing rejection of the emotions can be compatible with what is a human life. Emotions, for all their selectivity, intensity, and stirring, enable us, through those very vulnerabilities, to attend, see, know, and experience in a way that pure cognition cannot. Some of that way of knowing and being known anguishes beyond words. Poetry and literature can only begin to express the reality. But even if at times unruled by reason's measure, emotion must not, on that account, be an outlawed feature of human life. Nor must it be an outlawed feature of morality. How we care for others and what we notice and reveal both depend greatly on the subtlety, fineness, and often deep truth of our emotional readings of the world.

— NANCY SHERMAN

EPIDEMICS

Epidemics may be defined as concentrated outbursts of infectious or noninfectious disease, often with unusually high mortality, affecting relatively large numbers of people within fairly narrow limits of time and space. They probably emerged in human populations with the "Neolithic Revolution," roughly eight to ten thousand years ago, as humans began to domesticate animals, practice agriculture, and settle into towns and villages, with a corresponding increase in the density of population. This article will cover the history of epidemics with particular reference to their implications for bioethics, beginning with a survey of ancient and medieval times, moving on to responses to epidemics before the nineteenth century, then examining in more detail the impact of cholera and the bacteriological revolution. It will conclude with a discussion of the epidemiological transition and its aftermath, the emergence of new epidemics in the late twentieth century, and the ethical implications of the data surveyed. The focus will be mainly but not exclusively on Europe and North America, where historical source material is richest, and scholarly and scientific studies are most numerous.

Responses to epidemics before the nineteenth century

The ancient Greeks and Romans commonly, though not universally, believed that epidemics were brought into human communities from outside. Thucydides, for example, described the plague that struck Athens during the Peloponnesian War as having arrived by sea. This belief was the basis of official reactions to epidemics in medieval Europe. Following the closure of the port at Venice to all shipping for thirty days as the plague threatened in 1346, regulations imposed in Marseilles in 1384, and in other ports thereafter, prescribed the biblical period of isolation for a "quarantine" (forty days) outside the harbor for any ship thought to have called previously at a place infected with the plague. In 1423 the Venetians set up a hospital where plague victims were isolated, and by 1485 the city had a sanitary authority armed with wide-ranging powers during epidemics. In some epidemics, as in the Great Plague of London in 1665, victims were compulsorily isolated in their own houses, which were marked with a red cross to warn the healthy not to enter. Compulsory screening was not an issue before the late nineteenth century, however, because diseases were recognized as such only after the onset of obvious symptoms, and the concept of the asymptomatic carrier did not exist. In addition to these measures, the authorities in many medieval towns, working on the theory that epidemics were spread through the contamination of the atmosphere, ordered the fumigation of the streets to try to clear the air. Doctors and priests were expected to attend to the sick; and those who fled, as many did, are strongly criticized in the chronicles of these events.

Popular reactions to epidemics included not only flight from infected areas and evasion of public health measures, but also attacks on already marginalized and stigmatized minorities. As bubonic plague spread in Europe in 1348-1349, for example, rumors that the Jews were poisoning water supplies led to widespread pogroms. Over nine hundred Jews were massacred in the German city of Erfurt alone (Vasold, 1991). Such actions reflected a general feeling, reinforced by the church, that plagues were visited upon humankind by a wrathful Deity angered by immorality, irreligion, and the toleration of infidels. A prominent part in these persecutions was played by the flagellants, lay religious orders whose self-flagellating processions were intended to divert divine retribution from the rest of the population. Jews were scapegoated because they were not part of the Christian community. Drawing upon a lengthy tradition of Christian anti-Semitism, which blamed the Jews for the killing of Christ, the people of medieval Europe regarded Jews at such times as little better than the agents of Satan (Delumeau, 1990).

State, popular, religious, and medical responses such as these remained essentially constant well into the nineteenth century. The medical understanding of plague continued throughout this period to draw heavily on humoral theories, so that therapy centered on bloodletting and similar treatments designed to restore the humoral balance in the patient's body. They were of limited effectiveness in combating bubonic plague, which was spread by flea-infested rats. The isolation and hospitalization of victims also therefore did little to prevent the spread of plague. Nevertheless, the disease gradually retreated from western Europe, for reasons that are still imperfectly understood. The introduction of more effective quarantines with the emergence of the strong state in the seventeenth and eighteenth centuries was almost certainly one of these reasons, however, and helped prevent the recurrence of epidemics in the seventeenth and eighteenth centuries (Vasold, 1991).

State intervention also played a role in reducing the impact of smallpox, the other major killer disease of the age after bubonic plague. Its spread was first reduced by inoculation, before compulsory programs of cowpox vaccination brought about a dramatic reduction in the impact of the disease in nineteenth-century Europe. Despite the imperfections of these new methods, which sometimes included accidentally spreading the disease, vaccination programs in particular may be regarded as the first major achievement of the "medical policing" favored by eighteenth-century absolutist monarchies such as Prussia. Police methods that paid scant attention to the liberties of the subjects were used to combat the spread of epidemics. They included the use of troops to seal off infected districts, quarantines by land and sea, and the compulsory isolation of individual victims. Most of these measures had little effect, however, either because of lack of medical knowledge or because poor communications and lack of police and military manpower prevented them from being applied comprehensively (Rosen, 1974).

The impact of cholera

These theories and practices were brought into question above all by the arrival in Europe and North America of Asiatic cholera. The growth of the British Empire, especially in India, improved communications and trade, and facilitated the spread of cholera from its base in the Ganges delta to other parts of Asia and to the Middle East. Reaching Europe by the end of the 1820s, the disease was spread further by unsanitary and overcrowded living conditions in the rapidly growing towns and cities of the new industrial era. At particular moments of political conflict, above all in the European revolutions of 1830 and 1848, the Austro-Prussian War of 1866, and the Franco-Prussian War of 1870-1871, it was carried rapidly across the continent by troop movements and the mass flight of affected civilian populations (Evans, 1988).

Cholera epidemics affected the United States in 1832, 1849, and 1866, on each occasion arriving from Europe in the aftermath of a major conflict. State, popular, and medical responses in 1830-1832 were unchanged from earlier reactions to epidemics. Quarantine regulations were imposed, military cordons established, victims isolated, hospitals prepared. In Prussia, the breaching of such regulations was made punishable by death. But the opposition that such measures aroused among increasingly powerful industrial and trading interests, and the feeling among many liberals that the policing of disease involved unwar-

ANCIENT AND MEDIEVAL EPIDEMICS

Hippocratic texts indicate the presence of tuberculosis, malaria, and influenza in the population of ancient Greece, and the historian Thucydides provides the first full description of a major plague, the precise nature of which remains uncertain, in Athens (430-429 B.C.E.), in his history of the Peloponnesian War. The increase in trade brought about by the growth of the Roman Empire facilitated the transmission of disease, and there were massive epidemics in the Mediterranean (165-180 C.E. and 211-266 C.E.). The "plague of Justinian" (542-547 C.E.), which was said to have killed ten thousand people a day in Constantinople, is the first recorded appearance of bubonic plague (McNeill, 1979). In Europe and Asia, diseases such as measles and smallpox gradually became endemic, affecting virtually all parts of the population on a regular basis, with occasional epidemic outbursts. Periodic epidemics of bubonic plague continued, most seriously in the fourteenth century, when perhaps as much as one-third of Europe's population perished.

When Europeans arrived in the Americas, from 1492 on, they brought many of these diseases to native American populations for the first time, with devastating effects. The importation of African slaves introduced malaria and yellow fever by the seventeenth century (Kiple, 1984). The merging of the disease pools of the Old and New Worlds was completed by what appeared to be the transmission of syphilis to Europe from the Americas at the end of the fifteenth century, though the subject remains disputed by historians, some arguing that it was a recurrence or mutation of a disease that already existed on the Continent (Crosby, 1972).

— RICHARD J. EVANS

The belief that immorality is contagious often includes the belief that immorality causes disease.

PAGE 559

See Also

AIDS; Public Health and the Law

ranted interference with the liberty of the individual, forced the state to retreat from combating cholera by the time of the next epidemic, in the late 1840s. In addition, medical theories of contagion were brought into disrepute by the failure of quarantine and isolation to stop the spread of the disease in Europe. Until the 1880s, many doctors thought that cholera was caused by a "miasma" or vapor rising from the ground under certain climatic circumstances. It could be prevented by cleaning up the cities so as to prevent the source of infection from getting into the soil (Evans, 1987). This was a contributory factor in the spread of sanitary reform in Europe and the United States during this period. But its importance should not be overestimated. Boards of health established in American cities in the midst of the cholera epidemics of 1832 and 1849 were short-lived and of limited effectiveness, and even in 1866 the more determined official responses had less to do with the impact of cholera than with the changed political climate (Rosenberg, 1987).

"Sorrow and sadness sat upon every face; and though some parts were not yet overwhelmed, yet all looked deeply concerned."

DANIEL DEFOE
A JOURNAL OF THE PLAGUE YEAR, 1665
PUBLISHED 1722

The fact that cholera affected the poorest sectors of society most profoundly was the result above all of structural factors such as unsanitary and overcrowded living conditions, unhygienic water supplies, and ineffective methods of waste disposal. But state and public responses to epidemics in the nineteenth century, at least in the decades after the initial impact of cholera, were primarily voluntaristic. Religious and secular commentators blamed cholera on the alleged immorality, drunkenness, sexual excess, idleness, and lack of moral fiber of the victims. Fast days were held in eleven New England states in 1832, in the belief that piety would divert God's avenging hand. Once again, the socially marginal groups of industrial society, from vagrants and the unemployed to prostitutes and beggars—or, in the United States in 1866, the newly emancipated slaves and the newly arrived Irish immigrants—were blamed (Rosenberg, 1987).

SAFER INDOORS?
In a Madagascar village hit by pneumonic plague, two sisters and a child hope for safety indoors.

The rise of the medical profession, with well-regulated training and a code of ethics, ensured that doctors were more consistently active in treating victims of epidemics in the nineteenth century than they had been in previous times. Partly as a result, there were popular attacks on the medical profession in Europe during the epidemic of 1830-1832. Angry crowds accused doctors of poisoning the poor in order to be able to reduce the burden of support they imposed on the state or, in Britain, in order to provide fresh bodies for the anatomy schools (Durey, 1979). As late as 1892, doctors and state officials were being killed in cholera riots in Russia (Frieden, 1977). There were also disturbances in the United States, where a hospital was burned down in Pittsburgh and a quarantine hospital on Staten Island, in New York City, was destroyed by rioters fearing the spread of yellow fever. However, in most of Europe, public disturbances caused by epidemics had largely ceased by the middle of the nineteenth century. Fear of disorder was another reason for the state's withdrawal from policing measures (Evans, 1988). In Europe, too, religious responses to epidemics had become less important by the end of the century as religious observance declined. In 1892, however, as cholera once more threatened America's shores, it fed nativist prejudice and led to the introduction of harsh new restrictions on immigration.

The bacteriological revolution

Cholera was only the most dramatic of a number of infectious diseases that took advantage of urbanization, poor hygiene, overcrowding, and improved communications in the nineteenth century (Bardet et al., 1988). Typhus, typhoid, diphtheria, yellow fever, tuberculosis, malaria, and syphilis continued to have a major impact, and even smallpox returned on a large scale during the Franco-Prussian War of 1870-1871. Treatment continued to be ineffective. But the rapid development of microscope technology in the last quarter of the century enabled medical science to discover the causative agents of many infectious diseases in humans and animals. Building on the achievements of Louis Pasteur, Robert Koch identified the tubercle bacillus in 1882 and the cholera bacillus in 1884. These discoveries marked the triumph of bacteriology and completed the swing of medical opinion back from belief in "mias-

mas" as causes of epidemics toward a contagionist point of view.

From the 1880s, states once more imposed quarantine and isolation, backed by preventive disinfection. The greater effectiveness of state controls, compared with the earlier part of the century, was combined with the more precise focus on eliminating bacterial organisms. Once the role of victims' excretions in contaminating water supplies with the cholera bacillus became known, it was possible to take preventive action by ensuring hygienic water supplies and safe waste disposal. By the outbreak of World War I in 1914, the role of the human body louse in spreading typhus, and that of the mosquito in transmitting malaria and yellow fever, had been identified. Mosquito control programs were launched by the U.S. Army in Cuba following the Spanish-American War of 1898, and subsequently in the Panama Canal Zone, in order to reduce the incidence of yellow fever cases to an acceptable level. Regular delousing reduced typhus among armies on the western front in Europe during World War I. The Japanese army prevented casualties from typhoid and smallpox by a campaign of systematic vaccination during the war with Russia in 1904-1905 (McNeill, 1979; Cartwright, 1972).

The bacteriological revolution thus inaugurated an age of sharply increased state controls over the spread of disease. Laws were introduced in many countries making the reporting of infectious diseases compulsory. The growth of a comprehensive, state-backed system of medical care, working through medical officers, medical insurance plans, and the like, made comprehensive reporting easier. Hospital building programs in the second half of the nineteenth century facilitated the isolation of victims in hygienic conditions where they could be prevented from spreading the disease. The greater prestige of the medical profession in most industrialized countries by the late nineteenth and early twentieth century ensured that doctors were no longer attacked, and that the necessity of compulsory reporting and isolation was widely accepted by the public. However, a bacteriological understanding of disease causation also involved a narrowing of focus, in which increased emphasis was placed on the compulsory reporting of cases, followed by their isolation, at the expense of broader measures of public health and environmental improvement (Porter, 1993).

The epidemiological transition

Lower death rates from diseases such as cholera, typhoid, and tuberculosis were only partially the consequence of bacteriologically inspired state preventive measures, and the disease burden from acute infectious disease began to decline rapidly. The provision of clean, properly filtered water supplies and effective sewage systems reflected growing municipal pride and the middle-class desire for cleanliness. It made epidemics such as the outbreak of cholera that killed over eight thousand people in Hamburg, Germany, in little over six weeks in the autumn of 1892 increasingly rare. Just as important were improvements in personal hygiene, which again reflected general social trends as well as the growing "medicalization" of society in western Europe and the United States. Such developments reinforced the stigmatization of poor and oppressed minorities as carriers of infection, since they were now blamed for ignoring official exhortations to maintain high standards of cleanliness, even though their living conditions and personal circumstances frequently made it difficult for them to do so. Particular attention was focused on working-class women, who were held responsible by official and medical opinion for any lack of hygiene in the home (Evans, 1987).

The development of tuberculin by Koch in 1890 made possible the compulsory screening of populations even for asymptomatic tuberculosis. This was increasingly implemented after 1900, in conjunction with the forcible removal of carriers to sanatoria, although this was more effective in isolating people than in curing them. Educational measures also helped reduce the spread of the disease. The development and compulsory administration in many countries of a preventive vaccine against tuberculosis from the 1920s aroused resistance among the medical community, not least because by creating a positive tuberculin reaction in noncarriers, it made it impossible to detect those who truly had the disease, except where symptoms were obvious. These measures had some effect in reducing the impact of the disease. However, although the precise causes of the retreat of tuberculosis remain a matter of controversy among historians, the long-term decline of the disease from the middle of the nineteenth century was probably more the result of improvements in housing, hygiene, environmental sanitation, and living standards than of direct medical intervention. The introduction of antibiotics such as streptomycin after World War II proved effective in reducing to insignificant levels mortality from a disease that had been the most frequent cause of death or disability among Americans aged fifteen to forty-five (Dubos and Dubos, 1987).

Similarly, official responses to syphilis centered, especially in Europe, on the forcible confinement of prostitutes to state-licensed brothels or locked hospital wards, where they were subjected to compulsory medical examination. Before World War I, New York, California, and other states had introduced compulsory reporting of cases of venereal disease, and official concern for the health of U.S. troops led to the jailing of prostitutes. Measures such as these had no discernible

> *"Death was so always before their eyes, that they did not so much concern themselves for the loss of their friends, expecting that themselves should be summoned the next hour."*
>
> DANIEL DEFOE
> A JOURNAL OF THE PLAGUE YEAR, 1665
> PUBLISHED 1722

effect on infection rates, which rose sharply during the war. They also represented a serious restriction on the civil liberties of an already stigmatized group of women, while the men who were their customers, and equally active in the sexual transmission of disease, were regarded as irresponsible at worst, and were not subjected to similar measures. The development of Salvarsan (arsphenamine) by Paul Ehrlich in 1910 introduced the possibility of an effective treatment for syphilis. But here again there was resistance, both within the medical community and from outside, from those who considered that an increase in sexual promiscuity would be a result. This view became even more widespread following the use of penicillin on a large scale during World War II (Brandt, 1987).

"It could be said that the AIDS pandemic is a classic own-goal scored by the human race against itself."

PRINCESS ANNE
IN THE DAILY TELEGRAPH
U.K., 1988

Epidemics of the late twentieth century

In the West, epidemic infectious disease was regarded by the second half of the twentieth century as indicating an uncivilized state of mind, and was ascribed above all to nonwhite populations in parts of the world outside Europe and North America. This reflected structural inequalities in the world economy, as the great infections became increasingly concentrated in the poor countries of the Third World. By the middle of the twentieth century, however, rapidly increasing life expectancy was bringing rapid growth of noninfectious cardiac diseases, cancer, and other chronic conditions that posed new epidemic threats to an aging population in the affluent West. Under increasing pressure from the medical profession, the state responded not only with education initiatives but also with punitive measures directed toward habits, such as cigarette smoking, that were thought to make such conditions more likely. The arsenal of sanctions governments employed included punitive taxation on tobacco and the banning of smoking, under threat of fines and imprisonment, in a growing number of public places. Increasingly, institutions in the private sector also adopted these policies. They raised the question of how far state and nonstate institutions could go in forcing people to abandon pleasures that were demonstrably harmful to their own health. At the same time, they contrasted strongly with the reluctance of many states and companies to admit responsibility for cancer epidemics caused by factors such as nuclear weapons testing, the proximity of nuclear power stations to human populations, or the lack of proper precautions in dealing with radioactivity in industrial production.

Social disapproval or even indignation about a practice remains a potent ally of many public-health campaigns.

PAGE 559

In the 1980s, the identification of a new epidemic, known as acquired immune deficiency syndrome (AIDS), once more raised the ethical problems faced by state and society, and by the medical profession, in the past. Lack of medical knowledge of the syndrome and the danger of infection from contact with blood or other body fluids, posed the question of whether the medical profession had a duty to treat AIDS sufferers in the absence of any cure. The evidence of the overwhelming majority of past epidemics, for which there was also no known cure, seems to be, however, that medical treatment, even in the Middle Ages, could alleviate suffering under some circumstances, and was therefore a duty of the practitioner. In a condition that could prove rapidly fatal, the ethics of prolonged tests of a drug such as AZT, in which control groups were given placebos, was contested by AIDS sufferers anxious to try anything that might possibly cure the condition, or at least slow its progress.

If this was a relatively novel ethical problem, then the question of compulsory public-health measures was a very old one. Like the sufferers in many previous epidemics, AIDS victims tended to come from already stigmatized social groups: gays, drug abusers and prostitutes, Haitians and Africans. The ability to screen these high-risk groups for the presence of the causative agent, the HIV retrovirus, even at the asymptomatic stage, raised the possibility of compulsory screening measures, quarantine, and isolation. On the other hand, individuals publicly identified as HIV-positive generally found it difficult or impossible to stay employed, to obtain life or health insurance, or to avoid eviction from their homes. In the absence of adequate supportive measures, public-health intervention reinforces existing discrimination against these groups, as in many past epidemics.

An alternative state response has consisted of neglect, on the assumption that AIDS is unlikely to affect the heterosexual, non-drug-abusing, nonpromiscuous majority of the voting public. It is noticeable that, generally, politicians have invested resources in public education and other preventive measures only when they have believed that the majority population is at risk. These problems have been raised again by the recent resurgence of tuberculosis in Western countries, among the HIV-positive but also among the poor and the homeless. Drug-resistant strains of the disease are now common, and the transient, jobless, and destitute have neither the means nor the stability of life-style to complete the lengthy course of drugs that is necessary to effect a cure. The compulsory isolation of victims and their forcible subjection to a course of treatment is not a satisfactory long-term solution to the problem, since reinfection is likely upon release, unless the social and personal circumstances of the affected groups undergo a dramatic improvement.

Conclusion: Ethical implications

The history of epidemics suggests that society's responses have usually included scapegoating marginal and already stigmatized groups and the restriction of their civil rights. From the Jews massacred during the Black Death in medieval Europe, through the beggars and vagrants blamed for the spread of cholera in the nineteenth century, to the prostitutes arrested for allegedly infecting troops with syphilis during World War I, and the minorities whose life-styles were widely regarded as responsible for the spread of AIDS in the 1980s and 1990s, such groups have frequently been subjected to social ostracism and official hostility in times of epidemic disease. Frequently, though not invariably, they have been the very people who have suffered most severely from the disease they were accused of spreading. Doctors have sometimes been reluctant to treat them; the state has often responded with punitive measures.

At no time have public-health measures to combat epidemics been politically uncontested. Nineteenth-century feminists, for example, campaigned vigorously against the state's restriction of the civil liberties of prostitutes in the name of disease control. The fact that their male customers were left free to spread sexually transmitted diseases unhampered by the attentions of the state implied an official endorsement of different standards of morality for men and for women, and it was this major structural element of the social value system that the feminists were seeking to change. Without such change, not only was medical intervention ethically indefensible, but there would never be any likelihood of effective control of sexually transmitted diseases. Similarly, many nineteenth-century epidemics, such as cholera or tuberculosis, were spread by poor nutrition, overcrowded housing, and inadequate sanitation. Social reformers therefore regarded major improvements in these areas as more important than direct medical intervention through measures such as compulsory hospitalization.

Epidemics are frequently caused by social and political upheavals. In the past, movements of large masses of troops and civilians across Europe, from the Crusades to the Crimean War, brought epidemics in their wake. In the early 1990s, a major cholera epidemic broke out in Peru as the result of the flight of thousands of peasants from their mountain settlements, driven out by the pitiless armed conflict between the army and the "Shining Path" guerrillas, to the narrow coastal strip, where they lived in makeshift shantytowns with no sanitation. Economic crisis and the dismantling of welfare measures for the homeless, the mentally disturbed, and the destitute in many Western countries in the 1980s contributed to a massive increase in the transient population on the streets of the great cities. Discrimination against AIDS sufferers by landlords and employers has added to this problem. By the early 1990s there were an estimated ninety thousand homeless on the streets of New York City, half of whom were HIV-positive and several thousand of whom were suffering from tuberculosis. Any long-term solution to these epidemics must be more than merely medical, as must any explanation of their occurrence. Public-health measures are thus inevitably political in their implications, since they can be considered and administered only with reference to the wider social and cultural context within which the disease they seek to prevent or control has originated.

— RICHARD J. EVANS

ETHICS

TASK OF ETHICS

Ethics as a philosophical or theoretical discipline is concerned with tasks that concern ordinary, reflective individuals. Since its origins in classical and preclassical times, it has sought to understand how human beings should act and what kind of life is best for people. When Socrates and Plato dealt with such questions, they presupposed or at the very least hoped that they could be answered in "timeless" fashion, that is, with answers that were not dependent on the culture and circumstances of the answerer, but represented universally valid, rational conclusions.

In fact, however, the history of philosophical or theoretical ethics is intimately related to the ethical views and practices prevalent in various societies over the millennia. Although philosophers have usually

"The life which is unexamined is not worth living."

PLATO
THE SYMPOSIUM

sought to answer ethical questions without regard to (and sometimes in defiance of) some of the standards and traditions prevalent around them, the history of ethics as a philosophical discipline bears interesting connections to what has happened in given philosophers' societies and the world at large. Perhaps the clearest example of this lies in the influence of Christianity on the history of theoretical ethics.

Philosophical/theoretical ethics, of course, has had its own influence on Christianity, for example, Aristotle's influence on the philosophy of Thomas Aquinas and on the views and practices of the church. Nonetheless, to compare the character of the pre-Christian ethics of Socrates, Plato, Aristotle, the Stoics, the Epicureans, and other schools of ancient ethical thought with the kinds of ethics that have flourished in the academy since Christianity became a dominant social force is to recognize that larger social and historical currents play significant roles in the sphere of philosophical ethics.

Socrates, Plato, and Aristotle, for example, do not discuss kindness or compassion, moral guilt, or the virtue of self-denial, or selflessness. Christianity helped to bring these notions to the attention of philosophy and to make philosophers think that issues framed in terms of them were central to their task. By the same token, a late-twentieth-century revival of interest in ancient approaches to ethics may reflect the diminishing force and domination of Christian thinking in the contemporary world.

But if the concepts that ethics focuses on can change so profoundly, one may well wonder whether a single discipline of ethics can be said to persist across the ages, or even whether such a thing as "the task" of philosophical ethics can be said to endure. Socrates, and later Plato, were perhaps the first philosophers to make a self-conscious attempt to answer general ethical questions on the basis of reason and argument rather than convention and tradition. But was the task they accepted really the same as that of contemporary ethics? This issue needs to be addressed before the task of ethics can be described.

◆ **deontology**
Also called Kantian ethics, *stresses the rights of persons and the duties of others to respect persons as ends in themselves, and focuses on determining which choices most respect an individual's worth and value.*

Despite the fact that the concepts and problems of physics have varied over the last few centuries, it is still possible to speak of the history of a single discipline called physics. Moreover, we might say that the task of physics has been and remains that of developing physical concepts for the explanation and description of physical phenomena. Something similar can be said about theoretical ethics. Over the millennia, thoughtful people and philosophers have asked what kind of life is best for the individual and how one ought to behave in regard to other individuals and society as a whole. Although different concepts have been proposed to assist in the task of answering these questions, the questions themselves have retained an identity substantial enough to allow one to speak of the task of philosophical ethics without doing an injustice to the history of ethics.

See Also
Law and Bioethics

The history of ethical theories

There has been a good deal less variation in philosophical concepts between those Plato employed and those we employ than there has been in regard to physical concepts within the field of physics. Concepts in philosophical ethics are the instruments with which philosophers address perennial ethical questions, and the distinctive contribution of any given theoretical approach to ethics resides in how (and how well) it integrates such concepts into an overall ethical view.

The concepts of ethics fall into two main categories. The first category comprises notions having to do with morality, virtue, rationality, and other ideals or standards of conduct and motivation; the second, notions pertaining to human good or well-being and the "good life" generally. Notice that morality is only one part, albeit a major one, of the first category. Claims and ideals concerning how it is rational for us to behave are not necessarily "moral" within our rather narrow modern understanding of that notion. Prudence and far-sightedness, for example, are rational, but their absence is not usually regarded as any kind of moral fault; and since these traits are also usually regarded as virtues, it seems we have room for virtues that are not specifically moral virtues. In addition, questions about human well-being and about what kind of life is best to have are less clearly questions of morality, narrowly conceived, than of ethics regarded as an encompassing philosophical discipline. The two categories mentioned above basically divide the concepts of ethics understood in this broad sense, and all major, substantive ethical theories attempt to say something about how these two classes of concepts relate to one another. Since modern views employ concepts and ask specific questions that are more familiar to contemporary readers, these views will be discussed first.

DEONTOLOGY. Modern deontology treats moral obligations as requirements that bind us to act, in large measure, independent of the effects our actions may have on our own good or well-being, and to a substantial extent, even independent of the effects of our actions on the well-being of others. The categorical imperative of Immanuel Kant (1724-1804), in one of its main formulations, tells us that we may not use or mistreat other people as a means either to our own happiness or to that of other people, and various forms of moral intuitionism make similar claims (1964). Intuitionists typically differ from Kant in holding that there are several independent, fundamental moral requirements (e.g., to keep promises, not to harm others, to tell the truth). But they agree with Kant that moral obligation is not just a matter of good consequences for an individual agent or for sentient beings generally. Thus even though deontologists such as Kant and, in the twentieth century, W. D. Ross, have definite views about human well-being, they do not think of moral goodness and moral obligation as rooted in facts about human well-being (or the well-being of sentient beings generally); and here a comparison with Judeo-Christian religious thought seems not inappropriate.

The Ten Commandments are not a product of rational philosophy; they have their source in religious tradition and/or divine command. They do, however, represent a kind of answer to the question about how one should behave toward others; that is, they ask the question that philosophical ethics attempts to answer. Moreover, the way the Ten Commandments answer this question is somewhat analogous to the way moral principles are conceived by deontologists such as Kant and the intuitionists.

In religious thinking, the Ten Commandments are not morally binding through some connection to the well-being or happiness of individuals or even the larger community; they are binding because God has commanded them, and deontology seeks to substitute for the idea of a deity, the idea of requirements given by reason itself or of binding obligations perceivable by moral insight. The deontologist typically holds that one's own well-being and that of others are taken into account and given some weight by the set of binding moral requirements, but that these are not the only considerations that affect what we ought to do generally or on particular occasions. For deontologists, the end does not always justify the means, and certain kinds of actions—torture, betrayal, injustice—are wrong for reasons having little to do with good or desirable consequences.

CONSEQUENTIALISM. The contrast here is with so-called consequentialists, for whom all moral obligation and virtue are to be understood in terms of good or desirable consequences. Typically, this has meant framing some conception of human or sentient good or well-being and claiming that all morality is derivative from or understandable in terms such as "good" or "well-being." Thus Jeremy Bentham, Henry Sidgwick (1981), and other utilitarian consequentialists regard pleasure or the satisfaction of desire as the sole, intrinsic human good, and pain or dissatisfaction as the sole, intrinsic evil or ill, and they conceive our moral obligations as grounded entirely in considerations of pleasure and pain. The idea that one should always act to secure the greatest good of the greatest number is simply a way of saying that whether an act is right or wrong depends solely on whether its overall and long-term consequences for human (or sentient) well-being are at least as good as those of any alternative act available to a given agent. And since classical utilitarianism conceives human good or well-being in terms of pleasure or satisfaction, it holds that the rightness of an action always depends on whether it produces, overall and in the long run, as great a net balance of pleasure over pain as could have been produced by performing any of its alternatives.

This utilitarian moral standard is rather demanding, because it says that anything less than the maximization of overall human good or pleasure is wrong, and that means that if I fail to sacrifice my own comfort or career when doing so would allow me to do more overall good for humanity, then I act wrongly. But apart from the fact of how much it demands—there is nothing, after all, in the Ten Commandments or in the obligations defended by deontologists that requires such extreme sacrifice—what is most distinctive about utilitarianism is its claim that moral right and wrong (and moral good and evil) are totally, not merely partially, concerned with producing desirable results. The end, indeed, does justify the means, according to utilitarianism, and thus one might even be justified in killing, say, one innocent person in order to preserve the lives of two others.

Most deontologists would regard this as the most implausible, vulnerable feature of utilitarian and other consequentialist moral conceptions. But the utilitarian can point out that if you do not make human or sentient happiness the touchstone of all morality, but rely instead on certain "given" intuitions about what morally must or must not be done, you have given yourself a formula for preserving all the moral prejudices that have come down to us from the past. We require, Bentham argued, some external standard by which not only the state of individuals and society, but also all our inherited moral beliefs and intuitions can be properly evaluated. Bentham claimed that judging everything in terms of pleasure and pain can enable us to accomplish this goal. Historically, utilitarianism was conceived and used as a reformist moral and political doctrine, and that is one of its main strengths. If overall human happiness is the measure of moral requirement and moral goodness, then aristocratic privilege and the political disenfranchisement of all but the landed and wealthy are clearly open to attack, and Bentham and his "radical" allied did, in fact, make use of utilitarian ideas as a basis for making reforms in the British political and legal system.

But not all the reformist notions and energies lie on the side of consequentialism. The version of Kant's categorical imperative that speaks of never treating people merely as means, but always (also) as ends in themselves, was based on the idea of the fundamental digni-

See Also
Law and Morality

ty and worth of all human beings. Such a notion is clearly capable of being used—and, in fact, has been used—in reformist fashion to defend political and civil rights.

The debate between deontology and consequentialism has remained fundamentally important in philosophical ethics. Although there are other forms of consequentialism besides utilitarianism and other forms of deontology besides Kantian ethics, the main issue and choice has been widely regarded as lying between utilitarianism and Kant. This may be partly explained by the interest contemporary ethics has shown in understanding ethical and political issues as fundamentally interrelated; for both utilitarianism and Kantianism can claim to be "on the side of the angels" in regard to the large questions of social-political choice and reform that have exercised us in the modern period and may well continue to do so.

In the ancient world, the philosophical interest in ethics was also connected to larger political and social issues; both Plato (ca. 430-347 B.C.E.) and Aristotle sought to embed their ideas about personal morality within a larger picture of how society or the state should operate. Moreover, Plato was a radical and a reformer, though the *Republic* takes a direction precisely opposite to that of both utilitarianism and Kantianism. Plato was deeply distrustful of democratic politics and of the moral and political capacities of most human beings. His *Republic* (1974) advocates the rule of philosophers who have been specially trained to understand the nature of "the Good" over all those who have not attained such mystic/intellectual insight. Nor does Aristotle defend democracy. In somewhat milder form, he prefers the rule of virtuous individuals over those who lack—and lack the basic capacity for—virtue. If the ancient world contains any roots of democratic thinking, they lie in Stoicism, which emphasized the brotherhood of man (which seems to leave women out

VIRTUE ETHICS
Ego and the Common Good

All schools of ancient ethics defended one or another form of "virtue ethics." That is, they typically conceived what was admirable about individuals in terms of traits of character, rather than in terms of individual obedience to some set of moral or ethical rules or requirements. Ancient ethics was also predominantly eudaimonistic. *Eudaimonia* is the ancient Greek word for being fortunate or doing well in life, and eudaimonism is the view that our first concern in ethics is with the nature and conditions of human happiness/well-being and in particular our own happiness/well-being. This does not mean that all ancient ethics was egoistic, if by that term one refers to views according to which the moral or rational agent should always aim at his or her own (greatest) good or well-being. Aristotle is a clear example of an ethical thinker whose fundamental orientation is eudaimonistic, but who is far from advocating that people should always aim at their own self-interest.

For Aristotle, the question to begin with in ethics is the question of what is good for human beings. But Aristotle argues that human good or happiness largely consists in being actively virtuous, thus tying what is desirable in life to what is admirable in life in a rather distinctive way. For Aristotle, the virtuous individual will often aim at the good of others and/or at certain noble ideals, rather than seek to advance his or her own well-being, so egoism is no part of Aristotelianism.

But certainly most interpreters have regarded the Epicureans as having a basically egoistic doctrine. Epicureanism resembled utilitarianism in treating pleasure and the absence of pain as the sole conditions of human well-being. Rather than urge us to seek the greatest good of the greatest number, however, the Epicureans argued that virtue consisted in seeking one's own greatest pleasure/absence of pain. (Given certain pessimistic assumptions, the Epicureans thought this was best accomplished by minimizing one's desires and simplifying one's life.)

Although there are some notable modern egoists (e.g., Hobbes, Spinoza, and Nietzsche), most recent moral philosophers have assumed that there are fundamental, rational reasons for being concerned with something other than one's own well-being. Moreover, the eudaimonistic assumption that questions about individual happiness or well-being are the first concern of ethics has, in modern times, given way to a more basic emphasis on questions like, "How ought I to act?" and "What obligations have I?" The Jewish and Christian religious traditions seem to have made some difference here. In both traditions, God's commandments are supposed to have force for one independent of any question of one's own well-being (assuming that one is to obey because God has commanded, and not just because one fears divine punishment). For most Christians, moreover, Jesus sacrificing himself for our redemption places a totally non-egoistic motive at the pinnacle of the Christian vision of morality. So the notions that one should always be concerned with one's own well-being, and that ethics is chiefly about how one is to conceive and attain a good life, are both profoundly challenged by any moral philosophy that takes Judaism or Christianity, understood in the above fashion, seriously.

— MICHAEL SLOTE

of account), but also spoke of the divine spark in every individual (including women). (Kant took the idea that all human beings have dignity, rather than mere price, from the Stoic Seneca [4 B.C.E.—C.E. 65].)

Recent developments

Twentieth-century philosophical ethics bears the imprint of much of the history of the discipline, and many of the more current, prominent approaches to the subject represent developments of historically important views. But earlier in the twentieth century, ethics, at least in Britain and in the United States, veered away from its past in the direction of what has come to be called metaethics. The move toward metaethics and away from traditional ethical theory resulted, in part, from the influence of a school of philosophy called logical positivism. The positivists held up experimentally verifiable science as the paradigm of cognitively meaningful discourse and claimed that any statement that was not empirically confirmable or mathematically demonstrable lacked real content. Since it is difficult to see how moral principles can be experimentally verified or mathematically proved, many positivist ethicists began to think of ethical claims as cognitively meaningless and refused to advance substantive moral views, turning instead to the analysis of ethical terms and ethical claims. Issues about the meaning of moral terms have a long history in philosophical ethics, but the idea that these metaethical tasks were the main task of philosophical ethics gained a prevalence in the early years of the twentieth century that it had never previously had.

In the latter half of the twentieth century, substantive or normative ethics (that is, ethics making real value judgments rather than simply analyzing such judgments) once again came to the fore and tended to displace metaethics as the center of interest in ethics. In particular, there was a resurgence of interest in Kantian ethics and utilitarianism, followed by a renewal of interest in the kind of virtue ethics that dominated the philosophical landscape of ancient philosophy.

The revival and further development of Kantian ethics received its principal impetus from John Rawls and younger philosophers influenced by him. Rawls's principal work, *A Theory of Justice* (1971) represents a sustained attack on utilitarianism and seeks to base its own positive conception of morality and social justice on an understanding of Kant's ethics that bypasses the controversial metaphysical assumptions Kant was thought to have made about absolute human freedom and rationality. Other Kantian ethicists (Christine Korsgaard, Onora O'Neill, and Barbara Herman), however, have sought to be somewhat truer to the historical Kant while developing Kant's doctrines in directions fruitful for contemporary ethical theorizing.

Meanwhile, the utilitarians responded to Rawls's critique with reinvigorated forms of their doctrine, and, in particular, Derek Parfit's *Reasons and Persons* (1984) seeks to advance the utilitarian tradition of ethical theory within a philosophical perspective that fully takes into account the insights of the Rawlsian approach.

Finally, virtue ethics has been undergoing a considerable revival. In a 1958 article, Elizabeth Anscombe argued that notions like moral obligation are bankrupt without the assumption of God (or someone else) as a lawgiver, whereas concepts of character excellence or virtue and of human flourishing can arise, without such assumptions, from within a properly conceived moral psychology. This challenge was taken up by philosophers interested in exploring the possibility that the notions of good character and motivation and of living well may be primary in ethics, with notions like right, wrong, and obligation taking a secondary or derivative place or perhaps even dropping out altogether. Such virtue ethics does not, however, abandon ethics' traditional task of telling us how to live, since, in fact, ideals of good character and motivation can naturally lead to views about how it is best to treat others and to promote our own character and happiness. Rather, the newer virtue ethics sought to learn from the virtue ethics of the ancient world, especially of Plato, Aristotle, and the Stoics, while making those lessons relevant to a climate of ethical theory that incorporates what has been learned in the long interval since ancient times.

More recently, however, a radical kind of virtue ethics without precedent in the ancient world has developed out of feminist thought and in the wake of Carol Gilligan's groundbreaking *In a Different Voice* (1982). Gilligan argued that men tend to conceive of morality in terms of rights, justice, and autonomy, whereas women more frequently think of morality in terms of caring, responsibility, and interrelation with others. And at about the same time as Gilligan wrote, Nel Noddings in *Caring: A Feminine Approach to Ethics and Moral Education* (1984) articulated and defended the idea of a feminine morality centered on caring.

The ideal of caring Noddings has in mind is particularistic: It is not the universally directed benevolence of the sort utilitarianism sometimes appeals to, but rather caring for certain particular people (e.g., one's friends and family) that she treats as the morally highest and best motivation. Actions then count as good or bad, better or worse, to the extent that they exhibit this kind of caring. Clearly, Nodding's view offers a potential answer to the traditional question of how one should live, but since the answer seems to be based on fundamental assumptions about what sorts of inner motivation are morally good or bad, it is a

Renewed interest in the ethics of virtue has accompanied a renewed appreciation of the importance of community in ethics.

PAGE 685

See Also
Continuing Problems for an Ethics of Virtue

SEEKING SUPERMAN

Friedrich Nietzsche (1844–1900) viewed human life as characterized by a "will to power," a desire for individual achievement and power over others.

form of virtue ethics. Of course, her view can be stated in terms of the principle "Be caring and act caringly." But if we focus on conforming to the principle instead of on the needs of the individuals we care about, we risk falling short of what the principle itself recommends. It is the state or process of sensitive caring, rather than attention to principle, that generates what Noddings would take to be satisfying answers to moral questions and appropriate responses to particular situations.

Enriched by such feminine/feminist possibilities, ethical theory has been actively and fertilely involved with the perennial task(s) of ethics. But because few of the traditional questions have been answered to the satisfaction of all philosophers, one may well wonder whether philosophy will ever be able fully to answer those questions or even whether philosophers have, over the centuries, made real or sufficient progress in dealing with them. But it is also possible to attack the tradition(s) of philosophical ethics in a more radical fashion.

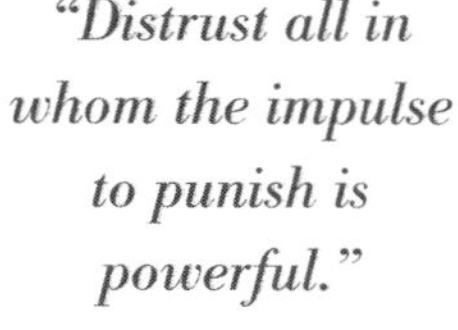

"Distrust all in whom the impulse to punish is powerful."

NIETZSCHE
THUS SPAKE ZARATHUSTRA
1878

Modern challenges to philosophical ethics

Some modern intellectual and social traditions have questioned the notion that ethics can validly function as a distinct sphere of rational inquiry. One example of such questioning was the widespread view, earlier in the twentieth century, that ethics should confine itself to the metaethical analysis of concepts and epistemological issues (and possibly to the sociological description of the differing ethical mores of different times and places) rather than continue in its traditional role of advocating substantive ethical views. (Metaethics has undergone something of a revival, but largely in a form regarded as compatible with substantive ethical theorizing.)

Historically, various forms of religion and religious philosophy have also posed a challenge to the autonomy and validity of traditional ethics. The claims of faith and religious authority can readily be seen as overriding the kind of rational understanding that typifies traditional philosophical inquiry. Thus, Thomas Aquinas believed strongly in the importance of the ethical issues raised by Aristotle and in Aristotle's rational techniques of argument and analysis; but he also permitted his Christian faith to shape his response to Aristotle and did not fundamentally question the superiority of faith to reason. He believed, however, that reason and philosophy could accommodate and be accommodated to faith and religious authority.

EXISTENTIALISM. But more radical religionists have questioned the importance of reason and have even prided themselves in flying in the face of reason. Religious views that stress our dependent, finite, sinful creatureliness can lead one to view philosophical ethics as a rather limited and even perverse way to understand the problems of the human condition. In modern times this religion-inspired critique of ethics and the philosophical received a distinctive existentialist expression in the writings of Blaise Pascal (1966) and Søren Kierkegaard (1960, 1983).

It is very difficult to give a completely adequate characterization of existentialism as a philosophical movement or tendency of thought. It cuts across the distinction between theism and atheism, and some of the most prominent existentialists have, in fact, been atheists. But the earlier theistic existentialism that one finds in Pascal and, more fully developed, in Kierkegaard is principally concerned with attacking rationalistic Western philosophy and defending a more emotional and individualistic approach to life and thought. Plato and Aristotle, for example, sought rationally to circumscribe the human condition by treating "man" as by his very essence a "rational animal" and prescribing a way of life for human beings that acknowledged and totally incorporated the ideal of being rational. But for Pascal, the heart has reasons that reason cannot know, and Kierkegaard regarded certain kinds of rationally absurd religious faith and love as higher and more important than anything that could be circumscribed and understood in rational, ethical, or philosophical terms.

The atheistic Nietzsche (1844-1900) also attacked philosophical ethics and rational philosophy generally by attempting to deflate their pretensions to being rational. Nietzsche saw human life as characterized by a "will to power," that is, a desire for power over other individuals and for individual achievement, and in *The Genealogy of Morals* (1956) he argued that Judeo-Christian ethics, as well as philosophical views that reflect the influence of such ethics, are based in debilitating and poisonous emotions rather than having their source in rational thought or enlightened desire. What comes naturally to man is, he thought, an aristocratic morality that is comfortable with power and harsh in regard to failure, and the idea that the meek and self-sacrificing represents the highest form of human being he took to be the frustrated and angry response of those who have failed to attain power, but are unwilling to admit even to themselves how they really feel.

Nietzsche clearly expressed an antipathy to the whole tradition of philosophical ethics, and even if he did defend an iconoclastic ethics "of the superman," his writings point the way to an attitude like that of the more recent existentialist Jean-Paul Sartre (1905-1980). In his *Being and Nothingness* (1956), Sartre argued that all ethics is based in error and illusion, and he attempted instead to describe the human condition in nonjudgmental, nonmoral terms. Sartre argued that human beings are radically free in their choice of actions and values, and he claimed that all value judgments, because they purport to tell us what we really have to do, involve a misunderstanding, which he called "bad faith," of just how free we actually are. At the end of his book, Sartre proposed to write a future book on ethics, but also set out, in compelling fashion, the reasons for thinking that any future ethics is likely to fall into error and illusion about the character of human freedom. Here, as in *Being and Time* of Martin Heidegger (1889-1976) which had a decisive influence on Sartre's existentialism, the existentialist philosopher is essentially critical of the role ethical thinking plays in philosophy and in life generally and says, in effect, that if we face the truth about our own radical freedom, we must stop doing ethics. Ethics may think of itself as a rational enterprise, but for Sartre, it was mainly a form of self-deception.

MARXISM. Existentialism has had a great influence on Western culture, but Marxism has probably had a much greater influence, and Karl Marx's writings (*Capital* and *The German Ideology*), like those of some of the existentialists, attempt to accustom us to the idea of taking ethics less seriously than practitioners of philosophical ethics have tended to do. According to Marx (1818-1883) (and Friedrich Engels), philosophical ethics and philosophy generally are best understood as expressions of certain class interests, as ideological tools of class warfare, rather than as independently and timelessly valid methods of inquiry into questions that can be settled objectively and rationally.

For example, intellectual, philosophical defenses of property rights can be seen as expressing and asserting bourgeois class interests against a resentful and increasingly powerful proletariat. All philosophy, according to such a view, is merely the expression of underlying economic forces and struggles. A truly liberated view of human history requires us to stop moralizing and start understanding and harnessing the processes of history, using the tools of Marx's own "scientific socialism." While Marx believed that a "really human morality" might emerge under communism, philosophical ethics is seen more as a hindrance than as a means to enlightened understanding of human society.

PSYCHOANALYSIS. In addition, psychoanalysis, as a movement and style of thought, has often been taken to argue against traditional ethics as an objective discipline with a valid intellectual task of its own. The psychoanalytic account of moral conscience threatens to undercut traditional ethical views and traditional views of ethics by making our own ethical intuitions and feelings seem illusory. In a manner partly anticipated by Nietzsche, Sigmund Freud's original formulation of psychoanalytic theory (e.g. in *The Interpretation of Dreams* and *Introductory Lectures on Psychoanalysis*) treat conscience and guilt as forms of aggression directed by the individual against himself (Freud, 1989). (Freud [1856-1939] tended to focus on the development of conscience in males.) Rather than attack parental figures he feared, the individual psychologically incorporates the morality of these seemingly threatening figures. If conscience is a function of hatred against one or more parental figures, then its true nature is often obscured to those who have conscience. According to classic psychoanalysis, the very factors that make us redirect aggression in such a fashion also make it difficult consciously to acknowledge that conscience has such a source.

If moral thought has this dynamic, then much of moral life and moral philosophy is self-deluded. However, for some more recent psychoanalysts, not all forms of ethical thinking are illusory. Followers of the British psychoanalyst Melanie Klein (1975) have said that various ethical ideals can and do appeal to us and guide our behavior, once "persecutory guilt" of the kind based in aggression redirected against the self is dissolved through normal maturation or through psychotherapy. Moreover, the analyst Erik Erikson (1964) gave a developmental account of basic human virtues that has clear, ethical significance.

In the end, perhaps it should not be surprising that many attempts to undermine ethics eventually reintro-

See Also
Marx and Engels
Freud and Psychoanalysis

E

ETHICS

Social and Political Theories

duce something like familiar ethical notions and problems. We have to live with one another, and the problems of making life together possible and, if possible, beneficial are problems that will not and cannot go away. Even if a given society and generation has settled on a particular solution to the problems of living together, new historical developments can make these solutions come unstuck, or at least force people to reconsider their appropriateness. And even if different societies and cultures have different moral standards, it is possible to overestimate the differences. For example, however much aggression societies may allow toward outsiders and enemies, no society has a moral code that permits people, at will, to kill members of that society. Moreover, the very fact of moral differences among different societies indicates a need for cooperative and practical ethical thinking that will enable people either to resolve or live with the differences.

"Man is born free, and everywhere he is in chains."

JEAN-JACQUES ROUSSEAU
THE SOCIAL CONTRACT
1762

APPLIED ETHICS. This is a point where the need for applied ethics most clearly comes into view. Whether it is in medicine, science, biotechnology, business, or the law, people have to come together to solve problems, and ethics or ethical thinking can play a role in generating cooperative solutions. If existentialism, religion, Marxism, and psychoanalysis all in varying degrees question the need for philosophical ethics, the practical problems of contemporary life seem to indicate some new ways and to highlight some old ways in which philosophical ethics has validity and value.

The explosive development of new knowledge and techniques in medicine and biology has made bioethics one of the central areas of practical, moral concern. And those seeking to solve moral problems in this area naturally appeal to philosophical ethics. To take just one controversial area, the question of euthanasia engages the ideas and energies of different ethical theories in different ways and often with differing results. Thus, the Kantian may focus on issues concerning the autonomy of the dying patient and the right to life, whereas utilitarians will stress issues about the quality of life and the effects of certain decisions on families and society as a whole, and defenders of an ethics of caring will perhaps see less significance in larger social consequences and focus on how a medical decision will affect those most intimately and immediately affected by it.

Applied ethics in our contemporary sense is not new: Socrates' discussion of the duty of obedience to unjust laws in the *Crito* and Henry David Thoreau's of civil disobedience are only two of countless historical instances of what we would call applied ethics. Today, we think, civilization is more complicated and our problems are more complex. Still, in facing those problems, bioethicists, business ethicists, and other applied ethicists typically look to philosophical ethics, to substantive theories like utilitarianism and virtue ethics and Kantianism, and to the criticisms each makes of the others, for some enlightenment on practical issues.

— MICHAEL SLOTE

See Also

Human Nature; Reproductive Technologies; Virtue and Character

SOCIAL AND POLITICAL THEORIES

Every social and political theory is entangled with ethics. The great political philosopher Jean-Jacques Rousseau proclaimed that the person who would separate politics from ethics will fail to understand both. Despite the efforts of practitioners of "value-free social science," the concepts and categories with which political theorists work—order, freedom, authority, legitimacy, justice—are part and parcel of competing ethical frameworks. It is very difficult to talk about justice without talking about fairness. What is fair is an ethical question that cannot be adjudicated without some reference to what is good for human beings or what kind of good human beings may strive to attain. Terms that circulate within ordinary discourse, such as "fairness" and "freedom," are also central themes within social and political thinking. The implication for bioethics is straightforward. No matter how strenuously the bioethicist may hope to isolate his or her perspective from metaphysical, ontological, epistemological, and civic imperatives, social and political theory frames and penetrates all bioethical considerations.

The human sciences cannot be value-free. In Charles Taylor's words, "they are moral sciences in a more radical sense than the eighteenth century understood" (Taylor, 1971, p. 51). There are, according to Taylor, inescapable epistemological arguments for what might be called an interpretive approach to the human sciences, for human beings are self-defining animals. These self-definitions, in turn, take place within a context that shapes our understanding of self and other as well as our appreciation of human possibilities and the need for constraint. We are caught in conceptual webs. It is the task of social and political theory to make more explicit the nature of the frameworks within which we think and act, and hence, the context within which bioethical imperatives make themselves felt, whether as advances in human freedom, triumphs of human control, or dangerous new forms of oppression. Based on an interpretive approach to political theory, this article will demonstrate why political theory must be normative and will go on to rehearse contemporary debates in social and political theory using the public/private distinction and the women's movement as illustrative examples.

Why social and political theory must be normative

Terms of ordinary discourse serve as a conceptual prism through which we view different human rela-

tionships, activities, and forms of life. Most of the time we take such terms for granted. We are all shaped by ways of life that are built upon basic notions and rules. Political theorists concern themselves with the ways in which a society's constitutive understandings either nourish or deplete human capacities for purposive activity. It is, therefore, one task of the political theorist to examine critically the resources of ordinary language, revealing latent meanings, nuances, and shades of interpretation others may have missed or ignored. When we examine our basic assumptions, we enhance our ability to sift out the most important issues (Elshtain, 1981).

The social and political theorist recognizes that no idea or concept is an island unto itself. Basic notions comprise a society's intersubjectively shared realm. "Intersubjectivity" is a rather elusive term referring to shared ideas, symbols, and concepts that reverberate within a society and help to constitute a way of life. The philosopher Ludwig Wittgenstein claims that when we first "begin to believe anything, what we believe is not a single proposition, it is a whole system of propositions. (Light dawns gradually over the whole.)" (Wittgenstein, 1969, p. 21e). Similarly, when we use a concept, particularly one of the bedrock notions integral to a way of life, we do not do so as a discrete piece of "linguistic behavior" but with reference to other concepts, contrasts, and terms of comparison.

As with the concepts of public and private, there are no neatly defined and universally accepted limits on the boundaries of politics. Politics, too, is essentially contested. An essentially contested concept is internally complex or makes reference to several dimensions, which are, in turn, linked to other concepts. Such a concept is also open-textured, in that the rules of its application are relatively flexible, and it is appraisive or normative. For example, one political theorist might claim that a given social situation is unjust. Another might argue that to label the situation unjust only inflames matters, because he or she believes that certain underlying cherished social institutions and relations should not be tampered with or eliminated in the interest of attaining a political or ideological goal. In another example, the feminist political theorist who believes that being born female in and of itself constitutes an injustice on the "biological" level may want to eliminate all sex differences and a public/private distinction as well, for she will see in distinctions themselves a ploy to oppress women (Firestone, 1970). Other feminist thinkers may find this view reprehensible, as it deepens rather than challenges societal devaluation of female bodies and a woman's central role in

"PUBLIC" AND "PRIVATE": Each Implies the Other

Society's understanding of the terms "public" and "private," for example, are always defined and understood in relationship to each other. One version of private means "not open to the public," and public, by contrast, is "of or pertaining to the whole, done or made in behalf of the community as a whole." In part these contrasts derive from the Latin origin of "public," pubes, the age of maturity when signs of puberty begin to appear: Then and only then does the child enter, or become qualified for, public activity. Similarly, *publicus* is that which belongs to, or pertains to, "the public," the people. But there is another meaning: public as open to scrutiny; private as that not subjected to the persistent gaze of publicity. The protection of privacy is necessary, or so defenders of constitutional democracy have long insisted, in order to prevent government from becoming all-intrusive, as well as to preserve the possibility of different sorts of relationships—both mother and citizen, friend and official.

Our involvement in one of a number of competing ethical or normative perspectives is inescapable. It is influenced by what we take to be the appropriate relationship between public and private life, for this also defines our understanding of what politics should or should not attempt to define, regulate, or even control. There is widespread disagreement over the respective meaning of public and private within societies. Brian Fay sees the public and the private as part of a cluster of "basic notions" that serve to structure and give coherence to all known ways of life. The boundaries between the public and the private help to create a moral environment for individuals, singly and in groups; to dictate norms of appropriate or worthy action; and to establish barriers to action, particularly in areas such as the taking of human life, regulation of sexual relations, promulgation of familial duties and obligations, and the arena of political responsibility. Public and private are embedded within a dense web of meanings and intimations and are linked to other basic notions: nature and culture, male and female, and each society's "understanding of the meaning and role of work; its views of nature; . . . its concepts of agency; its ideas about authority, the community, the family; its notion of sex; its beliefs about God and death and so on" (Fay, 1975, p. 78). The content, meaning, and range of public and private vary within each society and turn on whether the virtues of political life or the values of private life are rich and vital or have been drained, singly or together, of their normative significance.

— JEAN BETHKE ELSHTAIN

reproduction. This latter group sees injustice in inequalities that are socially and politically, not biologically, constituted. The point is not to eliminate a public/private distinction but to push for parity in male and female participation in both realms.

Boundary shifts in our understanding of "the political" and hence, of what is public and what is private, have taken place throughout the history of Western life and thought. Minimally, a political perspective requires that some activity called politics be differentiated from other activities. If all conceptual boundaries are blurred and all distinctions between public and private are eliminated, no politics can, by definition, exist (Elshtain, 1981). The relatively open-textured quality of politics means that innovative and revolutionary thinkers are often those who declare politics to exist where politics was not thought to exist before. Should their reclassifications remain over time, the meaning of politics—indeed of human life itself—may be transformed. Altered social conditions may also provoke a reassessment of old, and a recognition of new, "political" realities. Sheldon Wolin observes, "The concepts and categories of a political philosophy may be likened to a net that is cast out to capture political phenomena, which are then drawn in and sorted in a way that seems meaningful and relevant to the particular thinker" (Wolin, 1960, p. 21). Thus each social and political theorist must be clear about what rules he or she is employing to sort the catch and to what ends and purposes.

There have been few studies of the consequences for children of atypical family arrangements made possible by new reproductive technologies.

PAGE 601

Bioethical issues in the concepts of public and private

In the history of Western political thought, public and private imperatives, concepts, and symbols have been ordered in a number of ways, including the demand that the private world be integrated fully within the public arena; the insistence that the public realm be "privatized," with politics controlled by the standards, ideals, and purposes emerging from a particular vision of the private sphere; or, finally, a continued differentiation or bifurcation between the two spheres. Bioethics is deeply implicated in each of these broad, general theoretical tendencies that often touch on the private and the public, as in a case, for example, where a couple decides to conceive a child through artificial insemination by donor (AID). What happens to a society's view of the family and intergenerational ties if more couples resort to artificial insemination? What is the effect on the psychosocial development of donor children? What are the responsibilities, if any, of the donor father beyond the point of sperm donation for a fee? Do contractual agreements suffice to "cover" not just the legal but also the ethical implications of such agreements? Does society have a legitimate interest in such "private" choices, given the potential social consequences of private arrangements? Should such procedures be covered by health insurance, whether public or private?

Questions such as these pitch us into the world of social and political theory and the ways particular ideals are deeded to us. Thus, the social-contract liberal endorses a different cluster of human goods than the virtue theorist or the communitarian. Political and social theory yield ethical debates about these competing ideals of human existence. Moral rules—and whether they are to be endorsed or overridden—are inescapable in debating human existence and the human imperative to create meaning. "Public" and "private" and the relations of politics to each exist as loci of human activity, moral reflections, social and historic relations, the creation of meaning, and the construction of identity.

The ways in which our understanding of public, private, and politics plays itself out at present is dauntingly complex. Contemporary society is marked by moral conflicts. These conflicts have deep historical roots and are reflected in our institutions, practices, laws, norms, and values. For example, the continuing abortion debate in the United States taps strongly held, powerfully experienced moral and political imperatives. These imperatives are linked to concerns and images evoking what sort of people we are and what we aspire to be. The abortion debate will not "go away" because it is a debate about matters of life and death, freedom and obligation, and rights and duties.

Perhaps the intractability of many of the debates surrounding bioethics can best be understood as flowing from a central recognition that language itself has become a preoccupation for theorists and ethicists because of our growing concern for establishing norms, limits, and meanings in the absence of a shared ethical consensus. A persistent theme of contemporary social and political theory is that language helps to constitute social reality and frames available forms of action. We are all participants in a language community and hence share in a project of theoretical and moral self-understanding, definition, and redefinition. Our values, embedded in language, are not icing on the cake of social reasoning but are instead part of a densely articulated web of social, historical, and cultural meanings, traditions, rules, beliefs, norms, actions, and visions. A way of life, constituted in and through language, is a complex whole. One cannot separate attitudes toward surrogacy contracts, in vitro fertilization (IVF), use of fetal tissue for medical experimentation, sex selection as a basis for abortion, or genetic engineering to eliminate forms of genetically inherited "imperfection," from other features of a culture. These bioethical dilemmas do not take place in isolation but emerge from within a culture and thus engage in the wider contests over meaning that culture generates.

See Also

Assisted Reproduction: Psychology of Nontraditional Families

Contemporary debates in social and political theory

Current debate in social and political theory has focused on the question of whether to buttress or to challenge the liberal consensus that came to prevail in modern Western industrial societies. These broad, competing schools of thought are known as liberalism, civic republicanism, and communitarianism. A social movement informed by one or more of these traditions will exhibit conflicting tendencies and posit incompatible claims.

Liberalism comes in many different forms. Some liberal thinkers stress the individual and his or her rights, often downplaying notions of duty or obligation to a wider social whole. They assume, optimistically, that each individual's pursuit of self-interest will result in "good" for the society as a whole. Those whose analyses begin with the free-standing individual as the point of reference and the "good" of that individual as their normative ideal are often called individualists. In the nineteenth century, this standard of individualism was most cogently articulated by John Stuart Mill in his classic work, *On Liberty* (1859).

By contrast, communitarians begin not with the autonomous individual but with a social context out of which individuals emerge. They argue that the pursuit of individual self-interest is more likely to yield a fragmented society than a "good" and fair one. Communitarians insist that rights, while vital, are not the individual's alone. Instead, individual rights necessarily flow from rights recognized by others within a community of a particular sort in which responsibilities are also cherished, nourished, and required of individuals (Bellah et al., 1985).

FEMINISM. The contemporary women's movement and the way in which it reflects, deepens, and extends features of these traditions illustrate the range of social and political debate. There is no single ethics or moral theory of feminism. Liberalism, with its vibrant individualist strand, has been attractive to feminist thinkers. The language of rights is a potent weapon against traditional obligations, particularly those of family duty or any social status declared "natural" on the basis of ascriptive characteristics. To be free and equal to men became a central aim of feminist reform. The political strategy that followed was one of inclusion. Since women, as well as men, are rational beings, it followed that women as well as men are bearers of inalienable rights. It followed further that there was no valid ground for discrimination against women as women. Leading proponents of women's suffrage in Britain and the United States undermined arguments that justified legal inequality on the basis of sex differences. Such feminists, including the leading American

VOTING = CRIME?

Prominent suffragist Susan B. Anthony (1820–1906) argued against denying rights on the grounds of difference unless the difference was relevant.

suffragists Susan B. Anthony and Elizabeth Cady Stanton, claimed that denying a group of persons basic rights on the grounds of difference could not be justified unless it could be shown that the difference was relevant to the distinction being made. Whatever differences might exist between the sexes, none, in this view, justified legal inequality and the denial of the rights and privileges of citizenship.

Few early feminists pushed this version of liberal individualist universalism to its most radical conclusion of arguing that there were no bases for exclusion of adult human beings from legal equality and citizenship. Nineteenth-century proponents of women's suffrage were also heirs to a civic-republican tradition that stressed the need for social order and shared values, emphasized civic education, and pressed the importance of having a propertied stake in society. Demands for the inclusion of women often did not extend to all women. Some women, and men, would be excluded by criteria of literacy, property ownership, disability or, in the United States, race. Thus liberal feminism often incorporated the civic-republican insistence on citizenship as a robust, civically demanding, and limited privilege rather than a legalistic and universalistic standing.

At times, feminist theory turned liberal egalitarianism on its head by arguing in favor of women's civic equality on grounds of difference, an argument that might be called neo-Aristotelianism. Ronald Beiner writes,

> *"How can 'the consent of the governed' be given, if the right to vote be denied?"*
>
> SUSAN B. ANTHONY
> IS IT A CRIME FOR A CITIZEN OF THE UNITED STATES TO VOTE? SPEECH BEFORE HER TRIAL FOR VOTING, 1873

> *The basic conception of neo-Aristotelianism is that moral reason consists not in a set of moral principles, apprehended and defined through procedures of detached rationality, but in the concrete embodiment of certain human capacities in a moral subject who knows those capacities to be constitutive of a consummately desirable life.* (Beiner, 1990, p. 75)

Thus greater female political participation was promoted in terms of women's moral supremacy or characteristic forms of virtue. These appeals arose from and spoke to women's social location as mothers, using motherhood as a claim to citizenship, public identity, and civic virtue (Kraditor, 1971). To individualist, rights-based feminists, however, the emphasis on maternal virtue as a form of civic virtue was a trap, for they were, and are, convinced that only liberalism, with its more individualistic construal of the human subject, permits women's equality and standing.

"When a just cause reaches its flood tide . . . whatever stands in the way must fall before its overwhelming power."

CARRIE CHAPMAN CATT
SPEECH AT STOCKHOLM, "IS WOMAN SUFFRAGE PROGRESSING?" 1911

The diverse history of feminism forms the basis for current feminist discourse and debate. These debates are rife with ethical imperatives and moral implications. Varieties of liberal, socialist, Marxist, and utopian feminism abound. Sexuality and sexual identity have become highly charged arenas of political redefinition. Some feminists see women as universal victims, some as a transhistorical sex class, others as oppressed "nature." A minority want separation from "male-dominated" society. Others want full integration into that society, hence its transformation toward liberal equality. Others insist that the feminist agenda will not be completed until "women's virtues," correctly understood, triumph. Feminism, too, is an essentially contested concept.

Divisions among feminists over such volatile matters as AIDS, IVF, surrogate embryo transfer, surrogate motherhood, sex selection—the entire menu of real or potential techniques for manipulating, controlling, and altering human reproduction—are strikingly manifest. One broad general tendency in feminist theory might be called noninterventionist. Noninterventionists see reproductive technologies as a strengthening of arrogant human control over nature and thus over women as part of the "nature" that is to be controlled. Alternatively, the prointerventionist stance foresees technological elimination of males and females themselves. Prointerventionists celebrate developments that promise control over nature.

The prointerventionists, who welcome and applaud any and all techniques that further sever biological reproduction from the social identity of maternity, are heavily indebted to a stance best called ultraliberalism. This theory is driven by a vision of the self that exists apart from any social order. This view of the self, in turn, is tied to one version of rights theory that considers human beings as self-sufficient, promoting a view of society that sees itself organized around contractual agreements between individuals.

THE SOCIAL-CONTRACT MODEL. The contract model has its historical roots in seventeenth-century social-contract theory, and it incorporates a view of society constituted by individuals for the fulfillment of individual ends, with social goods as aggregates of private goods. Critics claim that this vision of self and society ignores aspects of community life, such as reciprocal obligation and mutual interdependence, thereby eroding the bases of authority in family and polity alike.

The pervasiveness of the individualist position is further evident in the prointerventionist stance on bioethical innovations in the area of reproduction. In this view, new reproductive technologies present no problem as long as they can be wrested from male control (Donchin, 1986). Women, having been oppressed by "nature," can overthrow those shackles by seizing the "freedom" offered by technologies that promise deliverance from biological "tyranny." Strong prointerventionists go so far as to envisage forms of biological engineering that would make possible the following: "One woman could inseminate another, so that men and nonparturitive women could lactate and so that fertilized ova could be transplanted into women's or even into men's bodies" (Jaggar, 1983, p. 132). The standard of evaluation concerning these technologies is self-sufficiency and control, paving the way for invasive techniques that break women's links to biology, birth, and nurturance, the vestiges of our animal origins and patriarchal control.

The prointerventionist position owes a great deal to Simone de Beauvoir's feminist classic, *The Second Sex* (Beauvoir, 1968). Beauvoir argues that the woman's body does not "make sense" because women are "the victim of the species." The female, simply by being born female, suffers an alienation grounded in her biological capacity to bear a child. Women are invaded by the fetus, which Beauvoir describes as a "tenant" and a parasite upon the mother. Men, by contrast, are imbued with a sense of virile domination that extends to reproductive life. The life of the male is "transcended" in the sperm. Beauvoir's negative appraisal of the female body extends even to the claim that a woman's breasts are "mammary glands" that "play no role in woman's individual economy: they can be excised at any time of life" (Beauvoir, 1968, p. 24). If to this general repudiation of female embodiment one adds strong individualism, the prointerventionist stand becomes clearer.

Opposed to the radical prointerventionist stance is the noninterventionist voice associated with feminism in a less individualist, more communitarian frame. The

See Also
Sexism
Women

noninterventionists ponder the nature of the many choices the new reproductive technology offers. They wonder whether amniocentesis is really a free choice or merely a coercive procedure with only one "correct" outcome: to abort if the fetus is defective. They speculate whether new reproductive technologies are an imposition upon women who see themselves as failures if they cannot become pregnant. Furthermore, noninterventionists reassess the values identified with mothering and encourage the growth and triumph of values they consider to be strongly, if not exclusively, female. They insist that technological progress is never neutral, stressing that "progress" requiring the invasion and manipulation of women's bodies must always be scrutinized critically and may need to be rejected.

Strong noninterventionists claim that women want nothing to do with new reproductive technologies. In the words of one, "The so-called new technology does not bring us and our children any kind of qualitative or quantitative improvement in our lives, it solves none of our basic problems, it will advance even more the exploitation and humiliation of women; therefore we do not need it" (Mies, 1985, p. 559). As with the prointerventionist posture, there are noninterventionists who maintain a critical stance but do not condemn all reproductive technologies outright. Moderate prointerventionists support some but not all of the technological possibilities presented by contemporary reproductive science.

These differences played themselves out in the quandaries confronted by feminists with the Baby M surrogacy-motherhood case, a situation in which biological motherhood and social parenting were severed—as feminists, especially strong individualist feminists, had long claimed they could or should be (*Baby M, in re*, 1988). It was also a case in which everyone presumably freely agreed to a contract. Baby M was born to Mary Beth Whitehead, who had contracted with a couple, the Sterns, to be artificially inseminated with Mr. Stern's sperm. She was to relinquish the baby on birth for $10,000. Ultimately, she could not give the baby up and refused the money. The Sterns sued on breach of contract grounds.

Although liberal feminism emphasizes contractarian imperatives, many liberal feminists, including such popular leaders of the women's movement as the liberal Betty Friedan, saw in the initial denial of any claim by Mary Beth Whitehead, the natural mother, to her child, "an utter denial of the personhood of women—the complete dehumanization of women. It is an important human rights case. To put it at the level of contract law is to dehumanize women and the human bond between mother and child" (Barron, 1987). Friedan implies an ethical limitation to freedom of choice and contract.

Clearly, feminist debates concerning reproductive technology and surrogacy inexorably lead feminists back into discussions of men, women, children, families, and the wider community. Once again we see that bioethical capabilities and possibilities cannot be severed from wider cultural and social surroundings, including our understanding of the human person and his or her private and public needs, identities, and commitments. One broad frame, the social contract, has been noted; it either assumes or promotes the image of the self-sufficient self and goods as the properties of individuals.

THE SOCIAL-COMPACT MODEL. A second model of social theory, that of the social compact, or social covenant, offers a more rooted and historical picture of human beings than that of the social contract. Compact, or covenant, theory does not recognize primacy of rights and individual choice as the self-evident starting point. The compact self is a historical being who acknowledges that he or she has a "variety of debts, inheritance, rightful expectations, and obligations" and that these "constitute the given of my life, the moral starting point" (MacIntyre, 1981). Modern uprootedness is construed as a problem in the social compact. To be cut off from a wider community as well as from the past, as required by strong individualist modes, is to deform present relationships. The argument here is not that the compact self is totally defined by particular ties and identities, but that without a beginning that recognizes our essential sociality, there is no beginning at all.

Some feminists argue that reproductive technologies demean women as "fetal containers."

PAGE 598

The world endorsed in the social-compact model is in tension with the dominant individualist mindset. For this reason, individualists sometimes claim that communitarians, who endorse a social-compact idea, express little more than nostalgia for a simpler past. But the compact defenders argue, in turn, that the past presents itself as the living embodiment of vital traditional conflicts. The social compact makes room for rebellion against one's particular place as one way to forge an identity with reference to that place. But there is little space in the compact frame for social revolt to take a form that excises all social ties and relations if the individual "freely chooses" to do so, a possibility the contractarian must admit. It follows that the familial base of the social compact is opaque to the standpoint of contract theory, given its individualist foundation. This difference about the family, the social institution that first introduces the child into the world, is the focus of political theory debates that bear important implications for bioethics.

The family as a theoretical battleground

Given their individualist starting point, contractarians tend to devalue women's traditional roles and identities as mothers and familial beings. Proponents of the social-compact model, by contrast, understand women's contributions as wives, mothers, and social benefactors as vital to the creation and sustenance of life itself and, beyond that, of any possibility for a "good life." The compact theorist argues that community requires that an important segment or significant number of its members be devoted to the task of caring for the young, the vulnerable, and the elderly. Historically, the work of care has been seen by ethicists, political theorists, and political leaders, including many prominent women, as the mission of women. They worry that in a world of individualism, an ethic of care will be repudiated or replaced by modes of intervention less tied to concrete knowledge and concern of those being cared for (Ruddick, 1989; Tronto, 1993). They also advocate a reevaluation of families that gives conceptual weight to the "private realm" by showing that this sphere is central to social and political life. They insist that our understanding of justice must include a notion of what it means to be a caring society and to honor the work of care.

The compact theorist regrets the lack of a descriptive vocabulary that aptly and richly conveys what we mean when we talk about families and what makes caring commitments different from contractual agreements. The intergenerational family, for example, necessarily constitutes human beings in a particular web of relationships in a given time and place. Stanley Hauerwas, for example, claims that, "Set out in the world with no family, without a story of and for the self, we will simply be captured by the reigning ideologies of the day" (Hauerwas, 1981). We do not choose our relatives—they are given—and as a result, Hauerwas continues, we know what it means to have a history. Yet we continue to require a language to "help us articulate the experience of the family and the loyalty it represents. . . . Such a language must clearly denote our character as historical beings and how our moral lives are based in particular loyalties and relations. If we are to learn to care for others, we must first learn to care for those we find ourselves joined to by accident of birth" (Hauerwas, 1981).

Moral conflicts, for Plato, suggest irrationalism. If one cannot be loyal both to families and to the city, loyalty to one must be made to conform to the other. For Plato, then, "Our ordinary humanity is a source of confusion rather than of insight . . . [and] the philosopher alone judges the right criterion or from the appropriate standpoint" (Nussbaum, 1986). Hence the plan of *The Republic*, which aims to purify and to control human relations and emotions. Later strong rationalists and individualists take a similar tack: They hold that all relationships that are not totally voluntary, rationalistic, and contractual are irrational and suspect. Because

"Woman stock is rising in the market. I shall not live to see women vote, but I'll come and rap at the ballot box."

LYDIA MARIA CHILD
LETTER TO SARAH SHAW
1856

PLATO'S SOLUTION
Ban the Family

Political theorists have grappled with the issue of the family's relationship to the larger society from the beginning: Where does the family fit in relation to the polity? In *The Republic*, Plato eliminates the family for his ideal city. The ruler-philosophers he calls Guardians must take "the dispositions of human beings as though they were a tablet . . . which, in the first place, they would wipe clean" (Plato, 1986). Women must be held "in common." A powerful, all-encompassing bond between individuals and the state must be achieved such that all social and political conflict disappears, and the state comes to resemble a "single person," a fused, organic entity. All private loyalties and purposes must be eliminated.

Plato constructs a meritocracy that requires that all considerations of sex, race, age, class, family ties, tradition, and history be stripped away in order to fit people into their appropriate social slots, performing only that function to which each is suited. Children below the ruler class can be shunted upward or downward at the will of the Guardians, for they are so much raw material to be turned into instruments of social "good." A system of eugenics is devised for the Guardians. Children are removed from mothers at birth and placed in a child ghetto, tended to by those best suited for the job. No private loyalties of any kind are allowed to emerge: Homes and sexual attachments, devotion to friends, and dedication to individual or group aims militate against single-minded devotion to the city. Particular ties are a great evil. Only those that bind the individual to the state are good.

No doubt the modern reader finds this rather extreme. Many contemporary theorists contend that Plato constructed his utopia in an ironic mode. Whether Plato meant it or not, his vision is instructive, for it helps us to think about the relation of the family to wider civic loyalties and obligations. Plato aspired to "rational self-sufficiency." He would make the lives of human beings immune to the fragility of messy existence. The idea of self-sufficiency was one of mastery in which the male citizen was imbued with a "mythology of autochthony that persistently, and paradoxically, suppressed the biological role of the female and therefore the family in the continuity of the city" (Nussbaum, 1986).

—JEAN BETHKE ELSHTAIN

the family is the ultimate example of embedded particularity, ideal justice and order will be attained only when "the slate has been wiped clean" and human beings are no longer limited by familial obligations.

Yet a genuinely pluralist civic order would seem to require diversity on the level of families as well as other institutions which, in turn, promote and give rise to many stories and visions of virtue. This suggests the following questions for social and political theory: In what ways is the family issue also a civic issue with weighty public consequences? What is the relationship between democratic theory and practice and intergenerational family ties and commitments? Do we have a stake in sustaining some models of adults in relation to children compared to others? What do families, composed of parents and children, do that no other social institution can? How does current political rhetoric support family obligations and relations?

Equality among citizens was assumed from the beginning by liberals and democrats; indeed, the citizen was, by definition, equal to any other citizen. Not everyone, of course, could be a citizen. At different times and to different ends and purposes, women, slaves, and the propertyless were excluded. But these exclusions were slowly dropped. Whether the purview of some or all adults in a given society, liberal and democratic citizenship required the creation of persons with qualities of mind and spirit necessary for civic participation. This creation of citizens was seen as neither simple nor automatic by early liberal theorists, leading many to insist upon a structure of education in "the sentiments." This education should usher into a moral autonomy that stresses self-chosen obligations, thereby casting further suspicion upon all relations, practices, and loyalties deemed unchosen, involuntary, or natural.

Within such accounts of civic authority, the family emerged as a problem. For one does not enter a family through free consent; one is born into the world unwilled and unchosen by oneself, beginning life as a helpless and dependent infant. Before reaching "the age of consent," one is a child, not a citizen. This vexed liberal and democratic theorists, some of whom believed, at least abstractly, that the completion of the democratic ideal required bringing all of social life under the sway of a single democratic authority principle.

COMMUNITARIAN VERSUS INDIVIDUALIST VIEWS OF FAMILY: MILL AND TOCQUEVILLE. In his tract *The Subjection of Women*, John Stuart Mill argued that his contemporaries, male and female alike, were tainted by the atavisms of family life with its illegitimate, or unchosen, male authority, and its illegitimate, or manipulative and irrational, female quests for private power (Mill, 1970). He believed that the family can become a school in the virtues of freedom only when parents live together without power on one side and obedience on the other. Power, for Mill, is repugnant: True liberty must reign in all spheres. But what about the children? Mill's children emerge as blank slates on which parents must encode the lessons of obedience and the responsibilities of freedom. Stripped of undemocratic authority and privilege, the parental union serves as a model of democratic probity (Krouse, 1982).

YOUNG AMERICANS

Alexis de Tocqueville (1805–1859) saw children as both ends and means to a well-ordered democratic family and polity.

Mill's paean to liberal individualism is an interesting contrast to Alexis de Tocqueville's observations of family life in nineteenth-century America, a society already showing the effects of the extension of democratic norms and the breakdown of patriarchal and Puritan norms and practices. Fathers in Tocqueville's America were at once stern and forgiving, strong and flexible. They listened to their children and humored them (Tocqueville, 1980). They educated as well as demanded obedience, promulgating a new ethic of child rearing. Like the new democratic father, the American political leader did not demand that citizens bow or stand transfixed in awe. The leader was owed respect and, if he urged a course of action upon his fellow citizens following proper consultation and procedural requirements, they had a patriotic duty to follow.

"Not only does democracy make every man forget his ancestors, but it hides his descendants and separates his contemporaries from him."

DE TOCQUEVILLE
DEMOCRACY IN AMERICA
1835

Tocqueville's discerning eye perceived changing public and private relationships in a liberal, democratic society. Although great care was taken "to trace two clearly distinct lines of action for the two sexes," women, in their domestic sphere, "nowhere occupied a loftier position of honor and importance," Tocqueville claimed. The mother's familial role was enhanced in her civic vocation as the chief inculcator of democratic values in her offspring. Commenting in a civic-republican vein, Tocqueville notes, "No free communities ever existed without morals and, as I observed . . . , morals are the work of women" (Tocqueville, 1945).

Clearly, Tocqueville rests in the social-covenant or communitarian camp; Mill, in the social-contract or individualist domain. In contrast to Mill, Tocqueville insisted that the father's authority in a liberal society was neither absolute nor arbitrary. In contrast to the patriarchal authoritarian family where the parent not only has a "natural right" but acquires a "political right" to command his children, in a democratic family the right and authority of parents is a natural right alone. This natural authority presents no problem for democratic practices as Tocqueville construed democracy, in contrast to Mill. Indeed, the fact that the "right to command" is natural, not political, signifies its special and temporary nature: Once the child is self-governing, the right dissolves. In this way, natural, legitimate paternal authority and maternal moral education reinforce a political order that values flexibility, freedom, and the absence of absolute rule, but requires order and stability as well.

"A youth, when at home, should be filial, and, abroad, respectful to his elders."

CONFUCIUS
THE ANALECTS

Popular columnists and "child experts" in Tocqueville's America emphasized kindness and love as the preferred technique of child nurture. Obedience was still seen as necessary—to parents, elders, God, government, and the conscience. But the child was no longer construed as a depraved, sin-ridden, stiff-necked creature who needed harsh, unyielding instruction and reproof. A more benign view of the child's nature emerged as notions of infant depravity faded. The problem of discipline grew more, rather than less, complex. Parents were enjoined to get obedience without corporal punishment and rigid methods, using affection, issuing their commands in gentle but firm voices, insisting quietly on their authority lest contempt and chaos reign in the domestic sphere (Elshtain, 1990).

FAMILY AUTHORITY AND THE STATE. In Tocqueville's image of the democratic family, children were seen both as ends and as means to a well-ordered family and polity. A widespread moral consensus reigned in the America of that era, a kind of Protestant civic religion. When this consensus began to erode under the force of rapid social change (and there are analogues to the American story in all modern democracies), certainties surrounding familial life and authority as a secure locus for the creation of democratic citizens were shaken as well. Tocqueville suggested that familial authority, though apparently at odds with the governing presumptions of democratic authority, is nonetheless part of the constitutive

FAMILY AUTHORITY
A Necessary but Risky Stewardship

What makes family authority distinctive is its sense of stewardship: the recognition that parents undertake continuing obligations and responsibilities. Certainly in the modern West, given the long period of childhood and adolescence we honor and recognize, parenting is an ongoing task. The authority of the parent is special, limited, and particular. Parental authority, like any form of authority, may be abused, but unless it exists, the activity of parenting itself is impossible. The authority of parents is implicated in moral education required for the creation of a democratic political morality. The intense loyalties, obligations, and moral imperatives nurtured in families may clash with the requirements of public authority, for example, when young men refuse to serve in a war they claim is unjust because war runs counter to the religious beliefs of their families. This, too, is vital for democracy. Keeping alive a potential locus for revolt, for particularity, for difference, sustains democracy in the long run. It is no coincidence, this argument concludes, that all twentieth-century totalitarian orders aimed to destroy the family as a locus of identity and meaning apart from the state. Totalitarian politics strives to require that individuals identify only with the state rather than with specific others, including family and friends.

Family authority within a democratic, pluralistic order, however, does not exist in a direct homologous relation to the principles of civil society. To establish an identity between public and private lives and purposes would weaken, not strengthen, democratic life overall. For children need particular, intense relations with specific adult others in order to learn to make choices as adults. The child confronted prematurely with the "right to choose" is likely to be less capable of choosing later on. To become a being capable of posing alternatives, one requires a sure and certain place from which to start. In Mary Midgley's words: "Children . . . have to live *now* in a particular culture; they must take some attitude to the nearest things right away" (Midgley, 1978). The social form best suited to provide children with a trusting, determinate sense of place and ultimately a "self" is a family in which parents provide ongoing care, protection, and concern.

— JEAN BETHKE ELSHTAIN

See Also
Family
'Family': Defining a Variable Term

background required for the survival and flourishing of democracy.

Family relations, so this politico-ethical argument goes, could not exist without family authority. These relations and responsibilities, in turn, remain the best way to create human beings with a developed capacity to give ethical allegiance to the principles of democratic society. Because democratic citizenship relies on the self-limiting freedom of responsible adults, a mode of child rearing that builds on basic trust, loyalty, and a sense of commitment is necessary. Family authority structures the relationship between adult providers, nurturers, educators, and disciplinarians, and dependent children, who slowly acquire capacities for independence. Modern parental authority is shared by mother and father.

The stance of the democratic political and social theorist toward family authority resists easy characterization. It involves a rejection of any ideal of political and familial life that absorbs all social relations under a single authority principle. Families are not democratic polities. The family helps to hold intact the respective goods and ends of exclusive relations and arrangements. Any further erosion of that ethical life embodied in the family bodes ill for democracy. For this reason, theorists representing the communitarian or social-covenant perspective are often among the most severe critics of contemporary consumerism, violence in streets and the media, the decline of public education, the rise in numbers of children being raised without fathers, and so on. They insist, against their critics, that a defense of the family—by which they mean a normative ideal of mothers and fathers in relation to children and to a wider community—can help to sustain a variety of ethical and social commitments, including providing a strong example of adults working together to create a home. Because democracy itself turns on a generalized notion of the fraternal bond between citizens (male and female), it is vital for children to have early experiences of trust and mutuality. The child who emerges from such a family is more likely to be capable of acting in the world as a complex moral being, one part of, yet somewhat detached from, the immediacy of his or her own concerns and desires.

Toward an ethical polity

All political and social theorists, whatever their particular philosophic frameworks and normative commitments, agree that social and political theories always embody some ideal of a preferred way of life. Although a handful of postmodern or deconstructive contemporary theorists disdain all normative standards, most social and political thinkers insist that no way of life can persist without a widely shared cluster of basic notions. Those who locate ethical concerns at the heart of their theories hope for a world in which private and public lives bearing their own intrinsic purpose are allowed to flourish. A richly complex private sphere requires freedom from some all-encompassing public imperative for survival. But in order for the private sphere to flourish, the public world itself must nurture and sustain a set of ethical imperatives, including a commitment to preserve, protect, and defend human beings in their capacities as private persons, and to allow men and women alike to partake in the good of the public sphere with participatory equality (Elshtain, 1981). Such an ideal seeks to keep alive rather than to eliminate tension between diverse spheres and competing ideals and purposes. There is always a danger that a too strong and overweening polity will overwhelm the individual, as well as a peril that life in a polity confronted with a continuing crisis of legitimacy may decivilize both those who oppose it and those who would defend it.

The prevailing image of the person in an ethical polity is that of a human being with a capacity for self-reflection. Such persons can tolerate the tension between public and private imperatives. They can distinguish between those conditions, events, or states of affairs that are part of a shared human condition—grief, loss through death, natural disasters, and decay of the flesh—and those humanly made injustices that can be remedied. Above all, human beings within the ethical polity never presume that ambivalence and conflict will one day end, for they have come to understand that ambivalence and conflict are the wellspring of a life lived reflectively. A clear notion of what ideals and obligations are required to animate an authentic public life, an ethical polity, must be adumbrated: authority, freedom, public law, civic virtue, the ideal of the citizen, all those beliefs, habits, and qualities that are integral to a political order.

Much of the richest theorizing of democratic civil society since 1980 has come from citizens of countries who were subjected for forty years or more to authoritarian, even totalitarian regimes. They pose alternatives both to collectivism and to individualism by urging that the associations of civil society be recognized as subjects in their own right. They call for a genuinely pluralist law to recognize and sustain this associative principle as a way to overcome excessive privatization, on the one hand, and overweening state control, on the other. Solidarity theorist Adam Michnik insists that democracy

> *entails a vision of tolerance, and understanding of the importance of cultural traditions, and the realization*

> *"I have never been more struck by the good sense and the practical judgment of the Americans than in the manner in which they elude the numberless difficulties resulting from their Federal Constitution."*
>
> DE TOCQUEVILLE
> DEMOCRACY IN AMERICA
> 1835

See Also

Family: Implementing Family Ethics

that cherished human values can conflict with each other. . . . The essence of democracy as I understand it is freedom—the freedom which belongs to citizens endowed with a conscience. So understood, freedom implies pluralism, which is essential because conflict is a constant factor within a democratic social order.

(Michnik, 1988, p. 198)

Michnik insists that the genuine democrat always struggles with his or her own tradition, eschewing the hopelessly heroic and individualist notion of going it alone. Michnik positions himself against contemporary tendencies to see any defense of tradition as necessarily "conservative"; indeed, he criticizes all rigidly ideological thinking that severs every political and ethical concern between right and left, proclaiming that "a world devoid of tradition would be nonsensical and anarchic. The human world should be constructed from a permanent conflict between conservatism and contestation; if either is absent from a society, pluralism is destroyed" (Michnik, 1988, p. 199).

A second vital political-ethical voice is that of Vaclav Havel, a playwright, dissident, political theorist, and, in the years following the "tender revolution" of 1989, the president of a then-united Czechoslovakia. In his essay, "Politics and Conscience," he writes:

We must trust the voice of our conscience more than that of all abstract speculations and not invent other responsibilities than the one to which the voice calls us. We must not be ashamed that we are capable of love, friendship, solidarity, sympathy and tolerance, but just the opposite: we must see these fundamental dimensions of our humanity free from their "private" exile and accept them as the only genuine starting point of meaningful human community.

(Havel, 1986, pp. 153–154)

To this end, he favors what he calls "anti-political politics," defined not as the technology of power and manipulation, of cybernetic rule over humans or as the art of the useful, but politics as one of the ways of seeking and achieving meaningful lives, of protecting them and serving them. "I favor politics as practical morality, as service to the truth, as essentially human and humanly measured care for our fellow humans. It is, I presume, an approach which, in this world, is extremely impractical and difficult to apply in daily life. Still, I know no better alternative" (Havel, 1986, p. 155). This is the voice of an ethical polity. Were this voice to prevail, the way in which our ethical dilemmas are adjudicated, including those emerging from bioethics, would be rich and complex enough to enable us to see the public and civic consequences of our private choices, even as it would guard against severe intrusion into intimate life from the outside.

Ethical dilemmas are inescapably political and political questions are unavoidably ethical. Bioethical matters can never be insulated from politics, nor should they be. But the way in which such matters are addressed will very much turn on the social or political theories to which the ethicist, the medical practitioner, the patient or consumer, and the wider, interested community are indebted.

— JEAN BETHKE ELSHTAIN

◆ **ethics**
The principles of conduct governing an individual or group; also a theory or system of moral values, or notions having to do with morality, virtue, rationality, and ideals of conduct and motivation.

See Also
Conscience

RELIGION AND MORALITY

In the minds of many people, religion and morality are closely connected. Even in secular discussions of ethics, law, and medicine, the presumption remains strong that religious beliefs are an important source of moral guidance, and that religious authorities have a significant influence in shaping attitudes toward biomedical research, new technologies, and medical interventions at the beginning and end of life. Both those who hold religious beliefs and those who do not expect that such beliefs will make a significant difference in the moral lives of their adherents.

When this commonplace assumption about the connection between religion and morality is subjected to examination, however, problems emerge. Although moral virtues and behaviors characteristic of Christian love or Buddhist compassion may be clearly associated with a specific religion, the human possibilities they describe are often familiar and admired, even among those who do not share the religious beliefs. Persons outside of a community of faith may display its characteristic virtues, and those who reject a particular religion may realize its moral ideals better than most of its adherents. For example, Christian writers often turn to Gandhi as the modern model of the love that Jesus preached, while Gandhi valued the life of Jesus as an example of the harmlessness he sought to encourage. This recognition of specific moral virtues in persons outside the community of belief in which those virtues are defined and taught is so common today as to be unremarkable, but it challenges the assumption that specific moral beliefs and practices can be tied to specific religious commitments.

The assumption that religion and morality are somehow related thus gives way to questions about exactly what forms this relationship may take and how it is understood. What claims are persons making when they relate a moral judgment to a religious belief, and how are we to understand the similar judgments that others make on nonreligious grounds? How will these different moral and religious orientations relate to the findings of the biomedical sciences? How should the providers of medical services relate to the diversity of these religious and moral orientations in a complex, pluralistic society?

Types of relationships

A first step toward answering these questions is to identify the variety of relationships between religion and morality that are found in the world's moral and religious traditions (Little and Twiss, 1978). In general, religion is an authoritative source of moral norms and a primary motivation for conformity to moral requirements. Significant variations on this general idea do, however, exist. Is religion the only source of the moral norms, or may those norms, or some of them, be discovered or created in other ways? Is the authoritative source the will of a divine lawgiver, or an intrinsic goodness in the nature of things themselves? Is the motive for moral action a religious love of the good for its own sake, or the hope for an ultimate compensation for the hardships that moral behavior sometimes requires?

Answers to these questions differ, both among different religious traditions and among different schools of thought within a single tradition. The major monotheistic traditions—Judaism, Christianity, and Islam—often represent key moral norms as direct commands of God. In the religions that originated in India—Hinduism, Jainism, and Buddhism—by contrast, the central concept is *karma*, a cosmic moral order that fixes inescapable consequences for any action (Green, 1978). Protestant Christianity has often stressed the word of God, the direct divine command that is independent of any human knowledge or wisdom, while Roman Catholic moral theology has relied more on the concept of "natural law," a moral order established by God, but knowable by human reason and apparent in the workings of the natural order (Gustafson, 1978).

While it would be possible to explore the relationships between religion and morality by surveying major religious traditions individually, that approach would quickly become a volume unto itself, and it would still do scant justice to the nuances and variety within each tradition. For present purposes, we must limit consideration to a typology of relationships that can be observed in a number of traditions, especially as these traditions come into contact with one another and with the forces of modern technological change. Examples of each type can be identified in a variety of religious traditions, but readers who seek a comprehensive understanding of morality in, for instance, Buddhism or Islam will need to consult other sources, some of which are identified in the bibliography for this article.

RELIGION AND MORALITY

Three Types of Relationships

1. *Cosmic unity*: Moral obligations derive from a natural or metaphysical order, understood in religious terms.
2. *Logical independence*: Moral norms not directly dependent on religion for validity; religious values must be distinguished from judgments of moral worth.
3. *Cultural interdependence*: Neither religion nor morality can be understood apart from the communities in which they developed.

This typology is derived from modern Western scholarship and reflects particularly the development of religion in modern, secular societies. Each of the types, however, has roots in earlier developments in Western theology and philosophy, and most have parallels in other, non-Western religious and cultural communities. While the emphasis in what follows will be on the modern West, much will be relevant to modern and modernizing cultures in other parts of the world, and analogies to the relationship between religion and morality in other cultural settings may illuminate both those settings and the West's.

COSMIC UNITY. Many cultures have conceived moral and natural orders as an undifferentiated unity. The rewards and punishments associated with moral action are as much a part of reality as the forces of wind and water or the patterns of growth and development observed in plants and animals. To put the matter another way, both the observable patterns of nature and the system of moral requirements are part of a larger order that encompasses all reality, seen and unseen. This unity, expressed both in myths and poetry and in speculative metaphysics, comes into question as science and philosophy develop, but it remains a powerful influence, even in modern, secular societies.

Sometimes, the power that requires moral conduct is thought of in impersonal terms, as a force to be reckoned with by humans and by more powerful beings as well. Early Greek philosophers and poets understood justice (*dikē*) in these terms. Justice keeps gods and humans from exceeding their limits, and those who ignore justice risk disaster for the whole community (Adkins, 1985). In ancient China, *tao* was a pervasive force that both regulated the order of natural events and set the standard for human conduct (Girardot, 1985). Similar concepts appear in other traditions.

In the Hebrew scriptures, the ultimate power is a personal God who is not subject to higher forces, but who addresses human beings in terms of moral commandments (Deut. 5:1-21). This God is also the creator of the natural forces with which humans must

◆ **morality**
A compromise between two inherently conflictual sides of nature, a code of conduct, for the sake of a semblance of decency in the social order.

See Also
Law and Morality
Population Ethics: Buddhist Perspectives

reckon. A somewhat later strand of the tradition represents wisdom (*hokmah*) as the pervasive, unifying power by which God both shapes the material world and directs the conduct of good persons (Prov. 8:1-31).

These early conceptions of a moral order inherent in the order of things often gave way to an understanding of laws and obligations as purely human creations, having power only so far as they are enforced. The development of these skeptical ideas often coincided with the breakdown of traditional social patterns, or with the discovery of other peoples and cultures who lived by quite different rules. Both Greek and Roman philosophers, however, retained the notion that some requirements are not conventional, but natural. However much Greece and Persia otherwise may have differed, some moral requirements remained the same in both places (Aristotle, 1962).

Natural law is perhaps the most ancient and historically persistent concept in Western ethics.

PAGE 481

This idea provided theologians with the basis for a concept of "natural law," through which God's commandments could be known by all rational persons. Thus, the same minimal requirements of morality apply to everyone, whether or not they share the same ideas about God. Both Judaism and Islam developed philosophical systems that transmitted the Hellenistic notion of natural law to the Christian West, and for a brief time in the Middle Ages, teachers in all three traditions could debate the relationship between God's will and the created order in a shared philosophical framework (Jacobs, 1978). In medieval Christian theology, natural law related all rational beings to God. Natural law was seen to be the way a finite, rational being participates in the eternal law by which God orders the universe.

The ever-present possibility of elevating a particular aspect of nature to the level of equality with God led, however, to widespread suspicion of natural law ideas among moral and religious reformers. The main line of development in Jewish ethics centered on observance of a code of law based on scripture and rabbinic interpretation, rather than on a rationalist moral philosophy (Lichtenstein, 1978). In Islam, the philosophical movement evolved in a more mystical direction, focused on the identity of the human spirit with the spiritual character of all reality, rather than on the moral requirements of a natural order (Rahman, 1979). In Western Christianity, the Protestant Reformation challenged all forms of religious legalism, including the precepts of natural law.

During the seventeenth century, however, a new group of legal and political theorists seized upon the concept of natural law as the key to understanding the relationships between nations as well as persons. While the religious significance of the natural law was not necessarily rejected, it was the universality of the obligation, not its divine origin, that attracted these jurists to the idea. In both legal and theological treatments of natural law, however, these highly articulated systems of moral thought share with the earliest myths of cosmic unity the notion that some moral requirements are inescapable because they are part of the structure of reality itself. Since World War II, renewed interest in theories of natural law as a starting point for an international recognition of basic human rights testifies to the continuing significance of this way of relating moral requirements to religious beliefs about the origin and end of the world in which the moral life is lived (Maritain, 1951).

The idea of a comprehensive order that encompasses both moral and religious requirements thus appears both in the most ancient religious traditions and in modern Western theories of natural law. Although reformers in many theistic traditions have sought to restore religious morality to a direct dependence on the will of God, the underlying idea that what God wills is also supported by the natural order that God has created never entirely disappears, even when the human ability to know God's will through the natural order is contested.

LOGICAL INDEPENDENCE. The fact that religion and morality are closely related in the history of Western thought does not, of itself, establish that their connection is important for contemporary moral decisions. The historical relationships might be viewed as accidental or contingent, subject to change without altering the basic requirements of morality. The links between religion and morality might even be points of confusion that obscure important features of both religious and moral truths. For some thinkers, then, it is important to establish the distinction between religious and moral evaluations, even though these may be commonly confused in practice, or integrally related in some more comprehensive system of ideas. Failure to make the distinction between religion and morality runs the risk of subordinating both to prevailing cultural practices, which may themselves be morally questionable.

By the eighteenth century, European philosophers had begun to advance theories about the historical development of religion that were not based on the history presented in the Bible. Religion could thus be given a "natural history," as opposed to the sacred history revealed in scripture. David Hume's "The Natural History of Religion," (Hume, 1927) postulated a primitive connection between fear of the awesome power of natural forces and dread of punishment for moral transgressions. Such fear may continue to serve as a useful inducement to moral conformity, but it leads only to confusion if the source of the moral imperatives is sought in a supernatural power. Against those who worried that a distinction between religion and moral-

See Also
Natural Law

ity would lead to a decline in moral standards, Hume argued that a sound logical connection between moral requirements and the public good was the only secure basis for morality. A utilitarian calculation of the line of conduct that will produce the largest social benefits is the final source of moral norms, and respect for that public good is the only secure ground of moral motivation.

In addition to the possibility that the connection between religion and morality is simply a residue of primitive superstitions, philosophers noted another point that seemed not only to distinguish religion from morality, but also to give a logical priority to morality. Religious traditions frequently praise a divine center and origin of moral goodness, or point to the lives of exemplary religious figures as examples to be followed. To recognize that goodness seems, however, to require a moral judgment that precedes the religious assent. We can only praise God or emulate the saints for moral goodness if we have an idea of what is morally good, by which we measure even these supreme examples. "Even the Holy One of the gospel," wrote Immanuel Kant, "must first be compared with our ideal of moral perfection before we can recognize him as such" (Kant, 1964, p. 76).

Clearly, whether one begins with Hume's "natural history" of religion or Kant's rational foundation for moral judgments, morality and religion cannot be simply identical. The Christian natural law tradition used reason to discern God's will in the order of the created world. In Kant and Hume, reason formulates its requirements independently, on the basis of social utility or of logical necessity. The resulting standard of morality is then applied to religion, which may or may not measure up.

This separation of moral requirements from religious belief does not, however, imply that religion has no connection to morality. Many who accepted a rational morality, the requirements of which did not depend on faith, continued to value religion as a motive for the moral life. Love of a God who is perfect in goodness, and reverence for saints who have upheld the requirements of morality in the face of severe temptations, provide powerful motives for people to live up to moral expectations in more ordinary circumstances. Indeed, Kant argued that some conception of God is ultimately required to make sense of the sacrifices that all moral action requires of us. The logical independence of morality from religion does not require that religion be abandoned, but it does require that moral actions be undertaken precisely because we are convinced that they are morally right, and not because we believe that God commands us to do them.

These philosophical developments coincided with important historical changes in European religious life. By the end of the seventeenth century, the normative requirement of religious conformity was rapidly being replaced by practices of religious toleration and, eventually, by a civic commitment to religious freedom. The logical separation of religion from morality became a sociological necessity as well, if citizens who were no longer united in their religious beliefs were to acknowledge moral obligations to one another. In the United States, especially, the idea developed that a variety of quite different religious beliefs could support a common moral consensus (Frost, 1990). Because morality and religion are independent, diversity of religious beliefs need not lead to moral conflict, and moral order does not require religious agreement.

In other cases, where the break with traditional forms of religious and social life was sharper, or where the conflict between religious groups was more intense, public moral expectations were reformulated in nonreligious terms. Where cooperation between religion and government proved difficult, or where the moral consensus between different religious groups was obviously lacking, the concept of a "secular state" provided the necessary basis for social unity. A secular state not only refuses to privilege one or another religious perspective among its people, it resolutely excludes religious considerations from the formation of policy and regulations. Religion and religious morality become private considerations, subject to regulation for the public good.

This understanding first emerges clearly in the French Revolution, but the idea of a secular state has also provided hope for civil unity for many twentieth-century leaders in countries deeply divided by religious strife or torn by controversy over modernizations that undermine traditional forms of religious life. In the United States, where the prevailing model has been the religious consensus on moral expectations, elements of the secular state concept have nonetheless been invoked to curb sectarian religious practices that differ sharply from those of the majority, or to exclude religious arguments from controversial questions of policy. Judicial limitation of a parent's power to withhold medical care from children on religious grounds and political arguments that Roman Catholic opposition to abortion violates the constitutional separation of church and state are two instances in which the apparent lack of religious consensus has prompted arguments for policies of a secular state.

The logical separation of morality from religion, then, provides an important intellectual starting point for the ordering of societies divided by religious differences or seeking to modernize in the face of opposition by traditional religious groups. The distinction between religion and morality does not, by itself, prescribe a role for religion in public life. Religion may be

"Morality is not properly the doctrine of how we may make ourselves happy, but how we may make ourselves worthy of happiness."

IMMANUEL KANT
CRITIQUE OF PRACTICAL REASON, 1788

See Also

Justice; Natural Law; Value and Valuation

one element in a powerful moral consensus that differs from the religious morality of a traditional society, or it may be virtually excluded from influence by a secular state that defines public morality in terms of a utilitarian calculation of the public good.

CULTURAL INTERDEPENDENCE. Although the logical separation of morality from religion is a premise for much of western European and North American thought in ethics, law, politics, and even theology, its relevance to other points in history and other parts of the world is less clear. The modern Western distinction between religion and morality is missing from many highly developed religious and cultural systems, which assign duties to persons on the basis of their position in society without obvious distinctions between what modern Westerners differentiate into moral requirements, common courtesy, religious obligations, and patriotic duties.

This is most clear in the traditional societies of India, China, and Japan. Hinduism recognizes few duties that correspond to the universal moral obligations of modern Western ethics. Specific persons owe duties to specific others, based on the place each occupies in a social, moral, and religious hierarchy, so that traditional Hinduism can hardly exist outside of the social system in which it originates. In China, a Confucian system of philosophical morality was tied to the details of the education and duties of an elite corps of governing intellectuals, while in Japan, the traditional religion of the people centered on the cults of specific ancestors and the spirits of specific places. Hinduism and, to a certain extent, Confucianism demonstrated in the nineteenth century that they could be reinterpreted in more universal philosophical terms, but the reconstruction of State Shinto in Japan during the same time period suggests that the unitary system of religion, state, and morals can also be adapted to the demands of modernizing societies (Hardacre, 1989).

◆ **moral principles**
Derived from actual practices, refined by reflection and experience, and always open to further revision and reinterpretation in new cases.

While the interdependence of religion and culture is most clearly seen in these highly developed national traditions, the missionary religions that have moved across large parts of the world also illustrate this interdependence, precisely in their adaptability to very different cultural settings. Christianity presents very different appearances in Moscow and in Dallas. Buddhism in Tokyo is distinctively Japanese, as it is distinctively Thai in Bangkok. The same might be said for Islam in Cairo and in Kuala Lumpur. Nor are these variations simply the result of a constant teaching consciously applied to different situations. Religious traditions develop by interacting with the economic life and productive systems by which their adherents meet their material needs, as well as by the inner logic of their spiritual teachings. The modern sociological study of religion rests on this awareness of the nonreligious forces that operate on religious communities and the unintended consequences that religious beliefs have in the world of economic life (Weber, 1958).

See Also
Population Ethics: Hindu Teachings
Sexual Ethics: Christian Traditions

Those who view religion from this perspective identify important changes that religions undergo in modern, technological societies. The institutions of religion no longer occupy the central positions of power and authority they once held. Wider knowledge of the world and more exposure to other cultures lead to an awareness of other religions beside one's own. These changes mark what sociologists call secularization, but the interactions of religion and culture are no less real in that context than they were when religion had a more dominant position.

Secularization may reduce the power of religious institutions and leaders, but it does not produce a neutral culture free of religious influences. A "secular" society is shaped in part by the historical interactions between the religion and culture that have shaped the particular place in which the society now exists. A modern economy influenced by a Confucian past differs significantly from one that has developed out of European Protestantism. The process of secularization, therefore, does not provide a neutral, universal standpoint from which to settle questions of morality and policy.

Since the 1970s, social scientists, philosophers, and theologians have widely accepted this contextualization of their work and have sought to explore its implications for their systematic thought (Stout, 1988). What was believed to be universal and rational is now widely seen to be particular. Notions of objectivity, tables of individual rights and duties—even, perhaps, the idea of rationality itself—are shaped by particular cultural starting points.

Where supposed neutrality and rational authority have been used to suppress religious conflict, the continuing influence of religion on culture sometimes results in violent rejection of the secular state and its institutions. Fundamentalist movements throughout the Islamic world and among Hindus in India reject modern secular culture as an alien Western imposition and reassert an identity of religion, morality, and culture. In the United States and elsewhere, renewed interest in the religions of indigenous peoples includes a rediscovery of their distinctive understandings of health and healing, which link religion, morality, and medicine in ways unfamiliar to modern medical science (Sullivan, 1988).

The implications of this reassertion of the cultural integrity of religion and morality are, however, variously construed by authors reflecting on modern pluralistic societies. One view suggests that the loss of community and the rise of social disorder is a direct result of the attempt to exclude from public discussion the religious values that are the only available foundation for moral-

ity. The social achievements that people in the United States most prize, including their individual rights and political freedoms, are simply the fruit of the Christian moral traditions that gave rise to them. If we hope to continue to enjoy them, we must restore those moral traditions in which they originate to a central role in shaping the life of society (Neuhaus, 1984).

Another point of view suggests, by contrast, that the public life of a pluralistic society can no longer provide a forum for genuine moral convictions, which always have a particular religious basis. If we seek to develop persons of moral character, we must do it within religious communities that have a distinctive identity. It may then be possible to translate some of these religious values into public policy through political action, but it will not be possible to offer a public argument for the values at stake. They can only be understood in a community where the way of life in which they originate is cherished and enacted (Hauerwas, 1981).

An understanding of the cultural interdependence of religion and morality thus calls into question both the cosmic order that sustains religion's requirements everywhere and the universal, rational morality that is characteristic of modern understandings of the independence of morality from religion. In this emphasis on cultural specificity that is sometimes called "postmodern," everything depends on the relationship between religion and morality in a particular place and time. Those who hold this view agree on the importance of the interaction of morality and religion. They differ over whether this interaction should take the form of cultural hegemony by a particular religious tradition, in order to provide the necessary foundation for public order, or should be practiced in small communities of shared faith, who venture into politics and public policy only for limited purposes and confine their virtues to their separated life.

Implications for bioethics

Perhaps the most striking result of this survey is the diversity of relationships between religion and morality that are held in different religious traditions and, indeed, within the same religious tradition, in different historical and cultural settings. In a pluralistic society, where researchers often work in global networks and medical-care providers deal with patients and families from many communities, many different understandings of morality and religion will impinge on their work, raising new issues in bioethics.

Questions of patient autonomy and appropriate respect for the human subjects of biomedical research become even more difficult when the parties have not only different religious beliefs about the nature of the human being, but also different understandings of how these beliefs appropriately relate to moral decisions that

CULTURAL COMPLEXITIES
How to Decide, and on What Basis?

Cultural interdependence opens up possibilities for serious conflicts between cultural perspectives in medical and scientific institutions. Often, research and clinical personnel do not share the commitments of universities or hospitals that have religious sponsorship. An ethical commitment to scientific objectivity or clinical autonomy, which is easy to sustain when religion and morality are believed to be logically distinct, may come into conflict with the view that sustaining a distinctive religious culture within the institution is the only way to sustain it as a moral community. Alternatively, religious views that stress the importance of distinctive moral communities may withdraw from the more complex, pluralistic world of the medical center or research institute, thus eliminating a possibly important mediating influence between the narrowly focused aims of medical practice and the values of ordinary Jews, Catholics, Muslims, or Baptists who happen for the moment to be patients in a medical facility.

The increasing cultural complexity of biomedical science and its institutions prompts the search for a core of morality that would provide the basis for policy decisions, without requiring unanimity on the religious reasons for those moral requirements. Logical independence of this common morality from particular religious commitments seems to be required, whether the morality is to be founded on a universal moral logic or, less ambitiously, on the necessary requirements of medical practice. Although the idea of a completely neutral, secular medical ethics may no longer be plausible, a standard of "secular arguments" for policy choices seems to some observers to solve the problem of moral and religious difference. By insisting that arguments for or against specific policy choices must be made for reasons accessible to all parties in the debate, we eliminate public choices based on specific religious convictions. Arguments for or against a program of acquired immunodeficiency syndrome (AIDS) education and prevention on ground of its effect on community health are acceptable. Arguments for or against it on grounds that it conforms to the requirements of a specific religious teaching are not.

— ROBIN W. LOVIN

◆ **cultural relativism**
A descriptive reaction, based on evaluations using internal (not external) criteria, to wide experience with other cultures.

See Also

Bioethics: When Values Conflict: Autonomy vs. Well Being

doctor and patient, researcher and subject, primary parties and review committees must make together. Conflicts may arise, for example, when medical personnel appeal for decisions on clinical or scientific grounds to patients and families whose beliefs do not admit nonreligious reasons for decisive personal choices. It is important in the first instance simply to be aware of this diversity of moral and religious perspectives and alert to their relevance to professional choices. Even specialists who are well trained in bioethics often uncritically accept the viewpoint that morality is logically independent of religion, because that is the position of the moral philosophy that has provided much of the theoretical framework for contemporary bioethics. Without awareness of the other possibilities this article has surveyed, significant moral issues may be overlooked until they become the subject of public controversy or undermine the relationship of trust between medical-care providers and patients.

"Father of Eugenics," Sir Francis Galton

PAGE 279

Investigations of the cultural interdependence of religion and morality may make us aware of serious moral claims. What a patient believes about ritual purity or about the fate of the soul after death deserves more than just respectful interest. It may determine what it means to treat that patient as a free person with an inherent dignity. In any case, the cultural specificity of all moral and religious perspectives should also alert us to the limitations of the claims of biomedical science.

While the standard of "secular arguments" or "publicly accessible reasons" is appealing, it presupposes a very large area of public moral consensus. Although some such consensus does exist, its scope is unclear, and there is no guarantee that it is actually broad enough to resolve the difficult bioethical issues that divide society today. In short, it may be that a strictly defined "secular argument" will be insufficient to yield a determinate solution to the problems, that some appeal to the religious convictions or other private views of the participants will be necessary if we are to settle the questions at all (Greenawalt, 1988).

Efforts to define an independent system of morality, in which bioethical issues could be resolved without reference to the diversity of religious moral positions, are thus subject to a variety of problems. The issues range from attacks on the supposed neutrality and objectivity of secular scientific inquiry, to the criticism that if it should achieve this neutrality, it would be unable to provide determinate solutions to policy questions that have been posed to medicine and science.

Another possibility, however, is to accept the unity of religious and moral discourse and ask whether biomedical science and clinical practice might participate in it. Physicians and other providers of medical services have ideas about human flourishing based on long experience with patients and clients. Scientific research may confirm or disprove widespread convictions about the best means to achieve and sustain a good life, and it may provide new evidence of causal links between choices and outcomes. Discussion of the human good typically takes quite different forms from the highly structured discourse of the biomedical sciences, but those sciences clearly do have a contribution to make to it.

Beliefs that hold that there is a cosmic unity of religion and morality, a single reality in which religious and moral truths make sense together, offer the clearest opportunities for biomedical participation. This openness is most apparent in contemporary formulations of natural law theory, which explicitly make use of biomedical knowledge as part of the determination of what is natural and what the conditions for human flourishing are. Even where religious traditions have not developed systematic statements, however, their narratives and rituals make implicit claims about the constraints that the world imposes on human life, and about what human beings must do to live well within those limits (Lovin and Reynolds, 1985).

Where these myths, narratives, hymns, and rites are taken to be rivals to a scientific account of reality, there will inevitably be conflicts between the biomedical sciences and the religious ideas about morality. But religious discourse is never simply an objective account of the way things are. It is always also an orientation of human life within that world of facts, and the physician's or the medical researcher's account of those facts may have a place in that orientation. Such an understanding neither separates religion from morality, nor links them both to a specific cultural system, but regards morality as an orientation of human life within a reality that is susceptible both to scientific examination and to the imaginative and liberating comprehension that religion offers.

Those who seek to join a discussion of the human good in which both religious wisdom and scientific discovery have a place must acknowledge that there are other views, religious and scientific, that will reject that collaboration. A moral realism that links religion, science, and morality may provide the best framework for biomedical researchers and clinicians to explain the ethical implications of their work in terms that many religious traditions can accept.

— ROBIN W. LOVIN

EUGENICS

HISTORICAL ASPECTS

The word "eugenics" was coined in 1883 by the English scientist Francis Galton, a cousin of Charles Darwin and a pioneer in the mathematical treatment of biological inheritance. Galton took the word from a Greek root meaning "good in birth" or "noble in heredity." He intended the term to denote the "science" of improving human stock by giving the "more suitable races or strains of blood a better chance of prevailing speedily over the less suitable" (Kevles, 1986, p. ix).

The idea of eugenics dated back at least to Plato, and discussion of actually achieving human biological melioration had been boosted by the Enlightenment. In Galton's day, the science of genetics had not yet emerged: Gregor Mendel's 1865 paper, the foundation of that discipline, was not only unappreciated but also generally unnoticed by the scientific community. Nevertheless, Darwin's theory of evolution taught that species did change as a result of natural selection, and it was well known that through artificial selection farmers and flower fanciers could obtain permanent breeds of animals and plants strong in particular characters. Galton thus supposed that the human race could be similarly improved—that through eugenics, human beings could take charge of their own evolution.

The idea of human biological improvement was slow to gather public support, but after the turn of the twentieth century, eugenics movements emerged in many countries. Eugenicists everywhere shared Galton's understanding that people might be improved in two complementary ways—to use Galton's language, by getting rid of the "undesirables" and by multiplying the "desirables" (Kevles, 1986, p. 3). They spoke of "positive" and "negative" eugenics. Positive eugenics aimed to foster greater representation in society of people whom eugenicists considered socially valuable. Negative eugenics sought to encourage the socially unworthy to breed less or, better yet, not at all.

How positive or negative ends were to be achieved depended heavily on which theory of human biology people brought to the eugenics movement. Many eugenicists, particularly in the United States, Britain, and Germany, believed that human beings were determined almost entirely by their germ plasm, which was passed from one generation to the next and overwhelmed environmental influences in shaping human development. Their belief was reinforced by the rediscovery, in 1900, of Mendel's theory that the biological makeup of organisms was determined by certain "factors," which were later identified with genes and were held to account for a wide array of human traits, both physical and behavioral, "good" as well as "bad."

In the first third of the twentieth century, eugenics drew the support of a number of leading biologists, not only in the United States and western Europe but also in the Soviet Union, Latin America, and elsewhere. Many of these biologists came to the creed from the practice of evolutionary biology, which they extrapolated to the Galtonian idea of taking charge of human evolution. One of the most influential was Charles B. Davenport, the head of the Station for Experimental Evolution, a part of the Carnegie Institution of Washington and located at Cold Spring Harbor, New York, where Davenport established the Eugenics Record Office. Other eugenic enthusiasts included, in the United States, the biologists Raymond Pearl, Herbert S. Jennings, Edwin Grant Conklin, William E. Castle, Edward M. East, and Herman Muller; in Britain, F. A. E. Crew, Ronald A. Fisher, and J. B. S. Haldane; and in Germany, Fritz Lenz, who held the chair of racial hygiene in Munich, and Otmar von Verschuer.

Some eugenicists, notably in France, assumed that biological organisms, including human beings, were formed primarily by their environments, physical as well as cultural. Like the early-nineteenth-century biologist Jean Baptiste Lamarck, they contended that environmental influences might even reconfigure hereditary material. Environmentalists were mainly interested in positive eugenics, contending that more attention to factors such as nutrition, medical care, education, and clean play would, by improving the young, better the human race. Some urged that the improvement should begin when children were in the womb, through sound prenatal care. The pregnant mother should avoid toxic substances, such as alcohol. She might even expose herself, for the sake of her fetus, to cultural enrichment, such as fine plays and concerts.

Individuals with good genes were assumed to be easily recognizable from their intelligence and character. Those with bad genes had to be ferreted out. For the purpose of identifying such genes, in the early twentieth century eugenics gave rise to the fist programs of research in human heredity, which were pursued in both state-supported and private laboratories established to develop eugenically useful knowledge. The Eugenics Record Office at Cold Spring Harbor was typical of these institutions; so were the Galton Laboratory for National Eugenics at University College (London), whose first director was the statistician and population biologist Karl Pearson, and the Kaiser Wilhelm Institute for Anthropology, Human Heredity, and Eugenics in Berlin, which was directed by the anthropologist Eugen Fischer. Staff at or affiliated with these laboratories gathered information bearing on human heredity by examining medical records or conducting extended family studies. Often they relied on field workers to construct trait pedigrees in selected populations—say, the residents of a rural community—on the basis of interviews and the examination of genealogical records. An important feature of German eugenic science was the study of twins.

However, social prejudices as well as dreams pervaded eugenic research, just as they did all of eugenics.

See Also

Race: European Concepts

Eugenic studies claimed to reveal that criminality, prostitution, and mental deficiency (which was commonly termed "feeblemindedness") were the products of bad genes. They concluded that socially desirable traits were associated with the "races" of northern Europe, especially the Nordic "race," and that undesirable ones were identified with those of eastern and southern Europe.

Eugenics entailed as many meanings as did terms such as "social adequacy" and "character." Indeed, eugenics mirrored a broad range of social attitudes, many of them centered on the role in society of women, since they were indispensable to the bearing of children. On the one hand, positive eugenicists of all stripes argued against the use of birth control or entrance into the work force of middle-class women, on grounds that any decline in their devotion to reproductive duties would lead to "race suicide." On the other hand, social radicals appealed to eugenics to justify the sexual emancipation of women. They contended that if contraception were freely available, women could pursue sexual pleasure with whomever they wished, without regard to whether a male partner was eugenically promising as a father. If and when a woman decided to become pregnant, then her choice of the father could focus on the production of a high-quality child. Sex for pleasure would thus be divorced from sex for eugenic reproduction.

Those with bad genes had to be ferreted out.

PAGE 175

In practice, little was done for positive eugenics, though eugenic claims did figure in the advent of family-allowance policies in Britain and Germany during the 1930s, and positive eugenic themes were certainly implied in the "Fitter Family" competitions that were a standard feature of eugenic programs held at state fairs in America during the 1920s. In the interest of negative eugenics, germ-plasm determinists insisted that "socially inadequate" people should be discouraged or prevented from reproducing themselves by urging or compelling them to undergo sterilization. They also argued for laws restricting marriage and immigration to their countries, in order to keep out genetically undesirable people.

In the 1930s, attempts to sanitize eugenics had been made by various British and American biologists. They wanted to maintain Galton's idea of human biological improvement while rejecting the social prejudice that had pervaded the conception. They realized that a sound eugenics would have to rest on a solid science of human genetics, one that scrupulously rejected social bias and weighed the respective roles of biology and environment, of nature and nurture, in the making of the human animal. They succeeded in laying the foundation for such a science of human genetics, and that field made great strides in the following decades.

The advances in human genetics boosted the new field of genetic counseling, which provided prospective parents with advice about what their risk might be of bearing a child with a genetic disorder. In the 1950s, the early years of such counseling, some geneticists had sought to turn the practice to eugenic advantage—to reduce the incidence of genetic disease in the population, and by extension to reduce the frequency of deleterious genes in what population geneticists were coming to call the human gene pool. To that end, some

SOCIAL CONSEQUENCES
How Eugenics Became a Dirty Word

In the United States, eugenicists helped obtain passage of the Immigration Act of 1924, which sharply reduced eastern and southern european immigration to the United States. By the late 1920s, some two dozen American states had enacted eugenic sterilization laws. The laws were declared constitutional in the 1927 U.S. Supreme Court decision of *Buck* v. *Bell,* in which Justice Oliver Wendell Holmes delivered the opinion that three generations of imbeciles are enough. The leading state in this endeavor was California, which as of 1933 had subjected more people to eugenic sterilization than had all other states of the union combined (Kevles, 1986).

At the time, a number of biologists, sociologists, anthropologists, and others increasingly criticized eugenic doctrines, contending that social deviancy is primarily the product of a disadvantageous social environment—notably, for example, of poverty and illiteracy—rather than of genes, and that apparent racial differences were not biological but cultural, the product of ethnicity rather than of germ plasm. In 1930, in the papal encyclical *Casti connubii*, the Roman Catholic church officially opposed eugenics, along with birth control. By the 1930s, a coalition of critics had helped bring a halt in most countries to the attempts of eugenicists to gain significant social and political influence. An exception to this tendency was Germany, where eugenics reached its apogee of power during the Nazi regime. Hundreds of thousands of people were sterilized for negative eugenic reasons and scientific authority joined with social hatred to send millions of the "racially unfit" to the gas chambers. Verschuer trained doctors for the SS in the intricacies of racial hygiene, and he analyzed data and specimens obtained in the concentration camps. In the years after World War II, eugenics became a dirty word.

— DANIEL J. KEVLES

claimed that it was the counselor's duty not simply to inform a couple about the possible genetic outcome of their union but also to instruct them whether to bear children at all. By the end of the 1950s, however, the informal standards of practice in genetic counseling were strongly against eugenically oriented advice—that is, advice aimed at the welfare of the gene pool rather than of the family. The standards had it that no counselor had the right to tell a couple not to have a child, even for the sake of the couple's welfare.

At first, genetic counseling could draw only on family histories and could tell parents nothing more than the odds that they might conceive a child with a recessive or dominant disease or abnormality. Since the 1960s, as the result of amniocentesis and advances in human biochemical and chromosomal genetics, genetic counseling has become coupled to technical analyses that can identify whether a prospective parent actually carries a deleterious gene and can determine prenatally whether a fetus truly suffers from a selection of genetic and chromosomal diseases or disorders. If the fetus is found to be at such a disadvantage, the parents have the option to abort—at least in countries where abortion is legal, which in 1993 included the United States, Great Britain, and France.

Reproductive selection on a genetic basis—by screening of parents, abortion of fetuses, or both—has found support among liberal religious groups, secular ethicists, and many feminists. They regard it as enlarging women's freedom to control their lives and as contributing to family well-being. However, reproductive selection has been contested by the Roman Catholic church and fundamentalist Protestants, mainly because of their opposition to abortion for any reason. Some feminists have interpreted such selection as yet another among several recent innovations in reproductive technology—for example, in vitro fertilization—that threaten to reduce women to mere reproductive machines in a patriarchal social order. Others have pointed to the heavy emotional and familial burdens placed upon women by prenatal diagnosis that reveals a fetus with a genetic disease or disorder. Genetic selection also has raised apprehensions among some members of minority groups and among disabled persons that it will lead to a revival of negative eugenics that may affect them disproportionately. Handicapped people and their advocates have attacked the attitude that a newly conceived child with a genetic affliction merits abortion, calling it a stigmatization of the living who have the ailment and the expression of a eugenics mentality (Stanworth, 1987; Rothman, 1986, 1989; Duster, 1989; Cowan, 1992).

The human genome project

These fears have been exacerbated by the Human Genome Project, the multinational effort, begun in the late 1980s, to obtain the sequence of all the DNA in the human genome. Once the complete sequence is obtained, it will in principle be easy to identify individuals with deleterious genes of a physical (or presumptively antisocial) type, and the state may intervene in reproductive behavior so as to discourage the transmission of these genes in the population. Such a policy could work special injury upon certain minority groups—for example, people of African origin, since the recessive gene for sickle-cell anemia occurs among them with comparatively high frequency. It could also threaten the disabled, since the only "therapy" currently available for most genetic or chromosomal diseases or disorders is abortion, and since identifying such fetuses as candidates for the procedure stigmatizes people who have been born with the handicap. In 1988, China's Gansu Province adopted a eugenic law that would—so the authorities said—improve population quality by banning the marriages of mentally retarded people unless they first submit to sterilization. Such laws have been adopted in other provinces and in 1991 were endorsed by Prime Minister Li Peng.

From the pyres of the 1930s and '40s the phoenix of eugenic thinking has risen; its resurrection is nearly complete.

PAGE 279

Negative eugenic intentions appeared to lie behind a July 1988 proposal from the European Commission for the creation of a human genome project in the European Community. Called a health measure, the proposal was entitled "Predictive Medicine: Human Genome Analysis." Its rationale rested on a simple syllogism—that many diseases result from interactions of genes and environment; that it would be impossible to remove all the environmental culprits from society; and that, hence, individuals could be better defended against disease by identifying their genetic predispositions to fall ill. According to the summary of the proposal: "Predictive Medicine seeks to protect individuals from the kinds of illnesses to which they are genetically most vulnerable and, where appropriate, to prevent the transmission of the genetic susceptibilities to the next generation." In the view of the European Commission, the genome proposal would make Europe more competitive—indirectly, by helping to slow the rate of increase in health expenditures; directly, by strengthening its scientific and technological base (Commission of the European Communities, 1988).

Economics may well prove to be a powerful incentive to a new negative eugenics. In the United States, the more that health care becomes a public responsibility, paid for through the tax system, and the more expensive this care becomes, the greater the possibility that taxpayers will rebel against paying for the care of those whose genetic makeup dooms them to severe disease or disability. Even in countries with national health systems, public officials might feel pressure to encourage, or even to compel, people not to bring genetically affected children into the world—not for the sake of the gene pool but in the interest of keeping public health costs down.

However, a number of factors are likely to offset a broad-based revival of negative eugenics. Eugenics profits from authoritarianism—indeed, almost requires it. The institutions of political democracy may not have been robust enough to resist altogether the violations of civil liberties characteristic of the early eugenics movement, but they did contest them effectively in many places. The British government refused to pass eugenic sterilization laws. So did many American states; and where they were enacted, they were often unenforced. Awareness of the barbarities and cruelties of state-sponsored eugenics in the past has tended to set most geneticists and the public at large against such programs. Moreover, persons with handicaps or diseases are politically empowered, as are minority groups, to a degree that they were not in the early twentieth century. They may not be sufficiently empowered to counter all quasi-eugenic threats to themselves, but they are politically positioned, with allies in the media, the medical profession, and elsewhere, including the Roman Catholic church, to block or at least to hinder eugenic proposals that might affect them.

In the United States, apprehensions of the ethical dangers in the Human Genome Project found expression in the Congress across the political spectrum—from liberals who had long been concerned about governmental intrusion into private genetic matters to conservatives who worried that the Human Genome Project might foster increased practice of prenatal diagnosis and abortion. Among the Americans most sensitive to the eugenic hazards and the ethical challenges inherent in the project were a number of its leading scientific enthusiasts, particularly James D. Watson, the first head of the National Center for Human Genome Research, who considered it both appropriate and imperative that the American genome program stimulate study and debate about its social, ethical, and legal implications. In 1988, Watson announced that such activities would be eligible for roughly 3 percent of the National Center's budget. He told a 1989 scientific conference on the genome: "We have to be aware of the really terrible past of eugenics, where incomplete

See Also

Race: European Concepts

EUGENICS RESTRICTIONS IN EUROPE

A Fear of "Biopolitics"

The European Commission's proposal for a human genome project provoked the emergence of an antieugenic coalition in the European Parliament that was led by Benedikt Härlin, a member of the West German Green Party. The Greens had helped impose severe restrictions on biotechnology in West Germany and raised objections to human genome research on grounds that it might lead to a recrudescence of Nazi biological policies. Guided by Härlin, the European Parliament's Committee on Energy, Research and Technology raised a red flag against the genome project as an enterprise in preventive medicine. It reminded the European Community that in the past, eugenic ideas had led to "horrific consequences" and declared that "clear pointers to eugenic tendencies and goals" inhered in the intention of protecting people from contracting and transmitting genetic diseases or conditions. The application of human genetic information for such purposes would almost always involve decisions—fundamentally eugenic ones—about what are "normal and abnormal, acceptable and unacceptable, viable and non-viable forms of the genetic make-up of individual human beings before and after birth." The Härlin Report also warned that the new biological and reproductive technologies could make for a "modern test tube eugenics," a eugenics all the more insidious because it could disguise more easily than its cruder ancestors "an even more radical and totalitarian form of 'biopolitics'" (European Parliament, Committee on Energy, Research, and Technology, 1988-1989, pp. 23-28).

The Härlin Report urged thirty-eight amendments to the European Commission's proposal, including the complete excision of the phrase "predictive medicine" from the text. As a result of the report, which won support not only from German Greens but also from conservatives on both sides of the English Channel, including German Catholics, the European Commission produced a modified proposal that accepted the thrust of the amendments and even the language of a number of them. The new proposal called for a three-year program of human genome analysis as such, without regard to predictive medicine, and committed the European Community in a variety of ways—most notably, by prohibiting human germ line research and genetic intervention with human embryos—to avoid eugenic practices, prevent ethical missteps, and protect individual rights and privacy. It also promised to keep the European Parliament and the public fully informed via annual reports on the moral and legal basis of human genome research. Formally adopted in June 1990, the European Community's human genome program will cost 15 million ECU (about $17 million) over three years, with some one million ECU devoted to ethical studies (Kevles and Hood, 1992).

—DANIEL J. KEVLES

knowledge was used in a very cavalier and rather awful way, both here in the United States and in Germany. We have to reassure people that their own DNA is private and that no one else can get at it" (Kevles and Hood, 1992, pp. 34-35).

Human genetics in a market economy

Despite the specter of eugenics that some see in the Human Genome Project, many observers hold that its near-term ethical challenges lie neither in private forays into human genetic improvement nor in some state-mandated program of eugenics. They lie in the grit of what the project will produce in abundance: genetic information. These challenges center on the control, diffusion, and use of that information within the context of a market economy.

The advance of human genetics and biotechnology has created the capacity for a kind of individual eugenics—families deciding what kinds of children they wish to have. At the moment, the kinds they can choose are those without certain disabilities or diseases, such as Down syndrome or Tay-Sachs disease. Although most parents would now probably prefer just a healthy baby, in the future they might be tempted by the opportunity—for example, via genetic analysis of embryos—to have improved babies, children who are likely to be more intelligent or more athletic or better-looking (whatever such terms might mean). People may well pursue such possibilities, given the interest that some parents have shown in choosing the sex of their child or that others have shown in the administration of growth hormone to offspring they think will grow up too short. In sum, a kind of private eugenics could arise from consumer demand.

Many commentators have noted that the torrent of new human genetic information will undoubtedly pose challenges to social fairness and equity. They have emphasized that employers may seek to deny jobs to applicants with a susceptibility—or an alleged susceptibility—to disorders such as manic depression or illnesses arising from features of the workplace. For example, around 1970, it came to be feared that people with sickle-cell trait—that is, who possess one of the recessive genes for the disease—might suffer the sickling of their red-blood cells in the reduced-oxygen environment of high altitudes. Such people were unjustly prohibited from entering the Air Force Academy, were restricted to ground jobs by several major commercial air carriers, and often were charged higher premiums by insurance companies. Life and medical insurance companies may well wish to know the genomic signatures of their clients, their profile of risk for disease and death. Even national health systems might choose to ration the provision of care on the basis of genetic propensity for disease, especially to families at risk for bearing diseased children (U.S. Congress, Office of Technology Assessment, 1990; Kevles, 1986).

In response to these threatening prospects, many analysts have contended that individual genomic information should be protected as strictly private. However, legal and insurance analysts have pointed out that insurance, and insurance premiums, depend on assessments of risk. If a client has a high genetic medical risk that is not reflected in the premium charged, then that person receives a high payout at low cost to himself or herself but at high cost to the company. The problem would be compounded if the person knows the risk—while the company does not—and purchases a large amount of insurance. In either case, the company would have to pass its increased costs to other policyholders, which is to say that high-risk policyholders would be taxing low-risk ones. Thus, insisting on a right to privacy in genetic information could well lead—at least under the largely private system of insurance that now prevails in the United States—to inequitable consequences.

American legislatures have already begun to focus on the genuine social, ethical, and policy issues that the Human Genome Project raises, particularly those concerning the use of private human genetic information. In the fall of 1991, a U.S. House of Representatives subcommittee held hearings on the challenge that such information posed to insurability. About the same time, the California state legislature passed a bill banning employers, health service agencies and disability insurers from withholding jobs or protection simply because a person is a carrier of a single gene associated with disability. Although California Governor Pete Wilson vetoed the bill, it was a harbinger of the type of public policy initiatives that the genome project no doubt will increasingly call forth. The Human Genome Project, like most of human and medical genetics, is less likely to foster a drive for a new eugenics than it is to pose vexing challenges to public policy and private practices for the control and use of human genetic information.

— DANIEL J. KEVLES

ETHICAL ISSUES

"Eugenics" (from the Greek for "wellborn") was coined in 1883 by Sir Francis Galton (1822-1911) to describe a form of applied heredity that could "improve the inborn qualities of a race" (Galton, 1869). The rationale for eugenic improvement came directly from the successes of animal breeders. Animal husbandmen who bred livestock and chickens discovered that they could increase the prevalence of desirable features (such as

◆ **eugenics**
A science that deals with the improvement (as by control of human mating) of hereditary qualities of a breed or ethnic group.

See Also

Confidentiality and the Control of Genetic Information

DNA Sequencing and the Origins of the Human Genome Project

exceptional fatback thickness or egg production) by selectively mating specimens with the desired trait. These observations suggested to Galton and his cousin Charles Darwin the possibility of human "improvement" through genetic means (see Darwin, 1871).

Even in its earliest conception, eugenics raised ethical issues because it presupposed the acceptability of social institutions that would favor one group over another. Galton's vision was to encourage judicious mating practices, control of social institutions, and other policies that gave procreative advantage to persons with "superior" traits over those deemed less genetically worthy. What constitutes a superior genetic trait is but one of the many ethical issues raised by eugenics.

While such intuitive observations provided the rationale for eugenics, both moral and practical reasons limited the achievement of eugenic ends. The justification for eugenic programs in the United States (Kevles, 1985) and Europe (Ludmerer, 1972) during the 1920s and 1930s was at best quasi-scientific and based on the crudest of political theory. Political eugenics in the Third Reich reached a scientific nadir in programs like the *Lebensborn* ("Spring of Life") movement, in which SS (*Schutzstaffel*) officers were "selectively" mated to idealized Aryan young women without regard to morality or genotype, and "biologically valuable" infants were kidnapped and placed in orphanages. Later, the children were assigned to "suitable" Aryan families (Lifton, 1986). Such heinous acts, coupled with the attempt to extirpate whole peoples in the Holocaust, led to public revulsion and the precipitous decline of eugenics after World War II.

Scientific considerations

The likelihood that any given trait can be augmented through controlled mating is called the "opportunity for selection." This opportunity depends heavily on the extent of genetic diversity—the frequency and number of different genetic variants maintained in a population—and on the degree to which a given trait is determined by genetic factors. Extensive human genetic diversity affords ample opportunity for selection. Even among groups with long histories of common lineages, such as certain South American Indian tribes, sufficient genetic variation and evolutionary potential continue to exist to permit genetic change (Salzano and Callegari-Jacques, 1988). These observations suggest that some form of human eugenics remains theoreti-

ETHICAL ISSUES
Types of Eugenics

Eugenic initiatives can be divided into two subcategories: *positive eugenics*, in which the frequency of presumptively desirable or beneficial genes is increased; and *negative eugenics*, in which deleterious genes are eliminated from the gene pool. Policies that reduce the frequency of desirable genetic combinations or increase those that are deleterious are said to be *dysgenic*. It is also useful to bifurcate eugenic policies into those that embrace whole populations or groups (*macro eugenics*) from those that affect only families or kinship groups (*micro eugenics*).

A program with a macroeugenic impact is one that gradually increases the frequency of presumptively beneficial genes over several generations. Positive macro eugenics occurs when whole cultural or ethnic groups with "desirable" genes are given incentives to adopt procreative methods that give them a selective advantage over other groups. Such a policy could result by default.

Simply discouraging certain forms of birth control or abortion in a targeted group, or providing tax advantages for procreation within certain social classes, offers a selective advantage to identified groups. While such policies do in fact occur, they are not at present linked to eugenic ends in any conscious way, largely because no "desirable" genotypes have been scientifically defined at a group level.

Similar macroeugenic impacts through negative eugenics are also possible: such ends were intended by the Nazi policies of forced sterilization and extermination of reproducing members of various ethnic groups, especially Jews. Today, no one would expect *intentionally genetic* macro policies to be countenanced in developed countries for both political and moral reasons; yet "ethnic cleansing" has occurred in regions of the former Yugoslavia, with little concerted opposition.

A program with a microeugenic impact is one in which an individual couple and their extended family are afforded access to greater genetic choice than is the norm. For instance, the early utilization of prenatal diagnosis was largely limited to certain high-income families (Lappe, 1981). Today, such a trend is evident in the selective availability and use of genetic tests by well-to-do couples during germ cell or zygote selection, in vitro fertilization, embryo transfer, and other forms of assisted fertility. These policies can in theory provide a microeugenic advantage to families that can afford these interventions by giving them some assurance of "genetic quality" in their offspring. This edge may be more imagined than real, depending on the actual ability of genetic testing to reduce the occurrence of abnormal or defective genes while not inadvertently introducing others. Because such policies are directed primarily at women, they raise special ethical issues discussed below.

— MARC LAPPÉ

cally possible, even in groups that have undergone evolutionary "bottlenecks" that in theory reduce their genetic variability.

In spite of genetic diversity, present patterns of human reproduction and demographics in most developed countries limit the opportunity for eugenics. Unlike the controlled breeding possible within domesticated animal populations or Nazi Germany, moral strictures on directed reproduction in most cultures make systematic control of reproduction infeasible. Where little variance exists in the numbers of children that families bear and low mortality across groups is the norm, genetic change is largely stifled. Thus, little intrinsic opportunity exists in most developed countries for the enrichment of certain genotypes over others. This is particularly true in the United States and Scandinavian countries, where the population replacement rate barely exceeds or equals the death rate (zero population growth).

Even where population growth has slowed or stalled, microdemographic conditions can have subtle genetic impacts. Under such circumstances, if only a few families leave many offspring over several generations, their genetic contributions to society will increase disproportionately. For instance, in America some families with the Huntington's chorea gene were uncharacteristically large as a result of some as yet unknown "reproductive compensation" in those carrying the responsible gene(s). Over several generations, these Huntington's family lineages have increased more rapidly than the surrounding population, thus increasing the frequency of Huntington's gene(s). Since Huntington's chorea is caused by a single gene, giving such families the choice of not reproducing or selectively aborting Huntington's disease-positive fetuses could reduce the frequency of the Huntington's gene. Would this program be desirable?

It is important to note that the full "adaptive value or disvalue" of this and many other genes is incompletely understood. Moreover, the Huntington's mutation(s), as well as those for hemophilia and other single-gene-determined conditions, are constantly reintroduced into the population at a relatively high rate through spontaneous mutation. In developed countries where the age of procreation is delayed and environmental mutagens are prevalent, high mutation "loads" in older sperm and eggs will tend to negate eugenic efforts. These factors increase the necessity for ethical analysis of various eugenic policies to include those designed to affect the occurrence of mutations as well as the transmission of genetic traits in populations.

Ethical perspectives

Proper ethical analysis of eugenic considerations is clouded by intrinsic uncertainties of the appropriate definition of the terms used in discussing eugenic initiatives. Each term carries poorly defined value connotations. Words like "normal," "deleterious," "desirable," "undesirable," and "improvement" are scientifically vague as they apply to the human genetic stock. A precise definition of a "deleterious genotype" remains unclear, in spite of our increased understanding of causation of genetic disease.

For instance, does a carrier of one or more recessive genes that in combination can cause genetic disease like sickle-cell anemia have a deleterious genotype? What about single genes, like those associated with colon cancer, that do not universally predict cancer occurrence when present? Often, carrier status is associated with heightened resistance to disease (as appears to be the case for several genetic loci and malaria) rather than with the selective disadvantage implied by a "deleterious genotype." The acceptability of moving from the "is" of this sort of human genetic variation to the "ought" of using this variation to effect eugenic ends is a critical ethical issue in eugenics.

Some people believe the idea that success in life derives from good genes is a self-serving ideology.

PAGE 280

The overall moral acceptability of implementing any eugenic strategy turns on the definition, human cost, and justification for using genetics to effect human "improvement." A naturalistic view in ethics is that the place of humans in the order of nature makes it clear that evolution has a direction and, by inference, that improvement is an imperative because it is an extension of the natural order (Sperry, 1974). At least one prominent evolutionary biologist contests this view (Simpson, 1974) by noting that nothing in the evolutionary program would suggest an innate tendency toward "progress." Religious scholars have observed that no reason exists to interpret human destiny as indicative of a divine imperative toward species improvement (Ramsey, 1970).

The same argument may not apply to preventing harm to the gene pool and, by inference, to the species from dysgenic trends. While no duty may exist to effect improvement, assuring that no harm occurs generally carries a stronger moral imperative in medicine than does beneficence. Thus, some have argued for the critical importance of maintaining the integrity of the gene pool by protecting it from accumulation of excessive mutations (see Lappé, 1981). Reduction of environmental mutagens coupled with an emphasis on procreation at earlier ages might be such a combination.

Because eugenic methods have historically been offered by those who are "best off" in terms of political power (not necessarily genotype), eugenics raises issues of justice and fairness to those who, through no fault of their own, receive a poorer share of the genetic lottery. Historically, sterilization policies have been directed at the poor, in the mistaken belief that they

See Also

Eugenic Thinking: Galton's Moral Crusade

EUGENICS

Ethical Issues

were the embodiment of defective genes (Reilly, 1977).

Eugenics provides a lens through which to see this and other forms of reproductive coercion. Ethicists have long questioned the acceptability of using coercion through officially sanctioned policies or social suasion to influence the reproductive choices in certain groups. This can occur when welfare recipients are penalized for having children, or when genetic policies are directed at members of one sex and not the other.

Issues affecting women

Since many eugenic policies entail the tacit or conscripted cooperation of women, they can be highly discriminatory by posing disproportionate risks—both physical and psychosocial—to women. Examples include female-centered sterilization programs and protracted contraception policies (Depo-Provera), the use of prenatal diagnosis and abortion, and welfare payments linked to procreative status. Some states, notably California, have policies that mandate, with only a modicum of informed consent, that all women undergo prenatal serum tests (for alpha-fetoprotein) to detect pregnancies at risk for neural tube defects or Down syndrome. While amniocentesis previously was used primarily for identifying seriously affected fetuses (e.g., those with Tay-Sachs disease), serum alpha-fetoprotein testing of prospective mothers prior to amniocentesis has a high false-positive rate and provides test results that embrace a range of conditions. Some of the "affected" fetuses so detected include less severely impaired ones (e.g., those with Down syndrome or minor neural tube defects) and a small percentage of otherwise normal fetuses.

The nearly universal participation of women in serum alpha-fetoprotein programs and their high acceptance rate of the subsequent "indicated" abortions approximates a eugenic program. Such genetically "selective" abortion and prenatal diagnosis generally are said to place a high psychosocial burden on women (Rothman, 1992), and are deemed to reduce rather than enhance genetic diversity (Bonnicksen, 1992).

◆ **negative eugenics**
Seeks to limit the socially unworthy's breeding and eliminate their deleterious genes from the gene pool.

The expansion of the use of genetic diagnoses to embrace the testing of embryos during in vitro fertilization and embryo transfer also impacts directly on women's reproductive freedom. The advent of a large spectrum of testable genotypes through the Human Genome Program, coupled with gamete choice, preembryo genetic testing, and selective in vitro fertilization will likely place social and psychological pressure on women to opt for "quality" and not merely reproductive success.

Such programs raise the specter of a eugenics program in which women serve as passive receptacles of artificially selected embryos (Lippman, 1990). Were such programs to conscript poor women and deny them both free and fully informed consent, as many claim surrogate mother programs initially did, they would be especially objectionable. The venue for the choices involved in such genetic selection would most likely be a genetic counseling clinic.

Genetic counseling and eugenics

Eugenic considerations are not usually overtly identified in programs that might influence reproductive decision making. American and European genetic counselors openly disavow any eugenic objectives to their practice (Wertz and Fletcher, 1988). The American Society of Human Genetics does not have any policy statement that implies a eugenic ideal. It is neither the primary nor the secondary objective of any medical society in the United States to adopt policies that impact on future generations or their genetic composition. These policies are often the result of reaction against a eugenic taint, and not necessarily a rational conclusion. For this reason, stated and actual policies may be inconsistent.

For instance, most counselors recognize that many existing genetic programs, including prenatal diagnosis, newborn screening, and carrier screening may have subtle or profound eugenic or dysgenic impacts. A value-neutral stance, such as that taken by genetic counselors regarding the impact of their genetic information, may be dysgenic, eugenic, or neutral, depending on the circumstances.

Because of value neutrality, genetic counseling as presently practiced does not usually protect certain families or ethnic groups from passing on deleterious genes. Groups that intermarry among close relatives (like the Amish) have higher than normal coefficients of inbreeding and therefore may transmit more deleterious genes in a double-recessive state (i.e., both parents pass on the same gene) than will other populations who intermarry more randomly.

A closer examination of the counseling process and content reveals that eugenic ends may be subtly incorporated into the options and disease entities chosen for inclusion as "suitable" for selective abortion (see Lippman, 1990). An example would be sex chromosome abnormalities that usually are associated only with minor physical and mental abnormalities. Revealing to anxious parents the genetic status of a fetus with Turner's syndrome (where the absence of an X chromosome leads to short stature, webbed neck, and subtle neurological deficits in girls) is a case in point, since the child's ultimate well-being is only marginally impaired.

The value-neutral counseling ethic leads to a noninterventionism that may of necessity permit dysgenic outcomes. The process of aborting a fetus with a deleterious recessive disease and then compensating for the

See Also
Maternal–Fetal Relationship: Ethical Issue
Genetic Counseling

loss of the expected child by trying to have more children ultimately results in a subtle increase in frequency of the recessive gene over many generations. This is true because with reproductive compensation, two-thirds of all of the live children will be carriers of the recessive gene at issue, instead of the one-half normally expected without prenatal diagnosis. (Such a dysgenic trend will not be true for prenatal diagnosis of dominant disorders. For example, selective abortion directed against a fetus carrying the gene for a dominant condition like polycystic kidney disease will lead to a rapid decline in the gene frequency.)

For prenatal diagnosis programs directed against X-linked conditions, such as Duchenne's muscular dystrophy or hemophilia A, aborting male fetuses will lead to more births of girls, half of whom will be carriers of the gene. A "eugenic" policy that aborted female carrier *fetuses* is considered morally unacceptable. But with the ability to test *pre-embryos* for their carrier status, their destruction in order to find a noncarrier replacement may be seen as morally acceptable. With the advent of these pre-embryo and related germ cell selection technologies, counselors who espouse a "no eugenics" view may not convince couples eager to improve the genetic status of their offspring.

Justifying eugenic policies

The appropriateness of providing state-sponsored services to encourage reproductive choices (for example, the screening programs for alpha fetoprotein and neural tube defects) is a more subtle ethical issue than that of forced sterilization, mandatory genetic testing, or state-encouraged selective abortion. The major ethical questions posed by intentionally adopting (or ignoring) potential eugenic or dysgenic impacts of these or related reproductive choices turn on the following considerations, among others: our duties to present versus future generations; the obligation not to do harm versus the duty to benefit; and the obligation of health professionals to provide for the needs of individuals or families versus that of protecting the gene pool as a whole.

These problems arise in the context of consanguinity. Marriage between related individuals can be considered genetically disadvantageous to the extent it brings together otherwise rare, recessive genes. But for

VALIDATING EUGENIC POLICIES
Acceptable in Some Cases?

Because genetic disease entails suffering, and minimization of suffering is a widely recognized and legitimate goal of medicine, all potentially eugenic policies that affect a whole population can be measured against this claim for legitimating genetic change. It is reasonable to ask if adopting a eugenic policy would materially reduce human suffering in the long run. Where and when does the current genetic status of a given group of extended family members warrant genetic intervention on this basis?

Eugenic interventions can be weighed against certain ethical tenets. While eugenic interventions are usually ethically suspect because they entail blunt and often coercive policies, there are special circumstances when such policies may be acceptable. Among the conditions that need to be met are at least the following:

1. The genetic condition of a particular group has been demonstrated to be sufficiently endangering to justify an intervention.
2. The persons who will be affected by the policy are given a voice in the decision making.
3. The ends sought are justified by the group's own standards and norms, at costs the group finds acceptable.
4. The means are necessary and ethically acceptable to the affected persons.
5. Policymakers can give reasonable assurances that both the risks and the benefits of the proposed policy will be equitably distributed.
6. Societal goals can be accomplished without infringing on other cultural or fundamental values.
7. The eugenic policy represents the least coercive option to attain the agreed upon objective.

To take the simplest example, an Indian population around Lake Maracaibo in Venezuela has one of the highest gene frequencies for Huntington's disease, a disorder that wreaks havoc in their indigenous cultural setting. This population also has an intrinsically high fertility rate, and hence could reduce or even eliminate most occurrences of the disease if restrictive reproductive policies were adopted for gene carriers. Would it be proper or acceptable to offer a populationwide program to identify and counsel persons with the Huntington's gene to not reproduce? Would such a policy be more acceptable than the present option of affording nondirective information through genetic counseling?

In the instance of the Maracaibo Indians, the conditions enumerated above could in theory be met, yet the question of respecting the cultural integrity of the group is not addressed. Eugenic questions almost always raise such political questions even after ethical issues are addressed.

— MARC LAPPÉ

E

EUGENICS

Ethical Issues

Eugenic thinking raises provocative questions about the type of social order most compatible with facts of human nature.

PAGE 280

ETHICAL ISSUES
Applying Ethical Principles to Eugenics

The major ethical issues surrounding eugenics should focus on integrating existing ethical principles with the new science of defined human genetics. Among the principles that can be invoked are the following:

1. *Intergenerational justice*. It is desirable not to leave the next generation worse off than the present one.
2. *Scientific responsibility*. Before genetic tests are put into commerce, it is incumbent on scientists and clinicians to use moral imagination to project the consequences of applying them.
3. *Not harming*. The duty not to harm takes precedence over the duty to benefit, suggesting that negative eugenics, in which certain deleterious genes are kept from reentering the gene pool, has priority over positive eugenics.
4. *Autonomy*. Respecting autonomy requires a continuation of the present policies of allowing reproductive freedom and privacy in individual decision making (Lappé, 1986).
5. *Justice*. Any benefits or risks of new genetic programs should be equitably distributed, and new policies adjusted in favor of the least well-off (Rawls, 1971) should be given priority over those that appear to afford social benefit at the expense of the genetically "handicapped."

With these policies in place, small-scale eugenic programs could in theory be instituted, albeit not without much public dialogue and legal protections to assure that discrimination and coercion are minimized. Ultimately, however, eugenic programs will continue to be ethically suspect because to work, they must favor or penalize extant or unborn human beings by virtue of their genetic and not their intrinsic social worth.

— MARC LAPPÉ

◆ **eugenics**
a science that deals with the improvement (as by control of human mating) of hereditary qualities of a race or breed.

some cultures, "desirable" marriages may involve first- or second-cousin matings, while in others, interbreeding within ethnic or religious lineages is expressly proscribed by scripture or common law. When, if ever, should society intervene to discourage such marriages?

From a purely theoretical perspective, it is possible to entertain the idea of eugenics on the premise that there is nothing intrinsically wrong with considering ways to improve the human condition as long as societal values are reinforced and overt harms to vulnerable populations are avoided. It has been argued (in Singapore) that a state that is not unnecessarily burdened by individuals with "avoidable" genetic diseases will be one that can compete more efficiently in international markets. Such a simplistic assumption belies the ethical tensions that arise when societal benefits accrue only at the expense of restricting individual reproductive and social freedoms.

Eugenic programs may compromise persons in other ways. The well-being of extant individuals may suffer when social policy permits prenatal diagnosis and abortion of fetal individuals with the same condition. This conflict is exemplified by the alphafetoprotein screening program in California, which was opposed by persons with neural tube-related disabilities, out of concern that it would diminish social acceptance of their normalcy.

In theory, reproductive freedom is protected by affording an informed consent mechanism before embarking on any genetic testing or selective abortion. In practice, the fact that a certain policy is state-sanctioned can be taken to imply an ulterior motive to reduce the overall birth incidence of a costly disorder and to replace affected individuals with others more socially or medically acceptable. Some observers (Duster, 1990) regard genetic screening policies as tantamount to a back door to eugenics, since their existence reflects a de facto acceptance of a social policy of genetic exclusion.

Ethical/political interface

Constitutional and ethical arguments against eugenics turn on the primacy of privacy in reproductive decision making. Any moral justification for a postmodern eugenics must establish the legitimacy of the state's claim of a right to limit fundamental reproductive freedoms based on individual differences. The necessity for making political judgments about reproductive choice may intensify as the real or perceived impact of deleterious genes on social institutions and health-care costs becomes more evident. With the advent of expanded genetic testing the workplace-based health insurance, the reproductive decisions made by employees may become the province of the employer. A carrier of cystic fibrosis, while not himself at risk of serious illness, may produce a child who will carry great costs to the insurer if he is married to another carrier and wants to have progeny. Hence, the possibility that employers may discriminate based on genetic status can occur and may have unintended eugenic consequences must be considered (see Draper, 1992).

Although ostensibly "eugenic" changes in gene frequency can occur through chance events or crude public policies (for example, the use of tax incentives in Singapore to encourage the breeding of well-to-do individuals), ethical issues arise most graphically under circumstances in which the distribution of genetic material is controlled intentionally. This can occur when carriers of genetic disease-causing genes are subjected to screening programs with implied social objectives of limiting procreation. Such an event occurred in the early 1970s when African-Americans with sickle-cell trait, who were themselves largely unaffected by their genetic status, were excluded from certain jobs or military service, and were required in some states to take genetic tests (for sickle-cell trait) as a condition for a marriage license.

When policy decisions restrict the reproductive options of certain groups, they constitute a kind of back door to eugenics. Such policies can carry a social connotation that diminishes the perceived worth of groups with certain genotypes. Policies of reproductive screening and/or exclusion can be mistakenly associated with "solutions" to societal ills. Such events as testing of newborns for an extra Y chromosome, mistakenly believed to be associated with criminality, are freighted with moral weight. This is especially true when socially identified or targeted genes are localized in certain ethnic or cultural groups with a long tradition of social exclusion or discrimination. The roots of such genetic lineages will become more evident as data are generated by the initiative to map and sequence the human genome. Such data raise questions about the potential misuse of genetics in forensic and other societally sanctioned activities especially where incorporating ethnic differences may be crucial for accurate testing.

The human genome program

Because of the greatly expanded net of genes identified through the Human Genome Program as it proceeds to describe the full sequence of the three billion bases on the human chromosomes, the opportunity for eugenic applications in setting diagnostic policies will undoubtedly increase. This program will provide a data base for genetic screening and testing that could provide couples with greatly enhanced knowledge of the genetic consequences of their reproduction, and for the potential to select sperm and/or eggs with certain genotypes prior to fertilization. The availability of new "nondestructive" genetic tests (for example, the use of the discarded polar body to assess the genetic makeup of a recently fertilized zygote) provides a still more radical opportunity for microeugenic choices. Issues of intentional killing or elimination of embryos or fetuses with certain genotypes (a key argument against germline engineering) ostensibly would be obviated by the use of such techniques.

The Human Genome Program would also provide a means of identifying groups of persons whose load of putatively adverse genetic mutations is disproportionately high compared with that of the surrounding population. Such populations probably exist generally, and high concentrations may be found among offspring whose parents were exposed to highly mutagenic chemicals (e.g., ethylene oxide) or ionizing radiation.

Such an eventuality suggests that ethical considerations of the eugenic impact of reproductive choices have a component of distributive justice. Deciding what groups benefit by virtue of their good "gene quality" and who may be hurt by continued neglect of their "genetic burden" are ethical dilemmas of the next century. With a font of genetic knowledge, ignoring genetic differences is itself a policy that requires justification.

— MARC LAPPÉ

EUGENICS AND RELIGIOUS LAW

JUDAISM

The laws against incest and consanguinity in the Old Testament would seem to have a rationale in eugenics, although this is never specified in the biblical text. The traditional commentators, too, advert only to the natural repugnance against incest. In the Talmudic discussion as well as in the legal codes, the subject is treated as a sexual offense, involving a breach of morality rather than a eugenic error. (The Talmud is the repository of rabbinic exposition of biblical law and teaching, spanning more than five centuries. The legal codes are based on the Talmud and on subsequent development of the law, such as in Responsa, formal opinions rendered by rabbinic authorities in response to new case-law inquiries.)

Even bastardy is a moral rather than a eugenic category. The *mamzer* (in Jewish law, the product of an adulterous or incestuous liaison, not of a relationship between two persons who are not married to one another) is not legally ill-born; his or her status is compromised only legally and socially, rendered so in punitive or deterrent judgment against parents not free to have entered the relationship. But no difference obtains between the *mamzer* born of adultery—even a technical adultery, such as when the document of divorce for the mother's previous marriage was impugned—and the

◆ **positive eugenics**
Aims to foster greater representation in society of socially acceptable people by increasing the frequency of their desirable genes.

See Also
DNA Sequencing and the Origins of the Human Genome Project

mamzer born of incest. Hence, no eugenic motive can be assigned here.

A man "maimed in his privy parts" bears the same legal disabilities as the *mamzer*. Thus, a man of "crushed testicles or severed member" is excluded from "the congregation of the Lord" (Deut. 23:2). This verse is interpreted to mean only that he may not enter into conjugal union with an Israelite woman. Thus, the castrated male is under the ban because the act of castration is forbidden. But one "maimed in his privy parts" as a result of a birth defect or disease, as opposed to one castrated by his own or another's deliberate assault, is free of this disability. The legal situations were thus analogized: "Just as the *mamzer* is the result of human misdeeds, so only the castrated one who is such as a result of human misdeeds is to be banned." Since that distinction is made in both cases, and since the banned *mamzer* and the castrated are permitted to marry, for example, another *mamzer* or a proselyte, it must be concluded that moral outrage and punitive judgment rather than eugenic considerations are operative.

Talmudic discussions raise the possibility of the moment—conception, birth, postbirth—at which the soul joins the body.

PAGE 26

Eugenics, in the sense of choosing a marriage partner with the well-being of progeny in mind, is more clearly present in Talmudic counsel and legislation. A man is counseled to choose a wife prudently, and guidance is offered in doing so in accordance with the intellectual and moral virtues of the prospective bride. And since, we are told, a son, for example, normally takes after his mother's brothers, a man should regard the maternal uncles in making his decision (Bava Batra, 110a). A hidden physical blemish in a spouse is grounds for invalidating a marriage, unless the other spouse can be presumed to have known of it in advance.

Heredity as a eugenic principle takes its legal model from rulings with respect to circumcision. A male infant whose two brothers died possibly as a result of this operation may not be circumcised. He is deemed to have inherited the illness (probably hemophilia) that proved fatal to his two brothers. The Talmud goes on to say that an infant whose two maternal cousins showed that weakness may not be circumcised either. That is, statistical evidence yielded by two sons from the same mother can also be reflected in two sisters of that mother (Yevamot, 64b). Coming from Talmudic times (before 500 C.E.), this is a remarkably early recognition that hemophilia is transmitted through maternal lineage—in itself a significant eugenic discovery.

The statistical evidence or the presumption of adverse hereditary factors in a third family member, when those factors are seen to exist in two others, thus becomes the basis of Talmudic laws of eugenics. With modern laboratory means to determine the presence of these factors, the principle of course operates even sooner, without waiting for statistical evidence in two members. The Talmud rules that one may not marry into a family of epileptics or lepers (Yevamot, 64b) or—by extension—a family in which tuberculosis or any similar disease appears in multiple members. This may be the first eugenic edict in any social or religious system.

The pure "heredity" underlying this recommendation is not unanimously agreed upon. While one view in the Talmud attributes the transmission of characteristics in the pre-Mendelian age to heredity, another view sees it as "bad luck." In a Responsum where the questioner considered abortion because the mother was epileptic, the rabbi responded that the latter of the two views stated above may be the right one, and that fear of bad luck is an inadequate warrant for abortion (Feldman, 1968).

In an earlier context, the Mishnah (the foundation layer of the Talmud) speaks of the faculties that a father bequeaths to his son: "looks, strength, riches, and length of years" (Eduyot, II, 9). Here, too, the commentaries align themselves on both sides: one sees the bequeathing of faculties as a natural hereditary process, the other sees them as divine reward for the father's virtues.

Two other Talmudic ideas with eugenic motifs are reflected in current practice. In the interests of fulfilling the injunction to "love one's wife as much as himself and honor her more than himself," a man is advised to seek his sister's daughter as a bride; his care for her will be the more tender due to his affection for his own sister. Yet in the thirteenth century, Rabbi Judah the Pious left a testamentary charge to his children and grandchildren that became a source of guidance to others on the level of precedent for subsequent Jewish law. In this famous testament, he advises against marriage with a niece because it may have adverse genetic results. Modern rabbinic authorities dismiss such fears as unjustified unless they are medically warranted.

A second point is a Talmudic notion that eugenic factors operate in intercourse during pregnancy. Conjugal relations, we are told, should be avoided during the first trimester as "injurious to the embryo"; but they are encouraged during the final trimester as desirable for both mother and fetus, for then the child is born "well-formed and of strong vitality" (Niddah, 31a). A medieval Jewish authority makes the matter a point of pride in comparative culture: the Talmud recommends coitus during the final trimester, whereas the Greek and Arab scholars say it is harmful. Do not listen to them, he says (Responsa Bar Sheshet, no. 447). Nonetheless, the Talmud prohibits the marriage of a pregnant or nursing widow or divorcee. In the case of a pregnant woman, the second husband, it is suggested, may be less considerate of a fetus fathered by another

See Also

Children; Family; Marriage and Other Domestic Partnerships

man and may inadvertently damage it through abdominal pressure during intercourse (Yevamot, 36a). In the nursing situation, the new father may fail to take the necessary steps to supplement the diet of his stepchild (it is assumed that a pregnancy diminishes the mother's milk). And a pregnant woman who feels an urgent physical or psychological need for food during the Yom Kippur fast is to be fed for the sake of her fetus's welfare as well as her own (Yoma, 82a).

More a matter of preaching than of law is the notion that defective children can be the result of immoral or inconsiderate modes of intercourse—an idea expounded but ultimately rejected by the Talmud (Nedarim, 20a). Yet in more modern times, the Hasidim (pietistic Jewish groups with a mystical orientation) maintain that spiritual consequences of the act are indeed possible; that if a man has pure and lofty thoughts during or preparatory to cohabitation, he can succeed in transmitting to the child of either sex an especially lofty soul. Hence dynastic succession of leadership, presuming the inheritance of that loftier soul, as opposed to democratic selection, obtains among Hasidic groups.

A study of biblical and Talmudic sources written by Max Grunwald in 1930, cited by Immanuel Jakobovits, discerns a broad eugenic motif. Grunwald writes that Judaism

> *quite consciously strives for the promotion of the quantity of progeny by the compulsion of matrimony, the insistence on early marriage, the sexual purity of the marital partners and the harmony of their ages and characters, the dissolubility of unhappy unions, the regulation of conjugal intercourse, the high esteem of maternity, the stress on parental responsibility, the protection of the embryo, etc. To be sure, there can be no question here of a compulsory public control over the health conditions of the marriage candidates, but that would positively be in line with the principles of Jewish eugenics: the pursuit after the most numerous and physically, mentally, and morally sound natural increase of the people, without thinking of an exclusive race protection.* *(Jakobovits, 1975, p. 154)*

Although abortion is warranted primarily for maternal rather than fetal indications, screening of would-be parents for actual or potential defective genes, such as in Tay-Sachs disease, would, like premarital blood tests, be much in keeping with the Jewish traditional eugenic concern. Such genetic screening is, in fact, facilitated by a unique computerized system under the auspices of the New York-based Dor Yesharim (Generation of Upright [Descendants], from Psalms 112:2). Young men and women diagnosed as Tay-Sachs carriers are identified by code number. When marriage is contemplated, the couple is alerted to the fact that both are carriers, with one chance in four of a homozygous fetus, so that marriage plans may be reconsidered. Besides Tay-Sachs, which is fatal to the child by about age five, nonfatal disabilities have been added to Dor Yesharim's data base.

Although surrogate parenting and artificial insemination create social and family problems, the conceptional procedures that make them possible are in and of themselves acceptable when natural means are ineffective. In vitro fertilization, to assist in a conception that might otherwise be thwarted by blocked fallopian tubes or by sperm inadequacy, has been accorded full moral and legal sanction. Genetic engineering that alters the germ line has been ruled out by Jewish ethicists, but gene therapy, removing or correcting defective genes, would be a proper extension of the mandate to heal. The newly announced technology for cloning embryos has been greeted with more caution than hope—hope for improved procreational prospects for couples otherwise limited to one or no progeny, but caution against creating multiple embryos deprived of their distinctiveness as individuals. Safeguards are called for against the dangers of genetic mutation, or of political or profit-motive "baby farming" that could result from abuse of broader eugenic techniques.

— DAVID M. FELDMAN

A hidden physical blemish in a spouse is grounds for invalidating a marriage.

PAGE 186

CHRISTIANITY

Christian religious laws historically comprehend a large spectrum of rules to guide individual conduct and social relationships among the baptized. The laws most likely to have eugenic significance are the canons prohibiting the marriage of relatives. These regulations also form the basis for the modern civil law prohibitions against the marriage of relatives in both the Continental legal systems and the Anglo-Saxon statutory scheme. Though the principal justification given for such prohibitions in Christian law has been ethical and social, there is substantial evidence that they also may reflect considerations classified as eugenic in contemporary scientific research.

The ecclesiastical regulations that forbid marriage between persons closely related by consanguinity are among the most ancient canons of the Christian tradition. Penalties attached to the violation of religious exogamic laws have varied historically in their severity, as, indeed, have the ways of measuring the degrees of kinship and defining within which degrees the crime of incest shall be punished. But the core of the tradition of canon law remains constant and reflects an extreme reluctance to accept the marriages of close relatives as humanly or religiously feasible.

For Roman Catholics all marriages within the

E

EUGENICS AND RELIGIOUS LAW

Christianity

direct line of blood relationship, that is, between an ancestor and a descendant by parentage, and within the collateral line to the fourth degree, that is, to third cousins, are forbidden (*Code of Canon Law*, 1983, canon 1091). The definition of marriages within four degrees of relationship as incestuous dates to the Fourth Lateran Council in 1215 (c. 50). In the Greek Orthodox tradition, marriage in the direct line and in the collateral line to the sixth or seventh degree by the Roman method of computation is prohibited in canon 54 of the Synod in Trullo, 691/692 (Hefele, 1896). All Oriental Christians forbid marriages in the direct line; Armenians, Jacobites, and Copts prohibit it in the collateral line to the fourth degree, Melkites to the sixth degree, Serbs and Chaldeans to the third degree, and Ethiopians without distinction. Among Protestant reformers the restrictions of the medieval canon law were accepted by some, such as Phillip Melanchthon and Martin Chemnitz (Kemnitz); only the Old Testament regulations of Leviticus 18:6-18 by others, such as Martin Bucer and, perhaps, Martin Luther; and only the closest ties of direct parental relationship by still others, such as John Wycliffe. In the Anglican community, The Book of Common Prayer contains a table drawn up by Archbishop Matthew Parker based on Leviticus in naming relatives incapable of marriage (Wheatly). Most Protestant churches today follow the prohibitions of civil law regarding incest and kinship marriage (Acte for Kynges Succession; Acte for Succession of Imperyall Crowne; Concerning Precontracte and Degrees).

The sources of and commentaries upon the Christian laws record debate about the extent of the prohibition, the possibility of dispensation within certain close degrees of kinship, and the related question of the divine or natural law origin of the laws (e.g., Burchard of Worms, *Decretum*, bk. 7, "De Incesto"; Burchard of Worms, *Collection in 74 titulis* 65.281-284). They reveal, however, only the most sketchy discussion of the foundations of the regulations themselves.

CONSANGUINEOUS MARRIAGES

Classical Prohibitions

1. Such marriage would undermine the respect due to parents.
2. Moral danger to family life arising from early corruption of the young dwelling in the same household in which marriage could be allowed.
3. Sexual competition would disrupt family; prohibition forces multiplication of friendships and spread of charity.

EUGENIC OBJECTIONS TO MARRIAGE BY BLOOD RELATIVES

It is only in comparatively modern times that an explicitly eugenic reason for the prohibition has received scientific attention. Writing in 1673, Samuel Dugard noted: "There is a *judgment* which is said often to accompany these Marriages, and that is *Want of Children* and a *Barrennesse*" (p. 53). "The Children are weak, it may be; grow crooked, or, what is worse, do not prove well; presently, Sir, it shall be said what better could be expected? an unlawfull Wedlock must have an unprosperous successe" (p. 51). Ambrosius J. Stapf's *Theologia moralis* in 1827 alluded to this possibility (p. 359). A fuller treatment is found in Dominic Le Noir's 1873 edition of St. Alphonsus's *Theologia moralis*. Edward Westermarck in 1889 and Eduard Laurent in 1895 spoke at length of a physiological justification of the canons to prevent indiscriminate inbreeding and the risk of a high incidence of deleterious genetic effects. Franz Wernz, in 1928 (n. 352 [70]), writing from a comprehensive knowledge of the canonical tradition, said the ancient writers also knew of the undesirable effects of excessive inbreeding. He noted reasons derived from contemporary medical science in the writings of Gratian (early twelfth century) (C.xx "Anglis permittitur, ut in quarta vel in quinta generatione cognibitur," c. 20, c. 35, q. 2), Pope Innocent III (1161-1216) (Schroeder, 1937), and Thomas Aquinas (*Commentum in libros IV Sententiarum*, dist. 40 and 41, q. 1, art. 4). Since the late nineteenth century nearly all commentators on the canonical rules speak of eugenic objections to marriages of blood relatives.

It is possible to find in the ancient ecclesiastical commentators an awareness of a eugenic foundation to the prohibition expressed in primitive and undifferentiated modes of speech. For example, a persistent belief was kept alive among theologians and canonists that children of incestuous relationships will die or will be greatly debilitated, or that the familial line will be cursed with sterility. Benedict the Levite (850?) wrote of these marriages: "From these are usually born the blind, the deaf, hunchbacks, the mentally defective, and others afflicted with loathsome infirmities" (*Capitularum collectio*). Furthermore, in the explanations of the name of the impediment (i.e., the impediment of consanguinity), if one traces their origins through medieval glossography to the *Etymologies* of Isidore of Seville (560?-636), there appears an awareness of a physiological factor in the blood bond of close relatives that must be weakened before marriage can be contracted safely.

— WILLIAM W. BASSETT

These three reasons seem to have been sufficient to justify the laws, so that most scholars did not go beyond them to seek a further justification. Adhémar Esmein, for example, said the laws arose out of an instinctive repulsion for incest and were not reflective of any known adverse physical consequences. Some modern authors speculate that the reason for strict enforcement of prohibitions against incestuous marriages was to force the breakup of landed family estates (Duby, 1983).

The antecedents of the Christian canons in the Mosaic law (Lev. 18:6-18) and the Roman law (Burge) were taken as expressions of natural law by the canonists and were continued in the barbarian codes (*Pactum legis salicae* 13.11; *Leges visigothae* 4.1.1-7; *Codex Euriciani* 2). In his *Ecclesiastical History* (I, 27), where the Venerable Bede (673-735) notes these laws, he records a quotation from a letter of Pope Gregory I to Augustine of Canterbury, written in 601 (*Responsa Gregorii*). The reason given by Gregory for forbidding marriages of close relatives is, "We have learned from experience that from such a marriage offspring cannot grow up." This letter and this reason not only are later picked up and cited by Gratian ("Anglis permittatur," c. 2, c. 35, q. 5) and Thomas Aquinas (*Summa theologiae suppl.* 54, 3), but may be found in virtually all the canonical collections of the early Middle Ages. Though comment on this passage is rare, comment was, perhaps, unnecessary. The passage from Gregory seems clearly to say that experience teaches that children from forbidden consanguineous marriages are affected or unable to grow up. There is thought to be a physiological consequence to incest. In the light of this it seems probable that the labored argumentation over the question of how close the relationship must be for marriage to be forbidden by natural law must have been conducted in some awareness of a popular belief in the biological consequences of such unions. The fear of genetic anomalies or biological debilitation from indiscriminate inbreeding may not be perfectly articulated. It is difficult to imagine, however, that warning of some physiological dangers to offspring may not have been intended in the frequent citation of Pope Gregory to sustain the severity of the prohibition.

Tomás Sánchez (1605), who wrote the greatest of the canonical commentaries on marriage, says that the most suasive ground for forbidding incestuous unions is that there is a sharing of the blood among close relatives and that the physical image of a progenitor (*imago, complexio, effigies, mores, virtus paterna*) passes to offspring, so that the blood must be weakened through successive generations before marriage should be contracted (7.50; 7.51.1-2). Thus, preventing marriages of close relatives to protect the offspring by allowing several generations to pass before procreation can be called a measure of eugenic foresight, however simple the scientific awareness to support it may have been.

In summary, a eugenic foundation to Christian religious laws forbidding the marriage of close relatives is clearly articulated and commented upon by modern scholars from the late eighteenth and nineteenth centuries. Evidence of this kind of awareness may be discovered earlier in the canonical sources, however, going back at least to the seventh century. It would seem consistent with the eugenic connotation of those laws rooted in antiquity, together with a Christian sense of responsibility for offspring that partly motivated them, to consider further eugenic restrictions on marriage in Christian communities today, in light of contemporary knowledge of genetics.

— WILLIAM W. BASSETT

ISLAM

The idea of eugenics is not well developed in the Islamic world. Both Islamic law and tradition generally condemn abortion, which is permitted only if the mother's life is endangered, so there is no genetic counseling that would lead to abortion. Both religious law and tradition do include references to a man's choosing an appropriate wife, but these concerns have been interpreted as moral and social, rather than eugenic.

Islamic religious-moral law, the Shari'a, deals with questions concerning laws of incest and consanguinity from the perspective of moral and social relationships rather than eugenic concerns. The general counsel of the Qur'an and the Prophetic traditions regarding marriage is promulgated in the laws that require a Muslim to marry within the community of believers. A Muslim is better than a non-Muslim as a spouse. "A woman may be married for four reasons: for her property, her status, her beauty, and her religion; so try to get one who is religious" (Muslim, 1956, tradition 3457). There is no law to suggest choosing a marriage partner with the intention of improving the progeny through the control of hereditary factors. With slight variations among the Sunni and Shiite schools, the law specifies that a woman may not marry a man who is not equal to her. The earliest ruling to require equality in matters of piety and freedom from physical defects detrimental to marriage is found among the Malikis (see al-Juzayri, 1969, for variations among the four schools of Sunni law).

In the Qur'an the main source for marriage law is book 4, verse 23. This prohibits marriage between persons closely related by blood, but this ban reflects ethical and social, rather than eugenic, considerations. Thus in Muslim jurisprudence a man and a woman may be forbidden to marry either because of blood relationship (e.g., a man may not marry his mother or

◆ **macro eugenics**
Policies, such as ethnic cleansing, used with whole populations or groups over several generations.

See Also

Islamic Views on Abortion: The Theological Context

E

EUGENICS AND RELIGIOUS LAW

Islam

It is God who brought you forth from your mothers' wombs.

QUR'AN (KORAN)

either of his grandmothers, etc.) or relationships established through marriage (e.g., he may not marry the mother or grandmothers of his wife, etc.). Moreover, there are women whom a man may marry singly, but not be married to at the same time (e.g., two sisters, a woman and the sister of her mother or father). This latter prohibition seems to be more for psychological than for eugenic reasons.

Evidence that the Qur'an (or Shari'a) considers nurture, or the environment, to have impact on a child perhaps comparable to that of nature, or genetic inheritance, comes from the Book of Marriage, which prohibits marriage not only between a man and the woman who gave birth to him but also between a man and the foster mother who breastfed him at least a certain number of times.

The ruling seems to indicate similar consequences for foster relations established through suckling: "What is unlawful because of blood relations, is also unlawful because of corresponding foster suckling relations" (al-Bukhari, 1986, tradition 46; al-'Amili, 7/281, tradition 2). In establishing unmarriageability, a foster mother who suckles an infant is regarded exactly as the infant's real mother.

There is further evidence of the Islamic tradition's lack of interest in eugenics. Islam abolished one of the four types of marriages among Arabs, the one described in Arab tradition in terms that may reflect eugenic concerns. The tradition says:

> *The second type [of marriage] was that a man would say to his wife after she had become clean from her period, "Send for so-and-so [whose nobility is well established] and have sexual relations with him." Her husband would then keep away from her and would not touch her at all till her pregnancy became evident from that man with whom she was sleeping. After the pregnancy was established her husband would sleep with her if he wished. However, he allowed his wife to sleep with that person being desirous of the nobility of the child* (najabat al-walad). *Such marriage was called "marriage seeking advancement"* (nikah al-istibda').
>
> *(al-Bukhari, 1986, sec. 37)*

Islam, which insisted that faith in God was the main source of all human nobility, was uninterested in this practice, traditional in the Arab tribal culture, for the improvement of the human race through the control of hereditary factors.

Other traditions counsel the believers to choose a partner for breeding (*al-nutaf*) "bravery among the people of Khurasan" [in Iran], sexual potency among the Berber [in North Africa], and "generosity and envy among the Arabs" (al-'Amili, 1965, 7/29, tradition #6). The Islamic traditions (hadith literature) do reflect explicit knowledge of eugenics in choosing a marriage partner. The source of these eugenic considerations seems to be the Irano-Semitic culture, in which such interests were commonplace. Although these traditions were never used as authoritative precedents for legislation in the Shari'a, they express the popular piety connected with marital relations. For example, the Prophet is quoted saying, "Anyone wishing to follow my tradition should know that among my traditions is marriage. Seek children [through it]. . . . Protect your children from the milk of the prostitute and the insane among women, because milk makes inroads [in the character of a child]" (al-'Amili, 1969, 7/4, tradition 6). Moreover, in the case of a person drinking wine, the Prophet regarded it permissible to annul the marriage contract, especially, if the person was alcoholic (literally, "sick" with alcohol) (al-'Amili, 1969). There also existed a warning against marrying fatuous individuals because their offspring would be a loss. However, it was acceptable to marry them for sexual reasons, as long as one did not seek children through such a union. These traditions reveal the concern about hereditary factors in the progeny.

Other traditions encourage marriages within one's own collateral line, to first cousins. The Prophet, who belonged to the Hashimite clan, at one time looked at the children of 'Ali and Ja'far, two brothers and his paternal cousins by relation, and said, "Our daughters for our sons, and our sons for our daughters" (al-'Amili, 1969, 7/49, tradition 7). This encouragement is contradicted by other traditions that recommend exogamous marriage and even intermarriage between Arab and non-Arab, and between a free person and a slave. There does not seem to be any awareness in these early traditions of deleterious genetic effects from excessive inbreeding. However, since 1970 there has been a growing debate among traditional Muslim jurists over the authenticity of the tradition that encourages endogamy indiscriminately. Certain injurious hereditary conditions have been detected in the fourth and fifth generations of some tribes in Muslim societies where endogamy is the norm.

Muslim traditions also speak about the negative impact on the fetus of "improper" modes of intercourse rejected by the Qur'an. Yet it was believed that special prayer when one intends to have intercourse with his wife keeps the devil away from what God has ordained to be created. The pure state of the parents' minds and bodies can be transmitted to the child through the invocation of the Divine Name before intercourse. In light of belief in the divine purpose and decree in the creation of offspring ("It is God who brought you forth from your mothers' wombs," Qur'an 16:78), either born with birth defects or normal, there does not seem to be any indication to support genetic diagnosis or screening that would justify abortion, which Islam permits primarily to safeguard the mother's health.

— ABDULAZIZ SACHEDINA

HINDUISM AND BUDDHISM

Because reproduction is one of the most important concerns of human life, most religions concern themselves with the regulation of sexual activity, marriage, and production of children. Hinduism and Buddhism also guide their followers in these matters, but in ways very different both from each other and from Western religions.

Eugenics might be defined as controlling human reproduction to modify or benefit the species. Prior to the present innovation of genetic engineering, eugenics meant restrictions on who could reproduce and with which partner. The recent development of methods of altering the human genome has opened a new area of ethical discussion: the propriety of voluntarily altering the human genome. Eugenics has also been used to excuse genocide, but this aspect will not be discussed here since nothing in Hinduism or Buddhism allows rationalization of genocide.

Although Hinduism and Buddhism have highly developed ethical philosophies, neither religion produces set positions on such contemporary matters as eugenics, nor is it likely that they will, given the nature and organization of the two religions. In both religions, ethics are developed by the individual or the social community; there is no official body that produces ethical statements. Hence there are no official Hindu or Buddhist positions on issues that were not envisioned when their scriptures were composed over 2,000 years ago. However, both religions have ethical ideas or methods that can be applied to modern problems.

Hinduism has its beginnings in the two millennia before the Common Era; the historical Buddha, Shakyamuni, died about 500 B.C.E. In those remote times there were no concepts akin to those of modern genetics and hence there could be no ethical discussions of genetic manipulation. Rather than a single scripture analogous to the Judeo-Christian Bible or the Koran, Hinduism and Buddhism have vast collections of diverse canonical texts that have appeared over millennia. Hinduism does have several authoritative legal texts, the most important of which, *The Laws of Manu*, was composed from about 200 B.C.E. to 200 C.E. These texts codify religious law (*dharma*) but are not regarded as the only legal or ethical authority. Buddhist texts are concerned with spiritual development and give only very general precepts for regulation of lay life. However, it is possible to develop Hindu or Buddhist positions on eugenics.

Hinduism and Buddhism both arose in India and share many common beliefs, such as the doctrine of *karma* (discussed below), yet the differences between the two religions must not be underestimated. Generally speaking, Hinduism is a legalistic religion and pays great attention to regulating life in the world. Buddhism sees worldly life as secondary in importance; attainment of release from suffering in this or subsequent existences is its central concern.

Reproduction in Hindu religious law

Although Hinduism recognizes a final stage of life in which the individual is released from domestic and social obligations in order to be able to pursue enlightenment (*moksha*), in the earlier, householder stage, detailed rules define acceptable behavior. Among the most important are those that regulate reproduction. The intent of these rules is to maintain the hereditary caste distinctions. Here Hinduism's outlook is very similar to that of nineteenth- and early twentieth-century Western eugenics, which proposed controlling reproduction to prevent what were considered undesirable unions. Although the specific rules for regulating marriage and reproduction were different from those proposed by Western eugenics, the spirit is the same: to protect the human species from degeneration due to unsuitable matches. Hinduism does not define suitability for marriage according to scientific understanding of genetics, but by caste membership, which is hereditary, and by physical traits, which are correlated with astrology. Traditionally, prospective brides were inspected undressed and an elaborate system of body divination existed for interpreting body markings, particularly on erogenous areas. Manu states, "A man should not marry a girl who is a redhead or has an extra limb or is sickly or has not body hair or . . . is too sallow . . . He should marry a woman who does not lack any part of her body . . . whose body hair and hair on the head is fine . . ." (Manu, p. 44). There are also rules for selecting the sex of children (males are conceived on even-numbered nights) and in all cases, the social class of husband and wife must match.

These procedures amount to methods of selecting marriage partners according to biological suitability, although the biological traits selected for concern may not seem very appropriate today. Marriage is discouraged if partners are not biologically and astrologically suited. In India, marriages have been and still are arranged by parents on the basis of social, economic, and reproductive suitability. Romantic interest is at best a very secondary consideration. The entire basis of marriage in Hinduism is eugenic, but the factors felt to predispose favorably to suitable offspring are quite different from modern Western ones. Marriage in Hinduism exists to ensure offspring and perpetuate family distinction and caste separation. These laws were

See Also

Hindu Traditions: Adapting in the U.S.

EUGENICS AND RELIGIOUS LAW

Hinduism and Buddhism

HINDUISM
Marriage as Conservation

Hinduism does not contemplate elimination of inferior castes, but simply limitation of physical contact between them and higher ones. The higher castes must preserve their purity, but all castes are necessary and have their place in the cosmos (Danielou, 1993). This contrasts with the extreme, modern racism, in which one group, which considers itself superior, aims at the elimination of others. There is no idea of altering the genetic or social situation of humanity as a whole. On the contrary, marriage rules attempt to maintain the status quo. Their rationale is not to improve the human species but to prevent its degeneration.

— GEOFFREY P. REDMOND

intended to regulate reproduction rather than sexuality. Sexual liaison outside of marriage and across caste, though not approved of, was not considered wrong so long as no offspring resulted.

In general, Hinduism has not been opposed to attempts to control reproduction. Female infanticide has been extensively practiced in India. An innovation is the use of ultrasound machines by entrepreneurs; at village marketplaces a pregnant woman can find out whether she is carrying a boy or girl, with abortion elected in the instance of the latter. A similar practice exists in China. Although the practice of female infanticide can be explained in economic terms (a girl's parents must provide a dowry if she is to be married), it represents a practice of controlling reproductive outcome for family or social goals. Infanticide has not been viewed with the same opprobrium as in the West, although it is certainly not fair to imply that the Hindu religion condones such acts.

The Indian concept of karma, which is fundamental to all its philosophical and religious systems, has some similarities to modern genetics. It is a law of moral cause and effect. The literal meaning of karma is action, and the theory holds that one's present state is the result of personal and collective actions in this and previous lives. Actions, like genes, have effects that persist across lifetimes. Much of each individual's present circumstances are the result of previous actions carried across generations. Karma and scientific genetics seek to account for the human experience that the past tends to repeat itself in the present. Both offer an explanation of how an individual comes to have certain traits.

◆ **karma**
The force generated by a person's actions held in Hinduism and Buddhism to perpetuate transmigration and in its ethical consequences to determine the nature of the person's next existence.

Buddhism and human reproduction

Buddhism, which abolishes the caste system, has no concern with the suitability of marriages. Indeed, its monastic nature has made Buddhism generally uninterested in family life and reproduction. Throughout Buddhist history, clergy were forbidden to solemnize marriages; this was seen as inappropriate involvement in worldly affairs. (Wedding ceremonies officiated by Buddhist monks are a recent innovation.) Nor does Buddhism have an elaborate ethical code for regulation of lay behavior. Throughout most of its 2,500-year history, Buddhism has been monastic; lay life was not considered conducive for progress toward enlightenment. However, the sangha, the order of monks and nuns, did try to inculcate simple moral understanding in the laity.

In the Theravada form of Buddhism, which most closely resembles early Buddhism, the laity is taught the Five Precepts, which call on the Buddhist to avoid

THE FIVE PROHIBITIONS OF THERAVADA BUDDHISM

1. unnecessary killing
2. taking what is not given
3. sexual misconduct
4. harmful speech
5. use of intoxicants

Although Buddhist teachers will offer their particular interpretations of these principles, detailed rules are not given in any canonical text. Sexual misconduct, for example, is rarely defined and there is no position on contraception. Nor are there specific rules on suitability of marriage or sexual partners. The first precept might be interpreted as discouraging abortion; however, termination of pregnancy is not absolutely forbidden, though it is considered highly undesirable. Buddhism would see the ideal situation as one in which the partners are mindful of the consequences of their actions and avoid a situation in which abortion is a consideration. If carried out, abortion should use a method that minimizes any suffering. (For Buddhist analyses of the abortion issue see Taniguchi, 1987, and Redmond, 1991.) In Japan, where abortion is used as a method of family planning, Buddhist monks are involved in practices that women use to atone for abortion.

In contrast to the religious law of Judaism, Christianity, and Islam, the Buddhist precepts are very general, expressing morality in spirit rather than letter. Nothing in the five lay precepts can be construed to oppose genetic manipulation, provided that it is not

See Also
Buddhist Views: Contraception and Karma

harmful. Buddhism does not try to regulate lay behavior by detailed codes of laws, but rather by teaching *sati*, "mindfulness" and *ahimsa*, "harmlessness." The ultimate value in Buddhism is not living in accordance with a code of religious laws but being aware of the effects of one's actions so as to minimize harm. In general, a Buddhist would be concerned that genetic knowledge not be used in a way that causes suffering, but would not be opposed in principle to the acquisition or application of such knowledge. Buddhism places its highest value on knowledge, which it sees as the sole vehicle for enlightenment and release from suffering. Ignorance, not sin or disobedience, is the cause of a human's unhappy state. Hence, Buddhism may be seen as favoring the acquisition and use of genetic knowledge, provided that it is applied in ways that help, rather than harm, living beings. Changing the genetic code so as to eliminate a disease in the offspring would be quite acceptable so long as it was carried out skillfully, that is, not harmfully. Partner selection for genetic or ethnic reasons is not supported by Buddhism, which abolished the Hindu caste system. However, such selection would not be ethically improper if it did not cause suffering to those involved.

Cosmology and eugenics

There are two commonly held contemporary Western positions about eugenics that Hinduism and Buddhism see rather differently from most Western ethicists. One position is that since the world and everything in it, including human beings, are held to be created by God according to a divine plan, then altering the human genome is altering the very basis of God's creation, which is impermissible. Thus the Vatican's statement on reproductive technology holds that "no biologist or doctor can reasonably claim, by virtue of his scientific competence, to be able to decide on people's origin or destiny" (Vatican, Congregation for the Doctrine of the Faith, 1992, p. 84). A similar but secular argument holds that we should not alter nature. Although altering nature may not be inherently wrong, pragmatically such alterations are much more likely to do harm than good. The only safe course is stringently to restrict novel technologies such as genetic engineering.

Neither Hinduism nor Buddhism conceives of a creator God whose divine plan might be altered by genetic manipulation. (Although Brahma is considered the creator in Hinduism, the metaphysics of creation are quite different. Creation occurs from moment to moment and not according to a perfect plan.) Far from seeing the world as divine or perfect, both religions regard the world as inevitably a place of suffering. The fundamental virtue in both Hinduism and Buddhism is practicing *ahimsa*, or harmlessness, which means to avoid making living beings suffer. For example, the environment should not be harmed because living

KARMA AND EUGENICS

The concept of karma can be interpreted, or sometimes misinterpreted, so that it appears to oppose eugenics. Karma holds that misfortunes in this life are due to harmful actions in a former life (although there are also social sources of unfavorable karma). By this interpretation, if a child is born with a genetic disorder, then the misfortune is due to previous voluntary actions that harmed others and hence is deserved. Furthermore, this karma must be worked off; the suffering must be endured to expiate the previous wrongdoing. If the suffering is prevented, it will simply occur later. Thus, if a fetus with Down syndrome is aborted, the same individual will simply be reincarnated later with a similar affliction.

The idea that suffering should not be relieved, because karmically deserved, is widespread in India and Buddhist countries and is sometimes articulated by Buddhist teachers in the West. It is a misunderstanding of the Buddha's teaching, which was concerned to explain the way of release from suffering. Although Buddhism teaches compassion, some Buddhists, in common with some followers of other religions, find interpretations that rationalize evasion of the ethical obligation to be kind to others. It is not consistent with Buddhist teachings on compassion to refrain from relieving another's suffering on the grounds that it is due to the operation of karma.

Buddhism, although not opposed to eugenics if it is skillfully applied, does not require it. In contrast to Hinduism, it does not establish rules regarding reproductive behavior. Some contemporary Buddhists believe that each individual has his or her tasks in life and that, although these might be different for someone with a birth defect, others should not assume that such a life is therefore less worthy. This has affinities with the idea that we should not interfere with nature because we may not fully understand the effects of what we do.

Hinduism, then, requires a form of eugenics, and Buddhism is essentially neutral on eugenics as such, but would be greatly concerned to ensure that eugenic practice decreased suffering rather than increasing it. Neither religion sees eugenics as in itself improper, but both concern themselves with how it is carried out. However, Hinduism and Buddhism produce no set positions, and individual Hindus and Buddhists may have views different from those summarized here.

— GEOFFREY P. REDMOND

creatures are dependent on it. Since the universe was not created by divine plan, altering it is not considered a repudiation of God. In this context genetic manipulation is perfectly acceptable.

As to the second argument, that humans cannot handle their power over the genome, neither Hinduism nor Buddhism can be held to have a clear position on this. Evil is the result, respectively, of delusion, *moha*, or ignorance, *avidya*. Ethical ignorance is simply an aspect of more general spiritual ignorance, which clouds perception of the true nature of existence. However, Buddhism and Hinduism conceive of ethical ignorance somewhat differently. In Hinduism, it is necessary to be aware of the complex laws, or *dharma*, regulating human behavior. In Buddhism, ignorance is lack of awareness of the law of cause and effect, for example, of knowing how one's actions will affect oneself and others (Taniguchi, 1994). Mindfulness shows that an action harmful to another will cause suffering just as it would if done to oneself. A unique moral insight of Buddhism is that ethical behavior requires factual knowledge (Redmond, 1989)—for example, what effects behavior will have on others—as well as knowledge of ethical precepts. The way to this knowledge is through self-cultivation such as meditation, study of religious texts, and, especially, the influence of a teacher. Ethical behavior results from personal moral development rather than detailed moral legislation.

— GEOFFREY P. REDMOND

FAMILY

Families have played a most important role in the history of medicine, tending the sick when doctors were unavailable or unavailing. These two ancient, and in some respects rival, systems of care for the very vulnerable—medicine and the family—are each in part shaped by the other and rely upon the other for certain kinds of help. When illness or injury exhausts a family's capacity for care, it looks to professional medicine for the necessary facilities and expertise; in turn, technological advances in medicine have driven the health-care system to depend on families for what can be enormous sacrifices of time, money, caring labor, and even spare body parts on behalf of its patients. Recent developments in medicine have not only expanded the options for forming families—for example, through in vitro fertilization and contract pregnancy—but they have also had an impact on familial demographics: artificial means of birth control have helped reduce family size, while improvements in health care have extended longevity, though they have not eradicated the ills of old age.

By and large, bioethics has had little to say about the moral significance of the family within the context of medicine. The explicit discussion of the family in the third edition of Tom Beauchamp and James Childress's *Principles of Biomedical Ethics* is confined to one paragraph stating that the burden on the family must not be determinative in decisions to refuse treatment (Beauchamp and Childress, 1989). The U.S. President's Commission for the Study of Ethical Problems in Medicine and Biomedical and Behavioral Research devotes no more than ten lines of text in 545 pages of *Deciding to Forego Life-Sustaining Treatment* to the family's role in medical decision making at the end of life (U.S. President's Commission, 1983). The Hastings Center's *Guidelines on the Termination of Life-Sustaining Treatment and the Care of the Dying* mentions families only in passing, in their role as surrogate decision makers or people who have feelings for the patient (Hastings Center, 1987). Allen E. Buchanan and Dan W. Brock's *Deciding for Others* views families as aggregates of competing individual interests and devotes much of its brief discussion of the family to the possibility of selfishness and disagreement among family members (Buchanan and Brock, 1989).

The nature of the family

This neglect admits of several different explanations. For some bioethicists, the family is such a commonplace moral entity that its significance is left tacit in their analyses; unargued assumptions about family form a strong subtext, for example, in many discussions of decision making for incompetent patients. For others, the dramatic shifts in the demographics of American families over the last several decades renders families deeply suspect: they have become so fragile and their configurations so arbitrary, compared with what they once were, that we do better to exclude them altogether from our bioethical accounts.

The first view obscures the moral character of families; as we will attempt to show, they are complex and puzzling entities. But the second view is problematic as well, substituting myth for history. American families have always been somewhat fragile and subject to rapid reconfigurations. Families in the Chesapeake colonies of Virginia and Maryland, to take only one instance, were so vulnerable to malaria and other fatal illnesses that it was not at all unusual for an adult, whether slave or free, to bury three or even four spouses, or for half-orphaned children to be reared by relatives other than the surviving parent. In the matrilineal Iroquois societies of that same period, divorce was quite common. It is true that middle-class families gained a certain solidity when they underwent a shift around 1800 to a sentimental, child-centered model of domestic life, but this was achieved through an arguably unjust gendered division of labor, in which the father was increasingly absent from home and the mother's work was narrowed principally to unpaid domestic concerns. For many poor young nineteenth-century mothers—whether black, Latina, Irish, or east European—this arrangement was not an option, and the long hours spent working outside the home left the care of their children a somewhat haphazard business. Death in childbed and other premature deaths once threatened the family's integrity as much as the divorce rate, which has risen by a steady 3 percent in every decade since the Civil War, does now. In short, there is good reason to think that stress, turmoil, and identity crises have long been a feature of American families (Mintz and Kellogg, 1988).

"[A toast] to the family—that dear octopus from whose tentacles we never quite escape, nor, in our inmost hearts, ever quite wish to."

DODIE SMITH
DEAR OCTOPUS, 1938

"FAMILY" Defining a Variable Term

A measure both of the importance of families to our lives and of our ambivalence about them is that any discussion of the topic quickly elicits a demand for an explicit statement of what is meant by "family." The most useful such account is perhaps a normative one, which identifies features of special moral significance in the clear paradigm cases. These features can then be used to determine what counts as a family in the less clear cases. Ludwig Wittgenstein's notion of family resemblances serves us here: any social configuration that incorporates at least most of the morally significant features of, say, marital and parent-child relationships can be thought of as a family for present purposes. These features include long-standing, committed relationships; blood ties; emotional intimacy; shared histories; shared projects that produce solidarity among family members. Other crucial features identify functions: families forge the selves of their youngest members and help maintain the selves of adults. Further, familial relationships go beyond the contractual and the voluntary; in them we incur responsibilities not of our own choosing.

Relationships within families will take on greater or lesser bioethical significance, depending on the familial question under consideration. If treatment decisions for a badly damaged neonate are at issue, "family" means the mother and father; if the issue at hand is pedigree testing for a genetic disorder, "family" means blood kinship; if the issue is determining the appropriate caregiver for a person with progressive dementia, "family" may mean spouse or child.

— HILDE LINDEMANN NELSON
JAMES LINDEMANN NELSON

◆ **family planning**
Planning intended to determine the number and spacing of one's children through birth control.

Family and the law

Discussions in family law echo the question of how we are to define families. While there was for many years no basis in common law for family members to make treatment decisions for incompetent adults, for example, a number of court decisions in the 1980s and recent legislative action now give families decisional authority in some twenty states (Areen, 1987, 1991). This makes it all the more necessary to know just who is entitled to count as family. A strictly biological definition does not capture what seems socially significant about single parenting, stepparenting, and contract pregnancy. The legal notion of marriage skips over "kith"—long-standing committed relationships resembling kinship that might give, say, a neighbor or housemate moral authority to speak on behalf of a patient who is too ill to make treatment decisions; the law also fails to recognize gay and lesbian relationships, which may be more significant than blood ties to a person with AIDS or a brain-injured person caught in a custody dispute between lover and parents. On the other hand, functionalist definitions of families require courts to determine whether a particular relationship closely enough approximates an accepted norm of "family" to count as one. This involves inquiry into such areas as sexual activity, management of finances, and degree of exclusivity and commitment—a profound intrusion into personal privacy.

When one compares the body of family law against the body of law dealing with, for example, commercial transactions, family law seems distinctly underdeveloped and lacking in detail. The reason for this, Lee Teitelbaum argues, is that families, incorporating "diffuse, particularistic, and collective values and relations," tend to reflect a wide-ranging set of circumstances and goals, while law is better suited to consider individuals as abstracted from these particulars, in public settings that can be assimilated into a formal, rational scheme (Teitelbaum, 1992, p. 789). There is a further problem. As Carl Schneider points out, in the last few decades family law has increasingly eschewed moral discourse. The temptation is understandable: the problems within families are complex and often "reduce to unresolvable disputes over unverifiable beliefs." But by avoiding the language of morality, family law has stripped itself of conceptual notions that might help resolve such bioethical perplexities as contract pregnancy and the family's role in decision making for incapacitated patients (Schneider, 1992, p. 822).

Challenges to an ethics of strangers

Bioethics, however, need not lie down with law. Because it can achieve a high degree of particularity, it is better suited than the law to use a working definition of families that identifies morally relevant features and notes family resemblances—so to speak—among various small-scale human groups that include some such features. While bioethics has been slow to take families seriously, there are signs that the period of neglect is over. Roughly speaking, two approaches have been used to incorporate into bioethics what is morally valuable about families.

The first approach assumes the moral framework characteristic of the Enlightenment, with its stress on the impartial and the universalizable. Within this tra-

See Also

Family Authority: A Necessary But Risky Stewardship

dition, Nancy Rhoden has criticized the suspicion of the motives and interests of family members that has opened to court review their decisions concerning nontreatment of incapacitated relatives. Arguing that because family members "are in the best position to reproduce the preferences of an incompetent patient," Rhoden concludes that the burden of proof should be on the physician rather than the family (as is currently the case) to convince a court of law that an unwise decision has been made (Rhoden, 1988). In a more radical departure from current practice, John Hardwig has attacked the exclusionary bias of the doctor-patient relationship, insisting that the interests of all those with a stake in a medical decision, not just the patient's, be honored impartially (Hardwig, 1990).

At the same time, the so-called personal turn in ethics explored by Bernard Williams, Lawrence Blum, Jeffrey Blustein, Margaret Urban Walker, and others has challenged the orthodox assumption that ethics has primarily to do with right conduct among strangers—an ethics that favors no one and has dictates that are universalizable. The personal turn might be said to have begun with Williams's (1981) germinal observation that impartialist dictates, if followed scrupulously, leave insufficient room for moral agents to pursue their own individual interests, desires, and projects—all the substance, in fact, that gives life its meaning, though such meaning is what motivates one to go on. The task of Williams and others has been to construct moral accounts that honor the particular and the personal but do so in a nonarbitrary way. Feminist ethical theory has devoted much attention to this task (Kittay and Meyers, 1987; Card, 1991).

In bioethics one can see the direct impact of the personal turn in the writings of Ferdinand Schoeman. He has argued that a Kantian ethics for strangers, which insists that medical decisions for an incompetent person can be made only in accordance with what is in that person's best interests, provides an inadequate basis for understanding the parent-child relationship. That relationship, because it is intimate, permits parents to compromise the child's interests to promote the family's goals and purposes. Parents could, for example, permit a child to donate bone marrow to save a sibling's life, even though donating the marrow is not in the child's medical interests. In Schoeman's view, then, the family is seen as an entity with an integrity of its own that is greater than the sum total of the interests of its members (Schoeman, 1985).

Rhoden's attempt to vindicate the decisional authority of families and Hardwig's challenge to the patient-centered focus of conventional bioethics use the relatively straightforward strategy of applying impartialist standards to a context—the doctor-patient relationship—where they have not been applied before. Both writers are concerned with decision making, and more particularly with the locus of the decision. The personal turn in bioethics, which is concerned with a more fine-grained understanding of the structures of interpersonal relationships and their importance for human action, is less developed. But attention to the personal suggests certain moral features of family life that might be used to construct an ethics of the family.

Some elements of an ethics of the family

Social critics from Plato through Shulamith Firestone have argued that the distinctive features of the family constitute moral liabilities, and that families ought to be altered or abolished. In *A Theory of Justice*, John Rawls notes quite explicitly that the family is always a problem for egalitarian social theory (Rawls, 1971). A more sympathetic approach would portray those features as morally valuable, but whatever one's basic stance toward families, they do possess features that require moral attention and analysis.

One rather marked characteristic of families is their tendency to favor members over nonintimates. A central question is whether this sort of bias can be adequately understood inside a universalizable, impersonal framework. For example, can the favoritism parents show their children be justified insofar, and only insofar, as it increases the overall utility? James Rachels has argued for a position he calls "partial bias," which allows the expression of particular regard for children (and presumably for one's intimates in general) in those cases where their needs are in conflict with similarly serious needs of others, but not otherwise; this approach, he suggests, allows the special goods of intimacy to flourish within the context of appropriate regard for the needs of all, impartially considered (Rachels, 1989). It is, however, questionable whether a truly disinterested regard for the needs of others, in a world where resources are so massively maldistributed as ours, would leave any appreciable room for special regard for the needs of our own, particularly for those of us living in affluence. But even if some measure of special attention to loved ones could be made consistent with general impartialist norms, unless family members favor their own to at least a slightly greater degree than impartialist considerations mandate, it would seem they express only an ersatz partiality, not true loyalty, love, or commitment. To feel the force of this point, consider our intuitive response to a father who, when his only daughter thanks him affectionately for taking her to a baseball game, tells her, "Oh, I would have had to do the same for any child of mine." Rather than attempt, as Rachels does, to assimilate personal loyalty into an impartialist framework, a

Parents' authority is essential to the ethical education required for a democratic political morality.

PAGE 166

See Also

Assisted Reproduction: Psychology of Nontraditional Families

It's no coincidence that 20th-century totalitarian regimes have aimed to substitute the state for the family as people's 'locus of identity.'

PAGE 166

promising strategy might be to put less emphasis on individual integrity and the separateness of individuals, and attend a little more to the connections among individuals. A careful attention to these interconnections offers a basis for just dealings with others that takes account of the difference between strangers and intimates.

A second notable feature of families is that not all of its relationships fit comfortably under what has come to be modern ethics' most favored image of relationship: the contract. Children notoriously "didn't ask to be born," and none of us has chosen our blood relations. This fact has important implications for any theory that bases duties solely on consent; indeed, families are perhaps the most plausible counterexample to such theories. It is sometimes claimed that parental duties toward children arise from the parents' having tacitly consented to the child's existence, first, by agreeing to have sexual intercourse and second, by choosing not to abort the fetus. But this analysis entails that where intercourse was forced or good-faith efforts at contraception failed, and where abortion is for ethical or economic reasons not an option, the parents are off the moral hook; many will be reluctant to pay this dearly to retain the contract as the model of obligation. Ordinarily, responsibilities can arise from causal as well as contractual relationships; a proximate causal role in putting another in danger, for example, obligates one to stand ready to provide aid. This suggests that parental responsibility may stem from the fact that parents caused the child's existence, and not because they contracted for the child (Nelson and Nelson, 1989). In fact it can be maintained that intimate living as such creates expectations and other vulnerabilities, which, as Robert E. Goodin has argued, carry with them certain prima facie noncontractual duties. Such an analysis would embrace family members other than parents in a web of moral but nonconsensual relationship.

ETHICAL FRAMEWORK OF THE FAMILY

Distinguishing Features

1. Families tend to favor their members over outsiders.
2. Members are bound in a web of moral but nonconsensual relationships.
3. Collective well-being comes before self-interest.
4. Endless uniqueness: families and their relationships are infinitely particular, with myriad differences.

A third feature of the ethos that typifies families is a less individualistic image of persons than is customary in impersonal ethics. Actions are often assessed in terms of their impact on the family overall, and there is a certain amount of collective responsibility for family members' well-being. A family of immigrants might, for example, devote its resources to settling other relatives in the new country, an enterprise that requires individual family members to subsume their own projects and goals to the familial one. While the communitarian feature of family ethics has often lent itself to abuse as repeated sacrifices are demanded of certain family members (particularly women) to carry out a family agenda set by its dominant members, it is also true that a family cannot function if its members are altogether unwilling to pull in common. An ethics of the family, in contrast to the broad ethical theories, will concern itself with interests that are essentially held in common, as well as with individual interests.

A fourth distinguishing feature of what might emerge as an ethics of the family is that it is particularistic. *Pace* Tolstoy, all happy families are not like one another; there are myriad differences among and within them—as there are, for that matter, among unhappy ones. Because familial relationships are not only intimate but also of long standing, family members can come to know each other in rich, particular detail and from a highly specific standpoint. This means that the principles governing their behavior toward one another can be fine-tuned to a pitch of precision that is impossible, say, in law, where individual differences are perforce flattened out. What Iris Murdoch (1970) has called loving attention, and Martha Nussbaum (1990) calls fine awareness, would likely play an important role in any ethics of intimacy, whether among friends or within families. Attention to the particulars is what allows people involved in intimate relationships to focus on who they are together. This self-awareness, guided by general moral ideas such as justice, permits intimates to arrive at ethical decisions that are highly sensitive to circumstances and persons; the ethical work can be done "close up." Further, as these ethical deliberations become a part of the history of the relationship, their results can be used to guide future decisions that will be just as sensitive to the particulars (Walker, 1987).

Implications for medicine

MEDICAL DECISION MAKING. When a patient is incompetent to decide about his or her own medical treatment, or when competence is intermittent, physicians turn to the family for help, since families are presumed to know best what the patient would want, and also to care about the patient's interests. Families are instructed to make their decision on the basis of what the patient would want—the "substituted judgment" standard established in the *Quinlan* case (1976)—or, if the patient was never competent, on the basis of what

See Also

Communication: Shared Decision-Making

is best for the patient—the "best interests" standard. Tightly focused on the patient, either standard is open to challenge.

Linda L. Emanuel and Ezekiel J. Emanuel (1992) observe that the "substituted judgment" standard has been objected to on both theoretical and empirical grounds. An important theoretical objection is that reconstructing what a patient would want in highly specific circumstances from a general knowledge of the person's values requires a tremendous imaginative effort that may be beyond most people, while the empirical objections are that patients do not in fact discuss their preferences with family members, that family members are not good at assessing a patient's quality of life, and that proxies' selection is not much better than random chance in predicting patients' preferences for life-sustaining interventions. As Patricia White (1992) points out, people often do not know what they themselves would want if seriously ill.

The "best interests" standard is open to the objection that it cannot be seen as a patient's exercise (by proxy) of his or her right to refuse or consent to treatment, but instead gives the family power to exercise its own authority over the incompetent patient—something our society is reluctant to do because of the fear of abuse. While there are certainly instances of familial abuse of patients, one might question whether we ought to base social policy on the assumption that abuse is the possibility most to be feared. Yet if this objection to the "best interests" standard is unpersuasive, there is another that may be less so: the standard is not suitable to families because they are not simply a group of people each seeking to maximize his or her own self-interest. There is a collective character to family life that is not easily accommodated by the notion of individual best interests, and so the "best interests" standard is a code of conscience that from the family's point of view is distinctly second best. In fact, the standard is invoked primarily in adversarial situations where the family's solidarity has broken down, as in child-custody disputes.

An ethics of the family might suggest that what family members owe each other is not the best, understood abstractly. If it were, each of us would have a duty to find better parents for our children than we are ourselves. Rather, what is owed is the good that inheres in this particular set of relationships. If this is right, then at the sickbed it is less important that a brother, lover, or daughter-in-law will correctly decide what is best for an incompetent patient than that the decision be made by this particular person, the person who stands as close to the patient as possible and so serves the patient as an extended self. Here, as well as where the patient is competent, decision making that recognizes morally salient features of family life might set the needs and desires of the patient into careful balance against the family's resources for care, bringing a nuanced understanding of all the relevant particulars to bear on the decision.

THE ELDERLY AND THE END OF LIFE. What, if anything, do adult children owe their frail elderly parents? Theories affirming a duty of reciprocity argue that our parents gave us life and cared for us when we needed care; in return, we owe them care when they are in need. The difficulty with such theories (held by Aristotle and Aquinas, and more recently by William Blackstone [1856]) is that they do not seem to recognize that parents owe their children a decent minimum of goods and services. If parents are merely paying what they owe, it is hard to see why the child need respond with anything more than a thank-you. Following this line of reasoning, Jane English (1979) and Norman Daniels (1988) cannot defend a duty of adult children to care for their parents: the child, not having contracted for the parental sacrifices made on his or her behalf, has no duty to reciprocate, since sacrifices that have not been requested require no return. A third view, shared by Joel Feinberg (1966) and Jeffrey Blustein (1982), distinguishes between duties of indebtedness and duties of gratitude, and concludes that duties of gratitude are owed even for those actions that are included in the parents' moral duties; children must help their parents when help is needed. And a fourth theory bases a duty to parents in the parents' own moral duties, for the parental duty consists in part in encumbering the child with a loving relationship that in the child's maturity will be mutual, and that cannot then legitimately be broken without cause (Nelson and Nelson, 1992).

Whatever the source of duties to frail elderly parents, the content of those duties is not easy to ascertain. If postindustrial societies do not set limits on the amount of increasingly costly medical care they offer the old as they leave this life, they may impoverish the young. Within a family, this dilemma might be played out in terms of nursing-home care for a grandparent (now costing upward of $35,000 a year) versus a child's college fund. Margaret Urban Walker (1987) has described such a decision as an opportunity for defining oneself morally, ratifying or breaking from a past course of action as one sets the course of one's future. Families, too, might be capable of strong moral self-definition of this kind.

◆ **persistent vegetative state (PVS)**
Existence only at the biological level with little quality of life.

REPRODUCTIVE ISSUES. Medical solutions to infertility are genetic solutions; there is an attempt to establish a genetic tie between the child and at least one parent. In "traditional" contract pregnancy (in which the birth mother's egg is used to produce a child for people who have paid her to have the baby on their behalf) the importance of the maternal genes is played

See Also

Life, Quality of

Decision Point: Who Decides When "No One's Home"? and "Caring at Any Cost?"

down, but the paternal genes—those of the contracting father—are considered crucial. In the far less common arrangement whereby the birth mother is hired to carry to term an embryo formed in vitro by the contracting couple's egg and sperm (this is called gestational contract pregnancy), the maternal genes regain their standard social meaning, designating the woman who will rear the child. In artificial insemination by donor, the paternal genes are seen to carry no social responsibility for the child. The model for all this is one of consumer choice, in which the infertile parties are at liberty to decide for themselves what weight to give genetic ties.

This model raises important questions about the moral significance of being a parent. If those who contribute genetically to a child can be said to cause that particular child to exist, and if an ethics of the family adopts a causal rather than a contractual model of responsibility, then the child's genetic parents would seem to have a prima facie obligation to remain in the child's life in an ongoing way; even if they delegate much of their responsibility for rearing the child, it does not follow that they may put themselves totally out of power to keep the child from harm. Thus lesbian or gay couples might have a duty to foster a loving bond between the child and the biological parent of the opposite gender.

Medicine invites a consumer-choice approach not only in the matter of genetic ties but also in the matter of genetic screening. While it is reasonable to protect one's family by trying to avoid giving birth to a child with a serious genetic defect, the choices made possible by genetic screening can be a burden as well as a benefit. An important mechanism for drawing new members into the family—the pregnant woman's continual process of making friends with her fetus—is distorted and interrupted by amniocentesis, endoscopy, chorionic villus sampling, ultrasound, alpha-fetoprotein assays. Such screening, along with the new possibility of fetal surgery, prompts the question, contrary to when the fetus becomes a human individual, of how and when the fetus joins the family. As Stanley Hauerwas and William Ruddick ask (Hauerwas, 1981; Ruddick, 1988), when is a fetus a child? At what point in the process of family creation ought the pregnant woman to make specific sacrifices on the fetus/child's behalf, and to what extent should these sacrifices be socially imposed?

ALLOCATION OF HEALTH-CARE RESOURCES. A major function of the family is the care of its sick and vulnerable members. Because the United States has not acknowledged a basic responsibility to provide a minimum of health care for all its citizens, the burden of providing that care has fallen disproportionately on families—and within families, on adult women. The difficulty in achieving gender justice with respect to health care is not conceptual but political: how can we

See Also

Family Authority: A Necessary But Risky Stewardship

FAMILY
Implementing Family Ethics

Just as medical care is ethically inadequate when the focus is on the organ to be treated rather than on the person in whom the organ resides, so it is likely to be inadequate when no notice is taken of the families in which patients reside. An ethics that treats people as if they were unconnected and self-centered is not up to the task of promoting either justice or human flourishing. Primary-care physicians—not only practitioners of family medicine but also pediatricians and internists—are often adept at seeing beyond the patient to the nest of relationships within which that patient lives. They, like nurses and social workers, although hampered by institutional pressures that push families into the background, tend to be attuned to these relationships even when they cannot give a formal moral account of them. That account has been slow in coming; the values of families remain much more diffuse and implicit than the well-articulated values of medicine. But the relationship between the two systems of care is beginning to receive systematic exploration.

As we continue to discuss what that relationship should be in the twenty-first century, we may discover that taking families seriously requires major institutional changes. Hospitals might need to be restructured so that patients are not so estranged from their families; hospital ethics committees might have to take on a mediator's role for disputes among family members concerning patient care; the moral significance of families might have to be better reflected in case law; the conditions under which care is delivered will certainly have to be more hospitable to an ongoing relationship between patients and those who care for them; there will have to be a greater acknowledgment that families—the true source of primary care—are as essential a source of health care as medicine is. The practical difficulties in implementing an ethics of the family as it relates to health care, while daunting, are surely counterbalanced by the importance of the enterprise to the larger task of bioethics: thinking well and carefully about the concrete human realities—our differences, our similarities, our particularities, our intimacies—that have a direct bearing on health, whether within a medical or a familial setting.

— HILDE LINDEMANN NELSON
JAMES LINDEMANN NELSON

reconfigure our society—and our families—to eliminate the bias that sees unpaid care as a natural task for women?

A further allocation issue concerns the range of the family's care. To whom is it owed, and when is it discretionary? What about adult siblings? Cousins? Grandparents? A lesbian daughter's partner? Need and the person's role in the family's history are both relevant considerations, as are the family's resources: If, after all, familial caregiving is exhausted, no further care will be forthcoming. What limits may the family set on the care it owes to its own? What limits may the family set on individual members' sacrifices? More particularly, in light of the fact that women assume a greatly disproportionate amount of the burden of care (Okin, 1989; Brody, 1990), what steps should be taken both within families and in the larger society to achieve gender justice? An ethics of the family might offer guidance in the notion of familial integrity: the particular way in which a given family strives to sustain a fruitful tension between intimacy and autonomy, and the way it engages in its characteristic projects and activities. Family integrity cannot, perhaps, be preserved at any price, but it is important to recognize that families as well as individuals can be destroyed unless justice forbids it.

— HILDE LINDEMANN NELSON
JAMES LINDEMANN NELSON

FERTILITY CONTROL

MEDICAL ASPECTS

The ability of individuals to regulate their own childbearing represents one of the great medical advances of the twentieth century. As a result of demographic trends, which indicate an earlier onset of sexual activity and smaller family size, a woman may spend as long as thirty-five years purposefully avoiding pregnancy. An array of contraceptive methods is necessary to provide individuals with options that are most appropriate to their lifestyle, motivation, desire for effectiveness and convenience, and acceptance of medical risk. Two fundamental trends have affected contraceptive practice since 1960: the development of safe, continuous, and highly effective hormonal contraception, and more recently, an increased awareness of the role of barrier contraceptives for the dual purposes of pregnancy prevention and protection against sexually transmitted infections.

Currently available contraceptive methods include permanent methods that cause sterility—such as vasectomy in men and tubal occlusion in women—and reversible methods. Reversible methods include oral contraceptives (OCs); subdermal implants (Norplant®); progestin injections (depot-medroxyprogesterone acetate; DMPA; Depo-Provera®); intrauterine devices (IUDs); barrier methods (male and female condoms, diaphragm, cervical cap, and spermicidal products); and "natural" methods such as celibacy, periodic abstinence (natural family-planning and fertility-awareness methods), and withdrawal.

General considerations

It is unreasonable to assume that there is an ideal contraceptive method for each couple; more commonly, couples alternate among various methods over time. A number of general considerations can help to guide an individual (or couple) in the selection of an appropriate contraceptive method.

FREQUENCY OF SEXUAL INTERCOURSE. Couples who have frequent intercourse (arbitrarily defined as more than two to three episodes of intercourse per week) should consider the more continuous, non-coitus-related methods of contraception: OCs, IUDs, implants, injectables, or if childbearing is completed, permanent sterilization. For less sexually active couples (those who have intercourse less than once per week), an episodic method, such as a barrier contraceptive, would provide protection without exposure to method-related risks at other times.

NUMBER OF SEXUAL PARTNERS. Individuals who have multiple sexual partners, or whose partners have other partners, should be advised to consider one or more barrier methods, with the dual purposes of protection against sexually transmitted infections (STIs) and prevention of pregnancy. For couples who desire an optimal degree of pregnancy prevention, a combined approach of a barrier method plus a highly effective contraceptive will compensate for the relatively high pregnancy rate associated with barrier methods. Additionally, women in this category should not wear an IUD, as the risk of pelvic inflammatory disease (PID) and tubal infertility in IUD wearers is increased significantly in women with multiple sexual partners. For couples who are involved in a mutually monogamous relationship, no method of reversible contraception, including the IUD, increases the risk of PID or tubal infertility.

USER ACCEPTABILITY. Personal attitudes regarding the acceptability of certain methods may influence the success of use. These include religious beliefs, which may preclude the use of "mechanical" and hormonal contraceptives; tolerance of "nuisance" side effects, such as breast changes and vaginal bleeding; willingness to touch the genitals (of self or partner); and aesthetic concerns, such as tolerance of the "messiness" of spermicidal creams and jellies.

◆ **spermicides**
Contraceptives that kill sperm and provide some protection against STDs.

See Also
Unplanned Birth Statistics

Pill users are screened for breast cancer more frequently than nonusers.

PAGE 553

MOTIVATION AND SELF-DISCIPLINE. The degree of motivation to avoid pregnancy has a strong impact upon the successful use of contraceptives. Women who contracept to "delay" pregnancy have a higher failure rate than those who are intent on pregnancy prevention. Self-discipline also must be assessed, as women who are highly motivated may do well with intercourse-related (barrier) methods, while individuals who are poorly motivated should choose continuous non-intercourse-related methods such as OCs, IUDs, implantable or injectable methods, or sterilization.

ACCESS TO MEDICAL CARE. Because of the risk of medical complications, certain methods should be used only on the condition of reasonable access to medical care. This concern centers mainly on IUDs and, to a lesser extent, hormonal methods. Users of barrier methods, natural methods, and those who have been successfully surgically sterilized have a negligible risk of life-threatening method-related complications.

EFFECTIVENESS. Desire for high effectiveness versus willingness to accept a degree of risk of failure is a primary concern for many contraceptors. Those who insist upon a high degree of efficacy are best advised to use a combination OC (discussed below), an IUD, an implantable or injectable method, or sterilization. Alternatively, for individuals who will accept a higher method failure rate, coupled with an understanding that such failures will result in a choice between delivery and abortion, less effective methods, including barriers and natural methods, may be used.

SAFETY. Medical safety is a major concern for most contraceptors, and concerns regarding health risks are a major reason for discontinuation of use. Paradoxically, adolescents are more likely to avoid or prematurely discontinue contraceptives for fear of adverse health effects, yet they comprise the age group least likely to experience them. The risks associated with contraceptive use are dependent on the following four variables, with an example of each:

1. *Age.* The risk of arterial complications (adverse effect on the heart and blood vessels, e.g., heart attack) of OCs is age-related; this risk is greatly compounded by cigarette smoking.
2. *Underlying medical conditions.* Women with underlying cardiovascular risk factors (e.g., hypertension, glucose intolerance, hyperlipidemia, cigarette use) are more likely to experience myocardial infarction (heart attack) while using OCs.
3. *Sexual behaviors.* A pattern of multiple sexual partners increases the risk of STIs. In particular, IUD wearers would have a greater risk of PID resulting in primary tubal infertility (fallopian tubes blocked by scar tissue).
4. *Method-specific risk.* Complications are intrinsic to the method, regardless of age, health, and sexual behaviors. Examples include the risk of hepatic adenomas (liver tumors that are noncancerous but that may hemorrhage) in OC users; and pelvic actinomycosis (infection) in long-term IUD users.

A key component of contraceptive efficacy and safety resides in the quality and clarity of instruction and counseling given to the user. Initial instruction should include a description of the methods of contraception currently available, their relative effectiveness, the advantages and disadvantages of each method, and, if appropriate, a comparison of short- and long-term costs. Once a method has been chosen, instruction should center on method-specific advice, such as information regarding method use and danger signals that should be reported to the provider. If the individual will be learning the use of a relatively complex method, or one with an increased likelihood of side effects, it is prudent to provide a simple backup contraceptive method, such as condoms, should the user decide to abandon the initial method. Method-specific counseling should be supplemented with a written fact sheet or other instructional material at a reading and comprehension level appropriate to the individual. Finally, the user should be encouraged to telephone or visit the office of the provider, as necessary, for further advice or modification of contraceptive use.

Oral contraceptives

The oral contraceptive (OC) is the method of reversible contraception used most widely in the United States. Two types are available: "combination" OCs, which contain fixed (monophasic) or variable (multiphasic) doses of synthetic estrogen and progestin, and progestin-only pills (POPs, mini pills). OCs primarily prevent pregnancy by preventing ovulation (release of an egg from the ovary). The estrogen and progestin in the pill exert negative feedback on the hypothalamus (the part of the brain that controls hormone production by the pituitary gland) to suppress the release of the hormone GnRH, which in turn decreases secretion of the pituitary hormones LH and FSH, preventing ovulation. OCs also thicken cervical mucus, which promotes an environment hostile to sperm and alters the endometrium (the lining of the uterus), so that implantation of an embryo is unlikely to occur even if an egg "breaks through" (is released) and is then fertilized. The failure rate of combined oral contraceptives when used correctly and consistently is 0.1 pregnancies per one hundred women per year. In typical use, the

See Also

The Pill and Cancer: What Are the Risks?

failure rate is three pregnancies per one hundred women per year.

ORAL CONTRACEPTIVES: ADVANTAGES AND RISKS

Beneficial Effects

- prevents pregnancy
- prevents acute salpingitis (or pelvic inflammatory disease)
- prevents genital tract cancers
- relieves menstrual symptoms
- reduces risk of benign breast disease
- prevents and treats functional ovarian cysts

Adverse Effects

- vascular complications
- hypertension
- carbohydrate intolerance
- breast cancer

BENEFICIAL EFFECTS OF OCS. *Prevention of pregnancy:* When used correctly, OCs are highly effective in preventing pregnancy. This includes ectopic pregnancies (those that implant outside the uterus), thus preventing an important cause of maternal morbidity and mortality. There is no increase in the rate of spontaneous abortion or fetal anomalies in former users of OCs, and no long-term reduction in fertility has been demonstrated.

Prevention of acute salpingitis (also called pelvic inflammatory disease, or PID): Even when controlled for sexual behavior and for the coincident use of barrier contraceptives, studies have shown that OC users have a decreased risk of acute salpingitis. It also appears that cases of salpingitis are less severe in OC users overall when compared to controls. Paradoxically, OC users seem to have a higher rate of chlamydial endocervicitis (an STI, with inflammation of the cervix, which may or may not progress to PID).

Prevention of genital tract cancers: Data from the Centers for Disease Control and Prevention's (CDCP) Cancer and Steroid Hormone (CASH) study show a 50 percent reduction in risk for the development of both endometrial and ovarian cancer. Past use of OCs appears to bestow this protective effect for as long as fifteen years after the user has discontinued OC use. The relationship of OCs and cervical dysplasia (abnormal cells of the cervix that, if not monitored, sometimes progress to cancer) and carcinoma is somewhat more complex because of confounding biases, but overall, OC use neither causes nor protects against cervical neoplasia (abnormal tissue formation).

Relief of menstrual symptoms: OCs provide excellent therapy for primary dysmenorrhea ("normal" painful or difficult menstruation that is not related to a disease) because they suppress the endometrium (the lining of the uterus). Consequently, the endometrium does not produce as much prostaglandin, the substance that produces cramping of the uterus. There is a more variable effect on premenstrual syndrome, in that while many women have a decrease in symptoms, others have no change, and a small percentage have worsening symptoms. Because of shorter and lighter menses, the incidence of iron deficiency anemia is reduced by 65 percent. There is also a reduced risk of toxic shock syndrome.

Reduced risk of benign breast disease: OC users have a significant reduction in the incidence of benign (noncancerous) breast conditions, including fibroadenoma and fibrocystic change.

Prevention and treatment of functional ovarian cysts: As a result of the pharmacologic suppression of GnRH release and consequent blunting of pituitary gonadotrophin release, women who use OCs are less likely to develop functional ovarian cysts than women who do not use hormonal contraception. This effect appears to be dose-related, and users of low-dose OC products have less protection than those using stronger formulations. If OCs are given in an attempt to suppress an existing ovarian cyst, it is necessary to utilize a relatively strong product (e.g., Ovral) in order to achieve an effective degree of hypothalamic/pituitary suppression.

Other beneficial effects: For reasons that are unclear, OC users also have a lower incidence of rheumatoid arthritis and peptic ulcer disease.

ADVERSE EFFECTS OF OCS. The most common OC-related side effects are relatively minor. However, the patient may perceive them as major, and this may result in OC discontinuation and subsequent pregnancy. Effective management of minor or "nuisance" OC side effects consists mainly of patient education, and occasionally, medical intervention. Side effects include nausea, weight gain, spotting or breakthrough bleeding between menstrual periods, failure to have a menstrual period during the seven days off OCs, new onset or exacerbation of headaches, and chloasma (darkening of facial skin). Complications, while rare on low-dose combined oral contraceptives, can be serious.

Vascular complications: While initial studies indicated a direct relationship between estrogen dose and an increased risk of deep vein thrombosis (clotting) and pulmonary thromboembolism, more recent studies with low-estrogen-dose products have demonstrated only a minimally elevated attributable risk of these complications. For this reason, OC products containing thirty-five mcg of estrogen or less should be used

◆ **birth control**
Contraception, or the control of the number of children born by preventing or lessening the frequency of conception.

See Also

Population Policies: Strategies of Fertility Control

routinely. In early studies of unselected women using relatively high-dose products, OC users also demonstrated an increased risk of myocardial infarction and stroke in comparison to controls. As a result of exclusion of women with major cardiovascular risk factors and a progressive trend toward the use of lower-dose products, OC users as a group no longer have an elevated attributable risk of OC-induced morbidity or mortality from arterial disease.

Hypertension: The estrogen and progestin components of OCs act in concert to occasionally cause the development of blood-pressure elevation in a small number of OC users. Hypertension is reversible with discontinuation of OCs.

Carbohydrate intolerance: The progestin component of OCs is known to cause peripheral glucose resistance and consequent elevation of insulin levels. In most cases, these effects are minor and are not clinically significant. If a diabetic woman is started on OCs, frequent blood glucose monitoring is necessary initially, as insulin requirements may change. OCs should not be given to diabetics who have clinically manifested vascular or kidney disease or to those with such cardiovascular risk factors as smoking, hypertension, hyperlipidemia (elevated fatty substances in the blood), or age over forty.

Breast cancer: The relationship between OC use and breast cancer has been studied extensively since the mid-1970s. In aggregate, the studies show that the relative risk of breast cancer in a present or former OC user is 1.0, implying neither protection nor increased risk. This relationship was present with a number of subgroups, including women who had initiated OCs at an early age, those who used OCs for longer than ten years, women with a history of benign breast disease, and those with a positive family history. However, a number of studies performed in the early 1980s demonstrated a possible association between OC use and breast cancer in other subgroups. The only thread of consistency in these studies was to show a small increase in the risk of breast cancer for recent OC users who developed breast cancer at an age younger than thirty-five. In that there seems to be a small reduction in breast cancers in past OC users older than thirty-five, it has been hypothesized that OCs, like pregnancy and exposure to other hormonal contraceptives, may be a weak breast cancer promoter, and that OCs may hasten the growth of a tumor already in existence.

◆ **conceptus**
Used to describe any stage of development from fertilization to birth.

DMPA

On October 29, 1992, the U.S. Food and Drug Administration (FDA) approved contraceptive labeling for depot-medroxyprogesterone (DMPA); commonly known by its trade name, Depo-Provera. This culminated a twenty-year effort to make a long-acting injectable contraceptive available to American women. Based upon the findings of extensive clinical research done outside the United States over a decade, the FDA determined that while some concerns remained, DMPA was considered to be as safe as other hormonal contraceptives already on the market.

DMPA's mechanism of action is quite similar to that of all other hormonal methods of contraception: inhibition of ovulation; thickening of cervical mucus, which makes sperm penetration through the cervical mucus more difficult; and induction of endometrial atrophy, which prevents implantation in the highly unlikely event of fertilization. The chemical structure of DMPA is much closer to that of natural progesterone than that of the 19-nortestosterone progestins used in oral contraceptives and Norplant. This may account for the fact that DMPA users have little, if any, change in a number of metabolic parameters over time. In particular, there is no change in clotting factors, globulin levels, or glucose metabolism in DMPA users when compared to pretreatment levels. The slight decrease in total cholesterol levels seen in DMPA users is the result of a minor drop in high-density lipoprotein, the "good" cholesterol, although neither change is clinically significant. Interestingly, DMPA positively affects the central nervous system, causing the seizure threshold to increase, thus making seizures less likely in women with seizure disorders (e.g., epilepsy). Estrogen levels in DMPA users remain at early follicular phase levels, and while other menopausal symptoms do not occur, there is a possibility that some DMPA users may lose a small amount of bone mass over time.

With DMPA there are 0.3 failures per one hundred women during the first year of typical use. This high efficacy is due both to DMPA's efficiency in inhibiting ovulation and the fact that it is a relatively "user friendly" method of contraception. The long interval between injections, a two-week grace period for injections given beyond twelve weeks, and the absence of need for any user or partner intervention at intercourse all contribute to DMPA's high effectiveness.

DMPA is given as a deep intramuscular injection into the deltoid (upper arm) or buttocks every twelve weeks. Since administration most optimally is provided with a $1^{1}/_{2}''$ needle, most DMPA users, particularly thin women, will prefer the buttocks site. The initial injection of 150 mg of DMPA must be given within the first five days after the onset of menses, unless the woman has effectively been using the pill or has an IUD, in which case the first injection can be given any time during the month. Subsequent 150-mg injections are given at twelve-week intervals, although pregnancy is highly unlikely during the following two-week grace period. If fourteen weeks or more have elapsed since the last DMPA injection, a negative highly sensitive

See Also

Fertility Control: Limitations Advocated by Environmentalists

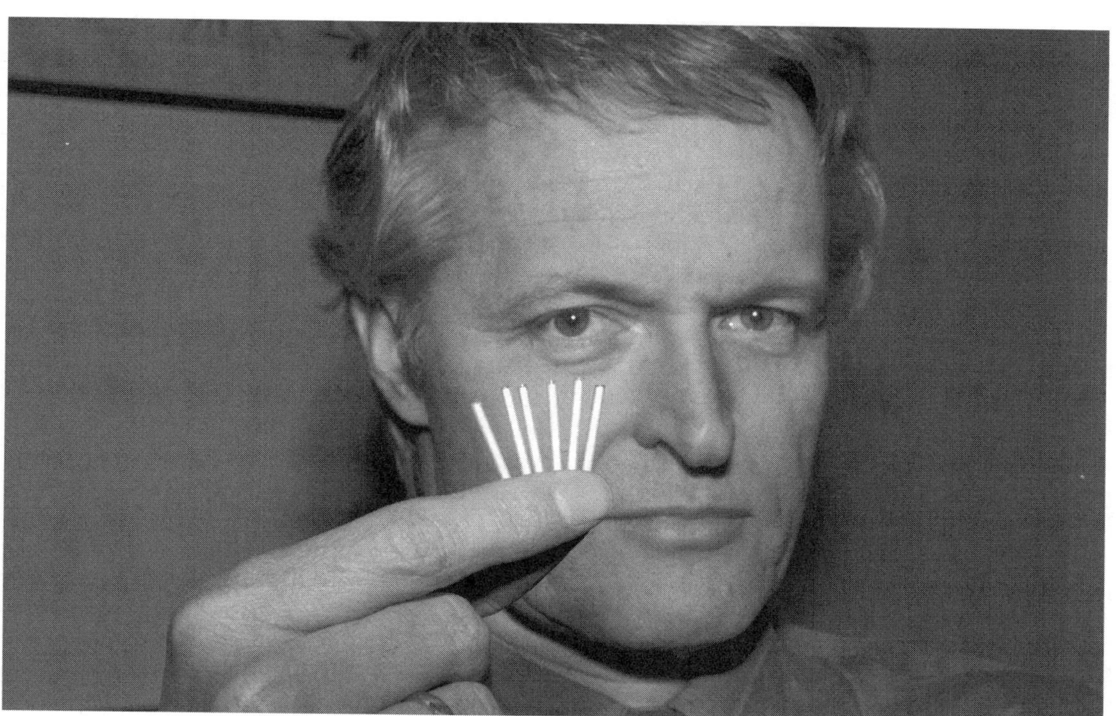

FIVE-YEAR FIX

Norplant is a sustained-release contraceptive in the form of six silicone rubber capsules surgically implanted in the upper arm.

urine pregnancy test must be documented before the next injection is given.

The ideal candidate for DMPA is a woman who is seeking continuous contraception; wants long-term birth spacing; desires a method that is neither coitus-dependent nor requires daily motivation; or who cannot use, or chooses not to use, a barrier method, an IUD, or an estrogen-containing method. It may be particularly appropriate for women who cannot use OCs because of a history of thrombophlebitis, hypertension, heavy smoking, or other cardiovascular risk factors. Women with sickle-cell anemia or seizure disorders actually may experience an improvement in their medical condition. DMPA is an excellent method for postpartum and post-abortal women and can be initiated immediately after completion of the pregnancy. Postpartum women who are lactating (nursing) should not be given DMPA until lactation has been established, usually one to two weeks after delivery. Women who desire a high degree of confidentiality in contraceptive use are attracted to DMPA because it does not require the personal possession of medications or devices, nor does it leave marks of administration or current use.

DMPA has few contraindications: active thrombophlebitis; undiagnosed abnormal genital bleeding; known or suspected pregnancy; active liver disease; a history of benign or malignant liver tumors; known or suspected carcinoma of the breast; and sensitivity (allergy) to the medication. Special conditions requiring more detailed medical evaluation and follow-up include a history of heart attack or stroke; diabetes mellitus; current migraine headaches; a history of severe endogenous depression; and chronic hypertension.

Menstrual changes are universal in women using DMPA and include episodes of irregular bleeding and spotting (lasting seven days or more during the first months of use) and amenorrhea (no menses). Sixty percent of women using DMPA for one year report amenorrhea, and the percentage increases with progressively longer use. Menstrual changes are the most frequent cause for dissatisfaction and discontinuation among women using DMPA, and appropriate patient education and selection and supportive follow-up measures can markedly reduce patient discontent. Medical intervention for irregular or heavy bleeding rarely is necessary, and anemia is uncommon. While counseling and reassurance are initial measures, medical therapy consisting of low-dose oral estrogen for one to three weeks may give temporary respite from bleeding. Women persistently dissatisfied may be better served by discontinuing this method and seeking alternative types of contraception rather than by repetitive medical or surgical intervention. In cases of heavy vaginal bleeding, gynecologic evaluation to rule out such unrelated conditions as vaginitis, cervicitis, or cervical lesions should be performed.

Another group of side effects that occur fairly frequently among DMPA users are pregnancy symptoms such as nausea, breast tenderness, abdominal bloating, and tiredness. While these symptoms are

prevalent in the first few months of DMPA use, persistence is uncommon and they rarely are cause for discontinuation.

Weight gain occurs in two-thirds of DMPA users owing to the drug's anabolic effect and its resultant impact on appetite. On average, DMPA users gain four pounds per year for each of the first two years of use. Women concerned or dissatisfied with weight gain should be counseled that it may be controlled with adequate exercise and moderate dietary restriction. Many women notice weight stabilization or improvement with time. If these measures fail and weight gain becomes problematic, DMPA discontinuation may become necessary.

Headache is a relatively common complaint in DMPA users, although not all headaches are necessarily related to the hormone in the drug. If the headaches are mild and without neurologic changes, treatment may be attempted with oral analgesics.

After a 150-mg injection of DMPA, the mean interval until return of ovulation is four to six months. Conception usually is delayed in former DMPA users when compared with women discontinuing oral contraceptives or IUDs. The median time to pregnancy following the last injection is nine to ten months, and studies have shown that almost 70 percent of former DMPA users conceive within the first twelve months following discontinuation, and over 90 percent conceive by twenty-four months, a rate comparable to that of oral contraceptive users. Nulliparous women (those who have never given birth to a child) and those using DMPA for many years experience the same return of fertility as other women studied.

Recent medical studies have addressed other safety issues regarding DMPA use. A large study conducted by the World Health Organization (WHO) showed that in aggregate, there is no overall increased risk of breast, cervical, or ovarian cancers in users of DMPA. DMPA users have a reduction in endometrial cancer for as long as ten years after discontinuation of the method. While there was evidence of a weak association between DMPA use and breast cancer in the subgroup of women under thirty-five who had used the drug within the previous four years, most experts feel that this represents a very weak promoter effect at a level similar to OC use. A single study showed a 7 percent reduction in bone density in premenopausal DMPA users compared to controls, but it is not clear whether this is a true biologic effect caused by low estrogen levels or due to selection bias. Until more work is done in this area, some believe that it is prudent to screen potential DMPA users for osteoporosis risk factors and to provide additional counseling or evaluation for those with multiple risk factors.

◆ **embryo**
The fertilized egg after fourteen days of development and the first sign of organ development.

See Also

Fertility Control as a Concern of Women

Norplant

Norplant is a sustained-release contraceptive system that acts continuously for five years. It consists of six silicone rubber capsules, each the length and diameter of a matchstick, which are surgically implanted under the skin of the upper arm. The synthetic progestin Levonorgestrel, a hormone found in many oral contraceptives, is slowly released into the bloodstream, resulting in a constant hormone level. The contraceptive effect of Norplant is due primarily to inhibition of ovulation, although secondary mechanisms include thickening of cervical mucus, and formation of an atrophic endometrium. Although 20 percent of Norplant users ovulate in year one and up to 50 percent ovulate by year five of use, studies suggest that when ovulation does occur, it is defective and the ovum is not subject to fertilization. The cumulative pregnancy rate of Norplant users is 3.8 pregnancies per one hundred women over five years; the first-year failure rate is only 0.09 per hundred women per year. Ectopic (tubal) pregnancies are reduced by two-thirds in comparison to noncontracepting women, although should Norplant fail, there is a greater conditional probability (proportionate risk) that the pregnancy will be located in the fallopian tube rather than in the uterus.

Studies that have evaluated the metabolic effects of Norplant have found minimal impact. There is no effect on cholesterol or lipoprotein metabolism, glucose metabolism, or propensity to blood clotting. Norplant is an appropriate method of contraception for women who desire long-term contraception, who have completed childbearing but do not desire permanent sterilization and have had problems with other methods of contraception (including combined OCs), and for postpartum women, whether nursing or not.

The technique of insertion of Norplant involves anesthetizing the skin with local anesthetic and creation of a four-millimeter incision, followed by placement of a twelve-gauge trochar to insert the capsules in a fan-shaped pattern. The procedure takes less than ten minutes and is well tolerated by most women. The method should be inserted within five days of the onset of the menses and provides a contraceptive effect within twenty-four hours. More problematic is Norplant removal, which requires substantially more skill and takes between fifteen and forty minutes. The ease of removal is related to a number of factors, including the correctness of the initial Norplant insertion, the amount of fibrous tissue that has developed around the capsules, and the skill of the clinician.

The most prevalent adverse effect of Norplant is the unpredictability and irregularity of menstrual cycles, especially in the first year of use. Cycles may be shorter or longer than usual and associated with more

or less bleeding; there may be bleeding between cycles, or no bleeding at all. Although there is no "cure" for irregular bleeding patterns, short-term palliation of the problem can be achieved by the use of low-dose oral estrogen therapy (e.g., ethinyl estradiol 20 mcg orally per day for two to three weeks). Other side effects include mild weight gain, headaches, hair loss, and new onset or exacerbation of depression.

Intrauterine devices (IUDs)

Although the IUD is used by only 1 to 2 percent of contracepting women in the United States, it is one of the most widely used methods worldwide. A popular method in the United States in the 1970s, IUD use dropped precipitously as a result of the high rate of pelvic infection and consequent tubal infertility experienced by women who used the Dalkon Shield IUD, which was removed from the market for this reason. Mainly because of business concerns related to the risk of product liability suits, manufacturers of most other IUDs voluntarily withdrew their devices over the next decade. The two IUDs currently available in the U.S. include a progesterone-releasing T-shaped IUD (Progestasert®), which must be exchanged yearly, and a copper-bearing T-shaped device called the Cu-T-380-A (ParaGard®), which exerts its contraceptive effect for eight years.

The IUD's mechanism of action is still a matter of conjecture. In copper IUDs, it is likely that copper ions released by the device have a toxic effect on sperm, rendering them incapable of fertilizing an ovum. Progesterone-releasing IUDs probably exert their contraceptive effect by converting the endometrium to a chronically atrophic state, preventing implantation of the zygote (fertilized egg). IUDs are known to be a relatively effective contraceptive, with failure rates in the range of 0.6 to 2.0 pregnancies per one hundred women per year. While many clinicians assume that the IUD increases a woman's risk of experiencing an ectopic (tubal) pregnancy, studies clearly show that users of progesterone-bearing IUDs have no increased risk of ectopic pregnancy when compared to nonusers of contraception, while users of copper IUDs experience profound protection.

Women best suited for the use of an intrauterine device are those who desire continuous contraception; who want long-term birth spacing or have completed their families but do not want to be sterilized; who require very high contraceptive efficacy; who desire a method that neither is coitus-dependent nor requires daily motivation; and who cannot use or choose not to use a barrier method or a hormonal method of contraception. IUD insertion and removal are simple office procedures that may result in temporary uterine cramping, but rarely require the use of local anesthesia or analgesia.

IUD use may result in relatively minor side effects such as heavy menstrual periods or cramping (less so with the progesterone-releasing type) and increased vaginal discharge. The relationship between IUD use and pelvic infection and consequent infertility has been studied in great detail. Early studies demonstrated that the major risk associations were recent insertion (within twenty days) and the type of IUD used (the Dalkon Shield bestowing the greatest risk). More recent studies have suggested that an IUD wearer's sexual behavior is the single most relevant risk factor for pelvic infection; a woman in a mutually monogamous sexual relationship has no increased risk of pelvic infection or tubal infertility ("blocked" or scarred tubes from PID) compared to the sexually active woman who uses no method. Conversely, women who have multiple concurrent sexual partners, or those who themselves are monogamous, but whose male partner has other sexual partners, appear to be at increased risk of IUD-associated pelvic infection.

POTENTIAL ADVERSE AFFECTS OF IUD USE

Contraindications to IUD use include:

- pelvic inflammatory disease within the past twelve months or recurrent PID (more than one episode in the past two years);
- post-abortal or postpartum endometritis or septic abortion in the past three months;
- known or suspected untreated endocervical gonorrhea, chlamydia, or mucopurulent cervicitis;
- undiagnosed abnormal vaginal bleeding;
- pregnancy or suspicion of pregnancy;
- history of impaired fertility in a woman who desires future pregnancy;
- known or suspected uterine or cervical malignancy;
- small uterine cavity;
- history of pelvic actinomycosis infection (not asymptomatic presence of the organism);
- known or suspected allergy to copper or, for copper IUD only, a history of Wilson's Disease (an inability to metabolize copper).

◆ **fertilization**

The union of two specialized cells—egg and sperm—produced by two individuals of one species but opposite gender.

See Also

Fertility Policy: Seeking Fairness across Genders, Generations, and Nations

While young age may be associated with certain risky sexual behaviors, young age alone is not an absolute contraindication to IUD use. Correspondingly, a history of previous childbearing should not be an absolute prerequisite for IUD use. If a young woman is involved in a long-term mutually monogamous relationship and has no other risk factors, she may be considered a candidate for an IUD.

Barrier methods

Barrier methods include mechanical barriers such as male and female condoms, the female diaphragm and cervical cap, and chemical barriers such as spermicidal products. Nonprescription barrier contraceptives are an important contraceptive option because of their wide availability, relative ease of use, and acceptably high efficacy when used correctly and consistently. While the contraceptive efficacies of the various barrier methods when used alone are comparable to each other (typically about twenty pregnancies per one hundred women per year), their use in combination adds significantly to their effectiveness. In addition, male latex condoms and female vaginal sheaths, when used consistently and correctly, provide a high degree of protection against both the acquisition and the transmission of a number of sexually transmitted pathogens, including gonorrhea, chlamydia, syphilis, and some viral pathogens, including hepatitis B virus and HIV (human immunodeficiency virus), the virus that causes AIDS (acquired immunodeficiency syndrome). Spermicidal products, in addition to their contraceptive effect, have in vitro microbicidal properties and appear to provide some protection against gonorrhea and chlamydia. Nonprescription barrier contraceptives include male latex and animal membrane condoms; female polyurethane vaginal sheaths; the contraceptive sponge; and spermicidal films, foams, jellies, creams, and suppositories. Contraindications include allergy to latex rubber (in the case of male condoms, diaphragm, or cervical cap), a history of significant skin irritation with acute or chronic exposure to spermicides, and inability to understand instructions for use.

Although new contraceptives give women reproductive control, they may also carry risks and side effects that may take years to discover.

PAGE 700

The contraceptive diaphragm is a dome-shaped latex device that serves as a mechanical barrier against the cervix and also holds a spermicidal preparation in place within the vagina. The diaphragm is one of the oldest barrier methods of the modern era, and has retained its popularity because of its nonhormonal nature, ease of use, and reasonable efficacy. It may be an appropriate method of contraception for women who prefer an intercourse-related nonhormonal method of contraception; desire a barrier method that can provide continuous protection over twenty-four hours; and feel that the diaphragm is less noticeable during intercourse than other barrier methods. The diaphragm should fit comfortably with the anterior (front) rim tucked behind the pubic bone in front and the posterior (back) rim seated deep in the vagina and behind the cervix, so that the cervix is covered by the dome of the diaphragm. The largest, most comfortable diaphragm that fits well should be chosen. Use of a backup method of contraception until the return visit, or until the patient is sure that the diaphragm is staying in place during intercourse, should be advised.

No attempt should be made to use the diaphragm if the woman cannot be fitted with the device due to physical characteristics of the vagina, cervix, or uterus that interfere with proper placement, or if the proper size diaphragm is not available. Other contraindications include a recent history of frequent lower urinary tract infections (e.g., cystitis), especially if associated with prior diaphragm use; less than three months since cervical surgery; less than two weeks since mid-trimester abortion or less than six weeks postpartum (after delivery of a child); allergy to rubber or to all spermicides; inability to understand instructions for use; and inability to insert, remove, and care for the device correctly.

The cervical cap is a thimble-shaped latex device that fits over the cervix and stays in place by mild suction. When used with a spermicide, it is a reliable barrier method of contraception that can be used continuously for up to forty-eight hours. In use in European countries since the 1930s, it was approved by the FDA for contraceptive use in the United States in 1988. The efficacy of the cervical cap in preventing pregnancy is similar to that of the diaphragm in nulliparous women, although the failure rate of the cap is greater in parous women.

The Prentif Cavity Rim Cervical Cap® is the only cap currently approved by the FDA. It is available in four sizes: 22-, 25-, 28-, and 31-mm internal diameter. Because cervix size may vary considerably, these sizes fit approximately 70-75 percent of women. The cap may be an appropriate choice for women who have experienced frequent urinary tract infections, especially if they occurred in association with the contraceptive diaphragm. Because there is less pressure on the urethra and bladder, the cap may be more comfortable than a diaphragm and less likely to predispose the user to a lower urinary tract infection.

Natural Methods

The most effective methods of fertility control are those in which sexual intercourse is avoided entirely. Abstinence is defined as a limited period of time in which intercourse is avoided, while celibacy refers to a

See Also

Health Effects of Fertility Control

lifestyle decision in which an individual chooses to avoid intercourse for a longer time interval, which may be lifelong in some cases.

Fertility awareness methods are those in which sexually active individuals avoid unprotected intercourse during the "fertile period," which is defined as the time in each cycle that ovulation is estimated to occur. Since the ovum survives for about 48 hours after ovulation and sperm can survive in the fallopian tubes for up to five days, the length of the fertile period is about seven days in most women. Couples who practice the fertility awareness method use a barrier method of contraception with intercourse during the fertile period and no method for the remainder of the cycle. In the "natural family planning" technique, a variant of fertility awareness, intercourse is avoided entirely during the fertile period and mechanical contraceptive methods are not used at any time in the cycle. The latter approach generally is endorsed by religious groups who object to the use of other birth-control methods, which they consider to be "artificial" in nature.

Four techniques, which can be used alone or in combination, are used to estimate the fertile period.

- The "calendar" method, in which previous menstrual cycling patterns are charted and from which future ovulatory patterns may be predicted. This method is comparatively inaccurate, as factors such as stress or illness can affect the time of ovulation and thereby shorten or lengthen a given cycle. In addition, many women have such variable cycle lengths that the estimated duration of the fertile period can be as long as two weeks.
- The "basal body charting" or "temperature" method, which is based upon the fact that a woman's basal temperature will increase by 0.5° to 1.0°F twelve to twenty-four hours after ovulation and will remain elevated until the next menstrual period. Women using this method are expected to check their temperature each morning upon arising until the temperature rise has been confirmed. Once two days have passed after the temperature rise, the fertile period is considered to be completed, and unprotected intercourse can resume until the next menstrual period.
- The "cervical mucus" method, also called the "Billings" or "ovulation" method, which relies upon the fact that a woman's cervical mucus becomes copious and watery in the few days before ovulation. The presence of characteristic mucus at the vaginal opening is a sign of impending ovulation and, hence, defines the existence of the fertile period.
- The "sympto-thermal" method uses a combination of two or more of the above techniques. The use of the cervical mucus to signal the beginning of the fertile period and the basal body temperature rise to predict its completion is the most accurate of the fertility awareness methods.

The effectiveness of the fertility awareness methods depends upon the couple's consistency of use and ability to avoid unprotected intercourse during the fertile period. When practiced correctly and consistently, the sympto-thermal method has a failure rate as low as two failures per one hundred women per year, while for the typical use failure rate for all methods of periodic abstinence is twenty pregnancies per one hundred women per year.

Most research and development of contraceptives has been on techniques for women.

PAGE 700

Sterilization

Voluntary surgical sterilization (VSS) is the most prevalent form of contraception in the United States; 60 percent of those surgically sterilized are women who have had tubal ligation, and 40 percent are men with vasectomies. Most couples who choose surgical sterilization have completed their families, although for some individuals this choice is prompted by an inability or unwillingness to use reversible methods of birth control. Criteria once used to determine the appropriateness of sterilization based on age and parity (number of children born) are no longer appropriate, and a woman's considered, informed decision should be respected by the provider, regardless of her age, parity, and social circumstances.

TUBAL LIGATION. The most important point to be made in counseling a woman regarding tubal ligation is that the procedure must be considered permanent and should be performed only when she is sure that she desires no further children. Alternative (reversible) methods of birth control should be discussed to ensure that these methods have not been rejected on the basis of misunderstanding or other biases. Other important aspects of counseling include a description of the surgical risks of tubal ligation, failure rates, and a comparison to the various methods of sterilization available, including vasectomy for the woman's partner. If consent cannot be obtained from a severely mentally disabled woman, a legal guardian may provide consent in some cases.

Both the federal government and individual states have regulations regarding minimum age requirements and waiting periods from the time of written consent until the date that the operation may be performed if federal or state funding is to be used. For this reason, women who plan to undergo postpartum tubal ligation should receive counseling and consent before thirty-four weeks gestation.

The surgical approach to tubal ligation is primarily dependent upon whether the procedure is performed in the postpartum period, or longer than six weeks after delivery, in which case it is considered to be an interval tubal ligation. In a postpartum tubal ligation, a minilaparotomy performed within four to twenty-four hours of delivery is the preferred approach subsequent to a vaginal delivery. After receiving a regional or general anesthetic, a three-centimeter curvilinear or vertical incision is made immediately under the umbilicus. Once the peritoneal cavity has been entered, either the operator's finger can be used to sweep each tube into the incision or each tube can be grasped under direct vision. In either case, positive identification of the tube can be made by visualizing the fringelike portion at the abdominal end of each tube and by demonstrating that the nearby round ligament is uninvolved. After completion of the tubal occlusion, each excised tubal fragment must be sent for histological confirmation. In a woman delivered by cesarean section, any of the three techniques described below can be performed after repair of the uterine incision has been completed.

A number of techniques are available when there is direct access to the fallopian tubes via minilaparotomy or cesarean section. They include the following methods:

- modified Pomeroy method, in which two ligatures (sutures, "ties") are placed in the midportion of each of the tubes and then the pieces of tube between the ligatures are removed. The closed ends retract, leaving a gap between the closed-off tubal segments.
- Irving method, whereby the tubal stump nearest the uterus is tucked into a tunnel made in the myometrium (muscular structure) of the large upper part of the uterus.
- Uchida method, which involves excision of a five-centimeter segment of tube, followed by burying the tubal stump farthest from the uterus within the mesosalpinx (the free margin of the upper part of the broad ligament).

While the failure rates of the Irving and Uchida techniques are exceedingly low (less than 1/1,000) in comparison to the Pomeroy method (1/250), the former take longer to perform and therefore are relegated to special cases.

◆ **gamete intrafallopian tube transfer (GIFT)**
Involves the transfer of freshly recovered ova and conditioned sperm into the fallopian tubes, thus resulting in in vivo *fertilization.*

Interval tubal ligation may be performed with a laparoscope (a narrow lighted tube) via a low minilaparotomy incision (a small horizontal incision, 2-5 cm long, just above the pubic hairline), the former being much more prevalent in the United States. Laparoscopic approaches ("band-aid" surgery) include either open or closed laparoscopy, and both one- and two-puncture instruments (laparoscopes) are available. While a large majority of laparoscopic tubal ligations are performed under general anesthesia, there is a growing trend to perform these procedures under local anesthesia, thereby reducing cost and avoiding the risk of general anesthetic complications, which is the most common cause of tubal ligation deaths. If local anesthesia is used, the tubes must be bathed in a long-acting local anesthetic, then banded or clipped, rather than electrocoagulated (coagulation or clotting of tissue using a high-frequency electric current).

Minilaparotomy for interval tubal ligation is performed via a three-centimeter low horizontal incision. Because of the difficulty entailed in working through a small incision, the procedure is facilitated by using a uterine elevator, an instrument placed in the vagina to lift the uterus. The procedure may be performed with general, regional, or local anesthesia. Minilaparotomy is contraindicated when the patient is obese, has an enlarged or immobile uterus, or when adnexal disease (in the areas adjacent to the uterus, e.g., ovaries and tubes) such as endometriosis is suspected. Nonetheless, minilaparotomy can be a safer, simpler, and less expensive procedure than laparoscopy, which requires more technical equipment and endoscopy experience.

If minilaparotomy is chosen, any of the occlusion techniques outlined above for postpartum tubal ligation may be used. In addition, spring-loaded tubal clips are available that can be easily applied through a minilaparotomy incision. With the laparoscopic approach, three methods of tubal occlusion are available:

- Electrocautery, with a coagulation or "blend" current, used at two or three sites along the mid-fallopian tube. Either unipolar or bipolar cautery may be used; while bipolar cautery is safer (since it is less prone to cause bowel burns), it takes longer and has a higher failure rate. Unipolar electrocautery is faster and more effective, but there is a risk of sparking between the electrode and the bowel, resulting in an unrecognized injury. Fallopian tubes occluded by electrocautery may be quite difficult to reanastomose (reconnect, in the event the woman changes her mind and wants to try to achieve pregnancy) because of extensive scarring.
- Silastic (silicone rubber) rings may be applied with a forceps-type applicator to a loop of mid-portion fallopian tube. This approach avoids the risk of electrical injury to the bowel and preserves much larger segments of healthy ends of the severed fallopian tube should later reversal be considered.
- Spring-loaded clips may be placed at a single site in the middle of the tube and can be used with double-puncture laparoscopy or at minilaparotomy.

See Also
Reproductive Decisions

The provider must explain that with tubal interruption alone, no organ is removed; tubal sterilization merely prevents conception. The operation is not "desexing" and will not reduce libido, vary the woman's menses, or alter her appearance. There is usually no adverse change in sexual function following tubal sterilization; on the contrary, many women who feared pregnancy before the operation report increased satisfaction in sexual intercourse and are pleased with the operative result. However, 2 to 5 percent report less frequent orgasm and a similar percentage have delayed regret that the procedure was performed.

Only hypophysectomy (excision of the pituitary gland), bilateral oophorectomy (removal of both ovaries), and ovarian damage by radiation are certain methods of sterilization. Abdominal and tubal pregnancies have occurred (rarely) even after total hysterectomy (removal of the uterus). Oophorectomy and sterilization by radiation are usually followed within four weeks by vasomotor reactions (symptoms associated with menopause such as "hot flashes") and a gradual diminution in libido or sexual satisfaction during the next six months.

VASECTOMY. Sterilization of the man by vasectomy is both less dangerous and less expensive than tubal ligation, as it is routinely performed as an office procedure under local anesthesia. Through one or two small incisions in the scrotum, the vas deferens (the tube or duct that carries sperm) is isolated and occluded and usually a small segment of each vas is removed. Neither physiologic impotence nor changes in libido result from the procedure. Sterility cannot be assumed until postoperative ejaculates are found to be completely free of sperm. Failure of the vasectomy, as manifested by pregnancy in a partner, occurs in 0.1 percent of patients. Medical risks of vasectomy include hematoma (blood clot or bruise) formation, epididymitis (congestion or inflammation of the epididymis, the coiled tubular structure where sperm cells mature), spontaneous recanalization of the vas (reconnection of the ends with restored patency) (incidence of less than 1 percent), and the development of a spermatocele (cystic nodule containing sperm). Atrophy of the testes very rarely results from ligation of excessive vasculature (blood supply). Vasectomy often is reversible—up to 90 percent in some reports—but requires expensive microsurgery and special skill with no guarantee of success. Pregnancy results in only about 60 percent of cases after reversal; factors that influence success include (but are not limited to) the surgeon's skill, the type of procedure used, and time interval since vasectomy.

— MICHAEL POLICAR

SOCIAL ISSUES

The status of birth-control, sterilization, and abortion services in the United States has always been linked to the various social movements that have been engaged with issues of reproduction and sexuality. Since the nineteenth century, different groups have advocated for and against family planning (used here to refer to both birth control and abortion) for different reasons, and with differing levels of success.

While issues pertaining to reproductive control have always caused some degree of social conflict, this has been especially true since the mid-1970s, when the polarization over the abortion issue became intense and spread to other reproductive health services (e.g., contraception and sex education). The emergence of AIDS and rising rates of sexually transmitted diseases (STDs) have also contributed to the controversy surrounding family planning in the United States in the late twentieth century. This article discusses various groups that claim a stake to "ownership" (Gusfield, 1981) of family-planning issues, indicates some of the specialized populations that require family-planning services, and speculates briefly about the uncertain future of birth-control and abortion services in the United States. Finally, the article touches on debates on family planning that are taking place in the developing world.

Interest groups and family planning

PROVIDERS OF FAMILY-PLANNING SERVICES. Family-planning services in the United States are offered by both private and public agencies. Public providers of family-planning services at the local level include public-health clinics in hospitals or neighborhood health centers, which often provide birth-control services along with other primary health services, and hospital-based clinics, which often specialize in family-planning delivery. At the county, state, regional, and national levels, various arms of government are involved with the setting of policy for these publicly supported clinics and in devising formulas to disburse funding. The major conduit for public funding of family-planning services is Title X of the Public Health Act of 1970. Title X has never allowed funding for abortion services.

In the private sector, abortion and birth-control services are offered both by for-profit and not-for-profit clinics, and by private physicians. The not-for-profit Planned Parenthood Federation of America, Inc., with some 170 affiliates across the country in the 1990s, has been the most important provider of family-planning services in the private sector.

In theory, the public and private components of the family-planning delivery system share similar goals:

◆ **gametes**
A mature male or female germ cell (sperm or egg) possessing a haploid chromosome set and capable of initiating formation of a new diploid individual by fusion with a gamete of the opposite sex.

See Also

Contraception: Reproductive Control—with Risks

the dissemination of contraceptive services and education under a public-health model, with the prevention of AIDS and sexually transmitted diseases a more recent addition to the previous agenda of fertility control. Yet the relationship between the private and the public components is quite complicated for two reasons. First, family-planning services, like other publicly provided social services in the United States, are typically delivered through a system that relies at least partly on private agencies, or "subcontractors," rather than directly by the government itself.

Second, the intense politicization of family-planning issues since the 1980 election of President Ronald Reagan has meant that often the agendas of public and private providers of family-planning services have been very much at odds. Title X—the major federal program for the provision of family-planning services—illustrates these contradictions. A significant proportion of Title X-funded services in many communities across the country is provided by Planned Parenthood, which is also a prime target of those who can be called "sexual conservatives" (see "Pro-Family Movement" below), because of the organization's visibility as an abortion provider. Political appointees within the U.S. Department of Health and Human Services, which oversees Title X and related services, have, at times, been aligned with political groups committed to the defunding of this program, because of some conservatives' opposition to birth-control programs. Between 1980 and 1990, the number of publicly funded family-planning clinics across the country declined 20 percent, from 5,000 to 4,000 clinics (Ettinger, 1992; Scott, 1991); this decline reflects the bitter ideological wrangling over the concept of publicly funded family planning.

THE WOMEN'S MOVEMENT. Since the reemergence of a visible women's movement in the United States in the late 1960s—the "second wave" of feminism—various groups associated with the movement have been forceful advocates for family-planning services, and particularly for abortion services. (Indeed, a significant difference between first- and second-wave feminists was the willingness of the latter to engage in issues of reproduction rights and sexuality [Joffe, 1986]). For example, the campaign to make abortion legal and accessible was a major focus of the feminist movement at the time of its reemergence in the late 1960s. During the 1980s, when legal abortion became threatened, women's organizations such as the National Organization for Women (NOW) played a highly visible role in pro-choice activities, and worked closely with such organizations as Planned Parenthood and the National Abortion Rights Action League (NARAL). Similarly, the National Women's Health Network and the Federation of Feminist Health Centers represent specialized interest groups within the larger women's movement that have focused on reproductive issues.

With respect to other reproductive issues, however,

SOCIAL ISSUES

The Future of Fertility Control

The future of family-planning services in the United States is unclear. The presidential election of Bill Clinton in 1992, in certain significant respects, muted the influence of conservatives in public-policy debates about family-planning issues. Clinton's appointments to key health-policy positions of individuals strongly committed to family planning, especially in the area of teenage pregnancy prevention, sharply reversed the trends of the Reagan-Bush era. Ideological battles may be temporarily muted, but they will not disappear entirely because of a change in presidential administration. At the state and local levels, many of the bitter struggles over the public provision of reproductive health services will continue. And given the salience of sexuality-related issues in U.S. political culture, future Republican presidential victories very likely will imply a return to some of the policies that characterized the Reagan-Bush era.

The major—and, at the time of this writing, unknown—factor in the status of these services in the near future will be the ultimate character of health-reform efforts initiated by the Clinton administration. Early drafts of proposed reform speak of coverage of "pregnancy-related services," but it is not clear what precisely will be made available. The abortion issue, of course, is among the most politically explosive items in this category, and many observers feel that disagreements about the inclusion of abortion have the potential to jeopardize the entire health-care-reform effort.

Beyond abortion, however, there are other important, as yet unanswered, questions. The Norplant insert, for example, when introduced in 1991, cost patients over $500, thus making this method accessible only to high-income women or those women whose incomes were low enough to qualify for Medicaid (Forrest and Kaeser, 1993). Thus it is not clear that all American women will have access to all contraceptive methods or to the more expensive fertility treatments, such as in vitro fertilization, under the new health measure. Generally speaking, however, we can assume that health-care reform will bring greater access to a broad range of family-planning services.

— CAROLE JOFFE

the relation of sectors of the women's movement to its abortion allies has been more complex. At times, the responses of some feminist health activists to prevailing contraceptive practices and new contraceptive innovations have conflicted with sometime allies, such as Planned Parenthood. These activists, for example, raised doubts early on about the safety of oral contraception ("birth-control" pills); objected to testing new contraceptive technologies on women in developing nations (Seaman, 1969; Gordon, 1976); and more recently, voiced reservations about the likely social abuses of Norplant, a contraceptive implant.

THE PRO-FAMILY MOVEMENT. Beginning in the 1970s, a movement of sexual conservatism—the "pro-family" movement—became a significant presence in family-planning politics (Petchesky, 1990; McKeegan, 1992). In broadest terms, this movement's main concern has been the breakdown of sexual morality in contemporary society, as evidenced by high rates of abortion, teenage pregnancy, out-of-wedlock births, and STDs. For sexual conservatives, widely available family-planning services—especially those supported by public funds—represent a temptation to break with traditional morality (Marshner, 1982). Though the pro-family movement is most visible in antiabortion activity, its interests and interventions extend to a broad range of reproductive and sexual matters—contraceptive services, sex education, teenage pregnancy prevention efforts, AIDS prevention services, and so forth (Joffe, 1986; Nathanson, 1991). Among the specific organizations affiliated with the pro-family movement that have engaged politically with family-planning issues are the Family Research Council, the Eagle Forum, the Moral Majority, the Concerned Women of America, and the Religious Roundtable. Some antiabortion groups, such as the American Life League, have recorded strong opposition to publicly funded birth-control programs.

Family-planning services for teenagers have been a major focal point of pro-family activity (Joffe, 1993). Conservative activists have persuaded legislators in a number of states to adopt parental notification and consent rules for teenagers seeking abortions, and have sought regulations that would include parental notification policies for federally funded clinics providing contraceptive services. Perhaps the key achievement of the pro-family movement has been the promotion of sexual abstinence as a major public-policy response to teenage pregnancy. One of the earliest and most controversial policy initiatives of pro-family political appointees was the establishment of so-called chastity centers. These centers, aimed at teenage females, focused exclusively on abstinence, and were forbidden by statute from mentioning abortion as an option in an unwanted pregnancy (Nathanson, 1991). Similarly, the Sex Respect curriculum, a sex-education program widely promoted by pro-family forces, contained no mention of birth control or abortion, focusing instead on abstinence.

The "gag-rule" controversy, which spanned the presidencies of Ronald Reagan and George Bush, is further illustration of the efforts of conservatives to link attacks on abortion and birth-control issues. Originally written as an administrative guideline during the Reagan administration, the gag rule forbade employees in Title X family-planning clinics to provide counseling about abortion options, even when clients asked. For many within the health-care community and the public at large, this ruling raised concerns about free speech for health professionals. In the space of several years, the gag rule was upheld by the Supreme Court and overturned by congressional legislation, which was promptly vetoed by then-President Bush, under intense pressure from conservatives. In one of his first acts after taking office in 1993, President Bill Clinton abolished the gag rule, under similar pressure from the pro-choice and family-planning communities.

The history of contraceptive research has been marred by ethical violations.

PAGE 700

WELFARE CONSERVATIVES. An interesting split within conservatism became increasingly evident in the early 1990s, with potentially profound implications for reproductive politics. "Welfare conservatives" differ from conservatives in the pro-family movement in arguing economic issues, especially issues of public spending (Nathanson, 1991). In contrast to the pro-family movement, whose defining issue is the breakdown of sexual morality, welfare conservatives are concerned about the rising welfare costs resulting from teenage pregnancies, out-of-wedlock births, and failure of fathers to make child-support payments. Welfare conservatives have made a number of policy proposals that either mandate use of contraception as a condition of receiving welfare or offer financial incentives for such contraceptive use, that penalize recipients financially for having additional children, and that forbid teenage mothers from receiving welfare assistance directly, providing instead that the grant go to their parents or guardians (Peirce, 1992).

The contraceptive implant, Norplant, introduced into the United States in late 1990, quickly became implicated in a number of policies advocated by welfare conservatives. Once inserted, the implant prevents pregnancy for up to five years. Both the insertion and the removal must be done by a health-care professional. After the patient has submitted to the insertion, no further "user compliance" is required, making this contraception far more effective than other birth-control methods. Within eighteen months of the introduction into the United States of this new method, virtually all states approved the public funding of Norplant inser-

Litigation over faulty contraceptives has caused a decrease in research and development of improved products.

PAGE 700

MINORITIES AND "BIRTH CONTROLLERS"

A History of Skepticism

Minority communities in the United States—most notably, African-Americans and Hispanics—have long had a wary relationship with family-planning services. The historical links between the first generation of "birth controllers," such as Margaret Sanger, and those in the eugenics movement with an avowedly racist ideology (Chesler, 1992; Gordon, 1976) created for many minorities a lasting sense of distrust as to the intentions of some within the family-planning movement (Gordon, 1976). Such distrust reached a height in the late 1960s and early 1970s when many of the new government-funded clinics appeared to be targeted specifically at African-Americans, leading some African-American leaders to accuse family planners of "genocidal" intentions (Littlewood, 1977). More recently, some leaders—most notably, clergy—within minority communities have joined forces with the pro-family movement, arguing against such measures as condom distribution in inner-city high schools.

At the same time, the rates of premarital sexual activity, STDs, teenage pregnancy, and abortion have been disproportionately higher for African-Americans and Hispanics than for others. Thus, a number of minority organizations argue forcefully for the retention and expansion of family-planning and abortion services in their communities. Perhaps the most prominent example of such minority advocacy for family planning has been the teenage pregnancy initiative of the Children's Defense Fund. Other relevant minority groups in this regard include the National Black Women's Health Project and Latinas for Choice.

— CAROLE JOFFE

tion for welfare recipients. The potential for coercion is evident. Already, there have been instances where judges have required Norplant use as a condition of probation or child custody for women convicted on drug-related charges or of child abuse (Forrest and Kaeser, 1993).

Services to specialized populations

TEENAGERS. In the early 1990s, teenagers were entitled to receive low-cost or free confidential contraceptive services at Title X sites. Teenagers as a class did not receive any public funds for abortion.

The rising rates of sexual activity among teenagers (Alan Guttmacher Institute, 1991), particularly among younger teens, increased concern within the family-planning community about teenage pregnancy and this group's vulnerability to AIDS and STDs. Starting in the 1980s, a major response to both these issues was the establishment of school-based clinics (Kirby et al., 1991), on the theory that while few teens would make their way to a free-standing clinic, clinics located within the school would reach a much larger public. Predictably, such school-based clinics were controversial from the start, strongly opposed by conservatives, and just as strongly advocated by health professionals who feared an epidemic of STDs among teenagers if such preventive measures were not taken. The movement to establish school-based clinics proceeded very slowly.

A number of school districts, particularly those in large urban areas, began distributing condoms to students in response to the AIDS crisis. Here, too, there has been massive controversy, with many parent and church groups opposing such efforts. Generally speaking, however, AIDS-related interventions in schools seemed more acceptable to the public and to educators than specific efforts for pregnancy prevention. A national study of sex education in U.S. schools in the late 1980s found far more attention paid to AIDS and STDs than to contraceptive education (Forrest and Silverman, 1989).

SERVICES TO THE DISABLED. Case law in the United States generally recognizes that developmentally disabled individuals have the same fundamental rights regarding procreative choice as nondisabled individuals. There are, however, difficulties in implementing family-planning services for disabled persons. The issue of informed consent—to birth control, abortion, or sterilization, for example—is particularly relevant. Is the individual in question capable of giving informed consent, and if not, who is the appropriate surrogate empowered to make such decisions (Stavis, 1991)?

In spite of legal decisions supporting provision of such services, relatively few disabled persons are served in Title X clinics (Moore and Lieber, 1988). Few clinic staffs have received the specialized training necessary to work effectively with this population. In addition, many caretakers, especially parents, seem reluctant to ensure that these individuals receive such services. Finally, would-be recipients and caretakers alike are typically not aware of the entitlement of the disabled to family planning, which implies a need for more outreach services to this population.

See Also

Population Policies: Strategies of Fertility Control

International issues

The highly politicized nature of family planning in the United States has had implications for the developing world. The Reagan-Bush era gave legitimacy to previously discredited theories of the relationship between population growth and economic growth, which argued the two were not incompatible. In response to pressures by conservatives, the emphasis of U.S. population programs abroad shifted heavily to programs promoting "natural family planning," rather than the more medically reliable methods of birth control, such as oral contraception. Most notably, the "Mexico City policy" adopted by the Reagan administration in 1984 stipulated that no U.S. aid would go to any international organizations that supported abortion, even if the U.S. funds were separated and used only for nonabortion purposes (McKeegan, 1992). The Mexico City policy was overturned in the early days of the Clinton administration in 1993, thus renewing a commitment on the part of the United States to international family-planning efforts, after a period of marked decline.

Family-planning issues appear increasingly to be a high priority for many developing nations. Concerns about the ability to feed fast-growing populations, the dramatic spread of AIDS in the Third World, especially in parts of Africa, and the estimated 200,000 to 250,000 deaths that occur each year from illegal abortions (United Nations, 1991) create constituencies for family-planning services within these countries—notwithstanding significant religious and cultural objections.

Finally, the rise of indigenous women's movements within the developing world has served as a particularly important stimulus for both additional family-planning services and the demand that such services be offered in a culturally appropriate manner (Bruce, 1987; Dixon-Mueller, 1993). The International Women's Health Coalition has been one of the most successful international population groups in terms of its ability to work closely with local, grass roots women's organizations in the design and delivery of family-planning programs.

— CAROLE JOFFE

ETHICAL ISSUES

Fertility control gives people the power and the means to limit and prevent the procreative aspects of human sexuality. Terminology prior to the mid-twentieth century often referred to birth control and family planning to describe the same basic reality. This article deals with the three means of fertility control most often used—contraception, sterilization, and abortion. Technological developments and contemporary theories blur the absolute distinction among these three means, but ethical perspectives both in the past and in the present recognize important differences among them.

Contraception

Contraception, in the strict sense, interferes with the sexual act in order to prevent conception. In the broad sense, contraception includes all the means that can be used to prevent conception, including sterilization, which interferes with the sexual faculty or power. A close, logical connection exists between the ethical evaluation of contraception and of contraceptive sterilization. Judgments about the morality of contraception have traditionally distinguished between contraception within marriage and contraception outside marriage, based on the moral principle, often challenged today, that condemns sexual relations outside marriage.

CONTRACEPTION WITHIN MARRIAGE. Most people today, along with philosophical ethicists, religious ethicists, and religious bodies, generally accept the morality of contraception within marriage, often appealing to the need for family planning. Most recognize a relationship between marital sexuality and procreation, but marital sexuality also has other significant purposes such as expressing and enhancing the love union of the partners and thereby the good of the marriage. Unlimited procreation, or at times any procreation, could be harmful to one of the spouses, the marriage relationship itself, the good of already existing children, or the needs of the broader society. No perfect contraception exists, but most ethical reasoning sees no significant moral differences among the various means, provided they are not harmful to the individuals who use them or to others. Logically, one could justify contraception on the basis of an absolute autonomy, giving the individual control over his or her body and the right to make all decisions concerning it; but most justifications of family planning, which by definition concerns more than the individual, avoid such a radical individual autonomy. The official teaching of the Roman Catholic church constitutes the strongest and the primary contemporary moral opposition to the use of contraception for spouses.

CONTRACEPTION WITHIN MARRIAGE

Significant Social Factors Influencing Widespread Acceptance

- increased life expectancy
- improvements in infant and child health care
- realities of urban, industrialized society
- women's changing roles and functions in society

Family-planning programs, like all modernizing and technical-aid-driven programs, have little interest in preserving indigenous cultures from change.

PAGE 540

Studies show that in the Third World, radio has more impact on family-planning practice than any other medium.

PAGE 539

Both Martin Luther and John Calvin followed the early Christian theological idea that divine ensoulment (the point at which God animates a human spirit) occurs at inception.

PAGE 32

The right to be born is relative—to the welfare of the mother, for example—while the right of existing persons to live is absolute.

PAGE 28

◆ **potentiality principle**
Conferring the moral status of a full-fledged adult with specific rights and responsibilities on a fertilized ovum since it has the potential of developing into an adult human.

- wider and more accurate understanding of physiology of human reproduction
- recognition of population explosion and need to limit growth
- development, availability, and active promotion of new methods of contraception

The Christian religion played a most significant role in the ethical approach to contraception in the West. John T. Noonan's writings (1978, 1986, 1987) constitute the best source for the historical development of moral approaches to contraception in Catholicism, in Christianity in general, and in the West.

The ancient world of both East and West knew the reality of contraception either by avoiding insemination of the female or by using potions or magic. In the Greco-Roman world, some philosophers (e.g., Plato, Aristotle) and some gynecologists (e.g., Soranos of Ephesus) apparently accepted contraception. The Roman Empire, however, tended to encourage childbearing. The influential Stoic philosophers insisted that procreation constituted the only purpose of sexual intercourse, and thus logically condemned contraception.

The Hebrew scriptures contain no law condemning contraception, but the concentration on Israel as God's people, the descendants of Abraham and Sarah, emphasized the need for procreation and fertility. Thus the scriptures were generally negative toward contraception. Onan merited God's punishment by spilling his seed and by failing to provide his brother's widow with offspring (Gen. 38:10). Onan's wrongdoing did not involve contraception as such but the refusal of family responsibilities, although some later Jewish writings used Onan's punishment to vindicate the wrongness of coitus interruptus. Some Jewish authorities came to recognize limits on procreation and in certain cases even approved a woman's using root potions as a contraceptive (Noonan, 1986).

The Christian approach to contraception developed in this milieu and also in the context in which contraception was associated with prostitution and extramarital sexuality, which Christians strongly opposed. In addition, the potions used for contraception could not clearly be differentiated from abortifacients. The Christian condemnation of contraception followed from its understanding of human sexuality. Clement of Alexandria (d. 215? C.E.), and the Christian tradition following him, adopted the Stoic rule that marriage and sexuality existed for the purpose of procreation—proposed as a middle position between the Gnostic right (opposing all sexual contact, in imitation of Jesus) and the Gnostic left (celebrating the freedom to use sexuality in any manner). The influential Saint Augustine of Hippo (d. 430 C.E.), in opposition to his earlier acceptance of Manicheanism, which excluded procreation but accepted sexual intercourse and contraception, strongly asserted the procreative rule condemning contraception. Augustine's negative view of sexuality (common to many in the early church and perhaps even stronger in others such as Jerome) strengthened his support of the Stoic procreative rule. According to Augustine, sexual intercourse transmits original sin, since concupiscence as the disordered inclination to sexual pleasure always accompanies sexual relations.

Medieval theologians (e.g., Thomas Aquinas) and their successors maintained that procreation did not constitute the exclusive lawful purpose for marital sexuality. The church, for example, accepted the marital sexuality of the sterile and those no longer able to procreate. The procreation of offspring also included responsibility for the well-being and education of the children. However, the condemnation of contraception remained, with emphasis on its violation of the order of nature calling for the depositing of male seed in the vagina of the female. This nature-based rationale also served as the basis for the condemnation of sodomy, oral and anal intercourse, and masturbation. The split between eastern and western Christianity in the eleventh century and the Protestant Reformation in the sixteenth century did not change the universal Christian condemnation of contraception within marriage. This teaching continued well into the twentieth century.

The impetus for change came not from religious bodies or philosophical ethicists in general, but from popular morality and especially from people committed to improving the human condition. In France, for example, the use of contraception brought about a precipitous drop in the birthrate between 1750 and 1800. At the end of the eighteenth century, Thomas Malthus, in *An Essay on the Principle of Population* (1993), recognized the problems caused by overpopulation and called for restraints on procreation but not contraception. Francis Place in England in 1820 first advocated birth control as a solution to economic and family problems. In the United States, Robert Dale Owens in 1830 advocated the use of contraception. A Malthusian League came into existence in England in 1878, proposing contraception as a solution to the problems connected with large families; similar groups were established in many other parts of the Western world (Noonan, 1986).

Early proponents of contraception and family planning ran into strong popular opposition. In the United States, Anthony Comstock (d. 1915), a Protestant moral reformer and crusader, succeeded in influencing Congress to pass the law bearing his name, prohibiting the use of the mails for obscene materials, including contraceptives. Many states passed even more restrictive laws, and the Comstock-inspired legislation had some effect in the United States until 1965. Early proponents of family planning included many urban radicals and anarchists. Margaret Sanger, who truly merits the title of mother and founder of the family-planning movement, came from such a background but soon made common cause with the medical profession and middle-class women. Sanger publicized family planning and set up clinics to educate and provide contraceptive help for the community at large, especially poorer women. The movement gained considerably from the amalgamation of rival factions into the American Birth Control Federation in 1939, which changed its name in 1942 to the Planned Parenthood Federation. Some charitable foundations (e.g., Rockefeller and Ford) became more interested in family planning and population problems. By 1970, family planning had become a successful popular movement enjoying widespread public support. People in general wholeheartedly accepted the morality of family planning and contraception (Back, 1989).

Although some Protestant laypersons were involved in the early birth-control movements in the Anglo-Saxon countries, the Christian churches remained firm in their condemnation of artificial contraception, as distinguished from abstinence, well into the twentieth century. The Church of England became the first Christian church to accept officially the morality of artificial contraception for spouses. Although the Lambeth Conferences of 1908 and 1920 (official meetings of the bishops of the Anglican Church) condemned birth control, some Anglican statements supportive of birth control appeared in the 1920s. In 1930, the Lambeth Conference, by a vote of 193 to 67, adopted a resolution recognizing a moral obligation to limit or avoid parenthood and proposing complete abstinence as the primary and most obvious way while also accepting other methods (Fagley, 1960).

The Committee on Marriage and Home of the United States Federal Council of Churches in March 1931 issued an influential statement in which the majority of its members accepted the careful and restrained use of contraception by spouses. However, the Federal Council of Churches did not act upon this report. Subsequently, the major Protestant churches and the most significant Protestant theological ethicists (e.g., Karl Barth, Reinhold Niebuhr) accepted contraception as a way to ensure responsible parenthood. The social, cultural, and historical conditions mentioned earlier obviously influenced this massive change in church teaching, but the proponents of change also pointed to aspects in the Christian tradition supporting such a move. Christians had gradually come to recognize the loving or unitive aspect of marital sexuality in addition to the procreative aspect. The procreative aspect itself included not only the procreation but also the education of offspring. The very possibility of procreation and education called for the good health of the parents. In this light, Protestantism in general justified the use of contraception as a way for spouses to realize responsible parenthood (Fagley, 1960).

Roman Catholic official teachings steadfastly opposed artificial contraception within marriage. In 1930, Pope Pius XI in his encyclical *Casti connubii*, in obvious reaction to the Church of England's moral stand, strongly reiterated the condemnation of artificial contraception. Some Catholic theologians even before that time had been advocating the use of the infertile period, or the so-called rhythm method. In a 1951 address to the Italian Catholic Union of Midwives, Pope Pius XII taught that serious medical, eugenic, economic, and social indications justified the use of the sterile periods even on a permanent basis.

Is it reasonable that the fetus should be treated as a "person" from conception onward if to do so would have dire consequences for the woman who bears it?

PAGE 31

The renewal of Roman Catholicism at the Second Vatican Council (1962-1965) created great ferment and introduced many changes in the church. Pope John XXIII established, and Pope Paul VI continued and enlarged, a commission to study the question of the church's teaching. The majority of the commission favored changing the teaching to allow for artificial contraception, but in July 1968, Pope Paul VI issued his encyclical *Humanae vitae,* reiterating the condemnation of artificial contraception (Kaiser, 1985); Pope John Paul II continued the same teaching.

Humanae vitae sets forth the rationale for the condemnation of artificial contraception. Paragraph 11 states that the natural law "teaches that each and every marriage act must remain open to the transmission of life." In the next paragraph the pope refers to "the inseparable connection, willed by God and unable to be broken by man on his own initiative, between the two meanings of the conjugal act: the unitive and the procreative meaning" (Paul VI, 1968).

According to official, hierarchical Roman Catholic teaching, couples can and, at times, should limit their family in the name of responsible parenthood. *Humanae vitae* implies that, although artificial contraception is morally wrong, in practice—because of all the pressures couples experience—the use of artificial contraception might not always involve grave sin (Paul VI, 1968). Rhythm (or natural family planning) is acceptable because it does not interfere with the natural act. Supporters of the Billings method—that is, rhythm based on observation of changes in the vaginal mucus—point out other advantages of their approach, especially the necessary cooperation of husband and wife and the fact that the method does not subject the wife to medical risks (Billings and Westmore, 1980).

Humanae vitae set off a lively discussion within

F

FERTILITY CONTROL

Ethical Issues

There are equity-based ethical issues in efforts to persuade another society to adopt measures to alter its demographic behavior.

PAGE 544

Roman Catholicism. Many theologians disagreed with the natural-law rationale proposed for the condemnation of artificial contraception and often argued that a loyal Roman Catholic could, in theory and in practice, legitimately dissent from such fallible teaching. Some theologians and ethicists continue to defend the hierarchical teaching (magisterium) and a few even claim that the teaching is infallible and no dissent is possible. The hierarchical teaching office, which continues to assert its position strenuously, has not claimed officially that the teaching is infallible but has sometimes taken actions against some theologians who dissent. In practice, the vast majority of Catholic spouses use contraception (Curran, 1979).

Other religious bodies today generally support artificial contraception in the context of responsible parenthood. The Eastern Orthodox church accepts responsible contraception while condemning abortion and infanticide. The multiple purposes of marriage, the lack of any definitive statement against contraception by the church, a synergistic cooperation between God and humans, and the need for responsible parenthood serve as the basis for the responsible use of contraception in marriage (Harakas, 1991; Zaphiris, 1974).

Orthodox Judaism gives a limited acceptance to some forms of contraception, based on the early Talmudic acceptance of the woman's using root potions. Jewish law puts the duty of procreation on the male, and this obligation militates against the use of condoms or coitus interruptus. In this view, the most acceptable contraception is that which interferes the least with the natural sexual act (Rosner, 1979). Conservative and Reform Judaism fully accept and endorse contraception provided it is not harmful to the parties involved.

Islam accepts contraception if it does not entail the radical separation of procreation from marriage. All forms of contraception are acceptable provided they are not harmful and do not involve abortion. Justification for contraception in Islam rests on reports that the Prophet Muhammad did not forbid the contraceptive practices of some of his companions (Hathout, 1991).

Ancient Hindu medicine and Hindu tradition did not contemplate contraception, but did sanction means to enhance conception. In time, medical texts such as the sixteenth-century *Bhavaprakasha* took the step toward contraception by advising a few oral preparations to prevent conception. When India embarked on a national family-planning program after its independence in 1947, the discussions accepted the morality of contraception but centered on the relative population sizes of the higher and lower castes (Desai, 1991).

Western philosophers today generally do not discuss in great detail the morality of contraception within marriage primarily because the basic issue is not controversial. Ethicists generally recognize that spouses have at times an obligation not to procreate, but they would not agree on the reasons for such an obligation.

Contemporary popular morality—the behavior and values of ordinary people—as well as contemporary philosophy, theological ethics, and religious bodies (with the major exception of Roman Catholicism), accept the morality of contraception for spouses in practicing responsible parenthood. General agreement exists that on the microlevel of the family, the decision about contraception should be made by the spouses themselves in the light of their own health, the good of their marriage, the education and formation of their children, and population and environmental needs,

FEMINIST INFLUENCES

Personal Is Political

Concerns of feminists have greatly influenced the contemporary discussion about fertility control in general and contraception in particular. The growing equality and full participation of women in marriage in the global context has definitely given impetus to a wider use of contraception. Feminist ethics starts from the experience of the oppression of women and seeks to unmask and do away with the patriarchal structures of society. Feminists see an important connection between the personal and the political. The practice of medicine involves patriarchal structures and practices that have oppressed women in general and especially in the matter of reproduction, which ordinarily takes place within the woman's own body. Feminists stress the need for women to control their own fertility and reproduction and to have the requisite freedom and autonomy to do so (Overall, 1987; Sherwin, 1992).

Contraception as a means of power, however, can be used by the strong against the weak. Population ethics deals with how contraceptive power has been used against the poor, the lower classes, and people of color, both within and across national boundaries. Feminists and others recognize the victimization of women by contraceptive power. Society has often forced women to bear the burden of contraception and especially to live with the medical risks of contraception. The contraceptive pill and the intrauterine device (IUD) definitely involve medical risks for women.

— CHARLES E. CURRAN

See Also

Population Ethics: Hindu Teachings

both local and global (Curran, 1979). Population ethics deals with the ethical question of what steps individual governments can and should take in educating, persuading, encouraging, and perhaps even coercing citizens in the light of the population situation of the particular country.

Efficient and effective contraception has been a boon to human existence by giving spouses the means to control their procreation. Like any human good, contraception can be abused, but such abuse does not cancel out the great good that it has provided for humankind.

CONTRACEPTION OUTSIDE MARRIAGE. Judgments about the ethical use of contraception outside marriage depend on one's understanding of the morality of extramarital sexual activity. As a matter of fact many unmarried people are sexually active. Truly there has been a sexual revolution. The majority of adolescents in the United States have had sexual intercourse by the time they are nineteen years old; the problem of teenage pregnancies continues to grow (Demetriou and Kaplan, 1989).

Many feminists with their emphasis on reproductive rights, freedom, control of one's body, and autonomy emphasize the right of individuals to make contraceptive decisions in all cases (Harrison, 1985). Although society at large in the United States no longer condemns all extramarital sexuality as immoral and irresponsible, the mainstream churches and religions still generally maintain the immorality of sexual relations outside marriage (Lebacqz, 1989). The use of condoms enters into the discussion of extramarital sexuality not only because of the desire to prevent procreation, but also because condoms can help to prevent the spread of AIDS and sexually transmitted diseases (STDs). If one believes that extramarital sexual relations are morally responsible, then the use of contraception to prevent unwanted procreation is morally acceptable.

Problems arise when one believes that extramarital sexual relations, especially among adolescents, are morally wrong. Two different positions exist. One position maintains that readily available contraception itself facilitates such morally wrong behavior, and that encouraging the use of such contraception contributes to this immorality. A second position holds that people are going to have sexual relations regardless, so it is better to make sure they do not conceive and do not transmit diseases. Many ethicists who hold this position have accepted the general precept of counseling the lesser of two evils when someone is determined to do the wrong in the first place. It is a lesser evil to have sexual relations in a way that prevents procreation and/or avoids the transmission of harmful diseases (Keenan, 1989).

The provision of contraception to adolescents involves other moral issues, especially parental consent. Parents have responsibility for their children and the right and the obligation to teach their children morality. Some people maintain that the rights and obligations of parents mean that no contraception should be dispensed to adolescents without the permission of the parents. Others maintain that contraception can be provided without parental consent and propose a variety of reasons: Some children do not and cannot communicate with their parents about sexuality; some are going to be sexually active anyway, and it is better for them to use contraception than not to use it; and some are mature enough to make their own decisions in this area.

The Committee on Adolescence of the American Academy of Pediatrics (1990) issued a statement that tries to balance the different ethical responsibilities. According to the statement, pediatricians should actively work to relieve the negative consequences of adolescent sexual activity. Preventive measures involve counseling on responsible sexual decision making—including the counseling of abstinence—and providing contraceptive services for sexually active patients. A general policy guaranteeing confidentiality to the adolescent patient should be clearly stated to the patient and the parent at the time of the initiation of the professional relationship. The goal is to enhance conversation between the adolescent and the parent and to enlist parental support for the adolescent's responsible sexual behavior, including contraceptive use, whenever possible.

Sterilization

Sterilization in the narrow sense is the procedure that takes away one's capacity to procreate. In this sense, sterilization differs from contraception, which interferes with the sexual act and not with the sexual capacity or faculty. According to this understanding, which was standard in Roman Catholic medical ethics and accepted by others, sterilization can be either temporary or permanent. The anovulant pill technically constitutes a temporary sterilization because the pill temporarily suppresses ovulation. This entry employs the broader description of sterilization as the permanent (or somewhat permanent because of some possibility of reversal) removal of procreative capacity. Older forms of sterilization include hysterectomy and castration, but tubal ligation and vasectomy, procedures that are less than a century old, have become comparatively simple and fairly common. The primary ethical distinction concerns voluntary and nonvoluntary sterilization.

VOLUNTARY STERILIZATION. Religions and religious ethicists generally recognize that individual human beings have stewardship over their bodies and that they should make the medical decisions that affect

See Also

Fertility Control:
Economic Incentives

their lives and health. Philosophers usually recognize the primacy of the person as the decision maker in matters affecting his or her human good. Voluntary consent, in general, has become a primary canon in medical ethics. Some feminists and others insist on an individual's total autonomy with regard to decisions involving reproductive capacity. Religious approaches, in general, and most philosophers as well as medical codes recognize that the individual makes the decision, but that justifying reasons are required to make the decision for sterilization a good and morally acceptable one. Sterilization is proposed for either contraceptive or therapeutic reasons.

Contraceptive sterilization has become increasingly common both in the United States and throughout the world. As the very name indicates, contraceptive sterilization logically follows the same moral judgments as contraception. The one significant difference concerns the somewhat permanent nature of the procedure because of which many ethicists require a more serious and permanent reason to justify it. A basic maxim of medical ethics insists that one should never do more than is necessary to overcome the problem. With a similar consistency, the official teaching of the Roman Catholic church strongly opposes contraceptive sterilization (O'Rourke and Boyle, 1989). Again, many Catholics dissent in theory and in practice from this position.

Therapeutic sterilization is done for the good of the individual and not for contraceptive reasons. The general literature does not frequently discuss therapeutic sterilization as such, because the same standards govern therapeutic sterilization as govern other therapeutic interventions—the procedure must ultimately be for the good of the person and the evil or loss involved must be proportionately less than the good attained. Official Roman Catholic teaching and ethics have treated therapeutic sterilization at length and have developed an elaborate casuistry—or method of resolution through discussion of cases—in distinguishing the morally accepted therapeutic sterilization from the morally condemned contraceptive sterilization. Since sterilization has two different effects—sterilization of the procreative power and protection of the health of the individual—Roman Catholic medical ethics traditionally has applied the principle of double effect, according to which direct sterilization is always wrong but indirect sterilization may be justified for a proportionate reason. Direct sterilization is that which aims at making procreation impossible either as a means or as an end. Therapeutic or indirect sterilization aims directly at the health or good of the individual. Thus, a cancerous uterus can be removed, but hysterectomy to prevent harm to the woman from a pregnancy involves a direct and morally wrong sterilization (Boyle, 1977).

The issue of informed consent, a basic principle in

NONVOLUNTARY STERILIZATION

Can some other purpose or goal ever override the important value of free consent? Population ethics considers the role of government, which can go from merely providing information to advocacy, providing incentives, or coercing with regard to sterilization. There has been some discussion of the ethics of eugenic and punitive sterilization.

Proposals (e.g., the Human Betterment Foundation) and even legislation for mandatory sterilization (thirty states in the United States passed such laws between 1907 and 1931) appeared in the early part of the twentieth century. Since mental disease and defects that are passed on by heredity create a menace for society and the state, advocates argued the good of the group can override the freedom of the individual. The Nazi eugenic laws and practices of this time have become notorious (Trombley, 1988).

In the second half of the twentieth century, only a few advocates have proposed some eugenic sterilization (e.g., Fletcher, 1960). The horrors occasioned by Nazi practice, the erroneous scientific foundation of the eugenic movement in the early part of the twentieth century, the fear of errors, the hubris of making eugenic decisions for others, the overly intrusive role of the state, and the continuing and growing emphasis on the freedom and rights of all, have contributed to the general consensus against eugenic sterilization. Some proposals have been made to cut off welfare funds to poor women who have children and refuse to undergo sterilization, but such proposals have not received much support (Lebacqz, 1978).

The fact that there is little or no discussion of punitive sterilization in the more recent literature hints at a consensus against the practice. However, Francis Hürth, a conservative Roman Catholic theologian in the 1930s, proposed limited cases in which punitive sterilization might be justified. Pope Pius XI went out of his way not to condemn punitive sterilization in his 1931 encyclical *Casti connubii*. Proponents maintain that if the state can inflict capital punishment for certain crimes, it can also inflict the lesser punishment of sterilization in limited, appropriate cases. Critics reply that punitive sterilization does not achieve the purposes of punishment and does not even inhibit future sex crimes (McCarthy, 1960). Punitive sterilization appears to be virtually unsupported (Mason, 1990).

— CHARLES E. CURRAN

contemporary bioethics, arises in different circumstances. Feminist literature, with its emphasis on reproductive rights and women's control over their bodies and because of many potential and actual abuses, strongly insists on informed consent. Until recently, women have borne the burden of sterilization much more than have men, even though female sterilization is a more difficult and risky procedure than male sterilization. Some poor women have been sterilized immediately after childbirth, having been "informed" about the sterilization and "given consent" just before the delivery of their children (Sherwin, 1992). Most people would also object to employers demanding that people, especially women, be sterilized as a precondition for certain types of employment.

Many writings deal with the sterilization of the mentally retarded who are somewhat incapacitated or even totally incapable of giving informed consent (Macklin and Gaylin, 1981). The Committee on Ethics of the American College of Obstetricians and Gynecologists (1988) issued a statement on "Sterilization of Women Who Are Mentally Handicapped," which urges all possible attempts to communicate with the person involved on whatever level is possible. In case the individual is mentally incompetent, the decision should be made by an appropriate surrogate or proxy, based on the best interests of the patient after considering alternative methods of dealing with the situation.

Abortion

Abortion, or the termination of pregnancy, also constitutes a means of fertility control. This section briefly explains the logical application of moral positions on abortion to judgments about abortion as a means of fertility control.

All those who oppose abortion as a general principle also oppose abortion as a means of fertility control. Those who hold that from the first moment of conception the zygote should be treated as an individual human being, or who attribute a high value to the early conceptus, oppose forms of contraception that work as abortifacients. Here again technological developments blur the clear distinction between contraception and abortion. Doubts about how the IUD actually works led some people to condemn it as an abortifacient because of the theory that the IUD prevents the implantation of the early conceptus in the endometrium of the uterus (McCormick, 1981). Those who hold this view of the early conceptus strongly oppose the RU-486 pill, which definitely works as an abortifacient. On the other hand, those who do not attribute any value or great value to the early conceptus have no moral qualms about the RU-486.

Many (e.g., Harrison, 1985) who advocate the morality of abortion in general recognize significant moral differences between abortion and contraception. Some attribute more value and worth to the fetus as it develops in the maternal womb. Consequently, abortion (at least after the first few weeks) should not be used as the regular and ordinary method of fertility control for a number of reasons—the danger of some risk to the mother, the problems caused by multiple abortions, and the value that is attributed to the fetus. However, many believe that abortion may still be used in the case of contraceptive failure.

Fertility control has always been significant for humankind, but contemporary scientific, social, philosophical, theological, and feminist developments have focused even more attention on this issue.

— CHARLES E. CURRAN

LEGAL AND REGULATORY ISSUES

A person's ability to control his or her fertility depends on available technology, moral and religious acceptability, and legal permissibility or the threat of sanction. A man or a woman's ability to prevent pregnancy when exercised knowingly and voluntarily enhances autonomy and liberty. Coercive control of fertility by the state or its agents poses a threat to dignity and reproductive freedom. The major fertility-control mechanisms are contraception and sterilization and, when neither is used or the chosen method fails, abortion. The mechanical and physiological characteristics of each method determine the ease and comfort of individual use, the likelihood of success, and the potential for coercion.

In many cultures men view children as proof of virility and power. They see attempts by women to limit or terminate pregnancy as an attack on male authority and reproductive potential, which in many societies equals wealth. For many women a desire to limit pregnancy must often be pursued furtively, with fear of violence and retaliation. Biology and the threat to a woman's independence, health status, and well-being make the control of fertility primarily a woman's concern. A woman's ability to limit and control her fertility may be a necessary precondition for equality and personal economic status. Control of fertility is central to modern notions of emancipated or liberated womanhood.

◆ **pre-embryo**
What the one-cell fertilized egg becomes after its first cell division and before it implants in the uterus.

Because they affect relationships between the sexes, population growth, and a woman's status, contraception, sterilization, and abortion are and have been problematic for many societies. Secular societies committed to individual rights and liberties are less likely to intervene in reproductive decisions. But all societies have tried in the past and still attempt, to some degree, to influence individual reproductive choices—especial-

See Also

After *Roe* v. *Wade*: New Choices, New Dilemmas

ly the choices of the less powerful, a status often identified with women of color.

History of contraception use and control

GENERAL. Various societies have for centuries interceded in the free use of contraception, largely for moral and/or religious reasons. Classical Islam permitted the use of birth control and even early abortion (Fathalla et al., 1990). Biblical Judaism, based on interpretations of the story of Onan in Gen. 38:8-10, condemned coitus interruptus and the use of male condoms. Christianity gradually evolved a doctrine, based on biblical references, interpretations of natural law, and the writings of Saint Augustine, that prohibited use of all contraceptive devices (St. John-Stevas, 1971). Widespread, class-linked knowledge of contraceptive practices was effectively withheld from most of the population following the condemnation of birth control by Thomas Aquinas in the mid-thirteenth century (Fathalla et al., 1990). As religion formed part of the basis for modern secular law, control of fertility became a subject of legal attention and regulation.

Both female and male condoms have been available for centuries. Roman women attempted to use goat bladders (Fathalla et al., 1990), and some African women hollowed out okra pods (Robertson, 1990). A picture of a penile sheath is recorded as early as 1350 B.C.E., although male condoms did not come into general use in Europe until 1671 and became reliable only with the vulcanization of rubber in 1843 (Robertson, 1990). Monitoring and prohibiting use of birth-control devices such as condoms are difficult because of the inherently private nature of their use. Manufacture, distribution, sale, and advertising are more easily regulated and prohibited.

Despite the long history and the private nature of fertility control, various legal and theological systems have attempted prohibition. The early Christian (Roman Catholic and Protestant) argument against contraception, influential as the model for legal regulation, holds that God's purpose for sex is conservation of the species, which is frustrated when people have intercourse for nonprocreative purposes (St. John-Stevas, 1971). The Catholic church first proscribed contraception in canon law in 1140 (St. John-Stevas, 1971). While not all religions have been as resistant to the idea of contraception as the Catholic church, contraceptive use has traditionally been considered an appropriate area for moral guidance and proscription and not until the beginning of the twentieth century did significant numbers of Protestant theologians provide moral approval (Larson, 1991).

Religious regulation has been selective. Some forms of birth control were interdicted, while others were and have remained relatively unnoticed. In addition, prolonged lactation, postpartum abstinence, delayed marriage, celibacy, and to some extent infanticide, are all

ABORTION AS FERTILITY CONTROL

International Perspectives

Abortion, as a method of fertility control, has always been especially controversial. Despite its morally and legally complex past and its tendentious present, there is evidence today that abortion remains a favored method of birth control for many women, both as a preferred method of fertility control and as a backup to failed contraception. Fifty million abortions are performed worldwide each year. In 1991, Romania, with little access to and inaccurate information about contraceptives, had the highest abortion ratio: three abortions for every one live birth, totalling 884,000 in 1991 (Stephen, 1992). In the United States 1.5 million abortions are performed per year, 25.9 per 1,000 women aged fifteen to forty-four; in China, ten million, one for every two live births (Preston, 1992).

While contraception and abortion address the prevention or termination of any specific pregnancy, sterilization terminates individual fecundity. With the development of modern, comparatively safe and effective means of sterilization (vasectomy, or surgical excision of the duct carrying sperm from the testicles; and salpingectomy, or surgical removal of one or both fallopian tubes), individuals can choose, by means of one medical intervention, to detach sexual intercourse from reproductive consequences. If chosen by individuals, these simple and almost always irreversible interventions extend autonomy; if imposed by the state, they can become instruments of repression.

Whether contraception, sterilization, and abortion should be permitted, prohibited, or coerced by government has generated intense controversy in countries as different as the United States, Romania, India, Ireland, and China. In each country, legislators, judges, individuals, and special-interest lobbies have struggled to affect how citizens will think about their options for controlling fertility, how the individual decision-making process will be informed and supervised, how access to contraception, abortion, and sterilization will be ensured or precluded, and whether coercion will be encouraged, permitted, or prohibited (Weston, 1990; Thomas, 1990).

— NANCY NEVELOFF DUBLER
AMANDA WHITE

techniques of fertility management that have been and continue to be used.

UNITED STATES HISTORY. Puritan theology dominated the early American colonists. The Puritans considered sex-related matters part of the devil's province, to be shunned and ignored, and they tolerated little open discussion (Robertson, 1990). In the 1830s some popular literature on contraception, such as Robert Dale Owen's *Moral Physiology*, began to be generally available (Robertson, 1990; Reed, 1978). Not until 1873 did law begin regulating distribution of contraceptives in the United States. The Comstock Act ("An Act for the Suppression of Trade in, and Circulation of, Obscene Literature and Articles of Immoral Use") equated contraception with obscenity and made it a federal offense to use the postal service for transporting obscene materials, defined to include contraceptive and abortion information and equipment. The act also banned importation and interstate transportation of such items (Sloan, 1988). After the act's passage, many states adopted their own regulations on the sale, advertising, and display of contraceptive devices.

Margaret Sanger, a nurse affected by her work in poor communities where morbidity (the incidence of disease) and mortality from abortion was high, was a vociferous advocate for birth control (Reed, 1978; *People* v. *Sanger*, 1918). She founded a monthly magazine, *The Woman Rebel,* for which she was arrested and indicted under the Comstock Act. She fled to Europe and returned in 1916 to establish the first American birth-control clinic in Brooklyn, a borough of New York City (Chessler, 1992). In 1918, she was convicted and sentenced to thirty days in the workhouse under New York State's Comstock law. Years later, a physician in one of Margaret Sanger's clinics who had ordered a package of contraceptives through the mail was charged with violating the Tariff Act of 1930, a statute based on the Comstock Act that prohibited importation of "any article whatever for the prevention of conception or for causing unlawful abortion" (Tariff Act, 1930). On appeal, the federal circuit court for the second circuit held that the act did not apply when the article imported was not intended for an immoral purpose. Judge Augustus Hand declared that the Tariff Act was part of a "continuous scheme to suppress immoral articles and obscene literature," and refused to find proper medical use of a contraceptive by a licensed physician to be immoral or obscene *(U.S.* vs. *One Package . . . ,* 1936, p. 739). Though the court did not invalidate the statute, its interpretation limited the sweeping definition of morality and obscenity that had previously held sway.

Statutes modeled after the Comstock Act continued to exist, however, until 1965, when the U.S. Supreme Court in the case of *Griswold* v. *Connecticut* invalidated a Connecticut statute prohibiting the use of contraceptives. The Court held, citing prior cases that had created a zone of privacy protecting certain personal behaviors, that these penumbral rights of "privacy and repose," based on several fundamental constitutional guarantees, protected the use of contraceptives by married persons (*Griswold* v. *Connecticut*, 1965, p. 481). *Griswold* was followed by *Eisenstadt* v. *Baird* (1972), extending this reasoning to nonmarried individuals. The statute that was invalidated in *Eisenstadt* prohibited single persons from obtaining contraceptives to prevent pregnancy, and permitted contraceptives only on a physician's prescription for the purpose of disease prevention. The statute was held to violate the equal protection clause of the Fourteenth Amendment:

> *[W]hatever the rights of the individual to access to contraceptives may be, the rights must be the same for the unmarried and the married alike. . . . If the right of privacy means anything, it is the right of the individual, married or single, to be free from unwarranted governmental intrusion into matters so fundamentally affecting a person as the decision whether to bear or beget a child.*
>
> (Eisenstadt *v.* Baird, *1965, pp. 452–453*)

Minors gradually attained access to contraceptive advice and devices. In 1977, in the case of *Carey* v. *Population Services International*, the U.S. Supreme Court invalidated a New York State statute that had banned the sale or distribution of contraceptives to persons below the age of sixteen and had prohibited the advertising or display of contraceptives by any person, including a pharmacist. In 1983, the Supreme Court struck down a federal statute prohibiting unsolicited advertisements of contraceptives (*Bolger* v. *Young Drug Products Corp.*, 1983). In addition, under Title X of the

PLAN THE PARENTHOOD

From her days as a nurse-midwife to her founding of Planned Parenthood, Margaret Sanger (1879–1966) led the fight for birth control.

> *"Tell me something to keep from having another baby. We cannot afford another yet."*
>
> MARGARET SANGER
> MY FIGHT FOR BIRTH CONTROL, 1931

FERTILITY CONTROL

Legal and Regulatory Issues

Public Health Services Act and Title XIX of the Social Security Act, receipt of federal funds prohibits a requirement of parental consent for services and requires confidentiality. Efforts to require parental notification under these acts have been held unconstitutional (*Jane Does 1 through 4* v. *State of Utah Dept. of Health*, 1985; *Planned Parenthood Association of Utah* v. *Dandoy*, 1987).

In 1988 the government attempted to impose a "gag" rule preventing providers at federally funded family-planning clinics from mentioning abortion as a possible solution to an unwanted pregnancy. The rule was reversed early in 1993, permitting federally funded clinics to provide a full range of advice and service for fertility control for men and women whether married, unmarried, or minors.

New contraceptive technologies

A revolution in birth control techniques has created new possibilities for individual choice and new dangers of coercive action by legislatures, bureaucrats, and judges. Additional dangers arise from inadequate new-product testing and from lack of information or misinformation about risks and benefits of use. Female condoms, Norplant, and Depo-Provera are increasingly available to women for contraception.

28% of women surveyed (aged 15–44 years) had an unintended birth; poor women and non-Hispanic black women were most likely to have had an unplanned birth.

NATIONAL SURVEY OF FAMILY GROWTH, 1997; NATIONAL CENTER FOR HEALTH STATISTICS

The female condom or vaginal pouch was approved by the U.S. Food and Drug Administration (FDA) in 1993. The device, developed and marketed by Wisconsin Pharmaceuticals, consists of a polyurethane sheath secured inside the vagina by a small metal ring and outside by a large metal ring. It is the only barrier contraceptive that is under the control of a woman, an increasingly important factor for women seeking to protect themselves from sexually transmitted diseases and human immunodeficiency virus (HIV) infection when their partners refuse or neglect to use condoms. The device was approved by the FDA despite concerns that it was not proved as effective as the male condom for prevention of pregnancy or prevention of transmission of infection.

Norplant (levonorgestrel), approved by the FDA in 1990, is a long-term implantable contraceptive comprised of six capsules that gradually release progestin, thereby providing effective contraception for five years. A two-capsule version provides protection for three years. Norplant, like other contraceptive devices, is morally neutral; it may enhance the range of individual choice or, because of its long-acting nature, lend itself to coercive action by others. It permits a woman to protect herself without conscious attention to contraception but makes her dependent on medical intervention for removal, a dependency many women resent.

Norplant suppresses ovulation, and changes the female physiology to discourage pregnancy. For women who choose this contraceptive technique, it offers 100 percent compliance and effectiveness without the need to attend to individual acts of intercourse or to daily medications. There are some side effects and contraindications for use, including the possibilities of weight gain, headaches, and a general feeling of malaise. A major problem in the United States is the cost, up to $700 to insert and remove (Board of Trustees, American Medical Association [AMA], 1992).

The only way to stop the contraceptive effect of the device is to have it surgically removed. Removal is more complicated than insertion and more than one session may be required to remove all the capsules; removal may also be painful. Norplant provides either long-acting contraception or time-limited sterilization (Mertus and Heller, 1992; Arthur, 1992).

Norplant presents an easy potential for coercive use by judges and legislatures. Problematic uses include requiring Norplant as a condition of parole following a conviction for child abuse, and paying women on welfare for consenting to initial and continued placement of the contraceptive. The first is clearly coercive. The second is potentially coercive depending on the context of a woman's poverty. Various state legislatures have considered statutes that would pay women receiving welfare to use Norplant or mandate its use by women convicted of child neglect and drug use, or both (Mertus and Heller, 1992; Board of Trustees, AMA, 1992).

Judicial or legislative imposition of Norplant may violate a woman's constitutionally protected rights to choose how to manage reproduction and to choose whether or not to consent to or refuse medical care (*Cruzan*, 1990). The U.S. Supreme Court has not yet ruled on this matter. Any long-acting male contraceptive would implicate these same rights. In addition, because long-acting contraception amounts to temporary sterilization, it raises the specter of eugenics—policies that are often directed at people of color, the poor, the retarded, the mentally ill, and other persons designated by those in power as undesirable. Norplant offers effective contraception when chosen voluntarily by a woman informed of the risks and benefits, and a potential for tyranny when imposed by judges or legislatures.

Regulation of contraceptive technologies

In addition to enhancing individual choice and restricting abuse, regulation of new technologies must ensure access and quality control. The development of new technologies is regulated formally by the approval process of the FDA, and informally by compensation awards under tort law for harm caused by defective products.

The FDA regulates the development of new drugs and contraceptive devices under the Federal Food,

Drug and Cosmetic Act of 1938. Under this law, a company interested in marketing new contraceptive drugs or devices must submit data, including results from various tests for safety, effectiveness, and dosage, as part of an extensive approval process. In addition to approving new drugs and devices, the FDA reviews labeling and assesses data in a postmarketing surveillance program. The FDA approval process has been criticized as expensive, time consuming, and a barrier to new techniques. It has also been praised for protecting consumers from the harm of untested substances.

The FDA approval process is not the sole factor dictating whether a reproductive technology reaches U.S. consumers, however. The American tort system is designed to compensate those injured, deter the marketing of dangerous and defective products, and resolve disputes between the injured person and the manufacturer.

A person may recover damages for dangerous or defective products, including contraceptive devices, if either negligence or a strict liability is established. Negligence requires proof that the manufacturer was at fault. However, sometimes the fault of a large company is difficult to establish, and therefore the interests of justice dictate that a victim should be allowed to recover damages without proving specific fault. According to the strict products-liability principle, if a product is sold in a defective condition, and is unreasonably dangerous to the consumer, there is liability regardless of the care taken, that is, regardless of negligence in any individual case. Strict liability may make manufacturers apprehensive about putting new contraceptive products on the market.

This is the case especially since the litigation experience of the A. H. Robins Company, developer and marketer of the Dalkon Shield, an intrauterine contraceptive device. In a series of court cases in the early 1980s, this device was proved to cause pelvic inflammatory disease, infertility, birth defects, perforated uterus, and spontaneous abortion. In a series of jury verdicts throughout the United States, A. H. Robins was forced to pay compensatory damages and punitive damages because plaintiffs proved that the company had understood the dangers of the device, withheld this knowledge from prospective users, and misrepresented the nature and safety of the device (Mintz, 1985). Despite this experience, cases brought by women seeking recovery for harm from contraceptive devices have usually found the manufacturer liable only under theories of negligence—for example, negligent failure to comply with the duty of care, negligent failure to warn of risks, or fraudulent misrepresentation (*Hilliard* v. *A. H. Robins Co.*, 1984; *Tetuan* v. *A. H. Robins Co.*, 1987). In fact, even those courts purporting to apply strict liability seem to be applying a theory of negligent failure to warn under the rhetoric of strict liability (Henderson and Twerski, 1990; Fox and Traynor, 1990). Some case law holds manufacturers liable for failure to warn of risks that were unknown; this more closely resembles strict liability, but few states have applied such a standard (Fox and Traynor, 1990).

How tort law is interpreted is in a state of flux. Some judges and juries appear to view manufacturers as "deep pockets" (Reilly, 1989) and to see tort law as a vehicle for providing social insurance for injury victims. Many critics of large jury awards argue that the size of jury awards often bears no relationship to actual economic loss or to pain and suffering, and that awards of punitive damages are arbitrary and unfair. Supporters of the present pattern of trial awards argue that claims of a law crisis in this area are exaggerated because of manufacturers' dislike for how the law determines their liability (Fox and Traynor, 1990). However, as long as manufacturers fear they will have to pay large financial penalties to women who suffer the consequences of their new products, many may be reluctant to market new products, a trend that may limit women's access to new contraceptive technologies.

Postcontraception, the "morning-after" pill, is widely dispensed on college campuses after unprotected intercourse and in emergency rooms for rape victims; it promises to be another barrier to unwanted pregnancy. The process generally entails two treatments of oral contraceptives within seventy-two hours of intercourse and is thought to prevent pregnancy either by blocking fertilization or by blocking implantation of the fertilized egg. An antihormone product called RU-486, discussed in the following section, has also shown promise as a "morning-after" pill.

Despite the convenience and desirability of postcontraceptive options, manufacturers of oral contraceptives have not sought FDA approval for use of drugs for this purpose. Their reluctance may be motivated by fear of liability, fear of anti-abortion publicity, or by the cost of financing the complex studies that are required for FDA approval.

20.4% of women surveyed reported having involuntary sexual intercourse at some time in their lives; of these women, more than one-fourth were under 15 when they were forced to have sex.

NATIONAL SURVEY OF FAMILY GROWTH, 1997; NATIONAL CENTER FOR HEALTH STATISTICS

Sterilization

Sterilization is a particularly useful technique for men and women who are certain that they have fulfilled their reproductive agenda. For these individuals sterilization provides an uncomplicated and generally certain method of limiting fertility. Whereas sterilization done competently is 100 percent effective, cases have claimed damages for children conceived as the result of incomplete sterilizations.

The key legal issues in sterilization involve the need to ensure that the choice is made by a compe-

tent adult who has chosen voluntarily; the need to decide for some persons, almost always women, who are clearly incapable of deciding for themselves; and the need to prevent notions of eugenics from dictating sterilization policy and practice. Sterilization, because it requires only one medical intervention, has been particularly susceptible to government abuse.

Women or men who choose sterilization must be counseled about the risks and benefits of the intervention itself and about the very slim chances for reversal if permanent infertility is no longer desired. Some localities have regulations requiring a waiting period between a request for sterilization and the actual procedure. Others preclude caregivers from soliciting consent for sterilization from women during the birthing process. Both restrictions offer protection against coercion, especially for low-income women and women of color who have been historically at risk for nonconsensual sterilization.

Sterilization has been used by physicians and by state and federal governments since the turn of the century (Mertus and Heller, 1992), in order to limit the reproduction of low-income women and women of color. It has also been used as a method of eugenics "to weed out traits or characteristics that are held to be undesirable. Further, sterilization was simultaneously discouraged among affluent white women" (Mertus and Heller, 1992, p. 377).

The history of involuntary sterilization of incompetent and developmentally disabled individuals in the first half of the twentieth century is a history of "wholesale violations of constitutional rights carried out with the approval of the highest judicial tribunals." Eugenic sterilization—the attempt to rid the collective gene pool of hereditary mental and physical defects—was the result of the "enthusiastic application of Mendelian genetics" to population policy (*Conservatorship of Valerie N.*, 1985, p. 148).

In the early twentieth century, thousands of young women and men were sterilized as the result of decisions by the directors of mental institutions or prisons in which they were housed, or by decisions of their conservators or guardians. The impulse to control the reproductive capacity of these people was fueled by the dual fears that children would perpetuate their parents' mental or physical "deformity" and would be a drain on state coffers. But there is another basis, never articulated as such in legislation or by the courts, and that is a general revulsion at the concept of mentally "defective" persons acting sexually. Indeed, a 1913 California statute granted authority to "asexualize" committed mental patients and develop-

See Also

Self-Induced Abortion: Difficulties of Enforcing Prohibition

RU-486: "THE FRENCH 'MORNING-AFTER' PILL"

While functioning as an abortion inducer, RU-486 (mifepristone) is thought of by many users as similar to oral contraceptives. RU-486 is a steroid analogue that, when used with prostaglandin (PG), is able to induce menses within eight weeks of the last menstrual period. It has been called a "menstrual regulator" in an attempt to distinguish it from contraceptives and abortion inducers, although to theologians the physiological function is clearly that of an abortion inducer. It was approved for use in France in 1988. Limited trials in the United States began in 1994. Shortly after its introduction in France, the manufacturer, Roussel Uclaf, attempted to halt distribution for fear of anti-abortion protests. The French government, a one-third owner of the company, ordered continued manufacture and distribution (Banwell and Paxman, 1992).

Whether RU-486/PG will become readily available will depend on each nation's interpretation of relevant abortion laws and regulations. If abortion "is defined to include techniques that operate before implantation is complete, RU-486/PG will be regulated by abortion law. If not, RU-486/PG might be considered similar to a contraceptive and could be made more widely available. This distinction is particularly important because abortion legislation generally imposes criminal penalties" (Banwell and Paxman, 1992, p. 1400).

While France considers RU-486/PG an abortion inducer, Germany, New Zealand, and Liberia use a definition of pregnancy in their abortion statutes providing that pregnancy begins only after complete implantation. In these countries, RU-486/PG and any other menses-inducing technique is regulated as a form of contraception. In countries with strict abortion laws in which pregnancy is defined as beginning with fertilization, even early use of RU-486/PG might be barred (Banwell and Paxman, 1992).

Many countries in Latin America and Africa have restrictive abortion statutes that require proof of pregnancy. Statutes that require proof of pregnancy will be difficult to use as a barrier to RU-486/PG. Other national statutes criminalize the intent to abort whether or not the woman is pregnant. In these countries, many of which are former French colonies, the widespread use of RU-486/PG is effectively precluded. In societies governed by Islamic law, where pregnancy may be terminated until quickening—when fetal movement is felt—RU-486/PG would likely be acceptable (Banwell and Paxman, 1992).

—NANCY NEVELOFF DUBLER
AMANDA WHITE

mentally disabled persons prior to their release from state institutions (*Conservatorship of Valerie N.*, 1985). Sexuality, as well as reproductive capacity, was at issue.

By the second decade of the twentieth century, twenty-two states had eugenic sterilization statutes. Between 1907 and 1921, 3,233 sterilizations were performed, of which California was responsible for 2,558. By 1927, California had performed over 5,000 sterilizations, four times as many as had been performed by any national government worldwide. By 1960, approximately 60,000 persons had been subjected to compulsory sterilization in the United States, with nearly 20,000 in California (Mertus and Heller, 1992).

In 1927, the U.S. Supreme Court upheld a Virginia statute permitting the sterilization of the "mental defectives" (*Buck* v. *Bell*, 1927). The Court based its decision on two lines of reasoning: that if rendered unable to procreate, the person might more easily become self-supporting; and that society can choose to protect itself from further dissemination of defective genes. Justice Oliver Wendell Holmes wrote, "The principle that sustains compulsory vaccination is broad enough to cover cutting the Fallopian tubes. . . . Three generations of imbeciles are enough" (*Buck* v. *Bell*, 1927, p. 207).

Buck v. *Bell,* though never overruled, has been severely limited by later decisions. In 1942, the U.S. Supreme Court invalidated the Oklahoma Habitual Criminal Sterilization Act, which ordered the sterilization of anyone convicted of three crimes involving "moral turpitude"; however, the contested law excepted certain white-collar crimes. In *Skinner* v. *Oklahoma* (1942), declaring the Sterilization Act unconstitutional on equal-protection grounds, the Court ruled that procreation is a basic civil right that can be abridged only by showing compelling state interest. The Court referred to the right to marriage and procreation as a basic liberty and as one of the basic civil rights. The Court's reluctance to approve the Oklahoma statute appears to reflect apprehension that sterilization could be used oppressively (*Skinner* v. *Oklahoma*, 1942).

The second half of the twentieth century has witnessed a revulsion against nonconsensual sterilization, based on the revelations of Nazi abuses and the emergence of various rights movements in the United States—civil, women's, welfare, mentally ill, the disabled, and prisoners. Sociological and medical research regarding the nature of mental illness and developmental disability also enlightened the public regarding the ability of developmentally disabled and mentally ill persons to lead constructive, competent, loving lives as partners and parents.

Beginning in the 1950s, numerous states repealed legislation permitting eugenic sterilization for institutionalized persons or limited the powers of conservators and guardians to procure individual sterilization. Yet in many states these statutes are still law. This has led to the ironic position, in many states, that no one can consent for the incapable, thus denying them access to sterilization even when sterilization is the only or arguably the best contraceptive solution—and even when it is required to protect health or life itself.

Arguments regarding sterilization for incompetent persons pit advocates of reproductive choice for the disabled against those who argue that the right to "bear or beget" a child includes the right to choose reproduction, contraception, or sterilization. Federal (*Hathaway* v. *Worcester City Hospital*, 1973; *Ruby* v. *Massey*, 1978) and state courts (*Moe*, 1982; *Grady*, 1981; *A.W.*, 1981) have generally held that developmentally disabled persons have fundamental privacy and liberty interests in making decisions about procreation and that these interests require sterilization to be an option for fertility control. Some state courts, however, have refused to authorize sterilization of an incompetent person unless the state legislature has specifically authorized the decision and specified a process (*Hudson* v. *Hudson*, 1979; *Eberhardy*, 1980). The U.S. Supreme Court has yet to examine the issue, but prior cases would seem to support a right of access to sterilization for incompetent persons.

Cases claiming rights of protection from sterilization most often involve consent for severely disabled young women for whom menstruation and pregnancy would be painful, provoking, upsetting, or possibly life-threatening (for example, one woman for whom the sight of her own blood caused a pattern of severe self-mutilation [*P.S.*, 1983]). In most states, courts appoint an independent guardian to protect the interests of the person and then base their decision on the standard of "best interest" (*P.S.*, 1983; *Hayes*, 1980) or substituted judgment (*Moe*, 1982; *Grady*, 1981).

The dangers of forced sterilizations are apparent outside the realm of prisoners, developmentally disabled, and incompetent individuals, largely where issues of race and class are present. The indigent, who are often persons of color, have been particularly subject to sterilization abuses by public officials and collaborating physicians. Numerous cases have been documented of coerced sterilization of Native Americans (Kelly, 1977), Latinos (particularly those who spoke little or no English), and African-Americans (*Relf* v. *Weinberger*, 1977). In response to one egregious incident (*Relf* v. *Weinberger*, 1977), the district court examined the practice of physicians at federally funded clinics who were using sterilization to limit the reproduction of African-American teenagers. The court invalidated federal regulations that permitted involuntary, coerced sterilization, including sterilization of minors or persons incapable of providing consent. The court further held that such sterilizations could not be

"Three generations of imbeciles are enough."

OLIVER WENDELL HOLMES
BUCK V. BELL, 1927

funded under the Social Security Act or the Public Health Service Act. The court found that minors and other incompetents had undergone federally funded sterilization and that an indefinite number of poor people had been improperly coerced into accepting sterilization operations under the threat that various federally supported welfare benefits would be withdrawn unless they submitted.

Local statutes and federal regulations have further limited the use of sterilization. In New York City, for example, statutes passed in 1985 require completion of a complicated informed-consent process and a thirty-day waiting period before sterilization is permitted (*New York City, N.Y., Charter and Administrative Code §17-401 et seq.*). Federal regulations also prescribe special informed consent procedures and waiting periods for federally funded sterilizations ("Sterilization of Persons," 1993; "Sterilizations," 1993).

Much current law attempts to protect vulnerable women and limit potential abuse by emphasizing voluntary, informed consent and limiting sterilizations to which individual, capable consent is not given. Even where there is no specific legislation to that effect, compulsory sterilization has become rare; those states that have retained compulsory sterilization statutes on the books have, for the most part, let them slip into disuse (Haavik and Menninger, 1981).

Discussion of eugenics as appropriate public policy for the protection of future generations has largely been discredited because of the Nazis' horrendous abuse of the concept, because of scientific and societal disaffection with eugenic theories, and because of increasing respect for those with developmental and other disabilities. Nonetheless, eugenics is not yet dead. Increasing knowledge about genetics and new reproductive technologies such as in vitro fertilization, artificial insemination, and surrogate motherhood, may allow people to selectively create babies of "higher quality," and may renew the specter of eugenics, albeit in a new light (Neuhaus, 1988).

◆ **primary tubal infertility**
Scar tissue blocks the fallopian tubes, resulting in sterility.

An ethical policy controlling reproduction must offer a range of contraceptive services to women and men and simultaneously protect adults with reproductive potential from state coercion. New technologies offer increased protection from unwanted pregnancy and increased potential for overriding individual preferences.

— NANCY NEVELOFF DUBLER
AMANDA WHITE

See Also
Maternal–Fetal Relationship

FETUS

The first of the following three articles describes human development from the initial meeting of ovum and sperm until birth; the second article presents and comments on the philosophical, ethical, and legal issues dealing with the human conceptus; and the third article deals in a special way with research utilizing the human fetus. The title of the entire entry is "Fetus" because that is the term most commonly consulted when information on ethical debates pertaining to prenatal stages of human development is being sought. A variety of accepted usages of the term "fetus" is found in the following articles.

HUMAN DEVELOPMENT FROM FERTILIZATION TO BIRTH

The overall developmental process that gives rise to a new human being is initiated by fertilization, the union of two specialized cells or gametes—egg and sperm—produced by two adult individuals of one species but opposite gender. The product of this union is the zygote (or fusion cell), which combines genetic information received from two hereditarily different parental lineages of the human species.

The word "zygote" is often used loosely. It is derived from the Greek *zygotos* (yoked together). In the strict sense, it should be applied to the one-cell fertilizing egg only after commingling of the genetic material from the mother and father, that is, after the dissolution of the membranes that surround and separate the two genetic messages—the two pronuclei. Prior to dissolution of the pronuclear membranes, the one-cell fertilizing egg is often called a prezygote. With the first cell division, the zygote gives way to the pre-embryo. The pre-embryo comes into existence with the first cell division and lasts until the appearance of a single primitive streak, which is the first sign of organ differentiation. This occurs at about fourteen days of development, after which the word "embryo" can be properly applied. The pre-embryonic interval can be further subdivided, depending upon the developmental state of the conceptus, as will be noted. For the purpose of this article, unless a technical meaning as just described is required, the generic word "conceptus" will be used. "Conceptus" can be used to describe any stage of development from fertilization to birth.

While these minutiae of definition are of interest mainly to the biologist, the details of the fertilizing process (which takes about twenty-four hours) and the pre-embryonic span (which lasts about fourteen days) have acquired moral significance. From a biological viewpoint, fertilization is a process, not an event; it is not possible to identify a biological moment of fertilization. The pre-embryonic span is marked by a biological instability, such as the possibility of tumor formation or twinning, so that biological individuation is not guaranteed until embryonic differentiation begins, marked by the appearance of the primitive streak. The complex interaction of these processes will be described below.

The cellular union takes place soon after the egg has been discharged (ovulated) from a mature ovarian follicle, usually into or near the funnel-shaped upper end of the oviduct (fallopian tube). The resulting conceptus is then propelled along the oviduct toward the uterus by ciliary action of the tubal lining.

During tubal transit the conceptus undergoes cleavage, a series of cell divisions that occur without significant intervening cellular growth. The cleavage process thus converts the single-celled zygote into a spherical cluster of smaller cells (blastomeres) making up the morula. Subsequently, a central cavity forms within the morula, converting it into the fluid-filled blastocyst. Still later a cluster of blastomeres at one pole of the blastocyst projects into the central cavity, or blastocoele. The cell aggregate thus produced from the blastocyst is referred to as the inner cell mass. It is the precursor to the entire later embryo.

The blastocyst and its immediately preceding and succeeding stages take place within the pre-embryo period. At this time the developing entity displays significant organization above the level of individual cells but has not yet begun formation of the recognizable organ rudiments characteristic of a typical embryo. In fact, the outer cellular layer of the pre-embryonic blastocyst never becomes part of the later embryo. Instead, it specializes as the peripheral trophoblast (feeding layer) of the developing entity. It is this outer trophoblast that makes first contact—on arrival of the blastocyst in the uterus—with the uterine lining, becoming incorporated into it in the process of implantation. Thus, none of the outer trophoblast cells participate in the embryo itself; rather, derivatives of these cells contribute to the later placenta, which is discarded as part of the afterbirth.

While these events are occurring, the inner cell mass organizes as the direct precursor of the entire new organism-to-be, first as the pre-embryo, then sequentially as the embryo, the fetus, and eventually the neonate. It is to be especially noted that the preliminary steps toward embryo formation are closely associated in time with implantation, thereby constituting the first stages of actual pregnancy in the mother. In this process, what in the earlier pre-embryonic stage was a helter-skelter "inner cell mass" begins to aggregate into two distinct and coherent cell layers, one within the other. The outer of these, in relation to the embryo-to-be, is referred to as the ectoderm; the inner one, as the endoderm.

A little later there can be observed in the transforming pre-embryo a linear "primitive streak" that is significant in several important ways. First, the streak corresponds in its location and orientation to the major

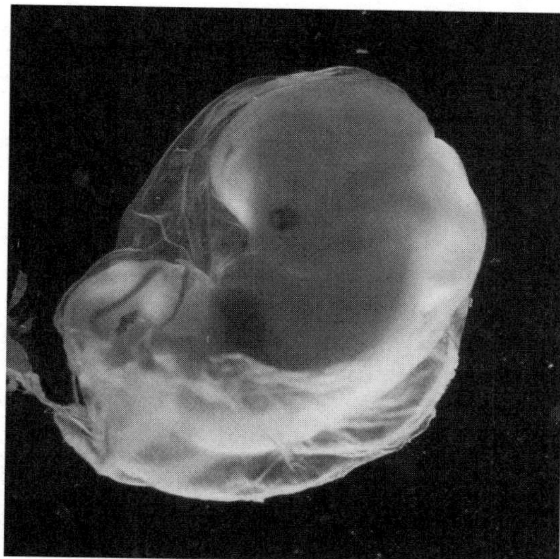

head-to-tail axis of the embryo-to-be—which will arise directly in front of and in line with the streak. This new axis provides the foundation of the embryo as a *single* multicellular individual. Second, the primitive streak turns out to be a thickening marked by inturning of surface cells into a new middle layer (the mesoderm), expanding as a third cellular sheet between the established ectoderm and endoderm. Third, later close interactions between the mesoderm and either the ectoderm or the endoderm are essential to subsequent embryogenesis, both of the embryo as a whole and in initiation and formation (morphogenesis) of individual embryonic organ rudiments.

Through these processes and events the pre-embryo transforms to a higher level of organization manifested as the embryo proper. The orientation (axiation) and development of organs (organogenesis) that mark the period of the embryo are regarded as terminating at about eight weeks after fertilization, when human bodily form and most major organs can be recognized as at least rudimentary precursors. Among the organs thus emerging are the heart and its major circulation, the tubular and elongating central nervous system, the segmented major skeletal axis and associated muscle groups, and the paired limbs. It should come as no surprise, therefore, that near the end of the embryonic period, limited bodily movements are detectable and visualized by ultrasonography. Indeed, it seems reasonable to interpret such bodily movements as indicators of the transition from embryo to fetus, where the latter exhibits increasing structural organization and functional maturation.

However, there are important caveats to be noted with regard to such simplifying generalizations. Primitive movement, such as the first turning of the head, observed six to eight weeks after fertilization, is certainly an indicator of deeper neuromuscular matu-

TOO EARLY TO TELL?

At what point in this human embryo's development is it to be regarded as a person? Does it have rights yet?

See Also

Fetal Rights? The Moral Status of the Unborn

The Legal Status of Human Fetuses

ration. But such movements do not require or demonstrate higher-order cognitive function—such as later-appearing sensation, pain, or intention. The latter require and are manifestations of significant brain function. But at eight weeks the brain is anatomically only a rudiment, without the differentiated cellular neurons essential to neural function. Movements at this stage, therefore, are important indicators of developing neuromuscular connection but offer no evidence of such cognitive activities as are known to be associated with the more mature and functional brain.

The lesson provided by this cautionary note can be generalized to other differences between embryonic and fetal properties and capabilities. In fact, the embryo can be regarded as occupied largely with generating new structures and their relationships—what embryologists call morphogenesis and construction workers speak of as "roughing out" a planned construction. The fetus, on the other hand, is largely involved with establishment and maturation of functional activity patterns—processes that will continue into and even beyond the newborn.

Thus, to say that by eight weeks the embryo has become a fetus is a legitimate broad generalization of an overall course. It does not, however, deny that a beating heart and early circulation of primitive blood were established considerably before eight weeks. Nor, on the other hand, does it convey the clear fact that fetal kidneys and lungs are still inadequate for effective extrauterine function even at twenty weeks.

Thus, the terms "embryo" and "fetus" are valid in distinguishing broadly different overall periods in a complex developmental continuum. The two periods are very different in their dominant developmental nature, particularly if one focuses on their initial states and their terminations. But the overall difference does not precisely apply to each and every time and aspect throughout the complex developmental course. The initiation of bodily movements, as now revealed by ultrasonography in the sixth and seventh weeks, is as good a marker as any other in defining the embryo-fetal transition.

◆ **stillbirth**
The delivery of a fetus who has already died.

Developmental stages and moral status

Why should the limits of particular developmental periods become the subject of vigorous and even contentious debate? Because such limits offer possibilities for dealing with a deeply divisive issue—the assignment of status and rights to human offspring during the course of their development. The problem is epitomized in the activist claim that the human conceptus has a right to life. To generalize the question thus posed:

- At what points in the course of development does human offspring acquire increasing value and entitlement rights as a person?
- Should such status be assigned at sharply delineated developmental times, technically defined and specified once and for all?
- Or should status arise—as realization itself proceeds in most gradual becomings—over extended periods that include and are influenced by changing circumstances?
- Should the defined circumstances be subject to judgments by evaluators who may take into account wider contexts, including ethical and religious teachings?
- And if such broader approaches seem reasonable or necessary, what are the critical developmental transitions that must be evaluated with respect to so central and complex a matter as personhood?
- And what contextual factors are to be taken into account in making such judgments?

Certainly a first step in any such difficult process is to establish which developmental transitions impinge critically upon the concepts of a person held by various informed parties. For example, fertilization restores an ovum to the diploid chromosomal state, in the process combining in a single cell what are the essentially equal but nonidentical genetic contributions from the two parental lineages. Few knowledgeable observers would doubt that when fertilization is completed, it has established the significant genetic foundation for the resulting person-to-be. On this basis, many argue that fertilization is, in fact, the definitive event in the process of human neogenesis.

But even this group would not seriously propose that zygotes should be counted as persons by the Census Bureau, or should be enfranchised to vote, or should be drafted into military service—all of these being reasonably applicable to the term "person" as it is variously defined in the law. Moreover, reestablishment of multicellularity in the course of cleavage of the zygote certainly makes a major contribution to essential aspects of a person—in this instance the unity of one individual despite a multiplicity of cellular components. In experiments on mice and other mammals, separation of blastomeres during the first several cleavages allows each blastomere to become a complete individual of the same genotype; that is, it produces identical twins. Identical human twins sometimes arise spontaneously, presumably by similar mechanisms. These observations suggest that multicellular singleness depends upon significant interactions among the early blastomeres, interactions that are, then, certainly prerequisite to the origin of a person.

See Also

The Moral Status of Human Fetuses

FETUS

Human Development from Fertilization to Birth

Moreover, such interactive cellular processes also occur in the later developmental course. In both the embryo and the fetus, genetic defects or exposure to toxic substances in the environment can disrupt normal development, leading to severe abnormality and even premature death. Thus development must be regarded as a series of sequelae to hereditary intergenerational messages played out in particular environments and circumstances, which can also influence the developmental course.

Indeed, in carefully tracing such developmental courses we become aware of a stepwise progression through which the realized, most significant properties of a human person evolve—until it is generally acknowledged as fully human and endowed with the rights and privileges respected and guaranteed by the entire company of persons. And is such a definition and its resultant not a shared goal of advocates of both the opposing positions in the abortion wars?

Can persuasive examples of such steps and processes be brought forward? Certainly fertilization involves some of the required characteristics and is regarded by some as having all that are necessary. During fertilization, hereditary entities (chromosomes) contributed by two previously unrelated individuals are combined in one new entity that has a unique hereditary constitution with characteristics traceable back to both parents. Such a unique individual stemming from human parentage certainly, it is argued, makes a strong claim to recognition as possessing moral status as a human person.

However, to others the case seems insufficient and far from fully convincing. Such a conceptus may be acknowledged as a step in the right direction, but the step is by no means fully determinative. For example, a person is a *single* individual, whereas a human pre-embryo is still potentially at least a pair of identical twins, that is, at least two individual persons. Indeed, in armadillos, the early conceptus regularly produces four individuals following regular separation of the first four blastomeres.

Therefore, the claim that fertilization immediately results in a single person in the full moral sense is unconvincing to those who defend a woman's right to choose what happens to her own body. Nonetheless, even this group has to acknowledge that significant steps toward a person occur during the course of fertilization, in particular formation of a new genetic entity—a zygote both developmentally activated and possessing established kinship with the two parental lineages that contributed to it. And the latter heritage includes not only the direct parental donors of the chromosomes but also the ancestral lineage network that contributed to each parent.

In consequence, it would seem, the zygote and its derivative pre-embryo should have a moral and legal status that acknowledges its complex biological genesis as well as its resulting developmental potential. Accordingly, the significance and value of pre-embryos should be recognized as more than that of individual gametes but less than that of fully developed, existential persons.

Following initiation by fertilization, a next major event requiring consideration for significant moral status is implantation and its associated complications. During implantation the pre-embryo—previously floating free and therefore at least physically independent—enters into intimately interactive coexistence with its female parent. Thanks to the erosive effects of its peripheral trophoblast on the uterine lining, the pre-embryo penetrates the underlying, highly vascular endometrium of the uterine wall.

Implantation, like fertilization, is a process, not an event. The pre-embryo attaches to the endometrial surface at about the fifth day after fertilization but is not completely within the endometrium; it is not completely implanted until about the twelfth day after fertilization. While this implantation process is under way or soon after completion, the conceptus is undergoing the other developmental events described here, such as the appearance of the primitive streak. Thus, the continuum of development and the changes in nomenclature from pre-embryo to embryo take place during or immediately after the implantation process.

Important support for this implantation process is provided by the maternal ovary, within which the ruptured follicle has transformed into the corpus luteum (yellow body). The luteal cells produce the pregnancy-fostering hormone progesterone. This hormone, on reaching the endometrium via the maternal circulation, stabilizes its highly vascular state; if progesterone is withdrawn or blocked in its action, the endometrium sloughs and bleeding occurs, as in monthly menstruation. Therefore, premature termination of the action of progesterone is contragestational, blocking implantation or terminating it (abortion) if it has already begun.

In a stable pregnancy, however, as noted, transformation of the pre-embryo into an embryo continues—as does expansion of the area of interaction between the trophoblast and the maternal endometrium. Thus, both embryonic organization and maternal adaptation to the presence and needs of the offspring significantly increase as implantation proceeds. In the case of the pre-embryo, it has now become established as a single individual in continuing development. In the case of the mother, she is now pregnant in the full sense. Her uterine lining has been invaded, and her hormonal status has been profoundly altered. Therefore, both mother and offspring have passed the point of high risk of biological error, and the reproductive process is fully under way.

◆ **viability**

The capability of a fetus to survive outside the womb with or without artificial support, variously fixed between twenty to twenty-eight weeks' gestation.

See Also

Body and Blood: Legal, Moral Obligations to Share?

These changes call for careful reconsideration of the status of the conceptus, now entering early embryonic stages (as evidenced by the soon recognizable primitive streak). Such conceptuses, unlike earlier stages, have become developmentally single—that is, so far as is known, they do not, and presumably cannot, undergo twinning. Their definitive singleness clearly constitutes an important step toward what we commonly think of as a single human individual. Achievement of this stage establishes a claim that the early embryo is entitled to some measure of personhood even if pre-embryonic stages are not.

However, also to be noted is the fact that developmental singleness is not characteristic only of the human species, nor even of mammalian lineages. Therefore, something further must be added before a developing *human* entity is clearly to be regarded as a person. This additional requirement is among the most difficult to define precisely. It clearly involves the behavioral realm but is more than the simple occurrence of behavior. It involves activities of the brain but not just any brain activity. Certain parts of the brain and their activities are especially relevant. Moreover, the necessary activities are among those that are regarded as most uniquely human—even though details of the activities are still an enigma. Stated synoptically, to be a person requires particular activities of the brain, activities at least on the way toward a self-image with some capacity to generate behavior on its own behalf.

This sketch of a concept and possible genesis of a person is hardly a satisfying or definitive answer to the question of when a human person comes into being, that is, becomes a human being, in the course of its development. But it suggests a process that is gradual and stepwise rather than a sudden transformation. It places special emphasis on maturation of the brain. In these terms, fertilization, implantation, embryonic morphogenesis, and fetal maturation all play roles in establishing the foundations of personhood. But the definitive realization of the moral status of a person would seem to await appropriate maturation of the brain, which is achieved only marginally even in the newborn. Thus, in this view, the immediate major substrate of what is diagnostic of a person lies in the brain and is not fully developed even in the newborn. Better understanding of this substrate requires greater knowledge of brain function and its maturation.

Conclusion

The genesis of a person begins at fertilization and proceeds stepwise throughout gestation. The generative process is not completed and terminated even at birth. An understanding of the moral significance of the various stages of prenatal human development requires further investigation and reflection. Meanwhile, practical policy governing the status and treatment of developing persons might recognize such subcategories as nonpersons, prepersons, protopersons, quasi persons, and neopersons—each meriting specification within the individual life history of human personhood.

— CLIFFORD GROBSTEIN

See Also

Maternal–Fetal Relationship: Biological Aspects

PHILOSOPHICAL AND ETHICAL ISSUES

Fetuses are generally defined as "the unborn young of a viviparous animal" (*Stedman's Medical Dictionary*, 1990, p. 573). Although the focus of this article is human fetuses, some morally relevant considerations, such as the ability to experience pain, apply to nonhuman fetuses as well.

The "viviparous [live-bearing] animal" in which the human fetus develops is female. Once removed or delivered from the body of a pregnant woman, it is no longer a fetus but an abortus or a newborn. Thus, the meaning and existence of human fetuses cannot be adequately understood apart from their crucial relationship to pregnant women.

While the end of fetal development is clearly marked by termination of pregnancy through birth or abortion, the origin of fetal development is more difficult to specify. In ordinary language, the term "fetus" is sometimes used to describe the developing organism from fertilization until birth. For opponents of elective abortion, for example, a "fetal right to life" is generally attributed to embryos as well as fetuses. If this usage were followed with regard to organisms whose development is initiated in the laboratory, it would be appropriate to speak of fetuses as existing apart from women's bodies.

Development of the embryo precedes that of the fetus, and the term "pre-embryo" has been used to characterize the developing organism from fertilization until implantation. Although the term "conceptus" is sometimes used for the developing organism from fertilization until birth, this term also applies to other products of conception, including the placenta and embryonic or fetal membranes. Some authors prefer the term "preimplantation embryo" for the period immediately following fertilization (Michaeli et al., 1990, p. 341).

In what follows, the term "embryo" refers to the developing organism from fertilization until fetal stage, regardless of whether development occurs in vivo or in vitro. The term "preimplantation embryo" identifies the organism prior to implantation, when pregnancy is established. The term "fetus" is used for organisms that have developed beyond the embryonic period but have not yet been born or aborted. Where developmental

stage is not pertinent to the discussion, the term "fetus" refers to the organism at any stage of its development, including the embryonic and preimplantation stages.

What kind of beings are fetuses?

The principal philosophical question to be addressed regarding fetuses is "What kind of beings are they?" Answers to this question determine the legal and moral status of the fetus, which is essential to resolution of a variety of ethical issues.

WHAT KIND OF BEING IS IT?

Four Questions to Weigh in Determining the Legal and Moral Status of the Fetus

1. its immaturity
2. its presence in, and dependence on, a biologically mature female
3. its species membership
4. its property of (or potential for) personhood

A mature human adult is capable of reproducing its own kind. Children as well as fetuses are immature by this standard, but most fetuses are also immature by a standard that measures maturity as ability to survive outside a woman's body, that is, viability. Prenatal tests for fetal maturity, for example, measure the ability of the fetus to breathe on its own. Fetuses are more mature or less immature by either standard than embryos, including preimplantation embryos, despite the ability of the latter to survive briefly in vitro. Some fetuses are more mature than some preterm or premature infants because the latter have not completed the duration of gestation that generally precedes birth.

The more immature the organism, the greater degree of maturation it is capable of achieving during its life span. At the same time, the probability of maturation is increased during the course of early development. It is estimated that up to 75 percent of all human conceptions and 15-25 percent of all physiologically recognized pregnancies are aborted spontaneously (Knight and Callahan, 1989). If a fetus is viable, its probability of survival approaches that of a newborn. Viability is morally significant because it reduces the dependence of the fetus on the pregnant woman. If the pregnancy is then interrupted, others may determine the fate of the newborn.

Neither embryonic nor fetal development is possible apart from a woman's body. Even preimplantation embryos can be sustained for only about two days in vitro. At that point they must be frozen or placed within a woman's body in order to survive. The woman who gestates the embryo or fetus need not be genetically related to the offspring to whom she gives birth. Freezing results in 25 to 50 percent loss of embryos; the process arrests development, which can recommence only if the embryo is thawed and placed within a woman's body (Bonnicksen, 1988).

Although some believe that the entire duration of embryonic and fetal development may someday take place in vitro, it is not clear that this is biologically possible. If such development were possible, the dependence on women that has characterized the developing organism from the origin of humankind would no longer hold. Pregnancy would no longer be necessary. Even if the definition of a fetus were expanded to accommodate that state of affairs, a morally relevant distinction would still obtain between fetuses that develop in vitro and those that develop in vivo. If the fetus could be brought to term in vitro, the claim of

IT'S HUMAN, BUT IS IT A PERSON YET?

Because an embryo or fetus develops from human gametes, it is human. However, this does not imply that the human fetus is a person or has rights. It may be argued that even if human fetuses are not persons, we are obliged to avoid killing or inflicting pain on them. The concepts of humanness, sentience (the ability to feel pain or pleasure), and personhood are thus separable in their application to human fetuses. Although humanness is a matter of fact and the onset of sentience is a matter of uncertainty, both concepts are empirically grounded and definable. Because personhood is not necessarily empirically grounded, its definition is more difficult and controversial.

While the question of whether human fetuses are persons is debated by philosophers and theologians, their potential for personhood is accepted even by those who deny that they are persons. The potential for personhood also distinguishes human fetuses from other human tissue and organs. R. M. Hare maintains that human gametes are potential human beings, thus attributing the potential to separate cells (ova and sperm) existing in different bodies (Hare, 1975). Unlike separate gametes, however, the human zygote is a single cell that will naturally develop toward birth and unquestionable personhood unless impeded by spontaneous or elective means.

— MARY B. MAHOWALD

See Also

Personhood: Central Yet Irresolvable

Is abortion the same thing as murdering a child, or is abortion not murder because the fetus really isn't a child?
Murder: 50%
Not murder: 38%

THE NEW YORK TIMES/ CBS NEWS POLL, JANUARY 16, 1998

women's right to determine the fate of the fetus would be considerably weakened.

While the in vitro status of the developing organism may seem to equalize the claims of men and women regarding the fate of externalized "fetuses," two factors argue against this: the fact that women experience both risk and discomfort in providing gametes, while men do not, and the fact that women are much more likely than men to be the principal caregivers of their offspring. It may further be argued that an externalized "fetus" capable of full development in vitro is comparable with a newborn, having rights of its own that supersede those of either genetic parent.

The legal status of human fetuses

Throughout the world, the legal status of fetuses is generally subordinated to that of pregnant women, but the degree to which women's interests or preferences are given priority varies from country to country, depending on the circumstances. Laws regulating abortion are generally indicative of the range of views. In countries such as Ireland and Honduras, for example, abortion is legal only if the woman's life is threatened by the pregnancy; the rationale for this position is that "the right to life [of the fetus] is inviolable" (Cook and Dickens, 1988, p. 1305). In countries such as Hungary, Norway, Taiwan, and Barbados, socioeconomic reasons are sufficient to override a fetal "right to life." In most countries, the legal status of the fetus is strengthened as gestation progresses. However, laws restricting or permitting abortion do not address the legal status of in vivo preimplantation embryos whose implantation may be prevented through use of contraceptive measures such as intrauterine devices. Neither do abortion laws address the legal status of in vitro preimplantation embryos.

In 1973, the *Roe* v. *Wade* decision of the U.S. Supreme Court maintained that "the word 'person,' as used in the Fourteenth Amendment, does not include the unborn" (*Roe* v. *Wade*, 1972, p. 158). Nonetheless, the Supreme Court affirmed that the states may prohibit abortion subsequent to fetal viability unless the pregnant woman's health is threatened by continuation of the pregnancy. Thus, although the fetus is not legally a person at any stage of its development, viability signifies a change in its legal status. Accordingly, some judicial rulings have compelled women to undergo surgery for the sake of a viable or possibly viable fetus (Kolder et al., 1987).

With the liberalization of abortion legislation in the United States in 1973, some feared that greater availability of abortuses might lead to widespread abuse involving fetal experimentation. The following year, a congressional moratorium was imposed upon federal funding of fetal research until the National Commission for the Protection of Human Subjects of Biomedical and Behavioral Research developed guidelines for such research. A fundamental principle of the commission was that fetuses to be aborted should not be subject to research procedures that were not also applicable to fetuses to be carried to term. Because fetuses in either category were to be treated in accordance with the same standard, this was called "the equality principle" (Fletcher and Ryan, 1987, p. 127). The commission's recommendations were partially codified in 1975 as federal regulations.

The regulations governing fetal research in the United States refer to the abortus as a "fetus ex utero" (Baron, 1985, p. 13). Requirements vary, depending on whether the experimental procedure is therapeutic to the pregnant woman or to the fetus, whether the procedure is performed in utero or ex utero, whether the fetus is living or dead, and if living, whether it is viable, nonviable, or possibly viable. Research involving pregnant women must have a therapeutic goal for the woman, or risks to the fetus must be minimal. Research with fetuses must be therapeutic or involve minimal risk for the fetus, and must be intended to provide significant knowledge that is inaccessible by other means. The last requirement is also applicable to research with nonviable and possibly viable abortuses. Additionally, research with nonviable living abortuses must avoid artificial maintenance of vital functions or deliberate termination of the abortus's heartbeat or respiration. Research with possibly viable abortuses must have a therapeutic goal and must avoid added risk for the abortus. Research with "viable abortuses" is subject to the same standard as research with newborns. Since abortion is clinically defined as termination of a pregnancy before viability, the term "viable abortus" is problematic. By that definition, a living human organism capable of surviving ex utero is not an abortus.

Research with dead fetuses in the United States is covered by the Uniform Anatomical Gift Act, which specifies that the "decedents" to which it applies include any "stillborn infant or a fetus" (Baron, 1985, p. 13). The act permits the gift of "all or part of the . . . body" of a dead fetus to be used for research or therapeutic purposes, so long as consent is obtained from "either parent" (Baron, 1985, p. 13). This act has been adopted in some form by all fifty states and the District of Columbia. Jurisdictions vary in their requirements for research with human fetuses, both living and dead. Some, for example, distinguish between the use of fetal tissue obtained from elective abortions and tissue obtained from spontaneous abortions: the latter is permitted, while the former is not.

Federal regulations governing fetal research in the United States virtually preclude research with preimplantation embryos developed through in vitro technol-

ogy. In contrast, the United Kingdom, following the recommendations of the Warnock Commission, enacted legislation that permits fetal experimentation until about fourteen days after fertilization. This point coincides with the formation of "the primitive streak" and the end of the possibility of twinning or recombination of the developing embryo (Glover, 1989, p. 100).

The moral status of human fetuses

Views about the moral status of human fetuses are even more far-ranging than views about their legal status. Because fetuses develop within women's bodies, some have characterized them as extraneous and sometimes unwanted tissue that women are as morally free to dispose of as they are free to dispose of growths or tumors. Because of the dependence of the fetus on the pregnant woman, some authors have characterized it as parasitic. On either of these accounts, the fetus has no moral status of its own.

At the opposite end of the spectrum is the view that the fetus has an independent moral status, despite the fact that it can exist only within the body of a pregnant woman. John Noonan, for example, maintains that the genetic humanity of the embryo, initiated at fertilization, gives it a right to life equal to that of any adult human being, including the pregnant woman (Noonan, 1970). Between these opposing views are positions that attribute to the fetus some moral status, but a status that is always subordinate to that of those who are unquestionably persons. As with its legal status, the moral status of the fetus is more likely to be supported late in its gestation. Carson Strong and Garland Anderson, for example, argue that the viable fetus has rights comparable with those of the newborn, while the nonviable fetus lacks those rights (Strong and Anderson, 1989). In contrast, Mary Anne Warren maintains that "the moral significance of birth" is such that the moral status of a developmentally younger newborn supersedes that of an older viable fetus. Her defense of this position is that "it is impossible to treat fetuses in utero as if they were persons without treating women as if they were something less than persons" (Warren, 1989, p. 59). Other authors place the point for affirming a fetal right to life earlier in gestation, some arguing that this occurs when individuation (the potential for separate existence) is established, others arguing that the onset of brain activity is the crucial threshold (Ford, 1988; Sass, 1989).

Another variable in views about the moral status of the fetus is an alleged distinction between those destined to be brought to term and those destined to be aborted. The argument here is that once a woman has declined the option of abortion, she is morally bound to make subsequent decisions that are protective of her developing fetus (Mattingly, 1992). Obviously, this distinction is at odds with the equality principle mentioned above, because obligations to fetuses destined to be born are more stringent than those toward fetuses destined to be aborted. It is also at odds with the principle of respect for autonomy, so long as that principle entails recognition of the fact that autonomous persons (including pregnant women) sometimes change their minds. The distinction is generally based on moral obligations to the potential child rather than to the fetus. On such an account we do not necessarily have responsibilities to fetuses as such.

It is not surprising that much of the debate about the moral status of the fetus focuses on the relevance of its potential for full or unquestionable personhood. Brian Johnstone supports the position that potential for personhood is morally compelling by distinguishing among three uses of the term "potential": a weak sense, in which one thing can be transformed into another by any kind of cause; a strong sense, in which something has the capacity for transformation within itself; and a statistical sense, which simply means that there is "high probability" that one thing will be transformed into another (Walters and Singer, 1982, pp. 49-50). Johnstone attributes all three of these senses to the human embryo, contrasting these with the absence of the strong or statistical sense of potential in human gametes. The implication is that human embryos, in virtue of their greater potential for personhood, have a moral status that lies somewhere between that of gametes and mature (born) human beings.

Like Hare, Helga Kuhse and Peter Singer argue that the potentiality argument is inadequate because all that can be said about the potential of embryos can also be said about the potential of ova and sperm (Walters and Singer, 1982). Consider, they suggest, a situation in which excess ova and sperm obtained for in vitro fertilization are disposed of by being flushed separately down the sink. No one, they believe, would find this action morally problematic. But suppose that after the ova and sperm are disposed of separately, a blockage in the sink occurs, and this causes them to remain lodged together, allowing fertilization to occur. According to Kuhse and Singer, "Those who believe that the embryo has a special moral status which makes it wrong to destroy it must now believe that it would be wrong to clear the blockage; instead the egg must now be rescued from the sink, checked to see if fertilization has occurred, and if it has, efforts should presumably be made to keep it alive" (Walters and Singer, 1982, p. 59). Assuming that reasonable people would not attempt such a rescue, they conclude that there is no sharp distinction between the moral status of human embryos and that of human gametes.

Do women who elect to abort have a familial, proprietary, or other interest in fetal tissue remains?

PAGE 24

FETUS

Philosophical and Ethical Issues

Specific issues

The preceding considerations are applicable to a broad range of ethical issues that involve human fetuses. These include abortion, coercive treatment during pregnancy, fetal therapy, custody disputes regarding extra embryos, fetal reduction, and fetal tissue transplantation. In what follows, each of these issues is considered with particular reference to the characteristics and status of the fetus.

ETHICAL ISSUES INVOLVING HUMAN FETUSES

- abortion
- coercive treatment during pregnancy
- fetal therapy
- custody disputes regarding extra embryos
- fetal reduction
- fetal tissue transplantation

Abortion may have three different meanings with regard to fetuses. First, it may mean termination of pregnancy, that is, the severance of the tie between the pregnant woman and her fetus. In some cases, severance of the tie has not resulted in fetal death, and the U.S. courts have held that the right to terminate the pregnancy does not imply the right to terminate fetal life in such circumstances. Second, abortion may mean termination of fetal life, which implies the intention of killing the fetus. In second-trimester gestations, different methods of abortion are more or less likely to accomplish that intent. Third, abortion may be defined as applicable not only to fetuses in utero but also to in vitro embryos. In this definition, the disposal of affected embryos after positive preimplantation genetic testing constitutes abortion. The second and third definitions are morally equivalent to feticide or embryocide.

◆ **breech presentation**
A fetus presents itself for birth hind end first.

Regardless of the definition and intention of abortion, the possibility of fetal sentience presents a moral consideration relevant to the selection of a method of abortion. Among techniques used in second-trimester terminations, for example, dilatation and evacuation (removal of fetal parts through the vagina) is more directly damaging to the fetus than other methods. Hysterotomy, the surgical removal of the fetus from the uterus, is least damaging to the fetus but most invasive for the woman. As already mentioned, the equality principle argues for providing comparable consideration to fetuses destined to be aborted and those destined to come to term. In the United States, this principle is not legally applicable to conflicts between the health of pregnant women and their fetuses because abortions are always permissible if the woman's health is endangered by the pregnancy.

Although most pregnant women willingly accept the inconveniences and discomforts of pregnancy, and some risk their own health in order to optimize fetal outcome, occasionally women refuse treatment recommended for the sake of the fetus. Pregnant women's refusal of hospitalization, intrauterine transfusion, or surgical delivery have been challenged on grounds of an obligation to the fetus or to the potential child (Kolder et al., 1987). Suits have also been brought against pregnant women for lifestyle decisions that endanger the fetus, such as drug and alcohol abuse. Most of these legal challenges have been unsuccessful because they are based on child abuse laws. Fetuses, even when viable, do not have equal legal standing with children. However, to the extent that human beings are responsible for others whose lives or welfare depend on them, a woman who has opted to continue her pregnancy may be morally responsible for avoiding behaviors that endanger the fetus.

When women accept treatment that jeopardizes their own health for the sake of their fetuses, their behavior may be considered virtuous rather than obligatory. However, their voluntariness in such situations may be compromised by social pressures that influence their decision making. George Annas suggests the possibility of such pressures when he compares the refusal of cesarean section recommended for treatment of fetal distress with a parent's refusal to donate an organ for his or her child (Annas, 1982). In both cases, parents may feel obliged to take risks in behalf of their offspring. Despite the fact that the personhood of the child is clearly established, while that of the fetus is controversial, judges have mandated that surgery be performed in the latter case but not the former (Annas, 1982). This implies that organ donation to one's child is superogatory, whereas cesarean section to benefit the fetus is obligatory.

Arguments in favor of overriding the pregnant woman's autonomy in behalf of the fetus have been made on grounds that harms to the developing organism are harms to the future child. Awards made to parents whose children were injured in utero are made on this basis. If a woman miscarries because of an accident or injury, an award may be made for the loss of the fetus, but this is not legally equivalent to the loss of a child. The duration of gestation and the possibility of viability are morally and legally relevant in such cases.

Advances in medical and surgical techniques for treatment of fetuses provide the prospect of women undergoing even more experimental and invasive procedures than they have accepted in the past. For example, it is possible to remove a nonviable fetus from a

See Also
Reproductive Technologies
Reproductive Technologies: Ethical Issues

woman's uterus, surgically repair problems such as a hernia in its diaphragm, and return the fetus to the uterus to continue gestation (Ohlendorf-Moffat, 1991). Such procedures are morally different from those that a newborn might undergo because they necessarily involve risk to the pregnant woman, for which her consent is morally and legally indispensable.

Advances in treatment of infertility have led to an increased incidence of multiple gestations. At times, the expectation of live birth is reduced or even negated because so many fetuses are not likely to survive in utero for the entirety of gestation. Fetal reduction, which is also called "selective termination," "selective abortion," "selective birth," and "selective feticide," may be performed in order to facilitate the birth of one or more healthy infants (Evans et al., 1988, p. 293). When the mortality and morbidity of a multiple gestation are high, the intention of the procedure is not to terminate the pregnancy but to promote the healthy live birth of one or more infants. Ordinarily, an attempt is made to reduce the pregnancy to twins rather than a single fetus. Whether to provide the procedure for triplet gestations is more controversial than for gestations of a greater number of fetuses, in part because the procedure carries a risk to the remaining fetuses. The recommended criterion for determining which fetuses to terminate is one of efficiency: those that can technically be most easily reached and effectively terminated. Unlike most abortion procedures, fetal reduction involves direct termination of fetal life. Although only a few centers in the United States perform this procedure, the number is growing.

The issue of fetal tissue transplantation exemplifies the apparently inevitable linkage between fetuses and concerns about abortion. Although fetal tissue has long been used in treatment of some diseases (such as DiGeorge's syndrome), its use for treatment of severe neurological conditions such as Parkinson's disease is new and experimental. The symptoms of patients suffering from Parkinson's disease have apparently improved through grafts of fetal tissue obtained through routine suction abortions at six to eight weeks' gestation (Widner et al., 1992). Fetal tissue can be transplanted with greater success than adult tissue because it is less immunologically reactive, reducing the incidence of rejection. It also has a greater capacity to develop than adult tissue. Most ethicists support the use of fetal tissue for transplantation as an issue separate from that of abortion. This view has been challenged by some on empirical as well as ethical grounds (Mahowald, 1991). Those who oppose the use of fetal tissue for transplantation claim that it unavoidably involves complicity in, and legitimation of, abortion.

To some, just as a parent's abuse of a child provides grounds for others to decide about the child's fate, so a pregnant woman's choice of abortion compromises her right to consent to transplantation of fetal tissue. To others, the fetus is the pregnant woman's property, and this gives her the right to dispose of it as she wishes, even when it is no longer within her body. As with custody disputes concerning frozen embryos, others in addition to the woman who is genetically related to the

EMBRYO CUSTODY DISPUTES

Tangled Claims

Custody disputes regarding embryos have arisen because of their in vitro status. So long as embryos remain within the woman's body, others' claims regarding their disposition are unlikely to be upheld. When embryos have developed and have been preserved in vitro, however, disputes about their fate have involved potential heirs, gamete providers, and institutions in which the embryos were developed or preserved. Claims by institutions have been rejected by the U.S. courts in favor of the gamete providers. A complicating possibility arises from the fact that the only claimant capable of both genetic and gestational relationship to the embryo is the woman who provided the ova. If she is unwilling to gestate one or more embryos, and her decision regarding its disposition is contested, the embryo can develop further only through involvement of a third party, that is, through contract motherhood or surrogate gestation. An offspring that develops from such an arrangement has in fact three biologically related parents. The development of the fetus is dependent on only one of these, the gestational parent. In situations where each of the biological parents desires, and is competent to raise, the offspring, their disparate risks and involvement with the fetus suggest an ordering by which to determine whose wishes have priority: first, the gestational parent; second, the ovum provider; third, the sperm provider (Mahowald, 1993). Some authors consider the genetic tie more compelling than the gestational relationship, and some give equal weight to claims of ovum and sperm provider. In the trial court decision regarding the case of "Baby M," Judge Harvey R. Sorkow gave greater weight to the sperm provider than to the woman who was both genetically and gestationally related to the offspring (Sorkow, 1988).

— MARY B. MAHOWALD

The initial ethical question created by these new reproductive technologies is whether they ought to be used at all.

PAGE 598

See Also

Ethical Questions Raised by the Use of the New Reproductive Technologies

fetus may claim ownership of the abortus. Institutions, for example, may argue that the abortus is discarded tissue, which they are legally entitled to dispose of as such; the sperm or ova providers may argue that they own the tissue generated by fertilization of their gametes. Conflicts are also possible between ova providers and gestational parents. The in vitro status of the abortus is critical to support of claims by those who are not gestationally related to it. Once the fetus is aborted or delivered, the pregnant woman's right to determine its fate is clearly less compelling.

In sum, human fetuses raise unique philosophical, legal, and ethical issues that are inseparable from their immature but human status, their relationship to pregnant women, and their potential for unquestioned personhood. All of these factors are relevant to issues that involve pregnant women: abortion, coercive treatment during pregnancy, possibilities for fetal therapy, custody disputes regarding embryos, fetal reduction, fetal research, and fetal tissue transplantation. Just as fetuses as such are inseparable from pregnant women, so the issues themselves inevitably overlap and are particularly likely to intersect with the controversial issue of elective abortion. So long as there are relievable threats to fetuses, and fetuses develop within women's bodies, this will continue to be the case.

— MARY B. MAHOWALD

There have been cases recognizing the right of the depositing couple to remove their frozen embryo from a bank against the bank's wishes.

PAGE 597

FETAL RESEARCH

All of the research discussed in this article involves women and men, as well as human embryos and fetuses. When implantation is a necessary condition for the research, as in the case of most fetal research, the fetus is implanted in the uterus of a woman. For all of the research considered in the article, the oocytes (eggs) of at least one woman are required; in cases involving in vitro fertilization, the oocyte retrieval process can be onerous for the woman involved. In addition, sperm from at least one man are required for fertilization. For reasons of brevity, this essay focuses primary attention on the developing human embryo and fetus, referring only incidentally to the woman and man who provide the gametes that give rise to the embryo and fetus or to the woman in whom gestation occurs.

FOUR MAJOR TYPES OF FETAL RESEARCH

1. preimplantation embryos
2. unimplanted embryos and fetuses beyond the fourteenth day of development
3. implanted embryos and fetuses
4. aborted, live embryos and fetuses

Preimplantation embryo research

The human preimplantation embryo can be defined as the developing organism from the time of fertilization to approximately the fourteenth day after fertilization, assuming a normal rate of development. The major preimplantation stages in human and other mammalian embryos are usually distinguished by such names as zygote, morula, and blastocyst. By the end of fourteen days the early human embryo has, except in rare cases, lost the capacity to divide into two individuals; it has also begun to exhibit a longitudinal axis that forms the template for the spinal column, an axis called the primitive streak (McLaren, 1986; Dawson, 1990a).

Preimplantation embryo research generally requires the associated procedure of in vitro fertilization (although it would in principle be possible to retrieve an early embryo by flushing it from the uterus of a woman following in vivo fertilization of an ovum). Thus, the question of research on preimplantation embryos did not arise until in vitro fertilization techniques had been developed and validated, first in laboratory animals, then in humans. M. C. Chang of the Worcester Foundation in Massachusetts was the first scientist to demonstrate unambiguously the fertilization of nonhuman mammalian oocytes in vitro (Chang, 1959). Chang's success was followed in 1969 by the first confirmed report of in vitro fertilization with human gametes by three British researchers (Edwards et al., 1969). Only nine years later the first human birth after in vitro fertilization—the infant's name was Louise Brown—was reported by members of the same British research team (Steptoe and Edwards, 1978).

There are two major contexts for research on preimplantation embryos. The first is one in which the transfer of the embryo into the uterus of a woman (or perhaps, in the future, into a device that can support full-term fetal development) is planned. In the second context, no embryo transfer is envisioned and, accordingly, the death of the embryo or later fetus at a stage before viability is intended. These two research contexts raise somewhat different ethical issues.

RESEARCH FOLLOWED BY EMBRYO TRANSFER. In the years preceding the birth of Louise Brown in 1978, researchers devoted substantial attention to improving the prospects for successful in vitro fertilization and embryo transfer. This research focused on methods for maturing oocytes, facilitating fertilization, and culturing or cryopreserving early embryos (Biggers, 1979). During the 1990s, researchers continued this type of research. New methods for assisting fertilization have been devised, including the drilling of a small hole in the outer shell of an oocyte or the injection of a sperm directly into an oocyte (Van Steirteghem, 1993). Similarly, researchers have developed methods for removing one or two cells from an eight- or sixteen-cell embryo in order to perform preimplantation diagnosis of genetic or chromosomal abnormalities (Edwards, 1993). In the twenty-first century, one can anticipate research that attempts to prevent the later development of a genetic disease (for example, cystic fibrosis) by treating an individual at the embryonic stage of life. If successful, this kind of disease prevention by means of gene modification would be likely to affect all of the cells of the person, including his or her reproductive cells (Wivel and Walters, 1993).

The ethical issues that arise with preimplantation embryo research when embryo transfer is planned are at least analogous to those that arise with fetal research in anticipation of birth, with research on infants, and with research on children. That is, one attempts to perform a careful analysis of the probable benefits and harms of the research to the individual and to others; one seeks an appropriate decision maker, usually a genetic parent or a guardian, who can represent the best interests of the potential research subject; and one looks for a disinterested mechanism for prior ethical review of the proposed research. This kind of embryo research, in which the research procedures are often designated "therapeutic" or "beneficial," is generally approved by commentators on the ethics of such research, even if they diverge widely in their attitudes toward in vitro fertilization, the moral status of preimplantation embryos, and abortion (see, e.g., Ramsey, 1970; Catholic Church, 1987; Singer et al., 1990).

RESEARCH NOT FOLLOWED BY EMBRYO TRANSFER. Research in this context may be proposed for a variety of reasons. The goal of the research may be to assess the safety and efficacy of clinical practices, for example, in vitro fertilization or the use of contraceptive vaccines. Alternatively, the goal may be epidemiological, for example, to estimate the frequency of chromosomal abnormalities in early human embryos. In other cases the research has little reference to clinical medicine or human pathology. That is, research with preimplantation embryos may be much more basic, seeking to compare early development in various species of mammals or to explore the limits of embryo fusion or hybrid creation among different species.

QUESTIONING THE ETHICS OF PREIMPLANTATION EMBRYO RESEARCH

- Is research on preimplantation embryos morally permissible if it has no intention of benefiting the embryos themselves?
- If yes, is it morally permissible to fertilize human oocytes for the sole purpose of performing research on the resulting embryos and in the absence of any intention to transfer the embryos for further development?

In their responses to the first question, proponents of nonbeneficial (to the embryos) research procedures adduce several arguments. First, the research may produce benefits, either for clinical practice or in terms of basic knowledge, that are not attainable by any other means (U.S. Department of Health, Education and Welfare, 1979; Warnock, 1984; Ethics Committee, 1990; Robertson, 1994). One variant of this argument asserts that it is morally irresponsible to introduce new techniques (for example, cryopreservation of embryos) into clinical practice without first performing extensive laboratory studies of the technique.

Second, proponents of preimplantation embryo research note that the biological individuality of the embryo is not firmly established until approximately fourteen (or perhaps twenty-one) days after fertilization. Before that time twinning can occur, or two embryos can fuse into a single new embryo called a chimera (Hellegers, 1970; Dawson, 1987; Grobstein, 1988). If developmental individuality does not occur until after the preimplantation stage, research proponents argue, the preimplantation embryo is not protectable as a unique human being.

Third, proponents of research cite the apparently high embryo loss rate that occurs in natural human reproduction. The most reliable estimates are that approximately 50 percent of the human eggs that are fertilized either fail to develop or die within two weeks after fertilization occurs (Chard, 1991). To this factual evidence is added the metaphysical assertion that entities with such a high rate of natural death within two weeks of coming into being cannot be morally significant at this early stage of their existence. Proponents of embryo research may acknowledge that adult persons have some moral obligations toward early embryos, but these obligations are viewed as relatively weak and are thought to be outweighed by, for example, substantial clinical benefits to many future patients.

Opponents of preimplantation embryo research have replies to these arguments and adduce other arguments of their own. In response to the first argument of proponents, the opponents assert that the end of desirable clinical consequences does not justify the means of performing research that seriously damages or destroys the embryo. To the consequential argument of proponents, conservatives may counterpose a consequential argument of their own, namely, that negative consequences will result from research on early embryos. For example, researchers may become desensitized to the value of human life, or bizarre human-nonhuman hybrids may be produced in the laboratory (Catholic Church, 1987; Dawson, 1990b).

The second and third arguments of the proponents are viewed as mere descriptions of natural phenomena that carry no particular moral weight. Twinning,

◆ **digoxin**
A medication administered to pregnant women for the benefit of a fetus with irregular heartbeats.

See Also
Pregnancy and Maternal Health

No longer is the fetus defined predominantly as a part of the pregnant woman.

PAGE 464

recombination, and embryo loss, if they occur naturally and are beyond human control, are in this view no more morally relevant than other natural evils like earthquakes or volcanic eruptions. For their part, opponents put forward two additional arguments. First, the genotype of a new individual is firmly established at the time when the pronuclei from the sperm cell and the ovum fuse. This fusion, sometimes called syngamy, occurs at the conclusion of fertilization. Thus, from a genetic standpoint, a new individual exists from syngamy forward. Second, opponents of preimplantation embryo research often adduce the potentiality argument: that the early embryo contains within itself all of the genetic instructions necessary for the development of a fetus, an infant, and an adult, provided only that the embryo is placed in an environment that will nurture its further development. Therefore, the person that the early embryo may one day become should be respected in an anticipatory way even at the early stages of development, when it lacks many of the characteristics of persons in the full sense.

Proponents of research do not deny that a new genotype is established at the time of fertilization. They simply point to other factual considerations that are in their view more relevant to moral judgments about the acceptability of embryo research. In response to the potentiality argument, research proponents note that a single sperm cell and a single oocyte have the potential to become an embryo, yet opponents of embryo research do not accord special moral status to reproductive cells. Further, only a few cells of the preimplantation embryo develop into the embryo proper; the rest become the placenta, the amniotic sac, and the chorionic villi (McLaren, 1986). In other words, potentiality is a continuous notion, or a matter of degree, not an all-or-nothing concept (Singer and Dawson, 1988).

Among proponents of research on preimplantation embryos there is a division of opinion on the second question noted above—whether the creation of human embryos specifically for research purposes is morally permissible. Proponents of the conservative answer to this question argue that only embryos left over from the clinical practice of in vitro fertilization and embryo transfer should be used in research (Steinbock, 1992). Such embryos might include those selected out when the number of embryos available for transfer exceeds a number that is considered safe for the woman (for example, more than four embryos). Leftover or surplus embryos might also become available in the context of cryopreservation, if a couple completes its desired family size or if both genetic parents die in an accident while some embryos remain in frozen storage.

The principal argument of conservatives on the deliberate-creation question is a Kantian argument against using early human embryos merely as means. In the opinion of conservatives, creating embryos with the prior intent of destroying them at an early stage of development is incompatible with the respect that should be accorded to human embryos. Conservatives can accept the use of leftover embryos for research because there was at least at one time an intention to transfer the preimplantation embryos to the uterus of a woman, where they could develop into viable fetuses. In their view, the research use of such "spare" embryos is a morally acceptable alternative to donation or discard (Steinbock, 1992). The primary argument of those who do not object to creating embryos for research is a composite. Proponents of this view argue, first, that our moral obligations to early human embryos are relatively weak. Further, proponents of the liberal view note that good research design may require either a larger number of embryos than the clinical context can provide or unselected embryos rather than those that have been rejected for embryo transfer, perhaps because they are malformed or slow in developing (Ethics Committee, 1990).

PRACTICE VS. ETHICS. In the 1990s international practice and ethical opinion regarding human embryo research diverged sharply. One polar position in practice was that of the United Kingdom, where research on preimplantation embryos was conducted in numerous laboratories under the supervision of voluntary and (later) statutory licensing authorities (United Kingdom, 1992). At the other pole was Germany, which prohibited the fertilization of ova for the practice of research, as well as any research that was likely to destroy or damage the embryo.

Ethics advisory bodies of the 1970s and 1980s were far from unanimous in their evaluations of research involving preimplantation embryos. The earliest report on this topic, produced by the Ethics Advisory Board for the U.S. Department of Health, Education, and Welfare (1979), judged embryo research to be ethically acceptable if it was designed primarily to "assess the safety and efficacy of embryo transfer" (p. 106). During the 1980s there emerged three general positions among such advisory bodies. Several Australian committees rejected the idea of any human embryo research. A few Australian committees and most of the committees based in continental Europe approved embryo research but rejected the deliberate creation of embryos for research purposes. In the Netherlands, the United Kingdom, Canada, and the United States, advisory committees tended to approve both human embryo research and the creation of embryos for research (Walters, 1987). The 1989 recommendation of the Parliamentary Assembly of the Council of Europe adopted the intermediate position, requiring as well the prior approval of the "appropriate public

See Also

Research on Aborted, Live Embryos and Fetuses

health or scientific authority" or "the relevant national multidisciplinary committee" (Council of Europe, 1989).

Research on unimplanted embryos and fetuses beyond the fourteenth day of development

The developing human organism is technically called an embryo during the first eight weeks following fertilization. It is called a fetus for the remainder of its development. In this section, prolonged in vitro culture of embryos and fetuses will be evaluated.

Prolonged embryo culture has been undertaken in several species of nonhuman mammals, especially rats and mice. In the early years of research, embryos at various stages of development were removed (or "explanted") from the uteri of pregnant females and sustained in various kinds of laboratory devices that delivered oxygen and nutrients (New, 1973). More recently, unimplanted mouse and cattle embryos have been sustained in culture to developmental stages more complex than those attained by preimplantation human embryos (Chen and Hsu, 1982; Thomas and Seidel, 1993).

At present, no researchers are proposing to perform studies of either of these types with human embryos. The explantation mode of research will probably not be undertaken in humans because of the risks to the pregnant woman and because the need is questionable. However, sustained culture of human embryos after in vitro fertilization would in principle be possible. It is not clear whether the current lack of proposals to culture embryos in vitro beyond fourteen days is based on technical or ethical considerations. The longest well-documented periods for human embryo culture are eight days and thirteen days (Fishel et al., 1984). Possible rationales for extending embryo culture beyond fourteen days could include studying differentiation, the anatomy and physiology of the embryo, the implantation process, or the effect of drugs or radiation on the developing embryo (Karp, 1976; Edwards, 1989; Sass, 1989).

There has been relatively little ethical discussion of embryo research beyond fourteen days. Most advisory committees have simply accepted the fourteen-day limit without extensive discussion. In the case of the Warnock Committee report from the United Kingdom, this limit was said to be appropriate because it correlates with the appearance of the primitive streak in the embryo (Warnock, 1984). The primitive streak is the first indication of the embryo's body axis. Several commentators have suggested that the justification for the fourteen-day limit is relatively weak and have proposed extending the limit for in vitro human embryo research to approximately twenty-eight days (Dawson, 1987; Edwards, 1989; Kuhse and Singer, 1990).

If embryo culture methods improve sufficiently, it may one day be possible to sustain either a nonhuman or a human embryo and fetus in vitro for an extended period, or even through an entire gestation. The technological support system that sustains such development will probably be called an artificial placenta. If prolonged embryo culture is employed with human embryos and fetuses, decisions will be required about whether to sustain development to the point of viability. At some point a transition will undoubtedly be made from laboratory research designed to test the technical feasibility of long-term culture to an actual attempt to produce a human child by means of ectogenesis (extrauterine development) (Kass, 1972; Fletcher, 1974; Karp, 1976; Walters, 1979).

Research on implanted embryos and fetuses

The ethical questions that surround research on implanted embryos and on implanted fetuses are virtually identical, except for the different stages of development involved. This continuity in biological development and similarity in ethical analysis is so striking that both the American National Commission for the Protection of Human Subjects and the British Polkinghorne Committee employed the term "fetus" to refer to the developing entity from the time of implantation through the whole of gestation (U.S. National Commission, 1975; Polkinghorne, 1989). In the following discussion the word "fetus" and its derivatives will be employed to refer to the embryo or fetus from the time of implantation in the uterus of a woman through the point at which physical separation from the woman occurs.

As in the case of preimplantation embryo research, one can distinguish two major contexts for fetal research. The first is one in which further development and delivery of an infant are anticipated. The second context is one in which induced abortion is either planned or in progress.

FETAL RESEARCH IN ANTICIPATION OF BIRTH. The ethical issues involved in fetal research conducted at any stage of gestation in anticipation of birth closely parallel the ethical issues in research on newborns. The main reason for the close parallel is that the further development of the fetus or newborn into an adult person is planned. No research procedure that is likely to threaten the life or damage the health of a future person would be either proposed or carried out by responsible scientists. For this reason, research not intended to benefit a particular fetus (in anticipation of birth) or a particular newborn is generally constrained by the no-risk or minimal-risk rule (U.S. National Commission, 1975; Polkinghorne, 1989). That is, the research must be judged to pose either no risk at all (as

The simplest fetal therapies are medications given to a pregnant woman for the benefit of her fetus.

PAGE 465

◆ fetal alcohol syndrome (FAS)
A condition found in the offspring of women who consumed excessive alcohol during their pregnancy that results in gross physical retardation; central nervous dysfunction, including mental retardation; and facial abnormalities.

in certain observational studies) or only minimal risk to the potential subject. For research intended to benefit a particular fetus or newborn, a careful weighing and balancing of likely benefits and harms to the subject is required (Polkinghorne, 1989).

The major difference between neonatal research and fetal research in anticipation of birth is that the fetus is contained within the pregnant woman's body, and any research intervention will require physical contact with, or at least physical proximity to, the pregnant woman. Thus, fetal research inevitably and simultaneously affects a pregnant woman. For this reason it requires a careful weighing and balancing of the risks to her, as well as her informed consent.

The most invasive fetal therapy is in utero fetal surgery.

PAGE 465

Many clinical procedures that are now routinely employed in obstetrical practice were first tested on pregnant women and fetuses in anticipation of birth. One early therapy was the use of exchange transfusions to overcome Rh incompatibility between a pregnant woman and her fetus. In the 1980s experimental types of fetal surgery were undertaken to correct problems like urinary-tract obstructions. The worldwide epidemic of HIV infection and AIDS provided the context for important fetal research in the 1990s. In one randomized clinical trial, the antiviral drug AZT (azidothymidine) was administered to HIV-infected pregnant women in an effort to delay the progression of disease in them, as well as to prevent the transmission of infection to their fetuses.

During pregnancy, almost every organ system in the mother undergoes adaptation to support the maternal-fetal unit.

PAGE 466

FETAL RESEARCH IN ANTICIPATION OF OR DURING INDUCED ABORTION. Fetal research conducted before or during induced abortion could have various aims. One possible goal would be to develop better techniques for prenatal diagnosis, for example, by means of fetoscopy or chorionic villi sampling. Another possible goal would be to study whether drugs, viruses, vaccines, or radioisotopes cross the placental barrier between pregnant woman and fetus. A third aim of such studies could be to develop techniques for induced abortion that are safer for pregnant women or more humane in the termination of fetal life. Fourth, during abortion by hysterotomy (a seldom-used procedure similar to a cesarean section), fetal physiology can be studied after the fetus has been removed from the uterus of the pregnant woman and before the umbilical cord has been severed (Walters, 1975).

◆ **fetal tissue research**

The use of abortion tissues and fetuses in research into the treatment of such diseases as diabetes, leukemia, Alzheimer's disease, and Parkinson's disease.

POSSIBLE GOALS OF FETAL RESEARCH DURING INDUCED ABORTION

1. to develop better techniques for prenatal diagnosis
2. to study whether drugs, viruses, or vaccines cross the placental barrier
3. to develop improved techniques for induced abortion
4. during abortion by hysterectomy, fetal physiology can be studied

Commentators on the ethics of fetal research in anticipation of induced abortion have always been aware that a pregnant woman who intends to terminate her pregnancy can change her decision about abortion even after a research procedure has been performed. In addition, in rare cases an attempt at induced abortion results in a live birth. Thus, except in the case of research procedures performed during the abortion procedure itself, the distinction between a fetus-to-be-aborted and a fetus-to-be-born is statistical rather than metaphysical. One study performed for the U.S. National Commission in the 1970s estimated the change-of-decision rate between a visit to an abortion facility and the scheduled time of termination to be in the range of 1-2 percent (Bracken, 1975).

The possibility that a pregnant woman may change her decision to undergo induced abortion after a research intervention sets an outer limit on the types of interventions that prudent researchers would be willing to perform. For example, it would be useful to know at what stages of pregnancy alcohol, drugs, or viral infections are most likely to produce malformations in human fetuses; however, in the view of most commentators on the ethics of fetal research, such studies ought not to be performed in humans. In the words of the Peel Committee report, "In our view it is unethical for a medical practitioner to administer drugs or carry out any procedures on the mother with the deliberate intent of ascertaining the harm that these might do to the fetus, notwithstanding that arrangements may have been made to terminate the pregnancy and even if the mother is willing to give her consent to such an experiment" (United Kingdom, 1972, p. 6).

Even if research likely to cause serious damage to the fetus is ethically proscribed, there are at least two different ethical standards that can be adopted with respect to fetal research in anticipation of or during induced abortion. The first standard asks for equal treatment of the fetus-to-be-born and the fetus-to-be aborted. In brief, this standard requires either that one should perform research procedures on fetuses-to-be-born concurrently with performing the same procedures on fetuses-to-be-aborted, or at least that one should be *willing* to perform the same procedure on both groups of fetuses. In practice, this standard would be virtually equivalent to the no-risk or minimal-risk rule discussed in connection with fetal research in anticipation of birth (McCormick, 1975; Walters, 1975; Ramsey, 1975; Polkinghorne, 1989).

An alternative standard would reject the equal-

treatment requirement. What is proposed instead is a kind of case-by-case approach to fetal research (U.S. National Commission, 1975; Fletcher and Ryan, 1987). For example, if the primary risk of a research procedure like chorionic villi sampling is that it will cause abortion in a small percentage of pregnant women, then it can be argued that research on this diagnostic procedure should be performed on women who plan to undergo induced abortion. If the research procedure itself is unlikely to injure the fetus, then the major remaining risk is that the abortion that the pregnant woman planned to have induced in the future would instead occur spontaneously. The major ethical questions remaining in a case of this kind have to do with the timing of abortion: Is a later rather than an earlier induced abortion less respectful of the developing fetus? Does a later abortion entail greater risks to the physical and mental health of the pregnant woman?

An important dimension of the fetal research discussion is the possibility that research procedures will cause pain to the fetus (Steinbock, 1992). One of the difficulties in coming to terms with this issue is that the word "pain" probably has different meanings at different developmental stages. The anatomical basis for simple spinal reflexes seems to be present in human embryos at about 7.5 weeks post fertilization. Between the ninth and twelfth weeks of development, the fetal brain stem begins to function as a rudimentary information processor. However, only at twenty-two–twenty-three weeks of gestation is the cerebral neocortex connected to the other parts of the brain (Flower, 1985). Presumably the fetal capacity to perceive pain would differ at each of these three steps, but it is difficult to know precisely to what extent painful stimuli would be felt or remembered.

Research on aborted, live embryos and fetuses

There are major conceptual difficulties involved in describing a previously implanted entity that is expelled or removed alive from a pregnant woman's body (or removed alive from attachment to an artificial placenta). One candidate term is "abortus"; another is "fetus ex utero" or "embryo or fetus outside the uterus." Adjectives applied to such entities include "previable" or "nonviable" and "viable." A "viable fetus outside the uterus" is in fact a newborn infant, albeit one that may be seriously premature. In addition, the notion of viability is elastic, sometimes seeming to mean the gestational age, weight, or length at which the smallest known infant has survived, at other times seeming to mean the stage at which a stipulated percentage of infants survive, given the assistance of technological means of life support.

Three circumstances can be envisioned in which the question of research on formerly implanted, living embryos or fetuses could arise. First, the surgical removal of an ectopic pregnancy could provide a still-living embryo or fetus. Second, a spontaneous miscarriage could result in the delivery of a live embryo or fetus. Third, an already implanted embryo or fetus could be aborted by means that make it either possible or likely that an intact, living embryo or fetus will result from the abortion procedure.

There is no clear consensus on the ethical justifiability of research on living human embryos or fetuses outside the uterus. In the United Kingdom, two official reports reflect a clear trend in a more conservative direction. In 1972, the Peel Committee affirmed the scientific value of research on clearly previable fetuses outside the uterus and permitted many kinds of research on such fetuses (United Kingdom, 1972). However, the Polkinghorne Committee report of 1989 expressly rejected the position of the Peel Committee, arguing that the only morally relevant distinction was between living and dead fetuses, not the distinction between previable and viable fetuses (Polkinghorne, 1989). In the United States, the National Commission for the Protection of Human Subjects allowed no significant procedural changes in the abortion procedure solely for research purposes and restricted what could be done with the live, delivered embryo or fetus to intrusions that would not alter the duration of its life (U.S. National Commission, 1975). Recommendation 1100 by the Parliamentary Assembly of the Council of Europe (1989) also discussed "the use of human embryos and fetuses in scientific research." Its recommendation clearly reflected the ambivalence of ethical opinion on research involving live embryos or fetuses outside the uterus. After stating that "Experiments on living embryos or foetuses, whether viable or not, shall be prohibited," the recommendation continued as follows: "None the less, where a state authorises certain experiments on non-viable foetuses or embryos only, these experiments may be undertaken in accordance with the terms of this recommendation and subject to prior authorisation from the health or scientific authorities or, where applicable, the national multidisciplinary body" (Council of Europe, 1989, p. 6).

Conclusion

Since André Hellegers's 1978 essay, the ethical discussion of research involving implanted fetuses and live, aborted fetuses has matured, but it has proceeded largely along the lines established in the 1970s. In contrast, the success of clinical in vitro fertilization has given new impetus to the ethical debate about research on preimplantation embryos. In the future it is at least possible that new methods for sustained embryo and

Ethics advisory bodies of the 1970s and '80s were far from unanimous in their evaluations of research involving preimplantation embryos.

PAGE 240

Coercion relies in some manner on force or threats.

PAGE 59

fetal culture in vitro will give rise to additional ethical challenges.

— LEROY WALTERS

The previous is an update of the first-edition article by the late André E. Hellegers—Ed.

FREEDOM AND COERCION

Freedom is a desirable component of human personalities, interpersonal relationships, and social and governmental arrangements, but the concept is difficult to define. To some, "What is freedom?" can seem a futile question (Arendt, 1968); but existentialists, pragmatists, linguistic analysts, deontologists, utilitarians, liberals, conservatives, and others have given many answers. Analyses of the idea of freedom and assessments of its value have sources in many disciplines. The great English poet John Milton's *Areopagitica* is a classic defense of freedom, and much other literature concerns itself with freedom (Bolt, 1962; Kazantzakis, 1953; Morrison, 1987).

Freedom is a complex notion, a family or cluster of ideas that applies to a wide range of phenomena. Isaiah Berlin said that there are more than 200 senses of the word "freedom" (Berlin, 1970). This entry concentrates on a few meanings that have, or that are easily mistaken to have, logical connections with "coercion."

Kinds of freedom

A number of ideas and terms that should be distinguished from freedom are often associated with it. "Liberty" seems at first to be synonymous with "freedom"; but we do not speak of an animal's liberty, although we may speak of its freedom. This suggests that freedom and liberty are not perfectly synonymous. Liberty refers primarily to political freedom, but there are many other kinds of freedom. Hanna Pitkin claims that liberty presumes a formal relationship with government (Pitkin, 1972); and Joel Feinberg defines liberty as "the absence of legal coercion" (Feinberg, 1984, p. 7), which means that options for individuals are left open by the state. "Liberation," as in "women's liberation" or "animal liberation," suggests a struggle to change the fixed values and practices of a culture. Being "at liberty" to do something means that we have no duty to refrain from it and have claims against others that they not interfere with our doing it (Feinberg, 1986). Point of view sometimes matters: Escaped prisoners say they are "free," while law enforcement officials say they are "at large." "A free country" can mean that no other country dominates it, but inside such a country individual persons may in fact be very unfree. One can feel unfree because of dependence on others. "Feeling free" denies feeling scrutinized, regulated, or out of control.

Freedom contrasts with restrictions. Limitations or constraints inhibit or negate different kinds of freedom, but only some kinds of restrictions are coercive. Some constraints are internal to persons, some external; some are negative, some positive.

FEINBERG'S FOUR CONSTRAINTS

1. internal negative (e.g., weakness)
2. internal positive (fear)
3. external negative (lack of money)
4. external positive (being handcuffed)

POSITIVE EXTERNAL FREEDOM. Positive external freedom consists in having the external means to achieve our ends and fulfill our desires or interests. It involves the availability of resources in the environment, such as schools open to all, or medical resources and personnel. Patients in great pain who desire medication may be fortunate to have compassionate doctors who give them the means to relieve pain; those with uncaring or inattentive doctors may be denied the means to pain relief and lack positive external freedom. A pregnant woman who wants an abortion but lacks the means to pay for it lacks the positive external freedom to have the abortion. Whether society should pay for abortions for the poor, thereby enhancing their positive external freedom, is highly controversial.

Isaiah Berlin (1970) and Frithjof Bergman (1977), among others, developed the distinction between internal and external freedom. They contend that the mere absence of external constraints and the presence of external means is not enough for freedom in the fullest sense. True freedom involves something internal to the person.

NEGATIVE INTERNAL FREEDOM. Negative internal freedom is the absence of internal psychological or physiological obstructions that inhibit the fulfillment of goals, desires, and interests. Persons so overcome by temptation, rage, jealousy, or sexual passion that they temporarily lose control of themselves or those confused or overwhelmed by unconscious processes, psychoses, neuroses, compulsions, addictions, and other nonvoluntary character defects and disorders generally lack negative internal freedom. Genetic and neuromuscular conditions involving pain, weakness, or hyperactivity also constrain negative internal freedom. Should the idea of negative constraints include internally functioning physical processes that have external causes? The answer is not completely clear; but if it is affirmative, then negative internal freedom is also lacking if individuals are temporarily stupefied by alcohol or by recreational or psychotropic drugs; if they are more permanently brain damaged or retarded; if they lose independence as a result of a degenerative disease; or if they are controlled and their options reduced by lobotomies, psychosurgery, hypnosis, behavior modification, or indoctrination. Used skillfully with the informed, voluntary consent of patients, many psychotherapies can increase human freedom rather than reduce it. Sigmund Freud thought that increasing the freedom of patients was the major purpose of psychoanalysis.

POSITIVE INTERNAL FREEDOM. Positive internal freedom consists in the effective presence of all internal factors that contribute to fulfilling one's goals, desires, and interests; to being self-reliant, one's own master; and to being in control of one's life. It requires the possession of certain elements of character, such as self-mastery—the ability to choose what to value, and having adequate mental resources and skills to choose rightly. Isaiah Berlin emphasized the presence of "my own, not other men's acts of will"; being "a subject, not an object"; being "moved by reasons, by conscious purposes, which are my own"; being "somebody, not nobody; a doer—deciding, not being decided for, self-directed, . . . conceiving goals and policies of my own and realizing them"; and being above all "conscious of myself as a thinking, willing, active being, bearing responsibility for my choices, and able to explain them by reference to my own ideas and purposes" (Berlin, 1970, p. 131). Being positively free is what most medical ethicists mean by being autonomous, or rationally autonomous.

Bergman's interpretation of positive internal freedom accentuates the ability to identify ourselves with our values and choices.

> An act is free if the agent identifies with the elements from which it flows; it is coerced if the agent dissociates himself from the element which generates or prompts the action. . . . *Freedom is a function of identification and stands in a relationship of dependency to that with which a man identifies. . . . The primary condition of freedom is the possession of an identity, or of a self—freedom is the acting out of that identity.* (Bergman, 1977, p. 37)

Bergman shows how the idea of freedom may be incorporated by its bearer, how a self might predicate freedom of itself. Positive internal freedom is the self's identification with its actions, feelings, thoughts, with its own nature. Bergman identifies three main models of free self-identification. One is Platonic, one Aristotelian, and one fashioned after the protagonist in Fyodor Dostoyevsky's *Notes from the Underground* (Dostoyevsky, 1960). Each model has implications for how patients experience elements of the medical world—the doctor-patient relationship, informed consent, the nature of their maladies, and the role of treatment.

A Platonic self identifies only with the purely rational, narrowly defined as products of mind that can be shown to be coherent and consistent. An Aristotelian self identifies with rationality but also with having an animal nature, and does not dissociate from all of its impulses and idiosyncratic desires. Underground selves do not identify with much of anything—not with rationality nor with any of their own impulses. They are inconsistent and undirected and can never achieve positive freedom.

Many ethicists believe that freedom of will is an essential part of positive internal freedom. Free will involves more than a capacity for making choices, for there may be both free and unfree choices. Free choices are creative, originative, or "contracausal"; and choices are not free if completely determined by antecedently existing desires, beliefs, or other conditions. Being responsible for decisions and actions depends on whether they originate with us, as opposed to being programmed into us by heredity, physical or social environment, fate, or God, even if we are influenced by them (Edwards, 1969; Erde, 1978).

Isaiah Berlin calls attention to problematic features of positive freedom. The idea of positive freedom may be developed in a way that splits the notion of the self into a higher real or true self and a lower apparent or experiential self. Positive freedom belongs only to the real or true self and involves suppressing or eliminating the apparent self, thus turning people against themselves.

From the time of the Stoics, many philosophers identified the true self with reason, and thus freedom was control of or complete escape from desires and feelings. The ascetic strain in Christianity found these themes congenial. For Immanuel Kant, only the real, rational lawgiving self was free, not the apparent self given in experience. Georg W. F. Hegel identified being rational with being free. Jean-Jacques Rousseau (1950) distinguished what the majority actually wants, "the will of all," from what it would want if it were well enough informed and sufficiently intelligent, "the general will." Rousseau contended that the general will for the common good should be forced on unwilling members of society (Berlin, 1970). But who or what is the proper interpreter of the general will? Rousseau's ambiguous answer waffled between the vote of the majority and the vote of enlightened legislators; but it was only a short step from the latter to the opinions of the self-appointed paternalist experts.

"Fear and freedom are mutually exclusive."

ERIC HOFFER
THE PASSIONATE STATE OF MIND, 1954

"Whatever crushes individuality is despotism, by whatever name it may be called."

JOHN STUART MILL
ON LIBERTY, 1859

When every person's true will is equated with the opinion of experts, positive freedom endangers negative freedom. Rousseau was willing to "force men to be free," which meant forcing them to obey laws expressing the general will for the common good. The enlightened expert would become the authentic spokesman for humanity's true, real, or general will (Berlin, 1970). Thus, by forcing men to be free, Rousseau meant forcing them to accept what experts (like himself, or enlightened legislators) believe to be best for them in ways that decrease their freedom of action. Such a theory of positive freedom enables elitists, paternalists, and totalitarians to turn freedom upon itself. Berlin says, "Once I take this view, I am in a position to ignore the actual wishes of men or societies, to bully, oppress, torture them in the name, and on behalf, of their 'real' selves . . . the free choice of [mankind's] 'true,' albeit often submerged and inarticulate, self" (1970, p. 133).

There are perplexities about the logical and moral structure of positive freedom, especially as it relates to other forms of freedom. In addressing some of these perplexities, Gerald MacCallum, Jr., proposes a schema for the concept of freedom. He follows Berlin's characterization of negative freedom as "freedom from" constraints, and of positive freedom as "freedom to" act because we have the necessary resources. MacCallum argues that both are aspects of a more complex, three-variable concept: "______ is free from ______ to do (or omit, or be, or have) ______" (MacCallum, 1967). Statements about freedom that omit the terms indicated by any of the blanks are incomplete. "Joe is free to vote Democratic" fails to mention what Joe is free from (threats, prejudices, or previous promises).

MacCallum's analysis helps clarify the logic of the concept of freedom, but it seems incomplete. The fullest schema should incorporate the perspective of positive freedom, as in "______ is free from ______ to do (have, etc.) ______ because (of) ______." The final blank makes a place for positive freedom. Consider: "Joe is free from prejudice to vote Democratic because he faced the influence of greed on the Republican way of thought." Here, having a reflective perspective fills in the final blank.

Some concepts of positive freedom may thus degenerate into a paternalistic or totalitarian elitism that rationalizes coercion of "inferiors" for their own good. To some theorists, negative external freedom for the masses is anathema (Popper, 1963). Dostoyevsky's Grand Inquisitor argues that most people lack both sufficient intelligence and fortitude (Dostoyevsky, 1960). The masses need a benevolent authoritarian because they are too weak to live with the horrible truth about suffering, death, and meaninglessness; they need miracles, mystery, and authority—a set of lies and enforced commands—in order to be happy. The Grand Inquisitor's paternalism is powerfully present in medicine's history, and the Inquisitor is an analogue for the physician in some models (Brody, 1991).

NEGATIVE EXTERNAL FREEDOM. Negative external freedom is the absence of external pressures and constraints. It is the most obvious contrast with coercion. Freedom is external to the individual person in relationship to external constraints; it is negative in the absence of external constraints, some of which are coercive. Negative freedom and lack of positive external constraints are equivalent: both consist in the absence of external restraining forces. "Joe jumped freely" alleges that Joe was not pushed, threatened, or drunk. "Joy entered the mental hospital freely" denies that she was committed or coerced by governmental power or family pressures.

Negative external freedom is often called freedom of action, the ability to do what we want or choose to do, unencumbered by external restraints such as chains, shackles, walls, or jails or by external constraints such as laws, institutional prohibitions, or coercive pressures from other people. Absence of encumbrances usually correlates with increased options for choice.

Many species of positive external freedom are recognized and cherished. The First Amendment to the U.S. Constitution distinguishes and affirms many kinds of freedom of action—freedom of religion, freedom of speech, freedom of the press, freedom to assemble peaceably, and freedom to petition government for a redress of grievances. As kinds of freedom of action, these constitutionally guaranteed rights mean that government, as are other institutions and individual persons, is forbidden to interfere with our choice of religion, with expressing our thoughts, with our efforts to communicate beliefs, knowledge, and ideas through the press and other media, and so on. Yet, all these kinds of freedom of action have their limits even in law; none is absolute or without qualification.

Historically, many classes of individuals were externally unfree in a great variety of ways. The fullest enjoyment of external positive freedom in the United States was once limited to competent landowning white males, while severe restrictions were imposed on the freedom of action of females, slaves, nonwhites, minors, mentally disabled persons, the landless, and other disfavored groups. Gradually, as prejudices waned, usually after prolonged and bitter struggles, both the socially allowable scope and the kinds of freedom of action were extended. In the latter part of the twentieth century, freedom found new foci. The civil rights movement that began in the United States in the 1960s led to the women's liberation and gay rights movements; a similar revolution led to the end of apartheid in the Republic of South Africa in 1994.

Worldwide, many groups advocate on behalf of animals. "Animal liberation" opposes killing animals for food or in medical experimentation and by hurtful uses in rodeos, zoos, and other forms of entertainment for humans. The scope of application for the concept of freedom of action is constantly evolving.

Coercion and freedom of action

Can morally legitimate limits to freedom of action be identified and distinguished from illegitimate limits? Is coercion always illegitimate, or is it sometimes morally justified? To answer, we must have a clear concept of coercion. According to Tom Beauchamp and James Childress, "Coercion . . . occurs if and only if one person intentionally uses a credible and severe threat of harm or force to control another. The threat of force or punishment used by some police, courts, and hospitals in acts of involuntary commitment for psychiatric treatment is a typical form of coercion. Society's use of compulsory vaccination laws is another" (Beauchamp and Childress, 1994, p. 164). Beauchamp and Childress capture the core of the concept of coercion, as ordinarily understood. Coercion is a relationship between at least two persons. Coercers may be acting as private individuals, or they may be playing an institutional role like law enforcement officer or functionary of a court or hospital. Coercers intentionally threaten those coerced with harm if they do not bend to the coercer's will. Those coerced clearly perceive that they are being threatened. Coercion restricts freedom of action, not by reducing the alternatives available to those coerced but by increasing the cost of pursuing the alternatives that they favor (Feinberg, 1986). When thieves say, "Your money or your life," they present their victims with an unwelcome forced choice. Their clear preference for saving their lives is not eliminated, but the cost of doing so dramatically increases. As Joel Feinberg says, "In general, effective coercion closes the [combined] option of noncompliance *and* avoidance of the threatened cost, while keeping open either without the other" (Feinberg, 1986, p. 192). Coercion can be resisted, nearly always at a very high price.

Coercive pressures come in degrees, depending on how much the victim values and disvalues the options allotted by the coercer. Under certain circumstances, a patient might lose control and consent to treatment (invalidly), almost as a reflex. If a patient refuses to have a broken leg pinned and, in an attempt to change her mind, someone pulls on her leg without her con-

FREEDOM AND COERCION

The Value of Freedom

What kind of value does freedom have? Philosophers distinguish between intrinsic values—things desirable for their own sake; instrumental values—things desirable as means to ends; and side constraints—things necessary for living together peacefully in a pluralistic society in which many people honestly disagree about values.

Positive internal freedom is perhaps the most plausible candidate for the status of an intrinsic good, for it consists of all the resources that constitute capable and responsible individual selfhood. Cherishing it for its own sake is prizing the fullness of our own unique individuality. Hedonistic utilitarians, who think that only pleasure is intrinsically good, are inconsistent if they value positive internal freedom as an end in itself. John Stuart Mill came very close to this inconsistency in his *On Liberty* (1947). As opponents see it, the fact that hedonistic utilitarians must treat even positive internal freedom as nothing more than a very great instrumental good for producing pleasure or happiness reveals a major inadequacy of their theory. Even if freedom is good in itself, Mill correctly noted the intrinsic satisfaction derived from acting freely.

Positive external freedom is by definition a means to other ends; and it would be peculiar, to say the least, if negativities or absences, whether those of internal or external freedom, are good in themselves. These forms of freedom seem more like instrumental conditions for the realization of the positive goods of life. All forms of freedom are immensely useful, indeed absolutely essential, in pursuing most human interests; but some freedom is also intrinsically good, most ethicists believe. Basic human welfare consists largely in being free in the fullest possible sense.

Ethicists like H. Tristram Engelhardt, Jr., emphasize the importance of negative external freedom as a side constraint, that is, as a "basic, minimum presupposition of ethics" to which all parties can commonly assent. It is the sole means for peaceable coexistence among persons in a pluralistic society who disagree about intrinsic values, including the value of freedom, but who are nevertheless committed to resolving disputes without resorting to force. A universal basic commitment to freedom generates a tolerant society in which many distinctive values and moral perspectives can flourish (Engelhardt, 1986). But do we have a common basic interest only in freedom?

— REM B. EDWARDS
EDMUND L. ERDE

sent, that is coercive if there is an implied threat to inflict more pain.

If this analysis of "coercion" is accepted, most constraints on freedom clearly do not count as coercion. Language is misused when anything that limits or constrains behavior is called coercive. If Beauchamp and Childress are right, only other agents can be coercers. Unless someone else deliberately deprives them of resources in order to control them, those who lack means to their ends are not coercively denied negative external freedom. Poor people who cannot afford to buy a new car are not coerced into carlessness by poverty itself. Poor women who cannot afford abortions are not coerced to have unwanted babies just because they are poor, and poor students who cannot afford advanced education are not coerced into a career choice. Internal constraints like rages, jealousies, passions, psychoses, neuroses, and so on definitely deprive persons of negative internal freedom; but these constraints are not coercive because they are not external, and there are not other persons making threats. Internal constraints that interfere with positive internal freedom are not coercive for the same reasons. External natural conditions like storms and earthquakes that constrain negative external freedom of action are not coercive because they are not agents, no matter how threatening they might be.

The Chinese family-planning program has used compulsion more extensively than has any other national program.

PAGE 548

Some philosophers suggest additional qualifications of the analysis of coercion. The concept is fuzzy at the edges. Disagreements about where to draw lines and how to deal with borderline cases are inevitable and are usually settled by stipulation. Consider the following proposed modifications.

Can nonpersonal external things like natural processes count as coercers? Unlike Beauchamp and Childress, Feinberg thinks that they can; threatened rock slides and hurricanes may exert pressures that significantly increase the costs of pursuing their interests on those making decisions about whether to travel (Feinberg, 1986). Similarly, for those who think before acting, the risk of getting acquired immunodeficiency syndrome (AIDS) can significantly increase the cost of pursuing some sexual interests.

Liberty is the absence of rule-imposed limitations on action . . . and freedom is the presence of open options.

PAGE 60

Must coercers use only the threat of force and not force itself? Like Beauchamp and Childress, Feinberg calls the actual use of force "compulsion" rather than "coercion" and insists that compulsion closes options, whereas coercion makes them more costly to pursue (Feinberg, 1986). However, others, like Michael D. Bayles (Pennock and Chapman, 1972) and the *Dictionary of the Social Sciences*, cited by J. Roland Pennock (Pennock and Chapman, 1972), have no difficulty in calling the actual use of force "coercion."

Must the mechanism of coercive pressure always be negative—like threats or the actual use of force? Or may the intentional use of intense positive pressures be coercive? Here there is much disagreement. Biomedical research on prisoners has been strictly supervised in the last few decades because prisons are considered to be highly coercive environments; protections for students, who are vulnerable to the graders' power, and for hospital patients, who are vulnerable to the physicians' power, issue from similar concerns.

If, to gain consent, vulnerable persons like prisoners, students, or patients are offered benefits or advantages to which they are not otherwise entitled, is that coercion, manipulation, or exploitation? When prisoners are enticed by drug companies to become subjects for testing new drugs by promises of better living conditions, early parole, more opportunities for entertainment, conjugal visits, and so on, are they thereby coerced into compliance in a manner that invalidates the voluntariness of informed voluntary consent? Besides coercion, deceit, exaggeration, manipulation, exploitation, enticement, or undue incentives may control persons and thereby invalidate informed voluntary consent. These incentives should be avoided by conscientious medical professionals. If anesthetized female patients are used without their knowledge or consent to teach medical students how to do pelvic examinations, these patients are not coerced, not conscious of a threat; but clearly they are wronged.

Are total institutions so inherently coercive that coercion invalidates voluntariness? The answer depends in part on the intensity or irresistibility of the positive inducements, but the crucial consideration is whether positive incentives, or only negative reinforcements, properly belong to the concept of coercion. Beauchamp and Childress (1994) exclude positive incentives, as do Robert Nozick (1969) and Bernard Gert (Pennock and Chapman, 1972). However, Feinberg clearly favors calling abnormally attractive offers coercive (Feinberg, 1986), as do Virginia Held (Pennock and Chapman, 1972) and Donald McIntosh (Pennock and Chapman, 1972). Those who include positive incentives in the concept of coercion usually argue that the crucial consideration is not whether the coercive mechanism is negative but whether it is the kind of thing that a normal or rational person might reasonably be expected to resist (Pennock and Chapman, 1972).

Morally acceptable and unacceptable uses of coercion

Is coercion always wrong or morally unacceptable? Beauchamp and Childress cite the use or threat of force by police, courts, and hospitals, and society's use of compulsory vaccination laws as typical examples of coercion; but they do not thereby mean to suggest that involuntary civil commitment and compulsory vaccination are morally wrong just because they are coercive. It is not always wrong to try to control others by coercive or other manipulative means.

Often there are valid moral justifications for using coercion. Parental coercion of children is inevitable at times, but not thereby wrong. Good laws, penalties for noncompliance, and proper enforcement mechanisms like the police, the courts, and the prisons exist for the sake of coercing lawless persons into behaving themselves. Coercive deterrents are perfectly in order when society confronts those who commit crimes such as murder, rape, or pillage. A defense force that is strong enough to be a credible and severe threat of harm to hostile nations serves a morally valid but coercive purpose. Rational persons do not want to live in a society without laws, police, prisons, and military protection; such a society would not last very long. Sometimes violent patients must be controlled coercively to protect other patients and members of the medical staff. Pedophiles and pyromaniacs do not live merely an "alternative lifestyle"; their predilections result in great harm to the persons and/or properties of others; and they must be deterred or stopped—coercively if necessary. With no qualms of conscience, college professors threaten students with bad grades to motivate them to improve their learning and performance; occasionally they promise better grades than earned in exchange for sexual and other favors.

Thus, using coercion is often, but not always, the morally right thing to do. Other human values besides freedom must be protected coercively. But when is coercion morally unacceptable? And how can we tell when it places morally unjustifiable limits on freedom?

We will consider a few of the most important and influential answers, beginning with the one accepted almost universally as most basic. In *On Liberty*, John Stuart Mill asked about the nature and limits of power that legitimately can be exercised over other individuals. He answered:

> *The sole end for which mankind are warranted, individually or collectively, in interfering with the liberty of action of any of their number, is self-protection. . . . The only purpose for which power can rightfully be exercised over any member of a civilized community, against his will, is to prevent harm to others. His own good, either physical or moral, is not a sufficient warrant.* *(Mill, 1947, ch. 1)*

Of course, the nature of "harm" and the relevant degree of its seriousness must be clarified, as Mill and others try to do (Feinberg, 1984, 1985, 1986).

Mill's "harm to others" principle justifies the use of coercion against those who would harm others, but not against those who would harm themselves, as long as

FREEDOM WRITER

In On Liberty, John Stuart Mill (1806–1873) questioned when and how power can legitimately be exercised over other individuals.

they are competent adults "in the maturity of their faculties." Mill accepted a weak paternalism designed to protect children, minors, and people who are not "capable of being improved by free and equal discussion" from self-harm. Unfortunately, the line between things that harm others and that harm the self is not always clearly drawn; many harms to the self often result in harms to others, as with drunk drivers; but this does not mean the distinction is useless.

Although Mill regarded the "harm to others" principle as the only consideration that legitimates coercive constraints on freedom of action, other ethicists propose additional liberty-limiting or coercion-legitimizing principles. Feinberg considers "the offense principle" that authorizes preventing serious offenses to others, the "legal paternalism" principle that would prevent self-harm by a competent self, the "legal moralism" principle that would prohibit inherently immoral conduct, and several others (Feinberg, 1984). He regards only the "harm to others" and "offense" principles to be valid (Feinberg, 1984).

Freedom, paternalism, and coercion in the practice of medicine

Many questions about negative freedom of action and its proper limits arise within the practice of medicine. Is it a legitimate restriction of the right to freedom of speech when government forbids medical professionals to inform patients about legal medical interventions that government officials oppose? What balances should be struck when physician freedom conflicts with patient freedom? Should medical professionals be free to abstain from providing services to which they have moral objections—like withholding nutrition and fluids from patients who will die without them, or participating in performing abortions? Should competent

See Also

Sociobiology: How 'Predestined' Are We?

FREEDOM AND COERCION

Freedom, Paternalism, and Coercion in the Practice of Medicine

"Debate on public issues should be uninhibited, robust, and wide open."

WILLIAM J. BRENNAN, JR.
NEW YORK TIMES CO. V. SULLIVAN, 1964

"The only index by which to judge a government or a way of life is by the quality of the people it acts upon."

ERIC HOFFER
THE PASSIONATE STATE OF MIND, 1954

adult patients be free to choose among and refuse treatments? Should terminally ill patients be free to refuse all life-sustaining procedures, including nutrition and fluids? Should a pregnant woman be free to demand that any qualified physician give her an abortion at any time during pregnancy and for any reason? Does academic freedom give medical researchers the right to investigate all questions of interest, no matter what happens to patients, and without any restrictions at all? Should pro-life groups be free to protest on the grounds of, or just outside, abortion clinics? Should anyone, including prisoners and persons who are mentally ill or retarded, be free to decide whether to enroll as subjects in experiments? Should persons with AIDS be free to enter into drug trials earlier than standard enrollment practices permit? In which of these situations is freedom of action morally justified, and in which is it not? On what grounds, if any, should the freedom of action of patients or of medical professionals be restricted? Do any of these situations involve coercion, justified or unjustified? In which, if any, of these situations should freedom of action be restricted by the "harm to others" principle or the "offense to others" principle? Do other liberty-limiting principles apply to these situations?

Mill and many contemporary medical ethicists find that strong paternalistic medical uses of coercion against competent adults are morally unacceptable. Paternalists believe that they know what is best for others and act upon this belief. In medicine, valid consent must be informed, competent, and voluntary. The ideal of informed voluntary consent requires that patients' own judgments about what is beneficial or best for themselves should prevail. Being informed is incompatible with passively accepting that others, like doctors, always know best. Informing patients properly requires effective communication with them concerning the nature of the relevant medical proceedings, their risks, benefits, alternatives, and the right to refuse. Ignorance, deceit, and misinformation can interfere significantly with freedom. Being competent is incompatible with severe mental encumbrances. Being voluntary is incompatible with coercion and requires that patients have negative external freedom of action. Valid consent is uncoerced. Ties between freedom and medical ethics are ancient; but they have changed greatly since the Hippocratic Oath avowed that the sick, whether slave or free, would be treated for their own benefit—as determined by physicians.

Is there any place for paternalism in medicine? Is freedom such a great good or strong side constraint that competent patients must be free to make even costly mistakes? Since physicians usually determine who is and who is not competent, does not freedom-limiting paternalism inevitably creep back in when determining competency? One of the most difficult questions of medical ethics is whether competent adult patients should ever be coerced into being free on the basis of the paternalistic judgment that being free is in their best interests. If freedom is such a strong requirement, should it ever be temporarily diminished coercively for the sake of its long-run enhancement, especially when it can be predicted that patients are highly likely to express retrospective gratitude for such coercion?

Occasionally, extremely passive patients, or those weakened by disease and pain, do not want to know the medical options or to make treatment decisions for themselves, so they say to their doctors, "Just do what you think is best for me." When treatment decisions that will have an enormous impact on their future lives must be made, should doctors allow these patients to choose freely not to exercise their freedom? Some ethicists believe in positive internal freedom to the extent that they reject a free or autonomous renunciation of choice. Others hold that forcing people to be free is always an unacceptable violation of their rights and selfhood (Feinberg, 1986).

Should doctors coercively threaten to withhold all treatment, including pain medication, from patients who abdicate freedom, until they are ready to act as responsible moral agents, to listen to a full explanation of the medical options, and to participate in making treatment decisions for themselves? Some ethicists insist that patients should not be allowed to abdicate being free moral agents, and that doctors are morally obligated to try to restore or enhance patients' freedom or autonomy—coercively if necessary (Komrad, 1983; Brock, 1983). Taking one side or another in this debate depends largely on one's judgment about whether the "real self" of the patients is present to refuse to exercise its autonomy, or whether in the future that self is likely to say, "Thank you, doctor, for coercing me into exercising my freedom!"

— REM B. EDWARDS
EDMUND L. ERDE

G

GENDER IDENTITY AND GENDER-IDENTITY DISORDERS

The term "gender" has a long etymological history in Latin roots signifying birth, race, and kind, and in Greek roots signifying birth, race, and family. In contemporary usage, the term generally signifies the male or female nature or identity of a person. That meaning, however, is more complex than might first appear. A satisfactory understanding of gender will contribute significantly not only to an understanding of gender-identity disorders but also to the ways in which the notion of gender is otherwise important to the theory and practice of medicine.

Despite the temptation to designate all human beings as either male or female, human sexual diversity is not easily confined by those simple categories. Human gender has at least chromosomal, hormonal, anatomical, psychic, and social components. Given the variability that is possible among such components, males are not all interchangeable replicas of one another, and neither are females. Neither are the male and the female always especially distinct from one another. The "male" and the "female" have fluid rather than fixed borders. For example, some human beings are born with an extra sex chromosome, resulting in XXY or XYY genetic complements; the former appear eunuchoid as adults and the latter appear male. In Turner's syndrome only a single X chromosome is present; individuals with this variation appear female though they will be infertile by reason of undifferentiated gonads. With regard to anatomy, some persons are born with both ovarian and testicular tissue or with ambiguous genitalia. Individuals within and between genders can vary, too, with respect to hormone traits that drive the development of bodily and behavioral traits. The range of human sexual traits extends even more widely in psychological qualities and social behavior inasmuch as cultural notions of masculinity and femininity—normative notions about how maleness and femaleness should be expressed—vary widely. Gender is thus a complex notion with both biological and cultural components.

Much contemporary feminist, anthropological, and gay and lesbian analysis has taken pains to differentiate biological components of sex and socially constructed components of gender. Attention to gender as an element of ethical analysis permits attention to matters that otherwise might be neglected: how notions of male and female are connected to matters of authority and power, how relations between genders are structured, how personal and social identities are constituted, and how justice may be analyzed in terms of gender. For instance, a number of scholars have shown that medicine has compromised women's interests. Women's lives have been medicalized much more than men's lives. Emotions, menstruation, and menopause, for example, have been subject to medical interpretations that have treated female traits as defects to be remedied (Apple, 1990). Women are often disproportionately hospitalized, medicated, and treated surgically, and they have been historically excluded from the professional practice of medicine (Walsh, 1977). Women also have been neglected in biomedical experimentation; consequently, biomedicine has assumed that males are an adequate research base for treating women and has ignored possible differences required in the health care of women. The treatment women have received often has been defined in relation to a gender "standard" based on male and female reproductive roles. Some feminist analysis has found that medical practices surrounding childbirth infantilize women (Laslie, 1982). Debates about "maternal-fetal" conflicts may mask a male valuation of children at the expense of the reproductive rights of women. Access to contraceptives, abortion, in vitro fertilization, and embryo implantation also have been criticized as exemplifying male mistrust of and hegemony over women (Smart, 1987). These examples make it clear that the theory and practice of medicine should not assume a neutral identity between the male and the female in the way health care is theorized or delivered.

What remains to be accomplished by greater attention to gender is the larger task of identifying ways in which biomedicine can accommodate the interests of persons regardless of gender-related differences and ways in which medicine can become less constrained by unjustifiable gender assumptions. This article takes up some of the representative ways in which the notion of gender is important to ethical analysis regarding gender identity, health, and sexual orientation.

◆ **gender**
Generally signifies the male or female nature or identity of a person, based on chromosomal, hormonal, anatomical, psychic, and social components.

See Also
Homosexuality

G

GENDER IDENTITY AND GENDER-IDENTITY DISORDERS

Gender-Identity Disorders

Gender-identity disorders

Gender-identity disorders are discordances between one's felt gender and one's assigned gender. These discordances may be especially acute in regard to expectations about appropriate behavior for a particular gender. Ordinarily, most persons experience themselves as male or female and express themselves in ways congruent with social expectations and roles accorded to that gender. At a very early age, however, small numbers of individuals discover themselves uncomfortable with the gender identity being imposed on them by virtue of their anatomy. This discomfort is not merely a sense of being inadequate in a particular gender role, it is discomfort with being identified as one gender rather than another. Such disorders range from comparatively mild discomfort to outright rejection of the designated gender.

Children may manifest gender disorders through rejection of stereotypic clothing or play activities, disavowal of actual anatomic characteristics, and, sometimes, assertions that they will grow up to be members of the opposite sex. The degree of severity varies, and some children eventually moderate or give up their determination to identify as members of the opposite sex. Rather more boys than girls with such childhood manifestations have homoerotic sexual orientations as adults, but neither males nor females usually retain in adulthood strong desires to be members of the opposite sex or beliefs that they are "trapped" in the wrong kind of body. Adolescents and adults, too, may have transient

GENDER ASSIGNMENT
Sometimes Not So Simple

A newborn's gender is a matter of concern for both parents and physicians, but sometimes a child's traits do not permit an easy classification as male or female. Children may be born with irregular gonads or, as mentioned above, ambiguous genitalia and atypical chromosomal traits. Gender assignment refers to the decision made to designate a newborn as either male or female. The traits that are taken as establishing a child's "real" gender reflect not only the state of biomedical knowledge but also cultural and moral standards about what traits are most important in gender identities.

Tests to determine the presence of testes, ovaries, and levels of various hormones in children with ambiguous genitalia are now available to physicians, as are surgical techniques to construct female genitalia and methods of enlarging some exceptionally small penises. Such tests were not always available, and these same methods may not be available even now in some regions of the world. Historically, children were matched to one gender rather than another on the basis of physical resemblance or the presence or absence of testes and ovaries. Such methods could not, however, distinguish humans with true intersexed conditions (in which both testicular and ovarian tissue is present), and they failed to be sensitive to the complexity of human sexual identity. Chromosomal and hormonal tests offer another way of characterizing the gender of children, but such methods still may presuppose that a child's gender is given as either male or female. Testing of this kind assumes that human beings are bifurcated neatly into male and female, and that children with ambiguous gender need only be studied carefully in order to determine their place in that order.

Gender-assignment decisions and therapy, however, make it clear that gender can be as much a product of human choice as of biological traits. Use of the term "assignment" suggests that gender is conferred rather than discovered. Even if the opportunity for postnatal assignment of the gender of children is not routinely offered to parents, prevailing theories of medical management of ambiguously gendered children suggest that any child's gender is moldable through early application of medical and psychological methods (Money and Ehrhardt, 1972). That gender assignment consists of more than mere discovery of gender as it has been obscured by ambiguous anatomy or genetics makes clear gender's connections to cultural standards of masculinity and femininity.

Suzanne J. Kessler has identified a number of ways in which cultural ideals about the male, the female, and a dimorphically gendered society influence the practice of gender assignment (Kessler, 1991). She has described how gender-assignment decisions sometimes are made primarily on the basis of the expected size and function of a child's genitalia rather than on more complex assessments of genetic and endocrinological tests. Kessler thinks that children may be assigned as female if physicians and parents view them as having an inadequately sized penis, a view that not only reduces male gender to genital appearance but also perpetuates a notion of femaleness as a kind of failed maleness. There is no question that biogenetic features shape the sexuality and behavior of each and every individual, but it appears just as true that social and moral judgments also profoundly influence an individual's gender identity. This is to say that gender is not merely a function of chromosomal, hormonal, or anatomical traits. Acknowledging that social influences, often unconsciously, play a role in gender assignment requires resisting the view that gender is merely given in the raw material of human biology. Acknowledging these social influences also requires paying attention to the way in which sexist or other prejudicial views may guide decisions about a child's "real" gender.

— TIMOTHY F. MURPHY

or lingering beliefs that they belong to the opposite sex, and in addition to declarations about the inappropriateness of their bodies and expected social roles, they may cross-dress, though not for purposes of sexual satisfaction and without the desire to achieve new anatomical sex characteristics. In the most extreme cases, however, some individuals retain a strong opposite-gender identification and do seek to conform their behavior and anatomy to the chosen gender. (This phenomenon of transsexualism is discussed in the next section.) Numerous and often competing theories have been offered to account for the occurrence of gender "dysphoria," as gender dissatisfaction has been called, and these theories variously suggest heritable traits, family dynamics, early physical illness, and early psychic events as among the causes (American Psychiatric Association (APA), 1987).

The nature of parental and health-professional response to gender dysphoria is of moral interest in a number of ways. It is interesting to note, for example, that the chief impairment attributed to gender-identity disorders is the generation of conflict between those affected and their peers and family. It is also recognized as impairing social and occupational functioning. While those affected may sometimes be depressed and may have other psychic disorders, many affected individuals claim that except for social difficulties, they are not especially disturbed by their felt gender preferences. The question may be posed, then, whose purposes treatment of gender-identity disorders serves.

Given a history in which moral preferences were sometimes encoded in psychiatric diagnoses, contemporary psychiatry has attempted to divest itself of responsibility for the enforcement of moral or political values. The APA has stated: "Neither deviant behavior, e.g., political, religious, or sexual, nor conflicts that are primarily between the individual and society are mental disorders unless the deviance or conflict is a symptom of a dysfunction in the person" that generates persistent stress, disability, or significant risk of suffering, death, pain, disability, or loss of freedom (1987, p. xxii). One may ask, in light of this definition, whether gender-identity treatments do in fact reinforce larger social expectations about appropriate gender identifications and behaviors. It may be replied that children and adolescents affected by gender dysphoria often face significant depression and restriction of opportunities as a result of their nonconforming beliefs and behaviors, and that for this reason treatment is morally appropriate because measures to protect a child from undue conflict and depression are a parent's prerogative. It does not follow, of course, that a parent might do anything at all in order to achieve a particular gender identity or behavior in a child. Insofar as social considerations are relevant to establishing the morality of a particular therapy, one would still need to consider the extent to which children and adolescents might be treated because they live in a society dominated by a view of mutually exclusive gender roles untrue to the diversity of human beings. The debate about the social influences on choices regarding gender dysphoria has thus far occurred primarily in relation to adults rather than children, and it will be profitable to consider the debate from perspectives on adult transsexualism.

Transsexualism

The term "transsexualism" was first used in the 1940s to describe adults who verbally and behaviorally identified themselves as male or female in contradiction to their anatomical sex and the behavior expected of that sex. (The term is to be distinguished from "transvestism," which describes persons who dress as members of the opposite sex but do not identify themselves as members of that gender. Some persons may dress thus for sexual satisfaction.) Historically, transsexuals were thought to suffer from psychological disorders, and some health-care practitioners still maintain this view. Transsexual therapy in the sense we know it today, however, more typically describes a range of surgical, hormonal, and psychological therapies whose goal is to conform anatomy, secondary sex characteristics, and behavior to those of the desired gender. Surgical efforts may involve mastectomy, the removal of penis and scrotum, the construction—to the extent this is possible—of a penis or vagina, and accompanying hormonal treatments to spur the appropriate characteristics in hair, voice tone, fat distribution, and so on. Such treatment cannot, however, achieve sexual fertility in the chosen gender. Various components of this therapy have been attempted since the 1930s. In the 1950s, Christine Jorgensen, formerly George, became famous as a male transsexed to a female. Since then the term "transgender therapy" has often been used to describe this overall type of therapy. It should be noted that transgender therapy does not impose a particular sexual orientation on an individual. A client who undergoes female transgender therapy, for example, may identify herself as lesbian or as heterosexual after the therapy. Certainly not all persons who consider themselves "trapped" in the wrong anatomy desire transgender therapy, given its costs and limitations. Neither do all persons who want such therapy qualify for it, since transsexualism may be accompanied by other psychic disorders that make the therapy unlikely to improve the lot of the person seeking it.

Transgender therapy has important implications for a person's legal and social standing in professional associations, entitlement to marry, legal rights to be recognized as a member of the chosen gender, and so on. Transsexed Renee Richards won the right to play in women's professional tennis, but other transsexuals

◆ **transsexual**
a person with a psychological urge to belong to the opposite sex that may be carried to the point of undergoing surgery to modify the sex organs to mimic the opposite sex.

ETHICAL COMPLEXITIES IN TRANSGENDER THERAPY

A number of ethical questions attend the practice of transgender therapy, especially since it challenges the expectation that congenital anatomy is gender destiny. First of all, there is the conceptualization of requests to be transgendered. Such requests presuppose that one's gender cannot be reduced to genitalia or chromosomal birthright. Indeed, to move away from seeing transsexualism as a psychological disorder is to acknowledge not only the separability of psychic identity and biological sex but also that some aspects of gender are subject to choice. Even if one acknowledges that gender is not reducible to any single trait, it does not automatically follow that transgender therapy and its surgery and lifelong hormonal treatments are ethically proper. One might object to transgender therapy from a natural-law perspective if one argued that such therapy violated that tradition's principle of bodily integrity because the significant bodily alterations do not confer an appropriate benefit important to other natural-law objectives. On the other hand, if one assumes that gender identity is not reducible to biological characteristics, it is possible to argue within the natural-law tradition, as Robert H. Springer has done, that transgender therapy serves an important moral good insofar as it protects psychic health (Springer, 1987).

— TIMOTHY F. MURPHY

have not been so successful in securing equivalent rights. Individuals undergoing such therapy often face legal difficulties insofar as they might violate laws regarding cross-dressing and the use of public washrooms. Prison housing also raises special problems, since persons in transgender therapy are especially vulnerable to contemptuous treatment and violence.

Some feminist analysis has seen in transgender therapy the extension of patriarchal privilege insofar as male-to-female transgenderism is much more common than its opposite. Janice Raymond has argued that transgenderism trivializes women insofar as the therapy reduces femaleness to a trait that men may or may not adopt, as they wish. By contrast, but still in support of her argument about patriarchal privilege, she characterizes female-to-male transgenderism as an attempt to bypass constraints on female participation in male-dominated society (Raymond, 1979). Raymond does not call for a ban on transgender therapy, but she does believe that greater social accommodation of gender diversity in the context of a greater social emancipation of women would eliminate the incentives to transgender therapy, with its attendant evils.

Because the ratio of men to women who seek transgender therapy is not constant around the world, it is unclear that transgender therapy represents primarily male interests (Godlewski, 1988). It is also hard to see how persons suffering with gender dysphoria from an early age can be accurately described as choosing transgender therapy for trivial or trivializing reasons. Even if transgender therapy were fully implicated in the evils Raymond ascribes to it, she would be right to seek recourse for those evils in something other than a ban on the practice. It is certainly desirable to eradicate social evils, but there is no ethical principle maintaining that the only legitimate way to remove unwanted personal suffering is through the moral correction of the entire social order that may be causing or contributing to it. Utilitarian theory would lend support to the pursuit of the therapy. Utilitarian ethics not only advocates the greatest happiness for the greatest number of people; in John Stuart Mill's formulation it also relies on the libertarian principle, a principle of noninterference with individual pursuits insofar as they do not harm others. Attempting to find ways to conform bodily and behavioral traits to a felt psychic gender might promote the general good insofar as it leads to important biomedical advances in addition to whatever benefits it confers on particular individuals. Moreover, it is unclear that transgender therapy affects others in ways sufficiently harmful to justify foreclosing the option through legal or medical consensus. Nor would there be anything in an ethical approach like that of John Rawls, who relies on a kind of social contractarianism that would preclude the practice of transgender therapy (Rawls, 1971). Indeed, it would appear that in formulating the principles and policies by which a just society ought to be governed, his original social contractors would have to envisage a place for transsexuals and accommodate in principle their therapeutic interests.

That a therapy is morally acceptable, of course, does not by itself establish what priority it ought to have in a health-care system. Some persons seeking transgender therapy have found private insurers and government health programs unwilling to pay for it because, it is said, such therapy is akin to cosmetic treatment and is in any case experimental and unproven. In response to claims of this kind, Eric B. Gordon has argued that the therapy meets an important psychic need of some persons, that it can work, and that its limitations can be overcome with better standards of determining eligibility. Gordon therefore concludes that public funding

See Also

Defining Terms: Sex and Gender

of transgender therapy ought to be provided according to the merits of the case (Gordon, 1991). To the extent this argument is successful, it would appear to extend to private insurers who offer coverage for similar psychic disorders, though the terms of such coverage might exclude preexisting conditions or might limit the amount of money paid to any individual, regardless of condition.

Sexual-orientation therapy

At least since the coining of the term "homosexuality" in 1869, a broad array of techniques has been used with men and women to redirect sexual orientation from homosexuality to heterosexuality. Much of this therapy has been based on a strict identification of male and female with opposite-sex desire: Maleness means attraction to women, and femaleness means attraction to men. Departures from this gender norm have been treated in a variety of ways that include moral censure, legal sanction, and formal medical declarations of pathology (Bayer, 1987). Techniques used to achieve a therapeutic goal of heterosexuality have typically reflected prevailing treatment methods: various forms of behavioral therapy, drug and hormone treatment, surgery, and a wide variety of psychotherapies (Murphy, 1992). While some therapy has been well-meaning and carried out with professional integrity, there also has been involuntary treatment, gruesome castrations in the Nazi camps, and abusive chemical and electrical aversive therapies.

Some commentators have argued that sexual-orientation therapy is immoral because it contributes to social prejudice against gay men and lesbians. Many gay men and lesbians see efforts designed to bring about sexual reorientation as an example of continuing disregard for their lives and as a falsification and devaluation of the integrity and worth of homoeroticism. Gerald C. Davison has argued that the mere availability of such therapy encourages its use, thereby perpetuating oppressive views about homosexuality (Davison, 1976). By contrast, Frederick Suppe has pointed out that such an argument is conclusive only if the therapy presupposes that homosexuality is inherently inferior to heterosexuality and that such therapy is socially influential in perpetuating injustice. A program that treated homosexuality merely as an unwanted trait would not be susceptible to Davison's objections (Suppe, 1984). Even if such therapy does not contribute to social injustice directly, social injustice regarding homosexuality may be a spur to such therapy, whether homosexuality is conceived as inherently inferior or merely an undesired trait; pursuit of sexual-orientation therapy may be an artifact of social injustice rather than an injustice in itself (Murphy, 1991).

Reports of success in reorientation come most typically from psychoanalysts, behavior therapists, and religious programs. However, these reports of success have been criticized on the basis of methodological problems including small sample size, success standards that measure behavior change but not psychic readjustment,

"TREATING" HOMOSEXUALITY
Social Attitudes in the Looking Glass

In 1973, the APA formally abandoned the view that homosexuality was necessarily pathological, a view it had held at least since its first formal diagnostic manual of 1952. The APA nevertheless maintains the diagnostic category "sexual-orientation distress" for those who suffer from unwanted sexual orientations. Though technically relevant to any sexual orientation, the diagnostic category is functionally limited to homosexuality, given the utter rarity of individuals professing distress from heterosexual orientation. Despite the formal declassification of homosexuality, some therapists still argue that homosexuality is pathological. Some other therapists wish to treat homosexuality, but they do not identify it as a disorder. These latter therapists approach homosexuality as an unwanted trait and justify their efforts as respecting the wishes of their clients. Some programs, for example, will enroll men and women only if they are "dissatisfied" with their sexual orientation (Schwartz and Masters, 1984). Some therapists practice from a religious perspective. Recovery from sin rather than from disease is the goal of religious reorientation programs (Pattison and Pattison, 1980), and they use Bible study, prayer, and group socializing to inaugurate or restore heterosexuality. It remains a matter of debate whether the extinguishing of unwanted traits is a legitimate objective for medicine and whether sexual-orientation therapy reveals social flaws in the treatment of homosexuality generally. Sexual-orientation therapy is an important opportunity to consider what such therapy suggests about a society's understanding of gender, difference, suffering, and medical collusion with larger social injustices. In this latter regard, sexual-orientation therapy can prove ethically instructive as to how homosexuality comes to be problematized as a deficit to be remedied rather than as a difference to be cultivated and nurtured.

— TIMOTHY F. MURPHY

◆ **gender-identity disorder**
Also called gender dysphoria, discordances between one's felt gender and one's assigned gender.

See Also

Theories on Causes: Is Homosexuality Genetic?

inadequacy of long-term assessment, and the uncontrolled nature of the studies. While there are reports of success in achieving heterosexual behavior and even heterosexual marriage, it is still unclear whether the therapies themselves have been responsible for those changes or whether and to what extent those changes will endure across a person's lifetime. Because of problems of these kinds, it is unclear that there is any generally effective therapy useful on randomly selected persons seeking sexual reorientation (Murphy, 1991). If this is so, it would follow that such therapy should be represented to patients or clients as experimental and unproven. In the past, some people were treated involuntarily for their homoerotic sexual orientation (Murphy, 1992). Certainly, any such coercive treatment could today only be seen as morally objectionable, given a principled respect for autonomous decision making in the absence of any consensus that homosexuality is a moral or medical evil.

There are many theories of the development of sexual orientation, but no one theory prevails.

PAGE 346

Since homosexuality is not confined to adults, it is also germane to consider the ethics of therapy with children. Given a confluence of scientific reports about possible biogenetic origins of homosexual orientation in males (Hamer et al., 1993; Bailey and Pillard, 1991; LeVay, 1991), discussions about the control of the sexual orientation of children are likely to come into greater prominence. In the past, parents turned to punishment, moral exhortation, religious counsel, reform school, and even electroshock therapy in order to bring their children to heterosexuality. Certainly one may expect that discussion about the control of sexual orientation not only will raise questions about the ethics of experimentation with children but also will engage ethical questions about the extent to which parents may properly attempt to control the characteristics of children (Crocker, 1979; Murphy, 1990).

Theorists have developed models suggesting that individuals acquire a homosexual identity in stages.

PAGE 346

Conclusions

The meaning of gender has become a focal point for moral and political analysis both in medicine and in the culture at large. This analysis typically focuses on the ways in which the biology and the cultural construction of gender are intertwined. It asks whether and with what consequences male gender stands paradigmatically for all human beings and whether the male is not preferentially treated. It asks whether biologically and socially polarized notions of gender are adequate to express the range of human gender variability. It asks whether the presumption of heterosexuality is normative and valid for judging the nature and destiny of all persons. It makes clear that treating gender, social roles, and sexual orientation as undivided in nature often has led to injustices against women, intersexed beings, and gay men and lesbians. A simplistic conflation of the biological and social roles of both males and females renders much more difficult the task of identifying and interpreting those social presumptions and moral values that impose oppression and disadvantage on the basis of gender. Appreciating the importance of gender to ethical analysis will offer biomedicine the opportunity to serve human beings as the persons they are and want to be rather than as the persons invidious gender presumptions would have them be.

— TIMOTHY F. MURPHY

GENE THERAPY

ETHICAL AND SOCIAL ISSUES

There are four possible types of human genetic intervention that can be performed on individuals. Such intervention can be targeted either toward an individual's somatic (nonreproductive) cells or toward germline (reproductive) cells. Similarly, the goal of genetic intervention may be the cure or prevention of disease or it may be the enhancement of human capabilities. These two pairs of alternatives can be represented schematically in a two-by-two matrix:

TYPES OF HUMAN GENE THERAPY

	Somatic	Germ-Line
Cure or Prevention of Disease	1	2
Enhancement of Capabilities	3	4

This article focuses on the first two of the four possible types of human genetic intervention.

Milestones in the public discussion of gene therapy

THE YEARS 1950 TO 1969. In the first half of the twentieth century imaginative anticipations of the human genetic future appeared in the writings of J. B. S. Haldane (1924), Aldous Huxley (1932), and Hermann J. Muller (1935). A qualitatively new phase in the public discussion began after World War II. Human genetics began to emerge as a distinct field; one concrete illustration of this emergence was the creation of a new journal, *The American Journal of Human Genetics*, in 1949. A decade later, the centennial of Charles Darwin's *The Origin of Species* gave biologists an opportunity to reflect on the past course of human evolution and on the likely future of the human race.

H. J. Muller's 1959 essay "The Guidance of Human Evolution" was almost certainly the most important stimulus to the genetic-intervention debate of the early 1960s. In the essay Muller, a classical geneticist, expressed doubt about the feasibility of "making direct alterations or substitutions of a desired kind in the genetic material itself" (Muller, 1959, p. 36). He expressed a strong preference for improving the human condition by the widespread, voluntary use of artificial insemination and other new reproductive methods. Muller's description of the human genetic load, or harmful mutations (Muller, 1950), and his self-consciously radical proposal for counteracting that load provided a major impetus for a series of conferences held in the 1960s (Hoagland and Burhoe, 1962; Wolstenholme, 1963; Sonnenborn, 1965; Roslansky, 1966). The important book by Theodosius Dobzhansky, *Mankind Evolving: The Evolution of the Human Species,* was also written at least in part as a response to Muller's views about the increasing burden of the human genetic load and to what Dobzhansky termed "Muller's bravest new world" (Dobzhansky, 1962).

The CIBA Foundation symposium held in London in November of 1962 on the theme "Man and His Future" provided an interesting snapshot of the then-prevailing views about human genetic intervention (Wolstenholme, 1963). At the symposium J. B. S. Haldane, Julian Huxley, Joshua Lederberg, and H. J. Muller (through a paper—he did not attend) shared ideas about both the goals and possible methods of deliberate genetic modification. Four strategies for achieving genetic change were considered by symposium participants: (1) voluntary artificial insemination using sperm from donors of "high genetic quality"; (2) direct intervention in the human germ-line to produce heritable changes; (3) genetic modification of somatic cells to achieve desired changes in the individual; and (4) clonal reproduction. Only the second and third of these techniques are pertinent to this article.

The CIBA Foundation symposium participants seemed to agree that germ-line intervention at the molecular level would be more difficult than the modification of somatic cells and that the enhancement of human capabilities would be more difficult than the cure of disease. The participants' anticipations of somatic-cell techniques are particularly interesting in the light of subsequent developments. J. B. S. Haldane envisioned "the deliberate provocation of mutations"; he also suggested that it might one day be possible to "synthesize new genes and introduce them into human chromosomes" or to "duplicate existing genes" for the same purpose (Haldane, 1963, p. 353). Joshua Lederberg asserted that "the ultimate application of molecular biology would be the direct control of nucleotide sequences in human chromosomes, coupled with recognition, selection, and integration of the desired genes . . ." (Lederberg, 1963, p. 265). Lederberg advocated that such techniques be employed either prenatally or in the early postnatal period to modify the phenotype (the external appearance) of the developing individual rather than its genotype (the genetic makeup) (Lederberg, 1963, p. 266).

The earliest extended commentary on the ethics of human genetic intervention was authored by theologian Paul Ramsey. In a lecture presented at a 1965 symposium (Roslansky, 1966), Ramsey saw parallels between Muller's pessimism about the human genetic load and a Christian understanding of history that acknowledges divine sovereignty. Ramsey argued that the Christian ethic should be oriented toward means rather than toward even the important end of preventing Muller's genetic apocalypse. The means of artificial insemination by donor (AID) advocated by Muller were viewed by Ramsey as ethically problematic because they would separate reproduction and the expression of love. On the other hand, Ramsey affirmed a belief in the potential value of "genetic surgery" to eliminate genetic defects, both in an individual and in the reproductive cells that would be passed on to future generations (Ramsey, 1966).

Between 1965 and 1969 the academic discussion of designed genetic change in humans abated somewhat. After H. J. Muller's death in 1967, Joshua Lederberg emerged as the most prominent scientist in the genetic engineering discussion. In Europe, Jesuit theologian Karl Rahner published a major essay entitled "On the Problem of Genetic Manipulation" in 1967. Despite the relative quiescence of academic debate, the first hints of political interest in human genetic intervention became evident in March of 1968, when Lederberg and Arthur Kornberg both testified before a U.S. Senate subcommittee considering Walter Mondale's proposal to establish a National Commission on Health Science and Society (U.S. Congress, 1968). Neither scientist saw a pressing need for a national commission to consider issues in genetic engineering. In fact, organ transplantation, the definition of death, and human experimentation received more attention at the hearings than did gene therapy. Meanwhile, molecular biologists made substantial progress, synthesizing a simple viral genome in 1967 (Goulian et al., 1967) and isolating important genes from the *E. coli* bacterium in 1969 (Shapiro et al., 1969). These successes and parallel developments in the laboratory made the technically complex task of performing genetic surgery seem more feasible.

At an interdisciplinary symposium held in December 1969, biologist Bernard Davis summarized the

Genetic linkage maps establish the relative position of genetic markers, detectable DNA sequences, along the chromosomes.

PAGE 325

◆ **gene therapy**
The insertion of normal or genetically altered genes into cells to replace defective genes in the treatment of genetic disorders.

See Also
Genome Mapping and Sequencing; Human Nature

prospects for genetic intervention in humans as of the end of the decade (Davis, 1970). Moral theologian James Gustafson responded to the Davis paper with a paper of his own, entitled "Genetic Engineering and the Normative View of the Human." In his paper, Gustafson noted Rahner's affirmation of the human capacity for self-creation (1967) and cautiously espoused "human initiative, human freedom (if you choose) to explore, develop, expand, alter, initiate, intervene in the course of life in the world, including his own life" (Gustafson, 1973, p. 57).

THE YEARS 1970 TO 1978. In the 1970s the ethical discussion of human genetic intervention was overshadowed by debates about two related but distinct topics: the ethics of genetic testing and screening, and the potential biohazards of a new form of laboratory research—recombinant DNA research. Nonetheless there were important publications on gene therapy during this time. Paul Ramsey's 1965 essay was incorporated into a 1970 book entitled *Fabricated Man: The Ethics of Genetic Control* (Ramsey, 1970). Joseph Fletcher responded to Ramsey and other cautious commentators with an article and a book advocating the widespread and vigorous use of many new genetic and reproductive technologies (Fletcher, 1971, 1974).

Most information in chromosomes is contained in the order of bases that make up the DNA chains.

PAGE 325

The first symposium to foreshadow the 1980s discussion of human gene therapy was held in May 1971 under the aegis of the National Cathedral in Washington, D.C. At this symposium, physicians W. French Anderson and Arno Motulsky, lawyer Alexander Capron, and theologian Paul Ramsey discussed somatic-cell gene therapy in categories that continued to be relevant into the 1990s (Hamilton, 1972). Several other authors also contributed to the evolving ethical literature during the decade (Friedmann and Roblin, 1972; Motulsky, 1974; Lappé and Morison, 1976; Baltimore, 1977; Howard and Rifkin, 1977).

THE YEARS 1979 TO 1985. The ethical discussion of human gene therapy took a decisively international turn at the end of the 1970s. The new phase of deliberation was initiated by a 1979 conference sponsored by the World Council of Churches. At the conference one working group focused its attention on "ethical issues in the biological manipulation of life." The group's final recommendation put forward what came to be the orthodox position on gene therapy during the 1980s—that somatic-cell gene therapy for the cure of disease (Type 1 in the matrix) is ethically acceptable, while germ-line intervention for prevention or cure of disease (Type 2) or enhancement of human capabilities (Types 3 and 4) is unacceptable (Abrecht, 1980, vol. 2).

◆ **genetics**
A branch of biology that deals with the heredity and variation of organisms.

In 1980 two U.S. developments stimulated the next stage of public debate. The first was a letter from leaders of Roman Catholic, Jewish, and Protestant religious groups to then-President Jimmy Carter. The letter argued that "we are rapidly moving into a new era of fundamental danger triggered by the rapid growth of genetic engineering" (U.S. President's Commission, 1982, p. 95). The second development was public disclosure in the *Los Angeles Times* of Martin Cline's unapproved gene-therapy experiments (Jacobs, 1980). One immediate response to the Cline study was a widely cited essay by W. French Anderson and John C. Fletcher entitled "Gene Therapy in Human Beings: When Is It Ethical to Begin?" (Anderson and Fletcher, 1980).

During the years 1981 and 1982, two major parallel studies of gene therapy were conducted, one in Europe by the Parliamentary Assembly of the Council of Europe, the other in the United States by a presidential bioethics commission. The culmination of these two study processes occurred in 1982. The Parliamentary Assembly acted first, adopting a position in favor of somatic-cell gene therapy in January 1982 (Council of Europe, 1982). On the question of germ-line intervention for the cure or prevention of disease, the Parliamentary Assembly opposed "tampering" with the human genetic heritage yet expressed an almost wistful hope that a list of legitimate target diseases for germ-line approaches might be drawn up. In November of the same year, at a congressional hearing, the U.S. President's Commission on Ethical Problems in Medicine and Biomedical and Behavioral Research released its report entitled *Splicing Life* (U.S. President's Commission, 1982; U.S. Congress, 1982). The major thrust of the report was to reassure the public that currently contemplated somatic-cell approaches were not qualitatively different from other widely accepted modalities of health care. In addition, the U.S. President's Commission put forward proposals for the public oversight of gene-therapy research.

From 1983 to 1985 major policy statements on gene therapy were compiled by various special committees in Denmark (Denmark, 1984), Sweden (Sweden, 1984), and what was then West Germany (Federal Republic of Germany, 1985). In addition, Pope John Paul II devoted a major lecture to the topic (John Paul II, 1983), and the Congressional Office of Technology Assessment in the United States produced an update of the 1982 *Splicing Life* report (U.S. Congress, 1984). All of these reports and the papal address were in agreement that somatic-cell gene therapy for the cure of disease was ethically acceptable.

A second development in the years 1983 through 1985 was the discussion and creation of a public review mechanism for human gene therapy protocols in the United States. In part as a response to the problems that had surrounded the Martin Cline study, and in part because of the recommendations in the *Splicing*

Life report, the Recombinant DNA Advisory Committee (RAC) of the National Institutes of Health agreed to provide review before the studies were carried out with human subjects. In the summer of 1984 the RAC created a special working group to provide initial review of such proposals, and by 1985 the RAC's working group had developed and published guidelines for somatic-cell gene-therapy protocols called "Points to Consider" (National Institutes of Health [NIH], 1985). At the end of 1985 the RAC and its working group were poised, waiting for the first clinical protocol to be submitted for public review (Walters, 1991a).

GENE THERAPY 1986–1994

Four Major Developments

1. proliferation of policy statements by nations and international organizations
2. revived discussions of germ-line therapy
3. gene-therapy protocols initiated in U.S. and abroad
4. expansion of clinical applications of somatic-cell gene-therapy techniques to new areas of medicine

THE YEARS 1986 TO 1994. After 1985, the public discussion of gene therapy was characterized by four important developments: (1) the proliferation of policy statements on gene therapy by nations and international organizations, resulting in the establishment of national guidelines and review processes in many countries; (2) the revival of the discussion of germ-line gene therapy in the wake of its universal proscription by those national guidelines; (3) the initiation of numerous gene-therapy protocols in the United States and several other nations; and (4) the expansion of the clinical applications of somatic-cell gene-therapy techniques beyond the treatment of paradigmatic genetic diseases like severe combined immunodeficiency to other areas of medicine. Each of these developments underscored ethical and social dimensions of gene therapy that continue to affect the evaluation of advances in genetic medicine.

Between 1986 and 1994 the number of national and international policy statements regarding the issues involved in human gene therapy increased dramatically. Particularly important were the 1987 German Committee of Inquiry report (cf. Sass, 1988), the statement by the European Medical Research Councils (1988), the 1989 Swiss Amstad Report (cf. Bourrit et al., 1989), the 1990 report from the Council for International Organizations of Medical Sciences (CIOMS) (Bankowski and Capron, 1991), the 1991 French National Ethics Committee's "Avis sur la thérapie génique" (France, 1991), the 1992 British Clothier Commission Report (Great Britain, 1992), and the final report of the Canadian Royal Commission on New Reproductive Technologies (Royal Commission, 1993). These reports reflected an international consensus that properly regulated research on somatic-cell gene therapy was appropriate to pursue. As a result, by 1994 a number of nations, including Australia, Canada, France, Italy, the Netherlands, Switzerland, and the United Kingdom had established national procedures for reviewing somatic-cell gene-therapy protocols.

The most important variation within the international response to gene therapy during this period occurred with the question of germ-line gene therapy. While no public group advocated the immediate pursuit of germ-line gene therapy, responses ranged from the legal prohibition of such research (Germany), to research moratoria on any human clinical trials (European Medical Research Councils), to calls for more policy discussion of the topic in anticipation of scientific progress (Bankowski and Capron, 1991).

These official expressions of caution in turn contributed to a resurgence in the academic and public discussion of germ-line gene-therapy research. Articles developing and defending the positive case for pursuing human germ-line gene therapy appeared in the mainstream bioethics literature (Zimmerman, 1991; Munson and Davis, 1992; Wivel and Walters, 1993). Public interest groups in the United States, following the lead of their European counterparts, released position statements condemning germ-line interventions in humans (Council for Responsible Genetics, 1992). This dialogue was facilitated by the founding, in 1990, of the journal *Human Gene Therapy*, which devoted space in each issue to articles addressing the ethical and regulatory aspects of gene therapy. The journal quickly became a principal locus of discussions of the merits of germ-line research and was quickly emulated by other journals, such as the British publication *Gene Therapy*.

These statements on and discussions of gene therapy emerged against a backdrop of vigorous scientific activity during this period. Early in 1990, Michael Blaese and W. French Anderson from the NIH introduced a proposal to treat severe combined immunodeficiency in children by means of somatic-cell therapy. This disease features the almost total inactivation of a child's immune system because of the malfunctioning of a single gene, which fails to produce an essential enzyme, adenosine diaminase (ADA). Between April and August of 1990, the NIH Recombinant DNA Advisory Committee examined the Blaese-Anderson protocol. Upon the approval of the protocol by the NIH director and the U.S. Food and Drug Administration, the experiment commenced in September 1990. The initial results from the study were quite encouraging. Meanwhile, the first European gene-therapy experi-

The term genetics *was not used until the first decade of the twentieth century.*

PAGE 325

A parent passes only one of each pair of chromosomes to each child.

PAGE 326

ment (also for ADA deficiency) was initiated in Milan in 1992.

In part because of this early success, the numbers of human somatic-cell gene-therapy protocols reviewed and approved in the United States rose dramatically during the following years. By early 1994, a total of forty-nine human gene-therapy protocols had been approved by the RAC and reviewing such protocols had become the committee's primary mission, collapsing any distinction between the RAC and its "Human Gene Therapy Subcommittee."

During the 1970s, biologists began to map DNA directly from the entire genomes of viruses and bacteria.

PAGE 326

Meanwhile, biomedical scientists were also taking the public discussion of gene therapy in another direction. Interestingly, only twelve of the first forty-nine RAC-approved gene-therapy protocols were intended to treat health problems that had been traditionally labeled as "genetic diseases." The range of clinical strategies utilizing recombinant DNA techniques expanded almost immediately to include a variety of gene-tagging and gene-transfer techniques that did not fit the traditional conception of gene therapy. By 1994 the public had learned about gene-transfer strategies to combat a variety of cancers, human immunodeficiency virus (HIV) infection, and arthritis (McGarrity, 1991), in addition to classic genetic diseases such as cystic fibrosis and Gaucher's disease (a disorder in which fats build up in the cells).

This expansion of the applications of gene transfer techniques had the effect of enmeshing gene-therapy protocols in much larger biomedical research contexts, which often involved their own ethical and social challenges. The fact that somatic-cell gene-transfer technologies were involved began to look like a side issue in the face of the other traditional questions of research ethics that gene transfer protocols faced. Thus, for example, this period saw the gene-therapy community begin to struggle with the translation of experimental interventions into clinical practice, through the provision of gene therapy as a form of innovative clinical care, outside the public research review process (Thompson, 1993). This development raised no issues peculiar to gene therapy, but it did return the discussion to the fundamental bioethical distinction between biomedical research and innovative clinical practice on which the RAC's gene-therapy review process was based.

Molecular genetic techniques can in some cases grab a molecular handle on diseases that otherwise elude study.

PAGE 326

Ethical issues in somatic-cell gene therapy

Because somatic-cell gene therapy is in many ways an extension of traditional medical approaches—especially the administration of drugs or biologics and cell or tissue transplantation—the ethical questions surrounding the practice closely parallel those that any innovative therapy must face. The major substantive ethical questions about gene therapy have to do with the anticipated benefits and risks of this new intervention, the selection of patient-subjects, the process of informing patient-subjects or their proxies, and the preservation of privacy and confidentiality.

The risk-benefit question examines the seriousness of the disease to be treated, the existence and effectiveness of alternative therapies, and the probable benefits and harms of the genetic approach. For gene-therapy protocols, this has also meant attempting to prepare for unforeseen as well as predictable risks in designing molecular genetic interventions. In particular, this concern has focused on anticipating possible risks involved in the delivery and integration of DNA into the subject's cells, including the risk of germ-line effects (Temin, 1990).

In the case of the Blaese-Anderson proposal to treat severe combined immunodeficiency in children, there was immediate agreement on the life-threatening character of the disease. For children with a matched sibling donor, a bone marrow transplant was often a permanently effective treatment. For other children there did exist an alternative but very expensive treatment: an enzyme treatment derived from cattle. However, the researchers argued that the genetic modification and reintroduction of a child's own T-lymphocytes might provide even greater benefit. The potential risks of genetically modified cells had been studied in mice and monkeys, as well as in the human subjects of a gene-marking study initiated in 1989. On the efficacy side, there were promising data from one study of mice performed in Milan, Italy.

The selection of patient-subjects was included as an ethical issue to be considered for reasons that stretch back to the early use of renal dialysis in Seattle, Washington. In the early 1960s, when renal dialysis was a scarce resource, a local review committee considered which patients with end-stage renal disease were the most fitting candidates for dialysis. In similar fashion, organ procurement agencies and transplant centers have, over time, developed guidelines for choosing among the large numbers of candidates for cadaver kidneys, hearts, and lungs. In the case of the Blaese-Anderson protocol, severe combined immunodeficiency caused by ADA deficiency was so rare that all children with the disorder who had no matched sibling donors were in principle eligible for the protocol. Yet, even within this group of eligible children, choices had to be made among children of different ages and differing disease severity.

The need for informed consent by patient-subjects is one of the central tenets of research ethics. Thus, it is no surprise that this issue would be considered in ethical discussions about gene therapy. A complicating factor with gene therapy is that the proposed intervention is technically at the cutting edge of research and requires that patient-subjects have at least a basic understanding of molecular biology. In the case of the Blaese-Anderson protocol, a basic knowledge of immunology was also important. Effective techniques for conveying complex technical information to laypeople do exist and should be employed in the consent process for these and all research protocols. One special issue in gene therapy is the fact that the subjects will often be in relatively desperate clinical circumstances, which can exert a powerful influence on the motivations of the subjects, their families, and their physicians. Since many potential gene-therapy subjects will be in quite vulnerable circumstances, extra review precautions may be required to ensure that their participation is voluntary. Thus, the influence of clinical desperation needs to be taken into account.

The protection of privacy and confidentiality for the pioneer patient-subjects in gene-therapy research is also important. In other cases involving innovative therapy—for example, in the early heart transplants, the first birth after in vitro fertilization, and the use of a baboon heart in a child—a virtual media circus has surrounded both the subjects and the research team. A proper approach to patient-subjects will not isolate them from public view but will attempt to strike a balance between disclosure to an interested public and respect for their privacy.

Finally, as somatic-cell gene-therapy techniques begin to show promise within the confines of the research setting, the process of their translation into clinical use will raise issues. Concern to prevent the premature adoption of unvalidated genetic interventions will increasingly have to be weighed against the claims of patients seeking access to the clinical benefits that new techniques might offer.

MAJOR ETHICAL CONCERNS ABOUT SOMATIC-CELL GENE THERAPY

- anticipated benefits and risks
- selection of patient-subjects
- process of informing patient-subjects (or proxies)
- preservation of privacy and confidentiality

These ethical considerations for human gene-therapy research are not unique to this practice. In fact, they can be viewed as derivations from, or approximations of, several venerable principles of biomedical ethics. The risk-benefit question is obviously related to the principle of beneficence. Both informed consent and the protection of privacy and confidentiality have their primary roots in the principle of autonomy. Fairness in the selection of patient-subjects is clearly an application of the principle of justice.

In addition to these substantive issues, there is an important procedural issue to be raised about gene therapy. Because special public concern seems to surround the genetic technologies, most countries have created national public review mechanisms to evaluate human gene-therapy protocols, at least during the early years of somatic-cell gene therapy. The result of this process has been both public education about and public confidence in this new approach to disease. It is possible that a similar approach would have been useful in the early years of past biomedical innovations, for example, cardiac transplantation and in vitro fertilization. In the future the evolving ethic of biomedical research may require a similar public review process for other major biomedical innovations, as a complement to the important work of local research ethics committees.

Ethical issues in germ-line gene therapy

The major difference between somatic-cell gene therapies and clinical techniques aimed at germ-line genetic intervention is that the latter would produce clinical changes that could be transmitted to the offspring of the person receiving the intervention. This simple difference is often the only consideration cited in the many official statements that endorse somatic-cell gene-therapy trials while proscribing or postponing research aimed at developing human germ-line gene-therapy techniques. Behind these official statements, however, lies a longer argument, revolving around four sets of concerns: scientific uncertainties; the need to use resources efficiently; social risks; and conflicting human rights concerns.

SCIENTIFIC UNCERTAINTIES. Even the proponents of germ-line gene therapy agree that human trials under our current state of knowledge would be unacceptable. In order for gene-therapy techniques to be effective, the genes must be stably integrated, expressed correctly only in the appropriate tissues, and reliably targeted to the correct location on a chromosome. If the intervention cannot eliminate the parents' risk of transmitting the alleles (alternative forms of a gene that can be located at a particular site on the chromosome) they carry, or can only do so by substituting other genetic risks, its promise remains weak. Critics maintain that, given the complexity of gene regulation and expression during human development, germ-line gene-therapy experiments will always involve too many unpredictable long-term iatrogenic (physician-caused) risks to the transformed subjects and their offspring to be justifiable (Council for Responsible Genetics, 1993).

Resource allocation emerged as the first science policy issue facing those who wished to pursue genome mapping and sequencing.

PAGE 327

◆ **genetic engineering** *the directed alteration of genetic material by intervention in genetic processes, esp. gene-splicing.*

Proponents, however, respond that our current ignorance only justifies postponing human trials of germ-line therapy techniques until their promise can be improved. A more optimistic reading turns the argument around: To the extent that the barriers to effective therapy can be overcome, its promise should encourage research to continue. Proponents add that, by focusing on the obvious barriers to performing clinical trials today, critics of germ-line therapy ignore the fact that it will take further research to determine whether or not current barriers should ultimately dissuade society from contemplating clinical trials in the future (Munson and Davis, 1992).

The main effect of mapping and sequencing technologies has been to accelerate the advance of human genetics.

PAGE 329

Proponents bolster their technological optimism with an argument from medical utility: that germ-line gene therapy offers the only true cure for many diseases. If illnesses are understood to be, at root, "molecular diseases," then therapeutic interventions at any level above the causal gene can only be symptomatic. From this perspective, all gene therapies involving simply the addition of genes are palliative measures on the road to complete "gene surgery," which could involve the excision of the pathological alleles from the organism (Zimmerman, 1991).

ALLOCATION OF RESOURCES. One common criticism of the argument from medical utility is that it betrays a reductionistic attitude that fails to appreciate approaches that could achieve the same ends more efficiently. Since it must become possible to identify target pre-embryos before their transformation, the argument goes, it would be more efficient to simply use the same techniques to identify healthy pre-embryos for implantation (Mauron and Thévoz, 1991). Many clinical geneticists argue that even our current methods of prenatal screening serve this function. Against these convenient, effective approaches, they conclude, germ-line gene-therapy techniques will never be cost-effective enough to merit high enough social priority to pursue.

The ability to identify individuals by sampling their DNA made forensic uses possible.

PAGE 329

One scientific rejoinder that is made to this argument is that screening will not help with all cases. Presumably, for example, as more beneficiaries of somatic-cell gene therapy survive to reproductive age, there will be more couples whose members are both afflicted with the same recessive disorder (Walters, 1991b). Gene-therapy strategies that affect the germ line may also be the only effective ways of addressing some genetic diseases, such as those with origins very early in development. And by preventing the transmission of disease genes, germ-line gene therapy would obviate the need for screening or costly and risky somatic-cell gene therapy in subsequent generations of particular families.

SOCIAL RISKS. Proponents of germ-line gene-therapy research also can point out that screening prevents genetic disease only by preventing the birth of the patients who would suffer from it. This, they point out, is a confusion of therapeutic goals that runs the long-term risk of encouraging coercive eugenic practices and tacitly fostering discrimination against those with genetic disease. By attempting to prevent disease in individuals rather than selecting against individuals according to their genotype, proponents argue, germ-line gene therapy would allow us to maintain our commitment to the value of moral equality in the face of biological diversity (Catholic Health Association, 1990).

Critics reply to this that, on the contrary, it is germ-line gene therapy that has the more ominous social implications, by opening the door to genetic enhancement. One line of argument recalls the historical abuses of the eugenics movement to suggest that, to the extent that the line between gene therapy and enhancement would increasingly blur, germ-line interventions would be open to the same questions about the proper vision of human flourishing that eugenics faced. Even those who dispute the dangers of the "slippery slope" in this context take pains to defend the moral significance of the distinction "between uses that may relieve real suffering and those that alter characteristics that have little or nothing to do with disease" (Fletcher, 1985, p. 303). Proponents must then argue that appropriate distinctions between these different uses can be confidently drawn (Anderson, 1989), and point out that the same eugenic challenges already face those engaged in preimplantation screening or prenatal diagnosis (Fowler et al., 1989).

HUMAN RIGHTS CONCERNS. Finally, however, some critics argue that the focus of germ-line gene therapy on the embryonic patient has other implications that foreclose its pursuit: If the primary goal of the intervention is to address the health problems of the pre-embryo itself, germ-line gene therapy becomes an extreme case of fetal therapy, and the pre-embryo gains the status of a patient requiring protection. Germ-line therapy experiments would involve research with early human embryos that would have effects on their offspring, effectively placing multiple human generations in the role of unconsenting research subjects (Lappé, 1991). If the pre-embryo is given the moral status of a patient, it would be very hard to justify the risks of clinical research that would be necessary to develop the technique. For example, would pre- or postimplantation screening be allowed in order to determine which attempts were successful?

This objection to human germ-line gene therapy research is couched in several ways. For the Europeans, it is often interpreted as the right to one's genetic patrimony (Mauron and Thévoz, 1991); germ-line gene-therapy interventions would violate the rights of subsequent generations to inherit a genetic endowment that has not been intentionally modified (Knoppers, 1991). For advocates of people with disabilities, this concern is interpreted in terms of the dangers to society's willingness to accept their differences (Asch, 1989). Interestingly, some feminists join this position as well, out of a concern for the impact on women of taking the pre-embryo too seriously as an object of medical care (Minden, 1987).

Proponents can offer several responses to these concerns. One is to argue that germ-line gene therapy is a reproductive health intervention aimed at the parents, not the fetus (Zimmerman, 1991). Its goal is to allow the parents to address their reproductive risks and have a healthy baby, in cases where the parents' own views of preimplantation screening prohibit preimplantation screening and selective discard of an embryo (Cook-Deegan, 1990). In taking this position, proponents acknowledge moral uncertainty over the status of the pre-embryo and defend parental requests for germ-line intervention as falling within the scope of their reproductive rights. Their argument is that, as a professional policy, medicine should continue to accept, and respond to, a wide range of interpretations of reproductive health needs by prospective parents, including requests for germ-line gene therapy (Fowler et al., 1989).

Conclusion

No other biomedical intervention in history has received as much international and interdisciplinary attention as human gene therapy (Fletcher, 1990). Three points of striking consensus have emerged from that global discussion:

The first point is that somatic-cell gene-therapy research does not constitute a major break with medical therapeutics, but that this technique should be regulated through public review processes. As somatic-cell gene-therapy techniques branch off into different medical domains, this policy raises hard questions about how seriously to take the public's involvement.

The second point of consensus is that current concerns about clinical risks and biohazards, research involving pre-embryonic subjects of uncertain moral status, and long-range social risks make human experimentation with germ-line interventions unacceptable for the time being. Beyond that, the discussion is flourishing about whether germ-line interventions could ever be ethically acceptable and, if so, under what circumstances.

The third point of consensus is less often directly stated but is nonetheless implied in much of the literature; it also animates the international discussion of these techniques. That is the view that gene therapy, both somatic and germ-line, should be evaluated solely as a clinical tool employed on behalf of presenting patients, and not as a eugenic public-health device designed to benefit the population. In contemporary political argot, genetic medicine should continue to be an empowering, not an exclusionary science. It should continue to be about helping living people address their individual health problems, and not about protecting the "gene pool" or society from the ebb and flow of human alleles in populations.

— ERIC JUENGST
LEROY WALTERS

GENETIC COUNSELING

PRACTICE OF GENETIC COUNSELING

Genetic counseling may be described as the interaction between a health-care provider and patient or family member on concerns about the birth of a child with medical problems, reproductive testing options, a family history of ill health, or the diagnosis of an inherited condition. There are over four thousand genetic conditions, chromosome disorders, and birth abnormalities that can result in miscarriage, stillbirth, death early in life or problems in childhood or adulthood. Those who seek this medical and psychological counseling service ask questions and have concerns about why a condition occurred, the chances that it may occur again in the future, and how they may be helped to cope with uncertainty, risk, or other ramifications of a diagnosis. These services are often provided by a team of clinical genetics specialists (physician geneticists and master's-level genetic counselors) in a medical genetics clinic within a hospital or in an outreach setting. Attention is paid to the medical, educational, and emotional needs of patients and their family members related to genetic conditions.

This article reviews the history of genetic counseling, the training of genetic counselors, and the practice standards and values inherent in the goal of nondirective counseling.

Genetics evaluation and counseling services

An accurate diagnosis must be established to address patients' needs. This is true even if the person seeking counseling is not affected with a genetic condition. The diagnosis of the patient or relative(s) in question determines the inheritance pattern in the family and thus the risk information that is provided. The diagnosis may be determined from family history information, pregnancy history, medical records, clinical examination, or test results. The physician geneticist

There is no evidence of widespread genetic screening by employers—possibly because the testing is expensive.

PAGE 324

G

GENETIC COUNSELING

Practice of Genetic Counseling

"Recessive" essentially means that both copies of the gene must be of the same allele in order to show the condition.

PAGE 275

HISTORY

Genetic Counseling

To appreciate the current standard of practice in genetic counseling, it is important to outline its history. In the United States, academic geneticists (nonphysicians), most of whom did not study humans, were the pioneers in addressing queries from affected family members about their risk of specific genetic conditions. From the early 1900s in Europe, Great Britain, and the United States, and particularly in the late 1930s and early 1940s in Nazi Germany, the practice of eugenics was widespread. This included the mass elimination of certain populations as well as forced sterilization of the mentally impaired. Because of their concerns about these eugenic practices, academics in subsequent years resisted providing childbearing advice to those who sought their expertise. This laid the groundwork for patient autonomy in reproductive decision making that has evolved over subsequent decades. This evolution of genetic counseling has been described as consisting of three paradigm shifts, from eugenics, to preventive medicine, and finally to psychologically oriented counseling (Kessler, 1979).

As human genetics developed into an academic field and medical information became available about inherited conditions, physician geneticists and smaller numbers of clinical Ph.D. geneticists became the primary communicators of information related to genetic conditions. Departments of Human Genetics became established in the 1940s and 1950s and led to the development of medical subspecialties. Practicing clinicians came to recognize the time-consuming and psychologically demanding aspects of communicating emotionally volatile information to families and began to involve nurses and social workers in the provision of services. Thus, a team approach to counseling ensued, yet nurses and social workers, at that time, had no formal education in genetics.

— BARBARA BOWLES BIESECKER

on the team typically performs this diagnostic aspect of genetic counseling. Medical and pediatric geneticists are physicians who have completed special postresidency fellowships in clinical genetics. Their expertise is to recognize rare patterns of physical features unique to particular genetic disorders; interpret molecular, biochemical, or chromosomal test results; and recommend management of related medical concerns.

The educational component of genetic counseling includes a wide range of information that stems from the diagnosis, including the inheritance pattern, the risk of recurrence, medical management or surveillance, prognosis, schooling needs, support groups, financial issues, reproductive options, and potential inherited and emotional ramifications to members of the patient's family. Genetic counselors and clinical geneticists are trained to address this spectrum of concerns, and most often, both participate in this portion of counseling sessions.

The psychosocial counseling component explores patients' emotional responses to the information discussed. It is provided in a supportive and nonjudgmental manner. Discussion of genetic conditions or risks often elicits feelings of lowered self-esteem, guilt, shame, loss, and blame, either on the part of patients or their family members. Genetic counseling in its most specific sense describes the psychodynamic process that occurs within a counselor-client relationship based on trust and rapport. The relationship borrows from clinical psychology its basic assumption that the client is capable of caring for his or her own emotional well-being. Exploration of the implications of genetic disorders assists clients in adjusting their expectations, coping with difficulty, and facing dilemmas. Empathic elucidation of the client's feelings conveys respect and benevolence and is not intended to be persuasive. Thus, the relationship is best described as client-oriented. Master's degree-level genetic counselors, in particular, have expertise in this aspect of genetic counseling.

Training and certification of genetic counselors

The first master's degree-level genetic counseling graduates entered the field in the early 1970s and became integrated into a clinical practice team alongside medical geneticists. There are now more than 1,300 of these health-care professionals throughout the United States and smaller numbers of nurses and social workers who have specialized in the area of clinical genetics. The vast majority of counselors are Caucasian females, and programs are actively recruiting applicants from diverse ethnocultural backgrounds (Rapp, 1988). As of 1994, eighteen master's degree graduate programs exist, including four clinical-nurse specialist programs. Two of these programs are in Canada, one is in South Africa, and one in Great Britain.

Persons who pursue genetic counseling often have undergraduate degrees in both biology or chemistry and the social sciences. Most successful applicants have participated in a community counseling endeavor prior to entering graduate school. Graduate programs are

See Also

The Idea of Eugenics: Three Strands

typically two years long and entail clinical, biochemical, and molecular genetics coursework coupled with psychology, public health, biomedical ethics, and social work. Genetic counseling students are trained in a variety of clinical settings throughout their studies; thus, there is a large experiential component to their education. Most programs limit the number of students enrolled to less than ten per year because this aspect of genetic counseling training is closely supervised and labor intensive. A master's degree in human genetics or genetic counseling is awarded.

In the past, the American Board of Medical Genetics has certified master's-level genetic counselors, as well as medical geneticists and several types of Ph.D.-trained geneticists. As of 1993, in the United States, genetic counselors are certified by the newly established American Board of Genetic Counseling (ABGC). Eligibility for certification requires stringent academic preparation as well as experience in counseling individuals for a variety of indications and in divergent settings. The ABGC also plans to certify graduate programs in genetic counseling in order to uphold professional standards for training and practice.

Standard of practice

Sheldon Reed (1974) stressed the importance of utilizing the term "counseling" in referring to this clinical genetics practice in an effort to distinguish it from genetic advice giving (eugenics). Reed also emphasized that patient autonomy in decision making (particularly with regard to reproduction) should be respected and upheld. A definition of genetic counseling, subsequently published by the American Society of Human Genetics Ad Hoc Committee on Genetic Counseling in 1975, emphasized the educational component to the service and thus, the importance of an effective communication process (Epstein et al., 1975). It implies (but does not state) the central dogma of genetic counseling, nondirectiveness, by describing patient autonomy in terms of individuals choosing their own course of action.

The term "nondirectiveness" was widely adopted in the genetic counseling literature in the mid-1970s. Although use and interpretation of the term varies dramatically, "nondirective" was borrowed from the writings of the psychologist Carl Rogers to describe a noneugenic counseling process. Rogers first coined the term in 1942 to describe his psychotherapeutic approach of not advising, interpreting, or guiding his clients. The concept led to confusion in the field of clinical psychology as Rogers realized that his very presence in a relationship had many "directive" aspects. By 1978, he had adopted the term "person-centered" to describe his therapeutic approach (Rogers, 1978). Clinical geneticists and genetic counselors often use the term to describe various aspects of their practice, but there has been debate about whether genetic counseling can be nondirective (Bartels et al., 1993).

Nondirectiveness should not be interpreted to mean that genetic counseling is value-neutral. Geneticists have long recognized that their values and ideas often are not identical to those of their patients. Rather, geneticists and counselors are explicit about certain values, such as the patient's role in making his or her own decisions, particularly about childbearing. It is impossible for geneticists and counselors to know

IN PRACTICE

Is "Nondirective" Counseling Possible?

Genetic counseling clearly has directive components. The education of patients is directive insofar as the counselor imparts certain information to the client. Since clients often come seeking such information, this activity is necessarily directed. Medical management and referrals to support groups or agencies are explicitly directive. A refusal to offer a carrier test to a minor or to offer prenatal testing for fetal sex selection are further examples of directive activities. Genetic counseling may even involve making recommendations.

There are also implicitly directive components to the counseling relationship conveyed through body language, emphasis, and time spent. These directive factors, however, do not diminish the need for client-oriented psychological counseling and autonomous decision making regarding reproduction. These aspects of genetic counseling are critical to the standard of practice often termed "nondirective." As Rogers discovered, the professional relationship does serve as a potent influence on the client; thus, what is reinforced by the counselor are the feelings and reactions expressed by the client without interpretation or judgment. The client is therefore empowered in his or her own central ability to develop further within the relationship. This approach defines a standard for practice. Because genetic counseling is a client-oriented service and inherently flexible, critics have stated that no standard of practice exists. This stems from confusing an outcome-based practice (eugenics) with a process-based standard (client-centered counseling).

— BARBARA BOWLES BIESECKER

Workplace genetic screening could give employers intimate information about employees that the individuals themselves might not have.

PAGE 324

See Also

Ethics: Nondirectiveness vs. Patients' "Dysgenic" Choices

In the population there are many recessive genes that cause various abnormal conditions.

PAGE 275

with any certainty what they would do if they were faced with others' circumstances. In one international survey, clinical geneticists identified patient autonomy as one of the most important values in the provision of services (Wertz and Fletcher, 1988).

Nondirectiveness was never intended to suggest a lack of provider bias. Biases are inherent to being human, and providers bring their own biases to the therapeutic relationship. The expression and discussion of such biases often may occur in a counseling session. Their acknowledgment actually defines genetic counselors as client-oriented. A common bias among counselors, for instance, is the assumption that clients are capable of self-growth following a tragic event or personal struggle. They value self-development, privacy, knowledge, and emotional revelation, and their relationship with their clients depends on their use or expression.

The National Society of Genetic Counselors adopted, in 1991, a code of ethics that outlines guidelines for the practice of master's-trained counselors. The code is based on an ethical framework called the ethics of care and addresses many of the important components of the relationship between the counselor and client. The following section discusses in more detail the ethical issues governing genetic counseling service provision.

Goals of counseling

The overall goal of genetic counseling is to reduce human emotional suffering or struggle related to genetic conditions and to address clients' concerns. Clinical genetics professionals who claim to know better than their patients what are "correct" or "good" decisions are practicing in direct conflict with the objective of patient-centered care. There is a critical need for research to evaluate the effectiveness of genetic counseling in addressing clients' needs and concerns. Previous investigation into the effectiveness of genetic counseling has often been limited to patients' retention of information, specifically risk factors (Sorenson et al., 1981). Although risk education is an important component of genetic counseling, families frequently do not make rational decisions based on critical interpretation of numbers. Outcomes for families are highly complex and it is often their psychological and social circumstances that determine their decision making and coping. Patients' expectations and desires, their interpretations of services, and their degree of satisfaction are all important sources of information to shape the approach and success of genetic counseling.

Conflicts arise in the provision of clinical genetics services when issues of serving the public good are introduced as a desired outcome. Genetic services are patently eugenic if the goal is to reduce the incidence of genetic disease. Several international genetic-screening programs exist that boast "successful" outcomes defined as the reduction of children affected with certain genetic disorders (by abortion or restricted matings). Such screening programs do not promote client-centered decision making and autonomy as important outcomes and may or may not include genetic counseling as a component of the service (Andrews et al., 1994). In addition, in times of increasing competition for health-care resources, it becomes increasingly difficult to justify expensive counseling services designed to help clients make autonomous, informed decisions. Pretest education and counseling are critical components of any genetic-testing or population-screening program. Without upholding this as a rigid practice guideline, clinical genetics professionals risk reverting to the tragedies of eugenic programs.

Settings

Genetic counseling occurs most often in obstetrical and pediatric genetics clinics. At least half of all genetic counselors practice some degree of prenatal genetic counseling. Typically this entails discussion with a woman or couple of their family histories and potential risks to a developing baby. Prenatal counseling usually involves decisions regarding the use of available testing options. When a test result indicates there is a problem or potential problem, then more extensive counseling ensues. Prenatal services are offered through university hospitals, private hospitals, and, increasingly, in private clinics or offices. Testing options may include amniocentesis, chorionic villus sampling, ultrasound, or preimplantation diagnosis. These techniques allow an opportunity to perform biochemical, cytogenetic, visual, or molecular evaluation on a developing fetus that may provide information about the likelihood that a genetic disorder or birth defect has occurred. None of these methods guarantees the arrival of unimpaired children, and the occurrence of many disorders is impossible to predict prior to delivery or onset of symptoms.

Because many birth abnormalities are unpredictable, pediatric clinics are also frequent settings for genetic counseling services. Most of these clinics are located in academic hospitals and focus on families' questions about the cause of a child's physical or mental maldevelopment. The sessions may address diagnostic, prognostic, or psychosocial issues. Certain chromosome or DNA testing (by obtaining a blood sample) may assist in making the diagnosis, but the essence of the evaluations is thorough physical examination and history taking. Emotional issues related to the child's prognosis often take precedence over more immediate issues, such as current school needs.

The financial aspects of genetic counseling services

have significant impact on service delivery. Genetic counseling is primarily a cognitive endeavor that is labor intensive. Counseling services historically have been reimbursed by third-party payers at a lower rate than medical services, particularly those involving a laboratory test. Prenatal testing procedures and accompanying laboratory services are one aspect of genetic services that has proved reimbursable. This differential creates conflicts of interest for geneticists and counselors, who often face administrative pressures to balance the expenditures of clinic services. It is incumbent upon both providers to ensure that financial needs are not met by directing patients toward more significantly reimbursable services.

In the United States, genetic services disproportionately serve persons with third-party coverage or who have other means to pay for services. Attempts have been made, initially by the federal government and subsequently by state governments, to support statewide genetic services for the geographically and economically underserved. Such programs have met with variable success. Many states provide funds for geneticists to travel periodically to outreach settings, such as public-health-department clinics, in more rural areas. Most often these services are pediatric genetic services since prenatal genetic services are time-dependent and require special equipment for patients who choose testing.

Genetic services have been described as a luxury, particularly in comparison to the significant need for more basic health services, such as, in the United States, prenatal care. In addition, racial minorities are underserved, as they are in most medical settings in the United States. More equitable genetic service delivery occurs in countries in which there is socialized medicine. Yet national health services place more emphasis on public-health outcomes and less on autonomous decision making and costly counseling services (Wertz and Fletcher, 1988). This suggests there will be challenges to the current mode of delivering genetic services if the United States adopts a similar health-care system in the future.

Future considerations

It is not currently possible, nor will it be possible in the future, for geneticists or genetic counselors to provide genetic counseling services to every person whose life is, or may be, touched by a genetic condition. The Human Genome Project in the United States, beginning in 1989, and genome research internationally have led to rapid identification of genes involved in the causation not only of single gene disorders, but also of more common diseases such as diabetes, cardiovascular disease, and cancer. With an abundance of new genetic tests expected, some aspects of genetic services must be integrated into primary-care settings. Because there are insufficient numbers of counselors and clinical geneticists to provide appropriate pretest education and counseling, new models of service delivery are needed.

Many of the education components to genetic counseling are and will continue to be provided not only by genetics specialists, but also by nurses and primary-care physicians. Education will need to be increasingly supplemented by interactive computer programs, videotapes, and written materials. The more complex the ramifications of genetic testing, or the more directly related to reproductive options, the more desirable it is that genetic counselors and medical geneticists play a role in the education and counseling in order to maintain the high standards of practice and noneugenic goals that currently govern genetics practice. Also, when the majority of patients' psychological needs stem from a genetic condition, genetic counseling by a certified counselor will continue to be desired. With significant professional education efforts and elegantly designed referral or triage mechanisms, services may be enhanced in the future. A significant goal for genetics providers is to more thoroughly meet the needs of a wider spectrum of the population with a broader array of services.

A variety of providers can and should respond to the increasing needs. Here, appropriate referral mechanisms will play an important role. For instance, if genetic testing becomes available to assist in predictions of cardiovascular disease, these tests may be offered in a primary-care physician's office. A nurse may provide the background information on what genetic information may be gleaned from the test and then what type of prevention program may be designed in conjunction with the results. There would seem to be little need for referral for genetic counseling in this scenario, or for other medical management uses of testing where the emotional issues are less likely to be profound.

On the other hand, cystic fibrosis gene testing illustrates the potential complexities of genetic testing. Test results can be ambiguous, there may be reproductive ramifications, and improvements in treatment of the disorder have increased longevity and quality of life. Even if cystic fibrosis carrier testing is offered in primary-care physicians' offices, the education component needs to be thorough and balanced; and referral for genetic counseling when the results indicate someone is a gene carrier will remain important.

When genetic testing becomes increasingly utilized as a tool for medical management, and not merely as a means to obtain risk information, there is likely to be less psychological turmoil for patients. Carrier testing or presymptomatic testing for a serious, late-onset disorder, however, illustrates the need

◆ **genetic counseling**
With pretest education and counseling, the interaction between a health-care provider and a patient or family member on concerns about the risks of bearing a child with a genetic disorder, reproductive testing options, or the diagnosis of an inherited condition.

See Also

Biomedical Technologies: "Factories" of Ethical Dilemmas

Trust and Communication: Shared Decision-Making

for client-oriented counseling. As the number and background of professionals providing genetic tests expand, there is a greater potential threat to autonomous, well-informed decision making. The maintenance of the current high standard of practice for genetic counseling is a key issue in considering the consequences of the diffusion and proliferation of these services.

— BARBARA BOWLES BIESECKER

ETHICAL ISSUES

Genetic counseling is a complex communication process that takes place between a genetic counselor and one or more counselees, also called clients. It may involve a single encounter lasting 30 to 60 minutes or multiple encounters over months or years. The type and duration of the encounter is determined by the nature of the condition that led to the encounter. This includes whether the condition under discussion is genetic or nongenetic, the mode of inheritance, and the severity of the disorder, including its prognosis. Therapeutic and reproductive implications play a significant role as well as the counselor's evaluation of the effectiveness of the counseling encounter.

Effective and helpful genetic counseling should be guided by several ethical principles and human values judged by most workers in the field to be of vital importance (Wertz et al., 1990). These include autonomy; beneficence and nonmaleficence; confidentiality; veracity and truth-telling; and informed consent. It is also crucial that varied cultural and ethnic factors be taken into account. The professional code of ethics for genetic counselors should also be considered (Palmer, 1992).

Since genetic counseling usually occurs in medical settings such as clinics, medical centers, or private offices, the ethical values that currently prevail in medical and nursing practice should also play a role in genetic counseling. These principles or values influence different aspects of the counseling process to different degrees. Their influence may also vary according to the cultural background, ethnicity, or religious beliefs of the counselees and their families. The latter factors should receive serious attention, since cultural, religious, or ethnic differences can profoundly influence the relative weight given to one value or principle over another. This is especially true when counseling involves individuals from other countries (Wertz et al., 1990). Counselees from the so-called Third World may cherish religious tenets and ethical values drastically different from those of the Jewish and Christian faiths that inform so much of Western medical ethics (Fisher, 1992).

◆ **genotype**
The genetic makeup of the developing individual.

See Also

Confidentiality

In Practice: Is 'Nondirective' Counseling Possible?

ETHICS
Nondirectiveness vs. Patients' "Dysgenic" Choices

An ethical dilemma may arise for the counselor if the counselee wants to make a decision that will have what the counselor strongly feels are mostly negative consequences. For example, a man and a woman are both affected by a serious homozygous recessive disorder (e.g., sickle-cell anemia) and are advised that all their children will be similarly affected. After being counseled, and with full knowledge of the genetic consequences, they decide to have their own biological children. This kind of decision is called dysgenic by some, because it has the potential of resulting in an increase in the number of deleterious genes in the next generation. This will be true if the couple has more than two children and they in turn live to reproduce in an environment where these genes have no selective advantage. Some counselors feel that the counselor may be justified in not honoring the principle of nondirectiveness because the net reproductive effect is likely to produce more harm than benefit (Yarborough et al., 1989). It further results in a situation in which children who are destined to live a life of pain and suffering are knowingly brought into the world. Furthermore, there is the possibility of genetic harm to this population if this practice becomes more common. These harms must be balanced against the benefit to these parents of having their own biological children, even if these children are much more likely to suffer or to die an early death.

The counselor who feels that the principle of nondirectiveness ought not be violated under any circumstances should at least explore with the counselees the psychosocial and emotional reasons that led them to this decision. The counselor should assist them in a careful and deliberate examination of the benefits and harms that may effect them and their offspring (Kessler, 1979). Strong arguments have been advanced suggesting that by applying the principle of beneficence, the counselor is justified in attempting to persuade counselees to reconsider their decisions in certain cases without violating the rule of nondirectiveness (Yarborough et al., 1989).

— ROBERT F. MURRAY, JR.

Autonomy and nondirectiveness

A major facet of the counseling process, and one important goal of a successful counseling process, is a course of action (or inaction) that is determined according to the best available evidence. Genetic counselors generally agree that this decision should be made by the counselee, and that it should be made freely and without coercion (Fraser, 1974; Ad Hoc Committee on Genetic Counseling, 1975). Counselors want to avoid, to the extent possible, being accused of "playing god" and to resist any temptation to practice eugenics, the process of manipulating genes in order to "improve" genetic makeup. The manipulation is accomplished by directing the counselees about what reproductive decisions they should or should not make. This is inappropriate because respect for autonomy should be a predominant ethical value guiding the counseling process and its outcome. This is the clear consensus of genetic counselors from all over the world (U.S. President's Commission, 1983; Wertz and Fletcher, 1988).

If counselees are to make autonomous decisions, they must be fully informed about the disorder in question, free of coercion, aware of all the possible choices, and have access to any facilities and/or services to implement their decision. In its purest sense and with only rare exceptions, the nature of the decision is not an issue as long as the counselee has decided that such a decision is in her or his best interest. In this model of counseling the counselor makes every effort to be "nondirective," that is, to refrain as much as possible from providing any suggestion directly or indirectly to the counselee as to what decision she or he should make (Fraser, 1974, 1979; Hsia, 1979). No counselor can be totally unbiased and without any interest in the decision that is made. However, the aim in counseling is to create "an accepting psychologic climate" and thereby the possibility of a nondirective relationship (Antley, 1979).

Beneficence/nonmaleficence: Whose needs come first?

When the counselee is trying to balance the benefits and harms of a particular decision against one another, there may be a tendency to emphasize the benefits over the harms. In some cases, the benefit or beneficence for the counselee(s) may mean maleficence or harm for the child. If parents who know they will have a child with a serious genetically determined disease decide to go ahead because they believe they have a "right to bear children," they may benefit in having their own biological children. At the same time they might not be judged "responsible parents" because they may not have given serious enough consideration to the suffering and discomfort their offspring will suffer. Even if this factor has been considered, the parents may justify their decision on the religious grounds that they are merely following the dictates of a higher power, leaving it to God to determine whether or not they have children.

In some cases it may be difficult for counselor and counselee to agree on what constitutes a benefit and what a harm, since such determinations are often rather subjective, governed primarily by the counselee's values. For example, abortion of an affected fetus might be considered a benefit to some and harmful to others, depending on whose needs are considered primary. Providing information that there is a high probability that a counselee at risk to inherit a serious genetically determined disease of late onset has in fact inherited it might seem a beneficent act by some who value knowledge of any sort, and a maleficent or harmful act by others who value information only when it leads to the prevention or correction of harm. In the tension between these contrasting ethical principles, medical ethical tradition suggests that nonmaleficence should be weighted more heavily than beneficence in cases where they are in conflict. This position is consistent with the maxim of *primum non nocere*, first do no harm (Beauchamp and Childress, 1989), since providing information without clear benefit has the potential for causing social and emotional harm.

Veracity and truth-telling in genetic counseling

A major part of the genetic counseling process is the exchange of information about the medical and family history provided by the counselee and comprehensive genetic and medical information about the disease in question provided by the counselor (Fraser, 1974; Hsia, 1979). The counselee needs accurate information, including the correct diagnosis, in order to choose a beneficial course of action. Truth-telling is an essential ingredient of the relationship between genetic counselors and counselees. Part of the trust that exists between them is based on this virtue. As a consequence, the genetic counselor should provide truthful, accurate, and complete information to the counselee concerning the genetic disorder being considered.

On some occasions the genetic counselor might have very good reasons for violating this important trust. Failure to tell the truth will most often involve withholding information rather than lying. But the counselor bears the burden of justifying failure to tell the whole truth. This is the case even if the counselor is keeping back some information until a time when it may be more readily received, that is, when the counselee is judged to be better prepared to accept negative information and its attendant consequences.

◆ **gene carrier**
An individual with one copy of a recessive allele that causes a particular trait.

See Also

Information Disclosure

Ethics of Disclosure: How—and How Much?—to Tell?

Ethics codes for psychotherapists, nurses, and other health professionals refer to protection of professional-client confidentiality.

PAGE 124

WHY WOULD A CLIENT WITHHOLD INFORMATION?

1. The information, if transmitted, is likely to cause permanent damage to the self-image of the counselee or result in a serious or severe emotional reaction. This is the case when a female is found to have an XY sex chromosomal constitution rather than the normal XX sex chromosomes.
2. Refraining from transmitting the information will not have a significant effect on the options open to the counselee or her or his family nor will it compromise any therapy the counselee or the family should receive.
3. The counselee has a history of serious depression and the information, if fully given, has a good chance of exacerbating the depression with a significant risk of suicide.
4. The information reveals evidence that the putative father in a family is not the biological father of a particular child; if this information is provided, it is likely to lead to the breakup of the family and the child will no longer have a father.
5. A young man or woman has been found to be a presymptomatic carrier of a late-onset, autosomal (related to chromosomes that are common to both sexes), dominant condition and does not want a fiance to be told because it is feared she or he might break off the relationship.

The latter two cases, in which information is withheld from third parties, raise the question of the counselor's obligation or "duty to warn" others who might be affected by the presence of the genetic condition in a spouse or significant other. For some counselors, the "right to know" or the "duty to warn" provides strong justification for telling the whole truth at all times during the counseling process, regardless of the potential consequences. At the same time, a minority of counselees feel they have a right "not to know." These people would rather not be told about a serious genetic condition of late onset, especially if there is no effective therapy or other maneuver that will forestall its onset or significantly reduce its symptoms. If counselees do not wish to know about their incurable condition, the information may nevertheless have to be placed in the medical record so that future health-care givers will be alert to the counselee's status. The information can also be provided if counselees should change their minds. In general, genetic counselors will withhold information only where there is a strong likelihood for serious harm to the family or to the self-image or status of the individual (Wertz et al., 1990).

Confidentiality and the control of genetic information

Medical genetics is more concerned with the family than almost any other medical subspecialty. As part of the evaluation of a clinically significant genetic disorder, the genetic counselor is required to collect detailed family data and record it in the form of a "pedigree." This enables the counselor and the medical geneticist to determine whether there is a pattern of occurrence in the family consistent with control by a single gene of major effect (often referred to as a "Mendelian" gene). The pedigree may also provide information that may indicate the presence of inherited chromosomal structural rearrangements called translocations. More often than not, the pedigree information is insufficient to make this determination. But when it does demonstrate the presence of an inherited defect, this knowledge can have serious, even grave, implications for the other genetically related members of the family. This is especially true when one is dealing with conditions that demonstrate autosomal or X-linked dominant or X-linked recessive modes of inheritance, because inheritance of a single mutant gene on an X or non-X chromosome can cause the full-blown clinical disorder.

Under the medical model that governs medical geneticists and genetic counseling, the counselee has the status of a patient. All information relative to his or her case is covered by the guarantee of privacy and confidentiality that is required of health professionals (Beauchamp and Childress, 1989). The medical geneticist or genetic counselor should get permission from the counselee to contact other family members to inform them that they are at risk for a serious genetically determined disorder. In general, this is not a problem; most counselees readily consent to having their relatives contacted or are willing to do this themselves. But in at least two instances the genetic counselor may face an ethical dilemma concerning the release of information to third parties.

1. The disorder is *not* treatable and can be diagnosed by prenatal diagnosis, so a couple at risk could theoretically avoid the birth of an affected child; or individuals at risk for this might wish to take special predictive tests and use the knowledge to get their affairs in order or in other ways to alter their life situation.
2. The disorder *is* treatable and can be cured or can have the symptoms and any complications significantly reduced by safe and readily available therapy; or the expression of the disorder can be prevented if it is detected before the symptoms have appeared.

See Also

Privacy: It's a Cultural Thing

ETHICAL ISSUES
Informed Consent in Genetic Counseling

Since a major component of genetic counseling is communication of information, and since the counselee is encouraged to make her or his own decision, problems or conflicts with informed consent are unusual. Informed consent is especially relevant in the counseling process when a procedure may result in potentially harmful or ambiguous outcomes, for example:

1. in connection with prenatal diagnosis, when the counselee or woman who is to undergo the test needs to understand its risks, benefits, errors, and limitations;
2. as a prelude to presymptomatic testing for a serious disorder without available treatment or methods of prevention, where a positive result can have profound implications for the individual's future life;
3. in connection with participation in a research protocol in which there may be questions about the future use of data or tissue or blood (especially DNA) in future studies or in the search for other genetic markers.

— ROBERT F. MURRAY, JR.

The obligation to maintain confidentiality of patient records and genetic information obtained in a medical setting is not absolute and may be breached when there is adequate justification. The exceptions may be invoked only if there are extenuating or overriding personal or social circumstances. The State of Texas statute on confidentiality, for example, allows confidential information to be disclosed if there is the probability of imminent physical injury to the patient or others (Andrews, 1987). In the case of genetic disorders, the most compelling argument for breaching confidentiality besides those instances where it is required by law is the protection of third parties from harm (Andrews, 1987). In ethical terms this is sometimes cited as "the duty or obligation to warn" when there is a clear or imminent danger.

In the cases shown above, there would appear to be clear justification for breaching confidentiality in the second case but not in the first. In the first example, useful information might be provided to third parties, but there is no evidence of harm because the condition identified is not treatable. In the second example, the fact that there is a treatment or a method of preventing the condition means that failure to warn would result in harm to a third party. Since the burden of justification would be on the genetic counselor to show that the harm, however conceived, is correctable or preventable, it makes sense not to breach confidentiality in instances where the potential harm is not clearly defined. The U.S. President's Commission for the Study of Ethical Problems in Medicine and Biomedical and Behavioral Research regarding confidentiality provided four conditions under which the requirements of confidentiality can be overridden and genetic information released to relatives or their physicians (1983).

Revealing genetic information, especially in cases of presymptomatic diagnosis, has other important implications for the counselee's eligibility for health insurance and possibly for life insurance. Depending on the condition involved, such information if revealed can also affect employability and opportunities for promotion. There is always a significant risk that sensitive information, if released, may find its way to individuals or agencies that might harm the counselee in the future.

Ethnic and cultural influences

The population of the United States and many other industrialized nations is becoming more diverse. It is estimated that by the year 2010 nearly one-third of the population of the United States will be made up of minorities. Genetic counseling that promotes individual autonomy and is consistent with the ethical values discussed here will require that counselors be aware of and responsive to a wide and growing range of ethnic and cultural variations among those who are now and will be seeking genetic counseling (Fisher, 1992). Conflicts are almost certain to arise when the values and decisions of the ethnically and/or culturally different counselees conflict with those of the counselors and the Western values derived from Jewish and Christian sources that in general govern the decision-making process. The value systems that have been used traditionally in counseling will probably have to be applied in significantly different ways if the process and outcome of counseling is to be helpful and effective.

— ROBERT F. MURRAY, JR.

GENETICS AND HUMAN BEHAVIOR

SCIENTIFIC AND RESEARCH ISSUES

One of the most difficult topics in philosophy and ethics is how to deal with individual differences. Why are some people good while others are evil by any stan-

The firmest grounding for the requirement to seek consent is the ethical principle of "respect for persons."

PAGE 397

See Also
Trust

G

GENETICS AND HUMAN BEHAVIOR

Scientific and Research Issues

BLURRED LINES
Genetic vs. Environmental Causes

There is a somewhat complicated history of philosophical misunderstanding of genetic science that has been covered by many people. Basically, what happened earlier in the twentieth century is that some influential people concerned about social reform and the betterment of mankind made the mistake of thinking that "genetically caused" meant a condition would be impossible to change. In their political writings they argued that if a condition was caused by the environment, then the condition would be easy to change if society wanted to change it (Degler, 1991). Thus, for many, "genetic" came to be associated with notions of social stagnation and cruel "social Darwinism," and "social" or "environmental" came to be associated with desirable social change and improvement of living conditions.

The fallacy is a simple one: "environmental cause" does not mean "easily changed," and "genetic cause" does not mean "unchangeable." Yet the misunderstandings resulting from this fallacy continue today. For example, it is "politically correct" today to claim that most social ills are caused by social conditions, and it is quite "politically incorrect" to maintain that some social realities might be caused by genetic conditions. It is often viewed as acceptable to suggest that conditions of poverty and social disorganization cause crime and stupidity. It is much less acceptable to suggest that genetic dispositions to impulsive criminality and stupidity might cause much poverty and social disorganization.

Most scientists interested in genetics and human behavior argue that knowledge of causes is important regardless of political or ethical pronouncements. At one time one could be burned at the stake for suggesting that the Earth was round rather than flat. Today scientists are sometimes attacked for suggesting that some socially important differences among people might be caused by genetic differences.

— GLAYDE WHITNEY

◆ **genetics**
A branch of biology that deals with the heredity, or genetic makeup, and variation of organisms.

dard? Why are some people smart, enthusiastic, and energetic while other people are severely mentally impaired? What makes someone crazy by any definition; alcoholic versus not alcoholic; or a murderer, arsonist, or upright citizen?

Not only are there individual differences, there are also average differences among various groups of individuals. People can be sorted into groups on the basis of many traits, and behavioral differences may be seen among the groups. People concerned with ethics and philosophy may sometimes have difficulty handling individual differences, and even more difficulty with group differences. In recent years discussions of group differences have become increasingly politically contentious. Nevertheless, group differences in behavior exist and are well documented; indeed, some are obvious to any impartial observer.

Consider sex differences. Among sexually mature humans, sexual aggression is almost exclusively a male-instigated behavior; cases of a woman raping a man are virtually unheard of. Indeed, physically assaultive crime is predominantly a male endeavor (Wilson and Herrnstein, 1985; Ellis and Hoffman, 1990). Consider an even more sensitive example, the link between race, sex, age, and crime. It is rare, for instance, to hear of an elderly woman mugging a stranger on the street or being the perpetrator of a murder. Group and individual differences in behavior are real, whether or not people wish to acknowledge them.

In order to understand the present status of our knowledge of genetics and human behavior, we must be careful not to confuse some issues of politics (or philosophical and ethical preferences) with some issues of scientific knowledge. Individual behavioral differences theoretically may result from different genetic inheritance. Just as one person inherits red hair and another person inherits blond hair, one person might inherit a genetic constitution that causes a certain brain chemistry predisposing that person to violent, impulsive criminal behavior (an example will be discussed further on). Charges of genetic determinism, sexism, racism, or political incorrectness in regard to investigation of genetic causes of behavior are political concepts, not scientific ones.

Early in the twentieth century, theories of genetic influence on behavior were popular. Then a number of political events occurred that resulted in many people becoming philosophically, ethically, and politically opposed to theories of genetic influences on human behavior. These historical developments include (1) the rise of Nazism in Germany, with scientifically incorrect theories of genetic determinism of racial differences; (2) the rise of Marxist-Leninism in the Soviet Union, with scientifically incorrect theories of environmental determinism of individual differences; (3) the elaboration of the civil rights movement in the United States, with scientifically incorrect theories denying the reality of individual differences (Whitney, 1990a). The political controversies (some continuing today) are so fundamentally important to society that

See Also
Behavior Control

many people are very sensitive about scientific knowledge concerning genetics and behavior (Davis, 1986; Pearson, 1991), making them unable to accept a differentiation between scientific and political inquiry.

In scientific investigations of individual differences, scientists attempt to discover the causes of individual differences, whatever they may be. Investigations of human behavior are perhaps always close to ethical concerns. However, many scientists believe that true knowledge of causes is important and in itself is ethically neutral. It is important to separate scientific knowledge from what a society decides to do with that knowledge.

Methods of study

A scientific approach to individual differences in behavior begins with a consideration of their fundamental causes. In scientific theory all causes of individual differences in human behavior can be placed in one of two categories: environmental effects or inherited (genetic) effects. Environmental effects include all experiences that could be different between two people and thereby influence their different growth and behavior, including nutrition, schooling, parental behavior, disease and accidents, and so forth. Genetic effects stem from inherited differences in the DNA, the basic material of the genetic code, which can cause two people to develop differently. It is a postulate of the scientific approach that all causes of individual differences can be understood as arising from either environment or genetic inheritance.

The main technical problem in understanding the role of genetics in human behavior is that genetic origin and rearing environment usually covary (go together) with human subjects. Children get their genes from their biological parents. Those same parents usually raise their children. If children then grow up to resemble their parents, and children of different parents grow up to be different, is it because of the shared genes or the shared environments? Somehow the scientist must overcome the usual family covariation of genes and environment in order to discover if inheritance (genetic differences) or environmental effects cause the individual differences in behavior that we see around us. Most of the general methods used to discover and separate genetic and environmental influences on behavior can be placed in one of three categories: (1) adoption method; (2) twin method; (3) genetic pattern method. These can be best understood by describing their application with real examples.

The major psychosis of schizophrenia presents many philosophical, ethical, and political dilemmas. It has many symptoms but can generally be characterized by sensory and cognitive hallucinations (for example, hearing voices of people who are not present, and experiencing delusional thoughts and beliefs). At the present time there is neither a medical cure for nor means of preventing schizophrenia, although the symptoms can often be treated. The existence of schizophrenia presents serious ethical issues to society because it is relatively common and often severely incapacitating.

GENETIC OR ENVIRONMENTAL?

Methods of Distinguishing Influences on Behavior

1. adoption method
2. twin method
3. genetic pattern method

Schizophrenia affects about 1 percent of the general population and about 10 to 15 percent of the biological children of a person with schizophrenia. If both parents have schizophrenia, about 40 percent of the children develop schizophrenia. This "familiality" (tendency to run in families) has been known for a long time.

Two major theories developed about the cause of schizophrenia. One was that it resulted from bizarre child-rearing behavior. According to this theory, if parents were inconsistent in their treatment of a child, then the child would grow up with a poor grasp on reality and, in extreme cases, develop the social withdrawal, hallucinations, and delusional thought that characterize schizophrenia. Because mothers traditionally spend more time with children than do fathers, this family-environment-cause theory became known as the theory of the schizophrenogenic mother ("genic" means "causing"). The second main theory about the cause of schizophrenia was that it was largely a genetic condition. The genetic theory was that if a person inherited a certain gene or set of genes, then that person would be susceptible to developing schizophrenia. If the person did not inherit the necessary genes, then the person would not develop schizophrenia.

A major problem with deciding between these two scientific theories about the cause of schizophrenia is that in most families, the parents who raise the children are also the genetic parents of the children. The source of the parenting and the source of the genes are the same, so simply observing that schizophrenia runs in families does not reveal anything about its cause. It was widely documented that strange parental behavior often occurred in families that produced schizophrenic children. But there was no clear interpretation for that observation. Did the strange behavior of the parent

◆ **genetic linkage**
The inheritance of one trait along with another that helps establish the relative position of genetic markers along the chromosomes.

See Also
Bioethics

cause the schizophrenia of the child? Or was the preschizophrenic child abnormal enough to cause the disruption in the family? Or did the strange behavior of the parent and the schizophrenia of the child result from the genes that they shared?

ADOPTION METHOD. The adoption method provides a way for the scientist to separate environmental parenting from genetic parenting. If scientists can find sets of biological (genetic) parents and their children who were separated at birth, then they will be able to look at the effect of genes without the added confusion of a shared family environment. Also, if they can study sets of adoptive parents and the children they have adopted, then they can look at the effects of the parenting behavior—the home environment—without the confusion of shared genes. Thus the adoption method provides an effective way to separate genetic from environmental causes.

As Abraham Lincoln observed, the signers of the Declaration of Independence "did not intend to declare all men equal in all respects."

PAGE 287

Leonard Heston reported the first modern adoption study of schizophrenia in 1966. He found that the adopted-away offspring of schizophrenic mothers, when raised in nonschizophrenic families, had a lifetime incidence of schizophrenia of about 16 percent; this outcome was essentially identical to that of natural offspring raised by a schizophrenic biological parent. Further, about half of the adopted-away children of schizophrenic mothers displayed some sort of psychiatric or criminal problems as adults.

Later studies excellently summarized by Irving Gottesman and Dorothea Wolfgram (1991) have confirmed and extended Heston's findings. Genes, not prenatal environment, are implicated because the results are about the same when the biological schizophrenic parent is the father. Being raised in a family environment that includes the bizarre behavior of schizophrenics does not induce schizophrenia in individuals without the predisposing genes. Schizophrenic genes appear to be necessary but are not alone always sufficient for the onset of the psychosis. This is most clearly illustrated by the incidence of schizophrenia among twins.

TWIN METHOD. The twin method is another important approach that helps a scientist decide between an interpretation of genetic causation or an interpretation of environmental causation. The basic logic of the twin method is straightforward. Twin pairs are one or the other of two types: identical or fraternal.

Identical twins (also called monozygotic, that is, one zygote) are genetically identical. They are created when one egg is fertilized by one sperm, giving rise to one individual. When, very early in development, that one individual divides into two separate embryos, the result is identical twins. Identical twins are genetically identical because early in development they actually were one individual. If the individual differences for any trait (such as eye color or schizophrenia) were 100 percent caused by genes, then identical twins should be identical for that trait. Fraternal twins (also called dizygotic, that is, two zygotes) are created when two separate eggs are each fertilized by a different sperm. Fraternal twins are thus genetically just like any other full siblings. They have both parents in common; they just happen to have been conceived and born at the same time. On average, full siblings, including fraternal twins, share half their genes. Since identical twin pairs share all their genes whereas fraternal twin pairs share half their genes, the essence of the twin method is to compare identical and fraternal twins. If a pair of identical twins are more similar to one another than are fraternal twins, that is strong evidence that the trait under consideration is influenced by the genes.

With regard to schizophrenia, members of identical twin pairs are concordant (that is, both show the condition) much more frequently than are members of fraternal twin pairs. That finding is consistent with the theory of genetic causation of schizophrenia. However, when one member of an identical twin pair is schizophrenic, the other twin is also schizophrenic in only about 50 percent of the pairs. An incidence of 100 percent would be expected if genes were the whole story.

Twin pairs are called "discordant" when one twin shows the trait and the other twin does not. When identical twins who are discordant for schizophrenia have children, the risk for the offspring is about 10-15 percent whether the parent is the twin with schizophrenia or the twin without it. The identical twin who does not display schizophrenia transmits the susceptibility to the child every bit as much as does the twin with blatant schizophrenia. Such transmission in the absence of schizophrenic behavior is further strong evidence for genetic transmission of susceptibility. What the causal factors are, in addition to the proper genes, is unknown. And although genes are clearly necessary for schizophrenia, exactly what the condition consists of genetically is unknown. Theories range from suggesting a single gene that disrupts brain chemistry, to suggesting that the simultaneous inheritance of many genes (at least more than two) is necessary in order to induce susceptibility to schizophrenia (Gottesman and Wolfgram, 1991).

GENETIC PATTERN METHOD. The third commonly used method is to look for genetic patterns of transmission for traits of interest. The genetic pattern method comes from almost a century of research into basic genetics. It has been discovered and repeatedly demonstrated that some basic patterns of inheritance are widely shared by plants and animals, including humans. If a trait of interest shows a pattern of occurrence that is identical to a known genetic pattern, that

See Also

Gene Therapy; Genetic Counseling; Value and Valuation

increases the likelihood that the new trait is influenced by genes. However, it is important to understand that consistency with a genetic pattern does not *prove* genetic causation. Further evidence confirmed by other methods is necessary for proof.

In order to illustrate the genetic pattern method with real human behavior examples, it is necessary to review some basic genetics. There are perhaps as many as 100,000 different genes. For creatures, like humans, that reproduce sexually, each individual has two copies of most genes, one from the mother and one from the father. Different copies of the same gene are called alleles. A particular allele may be dominant or recessive. The allele is said to be dominant if its effect is seen when only one copy is present. An allele is said to be recessive if two copies must be present in order to show the effect. In order to show a recessive characteristic, the individual must inherit copies of the same allele from the mother and from the father. To be a "carrier" of a genetic trait means that an individual has one copy of a recessive allele that causes the trait. With that we can illustrate some genetic patterns.

Dominant traits

Single-gene dominant inheritance means that only one copy of the allele is necessary to display the condition; thus everyone with the allele will display the condition. If the allele is rare in the population, then most individuals with the condition will have one copy of the dominant allele; their other allele for that gene will be the recessive allele. Huntington's disease is a well-known example of a dominant genetic disease. The disease's symptoms include degeneration of the nervous system, usually beginning in middle age, that results in death. In this devastating disease, as the nervous system degenerates, there is usually a gradual loss of intellectual ability and emotional control. The genetic pattern shown by Huntington's is that of a condition caused by a rare single dominant gene. Since affected people have one copy of the dominant disease gene and one copy of a recessive gene (for "normal nervous system"), half of their offspring develop the disease if they live long enough. Huntington's never skips a generation. Since the gene is dominant, the person who inherits it will manifest the disease (if he or she lives long enough). If one full sibling has the condition, there is a 50-50 chance that any other sibling will also get the disease.

Recessive traits

In contrast to dominant conditions, recessive conditions show a very different pattern of occurrence. To reiterate, essentially, "recessive" means that both copies of the gene must be of the same form (the same allele) in order to show the condition. Two parents, neither of whom shows a trait, can have a child affected by a recessive trait (this happens if both parents are carriers of one copy of the recessive allele; the child thus has two copies, one from each parent, and manifests the condition). Recessive traits can "skip generations" because parents and their offspring can carry one copy of the recessive gene and not display the associated trait. In the population there are many recessive genes that cause various abnormal conditions. Each particular recessive allele may be rare, but since there are many of them, their combined impact on a population can be substantial.

Among humans, a classic example of recessive inheritance is the condition of phenylketonuria (PKU). Individuals with PKU usually are severely mentally impaired. Most never learn to talk; many have seizures and display temper tantrums. PKU is a form of severe mental retardation that is both genetic and treatable. It is genetic in that it is caused by a recessive genetic allele. Without two copies of that particular allele, a person will not develop the set of symptoms, with mental impairment, that is characteristic of PKU. However, following scientific knowledge of the details of PKU, a treatment became available. It was discovered that the recessive gene prevents the normal metabolism of a substance that is common in food. Therefore many normal foods are toxic to the individual with two PKU alleles. Providing a special diet that is low in the offending substance can prevent or minimize the nervous system damage that leads to the profound intellectual disabilities of untreated PKU individuals.

The example of PKU demonstrates that inherited (genetic) conditions can be treated. Knowledge of specific causation can result in effective treatment. This is an extremely important point ethically and philosophically because it is often misunderstood and misinterpreted. This is why it was stated earlier that "genetic determinism" is a political, not a scientific, concept.

Today, well over 100 different genes are known for which relatively rare recessive alleles cause conditions that include among their symptoms severe mental impairment. The rapidly developing knowledge of basic genetic chemistry, from molecular genetics to biotechnology and the Human Genome Project, which is mapping human genes, holds out the hope that we may soon be able to treat many more of these devastating genetic conditions effectively.

Sex-linked traits

Not everyone has two copies of each gene. For genes that are technically "sex-linked" (genes in the X chromosome), women have two copies while men have only one copy. The basic biology of human chromosomal sex determination is that the vast majority of nor-

The most remarkable thing about the influence of genetics on human self-understanding is that it has been so small and limited.

PAGE 285

Eugenics may reenter public policy under the guise of "limited resources."

PAGE 304

mal women have two copies of the X chromosome. The vast majority of normal men have only one copy of the X chromosome. Instead of a second X chromosome, men have one copy of the Y chromosome. The X chromosome is a relatively large chromosome that contains many genes. The Y chromosome is one of the smallest chromosomes and contains relatively few genes. From this it follows that there are many genes (those on the X chromosome) for which women normally have two copies but men normally have only one copy. Also, there are some genes on the Y chromosome for which men normally have one copy and normal women have no copies.

One gene on the Y chromosome is sometimes called the tdf gene (testes determining factor) because early in embryological development, it causes the beginning of sexual differentiation of the male. Many of the anatomical and behavioral differences between the sexes can ultimately be traced to the effect of this one gene.

On the X chromosome there are many alleles that act as recessives in women (females need two copies to show the effect) but as dominant genes in men (males have only one copy of the X-linked allele, so they show its effect). Many more men than women will display the trait caused by a sex-linked recessive allele because every man with one copy of the allele will show the trait, but women need two copies of the same X-linked allele in order to show the trait.

Red/green color blindness and hemophilia are two well-known examples of sex-linked recessive conditions. Both can influence behavior in important ways. Although many affected men are not aware that they are color-blind until they are scientifically tested, that does not mean the condition is without effect on their behavior. Red/green color-blind men tend to confuse shades of red and green; to many, both appear brownish. Color blindness can have effects ranging from the humorously trivial to quite important. Color confusion can result in mismatched socks and weird shirt-slack combinations, or confusion of traffic signals (which is why the relative position of red/green traffic lights is standardized) and port/starboard lights on ships. A survey in Minnesota suggested that even with mandatory hunter orange clothing, it was a bit more dangerous to go hunting with a color-blind companion (Foltz, 1962).

It has been suggested that the sex-linked recessive hemophilia allele has had an influence on world history. Among European royalty, a number of the male descendants of Queen Victoria have been hemophiliacs. Did the worrisome effects of this "bleeding disease," which affected the tsarevich Alexei of Russia, contribute to the political downfall of the Romanov

GENES AND CRIME

What We Don't Study *Can* Hurt Us

There is a sex-linked recessive allele that apparently affects the likelihood of impulsive aggression. Biochemically, the X-linked allele affects an important chemical in the brain called monoamine oxidase (which is also involved in the effects of amphetamines and cocaine on the brain). All males known to have the particular X-linked allele display rather low intelligence and impulsive acting out. The impulsive criminal behaviors are reported to be most often triggered by anger, and the acts committed are out of proportion to the provocation. Behaviors noted include attacks with deadly weapons, such as stabbing a prison guard with a pitchfork, attempting to run over a complaining boss with a car, forcing women to undress at knifepoint. Some affected males are arsonists. Others have engaged in incestuous rape, exhibitionism, and voyeurism. Unaffected males and women from the same families are reported to be normal (Bruner et al., 1993).

The bioethical dilemmas facing modern society are starkly illustrated by the study of genetic influences on aggressive and criminal behavior. At essentially the same time that Han Bruner and his colleagues were publishing their scientific study, political pressure was being exerted in the United States to stifle such research. A scientific conference had been planned for October 1992 on the topic "Genetic Factors in Crime." One of the sponsors providing money for the conference was the National Institutes of Health (NIH). Under political pressure, the NIH first froze its support and then effectively prevented the conference by withdrawing support. As reported in *Science*, "the Congressional Black Caucus, among other mostly African-American critics, argued it was racist to suggest the existence of links between genes and crime" (1993, p. 619). Nancy Touchette (1993) points out that favorable scientific review had led NIH to support the conference on genetics and crime. It was strictly political pressure that led to its cancellation. Are there topics that are too controversial to be subjected to rational discourse and scientific investigation? Today it is common to hold up to ridicule the antiscientific nonsense of the Middle Ages while at the same time pretending to know the causes of some of today's most intractable social problems. A review of the substantial evidence concerning race differences in criminal behavior and possible genetic influences is available elsewhere (Whitney, 1990b).

— GLAYDE WHITNEY

dynasty? One source of Rasputin's influence was his ability to calm the tsarevich during bleeding episodes (Vogel and Motulsky, 1979).

Intelligence

There are more data about the inheritance of intelligence than about any other complex behavioral characteristic of humans. The notion of substantial genetic influences on individual variation in intelligence remains controversial even after almost a century of investigation.

Intelligence testing grew out of a societal problem: the failure of "universal education." When universal public education was first implemented in France during the latter half of the nineteenth century, it failed. Not everyone who went to school acquired an education. Alfred Binet and others invented intelligence tests in order to aid in the prediction of school performance (Boring, 1957; Fancher, 1985). Despite the controversies that continue to swirl around the applications of "standardized testing," intelligence tests remain among the best predictors of school performance (Jensen, 1980), and the original problem persists.

The level of intellectual functioning (abstract reasoning, ability to perform complex cognitive tasks, score on tests of general intelligence, IQ) is a strongly heritable trait. In 1963 Nikki Erlenmeyer-Kimling and Lissy Jarvik summarized the literature dealing with correlations between the measured intelligence of various relatives. After eliminating studies based on specialized samples or employing unusual tests or statistics, they reviewed eighty-one investigations. Included were data from eight countries on four continents spanning more than two generations and containing over 30,000 correlational pairings. The overview that emerged from that mass of data was unequivocal. Intelligence appeared to be a quantitative polygenic trait, that is, a trait influenced by many genes, as are such physical characteristics as height and weight.

The results did not suggest that environmental factors were unimportant. Rather, genetic variation was quite important. The less sensitive trait of height (or weight) can be used to illustrate this distinction. It is well known that an individual's height (or weight) can be influenced by nutrition. Inadequate diets during development can result in reduced height (or weight). The average height of whole populations has changed with changes in public health and nutrition. Yet at the same time, individual differences in height (or weight) among the members of a population are strongly influenced by heredity. In general, taller people tend to have taller children across the population as a whole, and the relative height of different people is strongly influenced by their genes. And that also appears to be the case with intelligence. The Erlenmeyer-Kimling and Jarvik survey data suggested that about 70 percent of the variation among individuals in measured intelligence was due to genetic differences. The remaining 30 percent of the variation was due to unspecified (and still unknown) environmental effects.

Thomas Bouchard and Matt McGue (1981) provided an updated summary of the world literature on intelligence correlations between relatives. They summarized 111 studies, fifty-nine of which had been reported during the seventeen years since the Erlenmeyer-Kimling and Jarvik review of 1963. Bouchard and McGue summarized 526 familial correlations from 113,942 pairings. The general picture remained the same. Roughly 70 percent of normal-range variation was attributable to genetic differences and about 30 percent appeared to be due to environmental effects.

Much is known about the genetics of mental retardation and learning disabilities. The most common single causes of severe general learning disabilities are chromosomal anomalies (having too many or too few copies of the many genes that occur together on the abnormal piece of chromosome). Among the many chromosomal anomalies that include mental retardation as a symptom, trisomy 21 is the cause of Down's syndrome, and the fragile X condition may by itself account for most, if not all, of the excess of males among people with severe learning disabilities (Plomin et al., 1990). A large number of rare single-gene mutations, many of them recessive like the PKU example already discussed, induce metabolic abnormalities that severely affect nervous system function and thus lead to mental retardation. Because the specific alleles involved are individually rare and recessive, such abnormalities of metabolism can cause learning-disabled individuals to appear sporadically in otherwise unaffected families (Vogel and Motulsky, 1979). The new molecular genetic technology holds future therapeutic promise for many learning disabilities.

Personality

Dimensions of personality tend to be familial (Eaves et al., 1989). Modern studies of twins and adoptees suggest that for adults, some major dimensions are influenced by differences in family environments, and some are not. For the dimension of extroversion, which encompasses such tendencies as sociability and impulsivity, genetic factors account for about 40 percent to 60 percent of the variation among adults in different studies. About 50 percent of the variation is environmental in origin. But, surprisingly to many people, none of the variation among adults appears to be related to environmental differences among families.

For neuroticism, which taps such traits as anxious-

Some have expressed fears about the use of preimplantation diagnosis to yield "designer babies."

PAGE 307

Preconception diagnosis may be ethically more acceptable to those opposed to the manipulation of human embryos.

PAGE 308

ness (a characteristic state of anxiety), emotional instability, and anxious arousability (a tendency to react with anxiety to events), 30 percent to 40 percent of the adult variation appears to be caused by genetic differences, and again none of the variation is from environmental differences that are shared by members of the same family. In contrast, social desirability, which measures a tendency to answer questions in socially approved ways, a tendency to want to appear accepted by and acceptable to society, does not show evidence of genetic causation. Essentially all of the measurable variation in social desirability appeared to be environmental, with about 20 percent due to family environment.

Some authors, including Robert Plomin, John DeFries, and Gerald McClearn in their 1990 textbook, suggest that because extroversion and neuroticism are general factors involved in many other personality scales or dimensions, most of the others also show moderate genetic variation. As an example, a twin study (Tellegen et al., 1988) involving eleven personality scales found genetic influence of various degrees for them all. On average across the eleven personality scales, 54 percent of the variation was attributable to genetic differences among the people, and 46 percent to environmental differences.

Tendencies toward affective (mood) disorders, including psychotic depression and bipolar disorder (manic depression), also are clearly influenced genetically. A lack of familial co-occurrence has established the separateness of schizophrenia from the affective psychoses. Unipolar depression and bipolar affective disorder do co-occur; in addition, there may be a genetically influenced major depressive syndrome distinct from manic-depression. The affective disorders probably include a diversity of genetic conditions.

Conclusion

To an extent that is truly surprising, even to many of the scientists conducting the studies, research indicates pervasive influences of genetics on human behavior. To a large extent many of the psychological differences among people are proving to be strongly affected by genetic differences. Intellectual ability, anxiousness, tendency to react with depression, impulsive violence, weight, height, hair color, and a host of other traits are strongly influenced by our genes. Genetic determinism? Of course not. But neither is it the simplistic environmental determinism that was so popular among academics only a few years ago. For instance, hair color, which is inherited, is not "genetically determined"; sophisticated coloring agents are readily available.

Understanding and accounting for individual and group differences requires an assessment of many of the mainstream philosophical and scientific theories that attempt to understand human behavior. In an excellent review of much behavior genetic research, David Rowe (1994) starts out by stating that "most people" believe that how children are raised has much to do with the differences in the way they turn out. Parents' behavior is thought to be a crucial determinant of the adult behavior of their children. He suggests that in important respects this widespread belief may be

See Also

Legal Moralism and Public Health

SCIENTIFIC AND RESEARCH ISSUES

Other Traits: Alcoholism, Crime, Obesity

Although data are sparse for many traits, modern studies are revealing genetic involvement in many conditions of importance to society. Robert Plomin and colleagues (1990) point out that the best single predictor of alcoholism is alcoholism in a first-degree biological relative. Alcoholism clearly runs in biological families. Severe alcoholism affects about 5 percent of males in the general population; among male relatives of alcoholics, the incidence is about 25 percent. The incidence remains about the same for adopted-away sons of male alcoholics. However, biological children of nonalcoholics are not at increased risk for alcoholism when raised by alcoholic adoptive parents.

Both adoption and twin studies of adult criminality suggest genetic involvement for serious crimes against persons and for property crimes. Large-scale adoption studies have suggested a genetic distinction between crimes associated with alcoholism and criminality not associated with alcoholism. Interestingly, socioeconomic status was found to be an interaction variable. Low socioeconomic status of the adoptive home was associated with an increased incidence of adult criminality only when the biological parent was also criminal or alcoholic (Whitney, 1990b).

In addition to twin studies that indicate obesity is highly heritable, a large adoption study of obesity among adults found that family environment by itself had no apparent effect. In adulthood, the body-mass index of the adoptees showed a strong relationship to that of their biological parents. However, there was no relationship between weight classification of adoptive parents and the adoptees. The relation between biological parent and adoptee weight extended across the spectrum, from very thin to very obese. Once again, cumulative effects of the rearing home environment were not important determinants of individual differences among adults (Stunkard et al., 1986).

— GLAYDE WHITNEY

wrong. He points out that it would not be the first time in history that whole cultures, both laypeople and experts, had been wrong in their beliefs. The theory of a flat Earth at the center of the universe would not have gotten us to the moon, and environmental determinist theories of human behavior have not yet solved most of our social problems.

— GLAYDE WHITNEY

PHILOSOPHICAL AND ETHICAL ISSUES

It is not the aim of this article to enter into any of several controversies that have been provoked by eugenic thinking, or to draw strong conclusions about the facts of nature and nurture, or to seek some kind of "biosocial" synthesis of opposite views (see Duster, 1990; Gould, 1981; Kevles and Hood, 1992; Nelkin and Tancredi, 1992; Suzuki and Knudtson, 1992; Lewontin, 1992). It is not the aim of this article to critique various models and conceptualizations of "heritability" or "kin selection" (Hamilton, 1964; Lewontin, 1976; Plomin, 1986).

It is not the aim of this article to assess the evidence in behavioral genetics and behavioral science for or against various kinds of genetic and environmental explanations of "altruistic" behavior, of gender differences, or of individual and group differences in health, intelligence, character, or criminality (Bem, 1993; Bowman and Murray, 1990; Elia, 1988; Herrnstein, 1990; Loehlin et al., 1975; Maccoby, 1974; Plomin, 1986; Rossi, 1977; Scarr, 1987; Wilson and Herrnstein, 1986). It is not the aim of this article to explain why adopted children are treated differently from blood kin, or why identical twins do not have the same fingerprints (Lewontin, 1992), or why identical twins reared together in the same home are less similar in their personalities and behavioral dispositions than one might suppose (Plomin and Daniels, 1987), or why heritability estimates derived from studies using an adoption design do not converge with heritability estimates derived from studies using a twin design (Plomin et al., 1990).

It is not the aim of this article to debate the cogency of various naturalistic and nonnaturalistic "resolutions" of the mind-body problem (Adams, 1987; Dennett, 1991; McGinn, 1991; Popper and Eccles, 1977), or to explain or explain away the appearance and function of "consciousness," "intentionality," and "free will" in the material world (see Churchland, 1986; Flanagan, 1992). It is not the aim of this article to reconsider the problem of universals, or the concept of innateness, or to address the Neoplatonic implications ("all learning is reminiscence") of the increasingly popular idea that "online" mental structures are not so much constructed as selected from a complex array of preexisting forms (Gazzaniga, 1993; Piatelli-Palmarini, 1989; Werker, 1989).

The aim is quite otherwise—to raise questions, as did Arthur Caplan in his earlier *Encyclopedia of Bioethics* contribution, "Genetic Aspects of Human Behavior: Philosophical and Ethical Issues," about the type of social order, understood as a moral order, that is most compatible with certain presumed facts about human nature, including our ability to alter our essential nature.

Historical background

The phoenix of eugenic thinking has risen up out of the pyres of the 1930s and 1940s, and its resurrection in our culture is nearly complete. Whether one toasts this regeneration of interest in the quality of each person's "natural" endowment or dreads it, it is hard to deny that eugenic thinking is very much with us today.

Not since the time of Sir Francis Galton in the late nineteenth and early twentieth centuries have so many prominent scientists held (and occasionally expressed) the view that successful people and their offspring do better in life because they have better genes, and that ethnic, racial, social class, and gender differences in, for example, health, intelligence, criminality, and interpersonal sensitivity are best understood in genetic terms (Freedman, 1979; Herrnstein, 1990; Jensen, 1969; Scarr, 1987; Wilson and Herrnstein, 1985). Not since Galton's time has there been such a strong undercurrent of informed opinion in our culture willing to "essentialize," "substantialize," or "naturalize" human abilities, mental capacities, behavioral dispositions, and

FATHER OF EUGENICS

Sir Francis Galton (1822–1911) coined the expression "nature-nurture" in an 1865 essay, and "eugenics" in 1883.

See Also

Genetic Studies: Under the Shadow of Eugenics

G

GENETICS AND HUMAN BEHAVIOR

Philosophical and Ethical Issues

"No eugenicist has publicly proposed sterilization as a remedy for defective kingship."

LANCELOT HOGBEN IN 1938, REFERRING TO HEMOPHILIA IN THE ROYAL FAMILIES OF EUROPE, PAGE 301

See Also

Race and Racism

life prospects (Buss, 1989; Degler, 1991; Gazzaniga, 1993; Symons, 1979; Wilson, 1975). Many people are willing to view everything from shyness to the ability to learn languages to the proneness to suffer from a particular physical or mental disease as the product of a genetic inheritance that can be analyzed alternatively at the level of the individual, the family, the social group, or the species.

Not since Galton's time have so many intellectuals been open to the findings of behavioral genetics and willing to accept the conclusion drawn by researchers like Thomas Bouchard and his colleagues in their study of identical twins reared in different home environments that "for almost every behavioral trait so far investigated, from reaction time to religiosity, an important fraction of the variations among people turns out to be associated with genetic variation" (Bouchard et al., 1990, p. 224). Not since Galton's time have the halls of science, medicine, industry, and government been so alive with the voices of ethically minded eugenicists eager to make the world a better place through selective alterations in the genetic endowment of particular members of our species (see Duster, 1990; Kevles and Hood, 1992; Lewontin, 1992).

Many people find these developments morally appealing. Eugenic thinking appeals to them because it brings to mind the image of a caring physician saving "defective" babies from Tay-Sachs disease or assisting a particular ethnic group in alleviating the suffering caused by some heritable disease to which that community is especially prone. Eugenic thinking excites their rational intuitions about the values of self-improvement, beneficence, protection of the vulnerable, justice, and control, while linking progress to something else that is good, the growth of knowledge. It appeals to them because they hope that one day, in the not-too-distant future, advances in science and genetic engineering will provide everyone with the means to be well-born. They picture a future in which human beings have created the secular equivalent of a heaven on earth. They surmise the progressive evolution of our species and suppose a state of organic grace in which everyone is free and equal, happy, healthy, responsible, and in the top 1 percent of the class.

Other people find the recurrence of eugenic thinking morally obnoxious. They think that the idea that "people do well in life because they have better genes" is a self-serving ideology designed to divert the community from promoting equality in the distribution of relevant human "goods," wealth, property, and education rather than genetic resources. They believe that successful individuals and groups are successful because they work long and hard at the things they do and because they have opportunities (financial resources, good coaching) to be successful. They are suspicious of scientific findings of genetically determined racial, ethnic, or class differences in school performance, criminality, or any other behavioral disposition or human ability. They view such "findings" as a loathsome expression of a dark desire to indict socially oppressed groups with the sin of inherent inferiority. In the context of a real world ripe with communal conflicts based on "ancient hatreds," they are made anxious by eugenic thinking. They remember the pyres of the 1930s and 1940s, and a time and a place when the utopian ideals of the government and its scientists, doctors, jurists, and intellectuals were not so humanitarian and egalitarian. They view eugenic thinking as a scourge.

The aim of this article is to understand these divergent moral intuitions about the implications of eugenic thinking by examining the qualities an action, policy, or practice must exhibit to make it right or good. One major view in moral philosophy argues that it is our beliefs about nature, including human nature, that set the standard for moral evaluation. Plato and Aristotle held this view when they asked whether monarchy or slavery or the institution of the family was in accord with human nature. Thomas Hobbes, Niccolò Machiavelli, Immanuel Kant, and Jean-Jacques Rousseau held this view. The challenge of eugenic thinking, like the challenge of moral philosophy itself, is that it raises provocative questions about the type of social order, understood as a moral order, that is most compatible with certain presumed or imagined facts about human nature, including our ability to choose to alter certain aspects of our essential nature. Should we exercise this ability, and if so, how?

Eugenic thinking: Galton's moral crusade

In 1865 Sir Francis Galton coined the expression "nature-nurture" in an essay entitled "Hereditary Talent and Character" published in *MacMillan's Magazine.* In 1883 he started using the word "eugenics," a Greek word meaning "well-born." By the turn of the twentieth century, the Greek word and the coined expression had become associated with an influential moral crusade whose aim was to increase the stock of basic human goods—intelligence, civility, and health—through the application to human beings of scientific principles of plant and animal breeding.

In 1911, the year Galton died, a veritable Who's Who of enlightened, ethically sensitive intellectuals, scientists, and politicians—among them Charles Eliot, president of Harvard University, Winston Churchill, and the British social reformers Sidney and Beatrice Webb—could be counted among those who were convinced that the aims of the eugenicists were noble and true, and that, through the intelligent application of

G

GENETICS AND HUMAN BEHAVIOR

Philosophical and Ethical Issues

THE IDEA OF EUGENICS
Three Strands

Eugenic thinking conjoins three types of theories: a theory of organic nature, a theory of human nature, and a theory of moral duty. The theory of organic nature asserts that the essence of an organism's nature (including its abilities, behavioral dispositions, and life prospects) is material (based in its genes). The theory of human nature asserts that since human beings are organisms, therefore individual and group similarities and differences in abilities, behavioral dispositions, and life prospects can be understood in material (genetic) terms. The theory of moral duty asserts that human beings can and ought to manage their own care and progress by altering their material nature. At the heart of eugenic thinking, then, there is a perceived ethical obligation to nurture our nature (our genetic resources) and to construct a social and political environment that makes it possible to bend nature in the direction of human values and ideals.

— RICHARD A. SHWEDER

scientific knowledge, we could increase the value of our collective genetic inheritance and rid the population of diseased bodies, wicked souls, and dull minds.

In Galton's time the only eugenic means to the moral end of promoting health, civility, and intelligence was regulation of the reproductive process via selective breeding and the crude all-or-nothing procedure of sterilization. In the United States, the forced sterilization of people with dull and criminal minds became legal in 1907 in the state of Indiana, and many other states followed suit. Judicial wisdom later upheld the constitutionality of sterilization laws ("Three generations of imbeciles is enough!" ruled Oliver Wendell Holmes, Jr., in 1927 in the U.S. Supreme Court decision *Buck* vs. *Bell*). But the ethical underpinnings of the case in favor of forced sterilizations had already been articulated by a voice of even greater authority, that of Galton's famous cousin, Sir Charles Darwin.

In *The Descent of Man*, Darwin expressed his concerns about the future of the genetic capital of our species in the following terms:

> *We build asylums for the imbecile, the maimed and the sick, we institutionalize poor laws; and our medical men exert their utmost skill to save the life of everyone to the last moment. Thus the weak members of civilized societies propagate their kind. No one who has attended to the breeding of domesticated animals will doubt that this must be highly injurious to the race of man. Both sexes ought to refrain from marriage, if they are in any marked degree inferior in body or mind, but such hopes are Utopian and will never be partially realized until the laws of inheritance are thoroughly known.*
> *(quoted in Degler, 1991, pp. 41–42)*

The implicit ethical logic of Darwin's argument seemed especially appealing to Galton and other eugenicists of his time. Indeed, the underlying logic of the argument—third-party effects, the social cost of unregulated individual choice, the social benefits of expert regulation—has from time immemorial seemed appealing to many ethicists and scientists. Twenty-five hundred years ago, in *The Republic*, Plato developed a rationale for state regulation of marriage choices. Social benefits, he argued, accrue from ensuring that individuals maximize the fit between their biologically inherited behavioral inclinations and their socially inherited occupational responsibilities.

Eugenics: The idea of the "primordial" in everyday thought

Any attempt to comprehend the "official" return of eugenic thinking in the late twentieth century must acknowledge the historical and cross-cultural pervasiveness of the idea of the "primordial" in everyday thought. The idea of the primordial is that people who are similar, proximal, emotionally and morally bonded to each other, or related as (or "as if") members of the same family are linked to each other by a common substance (e.g., "blood" and "bone"). It is the idea that what living things do is an extension of what they are, which is material or substantive, at least to some extent. Some social scientists have argued that the idea of "shared substance" and the tendency to equate "code with substance" and "fellow feeling" with "shared substance" is a fundamental feature of the human mind (Fiske, 1991).

Few of us are entirely free of this type of primordial or eugenic thinking in some aspect of our daily lives. Much of this thinking seems innocent or even beneficent, like breeding greyhounds to run fast or Tibetan terriers to be loyal, screening fetuses for defects, searching for the gene responsible for a dreaded disease, maintaining official records on the ethnic or racial distribution of lactose malabsorption or sickle-cell anemia, or wondering which characteristics of our mates (beauty, intelligence, self-confidence, a dislike of pudding) are likely to be reproduced in our children. In each case we reveal an intellectual inclination to substantialize the nature of life and of living things.

Yet, although few of us are entirely free of eugenic

◆ **heredity**
The sum of the qualities and potentialities genetically derived from one's ancestors.

See Also

Race Science: Bad Science Breeds Social Control

The Fatherland and the Motherland: Theories of Population in Totalitarian States

G

GENETICS AND HUMAN BEHAVIOR

Philosophical and Ethical Issues

Muller's "The Guidance of Human Evolution" (1959) was probably the most important stimulus to the genetic intervention debate of the early 1960s.

PAGE 257

thinking in everyday life, our eugenic reasoning rarely displays the marks of generality and consistency that we associate with a philosophy of life or an intellectual doctrine. In the United States, where human beings typically reproduce unregulated by any conscious system of eugenic control, it is commonplace to deliberately and systematically breed dogs, cows, horses, plants, and almost anything that is alive, except human beings. In India, on the other hand, where marriages are typically arranged by older (and as they believe, wiser) relatives, eugenic calculations are explicit and pervasive in the mating of human beings, while dogs, plants, and cattle reproduce unregulated by any conscious system of eugenic control. In everyday life, both cultures are eugenic, but not consistently so, and the two cultures do not display a eugenic regard for the same types of living things.

By conjoining a materialist theory of organic nature with a materialist theory of human nature with an interventionist theory of moral duty, Galton's eugenic thinking was more consistent and doctrinaire than everyday thought. Although there are significant elements of primordial thinking in everyday life, relatively few people are consistently eugenic in their thinking about these matters. To canvas everyday thought is to discover shards of eugenic thinking that do not coalesce into an integrated pattern.

For example, some people think that animal nature is essentially material (genetic) but that there is in the essence of human nature something more, something non-natural or spiritual. Some people extend this dualistic thinking to nonhuman animals, to their pets or, in the case of some vegetarians, to any living creature that nurses its young. (In India, among strict vegetarians, any species that has gender is prohibited as food because anything that has gender is thought to be a potential vehicle for an immortal reincarnating soul.)

Others think that human nature is essentially material (genetic), but they do not think that individual and group differences are part of human nature. Still others think that even if all similarities and differences between animals, human and nonhuman, are essentially material (genetic), human beings should not be so eager to bend nature to their will, and they dread the Faustian consequences of "playing God."

Some people think "playing God" is all right, as long as the God is a relatively minor deity with limited powers of control. They do not mind ceding to individuals, or even relatives, the right to influence marriage choices or the right to decide to abort a "defective" fetus, but they would not want to extend that right to a bureaucracy or to the state. And they worry about the limits of parental rights to mold the essential nature of an offspring and to act as guardian for its "interests." It is one thing—and "obviously good"—to alter the genetic code of a child so it will not be born with Down syndrome. It is quite a different thing—and not so obviously good—to genetically engineer a child to be patriotic and pious, or to redesign its genetic code so that the child lacks the capacity to experience "negative" emotions such as sorrow, anger, and fear. In everyday life, even those people who are totally at ease with the idea that everything about human and nonhuman animals and their behavior is material ("in the genes") may find themselves raising questions about the proper limits of rational planning and systems of control for managing human fate.

Indeed few people in everyday life are uniform or consistent in their thinking about the particular aspects of human nature to which eugenic doctrines might be applied. Height, skin color, sickle-cell anemia, and lactose intolerance? Sure. Intelligence? Well, maybe. Alcoholism, shyness, and fear of heights? I don't know. Morality, religious preference, musical interests, and a distaste for puddings? Really? Is that what the scientists say?

The recurrence of Galton's dream

Despite the prevalence of "primordialist" thinking in everyday life, Darwin's logic and Galton's movement experienced a setback during the 1920s, 1930s, and 1940s in the United States. The waning of the official influence of eugenic reasoning in the social, political, and scientific context of the Franklin D. Roosevelt presidency is a complex story (Degler, 1991). Suffice it to say that eugenic thinking temporarily lost its grip on the official and popular imagination even before it became associated with the evils of the Third Reich, the Nazi sterilization and extermination programs and experiments in the breeding of an Aryan "super-race."

Soon after World War II, however, the wind shifted again—back toward the eugenic ideas advocated by Galton and Darwin. Indeed, as we approach the turn of yet another century, the National Institutes of Health and the Department of Energy of the United States have committed nearly a billion dollars of public funds to the Human Genome Project in a state-sponsored effort to seek scientific knowledge of the material essence of human nature (Kevles and Hood, 1992).

This recent recurrence of a fascination with eugenic ideas has been stimulated, at least in part, by technological and scientific developments on various fronts. Major advances have occurred in the isolation and identification of genetic markers and in the screening of genetic defects and autosomal recessive disorders (recessive genes that are harmless to a single carrier yet are dangerous for an offspring if paired across both parents) like cystic fibrosis, sickle-cell anemia, and Tay-Sachs disease. There has been progress in the cloning of human genes and the application of recombinant DNA. Indeed, it has now become commonplace in the popular press to headline research findings

See Also
Race: European Concepts

in biochemistry and to feature stories about the latest discovery of a "long-sought" gene that is the cause of some dreaded disease. The stories invariably conclude with a visionary litany: "Scientists say that this discovery could lead to new therapies and even a cure."

Technological capacity to control and manipulate the human reproductive process has also expanded. Through sperm banking, in vitro fertilization, and artificial insemination, the means are at hand for the selective breeding of human excellences. Galton's dream of ridding the world of pathology and defective specimens through biochemistry has come to seem like a pending reality.

Each of these scientific and technological advances carries with it an atmosphere thick with moral implications. Information garnered through genetic screening makes it possible to abort fetuses doomed to a life of pathology and devastating disease. Yet it also has implications for decisions about marriage, childbearing and abortion, and for the control and regulation of these things by individuals or organizations with third-party interests and worries about social costs (e.g., insurance companies, the state). That a "public health policy" can be a moral minefield becomes apparent when one reads recommendations like this one from Linus Pauling:

> *There should be tattooed on the forehead of every young person a symbol showing possession of the sickle-cell gene or whatever other similar gene, such as the gene for phenylketonuria in a single dose. If this were done, two young people carrying the same seriously defective gene in a single dose would recognize this situation at first sight, and would refrain from falling in love with one another. It is my opinion that legislation along this line, compulsory testing for defective genes before marriage, and some form of semi-public display of this possession, should be adopted.* (Pauling, 1968)

Advances in extracorporeal fertilization make it possible for the egg of one woman to be fertilized in vitro and then gestated in the womb of another woman, a boon for some couples. Yet our very capacity to separate the identity of the "mother" as genitor (the person who contributes the egg) from the "mother" as gestator (the person who contributes the womb and goes through the labor of birth) raises new and difficult moral questions hitherto never imagined, except perhaps in mythology, in nightmares, or by Dr. Seuss.

Who is the "natural" mother of the child, the mother who lays the egg or the one who hatches it, the mother who contributes the genetic substance or the one who brings it to term? Imagine the effect on family life and on our sense of responsibility for the young when the notion of "shared substance" linking parent to child goes the way of "miasmas" and "ethers" and other notions that we now view as archaic. Imagine a world in which it is commonplace, through technological innovations, to redesign from scratch the genetic codes contributed by the genitors of a fetus, or to dispense with the need for genitors entirely. At that point the distinction between "natural offspring" and "adopted child" is likely to disappear. Perhaps that will be for the good, and everyone will come to view the old distinction as invidious and feel highly motivated to care for everyone else's children the way they once selectively cared for their own. Or perhaps the waning of the primordial idea of kith and kin, of kindred and kind, will lead to a disastrous weakening of the bond between generations and a diminishment in the inclination of adults to sacrifice for the young. Unintended consequences can be a worry when one has the power of "God" without divine foresight.

Many moral uncertainties and anxieties accompany technological change, and not every change in technological capacity is unequivocally an "advance." For example, the technologies associated with in vitro fertilization and cloning have even led one biological anthropologist to imagine a future world in which human cloning is commonplace and women are no longer needed for reproduction. "Why," she asks, "would the Nobel Prize-winning sex let the sex with the boring, meaningless lives eat up half the food if they are no longer needed for reproductive purposes?" (Elia, 1988, p. 272). To anticipate a battle of the sexes over scarce resources, and to fear gender genocide as the unintended consequence of the growth of knowledge, may seem extreme. Nevertheless, "slippery-slope" and "unintended-consequence" arguments abound in considerations of the ethics of bending the material essence of human beings to our own wills. (See Glover, 1984, for a series of philosophical arguments against slippery-slope reasoning and in favor of intelligent and moral human answers to the question, "What sort of people should there be?")

The current fascination with eugenic thinking—and, for some, the sheer horror of it all—cannot and should not be understood without an analysis of the moral, political, and social implications of advances in science and technology at particular times and in particular places and for particular individuals or groups of individuals within a society. Research on recombinant DNA, for example, holds out the promise that a "defective" fetus might one day, through human intervention, be transformed into an "excellent" fetus. Yet qualities of excellence such as "health," "civility," and "intelligence" are relatively abstract qualities; those in power versus those out of power, or those from different cultural or subcultural traditions, may disagree substantially on how such qualities should be defined.

In 1968, neither Lederberg nor Kornberg saw a pressing need for a national commission on genetic engineering issues.

PAGE 257

G

GENETICS AND HUMAN BEHAVIOR

Philosophical and Ethical Issues

BIOMEDICAL TECHNOLOGIES

"Factories" of Ethical Dilemmas

The question of what constitutes "defective" genetic material is going to impose itself on public policy debates with a force comparable to debates about affirmative action, the right to life, and the morality of capital punishment. The issue will not go away. Simple or inexpensive biomedical technologies will be used if they make it possible to eliminate "defective" genetic material without also eliminating "positive" genetic material or the potential for future reproductive success. They will be used even if they are illegal.

Advances in amniocentesis, for example, have made it possible to include gender among the potential criteria of a "defective" baby and to make abortion decisions accordingly. In South Asia and among many Americans and American residents of South Asian origin, what counts as a "defective" baby is, at times, gender-based. Given the financial burdens associated with the practice of dowry transfers at marriage, mothers who have already given birth to several girls are highly motivated to have a son. Consequently, in some clinics in India 95 percent of elected abortions involve a female fetus. If this practice of selective female abortion were to become widespread it would result in a relative scarcity of females, which, from a narrow economic point of view, ought to increase the perceived value of women which, ironically, might weaken the dowry system or at least increase the status of women in society. This is a difficult case for "pro-choice" advocates, many of whom are inclined to argue, somewhat inconsistently, that it is ethically acceptable to abort a healthy fetus that is unwanted but ethically unsound to abort a female fetus that is healthy, whether it is wanted or not. The difficulties are likely to grow. If detailed "personal" information about the characteristics of the fetus is made available in the first trimester of pregnancy, the argument that the fetus is not a person is going to seem increasingly questionable. Should such information be suppressed? Eugenic thinking is going to raise many challenging questions about the fabric of our constitutional liberties.

— RICHARD A. SHWEDER

Whoever has the power to define a human excellence in such cases will have the capacity to alter human fate. Within any complex, nonegalitarian society composed of diverse ethnic and racial groups (such as the United States), that power and the presumed authority on which it rests are likely to be contested.

Twenty-five hundred years after Plato's *The Republic* and 100 after Galton named the movement, eugenic thinking is very much with us. Eugenic thinking, whether it is concerned with individual and group differences in the distribution of inherited human excellences, or with an agenda for the alteration of the material essence of a single human being or a whole species, carries with it a set of provocative and controversial normative implications, which moral philosophers have a responsibility to address.

How our moral intuitions will be given historical and cultural definition in the light of eugenic thinking remains to be seen. Human nature is at least complicated enough to have two sides; we live, as Kant suggested, in "two worlds," a noumenal world and a phenomenal world. In the noumenal aspect of our nature, we are all free and equal, we recognize and respect each other as autonomous persons (or "spirits"), and we have high regard for all that is implied by the idea of autonomy. In the phenomenal aspect of our nature, however, we are unequal, and our autonomy is compromised to varying degrees. We are unequal in our material resources (both genetic and financial), in our motivations, in our bargaining power, in our foresight, in our vulnerability to duress, in the opportunities we are likely to have, given our location within the social order, and in our very capacity to act as autonomous agents.

There is thus an inherent tension in our nature and no easy reconciliation of noumenal and phenomenal claims. If we try to enforce noumenal liberty and equality in the phenomenal world, we introduce too many degrees of regulation and authoritarian control (communism, the "iron cage" of the bureaucratic liberal state), which is inconsistent with the very autonomy we seek to protect. If we fail to enforce nuomenal liberty and equality in the phenomenal world, we banish the "right" and the "good" from the natural world. If we throw up our hands and try to transcend or escape the phenomenal world in gnostic revulsion over the bleak absence of the divine in nature, we abandon society for the cave. Morality is a compromise we strike between these two inherently conflictual sides of our nature for the sake of a life in a social order that has some semblance of decency. And precisely because morality is a compromise it is composed of plural goods and obligations that cannot be reconciled or reduced to a single thing.

In the West, the current compromise between the noumenal and phenomenal sides of human nature is

◆ **heritability**
A technical concept designating a ratio of the contribution of heredity to the environment within a given population.

See Also
Reproductive Technologies

the "liberal expectancy," the moral idea of "equal life prospects." But the idea of "equal life prospects" is an abstract idea that needs to be filled in, implemented, and made relevant in the light of our beliefs about the sources of difference in the world, and in the light of what it is possible for us to accomplish technologically, and what is possible for us to afford.

Many classical societies of old subscribed to the idea of "god-gifts" (inherited qualities of excellence, a natural telos) and of a divine plan for their unequal distribution in the phenomenal world. They never considered the possibility that the state might level the genetic playing field. Their expectancy was that each person should have the opportunity to realize the full potential of his or her natural endowment, whatever that endowment might be. It was also their expectation that the fruits or products realized by each person, fulfilling his or her own peculiar nature, would be valued and esteemed by everyone else in society. In this way a balance was achieved between the moral qualities of self-improvement, fairness, respect, and community. That is what it meant for inherited differences to be part of a divine plan. That is what our liberal democracy will have to achieve if we are to convince ourselves and our offspring that our science, technology, and social and political institutions are really an extension of the mind of God.

— RICHARD A. SHWEDER

GENETICS AND HUMAN SELF-UNDERSTANDING

Sherlock Holmes once asked his friend and colleague Dr. Watson, "Did you notice the remarkable thing about the dog which barked in the middle of the night?" Watson replied, "I heard no dog barking in the middle of the night." Holmes's response to this was characteristic: "That was the remarkable thing."

And about the influence of genetics on human self-understanding the most remarkable thing is not that there has been absolutely no influence at all, but that that influence has been, and remains, so small and limited. The present entry, therefore, in the main will deal with the implications for human self-understanding of the discoveries of the geneticists, and with some of the sometimes extraordinarily widespread and stubborn refusals to take proper account of those discoveries. Little can be said about their extremely limited actual influence.

There is, however, one area in which genetic discoveries are already of enormous perceived importance for all those immediately concerned. Genetic defects in the fetus are with increasing frequency construed as indications for abortion. Consider, for instance, the case of the island of Sardinia, a strongly traditional Roman Catholic society in which until very recently many children were born with inherited anemia. Nevertheless, "Nine-tenths of couples at risk of having an affected child now know this, and when the woman becomes pregnant nine-tenths of them choose to end pregnancies which would have produced a genetically damaged infant" (Jones, 1993, p. 60). Although this is immediately a matter of a practical application rather than of any sort of theoretical self-understanding, in the longer term—if it becomes possible to produce "designer babies" by predetermining their genetic makeup—the impact upon human self-understanding is bound to be enormous.

Genetic facts ignored or outright repudiated

The system of hereditarian ideas that in the twentieth century have won by far the most numerous and powerful converts, and led to the most catastrophic consequences, was developed long before there was any concept of the gene. Nor did many of those converts, if any, later display much concern over the fact that the developing science of genetics provided no basis whatsoever for their cherished racial doctrines. The seminal figure here was a Frenchman, Arthur de Gobineau (1816-1882), who is now called "the Father of Racism." His master idea was that of a supposedly superior "Aryan" stock, which alone possessed true civilizing potential. That stock, he believed, had been irrevocably debilitated by miscegenation and was now under threat from lesser white elements within Europe and still more destructive nonwhite hordes beyond.

These ideas, mediated through Gobineau's friendship with Richard Wagner and his Bayreuth circle, had an immediate appeal in imperial Germany. British-born Houston Stewart Chamberlain (1855-1927), who had married Wagner's youngest daughter, acquired German nationality on the eve of World War I. He became a personal friend of Kaiser Wilhelm II and was recruited as an official propagandist for the German cause, a cause he presented as an attempt—made by the nation that was "manifestly superior" to all others in art, music, literature, philosophy, and science—to dominate the European heartland.

Chamberlain's magnum opus was *Die Grundlagen des 19ten Jahrhunderts (Foundations of the Nineteenth Century,* 1899). A monstrous book, it is a mixture of contorted pseudohistory and fanatical Germanic mysticism, presenting the world as a stage for a Manichaean conflict between an "Aryan" principle of good and the "Jewish" principle of evil. In October

Between 1986 and 1994 there was a dramatic increase in the number of human gene therapy policy statements.

PAGE 259

GENETICS AND HUMAN SELF-UNDERSTANDING

Genetic Facts Ignored or Outright Repudiated

1923, Adolf Hitler and Alfred Rosenberg visited Wagner's Haus Wahnfried, where they immediately recognized and accepted Chamberlain as the prophet and seer of the future Third Reich (Bullock, 1962). There is no reason to doubt that Alfred Rosenberg, official philosopher of the National Socialist German Workers' Party, considered his own *Der Mythus des 20ten Jahrhunderts (The Myth of the Twentieth Century)*, published in 1934, to have been erected upon *Foundations of the Nineteenth Century.*

Another tradition also originated long before genetics emerged as a science. Again the founding father was a Frenchman, albeit one writing a century earlier than Gobineau. Claude-Adrien Helvétius (1715-1771) was a philosopher and one of the Encyclopedists. In his *De l'Esprit (Concerning Mind*, 1758) he maintained that "All men are born equal in mental capacity; the manifold differences that seem so conspicuous result from nothing but the inequalities in men's social condition and opportunities." The book was, for reasons that are irrelevant here, condemned by the Sorbonne, and publicly burned. Fifteen years later, in his *De l'Homme (Concerning Man)*, the watchword of Helvétius became "l'éducation peut tout" (education can do everything).

Whereas the tradition stemming from Gobineau simply ignored the claims of genetic science, in its boldest form the tradition descending from Helvétius denies outright that there are or could be any relevant findings about hereditary factors in the production of different mental capacities. As his later statement makes clear, the prime purpose of this denial was to clear the way for a doctrine and program of environmental absolutism, according to which we are all, in all things, completely creatures of our several and usually different environments. The presumably unfulfillable promise of that program was epitomized in a famous behaviorist boast: "Give me a dozen healthy infants, and my own world to bring them up in, and I'll guarantee to take any one at random and train him to become any type of specialist you like to select—doctor, lawyer, merchant, soldier, sailor, beggar-man or thief" (Watson, 1925, p. 104).

◆ **human genetic intervention**
To cure or prevent disease, enhance human capabilities with therapies directed at a patient's somatic (nonreproductive) or germ-line (reproductive) cells.

Helvétius limited his environmentalism to the development of mental capacities. The author of the article "Behaviorism" for the *Encyclopaedia of the Social Sciences*, writing in the late 1920s, put no such limitations upon his contention that "At birth human infants, regardless of their heredity, are as equal as Fords" (Kallen, 1931, p. 498).

This assertion, as it stands, is so flagrantly false that we have to construe it as tacitly taking some crucial qualification for granted. For whereas it used to be notorious that customers could have their Model T in any color they wished, so long as they wanted it black, babies come in a variety of skin pigmentations. They also come in two sexes. Furthermore, whereas skin pigmentations are paradigmatically skin-deep, there are other physiological differences extending to the deeper structure. So perhaps we should charitably construe Kallen as contending not that there are in fact no discernible differences, since very obviously there are; but that these observed differences, along with all other genetically determined differences, however obvious or however far from obvious, are actually unimportant and/or irrelevant.

There are two common mistakes. The first is to assume that anything innate must be manifest at birth. That is quite wrong. For instance, although human males do not display facial hair on the delivery table, they do begin to do so, in an extremely wide range of environments, in their early teens. The second mistake is to assume that it is possible to determine a priori that some difference is too small to be relevant and important. This is a point that can be most effectively enforced by drawing an example from the natural rather than the social sciences. Even though the difference between the two natural isotopes of uranium is only three neutrons—about 1 percent of the atomic weight of uranium—those three neutrons make the difference between being able and being unable to sustain an explosive chain reaction.

Even supposing that all human beings were at birth as similar to one another as Model T Fords, it still would not necessarily follow that our innate human nature could, given the appropriate environment, be molded into any shape desired. To establish this possibility decisively in any particular case—and it is, surely, only case by particular case that this could be done—it is necessary to show that molding of the kind desired has on some occasion actually been achieved. For, as Aristotle rightly remarks, the argument from actuality to possibility always goes through. That is, if anything is actual, then it must be possible.

It was in hopes of establishing just how completely the behavior of adolescents is shaped by the cultures in which they have been socialized that in 1925 Franz Boas—a protagonist of nurture in the great nature/nurture controversy of the 1920s—sent his doctoral student Margaret Mead to the South Seas. Her mission resulted in the publication three years later of the all-time anthropological best-seller *Coming of Age in Samoa*, significantly subtitled *A Psychological Study of Primitive Youth for Western Civilization* (Mead, 1928).

Although Mead's findings have been discredited (Freeman, 1983, 1991)—many of the most exciting were the diametric opposite of the truth—there can be no question that in its day (a day lasting several decades) her book had a very substantial influence upon a great many people's self-understanding. That

See Also
Race: European Concepts

substantial influence, however, was not exercised against the acceptance of the discoveries of geneticists but, rather, through a reaction against the perceived threat arising from their previous and possible future discoveries. The threat was to the protagonists of nurture in the nature-nurture controversy. They maintained that the prime determinant of all human behavior is the environment, whereas their opponents contended that, on the contrary, it is our innate nature.

Implications of basic general facts of human genetics

An exploration of the true implications of genetic discoveries for a late-twentieth-century understanding of human nature must begin from a statement of two fundamental and complementary facts.

The first of these is the fact of genetic diversity. Except for identical twins—monozygotic (one-egg) as opposed to dizygotic (two-egg) twins—no two people who have ever lived or ever will live have been, are, or will be built on the same genetic plan; the chance that any particular existing array of particular genes either has occurred in the past or will occur in the future is for all practical purposes nil. Furthermore, this genetic uniqueness is compounded by environmental uniqueness, because the phenotypic expression is conditioned at every step in development by environmental forces that are forever changing: Even identical twins become different persons because, during intrauterine life and increasingly after birth, they are exposed to different environmental conditions.

Leo Loeb, whose life's work was a study of biological individuality, put this first fundamental fact into an evolutionary perspective: "We find, phylogenetically, a progressively increasing complexity in the activities of organisms and increasing differences between members of the same species, an increasing individualization which reaches its highest development in man" (quoted in Williams, 1979, p. 45).

The second fundamental and complementary fact is that, along with this enormous genetic diversity *as individuals*, we nevertheless have *as a species*—presumably because our species evolved so recently—an equally remarkable genetic homogeneity: "This means that if, after a global disaster, only one group—the Albanians, the Papuans or the Senegalese—survived, most of the world's genetic diversity for functional genes would be preserved. . . . Other creatures vary much more from place to place. . . . The difference between the highland and the lowland populations of the mountain gorilla a few miles apart in central Africa is more than that between any two human groups" (Jones, 1993, p. 51).

To deduce normative and prescriptive conclusions directly from such purely factual and neutrally descriptive premises would be to commit the naturalistic fallacy. (This fallacy is perhaps most commonly committed in attempts to derive such normative conclusions directly from allegations about human nature or from statements of laws of nature.)

ATTENTION, EGALITARIANS
"Equality" in the Context of Genetic Diversity

To those for whom a main, if not the supreme, political objective is raising (or reducing) everyone to the same equal condition, the facts of our genetic diversity must constitute a formidable embarrassment: "For . . . a thoroughgoing egalitarian . . . inequality that derives from biology ought to be as repulsive as inequality that derives from early socialization" (Jencks et al., 1972, p. 73). Presumably under pressure of that embarrassment, the distinguished social scientist who wrote the sentence just quoted refrained from speculating about the eventual, no doubt extremely long-term, possibilities of reproducing human populations by big-batch clonings, and instead proceeded to discuss approaches to the ideal of "cognitive equality" (Jencks et al., 1972, pp. 54, 109). Thanks to the general genetic diversity and the limited intellectual capacities of many, the cost of realizing this ideal might be universal, nearly total nescience.

These same facts of genetic diversity and genetic homogeneity are comfortably conformable with the rights claims of the American Declaration of Independence; and this notwithstanding that those claims have sometimes been misunderstood to have been grounded upon a denial of that diversity. Certainly the signers of that document held it "to be self-evident, that all men are created equal. . . ." But there is no full stop at the word "equal." For, as Abraham Lincoln once explained, the signers "did not intend to declare all men equal in all respects. They did not mean to say that all men were equal in color, size, intellect, moral development, or social capacity. They defined with tolerable distinctness in what respects they did consider all men created equal—certain inalienable rights, among which are life, liberty and the pursuit of happiness." These equal rights, therefore, are grounded not in any mistakenly assumed equality of ability or inclination but in our common humanity; not, as we might say, in our genetic uniformity but in our genetic homogeneity.

— ANTONY FLEW

◆ **pluralism**
A state of society in which members of diverse ethnic, racial, religious, or social groups maintain an autonomous participation in and development of their traditional culture or special interest within the confines of a common civilization.

See Also

Genes and Crime: What We Don't Study *Can* Hurt Us

G

GENETICS AND HUMAN SELF-UNDERSTANDING

Implications of Genetic Facts about Individuals and Collectives

"There is a taboo on open-minded investigation . . . at least as strong as the resistance in Darwin's day to questioning the authority of the Bible."

SIR ANDREW HUXLEY

We cannot, therefore, validly deduce from the facts of genetic homogeneity any doctrine of the moral unity of humankind. Nevertheless, it does become very awkward to insist, in the face of these facts, that there are fundamental and innate differences between Greeks and barbarians or between blacks and whites that justify treating members of such contrasting groups in importantly different ways. Again, while we cannot validly deduce any prescriptive conclusions from the facts of genetic diversity, these facts are very congenial to people who want to maximize the number and variety of alternatives between which individuals can choose. For they make it likely that a variety of different alternatives will be chosen by the variety of different individuals. Similarly, were it not for this diversity of talents and inclinations, the possibilities of a wealth-creating division of labor combined with a free and effective market for labor would not be nearly so great as they in fact are (Williams, 1979).

Implications of genetic facts about individuals and collectives

Thomas Jefferson—the man who, thanks to his "peculiar felicity of expression," was asked to draft the Declaration of Independence—was under no illusions about equal talents. On the contrary: In his sole published book, *Notes on the State of Virginia*, he developed a scheme for a fiercely selective system of primary education, in the course of which "twenty of the best geniuses will be raked from the rubbish annually." After six further years of schooling, ten of those twenty "are to be chosen, for the superiority of their parts and dispositions," and sent to study "at William and Mary College" (Jefferson, 1955 [1787], p. 143; cf. pp. 137-142).

In this, as no doubt in many other ways, Jefferson was by today's standards in the highest degree "politically incorrect." Certainly Sir Andrew Huxley—a great-grandson of Thomas Henry Huxley—was in his 1977 Presidential Address to the British Association for the Advancement of Science constrained to speak of "the assumption of equal inherited ability as something which . . . does not require experimental evidence . . . and which it is politically wicked to question." He went on to complain: "There is in fact a taboo on open-minded investigation . . . at least as strong as the resistance in Darwin's day to questioning the authority of the Bible." This taboo appears to be stronger in the United States, where the media systematically misrepresent what seems to be the contrary if largely tacit consensus of the researchers (Snyderman and Rothman, 1988; cf. Fletcher, 1991). If and insofar as the truth is that inherited abilities are extremely unequal, then any such failure or refusal to take account of the genetic facts must contribute substantially to human self-misunderstanding.

Nor is there any reason to believe that Jefferson, having rejected the notion that talent is distributed equally among individuals, would nevertheless have been content to concede that among different collections of unequally talented individuals, such unequal talents are always distributed in the same way. He would not, for instance, have accepted uncritically the categorical pronouncement issued in 1965 by the U.S. Department of Labor: "Intelligence potential is distributed among Negro infants in the same proportion and pattern as among Icelanders or Chinese, or any other group. . . . There is absolutely no question of any genetic differential."

Whether or not that pronouncement is true, there is no question that it does not follow from the previously quoted assertion "that if, after a global disaster, only one group . . . survived, most of the world's genetic diversity for functional genes would be preserved." For even if all the genetic diversity was preserved—even if, that is, at least one single specimen of every functional gene was preserved—this would not begin to show that the distribution within the surviving group was the same as that within all those others that, by the hypothesis, did not survive.

On the other hand, the truth of that assertion about the survival of most, if not all, "the world's genetic diversity for functional genes" does carry some practically important implications. In the first place, it means that to be true, statements about the genetically determined abilities or inclinations of particular subsets of the total human population must be statements about averages rather than categorical statements to the effect that either all or no members of that subset are either able to do this or are strongly inclined to do that. From statements about the average characteristics of any set, it is impossible immediately to infer any conclusion about the characteristics of a particular member of that set. Thus, from the statement that the members of some set are on average five feet, nine inches tall, we are certainly not licensed to infer that any single member of that set is either five feet nine inches tall or is of any other particular height.

The practical importance of this elementary logical truth is that people cannot properly be ruled out of consideration for appointments on the ground that some set to which they belong is on average deficient in characteristics essential in those appointments. So we can be reassured that even if that pronouncement by the U.S. Department of Labor were shown to be false, and so long as the assertion about the survival of most, if not all, of "the world's genetic diversity" for fundamental genes was known to be true, this falsification would not provide any justification whatsoever for hostile discrimination against the members of any of the subsets concerned.

But, granted that that assertion is indeed known to be true, we still need to appreciate something that holds for differences on average between sets of all sorts. We have here another of those cases in which what seems comparatively small can turn out to make a very large difference. For where a characteristic is normally distributed—as is the case with most characteristics measured by psychologists—a difference between two averages of only a single standard deviation will produce quite dramatic changes in the numbers at the extremes. Take, for instance, the much-measured characteristic of IQ, which certainly is both normally distributed and at least in part genetically determined. And suppose that we have two sets of people differing by one standard deviation in respect of that characteristic. Then, all other things being equal, we should expect—absent either substantial hostile discrimination or gross social disadvantage—that the set with the higher average IQ will by comparison be heavily overrepresented in whatever sorts of occupations and achievements demand very high IQs. On the same assumptions we should also expect that set to be correspondingly underrepresented among those rated, by whatever are the prevailing standards, as educationally subnormal (ESN). In this area, as in others, the operation of policies founded upon false assumptions can have extremely disturbing, unintended consequences (Jensen, 1972).

The challenge of sociobiology

Any consideration of the influence of genetics upon human self-understanding has to attend to E. O. Wilson's *Sociobiology: The New Synthesis*, "sociobiology" being defined as "the systematic study of the biological basis of all social behaviour" (Wilson, 1975, p. 4). In the final chapter of an earlier treatise, *The Insect Societies*, Wilson had envisaged that "the same principles of population biology and comparative zoology," which had "worked so well in explaining the rigid systems of the social insects, could be applied point by point to vertebrate animals" (Wilson, 1971).

In the case of human societies this application will apparently involve a takeover by evolutionary genetics. For

> *Sociology* sensu stricto . . . *still stands apart from sociobiology because of its largely . . . nongenetic approach. . . . Taxonomy and ecology . . . have been reshaped entirely . . . by integration into neo-Darwinist evolutionary theory—the "Modern Synthesis" as it is often called*—in which each phenomenon is weighed for its adaptive significance and then related to the basic principles of population genetics. *(Wilson, 1975, p. 4; emphasis added)*

This particular statement, however, concludes cautiously: "Whether the social sciences can be truly biologicized in this fashion remains to be seen."

In subsequent writings Wilson has been less cautious and more explicit in his reductionist ambitions. The issue at stake is the extent to which human cultures, and the behaviors that are a part of them, can be accounted for by "genetic determinism." Thus, in his treatise *On Human Nature*, Wilson stresses that it is on the interpretation of this "key phrase" that "the entire relation between biology and the social sciences depends" (Wilson, 1978, p. 55).

The final chapter of *Sociobiology: The New Synthesis* gets off to a splendid start with this sentence: "Let us now consider man in the free spirit of natural history, as though we were zoologists from another planet completing a catalog of social species on Earth." Suppose that we actually do begin in this way, as Wilson in fact did not. Then the first peculiarity we have to pick out is, surely, the extended period between birth and maturity, the incomparable capacity for learning, and the importance of learned (as opposed to instinctual) behavior.

This unrivaled capacity for learning—together with its instrument and expression, developed language—provides our species with a serviceable substitute for the (genetic) inheritance of acquired characteristics. It is this serviceable substitute for the (genetic) inheritance of acquired characteristics that constitutes the first threat to the project for a reductionist human sociobiology. For it makes it impossible fully to understand the workings of human societies, as it is certainly not impossible to understand those of insect societies, without constantly taking account of their pasts as well as of the previously acquired information stocks to which their members have access. (What is peculiar to our species, it must be emphasized, is not the exogenetic [nongenetic] transmission of specific possible behaviors from one generation to the next, as such, but the enormous number and variety of possible behaviors that, thanks to the hypertrophy of the human brain and to the presumably concurrent and connected development of language, can now be transmitted exogenetically.)

No doubt this "unrivaled capacity for learning," like all our other innate capacities and dispositions, is itself genetically determined. But—and here we come to the second of the peculiarities that threaten the project for a reductionist sociobiology—the directions to which we turn such capacities, and how far *we* inhibit or pursue such inclinations, is not already determined by our genes. It is instead for us to decide. For we are creatures of a kind whose members are all, to a greater or lesser

◆ **sociobiology**
The systematic study of the biological basis of all social behavior.

See Also

Human Sociobiology: Hot Topic, Controversial Ideas

SOCIOBIOLOGY

How "Predestined" Are We?

The issue at stake is the extent to which cultures, and the behaviors that are a part of them, can be explained in terms of a "genetic determinism." It is on the interpretation of this "key phrase," as Wilson stresses, that "the entire relation between biology and the social sciences depends" (Wilson, 1975, p. 532). So, as an example of an organism whose behavior is genetically "predestined," he instances the mosquito: "The mosquito is an automaton," with "a sequence of rigid behaviors programmed by the genes to unfold swiftly and unerringly from birth to the final act of oviposition" (Wilson, 1978, p. 55).

Wilson then offers one of an abundance of possible examples of a "restricted," as opposed to a "rigid," behavior, in which "the genes have their way unless specifically contravened by conscious choice." Yet it will not do, as Wilson does, to leave it at that. For whenever genes have causally necessitated their—shall we say owners, or subjects, or whatever else?—to have not uncontrollable reflexes but inhibitable and controllable desires or dispositions or orientations or inclinations, then this must open the possibility that choice will intervene to contravene.

— ANTONY FLEW

extent, agents; and insofar as we are, we can and cannot but make choices between alternative courses of action. Agents as such always could have done, and could do, other than they did or will do—in a strong sense that can, and perhaps can only, be explained ostensively.

Presumably there are in some nonhuman mammals embryonic developments on these lines, just as there certainly are, in several species other than ours, cases of the exogenetic inheritance of the acquired characteristic of a learned behavior. In both instances, however, the prehuman anticipations of what has in our species become a vastly extended and elaborately sophisticated development appear to be comparatively minor. It is this second peculiarity of our species, even more than the first, that makes the human sciences irreducibly different from the natural sciences. Wilson does in his own way recognize the reality of choice. But, once again, he fails to appreciate its revolutionary and relevant significance.

◆ **predestination**
A theological doctrine that holds people are all creatures of an omnipotent creator who guides those who, with divine grace and forgiveness, are destined for salvation.

See Also

Scientific and Research Issues: Other Traits: Alcoholism, Crime, Obesity,

Freedom and Coercion

A scientific Calvinism?

In 1932, in an essay published under what would now be deemed a provocative title, *The Inequality of Man*, J. B. S. Haldane, at that time Britain's leading geneticist, told how his distinguished predecessor William Bateson had, during World War I, lectured about innate differences. A Scottish soldier commented: "Sir, what you're telling us is nothing but scientific Calvinism."

Haldane then proceeded to develop this theme by reference to *Crime as Destiny: A Study of Criminal Twins* (Lange, 1931). This book, which Haldane thought might one day be seen as "the most important . . . of this century," reported the results of a study of pairs of brothers at least one of whom was incarcerated in a south German jail. Of the 428 nontwin brothers of prisoners, only about one in twelve had a record of criminal imprisonment.

Of the sixteen undoubtedly dizygotic twins, only two of the incarcerated men had criminal brothers, and in one of these cases one brother was a habitual criminal while the other, after engaging in criminal behavior for one year, had been law-abiding for the following fifteen. So the record of the dizygotic twins seems very similar to that of the nontwin brothers.

But the case of the thirteen monozygotic pairs was very different. Ten of these pairs were both criminals. The stories of these ten pairs are told in great detail, and the behavioral resemblances of each set of twins are often extraordinarily close. Haldane, echoing Lange, construed these findings as counting against a doctrine of the freedom of the will. They tend to show that most, if not all, "of those moral decisions that land us in jail or otherwise are predetermined."

So what do these and similar, more recent findings, including the claims about supposedly "criminal" chromosomes, actually tend to show? Since there is no reference here, either explicit or implicit, to a creator God, these findings can at most be compatible with (without in any way providing positive support for) the specifically theological doctrine of predestination—a doctrine that, though commonly identified with Calvin and Calvinism, was in fact substantially shared by Thomas Aquinas, Martin Luther, and other classical theologians. It is important to be clear about this. For the doctrine is that specifically theological one that carries the infinitely appalling implication that we are all creatures of an omnipotent creator God who secretly makes us behave in ways that, absent gratuitous exercises of divine grace and forgiveness, must earn the punishment of eternal torment.

Do such genetic findings, considered in an entirely secular and this-worldly context, constitute anything more than an approach to a genetic explanation of something that everyone knew to be the case long before there was such a thing as a science of genetics or any science at all—namely, that most of us have some, though by no means in everyone the same, natural inclinations? Surely they do not even begin to show that none of our behaviors are—to reemploy Wilson's terminology—"restricted" as opposed to "rigid." The former behaviors are those in which agents are strongly inclined to behave in particular ways yet could do differently if they so chose.

It is necessary to distinguish more from less fundamental senses of "having a choice" and "could have done otherwise." When Martin Luther protested before the Diet of Worms, "Here I stand. I can no other. So help me God," he was not asserting that he had been afflicted with a general paralysis that left him physically incapable of withdrawing to his Saxon refuge. In the more fundamental sense he certainly could have done that, but for him any such alternative was intolerable. When some unfortunate businessman receives from a "godfather" an "offer he cannot refuse," we may say that he has no choice but to sign a document transferring his property to the Organization. But the fact that in the more fundamental sense he did have a choice can be brought out by comparing his situation with that of the treacherous Mafioso who without warning is gunned down from behind. And to anyone who nevertheless tries to deny that those who, in this fundamental sense, did have choices and could have done otherwise, what can be said but that those expressions are definable only by reference to the sorts of situations to which they are conventionally applied? For how can we understand what is meant by "having a choice" or "being able to do other than we do" if not by reference to the sorts of situations to which we have learned to apply such expressions as "He had a choice" or "She could have done something else"?

— ANTONY FLEW

GENETICS AND THE LAW

The interaction of genetics with law is driven by the powerful information that can be discerned about individuals by genetic testing. In general, genetic data can be divided into two broad categories: information that determines identity or biological relationship, and information that has diagnostic or predictive value about one's health or the health of one's potential children. As we have entered an era where genetic testing can make definitive statements about identity and discern critical facts about health, it is crucial that societies develop rules to regulate the use of these data. The possibility that genetically engineered organisms could create biohazards also has stimulated much public discourse and some legal activity.

Advances in genetics have stimulated legislative interest and judicial attention for several decades. Analysis of how legal systems use genetic (and other scientific) information to help order society suggests that too often lawmakers and judges are not provided with an adequate technological primer to enable them to properly use new knowledge. Lawmakers and judges need routine access to institutions that can neutrally and competently evaluate genetic data. Work performed by the Office of Technology Assessment for Congress is an apt model.

Courts have long recognized the value of biological markers to determine identity. Blood-group analysis was first used more than fifty years ago to exclude wrongfully accused males in paternity disputes; subsequently, human leukocyte antigen (HLA) testing and, since 1986, deoxyribonucleic acid (DNA) based approaches, have been used widely in Europe and the United States in both civil and criminal proceedings to determine alleged familial relationships or to decide whether biological samples from crime scenes match those from a particular individual. DNA forensics has revolutionized the investigation of violent crimes (Committee on DNA Technology in Forensic Science, 1992).

The legislative and executive branches of governments have often been eager (sometimes too eager) to translate advances in genetic knowledge into progressive public-health policy. During the first half of the twentieth century, now-repudiated eugenic theories that claimed a factual foundation in genetics were used to rationalize the involuntary sterilization of institutionalized retarded and mentally ill persons in the United States and several European countries, particularly Germany (Reilly, 1991). Since the early 1960s the United States and European nations have conducted mass genetic screening of newborns to detect rare but ameliorable forms of genetically caused mental retardation. During the 1970s the first carrier-screening programs were launched, often with government support, to identify otherwise healthy individuals who carried particular disease genes placing them at high risk of bearing a child with a recessive disorder if the child were conceived with a person who carried the same disease gene.

The unprecedented ability to learn genetic facts about individuals creates a fundamental tension between the right to privacy and the competing interests of the state and other social institutions. In the United States and in many other nations there is a constitutional right to privacy. Many of the U.S. Supreme Court opinions that initially articulated this right arose from challenges to the state's power to restrict access to contraception and abortion (*Roe* v. *Wade*, 1973), areas of crucial importance to genetic counseling.

Fueled by the Human Genome Project—a feder-

◆ **regulatory and policy ethics**

To fashion legal or clinical rules and procedures designed to apply to types of cases or general practices.

See Also

Theory Fashion: In and Out with Biological Determinism

DNA Sequencing and the Origins of the Human Genome Project

G

GENETICS AND THE LAW

Who Should Have Access to Genetic Information?

Genetic testing eliminates the possibility of terminating at later stages a pregnancy diagnosed as affected.

PAGE 307

ally funded effort begun in 1991 to map and, ultimately, to sequence every human gene—the array of clinically useful genetic tests will increase substantially in coming years. This has raised fears of genetic discrimination. As is demonstrated by the introduction of involuntary eugenic sterilization in the People's Republic of China, genetic information can be used to limit fundamental rights. In the United States and Europe, some are concerned that genetic data will be used to rationalize discriminatory treatment by insurers, employers, and other social institutions. No technologically advanced nation has yet fully explored the social consequences of having a large amount of genetic information available about its citizenry.

Who should have access to genetic information?

The most important legal issue that arises from our growing power to read the genetic code is summarized in a single question: Who should have access to genetic information about ourselves? The response each society develops will reflect the dimensions of the individual's right of privacy, which vary widely. In the United States, Canada, the European Union, Australia, and Japan, discussion of the need to develop rules on the acquisition, storage, and control of genetic information is underway and guidelines are beginning to emerge.

Genetic testing raises challenging privacy conflicts between individuals. Depending on the context, spouses, parents, children, siblings, and even members of one's extended family may have powerful claims to know genetic facts about an individual. For example, when a physician determines that a child is suffering from a genetic disorder, that information may be extremely important to the reproductive planning of the child's aunts and uncles. If the child's parents refuse to communicate with relatives, are there circumstances that would justify the decision by the physician to warn relatives? The common-law expectation that the physician-patient encounter will be conducted in confidence offers some guidance about how to regulate the flow of genetic information within families (Andrews, 1987), but novel questions remain. For example, how should a physician respond to a request for genetic testing from an identical twin? There is virtually no case law concerning the duty of an individual to share genetic information with relatives, but this topic has been explored by several national committees (e.g., U.S. President's Commission for the Study of Ethical Problems in Medicine and Biomedical and Behavioral Research, 1983; Committee on Assessing Genetic Risks, 1994) that have strongly valued the protection of personal privacy, while acknowledging that situations might arise that would justify a disclosure to a third party.

GENETIC TESTING

The Decision to Undergo Genetic Testing

In democratic societies an individual has the right to determine whether or not he or she will undergo genetic testing. The exception, now widespread in the Western world, is newborn screening; these programs test infants for several rare, severe, treatable genetic diseases, usually without giving parents an opportunity to decline. In the United States compulsory newborn screening has never been challenged in court, but would likely be upheld as a valid exercise of the public-health power. However, state-based compulsory screening to identify children with genetic conditions that are not associated with obvious disease are less likely to pass constitutional muster.

— PHILIP R. REILLY

Beyond the family, genetic information may be of interest to public-health authorities, insurers, employers, school systems, child welfare agencies, law enforcement officials, the courts, and the military. In the United States there is growing discussion about whether existing legislation and common law are sufficient to guide the nonclinical uses of genetic data, such as in the underwriting practices of insurers, the hiring practices of employers, and by adoption agencies (McEwen and Reilly, 1992) so as to minimize improper discrimination based on genotype. Constitutional law, especially in determining the limits on state action to further the public health, is relevant to the implementation of mass genetic screening programs and the development of DNA data banks.

Informed consent

In noncompulsory situations, decisions about whether to undergo genetic testing are governed by the doctrine of informed consent, derived from case law and medical literature that developed largely in the United States from the 1960s on (U.S. President's Commission, 1982a). The term "informed consent" first appeared in the case law in 1957 (*Salgo* v. *Leland Stanford Jr. Univ. Bd. of Trustees*), and the concept was developed at length three years later by the Supreme Court of Kansas (*Natanson* v. *Kline,* 1960).

An informed choice presumes that the individual has had an opportunity to become educated about the relevant issues. At a minimum, the physician or genet-

See Also
Confidentiality

ic counselor should inform the individual about the nature and purpose of the test, any significant risks associated with it, and foreseeable problems that may arise from undergoing the procedure or learning the result (*Canterbury* v. *Spence*, 1972). The individual should be informed that test results could discern that assumed biological relationships are incorrect (e.g., nonpaternity or undisclosed adoption). Some commentators advocate informing persons that the presymptomatic diagnosis of disease or recognition of increased risk for a serious disorder could compromise access to health and life insurance and restrict employment opportunities (Billings et al., 1992).

Liability for failure to inform about relevant genetic tests

Most of the litigation concerning genetic information has focused on whether or not a physician owed a duty to warn a patient that she was at increased risk for having a child with a serious genetic disorder. This litigation has given rise to the concepts of "wrongful birth" and "wrongful life." The notion of wrongful life arose in a discussion of whether children should have legal recourse for the stigmatization of illegitimacy; the concept of wrongful birth was developed from about 1975 to 1985 as a number of court decisions (e.g., *Becker* v. *Schwartz*, 1978) and law review articles considered the dimensions of a physician's duty to inform women about reproductive risks (Capron, 1979).

In the United States most jurisdictions will not permit children with birth defects to bring wrongful-life lawsuits against physicians. Such suits typically allege a failure to warn parents about a reproductive risk that subsequently occurred. Judges have been unwilling to permit the child plaintiff in a wrongful-life suit to argue that but for the warning that a physician failed to give, he or she would not have been born. To do so would require the jury to measure the value of an impaired life (due to a serious birth defect) against nonexistence.

In contrast, many jurisdictions do permit wrongful-birth lawsuits brought by the parents of children with birth defects, arguing that the physician's failure to warn breached a duty of care and deprived them of an opportunity to avert the birth of an affected child. If a jury decides that such a duty exists, that the physician breached it, and that an injury occurred, then the jury must decide the damages. Virtually all jurisdictions permit the jury to calculate the special costs of raising a child with the particular disorder; some permit additional damages to be awarded to the parents for loss of economic productivity, and a few permit damages to be awarded for emotional harm (Andrews, 1987).

The availability of ever more genetic tests, some intended to diagnose only mild to moderately severe disorders, will eventually define the limits of the duty to warn. It is likely that actions for wrongful birth will be limited to situations where the physician knew or should have known of the availability of a test for parents who have a significantly increased risk of bearing a child with a serious disease that manifests at birth or in childhood.

Regulation of genetic services

In many nations, education and counseling about genetic disorders is provided through a network of state-supported family-planning clinics. For example, pursuant to Article 20 of its Eugenic Protection Law (1949), in Japan every local government must set up a Eugenic Protection Counseling Center. In 1989 there

GENETIC SERVICES
A Brief History of Legislation

In the United States perhaps the first federal law pertaining to genetic services was the Sickle Cell Anemia Control Act, which in 1972 made funds available to state-based voluntary screening programs that provided access to appropriate genetic counseling. The federal statute, which reduced concerns about poorly drafted state legislation, stimulated a wave of interest in disease-specific legislation. In 1973 the National Cooley's Anemia Control Act appropriated $11 million to support state and local screening programs for beta-thalassemia, an incurable, fatal blood disease of childhood. The Department of Health, Education and Welfare then developed a comprehensive approach to genetic services.

The most significant federal legislation pertaining to the provision of genetic services in the United States was the National Sickle Cell Anemia, Cooley's Anemia, Tay-Sachs, and Genetic Diseases Act, which amended Title XI of the Public Health Service Act. During fiscal 1978, the first year in which funds were appropriated, the Bureau of Maternal and Child Health (MCH) divided $6.8 million about evenly between genetic services grants to individual states and the funding of sickle-cell screening and education clinics. In 1983 MCH began using Title XI dollars to support regional genetic networks that operate under the aegis of a Council of Regional Networks for Genetic Services. Since 1985 MCH has supported the development of newborn screening programs for sickle-cell anemia.

— PHILIP R. REILLY

◆ **common law**
A body of judicial resolutions based on custom and precedent and constitutes the basis of the English legal system.

See Also

Informed Consent and Special Situations: Pregnant Patients

were 836 such centers, most staffed by the Japan Family Planning Association and subsidized by the Ministry of Health and Welfare. The law lists more than twenty hereditary disorders for which abortion may be permitted, but does not have a general provision to cover elective termination of any fetus with a serious hereditary disorder (Takagi, 1991).

In the United States during the 1980s, a federal rule prohibited federally funded family-planning clinics from counseling about abortion. This had a chilling effect on discussions about genetic screening and testing as well. The rule survived constitutional attack (*Rust* v. *Sullivan*, 1991), but was rescinded by an executive order in 1993.

A growing number of nations have limited the use of certain technologies that are relevant to clinical genetics. Alarmed by the use of amniocentesis and karyotyping to identify fetal sex and abort females, India has prohibited prenatal sex selection. Germany, Austria, and Switzerland have forbidden surrogate pregnancies, and France has ruled that the surrogacy contract is unenforceable. These nations also prohibit embryo donation. Preimplantation diagnosis for X-linked disorders is permissible (Knoppers and Le Bris, 1993).

Advances in molecular genetics have spawned a new interest in DNA-based diagnostics. This in turn has raised concerns, particularly among academically based physicians and state regulatory officials, about the quality of the testing services that laboratories will provide. A few states, notably New York and California, have well-developed approaches to evaluating and monitoring genetic testing laboratories, but most do not. A committee of the Institute of Medicine has concluded that the Clinical Laboratories Improvement Act of 1988 and the Medical Devices Act of 1976 grant the Food and Drug Administration sufficient authority to oversee DNA diagnostic facilities, but that the relevant regulations have not yet been applied to these new labs (Committee on Assessing Genetic Risks, 1994).

◆ **health screening**
Tests to detect potential diseases in asymptomatic people.

Until the early 1990s, most genetic testing was performed in medical centers, and most individuals had assistance from genetic counselors. In the United States these counselors had master's-degree training and obtained certification from the American Board of Medical Genetics. No state required that genetic counselors be licensed. In the future most counseling will be done by persons without such specialized training. This raises the need to develop alternative training programs and mechanisms to ensure competence.

NEWBORN SCREENING. Beginning in 1962 with the first law to mandate newborn screening for phenylketonuria (PKU), a disease leading to brain damage and mental retardation, there has been a steady growth of state-operated, population-based newborn screening in the Western world. In the United States every state participates in newborn screening, most as mandated by state law. The programs were originally aimed at identifying children with treatable inborn errors of metabolism; they now include screening for sickle-cell anemia and (in a few states) congenital adrenal hyperplasia, two other disorders where early diagnosis can be lifesaving.

Screening statutes and regulations typically mandate testing, but exempt children whose parents object on religious grounds. In a few states, notably Maryland, the parent is routinely given an opportunity to refuse the test. A report by the Institute of Medicine has concluded that newborn screening can be safely and efficiently conducted on a voluntary basis, and has recommended that new tests be added only when pilot studies have confirmed their potential benefit (Committee on Assessing Genetic Risks, 1994).

CARRIER SCREENING. Carrier screening is intended to identify otherwise healthy persons who, depending upon whom they marry, may be at high risk for having children with a severe genetic disorder. In the United States population-based screening programs have been undertaken to identify carriers for sickle-cell anemia and Tay-Sachs disease. Since its start in the mid-1970s, Tay-Sachs screening has been community based, conducted without state intervention, and highly utilized by the Ashkenazi Jewish population in which the disease is relatively common. In contrast, sickle-cell screening programs were often implemented by law. Between 1970 and 1972 twelve states and the District of Columbia enacted statutes that mandated carrier screening of African-Americans, usually by tying it to entry into the public schools or to obtaining a marriage license. Most state laws failed to offer pretest education or to provide access to genetic counseling. Concerns about genetic discrimination provoked a strong outcry from the African-American community and led to corrective federal legislation (Reilly, 1975).

Voluntary mass screening for beta-thalassemia has been conducted in Sardinia, Cyprus, and Greece. In 1975 geneticists in Sardinia initiated a screening program, heavily endorsed by prominent social institutions, that has had a remarkable impact. By 1991 more than 167,000 people had been tested and about 90 percent of carrier couples had been identified. The vast majority of at-risk couples chose prenatal diagnosis; most of the women with affected fetuses had them aborted. In fifteen years the number of children born with beta-thalassemia in Sardinia declined by 90 percent (Cao, 1991).

The cloning of the cystic fibrosis gene in 1989 sparked debate over the criteria that should be met

See Also
Preimplantation Diagnosis: Ethical Considerations

before mass carrier screening could be offered. One in twenty-five white persons of northern European extraction is a carrier. In England several population-based cystic fibrosis screening programs have been introduced regionally, and a large voluntary effort was undertaken in Denmark. In the United States there is general agreement that population-based cystic fibrosis screening efforts must be voluntary, preceded by adequate education, and anchored to the availability of competent genetic counseling.

PRENATAL SCREENING. Prenatal genetic screening is widely practiced in the United States and Europe. In the United States it is now standard practice for physicians to inform women who will be thirty-five at the time of delivery that they are at a relatively high risk (1 in 270) for having a fetus with Down syndrome. The age of thirty-five was chosen based on studies showing that among women thirty-four and under who had amniocentesis, the risk of miscarriage after the procedure was greater than the risk of bearing a child with Down syndrome. The requirement that women be informed is not statutorially imposed; it reflects clinical consensus and court decisions.

Screening programs that measure the concentration of alpha-fetoprotein (AFP) in maternal serum (MS) to identify women at increased risk of having a child with a neural tube defect (anencephaly or spina bifida) were first used in England and Wales in the 1970s (U.K. Collaborative Study, 1977). In the United States from 1978 to 1983, the Food and Drug Administration hesitated to license the test reagents for sale in interstate commerce. Opponents of licensing argued that the test generated too many false positives, that some laboratories would perform it inaccurately, and that adequate counseling would not be available to assist women in understanding the results. For a time the American Medical Association opposed routine prenatal screening of maternal serum alpha-fetoprotein (MSAFP) (Council on Scientific Affairs, 1982). In 1983 the FDA withdrew a conservative proposal that would have sharply limited use of the reagents, setting the stage for widespread use. In 1986 California enacted a law that required physicians to inform women about the availability and purpose of MSAFP screening, but through 1993 only the District of Columbia had enacted a similar rule. About 70 percent of women in California chose to be tested (Cunningham and Kizer, 1990).

During the late 1980s in the United States, MSAFP screening grew rapidly. This was partly the result of reports on successful screening experiences, but a bulletin published by the legal department of the American College of Obstetricians and Gynecologists warning physicians of a liability risk if they did not inform their patients about the test also had a substantial impact. The rapid growth of MSAFP testing stimulated the American Society of Human Genetics to develop a policy statement on laboratory practices (American Society of Human Genetics, 1987). California controls this technology by limiting testing to six regional laboratories within the state. Elsewhere most MSAFP tests are performed by commercial laboratories operating under standard state public health and federal Clinical Laboratory Improvement Act licenses.

Clinical standards of practice evolve as physicians gain experience with new diagnostic or therapeutic methods. In contrast, medicolegal standards of care develop jurisdiction by jurisdiction as appellate courts consider arguments about whether an act or omission breached a duty owed to a patient. The duty of the physician to inform women who will be thirty-five or older at delivery of the age-associated risk of Down syndrome, and of the existence of a test to diagnose that condition in the fetus, is well established. With the exception of California, where they are statutorially required to do so, it is not yet clear whether physicians have a legal duty to inform pregnant women about MSAFP screening, but it is likely to become established. Similarly, neither the medical literature nor court decisions suggest that there is a duty to inform women about the "triple marker" screen to detect fetuses with Down syndrome; but, given the growing use of this test, courts could decide that physicians have a duty to inform women about it.

During the late 1980s and 1990s a number of feminist scholars scrutinized prenatal screening and testing. They challenged others to reconsider whether prenatal screening confers a net social benefit, to assess its impact on persons with developmental disabilities, and to reflect on how it affects the very notion of pregnancy (Lippman, 1991). MSAFP screening, for example, has been criticized because of a high false positive test rate that generates anxiety in women who initially test positive but turn out on further testing not to be carrying an affected fetus (Press and Browner, 1993).

Laws to curb genetic discrimination

There is growing concern that genetic data acquired to assist in the resolution of a clinical problem or in the course of screening might be used in nonclinical contexts that may harm the economic or social interests of the individual or his or her relatives. The origins of this concern can be traced to the eugenics movement that flourished in the 1920s and 1930s, during which many states in the United States and some European nations enacted involuntary sterilization laws targeting institutionalized persons. U.S. immigration law from 1921 until 1968 favored entry by immigrants from northern and western Europe over eastern and southern Europe,

Modern prenatal diagnosis began in the late 1960s with the development of laboratory techniques for culturing amniotic fluid cells.

PAGE 308

See Also

When is Prenatal Diagnosis Recommended?

G

GENETICS AND THE LAW

Regulation of the Introduction of New Life Forms into the Environment

Discrimination from disclosure of genetic status may result from misunderstanding information.

PAGE 321

GENETIC RESEARCH
Some Protective Regulations

Accelerating efforts to find the genes that contribute to particular illnesses has led the Office for Protection from Research Risks (OPRR) of the National Institutes of Health to issue guidelines for use by local institutional review boards (IRBs) in their assessment of grant applications that would involve genetic testing of human subjects. Although they are advisory in nature, the OPRR guidelines shape the conduct of research and have substantial regulatory weight. They stress that the decision to participate in human genetic research requires an informed consent, that subjects must have access to adequate genetic counseling, and that participants must be told that should they enter and then withdraw from a study, the researcher is not required to purge existing data or destroy cell lines or DNA derived from them. The OPRR has instructed local IRBs that in gathering family histories, investigators may seek information that is routinely available from other public sources (such as names and addresses), but may not seek nonpublic information, for example, about illnesses or adoptions, a position that could impede data gathering (Office for Protection from Research Risks, 1993).

— PHILIP R. REILLY

a pattern rationalized in part by eugenic beliefs (Reilly, 1991).

During the early 1970s in the United States, some persons who participated in sickle-cell screening programs and were found to be carriers experienced employment discrimination. For a short time a few life insurance companies placed persons with sickle-cell trait outside the normal risk pool (Reilly, 1975). This led several states to enact legislation that specifically forbade the use of sickle-cell testing to determine insurability and employability.

Concerns about genetic discrimination as a consequence of screening and testing have grown among geneticists since the mid-1980s (Billings et al., 1992). The possibility that genetic data could be used to deny individuals access to health insurance has become a major topic (Task Force on Genetic Information, 1993).

In 1989 Representative John Conyers introduced the Human Genome Privacy Act. It was reintroduced in 1990 (H.R. 2045, 1991), and hearings were held in 1991, but the bill, which pertained only to the protection of genetic data derived through the use of federal funds, did not become law. Since 1991 several states have considered, and some have adopted, laws that specifically prohibit the use of genetic data in certain contexts, usually underwriting life insurance or hiring. Wisconsin prohibits employers from requiring or administering a genetic test without first obtaining the subject's prior written informed consent. California forbids insurers from charging discriminatory rates to persons solely because they carry a disease allele that may be associated with disability in their offspring. Montana forbids life insurers from refusing applicants on the basis of a "specific chromosomal or single-gene genetic condition" (McEwen and Reilly, 1992).

The enactment of the Americans with Disabilities Act (ADA) of 1990, which covers persons who can demonstrate that they have been discriminated against because they are perceived to be disabled, has raised the possibility that otherwise healthy persons who carry a gene that will eventually cause a disease or increase their risk of becoming ill may invoke the law to seek redress of employment discrimination (Gostin, 1991). The courts will ultimately decide the scope of coverage. One court has held that severe obesity, a genetically influenced condition, may qualify for protection under Section 504 of the Rehabilitation Act, which uses the same definition of disability as does the ADA.

Genetic discrimination in determining access to health insurance is a problem of significant size only in the United States and South Africa, nations that have not provided guarantees to their citizens of universal access to a basic package of health care. In the United States the problem is further exacerbated by the federal Employee Retirement Income Security Act (ERISA), which permits employers to self-insure and thereby circumvent state regulations intended to provide coverage for individuals at higher than average risk (*McGann* v. *H & H Music Co.*, 1991).

Regulation of the introduction of new life forms into the environment

The ability to recombine DNA from widely divergent species raised the possibility that genetic engineering could create serious biohazards. In 1973 the National Academy of Sciences formed a committee to evaluate the safety of this research. The committee called for a voluntary moratorium until safety issues could be evaluated, and recommended that the National Institutes of Health (NIH) establish a committee to oversee the evaluation and develop guidelines for conducting the research. After extensive discussions at the International Conference on Recombinant DNA Molecules held in Asilomar, California, leading scientists issued a statement of principles that advocated stringent research practices until safety issues had been fully explored (Berg et al., 1975).

In 1976 the newly formed Recombinant DNA Advisory Committee (RAC) of the NIH published its first guidelines, focusing on laboratory safety and containment issues. As the evidence mounted that safety concerns were not as dangerous as had been feared, the guidelines were relaxed. The RAC guidelines have been widely replicated by other federal agencies, state and local governments, universities, the industrial community, and other nations (Committee on Scientific Evaluation of the Introduction of Genetically Modified Micro-Organisms and Plants into the Environment, 1989).

Requests to field-test microorganisms were first proposed to the RAC in the early 1980s. In 1983 the RAC approved the first such test (to determine if a genetically engineered bacteria could protect plants against frost damage). This prompted a legal challenge, arguing failure to comply with the National Environmental Protection Act (NEPA). A federal district court ruled that the RAC approval process required assessment of an environmental impact statement; an appelate court reversed the requirement of an impact statement, but upheld the injunction pending NEPA review.

During the 1980s Congress held several hearings on the environmental release of genetically engineered organisms, but it did not enact new legislation. In 1986 the Office of Science and Technology Policy (OSTP) issued the Coordinated Framework for Regulation of Biotechnology, which identified the agencies responsible for approving biotechnology products and their respective jurisdictions for regulating planned introductions (OSTP, 1986). It concluded that existing laws were sufficient to regulate release issues. In the 1980s, as experience with controlled environmental releases of genetically modified microorganisms and plants mounted, reports by the National Academy of Sciences, the Office of Technology Assessment, and the General Accounting Office concluded that there was no significant evidence that the environmental release of organisms modified by recombinant DNA constituted unique hazards (Committee on Scientific Evaluation of the Introduction of Genetically Modified Micro-Organisms and Plants into the Environment, 1989).

During the early 1990s economic and safety issues arose over requests to the FDA to license the use of recombinant bovine somatotropin (growth hormone) as a means to improve milk production by dairy cows. After a full review, the FDA licensed the hormone, which is chemically identical to the naturally occurring substance. This was the first of many genetically engineered agricultural products that will enter the marketplace. Despite the evidence that bioengineered milk poses no discernible risk, it is likely that it and other food products will be labeled, partly out of an effort to respect religious traditions concerning food purity.

DNA forensics

During the 1980s molecular biologists developed techniques to compile a unique DNA profile of every human being (except for identical twins), a technology that has fostered a revolution in forensic science (Jeffreys et al., 1985). Law enforcement officials in England first used DNA evidence to resolve violent crimes in 1986, and the techniques are now used in many nations. In the United States since 1987, DNA evidence has been widely used, usually in the prosecution of rape. In these cases DNA is extracted from semen, blood, or other tissue found at a crime scene and compared to DNA taken from a suspect. The evidence has usually been admitted after a *Frye* hearing, a proceeding by which a judge decides whether the evidence in question is based on theories and practices that have reached general acceptance in the relevant scientific community. Courts in jurisdictions that follow the more liberal Federal Rules of Evidence, which permit the judge to admit any information that is relevant and not unduly prejudicial, also admit this evidence.

The introduction of DNA forensic evidence occurred as courts in the United States followed the lead of European courts in permitting the use of human leukocyte antigen (HLA) testing to inculpate accused males in civil paternity suits. DNA-based paternity testing evidence has since been admitted in many states (Committee on DNA Technology in Forensic Science, 1992).

In 1989 controversy erupted over a number of aspects of how DNA evidence was generated. The core problem has been to determine the likelihood that a crime scene sample could match that taken from a randomly selected individual—in essence, the chance of erroneously convicting the wrong suspect. The debate over this question turns on statistical arguments over whether DNA markers are inherited independently through the generations and uncertainty as to their distribution in different ethnic groups. After reviewing objections from expert witnesses, several courts have refused to permit the use of DNA evidence (e.g., *Commonwealth* v. *Curnin*, 1991), but most are convinced of its utility.

In 1992 a committee of the National Academy of Sciences recommended that the independence of the DNA markers should not be assumed. The committee suggested that until the statistical argument was resolved, experts testifying in court should limit them-

Using standard techniques of molecular genetics, investigators can compare variable loci in DNA taken from different sources.

PAGE 135

selves to stating whether or not a DNA profile of tissue found at the crime scene that matched the profile of the suspect was or was not present in a randomly selected data base of DNA samples. If it was not, then the expert could state, for example, that among a population of 300 randomly selected white males not one had a DNA profile like that of the suspect (Committee on DNA Technology in Forensic Science, 1992). The committee's recommendation has been criticized for being overly cautious.

In 1993 the U.S. Supreme Court, considering the question of standards of admissibility of scientific evidence for the first time, held that the *Frye* standard was too restrictive, and that the judge, applying the Federal Rules of Evidence, must decide whether the evidence offered was based on a sufficiently solid scientific basis (*Daubert* v. *Merrill Dow Pharmaceuticals, Inc.*, 1993). This decision may ease the debate over the admissibility of DNA-based forensic evidence. Scientific consensus over the proper statistical approach in using DNA evidence to make statements about identity will eventually be achieved. DNA evidence will continue to be widely used, for it constitutes a powerful means to exonerate wrongfully suspected individuals and to support the prosecution of perpetrators.

DNA banks

By 1993 eighteen states had enacted laws that require convicted felons (typically, those convicted of sexual offenses) to provide a tissue sample prior to parole. DNA extracted from these samples is being used to create a reference base with which to compare biological samples taken from rape victims or from crime scenes. Because of the high rate of recidivism among sexual offenders, the possibility that a crime scene sample will be found to match a sample in a state data base is reasonably high, especially since investigators will be able to query all state data bases through a system organized by the Federal Bureau of Investigation. In 1993 murders in Minnesota and Virginia were solved by comparing crime scene samples to DNA profiles located in data bases compiled on felons before parole. DNA data bases composed of samples from unidentified bodies and of samples from unknown persons found at crime scenes are also being established. In the former case comparison of the banked DNA and DNA from relatives of a missing person may conclusively identify the remains; in the latter case sample comparisons may indicate whether a series of rapes are the work of one or several criminals (McEwen and Reilly, 1994).

◆ **recombinant DNA (r-DNA) techniques**
The investigation of the nature and composition of the basic molecular building blocks of organisms to gain more insight into the functioning of the cell and how to fabricate new organic forms. Includes gene-tagging and gene-transfer techniques.

A federal appellate court has held that taking DNA samples from convicted felons prior to parole does not violate the Fourth Amendment prohibition against unreasonable searches (*Jones* v. *Murray*, 1992). Further constitutional challenges are likely to argue that DNA data-banking laws should not require tissue samples from convicted felons who have no history of crimes against the person.

DNA BANKS
Prepare to Register

The collection and storage of DNA samples from large populations, possibly even entire populations, is likely to occur routinely in coming years. The two rationales for such an undertaking are to create a DNA data base for identification purposes and to promote the scientific study and clinical use of genetic information, particularly in regard to preventing the onset of genetically influenced diseases. The U.S. military collects tissue samples on new recruits. Researchers in many nations have established small DNA banks in the course of searching for disease genes. As of the mid-1990s, this conduct was unregulated, but concern for the interests of the individuals whose samples are stored suggests that it is likely that the state will eventually regulate academically based and commercial DNA storage facilities (Annas, 1993).

— PHILIP R. REILLY

Gene therapy

In the United States, experiments in which recombinant DNA is introduced into cells of a human subject with the intent of modifying a gene are regulated by the NIH Guidelines for Research Involving Recombinant DNA molecules (National Institutes of Health, 1984), and its subsequent amendments. In Canada the Medical Research Council Standing Committee on Ethics in Experimentation has taken a similar approach, one that requires both local and national review.

Research to treat disease by the reintroduction of genetically modified cells or the use of DNA sequences as drugs, "somatic-cell therapy," has been fully reviewed by several national commissions (U.S. President's Commission, 1982b), and Congress has held hearings about it. The civic, religious, scientific, and medical groups that have studied the topic have concluded that this therapy does not present unique ethical problems (Office of Technology Assessment, 1984). Commentators in Canada and the European

See Also
DNA Typing

Medical Research Councils have also concluded that the therapy is not fundamentally different from other medical therapies ("Gene Therapy," 1988).

Unlike somatic-cell therapy, in which the impact of the intervention is limited to an individual patient, germ-line therapy—the manipulation of the genome in cells that are the progenitors of egg or sperm cells—affects the patient's descendants. This fact, coupled with the concern that genetic engineering may someday permit germ-line enhancement—the introduction of DNA sequences intended to increase the likelihood of having a child with desired traits rather than to avert disease—has provoked much concern. Religious and civic groups have urged a ban on such germ-line manipulations, and the RAC has stated that it would not approve proposals to do research intended to further this goal in humans. The Parliamentary Assembly of the Council of Europe has recommended that the Committee of Ministers provide in the European Convention on Human Rights an explicit recognition of the right to a genetic inheritance that has not been artificially interfered with, unless it is in accord with principles that are compatible with respect for other human rights, language that would permit interventions to prevent disease (Knoppers, 1991).

The individual human genome and the collective human gene pool deserve special protection. We have entered an era in which relatives, insurers, employers, school systems, and the state may be able to acquire ever more genetic information about individuals. We must ensure that genetic testing confers benefits rather than causing injuries. The means to accomplish this will almost certainly be legislation that reasonably subordinates the interests of third parties in the data to the individual's right to privacy. We also possess the power, through massive environmental pollution, to threaten our gene pool and those of other species. We must act as responsible caretakers, a duty that demands a global vision.

— PHILIP R. REILLY

GENETICS AND RACIAL MINORITIES

People are not born equal, nor do they live or die equal. Religion, race, class, and nationality have been a perennial source of stigmatization and discrimination. Racial minorities (herein abbreviated as "minorities") are particularly at risk. In this entry, minorities are categorized as subset populations of a state that have relatively little power and are discriminated against. Hence, the white minority population of South Africa is not a minority, even though numerically they are a minority. Examples of minorities include the Ainu and Koreans of Japan, Australian Aborigines, the Palestinians in Israel, the Catholics in Northern Ireland, Africans and Algerians in France, Africans and their descendants and Asian Indians in Great Britain; and, in the United States, African-Americans, Hispanics, peoples of Asian-Pacific Islander and American Indian-Alaskan Native origin, and the poor.

Jews in the United States are not included here as a racial minority because Jews are not a race. Judaism is a religion and includes such disparate peoples as the Falasha of Ethiopia and Yemenites and Jews of Iraq, Iran, and China. Reference, however, will be made to Tay-Sachs disease screening in Jews in the United States for the purpose of comparison.

Distribution of genetic diseases among minority and nonminority groups

Diabetes is divided into insulin-dependent diabetes mellitus (IDDM) or Type I, and non-insulin-dependent diabetes mellitus (NIDDM) or Type II (Bowman and Murray, 1990). Type I diabetes is uncommon in tropical regions, and accordingly is less common in Africans than in African-Americans, but the prevalence of Type I diabetes is higher in European Americans than in African Americans. The reverse is true with Type II diabetes, which has a higher frequency in African Americans than European Americans.

Certain Asian, Pacific, and Amerindian populations are at increased risk of Type II diabetes. The Pima Indians of the United States have one of the highest world frequencies (35 percent of the adult population) (Polednak, 1989). As one would expect, Type II diabetes is higher in Mexican Americans (because of their Amerindian component) than in Anglo-Americans. Unfortunately, in Mexican Americans the incidence of diabetes-related end-stage renal disease is greater than that predicted from their excess of Type II diabetes. The disease also has an earlier age of onset, greater severity, and poorer control of diabetes than that of other groups (Polednak, 1989). Unfortunately, the higher morbidity and mortality of diabetes in the Mexican American group could also be a reflection of inadequate medical care. The ethical consequences of the market health care system and poverty in the United States are once more quite evident.

TWO TYPES OF DIABETES

Type I:	insulin-dependent diabetes mellitus (IDDM)
Type II:	non-insulin-dependent diabetes mellitus (NIDDM)

◆ **race**

A putative cultural-based explanation for observed human variation in appearance, origin, language, religion, and behavior, but such observation of differences depends not on biology but on local context and social history.

See Also

Race and Racism

Predispositions: Genes, Race, and Violence

G

GENETICS AND RACIAL MINORITIES

Distribution of Genetic Diseases among Minority and Nonminority Groups

In one study of forced C-sections, 81% of the women belonged to a minority group and 24% did not use English as their first language.

PAGE 469

Let us now look at screening and prenatal programs for hemoglobins in Canada, Italy, and Cuba. A population survey in Vietnam is also mentioned because many Vietnamese populations form minority communities in the United States.

H. Granda and colleagues (1991) conducted an extensive nationwide sickle hemoglobin screening program in Cuba, which involved education, couples at risk counseling, and prenatal diagnosis. Blood was obtained from mothers when they attended for prenatal care. If the mother was positive for sickle hemoglobin, couples were given an appointment at a genetics center, where fathers were tested and counseled. The counseling was nondirective and decisions were made by the couples. The author indicated that about one hundred children with sickle-cell disease (HbSS or HbSC) are expected to be born yearly in Cuba. In 1989 this number was reduced by about 30 percent. "Ninety-eight affected fetuses were found. In seventy-two cases the pregnancy was terminated" (p. 153).

James Bowman and colleagues (1971) studied red cell enzyme variation and hemoglobins in populations of Vietnam. The prevalence of glucose phosphate dehydrogenase deficiency was lowest in the Sedang, the Vietnamese, and the Rhade. The highest prevalence of glucose-6-phosphate dehydrogenase deficiency was in the Stieng (0.153). The lowest frequencies of hemoglobin E were in the Vietnamese and the Sedang, and the highest in the Stieng (0.365). Unfortunately, it was not possible to test for alpha thalassemia or beta thalassemia, hereditary markers that are known to be in high frequency in these populations. These studies point to the difficulty of screening for hemoglobins and thalassemias in the United States in these populations. Ethnic groups and language must be identified and appropriate educational and counseling material and counselors with a variety of languages must be required for first generation peoples from Vietnam.

Charles Scriver and colleagues (1984) described a beta-thalassemia disease prevention program in communities in Quebec at highest risk. The populations were of Greek, Italian, Asian, and Oriental, and French Canadian descent. A total of 6,748 persons were screened from December 1979 to December 1982 using MCV/Hb A2 indices. This group included 5,117 senior high school students with a participation rate of 80 percent. (In Canada, parental permission is not needed for screening of students.) The prevalence of beta-thalassemia carriers was 4.7 percent, with a tenfold variation among the various ethnic groups. A total of 60 carriers and 120 unaffected individuals were surveyed. Eleven fetal diagnoses were performed during the study period, either by fetoscopy and globin chain analysis or by amniocentesis and DNA analysis. There was one spontaneous abortion following fetoscopy and seven live births. The economic cost of the program (cost per case prevented) was $6,700, which was slightly less than the average cost of treatment of one patient in one year. A preprogram survey showed that even though 88 percent of those ascertained favored a program, only 31 percent considered fetal diagnosis an acceptable option. Nevertheless, when faced with the actual decision, *all of the couples at risk* took the option of fetal diagnosis.

These figures resemble those found by Rowley and colleagues (1991) for Southeast Asians in the United States, but are unlike those for blacks in a prenatal diagnosis program, all of whom stated that they could not terminate a pregnancy for any reason. Other important facts emerged. The couples who were at risk claimed that they would not have considered pregnancy without the availability of fetal diagnosis. Only one couple with an affected fetus refused abortion. The authors concluded that their findings indicated acceptance of the program, relative absence of stigmatization of carriers, acceptance of the efficacy of fetal diagnosis, and cost-effectiveness.

Extensive surveys for abnormal hemoglobins and thalassemias have been reported in Italy (Tentori and Marinucci, 1983). This analysis will concentrate, however, on the outcome of a screening program for the prospective prevention of thalassemia in the province of Latium, Italy. The average frequency of heterozygous alpha- or beta-thalassemia was 2.4 percent. This figure was ascertained from a study of 289,763 students. In a region of 17,000 km2, a single center was able to examine about 50,000 students per year, which is about 80 percent of all intermediate school children. In this region, couples at risk of childbearing age since 1980 were analyzed. Some of these couples (51 out of 161) had already had an affected child and came to the center during or before a new pregnancy, but the majority (110 out of 161) had no affected children and came for counseling before conception as a consequence of the school screening program. Of the 94 prospective couples, 35 were former students identified in the school screening program or through one of their close relatives. From January 1980 to April 1983, 37 of the 110 prospective couples became pregnant and 6 of 31 monitored pregnancies had a homozygous fetus that was aborted. Further evidence was given to show that the population approved of the screening program and at-risk couples accepted prenatal diagnosis and abortion.

At this point some comparisons may be made from the international experience. Evidently, in the most Catholic of countries, Italy, prenatal diagnosis for thalassemia was accepted to such an extent that if generalizations can be made from this study, the disease may be expected to almost disappear in the next generation.

The acceptance of prenatal diagnosis is also high in Canada among populations at risk for thalassemia. It would appear that at present, the black minority population in the United States is most reluctant to accept prenatal diagnosis and abortion. The reasons have not been documented. Education, religion, suspicion of the health-care system are all conjecture, and not supported by other statistics. The U.S. National Center for Health Statistics in 1990 recorded that in the white population there were 17.5 abortions in 1973 and 30.0 abortions in 1987 per 1,000 live births. Blacks were classified in the "all other" group and undoubtedly consisted of the majority. In this population there were, per 1,000 live births, 28.9 abortions in 1973 and 55.7 in 1987. The figures that show black women aborting fetuses at a higher rate than white women are inconsistent with those that show black women declining to abort fetuses with sickle-cell disease. This suggests a need for further study.

Eugenics

A major scientific and pseudoscientific weapon for discrimination against minorities has been eugenics, a political, economic, and social policy that espouses the reproduction of the "fit" over the "unfit" (positive eugenics) and discourages the birth of the "unfit" (negative eugenics) (Haller, 1963; Ludmerer, 1972). Sir Francis Galton (1871) introduced the word *eugenics* in nineteenth-century Great Britain. He documented the concentration of genius and high achievement in his family and in families of his peers, and disparaged the intellectual abilities of the "masses," and even the peoples of nations such as Spain and France.

The "fit" and "unfit" have been variously defined. The earlier eugenics movement in the United States targeted as "unfit" individuals with epilepsy, criminals, crippled and deformed peoples; persons who were mentally defective, or who had low intelligence; patients with communicable diseases such as syphilis, tuberculosis, or leprosy; alcoholics and drug abusers; poor people; and Eastern European immigrants to the United States. The Nazis marked Jews, Gypsies, and other so-called non-Aryan peoples as individuals who were incurably mentally defective. In the heyday of eugenics, sterilization, infanticide, euthanasia, or a variety of "final solutions" were tools for the prevention or elimination of the "unfit" (Haller, 1963; Ludmerer, 1972).

But who are the "unfit" today, and how are they dealt with? Today, scientific advances in prenatal diagnosis—with the option for abortion—have broadened the "unfit" base to identify early in pregnancy fetuses with hereditary disorders such as Tay-Sachs disease, neural tube defects, Down syndrome, sickle-cell anemia, and cystic fibrosis. These fetuses are placed in the unfit category because abortion is offered as an option in genetic counseling. If they were not "unfit," abortion would not be offered. There also have been repeated attempts to link genetics with abusers of alcohol or drugs and with perpetrators of violent crime since the beginning of the eugenics movement in the United States.

However, "white collar" criminal activities such as embezzlement, insider trading in the stock market, and the savings and loan associations' siphoning of hundreds of millions of dollars from their members have not been objects of study, which suggests that classism, or racism, or both are contributory factors to the linking of genes with crime. Neil Holtzman and Mark Rothstein (1992) perceptively alluded to an example of the selectivity of eugenicists. They quoted Lancelot Hogben's (1938) reference to hemophilia in the royal families of Europe: "No eugenicist has publicly proposed sterilization as a remedy for defective kingship" (p. 457).

Consequently, eugenics is invariably directed to those minorities who have relatively little power, without regard to race, ethnic group, or religion. This entry does not classify most middle- and upper-class African-Americans as minorities because pressures on health-care resources place the poor in all populations at risk for genetic discrimination.

There also operates what could be called "passive eugenics." Passive eugenics is the societal acceptance of infant and maternal mortality rates in the United States that exceed those of any industrialized country. Passive eugenics is an inequitable system of health care. A recurring shibboleth, "health-care resources are scarce," is incomplete. Health-care resources are scarce only for the poor. A society that passively accepts deaths by preventable social and economic inequities will also tolerate the discouragement of the birth of children with "preventable" genetic disorders.

Mandatory sterilization

To compound the problem, at least thirteen states (Reilly, 1991) still have mandatory sterilization laws on their books, all under the aegis of the police power of the State, and affirmed by the landmark Supreme Court decision of *Buck* v. *Bell* (1927), which legalized mandatory sterilization for eugenic reasons. Carrie Buck was alleged to be the feebleminded mother of a feebleminded child. She was a ward of the State Colony of Virginia for Epileptics and the Feeble-Minded. Carrie Buck's mother was also confined to the same institution and was said to be feebleminded. James E. Coogan (1953) disputed the diagnoses of both Carrie Buck and her daughter. J. H. Bell was the superintendent of the State Colony and had been looking for a test case in order to prevent the birth of mentally deficient children by mandatory sterilization. Even though Carrie Buck's

In considering the referents of the term "race," no fixed criterion exists even within the U.S.

PAGE 568

See Also

Melting Pot: Racial Theories in the United States

G

GENETICS AND RACIAL MINORITIES

The Police Power of the State

> ### IMMANUEL KANT
>
> Eugenics is incompatible with Immanuel Kant's dictum that one should treat humanity always as an end and never as a means (Kant, 1964). He maintained that the supreme principle of morality cannot be obtained by studying generalizations from examples derived from experience. Examples cannot replace moral principles and they cannot be a foundation on which moral principles are derived.
>
> — JAMES E. BOWMAN

Because racism clearly influences cognition, perception, and emotion, it could well appear in psychiatric classifications as a specific disorder.

PAGE 568

attorney was appointed by those who wanted Carrie Buck sterilized, he eloquently warned, in part, "A reign of doctors will be inaugurated and in the name of science new classes will be added, even races may be brought within the scope of such regulation, and the worst form of tyranny practiced" (Reilly, 1991, p. 87). While Carrie Buck's attorney was predicting the dangers of compulsory sterilization, Hitler and his colleagues were laying the groundwork for National Socialism with the earlier eugenics movement in the United States as a model (Ludmerer, 1972). In their rush to judgment, it is likely that those who were intent on sterilizing Carrie Buck were also guided by prejudice against the poor. Dr. Harry Laughlin's "expert" testimony in Virginia against Carrie Buck substantiates this premise. Laughlin asserted, "These people belong to the shiftless, ignorant, and worthless class of anti-social whites of the South" (Coogan, 1953, p. 45). The most powerful condemnation of eugenics is revealed in Laughlin's statement. The poor are also selectively affected by passive eugenics. Consequently, the "slippery slope" from passive to active eugenics may be an inexorable continuum.

The police power of the state

The police power of the state is based on utilitarian ethics in that the Supreme Court in *Munn* v. *Illinois* (1877) supported a fundamental precept of both democratic and totalitarian societies: The private interests of the individual must be subservient to the public interest. The threat of eugenics today lies not in blatant criminal behavior like that associated with Nazi Germany but in subtle social and political precepts. In fact, some of the court decisions that may lead to eugenics are even based on liberal ethical views of autonomy, and the right to privacy as found in *Roe* v. *Wade* (1973). Discrimination is cryptic, however, even in the field of ethics, which like economics, provides principles for the allocation of "scarce resources." The canon of "scarce resources," like so-called just wars, is repeated by countless philosophers, but both doctrines have killed millions of innocent people through the centuries. In this discussion of the relationship of ethics to eugenics, it is important to remember a major thesis of this presentation: All propositions that have been used to foster eugenics were not necessarily developed with eugenic intent.

John Rawls and "a theory of justice"

"People are poor because they have defective genes" is a recurring catch phrase. John Rawls (1978) is particularly concerned about the disadvantaged members of society and has developed an important theory of justice in an attempt to resolve some of the major objections to utilitarianism. In so doing he examined a social contract mechanism, which in a way was an outgrowth of previous social contracts outlined by John Locke (1632-1704), Jean-Jacques Rousseau, and Kant. Rawls argued that justice denies that the loss of freedom for some is compensated by a greater good shared by others. A just society not only is designed to foster the good of its members but also is regulated by a public impression of justice.

The heart of Rawls's theory is that the participants must begin under a veil of ignorance. If one were to know in advance one's position in society, it would be the unusual person who would choose a position that jeopardizes his or her self-interest. Rawls provides examples: "[I]f a man knew he was wealthy, he might find it rational to advance the principle that various taxes for welfare measures be counted unjust; if he knew that he was poor, he would most likely propose the contrary principle." "To represent the desired restrictions one imagines a situation in which everyone is deprived of this sort of information" (pp. 18-19). Since utilitarianism espouses the sacrifice of some persons in order to promote the happiness of others, or the majority, Rawls's precepts are patently in opposition to utilitarianism and to eugenic proscriptions against minorities.

Situation ethics

Joseph Fletcher (1979) fostered situation ethics as more useful in resolving moral dilemmas. He postulated that moral judgments are made by following one of two choices: rule ethics or situation ethics. Rule ethics involves what one ought to do. A priori examples are various divine command philosophies or deontological ethics as espoused by Kant. In situation ethics, the agent is central. It is up to the individual to judge what is best under the circumstances and make a decision. This is the a posteriori approach—collect the facts; examine the circumstances; look at the individual, the family, the economic circumstances, society and any other factors that may bear on the situation. One seeks, as in utilitarianism, the greatest good for the greatest

See Also

Genetics and Human Behavior

UTILITARIANISM

If minorities accept utilitarianism as a philosophy, it subjects them to "the greatest good for the greatest number." But here is the dilemma: To reject this concept would be to negate marriage laws, compulsory vaccination for communicable diseases, seat belt laws, and most public health measures.

— JAMES E. BOWMAN

number. A correct decision in one situation may be nonsensical in another. As Fletcher pointed out, physicians are probably more comfortable with situation ethics, for its precepts are what the clinician subscribes to in daily practice. Most physicians do not judge what is best for their patients according to Kant's "categorical imperative."

With the advent of new technology, considerable attention is directed to the question: "What is a person?" Fletcher believed that in order for one to qualify as human, or a person, the following criterion should be taken into account: minimum intelligence (an IQ of less than 40 places the individual in the questionable category; an IQ of less than 20 indicates that the individual is not a person). To quote an aphorism from Fletcher, "*Homo* is indeed *sapiens*, in order to be *Homo* (Fletcher, 1979, p. 12). A person is judged by the following attributes: self-awareness; self-control; a sense of time; a sense of futurity; a sense of the past; the capability to relate to others; concern for others; communication; control of existence; curiosity; change and changeability; balance of rationality and feeling; idiosyncrasy; being idiomorphous, a distinctive individual; neocortical function (pp. 12-16). It follows that if an individual is not a person he or she is "unfit" and a eugenic target.

Albert Blumenthal

Albert Blumenthal (1977) exceeded the fondest hopes of the eugenics movement in the United States in the 1920s:

> *There are no intrinsic moral rights, hence people do not have an inherent moral right to reproduce. The unborn child has a moral right not to be born to parents who have serious genetic deficiencies or who are likely to be unable or unwilling to care for him so that he can develop into a good citizen. Other people have moral rights not to be burdened by obligations to care for the children which improvident, neglectful and incompetent parents produce and by the deficient adults which these children so often become.* (pp. 203-204)

Blumenthal felt that all prospective parents should be licensed according to their parental fitness: some "to reproduce but not to rear children, others to rear but not to reproduce and still others both to beget and rear children." Parents licensed for all functions should be free of serious genetic defects and dysfunctional habits, should love children, should be knowledgeable about nutrition, child psychology, and education, and should be able to provide sufficient economic support. The state would determine a couple's permissible number of children.

Critical theory

Critical theory, critical legal theory, and critical social science (Unger, 1986; Kairys, 1982) have meaningful implications for minorities but for some reason are not alluded to in publications on ethical issues in genetics. Humans are dominated and oppressed because they uncritically accept social roles allotted to them. Established power and organizations shape people's lives because they are accepted as given, beginning in the elementary schools and continuing throughout formal education. Critical theory forces an analysis of the sources of power. But even this may be impossible. People are confronted with repeated dilemmas brought about by a latticework of interrelated events and objects over which they have no control. Critical science questions that an increase in human power over nature will produce human betterment or progress. A major tenet is that power is differentially distributed and frequently used by those who possess it to oppress those who are powerless. Consequently, an increase in scientific knowledge may not rebound to the welfare of the less powerful in a society. Indeed, it may be used to dominate them. In addition to branches of the state and federal governments, the Church, universities, medical centers, scientific, social, economic, political, and philosophical organizations, the Institute of Medicine, the American Medical Association, the American Hospital Association, and many other self-appointed authorities are often major sources of power—and more often, the oppressors.

David Kairys (1982) disagreed with the ideal model that a particular legal mode of reasoning or analysis characterizes the legal process. Kairys further related that the economic decisions that shape our society and affect our lives on the most basic of social issues are not made democratically, or even by our elected government officials. The law is not neutral, value free, or independent of and unaffected by social and economic relations, political forces, and cultural phenomena. The law enforces and legitimizes dominant social and power relations without a need for or the appearance of control from outside and by individuals who *believe in their own neutrality* (a most danger-

◆ **minorities**
Subset populations of a state that have relatively little power and are discriminated against.

See Also

Genes and Crime: What We Don't Study *Can* Hurt Us

Race: European Concept

ous situation for the powerless) and the myth of legal reasoning. It is most difficult to counter individuals who do not know that they are harmful. Furthermore, in the United States at least, the law is a highly respected force for the perpetuation of existing power. Accordingly, the law confers a legitimacy on a social system and ideology that is dominated by a corporate elite that cloaks itself under the mantle of science, with an occasional reference to God.

Public policy

What is public policy? From early childhood we are taught that the "people" decide in a democracy. A contradictory view is that public policy is merely what those who have power decide. Even morality has been placed in this category. Variations of this theme are ancient and recur throughout history. In Book I of Plato's *The Republic,* the Sophist, Thrasymachus, maintained that laws serve only to protect the interest of those in power. A Marxist view (Lavine, 1984) is that morality is contrived and dictated by the ruling elite to control the masses: All morality is class morality. Scholars of the Critical Legal Issues Movement (Unger, 1986) profess that the law is not neutral, but is guided and dictated by political considerations. Accordingly, some expressions like common values and public policy—though sacrosanct to some—have disparate interpretations. Needless to say, this view of the law and public policy has ominous implications for those who believe that eugenics is dead. It should also be a reminder to geneticists that they may be only minor players in the determination of public policy.

Health-care inequity

As noted earlier, laws and practices with eugenic implications are often designed for other purposes. For instance, universal health care may operate to discourage the birth of children with genetic defects, because of their perceived burden on public funds. Limits to state support of children born of mothers who are on welfare is a policy that has eugenic implications for poor mothers who repeatedly bear children with "preventable" genetic disorders. Scientific advances in genetics create a fertile ground for eugenics, because inequities in the delivery and costs of health care have led to plans for additional rationing of health care under the rubric of broadening the base of the U.S. market health-care system to include those 37 million Americans who are merely bystanders to decent preventive health care and health. If health-care resources are indeed scarce for the poor, economic pressures to reduce health-care costs may one day restrict the birth of children with "preventable" severe genetic disorders by indirect coercion or by mandatory legislative and court prohibitions. Accordingly, eugenics may reenter public policy under the guise of "limited resources." The recurring theme of "limited resources" coincides with an explosion of scientific advances in genetic testing from ova to spermatozoa, from blastulae to fetal and

GENETICS AND THE POWER OF THE STATE

Eugenic precepts in the United States are embedded in constitutional rights. The landmark Supreme Court decision of *Munn* v. *Illinois* (1877) established that the private interests of the individual must be subservient to the public interest, and formed the basis for the constitutionality of such diverse edicts as mandatory vaccination, and seat belt and sterilization laws. In short, whatever the state deems critical for the public good is supported by the umbrella of the police power of the state, provided, of course, that the law does not negate the Constitution. Paradoxically, the doctrine that the private interests of the individual must be subservient to the public interest is similar in both totalitarianism and democracy. Consequently, eugenics may prosper under disparate systems of government.

The police power of the state also invades marriage and the family. Family definitions and marriage restrictions open the door to eugenics because many of the prohibitions against marriage—particularly those against consanguineous mating—are far less defensible, genetically, than the mating of carriers with identical traits for genetic disorders. The banning of consanguineous mating facilitates the interdiction of mating of carriers for sickle-cell disease, Tay-Sachs disease, cystic fibrosis, and eventually the mating of carriers of several thousand genetic disorders, once the techniques for early diagnosis in utero are developed.

The expanding field of prenatal diagnosis could not have been developed without the landmark Supreme Court decision of *Roe* v. *Wade* (1973), which established the right of a woman to have an abortion—under certain conditions. This decision was preceded by *Griswold* v. *Connecticut* (1965), which established the right not to procreate. Although abortion is legal, the Supreme Court decisions of *Maher* v. *Roe* (1977) and *Harris* v. *McRae* (1980) and the Congressional legislation known as the Hyde Amendment affirmed that even if abortion is legal—under certain conditions—the state has no obligation to pay for it.

— JAMES E. BOWMAN

trophoblastic cells in pregnant women, to fetuses, to newborns, to children, and to adults. Blastulae are embryos in the early stages of development in which a vesicle is surrounded by a single layer of cells. One of these cells may be extracted and studied for genetic defects without harm to the developing embryo.

Wrongful birth, wrongful life

Once scientific advances become part of the public domain, the courts have invariably supported their use, and expect patients to be made aware of them. Accordingly, failure to inform patients of medical advances has been a source of litigation in the form of wrongful birth and wrongful life suits. One of the first wrongful life cases, *Gleitman* v. *Cosgrove* (1967), rejected a woman's plea that she would not have borne a child blinded by rubella if she had known that rubella early in pregnancy could affect the fetus. The reason for the rejection of her argument was that abortion was illegal, and therefore the physician was under no obligation to suggest an illegal act. Even though abortion is now legal under certain conditions, the Supreme Court has decreed that the state is under no obligation to fund abortions for poor women (*Harris* v. *McRae,* 1980). Nevertheless, the states generally pay for voluntary (indirect coercive) sterilization for poor women. Accordingly, sterilization as an option to prevent future children with genetic disorders now has a more scientific rationale, but, as always, will disproportionately be limited mainly to poor women.

Wrongful birth and wrongful life decisions have formed the basis for litigation to ensure that women will be informed of the availability of genetic and other tests in early pregnancy, and to alert women of the risk of bearing a child with a genetic or other disorder. Wrongful life and wrongful birth litigation led also to assaults on the autonomy of women. Women are now at risk of incarceration for fetal abuse and of discrimination in the workplace, under the aegis of protection of the fetus. The rights of the fetus are often pitted against maternal duties and rights. It even has been suggested that charges of genetic neglect may follow women who elect to bear children affected with preventable congenital and genetic disorders (Shaw, 1984), a policy which patently would be eugenic. Pregnant women who drink alcohol or who are cited for drug abuse have been censured, and even incarcerated (Tanne, 1991). Fetal abuse is equated with child abuse. It is inescapable, however, that there is no greater fetal abuse than abortion. Accordingly, family, community and societal pressures could open a path to eugenics by questioning the discretion of women who elect to have children with preventable genetic disorders. Not surprisingly, since risk analysis is a major factor in insurance and employment, recent advances in genetic prediction may be taken into account in considerations for health, life insurance, and employment. Interestingly, even though the Americans with Disabilities Act of 1990 was passed to protect disabled persons from the private insurance system, the act specifically does not interfere with state laws that allow insurance companies to place restrictions on claims from disabled persons (Natowicz et al., 1992).

Interestingly, the right-to-life (anti-choice) and the opposing pro-choice movements may serve as a needed balance. Paradoxically, these opponents serve as buffers to eugenics. The right-to-life movement opposes abortion, a modern tool to eliminate the "unfit," but the pro-choice movement fosters autonomy and freedom for the women to choose or not choose abortion, and if autonomy prevails, society will not be able to mandate abortion.

Genetic testing

In the early 1970s many mistakes were made in genetic testing programs for sickle hemoglobin. These mistakes led to state-mandated screening, insurance company and employee discrimination, and widespread stigmatization (Bowman, 1977). It may be widely believed that genocide and other motives were responsible for the mandatory laws and discrimination of carriers for sickle hemoglobin (Bowman, 1977). However, it has been asserted that the principal reasons for discriminatory laws and insurance restrictions of carriers of sickle hemoglobin were misinformation in brochures from the National Institutes of Health; pressure for the use of a solubility test by the Ortho Pharmaceutical Company; the proliferation of black community organizations in sickle hemoglobin screening programs with improper educational materials; inadequate testing procedures; and little or misinformed counseling. Further, most, if not all, of the state and District of Columbia mandatory sickle hemoglobin laws were instigated by black physicians, state legislators, or community groups. Jews, on the other hand, knew their history and its tragic consequences in Nazi Germany. *All* programs for Tay-Sachs disease were voluntary, and directed by experienced geneticists, with the cooperation of rabbis and the community (Kaback and O'Brien, 1973).

The lessons to be learned from sickle-cell screening in the black community and Tay-Sachs disease screening in the Jewish community include (1) involving the community first in any widespread genetic screening program; (2) contacting religious and community leaders, physicians, insurance companies, and other concerned parties in a program of community

Imputing wildness and irrationality is doubtless a defensive projection of aggression that actually exists in the dominant group.

PAGE 572

See Also
Blurred Lines: Genetic vs. Environmental Causes

GENETIC COUNSELING
Education Is Essential

All publications on genetic counseling emphasize the importance of education of the community before genetic screening is instituted, as well as accurate testing and counseling that is sensitive to the racial, class, and religious characteristics of the community (Bowman and Murray, 1990). Whenever possible, counselors should be of the same ethnic group as the counselees. Language is important. Today, efforts are made to produce educational and counseling material in the language of the counselees. This may be impossible, particularly when dealing with communities such as those from Vietnam and Laos, where many languages are used. Other writers such as Peter Rowley, Starlene Loader, Carol Sutera, Margaret Walden, and Alyssa Kozyra (1991) found that in a prenatal diagnosis program obstetricians were reluctant to provide education before pregnant woman were tested for hemoglobins. Such practice is contrary to accepted practice in genetic programs. It is paternalistic and denies autonomy to the pregnant woman, placing her at risk for stigmatization for employment, life, and health insurance, without her consent. On the other hand, in the real world of practice in a busy obstetrician's office, other means of counseling may have to be found, such as ethnically relevant educational materials, recordings, and office or home videos.

— JAMES E. BOWMAN

◆ **biological psychiatry**
A racially based comparative psychology that established a biological basis for major mental diseases.

education so as to minimize misinformation, with its discriminatory and stigmatizing consequences; and (3) emphasizing voluntary genetic screening instead of mandated state laws. There have never been recommendations for either federal or state mandatory programs for Tay-Sachs disease. As of mid-1994, however, mandatory newborn screening for sickle hemoglobin was the law in over thirty-nine states in order to decrease morbidity (incidence of disease) and mortality early in life from pneumococcal disease (bacterial pneumonia) by the early introduction of prophylactic penicillin.

A recapitulation and challenge

The prospects of eugenics are anathema to most geneticists and ethicists. Nevertheless, consider the plight of poor women in the United States. Several states have decreased benefits for parents receiving Aid to Families with Dependent Children (AFDC) (Jencks, 1992). For example, in 1951, Georgia became the first state to deny welfare grants to more than one illegitimate child of a welfare mother. Louisiana followed in 1960 by denying public assistance to 23,000 children born out of wedlock on the same basis. Twelve states supported punitive action against those who might in the future conceive a child out of wedlock, and some even attempted to mandate the imprisonment or sterilization of women who bore more than one child out of wedlock (Solinger, 1992). The Supreme Court decision of *Dandridge* v. *Williams* (1970) restricted total state Aid for Dependent Children (AFDC) to a maximum of $250 per month per family, no matter how large the family. The state of Wisconsin in 1992 embarked on an "experiment" in which a limit would be placed on public funding of women on welfare who bear children out of wedlock; New Jersey has decided not to increase AFDC recipient benefits if a woman has a child while on welfare (Jencks, 1992). President Bill Clinton suggested during his campaign that no one be allowed to collect AFDC for more than two years (Jencks, 1992). As a follow up, Clinton gave Wisconsin permission to impose a two-year limit on indigent families with children. One may conclude that if legislators are so draconian as to attempt to mandate incarceration or sterilization for women who have more than one child out of wedlock, poor women who have children with "preventable severe genetic disorders" are at risk for mandatory sterilization or other coercive means to prevent the birth of such children.

In summary, scientific, economic, social, and legal forces may eventually restrict the birth of children with severe genetic disorders, particularly those who are members of poor racial groups. The scientific advances include developments in prenatal diagnosis and the eventual deciphering of the human genome. The legal precedents are based on the police power of the state (the doctrine that the private interests of the individual must be subservient to the public interest), mandatory sterilization laws, and the legalization of abortion. The social pressures include the dictum that health-care resources are scarce and the fact of widening gap between the haves and the have-nots.

Today, however, we are concerned not only with those with genetic disease who may be stigmatized as unfit but also with individuals who carry a single dose (carriers) of a genetic defect, which causes little if any effect. Since all people have at least five recessive genes, all of us are at risk for having "unfit" children. Five

See Also
Genetic Counseling

recessive genes may, however, be just the tip of the iceberg. When the human genome is mapped, many more potentially harmful genes—recessive and otherwise—may be unveiled in each of us. Consequently, in this day of rapid advances in genetics, we all are potentially able to pass "unfit" disorders to the next generation. Since we are all in the same position, scientific advances in the understanding of the human genome *may* be one of the best defenses against subjecting minorities to eugenic discrimination. We rarely discriminate against those who are "like ourselves."

JAMES E. BOWMAN

GENETIC TESTING AND SCREENING

PREIMPLANTATION DIAGNOSIS

The detection of genetic defects that cause inherited disease in human embryos before implantation (preimplantation diagnosis) has a number of advantages for couples known to be at risk of having affected children (Handyside, 1992). The main advantage is that selection of unaffected embryos for transfer to the uterus means that any resulting pregnancy should be normal. It eliminates the possibility of terminating by conventional methods at later stages a pregnancy diagnosed as affected. Another advantage relates to the use of superovulation and in vitro fertilization (IVF) for access to embryos at the early stages. Superovulation increases the number of eggs that reach maturity in a single reproductive cycle. After IVF, an average of five or six embryos can be screened simultaneously, increasing the chance of identifying unaffected embryos. Although several IVF cycles may be necessary, since pregnancy rates average only one in three to four embryo transfers (Hardy, 1993), establishing a normal pregnancy may in many cases take less time than following a series of terminations of affected pregnancies diagnosed at later stages.

For deoxyribonucleic acid (DNA) analysis, cells are removed or biopsied from each embryo at about the eight-cell stage, early on the third day after insemination. The DNA analysis is then carried out, if possible

PREIMPLANTATION DIAGNOSIS
Ethical Considerations

The ethical issues raised by preimplantation diagnosis are concerned first with the manipulation of human preimplantation embryos and, second, with the use of this approach to screen for genetic defects that would not justify terminating established pregnancies. Ethical objections to the manipulation of human preimplantation embryos are generally based on the view that there is in principle no difference between an eight-cell embryo, for example, and a midgestation fetus or a child. They are all human individuals, and since informed consent is not possible, should not be interfered with. On this basis, terminating an affected pregnancy in midgestation is no more or less acceptable than discarding affected preimplantation embryos. The opposing view draws a sharp distinction between these stages of a human's development and consequently argues that the ethical constraints are different at each stage. In this case, manipulation of early embryos to remove cells for genetic analysis is acceptable; some would argue that discarding affected embryos is preferable to termination at later stages. Even after normal conception with fertile couples, it is known that many fertilized embryos are often lost before implantation because they have gross genetic, usually chromosomal, defects (Burgoyne et al., 1991).

The other ethical issue arises out of the possibility that preimplantation diagnosis might be used to screen for genetic characteristics associated with only mild non-life-threatening conditions, for example, for the health of the individual, or indeed, simply for physical characteristics. Examples of milder inherited conditions include detection of the premutation predisposing to the fragile X syndrome, hereditary blindness or deafness, and Huntington disease, which causes dementia in later life. In these cases, the principle that a couple has the right to choose prenatal screening may still be a sufficient safeguard. After all, a couple is unlikely to elect IVF and preimplantation diagnosis unless they feel strongly about the effects of any condition and often know firsthand exactly what is involved because they already have affected children or relatives. Of more concern is the identification of single genes, segregating in families, that predispose to cancer or heart disease. Also, with so much worldwide effort directed toward mapping the human genome, fears have been expressed about the use of preimplantation diagnosis to yield "designer babies." This is not a realistic prospect, however, since it overlooks the fact that even with complete knowledge of the human genome, geneticists would be able to identify embryos with the desired characteristics only if the parents had passed on the right combination of genes.

— ALAN H. HANDYSIDE

Ethical discussion human gene therapy took a decisively international turn at the end of the 1970s.

PAGE 258

The need for informed consent by patient-subjects is a central tenet of research ethics.

PAGE 260

within eight to twelve hours, and unaffected embryos are transferred to the uterus later the same day. The embryos are apparently unharmed by this process since the cells have not become specialized at this early stage (Hardy et al., 1990). As an alternative, the first polar body (a small nondividing cell produced during egg formation and containing one set of discarded chromosomes) is removed from eggs before fertilization to test (indirectly) whether the egg itself has inherited the genetic defect from women carriers (Verlinsky et al., 1990). Preconception diagnosis may be ethically more acceptable to those opposed to the manipulation of human embryos. However, it is limited to the analysis of maternal genetic defects, is less efficient, and has so far failed to establish a pregnancy after diagnosis.

To date, pregnancies (and in some cases births) have been achieved mainly after preimplantation diagnosis to identify the sex of embryos and to transfer females in couples at risk of diseases affecting only boys (Handyside et al., 1990). However, specific diagnosis of embryos affected by cystic fibrosis (Handyside et al., 1992) and several other diseases has recently been achieved. This is accomplished by amplifying DNA specific for the male Y chromosome or for the cystic fibrosis gene, for example, from the single cells biopsied from each embryo. In principle, similar strategies can be used for the detection of almost any genetic defect that has been characterized at the DNA level (Hardy and Handyside, 1992). Examples include Duchenne muscular dystrophy, Tay-Sachs disease, hemophilia A and B, beta-thalassemia, sickle-cell disease, alpha$_1$-antitrypsin deficiency, and Lesch-Nyhan syndrome. Another technique for identifying the sex of embryos is the use of fluorescent DNA probes that recognize the sex chromosomes. This approach also enables embryos with abnormal numbers of chromosomes to be identified in carriers of chromosome abnormalities or in older women at increased risk of Down syndrome (Griffin et al., 1991, 1992).

Preimplantation diagnosis is rapidly becoming an established procedure and many clinics will be starting their own programs over the next few years. In the United Kingdom, legislation regulates the use of any procedure involving human fertilization and embryo manipulation, including preimplantation diagnosis. The alteration of an embryo's genes, for example, even for gene therapy or for cloning of embryos, is illegal. In addition, all IVF clinics must be licensed by a government-appointed authority with both specialist and nonspecialist members. This authority has the power to withhold a license if a clinic has not demonstrated minimum standards of competence or if the proposed purpose is not considered ethically or otherwise justified. For example, the authority does not allow the identification of an embryo's sex simply to allow couples to choose the sex of their child. It is important that similar initiatives be taken in other countries to ensure that clinics have the necessary expertise to attempt preimplantation diagnosis and prevent its misuse.

— ALAN H. HANDYSIDE

PRENATAL DIAGNOSIS

Modern prenatal diagnosis began in the late 1960s and early 1970s with the development of laboratory techniques for the culturing of amniotic fluid cells (Fuchs and Riis, 1956; Steele and Breg, 1966). As with many new technologies, priority was given to patients believed to be at highest risk—and, in this case, those willing to consent to abortion if an abnormality were detected. Before the risks of prenatal diagnosis were known and the resource was very scarce, this priority was understandable, but it is now an unacceptable standard of care in the United States (Eden and Boehm, 1990). Since the literature on prenatal diagnosis is vast, the interested reader is referred to other materials (Evans, 1992; Evans et al., 1989; Fleischer et al., 1991).

Reproductive risks and indications

From 2 to 4 percent of all infants are born with a serious defect. If minor defects are included, the rate can reach 8 to 10 percent. Of serious abnormalities, approximately half are genetic. The remainder can be attributed to drugs, alcohol, infections, or other nongenetic causes.

WHEN IS PRENATAL DIAGNOSIS RECOMMENDED?

Risk Indications

1. advanced maternal age (usually over 35)
2. genetic history of abnormalities
3. belonging to an ethnic group known to be at risk
4. previous poor reproductive outcomes
5. family history of infants with birth defects
6. multiple miscarriages
7. documentation in a current pregnancy of a problem or abnormality

Advanced maternal age is still the most common indication for prenatal diagnosis; worldwide, it accounts for more than 90 percent of all prenatal diagnostic procedures. Although it is a standard of care in the United States to inform pregnant women over the age of thirty-five as to the availability of prenatal diagnosis, the choice of that age as the cutoff is entirely arbitrary (ACOG, 1987). In fact, the risk of a child with a chromosome abnormality begins to increase prior to age thirty, then continues to rise at an accelerated rate (Hook et al., 1983).

Couples who already have had a child with Down syndrome or another chromosomal abnormality face a recurrence risk of 1 percent or more in each subsequent pregnancy (Stene et al., 1984). They are candidates for prenatal diagnosis regardless of age.

A known cytogenetic abnormality (i.e., a balanced translocation) in one of the parents is a less frequent but important indication for prenatal diagnosis (Boue and Gallano, 1984). Such balanced translocations typically come to light after the birth of a child with an "unbalanced" chromosomal rearrangement. Parental balanced translocations may also be uncovered as part of the diagnostic evaluation of multiple spontaneous first-trimester abortions.

Some abnormalities are significantly linked to certain ethnic groups. For example, Tay-Sachs disease is seen mostly in Ashkenazi Jews, sickle-cell anemia in African-Americans, and beta-thalassemia in Mediterranean peoples.

A previous child or first-degree relative with a neural tube defect is an indication for amniocentesis. Such a defect is inherited in a multifactorial pattern. A couple who has had a child with anencephaly or meningomyelocele faces approximately a 3 percent risk of having a second affected child. At least 90 percent of open defects (those in which there is communication between the subarachnoid space and the amniotic cavity) can be detected by measurement of alpha-fetoprotein in the amniotic fluid. Amniotic fluid acetylcholinesterase is also elevated in the presence of these defects and has proven to be a very useful diagnostic adjunct.

Women who have had elevated serum alpha-fetoprotein levels on two occasions during pregnancy, and whose gestational timing has been confirmed by ultrasound examination, are at markedly increased risk of having a child with a neural tube defect and are candidates for amniocentesis for definitive diagnosis.

Procedures for prenatal diagnosis

There are three basic approaches to identifying fetal defects: visualization, analysis of fetal tissues, and laboratory studies.

PRENATAL DIAGNOSIS

Three Basic Approaches

1. visualization
2. analysis of fetal tissues
3. laboratory studies

VISUALIZATION. The application of ultrasonographic methods to the study of human anatomy has had a tremendous impact on all areas of medicine. The development of high-resolution, real-time scanners has made it possible to visualize essentially any part of the fetal anatomy in exquisite detail (Romero et al., 1988; Fleischer et al., 1991).

Second-trimester ultrasound examinations are performed in 30 to 50 percent of all pregnancies in the United States, frequently in the obstetrician's office. More detailed examinations are best performed by ultrasonographers with special interest and expertise in fetal anatomy, pathology, and physiology. Prenatal diagnosis may be most successful when a particular defect is sought. A thorough examination includes a variety of measurements to assess intrauterine growth and gestational age, and to identify skeletal disproportions. In addition, each part of the fetal anatomy (face, intracranial structures, chest, heart, abdomen, genitourinary system, and extremities) is examined in detail.

ANALYSIS OF FETAL TISSUES. Because visualization techniques do not provide genetic information about the fetus, amniocentesis or chorionic villus sampling may be indicated where a fetus is at risk for genetic abnormality.

Amniocentesis. Transabdominal amniocentesis (needle puncture of the uterus) is the most widely used invasive technique for prenatal diagnosis because of the wealth of information that can be derived by studying cells in the amniotic fluid and the fluid itself.

Amniocentesis should be performed by an obstetrician skilled in the technique. It is commonly performed with ultrasonographic guidance (Benaceraff and Frigoletto, 1983; Romero et al., 1985), although many thousands of procedures have been performed without it. In skilled hands an adequate sample is obtained on the first attempt in over 99 percent of cases, and successful fluid cell cultures are established in 98 to 99 percent of these. The major risk of amniocentesis is fetal loss. In the 1976 National Institute of Child Health and Human Development study the rate of loss (spontaneous abortion, fetal deaths in utero, and stillbirths) was 3.5 percent in the subjects and 3.2 percent in the controls; after adjustment for maternal age, the rates were 3.3 percent and 3.4 percent, respectively. This loss rate of approximately 1 in 200 is widely believed to have decreased in major centers to about 1 in 300.

With increasing experience and confidence of needle placement under ultrasound guidance, it has become possible to perform amniocentesis earlier and earlier. Motivated by the desirability of completing prenatal diagnostic studies as early as possible, and by the limited availability of chorionic villus sampling (CVS) in many areas, several prenatal diagnosis pro-

Both informed consent and the protection of privacy and confidentiality are rooted in the principle of autonomy.

PAGE 261

See Also
Confidentiality; Informed Consent

grams have begun offering amniocentesis as early as 10 to 14 weeks' gestation. Limited experience in the last few years suggests that the safety of the procedure will likely become comparable with that of traditional amniocentesis, but long-term outcome studies are not yet available.

Early amniocentesis still does not enable chromosome analysis or biochemical analyses to be performed as quickly as they can be after a chorionic villus sample. However, it may be useful in some twin pregnancies (if there is a single fused placenta or if sampling both fetuses may not be possible by CVS) or other circumstances in which CVS is contraindicated.

Chorionic villus sampling. Although amniocentesis has proven to be very safe and highly reliable, the desirability of a procedure that can provide information prior to eighteen or twenty weeks' gestation is obvious. Although the decision to terminate a pregnancy is rarely (if ever) easy, it is perhaps more easily made earlier in pregnancy.

Chorionic villus sampling (CVS) is a first-trimester alternative to amniocentesis. The chorionic villi are the forerunners of the placenta and can be obtained by aspiration, usually between nine and twelve weeks' gestation. The most common technique relies entirely on ultrasound guidance. A metal sound is introduced through the internal cervical os to chart the path for the catheter on the ultrasound, and to determine the degree of curvature between the cervical canal and the placenta. A malleable catheter (usually plastic with an aluminum guide) one to two millimeters in diameter is then bent to permit easy passage through the cervix and maneuvering to the implantation site. The tip of the instrument is advanced through as much of the placenta as possible. The metal guide is removed, a 20 cc syringe is attached to the catheter, and suction is applied. The catheter is then slowly pulled back, with some rotation, to increase tissue aspiration. The villi that are torn from the chorion are taken up in tissue culture medium and examined under the dissecting microscope to determine the adequacy of the sample. An adequate sample is successfully obtained on the first attempt by an experienced operator in 85 percent of cases, and after two attempts in 98 percent of cases. Alternatively a needle can be passed transabdominally into the placenta, and villi then aspirated. The choice of approach (transcervical or transabdominal) depends on placental location and the experience of the opera-

PRENATAL DIAGNOSIS

Ethical Implications

It has become a fundamental tenet of genetics that there is no linkage between the offering of prenatal diagnosis, the documentation of fetal abnormalities, and the decision of whether to have an abortion. *Prenatal diagnosis is for the purpose of providing information to couples about what they can expect.* Even for couples who would not under any circumstances consider termination of pregnancy, the knowledge gained can be extremely valuable. In the vast majority of cases, general levels of anxiety can be considerably decreased, since a normal result will be found. In the event that an abnormality is detected, the patients then have the ability at least to be prepared for what is coming, and perhaps significantly to alter the way in which the obstetrical care of the patient is handled. For example, patients with ventral wall defects such as omphaloceles or gastroschises are best delivered in a tertiary-care center where an immediate repair of the defect can be undertaken. Patients with neural tube defects are best delivered by cesarean section, to avoid trauma to the open neural tube, which appears to decrease motor function. Fetuses with lethal disorders, such as trisomy 18, can be managed conservatively. Over 50 percent of fetuses with undiagnosed trisomy 18 have been delivered by emergency cesarean section, only to have the baby die and thus to have subjected the mother to a futile major operation.

The use of screening technologies, such as routine ultrasound and maternal serum alpha-fetoprotein screening, has brought many couples to prenatal diagnosis who otherwise would never have been seen. This is important from a public-health viewpoint, since if prenatal diagnosis were offered only to women age thirty-five or older, less than 20 percent of all chromosome abnormalities would be detected. The use of such tests as MSAFP screening was originally met with considerable skepticism and anxiety by women who previously were considered low risk and suddenly shifted to being high risk. However, after several years of experience, patients have learned to cope with the alteration in anxiety and, by and large, to undergo the further testing necessary to clarify their situations. In most cases these patients return to a lower state of anxiety with diagnoses of normal pregnancy.

Obstetricians have long held the concept of having two patients—mother and fetus. Only in recent years, with the advent of ultrasound and fetal treatments, has the distinction between mother and fetus become generally understood—elevating the standing of the fetus ethically and sometimes legally. Predictably, there are sometimes conflicts of interest between the two that have profound legal and ethical implications.

— MARK I. EVANS
MORDECAI HALLAK
MARK P. JOHNSON

tor. The ability to utilize both approaches is necessary for optimum efficiency and safety. Use of transabdominal CVS does increase with advancing gestational age, which is a function of placental accessibility. After fourteen weeks' gestation most procedures are performed transabdominally, since the placenta gains bulk and moves away from the cervix.

As with amniocentesis, there has been great concern about the risk of spontaneous abortion or fetal injury as a result of CVS. The first major problem in determining the loss rate, however, was differentiating the true procedure-related losses (added) from the spontaneous losses. Overall, the fetal loss rate after a normal ultrasound at eight to ten weeks has been estimated to be 1.4 to 2.7 percent. However, the spontaneous abortion rate increases with maternal age (and other factors, such as tobacco and alcohol consumption). Since 80 to 90 percent of CVSs are performed in women over the age of thirty-five, the spontaneous abortion rate at this age (4.0-4.3%) is also more relevant than lower spontaneous risks in younger women.

Published data on the safety and efficacy of CVS have begun to emerge, but reflect data two to three years old (Cole, 1987; Wilson et al., 1989; Rhoads et al., 1989; Jackson et al., 1992). Most studies showed no statistical difference between procedure-related fetal loss and spontaneous losses. Patients are usually informed, however, that CVS is believed to carry between a 1 percent and a 0.5 percent risk of fetal loss due to the procedure.

LABORATORY STUDIES. Neural tube defects (spina bifida and anencephaly) occur in about one in 700 white and one in 1,000 black pregnancies. Amniocentesis to measure alpha-fetoprotein (AFP) and sometimes acetylcholinesterase (fetal enzymes found in higher elevations when the fetus is affected) is used for the definitive diagnosis for patients at high risk. However, the vast majority (about 95%) of all infants with neural tube defects are born to couples unaware of any increased risk. Thus, inherent in a program to detect the vast majority of neural tube defects is the necessity to test *all* pregnancies. Clearly it is impossible to offer amniocentesis to all patients. Thus, the concept of testing for AFP in maternal serum (MSAFP testing) was developed in the mid-1970s (Brock et al., 1973). For neural tube defects, approximately 3 percent of patients will have either one blood test with very significantly elevated MSAFP or two tests, both of which are slightly elevated. Of these patients, ultrasound will find an obvious explanation for the elevations in approximately half the cases: twins, anencephaly, severe neural tube defect, or, most commonly, incorrect assessment of gestational age. The remaining 1.5 percent of patients are offered a genetic amniocentesis. In most large programs the detection rate for abnormalities is approximately 5 percent of patients who have the amniocentesis.

The chance of finding that babies born with chromosome anomalies such as Down syndrome tended to have lower-than-normal MSAFP values has led to a reevaluation of assessment of genetic risk (Cuckle et al., 1984; Merkatz et al., 1984). The definition of a low MSAFP is a value at which the adjusted risk for the given patient is equal at least to the risk of a thirty-five-year-old, regardless of her actual age. Through this test, thousands of women thought to be low risk have been identified as high risk and offered amniocentesis.

The potential benefits of mass screening for chromosomal abnormalities are obvious. If only women thirty-five years of age and older were offered amniocentesis or CVS, only about 12 to 20 percent of chromosome abnormalities would be detected. MSAFP, when properly performed, raises the detection rate to between 40 and 50 percent. In an effort to increase the detection rate beyond 40 to 50 percent, there has been research looking for additional serum markers.

There are vociferous arguments as to the best combination of markers, but the trend is toward multiple markers and attempts to move screening into the first trimester. It is very likely that the specifics, timing, and efficacy of screening will change rapidly in the next several years.

— MARK I. EVANS
MORDECAI HALLAK
MARK P. JOHNSON

NEWBORN SCREENING

Phenylketonuria (PKU) is a genetic disease that, if undetected and untreated, can lead to often severe mental retardation. Each parent of the affected child carries a single PKU gene in his or her sex cells, giving the parents a one-in-four chance in every pregnancy of conceiving a child with this recessively inherited disorder. Carrier status is not harmful to the parents. The affected condition of the child, however, produces a biochemical defect in the body's ability to metabolize phenylalanine, an amino acid essential to nutrition. The result is a markedly increased level of phenylalanine and brain damage due to this accumulation or to an organic by-product of the body's abnormal biochemical processing of phenylalanine (Scriver, 1990).

The course of PKU can be altered by treating with a special diet low in biochemical and clinical phenylalanine, which controls the biochemical abnormalities (Hudson, 1970; Smith, 1970). Nevertheless, when this diet begins after mental retardation is present, the mental retardation cannot be reversed.

The need to initiate diet before mental retardation appears led to newborn screening for PKU. This was

Pharmacologic fetal therapies benefit the fetus and are minimally invasive.

PAGE 465

See Also
Infants; Maternal-Fetal Relationship

developed in the early 1960s by Robert Guthrie (Guthrie and Ada, 1963) as a test to measure phenylalanine in a dried blood specimen. The specimen was collected by pricking the newborn's heel with a lance and blotting the drops of blood on filter paper. These dried blood spots were sent to a laboratory for testing. This process resulted in the rapid and early diagnosis of PKU in the infant and could be followed quickly by initiation of the diet. Soon after development of the test, all fifty states in the United States and many countries throughout the world began routine screening for PKU in newborn infants (Therrel, 1987). In this early period, mistakes were made in a general rush toward newborn screening. A 1975 report of the National Research Council's Committee for the Study of Errors of Inborn Metabolism concluded that "hindsight reveals that screening programs for phenylketonuria were instituted before the validity and effectiveness of all aspects of treatment, including appropriate dietary treatment, were thoroughly tested" (p. 2).

Some people think "playing God" is all right as long as the God is a relatively minor deity.

PAGE 282

Biomedical research led to tests and treatment for other genetic and partially genetic disorders besides PKU and these were gradually added to mandatory screening programs (Seashore, 1990). Among these disorders were (1) galactosemia, a disorder affecting the body's ability to process galactose, which comes from the lactose of milk; (2) congenital hypothyroidism, an endocrine disorder that results from aberrant development or function of the thyroid gland; and (3) sickle-cell disease, a genetic abnormality in hemoglobin, a component of human blood, that can cause serious crises and death even before one year of age. Most states have laws that require newborn screening for one or more of these three disorders. Some states also screen for other rare genetic disorders of metabolism. The American Academy of Pediatrics (1992) recommends that blood samples be taken from all infants prior to their discharge from the hospital; most states assign this duty to the hospital.

Galton's dream of ridding the world of pathology and defective specimens through biochemistry has come to seem like a pending reality.

PAGE 283

Technical and ethical issues

More than four million babies are born in the United States each year. Public policy, embodied in state laws and federal programs (National Institutes of Health, 1987), increasingly recognizes that newborn screening tests play an important role in safeguarding child health and development. The ethical principle at work behind such laws obligates society and its members to prevent harm wherever possible. Newborn screening is the use of knowledge to prevent serious harm in cases where parents may be completely unaware of their genetic risks. In this framework, newborn genetic screening is a medical act in the context of preventive medicine, intended to be followed by medical intervention for the benefit of the newborn. A medical act creates a relationship with obligations between the participants, that is, the states, laboratories, physicians, and the parents (Knoppers and Laberge, 1990).

TECHNICAL ISSUES. Challenging technical and ethical issues arise in newborn screening. Technical issues begin with accuracy and precision of testing. Large numbers of samples need to be tested quickly and inexpensively. Whether the laboratories where samples are tested should be centralized or dispersed depends on population size and density; it also depends on the availability of experts to perform and interpret several tests requiring state-of-the-art knowledge in measuring metabolites (PKU) and enzymes (galactosemia), and identifying proteins (sickle hemoglobin). Other important technical issues involve reporting, tracking, and monitoring the outcomes of treatment. States and nations differ as to whether all results or only abnormal results must be reported to attending physicians. Variation also exists in whether reports must be sent to the child's pediatrician, the physician in the hospital who authorized the test, or the hospital itself.

THE FUTURE OF NEWBORN SCREENING

As the Human Genome Project unfolds, difficult ethical and public policy challenges will face newborn screening programs (Seashore, 1991). The blood spots on Guthrie cards are an excellent source of DNA that can be easily stored. New approaches to DNA testing will make it possible to identify the molecular basis for many more genetic conditions and also whether the child is a carrier of recessive genes. Issues of privacy will become increasingly significant because so much more can be known about each individual. Some of the information available will not predict disease but will bear upon such sensitive areas as susceptibility to diseases and personality traits.

Ought societies encourage research in these directions, especially in the case of conditions that cannot now be treated or are only of indirect or no immediate benefit to the child? Such questions are appropriate for professionals involved with newborn screening (Knoppers and Laberge, 1990) and at the highest level of national bioethics consideration. The answers potentially affect the well-being of every child screened at birth.

— MARGARETTA R. SEASHORE

States also vary in strategies to track affected children, whose families may move several times. Following those treated for PKU through their reproductive years is important, because a female treated for PKU needs to resume the diet therapy before becoming pregnant, or the fetus can suffer serious brain damage (Koch et al., 1993). Some states have PKU and other registries, but some do not. The outcomes of treatment need to be monitored to assure a high degree of certainty that newborn screening is effective and to develop new treatment strategies. These outcome studies also broaden knowledge of these genetic disorders.

ETHICAL ISSUES. Ethical problems in newborn screening have to do with access, informed consent of parents, confidentiality and privacy, and the interests of third parties. Unfairness of access results from policy and resource allocation decisions. Where a child happens to be born may determine whether an infant is screened for a given disorder. Attaining an adequate and ethically valid informed consent is a complex process under any circumstances, but especially in the context of labor and childbirth, with their attendant anxieties and pressures. The state of Maryland tried to adopt a voluntary ("opt-in") approach to newborn screening, with a required informed-consent process for parents (Holtzman et al., 1983). Other states take either a strictly mandatory approach or legally permit an informed refusal ("opt-out") to newborn screening; if parents are advised of this option during the perinatal period, they may choose not to participate.

The privacy and confidentiality of the parents and the child need to be respected, a difficult task in the context of computerized record keeping and electronic access to information. Third parties with legitimate interests include both family members and insurers expected to cover treatment costs resulting from a disorder discovered through a screening program. Other family members who may be unaware of their genetic risks have a need to know that cannot be given priority unless the parents choose to cooperate and release the information. Agencies responsible for tracking affected children must zealously guard the privacy of these children.

CARRIER SCREENING

Carriers are people in whom one copy of a gene varies from the normal. Since carriers also have one normal copy of the same gene, they do not ordinarily exhibit symptoms of a genetic disorder. Sometimes the variant (mutant) gene is beneficial for the carrier. Having one gene that causes some, but not all, red blood cells to take a sickle shape protects the carrier from malaria. Having two such genes, however, leads to a severe, painful blood disorder called sickle-cell anemia.

There are two types of carriers. First, carriers of genes for autosomal recessive (AR) disorders have one normal and one variant gene at the same place on one of the forty-four autosomes (chromosomes common to both sexes). The normal gene takes precedence over the variant gene, so the carrier has no symptoms. The carrier can transmit only one copy of the variant gene to children. The children cannot have the disorder unless they receive a second copy of the variant gene from the other parent. If two carriers mate, each of their children has a one-in-four chance of having the disorder. Examples of AR conditions are cystic fibrosis (CF), which affects lungs and digestion, greatly shortens life expectancy, and is found primarily among whites of European descent; sickle-cell anemia, a blood disorder with severe, painful crises, found primarily among people of African descent, though it also occurs in Mediterraneans and Asians; beta-thalassemia, a blood disorder causing anemia and early death, found among people of Mediterranean, African, and Asian descent; and Tay-Sachs disease, a disorder leading to profound mental retardation and death before age five, found primarily among people of eastern European (Ashkenazic) Jewish descent. In the United States, an estimated one in twenty-five whites carries a gene for CF, one in ten or eleven African-Americans carries sickle-cell trait, and one in thirty-one Ashkenazic Jews carries a gene for Tay-Sachs disease. Beta-thalassemia is a major world health problem. In Cyprus, one person in eight is a carrier, and in Sardinia, one couple in eighty is a carrier-carrier couple with a one-in-four risk, with each pregnancy, of having an affected child.

Second, carriers of X-linked recessive disorders are women with a variant gene on one of their two X (sex-determining) chromosomes. The woman, although not ordinarily affected herself, has a 50 percent chance of transmitting the variant gene to each child. Daughters receive a normal gene on the X chromosome from their father and are not usually affected. Since males have only one X chromosome, sons who inherit one copy of the variant gene will have the disorder. Examples of X-linked disorders are Duchenne muscular dystrophy, which usually confines a boy to a wheelchair by the age of ten and leads to death by the mid-teens, and fragile X syndrome, a leading cause of mental retardation.

The stated purpose of carrier testing and carrier screening is to inform potential parents of their genetic status so that they can make informed reproductive decisions. A couple who are both carriers of an AR disorder may decide not to marry, or to adopt, to use artificial insemination by a noncarrier donor, to have prenatal diagnosis and selectively abort affected fetuses, or simply to take their one-in-four chance of having a child with the disorder. A woman carrying an X-linked disorder might consider adopting, using an egg from a noncarrier donor, using a surrogate mother,

"Slippery-slope" arguments abound in considerations of the ethics of bending the material essence of human beings to our own wills.

PAGE 283

Even after a century of study, the notion of substantial genetic influences on intelligence remains controversial.

PAGE 277

having prenatal diagnosis and selective abortion, or taking her chances of having an affected son.

From a public-health point of view, especially in nations with national health insurance, the purpose of screening is to avoid the births of children with serious, costly, or untreatable disorders. Cost-benefit calculations are used to justify national screening programs.

Testing differs from screening. The word "testing" usually describes procedures performed at the request of individuals or families known to be at high risk, such as the siblings of persons with CF. Testing should always be voluntary (Wertz and Fletcher, 1989). Screening is a public-health concept. It applies to entire populations or to subsets of populations (e.g., pregnant women, newborns, or job applicants) without a known family history of a disorder. Screening may be voluntary or mandatory. The U.S. President's Commission (1983) recommended that all screening be voluntary, with the exception of newborns if, and only if, early treatment will benefit the newborn. Some believe that newborns should be screened, in the absence of available treatment, primarily to identify and inform parents of their carrier status before they conceive another child. Any such screening should be voluntary and should be carried out only after full information and informed consent. Mandatory or routine screening solely to identify carriers could lead to coercive eugenics.

About half the adopted-away children of schizophrenic mothers displayed some sort of psychiatric or criminal problems as adults.

PAGE 274

Ordinarily no benefit is gained from testing or screening children for carrier status before they reach reproductive age. Testing at younger ages can lead to stigmatization and a poor self-image, or test results may be forgotten. Testing is best carried out in the context of reproduction, but preferably before marriage or pregnancy, so that people will have the maximum range of choices.

Testing and screening should be preceded by full information about the disorder and the various decisions, including the possibility of abortion, that an individual or couple may face if found to carry the gene. Screening in the absence of full information and support from the community can lead to misunderstanding and to accusations of genocide. The sickle-cell screening introduced in the United States in the early 1970s as the first public-health genetics program is an example of a poorly designed endeavor with little effect on reproductive decisions. In contrast, a Tay-Sachs screening program introduced with the support of Jewish community leaders led to 90 percent reduction in the births of children with Tay-Sachs, mostly through use of prenatal diagnosis (U.S. President's Commission, 1983; U.S. Congress, Office of Technology Assessment, 1992a). Orthodox Jewish communities, which opposed abortion but favored arranged marriages, developed a system for premarital carrier testing that would enable a rabbi to declare a match unsuitable if both persons were carriers while preserving individuals' anonymity. Carrier screening programs for beta-thalassemia in Cyprus and Sardinia and among Cypriots in London have reduced the births of affected children by 90 to 97 percent, largely through prenatal diagnosis (Cao et al., 1989; Angastiniotis, 1990; Modell and Petrou, 1988). Most people in these communities had seen children with thalassemia and wished to avoid it. The Greek Orthodox and Roman Catholic churches, while not approving abortion, did not condemn women who did not carry affected fetuses to term. In Cyprus, the church requires carrier testing before marriage but does not prohibit marriages between carriers.

The overall goal of genetic counseling is to reduce emotional suffering related to genetic conditions.

PAGE 266

In the next few years, CF testing of pregnant women will probably become routine. CF carrier screening in the general population, however, could be introduced only after extensive education of the target population, and only after ongoing pilot screening programs demonstrated public interest and lack of adverse effects. It is also possible that new treatments for CF will diminish public interest.

Fragile X may be the next major carrier test offered. Eventually carrier testing may become possible for predispositions to cancer and heart disease (Holtzman, 1989). These are multifactorial diseases (partly genetic, partly environmental), so risks will be less exact than with AR or X-linked disorders.

Protection of privacy is the primary ethical issue. Health insurers have misused information to deny coverage to families at risk of having children with costly disorders (U.S. Congress, Office of Technology Assessment, 1992b, 1992c). Employers have required carrier testing (notably for sickle-cell trait) as a precondition of hiring, even though there is usually no proven link between carrier status and susceptibility to occupational hazards (U.S. Congress, Office of Technology Assessment, 1990). Carrier testing has been applied disproportionately to ethnic groups new to an industry (Draper, 1991). Sometimes carriers become objects of discrimination. In the 1970s the U.S. Air Force Academy rejected candidates with sickle-cell trait. The Italian army rejects carriers of beta-thalassemia. To avoid discrimination, access to information by insurers, government agencies, and employers should be forbidden by law.

Carriers have ethical obligations of disclosure to family members. They should tell close blood relatives that the relatives may also be carriers. If a couple intends to have children, the carrier should tell the spouse or partner. If a carrier refuses to tell a partner and they intend to have children, the professional should be legally permitted to inform the partner.

— ANTONIO CAO

LEGAL ISSUES

"Genetic screening" refers to programs designed to canvass populations of healthy individuals to identify those with genotypes that place them or their offspring at high risk for disease or defect. "Genetic testing" refers to diagnostic procedures offered to individuals or families who are at increased risk for developing specific disorders or for bearing affected children. This article provides an overview of U.S. law governing newborn screening, prenatal screening, carrier screening, and occupational screening programs; it then discusses access to genetic testing, malpractice, informed consent, confidentiality and disclosure issues, and special testing situations. It also discusses laws governing DNA forensic testing and the regulation of DNA forensic data banks.

NEWBORN SCREENING. The vast majority of states require the screening of infants for treatable inborn errors of metabolism, particularly phenylketonuria (PKU) (Andrews, 1985). Although most states make such screening compulsory, many permit parental refusal on religious or other grounds. Some statutes explicitly make newborn screening voluntary, but it often is done without obtaining informed consent.

Mandatory newborn screening programs have not been constitutionally challenged, but they would probably be upheld based on the state's police power—the same power that justifies vaccination and disease reporting requirements. The courts might recognize a limited right to refuse newborn screening under the First Amendment, which protects freedom of religious belief, and in accord with the right of parents to make decisions about rearing children without unnecessary state interference. The likelihood that a child who is not screened will actually be affected with an inborn error of metabolism (assuming there is no family history for the disorder) is extremely low (1:10,000), and the risk associated with a refusal of screening is significantly less than the risks inherent in many other decisions about children that parents normally make.

PRENATAL SCREENING. Prenatal screening is intended to detect genetic (or genetically influenced) disorders in fetuses. Obstetricians routinely inform certain groups of women about specific genetic tests, such as fetal karyotyping for women who will be 35 or older when they deliver and who therefore have an increased likelihood to be carrying a fetus with Down syndrome. Except for laws that require Rh testing, however, no state at present mandates any type of prenatal screening (Powledge and Fletcher, 1979). Were a state to enact such a law—for example, mandatory screening for maternal serum alpha-fetoprotein (now routinely used to identify women at increased risk of having a child with a neural tube defect)—a court would probably strike it down as an impermissible invasion of a pregnant woman's physical integrity and a violation of her constitutional right of privacy.

California and the District of Columbia have mandated that health-care workers inform pregnant women of the availability of prenatal screening for neural tube defects; the women are free either to undergo or to refuse the procedure (Cal. Health and Safety Code, 1991; District of Columbia Laws, 1985).

CARRIER SCREENING. Carrier screening generally involves testing healthy people to determine whether they are carriers of genes for recessive disorders, in order to provide them with information about potential childbearing risks. Since the early 1970s the Ashkenazi Jewish population has operated a number of highly successful, community-based, voluntary screening programs to identify carriers of the gene for Tay-Sachs disease. Also during the 1970s, a number of states enacted sickle-cell testing statutes to identify carriers of the sickle-cell trait. Many of these were based on erroneous clinical assumptions, targeted inappropriate groups (for example, children entering public schools), and made no provision for counseling or confidentiality (Reilly, 1977). These laws led to public outcry, resulting in the enactment of corrective federal legislation (National Sickle-Cell Anemia Control Act of 1972). Today, several states explicitly forbid using sickle-cell test information to make decisions about employment and related matters.

Much attention has centered on whether to develop population-based screening for the cystic fibrosis gene. Given the high frequency of the gene and increasingly accurate test methods, genetic counselors and physicians may soon begin to inform persons of reproductive age about this test. This could alter the prevailing standard of care—what "reasonable practitioners" should do—in effect requiring physicians and genetic counselors to inform patients about the test.

OCCUPATIONAL SCREENING. Genetic screening can also occur in employment settings. If low-cost predictive tests become available to identify persons genetically predisposed to common chronic diseases such as cancer, diabetes, and coronary artery disease, some employers concerned about spiraling health costs may try to screen out high-risk workers. Industrial employers may also seek to detect those with heightened susceptibilities to the adverse effects of exposure to certain chemicals (*International Union, UAW* v. *Johnson Controls, Inc.*, 1991). Although very few companies currently operate screening programs, recent surveys suggest that a number of large companies would be interested in the eventual implementation of genetic screening programs (U.S. Congress, Office of Technology Assessment, 1991).

There are legal restrictions on the extent to which

There is a critical need for research to evaluate genetic counseling's effectiveness in addressing clients' needs.

PAGE 266

Because genetic counseling is client-centered and inherently flexible, critics have charged that no standard of practice exists.

PAGE 265

Proponents argue that germ-line gene therapy offers the only true cure for many diseases.

PAGE 262

GENETIC TESTING
Legal Issues to Access

ACCESS TO GENETIC TESTING. In the United States, while the federal government plays a role in determining access to genetic services by funding some genetics programs, the states bear primary responsibility for providing genetic services. Some states directly provide or subsidize genetic services and have comprehensive statutes or regulations with commissions or advisory boards to oversee service delivery and the use of genetic data. Other states take a piecemeal approach, with laws that refer to only a limited set of genetic conditions or that merely require giving applicants for marriage licenses educational materials about particular disorders. Most states have no statutes relating to genetic services (apart from their newborn screening laws), apparently providing such services, if at all, only in reliance on a general constitutional mandate to provide for the health of their population. No state's failure to provide access to adequate genetic services has yet been legally challenged.

Canada and the European nations have significantly greater control over access to services through national health policies and programs. For example, the Norwegian Parliament has placed legal restrictions on access to prenatal diagnosis, strictly limiting the procedure to women over age thirty-eight or those with other specific medical indications (Fletcher and Wertz, 1989). Similarly, in Japan the Eugenic Protection Act has the effect of limiting rather than encouraging the use of genetic testing.

— JEAN E. MCEWEN
PHILIP R. REILLY

employers may ask prospective and current employees to submit to genetic tests. Both the Rehabilitation Act of 1973, applicable to federal agencies, and the Americans with Disabilities Act of 1990 (ADA), applicable to private employers, specifically prohibit preemployment inquiries about health or disability status. While an employer may make an offer of employment contingent on genetic testing, the testing must be required of all applicants, and cannot be performed until after the offer has been made. In addition, employers who use genetic testing to exclude current workers from their jobs must offer them alternative employment.

MALPRACTICE AND THE DUTY TO WARN. Advances in genetic testing and counseling alter the standard of care expected of health-care professionals. Malpractice lawsuits have been brought, particularly against obstetricians, alleging breaches of the duty to warn (that is, failure to alert individuals or couples of their increased risk of a fetus with a genetic disease) (Elias and Annas, 1987). These negligence suits fall into two major categories: wrongful birth claims brought by parents of children born with genetic diseases who were not alerted to the risk, and wrongful life claims brought on behalf of children with genetic diseases (Wright, 1978).

Most jurisdictions recognize at least a limited cause of action for wrongful birth, with the major conceptual struggle involving the calculation of damages once negligence is established. However, most courts have rejected wrongful life claims, refusing to weigh the value of nonlife (the consequence of abortion) against the value of a "defective existence." A few states have enacted statutes that prohibit parents from filing wrongful life suits on behalf of their children or that forbid children from suing their parents for wrongful life. Advances in genetic testing will probably lead to novel negligence suits—for instance, claims for "wrongful abortion" based on an erroneous diagnosis of genetic disease in a fetus that, after termination, proves not to have been affected.

THE REQUIREMENT OF INFORMED CONSENT. The consent of the patient is a prerequisite to genetic testing. This requires explaining to the patient, prior to the test, the nature and scope of the information to be gathered, the significance of positive test results, the nature of the disease in question, and, if relevant, the risks involved in procreation and the availability of reproductive alternatives (Andrews, 1987). To this list may soon be added the duty to warn about the possible interests of insurers and employers in test results. This process allows patients to weigh the benefits of testing against the possible risks, reduces misunderstandings, and minimizes potential legal liability.

In some situations (where a routine blood sample is taken from a pregnant woman for a battery of tests), consent to a particular genetic test may arguably be implied. For both ethical and legal reasons, however, eliciting a subject's full informed consent is ordinarily the proper course.

The advent of presymptomatic testing of persons at risk for Huntington disease and other disorders that depend on the participation of several family members for diagnosis (linkage testing) raises the question of whether one individual may compel another to submit to genetic testing. Although there exists no case law directly on this point, it is unlikely that a court would compel a relative to undergo such testing. To do so would be inconsistent with the concept of protecting bodily integrity and would violate the principle of informed consent.

Obtaining informed consent to genetic testing of children or adults who lack legal competency generally requires that a parent or guardian decide by proxy. However, legitimate conflicts between parent and child may arise. In general, as the child matures, his or her views should be given more weight. Many states have statutes that authorize the provision of some types of medical care to adolescents without parental consent. Some may protect health-care professionals from liability for testing or counseling an adolescent where the parents oppose such action.

Stringent informed consent procedures are required for genetic testing in research settings. The U.S. Department of Health and Human Services has promulgated regulations applicable to all federally funded research with human subjects. These regulations provide explicit guidelines for ensuring that participation in the research is voluntary and that the research risks are minimized.

CONFIDENTIALITY OF GENETIC INFORMATION. There is a strong presumption in clinical practice that medical information should remain confidential. Nonetheless, state laws addressing this subject are riddled with exceptions authorizing disclosure in a variety of circumstances. Moreover, except for a handful of statutes relating to birth defects registries, sickle-cell anemia, and a few other diseases, these laws were not drafted to consider the familial nature of genetic information. Although some statues make wrongful disclosure of DNA-based data held by state agencies a criminal offense, individuals must rely primarily on traditional common law tort and contract principles to obtain redress for confidentiality breaches.

Disclosure to relatives. Physicians and genetic counselors frequently acquire genetic information from one patient that may be extremely important to other family members. This raises the question of whether there is a right—or even an obligation—to disseminate such information to a patient's relatives despite the general presumption of medical confidentiality. Disclosing the results of a genetic test stored in a person's medical record is different from compelling him or her to be tested, because it involves no invasion of bodily integrity. Disclosure of genetic data within families also does not typically expose patients to the type or degree of harm from which the common law of privacy traditionally has sought to protect people. In addition, the potential benefit of the information to a relative can sometimes be substantial.

Case law provides no specific guidance on the circumstances under which genetic data may be disclosed to a relative over a patient's objection. The 1983 U.S. President's Commission for the Study of Ethical Problems in Medicine and Biomedical and Behavioral Research took the position that confidentiality may be overridden where (1) reasonable efforts to elicit consent to disclosure by the test subject have failed; (2) there is a high probability both that harm will occur if the information is not disclosed and that the disclosure can be used to avert that harm; and (3) the disclosure is made in as limited a manner as is reasonably possible (U.S. President's Commission, 1983). This approach is consistent with judicial reluctance to impose liability against physicians who warn individuals that their spouses or potential spouses have serious infectious diseases.

The question of whether a health-care professional in some circumstances must disclose genetic data to a patient's relatives has never been decided in court. The recognition of a possible obligation to breach confidentiality to protect third parties derives in part from a 1976 California case holding that a psychotherapist had a duty to warn a woman that the therapist's patient had threatened her life when the therapist should have had reason to believe that the threat would be carried out (*Tarasoff* v. *Regents of the University of California*, 1976). Some argue that this case suggests there is a duty to warn a patient's blood relatives about important facts that may affect their health or reproductive plans. Others contend that the risk of someday parenting a child with a genetic disease is not analogous to an immediate threat of violence.

Disclosure to spouses. Physicians and genetic counselors may discover nonpaternity in the course of genetic testing. The majority view has long been that disclosing the fact of nonpaternity to a husband is likely to cause more harm to the family than good (Andrews, 1987). Of course, selective nondisclosure stands in conflict with the expectation of both wife and husband that they will be told the truth. The current approach requires redefining the "client" (in whose best interests the health-care professional must act) as the couple rather than as two separate individuals. This may be sound ethical reasoning, but it lacks solid legal foundation.

Disclosure outside families. Unlike disclosure within families, where the damage caused by the disclosure, compared with the benefit, is likely to be relatively small, disclosure of genetic data to other third parties can seriously harm individuals. Life, health, and disability insurers, employers, educational institutions, law enforcement agencies, the military, and other institutional entities routinely acquire genetic data through their review of medical records and communications with physicians. The risk thus arises that individuals will be mislabeled, stigmatized, or discriminated against on the basis of real or perceived differences in their genetic constitution (Gostin, 1991). When genetic information begins to be stored in large data banks, the risk of additional abuses will be magnified.

A proposed federal bill, the "Human Genome Priva-

Critics reply that by opening the door to genetic enhancement, germ-line gene therapy has ominous social implications.

PAGE 262

See Also

Protective Privilege and Public Peril: The *Tarasoff* Case

No other biomedical intervention in history has received as much international and interdisciplinary attention as human gene therapy.

PAGE 263

A 1979 conference sponsored by the World Council of Churches focused on "ethical issues in the biological manipulation of life."

PAGE 258

cy Act" (1991), sought to address this problem by limiting third-party disclosure of genetic information without the consent of the individual to whom the data relates. That bill was not enacted. Bills considered in several states would specifically prohibit the disclosure of genetic information to insurers and employers. Currently, however, few explicit legal safeguards exist to ensure that genetic data, once gathered, will not fall into the hands of third parties who will use it for nonmedical reasons.

Although no European nation has yet enacted a law that directly addresses the problem of genetic discrimination, in its 1991 report a committee convened by the Council of Europe recommended studying this issue (Council of Europe, 1991). In 1990 the Danish Parliament adopted a resolution that advocated a ban on the use of genetic data in employment decisions.

In the United States the Rehabilitation Act of 1973 and the Americans with Disabilities Act of 1990 (ADA) prohibit employment discrimination against otherwise "qualified" handicapped persons, and it is arguable that these statutes (along with similar state laws) can be interpreted to prohibit most types of genetic discrimination in employment. However, the extent to which the ADA will prove a means of redressing genetic discrimination must await judicial interpretation.

In this regard the U.S. Supreme Court decision that restricting the working of women of childbearing age in dangerous environments because of the risk of injury to their fetuses constitutes unlawful sex discrimination under Title VII of the Civil Rights Act of 1964 is important (*International Union, UAW* v. *Johnson Controls, Inc.*, 1991). Title VII, which also prohibits employment discrimination based on race, religion, and pregnancy, may be invoked in genetic discrimination lawsuits by women and members of minority racial groups where certain genetic conditions are unusually prevalent.

SPECIAL TESTING SITUATIONS. A few laws concerning adoption recognize the importance of acquiring a full family history from the child's biological parents and of sharing that information with the adoptive parents at the time of placement. A situation may arise where genetic information derived from a biological parent could be important to the health of an adopted child, or vice versa, years after the adoption (American Society of Human Genetics, 1991). A legal justification may exist for breaching secrecy so that the appropriate agency may contact the adoptive family, or biological parent, and communicate the data. Alternative reproductive methods, such as artificial insemination or surrogate motherhood, can give rise to similar testing and disclosure problems.

DNA FORENSICS. In recent years the discovery that certain short repetitive sequences of DNA vary greatly in length among individuals (except for identical twins) has become the basis for DNA-based identification technologies. This has had an extraordinary impact on criminal law. It is now possible to create a DNA profile of biological specimens from a crime scene and compare it with a similar profile prepared from the blood of a suspect or from biological specimens found in the suspect's possession. If these two samples do not match, the finding tends to exonerate the individual; if they match, the finding may be powerful evidence of the suspect's presence at the crime scene (U.S. Congress, Office of Technology Assessment, 1990; National Research Council, 1992). DNA identification evidence is widely used in both European and U.S. courts. The decision by the Pentagon to collect blood from military recruits to create a repository upon which DNA analysis could be used to resolve most personnel identification issues arising out of combat indicates the value of this technology.

DNA identification technology—also known as "DNA fingerprinting"—has stimulated a wave of genetic testing laws. In the United States a number of states have enacted laws that require blood samples to be taken from convicted felons at parole. The DNA

GENETIC TESTING
Insurance Ramifications

Fewer safeguards exist to prevent life, health, or disability insurers from refusing to write policies or rating applicants on the basis of genetic test results. A health maintenance organization, under general contract law principles, may presumably require submission to genetic testing as a condition of entry into a plan or exempt particular genetic diseases from coverage. A number of states have considered legislation to curtail genetically discriminatory underwriting practices, but few such laws have been passed.

Because much health insurance at present is tied to employment, complex relationships exist among the many laws regulating employers and insurers. For example, the ADA exempts insurance companies from its reach, leaving them free to discriminate against applicants based on perceptions of genetic risk. An employer may not, however, use the existence of genetically discriminatory insurance practices as a pretext for refusing to hire, for firing, or for taking other adverse action against an applicant or employee.

—JEAN E. MCEWEN
PHILIP R. REILLY

profiles prepared from this blood will be stored and used as a data bank against which DNA samples from future crime scenes can be compared. Felon DNA data banks are premised on the high rate of recidivism, especially for rape. Federal legislation is pending that would provide federal funds to support DNA-based forensic laboratories that meet certain quality control standards and establish privacy standards for forensic DNA data banks (DNA Identification Act of 1991).

THE IMPACT OF ABORTION LAW. Resolution of the many legal issues generated by the increasing use of genetic screening and testing will be determined by an evolving societal discourse. The enactment by some states of laws that sharply limit access to abortion and the possibility that the U.S. Supreme Court will continue to interpret conservatively the constitutional right of privacy regarding abortion are important aspects of this dialogue. Laws have been enacted in a few states that deprive women of the abortion option even where tests indicate that the fetus is likely to have a serious genetic disorder. The U.S. Supreme Court has upheld federal regulations that prevent physicians in federally funded facilities from discussing abortion with their patients, thus affecting their ability to provide genetic counseling that includes consideration of prenatal diagnosis (*Rust* v. *Sullivan,* 1991). Although the Supreme Court has reaffirmed the decision in *Roe* v. *Wade* (1973) recognizing a woman's right to choose an abortion before fetal viability, it has upheld a variety of other restrictions on the procedure's availability (*Planned Parenthood of Southeastern Pennsylvania* v. *Casey*, 1992).

Conclusion

Genetic testing and screening raise numerous legal issues, and are likely to be the focus of much legal activity—in both the courts and the legislatures—well into the future. Apart from the abortion debate, the primary areas of activity involving genetics are likely to be legislative efforts to regulate the conditions under which genetic data—and DNA itself—may be acquired, stored, studied, and used. A related area will probably focus on the passage of laws designed to prevent genetic discrimination. Here, the current debate over national health insurance is likely to assume increasing importance. National health insurance will mitigate, although not completely resolve, some of the difficult legal issues that genetic screening and testing raise.

— JEAN E. MCEWEN
PHILIP R. REILLY

ETHICAL ISSUES

The ethical issues raised by genetic testing and screening fall into three major categories: issues concerning education and counseling; problems involving confidentiality; and issues of justice. This entry discusses four main applications of genetic testing and screening: prenatal screening, including preimplantation embryo diagnosis; diagnosis of genetic disorders in newborns; identifying individuals who are at risk of having children with symptomatic genetic disorders; and the use of genetic information by employers and insurers.

Special moral features

There is a tendency to regard the ethical issues raised by genetic testing and screening as new and fundamentally different from those raised by other kinds of health care. Although the ethical concerns raised by genetic testing and screening are not entirely novel, there are a number of factors inherent in genetics that should heighten our sensitivity to the human values involved. Seven factors deserve mention.

PROPHECY PRECEDES CURE. In the foreseeable future, genetics is likely to give us the ability to predict diseases long before it will help us to prevent, treat, or cure them. Huntington disease and sickle-cell disease are two of many examples.

AMBIGUITIES IN THE CONCEPT OF GENETIC DISEASE. Presymptomatic testing, which can uncover incipient genetic disease before any symptoms appear, and carrier testing, which can aid in the search for genes in potential parents who might have offspring with a specific disease, challenge our everyday notions of disease. The prospect of prenatal testing for late-onset diseases such as Alzheimer's disease or Huntington disease poses an interesting conceptual question: Should we regard as ill a fetus or person who is likely to develop symptomatic disease in forty to seventy years? Individuals who carry a gene for a recessive disease generally are not themselves affected but may have affected children: Do such carriers have a genetic disorder? Also, people may wish that their offspring not have certain genetically determined traits, including eyes or hair of a certain color, or an undesired sex. What limits, if any, should be placed on parents' power to determine their offspring's characteristics?

CONCEPTS OF GENETICS AND OF RISK ARE POORLY UNDERSTOOD. The public and, to a distressing extent, health professionals have a poor grasp of the basics of genetics, of probability, and of risk. Because so many of the putative benefits from genetic information hinge on understanding basic genetics and risk probabilities, it is imperative to ensure that the public and the experts to whom they will turn have the knowledge they need.

EMPHASIZING RACIAL AND ETHNIC DIFFERENCES. An emphasis on genetic differences is at the same time an emphasis on the differences among racial and ethnic groups. History is replete with examples of

In 1980 a letter to President Carter from Catholic, Jewish, and Protestant leaders warned of "a new era of fundamental danger" resulting from genetic engineering.

PAGE 258

Advances in amniocentesis have made it possible to include gender among the potential criteria of a "defective" baby.

PAGE 284

G

GENETIC TESTING AND SCREENING

Ethical Issues

presumed racial or ethnic differences that were used as excuses to treat people badly. Especially when attention turns to the genetics of socially significant behaviors and traits, such as propensity toward violence or intellectual capacity, there will be temptations to claim that there are differences among groups, and that those differences are genetic in nature. When such differences are used as reasons for treating people differently or as explanations for enduring inequalities, the potential for injustice is great.

GENETICS AND PERSONAL IDENTITY. Our genetics affect our identity by influencing our physical attributes and traits, and our propensities toward disease. Genetics also ties us to our ancestors and our descendants, who shape the persons we are. Genetic inheritance is intimately connected with our personal identity.

GENETIC INFORMATION IS ALSO INFORMATION ABOUT OTHERS. The information that one is a carrier of or afflicted with a genetic disease is also information relevant to one's biological relations, who may also be carriers or at risk of the same disease. A sister could receive the unwanted knowledge that she and her children are at risk of a serious genetic disease because a genetic test revealed her brother to be at risk of the same disease. Confidentiality can be difficult to maintain within a family, especially with certain forms of genetic testing that require obtaining tissue samples from biological relatives of the person being tested.

A DISPROPORTIONATE BURDEN ON WOMEN. In carrier screening programs especially, though potentially also in presymptomatic screening, women typically bear a disproportionate burden. They often are tested first, with men tested later if at all; when decisions are made whether to continue a pregnancy, women must bear the direct consequences, whatever choice is made.

One of the most important distinctions between genetic testing technology and other areas of medical diagnosis is the gap between the ability to identify the molecular basis for a genetic condition and the ability to do something about it. This gap is due to our current lack of understanding of how genes function in their complex interactions with other genes and the intracellular and extracellular environments. This discrepancy between diagnostic abilities and treatment abilities raises a number of ethical issues in different applications of screening and testing.

Our technology allows us to detect sequences of DNA that are associated with medical conditions. But locating an abnormal gene is only the first step in understanding the condition. The function of the gene must then be determined. Next, the connection between the alteration of the normal gene and the dysfunction at the cellular and tissue level must be worked out. Finally, the connection between cell and tissue dysfunction and the problems experienced by the affected person must be appreciated. The full under-

See Also
Informed Consent

ETHICAL ISSUES

Education and counseling

Enabling informed choice is a principal goal of many clinical applications of genetic technology. Particularly in prenatal screening, carrier screening, and presymptomatic testing and screening, individuals may be interested in their genetic status in order to make decisions about reproduction, lifestyle changes, or other personal plans. The results of genetic tests often have profound implications for people's lives; therefore, a reasonable understanding of the results is essential. In addition, technical limitations of the tests require that patients and physicians be appropriately educated about the possibilities of false positive or false negative results. Appropriate education and counseling of both health professionals and the public are an important part of any screening and testing service.

The sickle-cell and the Tay-Sachs screening programs illustrate the influence of education and counseling on the efficacy and acceptance of a program (U.S. President's Commission, 1983). The confusion between sickle-cell disease and sickle-cell trait led to unnecessary screening, inappropriate fears, and discrimination. The Tay-Sachs program was more carefully instituted with efforts to foster broad community understanding and support in its early stages.

Unfortunately, the general level of education in human genetics is relatively poor for both the medical profession and the lay public. This raises significant concerns, since there are too few trained genetic counselors to fully support the use of new genetic technology (Holtzman, 1988). Expanding the use of testing or screening beyond experimental protocols may significantly increase the risk of misuse and harm. For example, the early protocols for presymptomatic testing for Huntington disease entailed five to six sessions for counseling prior to providing diagnostic information, and subsequent follow-up for one to two years. Now that testing for Huntington is commercially available, there is no assurance that patients are being appropriately counseled and supported. The potential influence of genetic information on crucial decisions in patients' lives requires that screening and testing be performed in an environment that ensures informed decisions, emotional support, and available guidance.

—THOMAS H. MURRAY
JEFFREY R. BOTKIN

standing of a disease may be greatly enhanced by DNA technology, but genes are only part of the full story. While it is not necessary to fully understand a disease before effective treatments can be developed, much more must be learned than what genetic technology alone can tell us.

Perhaps the best illustration of this gap is sickle-cell anemia. This genetic condition is well understood (although not fully understood) at the genetic, cellular, and tissue levels, but there is little that medicine has been able to offer affected individuals beyond supportive care. Therefore, genetic technology will give medicine some powerful tools to diagnose conditions at a molecular level, and some critical information that will unravel the mysteries of many diseases, but we should recognize that years of hard work will be necessary before patients can be offered effective treatments based on this knowledge.

From an ethical perspective, this means that the benefits of genetic testing and screening for many conditions will be indirect—focusing on preventive measures in many cases. This contrasts with medical testing for such conditions as strep throat, coronary artery disease, and breast cancer, where the results of the test may result in immediate interventions to ameliorate or cure the condition. For genetic testing and screening of untreatable conditions, a more subtle ethical balancing of the benefits and risks must be undertaken. This is particularly true because many preventive measures require lifestyle changes. Human behavior is remarkably difficult to alter. This problem is illustrated in the efforts to find a gene associated with alcoholism. It has been suggested that if such a gene were to be found, we could test adolescents for the gene and counsel those who were positive to avoid alcohol. While reasonable on the surface, we must recognize that changing the behavior of teenagers (or anyone else) through warnings about health risks has not been very successful. If preventive measures rely heavily on long-term behavior changes, we must look carefully at whether predictive testing and screening offer real benefits.

There is enormous pressure to bring discoveries in molecular genetics into the clinical realm. This pressure, combined with our limited knowledge of human biology, will encourage an initial focus on disease prevention rather than on treatment. The pursuit of prevention in the absence of treatment for many genetic conditions raises a number of important ethical issues in genetic testing and screening.

Confidentiality

The personal nature of genetic information makes confidentiality a particularly important consideration in genetic testing and screening. Results of tests that reveal probabilities about future health may hold significant interest for an individual's family, employer, and health and life insurance companies, all of whom may claim a "right to know." The injustice of discrimination from the disclosure of genetic status may result from misunderstanding information. Again, the sickle-cell screening program is a prime example: Asymptomatic carriers of the gene were often labeled as ill or potentially ill, and deprived of insurance and job opportunities. In the future, disclosure of genetic information to certain institutions, such as employers or insurance companies, may be more carefully regulated by legislation to prevent discrimination.

Disclosure of health information in private relationships is less amenable to regulation. Reproduction raises some of the thorniest issues of confidentiality. Does a spouse have a right to know a mate's genetic status in order to make an independent, informed decision about reproduction? This issue has been discussed in the context of Huntington disease (Shaw, 1980), although the problem may become more common as screening and testing capabilities expand. A problem of confidentiality also arises in prenatal diagnosis and newborn testing when nonpaternity is discovered. Disclosure of this information to the husband may be devastating to the family, yet this information may be important for the husband's future reproductive choices. Some genetic counselors maintain confidentiality in this circumstance by deception, through the suggestion that the child's condition is due to a new mutation and that the husband will not be at risk of fathering a similarly affected child in the future. These dilemmas are an inherent part of pursuing genetic information.

Issues of justice

Justice becomes an issue for genetic testing and screening in two ways: access to genetic services and the allocation of health-care resources. Most, though not all, accounts of justice in health care make the *need* for such care a crucial factor in deciding what constitutes a just distribution of health care.

To the extent that genetic testing and screening become valued for their contribution to human well-being and the satisfaction of human need, access to them and to other health services to which they provide entry will become a matter of justice. To the extent that such tests and services are linked to human well-being but are made available on some basis other than need—for example, to those who can afford them—injustice will arise. Genetic services are likely to be treated like other health-care services. A health-care system that does not provide equitable access to most services is unlikely to do so for genetic services. The problem, then, is with injustice in the health-care system itself, not with genetics alone.

◆ **genetic testing** *Diagnostic procedures offered to individuals or families who are at increased risk for developing special disorders or for bearing affected children.*

See Also
Justice
Confidentiality

G

GENETIC TESTING AND SCREENING

Ethical Issues

No society has unlimited resources to spend on genetic testing, screening, and other services. Just as genetics must compete for resources with other forms of health care, so health care must compete with other sectors of each nation's economy, including such social goods as education, housing, and food. Large-scale genetic screening programs, such as screening for carriers of cystic fibrosis (CF), could be very expensive. One study estimates a cost of U.S. $2.2 million for every CF birth avoided (Wilfond and Fost, 1990). Genetic screening and testing have no claim to primacy for health-care resources. One concern is that the combination of enthusiasm over genetics resulting from the Human Genome Project and the rapid development of tests by commercial laboratories will result in much broader testing than is medically advisable, ethically sound, or fiscally prudent.

Preimplantation embryo diagnosis and prenatal screening

There are a number of ethical issues in prenatal diagnosis that can be distinguished from the ethics of abortion more generally considered. Merely asking "To whom should prenatal diagnosis be offered?" raises a complex set of considerations. Traditionally, prenatal diagnosis has been offered to those in specific "high risk" groups, such as older mothers and those with a family history of congenital or genetic impairments. But "high risk" is itself a value-laden concept. For example, a pregnant woman thirty-five years of age has one chance in 300 of bearing a child with Down syndrome, while a thirty-year-old woman has a risk of one in 900. It is not clear why the thirty-five-year-old woman should be considered "high risk" based on these numbers alone. Conversely, it is not clear why a thirty-year-old woman's interest in amniocentesis should be discouraged with the argument that "maternal anxiety" is an inappropriate indication.

◆ **genetic screening**
Programs designed to canvass populations of healthy individuals to identify those with genotypes that place them or their offspring at high risk for disease or defect.

Defining when prenatal diagnosis is considered "indicated" has two components. The first is deciding what risk levels for serious conditions justify discussing prenatal screening. An emerging example is the question of whether to offer carrier screening for CF to African-Americans, whose risk is significantly less than for Caucasians but not zero. Do considerations of justice require us to provide full information about disease states and risk levels to all, or is it justified to restrict disclosure to those in whom screening would be cost-effective? How should cost-effectiveness be determined?

The second issue is to define conditions that are sufficiently severe to warrant prenatal diagnosis. Prenatal diagnosis for sex selection is an extreme example, but there are a host of genetic conditions that have less-than-severe health implications and/or a later age of onset. In an international survey of genetic counselors, Dorothy Wertz and John Fletcher (1989) found substantial variation between nations on the discussion with prospective parents of "low-burden" disorders, such as Turner syndrome and XYY. Professionals will need to develop more explicit standards for when to inform patients about genetic risks, and when to provide prenatal diagnostic services. Our answer as a society may depend on how much control we believe parents should have over the genetic composition of their children.

The guiding principle in genetic counseling, at least in the United States, has been autonomous choice—a value promoted by nondirective counseling. However, a number of important questions have been raised about the degree of autonomy that exists in prenatal screening and diagnostic services. The very availability of these services, in conjunction with society's ambivalent attitude toward those with disabilities, may carry an implicit message to couples about appropriate or responsible behavior during pregnancy (Lippman, 1991). Within the context of the patient-counselor relationship, nondirective counseling may be undermined by unintended verbal cues that promote the counselor's values on the use of prenatal diagnostic services (Rothman, 1986; Duster, 1990).

Finally, some call for explicit "guidance" on decisions about selective abortion. Margery Shaw draws the analogy of child abuse in claiming that knowingly giving birth to a seriously impaired child could be considered negligent fetal abuse by the parents (Shaw, 1980). She suggests that courts and legislatures should develop standards by which parents will be held accountable for the genetic health of their children.

There is also an important emerging set of issues in prenatal diagnosis that does not relate to selective abortion. As our therapeutic measures improve, we will be able to treat a wider variety of genetic and congenital conditions in utero with fetal surgical techniques and, perhaps, gene therapy. If these approaches pose a risk or burden to the mother, a conflict will arise between responsibility to treat the fetus and respect for the autonomous refusal of the mother. Fortunately, the typical desire of parents to promote the welfare of their children despite personal sacrifice should make such conflicts rare.

Neonatal screening

Newborn screening is largely uncontroversial when used to detect conditions that pose a serious threat to the welfare of the child but can be ameliorated through early intervention. This is the case with such conditions as PKU, hypothyroidism, and sickle-cell disease. For other conditions, the benefit of early detection remains unclear. Examples here include maple syrup urine dis-

See Also
In Practice: Is "Nondirective" Counseling Possible?

ease and galactosemia, both of which may produce serious harm or death shortly after birth, before the results of screening tests are available. In such cases, the burdens of mass newborn screening need to be more carefully considered. One of the burdens of screening is false positive and false negative results that occur with all tests that are not 100 percent sensitive and specific. For many of the present techniques, false positives outnumber true positives by ten to one. Repeat testing is then required to identify those who are truly affected.

False positives may harm parents by creating anxiety that may not be dispelled entirely by subsequent testing and counseling (Holtzman, 1991). In addition, there is a small but potential risk that the physician will misinterpret the results and begin unnecessary and potentially harmful treatments. In general, documentation of the extent of these problems in newborn screening has been poor.

A second set of issues arises when newborn screening techniques allow the identification of newborn carriers of genetic conditions, as well as those affected with the disease. This is presently the case with sickle-cell disease. Should parents be informed of the infant's carrier state in order to warn them that they may be at risk of having a future child with the disease? In essence, this is using newborn screening as a surrogate method of parental carrier screening.

On the one hand, this information about the infant may be useful for the child when he or she is considering reproduction in the future, and some parents will be alerted that future children are at risk. On the other hand, the difficulty in explaining the distinction between the carrier state and the disease may confuse many parents, leaving them with the impression that their infant is not healthy. In addition, questions should be raised about screening parents (without consent) through an unconsenting infant when the parents themselves could be directly offered carrier screening.

Finally, newborn screening programs raise the issues of freedom of choice and informed consent by parents. In the United States, newborns are generally screened within state-run programs that are designed to obtain

RISKS OF CARRIER SCREENING

Can't Please Everyone

Ethical issues raised by carrier screening include the possibility of coerciveness, the risks of focusing on at-risk populations, the need to create acceptable choices, and the consequences of introducing new tests.

Though most carrier screening is voluntary, some programs have relied on formal or subtle coercion. By June 1974, seven states in the United States mandated screening for sickle-cell trait (National Research Council, 1975). The U.S. screening program for Tay-Sachs disease has been criticized for more subtle forms of coercion, such as community pressure on individuals and couples (Goodman and Goodman, 1982). In Cyprus, the Church of Cyprus requires couples who wish to marry to be tested for the beta-thalassemia gene. The policy appears to have drastically reduced the number of children born with the disease (Angastiniotis et al., 1986). If, as seems likely, screening programs that might save money, like the one in Cyprus, are developed, the possibility of some degree of coerciveness grows.

Screening programs directed at populations at risk can be more efficient than screening the general population. Such targeting, however, can create its own ethical problems. Sickle-cell carrier screening in the United States was directed at people of African heritage. Some in the African-American community saw the program as a thinly disguised effort at eugenics. Recent programs in CF carrier screening focus on women likely to bear children. Though a woman can contribute only one of the two copies of the gene necessary to cause CF, programs have chosen to target women's reproductive capacity, compelling them to bear the heavier share of the burdens of testing.

Carrier screening can result in unacceptable choices available to people found to carry a disease gene. Individuals may have the option of choosing a mate who is not also a carrier, choosing not to have children, or, if the techniques are available, using prenatal testing and possibly abortion for affected fetuses. How acceptable each of these options is will depend on the individual's own life plans and ethical convictions, and on the practices and laws of his or her particular culture. Carrier screening programs should be designed to ensure that they provide ethically acceptable choices for people in that culture.

Whether new tests to identify carriers result in more benefit or harm depends upon many factors. A common means to manage such new technologies has been to have experts set a standard of good practice, taking into account the relevant factors. Shortly after the test for CF carriers was introduced, such a standard was articulated, calling for use of the test only in specific, limited circumstances (Beaudet et al., 1990). In contrast, commercial biotechnology companies might find it in their interest to promote the widest possible use of new tests. Finding ways to minimize the harms of premature use and overuse of carrier screening tests will be a priority for the future.

—THOMAS H. MURRAY
JEFFREY R. BOTKIN

Whoever has the power to define a human excellence will have the capacity to alter human fate.

PAGE 284

2,500 years after Plato's The Republic *and 100 after Sir Francis Galton, eugenic thinking is very much with us.*

PAGE 284

blood from all newborns within a few days of delivery (Clayton, 1992). In only one state (Wyoming) is there any legislative requirement for informed consent. A few states will permit refusal of testing on religious grounds, and a few others permit refusal for any objections raised by the parents. In most circumstances, screening is done routinely, with little discussion of the pros and cons with the parents. Some commentators believe mandatory screening for PKU is justified on the basis of the substantial benefit for infants who are detected and promptly treated, particularly given the minimal risks involved in the blood test (Faden et al., 1982). Other commentators argue that the risk to an individual child is remote (PKU occurs in approximately one in fourteen thousand infants), and that voluntary screening is likely to be as effective as mandatory programs, as long as adequate informed consent is provided (Annas, 1982). The appropriate role of government in providing genetic testing and screening is clearly at issue here. All of these issues are likely to be the subject of debate as the number of genetic conditions detectable in the newborn expands.

Predictive testing in the workplace and insurance

The idea of using genetic tests to identify individuals with heightened susceptibility to workplace exposures was introduced in 1938 by the eminent geneticist J. B. S. Haldane. Haldane's goal was to reduce the incidence of workplace-induced illness and death—a familiar public-health aspiration. The greatest ethical difficulties such screening poses are its potential coerciveness, its use as an alternative to reducing hazardous exposures, and the possibility that people of disfavored ethnic or racial groups might be disproportionately denied employment (Murray, 1983).

Workplace genetic screening, if imposed on workers and prospective workers by employers, would give employers intimate and potentially very important information about individuals that the individuals themselves might not have. It could, alternatively, force unwanted information on people. If most people would choose to work elsewhere if their health was at special risk in a particular work environment, and if they had a choice, virtually all of the benefits of a coercive program could be obtained with a voluntary program.

Employers might view screening out susceptible workers as a less expensive option than purchasing safer equipment or changing manufacturing processes or work practices. The specter of racism hangs over the discussion of workplace genetic screening, principally because the only publicized case involved African-American workers tested for sickle-cell trait.

In the mid-1980s a new rationale for workplace genetic testing emerged. Although its putative public-health purpose had not materialized, in part because hazardous exposures were diminishing and epidemiologic evidence linking genes to exposures to disease was lacking, a new potential use emerged. The ever-increasing cost of health care in the United States, much of it borne by employers, prompted people to think of ways to trim costs. Hiring workers unlikely to become ill or disabled, if screening could identify them, might be an attractive means of saving money. Genetic tests that predict the likelihood of common—and expensive—diseases such as coronary artery disease, cancer, and stroke were suggested as one way of accomplishing this. If such testing were widely used, it could result in substantial numbers of people becoming essentially unemployable. In contrast to genetic testing for susceptibility to workplace disease, there is no intent to reduce the incidence of disease and early death in screening for nonworkplace diseases. There is no evidence at this time of widespread genetic screening by employers, but that may be because the tests have been too expensive to make such screening cost-effective. As the price of testing drops, the incentive to use genetic tests may grow.

Genetic tests that predict risks for common diseases have other potential applications with substantial ethical problems. Insurance may well be affected. As individuals learn more about their own genetically predicted health risks, their insurance-purchasing behavior is likely to change in a pattern known in the industry as "adverse selection"—those most likely to file a claim are most likely to buy insurance. Insurers argue that "actuarial fairness" requires that every person pay according to his or her particular risks (Clifford and Iuculano, 1987). This notion of fairness appears to work well enough in dealing with commercial insurance, such as policies for oil tankers. It is less obviously appropriate for health, disability, or life insurance (Daniels, 1990). Reassessments of the social purpose of each form of insurance and of underwriting will help clarify what role, if any, predictive genetic testing ought to play.

Conclusions

The widespread ignorance and misunderstanding about genetic disorders make it important to include adequate education and counseling as a constitutive part of genetic testing and screening programs. The sensitivity of genetic information and the fact that genetic information about an individual is also information about biological relatives mean that great care and thought need to be given to confidentiality when genetic information is generated. Finally, there must be continual vigilance to guard against unjust misuse of genetic information against individuals or groups of people.

— THOMAS H. MURRAY
JEFFREY R. BOTKIN

GENOME MAPPING AND SEQUENCING

Biomedical research was transformed in the 1980s by human genetics, which was itself transformed by molecular biology during the same period. New techniques to construct maps of the human chromosomes lay at the center of these transformations. While for decades those studying genetic disease engaged in searches for disease-associated genes, technological advances in the 1980s shifted the scale to the full complement of genes—the genome. Advancing techniques to study deoxyribonucleic acid (DNA) directly opened new frontiers for genetic exploration.

Genetics is largely a twentieth-century science. The term itself was not used until the first decade of the twentieth century. Genetics grew out of theoretical and experimental work that observed how characters, or traits, were inherited from generation to generation. The Austrian monk Gregor Mendel performed masterful experiments on inheritance in plants during the 1860s, but this work remained obscure, in part because its relevance to the central biological questions of the day—evolution and natural selection—did not become clear for many decades. The rediscovery of Mendel's principles at the turn of the twentieth century was the first of many giant strides taken by geneticists.

Gene maps

The central thrust of human genetics was finding disease-associated genes. The process typically involved several steps, each requiring a different kind of map. All genetic maps ultimately refer to the DNA constituting the chromosomes, but different maps are used for different purposes.

Genetic linkage maps establish the relative position of genetic markers, detectable DNA sequences, along the chromosomes. "Genetic linkage" refers to the inheritance of one trait along with another. A map of detectable variations using standard markers can be used to trace the inheritance of chromosome regions. By correlating the inheritance of chromosome regions to the inheritance of characters, such as specific genetic diseases, the approximate location of a gene can be determined. This narrows the chromosomal region

DNA SEQUENCING AND THE ORIGINS OF THE HUMAN GENOME PROJECT

In the mid-1980s, groups in the United States and Europe began the task of fragmenting the entire genomes of yeast and C. *elegans*, cloning the fragments, and reconstructing the order of DNA fragments into maps of their entire genomes (Coulson et al., 1986; Olson et al., 1986). Decades of work had produced mutant strains in both organisms, whose biology was under intense study. Strains of yeast had well-characterized metabolic defects, for example, whose genes were precisely known. In C. *elegans*, there were mutations in which specific cell types failed to develop. The effects from loss of the cell could be directly observed, and correlated with specific genetic defects. Genes corresponding to these mutations could be directly mapped. Mapping the entire genome was intended to make this process far more efficient. The Human Genome Project grew, in part, from a desire to have similarly powerful physical maps to study human disease and normal physiology.

DNA sequencing is a physical mapping at its ultimate resolution. DNA sequence is, in a genetic sense, the territory to be mapped. Most information in chromosomes is contained in the order of bases that make up the DNA chains. In the mid-1970s, two groups independently discovered how to determine the sequence of DNA bases (Maxam and Gilbert, 1977; Sanger, 1988). As techniques became faster and less costly, the power of DNA sequence information as an analytical tool became apparent. Three individuals independently proposed to determine the DNA sequence of the entire human genome (that is, a reference sequence to be used for study, not the entire genome of a particular individual) (DeLisi, 1988; Dulbecco, 1986; Sinsheimer, 1989). Proposals to sequence the human genome provoked a controversy.

The Human Genome Project grew from the ensuing debate. The original proposals for DNA sequencing were broadened to encompass physical and genetic linkage maps, to analyze nonhuman organisms as models of human genetics, and to emphasize the development of new technologies for DNA analysis and its interpretation (Cook-Deegan, 1991). In the first five-year plan for the project, the goals of finding and mapping chromosomal markers for linkage studies and of assembling large-scale physical maps became primary. The ultimate goal almost imperceptibly shifted from a complete sequence to a complete structural catalog of genes in humans and selected nonhuman organisms.

The products of the Human Genome Project thus included not only maps of humans and other organisms but also new technologies for direct analysis of DNA. This included technologies to derive DNA sequence information, emphasizing automation and robotics. Just as important, it also included new computer methods to analyze map and sequence information, and complex pedigrees. Data bases to store the structural data had to be enlarged and refined, and made accessible to a broader range of users.

— ROBERT MULLAN COOK-DEEGAN

G

GENOME MAPPING AND SEQUENCING

Gene Maps

whose DNA must be thoroughly scrutinized to look for the gene, and brings to bear the precise tools of direct DNA analysis. Genetic linkage is thus a bridge from the study of inherited characters that run in human families to the realm of molecular genetics.

A landmark 1980 paper described how DNA sequence differences among individuals could be used to construct a genetic map of the entire human genome (Botstein et al., 1980). A genetic linkage map could be assembled by systematically searching for minor sequence differences. DNA sequence differences occur once in every 200 to 1,000 bases when comparing any two persons, on average. The variation is minuscule in comparison with the size of the genome, but millions of these generally "silent" differences can, in theory, be detected. The vast majority have no observable effects, but they can nonetheless be used as chromosome markers. The key is to find regions of the genome likely to differ among individuals in a family.

A parent passes only one of each pair of chromosomes to each child. A sequence difference that distinguishes the two copies of chromosome 7 inherited from the mother, for example, can identify which copy of that chromosome went to which children. If the father has yet another two variations at the same marker site, then the copy of chromosome 7 coming from each parent can be unequivocally traced through the family.

If a disease is consistently inherited along with a marker for a specific chromosome region among individuals in many different families, it is quite likely that a gene in that region causes the disease in those individuals. Chromosome marker studies were used to locate the cystic fibrosis gene in an early success story of modern human genetics. Children who developed cystic fibrosis consistently inherited a different chromosome 7 from their parents than did their unaffected siblings. The specific region of chromosome 7 containing the gene was narrowed by studying many different families (Knowlton et al., 1985; Tsui et al., 1985; Wainwright et al., 1985; White et al., 1985). Genetic linkage to a region on chromosome 7 began an intense investigation of the DNA from that region in search of the gene. The next step was to clone DNA taken from children with the disease, and to compare it against DNA lacking the mutation. This process involved construction of a different kind of map, a physical map of ordered DNA clones, and extensive use of direct DNA sequence comparisons (Kerem et al., 1989; Riordan et al., 1989; Rommens et al., 1989).

◆ **genome**
Unique to each person, the entire genetic sequence.

Physical mapping is a critical element in the direct analysis of DNA from a chromosome region. The most generally useful form of a physical map is a set of ordered clones that contain DNA spanning an entire region of the chromosome. The chromosomal DNA is, in essence, fragmented into a size that can be copied in yeast or bacteria. The fragments are replicated manifold and then reassembled. A contiguous map of a chromosome region is complete when the DNA from any part of the entire region is contained in at least one such clone whose order is known relative to others on the map. Ultimately, when a gene has been located to a region between genetic markers A and B on a genetic linkage map, investigators will know that the DNA between markers A and B is contained in clones 12,312 through 12,543, for example.

During the 1970s, biologists began to map DNA directly from the entire genomes of viruses and bacteria, and learned the enormous power of working from this molecular foundation. The genetics of viruses, bacteria, fruit flies, yeasts, nematodes, and mice were particularly sophisticated. Among these, yeasts and nematodes emerged as the prototypes for the Human Genome Project—starting from the structure of chromosomal DNA and progressing toward the underlying biology.

Yeasts live as single cells whose genes are enclosed in a cell nucleus, in contrast to bacteria and viruses, which lack a cell nucleus. The yeast genome contains over twelve million base pairs, roughly one-fourth of one small human chromosome. Since many genes are shared among all organisms, the study of yeast is a rapid and efficient way to test their functions (Botstein and Fink, 1988).

Caenorhabditis elegans is a soil-dwelling nematode. If molecular genetics is the reductionist core of biology, C. *elegans* is the reductionists' paradise. Sydney Brenner explicitly selected it in the early 1970s, to study the biological complexity of development and behavior. Its small size, rapid reproductive cycle, relatively small number of cells, and nearly transparent cell body make C. *elegans* an ideal model to study the development of multiple organs, including the nervous system. Enormous energy was invested over more than two decades to build up the informational base for nematode biology. The lineage of every cell was traced, and the interconnections among the cells of the nervous system were mapped (Sulston, 1983; Sulston and Brenner, 1974; Sulston and Horvitz, 1977; Sulston et al., 1983; White et al., 1986). The genome of its six chromosomes, containing approximately one hundred million base pairs, is in aggregate roughly comparable to a single human chromosome.

Genetic analysis extends well beyond the diseases inherited according to simple Mendelian patterns. Molecular genetic techniques can in some cases grab a molecular handle on diseases that otherwise elude study. Most common diseases have genetic forms. Atherosclerosis, arthritis, Alzheimer's disease, hypertension, diabetes mellitus, immune disorders, and many

See Also
DNA Typing

kinds of cancer at least occasionally run in families. When such inheritance is Mendelian (explained by a single gene), then finding that gene establishes one link in the causal chain leading to disease. Families with a single-gene form of disease may be rare, but they provide a valuable glimpse of molecular mechanisms. The mechanism found in one family may disclose clues about the cause of more common forms of the same disease. With complete genetic maps, finding the genes responsible for Mendelian traits is, theoretically, a matter of persistence. Molecular genetics should eventually find a gene whose function can be studied directly.

Complete genetic maps also enable investigators to search for multiple genes that must work in concert to produce disease. Hypertension and insulin-dependent diabetes are two diseases in which constellations of genes are at play. Many common diseases will similarly be explained as genes interacting with other genes and environmental factors. The study of animal models reveals specific genes that influence the course of a disease, that increase or diminish the risk of developing symptoms, or that point to specific environmental insults involved in disease expression. Genetic maps of various kinds are thus becoming essential tools in biomedical research.

Science policy issues

Resource allocation emerged as the first science policy issue facing those who wished to pursue genome mapping and sequencing. Consensus that genetic maps and technology development were important did not extend to agreement on how important the Human Genome Project was relative to other biomedical research opportunities. Whether the Human Genome Project deserved specific additional funding became the central question. The initial response of the biomedical research community was concern that the Human Genome Project would detract from other research by siphoning off monies better devoted to undirected basic research.

Three advisory groups convened to consider this question all reached the same conclusion: that a systematic mapping and sequencing program was likely to be far less costly and more powerful in the long run than a less organized effort (Health and Environmental Research Advisory Committee, 1987; National Research Council, 1988; U.S. Congress, 1988). Each of these committees reached a consensus that genetic strategies were becoming central to all biomedical research, and the work entailed in the Human Genome Project would have to be done eventually. The argument boiled down to a shared belief that mapping and sequencing at the scale of entire genomes was progressing with sufficient speed to justify a concerted research program. Constructing maps and developing technologies in an organized fashion would prove far more efficient than hoping that complete maps would emerge from thousands of uncoordinated searches for individual genes.

The three committees used somewhat different methods to project budget needs, but all agreed on the need for a project of roughly fifteen years' duration and approximately $200 million annual budget. Efficiency of resource allocation was invoked as the principal justification for the Human Genome Project. Those promoting the project argued that it would not displace other science of equal merit, but instead would free up resources by making available maps and technologies that would otherwise be assembled haphazardly and inefficiently. The question was not whether to construct maps and develop technologies but, rather, how to organize the effort and how quickly to proceed. These arguments convinced those in Congress and the executive branch, who allocated dedicated funds for genome mapping and sequencing programs.

The debate first surfaced in the United States, and the first formal reports were American in origin. The U.S. Department of Energy commenced its Human Genome Initiative in fiscal year 1987, and was joined by the National Institutes of Health in 1988. Italy also began a genome project in 1988; the United Kingdom and the Soviet Union followed suit in 1989. (The Soviet program was transferred to the Russian Republic in 1991 and 1992.) These efforts were soon joined by genome research programs of the European Community and the United Nations Educational, Scientific, and Cultural Organization (UNESCO). France, the Netherlands, and Denmark also mounted human genome programs by the end of the 1980s. In Japan, the Ministry of Education, Science and Culture began a human genome program in 1989. The Japanese Science and Technology Agency supported a pilot project to automate DNA sequencing beginning in 1981. In 1988 and 1989, this was augmented and expanded into a genome mapping and sequencing effort. The Ministry of Health and Welfare began a program aimed at human genetic diseases during this period, and the Ministry of International Trade and Industry seriously considered joining the fray. Scientists in several Latin American countries formed a collaborative network. Scientists in Canada, Australia, New Zealand, the People's Republic of China, and other nations petitioned their governments to implement human genome research programs.

This profusion of programs pursued similar but somewhat different goals. The Danish program, for example, was an incremental augmentation of ongoing disease-oriented research, while the U.S. efforts were largely focused on map construction and technology

◆ **Human Genome Project (HGP)**

A multinational effort to catalog all possible human genetic characteristics by obtaining the sequence of all the DNA in the human genome.

See Also

Asexual Reproduction: Cloning: 'Hello, Dolly,

Cloning: Fears of Abuse

G

GENOME MAPPING AND SEQUENCING

Science Policy Issues

development. The Soviet genome budget funded much of all molecular biology in the U.S.S.R., while the U.S. program constituted less than 2 percent of the National Institutes of Health research budget. The budgets also varied widely, from a few million dollars to over one hundred million dollars in the United States. The programs were, moreover, administered by many different agencies and organizations with largely independent planning and advisory processes. While the ends were largely similar, the means were disparate. The purpose of the Human Genome Project was to produce information tools that contained information from many different sources. Genetic linkage maps, physical maps, and DNA sequencing information would be contributed by thousands of laboratories throughout the world, but transforming this information into useful maps and data bases required collective efforts.

The main argument for organized work at the scale of entire genomes was its efficiency. Such efficiency necessitated more systematic organization of effort than existed in most biomedical research. Coordination thus emerged as a central policy concern—interagency coordination within countries and international collaboration around the globe. Most European countries centralized their research in ministries. The more decentralized organization in the United States and Japan raised greater barriers to coordination. In the United States, the Department of Energy and the National Institutes of Health jointly forged a five-year plan, intended to be revised every three to four years, and a coordinated planning apparatus (U.S. Department of Health and Human Services and U.S. Department of Energy, 1990). Coordination of the Japanese ministries was more informal.

Orchestrating collaboration across international borders proved more difficult. The Human Genome Organization (HUGO) was formed in April 1988 specifically to mediate international cooperation, and to harness various national programs into a coherent team. The task proved more difficult than its founding scientists anticipated. HUGO, intended to be a "United Nations of the human genome," in the words of founding president Victor McKusick, instead resembled the League of Nations—more a congeries of independently planned national efforts than the hoped-for coherent plan. The principal coordination mechanisms remained ad hoc arrangements among national programs and private philanthropic organizations, publication in the open scientific literature, and periodic

ELSI
Seeking Accountability and Foresight

Leaders of the effort to create the Human Genome Project recognized the need for national attention to social, legal, and ethical issues as scientific planning proceeded. The National Research Council report and the Office of Technology Assessment report stressed the need for a mechanism to address the social implications of applying knowledge gained through genome mapping and sequencing (National Research Council, 1988; U.S. Congress, Office of Technology Assessment, 1988). The Department of Energy took preliminary steps to support ethical analysis of its research program as early as 1986, but these failed to translate into specific grants or research activities for several years. At a September 1988 press conference to announce that he would direct an office for human genome research at the National Institutes of Health, James D. Watson indicated that part of that program's budget should be dedicated to analysis of ethical, legal, and social issues. Following a Senate hearing in October 1989, the Department of Energy followed suit, and the joint NIH-DOE Working Group on Ethical, Legal, and Social Issues (ELSI) was established, chaired by Nancy Sabin Wexler.

ELSI was responsible for providing advice to both the NIH and DOE on research strategies, and for sponsoring a program of activities to promote outreach and public education and to produce policy options for Congress and the executive branch to consider. Within a year, the ELSI programs more than doubled the direct federal support of bioethics, then doubled it again by the end of fiscal year 1990.

The ELSI program was an unprecedented effort by a scientific research initiative to analyze its impact on social issues. The program, established by executive fiat, was quickly ratified by Congress. Once formulated, the strategy quickly spread abroad. The genome mapping and sequencing programs sponsored by Italy, France, the European Community, the Russian Republic (originally the Soviet Union), UNESCO, and Japan all explicitly included a component devoted to analysis of social and ethical issues. The British program was alone in being focused solely on the science, although even in the United Kingdom, the private Neufield Council evinced an interest in bioethical issues related to genome research. With the creation of the ELSI program, government science agencies acknowledged responsibility not only to support science but also to assess its social impact. This reflected a shifting social contract in which the biomedical research enterprise was increasingly expected to account for itself.

—ROBERT MULLAN COOK-DEEGAN

international meetings, as in fields in biomedical research.

Social policy issues

Policymakers and the general public welcomed the possibility of understanding many diseases through genetics but greeted the genetic revolution with some trepidation. Public support was strong for biomedical research, and genome mapping promised to expedite biomedical research. Print, radio, and television news media reported a long succession of successful hunts for disease genes and the genesis of the Human Genome Project. Most of the coverage was quite favorable, but there were nagging doubts about potential misuse of the new technologies.

In the United States, many issues stemming from progress in human genetics were left to fester in the absence of a national forum in which to discuss issues related to bioethics. The National Commission for the Protection of Human Subjects of Biomedical and Behavioral Research operated from 1973 to 1978, laying a foundation for human subjects' protection. The National Commission demonstrated a welcome ability to mediate debate over difficult policy questions that involved scientific, legal, and social issues. The Ethics Advisory Board within the Department of Health, Education and Welfare was transiently active from 1978 to 1980. Its role included reviewing specific protocols that raised ethical or legal issues or that required waivers of usual human subjects' regulations. The U.S. President's Commission for the Study of Ethical Problems in Medicine and Biomedical and Behavioral Research operated from 1980 until 1983. A successor to the National Commission, its principal function was to serve as a national forum to discuss policy issues. The U.S. President's Commission issued two prescient reports on genetics, a 1982 report on recombinant DNA research and gene therapy and a 1983 report on genetic screening and counseling.

In 1985, Congress established the Biomedical Ethics Board and Biomedical Ethics Advisory Committee as congressional successors to the U.S. President's Commission. A report on implications of human genetics was the first of three mandated activities for the new body. Its structure was modeled on the Office of Technology Assessment, and it operated briefly from 1988 to 1989; then it ran aground on the shoals of abortion politics. While none of its mandated studies dealt directly with abortion, several topics nonetheless touched on interests of groups on both sides of the extremely divisive abortion debate. In March 1989, senators on the Biomedical Ethics Board found themselves completely deadlocked, and the Biomedical Ethics Advisory Committee could not operate in the face of this paralysis. Its ability to expend funds was terminated six months later, and its statutory authorization expired September 30, 1990.

Most of the social policy issues posed by genome mapping and sequencing arose from application of knowledge or new technologies rather than in the conduct of research. Many of these application areas are briefly summarized here. The main effect of mapping and sequencing technologies was to accelerate the pace of the advance of human genetics. They also expedited the development of analytical methods useful in medicine and forensic science. The same techniques used to construct maps in most cases could be readily translated into new methods for DNA-based diagnosis, or to identify individuals by analyzing their DNA.

The first wave of concern stemmed from policy problems that had arisen in the 1960s and 1970s, when genetic screening for phenylketonuria and sickle-cell disease began. By producing vastly greater detail about the human genome and by augmenting diagnostic technologies, genome mapping and sequencing raised the prospect of more widespread genetic testing and screening. The ethical and legal concerns related to genetic testing centered on the confidentiality of information about individuals' disease susceptibility or other genetic data. The core issue was genetic discrimination; identifying the genes that caused disease, and discovering technologies to detect them, threatened discrimination against those carrying particular genes. Opportunities for discrimination abound when individuals at risk seek jobs, health insurance, life insurance, and other social benefits.

The ability to identify individuals by sampling their DNA enabled forensic uses of DNA tests. Genetic markers were useful not only in tracing the inheritance of chromosomal regions through families but also could serve as unique genetic identifiers, except in the case of identical twins. (Identical twins should, in theory, be genetically identical except in cells undergoing DNA rearrangement during development.) DNA testing could thus be used to establish paternity or to investigate violent crime (Committee on Forensic Uses of DNA Tests, 1992; U.S. Congress, Office of Technology Assessment, 1991). One common application, for example, was to compare sperm taken from a rape victim against DNA from a suspect in the crime. Another was to analyze hair and blood samples at the scene of a murder, and to look for matches with a suspect's DNA. DNA typing even became part of a human-rights investigation, when DNA sequencing of variable regions was used to trace possible genetic relationships between grandmothers and the children of parents who had been tortured and murdered in Argentina. These children had been separated from their families, and geneticists aspired to reunite the families (King, 1991). On the other hand,

A previous child or first-degree relative with a neural tube defect is an indication for amniocentesis.

PAGE 309

Most states have laws requiring newborn screening for certain disorders, including galactosemia and sickle-cell disease.

PAGE 312

GENOME MAPPING AND SEQUENCING

Social Policy Issues

the forensic uses of DNA testing that grew from these powerful techniques of DNA analysis raised questions of civil liberties, due process of law, and international exchange of information between governments with widely differing criminal-justice codes and human-rights standards.

Public concern grew not only from applications of genetic technology but also from the troubled history of human genetics. Geneticists labored under the long shadow of eugenics. A wave of enthusiasm about prospects for human genetics crested in the 1920s and 1930s, as genetics entered the mainstream of science. The nascent field of human genetics became inextricably entangled in the parallel political movement that led to eugenic policies such as mandatory sterilization, immigration restriction, and antimiscegenation statutes. The eugenics movement started in the United Kingdom and the United States, and eventually merged with the racial hygiene movements in Nazi Germany and elsewhere (Adams, 1990; Gallagher, 1990; Kevles, 1985; Lifton, 1986; Muller-Hill, 1988; Proctor, 1988; Smith and Nelson, 1989).

Medical genetics in the postwar era explicitly rejected the coercive social policies of eugenics and concentrated on nondirective counseling to individual clients. Controversies about genetic determinism and sociobiology concerned principally those studying population genetics and evolution rather than medical genetics. Many human geneticists and molecular geneticists were largely oblivious to the social history of eugenics and the ongoing nature-nurture debate. Medical geneticists had traditionally concerned themselves primarily with Mendelian diseases, and were only beginning to deal with conditions in which the genetic basis was less clear. They were bewildered by claims that their science had inherent eugenic intentions. When a debate began about how the fruits of the Human Genome Project would be distributed and controlled, however, the project was ineluctably drawn into the cross fire.

The technologies of DNA sequencing and mapping made the discovery of new genes faster and more straightforward. Starting from genetics, however, turned the normal course of research on its head, since

See Also

Race Science: Bad Science Breeds Social Control

GENETIC STUDIES
Under the Shadow of Eugenics

Human molecular genetics historically grew from the molecular biological study of non-human organisms, on the one hand, and the study of human genetic disease, on the other. Medical genetics reacted strongly against eugenic ideology in the postwar era. The ethical norms of medical genetics were widely shared throughout the world (Wertz and Fletcher, 1989). Respect for the views of clients produced the ideal of "nondirective counseling" and explicit rejection of coercive social policies such as those espoused by eugenicists. Molecular biology concerned itself primarily with the detailed mechanisms of biology, and came to confront broad social issues only when molecular genetics began to find application in humans.

Molecular genetics might have more scientific depth than the facile interpretations of pedigree data that undergirded most eugenic thinking, but the public harbored a healthy skepticism about the facile prognostications of scientific elites, particularly regarding human genetics. While molecular genetics might prove more scientifically robust than eugenics, its potential for social mischief remained potent. The degree to which gene-mapping efforts provoked genetic discrimination and imposition of social stigma hinged on how accurately genetic tests could predict important characteristics of individuals.

Eugenic policies presumed genetic determinism. Eugenic ideology viewed genes as powerful determinants of behavior, intelligence, perception, athletic ability, moral stature, and even social class. Socially desirable or undesirable characteristics were foreordained at the time of conception. In the late 1970s and into the 1980s, debate about sociobiology rekindled this decades-old debate about nature versus nurture. Genetic determinism provoked a vigorous reaction. Geneticists concerned about the past abuses of human genetics rejected the central claims of strong genetic determinism, viewed correlations between genes and behavioral traits with great skepticism, and found policy implications of deterministic genetics particularly suspect (INSAN, 1984; Lewontin et al., 1984).

Molecular genetics focused on elucidating causal chains and physiological mechanisms, and was thus inclined to reductionist explanations of detailed molecular phenomena. It was, on its face, inclined to determinism. Molecular genetics aspired to explain behavior, and made some progress toward this end by illuminating behavior mutant organisms of the sea hare Aplysia, fruit flies, nematodes, and mice. It was clear that molecular defects could inhibit development of the nervous system, impede the transmission of neural impulses, and cause behavioral changes. This was a far cry, however, from establishing the primacy of genetics in determining behavior. Indeed, the complexity of behavior made it likely that the genetic dissection of most functions in the nervous system would be more readily understood as highly complex networks of genetic and nongenetic factors rather than linear causal chains.

—ROBERT MULLAN COOK-DEEGAN

investigators were starting from genes of unknown function and looking for functional correlations, rather than starting from a known protein and looking for the genes encoding it.

This reversal of traditional research strategies induced confusion about how to interpret patent law. Exactly how did map and sequence information influence what could be patented? If one had, for example, sequenced all or part of a gene but had no idea what it did, could the gene's sequence nonetheless be patented? If so, a rapid survey of gene-bearing regions linked to a patenting strategy was central to developing new pharmaceutical and agricultural products using biotechnology. If genes of unknown function were not patentable, how would private biotechnology, pharmaceutical, agricultural, and other private firms protect their investments in research and development? Yet commercial attachments to such work might hinder the free exchange of scientific data. Genetic data were the essence of international genome mapping efforts; maps were constructed from collective data pooled from around the world. The new technologies thus raised a thorny and controversial issue that could be resolved only through a welter of legal activity, including patent applications, approvals or rejections of patent claims, litigation over patent infringements, possible new patent legislation, and accumulated judicial interpretations of patent law and DNA technologies.

— ROBERT MULLAN COOK-DEEGAN

H

HEALTH CARE, QUALITY OF

Quality of health care is a measure of the extent to which health services increase the likelihood of desired health outcomes and are consistent with current professional knowledge (Institute of Medicine, 1990). This idea applies to a broad range of services, many types of health-care professionals (such as physicians, nurses, dentists, and certain others), and all settings of care (from hospitals and nursing homes to physicians' offices and private homes). The definition covers populations as well as individual patients; it therefore emphasizes access to health care and suggests that the perspectives of both individuals and society are important.

The definition's stipulation of desired health outcomes draws attention to a link between the processes of health care and outcomes of that care, to patient well-being and welfare, to the importance of being well informed about alternative health-care interventions and their expected outcomes, and to the need for health-care professionals to take their patients' preferences and values into account. The emphasis on current professional knowledge underscores the need for health professionals to stay abreast of a dynamic knowledge base in health care and to take responsibility for clarifying for their patients the processes and expected outcomes of care.

By the sixth century C.E., quality of health care was already linked to the idea of profession. Notions about the responsibilities of the professions, such as

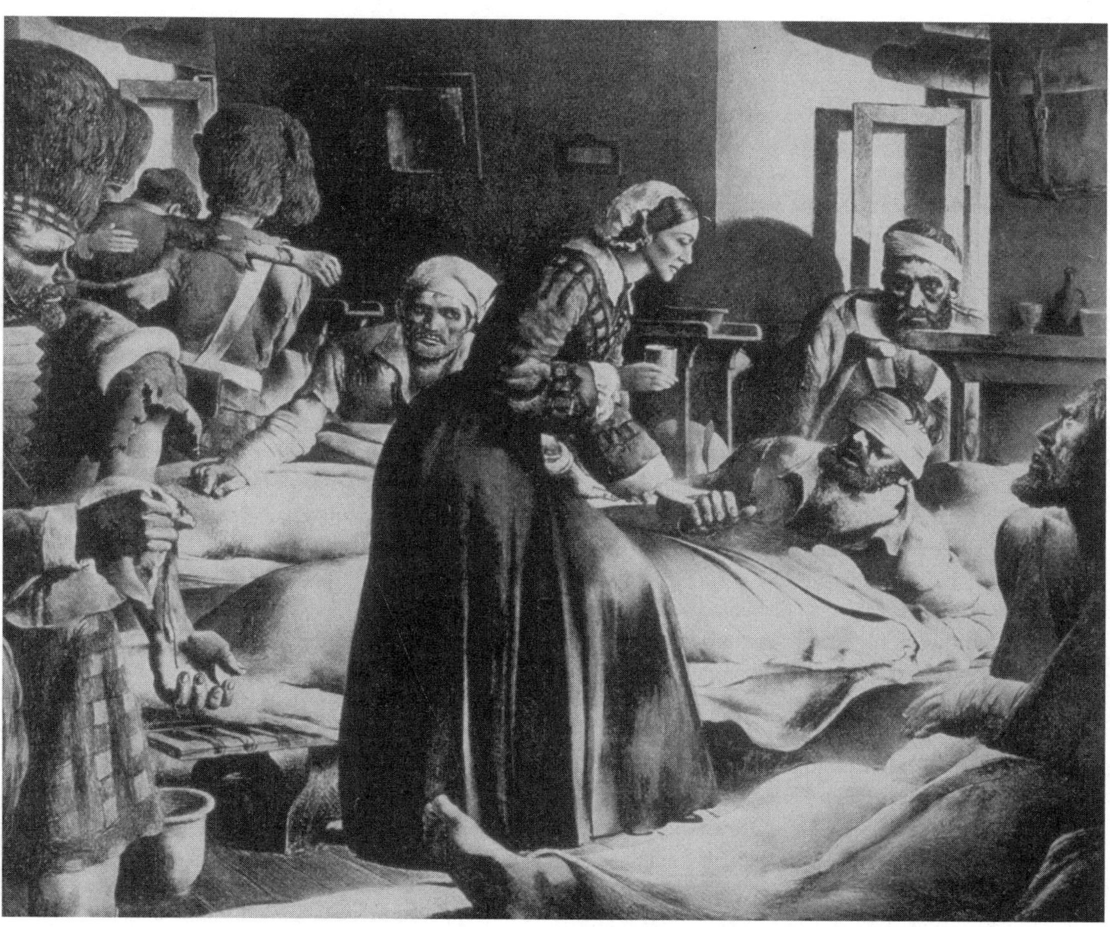

PROFESSIONAL NURSE

British nurse and humanitarian Florence Nightingale (1820–1910) was a pioneer in professionalizing the training of nurses.

H

HEALTH CARE, QUALITY OF

"It may seem a strange principle to enunciate as the very first requirement in a Hospital that it should do the sick no harm."

FLORENCE NIGHTINGALE
NOTES ON HOSPITALS
1859

the healing arts, date at least to St. Benedict (c. 480-547). The Rule of St. Benedict required new members of the order to make solemn profession of their intention to live the rule and to advance in that profession by way of their vows, in the manner of "continuous improvement." This Benedictine notion of profession—professing before peers—together with the attendant requirements of self-examination and self-regulation, provided a model for all the professions. According to this model, health care professionals would profess their responsibility for assuring the continued improvement of the quality of care they give.

The relationships of quality of care to ethical principles such as beneficence, nonmaleficence ("first, do no harm"), and patient autonomy are clear. The medical profession, as other professions, functions under a form of social contract in which it enjoys certain privileges, such as self-governance, in return for meeting certain obligations, such as stewardship of the public interest. In the nineteenth century, pioneers such as the nurse Florence Nightingale (for British troops in the Crimean War) and the surgeon Ernest A. Codman (for hospitalized patients in Boston, Massachusetts) led the way in studying outcomes of care. By the middle of the twentieth century, concerns about quality of care were more frequently voiced; concepts such as quality assessment and quality assurance, and ways to put them into practice, were being developed, most often under the leadership of physicians and nurses.

PRIMARY FRAMEWORK FOR QUALITY OF CARE

- structural measures
- processes of care
- outcomes

In the 1960s, the physician-philosopher Avedis Donabedian offered a unifying concept of "structure, process, and outcome" that became the primary framework to guide those concerned with quality of care in the latter part of the twentieth century. *Structural measures* are the characteristics of the resources in the health-care delivery system and are assumed to reflect the capacity of a practitioner or institutional health-care provider to deliver good-quality care. *Processes of care* consist of what is done to and for the patient, from screening and prevention of disease, through diagnosis and treatment of illness, to counseling and palliation of symptoms. A further distinction is sometimes made between the technical or skill-based aspects of care (the "science" of care) and the interpersonal, or humanistic, aspects of care (the "art" of care). *Outcomes* are the end results of care—that is, the effect of the care processes on the health and well-being of individuals and populations.

The notion of outcomes has evolved from a fairly narrow concern with death and disease to recognition that a much broader set of measures must be used as quality indicators. These concepts are sometimes referred to as health status or health-related quality of life. They include, in addition to survival, such dimensions of health as physical functioning, mental and emotional well-being, cognitive functioning (ability to think and reason), social and role functioning (ability to engage in social and other activities, such as work or school, that are usual for a person of a given age or other characteristics), activities of daily living (ability to perform at least simple activities to care for oneself and to live independently outside of an institution). Sometimes other measures—such as energy, vitality, pain, and satisfaction with life (or with health care)—are included in the broad concept of outcomes. Thus, quality of care implies that judgments are made both about how well health care has been handled technically and about how well from a standpoint of interpersonal exchanges; those judgments may be made using explicit, objective criteria or implicit, subjective criteria, or both.

Quality assessment is the act of measuring quality of care—that is, detecting problems with quality and finding examples of good performance and good outcomes. *Quality assurance* is a more complete cycle of assessment and intervention: detecting a problem, verifying that it truly exists and is important, identifying what might be correctable about the problem, intervening to correct it, studying further to ensure that the problem has been corrected, and making certain that no further problems have been generated as a side effect of the intervention. Quality assessment and assurance tend to be concerned with three major problems regarding quality of care—poor technical or interpersonal performance, overuse of unnecessary or inappropriate services, and underuse of needed or appropriate services—with most attention going to the first two.

Concerns about quality of care can relate to other health policy concerns, such as overly high expenditures on health care (for example, when unneeded, inappropriate, or ineffective services are provided) and poor access to care (for example, when people do not receive needed care at all or obtain it only after inappropriate delay or in unsuitable circumstances). In practice, traditional quality assessment and assurance efforts have tended to focus on individuals rather than systems and to emphasize identifying and correcting or disciplining poor performers rather than finding and rewarding superior performers.

In the 1980s in the United States, concepts of *con-*

tinuous quality improvement* and *total quality management* began to be popular in the manufacturing and service sectors, and later in health care. These programs are based on statistical quality-control models designed for manufacturing industries by American statisticians such as W. Edwards Deming and applied mainly after World War II in Japan. Like traditional quality-assurance programs, they entail a cycle of system design, examination, action, and redesign. The underlying philosophy and analytic methods differ somewhat from the traditional approaches. They are oriented toward systems and organizations rather than individuals, emphasize "customer-supplier" relationships, focus on improving performance as a goal rather than simply on finding poor performers, and seek out excellence as a benchmark against which to measure performance. Also, they employ formal, although relatively simple, statistical concepts and methods for continuously collecting and analyzing data on processes and outcomes of care.

Monitoring the quality of care is typically seen as an endeavor of the professions and the private sector in the United States. This is reflected, for example, in specifications for education, training, and professional certification for members of the health-care professions that date to the early part of the twentieth century and continue to the present; in requirements for hospital accreditation that have been specified and refined by the Joint Commission on Accreditation of Healthcare Organizations for several decades; in professional peer review programs, such as Foundations for Medical Care, that emerged in the middle of the century; and in various committees and other programs of individual hospitals, health maintenance organizations, and other health-care delivery institutions. The regulatory aspects of quality assurance are seen most clearly in the establishment of Professional Standards Review Organizations (in the 1970s) and Utilization and Quality Control Peer Review Organizations (in the 1980s) for the Medicare program (which finances health care for the elderly in the United States). The many state and federal laws and regulations concerning accreditation, licensure, and certification for health-care professionals, facilities, and institutions also speak to governmental or public sector concern with quality of care.

Several trends in the late twentieth century may draw yet more attention to quality of care and make quality assurance and quality improvement far more complex to manage than in previous decades. These trends include efforts to control excessive costs and expenditures on health; new ways to pay hospitals and physicians; growth of hybrid health-care financing and organization schemes; malpractice litigation and efforts to reduce the risk of malpractice liability; movement of complex technologies outside institutions and into outpatient and home settings; and changing demographics of populations. Both professional and regulatory perspectives are likely to be reflected as quality assurance and improvement programs grow in number and in complexity. Because quality assurance and improvement are better developed for hospitals than for outpatient settings, and because more is known about how to identify good or poor care and performance than about how to change the attitudes, behaviors, and performance of individual clinicians or institutions, a considerable agenda of research and development is still needed.

The United States is seen as the world leader in organized quality-assessment, quality-assurance, and quality-improvement programs for health-care professionals and institutions. Some efforts outside the United States took hold in the late 1980s; these include programs in several postindustrial Western countries, especially the Netherlands, and the organization of the International Society of Quality Assurance in Health Care.

— KATHLEEN N. LOHR

HEALTH POLICY

POLITICS AND HEALTH CARE

At the heart of the health-policy debate in the United States has been the question of health care as a basic human right. The concept of a right to needed services is not new to America; for instance, the constitutional right to legal representation establishes that all individuals are entitled to at least some basic services. However, the Constitution does not provide for a clear right to health care, in contrast to the constitutions of many other countries (Fuenzalida-Puelma and Connor, 1989).

The United States and the Republic of South Africa are the only two economically developed countries in the world without a national policy that accepts the principle of universal entitlement to basic medical care. Many observers believe, however, that the American system has become ethically intolerable. This article analyzes American health policy and some proposed directions of policy change.

Gaps in public coverage

Medicaid and Medicare were created in 1965 to improve the accessibility of medical services to the poor and the elderly. However, major problems have remained. Federal Medicaid payments go to limited categories of the poor and therefore exclude about one-

See Also
Value and Valuation

third of American citizens with incomes below the poverty level; provisions vary from state to state. The elderly, on the other hand, have experienced erosion in Medicare coverage, with increasing copayments and deductibles on covered services, as well as continued noncoverage for nursing-home care and prescription drugs. Historically, individuals with Medicare have paid out of pocket for more than half of all medical expenses, a higher proportion than before the inception of Medicare (Minkler and Robertson, 1991).

The number of uninsured rose steeply after 1980, reflecting changes in the labor force, as more people were employed without benefits in service industries and many companies eliminated benefits due to the escalating cost of health insurance. Indeed, by the early 1990s, more than 37 million people were without insurance. During the 1980s, 13 percent of the American population, representing more than 11 million individuals, lost private insurance. African-American and Hispanic populations have remained disproportionately uninsured. Employed people and their dependents comprise approximately three-quarters of the uninsured. More than half of these employed uninsured earn middle-income or high-income wages but have no health benefits provided by their employer, nor do they purchase health insurance on their own. Working-age persons with private insurance face deductible provisions and limited coverage that frequently create major financial difficulties as well as frustrating complexities in obtaining benefits (Himmelstein et al., 1992).

Health screening is intended to identify from a large population those who in some way deviate from a statistically derived norm.

PAGE 344

Because there is no universal entitlement to basic health care, the availability, quality, and utilization of services depend on local conditions. In some geographical regions, there is a surplus of health professionals; in others, a shortage. Access differs according to patients' personal finances, initiative, and linguistic abilities. Mechanisms to ensure quality of care are insufficient, and malpractice litigation is extensive. In different localities, the utilization of expensive medical procedures varies widely, indicating wasteful practice patterns (National Leadership Commission on Health Care, 1989). A laissez-faire approach to planning and organization has created a situation in which very high-quality medicine is available for part of the population, while others cannot receive the most basic services. Patients frequently face the frustrations of high costs, complex administrative procedures, inaccessible services, and variable quality. Due to cutbacks at the federal, state, and county levels, practitioners frequently cannot arrange for needed hospitalization, diagnostic procedures, or treatments when patients are uninsured or underinsured. As a result, patients frequently utilize emergency rooms for primary health-care needs at substantially higher cost to hospitals and society than if they were treated in less costly outpatient clinics.

Policy options

COMPETITIVE STRATEGIES. Since the 1980s, competitive strategies have achieved prominence in health-policy circles. Such proposals aim to foster competition among providers, and thus to lower costs (Enthoven and Kronick, 1991). Competitive strategies culminated in "managed competition," a policy option favored initially by the Clinton administration (elected in 1992). The basic assumption of managed competition is that allowing competitive forces of the market to control health-care delivery will result in a high-quality, cost-effective system. Under such a system, two or three large managed-care providers operated by insurance companies would provide a government-determined basic package of health care to a specified region.

Competitive strategies have received major criticism. Forces of competition historically have not controlled health-care costs, as illustrated by the rise in overall costs at a rate higher than general inflation and by higher costs in regions with keen competition among health-care providers (Robinson and Luft, 1988). Further, medical services never have shown the characteristics of a competitive market, since government pays for more than 40 percent of health care and since the insurance, pharmaceutical, and medical-equipment industries all manifest monopolistic tendencies that inhibit competition. Hospitals and physicians maintain political-economic power through professional organizations that reduce the impact of competitive strategies. Physicians also affect the demand for services through recommendations about referrals, diagnostic studies, and treatment. Analytically, the effects of competition on costs are difficult to separate from other important changes, especially the effects of general inflation, the requirement of major copayments by patients, and the impact of prepayment (Siminoff, 1986).

Such competitive strategies also have led to major dislocations and gaps in services. For example, competitive contracting and prospective reimbursement under Medi-Cal (California's Medicaid system) have worsened the financial crises of hospitals with a large proportion of indigent clients. The resultant disruption in services due to underfunding of Medicaid has led to a measurable worsening of some patients' medical conditions (Lurie et al., 1986). In other states, competitive health plans have suffered severe and unpredicted financial problems, and patients have encountered major barriers to access, including direct refusal of care by providers (Freeman and Kirkman-Liff, 1985).

Several ethical issues also arise with "managed competition." On an individual level, autonomy may be compromised through elimination of a consumer's free choice of physicians and hospitals. Increased out-of-pocket costs may further impair autonomy by restricting access to care, especially among the poor. On the societal level, a two-tiered system remains in place, with the working poor and unemployed receiving minimum health care compared with more extensive coverage enjoyed by a relative few in the upper classes who can afford to pay out of pocket for additional coverage. Furthermore, managed competition does not curtail administrative waste, which has been estimated at approximately 15 percent of health-care expenditures, or about $120 billion annually (Woolhandler and Himmelstein, 1991).

PUBLIC-SECTOR PROGRAMS. Policies enacted between 1980 and 1992 greatly reduced public-sector health programs. Cutbacks occurred in the national Medicaid program; Medicare; block grants for maternal and child health, migrant health services, community health centers, and birth-control services; health planning; educational assistance for medical students and residents (affecting especially minority recruitment); the National Health Service Corps; the Indian Health Service; and the National Institute of Occupational Safety and Health. Many federally sponsored research programs also have been cut.

During this same time period, measures of health and well-being in the United States either stopped improving or actually became worse. For example, a marked slowing in the rate of decline in infant mortality coincided with cutbacks in federal prenatal and perinatal programs; in several low-income urban areas, infant mortality increased (U.S. Department of Health and Human Services, 1987). Among African-Americans, postneonatal and maternal mortality rates stopped falling, after decades of steady decline, and a growing proportion of African-American women have not been able to receive adequate prenatal care (Hughes et al., 1988). These reversals in health status and health services, emerging as direct manifestations of changes in federal policies, have been unique among economically developed countries (World Bank, 1993; Cereseto and Waitzkin, 1986).

Alongside these programmatic cutbacks, bureaucratization and regulation in the health-care system

CORPORATE HEALTH CARE
Best for All Concerned?

Various policies have encouraged corporate expansion in the medical field. By the mid-1970s, private insurance companies, pharmaceutical firms, and medical-equipment manufacturers had achieved prominent positions in the medical marketplace. In the 1980s, multinational corporations took over community hospitals in all regions of the country, acquired and/or managed many public hospitals, bought or built teaching hospitals affiliated with medical schools, and gained control of ambulatory-care organizations (Gray, 1991; Relman, 1980).

Despite concerns about cost containment, corporate profitability in health care has encountered few obstacles. In the early 1990s, after-tax profits for corporations with direct activities in health care ranked the third highest among American industrial groups ("Forty-Fifth Annual Report," 1993). Nationally, for-profit chains control about 15 percent of all hospitals, but in some states (for example, California, Florida, Tennessee, and Texas) the chains operate between one-third and one-half of hospitals. Ownership of nursing homes by corporate chains has increased by more than 30 percent. For-profit corporations have enrolled about 70 percent of all health-maintenance organization subscribers throughout the country.

While proponents perceive several economic advantages of corporate involvement in health care, substantiation of such claims is limited. For example, it is argued that tough-minded managerial techniques increase efficiency and decrease costs, although several studies have shown that for-profit health-care organizations are no more efficient than nonprofit ones (Watt et al., 1986). Similarly, research on corporate management has not supported the claim that corporate takeover can alleviate the financial problems of hospitals serving indigent clients (Lewin et al., 1988).

Corporate involvement in health care also has raised ethical questions. There is concern that corporate strategies lead to reduced services for the poor. While some corporations have established endowments for indigent care, the ability of such funds to ensure long-term access is doubtful, especially when cutbacks occur in public-sector support (Feder and Hadley, 1985). Other ethical concerns have focused on physicians' conflicting loyalties to patients and corporations, the implications of physicians' referrals of patients for services to corporations in which the physicians hold financial interests, the unwillingness of for-profit hospitals to provide unprofitable but needed services, and similar issues (Mitchell and Scott, 1992). These observations lead to doubts about the wisdom of policies that encourage corporate penetration of health care.

—NANCY E. GIN
HOWARD WAITZKIN

Interpreting health-screening tests involves assumptions about the accuracy and reliability of the instruments.

PAGE 344

have grown rapidly (Stern and Epstein, 1985). A distinction between the rhetoric of reduced government and the reality of greater government intervention is nowhere clearer than in the Medicare diagnosis-related group (DRG) program. Intended as a cost-control device, DRGs introduced unprecedented complexity and bureaucratic regulation. By providing reimbursement to hospitals at a fixed rate for specific diagnoses, DRGs encouraged hospitals to limit the length of stay, since the hospital receives the same amount whether a patient stays one day or five days. The same disincentive exists for providing services during the hospitalization, since fewer services translate into higher income for the institution. Hospitals responded to DRG regulations with an expansion of their own bureaucratic staffs and dataprocessing operations, more intensive utilization review, and a tendency to discharge patients with unstable conditions when DRG payments are exhausted. Private hospitals admitting a small proportion of indigent patients profited under DRGs; public and university hospitals that serve a higher percentage of indigent and multiproblem patients faced an unfavorable case mix within specific DRGs and thus fared poorly. The extensive utilization review that DRGs encouraged focused on cost cutting rather than on ensuring quality of care. Moreover, DRGs' contribution to cost controls remains unclear, in comparison with other factors, such as reduced inflation in the economy as a whole.

A national health program for the United States

HISTORY OF PRIOR PROPOSALS. Although advocacy for a national health program (NHP) dates back to the mid-1920s, with the proposal of the Committee on the Costs of Medical Care (an independent body funded by private foundations), the most intense efforts occurred during the 1970s, when Congress considered at least eighteen separate proposals. The supporters of these measures ranged across a wide political spectrum, including the Nixon administration, the American Medical Association, and both liberal and conservative legislators. During the Carter administration of the late 1970s, conflicts within the Democratic Party over reforms in health care helped prevent enactment of an NHP. Later, during the Reagan and Bush administrations (1981-1993), the support for an NHP from the legislative and executive branches of government seen during the 1970s was replaced by a policy of cutbacks in health and welfare programs, effectively eliminating the possibility of enactment. An NHP again emerged as a priority during the 1992 presidential campaign.

Within the range of NHP proposals considered during the late 1970s, several problems became clear. First, the NHP would have changed payment mechanisms rather than the organization of the health-care system. Under these proposals, the federal government would have guaranteed payment for most health services. However, the NHP would not have ensured that practitioners would work in different ways, in different areas, or with different patients.

Most of these plans for the NHP would not have covered all needed medical services. Copayment provisions would have required out-of-pocket payment by each person for some fixed percentage of health costs. While such copayments might have helped control costs, coinsurance predictably would have had a detrimental impact on the poor and other vulnerable groups, for whom such out-of-pocket payments are deterrents to obtaining needed care.

New and compulsory taxation, usually as fixed payroll deductions, would have paid for the NHP. The financing arrangements therefore would have been regressive; that is, low-income people would have paid a proportionately higher part of their income for health care than would the wealthy. Although various tax mechanisms could relieve the burden of health insurance for low-income persons, legislators devoted little attention to this issue (Mitchell and Schwartz, 1976).

In most NHP plans, private insurance companies would have served as the fiscal intermediaries. They would have received compensation for distributing NHP payments from the government to health providers. Such provisions thus would have assured continued profits for the private insurance industry and would have done little to reduce the administrative waste that has characterized this industry (Woolhandler and Himmelstein, 1991). Administrative costs account for approximately 25 cents of every health-care dollar spent in America, compared with approximately 10 cents in countries with NHPs. That translates to 15 percent less money available for direct patient care in America.

Regarding accessibility, NHP proposals would have contained few provisions for improving geographical maldistribution of health professionals. Fee schedules might have been higher in some proposals for doctors who practiced in underserved areas, but such incentives could not ensure that physicians actually would work in these areas.

PERSPECTIVES FROM OTHER COUNTRIES. Planning for an NHP in the United States would require open-minded consideration of the strengths and weaknesses of existing NHPs around the world. For instance, most countries in western Europe have initiated NHP structures permitting private practice in addition to a strong public sector. Canada has achieved universal entitlement to health care through an NHP that depends on private practitioners, private

hospitals, and strong planning and coordinating roles for the national and provincial governments (Evans et al., 1991).

NHPs vary widely in the degree to which the national government employs health professionals and owns health institutions. For example, the NHPs of Great Britain, Denmark, and the Netherlands contract with self-employed general practitioners for primary care; Canadian private practitioners receive insurance payments mainly on a fee-for-service basis; in Finland and Sweden a high proportion of practicing doctors work as salaried employees of government agencies. In the United Kingdom, the national government owns most hospitals; regional or local governments own many hospitals in Sweden, Finland, and other Scandinavian countries; and Canada's system depends on governmental budgeting for both public and private hospitals.

The Canadian system is very pertinent to the United States, because of geographical proximity and cultural similarity. Canada assures universal entitlement to health services through a combination of national and provincial insurance programs. Doctors generally receive public insurance payments through fee-for-service arrangements. Hospitals obtain public funds through annually negotiated contracts based on projected costs, eliminating the need to bill for specific services. Progressive taxation finances the Canadian system, and the private insurance industry does not play a major role in the program's administration. Most Canadian provinces have initiated policies that aim to correct remaining problems of access based on geographical maldistribution. Cost controls in Canada depend on contracted global budgeting with hospitals, limitations on reimbursements to practitioners, and markedly lower admin-

PRINCIPLES AND PROSPECTS FOR A U.S. NATIONAL HEALTH PROGRAM

NHP proposals can be appraised against several basic principles:

1. The NHP would provide for comprehensive care, including diagnostic, therapeutic, preventive, rehabilitative, environmental, and occupational-health services; dental and eye care; transportation to medical facilities; social work; and counseling.
2. These services generally would not require out-of-pocket payments at the point of delivery. While carefully limited copayments for certain services might be appropriate (as in Canada), copayments would be implemented in such a way as to ensure that they do not become barriers to access.
3. Coverage would be portable, so that travel or relocation would have no effect on a person's ability to obtain health care.
4. Financing for the NHP would come from a variety of sources, including continued corporate taxation, "health taxes" on cigarettes and alcoholic beverages, "conservation taxes" on fossil fuels and other energy sources, "pollution taxes" on known sources of air and water pollution, and a restructured individual tax. Taxation would be progressive, in that individuals and corporations with higher incomes would pay taxes at a higher rate.
5. The NHP would reduce administrative costs, private profit, and wasteful procedures in the health-care system. A national commission would establish a generic formulary of approved drugs, devices, equipment, and supplies. A national trust fund would disburse payments to private and public health facilities through global and prospective budgeting. Profit to private insurance companies and other corporations would be closely restricted.
6. Professional associations would negotiate the fee structures for health-care practitioners regionally. Financial incentives would encourage cost-control measures through health-maintenance organizations, community health centers, and a plurality of practice settings.
7. To correct geographical maldistribution of health professionals, the NHP would subsidize education and training, in return for required periods of service by medical graduates in underserved areas.
8. The NHP would initiate programs of prevention that would emphasize individual responsibility for health, risk reduction (including programs to reduce smoking, alcoholism, and drug abuse), nutrition, maternal and infant care, occupational and environmental health, long-term services for the elderly, and other efforts to promote health.
9. Elected community representatives would work with providers' groups in local advisory councils. These councils would participate in quality-assurance efforts, planning, and feedback that would encourage responsiveness to local needs.

— NANCY E. GIN
HOWARD WAITZKIN

By the early 1990s, more than 37 million people were without health insurance.

PAGE 336

istrative expenses because of reduced eligibility, billing, and collection procedures.

Since the structure of the economy in the United States is very similar to that of Canada and western European countries, which have established and comparatively successful NHPs, the feasibility of implementing such a program in America is high. As in these other countries, private hospitals, private practitioners, pharmaceutical companies, and other corporations involved in health care would remain in place. The systems in Canada and several European countries achieve their cost savings through drastic reductions in administrative activities, made possible by the use of a government agency as the only payer for needed health services. This type of monopsony financing allows private insurance for nonessential services and amenities, like cosmetic surgery or a private hospital room, but does not permit duplicating private insurance coverage for essential services. Curtailing the role of private insurance companies in health care could become the most important modification, under a single-payer system, of current financing policies in the United States.

Because of the commonly expressed concern about costs in the United States, the experiences of existing NHPs are instructive. American health-care expenditures, already the highest in the world, account for (as of 1993) approximately 14 percent of the gross national product. The presumption that an NHP would increase costs is not necessarily correct; depending on how an NHP is organized, costs might well fall below their prior level. First of all, major savings would come from reduced administrative overhead for billing, collection procedures, eligibility determinations, and other bureaucratic functions that no longer would be necessary. In the Canadian NHP, for instance, global budgeting for hospitals has greatly reduced administrative costs, and a much smaller role for the private insurance industry has lowered costs even further by restricting corporate profit. An analysis by the U.S. General Accounting Office (1991) showed that, due to savings from reduced administrative functions and entrepreneurism, a single-payer NHP like Canada's, if introduced in the United States, would lead to negligible added costs despite achieving universal access to care. For comparison, the cost of instituting a single-payer NHP is one order of magnitude less than expenditures on military systems like the Stealth bomber or government support for the financial sector in the savings and loan bailout.

There is and has been wide support for an NHP in the United States. Public opinion polls consistently have shown that a majority of the American population favors an NHP that assures universal entitlement to basic health-care services (Blendon and Edwards, 1991). Major professional organizations, including the American Medical Association (Todd et al., 1991), the American College of Physicians (Scott and Shapiro, 1992), the American Public Health Association, and a major physicians' organization favoring a single-payer option (Himmelstein and Woolhandler, 1989), have called for an NHP. Leaders and members of corporations, senior citizens' groups, and a large number of civic organizations have pressed Congress to create an NHP, although specific proposals have varied. Likewise, many state legislatures have considered setting up state health programs to provide universal access to care.

Strong opposition to an NHP will come from the corporations that currently benefit from the lack of an appropriate national policy: the private insurance industry, pharmaceutical and medical-equipment firms, and the for-profit chains. While corporate resistance should not be underestimated, there is also growing support for an NHP from the corporate world. The costs of private-sector medicine have become a major burden to many nonmedical companies that provide health insurance as a fringe benefit to employees. Corporations that do not directly profit from health care have influenced public policy in the direction of cost containment. In western Europe, corporations have come to look kindly on the cost controls and services that NHPs provide, even when corporate taxation contributes to NHP financing.

Conclusion

Ultimately, policies for health care are shaped by a multitude of forces, including ethical, economic, and political forces. Through research and analysis, the intellectual discipline of health policy contributes to national debates. There is no assurance, however, that the views of health-policy experts based in academia, government, or foundations will prevail. Knowledge generated from research and analysis enters a political process in which health-policy decisions are determined by political power as well as rational deliberation (Waitzkin and Hubbell, 1992).

With increasing discontent among the general public and practitioners, health-policy debates take on a certain urgency. While an ethical perspective tells us that basic health care for all is an individual right and a societal obligation, the burgeoning costs of the American health-care system hamper domestic economic growth and stability. Meanwhile, millions of people face major access barriers. Change in health policies to address these problems doubtless will occur during the 1990s, but the specifics of change remain difficult to predict with certainty in the complex political terrain of the United States.

— NANCY E. GIN
HOWARD WAITZKIN

HEALTH PROMOTION AND HEALTH EDUCATION

Governments promote health by financing medical research and care, by ensuring safe and clean workplaces and environments, and by encouraging healthy behavior. The last (and not necessarily the most important) of these is the focus of this entry.

On the surface, health promotion and health education would seem to pose few ethical problems. Governments that draw on research in medicine and public health have knowledge to impart to the population about the health effects of particular behaviors; members of the public value their health and welcome attempts to provide this information.

Health education and promotion is a beneficial and necessary element of national health policy. Nevertheless, health promotion has always engendered controversy. Those who urge changes in behavior, such as quitting smoking or reducing alcohol consumption, implicitly condemn chosen ways of living. The ascription of personal responsibility can be understood as an insult—and perhaps, if the target is a member of a particular class or ethnic group, a deeply resented insult. The behavior in question may be highly personal, as with sexually transmitted diseases. Health promotion can thus conflict with other deeply held values. In the guise of promoting health, moreover, the authorities may resort to coercion, setting up a conflict between the values of good health and personal liberty.

The politics of health promotion

Health promotion may be engaged in for purely benevolent reasons, but other motivations may be present. By singling out the individual as an agent of change, health promotion may become a substitute for government action on other determinants of ill health.

For example, "wellness" initiatives at the workplace, which involve such interventions as drug counseling and exercise and are marketed to employers as enhancing productivity and reducing costs, are conducted in isolation from traditional occupational safety and health programs that typically call for remedial action by the employer as well as the worker. Seen in the worst light, wellness programs generally call upon workers to adapt to unhealthy environments; the employees, not the employer, bear the burden of protection.

Health promotion can substitute for effective action in response to public pressure for governmental responses to health risks. In place of instituting prod-

HEALTH EDUCATION AND PERSONAL LIBERTY

Insofar as health promotion and health education are understood as alternatives to coercive regulation of behavior, they uphold rather than threaten the goal of self-determination. Indeed, education increases autonomy, for it points out consequences of one's behavior and the possible alternatives to it. There is a gray zone, however, between the innocuous provision of information and blatant coercion, and in this category are some of the tools used by health educators.

There may be no such thing as the neutral presentation of "facts," for some selection must be made among the facts, and this will be done with a goal in mind. Health education campaigns, however, differ in the extent to which neutrality is an ideal. Health educators may frequently manipulate the public

- by designing "education" programs that produce behavioral changes by inducing individuals to feel shame when contemplating the unhealthy behavior (as when smoking is paired with being a social outcast responsible for endangering others with passive smoke);
- by overestimating the risk faced by individuals in order to promote healthy behavior, as with attempts to secure voluntary vaccinations even where those who are not vaccinated are generally protected by the vast majority of individuals who are;
- by concealing the degree of behavioral change necessary to promote good health if full candor seems likely to result in total noncompliance (e.g., by recommending a reduction of fat consumption to 30 percent of daily caloric intake instead of a healthier 10 to 15 percent of intake).

Manipulative health promotion might be defended, sometimes successfully, on any number of grounds: the individual's benefit; the fact that the pressure is mild and easily resisted by those determined to take risks; and the fact that the behavior in question may not be voluntary to begin with. Nevertheless, recourse to manipulation forfeits the claim of being purely informative, and stands in need of justification.

— DANIEL WIKLER, DAN E. BEAUCHAMP

During the 1980s, more than 11 million—13% of the population—lost their health insurance.

PAGE 336

HEALTH PROMOTION AND HEALTH EDUCATION

Health Promotion and Other Values

uct-safety regulations, government can coach consumers to be careful in using the products; instead of restricting toxic substances, such as tobacco, government may simply warn the public not to abuse them. Reliance on health education permits the government to claim that it is taking action to preserve health, even while refraining from any genuinely effective action that would impinge on the interests of those who may be profiting from the unhealthy behavior. The very fact that health education is compatible with freedom of choice can camouflage this strategy: For many years, American automobile manufacturers successfully opposed regulations mandating such safety equipment as seatbelts and airbags, while driver education programs in the schools encountered little opposition.

Health promotion and health education can run afoul of persistent class and racial divisions. The newspaper of America's educated elite, the *New York Times*, in 1966 called cholera "the curse of the dirty, the intemperate, and the degraded." The beneficiaries of health education, on the other hand, are likely to be those who have access to it and who have the psychological disposition and practical opportunity to take advantage of it. In many cases, this has meant that public-health education campaigns have benefited mainly the middle and upper classes, who are healthier to begin with. Poor Americans are almost three times more likely than rich Americans to smoke, although the numbers were equal in 1960, before the antismoking campaigns began in earnest. Urgent public-health advice on avoiding AIDS has largely been heeded by well-educated gays, but has had much less impact on poor drug abusers. Correction of this class bias may require that the authorities choose between expending much greater sums to reach the poor, who may be difficult to reach, and diverting existing funds from education of the better-off, where results per dollar would have been greater.

◆ **health-care option, equal**

The option of specifying an optimal and affordable level of health care and then guarantee this level of health care to all legitimate claimants.

Health promotion and other values

The central objective of health promotion and health education is health, but the behavior targeted for change might be serving other valued ends. Indeed, the behavior promoted by health authorities may be offensive in its own right.

In the present era, the chief conflicts occur with AIDS. Provision of sterile needles for drug abusers can prevent the spread of AIDS in this vulnerable population, but to the extent that the difficulty of obtaining needles inhibits drug use, providing free needles may conflict with national drug policy; even if distributing free needles does not appear to increase drug abuse, some shrink from the alleged symbolic acceptance of drug use that providing needles may signal.

Promotion of safe sex, the key AIDS strategy (other than research toward a cure) of public-health authorities, has faced strong opposition. Supporters of traditional sexual mores dislike promotion of any sexual behavior other than that in marriage, even if the educators mention the superiority of abstinence. Condom use is specifically condemned by the Roman Catholic church, and in Latin America, where the church's influence is strong, public-health officials have had to fight AIDS in other ways. Even in the United States, squeamishness about sex has inhibited candid and direct public education on safe sexual practice; condom advertisements, for example, are still rare on television.

Ideologies of health promotion

Health promotion is a heterogeneous field, and there is no single ideology underlying its many manifestations. Perhaps the common element in all health promotion is the incontestable premise that health is valuable in its own right. No further motivation need be cited to explain the dedication and enthusiasm of health educators for their work.

Throughout its long history, however, health promotion has often been married to ideologies and fads of the day. Nineteenth-century American health promotion was linked to social Darwinism, while today it is often packaged with near-mystical faith in the power of attitudes and diet and the enshrinement of healthful living as a moral virtue.

The belief that individual beliefs, efforts, and attitudes can overcome nearly all threats to health, implicit in some contemporary health promotion, carries both the promise of freedom from disease and the burden of guilt and blame for those who do succumb. Although many authors who promote the concept of personal responsibility for health disavow any intent to penalize or stigmatize those who cannot or will not adopt healthful living habits, the promotion of "wellness" is coincident with increased resentment of those whose lifestyles impose financial and other costs on others. The individual who tries but fails to lose weight or stop smoking risks being burdened not only by increased risk of serious illness but also with a loss of sympathy and support. Eventually, the illness might incur resentment and, as in Butler's Erehwon, even punishment. Health educators face the challenge of pointing out the individual's contribution to his or her own disease and disability without unduly diverting attention from the contributions of both nature and the social environment.

— DANIEL WIKLER
DAN E. BEAUCHAMP

See Also
Public Health and the Law; Sexuality in Society

HEALTH SCREENING AND TESTING IN THE PUBLIC-HEALTH CONTEXT

Health screening, used predominantly to detect potential diseases in asymptomatic people, came into practice in the nineteenth century, when progressive reformers promoted the idea that adults should have regular precautionary medical examinations. Later the growing use of the automobile, which needed regular checkups, suggested that the human "machine," too, could benefit from regular inspection (Reiser, 1978).

The military employed health screening on a large scale during World War I to discover who should be disqualified from the draft (Yerkes, 1921). Tests were administered to establish both the medical suitability and the intellectual competency of potential draftees. Of the 2.7 million men called into service, 47 percent were found to have previously undetected physical impairments. Since many of these impairments could have been prevented, preventive health examinations became a major objective of public-health organizations in the 1920s, when syphilis was a major concern (Brandt, 1985). The initiative came primarily from consumers, but physicians, too, took an interest in mass screening programs, and the American Medical Association endorsed regular examinations for those "supposedly in health."

Interest in preventive health declined after the 1920s when the control of disease through mass screening appeared economically impractical, especially during the Great Depression. It revived again in the late 1950s and 1960s, when the federal government supported multiphasic screening programs that would identify a variety of conditions. These programs consisted of routine urine and blood tests and, in some circumstances, X rays and electrocardiograms. They became possible on a large scale with the introduction of efficient automated laboratory analyzers in the late 1960s (Rushmer and Huntsman, 1970). Subsequently, in the context of growing concern about national health-care costs, preventive screening has become increasingly important and, indeed, the basis for a burgeoning industry.

The screening of targeted groups has become a major aspect of predictive medicine, and the range of tests has expanded with technological advances. Adults believed to be vulnerable are routinely tested for their predisposition to diseases such as breast, colon, cervical, and prostate cancer and diabetes; for risk factors such as hypertension, cholesterol level, and HIV status; and for genetic diseases such as Tay-Sachs disease and sickle-cell anemia. Despite the expansion of testing, however, there has been limited development of tests for the specific conditions of women and minorities.

HEALTH SCREENING
Institutional Benefits

The growing availability of computers and automated diagnostic systems has encouraged the expansion of screening in many nonclinical contexts: for example, in the military, to test for drug abuse; in prenatal clinics, to test for genetic disease; in schools, to discover learning disabilities; and in the workplace, to define the health status of prospective employees. In these settings, however, tests have often focused on intelligence and personality traits, where indicators are less precise and predictions unreliable. The tests have included ALPHA, used in the military to test intelligence (Anastasi, 1976; Gould, 1981); the Minnesota Multiphasic Personality Inventory, used in industry for personality assessment (Friedman et al., 1989); and instruments such as the Statistical Assessment of Diagnostic Syndromes, for detecting psychopathology (Kaplan et al., 1991).

Individuals may benefit from the identification of a hidden health risk if there are available preventive strategies. But it is mainly institutions such as schools, employers, and insurers that stand to gain from better understanding of the present and future health status and behavioral syndromes of their clients. In these contexts, diagnostic screening is a means to facilitate planning and reduce costs by predicting future risks. Tests can provide predictive parameters for insurance companies designing premiums, for schools attempting to assess the potential of students before admitting them to lengthy and costly special-education programs, for health maintenance organizations seeking to anticipate the possible development of disease among their clients—indeed, for any organization concerned with problems of health and behavior that might contribute to future costs (Nelkin and Tancredi, 1989).

— DOROTHY NELKIN
LAURENCE TANCREDI

Assumptions underlying screening practices

The expansion of screening from clinical to nonclinical contexts is a source of growing controversy that must

◆ **carrier screening**
Methods to identify an otherwise healthy person who may be at high risk for having children with a severe genetic disorder.

See Also
Genetic Testing and Screening

be understood in terms of the nature and purpose of tests. Health screening differs from clinical diagnosis in significant ways. A clinical test is intended to obtain data about an individual's health status in response to a specific complaint. Accuracy of diagnosis is the primary goal. In contrast, health screening is intended to identify from a large population those individuals who in some way deviate from a statistically derived norm (Morton and Hebel, 1979). Individuals with latent conditions are identified as problematic because in the future they may be at risk for developing a serious condition (Thorner and Remein, 1961).

The use of diagnostic tests for public-health screening is directly linked to social or medical intervention through therapy, prevention, or exclusion. For example, genetic screening of potential carriers of Tay-Sachs disease (a hereditary disorder resulting in serious retardation and early death) is a way to identify those who may perpetuate the trait, in order to provide genetic counseling prior to pregnancy. Prenatal screening for genetic disorders is a way of providing parents with the option of terminating a pregnancy if the predicted condition is sufficiently serious (Elias and Annas, 1987). Genetic screening in the workplace is a way of identifying those predisposed to illness from exposure to toxic chemicals so as to prevent potential harm to the individual, which could lead to legal actions and compensation (Draper, 1991).

There are many public-health benefits to be gained by the expansion of screening of targeted groups with a suspected predisposition to specific diseases. Such screening may point the way to particular preventive or therapeutic measures. It can provide families with the opportunity to avoid the anxiety and cost of bearing a child with an untreatable disease. It can identify potential health or behavioral problems for remedial or preventive action through diet. It can help in the early recognition of learning-disabled children. It can protect vulnerable workers from exposure to toxic substances.

Nevertheless, screening has become increasingly controversial. This reflects, in part, discomfort regarding the significant possibilities for error—especially in screening programs involving large numbers of people, where there are many areas ripe for interpretive bias (Tversky and Kahneman, 1974). Interpreting tests involves assumptions about the accuracy and reliability of the instruments and about the validity of the theories relating biological conditions to their expression in disease. For example, screening for mental illness—in particular, schizophrenia—would be especially problematic in view of changing diagnostic criteria. Correlations can easily be misperceived as causation and exploited to meet economic or policy agendas. Some tests are so sensitive that they pick up indicators that may in fact have no predictive relevance, while others may miss relevant indicators.

The question of health care as a basic human right has been at the heart of the health-policy debate in the U.S.

PAGE 335

Such questions of uncertainty have different meanings in screening than they do in individual diagnosis. Because cost and administrative efficiency are essential in the effective screening of large populations, certainty is necessarily compromised, and the extent of compromise will depend on the purposes of a test. A high degree of false positives may be tolerated if the goal is to detect all cases of a condition—for example, in the early efforts of some companies to screen for drug abuse. In calibrating the level of acceptable diagnostic certainty, the goals of institutions may override the interests of affected individuals. This is the source of many of the ethical dilemmas inherent in screening practices.

Ethical issues

The problems of diagnostic uncertainty are greatest when a technology developed in the context of clinical care is transferred to another setting for use as a screening tool. This is the case when tests are used by the institutions that oversee health-care financing, education, or work. Genetic tests, such as those for sickle-cell anemia, were developed to help carriers of the disease make informed family-planning choices. But some of these tests have been used in the workplace to identify those susceptible to illness resulting from exposure to chemicals (U.S. Congress, Office of Technology Assessment, 1983). In this context they can limit opportunities, as when identified carriers are excluded from the military. Genetic information, mainly intended as a basis for genetic counseling, can be used to identify those at risk for a condition that may be too costly for an insurance plan (Karjala, 1992).

In a clinical situation, inconsistencies and errors are easily discovered because the purpose of a test is to discover the abnormalities underlying a single individual's overt symptoms. But when tests are used for screening purposes, or when the objective is to deduce statistical levels of disease in a large population, individual inconsistencies can remain undetected and the potential for misdiagnosis, with all its problematic consequences, is far greater. Moreover, the pressures for efficiency and cost control that encourage efforts to predict the potential diseases of a client population can overshadow the uncertainties of screening techniques. For example, test results that detect very small deviations, such as a minor amount of blood in urine or slightly high blood pressure, may have minimal consequences for a person's health but can be used to exclude that person from insurance or employment.

For the institution carrying out the screening test, a

low level of reliability may be adequate to meet its needs for long-term planning or for the allocation of resources. But for the individual being screened, errors may have very high costs. A false positive diagnosis of AIDS, for example, would be devastating, since persons falsely diagnosed as seropositive would experience not only emotional and psychological distress but also the social stigma attached to the disease. A test that identifies those with genetic vulnerability to heart disease may encourage a preventive lifestyle, but the prediction itself could affect a person's career. Tests have often been abused, serving not only as a basis for preventing harm but also as a means to justify racial or gender biases, to legitimate arbitrary exclusionary practices, and to enhance institutional power with little regard for the rights or personal fates of individuals (Duster, 1990).

The expansion of screening techniques and their extension outside the clinical context introduce a host of ethical dilemmas that are currently under debate: What is the institutional obligation to inform a person that his or her body fluids may be used for screening? Who has a right to know the information available from test results, and what is the bearing of such information on racial and gender discrimination? What are the obligations of an institution to inform the screened person of a positive result? Does the obligation extend to family members or other affected persons? How much reliance should be placed on screening for emotional and personality characteristics when indicators are relatively subjective? Is the use of blind screening for epidemiological studies ethically appropriate? Such questions will have to be addressed with the expansion of screening programs.

The potential abuses of public-health screening are beginning to generate legislative initiatives to assure the confidentiality of medical records and the protection of individual privacy (Westin, 1993); and there is increased awareness of the need to control institutional uses that would infringe on individual rights. Meanwhile, improvements in diagnostic predictability allow detection of very early biological changes, expanding the number of people defined as vulnerable, predisposed, or at risk. Measures to protect the public health are inextricably connected to the search for efficiency and cost-effective practices. Advances in screening technologies and their increasing use by diverse social institutions may expand the number of people considered uninsurable and unemployable. This could, in effect, create a genetic underclass—a class of individuals excluded from critical social benefits on the basis of their predicted biological characteristics.

— DOROTHY NELKIN
LAURENCE TANCREDI

HOMOSEXUALITY

CLINICAL AND BEHAVIORAL ASPECTS

In order to understand the clinical and behavioral aspects of homosexuality, it is important to recognize that terms such as homosexual, bisexual, and heterosexual are constructed within a sociopolitical and cultural climate. As this climate changes, our understanding of the meaning of such labels changes, too. This point is important for clinicians to keep in mind when assessing an individual's sexual orientation and in choosing the terms to describe it. Historically, clinicians have assessed sexual orientation (e.g., Kinsey et al., 1948) based upon the assumption that sexual orientation is determined by one's sex or genitalia and the sex or genitalia of the individual to whom one is erotically attracted. Many clinicians have also assumed that a person's sexual orientation is fixed and immutable.

Recent research, however, has challenged these assumptions. We now recognize that biological sex is only one of the many components of the attraction or orientation two individuals experience in relation to one another. Sexual orientation must be understood as multidimensional, incorporating the various components of a person's sexual identity (male or female physical characteristics, male or female gender identification, traditional masculine or feminine sex-role characteristics) and various dimensions of sexuality (behavior, fantasies, and emotional attachments). Recognizing multidimensional complexity, clinicians and their clients are finding that sexual orientation identities (homosexual, bisexual, and heterosexual) are no more important than any other single aspect of overall identity.

MY TWO DADS

Studies of influences of homosexual parents on children have looked more at lesbian couples than gay men.

H

HOMOSEXUALITY

Clinical and Behavioral Aspects

Beyond the illness paradigm

Since Alfred Kinsey's pioneering work in the 1940s and early 1950s, the association of homosexuality with illness has been gradually but thoroughly refuted by scientific research (see Gonsiorek, 1991, for a review of these studies). This scientific evidence led to the American Psychiatric Association's 1973 decision to declassify homosexuality per se as an illness in their diagnostic manual of mental disorders (DSM-II). Some psychiatrists still dispute whether this decision was based upon science or politics. The concept of illness was nevertheless retained (American Psychiatric Association, 1973) by the introduction of the disorder "ego-dystonic homosexuality" to describe individuals who had persistent homosexual desires but were troubled by them and desired a change in sexual orientation. This category was finally eliminated in DSM-III-R (American Psychiatric Association, 1987) and DSM-IV (American Psychiatric Association Task Force, 1991), but a vestige of the illness notion could still be found as an example of "Sexual Disorders Not Otherwise Specified" (DSM-IV, p. 538). But the fundamental change declassifying homosexuality per se as a mental disorder has been upheld in revisions of the DSM.

In spite of these changes in scientific opinion and the removal of homosexuality as a mental disorder, there is no complete consensus on this matter. Some professionals and laypeople still view homosexuality as the result of an abnormal process of development that is driven by some type of pathology (e.g., Aardweg, 1986; Society of Medical Psychoanalysts, 1988; Socarides, 1988).

The development of sexual identity and sexual identification

While the process of developing sexual identity is most probably a complex interaction of biopsychosocial influences of which we have very little understanding, theorists have developed various models that suggest that individuals acquire a homosexual identity in stages (e.g., Cass, 1979; Coleman, 1981-1982). The developmental stages illustrate how individuals who are pre-

THEORIES ON CAUSES

Is Homosexuality Genetic?

Many theories of the development of sexual orientation have been articulated, but no current one prevails. Traditional psychoanalytic theorists have believed that homosexuality is a result of childhood trauma that causes intrapsychic conflict and an arrested psychosexual development (e.g., Socarides, 1968, 1988); many psychoanalysts still hold this view. This traditional view of the cause of homosexuality has been challenged by many sexual scientists and by gay-identified and some other psychoanalysts. For example, the psychoanalyst Richard Isay (1989) believes that homosexuality is innate and influenced by prenatal biological influences.

Learning theorists and behavior therapists have traditionally seen homosexuality as a maladaptive learned behavior. Behaviorists hold the belief that sexual deviations are learned through operant and classical conditioning mechanisms.

Both psychoanalytic and behavioral theories have held that homosexuality is an illness or a maladaptive behavior. In contrast, John Money (1988), a sexologist who has studied the origins of sexual attractions for over forty years, believes that homosexuality is a normal variation of sexual expression and develops along a nature/critical period/nurture pathway (i.e., prenatal influences interact with environmental events at critical periods)—although the exact mechanisms are still unknown. In a major study of the development of sexual orientation, Alan Bell, Martin Weinberg, and Sue Hammersmith (1981) were unable to confirm any of the psychoanalytic or behavioral theories among their large sample of participants. While unable to find an environmental influence, the authors suggested that research might focus on biological factors to find the etiology heterosexuality and homosexuality.

In the 1980s and 1990s, a few studies focused on biological correlates (hormonal, neuroanatomical, genetic) of adult sexual orientation (Gladue et al., 1984; Swaab and Hoffman, 1990; LeVay, 1991), and a few studies identified a substantial genetic component (Bailey and Pillard, 1991; Bailey et al., 1993). These studies attracted significant media attention and have promoted a belief in biological factors as the basis of sexual orientation.

Without solid replication studies, the relative influence of biological factors is still unclear (Coleman et al., 1989). If these recent findings follow other biological research in the complex area of human sexuality, William Byne and Bruce Parsons have argued, answers regarding a biological cause of homosexuality are unlikely in the near future (Byne and Parsons, 1993).

Apart from the contributions such biological studies may make to our understanding of how we come to be the sexual persons we are—whether hetero-, bi-, or homosexual—their findings have significant implications for how society treats persons identified as homosexual. Some argue that if "biology made them do it," homosexual men and women cannot be held responsible for their behavior, should not be seen as morally depraved, and should be given the same legal and social rights as heterosexual individuals. But some people fear that evidence of a biological basis will strengthen the hand of those who would use medical or psychological treatment to correct the biological "mistake" of homosexuality.

— ELI COLEMAN

dominantly homosexual construct their identity in a positive, self-affirming manner, despite living in a society that stigmatizes homosexuality.

After a period of confusion and a sense of "differentness," an individual adopts a homosexual label and begins a process of exploring his or her sexual identity and sexual relationships, learning about intimacy, and finally reaching a stage of self-acceptance and integration (Coleman, 1981-1982). Adopting the label "gay," "lesbian," or "bi" is often a means of developing more positive attitudes about one's homosexual behavior and identity. These labels are positively construed and help counteract negatively construed labels such as "faggot," "dyke," and "queer." Although this process of identity formation is similar for men and women, sex-role socialization makes for gender differences. Men are likely to experience more sexual relationships during their exploration stage and women are more likely to define their identity based upon awareness of their emotional attachments (Coleman, 1981-1982).

The psychological problems that homosexual men and women face result from social stigma rather than from their sexual orientation. The effects of stigmatization on psychological well-being are well understood. As long as homosexuality is stigmatized in a society, homosexual men and women are at risk for psychological maladjustment, impaired psychosocial development, family alienation, inadequate interpersonal relationships, alcohol and drug abuse, and depression and suicidal ideation, in addition to the inevitable anxiety about AIDS and other sexually transmitted diseases (Coleman, 1988). Conversely, affirming sexual diversity is linked to psychological and physical health. Social attitudes profoundly affect individuals with same-sex attractions either by assisting them in the development of a positive and integrated sexual identity or by thwarting such development. Psychotherapy is often needed to help individuals whose development has been thwarted by negative societal attitudes.

Medical and social attitudes toward homosexuality

Medical professionals have participated in the widespread discrimination against individuals who identify themselves as gay or lesbian. In one study of 1,000 physicians, three-quarters acknowledged that knowing that a male patient was homosexual would adversely affect their medical management (Pauly and Goldstein, 1970). More recent studies are lacking, but there is anecdotal evidence that irrational fears of homosexuality and negative attitudes toward homosexuality among physicians compromise comprehensive and quality health care of homosexual men and women. On the other hand, as more and more physicians acknowledge their homosexuality to their colleagues, it becomes increasingly difficult for the latter to maintain discriminatory attitudes and irrational fears, at least openly. It is more difficult to hold these attitudes and views about people one knows and respects than about a class of people or abstractions of people portrayed in the media. Some professional medical organizations have taken active responsibility to help dispel prejudice. The American Academy of Pediatrics (1983), for example, has provided a positive policy statement:

> *Teenagers, their parents, and community organizations with which they interact may look to the pediatrician for clarification of the medical and social issues involved when the question or fact of adolescent homosexual practices arises. . . . The American Academy of Pediatrics recognizes the physician's responsibility to provide health care for homosexual adolescents and for those young people struggling with the problems of sexual expression.* (pp. 249–250)

These changes in the medical world reflect societal changes. Numerous social, political, and religious organizations have legitimized homosexual behavior. New laws in some cities and states of the United States and in other Western countries prohibit discrimination based on homosexual behavior or sexual orientation. Personnel policies of many corporations prohibit discrimination on the basis of sexual orientation. Public and private institutions provide health-care and other personnel benefits to the partners of gay men and lesbians (Jefferson, 1994). At the same time, antihomosexual prejudice and discriminatory practices persist. Even as the civil rights of gay and lesbian persons are explicitly guaranteed, there has been an escalation in the number of "hate crimes" against people identified as gay or lesbian. Unfortunately, society still struggles with accepting its diversity. However, the overall social trend indicates less fear, prejudice, bigotry, and discrimination and greater understanding and respect for individual differences.

Ethical issues in psychological or psychiatric treatment

The ethical issues in the treatment of gay men and lesbians are for the most part no different from the ethical issues a psychotherapist encounters in treating those who seek his or her help. The issue of "conversion" to heterosexuality remains an ethical issue principally for those who view homosexuality as an illness. There is no evidence that adults sustain long-term change in sexual orientation through therapy (Coleman, 1978). Behavior modification, for example, has had limited success and is generally not sustainable over time. Still, some individuals who have homosexual attractions seek a "conversion" to heterosexuality. Parents who are concerned that their children might be gay or lesbian often will encourage them to seek

In 1973 the APA formally abandoned the view that homosexuality was necessarily pathological.

PAGE 255

See Also
Domestic Partnerships: Some Historical Reflections

psychotherapy to ensure a heterosexual outcome. And some therapists continue to accept patients into therapy with the goal of changing their sexual orientation. But authorities have rejected pursuit of these goals of treatment as unscientific, unjustified, unethical, and psychologically scarring (Gonsiorek, 1988; Isay, 1989). Nevertheless, some psychoanalysts still consider it possible to change a person's sexual orientation and see pursuing this goal as ethical as long as the individual desires this change (Aardweg, 1986; Society of Medical Psychoanalysts, 1988; Socarides, 1988). This issue remains controversial.

In reviewing this ethical controversy, Gerald C. Davidson, one of the pioneers of "conversion therapy" who used behavior therapy approaches, concluded:

> *Change of orientation therapy programs should be eliminated. Their availability only confirms professional and societal biases against homosexuality, despite seemingly progressive rhetoric about its normalcy. Forsaking the reorientation option will encourage therapists to examine the life problems of some homosexuals, rather than focusing on the so-called problem of homosexuality.* (1982, pp. 97–98)

It remains a matter of debate whether the extinguishing of unwanted traits is a legitimate objective for medicine.

PAGE 255

Consequently, most therapists focus upon improving the psychological and interpersonal functioning of homosexual men and women rather than on changing their sexual orientation (e.g., Coleman, 1988; Friedman, 1988; Isay, 1989).

But the issue of sexual orientation is not moot. Because sexual orientation is still salient to overall identity, psychotherapists can and do help people define themselves in terms of their sexual orientation, recognize and value the complexity of that sexual orientation, and further their overall sexual identity development and satisfaction.

Health professionals can create for their patients an atmosphere in which sexuality can be discussed openly. By raising the issue of sexual orientation, related problems and concerns can be addressed and resolved. Health professionals' attitudes toward homosexuality greatly influence their ability to be helpful. They, too, are affected by societal attitudes and values concerning homosexuality. And, while some health professionals hold intellectually positive attitudes, their emotional responses can hinder them from conveying full acceptance and from encouraging the exploration of a positive and integrated homosexual identity.

Psychotherapists are sometimes called upon to offer opinions to clients or to appear as expert witnesses in family courts that are assessing whether homosexual men and women are fit parents. Most of the research in this area pertains to lesbian mothers and their children and has been extrapolated to gay men. There has been no evidence that children develop sexual orientation conflict, intra- or interpersonal conflict, or any other significant mental-health concern when raised by their lesbian mothers in the absence of the biological father (see Kirkpatrick, 1988, for a review of these studies). Given the continued societal stigma of homosexuality, however, these children, like gay and lesbian individuals, are especially vulnerable to societal stressors. Further research (especially longitudinal) is needed in this area because of the growing number of gay, lesbian, and bisexual individuals who are choosing to become parents through adoption and foster care or through retaining custody of their biological children.

See Also
Treating Homosexuality: Social Attitudes in the Looking Glass

Another ethical issue involves the objectivity and the capacity for empathy and understanding of a clinician having a certain sexual orientation. Should the sexual orientation of the clinician be a factor in selecting a health-care provider? Further, should a clinician disclose his or her sexual orientation as part of the therapeutic process? There is little scientific research on which to base consideration of these questions. Training and experience should probably be the most salient variables in selecting a clinician—regardless of the client's sexual orientation. Self-disclosure is a therapeutic intervention and should be applied when it seems to be in the client's best interest and to have potential therapeutic value. By following these general ethical principles of health care, the clinician can resolve these ethical dilemmas.

— ELI COLEMAN

ETHICAL ISSUES

Scientists and historians have produced a large body of research that has significantly improved our understanding of all aspects of homosexuality. Despite this research, the precise definition of homosexuality is still controversial. One approach to the problem of definition distinguishes four components of sexual identity: biological sex, gender identity, social sex role, and sexual orientation (Gonsiorek and Weinrich, 1991). (For alternative definitions of sexual identity, gender identity, or gender identity/role, and discussion of terminological divergence; see Pleck, 1981; Weinrich, 1987; Money, 1986, 1988; Friedman, 1988.)

Sex researchers generally agree that no necessary relationship exists among the components of sexual or gender identity. Homosexuals as a group are unique only in their sexual orientation; they are erotically attracted to members of their own sex. Strong evidence that erotic attraction is relatively permanent after a critical period early in a person's life has led scientists to adopt the term "sexual orientation." The term "sexual preference" implies greater volitional capacity to change erotic disposition than seems to exist (Green, 1988).

Although the bipolar distinction between homosexuality and heterosexuality has heuristic value in describing behavior, it is not adequate to understand the complexity of sexual orientation. There are some persons who are bisexual in the sense that they are able to respond erotically to qualities in their partners regardless of biological sex. Current thinking recognizes that sexual orientation is multidimensional and specific to the person (Money, 1986).

Moral disagreement about homosexuality can be traced to different interpretations of the facts, different definitions of the meaning and scope of concepts, and different assumptions in ethical theory about what constitutes good sexuality and right sexual conduct. Disagreements are often difficult to clarify and resolve because of unacknowledged differences in factual interpretation, the meaning of concepts, and ethical theory. Many moral disagreements might be resolved by information if the reason for the disagreement is only factual or conceptual. But no amount or kind of information will resolve a disagreement if the reason for the disagreement is a fundamental difference in ethical assumptions.

Premodern approaches

Premodern European society did not evaluate the goodness or badness of homosexuality in terms of sexual orientation. People may have recognized that categories of persons with a homosexual orientation exist, but they did not attach moral significance to the categories or their mutability. Sexuality was evaluated in terms of its expression in prescribed social roles and behaviors.

In ancient Greece, various patterns of same-sex intimacy were permitted and in some cases prescribed. For example, in the city-state of Athens, during the classical period and among the educated, good homosexuality was defined as a tutorial relationship between an older and a younger male citizen of equal status, expressed through intercrural (between the thighs) "intercourse." Sexual activity between persons of the same age was sometimes cause of laughter. In Sparta, however, pairs of soldiers were often lovers (Dover, 1980; Lewis, 1983; Halperin, 1989).

The early Christian approach did not depart from the Greek and Roman practice of evaluating sexuality in terms of social role and not in terms of the biological sex of the persons in a relationship. Christian criticisms were directed at promiscuous forms of sexual expression or ones that involved participation in idolatrous cultic practices. Christian constraints on sexuality probably were related to the assumption, also present in Hellenistic culture, that sex is a potentially dangerous force requiring careful control. Celibacy was seen either as an ideal or as the best option for those who could not control their sexuality. For others, regardless of erotic disposition, sexuality should be confined to relationships marked by permanence and fidelity.

The history of Christian sexual ethics can be understood as a development of restrictions on the role of sexuality and not as a radical departure from previ-

MORAL ISSUES
Basic Questions

In evaluating homosexuality, moral philosophers assume that the questions we are trying to answer are moral questions. We make many judgments that do not seem to be morally significant: For example, "That is a good television." Or, "You should tie your right shoe before your left." Such judgments may have practical importance in our daily lives, but they do not necessarily involve moral matters. Our task, then, is to determine why and under what circumstances homosexuality is a moral matter.

The distinction between homosexual orientation and behavior implies two general questions, one concerning the quality of being and the other the quality of action: Is homosexuality morally good sexuality? What kinds of homosexual activity, if any, are morally right? We cannot simply assume that all judgments about homosexual orientation and behavior are moral judgments. An ethical theory is required in order to decide which judgments about homosexuality are moral judgments.

These general questions involve the good and the right, two basic ethical concepts. Ethical theories provide a structural definition of the relationship between value (the good) and obligation (right and wrong conduct). How the basic concepts of good and right are defined and related determines the structure of an ethical theory. Structurally, ethical theories can be divided into either teleological or deontological types. In teleological theories, some nonmoral good or value (e.g., pleasure, health, or happiness) is defined independently of the right. Right is based on the good, that is, the promotion or maximization of this value. In deontological theories, the good is not defined independently of the right. Right depends on some characteristic of an action itself (e.g., that it can be universalized or that it involves appropriate treatment of persons).

—LOUIS TIETJE
JAMES HARRISON

◆ **homosexual**
A person who is erotically attracted to members of the same sex.

See Also
Sex in Antiquity: Same-Sex Relationships

ous views. The most restrictive position, that only a sexual act with procreative purpose could be sinless, existed early in Christian thought. The development is toward a gradual elimination of all other possibilities. This position "gradually spread throughout the Christian world and became the favored position of ascetics in the West since it both limited sexuality to the smallest possible arena and appealed to an easily articulated and understood principle. Ultimately, it became the standard of Catholic orthodoxy, although hardly inevitably: Not for a millennium after it first appeared did it sweep all other approaches before it." (Boswell, 1990, pp. 18-19. See also Boswell, 1980, for a detailed historical analysis.)

Natural-law theory

Thomas Aquinas (1225-1274) gave the restrictive position its most systematic theoretical formulation. His argument rests on two assumptions. His implicit assumption is that good sexuality cannot be determined by asking what social role sexuality plays in human affairs. His explicit theological assumption is that the world was created and is governed by divine reason. Human beings participate in divine reason through their own reason, which gives them access to the eternal law, the natural law, or God's plan for the world.

We can uncover God's sexual plan by asking what the purpose, goal, or function of sexuality is. Aquinas argued that the purpose of sexuality is reproduction or procreation. Sexual activities are natural if they fulfill this purpose and thus accord with the eternal or natural law. All nonprocreative sexual activities are unnatural (Aquinas, 1980).

Critics of natural-law theory do not challenge the view that procreation and interpersonal love are purposes of sexuality or deny that these purposes are good. Rather, they challenge limiting good sexuality to these purposes. A theological commitment to physical and biological complementarity is the only justification for the limitation. This limitation disavows the spiritual dimension of a loving relationship that may be possible for all persons, regardless of sexual orientation. (McNeill, 1976, 1988. See Batchelor, 1980, for a selection of traditional Roman Catholic and Protestant positions and critiques based on various moral norms in the scriptural tradition.)

In sum, premodern European ethical thought appears to begin with the question, "What is good sexuality?" Sexual orientation probably did not exist as a concept. The goodness or badness of sexuality was evaluated according to prescribed social roles. The biological sex of persons in a sexual relationship was not a primary consideration until Aquinas shifted the focus of evaluation from social role to an account of natural

Lesbian relations in ancient Greece counted as adultery, since women belonged to their husbands.

PAGE 642

See Also
Natural Law

NATURAL-LAW THEORY
Challenges and Responses

The argument from natural law has faced two major challenges. The first is a challenge to the idea that procreative purpose is disclosed in the design of the sexual organs. Skeptics point out that most organs of the body have multiple purposes. A mouth is used for the purpose of speaking, eating, and tasting. Which of these is its proper function? The design of the sexual organs includes a large concentration of nerve endings that provide pleasurable sensations. Why is the production of pleasure not a proper function of the sexual organs? A second challenge concerns the implication that interpersonal purposes of sexuality are not proper purposes. Why should the purpose of expressing affection, nurturance, or love of one person for another be excluded as proper purposes?

Modern traditional Roman Catholic theologians have responded to these challenges by expanding the range of proper purposes to cover interpersonal love as well as procreation. They have not conceded, however, that the expanded range of purposes extends beyond the context of fidelity in heterosexual marriage or to persons of the same sex. Homosexuals are excluded because their sexual relationships cannot include physical complementarity, "the structural and systemic receptivity of the female vagina for the male sexual organ," and biological complementarity, "the mutual contribution of male and female to the procreation of new life" (Hanigan, 1988, p. 87). That persons of the same sex do express love for each other in a sexual act and do have committed relationships is not given moral significance because these are not relationships of physical and biological complementarity. Physical and biological differences are given moral significance because they have been interpreted in a theological framework of complementarity. These modes of complementarity disclose to human reason God's purposes for sexuality. Celibacy is the only moral option for homosexuals, even if sexual orientation is immutable (Hanigan, 1988).

—LOUIS TIETJE
JAMES HARRISON

purpose. It was assumed that all individuals could participate in prescribed social roles and voluntarily control their sexual behaviors. The question of the mutability of sexual orientation, therefore, did not arise. Premodern ethical thought was teleological in structure. Right or wrong sexual conduct depended on an answer to the prior question of good sexuality. Aquinas did not change the structure of ethical reasoning in premodern Europe. He only changed the basis for the answer.

Modern approaches

Modern ethical theories emerged in a context of social instability and religious intolerance and warfare. John Locke (1632-1704) suggested a solution to religious and moral disagreement that became the foundation of constitutional democracies in the West. Locke believed that, as a moral minimum, rational people agree that individuals have rights to life, liberty, and property. He proposed that the rules of social and political life be based on this consensus. His solution means that, in the course of their cooperative endeavors, individuals must be willing to exercise considerable tolerance of religious and moral opinions outside this minimal consensus (Locke, 1980).

The theoretical assumption of Locke's proposal is that liberty is the fundamental moral characteristic of individuals. Individual liberty is natural, since it exists prior to and independent of particular social laws and customs. Individual rights to life, liberty, and justly obtained property are grounded in this moral assumption. The existence of individual rights implies the existence of obligations to respect these rights. Rights entail obligations to refrain from interfering with individual liberty. The conviction that individuals have a right to live as they choose, compatible with the same right of all other individuals, is central to all natural-rights theories.

In the natural-rights approach, individuals are free to choose the sexual activities in which they want to participate. A wide variety of these activities is morally right, or at least morally neutral. Only those activities that are coercive or injurious to others are morally wrong. Coercive or injurious sexual activities violate the rights of others. Sexual conduct that violates individual rights, not an evaluation of good sexuality, is morally significant. Natural-rights theories are deontological. Right and wrong homosexual conduct depends on free consent and respect for the rights of others.

The natural-rights perspective has been called "libertarian," not to be confused with "libertine." In this tradition, it is not as if anything goes. It is true that libertarians define a wide zone of permissible sexual behavior. For libertarians, the normative question of good sexuality is important, although the answer is left to individual choice. Homosexual activities that violate individual rights, however, are clearly wrong. The major problem for libertarians is how and under what circumstances to limit sexual conduct between consenting adults. (An example of a contemporary libertarian approach to homosexuality is Mohr, 1988, 1994.)

The theory of Immanuel Kant (1724-1804) is also deontological in structure and coincides with the libertarian supposition that right and wrong sexual conduct does not depend on an independent evaluation of good sexuality. Kant, however, did not argue from the primacy of individual rights. Rather, he argued that moral judgments depend on a maxim of action determined by the categorical imperative: "Act only according to that maxim by which you can at the same time will that it should become a universal law" (Kant, 1959, p. 39).

Kant concluded that homosexual conduct is morally wrong because it cannot be universalized without contradiction. Perhaps he reached this conclusion by reasoning that the universalization of homosexual conduct involves the exclusion of heterosexual intercourse. If all persons were homosexual, the human species would not survive (Kant, 1963).

Many Kantian philosophers think that Kant's reasoning in condemnation of homosexuality is flawed and that the universalization formula does not support his conclusion. They maintain that the distinctive content of Kantian ethics is contained in another formulation: "Act so that you treat humanity, whether in your own person or in that of another, always as an end and never as a means only" (Kant, 1959, p. 47).

According to this formulation, respect for autonomy is the standard of moral evaluation. Sexual orientation in itself is not a moral issue. For either heterosexuals or homosexuals, the danger is that a person in an erotic relationship will be objectified and will be used merely as a means to another's end. The end might include a desire to control, manipulate, dominate, or simply to experience sexual pleasure. In any of these instances, persons are not treated as ends in themselves. The Kantian understanding is expressed in the judgment that sexual relationships ought to be characterized by mutual respect, trust, and love. Another judgment—that using persons as sex objects is dehumanizing and morally wrong—expresses the same Kantian position on how persons ought to be treated.

The Kantian and natural-rights approaches concur that voluntary, free consent in sexual relationships is a moral minimum, but, for Kantians, free consent is not sufficient. The way in which persons treat each other is also morally significant. A Kantian could not sanction a mutual agreement between persons to use each other only as a means to sexual pleasure, even if the agree-

"Act only according to that maxim by which you can at the same time will that it should become a universal law."
IMMANUEL KANT

ment were entered into freely. Kantians are therefore inclined to see permanence, stability, and commitment as conditions of the proper treatment of persons in sexual relationships. Anonymous sex is suspect. (See O'Neill, 1985 for a contemporary Kantian interpretation.)

Since modern utilitarian theories are teleological in structure, they must answer the question of what nonmoral value defines good sexuality. Jeremy Bentham (1724-1832) undoubtedly imagined that this question is not difficult to answer. He thought that pleasure is a value everyone accepts. Sexual activities that promote pleasure are right; those that promote pain are wrong. Bentham's approach suggests that homosexuality cannot be bad sexuality because many people take pleasure in homosexual activities. He would agree with libertarians and Kantians that sexual orientation itself is not a morally significant issue (Bentham, 1984).

Some commentators have argued that sexual-orientation therapy is immoral because it contributes to social prejudice against gays and lesbians.

PAGE 255

Even in his own time, Bentham's simple answer to the question of right conduct was met with criticism. The value of pleasure may be a sufficient criterion for animals, but not for human beings. Bentham's concept of sensuous pleasure seemed too narrow. John Stuart Mill (1806-1873) agreed that elementary sensuous pleasures such as eating, drinking, and sexuality are valuable to humans. But he noted that, as creatures with higher-order faculties, they also take pleasure in a variety of intellectual, aesthetic, and social activities. Mill argued that happiness, defined in terms of both lower- and higher-order pleasures, is the inclusive norm of the good for humans on the basis of which right and wrong conduct ought to be evaluated (Mill, 1979). Mill's amendment, however, does not alter Bentham's apparent position on the moral significance of sexual orientation.

Mill believed that freedom is a constituent element of happiness. He was antipaternalistic, arguing that, as a matter of law and public policy, government should not limit what might be considered behavior harmful to self. He argued that only behavior harmful to others is the basis for limiting individual liberty (Mill, 1978). In affirming Mill's harm principle, libertarians and utilitarians are classical liberals. Either can support the recommendation of the English Wolfenden Report in the 1950s to lift the legal ban on homosexual activities between consenting adults in private.

Utilitarians, however, confront a major problem in defining what counts as harm. This difficulty is illustrated in English judge Patrick Devlin's famous response to the Wolfenden Report. Lord Devlin did not dispute Mill's harm principle, but he argued that society's deeply felt moral revulsion is also a valid reason for the legal restriction of homosexual behavior, even between consenting adults in private. Disagreement over the definition of harm has been repeated in a number of court cases. The United States Supreme Court case of *Bowers* v. *Hardwick* (1986), in which the Court upheld Georgia's sodomy statute, is a good example. In this case, the Court supported its majority ruling by appealing to an alleged consensus in the Judeo-Christian tradition on the immorality of homosexuality and its presumed threat to the American family as the legitimate basis of legal restriction. (For a critical analysis of the issues raised by Lord Devlin's response to the Wolfenden Report, see Feinberg, 1990, Chapter 30; see also Mohr, 1988, especially Chapters 2 and 3.) Seidman (1992) outlines a "pragmatic formalistic sexual ethic" based on moral criteria of consent and responsibility for the consequences of sexual acts. Seidman's proposal begins with minimal libertarian and utilitarian criteria of individual free choice and harm to other individuals but expands their meaning and scope to take account of the interrelational, social-communitarian context in which individuals act. His proposal is designed for what has been called the "postmodern" situation, in which a plurality of moral approaches exists and moral disagreement prevails.

The medical model

The advance of modern science and medicine opened the possibility of evaluating homosexuality in nonreligious and nonmoral terms. In the nineteenth century, physicians such as Sigmund Freud, Magnus Hirschfeld, and Carl Westphal thought that this new evaluation would help rather than hurt persons whose sexual practices departed from accepted norms (McWhirter et al., 1990; Bullough and Bullough, 1993). The terms changed from "good," "bad," "right," and "wrong" to "health," "disease," "illness," and "pathology." This change created a new debate over the value-neutrality of medical categories. The debate has been conducted theoretically and in the context of scientific research. Theoretically, the burden of proof seems to be on those who advocate that categories of health and disease are objective and value-neutral in light of modern historical awareness of cultural and cross-cultural diversity.

Some contemporary heterosexual couples choose not to be married because they want to avoid state intervention into their interpersonal relationship, not because they lack commitment to each other or an intention to parent. Similarly, many lesbians and gay men choose committed relationships that at this time are not sanctioned by the state. Some lesbians and gay men also choose to become surrogate parents or to parent through adoption or alternative insemination. In addition, numerous married persons of both sexes who are already effective parents realize their homosexual orientation later in life and redefine their conjugal relationships while continuing to affirm their parental

IS IT AN ILLNESS? The Value-Neutral Perspective

Christopher Boorse is often cited as one of the most articulate recent spokespersons for the value-free position (Boorse, 1987). His position resembles natural-law theory in that what appears to be a value-neutral, descriptive state of affairs is grounded in an answer to the question of purpose or function.

In Boorse's account, the natural and the normal are associated with health, and abnormality and pathology are associated with disease. For Boorse, definite standards of health can be identified by reference to the full number of biological capacities members of the human species possess on average. These capacities are defined by their functional contribution to survival and reproduction. Diseases represent some deficiency in, or lack of, functional capacity. Boorse advises us to distinguish between disease and illness. Disease is a descriptive biological concept; illness is a value judgment of desirability. A person whose reproductive organs are deficient has a disease. Classifying this person as ill is a value judgment.

Boorse concludes that exclusive homosexuality is probably a form of pathology, which apparently means a functional disease, because of reproductive failure. This conclusion, however, is difficult to understand. Although sexual orientation is not chosen, homosexuals, heterosexuals, and celibates may choose their reproductive behavior. Heterosexuals may choose not to have children without a diagnosis of functional incapacity.

—LOUIS TIETJE
JAMES HARRISON

responsibility. It seems that in the final analysis, Boorse's distinction between disease and illness, at least concerning homosexuality, collapses into a subjective judgment of desirability. (For a positive, sociobiological interpretation of the ways in which gay men and lesbians may have contributed to survival, reproduction, and parenting in the human species, see Weinrich, 1987. See also Ruse, 1985, 1988.)

Researchers, using accepted measures of mental disorder, have not found valid evidence that homosexuality per se is related to psychopathology or psychological adjustment. (For a review of the evidence, see Gonsiorek, 1991.) This does not mean that there are no psychologically disturbed homosexuals or that no homosexuals are disturbed by their sexual orientation. It would be unusual if some homosexuals did not experience psychological distress in an environment of negative stigma and social prejudice. Research has uncovered more alcohol and drug abuse, attempted suicides, use of mental health services, and troubled adolescent years in a subgroup of gay and lesbian people. Nevertheless, those who survive the stigma may demonstrate a trend toward superior adjustment (Hooker, 1957; Harrison, 1987; Gonsiorek and Rudolph, 1991).

Developmental issues

Although scientific research does not support a connection between homosexual orientation and psychopathology or psychological adjustment, many people continue to believe that homosexuality is a problem. As parents, they hope that their children will grow up to be heterosexual and worry about why they might not. At the same time, many parents think that sexuality is a topic children should not be aware of until they mature enough to understand and manage it. Paradoxically, it is not assumed that heterosexuality develops naturally, but its development is precarious and may be derailed by minimal interference (Pleck, 1981).

In our society, therefore, all the developmental questions are related to a single concern about how sexual identity and orientation are influenced. The first question involves the influence of homosexual parents on their biological or adopted children. There is reason to believe that the biological children of homosexual parents are more likely to be homosexual than children whose parents are heterosexual (Kirsch and Weinrich, 1991). However, the sexual orientation of adoptive children raised by homosexual parents seems to reflect the same distribution rates as sexual orientation in the population (Green and Bozett, 1991). Children of any sexual orientation raised in happy and secure environments tend to share the values and beliefs of their parents. Children raised in unhappy homes either identify with or develop reaction formations against violent parental behavior and negative or prejudicial parental values and opinions.

Another question involves the influence of teachers on the sexual orientation of their children. Teachers may be competent, benevolent, and heterosexual, but, despite great respect and admiration, students do not emulate the sexual orientation of their teachers. There is no known instance of a student's becoming homosexual because of identification with a teacher.

However, the needs of young people who have emerging homosexual identities are rarely considered. Instead of receiving sympathetic attention and accurate information about how to live responsible lives with homoerotic desire, they are often given inaccurate

Despite the temptation to designate all human beings as either male or female, sexual diversity is not easily confined by those simple categories.

PAGE 25

information, encouraged to feel ashamed of their emotions, and expected to take responsibility for sexual desire, which is not under their conscious control. Most homosexual teachers are so fearful of the accusation of inappropriate conduct that they are likely to abandon the perceived needs of some of their students to avoid the accusation.

Another question frequently asked is, "Does seduction by an adult influence the sexual orientation of a young person?" Since one of the terms for intergenerational sex in our language is "pederasty," the background of this question may be some awareness of the educational context of homosexual expression in Classical Athens. There is no evidence to support the view that seduction alone affects sexual orientation. Clinicians report that many young people say they would like to be seduced by an admired adult, and some say they initiated sexual activity with an older person (Silverstein, 1977, 1981).

Sexual-orientation therapy is an opportunity to consider what such therapy suggests about a society's understanding of gender.

PAGE 255

People also wonder if influencing the "feminine" or "masculine" characteristics of children might alter sexual orientation. Developmental research indicates that most "feminine" boys grow up to be homosexual men. Similar studies on women are not available, perhaps because greater tolerance of "tomboy" behavior in girls exists in our society (Green, 1987; Friedman, 1988). Research does not support the efficacy of early intervention to influence the development of a heterosexual orientation in "feminine" boys. However, clinical evidence suggests that early intervention with "feminine" boys who are having difficulty in social adjustment is effective in helping them develop self-esteem, a wide range of coping skills, and satisfactory peer relationships (Coates, 1992; Coates and Wolf, 1994).

In ordinary cases, all moral theories assume that moral agents are normal, competent adults who are able to deliberate rationally about alternative courses of action and control their behavior in a way that is typical for members of the society as a whole. Decisions and control shift to surrogates for individuals who do not meet typical standards. Moral theories cannot tell us when, in fact, individuals are rational and capable of controlling their behavior. For this reason, the age of consent is in some sense arbitrary and has changed historically.

In the case of children, and young people before the age of consent, parents are usually the surrogates. In our society, the natural-rights tradition is the origin of the minimal moral criterion of individual free choice for competent adults and surrogates. By extension, the autonomy of the family, for practical purposes, is considered to be a sacrosanct zone. We are reluctant to authorize the state to interfere in family affairs except in extreme cases of neglect or harm. Short of neglect or harm, parents should have the right to raise their children in the way they choose, transmit the values they uphold, decide how their children should be educated, and decide how and when children should be treated medically and psychotherapeutically.

Kantians, utilitarians, and natural-law theorists support the minimal criterion of free choice. These theorists, however, do not believe that the minimal criterion is sufficient. They add an additional moral criterion of respect or some concept of the good. The problem is what additional moral criteria can be imposed, and under what circumstances, on all members of a democratic society. This problem becomes acute and a matter of dispute in public institutions such as education because parents fear that the values they want to transmit or the ways in which they have parented their children in the home will be negatively influenced by teachers and other adults who are surrogate role models.

Most of the influences that some parents fear are not supported by scientific evidence. For healthy development, children require loving and supportive environments, at home and in public institutions with surrogates. Beyond this, scientists cannot tell us how to ensure that children become heterosexual or homosexual, even if one outcome or another is desired by the parent. What scientists do know, however, is that neglectful, violent, or punitive parental behavior—that is, behavior most people consider harmful to any person—is likely to damage the psychosexual development of children and deny a child the possibility of loving, intimate interpersonal adult relationships, regardless of sexual orientation.

"Diagnosis" and "treatment"

Recognizing a need to amplify the World Health Organization's *International Classification of Diseases* for the practice of psychiatry in the United States, the American Psychiatric Association began production of a series of diagnostic manuals. The first edition of its *Diagnostic and Statistical Manual of Mental Disorders* (DSM, 1952) was essentially a compilation of diagnostic categories used by practicing psychiatrists at the time. The second edition was a more comprehensive and better-organized manual based on psychoanalytic theory, broadly defined. (See Friedman, 1988, for a sympathetic critique of the psychoanalytic tradition informed by social science research.)

The association was challenged by gay activists and some psychiatrists and psychologists such as George Weinberg, Judd Marmor, Richard Pillard, and Charles Silverstein to recognize that categorizing homosexuality as a personality disorder or sexual deviation in the first two editions of its manual had no scientific basis. In the third edition, the association attempted to circumvent the debate over the value-neutrality of concepts of health and disease by developing a phenomenological, atheoretical, nosological system. Homosexuality was declassified as a mental disorder, but, in order to account for the experience of persons who have difficulty affirming their sexual orientation, the concept of ego-dystonic homosexuality was retained and defined as "a sustained pattern of overt homosexual arousal that the individual explicitly states has been unwanted and a persistent source of distress" (DSM-III, 1980, p. 281). In this edition, the remaining sexual deviations were called "paraphilias," in which "unusual or bizarre imagery or acts are necessary for sexual excitement" (DSM-III, 1980, p. 266). For an historical account of the highly politicized classification debates, see Bayer, 1987; see also Conrad and Schneider, 1992. In a revision of the third edition (DSM-III-R), ego-dystonic homosexuality was removed as a diagnostic category. In the fourth edition (DSM-IV), homosexuality is not mentioned under any diagnostic category.

Without a theory of health and disease, however, it is not clear what the criterion of inclusion or exclusion should be. The difficulty of formulating a value-neutral nosology has convinced many that categories of mental disorder are only a codification of prevalent social mores. In this view, the list of paraphilias retained in the *Diagnostic and Statistical Manual* cannot be justified and should also be removed (Suppe, 1984).

The codification view of the categories of mental disorder is called "social constructionist." Social constructionists believe that all categories of human understanding, even categories of moral judgment and the category of sexual orientation, develop and have meaning only within particular historical constellations of power. In contrast, those who are labeled "essential-

SEXUAL COMPULSIVITY
Paraphilia

Sex researcher John Money, a psychologist working within the medical model, has been critical of the view that categories of mental disorder are only a codification of social mores. Money supports the movement to secure civil rights for gay people, but he argues that prior medical mistreatment of persons does not invalidate biomedical research that is conducted with fully informed and knowledgeable consent and with independent protection of individual rights. The scientific search for criteria to differentiate conditions that produce individual suffering and are potentially dangerous to others is essential. Money's research indicates that paraphilia occurs among both heterosexuals and homosexuals and that sexual compulsivity is a real, though rare, clinical entity.

A paraphilia entails an individually or socially unacceptable obligatory stimulus, for example, types of clothing, an amputated limb, or activity such as receiving an enema, which must be present for sexual arousal and orgasm and over which individuals often have little control. It is not addiction to sex in general but dependence on a unique stimulus that is the problem. Individuals with paraphilias may suffer from loneliness because idiosyncratic erotic objects and activities and not relationships with persons predominate in their lives. If the stimulus is an activity such as rape, paraphilic compulsion obviously becomes a threat to society.

Money admits that what is defined as sexuoerotically normal and acceptable varies historically according to ideological norms. Who is to say, then, what is good sexuality and right and wrong sexual conduct? Money is not reluctant to say that good sex is sex that leads to the integration of lust (erotic desire) and love in a reciprocal, mutually responsive, pairbonded relationship between persons. Loving, pairbonded relationships are possible for homosexuals. People with restrictive paraphilic conditions have disorders of love, not sex. They experience a cleavage between lust and love that resists integration in therapy and usually results in a failure to achieve personally satisfying sexuoerotic relationships.

Money's attention to the quality of sexual relationships, not sexual orientation, is reminiscent of the Kantian approach to moral evaluation of sexual conduct. Money's thesis that paraphilia inevitably leads to sexual objectification suggests a formulation of the Kantian injunction not to treat persons as mere means. Persons with paraphilias are compelled to seek sexual satisfaction in unique objects and activities and not in pairbonded relationships.

Money, however, does not attribute moral significance to the inability to form a pairbond; he calls this inability an "unfortunate affliction." Instead, he recommends libertarian criteria of "personal inviolacy" and "subjective discontent." According to the first criterion, "no one has the right to infringe upon someone else's personal sexual inviolacy by imposing his or her own private ideological version of what is or is not erotic and sexual, without the other person's informed consent" (Money, 1988, p. 140). The second criterion is "the personal and subjective discontent with having one's life dictated by the commands of a paraphilic lovemap" (Money, 1988, p. 142). Money defers here to the moral minimum of the natural-rights tradition. He believes that these are the only criteria possible that guarantee both societal rights and equal sexual rights for everyone in a "sexual democracy."

—LOUIS TIETJE
JAMES HARRISON

Gender assignment decisions and therapy make it clear that gender can be as much a product of human choice as of biological traits.

PAGE 252

ists," and are often classified under "the medical model," hold that the objective validity of categories across historical periods and cultures can be established scientifically. The postmodern debate between social constructionists and essentialists has been conducted under various banners in all scholarly disciplines. (See Stein, 1992, for a survey of the debate on sexual orientation. See Boswell, 1983, who interprets the debate in terms of the nominalist-realist controversy in philosophy.)

Proponents of the constructionist perspective argue that diagnostic categories are relative to social rules and function to maintain conformity and to prevent and control nonconformist sexual behavior. Therapists construct both what is to be understood as a psychological problem and what is to constitute a cure. Therapeutic interventions are therefore also guidelines for how clients ought to shape their lives in a moral sense. The therapeutic objective for gay people should be the alleviation of shame and low self-esteem due to social stigma. Therapists should assist the integration of gay people into society (Silverstein, 1991, and Davison, 1991).

These proponents believe that the value of a new egalitarianism, reflected in the black civil rights and women's liberation movements, contributed to social change in the 1960s and 1970s. Social, economic, and political conditions did not support the value of conformity and the need for strong social control. Conditions changed in the 1980s with the emergence of the AIDS crisis and resurgence of conservative religious ideas. Anonymous sex with a large number of partners became problematic for both individuals and society; it represented a threat to life for individuals and a public health disaster of unprecedented magnitude.

In this threatening environment, it is not surprising that some mental-health practitioners "discovered" the new pathologies of sexual addiction and compulsivity. The need for individual self-control seemed urgent. Advocates of the constructionist perspective claim that the clinical entities of pathological addiction and compulsivity were invented to support moral judgments. These "value-neutral" clinical entities only conceal the judgment that nonrelational sex is bad and that individuals should exercise more control over their sexual behavior (Levine and Troiden, 1988).

Many kinds of therapy, even sexual orientation conversion therapies, are permissible under libertarian criteria. Some critics charge that conversion therapies do not support human dignity, may involve consumer fraud, and potentially harm clients because there is no evidence that they are effective (Haldeman, 1991). These charges presuppose the moral criteria of respect and harm endorsed by modern ethical theories.

An important question is whether it is morally wrong for therapists to offer treatments of dubious efficacy and safety. Libertarians and utilitarians would not morally disapprove of the provision of conversion therapy if individuals are adequately informed about the unlikely prospect of success and potential harms. Kantians might be more hesitant. They would be fearful that informed consent is not sufficient to protect individuals from improper treatment by therapists. Natural-law theorists would be the most willing to approve of conversion therapy for homosexuals because a change in sexual orientation means that a moral alternative to celibacy becomes available in heterosexual marriage.

Conclusion

All the traditions of ethical thought coexist in modern liberal societies. Some moral disagreements about homosexuality derive from the teleological or deontological structure of ethical theories. In natural-law and utilitarian theories, moral judgments of right and wrong conduct are based on an account of good sexuality. The problem is that people do not agree on whether good sexuality should be defined in terms of the purposes of procreation, interpersonal love, pleasure, or happiness. Utilitarians approve of homosexual activities that promote pleasure and happiness, whereas natural-law theorists disapprove of these activities because they do not have a procreative purpose. Libertarians and Kantians do not confront the problem of defining good sexuality because they base their moral judgments on respect for individual rights and autonomy. Kantians, however, disagree that respect for individual rights is a sufficient moral criterion.

Other moral disagreements derive from differences in factual interpretation. Libertarians, Kantians, and utilitarians agree that the biological sex of a partner is not morally significant. The morally relevant facts involve free consent, harmful conduct, and the treatment of persons. Their disagreements are over what counts as free consent, harmful conduct, and the proper treatment of persons in sexual relationships. They also disagree about what kinds of sexual behavior ought to be legally sanctioned. For natural-law theorists, however, facts about the harmlessness of homosexual behavior or even the proper treatment of persons are not the only relevant facts. For them, physical and biological complementarity have normative implications that are morally significant. Natural-law theorists are bound to complain that the tolerance of what some regard as harmless homosexual behavior in modern liberal societies encourages what they believe is immoral conduct.

—LOUIS TIETJE
JAMES HARRISON

HUMAN NATURE

Theories of human nature offer systematic and comprehensive accounts of human beings' most significant distinguishing characteristics. Such accounts are central in people's perennial attempts to organize their understandings of the cosmos; to figure out their relation to God, to nature, and to each other; and to uncover the possibilities, meanings, and purposes of human life.

Western understanding of human nature

Modern Western theories of human nature, which will be the focus of this essay, typically differ from their classical and medieval predecessors in appealing to the findings of a variety of life and social sciences, including anthropology, medicine, physiology, psychology, economics, sociology, and even ethology. Nevertheless, although these sciences undeniably help us to understand specific aspects of human life, even contemporary theories of human nature are never simply summaries of the results of empirical research—despite their frequent claims to scientific authority.

One reason that theories of human nature are not simply generalizations from the conclusions of scientific study is that they enter into empirical investigations not only as conclusions but also as presuppositions, structuring the conceptual frameworks within which research programs are conducted. Contemporary psychological investigation, for instance, proceeds with a variety of models of the human mind, including the Freudian, the behaviorist, the existentialist or humanist, and the computer models. Empirical research cannot fully evaluate the adequacy of its own framework relative to others; determining the adequacy of an entire framework requires reference to considerations beyond empirical data, including how the framework coheres with other respected theories and even its moral and political implications.

A related reason that theories of human nature go beyond ordinary scientific claims is that typically they aspire to provide a comprehensive conceptual framework that will render coherent the contributions of all those disciplines and discourses that investigate various aspects of human life. These often represent human beings in ways that, at least on the surface, appear quite incompatible with each other; for instance, lawyers assume that people ordinarily are responsible for their actions, while psychologists may suggest that people's behavior is determined ultimately by factors outside their control. Theories of human nature endeavor to resolve these incompatibilities in a variety of ways, ranging from reinterpreting the meaning of a discourse, such as the religious, to setting limits on the domain within which its claims are accepted; occasionally, a theory of human nature may even proclaim the invalidity of a whole realm of discourse, such as the parapsychological. Rather than simply summarizing the conclusions of the various life and social sciences, therefore, theories of human nature typically perform a regulatory function, authorizing some methodological approaches while delegitimating others.

Yet another respect in which theories of human nature differ from scientific theories, at least as science is ordinarily understood, is in the prominence of their normative or evaluative component. Even if one contends that all knowledge is to some degree value-laden, the evaluative element is far more evident in theories of human nature than it is, for instance, in modern theories of the physical universe. All theories of human nature provide a general account of human capacities and human needs, human potentialities and human well-being, and thus contain at least an implicit, and often an explicit, diagnosis of human malaise and a prescription for human flourishing.

"And they were both naked, the man and his wife, and were not ashamed."

GENESIS 2:24–25

Like all theoretical constructions, theories of human nature are developed in specific historical circumstances and are designed to address specific conceptual puzzles or practical concerns; consequently, they shift their emphasis according to the scientific, moral, and political preoccupations of the time. Despite variations in focus and emphasis, however, the Western project of understanding human nature his-

BEFORE THE FALL

The parents primeval, Adam and Eve stand as archetypes of human nature in all its innocence, fertility, curiosity, and weakness before temptation.

H

HUMAN NATURE

Three Classic Western Approaches

"And Adam called his wife's name Eve; because she was the mother of all living."

GENESIS 3:19–20

"Adam was but human—this explains it all. He . . . wanted [the apple] only because it was forbidden."

MARK TWAIN
PUDD'NHEAD WILSON
1894

torically has centered on two questions. The first of these addresses the human aspect of "human nature": How can human be distinguished from nonhuman nature? The second addresses the natural aspect: How can what is natural for humans be distinguished from what is unnatural, abnormal, or artificial? The concerns inherent in these two questions constitute continuing themes that link the variety of Western inquiries into the nature of human beings.

Reflection on these themes reveals that the Western project of providing a systematic theory of human nature has been predicated historically on certain assumptions. They include the following: (1) that it is possible to discover specific qualities or features that characterize human beings universally and transhistorically; (2) that these characteristics decisively distinguish humans from all other beings, notably nonhuman animals; and (3) that, from the discovery of these characteristics, it is possible to derive specific prescriptions about the proper conduct of human life. In other words, the Western project of understanding human nature generally has been motivated by a desire to derive from it universal and unchanging values.

These assumptions went unquestioned and often unarticulated throughout most of Western history. Once they are made explicit, however, it is easy to see that they are all contestable; and we shall see how, in the nineteenth and twentieth centuries, each of them was contested. For instance, Karl Marx (1818-1883) and John Dewey (1859-1952) challenged the first assumption; Charles Darwin (1809-1882) and the twentieth-century sociobiologists challenged the second; and the theorists of positivism and neopositivism challenged the third.

Since the 1970s not only these assumptions but the whole project of developing a comprehensive theory of human nature has been subjected to more fundamental critiques, launched by poststructuralist or postmodern French writers such as Michel Foucault (1926-1984), Jacques Derrida (1930-), and Jean-François Lyotard (1924-). While these authors differ on many points, they are united in rejecting the possibility of any overarching philosophical framework capable of unifying and legitimating the specific disciplines. Such totalizing frameworks or discourses, they claim, reflect unrealizable aspirations to discover universal and absolute truths in morals, politics, or science. These authors deny that any genuinely universal truths can be found, and assert that claims to them typically are propounded by groups who wish to use them for promoting their own political agendas. Truth, they argue, is relative to specific discursive practices that are historically contingent and self-justifying. Consequently, there is no need for, as well as no possibility of, a "master" discourse designed to be the ground or foundation of these more specific discourses.

As described so far, the dominant tendency in Western thought has been to conceptualize human nature as both *universal* and *transhistorical*. Its conceptualizations typically take the form "All human beings throughout history have characteristics x, y, z," implying that x, y, and z are necessary, as well as universal, characteristics of human nature. However, the Western tradition also includes conceptions of human nature that are not universalistic although they are transhistorical. These *relational* theories take the form "Group x is inferior to group y with respect to characteristics x, y, z"; typically, relational theories are used to justify the dominance of one group over another. Finally, some Western conceptions of human nature are *historical* rather than transhistorical, used within theories that claim that as human cultures change, so do certain important human characteristics. Some theories contain elements both universal and relational—for example, the theories of Aristotle and the sociobiologists—or both transhistorical and historical—for example, the theories of Karl Marx and John Dewey.

Three classic Western approaches

ARISTOTLE. The origins of Western philosophy, in the sense of systematic and rational inquiries into the nature of reality, knowledge, and value, are often traced to the reflections of ancient Greek thinkers in the fifth and fourth centuries B.C.E. Plato (ca. 428-347) and Aristotle (384-322), two of the three philosophical giants of this period (the third being Socrates, ca. 470-399), developed systematic theories of human nature. Aristotle's view has been particularly influential on the Western tradition because it was incorporated into the Scholastic philosophy that dominated Europe in the Middle Ages and early Renaissance, and continues to shape the thinking of the Roman Catholic Church.

Aristotle (1947) conceptualized human beings as complexes of soul and body. The soul was the distinctively human element—the essence or form or intelligible principle of the body—but it existed only in conjunction with a living human body. Aristotle's conceptualization of the soul as inseparable from its body contrasted with Plato's view that human beings were souls united only temporarily with bodies, but Aristotle also acknowledged the possibility of the actively knowing and thinking part of the soul, the mind or intellect, being "set free from its present conditions . . . immortal and eternal." When this happened, however, Aristotle asserted that the mind remembered nothing of its former embodied activity and, because all connection with a specific human body was thus lost, he did not regard the human soul as personally or individually immortal.

Aristotle's view of human nature, like Plato's, was

teleological, which is to say that he regarded human beings, like other things in the world, as having a "function" or activity peculiar to them. He further assumed, again like Plato, that the good life, or *eudaimonia,* consisted in the successful or efficient performance of that function. For Aristotle, the distinctive function of human beings was reasoning, or "an active life of that which possesses reason," and so he inferred that the good life was one in which the rational part of the soul governed the appetitive or desiring part, thus avoiding excess and living in accordance with virtue.

For Aristotle, human beings were, by nature, political animals who needed to live in a community: "He who is unable to live in society, or who has no need of it because he is sufficient to himself, must be either a beast or a god." Within human communities, however, not everyone was capable of citizenship: The nature of some was to rule and of others to be ruled. Among those whose nature was to be ruled were children, barbarians, and Greek women; thus, while Aristotle posited a universal standard for human nature, he simultaneously asserted that some groups of humans were less than fully human. The theme of dominance and subordination runs not only through Aristotle's account of the relations between human beings but even through his account of the nature of individual humans. He compared the controlling relation between form and matter with the relation between male and female, and he asserted that the proper relation between mind and body was like that of master to slave.

AQUINAS. The dominant philosophical figure of the Middle Ages was Thomas Aquinas (1226-1274), later Saint Thomas, who synthesized Greek thought and church doctrine into a Christian philosophy (1962). He conceptualized human nature in terms that were basically Aristotelian, with some (often Platonic) modifications made in order to adapt Aristotelian views to church doctrine.

Aquinas believed, like Aristotle, that there was a distinctive and essential human nature that could be understood teleologically; he also shared the Aristotelian belief that the good life or *eudaimonia* was action in accordance with this function. A proper understanding of the ends or purposes of human life was therefore essential to morality and should be achieved by discovering the precepts of *natural law.* Natural law, as Aquinas conceptualized it, was universal and unchanging. It described supposedly universal human tendencies, such as preserving life, but presented them not simply as empirical facts about human nature but also as manifestations of God's design for humanity. For Aquinas, therefore, natural law simultaneously described how things were and prescribed how they should be. It was discoverable by reason, which, because it gave insight into God's purposes, provided guidance on how humans should live.

ON HUMAN NATURE

Saint Thomas Aquinas (1225–1274) viewed human life on earth as a preparation for life everlasting in heaven.

Like Aristotle, Aquinas saw humans as combinations of soul and body, with the soul as the form of the body. To allow for the possibility of personal or individual immortality, however, Aquinas diverged from Aristotle, declaring that the soul was a "substantial" form, capable of existing separately from matter. Not only was personal immortality conceptually possible, according to Aquinas; it was humans' destiny. God would not have implanted the universal—and therefore natural—human desire to live forever unless this desire had an object.

"Three things are necessary for the salvation of man: to know what he ought to believe; to know what he ought to desire; and to know what he ought to do."

SAINT THOMAS AQUINAS
TWO PRECEPTS OF CHARITY, 1273

While Aquinas shared the Aristotelian view that human nature had an end or purpose, he believed, in accordance with church doctrine, that this end was supernatural rather than natural: It was to spend eternity united with God in heaven, where alone perfect happiness might be enjoyed. Human life as we know it was no more than a preparation for life after death, and this world was simply a testing ground for the next. So long as humans inhabited this world, however, they should strive to live in accordance with natural law, which provided a test for the moral validity of the laws of the state.

DESCARTES. The thought of René Descartes (1596-1650) is generally considered to mark the beginning of modern philosophy. Refusing to accept the authority of tradition, Descartes developed "rules

H

HUMAN NATURE

The Materialist Tradition and the Darwinian Pivot

"Reason in man is rather like God in the world."

SAINT THOMAS AQUINAS
OPUSCULE II, DE REGNO

"It is human nature to think wisely and act foolishly."

ANATOLE FRANCE

for the direction of the understanding" and a "method for rightly conducting reason" designed to enable each individual to establish certain truth in science and philosophy (1931). He wrote in the vernacular (French) as well as in Latin, in order to reach lay as well as clerical readers.

Descartes's conception of human nature was even more *dualistic* than that of Aristotle and Aquinas. Living human beings, for Descartes, were composed of two entirely different kinds of entities: souls, which were active, intellectual substances, immaterial and immortal; and bodies, which were unthinking, passive mechanisms, spatially extended and temporally finite. Individual humans were to be identified not with their bodies but with their souls, which were able to survive the death of the body. While Descartes's model allowed for the soul's separation from the body after death, it rendered problematic the relation of the soul to the body during life, since it was unclear how material and immaterial substances could have a causal influence on each other. Descartes never succeeded in providing a satisfactory explanation of mind-body interaction.

As a scientist, Descartes wanted his theory of human nature to be compatible with both the new developments in physical science and the doctrines of the Roman Catholic Church. He attempted to reconcile these two worldviews by postulating two spheres of reality, each governed by entirely different laws or principles. The laws of God governed spiritual or mental reality; the laws of science governed physical reality, understood by Descartes in mechanical terms. Although Descartes never developed a systematic moral philosophy, his assertion that all "men" were potentially equal in their capacity to reason laid the foundation for later egalitarian moves in ethics and politics. Simultaneously, his conceptualization of animals as mere stimulus-response mechanisms, lacking consciousness because they lacked souls, justified the exclusion of animals from moral consideration. Cartesian biologists, in defense of vivisection, have compared the howls of cut-up dogs to the squeaks of unlubricated machines.

ON HUMAN NATURE
The View before Darwin

There are at least six common features of pre-Darwinian conceptions of human nature:

1. Human nature is the same transhistorically.
2. It is distinguished primarily by possession of a soul.
3. Human souls are characterized by their capacity to reason. This capacity exists, perhaps in varying degrees, as a potential innate in all humans, sharply distinguishing them from all other beings, including animals.
4. Humans' possession of a rational soul gives them special moral worth.
5. Lacking such a soul, animals lack comparable moral worth or value. Those biological features that are similar in humans and animals comprise humans' "lower" nature, which humans should strive to rise above.
6. Developing our potential to reason is a key to the good life for humans. Reasoning not only tells us how to live well but actualizes our distinctively human potential. Thus, the concept of human nature is clearly normative: Our task is to realize our humanness by fulfilling our potential for rationality; those who are incapable of fulfilling this potential are less than human.

— ALLISON M. JAGGAR
KARSTEN J. STRUHL

The materialist tradition and the Darwinian pivot

The features listed above as characterizing pre-Darwinian conceptions of human nature represent the dominant Western tradition prior to the nineteenth century. Running counter to this *rationalist* and dualist tradition, however, Western thought also includes a less prominent *materialist* or naturalist tradition.

Anaximander (ca. 500 B.C.E.), an early pre-Socratic philosopher, developed a speculative theory of evolution in which human beings were descended from lower forms of animal life. Democritus (460-370 B.C.E.), a contemporary of Socrates, developed a speculative atomic theory in which even the human soul was composed of atoms. The English philosopher Thomas Hobbes (1588-1679) assimilated individual behavior and politics to the laws of mechanics, regarding desire as motion toward an object, and human beings as motivated entirely by self-interest. The French philosopher Julien de La Mettrie (1709-1751) accepted Descartes's assertion that animals were like machines but insisted that so, too, were human beings. The German philosopher Baron Paul Henri d'Holbach (1723-1789) argued that thinking could be reduced to the functioning of the brain and explicitly denied the existence of a soul. Another of the French philosophes, Claude-Adrien Helvétius (1715-1771), argued that all mental faculties were ultimately reducible to physical sensation and that all humans were motivated by the desire to achieve physical pleasure and reduce pain. This latter idea was developed into an elaborate ethical calculus by the nineteenth-century British utilitarians, Jeremy Bentham (1748-1832), James Mill (1773-1836), and the latter's more famous son, John Stuart Mill (1806-1873). Collectively, these philosophers suggested an alternative understanding of human nature—one that focused more on the body than on the soul, on the emotions and desires more than on reason, and on the similarities rather than the differences between humans and animals. It remained for Charles Darwin to give this materialist tradition a scientific basis by providing a naturalistic analysis of the relations between humans and animals.

In his landmark work, *On the Origin of Species* (1859), Darwin argued that the distinctive features of human nature were not divinely created in an instant but had evolved over many millennia through a process he called "natural selection" (Darwin, 1936). Although the word "selection" suggested conscious purpose, Darwin's use of it was metaphorical, since nature "selects" only in the sense that certain new traits or mutations that appear accidentally are sufficiently adaptive to the environmental conditions within which the organism lives for the new organism to survive. The view that human beings had evolved through accidental mutations implied that there was no preordained nature, no ultimate meaning or cosmic purpose for human life to fulfill. In an attempt to escape this conclusion and reconcile science with Christianity, some later theorists postulated a direction and a goal in evolution, characterizing more recently evolved species as "higher" or otherwise superior; but such teleological and evaluative interpretations were ultimately alien to the basically antiteleological spirit of the concept of natural selection.

When Darwin first proposed his theory of evolution, the wife of the canon of Worcester Cathedral was said to have remarked, "Descended from the apes! My dear, we will hope it is not true. But if it is, let us pray that it may not become generally known." Indeed, the church denounced Darwin, recognizing that his theories challenged not only the beliefs in divine creation and a radical discontinuity between humans and animals but also the idea of an immortal soul with special moral worth. Darwin argued that morality had developed from the social instincts of animals; and he construed the uniquely human capacity for rationality, which Aristotle had seen as the telos of human existence, as the outcome of natural selection operating on accidental mutations.

Biological determinism: A critique

Once Darwin had demonstrated an evolutionary continuity between humans and other animals, questions arose about the causal role of human biology in relation to other aspects of human life. For many scientists, the project became the *reductionist* one of showing how the various psychological and social characteristics of human beings were causally determined by human biology.

Many *biological determinist* theories have negative social implications because they present human characteristics like aggression and dominance as biologically determined and therefore inescapable. For instance, Sigmund Freud (1856-1939), the founder of psychoanalysis, insisted that all human motivation could be reduced to two basic drives—the sexual drive, or libido; and the aggressive drive, an ineradicable instinct to hurt, torture, or kill other human beings (Freud, 1962). The German ethologist Konrad Lorenz (1903-1989) also posited an aggressive instinct in humans similar to that he found in his study of various animal species in their natural habitats. In each species, the instinct had evolved to serve one or more life-preserving functions, such as territorial dispersion, selection of the strongest for reproduction, defense of the young, and the establishment of a hierarchy that could provide the group with social cohesion. In species armed with sharp teeth, claws, or beaks, the aggressive instinct was generally coupled with an inhibitory mechanism preventing fighting animals from killing each other; Lorenz argued that there had been no need for such an inhibitory mechanism to evolve in humans because they were not naturally armed. With the development of weaponry, however, the absence of such a mechanism was often lethal, and the advent of nuclear weapons made it a threat to the survival of the species (Lorenz, 1974).

More recent studies of animal behavior have generated a new form of biological determinism called *sociobiology*. Two precursors of sociobiology, anthropologists Lionel Tiger (1937-) and Robin Fox (1913-1971), proposed the concept of a "biogram," a code or program genetically "wired" into the brain that produced certain forms of social behavior, including patterns of dominance and submission—hierarchy among males and dominance of males over females. Both of these were assumed to be the evolutionary heritage of the hunting life of early hominids (Tiger and Fox, 1974). The same general line of thinking was employed by entomologist Edward O. Wilson (1929-), who first coined the term "sociobiology." Wilson insisted that "genes hold culture on a leash" and play a significant role in determining such human social behavior as altruism toward kin, communal aggression, nationalism, racism, homosexuality, and the dominance of males over females. Wilson has conceded that these biologically based tendencies might be counteracted through extreme social measures, but he

"The thief and the murderer follow nature just as much as the philanthropist."

THOMAS HENRY HUXLEY
EVOLUTION AND ETHICS
1893

H

HUMAN NATURE

Biological Determinism: A Critique

argues that humans would pay a high price for doing so (Wilson, 1977).

While Wilson's assertion of a universal genetic tendency toward ethnocentric and racist attitudes was not an attempt to justify racism, there is a long Western tradition of using evolutionary theory to denigrate certain racial or ethnic groups. In the nineteenth century, some scientists in this tradition asserted that Caucasians and Orientals had crossed the *Homo sapiens* threshold before "Negroes," or that *Homo sapiens* had begun in Asia and migrated to Africa, where the original stock had degenerated. Others sought to prove racial, ethnic, and class inequalities in intelligence through the use of IQ (intelligence quotient) theory. Frances Galton (1822-1911), a cousin of Darwin who coined the term "eugenics," attempted to show that the upper classes had superior intellectual capacities and that blacks were "two grades" below whites. Many of the early IQ theorists in the United States made similar claims about various immigrant groups.

After World War II, when the Nazis had shown the possible social consequences of eugenic ideas, such theories fell into disrepute. They were revived in 1969 when educational psychologist Arthur Jensen (1923-) published an article in the *Harvard Educational Review* arguing as follows: Intelligence testing has demonstrated that whites score on average about fifteen IQ points above blacks; IQ is 80 percent "heritable"; therefore, the mean difference between the scores proves a hereditary difference in innate intelligence between the two groups (Jensen, 1969). Shortly after Jensen's article appeared, Harvard psychologist Richard Herrnstein (1930-) made a similar argument concerning the difference in IQ scores between "upper-class" and "lower-class" people. He concluded that humans should give up any aspirations to democratic equality and accept the idea of a natural meritocracy (Herrnstein, 1973).

Biological determinist theories of human nature are not just empirically unconfirmed; they also fail to acknowledge what is most distinctive of our species. The human genetic constitution determines highly developed learning and cognitive capacities that allow

THEORY FASHION
In and Out with Biological Determinism

Biological determinist theories were highly controversial in the late 1960s and 1970s, but in the 1980s and 1990s they became increasingly fashionable—claiming, for instance, genetic factors in alcoholism; locating homosexuality in the structure of the brain; and asserting that men with XYY chromosomes have a tendency toward criminal violence. However, biological determinist theories of human nature are problematic in a number of respects.

Empirically, the evidence for such theories is at best inconclusive. Even within the psychoanalytic tradition, some theorists have argued against Freud that aggressive desires may be explained as derivative manifestations rather than primary instincts, resulting from situations that frustrate other, nonaggressive desires. Ethologists and sociobiologists typically move incautiously from observations of certain animal species or conjectures about early hominids to claims about modern human beings. Sometimes, like Lorenz, they focus on the behavior of fish, birds, and other animals considerably removed from humans—while they ignore studies indicating that many higher mammals, especially primates, display almost no hierarchical organization or intraspecies aggression, being instead peaceful and cooperative. Finally, regardless of how nonhuman species behave, similarities in behavior between humans and nonhuman animals do not establish that the human behavior in question is biologically determined; it may still be a learned response.

Claims for the universality of human aggression, hierarchy, and male dominance also are not confirmed by anthropological evidence. Many hunter-gatherer societies are reported to be remarkably lacking in aggressive behavior, and some enjoy an exceptionally high degree of social equality. Assertions of women's "natural" dependence on men are undermined by evidence that gathering, a task often performed predominantly by women, is a more reliable food source than hunting in many hunter-gatherer societies. The sexual division of labor varies widely cross-culturally, and even where certain constants are observed, such as a tendency for women rather than men to care for young children, this may be a social adaptation to prevailing conditions rather than a biological predetermination.

Claims about the genetic basis of racial and ethnic differences in IQ are equally suspect. The idea of different evolutionary paths for different races is contradicted by the paleontological evidence; indeed, the concept of race itself is now widely discredited, with anthropologists preferring instead to talk about the statistical frequency of certain characteristics within a geographical population. Further, the idea that IQ tests measure innate intelligence is undermined by the recognition that all tests are culturally biased, since they all require prior learning, and that learning experience can significantly raise IQ. Finally, the very concept of "heritability" is a technical one, designating a ratio of the contribution of heredity to environment within a given population; it cannot be used, therefore, to compare one population against another.

— ALLISON M. JAGGAR
KARSTEN J. STRUHL

humans to respond flexibly rather than instinctively to environmental problems, as well as to develop a range of distinctively human cultural characteristics. The implications of this were noted by one of the world's foremost geneticists, Theodosius Dobzhansky (1900-1975), who wrote, "In a sense, human genes have surrendered their primacy in human evolution to an entirely new, nonbiological or superorganic agent, culture. However, it should not be forgotten that human culture is not possible without human genes" (Dobzhansky, 1966, p. 113). In short, what has developed in the human evolutionary process is a primate with a genetic structure capable of a new kind of evolution, cultural evolution.

Biological determinist theories of human nature contrast sharply in content with their pre-Darwinian counterparts, but they are often inspired by the same motivation of discovering universal and unchanging social values. Typically, they describe as "natural" aspects of behavior thought to be biologically determined; though few would assert that natural behavior is always to be encouraged or even permitted, characterizing some behavioral tendencies as natural provides a certain legitimation for them. Because they are understood as resulting from natural selection, such tendencies are regarded as having been necessary at least at some time for human survival; in consequence, they cannot be entirely deplored, and they may even be romanticized as clues to a more "natural" way of life. Thus, biological determinist approaches to understanding and evaluating human nature may be seen as secular analogues of Aquinas's theory of natural law.

It may be the social function of biological determinist theories of human nature, rather than their scientific credentials, that accounts for their continuing popularity. Put simply, these theories tend to rationalize existing manifestations of aggression and inequality: Biological determinist analyses of violence, war, and crime tend to deflect attention from the social and economic causes of these phenomena, just as theories about the biological determinants of male and female behavior distract us from the ways in which men and women are socialized for their respective roles. The implication often drawn from biological determinist theories is that significant social movement in the direction of peaceful cooperation and equality is impossible because it is alleged to go against "human nature." Clearly, those in power benefit from such an assumption and are likely to encourage the development of such theories.

Behaviorism: Another form of post-Darwinian reductionism

The Western materialist or naturalist tradition has not always moved in a biological determinist direction. It also includes thinkers who claim that environmental or cultural factors are the primary determinants of the human mind or behavior. The philosopher John Locke (1632-1704) saw the human mind as a kind of blank tablet to be written upon by sensory impressions, while Enlightenment figures like Helvétius assumed that education could shape human beings into almost any form.

In the first part of the twentieth century, environmentalist ideas became popular in the United States through a psychological movement known as behaviorism. John B. Watson (1878-1958), who first systematically developed the theory, insisted that in order for psychology to become a rigorous experimental science, it must give up its introspective orientation. It should no longer take its task to be analyzing private mental states, such as feelings, desires, and thoughts, but instead should study the relation between publicly observable behavior and the environment. For Watson, the two basic forms of this relation were the *unconditioned* and the *conditioned reflex*. The former was the basic human physiological endowment, consisting of automatic responses to environmental stimuli, such as salivating in the presence of food and contracting pupils in the presence of light. Watson based his analysis of the conditioned reflex on the work of the Russian experimental psychologist Ivan Petrovich Pavlov (1849-1936), who had demonstrated that a hungry dog, repeatedly presented with both food and the ringing of a bell, would eventually salivate at only the bell-ringing. The sound of the bell had become a *substitute stimulus*, and the salivation was now a *conditioned response*. For Watson, all human behavior could be reduced to these two kinds of reflexes (Watson, 1925).

Watson's version of behaviorism was superseded by that of B. F. Skinner (1904-1990), who argued that reflex action could account for only a small part of human behavior. For Skinner, human behavior was primarily shaped by what he called *operant conditioning*, which *reinforced* certain spontaneous movements of the organism. For example, when a pigeon raised its head above a certain height and food was released into its cage, the result was a higher frequency of that behavior. Unlike the stimulus in Watson's model, the "reinforcer" (the food) was introduced *after* the "response" (the raising of the head to the desired height) occurred. For Skinner, most human behavior other than automatic reflex action, even human language, could be explained as the result of *positive* or *negative reinforcement*, which, by adding something to the situation (food, sex, money, praise, etc.)—or by removing something from it—increased the frequency of some behavior. While not denying that feelings and thoughts existed, Skinner refused to characterize them as residing in a special mental domain, consciousness, and claimed that they

There is perhaps no better way of measuring the natural endowment of a soul than by its ability to transmute dissatisfaction into a creative impulse.

ERIC HOFFER
THE PASSIONATE STATE OF MIND, 1954

See Also
Sociobiology: How 'Predestined' Are We?

SPECTERS HAUNTING EUROPE

Karl Marx (1818–1883) and Friedrich Engels (1820–1895) viewed human nature as driven by the primary need to satisfy basic biological requirements.

had no causal effect on human behavior (Skinner, 1953).

Both Watson and Skinner believed that human beings could be conditioned to develop almost any pattern of behavioral responses. Watson boldly declared that he could take almost any infant "at random and train him to become . . . doctor, lawyer, artist, merchant-chief, and, yes, even a beggar man and thief." Skinner insisted that operant conditioning "shapes behavior as a sculptor shapes a lump of clay." One evident consequence of the behaviorist program was that human freedom was an illusion. For Skinner, in particular, such concepts as freedom, moral responsibility, and human dignity were the conceits of a prescientific age (Skinner, 1973).

"The history of all hitherto existing society is the history of class struggles."

MARX AND ENGELS
THE COMMUNIST MANIFESTO, 1848

Behaviorism, just as much as biological determinism, is heir to the evolutionary paradigm because human behavior is still explained in terms of genetic dispositions regarded as having survival value. For behaviorism, however, these predispositions are not instincts or drives. Instead, specific unconditioned reflexes have evolved in the human species because they have survival value, while the human organism's susceptibility to conditioning helps it survive by allowing it to adapt to environmental changes more rapidly than its genetic structure could.

There are a number of difficulties with the behaviorist conception of human nature. First are the primary data of consciousness, such as desires, feelings, reflection, and decision making; it is hard to believe that these do not have at least some causal influence on human activity. Second, the fact that pigeons, rats, and human beings can sometimes be controlled by operant conditioning does not mean that all human behavior can be understood in this way. Linguist Noam Chomsky (1928-), for example, has argued against Skinner that linguistic competence requires creativity that goes beyond responses to prior conditioning because we are constantly constructing sentences that we have never before encountered (Chomsky, 1959). Finally, there is no room in the behaviorist model for human agency: The environment acts, human beings merely react. In this, behaviorism may be seen as ideologically reflecting a world in which people are continually managed and manipulated by technocratic and bureaucratic elites.

Social and historical conceptions of human nature

Social and historical conceptions of human nature offer an alternative to seeing human beings either as primarily determined by their biological drives or as passive clay to be molded by their physical and social environment. These approaches, while not ignoring human biology or the role of social conditioning, emphasize the importance of human social activity within specific historical contexts. The work of the revolutionary social theorist Karl Marx, together with his collaborator Friedrich Engels (1820-1895), and of the U.S. pragmatist philosopher John Dewey, provides two examples of this approach.

Marx and Engels's view of human nature (Schmitt, 1987) was embedded in their more general theory of human history, *historical materialism.* Human history, they contended, began with humans' attempt to satisfy their basic biological needs through producing their means of subsistence, so that human beings were, first and foremost, producers. Human production differed from that of nonhuman animals in that it was deliberate rather than instinctive, involving imagination, planning, and tool use. It was also inherently social, not only in requiring the coordination of human effort but also in utilizing skills and knowledge transmitted from one individual, group, or generation to another. In societies producing a surplus beyond that needed for immediate survival, human production typically involved a division of labor going beyond a division into separate tasks, to a division between intellectual and physical work and between work considered appropriate for men and for women. Most important for Marx and Engels was the class division of labor between those groups who owned the means of production and those who had to work for them, a division generating the class struggles regarded by Marx and Engels as the motor force in history.

Different economic systems, or what Marx and Engels called modes of production, established forms of social life through which human beings individuated and understood themselves. Peasants and artisans, "ladies" and "gentlemen," merchants and professionals, corporate capitalists and industrial workers would tend to think and act differently from each other. Changes in the mode of production would generate new forms of social life, new ways of understanding the world, and new ways of thinking and acting—in effect, new kinds of "individuals." Thus, human nature itself would change. Since human beings were active in the class struggle that caused these social and economic changes, however, it could also be said that human beings actively changed their own natures over the course of history.

For John Dewey, as for Marx and Engels, human beings were neither governed by instincts nor passive recipients of environmental forces; rather, they were social agents who changed their own natures in the process of changing their societal conditions. However, in contrast to Marx and Engels, Dewey regarded the motor force of social change not as class struggle but as the product of reflective intelligence (Dewey, 1957, 1963).

Dewey acknowledged that human beings had instincts—or impulses, as he preferred to call them in order to discourage associations of inflexibility. Impulses, in his view, were extremely flexible in that they could take on a variety of meanings, depending on the social context. Thus, the impulse of fear might become cowardice, caution, reverence, or respect; while the impulse of anger might become rage, sullenness, annoyance, or indignation. Impulses took on these meanings as habits, predispositions to certain kinds of thinking and acting, ultimately embodied in social customs and institutions. The content of these habits constituted our historical nature. However, when the habits proved inadequate to new social problems, humans could employ their reflective intelligence to redirect their impulses into new habits. For example, as war became increasingly problematic or as certain economic institutions become increasingly outmoded, human impulses could be rechanneled, creating new institutions embodying new habits.

To make sense of the claim that human nature changes, we need to remember the distinction between transhistorical and historical conceptions of human nature. For both Dewey and Marx, it is precisely because a certain transhistorical human nature exists—socially productive and reflectively intelligent—that the content of human nature can be changed historically. To put this point in a more contemporary idiom: Our distinctively human capacity to transform social institutions transforms social roles and, in so doing, transforms historically specific character structures.

Giving more weight to the social and historical aspects of human nature offers a new model of the relation between genetic determination and social conditioning, on the one hand, and social behavior, on the other. What is determined by our genes is our capacity to learn, reflect, and work for change. Humans can, thus, be agents of their own history. Biology determines certain potentialities, but it is only through concrete historical activities that humans develop certain specific cultural and psychological characteristics. Genes dictate the ability to develop general modes of response, such as learning languages, engaging in productive labor, and developing forms of social relatedness; but they do not dictate that humans learn English, produce nuclear weapons, or become selfish and competitive as opposed to altruistic and cooperative. Thus, historical and social conceptions of human nature do not deny biology but refuse to privilege it as the primary cause of human action. Similarly, they do not deny conditioning but equally refuse to privilege it in explaining human action. Certain social conditions undoubtedly encourage the development of certain habits, but these are not merely behavioral responses; instead, they are social patterns of meaning that connect thought to action. Furthermore, human beings do not merely react to social conditions but individuate themselves within them and can reflect intelligently on them. Thus, both individually and collectively humans can decide to change their habits and work to transform the social conditions from which they arose.

Ethical implications for the life sciences: A cautionary tale

What are the bioethical implications of these various conceptions of human nature? First, a cautionary note. Practical ethics reflects on a host of considerations in practical contexts and cannot simply deduce specific moral conclusions from general ethical principles, let alone from some general conception of human nature. Thus, the relation between the various conceptions of human nature and any specific bioethical position is unlikely to be one of logical entailment. This does not mean, however, that concepts of human nature have no relevance to bioethical issues. They may serve as starting points for bioethical analysis, raise suspicions about certain bioethical claims, or even rule out certain bioethical positions. In general, certain conceptions of human nature may be said to cohere, or provide a better "fit," with certain bioethical stances than with others.

The dominant pre-Darwinian conceptions of human nature view physical nature, including the human body, as the realm of the material, the immanent, and the profane, and identify God with the spiri-

"From each according to his abilities, to each according to his needs."

KARL MARX
CRITIQUE OF THE GOTHA PROGRAM, 1875

H

HUMAN NATURE

Ethical Implications for the Life Sciences: A Cautionary Tale

tual, the transcendent, and the sacred. It is only because human beings are endowed with a soul that they are regarded as capable of partaking in the sacred, and their mission is to transcend their bodies and realize their spiritual nature. Insofar as they are part of God's creation, nonhuman animals are sometimes assigned a degree of moral worth, but the view that they lack souls typically rationalizes the claim that nonhuman animals are merely resources to serve human purposes. Saint Francis of Assisi notwithstanding, the dominant view of the Judeo-Christian tradition is that God created nonhuman animals and, indeed, all of nonhuman nature, primarily for the use of human beings. This sharp bifurcation between human and nonhuman nature not only permits but even legitimates the human subjugation and exploitation of all nonhuman nature, and may therefore contribute to the contemporary ecological crisis.

Within this ontology, the human body occupies a unique and somewhat ambiguous moral status. Although material, and therefore a source of temptation, the body is nevertheless sacrosanct because it is

"MADE OF CLAY"
The Malleable Human Body

Although many theorists are willing to acknowledge that people's character or personality or behavior is socially shaped, at least to some degree, the biological constitution, the body, is often viewed as a presocial given, the universal and unchanging foundation on which elaborate cultural edifices are erected. According to this way of thinking, the body constitutes the most natural aspect of human nature. Itself a product of natural selection, the body sets the "natural," that is, biologically determined, limits of social variability.

While it may be true that there is less systematic cross-cultural and transhistorical variation in people's bodies than there is in their personalities and social institutions, it is too simple to regard the human body as a presocial given. Although the human body may sometimes be experienced as a given, in fact, like the mind or the personality, bodies are socially and historically shaped on several levels.

It is not difficult to recognize some of the ways in which human bodies are influenced by their social context. Different kinds of work and living conditions develop or distort the body in various ways. For instance, scarcity of food results in stunted growth, so that body size and development vary systematically not only between cultures but often also between social classes. While many of these bodily marks are unintended side effects of social practices, others are deliberately induced. Social norms are consciously inscribed on the body in a variety of ways, ranging from footbinding and circumcision to diet clinics and cosmetic surgery. The varying social meanings assigned to bodily characteristics and functions influence a person's experience of his or her body, which, depending on the social context, may become a source of pride, joy, pain, or embarrassment.

Social influences on the human body operate not only on the level of observable physical structure, the phenotype; in the past, they have also influenced the genotype, our genetic inheritance, and they continue to do so. While human prehistory is highly speculative, it seems likely that some genetically heritable characteristics have been selected not only "naturally," as adaptive to such nonsocial circumstances as climate and food availability; but also socially, as adaptive to certain forms of social organization or perhaps even as the results of conscious social preferences. For instance, the average size difference between human males and females may have been a consequence as much as a cause of male dominance: If the dominant males fed first and most, only smaller-framed women could survive on the leftover food. Even today, the human gene pool continues to be influenced by social factors. For instance, exposure to environmental pollutants sometimes leads to genetic mutations, and modern medicine now makes it possible for people to survive and reproduce with genetic conditions that otherwise would have led to their early deaths. Finally, genetic engineering is rapidly becoming a real possibility.

The recognition that even the genetic constitution is influenced by social factors has far-reaching consequences for understanding human nature. The point is not simply that most versions of biological determinism are false because they fail to give sufficient weight to the social determinants of human characteristics. It is, rather, that the usefulness of the whole nature-culture distinction as an analytical framework for understanding human beings comes into question. Just as we cannot identify any cultural or social phenomena uninfluenced in some way by human biology, neither can we identify any human biological or "natural" features that are independent of social influence. The biological and the social are so intertwined in the human past and present that it becomes impossible in principle to distinguish the natural from the social or cultural components in the constitution of human beings. As far as human beings are concerned, the relation between nature and culture is mutually constitutive: To oppose one to the other is incomprehensible. Everything that we are and do is revealed as simultaneously cultural and natural.

— ALLISON M. JAGGAR
KARSTEN J. STRUHL

indispensable to human life. God is thought to have a divine plan for humanity, and any attempt to subvert this plan by tinkering with the human body is regarded as at least prima facie wrong. When applied to humans as opposed to nonhuman animals, therefore, reproductive technology, genetic engineering, and euthanasia are viewed with suspicion, if not censure; and "brain death" may not be considered sufficient reason to switch off a life-support system, depending on when the soul is believed to leave the body. If, for example, the soul is thought to remain in the body until the last breath of life, then euthanasia can never be justified: Even the suffering and dying body must be revered as the house of the soul. Finally, because humans are morally distinguished by the possession of a soul, abortion is condemned at whatever point the fetus is believed to acquire a soul. It is interesting to note that the Catholic Church has not always held that fetal ensoulment occurs at the moment of conception: Saint Thomas Aquinas (1962), for instance, argued as an Aristotelian that the fetus did not have a soul until it assumed human form, which he thought occurred after three months' gestation for the male fetus and six months' for the female.

In contrast with the pre-Darwinian dichotomies between human and nature, spiritual and material, sacred and profane, post-Darwinian conceptions of human nature posit an evolutionary continuity between human and nonhuman animals. This continuity is sometimes used as a basis for moral challenges to the human exploitation and domination of animals, especially animals that are close to human beings in evolutionary terms. It is precisely those nonhuman animals most like humans, however, that are most useful for many purposes, such as medical experiments and organ transplants; in consequence, some philosophers have sought to undercut moral challenges to the human exploitation of nonhuman animals by arguing that beings "lower" on the evolutionary scale may be sacrificed for the good of "higher" species. Opposing this position is a growing minority in the bioethics community which argues that such a position is an example of unwarranted human chauvinism or "speciesism," a term invoked to suggest parallels with racism and sexism.

Although post-Darwinian assumptions of an evolutionary continuity between humans and nonanimals may be used to challenge the view that animals are simply a resource for human use, they have also been used to justify radical interventions in human life processes. If it is legitimate to experiment on nonhuman animals, for instance, it may be equally legitimate to experiment on human beings. If *Homo sapiens* is the accidental outcome of natural selection, if there is no inherent purpose for which we are created, then there is no a priori reason to assume that further modifications in human biological processes should not be made via reproductive technologies or even genetic engineering. Since the human nervous system is a defining component of human life, the fetus at an early stage of brain development is likely to have a different moral status than it does once the brain has developed. Certainly, the post-Darwinian conception of human nature would generally assume that "brain dead" means dead.

These conclusions reflect the absence of the concept of a soul in post-Darwinian views of human nature, since it was the soul that, in earlier conceptions, provided the philosophical grounding for human dignity. Unless an adequate substitute for the concept of the soul can be found, post-Darwinian conceptions of human nature may permit the drastic manipulation of human beings. Behavior regarded as undesirable may be treated either as a biological abnormality or as a failure of social conditioning. Biological determinists may regard alcoholism, addictive gambling, violent criminal behavior, schizophrenia, depression, and even homosexuality as candidates for treatment with a variety of biological techniques: psychosurgery, shock therapy, hormonal therapy, psychopharmacological interventions, and perhaps, in the future, even genetic manipulation. Behaviorists, of course, emphasize the use of various conditioning techniques to modify human behavior, raising the prospect of a *Clockwork Orange* world. Skinner, in fact, wrote a utopian novel, *Walden Two* (1948), in which behavioral managers conditioned people from birth to make choices in accord with the goals and institutions of that society. Both biological and behavioral interventions often work toward the same goal—direct control of human behavior.

But who will control the controllers, and how far will such control be allowed to extend? There are already biological determinists who advocate the use of genetic manipulation to raise IQ or to alter certain "undesirable" tendencies in the human species, perhaps to create a Superman. Others would clone the embryo and store it for future use, perhaps in case of some failure of the original stock. Brave New World may be just around the corner unless we can reclaim the concept of human dignity. Social and historical conceptions of human nature offer a secular basis for doing so.

Although people who accept a social and historical conception of human nature may still utilize some concept of naturalness in describing various human activities, such as conceiving or giving birth, they recognize that what is taken to be natural or unnatural changes historically and culturally, so that ethical decisions cannot be grounded in some unchangeable concept of human nature. However, this does not prevent us from ethically evaluating various attempts to manipulate and

"It is to the credit of human nature, that, except where its selfishness is brought into play, it loves more readily than it hates."

NATHANIEL HAWTHORNE
THE SCARLET LETTER
1850

See Also
Body

"Nature her custom holds, Let shame say what it will."

SHAKESPEARE
HAMLET, 1600

control human nature. Indeed, those who accept social and historical conceptions of human nature are likely to urge caution in the use of biological interventions and conditioning techniques for the purposes of altering human behavior. They will be suspicious of all treatment and research modalities that fail to respect human agency, reflective intelligence, and decision-making capabilities, since it is precisely these transhistorical capacities that make possible the continuous transformation of our historical natures. In short, social and historical conceptions of human nature will tend to reaffirm the concept of human dignity. In the sphere of medicine, for instance, they are likely to insist on the dignity of medical subjects and emphasize informed consent and coparticipation in physician-patient relationships.

The recognition that human beings individuate themselves within and through social processes may also have implications for the abortion controversy; at the very least, it suggests that women and fetuses cannot have the same moral status. Moreover, social and historical conceptions of human nature emphasize that consideration of bioethical problems must be sensitive to concrete social and political contexts; in a society with an expressed commitment to human equality, for example, questions like procreative technology or contract parenting must be evaluated with special reference to their implications for people of different classes, genders, abilities, races, and ethnicities. Finally, social and historical conceptions regard human beings as transhistorically creative, productive, social, and capable of reforming their habits through reflective intelligence; and people who accept these conceptions are likely to valorize those capacities and seek to develop social institutions—including health-care, psychiatric, and research institutions—through which they would be enhanced.

The open-ended nature of these last implications serves as a reminder that ethical conclusions are not strictly entailed by any general conception of human nature, especially by social and historical conceptions. In addressing particular bioethical problems, therefore, the values implicit in these conceptions must be supplemented by explicitly ethical criteria, such as historically specific understandings of justice, freedom, and human well-being.

— ALLISON M. JAGGAR
KARSTEN J. STRUHL

I

INFANTS

HISTORY OF INFANTICIDE

In many societies infanticide, the deliberate killing of infants, was not only tolerated but also sometimes promoted as a solution to the problem of unwanted infants, whether deformed or healthy. This article provides a historical account of infanticide in Western societies, beginning with its practice in Graeco-Roman antiquity and concluding with modern evidence for infanticide.

Infanticide in antiquity

In Greek society, an infant's worth was measured by its potential to fulfill a useful function in society. Thus, Plato maintained that society was better served if deformed newborns were "hidden away, in some appropriate manner that must be kept secret," a practice that likely included infanticide (Plato, *Republic*, 460). Similarly, Aristotle wrote in *Politics*: "As to the exposure and rearing of children, let there be a law that no deformed child shall live." Aristotle also condoned abandonment as a method of population control, although he recommended early abortion in regions where the "regular customs hinder any of those born being exposed" (Aristotle, *Politics*, 1335b). In Sparta, where military strength was highly valued, infanticide may have reached its zenith. Plutarch gives an account of the Spartan custom: "But if it was ill born and deformed they sent it to . . . a chasm-like place at the foot of Mount Taygetus, in the conviction that the life of that which nature had not well-equipped at the very beginning for health and strength, was of no advantage, either to itself or to the state" (Plutarch, *Life of Lycurgus*, 16).

It is difficult to distinguish between infanticide, with the intent to kill the infant, and abandonment, which may or may not have involved this intention. Failure to distinguish between the two has made accurate assessment of each difficult (Boswell, 1988). Historians have generally interpreted the Greek word for abandonment, translated as "exposure, putting out, or hiding away," as equivalent to infanticide. However, the Greek terms for abandonment do not convey the sense of injury or harm associated with infanticide. Historical evidence is not clear as to whether abandoned infants usually died or if those who abandoned them intended their death. Often abandonment was viewed as an alternative to infanticide. Nevertheless, it is reasonable to infer that some deformed and healthy infants, particularly females, were exposed with the intent that they would not survive. Further, it is likely that direct infanticide was practiced for both eugenic purposes and population control. Laws neither prohibited the killing of defective infants nor protected healthy infants from death by exposure.

Evidence from classical sources suggests that infanticide was practiced widely and with impunity in Roman society. While Romans continued the practice of disposing of defective infants for eugenic and economic reasons, an additional motivation stemmed from the Roman belief in the phenomenon of unnatural events, or *prodigia* (Amundsen, 1987). The Greeks saw deformities in newborns as natural occurrences. In contrast, the Romans viewed portentosi, meaning "unnatural" or "monstrous" births, as ominous or numinous signs that needed to be destroyed in order to rid the community of guilt and fear. The historian Livy of the first century B.C.E wrote about the birth of an infant who was both unusually large and of indeterminate gender:

> *[M]en were troubled again by the report that at Frusino there had been born a child as large as a four year old, and not so much a wonder for size as because . . . it was uncertain whether male or female. In fact the soothsayers summoned from Etruria said it was a terrible and loathsome portent; it must be removed from Roman territory, far away from contact with earth, and drowned in the sea. They put it alive into a chest, carried it out to sea and threw it overboard.*
>
> *(Livy,* Histories, *37.27)*

Roman literature is rife with testimony to such killings. According to the Laws of the Twelve Tables (5th century B.C.E, considered to be the basis of Roman law), deformed children, *puer ad deformitatem*, were to be killed quickly. Historians disagree whether the law required that these infants be killed or whether it merely allowed infanticide. In any case, Roman society appears to have accepted infanticide as a reasonable solution to the problem of deformed infants both for eugenic and superstitious motives. In a gynecological

"If pregnancy were a book they would cut the last two chapters."

NORA EPHRON
IN THE PORTABLE CURMUDGEON
1987

treatise entitled "How to Recognize a Newborn Worth Rearing," the Graeco-Roman physician Soranus (1st-2nd century C.E.) specifies that such an infant "immediately cries with proper vigor, is perfect in all its parts, members and senses [and] has been born at the due time, best at the end of nine months. And by conditions contrary to those mentioned, the infant not worth rearing is recognized" (Soranus, *Gynecology*, pp. 79-80).

Seneca argued that the practice of infanticide is rationally motivated: "Mad dogs we knock on the head; the fierce and savage ox we slay; sickly sheep we put to the knife to keep them from infecting the flock; unnatural progeny we destroy; we drown even children who at birth are weakly and abnormal. Yet it is not anger, but reason that separates the harmful from the sound" (Seneca, *Moral Essays*, 1.15). Even if it were not legally mandated, it is unlikely infanticide was penalized in Roman society given the tradition of *patria potestas*, which granted fathers absolute authority over other members of the family. Roman fathers had power of life and death over their children and were allowed to execute even a grown son (Boswell, 1988). The most likely victims, however, were infants, especially deformed ones, or female children who—even when healthy—were considered of little social value.

Some Roman philosophers objected to abandonment and infanticide. Musonius Rufus, writing in the first century C.E., opposed infanticide because it reduced the population. Epictetus, a Stoic philosopher and a contemporary of Musonius, condemned abandonment as a violation of the natural affection that parents should have for their offspring. Such apparent concern for the infant was not based on a belief in the child's intrinsic right to life, but was motivated by the desires to follow natural law and to increase the population. Thus, although evidence for the practice of infanticide under the Roman empire is somewhat inconclusive, Roman law and custom apparently did not prohibit parents from killing their children.

◆ **infanticide**
The deliberate killing of infants.

Early Jewish and Christian traditions

Jewish scholars were among the first to clearly condemn the killing of infants. Jews believed that humans were created in the image of their creator, Yahweh. Hence, all human life was sacred from the moment of birth. The Torah speaks of defective individuals as Yahweh's creations and it mandates protection to the blind, the deaf, the weak, and others who are needy (Lev. 19:14). Human life had intrinsic value by virtue of divine endowment, not merely instrumental value by virtue of social utility, as in classical Greek and Roman society.

The first-century Jewish philosopher Philo denounced infanticide and emphasized adults' duties toward children. His account equated abandonment with infanticide:

> *Some [parents] do the deed with their own hands; with monstrous cruelty and barbarity they stifle and throttle the first breath which the infants draw or throw them into a river or into the depths of the sea, after attaching some heavy substance to make them sink more quickly under its weight. Others take them to be exposed in some desert place, hoping, they themselves say, that they may be saved, but leaving them in actual truth to suffer the most distressing fate. For all the beasts that feed in human flesh visit the spot and feast unhindered on the infants, a fine banquet provided by their sole guardians, those who above all others should keep them safe, their fathers and mothers.*

Philo further condemned the practice by claiming, "Infanticide undoubtedly is murder, since the displeasure of the law is not concerned with ages but with a breach to the human race" (Philo, *Works*, vol. 7).

However, it was the advent of Christianity, rooted in Judaism, that significantly altered public attitudes toward the practice of infanticide. Christians inherited the Jewish doctrine that humans were divinely created, including the emphasis on the sanctity of all human life. Believers were urged to emulate Christ's self-sacrificing love through benevolence and charity, providing a new rationale for philanthropy (Ferngren, 1987a). The consequences of this philanthropy were seen in Christian charities and endeavors for the poor, the sick, and the needy. Rescue and care of exposed infants was viewed as a special Christian duty. During the medieval period through the nineteenth century, Christians established foundling hospitals, institutions for abandoned and unwanted children.

Two other Christian concepts important for their effect on the practice of infanticide were original sin and its correlative ritual of infant baptism, thought to have become common during the third century. Christians believed that infants who died without baptism were condemned to eternal hell. Because baptisms were performed only on holy days, not necessarily soon after birth, many parents already were committed to raising the child by the time of the ritual. Thus, baptism served as an important deterrent to both abandonment and infanticide.

Although Jews and Christians vigorously opposed infanticide, their opposition had little impact until Christianity became widespread and officially recognized in the fourth century. A church council in Spain issued the first canon against infanticide in 305 C.E.,

See Also

Fetus; Maternal-Fetal Relationship

and soon after, both local and ecumenical councils throughout Europe took similar actions. The penalty prescribed by the church for infanticide was either penance or excommunication.

The first secular law concerning the killing of children was issued in 318 C.E. by Constantine, the first Christian emperor. However, the law mentions children killing parents as well as parents killing children and thus was not directed specifically against infanticide. In 374 C.E., Valentinian enacted legislation declaring infanticide to be murder and punishable by law. Soon after, a statute was issued that appears to have prohibited exposure of infants. Although Christian emperors promulgated many laws reflecting Christian morality, fear of losing salvation made the penitential system of the churches far more effective in influencing moral behavior than did state legislation. Church leaders continued to put pressure on the state, bringing about a series of legal codes aimed at protecting newborn children.

Although the laws did not distinguish between healthy and defective infants, one may assume that Christian condemnation of infanticide extended to all infants. Early Christian apologists reflect this position. Saint Augustine argued that differences between healthy and deformed people should be seen in the same light as racial and ethnic diversity:

> *If whole peoples have been monsters, we must explain the phenomenon as we explain the individual monsters who are born among us. God is the Creator of all; He knows best where and when and what is, or was, best for Him to create, since He deliberately fashioned the beauty of the whole out of both the similarity and dissimilarity of its parts. . . . It would be impossible to list all the human offspring who have been very different from the parents from whom they were certainly born. Still all these monsters undeniably owe their origin to Adam.* *(Augustine,* City of God, *16.8)*

Augustine's writings show a concern for children unusual in his time, placing the infant and the child under the protection of the Lord.

Despite decisive changes in attitudes and laws, infanticide persisted even after the official triumph of Christianity as the imperial religion. While the practice may have diminished, episodic killing of infants continued throughout Western history. What changed in subsequent periods were the motivations, methods, and penalties associated with infanticide as well as the options available to parents of unwanted children.

Medieval period

Throughout most of the medieval period, infanticide was regulated largely by church courts rather than civil

MEDIEVAL PRACTICES
A Dangerous Mix of Religion and Folk Superstitions

Christianity's beliefs mixed with pagan myth, superstition, and folklore during Europe's medieval period. This commingling had significant implications for deformed infants and the practice of infanticide. Some thought, for example, that parental sexual behavior or "ill-timed passions" generated abnormal births or that sexual relations during menstruation, pregnancy, or lactation resulted in dire consequences for the unborn. In addition, the birth of an anomalous infant was sometimes attributed to demonic intervention: Such births were seen as the product of either a sexual liaison between the mother/witch and the devil or a changeling left by the devil as punishment for parental sins. Parents, particularly mothers, were held morally responsible for their infants' abnormalities.

The changeling myth, derived from pagan sources, maintained that fairies, motivated by jealousy, substituted an elf child for the real child (Haffter, 1968). This version did not impute guilt to the parents; instead, blame was placed on demon fairies of the underworld and their envy of humans. Once the myth was Christianized, however, it became the devil who stole the real child and left a demon-child in its place. Thus, God allowed parents to be punished for impiety or for bearing children outside matrimony. This change transformed the rationalization for the birth of defective infants from external forces to parental responsibility. Brutal and frequently lethal methods were employed either to exorcise the devil from the child or to compel the devil to return the normal child. Few infants survived the ordeal. However, violent infanticide of this sort was probably the exception rather than the rule, even during the Middle Ages.

There was some secular legislation against infanticide, particularly in the later medieval period, and the crime was usually considered to be homicide. But overlaying (suffocation in the parental bed), the most frequent cause of infanticide, was easy to conceal and intent was nearly impossible to establish, thus making prosecution extremely difficult. When cases of infanticide did reach secular courts, the accused were readily acquitted on pleas of insanity or poverty. Secular authorities displayed remarkable ambivalence toward the killing of infants. By law it was considered a serious crime, yet in practice it was generally excused (Damme, 1978).

— CINDY BOUILLON-JENSEN

Fetal therapies and neonatal advances have improved the chances for babies previously at high risk of stillbirth, birth trauma, hypoxia, and neonatal death.

PAGE 467

courts. Ecclesiastical penalties for married women convicted of infanticide were also remarkably light, considering the Church's position. Punishment involved penance and was comparable to that imposed for sexual offenses such as adultery and fornication. Once the penance had been performed, the guilty person was not prosecuted in civil courts. The relatively light penance and the failure of secular authorities to prosecute cases of infanticide suggests that the crime was considered something less than homicide (Helmholz, 1974). Cases involving unwed mothers, however, were treated differently. Unmarried mothers who killed their infants were often accused of being witches. In fact, infanticide was the most common charge brought against "witches" during the Middle Ages. Unlike their married counterparts, alleged witches were punished severely, usually by drowning, burial alive, or impalement.

The only reference to the status of infants under medieval secular laws was a civil law definition of a freeman, which appears to have excluded both illegitimate and seriously deformed infants from what little protection the law offered: "Among freemen there may not be reckoned those who are born of unlawful intercourse . . . nor those who are created pervertedly, against the way of human kind, as for example, if a woman bring forth a monster or a prodigy" (Fleta 1.5, "Of Different Kinds of Children"). As legal historian Catherine Damme comments, "Clearly, these pitiful non-persons were vulnerable to the murderous attacks of their progenitors" (Damme, 1978, p. 7).

Although direct infanticide was practiced to some extent, the more common and insidious cause of infant death during the Middle Ages was abandonment. The distinction between infanticide and abandonment became increasingly important because abandonment was generally regarded as a venial offense, punishable only if the child died. In the early Middle Ages, abandonment was widespread, motivated primarily by poverty and illegitimacy. Although a few churchmen believed it was equivalent to infanticide, two forms of abandonment were virtually institutionalized: oblation (or donating infants to the Church) and leaving infants at foundling hospitals. From a Christian point of view, both were improvements over the morally objectionable practices of exposure and infanticide. A canonical decree of the tenth century urged women to leave their illegitimate infants at the church rather than kill them (Boswell, 1988). Although oblates were tied irrevocably to the Church for life, the Church provided food, clothing, and a secure monastic life.

Foundling homes were established to diminish the practice of exposure and to provide a humane solution to infanticide. In reality, however, the foundling home often was equivalent to consigning the child to death through neglect, disease, and sometimes more direct action. Once infants arrived at a foundling home, they frequently were sent to the country with a wet nurse who was likely to be negligent and more interested in a steady flow of babies than in nurturing. Death rates were high, especially for female infants (Trexler, 1973). Markedly high demographic ratios of males to females throughout Europe during this period suggest that selective female infanticide may have been widely practiced. The disparity between male and female deaths was probably due to greater social value for males and a greater likelihood that, when put into foundling homes, they would be reclaimed by their parents. Thus, such institutions did little to secure the lives of unwanted infants. They were successful only in transferring the problem of unwanted infants from a public arena to an institutional one, shielding society from the realities of abandoned children and possibly encouraging the very practice they were intended to alleviate.

Renaissance and Reformation

During the sixteenth and seventeenth centuries there was a concerted effort to stem the practice of infanticide throughout Europe. Despite a dramatic surge in reported cases, it is not clear whether or not the increase meant more frequent practice; urbanization undoubtedly made it more difficult to destroy infants secretly. Authorities were more successful at promulgating harsh legislation aimed at ending the practice and were also increasingly vigilant in prosecuting murdering mothers. An intense focus on the problems of poverty and sexual promiscuity and their purported ties to infanticide led to laws that were strongly moral in tone and selective against unmarried mothers.

The first attempt to strengthen and unify infanticide laws under the Holy Roman Empire was a statute known as the Carolina, issued in 1532 by Emperor Charles V. The law decreed that those found guilty were to be buried alive, or impaled, or drowned. The law also made concealment of pregnancy a crime, as it was presumed that such secrecy indicated infanticidal intentions. Many judges, under the pretext of the Carolina, "engaged in a policy of terror," the most notorious being the Saxon jurist Benedict Carpozof, who claimed that he assisted in the executions of 20,000 women (Piers, 1978, p. 69). The Carolina was only the first in a series of laws over the next few centuries that dealt severely with alleged infanticidal mothers.

In England, Henry VIII's split from the Roman Catholic church resulted in increased secular control. Growing concern about sexual immorality and criminality among the swelling numbers of urban poor led to the enactment of several social control laws. The Poor Law of 1576 (18 Eliz. I, c.3) made bearing bastard children a crime. The fact that punishment was severe and involved substantial social disgrace for the mother increased the incentive for these women to commit infanticide. It is not surprising, therefore, that English criminal court records show that the number of indictments and guilty verdicts for infanticide rose dramatically after 1576. Most cases involved bastard children, and concealment of pregnancy was mentioned frequently (Hoffer and Hull, 1981).

The reasons for the increased zeal in punishing illegitimacy are somewhat obscure, but Puritan interests seem to have played a role. The 1623 Jacobean infanticide statute (21 Jac. I, c.27), influenced by the Puritan element in parliament, allowed courts to convict on the basis of circumstantial evidence of concealment and prior sexual misconduct. The law presumed that the child was born alive and then killed unless the mother could prove otherwise. Prosecutions of infanticide showed a fourfold increase immediately following its enactment (Hoffer and Hull, 1981).

Ideas about the role of witches in the death of infants, even the deaths of children in foundling hospitals, persisted. Infanticide and witchcraft were so strongly interrelated during this period that their rates of indictments rose and fell in parallel. Witchcraft continued to play a major part in the drama of infanticide until the early 1800s.

Foundling hospitals continued to remove unwanted and abandoned children from public view throughout the sixteenth and seventeenth centuries. As in earlier centuries, the fate of these children was precarious. Overcrowded conditions, disease, lack of enough wet nurses, and general neglect continued to claim the lives of many of the institutions' charges.

The overwhelming majority of the victims of infanticide during this period were children born out of wedlock. Demographic information does not show the strong gender bias seen in the medieval years, nor is there evidence that defective newborns were consistently selected out. Apparently the shame associated with immoral sexual behavior was the primary selective force associated with the killing of infants.

Eighteenth and nineteenth centuries

In the eighteenth century, a steep decline occurred in indictments for infanticide; the courts showed greater leniency toward those accused of killing their children. In addition, illegitimacy was more common; as a result the stigma associated with it lessened and its strong correlation to infanticide began to diminish. Attitudes toward parenting changed as well, with a new emphasis on the emotional nurturing of children. Wet-nursing lost popularity, and it became more common for children to spend their early months with their mothers. The greater value placed on children resulted in increased beneficence in child rearing, and so parents were probably less likely to kill their offspring. In any case, juries were less willing to convict parents of infanticide solely on the basis of concealment.

New defenses for the suspected infanticidal mother were developed and more readily accepted by juries. One of the first of these defenses, known as "benefit of linen," was based on evidence that the mother had made linen for the baby before its birth and therefore had no intention to kill it. This line of argument became very popular after 1700 and virtually guaranteed acquittal. Another major defense commonly used was the "want of help" plea. Various accidents and calamities, such as failure to tie the umbilical cord, falls of either the mother or baby, illness of the mother, and unheeded cries for help, all effectively helped to sway jurors.

Efforts to reform the English infanticide statute of 1624 began in 1773 but were not successful until 1803. In the ambivalence of eighteenth-century English society, infanticide was considered homicide yet somehow not quite the equivalent of killing an adult. Despite the failure of reform resolutions until the nineteenth century, juries tended to ignore the severe infanticide law aimed selectively at unwed mothers.

A similar trend occurred in Prussia during the reign of Frederick the Great. In his *Dissertation sur les raisons d'établir ou d'abroger les lois* (1756), Frederick argued that the prevalence of infanticide was due to the harsh penalties for illegitimacy. He therefore abolished laws penalizing pregnancies out of wedlock and eventually provided legal protection for unwed mothers. Scholars throughout Europe, including Cesare Beccaria, Voltaire, Johann Heinrich Pestalozzi, and Johann Wolfgang von Goethe, also called for legal

SOCIAL REFORMER

Frederick the Great (Frederick II) of Prussia (1712–1786) sought to discourage infanticide by abolishing laws that penalized pregnancies out of wedlock

"The prince is the first servant of his state."

FREDERICK THE GREAT
MEMOIRS OF THE HOUSE OF BRANDENBURG, 1758

reform and urged authorities to prevent the circumstances leading to infanticide.

Despite moderately successful reform efforts, however, infanticide did not disappear. During the nineteenth century high rates of illegitimate births continued; so, consequently, did infant killing. Corpses of infants found in privies, parks, rivers, and other public places fueled the perception that infanticide was reaching intolerable proportions. This perception may or may not have represented an actual increase in the incidence of the crime, but it did serve to stimulate an unprecedented public outcry. By the mid-nineteenth century, the concern over the "slaughter of innocents" appeared in the press (Behlmer, 1979). The British newspaper *Morning Star* (June 23, 1863) declared, "This crime is positively becoming a national institution"; and the *Pall Mall Gazette* (April 30, 1866) protested, "It is exceedingly unpleasant to find ourselves stigmatized in foreign newspapers . . . as a nation of infanticides. . . . 13,000 children are yearly murdered by their mothers in heretical England." The *Saturday Review* (1865, pp. 161-162) asserted that infanticide "is the characteristic at once of the rudest barbarism and of that more terrible epoch of national life when the wheel has gone its full circle, and society falls to pieces by the vices of civilization."

Physicians were among those who led reform efforts. In his essay on infanticide in 1862, William Burke Ryan wrote passionately against the horrors of infant murder; he and several colleagues formed the Infant Life Protection Society. By 1870 the group had achieved many of its goals, including mandatory registration of all births. In 1872, Parliament passed the first Infant Life Protection Act requiring registration of all "baby farms," houses with more than one child under the age of one.

Legal prosecution of infanticide also underwent significant changes. Ellenborough's Act of 1803, which replaced the Infanticide Act of 1623, reinstated the common-law presumption of stillbirth, shifting the burden of proof from the defendant (mother) back to the prosecutor. In 1828 the law was expanded to include legitimate as well as illegitimate births, removing the obvious selection against unwed mothers. The fact that courts consistently acquitted the accused or mitigated penalties on the basis of insanity is testimony to the court's continued hesitancy to consider infanticide the moral equivalent of murder. There was a "visceral feeling that such a crime simply could not be a rational act. . . . the minds of the jury and jurist could not accept that such a heinous act could be committed by a rational person—the accused's mind had to be deranged, if only temporarily" (Damme, 1978, p. 14).

TWENTIETH-CENTURY PRACTICES

A More Englightened Age?

The most notorious instances of infanticide in the twentieth century were committed secretly in Nazi Germany, under the auspices of the Committee for the Scientific Treatment of Severe, Genetically Determined Illness. Doctors, nurses, and teachers were required to register all children with congenital abnormalities or mental retardation. Failure to comply meant civil penalties or imprisonment. Defective children were removed from their homes and routinely euthanized at hospitals by morphine injection, gas, lethal poisons, or sometimes starvation. To ensure secrecy, the bodies were cremated immediately. Parents who protected their children were sent to labor camps and their children were taken from them. Documents reveal substantial public support for the euthanasia of defective children, even from parents with abnormal children (Proctor, 1988).

Calls for legalized euthanasia also arose from the United States, where it was justified primarily as a way of limiting the social costs associated with defective infants. W. A. Gould, writing in the *Journal of the American Institute of Homeopathy*, cited the "elimination of the unfit" in ancient Sparta as a defense of the economic arguments for euthanasia in the twentieth century (Gould, 1933). In 1938, W. G. Lennox advocated the "privilege of death for the congenitally mindless and for the incurable sick who wish to die" because saving these lives "adds a load to the back of society" (Lennox, 1938, p. 454). But as the realities of the Nazi extermination programs began to surface in the United States in the 1940s, promotion of euthanasia in general began to decline.

Yet in 1942, Foster Kennedy, professor of neurology at Cornell Medical College, wrote an article entitled "The Problem of Social Control of the Congenital Defective" advocating "euthanasia for those hopeless ones who should never have been born—Nature's mistakes." Kennedy believed "we have too many feebleminded people among us," and it was most humane to relieve defective individuals of their tortured and useless existence. Furthermore, he maintained that in diagnosis and prognosis there could be no mistakes in this "category" of children. A Gallup poll conducted twelve years earlier indicated that Kennedy's position probably was not without support within the American community. According to the poll, 45 percent of Americans in 1930 favored euthanasia of anomalous infants (Proctor, 1988, p. 180).

— CINDY BOUILLON-JENSEN

Conclusion

Authors who have explored the ethical dimensions of infanticide have frequently prefaced their discussions with surveys of its practice throughout history. The ostensible purpose of these discussions generally has been to provide a broader, less culturally bound perspective. However, Stephen Post argues that many writers selectively present "a one-sided and reductionist view of the history of infanticide to support their position . . . that active killing of neonates is morally acceptable" (Post, 1988, p. 14). He contends that the extent of infanticide has been misrepresented and overstated. The argument is that commentators on the history of infanticide have drawn, at least to some extent, from historical surveys plagued by interpretations that tend to view history in a positivist or linear fashion. The French historian Phillipe Ariès maintains that the idea of a separate childhood was unknown until the later Middle Ages (Ariès, 1962). Similarly, Lloyd DeMause contends: "The further back in history one goes, the lower the level of child care, and the more likely children are to be killed, abandoned, beaten, terrorized, and sexually abused" (DeMause, 1974, p. 1).

Revisionist historians, focusing on social, economic, and cultural forces, offer a significantly altered perspective on infanticide. While infanticide has been practiced continuously throughout Western history, it is not obvious that filicidal tendencies are widespread among parents. On the contrary, parents have usually resorted to infanticide only in exceptional circumstances. Although accurate estimates of the frequency of infanticide are almost nonexistent (largely due to inadequate and inconsistent recordkeeping), the prevalence of infanticide throughout Western history seems to have been episodic. Rates of infant killing have shown a tendency to rise and fall depending on prevailing economic and social forces. There have been striking discrepancies between the official position of the law, the frequency of the crime, the rate of prosecutions, the severity of punishment, and public sentiment concerning infanticide. Although the law has been relatively consistent in prohibiting its practice, the law has not always been an accurate gauge of societal values. Finally, the availability of alternatives to infanticide—including abandonment, foundling hospitals, oblation, contraception, and abortion—appears to have had more impact on its practice than have official prohibitions.

— CINDY BOUILLON-JENSEN

ETHICAL ISSUES

The birth of a baby can be one of the most satisfying, fulfilling experiences of a parent's life or a couple's marriage. After months of "infanticipating," the experiences connected with the first few hours and days of the baby's life can be intensely rewarding for the parents, providing them with joy, gratitude, and perhaps humility as they contemplate the new life that is now entrusted to them for care and support. If they are religious believers, they may be inclined to think of the baby's life as a divine gift and to regard their parental role as involving responsible stewardship over that gift. At the very least, they will probably be thankful that the baby has a normal brain, the correct number of fingers and toes, and the rest of a physical endowment that would suggest normal human development.

Unfortunately, in a small minority of cases the months of parental dreams and plans for a normal baby turn out to be false hope. In some instances, even when prenatal diagnosis has already indicated that the baby will not be normal, there may still be parental surprise and disappointment at the range of medical problems and the degree of neurologic impairment the child has. In other instances, when prenatal diagnosis was not done and the potential parents had no opportunity for anticipatory grief over the loss of a normal baby, the birth of a premature and/or congenitally disabled infant can have an enormous emotional impact on the parents that severely tests their most deeply held beliefs, values, and hopes for the future.

The birth of such a baby can also reflect the diversity of ethical perspectives that exist among parents, physicians, and other persons regarding the value of infants with life-threatening medical conditions, especially when the projected future lives of these children are filled with a mixture of neurologic impairments, mental and physical disabilities, and, sometimes, considerable medical uncertainty regarding the degree of those disabilities. For many persons, such cases raise important substantive questions: What is the moral status of infants with mental and physical disabilities? Should all of these infants receive life-sustaining medical interventions regardless of the severity of their medical conditions? What should be the ethical standard according to which a few infants would not receive life-sustaining efforts? Is there any moral difference between withholding and withdrawing life-sustaining treatments? Are there important moral differences between decisions about life-sustaining treatment in cases of severely disabled infants compared with cases of adults who have never been autonomous because of severe mental retardation? Would it be justifiable, in rare cases, intentionally to kill any of these infants?

Cases of premature and disabled infants also raise important procedural questions: Who should have the authority to make these life-and-death decisions? Should physicians, and in particular neonatologists, make these decisions because of their greater technical knowledge and experience with similar cases? Should

The longest well-documented periods for human embryo culture are 8 days and 13 days.

PAGE 241

There has been little ethical discussion of embryo research beyond 14 days.

PAGE 241

I

INFANTS

Ethical Issues

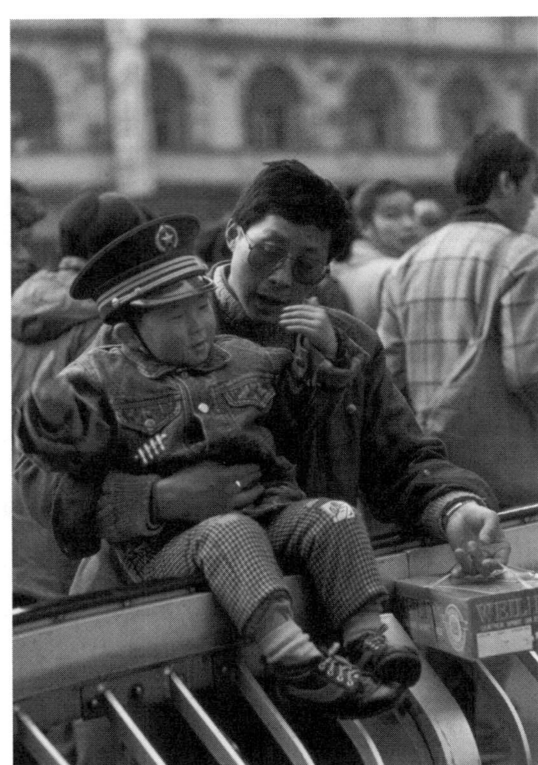

FAMILY FIRST

Parental decisions about keeping a child (or authorizing lifesaving measures) often first involve concerns about the family's welfare, and then the child's.

the infant's parents decide because of their roles in conceiving and caring for the child, and because of their greater emotional and financial stake in the child's death or disabled life? Should a collective body (e.g., a pediatric ethics committee) make the borderline decisions?

In addition, important questions are sometimes raised about contextual and methodological matters related to decisions about the care of infants: What lessons can we learn about caring and nurturing from parents who have learned to cope with and transcend one of life's personal tragedies? Is a philosophical approach that focuses on principles, rights, interests, and obligations the correct model for ethical analysis? Do theological claims about the sanctity of life, the meaning of suffering, and the importance of stewardship over life have a significant place in decisions about the appropriate level of care for infants, whether normal or abnormal in some way? To what extent should the realities of medical economics influence the decision about whether a premature and severely disabled infant lives or dies? How much should decision makers in individual cases consider the implications of their decisions in terms of public policy?

This article has five parts: (1) a brief historical overview; (2) international perspectives among pediatricians; (3) alternative perspectives on the moral status of infants; (4) perspectives on abating life-sustaining treatment; and (5) the emerging mainstream ethical perspective. Additional information on some of these points is found in the other articles in this entry.

Historical overview

Throughout history, as at the present time, the birth of a baby has often been the occasion for joy, celebration, and thanksgiving. In earlier centuries, the birth of a healthy, normal baby was frequently the occasion for celebration because the baby, especially if the infant was male, offered future promise for the family: another hunter for food supplies, another worker for the field or factory, another opportunity for continuing the family lineage. The birth of a baby was often an occasion for celebration for another reason: the mother had survived the dangers inherent in pregnancy and childbirth, dangers that posed a significant risk to maternal health and life in every pregnancy before the advent of modern medicine.

However, not all births were celebratory occasions. In many societies and in virtually all historical periods, very young infants, female infants, bastards, and infants and older children believed to be "defective" in some way were frequently killed. The intentional destruction of infants and children through starvation, drowning, strangulation, burning, smothering, poisoning, exposure, and a variety of lethal weapons was a tragically common practice. Such practices were widely accepted ways of dealing with unwanted children, with the responses of governments varying from required infanticidal practices (e.g., in Sparta), to acceptance of or at least indifference to the killing of female infants (e.g., in China and India), to considerable uncertainty as to how to punish parents who may have committed an illegal act by killing one of their children under questionable circumstances.

Mothers and fathers have historically had several possible reasons for killing one or more of their children. Some of them have killed for economic reasons: A dead child would mean one less mouth to feed. Others have killed their infants because of social customs and pressures: An illegitimate child, an "extra" child beyond a certain number, or another female child was especially vulnerable. Still other parents have killed their children because the infants were physically or mentally abnormal, with their congenital abnormalities being interpreted as works of the devil, signs of fate, punishment for the sins of the parents, or tricks played by witches (Weir, 1984).

Some of these older explanations of congenital disabilities seem strange now, but two features of traditional infanticidal practices remain a part of the modern world. First, infants are still sometimes killed by their parents or, perhaps more commonly, abandoned without food, shelter, or parental protection. No society is exempt from such events, with media reports of dead or abandoned babies coming from China, India, Brazil, the United States, Romania, and

See Also

Coercive Policies: China's Missing Girls

other countries. Second, even for parents who cannot imagine killing their own children, the birth of an extremely premature and/or severely disabled infant is a mixed blessing. For that reason, parental decisions about medical efforts to prolong a child's life frequently involve concerns about the future of the family as well as considerations about the welfare of the child.

In many parts of the world, such decisions, whether made by a child's parents or physicians, are strikingly similar to decisions made about sick and disabled children in earlier historical periods because many countries still lack the medicines, the medical and nursing personnel, and the medical technology that are common to the rest of the world. In technologically developed countries, by contrast, the development of neonatal intensive-care units (NICUs), neonatologists and other pediatric subspecialists, sophisticated medical technology, new medicines, and new surgical techniques has brought unprecedented opportunities and challenges to physicians, parents, nurses, and all other persons interested in prolonging the lives and improving the health of critically ill children. Likewise, changes in neonatal medicine since the 1970s have meant that physicians, parents, or some combination of health-care professionals in a hospital can sometimes decide that the appropriate course of moral action in a case is not to initiate or continue life-sustaining treatments, given the child's severe neurologic impairments and likelihood of continued suffering.

Such decisions—not to use medical technology to sustain an extremely premature or severely disabled infant's life—are usually difficult and sometimes controversial. In the United States, public and professional responses to publicized pediatric cases in the 1980s generated two efforts at regulating selective nontreatment decisions. The two attempts at regulation, while not always in conflict, reflected two quite different eth-

ETHICAL ISSUES
Technologically-Induced Challenges

Some themes and problems are common as decision makers in technologically advanced countries confront the difficult choices presented by premature and disabled infants:

1. The ongoing technological development of pediatrics (e.g., the use of exogenous surfactants and high-frequency oscillatory ventilation for treating pulmonary problems) has resulted in improved mortality and morbidity rates for numerous infants and young children.
2. Unprecedented surgical techniques (e.g., surgery for short-bowel syndrome and for hypoplastic left ventricle) have resulted in the prolongation of life for many infants who would have died without surgery only a few years ago.
3. These technological and surgical achievements have created a trend in some pediatric subspecialties toward overtreatment of premature and disabled infants, a trend that seems to be contrary to the best interests of some of these children (Caplan et al., 1992).
4. Even with the technological progress in pediatrics, neonatologists and the parents with whom they work in individual cases are still frequently confronted with an inescapable problem: medical uncertainty regarding the degree and range of disability a neurologically impaired child will have, if the child survives with medical treatment (Hastings Center, 1987).

Compared with earlier historical periods, the period of technological medicine has produced unprecedented changes and challenges for parents, physicians, and other persons concerned about the care of infants. The rapidity and extent of the change is noticeable in the types of cases that now present the greatest ethical challenges for parents and physicians in NICUs. In the 1970s and 1980s, considerable debate centered on whether infants with Down syndrome plus complications and infants with myelomeningocele should receive surgical correction of their physical abnormalities. In the 1990s these types of cases have largely been replaced as ethical challenges by other kinds:

1. cases of extremely premature neonates with birth weights below 600 grams, gestational ages of approximately twenty-four weeks, and severe cardiac, pulmonary, and neurologic impairments;
2. cases of very small and disabled neonates whose low birth weights and disabilities are the result of factors during pregnancy, such as maternal malnutrition, infection (e.g., HIV and AIDS), smoking, consumption of alcohol, or use of cocaine and other drugs; and
3. cases of neonates with anencephaly whose organs could be transplanted into other infants, if the parents of the anencephalic infants were to consent and the law were to permit the transplantation (Walters, 1991).

— ROBERT F. WEIR

ical perspectives regarding how and by whom selective nontreatment decisions should be made.

One effort at regulation took the form of two sets of published federal regulations during the administration of President Ronald Reagan. The "Baby Doe" regulations, first proposed in 1983, and the subsequent child-abuse regulations, established in 1985, differed in legal philosophy, implementation, and influence. Yet both agreed on the ethical perspective that should govern life-and-death decisions made in NICUs and pediatric intensive-care units (PICUs): Every infant, unless permanently unconscious, irretrievably dying, or salvageable only with treatment that would be "virtually futile and inhumane," should be given life-sustaining treatment, no matter how small, young, or disabled the infant might be.

The other effort at regulation was made by the U.S. President's Commission for the Study of Ethical Problems in Medicine (1983), the American Academy of Pediatrics, and numerous writers on ethics in pediatric medicine. Given the complexity of some pediatric cases and the life-and-death nature of selective nontreatment decisions, the common recommendation was to have an ethics committee consult on the cases and give advice to the physicians in the cases. The ethical perspective at the heart of this recommendation was straightforward: In truly difficult cases, the most prudent procedure for decision making is the achievement of consensus by a multidisciplinary committee that is knowledgeable, impartial, emotionally stable, and consistent from case to case.

Similar efforts at regulating selective nontreatment decisions in NICUs and PICUs have not occurred in other countries having technological medicine. In Britain and Australia, for example, governments interested in regulating assisted reproduction technologies to protect pre-embryos have not had a similar interest in regulating selective nontreatment decisions to protect young infants, either from premature deaths or from profoundly impaired lives. Likewise, neither the governments nor the medical societies in these countries have chosen to establish pediatric ethics committees, preferring instead to leave decisions to abate life-sustaining treatment for young infants to the discretion of the physicians and parents of the children.

◆ **vertical transmission**
An infection that is passed from mother to infant.

International perspectives among pediatricians

The roles of physicians, parents, and nurses in the care of premature and disabled infants vary significantly from country to country. In general, pediatricians in countries that in recent decades have been characterized by authoritarian or totalitarian political regimes tend to take a similar approach to decisions made in NICUs: The decisions to treat or not to treat are made by physicians with only minimal participation by parents, nurses, or other health professionals. By contrast, pediatricians in democratic societies tend to have a more democratic attitude toward decisions made in NICUs: With some variation from physician to physician, the decisions to treat or not to treat are often made in consultation with the parents of the imperiled infants, with some physicians also finding merit in having pediatric ethics committees consult on some of the truly difficult decisions.

For example, one study indicated significant differences between pediatricians in Poland and pediatricians in Australia. The majority of both groups of physicians indicated that they had been confronted with the necessity of making decisions regarding the withholding or withdrawing of life-sustaining treatment from severely disabled infants. However, their views regarding the substantive and procedural features of such decisions were quite different. Whereas virtually all the pediatricians surveyed in Australia (98.2 percent) indicated that they did not believe that "every possible effort" should be made to sustain life in every case, half of the pediatricians surveyed in Poland (50 percent) stated that they thought that all possible efforts at sustaining life should be made in every case. Regarding specific diagnostic cases, significant numbers of Australian pediatricians thought that life-sustaining treatment could be withheld or withdrawn in cases of anencephaly and microcephaly (29.7 percent of the responding physicians), spina bifida and myelomeningocele (25.2 percent), extreme prematurity (9.0 percent), Down syndrome with complications (16.2 percent), and brain damage with projected mental retardation (26.1 percent). By contrast, the pediatricians in Poland, while agreeing with the Australian physicians regarding cases of extreme prematurity and brain damage, were much more reluctant to abate life-sustaining treatment for infants having microcephaly, spina bifida, or Down syndrome (Szawarski and Tulczynski, 1988).

The differences between the Australian and Polish pediatricians were even more significant when they were asked about the procedural aspects of decisions that would probably result in an infant's death. The majority of responding Australian pediatricians indicated that they discussed such decisions with other physicians (90.9 percent), the parents of the infant (90.1 percent), and nurses (84.7 percent). The Polish pediatricians, by contrast, almost always consulted with other physicians (99.0 percent) but rarely discussed the decisions with the parents (8.1 percent) or nurses (4.3 percent).

Another study suggested that there are differences among pediatricians in the United States, Sweden, Britain, and Australia on both substantive and proce-

See Also
Reproductive Technologies
Fetus

dural aspects of selective nontreatment decisions. According to this interpretive study, the dominant practice among American pediatricians, especially neonatologists, is to initiate aggressive life-sustaining treatments early, continue those medical interventions while diagnostic tests are being done and various pediatric specialists are consulted, and talk with parents about the alternative of abating treatment only when the parents bring up the subject or when a grim prognosis becomes increasingly clear. This perspective is described as a "wait until certainty" approach, an approach involving a clear ethical choice: Saving an infant who will have severe-to-profound disabilities is preferable to permitting the death of an infant who could have lived a tolerable life. This strategy ensures that all errors are in one direction: the promotion of the infant's life, even a severely disabled life. Treatment that sustains the infant's life can therefore be terminated only when death or profoundly impaired life is inevitable (Rhoden, 1986).

This study suggests that pediatricians in Sweden have a different perspective, one that is described as a "statistical prognostic" strategy. This approach seeks to minimize the number of infants whose deaths would come slowly as well as those whose lives would be characterized by profound disabilities. At the risk of sacrificing some potentially normal infants to avoid prolonging the lives of severely impaired infants, this approach uses statistical data, like birth weight, gestational age, and early diagnostic tests, to make selective nontreatment decisions. This strategy also ensures that all errors are in one direction: the promotion of healthy life, even at the cost of allowing some infants to die who could have lived with disabling conditions.

Pediatricians in Britain and Australia are described in the study as having medical and ethical perspectives that frequently differ from those of their American and Swedish counterparts. In contrast to many pediatricians in the United States, pediatricians in Britain and Australia are willing to withhold or withdraw treatment with much less prognostic certainty. Yet in contrast to many pediatricians in Sweden, British and Australian pediatricians are willing to engage in time-limited trials to give various treatments a chance to work, even when the child being treated is likely to have ongoing disabilities. Called an "individualized prognostic" strategy, this approach reflects an ethical perspective that realizes the inherent uncertainty in medicine, permits some role for parental discretion, and affirms the appropriateness of selective nontreatment decisions once a child's prognosis appears poor (Rhoden, 1986).

In much of the world, the ethical perspectives among physicians are quite different from the approaches described above because the provision of care to infants takes place outside the confines of technological medicine. In the People's Republic of China, India, the countries of the former Soviet Union, and many of the other countries in the world, the differences in medical management that have just been described have no significance. The shortages of medicine, the obsolescence of medical equipment, the inadequacies of prenatal care, the limited number of pediatricians, and the ongoing problems of malnutrition and infectious disease contribute to a social context in which the lives of infants are frequently short and often characterized by disease and disability.

Alternative perspectives on the moral status of infants

THREE POSITIONS ON PERSONHOOD OF NEWBORNS

1. All neonates count as actual persons in the same way adults do.
2. In order to count as a person, an infant must possess the intrinsic qualities of consciousness, self-awareness, and rationality.
3. Neonates are to be regarded as potential persons, not yet possessing the ontological status of actual persons, but on the way toward development.

Ethical perspectives on the care of infants are significantly influenced by views that are held regarding the ontological status and moral standing of infants, whether premature, disabled, or normal. What kind of entity is it whose life, health status, or death is at stake in the decisions made by physicians and/or parents? Is a neonate, in terms of ontological status, the same as an older child and an adult? Does an infant count as a person, in the same way that you and I count as persons? Or are questions about personhood irrelevant in terms of the moral standing that adults choose to grant infants? In terms of moral standing, what kinds of moral rights do infants possess? Do human infants possess full moral standing, making them morally equal to adult persons? Is the moral standing of neonates to be understood as somehow less than that of human adults but more than of human fetuses, or are fetuses, neonates, and adults to be understood as morally the same?

For many philosophers in recent years, questions related to the moral standing of infants have been addressed in the broader context of a discussion about ontological status and, more specifically, the meaning of personhood. One approach is to define "person" as meaning "a living being with full moral standing." According to this definition, all persons have such

◆ **Baby Doe guidelines**
Rules (1984) that forbid withholding or withdrawing lifesaving care, even those that are deemed inhumane, from a sick infant unless the care can be deemed virtually futile.

See Also
Personhood: Central Yet Irresolvable

standing, leaving open the question of just which characteristics give that standing.

Given this general philosophical perspective on personhood, at least three positions can be identified that link the ontological status of neonates with the moral standard granted to infants. The first position holds that all neonates, whether normal or neurologically impaired, count as actual persons in the same way that you and I count as persons. According to this view, the personhood of neonates is merely an extension of the personhood possessed earlier by fetuses. With this ontological status, neonates, like all other actual persons, have the moral right not to be killed or prematurely allowed to die, since the possession of personhood entails full moral standing, regardless of the age of the person. Personhood, according to this view, is based on genetic code or some other characteristic possessed at conception, not on possession of consciousness, self-awareness, rationality, or any other neurological characteristic.

The second position holds that in order to count as persons, infants (and other beings, whether human or nonhuman) must possess the intrinsic qualities or traits often defined by philosophers as being the threefold combination of consciousness, self-awareness, and at least minimum rationality (Feinberg, 1986). If infants lack these core properties, they have an ontological status that is more similar to the status of human fetuses than to the status of older children or adults. Holders of this view claim that all neonates, including normal babies, fail to pass the neurologic tests for personhood and are thus to be classified as nonpersons. In this view, all neonates lack the cognitive qualities that make a human into a person. In addition, the notion of potential personhood is discarded as flawed, largely because the advocates of this second position argue that personhood cannot be possessed in varying degrees. Holders of this second view also claim that only those who have the neurological characteristics of persons possess the rights of persons, including the right not to be killed or prematurely allowed to die. The result, in terms of the moral standing of neonates, is straight forward: Neonates do not possess the moral rights of persons, leaving them at risk of being killed or prematurely allowed to die unless their parents and physicians are motivated by psychological or legal considerations to sustain their lives (Tooley, 1983).

◆ **feticide**
Surgery performed to remove fetuses from the womb and to facilitate the birth of one or more healthy infants when multiple gestations appear.

The third position stands between the other positions. It identifies the same neurological characteristics of personhood, but according to this view, most neonates (those lacking severe neurologic impairment) are to be regarded as potential persons, not yet possessing the ontological status of actual persons but on the way to the possession of the core properties of personhood through the normal course of human development. Agreeing with advocates of the first two positions on the linkage between ontological status and moral standing, philosophers holding the third position maintain that when infants develop and subsequently become persons, they will acquire full moral standing. Until that time, including during the neonatal period, they are regarded as having a prima facie claim not to be killed, prematurely allowed to die, or significantly harmed in some other way, precisely because they will subsequently and naturally become actual persons.

The differences in these philosophical views have practical consequences in terms of the ways that adults value the lives of infants, including infants who may be extremely premature or severely disabled. Advocates of the first position tend to call for life-sustaining treatment to be administered to all infants in NICUs regardless of birth weight, gestational age, or neurological status, because all infants are actual persons in possession of the full panoply of moral rights common to persons. By contrast, any parents or physicians in NICUs who regard neonates as nonpersons (and who believe that only persons bear the rights borne by persons) are likely to be ready to withhold or withdraw treatment much more quickly, if the law permits them to do so, because the infant lives that are lost do not yet count for much morally. For advocates of the third position, the concept of potential personhood provides an intellectual framework in which difficult prognostic judgments make some sense. In this view, at least part of the difficulty in making decisions to provide life-sustaining treatment or to abate treatment, especially in cases of severe neurologic impairment, has to do with judgments about whether a particular baby has the potential even to become a person in the normal course of his or her development.

Other perspectives on the moral status of infants, some of which are grounded in theological ethics, suggest that the philosophical debate about the personhood of infants is intellectually restrictive and of little practical significance. For example, one fairly common view is that the moral standing of infants cannot depend on whether they meet a philosophically strict definition of personhood, because all infants fail to meet that standard. Rather, what is important is a social understanding of "person" according to which infants are regarded by their parents, physicians, and others "as if" they were persons. This social sense of personhood involves the imputing of personlike rights to infants because of their special roles in families and in society. The practical consequence of this view is that infants, who are given the imputed status of "person" in a social sense, have the same kind of moral standing as older human beings who are persons in a more formal sense (Engelhardt, 1978).

See Also

It's Human, But Is It a Person Yet?

Another widely held view is that the personhood question simply does not apply to infants, either in a strict sense or in a social sense. Rather, what is important is that infants are understood to have moral standing as "fellow human beings." Advocates of this view may regard fetuses and infants as having equal moral standing as human beings, or they may have a developmental view in which viable fetuses and infants, but not nonviable fetuses, have equal moral standing as human beings. Either way, infants are regarded as having the same kinds of moral rights that older human beings have, including the right not to be killed or allowed to die prematurely unless, in unusual cases, the burdens of continued life are regarded as outweighing the benefits of that life to the child (Fletcher, 1975). Holders of this view give the same moral standing to infants and fetuses as do holders of the first position above, but deny that these beings have to be called persons.

The personhood approach to the moral status of infants, according to another theological view, is unrelated to the possession of the neurological characteristics identified with personhood discussed above for another reason. The limiting of an infant's value to the question of whether that infant possesses the intrinsic properties of personhood entirely omits another approach to the understanding of the value that infants have: namely, a relational view of value that results from interpersonal bonding, affection, and care by parents and other adults. Even when an infant has a future that will, because of neurologic impairments, be characterized by developmental delay and mental retardation, the parents of the child still usually go through a process of bonding with the child. That process of bonding, which involves the replacement of a hoped-for child with a healthy attachment to the child one has been given, results in a valuing of the child by parents that is surely equal to the valuing of normal children by their parents (May, 1984).

A related view is that philosophical arguments about the moral status of infants need to be supplemented, if not replaced, by an experiential ethic of care. This view emphasizes the importance of the various perspectives that parents, physicians, nurses, and other persons bring to pediatric cases. Rather than focusing on the ontological and moral status of infants, most commonly with questions related to the possession of personhood and moral rights, this approach concentrates on the various values and virtues present, or possible, in the context of decision making about an infant's impending death or projected life with disabilities. The practical result is that questions in difficult cases are raised not only about what should be done for the patient but also about what kinds of moral agents the parents, physicians, and nurses should be as they provide care for an imperiled infant (Reich, 1987).

Ethical perspectives on abating life-sustaining treatment

The ethical perspective that became enacted into the "Baby Doe" regulations and child abuse regulations was only one of the ethical perspectives on the medical care of infants that received considerable attention in the United States in the 1970s-1990s. Other ethical perspectives have also been widely held, both before and after the federal regulations became policy.

For example, for some persons the important ethical question is not whether a given infant can be salvaged through medical treatment. Rather, the important question is what quality of life the child will probably have later, especially if the child's future is predicted to be dominated by severe-to-profound neurologic impairments, multiple surgeries, and numerous other medical problems. The question is sometimes posed in terms of the future relational potential possessed by a child with severe neurologic impairments, with the moral judgment being that an infant who lacks relational capacity will never have the quality of life that would justify the continuation of the child's life (McCormick, 1974).

A closely related ethical perspective focuses on a child's best interests. For persons holding this position, the important question is whether the life-sustaining treatment that could be given to imperiled newborns will, on balance, provide the infants with more benefits than burdens. Since quality-of-life projections can sometimes extend to include persons other than the patient, this position's strength is in framing the ethical debate primarily in terms of the patient's best interests, not the interests of the family or society (U.S. President's Commission, 1983).

Another ethical perspective emphasizes procedural issues. According to this view, the most important aspect of decisions not to sustain some infants' lives is the question of who should make these difficult decisions. Advocates of this position maintain that in most cases, the parents of a premature or disabled infant are the appropriate decision makers.

A very different ethical perspective on selective treatment decisions also has some advocates. As described in the previous section, some philosophers hold that life-sustaining treatment can morally be withheld or withdrawn from any infant, regardless of birth weight or disability, because the only deaths that matter are the deaths of persons, and no infants meet the requirements of personhood.

The emerging mainstream perspective

If any of these positions can be correctly designated as the mainstream ethical position, at least in the United

◆ **fetoscopy**
Examination of the pregnant uterus by means of a fiber-optic tube.

See Also
The Legal Status of Human Fetuses
The Moral Status of Human Fetuses

States, it is the patient's-best-interests position. Advocates of this position are concerned about the treatment-related harms that sometimes occur when neonatologists and other pediatric subspecialists persist, perhaps under the influence of the federal regulations, in overtreating infants who have extremely low birth weights and severe disabling conditions but who are neither unconscious nor dying. At the same time, proponents of the best-interests view are reluctant to grant the parents of premature and disabled infants as much discretion in deciding to abate life-sustaining treatment as some parents would like to have.

In clinical cases, the best-interests position relies on eight variables that help to determine whether to initiate, continue, or abate life-sustaining treatment: (1) the severity of the patient's medical condition, as determined by diagnostic evaluation and comparison with (a) all infants and (b) infants having the same medical condition; (2) the achievability of curative or corrective treatment, in an effort to determine what is meant by "beneficial" treatment in a given case; (3) the important medical goals in the case, such as the prolongation of life, the effective relief of pain and other suffering, and the amelioration of disabling conditions; (4) the presence of serious neurologic impairments, such as permanent unconsciousness or severe mental retardation; (5) the extent of the infant's suffering, as determined by the signs of suffering that infants send by means of elevated blood pressure, elevated heart rate, degree of agitation, and crying; (6) the multiplicity of other serious medical problems, with the most serious cases usually involving a combination of neurologic, cardiac, pulmonary, renal, and other medical complications; (7) the life expectancy of the infant, because some of the severe congenital anomalies involve a life expectancy of only a few weeks or months; and (8) the proportionality of treatment-related benefits and burdens to the infant, a medical and ethical "bottom line" for deter-

See Also

Doctors Refusing the Risk: A Neglect of Duty?

ETHICS OF NONTREATMENT

Three Perspectives

Three ethical perspectives cotinue to play major roles in selective nontreatment decisions, with the dominant perspective in individual cases varying from hospital to hospital, physician to physician, parent to parent, case to case. The perspective that calls for life-sustaining treatment to be administered to all infants who are conscious, not dying, and for whom treatment is not "virtually futile and inhumane" remains influential, even if the federal regulations that reflect this perspective have been largely unenforced throughout the country. The reasons for its continuing influence are twofold. First, this perspective is consistent with the reasons that motivate neonatologists to do the work they do: to prolong and enhance the lives of the youngest, smallest, most disabled, and most vulnerable human beings among us. Second, this perspective offers the simplest way of dealing with the multiple problems that constitute the "ethics lab" known as the NICU: It minimizes the factor of medical and moral uncertainty in cases, the role of parents as decision makers, and any considerations of the harm that may be done through prolonged, aggressive efforts to salvage imperiled young lives.

The second perspective that remains influential is the position that emphasizes the role of parents as decision makers. Advocates of this view rarely suggest that parents alone should make the selective nontreatment decisions that could result in the deaths of their children, or that parents should be given unlimited discretion in making such decisions. Rather, the claim that is often made is that parents should, in response to appropriate medical information and advice, have reasonable discretion in making a life-and-death decision regarding their child in the NICU, subject to certain ethical and legal constraints. They are the ones, after all, who may be saddled with the enormous financial costs of neonatal intensive care. They are the ones, in addition to the child, who will have to deal with the child's ongoing medical problems, repeated hospitalizations and surgeries, neurologic abnormalities, and developmental delays. They are the ones who will have to struggle to sustain their marriage, their family life, their careers, and their own physical and mental health.

The third perspective that remains influential is the patient's-best-interests position. Advocates of this position acknowledge the medical and moral uncertainty inherent in many cases, affirm an important role for parents as decision makers, and recognize that the same medical and surgical interventions that produce great benefit for some patients can produce undue harm for others. In contrast to the parental perspective, proponents of this view emphasize that the focal point of decision making in neonatal and pediatric cases should be the best interests of the patient, even when the patient's interests conflict with the interests of the parents. In this manner, the patient's-best-interests position emphasizes the linkage between life-sustaining medical treatment and patient-centered considerations regarding the quality of life—without broadening quality-of-life judgments to include the family, the society, or arbitrary standards for normalcy and acceptability, as quality-of-life projections sometimes do.

— ROBERT F. WEIR

mining whether life-sustaining treatment or the abatement of such treatment is in a particular infant's best interests (Weir and Bale, 1989).

Even with these variables, the ethical analysis of cases involving neonates or other young pediatric patients is anything but easy. Although there are numerous cases about which almost everyone agrees, there continue to be many cases that combine unprecedented medical and moral territory, advances in medical management and technology, medical uncertainty, and ethical conflicts between physicians and parents in such a way as to present serious ethical challenges to all the parties involved in the cases. In such instances, the discernment of the infant's best interests can be a challenging and humbling experience.

— ROBERT F. WEIR

PUBLIC-POLICY AND LEGAL ISSUES

Medical decisions regarding infants vary in the seriousness of their consequences for infants, families, health providers, and society. They range from decisions about home birth and male circumcision—debatable but generally agreed to be matters of private choice—to vaccination, genetic screening, female genital mutilation, and artificial life support for a critically ill newborn. In the United States, parents' legal right to select even the most invasive treatment—or to refuse lifesaving measures—was nearly unquestioned until recently; it has become the subject of litigation, extensive scholarly comment, and public concern. Because much of the legal and public-policy debate has focused on infants who require life support, decision making will be discussed here in that context.

The infant's interests

The increasing complexity of decisions about the treatment and nontreatment of infants has exacerbated the struggle over who may decide these issues. Advances in medical technology, surgical procedures, and pharmaceuticals allow severely compromised infants to survive, often for prolonged periods of time. These new technologies also usually entail painful, invasive procedures for the infant and the possibility of adverse effects that further attenuate the infant's already fragile hold on life. For example, medical expertise allows the resuscitation of many more premature infants than would have survived in the past; but these infants frequently need prolonged ventilatory assistance and frequent invasive tests. They are also at increased risk both for cerebral hemorrhages, which create severe neurological and mental deficits, and for serious adverse effects of treatment, such as blindness and deafness.

Decisions on treatment have traditionally rested with parents, health-care providers, or some combination of the two. Since the 1980s, the decision-making powers of these parties have been challenged. In the United States, the older body of law has been partially eroded by legislative enactments and court decisions that focus instead on the rights of the infant (Cooper, 1992). Indeed, recognition of the infant's individual rights arising from the celebrated 1982 Baby Doe case became the basis for substantial federal intervention in medical practice and family life.

— ANNE M. DELLINGER
PATRICIA C. KUSZLER

Ascertaining the infant's best interests generally falls to the primary caregivers—in most cases, the parents, who, although assisted by numerous directors, nurses, and social workers, frequently must make and bear the brunt of these difficult decisions. Unfortunately, the guidelines available to decision makers from the commission and subsequent case law are far from concrete. In describing the "best interests" standard, the commission stressed that normal adults must not impose their values or external concerns upon the beleaguered infant. In its guidelines, the commission stated that futile treatment for severely compromised infants with a life span of hours or days, such as anencephalics, need not be provided; at the other end of the spectrum, the commission condemned the withholding of treatment for a correctable problem when the infant was afflicted with an unrelated, non-life-threatening disorder, such as Down syndrome (U.S. President's Commission, 1983). However, for the vast territory in between, there is little guidance.

Determining the best interests of a compromised infant using the commission's guidelines presents considerable problems of interpretation (Rhoden, 1985). Some, including C. Everett Koop, former U.S. Surgeon General, believe that the best interests of the infant require providing maximum treatment in virtually all cases (Smith, 1992; Wells, 1988; Wells et al., 1990). In this view, infants express their interest in surviving by responding positively to treatment (Cooper, 1992). Others believe that nontreatment may be justified when the infant's life can be viewed as an injury rather than a gift to the infant; an "injury" is inferred when there is no prospect of meaningful life, which might occur because life expectancy is very short, there are severe mental deficits, and no curative or corrective treatments are available (Weir, 1994).

◆ **passive eugenics**
The societal acceptance of deaths by preventable social and economic inequities, such as infant mortality rates.

Some argue that the rational interests of the infant in treatment or nontreatment should not be limited to avoiding suffering (including the pain of treatment) and to minimizing physical and mental deficits, but should also include factors such as the burden of treat-

See Also
Maternal–Fetal Relationship

ment on family and society (Wells et al., 1990; Smith, 1992). Such a view holds that when an infant's condition lacks any "'truly human' qualities" or "relational potential," the best decision is not to treat (Smith, 1992, p. 56). Certainly, one can presume that an infant has an interest in his or her "standing and memory within the family" (Mitchell, 1989, p. 341). If so, the infant's best interests cannot be determined in isolation from the feelings and concerns of others. Although such "quality of life" considerations are given short shrift under the current federal law and under the President's Commission's best-interests standard, they may well be inevitable (Rhoden, 1985). Heretofore the courts have both embraced and enhanced quality-of-life concerns in deciding controversial issues. No consensus has yet emerged.

Parents' interests

U.S. jurisprudence still strongly favors parents as decision makers for children's medical care, although it does not accord the preference constitutional status (*Cruzan* v. *Director, Missouri Department of Health*, 1990). Though some dispute the basis for a parental preference—asking whether it is for the parents' sake, the children's, or society's (Schneider, 1988)—the law is willing to assume that parents, with physicians' help, can best judge the child's interest and will best protect it. Moreover, it seems fair to defer to those who will live intimately with the results of the decisions. As explained below, however, the wisdom of this presumption is challenged on many fronts, both from within and outside the legal establishment. In any case, parental authority is conditional. It is settled law that the state may intervene if necessary, superseding parents' authority by proving them unable or unwilling to guard the child's welfare. In extreme cases, parents may be criminally liable for failing to fulfill the responsibility to provide ordinary care.

Critics of leaving decisions about the treatment for dangerously ill newborns solely or primarily to parents question how well parents are able to judge an infant's needs. Certainly the task is daunting, since the medical specialists on whom parents depend often cannot predict a child's chances of survival or normality with any certainty at the point when decisions must be made, nor adequately warn of the suffering that treatment may eventually entail (Bouregy, 1988). In addition, parents come to the task exhausted by childbirth and the child's medical crisis, grief-stricken and in near shock (Jellinek et al., 1992). There is evidence that

See Also

Fighting over "Life": Arguments Based on Rights and on Biology

INFANTS' RIGHTS
The Baby Doe Case

Baby Doe was afflicted with Down syndrome, a chromosomal abnormality resulting in mental retardation and a propensity for cardiac and other congenital malformations. The infant had such a congenital defect, a tracheo-esophageal fistula (an abnormal passage connecting the trachea and esophagus), which if not surgically corrected results in death. The parents, after consultation and with the concurrence of their attending physician, refused to consent to the surgery, primarily on the ground that a child with Down syndrome could not attain a "minimally acceptable quality of life." That conclusion was, and continues to be, strongly disputed. A trial court, however, ruled that the parents had the right to refuse surgery for their child (*In re Infant Doe*, 1982).

Immediately after the infant's death, President Ronald Reagan directed the U.S. Department of Health and Human Services (DHHS) to issue regulations protecting handicapped infants from treatment discrimination by parents, health-care providers, or both. Through the regulations, issued in March of 1983, DHHS claimed authority under the Rehabilitation Act of 1973 to order health-care facilities receiving federal assistance to provide sustenance and aggressive medical treatment to handicapped infants. The regulations required posting signs announcing the new federal protection in treatment areas of hospitals; established teams, soon nicknamed "Baby Doe Squads," to investigate alleged instances of treatment discrimination; and provided for a toll-free hotline to facilitate the reporting of discrimination (Lawton et al., 1985). Most health-care providers, as well as many members of the public and of Congress, reacted negatively. A prestigious national group studying health-care decisions—the U.S. President's Commission for the Study of Ethical Problems in Medicine and Biomedical and Behavioral Research—and the American Academy of Pediatrics (AAP) strongly criticized the regulations. The AAP, along with several other parties, sought help from the federal courts, which invalidated the regulations only a few weeks after they became final (*American Academy of Pediatrics* v. *Heckler*, 1983).

DHHS next produced the "Baby Doe II" regulations, modifying the requirements for signs and providing for an infant-care review committee in each hospital in place of the outside investigative team. These regulations too were rejected—ultimately by the U.S. Supreme Court—on the ground that the Rehabilitation Act did not give DHHS any authority to regulate parental decisions about infant treatment (*Bowen* v. *American Hospital Association*, 1986).

In a final effort to influence the care of

(continued)

physicians do not always share essential information with parents and that parents often absorb poorly the limited information they receive (Perlman et al., 1991). Even observers who find parents the best possible decision makers speak of their vulnerability during the crisis, especially to manipulation by others (Rushton and Glover, 1990). On the other hand, parents may wholly reject medical guidance. Several have protested the removal of a dead infant from life support; and in one notorious incident, a father, Rudy Linares, disconnected his infant son's respirator and held off nurses at gunpoint until the boy died. (For an excellent analysis of the issues discussed in this article, see Gostin, 1989.)

A second criticism of giving parents authority is that they may deliberately elect not to satisfy an infant's dire needs. In this view, it is naive to posit an identity of interest between infant and parent. Parents guard their own interests, those of the family as a unit, and those of current and future siblings—all of which may be gravely threatened by the newborn. Some observers of such behavior describe it neutrally. To a sociobiologist, "individual infants may attempt to extract greater investment from their parents than the parents have been selected to give," causing parents to reduce their investment in the child (Hrdy, 1992, p. 410). A philosopher writing on the subject actively encourages parents to weigh the child's interests, including life itself, against others' needs: "The neonate is not born into the family circle so much as outside it, awaiting inclusion or exclusion. The moral problem the parents must confront is whether the child should become a part of the family unit" (Blustein, 1989, p. 166). But other commentators condemn any deviation on the part of parents from pursuit of the child's interest. Among these were the proponents of the Baby Doe regulations and, later, a majority of the U.S. Supreme Court, which noted that family members "may have a strong feeling—a feeling not at all ignoble or unworthy, but not entirely disinterested either—that they do not wish to witness the continuation of the life of a loved one which they regard as hopeless, meaningless, and even degrading" (*Cruzan* v. *Director, Missouri Department of Health*, 1990, p. 286).

Practitioners—doctors, lawyers, and social workers—also observe parents acting from mixed motives in accepting or rejecting medical care. By forgoing treatment, they may hope to spare the infant suffering and lessen their own, avoid financial and other burdens on the family, and prevent the child's eventual institutionalization (Newman, 1989). They may instinctively—

See Also
Informed Consent

INFANTS' RIGHTS

(continued)

newborns, even if indirectly, Congress enacted the Child Abuse Amendments of 1984, which directed DHHS to develop regulations governing infant care and guidelines for hospital infant-care review committees. As of 1985, federal funding for state child-abuse prevention and treatment efforts was conditioned on compliance; only a few states had declined the funding. Under the amendments, the Child Protection Service of a state is the only party that may initiate an action of neglect. Still, the fact that the act broadened the definition of child abuse to include "withholding of medically indicated treatment" affects physician practice standards. The amendments require that a disabled infant receive appropriate nutrition, hydration, medication, and the "most effective" treatment according to the reasonable judgment of the treating physician. In only three situations may treatment be withheld: (1) when the child is chronically and irreversibly comatose; (2) when treatment could not save the child's life for any substantial length of time; or (3) when the treatment would be inhumane and "virtually futile" with respect to survival. The distinction between inability to save the life (situation 2) and "virtually futile" (situation 3) lies in the "degree of probability or uncertainty in determining the futility of treatment" (Boyd and Thompson, 1990). This distinction has become increasingly difficult to draw, in the context of both withdrawal and continuation of treatment. With respect to the latter, for example, in the case of Baby "K," a mother fought successfully to continue extraordinary medical intervention to preserve the life of her irreversibly comatose anencephalic child, despite the fact that such treatment is virtually futile in terms of ultimate survival (Baby "K," 1994).

The U.S. President's Commission disagreed with the Reagan administration on its Baby Doe regulations and proposed that the standard for infant treatment or nontreatment be based on the "best interests" of the infant. This standard was a variation of the substituted judgment standard that is often applied to incapacitated but once competent patients. In such cases, a proxy attempts to make treatment decisions as she or he believes the patient would, if able. For newborns, the commission recommended that decision makers attempt to assess the best interests of the infant "by reference to more objective, societally shared criteria." In sum, the commission recommended that decision makers "choose a course that will promote the patient's well-being as it would be conceived by a reasonable person in the patient's circumstances" (U.S. President's Commission, 1983, pp. 135-136). Numerous courts have since adopted the "best interests" standard in making infant treatment decisions.

— ANNE M. DELLINGER
PATRICIA C. KUSZLER

and with good reason—fear the damage to parent-child relations created by medicine's lifesaving technology (Boyce, 1992; Kratochvil et al., 1991). Not infrequently, the parents' religious beliefs discourage medical intervention. On the other hand, a parent may insist on extraordinary measures in an attempt to be faithful to their understanding of their religion's tenets, as well as to assuage perceived guilt; or to please the other parent, friends, and family; or from selfless devotion to the child that the parent cannot reconcile with consenting to death (Nelson and Nelson, 1992).

By whatever means and for whatever reasons, parents usually prove effective advocates for their treatment preference. (An exception is where parents cannot agree on treatment. When this occurs, neither is likely to remain the primary decision maker [*Jane Doe*, 1992].) Deference to parents was especially prevalent before Baby Doe. Surveys of physicians in the 1970s suggest either their deference to parents or a marked congruence between parents' and physicians' choices for infants. Three studies are particularly revealing because they ask the very question later placed in issue by Baby Doe: whether lifesaving treatment that would be given to other newborns may be withheld from a child with Down syndrome. In each survey, most physicians either would not recommend treatment or would acquiesce in a parental decision to reject it (U.S. President's Commission, 1983). According to Angela Holder, when courts review parents' decisions, parents usually lose if they stand alone against physicians; but bolstered by respectable medical advice, they generally prevail against legal challenges from other physicians, health-facility administrators, lawyers, or government agencies (Holder, 1985).

However, the differing views of the intrinsic value of the infant's life described above are not mirrored in the law. The law is relatively clear in its expectation of parents, though the mandate may be excruciatingly difficult to follow. Firmly rejecting any intermediate status for newborns, federal and state constitutions, as well as statutory and decisional law, accord equal status to all living human beings. Parents must act in their child's interest, weighing the immediate physical and long-term emotional suffering for the infant to be expected from aggressive treatment against the consequences of no or lesser treatment. Thus, while some object to consideration of the infant's quality of life in these decisions, such factoring is central to the parents' legal duty.

◆ **statistical prognostic strategy of treatment**
Seeks to minimize the number of patients (especially infants) whose deaths would come slowly as well as those who would be profoundly disabled, using statistical data to make selective nontreatment decisions.

Health-care providers' interests

Historically, treatment decisions rested with the midwife or physician caring for the newborn and its mother. Although parents ostensibly "owned" their children, they routinely ceded control to the health-care provider. During the twentieth century, the decision-making model shifted to one in which the parent and the provider jointly decided on medical intervention for the infant. In recent decades, the parents' role has markedly increased as a result of a greater number of treatment options and increased parental knowledge and awareness (Cooper, 1992).

Organized medicine has not opposed this development. A 1975 AAP survey indicated broad support among pediatricians for the proposition that infant treatment decisions should be made jointly by the parents and physician, with the parents taking the pivotal role. The Society of Critical Care Medicine's Task Force on Ethics recommends that parents set priorities for treatment of critically ill pediatric patients (Task Force on Ethics, 1990). The American Medical Association also defers to parents but would require them to decide on the basis of the best-interests standard proposed by the President's Commission.

Physicians readily acknowledge the frequent conflicts between their dual commitment to save lives and to alleviate suffering. In reality, these factors are rarely the only ones that affect the physician treating a critically ill infant. Health-care providers may have varying philosophies with respect to treatment of infants afflicted with certain disabilities; they may also be influenced by their research agendas, possess insufficient knowledge to assess accurately the infant's disability and prognosis, or be influenced by real or perceived risk of legal liability (Rushton and Glover, 1990). In addition, physicians focus on the diagnosis, rather than on the prognosis and long-term care of their infant patients (Perlman et al., 1991). As a result of all these factors, physicians may not be optimally effective partners for the parents in the decision-making process. For example, an obstetrician may act in a paternalistic fashion toward his or her patient, the mother, seeking to protect her from the tragedy of dealing with the fate of an impaired infant. Alternatively, a neonatalogist may be overly optimistic in judging and discussing with the parents the infant's potential for meaningful life (Cooper, 1992).

Frequently, nurses serve as the primary information conduit between doctors and parents, and naturally there are biases inherent in their perspective, too. Because they are the health-care providers who care for patients most intimately, they may personalize severely disabled infants beyond reality in order to deal with the burden of nursing them on a day-to-day basis. As a result, nurses may be incapable of advocating against treatment when it is futile and thus be unable to serve as effective advocates for either the infant or the family. In addition, they are limited by the practical realities of their role in the employment hierarchy of the hospital (Mitchell, 1989).

See Also
Pregnancy and Maternal Health

In some cases, health-care facilities and providers may overtreat a severely compromised infant to avoid legal liability. The Linares case, while an extreme example, arose from tensions that are often present. There, despite their acknowledged sympathy and agreement with the father's desire for his son's death, the health-care providers insisted for many months on treating the infant. They did so, they said later, because they believed that state law required continued life support. Critics alleged that individual health-care providers and the facility (through its lawyer) had abandoned the best interests of both the child and the family to protect themselves. Indeed, some see an "overwhelming fear of possible, indeed theoretical, adverse legal repercussions" among health-care providers (Nelson and Cranford, 1989, p. 3210). The Baby "K" case, which casts doubt on the physician's freedom to refuse to provide treatment he or she considers futile, suggests that fear of legal reprisal is not unfounded.

Providers are also strongly motivated by sympathy. Some physicians assert that when patients' lives are extended beyond hope of recovery, it is usually because the patient's family is unwilling to accept the inevitability of death (Emanuel, 1994). When this occurs, although it may be ethically justifiable and legally defensible for a physician to withhold or withdraw treatment, physicians frequently accede to parental demand (Nelson and Nelson, 1992).

Society's interests

Two of these issues, cost and the social effect of litigating treatment decisions, are discussed below.

INFANT HEALTH CARE

Society's Overlapping Interests

- preserving life and health of the next generation
- guaranteeing rights to individuals
- support of families
- wise use of economic resources
- maintaining a just and predictable legal system
- compromising of clashing values of groups within society

Concern for the cost of neonatal intensive care—the most expensive element in the care of infants—preceded the currently intense focus on health costs in general. This treatment is the exception to the rule that the United States directs resources disproportionately to adults, especially the elderly. Technological advances in the treatment of newborns halved the neonatal death rate between 1970 and 1980 (U.S. President's Commission, 1983). Since then, the extraordinary cost of the technology has helped to focus attention on how many and which infants should be treated.

Many families cannot cover the cost, and there is debate over whether the resources available for a particular infant should be taken into account by decision makers. Most commentators share the view expressed in a seminal article on the subject: "Just as a parent is not obligated to attempt to save a drowning child if the parent cannot swim, neither is he obligated to incur enormous expense in providing treatment with a slight chance of success" (Robertson, 1975, p. 236; see also Newman, 1989). No judicial decision, however, accepts the proposition that personal resources should dictate life or death. Usually, the issue is avoided in litigation. When it is specifically cited, a typical court reply is that the "cost of care in human or financial terms is irrelevant" (*Beth, Care and Protection of*, 1992, p. 1383).

Whether or not cost should affect decisions on treatment, there is evidence that it does. Although providers may not abandon a patient without incurring liability, a study comparing medical need to the services sick newborns receive indicates that health-care providers do not allocate services solely according to need, but are instead influenced by the newborn's insurance coverage—private, governmental, or none (Braveman et al., 1991). Governmental insurance is less attractive to providers than private insurance because government does not reimburse the full cost of care. Thus, at times it appears that while society insists on extending the life of premature and seriously ill infants, it simultaneously refuses to absorb the cost of their immediate and long-term care—a result described as "political hypocrisy in its cruelest form" (Holder, 1985, p. 113).

A second salient issue for society is whether it has erred by assigning this category of treatment decisions increasingly to the courts. Criticism of the failure to treat Baby Doe was widespread and severe, but the legal processes that ensued were also criticized. Numerous objections are raised to the removal of medical decisions from the private sphere. The judicial system may be too cumbersome and costly and may further traumatize family members and invade their privacy. The publicity surrounding infant-care cases may prevent other parents from exercising their right to forgo treatment. In addition, the practice of medicine is negatively affected. Explicit direction from some courts to extend life whenever possible and the implicit threat of litigation reinforce U.S. medicine's alleged tendency to overtreat (Newman, 1989). For example, one in three neonatologists state that the Baby Doe regulations require treatment not in an infant's best interest (Fost, 1989). Finally, in investigat-

◆ **amniocentesis**
Commonly performed with ultrasonographic guidance, an invasive technique—needle puncture of the uterus—to study cells in the amniotic fluid and the fluid itself for fetal abnormalities.

See Also

Ethics of Access: Is Infertility a Disease?

ing and deciding these cases, judges and other officials must choose among competing moral and religious philosophies, a problematic choice in a society that values diversity (Newman, 1989).

Obviously, the law is disadvantaged in attempting to supervise medical care for particular infants. In most jurisdictions, understanding of the legal requirements for forgoing treatment is imperfect, even among lawyers (see Gostin, 1989). The scarcity of prosecutions and precedents suggests a high degree of social ambivalence on this subject—"a troubling disjunction between the law on the books, which seems to make neonatal euthanasia criminal, and the law in action, which does not punish it" (Schneider, 1988, p. 152). According to Carl Schneider, there is no social consensus on the central questions: What is human life? When is death preferable to life? What do parents owe their children? What does society owe the suffering? As a result, he and others see a tendency to abandon the search for substantive principles in the law and instead adopt procedures for reviewing individual cases (Schneider, 1988).

One such procedure is the assignment of a role in decision making to institutional ethics committees. Virtually unknown before 1983 (fewer than 1 percent of U.S. hospitals had committees), they came to prominence through two avenues. First, the influential U.S. President's Commission report in 1983 recommended their use; second, the establishment of committees became a major point of compromise in negotiations between the government and health-care providers over the Baby Doe regulations (Lawton et al., 1985). By 1986 the American Academy of Pediatrics, which had strongly endorsed the committees, found them in 60 percent of hospitals.

In some instances, the committees have functioned as it was hoped they would. For example, in the case of Baby "L," a physician applied to the hospital's ethics committee for permission to cease extraordinary treatment of an infant who was capable only of pain perception and to transfer the infant to another facility and provider. The parent opposed this action and sought an opinion from the courts. The court upheld the hospital and physician's decision and allowed transfer of the child to a facility willing to continue treatment (Paris et al., 1990). In the case of Baby "K," however, a hospital's ethics committee failed to persuade either the parent or the trial court that treatment was futile.

◆ **required reporting**
Legally required disclosures of otherwise confidential information.

Concerns are expressed about the committees' role, makeup, criteria for decision making, influence, results, and effectiveness. Are they intended to advise or to bind? If the latter, do they deprive parents or infants of constitutional rights? Are they instruments of the medical establishment rather than havens for patients? How reflective of the entire community is their membership? Do they diffuse moral responsibility? Do they—and should they—help to reduce liability? (Newman, 1989; U.S. President's Commission, 1983). Despite such questions, ethics committees appear entrenched as a visible representative of society in controversies over care for infants.

Conclusion

Long-standing respect for parent and health-care provider discretion in making infant treatment decisions has been partially replaced by a greater emphasis on the rights of the infant. As a result, the roles of the infant, parents, health-care providers, and, in the larger context, society, in making these difficult decisions are undergoing reexamination. Although institutional infant-care review committees occasionally serve as forums for such decision making, a number of these cases continue to be referred to the courts, where little, if any, consensus has emerged.

— ANNE M. DELLINGER
PATRICIA C. KUSZLER

INFORMATION DISCLOSURE

See Also
Confidentiality
Trust

ATTITUDES TOWARD TRUTH-TELLING

Ethicists, health professionals, and social scientists have paid considerable attention to the issue of information disclosure in clinical settings worldwide. Attitudinal research involving innumerable samples of clinicians, patients, families, and the public has examined the questions of whether "truth" should be told to patients, and if so, what truths, how much, by whom, when, and how. Opinions about how these questions should be answered have been assessed and analyzed in regard to an array of circumstances, illnesses, and conditions, each presenting special considerations. For instance, patients and practitioners have been asked about the wisdom and desirability of disclosing the risks of experimentation, terminal prognoses, or specific diagnoses—including but not limited to cancer, mental illness, HIV, and genetic predispositions. Whether revealing such information is a benefit or a burden to patients may be a question as old as the healer-patient relationship. Even as this ancient question remains unsettled, however, new puzzles about disclosure are created by new diseases, health-care technologies, roles, and organizational structures. This article reviews recent attitudinal trends regarding information disclosure in a number of areas of clinical concern.

To tell or not to tell?

Many of the attitudinal surveys about information disclosure in clinical settings have focused on whether physicians should reveal diagnoses to patients, particularly when the diagnosis implies a terminal prognosis. These studies have documented a marked difference in physicians' attitudes over time. Until the 1970s, surveys of U.S. physicians indicated their clear preference for protecting patients from the news of impending death from cancer. Then, beginning in the 1970s, there was evidence of a shift. Dennis Novack and his colleagues (1979), replicating a 1961 study by Donald Oken, found a complete reversal of the earlier findings. Ninety-seven percent of these physicians, compared with 10 percent in the first sample, reported that it was their general policy to provide patients with the full details of their condition.

Other countries have witnessed similar, although not as dramatic, trends indicating an increasing willingness of physicians to talk with patients about their impending death. A study of family practice physicians in the United States, Canada, and Britain provides a useful comparison of current practice in these three countries. Responding to hypothetical vignettes, physicians indicated their relative willingness to divulge information about the possibility of multiple sclerosis and cancer to patients. In general, the U.S. sample was most likely to tell patients about the suspected diseases (55 and 79 percent), Canadian physicians were moderately likely to tell patients (49 and 67 percent), and British physicians least likely to do so (45 and 44 percent). Even in Japan, where the majority of physicians remain hesitant to reveal diagnoses of malignancy (especially cancers) to patients, there is increasing public and professional debate about this traditional practice (Hattori et al., 1991).

Of course, what survey respondents say they do is not always a measure of actual behavior. This methodological shortcoming is well illustrated by Kathryn Taylor's (1988) study of Canadian oncologists who reported they routinely discuss the results of breast biopsies with patients. A comparison between observational and interview data revealed that despite their perceptions of their behavior, very few of the physicians actually communicated positive biopsy results to patients in a clear and direct manner.

Since the 1960s legal requirements for informed consent have undoubtedly influenced the change in physicians' attitudes toward disclosure of information to patients. These laws generally require that patients be given explicit information about the risks and benefits of procedures, drugs, and clinical trials. However, even where the practice of informed consent is law, physicians vary in terms of what information is revealed and how it is disclosed. An international study (Taylor and Kelner, 1987) polling oncologists in Canada, Australia, France, Sweden, the United States, England, and Italy about their attitudes toward informed consent for breast cancer treatment trials found that these physicians used a wide range of discretion in the amount of detail they gave to patients; their disclosures depended more on their assessments of patients' needs than on regard for legal regulations pertaining to disclosure. Other studies document a similar pattern of clinicians' preference for discretionary use of partial disclosure of drug side effects (Keown et al., 1984) or the possible complications associated with a medical procedure (Kessler, 1977).

The patient's perspective

In contrast with the variable nature of physicians' attitudes about disclosing terminal diagnoses, many surveys of patients over time and across cultures indicate they would prefer to have knowledge of their diagnosis, treatment course, and prognosis. As early as 1950, William Kelly and Stanley Friesen found that 89 percent of their respondents in the United States wanted to know their diagnosis of cancer. Subsequent studies in the United States (Blanchard et al., 1988), Australia (Reynolds et al., 1981), Scotland (Reid et al., 1988), and Canada (Sutherland et al., 1989) report that similarly high proportions of patients with cancer would like to hear from their physicians about the nature of their malignancies.

Many patients seem to want information about other diagnoses besides cancer. For instance, a 1988 study of ambulatory patients in the United States reported that over 90 percent would want to know if they were found to have Alzheimer's disease (Erde et al., 1988). Cross-national studies report that parents want to know information about the diagnoses and prognoses of their children's diseases, including leukemia (Greenberg et al., 1984), spina bifida and Down syndrome (Murdoch, 1983), and severe mental handicaps (Quine and Pahl, 1986). Highlighting the difference between patients and physicians, Ruth Faden and her colleagues found that patients' parents in the United States wanted "far more detailed disclosures than physicians routinely offer[ed]" about epilepsy medication (1981, p. 718). This patient-parent sample wanted detailed information even if it would make them feel anxious, and they were willing to take and pay for the extra time required during an office visit for this depth of information.

However, not everyone desires complete disclosure of diagnoses, prognoses, or risks inherent in their medical choices. Circumstances and cultural interpretations influence what patients and families desire to know and how they want to be told. For example, the

◆ **informed consent**
Requires that physicians must disclose to patients information that reasonable persons need to decide on a course of treatment, thus ensuring the patients' autonomy, and letting the patients' own judgments prevail.

See Also
Trust

context of disclosure was significant to a sample in the United States who reported that they would prefer that the news of the unexpected death of a relative be couched in a temporary lie if they received it from a physician by telephone; in person, they would prefer immediate and full notification (Viswanathan et al., 1986). A study about informed-consent practice associated with elective circumcisions on male newborns in the United States showed that parents' commitment to traditional, religious, and social values superseded their interest in hearing about medical risks of this surgery (Christensen-Szalanski et al., 1987).

In companion articles, Antonella Surbone and Edmund Pellegrino reason that variation in our expectations for disclosure of information is based on different cultural understandings of patient autonomy as it relates to truth-telling. Surbone observes, "In Italian culture autonomy (*autonomia*) is often synonymous for isolation (*isolamento*) . . . [so] protecting the ill family member from painful information is seen as essential for keeping the family together and not allowing the ill member to suffer alone" (1992, p. 1662). Given such an interpretation, Pellegrino advises that "to thrust the truth or the decision on a patient who expects to be buffered against news of impending death is a gratuitous and harmful misinterpretation of

RESEARCH STUDIES
Why Tell a Lie?

A number of studies have investigated different reasons why physicians equivocate to patients with lies, half-truths, vague accounts, or avoidance, especially when it comes to the disclosure of bad news. A common explanation for such behavior derives from the belief that disclosure can set off a destructive interplay of psychological and physical processes that result in worsening of patients' conditions (Meador, 1992). In the case of informed consent for a painful procedure or risky clinical trial, some authors warn that the power of suggestion can exacerbate pain and side effects unnecessarily or that the truth will lead subjects to decline to participate in randomized treatment (Simes et al., 1986). Other studies contradict this reasoning with evidence that patients' coping skills are enhanced, cooperation with treatment is increased, and levels of anxiety are reduced when they are provided with adequate information about their condition (Ell et al., 1989).

Several authors focus on the importance of the context of disclosure to explain clinicians' decisions about what to tell patients and others. For instance, Dennis Novack et al. (1989) found that most in their sample of U.S. internists would willingly engage in deception if, in their judgment, circumstances called for it. Responding to hypothetical cases, these physicians said they would misrepresent facts if to do so would benefit a patient or circumvent a stupid regulation; one-third of the sample answered that they would evade or mislead in order to protect themselves if they had mistakenly contributed to a patient's death. Another study reported that opinions regarding when it is best to tell patients about genetic predispositions or anomalies will vary if the information is relevant to imminent reproductive decisions (Wertz and Fletcher, 1987). Haavi Morreim raises important questions about whether and how new practice arrangements and reimbursement procedures in the United States will affect "physicians' obligations to discuss these economic changes openly with patients and to help them find their way through an increasingly complex maze of resource rules and restrictions" (1991, p. 276).

Physicians often express confidence in their "gut reactions" to assess their patients' ability and desire to hear bad news (Still and Todd, 1986). Consequently, they are apt to recommend flexibility and individualized consideration of patients' needs. Given the psychological, clinical, and linguistic complexity of communication about illness, it is important to honor this sentiment.

However, a number of researchers have shown that physicians' decisions regarding information disclosure may well be influenced by their culturally constructed role expectations and rules for communication (Todd and Still, 1984; Takahaski, 1990). In pluralistic societies, physicians and patients may not share assumptions about appropriate disclosure. Moreover, role expectations are subject to change over time, creating confusion about what is to be revealed and by whom. Research has shown that the introduction of new clinical roles (e.g., radiologists; Vallely and Mills, 1990) and the expansion of old ones (e.g., nurses; Davis and Jameton, 1987) can complicate role expectations and raise questions about who on the clinical team is or should be responsible for giving information to patients.

Furthermore, the asymmetry of power and knowledge inherent in the physician-patient relationship can confound communication efforts (Waitzkin, 1985), especially when it is exaggerated by social class differences (Mathews, 1983). In addition, physicians' own discomfort with death (Eggerman and Dustin, 1985) and their lack of explicit training in communication skills can limit their effectiveness in breaking bad news and handling patients' reactions to it. To the extent that these factors cloud clinical judgment about disclosure, physicians may not be serving their patients' interests when solely relying on their intuition and medical expertise.

—KATE H. BROWN

the moral foundations for respect for autonomy" (1992, p. 1735).

Similar reasoning informs Nicholas Christakis's recommendation that researchers be sensitive to cultural definitions of personhood and ethical norms governing informed consent for AIDS vaccine trials in Africa (1988). On the other hand, Carel IJsselmuiden and Ruth Faden (1992) caution against the use of cultural arguments supporting the wholesale disregard of informed consent, especially in the context of contemporary African society, where radical changes have restructured traditional communal beliefs and social organization. They argue that the appeal to cultural sensitivity may well mask other, less benign motives related to expediency of experimentation and development of pharmaceutical markets among African populations.

HIV/AIDS and information disclosure

The AIDS epidemic has brought additional challenges to the issue of truth-telling in clinical settings. Until effective pharmaceutical therapies are developed, HIV will remain a fatal condition and thus will bear the psychological and social weight of this prognosis. Furthermore, in the United States and elsewhere, the virus carries a stigma due to its association with socially marginalized populations: homosexuals, illegal intravenous drug users, and prostitutes. The very real threat of discrimination and abuse of persons who are HIV-positive has brought renewed seriousness to the need for safeguarding patient confidentiality and has necessitated careful examination of decisions to disclose patients' HIV status to patients and others. At the same time, however, clinicians often must balance this concern for patient confidentiality with their duty to warn others who may be at risk of unprotected exposure to the virus.

A number of studies have explored the question of who should know someone's HIV status. The patient? Not all patients who are tested for HIV want to know their test results (Lyter et al., 1987). Nor is it clear whether children with HIV will benefit from learning about their diagnosis, and if so, at what age.

Attention has also been paid to the question of who, besides the person with HIV, needs to be informed about that person's infection. Samuel Perry and his colleagues (1990) surveyed forty gay men in New York about whom they voluntarily told when they learned of their positive test results. Most of the sample had told their personal physicians and current sexual partners; however, most had not tried to contact their former sexual partners. A Los Angeles study of men with HIV reported that half of those who had been sexually active since learning of their condition had kept their infection secret from one or more partners (Marks et al., 1991). If patients with HIV are reluctant to talk about their infection, who should disclose this information to those at risk? A South Carolina study of sexual partners showed that a contact-tracing program through the health department was acceptable to that research sample (Jones et al., 1990).

Health providers do not agree on the issue of who should know someone's HIV status. According to a study of mainland United States and Puerto Rican health providers' opinions, the range of people who should know about a mother's or infant's HIV is subjective and seemingly without limit, potentially including many clinical and administrative hospital personnel, as well as patients' formal and informal support systems (Dougherty et al., 1990). The issue of whether health providers with HIV should disclose this information to their patients raises special concern among health providers, their patients, and the public (Gramelspacher et al., 1990).

Conclusion

This review of research about attitudes toward information disclosure reveals a diversity of opinion on the subject. Numerous factors enter into considerations of whether and what to tell patients and research subjects about their conditions, treatments, or risks of experimentation. Variation in cultural expectations for patients and their caregivers influences what information will be told, to whom, and in what manner. Personal and social characteristics of providers and patients, such as their age, social class, and orientation to death, also shape the content and process of communication in clinical encounters. The specific clinical, environmental, and economic circumstances of such encounters can further define preferences for what is told and how it is told. Given this contextual complexity, ethical concerns regarding information disclosure are likely to continue to demand sensitivity, thoughtfulness, and skillful communication from clinicians, patients, and ethicists in the future.

— KATE H. BROWN

◆ **therapeutic privilege exception to informed consent**

Permits a doctor to withhold information when, in the doctor's opinion, disclosure would be detrimental to the patient's interests or well-being.

ETHICAL ISSUES

Since 1970, ethically recommended health-care practice in the United States has increasingly supported a high level of information disclosure to patients. This article reviews the change, notes some reasons for it, and explores several concerns about disclosure and its implications for particular information types.

Philosophical background of current opinion

Generally, philosophical discussion has supported veracity as a moral principle, obligation, or virtue.

See Also
Abortion: Model of Privacy
AIDS and Confidentiality

I

INFORMATION DISCLOSURE

Ethical Issues

There is virtually no case law on the basis of which legal standards for consent to research might be defined.

PAGE 398

Veracity draws its strength from the complex support it provides to diverse values—respecting others, avoiding coercion and manipulation, supporting community, maintaining reciprocity in relationships, supporting the value of communication generally, eliminating the costs and complexities of deception, refraining from unduly assuming responsibility, and maintaining trust.

Philosophers have generally treated veracity as an obligation flowing from more fundamental theoretical principles, such as utility, religious duty, respect for persons, or some combination of beneficence, fidelity, and autonomy. John Stuart Mill, for instance, regarded truth-telling as justified by utilitarian considerations, and W. D. Ross included honesty among the duties of fidelity. A few have given it more basic status. Some theologians, such as Dietrich Bonhoeffer, have set truth telling in the context of greater religious truths and treated false doctrines as forms of deception. Aristotle described falsehood as "in itself mean and culpable" (Bok, 1978, p. 24); G. J. Warnock listed veracity as a major virtue with the same status as beneficence and justice. Immanuel Kant and Augustine are notable for having defended truth-telling most strongly. In a brief article, Kant argued that it would be wrong to lie even to a murderer seeking the hiding place of an intended victim.

However, not all theorists have defended veracity; Henry Sidgwick denied that it could stand as a "definite moral axiom" because of its variable applications and numerous exceptions (Bok, 1978, p. 293). David Nyberg argued that trusting relationships among people normally require "the adroit management of deception" (Nyberg, 1993, p. 24). Moreover, most philosophers have defended deception in at least some cases. Plato defended lying to the public for the sake of society as a whole, and many philosophers have warranted deception when truthfulness might result in serious harm (Bok, 1978).

Application to health care

Until the late twentieth century, philosophers often regarded a physician's withholding a fatal diagnosis from a patient as a stock exception to general precepts of veracity. Philosophers and physicians regarded the distress expected from such news as sufficiently harmful to outweigh the presumption favoring disclosure. Withholding a fatal diagnosis functioned as a paradigm for sharing other medical information with patients. The ethical tradition concerning the doctor-patient relationship thus tended, with some notable exceptions such as Worthington Hooker and Richard Cabot, to emphasize the obligations of confidentiality and to ignore and even deprecate disclosure (Radovsky, 1985). Oaths and codes omitted truth-telling, and precepts and discussions of talking with patients tended to recommend caution in revealing information. Ethicists perceived the doctor-patient relationship as oriented to therapy, reassurance, and avoiding harm; physicians were to provide lies and truth instrumentally only insofar as they aided therapy.

Since the 1960s, opinion on the role of disclosure in health care has changed rapidly in the United States. The patients' rights movement and the rise of bioethics have created a climate of opinion supporting honest disclosure of medical information. The affirmation in 1972 of "A Patient's Bill of Rights" by the Board of Trustees of the American Hospital Association notably marked this shift in opinion. The bill stated, "The patient has the right to obtain from his physician complete current information concerning his diagnosis, treatment, and prognosis in terms the patient can be reasonably expected to understand" (Lee and Jacobs, 1973, p. 41).

These changes in opinion developed in concert with the spread of informed consent as standard practice in research and therapy. Informed consent derived from a view of respect for persons that emphasized an individual's power to make decisions adequately. This view required honest disclosure. Thus, most ethicists in the 1970s and 1980s supported fuller disclosure as a means of respecting patient autonomy (Katz, 1984).

The patients' rights movement favored empowering patients and increasing their control over medical care. As Howard Waitzkin argued in his observations of physicians' communications with patients, the traditional pattern of withholding information reflected a habit of dominating patients and keeping the course of therapy firmly under professional control (Waitzkin, 1991). Reformers saw a wider patient understanding of care as supporting a less paternalistic and more contractual relationship, as well as empowering particular classes of patients, such as women and people of color. Susan Sherwin, for example, identified one of the main tasks of feminist health-care ethics as being to increase equity "by distributing the specialized knowledge on health matters in ways that allow persons maximum control over their own health" (Sherwin, 1992, p. 93).

The codes of ethics of the health professions began to reflect this important shift in opinion. The American Nurses' Association's Code for Nurses linked disclosure with truth-telling and self-determination: "Clients have the moral right . . . to be given accurate information, and all the information necessary for making informed judgments." The code counseled nurses to avoid "claims that are false, fraudulent, misleading, deceptive, or unfair" in their relations with the public (American Nurses' Association, 1985, p. 2). The 1980 revision of the American Medical Association's "Principles of Medical Ethics" included the principle, "A physician shall deal honestly with patients and colleagues, and strive to expose those physicians deficient in character or competence, or who engage in fraud or deception" (Council on Ethical and Judicial Affairs, 1989, p. ix). The American College of Physicians' (ACP) Ethics Manual recommended that patients be "well informed to make health care decisions and work intelligently in partnership with the physician." The manual advised that communication can "dispel uncertainty and fear and enhance healing and patient satisfaction." In general, the ACP held, "disclosure to patients is a fundamental ethical requirement" (1992, p. 950). Subspecialty ethics codes—such as those of the American Academy of Orthopaedic Surgeons, the World Psychiatric Association, and the American College of Obstetricians and Gynecologists—also began to include recommendations supporting veracity.

Changing contexts for veracity in health care

While a high level of disclosure became the recommended practice, cross-currents of thought emerged regarding the motivations for informing patients. First, observers discussed the psychological benefits and risks of giving patients bad news. Second, the increasingly institutional setting of health-care practice influenced patterns of disclosure. Third, discussion distinguished the obligation to disclose information from the obligation to refrain from lying. Fourth, the uncertainty of medicine modulated the obligation to disclose. Finally, an increasing philosophical emphasis on relational aspects of practitioner-patient ethics broadened the foundations for veracity beyond the single element of respect for autonomy.

HEALTHY DISCLOSURE. Medical works prior to the 1970s tended to assume that revealing a fatal diagnosis would cause patients to experience painful emotions, commit suicide, refuse needed care, or give up hope and die more swiftly. In her important work *Lying: Moral Choice in Public and Private Life*, Sissela Bok argued that traditionalists exaggerated such problems. Patients generally want to be informed, and the benefits to a well-informed and cooperating patient outweigh the risks of disclosure (Bok, 1978). Others supplied case histories illustrating the emotional perils of withholding a terminal diagnosis from vulnerable and trusting patients (Dunbar, 1990; Sherwin, 1992).

Elisabeth Kübler-Ross provided crucial support for the psychological benefits of disclosure by her research on the emotional processes of coming to terms with expected death. In extensive interviews with dying cancer patients, she observed that patients' initial negativity was normally followed by a staged sequence of feelings resolving in acceptance with hope. She regarded disclosure as part of the healthy process of maintaining ongoing communication with dying patients, and her stage theory permitted clinicians to engage in a therapeutic process around disclosure of a fatal diagnosis. The hospice movement accepted this perspective as key to humane care of the dying. Kübler-Ross nevertheless strongly opposed disclosing detailed predictions of life expectancy (Kübler-Ross, 1969).

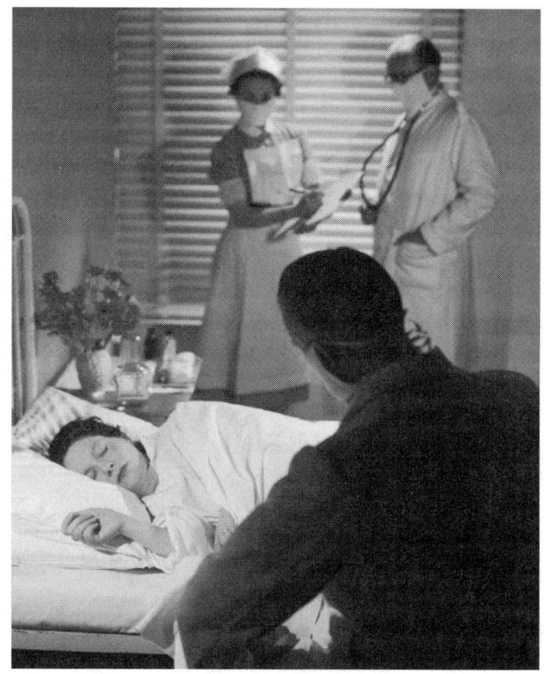

Patients' powerful emotional reactions and personal transformations during grave illnesses involve caregivers in intimate, significant connections with patients. The belief that knowledge of death is healthy has changed the image of the clinician from that of maintaining a cool distance to one of performing emotional work with patients (Hochschild, 1983). Ethicists often suggested that health professionals who withheld information from patients reflected several concerns: denial of their own and the patient's fear of dying, unconscious wishes to foster dependency in their clients, concern that discussing death constituted admitting failure, and manipulation of hope to encourage more extensive treatment choices.

Some commentators have challenged the positive emotional benefits of discussing death. Ernest Becker argued that the fear of death is too powerfully terrifying to permit most people to accept it (Becker, 1973). Some studies have found at least a few patients showing regret over being informed (Temmerman, 1992). Others have criticized the cold delivery of information, the image of the physician "bearing down" on the patient with bad news (Byrne, 1990). But in most of the literature, the question has become not whether to tell but how to tell; sharing bad news involves timing and a commitment to continuing empathy, compas-

"FULLER" DISCLOSURE

In recent years, many ethicists and physicians' associations have encouraged physicians to be "compassionately truthful" with their patients.

To treat competent persons against their will is considered battery, in legal terms.

PAGE 674

sion, reassurance, and conversation (Buckman, 1992; Kessel, 1979; Kübler-Ross, 1969; Radovsky, 1985).

THE INSTITUTIONAL CONTEXT. Expanding health-care delivery organizations and complex technologies have multiplied the number of personnel providing patient care. These changes have magnified the obstacles to easily orchestrated and effective deception; a physician must not only deceive the patient and family but also involve dozens of other staff in the process. Institutional growth has also increased the need for accurate recordkeeping to cope with the expanding quantity of information.

In practice, information is often given only for major procedures, and practitioners tend to assume consent for lesser interventions.

PAGE 674

Although information flow to patients has traditionally been the responsibility of physicians, other health-care team members spend more time with patients, have the knowledge and opportunity to disclose information to patients and their families, and belong to professions assuming responsibility for educating patients. Coordinating communication has become an organizational challenge as hospital staffing has become more efficient, patient acuity greater, and lengths of stay shorter (Zussman, 1993). Who should talk with the patient when the physician is absent poses ethical questions for staff members, who may feel reluctant to provide information without explicit delegation even though disclosure may be timely for the patient. Nurses experience ethical conflicts when physicians order them to withhold information to which patients are entitled (Chadwick and Tadd, 1992). Staff members may make promises to patients and their families about disclosure, promises that other staff members cannot keep.

Legally, the information in the hospital record belongs to the patient (Annas, 1992), but patients are not employees, and so patients' rights are hard to define procedurally. Patients' responsibility to provide honest disclosure to health-care staff similarly lacks explicit definition. Thus, although large health-care institutions have fostered a need for improved communication with patients and made systematic deception difficult, smoothing the flow of appropriate information to patients presents a daunting institutional task.

DOUBTS AND UNCERTAINTIES. The phrase "information disclosure" connotes a level of certainty absent from many diagnoses, prognoses, and therapeutic options. Do guesses and projections "belong" to the patient as much as the contents of the case record? Kathryn Taylor observed that physicians diagnosing cancer often exaggerate their uncertainty in order to soften the blow of a diagnosis or suppress it in order to hide feelings of doubt (Taylor, 1988). Physicians diagnosing symptoms often consider unlikely possibilities, which would frighten patients if shared unnecessarily with them. Nurses may discover or obtain information about which they are uncertain or lack authority to know and wonder whether or not to share it with patients.

ETHICS OF DISCLOSURE
How—and How Much—to Tell?

DISCLOSURE AND DECEPTION. The principle of veracity suffers ambiguity; it may simply prohibit lying and deception, or it may express a broader obligation to disclose information. Ethicists have tended to deploy arguments against lying and deception to support a high level of disclosure in health care, because lying and deception have often accompanied withholding information in maintaining illusory hopes. But, one can avoid lies and deception and yet disclose scant information. Since the obligation of full disclosure is role-dependent, supporting it involves considerations beyond criticizing deception. Arguments for full disclosure require normative arguments concerning appropriate relationships of health-care professionals and institutions to patients in their service.

In health care, the principle of full disclosure stands in a reciprocal relationship to the obligation to keep confidentiality. Clinicians often have an obligation to disclose information to the patient, and at the same time, keep the same information from others. Moral judgment requires appreciating the range of application of both principles, that is, knowing which information should be disclosed or withheld in what circumstances (Jonsen and Toulmin, 1988). The more formal arguments justifying disclosure parallel the arguments for informed consent by appealing to autonomy, but broader notions of serving patient psychological good and building relationships provide less clear guidance as to the full extent of disclosure. Although favoring disclosure of a fatal diagnosis, as the worst possible news, has tended to encourage wide disclosure of less frightening information, it is still unclear what patients should or should not be told about hospital procedures, student participation in procedures, financial information, names of manufacturers, opinions on the skills of clinicians, personal information about practitioners, mistakes, and so on.

— ANDREW JAMETON

Prevailing uncertainty has motivated some physicians to argue that the truth is so uncertain and variable that veracity is irrelevant to patient care. They argue that prospects and options can be framed in so many ways that clinicians inevitably control patient decisions. Even in the relatively well-studied area of informed consent, what to tell about unlikely dangers remains a contested area. Although some physicians have chosen to limit disclosure on the grounds of uncertainty, David Hilfiker characterized giving false reassurances and concealing uncertainty as forms of dishonest misrepresentation (Hilfiker, 1985).

BUILDING RELATIONSHIPS. Although bioethics in the 1970s and 1980s rooted disclosure in autonomous decision making, the practice of disclosure has become so widespread in the United States that it has received support on broader grounds. Feminist ethics began to shift the basis of philosophical discussion from the language of autonomy to the language of caring and community. This trend, by diminishing the use of rights language, might have relaxed the new emphasis on disclosure; however, the trend expanded grounds for it, and a conception of the practitioner-patient relationship developed that sees disclosure as a key element in a good professional-patient relationship, apart from its role in decision making.

Lorraine Code, for instance, noted that there is "no stark dichotomy between interdependence and autonomy" (Code, 1991, p. 74). Howard Brody recommended that as part of the ongoing "conversation" between physicians and patients, physicians should "think out loud" (Brody, 1992, p. 116) in order to share medical reasoning more fully with patients. Charles Lidz and his colleagues found that patients generally wanted procedures explained to them, not to participate in decision making, but as a sign of respect and to assist in therapy (Lidz et al., 1983). Annette Baier advocated the necessity of going beyond the contract model and of appreciating disclosure in a context in which power relationships are unequal (Baier, 1986). Baier emphasized trust in relationships as a priority over decision making. Trust thrives most readily in relationships free of deception and where good mutual communication maintains connections between people.

Specific concerns in disclosure

Although terminal diagnoses have served as the paradigm for exploring disclosure, they cover only a portion of the possible concerns involving communication with patients. This section briefly describes a few of the other concerns. Many can arise, such as using placebos; therapeutic privilege; giving patients information about the costs of care; disclosing brain death to the family; lying to an insurance company to obtain coverage for a treatment or diagnostic test; falsifying records to help patients escape war service or school busing; reporting an accidentally discovered serious condition to the patient when the doctor-patient relationship is undefined; offering information to patients concerning futile therapeutic options; deceptively introducing medical students to patients as "doctor"; concealing the histocompatibility (mutual tolerance of tissues or organs to be grafted) of an unwilling potential organ donor; revealing to patients that a caregiver has tested positive for the human immunodeficiency virus (HIV); revealing HIV diagnoses to patients; encouraging patients to disclose HIV diagnoses to sexual partners; communicating psychiatric interpretations to patients; expecting disclosure by patients to health professionals; and disclosing genetic information to patients.

DISEASES LACKING EFFECTIVE TREATMENT. When a diagnostic test can predict a dread and incurable disease—such as Huntington or Alzheimer's disease—some physicians consider the possibility of withholding the diagnosis. An instrumental view of communication tends to support the view that the burden to the patient of knowing outweighs the value of disclosure. This concern arose with regard to Huntington disease when a levodopa test became available in the early 1970s; the concern was renewed when genetic marker tests became available in 1983. Although some critics continued to express reservations, genetic counselors tended to find that disclosure helped both patient and family to make long-range plans. Gwen Terrenoire emphasized that a consensus favoring testing and disclosure resulted from counselors working with organized patient groups involved with Huntington disease (Terrenoire, 1992). In 1989, the Huntington Disease Society of America published guidelines for testing for the condition. They recommended counseling patients prior to the screening decision and before disclosing results. They also recommended against screening patients who have conditions that diminish judgment, while thoroughly evaluating them for suicide risk (DeGrazia, 1991).

DISCLOSING DIAGNOSTIC TESTS. Hospitals and clinics often screen patients upon admission for a wide range of conditions without informing them of the reasons for testing. Services may standardly screen for HIV, sexually transmitted diseases, or pregnancy without informing the patient. They may also wish to make surreptitious tests when they believe a patient is claiming false symptoms. One case study described a patient as suffering from mysterious bruising, which could most probably be explained by drug abuse; she denied taking drugs and refused to permit a blood test. Physicians considered whether to administer the diagnostic test without informing her of its purpose. The discussants of the case argued that a contractual model of the doctor-patient relationship is inadequate because patients frequently lie to physicians and are poor historians. They suggested also that such tests

At a minimum, the surgeon depends on the patient to disclose all information relevant to the case so as to minimize the risks of unexpected events in the operating room.

PAGE 674

need not be disclosed since they yield such diverse results; they are often based on guesses; and their interpretation depends on patient histories (Vanderpool and Weiss, 1984).

REVEALING MISTAKES TO PATIENTS. Surely, practitioners should tell patients of mistakes pertinent to their welfare or requiring changes in treatment plans. However, the possibility of lawsuits, the fear of losing patient confidence, painful feelings of incompetence, and solidarity between health-care team members often outweigh patient benefits in frankness regarding errors. Charles Bosk observed that discussion of medical errors tends to be highly ritualized, confined to well-defined hospital subgroups, and used to reaffirm a strong collective sense of competence (Bosk, 1980). Hilfiker, however, in a remarkably frank discussion of his own errors, recommended that patients can be accepting of physician limitations, that maintenance of illusions about competence tends ultimately to undermine trust in physicians, and that hiding mistakes tends to alienate caregivers from the healing process of confessing and handling mistakes (Hilfiker, 1985). The ACP Ethics Manual also recommends disclosing significant "procedural or judgment errors" (ACP, 1992, p. 950).

PATIENT REFUSAL OF INFORMATION. The bioethics literature has debated the proper handling of patient refusals of information (Ost, 1984; Strasser, 1986). On the one hand, the literature usually has regarded refusing information as an autonomous choice and therefore has supported it: A caregiver may ethically choose to respect a patient's wish to rely more heavily on the caregiver. Raanan Gillon argued that "forcing" information on a patient is both harmful and disrespectful of autonomy (Gillon, 1990). The issue can also be regarded as a feature of relational style; Edmund Pellegrino noted that "some patients need a more authoritative approach than others" (Pellegrino, 1992, p. 1735).

◆ **valid consent**
The principle that a physician must only impart that information that the patient/subject needs to make a responsible and voluntary decision and not all the information available.

On the other hand, autonomy is not the only basis for disclosure; caregivers have some role-dependent duties to disclose information to the reluctant; and patients have responsibilities as well as rights to use information on their own behalf. Some information may be so surprising and crucial for patients or so necessary for a working partnership that caregivers have an obligation to disclose despite patient protests. Caregivers may feel that a patient's denial is slowing recovery, or that patients may have a duty to act on information, such as that they are HIV-positive, in order to protect others. It is thus doubtful that the question of refusals can be answered generally.

DISCLOSURE TO FAMILY MEMBERS. Kübler-Ross suggested entrusting some information to family members rather than the patient (Kübler-Ross, 1969); this has also been the pattern reported in several countries, such as Hungary, Italy, Japan, and China. This approach may result from seeing the patient as "an extension of the family" (Christakis and Fox, 1992, p. 1101), respecting the family as a strongly interdependent unit, or wishing others to carry the burden of knowledge. Yoshitomo Takahashi reported that some Japanese practitioners consider talking about death as threatening family relationships and separating the patient from others (Takahashi, 1990), and Eric Feldman noted that many Japanese practitioners perceive disclosing terminal diagnoses as "a callous practice" (Feldman, 1985, p. 21). However, supporters of patient autonomy have expressed concern that leaving the patient uninformed is more likely to isolate the patient psychologically (Quill and Townsend, 1991). From both perspectives, the main concern appears to be to include the dying patient in the community, but it is difficult to make reliable cross-cultural generalizations because recommended practices, actual practices, and patient attitudes often vary widely within each culture.

Difficult questions balancing disclosure and confidentiality arise in keeping family members appropriately informed along with the patient. The family may be the recipient of disclosure when an unconscious patient is admitted to the hospital; when the patient recovers competency, the pattern of leaving the family in charge may continue or the family may become excluded from communication. Or family members may give clinicians important information about the patient and ask that the patient not be told; however, the ACP Ethics Manual holds that practitioners are "not obliged" to keep such secrets and should "use sensitivity and judgment" in disclosing such information (ACP, 1992, p. 949).

DISCLOSURE IN THE SOCIAL ARENA. Although bioethical discussion has focused primarily on disclosure and honesty at the bedside, similar issues arise in the larger health-care arena. For instance, a study of advertising in medical journals showed that a high proportion of pharmaceutical advertisements failed to meet U.S. Food and Drug Administration standards for honesty (Wilkes et al., 1992). Many physicians rely on advertisements and pharmaceutical representatives for their information. Consequently, deceiving physicians leads to misinformed patients.

Occupational and public-health physicians face conflicts affecting disclosure. For instance, some clinicians and medical researchers cooperated for many years in industry suppression of information on the carcinogenicity of asbestos (Lilienfeld, 1991); other health professionals have been active in political struggles over posting health warnings on cigarette and alcohol labels. In recent years, the U.S. Occupational Safety and Health Administration has expanded work-

See Also
Communication: Shared Decision-Making

ers' rights to know about their exposure to toxic materials in the workplace, although the complexity of state and federal regulations makes application difficult. Pressures arising from fear of litigation, protection of trade secrets, and concern for individual confidentiality create tensions in pursuing public-health goals of improving public health by keeping workers and the public better informed of their exposure (Ashford and Caldart, 1985).

Conclusion

Beneath this sketch of disclosure lie a number of ethical concerns of great subtlety and depth. Brief reflection on honesty links veracity primarily to telling others what one believes. But, the complex interactions between clinicians and patients require clinicians to consider carefully how patients interpret their words; skill in listening to patients has often been identified as the key element in effective patient teaching. Moreover, health professionals bear serious duties to service and science that require them to examine honestly the limits of their knowledge, the help they can promise, and their insights into the meanings of illness and death. Thus, accepting honest disclosure calls upon professionals to reflect deeply on the relationship of medical science to health, the consequences of individual service to public health, and the impact of health-care institutions and practices on the public's understanding of health, illness, and death.

— ANDREW JAMETON

INFORMED CONSENT

CONSENT ISSUES IN HUMAN RESEARCH

"The voluntary consent of the human subject is absolutely essential." This, the first sentence of the Nuremberg Code, signals the centrality of the consent requirement in research involving human subjects (Germany [Territory Under Allied Occupation], 1947, p. 181). Before the Nuremberg Code was written in 1947 as a response to the atrocities committed in the name of science by Nazi physician-researchers, statements of medical and other professional organizations apparently made no mention of the necessity of consent. Ironically, the only nations known to have promulgated regulations that established a requirement for consent to research were Prussia and Germany (Perley et al., 1992). Subsequently, the tendency to focus on informed consent has been reinforced by public outcry over the inadequacy of consent in certain U.S. judicial landmark cases, such as *Willowbrook*, *Jewish Chronic Disease Hospital*, *Tea Room Trade*, and *Tuskegee* (Katz et al., 1972; Levine, 1986). Indeed, the issue of informed consent has so dominated recent discussion of the ethics of research that one might be led to think erroneously that other ethical issues (e.g., research design, selection of subjects) are either less important or more satisfactorily resolved.

Grounding of informed consent

PHILOSOPHICAL BASIS. The philosophical foundations of the requirement for informed consent may be found in several lines of reasoning (Veatch, 1981; Faden et al., 1986; Brock, 1987). Based upon the Hippocratic admonition "to help, or at least, to do no harm," one can justify seeking consent for the benefit of the patient; to do so provides a mechanism for ascertaining what the patient would consider a benefit. Allowing the individual to decide what he or she considers beneficial is consistent with the perspective affirmed in U.S. public policy that competent persons are generally the best protectors of their own well-being (Brock, 1987). However, a focus solely on patient benefit would allow physicians and scientists not to seek consent when they judge that doing so might harm patients or subjects. Thus this justification alone does not suffice to establish a requirement to seek consent.

The requirement can also be justified on grounds of social benefit: The practice of seeking consent may contribute to producing the "greatest good for the greatest number" by forestalling suspicion about research, thus ensuring a subject population and increasing the efficiency of the research enterprise. Again, however, the justification fails to stand alone, since it can also be used to justify not seeking consent; the social good might be better served by avoiding the inefficient and frequently time-consuming consent process. Some commentators express concern that, carried to its extreme, the social-benefit argument might support the use of unwilling subjects, as in Nazi Germany (Caplan, 1992); such a position would necessarily rest on a very limited vision of the relevant social consequences.

The firmest grounding for the requirement to seek consent is the ethical principle "respect for persons," which according to the U.S. National Commission for the Protection of Human Subjects of Biomedical and Behavioral Research (hereafter, U.S. National Commission) "incorporates at least two basic ethical convictions: first, that individuals should be treated as autonomous agents, and second, that persons with diminished autonomy and thus in need of protection are entitled to such protection" (U.S. National Commission, 1978, p. 4). Although this term suggests a

Most patients are well informed only about the risk of death or significant permanent injury in circumstances in which informed consent is legally or institutionally mandated.

PAGE 674

Kantian or deontological grounding of the principle, this was not the intent of the commission; a substantially similar principle, self-determination, may be grounded in rule utilitarianism (Brock, 1987). In a legal context, Justice Benjamin Cardozo in 1914 stated that "every human being of adult years and sound mind has a right to determine what shall be done with his own body" (Katz, 1984, p. 51). To return to the Kantian terms that will be used often in this article, this principle ensures that the research subject will be treated as an end and not merely as a means to another's end (Beauchamp and Childress, 1989). Thus the purpose of the consent requirement is not to minimize risk but to give persons the right to choose.

RELIGIOUS BASIS. Several fundamental tenets of the Judaeo-Christian tradition also provide grounding for the requirement to seek consent. This tradition affirms that each human life is a gift from God and is of infinite and immeasurable worth (the "sanctity of life"). The infinite worth of the individual requires that persons treat each other with respect and not interfere in each other's lives without consent. The consent requirement can also be grounded explicitly in the notion of covenant. Seeking consent is an affirmation of the basic faithfulness or care required by the fundamental covenantal nature of human existence (Ramsey, 1970).

Functions of informed consent

Jay Katz and Alexander Capron identified the following functions of informed consent: to promote individual autonomy; encourage rational decision making; avoid fraud and duress; involve the public; encourage self-scrutiny by the physician-investigator; and reduce the civil and/or criminal liability of the investigator and his or her institution (Katz and Capron, 1975).

In general, the negotiations for informed consent are designed to safeguard the rights and welfare of the subject, while documentation that the negotiations have been conducted properly safeguards the investigator and institution (Levine, 1986). The net effect of the documentation may, in fact, be harmful to the interests of the subject. Retaining a signed consent form tends to give the advantage to the investigator in any adversary proceeding. Moreover, the availability of such documents in institutional records may lead to violations of privacy and confidentiality. Consequently, federal regulations permit waivers of the requirement for consent forms when the principal threat to the subject would be a breach of confidentiality and "the only record linking the subject and the research would be the consent document" ("Documentation of Informed Consent," 1993, 46.117c).

Those who are interested in making operational the requirement for consent have a tendency to focus near-

◆ coercion
Controlling a patient and restricting the patient's freedom of action by intentionally using credible and severe threats of harm or force or by pressuring a patient to comply, thus making his action costly to pursue and undermining his informed consent.

CONSENT REQUIREMENT
A Twofold Legal Basis

The legal grounding for the requirement for consent to research (Annas et al., 1977; Fried, 1974) is based on the outcome of litigation of disputes arising almost exclusively in the context of medical practice. There is virtually no case law on the basis of which legal standards for consent to research, as distinguished from practice, might be defined (there is one Canadian case, *Halushka v. University of Saskatchewan*). The law defines, in general, the circumstances under which a patient, or by extension, a subject, may recover damages for having been wronged or harmed as a consequence of failure to negotiate adequate consent.

The legal bases for the consent requirement—which also shed light on the ethical dimensions of consent—are twofold (Annas et al., 1977). First, failure to obtain proper consent was traditionally treated as a battery action. Closely related to the principles of respect for persons and self-determination, the law of battery makes it wrong a priori to touch, treat, or do research upon a person without the person's consent. Whether or not harm befalls the patient/subject is irrelevant: It is the unconsented-to touching that is wrong.

The modern trend in malpractice litigation is to treat cases based upon failure to obtain proper consent as negligence rather than battery actions. The negligence doctrine combines elements of patient benefit and self-determination. To bring a negligence action, a patient/subject must prove that the physician had a duty toward the patient; that the duty was breached; that damage occurred to the patient; and that the damage was caused by the breach. In contrast to battery actions, negligence actions remove as a basis for the requirement for consent the simple notion that unconsented-to touching is a wrong. Rather, such touching is wrong (actionable) only if it is negligent and results in harm; otherwise, the patient/subject cannot recover damages. Under both battery and negligence doctrines, consent is invalid if any information is withheld that might be considered material to the decision to give consent.

— ROBERT J. LEVINE

See Also
Confidentiality

ly all of their attention on the consent form. Federal regulations prescribe what information must be included in and excluded from these forms. Members of institutional review boards and researchers collaborate in a struggle to create reproachless forms. This seems to reflect an assumption that the consent form is an appropriate instrumentality through which researchers might fulfill their obligation not to treat persons merely as means. Most commentators on informed consent disagree, however, seeing consent as a continuing process rather than an event symbolized by the signing of a form; for example, Robert Levine (1986) characterizes informed consent as a discussion or negotiation, while Katz (1984) envisions consent as a searching conversation.

Whether or not negotiations for informed consent to research should be conducted according to different standards than consent to practice is controversial. Alvan Feinstein observes that it is the custom to adhere to a double standard: "An act that receives no special concern when performed as part of clinical practice may become a major ethical or legal issue if done as part of a formally designed investigation" (Feinstein, 1974, p. 331). In his view there is less need for formality in the negotiations for informed consent to a relationship where the interests of research and practice are conjoined—for example, as in research conducted by a physician-investigator who has the aim of demonstrating the safety and/or efficacy of a nonvalidated therapeutic maneuver—than when the only purpose of the investigator-subject relationship is to perform research. Capron, on the other hand, asserts: "Higher requirements for informed consent should be imposed in therapy than in investigation, particularly when an element of honest experimentation is joined with therapy" (Capron, 1972, p. 574). Levine (1986) concludes that patients are entitled to the same degree of thoroughness of negotiations for informed consent as are subjects of research. However, patients may be offered the opportunity to delegate some (but not all) decision-making authority to a physician, while subjects should rarely be offered this option. The most important distinction is that the prospective subject should be informed that in research, in contrast with practice, the subject will be at least in part a means and perhaps primarily a means to an end identified by someone else.

Two interpretations of the consent requirement

Interpretations of the meaning and application of informed consent reflect a tension between respecting the autonomy of persons and protecting them from harm. Hans Jonas (1970) and Paul Ramsey (1970) have developed a covenantal model in which subjects are respected and protected by ensuring that they give truly informed consent. Benjamin Freedman (1975) stresses the individual's freedom of choice, whether or not the choice is informed.

For Jonas and Ramsey, the consent requirement is derived from the duty to treat persons as ends, not merely as means. In research, subjects are "used" as means to the end of acquiring knowledge. (In Jonas's terms, they are "sacrificed" for the collective good.) Such "use" of persons is justified only if the subjects so identify with the purposes of the research that they will those purposes as their own ends. Only then are they not being "used," but instead they have become, in Ramsey's term, "co-adventurers." The consent requirement thus affirms a basic covenantal bond between the researcher and the subject and ensures respect for the subject as an end, not merely a means.

To establish a true covenant, the subject's consent must be informed. Only subjects who genuinely know the purposes and appreciate the risks of research can assume those risks and adopt those purposes as their own ends. Ideal subjects, therefore, would be researchers themselves (Jonas, 1970). The less one understands the risks and identifies with the purposes of research, the less valid is one's consent. Jonas therefore established a "descending order of permissibility" for the recruitment ("conscription") of volunteers. Both Ramsey and Jonas restrict the use of subjects unable to consent or to understand what is involved, permitting the use of such subjects only in research directly related to their own condition (Jonas) or their own survival and well-being (Ramsey).

This interpretation reflects certain assumptions that can be challenged. First, while neither Jonas nor Ramsey focuses exclusively on patients as subjects, their approach appears to be influenced largely by the medical practice model. That approach may not be adequate to deal with research not based on the medical practice model—for example, social-science research.

Second, while Ramsey argues that it is wrong to use a person in research without consent irrespective of risk (because one can be "wronged" without being "harmed"), he nonetheless appears to share with Jonas the assumption that most research is risky and involves "sacrifice" on the part of the subject. In fact, most research does not present risk of physical or psychological harm; rather, it presents inconvenience (e.g., of urine collection) and discomforts (e.g., of needle sticks) (Levine, 1986). Even Phase I drug testing, involving the first administration of new drugs to humans and usually assumed to be highly risky, has been estimated to present subjects with "risks" slightly greater than those involved in secretarial work and substantially less than those assumed by window washers and miners (Levine, 1986).

"The voluntary consent of the human subject is absolutely essential."

FIRST SENTENCE OF THE NUREMBERG CODE, 1947

See Also

Trust

But the most important challenge is Freedman's (1975) alternative interpretation and use of the basic principles. Like Jonas and Ramsey, Freedman derives the consent requirement from the duty to have respect for persons. Unlike Jonas and Ramsey, however, he interprets the requirement of respect for persons to allow the possibility of a "valid but ignorant" consent.

Freedman proposes that striving for "fully informed consent" is generally undesirable, and that what is required is "valid consent," not necessarily "informed consent." To be valid, consent must be responsible and voluntary. Thus valid consent "entails only the imparting of that information which the patient/subject requires in order to make a responsible decision" (Freedman, 1975, p. 34). A choice based upon less or other information than another responsible person might consider essential is not necessarily a sign of irresponsibility. Overprotection is a form of dehumanization and lack of respect; for example, to classify persons as incompetent in order to protect them from their own judgment is the worst form of abuse.

This approach also has several weaknesses. Much hinges on what is taken to be a responsible choice. Freedman suggests that responsibility is a dispositional characteristic and is to be judged in terms of the person, not in terms of a particular choice. However, there is still an element of paternalism introduced in judging another to be a responsible person. Moreover, this approach may not provide sufficient protection for those subjects who tend too readily to abdicate responsibility for choice.

It is clear that debates over the interpretation of informed consent depend on interpretations of the basic ethical principle of respect for persons and the extent to which that principle requires protection from harm or respect for autonomy.

◆ **law of battery**
Makes it wrong to touch, treat, or do research upon a person without the person's consent, which could become invalid if any information considered material to the decision is withheld from the patient.

Informed consent: Conditions and exceptions

Recent discussion emphasizes the knowledge or information component of consent—hence the term "informed consent" (Katz, 1984). Nuremberg's focus on freedom of choice rather than on the quantity or quality of information transmitted is represented by its use of the term "voluntary consent," not "informed consent." It is worth recalling that a demand for informed consent at the expense of other styles of self-determination such as Freedman's responsible choice is not necessarily respectful of persons. Most commentators agree that compromise of any one of the four conditions specified by the Nuremberg Code jeopardizes the ethical acceptability of the consent.

See Also

Communication: Shared Decision-Making

INFORMED CONSENT TO PARTICIPATION IN RESEARCH

Four Conditions According to the Nuremberg Code (1947)

1. One must be able to exercise free power of choice.
2. One must have the legal capacity to give consent.
3. One must have sufficient comprehension to make an informed decision.
4. One must have sufficient knowledge on which to decide.

"FREE POWER OF CHOICE." The Nuremberg Code proscribes "any element of force, fraud, deceit, duress, overreaching, or other ulterior forms of constraint or coercion" (Germany [Territory Under Allied Occupation], 1947, p. 181) in obtaining consent. Any flagrant coercion—for instance, when competent, comprehending persons are forced to submit to research against their expressed will—clearly renders consent invalid. There may be more subtle or indirect "constraints" or "coercions" when prospective subjects are highly dependent, impoverished, or "junior or subordinate members of a hierarchical group" (Council for International Organizations of Medical Sciences [CIOMS], 1993, p. 30). Some argue that consent obtained from such persons violates the intent of the Nuremberg Code. This argument has been posed most sharply with respect to prisoners and other institutionalized populations, since institutionalization often involves both dependency and impoverishment. (Biomedical research involving prisoners as subjects has become quite rare since 1976 when the U.S. National Commission recommended very stringent standards for its justification [Dubler and Sidel, 1989].) Some argue that consent to participate in research is not valid when it is given (1) to procure financial reward in situations offering few alternatives for remuneration; (2) to seek release from an institution either by evidencing "good behavior" or by ameliorating the condition for which one was confined; or (3) to please physicians or authorities on whom one's continued welfare depends (Branson, 1977).

Cornel West (1976) argues, however, that such indirect forms of constraint do not constitute coercion in a strict sense and thus do not render consent involuntary. "Coercion," says West, consists in a threat to render one's circumstances worse if one does not do something. Hence, a threat to withdraw basic necessities of existence, or in some other way to render a prison inmate's situation worse if he or she declines to participate in research, would constitute coercion and render consent invalid. Similarly, to condition release from prison upon participation would constitute coercion, since it would make the inmate's situation worse by removing normal alternatives for seeking release. But the provision of better living conditions in exchange for participation in research does not constitute a threat to make conditions worse; rather, it is an enticement to make conditions better. While enticement and bribery can invalidate consent by undermining the rational grounds for choice, they do not undermine the voluntariness of the choice (Cohen, 1978). Similarly, a desire to "get well" or to favorably influence institutional authorities is not an "ulterior" constraint in the strict sense of the Nuremberg Code, though it may be a very real psychological constraint.

Other commentators, however, are less concerned with a sharp distinction between coercion and other forms of constraint or undue influence (Levine, 1986; CIOMS, 1993). Even outside such total institutions as prisons there are many situations in which junior or subordinate members of hierarchical groups may be exploited or manipulated. Such persons may assume that their willingness to consent to research may be rewarded by preferential treatment or that their refusals could provoke retaliation by those in positions of authority in the system. Whether or not such assumptions are justified, it is the assumptions themselves that make such persons susceptible to manipulation. Examples of such persons are medical or nursing students, subordinate hospital and laboratory personnel, employees of pharmaceutical firms, and members of the military services. Other persons whose dependency status can be exploited include residents of nursing homes, people receiving welfare benefits, patients in emergency rooms, and those with incurable diseases.

Apart from those populations identified by regulations and ethical codes as requiring "special protection"—fetuses, children, prisoners, and those who are incompetent by reason of mental incapacity—there is no clear consensus about how to respond to the problems presented by those whose capacity to consent may be limited by virtue of their dependency status. For example, while some medical schools have policies that forbid the involvement of medical students as research subjects, others have required investigators to invite them to participate in certain complex projects, reasoning that their highly sophisticated understanding of the risks, benefits, and purposes of such projects ensures a high quality of consent (Levine, 1986). Involvement of medical students, it is further argued, is consistent with Jonas's "descending order of permissibility" and contributes to their socialization into the medical profession.

While most regulations and ethical codes proscribe undue material inducements, there is no consensus on what this means. Some commentators argue that in most cases in which competent adults are recruited to serve as subjects in research that presents only slight increases above minimal risk, the role of the research subject is similar to that of an employee (Levine, 1986). Consequently, the amounts of cash payments or other material inducements can be determined by ordinary market factors. Others protest that because participation in research entails "selling one's body" as opposed to "selling one's labor" the role of the research subject might be considered more akin to prostitution than to any other type of employment (Wartofsky, 1976). According to this view, research subjects should not be paid at all; rather they should be motivated by altruism.

Attempts to regulate the amounts of permissible material inducements are inevitably problematic (Levine, 1986). Setting the rates at a low level results in inequitable distribution of the burdens of participation among those who have no opportunities to earn more money for each unit of their time. Higher rates may overwhelm the capacity of the impoverished to decline participation.

COMPETENCE AND COMPREHENSION. The Nuremberg Code requires both "legal capacity" to consent (often called "competence") and "sufficient understanding" to reach an "enlightened" decision. Definitions of competence often include elements of comprehension, for example, to evaluate relevant information, to understand the consequences of action, and to reach a decision for rational reasons (Stanley and Stanley, 1982).

Joseph Goldstein charges that linking determinations of competence to assessments of comprehension is "pernicious," since refusal to participate in research might be judged "irrational" by the investigator and then used as grounds for declaring the person incompetent. Because the purpose of the informed consent requirement is to guarantee the exercise of free choice, not to judge its rationality, Goldstein argues, competence should be presumed; only a "showing that the patient is comatose" should ordinarily be accepted as proof of incompetence (Goldstein, 1978).

ASSESSMENTS OF INCOMPETENCE. The various standards employed for assessing competence are variations of four basic themes (Stanley and Stanley, 1982).

1. *Reasonable outcome of choice.* This is a highly paternalistic standard in that the individual's right to self-determination is respected only if he or she makes the "right" choice—that is, one that accords with what the competency reviewer either considers reasonable or presumes a reasonable person might make.

See Also

Contemporary Ethics of Care

2. *Factual comprehension.* The individual is required to understand, or at least be able to understand, the information divulged during the consent negotiation.
3. *Choice based on rational reasons.* Individuals must demonstrate a capacity for rational manipulation of information. They may, for example, be required to show that they not only understand the risks and benefits but also have weighed them in relation to their personal situations.
4. *Appreciation of the nature of the situation.* Individuals must demonstrate not only comprehension of the consent information but also the ability to use the information in a rational manner. Furthermore, they must appreciate the fact that they are being invited to become research subjects and what that implies.

While there is disagreement as to the grounds for assessing incompetence, most commentators agree that such assessments are limited in several ways (Faden et al., 1986). First, a judgment of incompetence may apply only to certain areas of decision making, for example, to one's legal but not to one's personal affairs. Second, confinement to a mental institution is not in itself equivalent to a determination of incompetence. Third, some who are legally competent are functionally incompetent, while some who are legally incompetent are functionally competent.

The Nuremberg Code does not permit the use of subjects lacking legal capacity or comprehension. Most subsequent codes and discussions allow their use with certain restrictions: for example, that mentally competent adults are not suitable subjects, that the veto of a legally incompetent but minimally comprehending subject is binding, and that consent or permission of the legal guardian must be obtained (Levine, 1986).

◆ **Nuremberg Code**
Written in 1947 in reaction to the Nazis' eugenics policies, it prohibits research unless the subjects can give informed, mature, voluntary consent.

According to the U.S. President's Commission for the Study of Ethical Problems in Medicine and Biomedical and Behavioral Research (hereafter, U.S. President's Commission), "decision-making capacity requires, to a greater or lesser degree: (1) possession of a set of values and goals; (2) the ability to communicate and understand information; and (3) the ability to reason and deliberate about one's choices" (U.S. President's Commission, 1982, p. 57). Moreover, individuals may have sufficient capacity to make some decisions but not others (Brock, 1987; Kopelman, 1990). In the words of the U.S. President's Commission:

> *Since the assessment [of capacity] must balance possibly competing considerations of well-being and self-determination, [one should] take into account the potential consequences of the patient's decision. When the consequences for well-being are substantial, there is a greater need to be certain that the patient possesses the necessary level of capacity.... Thus a particular patient may be capable of deciding about a relatively inconsequential medication, but not about the amputation of a gangrenous limb.*
> *(U.S. President's Commission, 1982, p. 60)*

PROXY CONSENT. The debate between Paul Ramsey and Richard McCormick over the legitimacy of proxy consent to authorize the participation of an incompetent person in research is one of the classics in the brief history of bioethics. Adopting the battery argument, Ramsey claimed that the use of a nonconsenting subject is wrong whether or not there is risk, simply because it involves an unconsented touching. Unconsented touching is not wrongful, however, when it is for the good of the individual. Hence, proxy consent may be given for the use of nonconsenting subjects in research only when it includes therapeutic interventions related to the subject's own recovery (Ramsey, 1970).

However, Ramsey acknowledged that benefit does not always justify unconsented touching; such touching of a competent adult is wrong even if it benefits that person. Why, then, can benefit be presumed to justify such touching for a child (or other subject unable to give consent)? McCormick proposed that the validity of such interventions rests on the presumption that the child, if capable, would consent to therapy. This presumption in turn derives from a child's obligation to seek therapy, an obligation that the child possesses simply as a human being (McCormick, 1974). Because children have an obligation to seek their own well-being, we presume they would consent if they could, and thus presume also that proxy consent on their behalf would not violate respect for them as persons.

By analogy, McCormick suggested that, as members of a moral community, children have other obligations to which one would presume their consent and give proxy consent on their behalf. One such obligation is to contribute to the general welfare when such contribution requires little or no sacrifice. Hence, nonconsenting subjects may be used in research not directly related to their own benefit so long as the research fulfills an important social need and involves no discernible risk. Ramsey countered this argument with respect to children, claiming that McCormick's position fails to recognize that children are not adults with a full range of duties and obligations. Instead, they have rights that must be protected by adults (Ramsey, 1976).

Adopting this premise about the nature of the child

See Also

Confidentiality; Gene Therapy; Genetic Testing and Screening; Maternal-Fetal Relationship as a moral being, Freedman drew different conclusions. Since a child is not a moral being in the same sense as an adult, he argued, the concept of wrongful touching does not apply. The child has no right to be left alone but only a right to be protected. Hence, Freedman concludes that the only relevant moral issue is the risk involved in the research, and, like McCormick, that children could be used in research unrelated to their therapy, provided it presents them no discernible risk (Freedman, 1975). Thus, the debate centers on the status of the child (a paradigmatic incompetent) as a moral being and on interpretations of the requirements of respect for persons.

Although disagreements persist over both standards of competence and the use of incompetent subjects, one issue seems to have been settled by the U.S. National Commission in several of its reports (Levine, 1986). Parents, guardians, and, in some cases, other "responsible relatives" may give "permission" (a term that replaces "proxy consent") to involve an incompetent in research if there is no more than minimal risk, if incompetents who are capable of giving their "assents" (knowledgeable agreements that do not meet the legal standards for informed consent) do so, and if certain other criteria are satisfied. If there is more than minimal risk, the standards for ethical justification of the involvement of incompetents are more stringent.

DISCLOSURE OF INFORMATION. The Nuremberg Code requires that the subject be told "the nature, duration, and purpose of the experiment; the method and means by which it is to be conducted; all inconveniences and hazards reasonably to be expected; and the effects upon his health or person which may possibly come (Germany, [Territory Under Allied Occupation], 1947, p. 182)." These requirements have been modified by subsequent codes and regulations. U.S. federal regulations require:

1. a statement of the purpose of the research and a description of its procedures;
2. a description of foreseeable risks and discomforts;
3. a description of benefits;
4. disclosure of appropriate alternatives, if any;
5. a statement of the extent of confidentiality;
6. an explanation of the availability of medical treatment for injury and compensation for disability;
7. an explanation of whom to contact for answers to questions; and
8. a statement that participation is voluntary and that neither refusal to participate nor withdrawal at any time will result in a loss of benefits to which the subject is otherwise entitled ("General Requirements," 1993).

The regulations further specify six additional elements of information to be provided when appropriate:

1. additional risks to the subject or to the fetus if the subject becomes pregnant;
2. circumstances in which a subject's participation may be terminated without his or her consent;
3. additional costs to the subject that may result from participation;
4. the consequences of a subject's decision to withdraw and procedures for orderly termination of participation;
5. a commitment to divulge significant new findings developed during the research that may relate to the subject's continued willingness to participate; and
6. the approximate number of subjects in the study.

Finally, the regulations forbid requirements that subjects waive any of their legal rights as well as releases of the investigator, sponsor, or institution from liability for negligence.

While these requirements have the force of law, they are by no means exhaustive of possible standards for disclosure. To them one might add the following: a clear invitation to participate in research, distinguishing maneuvers required for research purposes from those necessary for therapy; an explanation of why that particular person is invited (selected); a suggestion that the prospective subject might wish to discuss the research with another person; and an identification of the source of funding for the research. Robert Veatch would add the names of members of any review boards that had approved the research and an explanation of the right, if any, to continue receiving treatments found useful (Veatch, 1978). In short, there is no universal agreement on standards for disclosure of information or on what it takes for a person to have "sufficient knowledge" to give "informed" consent.

Those who agree on the need for disclosure of information in a particular category—the risks, for example—often disagree on the nature of the information that must be made known. The Nuremberg Code requires explication of hazards "reasonably" to be expected. Does this include a very slight chance of a substantial harm, or a substantial chance of a very slight harm? Neither the quality nor the probability of the risks to be divulged has been clearly determined legally.

Privacy in law is linked to freedom from intrusion by the state or third persons.

PAGE 123

Privileged communications are those of a confidences protected by law against disclosure in legal settings.

PAGE 123

Disagreements over particulars arise in part from disagreements about underlying standards: Is disclosure to be determined by:

1. general medical practice or opinion;
2. the requirements of a "reasonable person"; or
3. the idiosyncratic judgment of the individual?

While the legal trend may be shifting from the first to the second, it may be argued that only the third, the "subjective standard," is truly compatible with the requirement of respect for the autonomy of the individual person (Faden and Beauchamp, 1986; Veatch, 1978).

Yet even those who adopt the subjective standard disagree as to its implications. As noted earlier, Freedman (1975) holds that the idiosyncratic judgment of the individual is overriding, to the point that the prospective subject can choose to have less information than a "reasonable" person might require. Veatch, however, argues that anyone refusing to accept as much information as would be expected of a "reasonable person" should not be accepted as a subject (Veatch, 1978).

In the context of medical practice, two exceptions to the requirement for informed consent are recognized—"emergency exception" and "therapeutic privilege." The former, which permits the doctor to proceed without delay to administer urgently required therapy in emergencies, is included in a limited form in the regulations of the U.S. Food and Drug Administration; in some "life-threatening" emergencies in which informed consent is "infeasible," physician-investigators are authorized to employ investigational drugs and devices (Levine, 1986). There is continuing controversy over whether the emergency exception can be invoked to justify "deferred consent," that is, postponement of soliciting the consent of the subject or permission of the next-of-kin for up to several days after the subject has been enrolled in a research protocol in an emergency (Levine, 1991; Prentice et al., 1994). The therapeutic-privilege exception to the informed-consent rule permits the doctor to withhold information when, in his or her judgment, disclosure would be detrimental to the patient's interests or well-being (Levine, 1986). Most commentators agree that invoking the doctrine of therapeutic privilege to assure a subject's cooperation in a research project is almost never appropriate; it gives the investigator entirely too much license to serve vested interests by withholding information that might be material to a prospective subject's decision. U.S. federal regulations do not explicitly endorse the use of the therapeutic-privilege exception in research, although some authors have suggested that they could be interpreted as an implicit endorsement (Levine, 1986).

The success of some research activities is contingent upon withholding from the subjects information about their purposes or procedures or, in some cases, by deliberate deception (providing false information). U.S. federal regulations permit "waivers and alterations" of consent requirements if there is no more than minimal risk; if the waiver or alteration will not adversely affect subjects' rights or welfare; if without the waiver or alteration the research "could not practicably be carried out"; and if the subjects will be debriefed (given a full and accurate explanation afterward) when appropriate ("General Requirements," 1993, 46.116d). Diana Baumrind opposes deceptive practices, arguing not only that they violate the principle of respect for persons but also that in the long run they will invalidate research on scientific grounds (Baumrind, 1979). Various proposals have been made to minimize the need for and harmful effects of deceptive practices: Subjects might be invited to consent to incomplete disclosure with a promise of full disclosure at the termination of the research; subjects might be told as much as possible and asked to consent for specified limits of time and risk; or approval of the plans to withhold information from or to deceive subjects might be sought from "surrogate" populations that resemble the actual intended subject populations in relevant respects (Levine, 1986).

Conclusions

The use of a person as a research subject can be justified only if that person, or one authorized to speak on his or her behalf, consents to such use. The legal and ethical requirement for consent is grounded in fundamental tenets of the Judaeo-Christian religious tradition as well as in basic ethical principles that create the universal obligation to treat persons as ends and not merely as means to another's end. The consent requirement also reflects the perspective that competent persons are generally the best protectors of their own well-being. Most major disagreements over the form and substance of the consent requirement derive from conflicting interpretations of one or more of the basic principles.

A widespread tendency among researchers to focus on consent forms seems to reflect an assumption that the consent form is an appropriate instrumentality through which they might fulfill their obligation not to treat persons merely as means. Most commentators on informed consent disagree, however, seeing consent as a continuing process rather than a single event consummated by the signing of a form. Moreover, while the primary purposes of informed consent are to foster self-determination and to empower prospective subjects to protect their own well-being and other interests, the primary purpose of its written documentation is to protect the investigator, the institution, and the research sponsor from legal liability.

— ROBERT J. LEVINE

LEGAL AND ETHICAL ISSUES OF CONSENT IN HEALTH CARE

The doctrine of informed consent, introduced into U.S. case law in 1957, represents judges' groping efforts to delineate physicians' duties to inform patients of the benefits and risks of diagnostic and treatment alternatives, including the consequences of no treatment, as well as to obtain patients' consent (*Salgo* v. *Stanford University*, 1957). The doctrine's avowed purpose was to protect patients' right to "thoroughgoing self-determination" (*Natanson* v. *Kline*, 1960). The legal implications of informed consent, however, remain unclear. The doctrine is in fact more of a slogan, which judges have been too timid or too wise to translate into law, at least as yet. It has been employed with little care but great passion to voice a dream of personal freedom and individual dignity. Though its legal impact in protecting patients' right to self-decision making has been scant, the threat of informed consent has opened profound issues for the traditional practice of medicine.

The medical framework

It has been insufficiently recognized, particularly by judges, that disclosure and consent, except in the most rudimentary fashion, are obligations alien to medical practice. Hippocrates' admonitions to physicians are still followed today: "Perform [these duties] calmly and adroitly, concealing most things from the patient while you are attending to him. Give necessary orders with cheerfulness and serenity, turning his attention away from what is being done to him; sometimes reprove sharply and emphatically, and sometimes comfort with solicitude and attention, revealing nothing of the patient's future or present condition" (Hippocrates, 1923). Thus it is not surprising that the Hippocratic oath is silent on the duty of physicians to inform, or even converse with, patients. Similarly Dr. Thomas Percival, whose 1803 book *Medical Ethics* influenced profoundly the subsequent codifications of medical ethics in England and the United States, commented only once on the discourse between physicians and patients, restricting his remarks to "gloomy prognostications." Even in that context he advised that "friends of the patient" be primarily informed, though he added that the patient may be told "if absolutely necessary" (Percival, 1927, p. 91). The Code of Ethics of the American Medical Association, adopted in 1847, and the Principles of Medical Ethics of the American Medical Association, adopted in 1903 and 1912, repeat, in almost the same words, Percival's statement. The AMA Principles of Medical Ethics, endorsed in 1957, delete Percival's wording entirely and substitute the vague admonition that "physicians . . . should make available to their patients . . . the benefits of their professional attainments." The pertinent sections of the *Opinions of the Judicial Council* of the AMA, interpreting the principles, note only the surgeon's obligation to disclose "all facts relevant to the need and performance of the operation" and the experimenter's obligation, when using new drugs and procedures, to obtain "the voluntary consent of the person" (American Medical Association Judicial Council, 1969). Nine years later, the AMA House of Delegates in endorsing, with modifications, the Declaration of Helsinki, asked that investigators, when engaged "in clinical [research] primarily for treatment," make relevant disclosures to and obtain the voluntary consent of patients or their legally authorized representative.

Thus in the context of therapy no authoritative statement encouraging disclosure and consent has ever been promulgated by the medical profession. The AMA's tersely worded surgical exception was compelled by the law of malpractice. Its experimental exception represented primarily an acquiescence to the U.S. Public Health Service and the U.S. Department of Health, Education, and Welfare requirements, which in turn were formulated in response to congressional concerns about research practices. When disclosure and consent prior to the conduct of therapeutic research were endorsed by the AMA, it did not extend those requirements to *all* patient care but limited the exception to "clinical [research] primarily for treatment."

Two significant conclusions can be drawn:

1. "Informed consent" is a creature of law and not a medical prescription. A duty to inform patients has never been promulgated by the medical profession, though individual physicians have made interesting, but as a rule unsystematic, comments on this topic. Judges have been insufficiently aware of the deeply ingrained Hippocratic tradition against disclosure and, instead, seem to have assumed that individual physicians' lack of disclosure was aberrant with respect to standard medical practice, and hence "negligent," in the sense of "forgetful" or "inadvertent," conduct.
2. When judges were confronted with claims of lack of informed consent, no medical precedent, no medical position papers, and no analytic medical thinking existed on this sub-

◆ **Helsinki solution**
Found in the World Medical Association's 1991 Declaration of Helsinki, the view that persons who lack the capacity to give informed consent may be enrolled only in therapeutic studies.

See Also
Rights of Patients/Clients

I

INFORMED CONSENT

Legal and Ethical Issues of Consent in Health Care

ject. Thus physicians were ill prepared to shape judges' notions on informed consent with thoughtful and systematic positions of their own.

The legal framework

With the historical movement from feudalism to individualism, consent, respect for the dignity of human beings, and the right of individuals to shape their own lives became important principles of English common law and, in turn, of American common law. Yet, as these principles gained greater acceptance, questions arose in many areas of law about the capacity of human beings to make their own decisions and about the need to protect them from their own "folly." The tug of war between advocates of thoroughgoing self-determination and those of paternalism has continued unabated. The informed-consent doctrine manifests this struggle. While in physician-patient interactions the legal trend during the past two decades has been to increase somewhat the right of patients to greater freedom of choice, the informed-consent doctrine has not had as far-reaching an impact on patients' self-determination as many commentators have assumed. This fact has been insufficiently appreciated and has led to confusion, further compounded by the courts' rhetoric that seemed to promise more than it delivered.

Consent to medical and surgical interventions is an ancient legal requirement. Historically an intentional touching without consent was adjudicated in battery. The law has not changed at all in this regard, and a surgeon who operates on a patient without permission is legally liable, even if the operation is successful. In such instances any inquiry into medical need or negligent conduct becomes irrelevant, for what is at issue is the disregard of the person's right to exercise control over his body. The jurisprudential basis of these claims is personal freedom:

> *. . . under a free government at least, the free citizen's first and greatest right, which underlies all others—the right to himself—is the subject of universal acquiescence, and this right necessarily forbids a physician or surgeon, however skillful or eminent . . . to violate without permission the bodily integrity of his patient by . . . operating on him without his consent. . . .*
> (Pratt *v.* Davis, *1906*)

◆ patient-centered approach
A process of shared decision making in which competent patients retain authority over their treatment, with providers recommending and explaining alternatives and allowing patients informed consent and the right to refuse treatment.

But what does consent mean? In battery cases it means only that the physician must inform the patient what he proposes to do and that the patient must agree. Medical emergencies and patients' incompetence are the only exceptions to this requirement.

In mid-twentieth century, judges gradually confronted the question whether patients are entitled not only to know what a doctor proposes to do but also to decide whether the intervention is advisable in the light of its risks and benefits and the available alternatives, including no treatment. Such awareness of patients' informational needs is a modern phenomenon, influenced by the simultaneous growth of product liability and consumer law.

The law of fraud and deceit has always protected patients from doctors' flagrant misrepresentations, and in theory patients have always been entitled to ask whatever questions they pleased. What the doctrine of informed consent sought to add is the proposition that physicians are now under an affirmative duty to offer to acquaint patients with the important risks and plausible alternatives to the proposed procedure. The underlying rationale for that duty was stated in *Natanson* v. *Kline*:

> *Anglo-American law starts with the premise of thorough-going self-determination. It follows that each man is considered to be master of his own body, and he may, if he be of sound mind, expressly prohibit the performance of life-saving surgery, or other medical treatment. A doctor might well believe that an operation or form of treatment is desirable or necessary but the law does not permit him to substitute his own judgment for that of the patient by any form of artifice or deception.*
> (Natanson *v.* Kline, *1960*)

The language employed by the *Natanson* court in support of an affirmative duty to disclose derives from the language of the law of battery, which clearly makes the patient the ultimate decision maker with respect to his body. Thus the courts reasoned, with battery principles very much in mind, that significant protection of patients' right to decide their medical fate required not merely perfunctory assent but a truly "informed consent," based on an adequate understanding of the medical and surgical options available to them.

Yet in the same breath judges also attempted to intrude as little as possible on traditional medical practices. In doing so their impulse to protect the right of individual self-determination collided with their equally strong desire to maintain the authority and practices of the professions. Law has always respected the arcane expertise of physicians and has never held them liable if they practiced "good medicine." The law of consent in battery represented no aberration from this principle since most physicians agree that patients at least deserve to know the nature of the proposed procedure. However, the new duty of disclosure that the law, in the name of self-determination, threatened to impose upon physicians was something quite different. For the vast majority of physicians significant disclosure is not at all part of standard medical practice. Most doctors believe that patients are neither emotionally nor intellectually

See Also
Treatment Questions: Access to Unproven Drugs

equipped to be medical decision makers, that they must be guided past childish fears into "rational" therapy, and that disclosures of uncertainty, gloomy prognosis and dire risks often seriously undermine cure. Physicians began to wonder whether law was now asking them to practice "bad" medicine.

In the early informed-consent cases, judges simply did not resolve the conflict between self-determination and professional practices and authority. The result was distressing confusion. In obeisance to the venerable ideal of self-determination, courts purported to establish, as a matter of law, the physician's

> ... *obligation ... to disclose and explain to the patient in language as simple as necessary the nature of the ailment, the nature of the proposed treatment, the probability of success or of alternatives, and perhaps the risks of unfortunate results and unforeseen conditions within the body.* (Natanson *v.* Kline)

The threat of such an obligation greatly disturbed the medical profession. It recognized that serious implementation of such a standard would significantly alter medical practice. Physicians argued that in order fully to serve patients' best interests, they must have the authority to exercise medical judgment in managing patients. Courts likewise bowed to this judgment. In the very sentence that introduced the ambiguous but exuberant new phrase "informed consent," the court showed its deference to medical judgment and its hesitancy to disturb traditional practice:

> ... *in discussing the element of risk a certain amount of discretion must be employed consistent with the full disclosure of facts necessary to an informed consent.*
> (Salgo *v.* Stanford University)

Thus the extent to which evolving case law, under the banner of individualism, was challenging traditional medical practice—which for millennia has treated patients paternally as children—remained confusing. In those earlier cases (*Salgo* v. *Stanford University*, *Natanson* v. *Kline*) judges were profoundly allegiant to both points of view, but the balance was soon tipped decisively in favor of protecting medical practices.

BATTERY OR NEGLIGENCE? The striking ambivalence of judges toward the doctrine of informed consent manifested itself in the competition between battery and negligence doctrines as a means of analyzing and deciding the claims of lack of informed consent. Battery offered a more rigorous protection of patients' right to self-determination. The inquiry into disclosure and consent would not be governed by professional practices but instead would rest on the question: Has the physician met his expanded informational responsibility so that the patient is able to exercise a choice among treatment options? A negative answer to this question would show that the physician's actions constitute trespass, rendering him liable for an unauthorized and "offensive" contact (*Dow* v. *Kaiser Foundation*).

However, in virtually every jurisdiction judges resolved the competition in favor of negligence law. In doing so, judges were able to defer to medical judgment by evaluating the adequacy of disclosure against the medical professional standard of care, asserting that this standard will govern those duties as it does other medical obligations. As a consequence, physicians remain free to exercise the wisdom of their profession and are liable only for failure to disclose what a reasonable doctor would have revealed. Furthermore, negligence theory does not redress mere dignitary injuries, irrespective of physical injuries, and requires proof that the patient, fully informed, would have refused the proposed treatment. Interferences with self-determination, standing alone, are not compensated.

In rejecting battery, judges made much of the fact that such an action required "intent," while negligence involved "inadvertence"; it was the latter, they believed, that accounted for the lack of disclosure. They overlooked that the withholding of information on the part of physicians is generally quite intentional, dictated by the very exercise of medical judgment that the law of negligence seeks to respect. In stating that the nondisclosures were "collateral" to the central information about the nature of the proposed procedure and hence not required for a valid consent, judges discarded the very idea of informed consent—namely, that absence of expanded disclosure vitiates consent. They refused to extend the inquiry to the total informational needs of patients, without which patients' capacity for self-decision making remains incomplete. At bottom, the rejection of an expanded battery theory and of its proposed requirement of informed consent followed from the threat they posed to the authority of doctors and traditional medical practice.

Thus informed consent, based on patients thoroughgoing self-determination, was a misnomer from the time the phrase was born. To be sure, a new cause of action has emerged for failure to inform of the risks of, and in most jurisdictions alternatives to, treatment. Some duty to disclose risks and alternatives, the courts were willing to say, exists; the extent of that duty is defined by the disclosure practice of a reasonable physician in the circumstances of the case. The new claim is firmly rooted in the law of negligent malpractice, in that plaintiffs are still required to prove the professional standard of care by means of medical expert witnesses. In these, the majority of jurisdictions, traditional medical practice—which generally opposes dis-

In exchange for the loss of privacy, clients expect and are promised some degree of confidentiality.

PAGE 123

closure—has scarcely been threatened at all in legal reality. The legal life of informed consent, except for dicta about self-determination and the hybrid negligence law promulgated in a handful of jurisdictions, was almost over as soon as it began. Judges had briefly toyed with the idea of patients' self-determination and then largely cast it aside. Good medicine, as defined by doctors, remains good law almost everywhere.

TENSIONS BETWEEN SELF-DETERMINATION AND PATERNALISM. Beyond its allegiance to medical paternalism, the *Canterbury* court showed its preference for paternalism in another way. Under negligence law, the courts have stated that lack of disclosure cannot be said to have caused the patient's injury unless the patient, if adequately informed, would have declined the procedure; this is the crucial problem of causation in informed-consent cases. Such an approach to causation is quite appropriate where law seeks not to compensate interference with self-determination, but only physical injuries resulting from inadequate disclosure. Yet the *Canterbury* court, and every court that has considered the matter subsequently, held that the decision whether or not to undertake therapy must be examined not from the point of view of the patient-plaintiff but from that of a "prudent person in the patient's position," limiting the inquiry to whether a "reasonable patient" would have agreed to the procedure. This substitution of a community standard of a "reasonable" person cuts the heart out of the courts purported respect for individual self-determination.

CANTERBURY V. SPENCE

Paternalism Meets Self-Determination

In a few jurisdictions, beginning in 1972 in the District of Columbia with the decision in *Canterbury* v. *Spence,* the new cause of action for failure to inform combined elements of battery with negligence, creating a legal hybrid. The court purported to abandon the professional standard of care with respect to disclosure, asserting that

> *. . . respect for the patient's right of self-determination on particular therapy demands a standard set by law for physicians rather than one which physicians may or may not impose upon themselves.*
>
> (Canterbury *v.* Spence)

Thus the court laid down a judge-made rule of disclosure of risks and alternatives, which for all practical purposes resembled an expanded battery standard of disclosure.

The preoccupation with risk disclosure, however, continued unabated. From the very beginning, despite all the talk about "informed consent," judges did not lay down any rules for a careful inquiry into the nature and quality of consent, which on its face any meaningful implementation of the doctrine required. Instead major emphasis was placed on risk disclosures. Since in the cases before courts plaintiff-patients only complained of the injurious results of treatment, this emphasis is understandable. Yet to focus solely on risks is to bypass the principal issue of self-determination—namely, whether the physician kept the patient from arriving at his own decision. The *Canterbury* court, too, restricted its concerns largely to risk disclosures and added the requirement that

> *an unrevealed risk that should have been made known must materialize for otherwise the omission, however, unpardonable, is legally without consequence.*
>
> (Canterbury *v.* Spence)

Thus the court foreclosed legal redress for the patient who, fully informed of the potential effects of, for example, a maiming operation, would have chosen an alternative medical course, even though some of the risks did not materialize.

But to the extent these jurisdictions have abandoned the professional standard of disclosure, traditional medical practice has been challenged; "good medicine," in the eyes of the profession, may no longer be a sufficient defense. Seemingly, in these jurisdictions self-determination has begun to encroach upon the province of medical paternalism. That encroachment, however, may be substantially an illusion, for the touted abandonment of the professional standard of disclosure in *Canterbury* was far from complete. Medical judgment to truncate full disclosure must be "given its due," the court said, when "it enters the picture." The court left ambiguous when the plaintiff must establish the appropriate standard of disclosure by an expert witness, or when he must produce such a witness in order to rebut a defendant-physician's claim that good medical judgment was exercised.

What is clear is that the physician has a "therapeutic privilege" not to disclose information where such disclosure would pose a threat to the "well-being" of the patient. But the ambit of this privilege as well as the relationship of its invocation to a directed verdict is not clear, and this for "good" reasons: Even in these most liberal jurisdictions with respect to patients' rights, courts still cannot face squarely the question of how much they are willing to challenge the traditional medical wisdom of nondisclosure. The law remains ambiguous with respect to this, the core issue of informed consent.

— JAY KATZ

Questions of the influence of hindsight and bitterness are familiar to juries, as is the problem of self-serving testimony generally. While those are delicate problems, they do not justify abrogating the very right at issue in cases of informed consent: the right of individual choice, which may be precisely the right to be an "unreasonable" person.

EPILOGUE ON LAW. Thus law has proceeded feebly toward the objective of patients' self-determination. While a new cause of action, occasionally hybridized with battery, has emerged for the negligent failure to disclose risks and alternative treatments, it remains a far cry from the avowed purpose of the informed-consent doctrine, namely, to secure patients' autonomy and right to self-determination. In not tampering significantly with the medical wisdom of nondisclosure, yet creating a new cause of action based on traditional disclosure requirements, courts may have accomplished a different result, very much in line with other purposes of tort law—namely, to provide physically injured patients with greater opportunities for seeking compensation whenever it can be argued that disclosure might have avoided such injuries. In doing so judges may have hoped, through the anticipatory tremors of dicta, to urge doctors to consider modifying their traditional disclosure practices. But judges have been unwilling, at least as yet, to implement earnestly patients' right to self-determination.

Whither informed consent?

The disquiet that the doctrine of informed consent has created among physicians cannot be fully explained by the small incremental step courts have taken to assure greater patient participation in medical decision making. More likely it was aroused by the uncertainty over the scope of the doctrine and by an appreciation that medical practice, indeed all professional practice, would be radically changed if fidelity to thoroughgoing self-determination were to prevail. In what follows, some of the issues raised by the idea of an informed-consent doctrine, based on a premise of self-determination, will be discussed.

PATIENTS. Traditionally patients have been viewed as ignorant about medical matters, fearful about being sick, childlike by virtual of their illness, ill-equipped to sort out what is in their best medical interest, and prone to make decisions detrimental to their welfare (Parsons). Thus physicians have asserted that it makes little sense to consult patients on treatment options: far better to interact with them as beloved children and decide for them. In the light of such deeply held convictions, many physicians are genuinely puzzled by any informed-consent requirement. Moreover, its possible detrimental impact on compassion, reassurance, and hope—ancient prescriptions for patient care—has raised grave ethical questions for the medical profession.

Those concerns should not be dismissed lightly. What may be at issue, however, is not an intrinsic incapacity of patients to participate in medical decision making. For not all patients, and probably not even most, are too uneducated, too frightened, or too regressed to understand the benefits and risks of treatment options available to them. Moreover, their capacities for decision making are affected to varying degrees, for example, by the nature of the disease process, its prognosis, acuteness, painfulness, etc., as well as by the personality of patients. The medical literature is largely silent on the question of who—under what circumstances and with what conditions—should or should not be allowed to participate fully in medical decision making.

But why has not the sorting-out process, distinguishing between those patients who do and those who do not have the capacity for decision making, been undertaken long ago? One answer suggests itself: Once those patients have been identified who, in principle, can make decisions on their own behalf, physicians would be compelled to confront the questions of whether to interact with them on a level of greater equality; whether to share with them the uncertainties and unknowns of medical diagnosis, treatment, and prognosis; and whether to communicate to them their professional limitations as well as the lack of expert consensus about treatment alternatives. Such an open dialogue would expose the uncertainties inherent in most medical interventions; and to the extent medicine's helpful and curative power depends on the faith and confidence which the physician projects, patients may be harmed by disclosure and consent.

Physicians' objections to informed consent, therefore, may have less to do with the incompetence of patients as such than with an unrecognized concern of the doctrine's impact on the dynamics of cure. Put another way, the all too sweeping traditional view of patients has misled doctors into believing that medicine's opposition to informed consent is largely based on patients' incompetence, rather than on an apprehension, however dimly perceived, that disclosure would bring into view much about the practice of medicine that physicians seek to hide from themselves and their patients; for example, the uncertainties and disagreements about the treatments employed; the curative impact of physicians' and patients' beliefs in the unquestioned effectiveness of their prescriptions rather than the prescriptions themselves; the difficulty in sorting out the contributions that *vis medicatrix naturae* ("the healing power of nature") makes to the healing process; the impact of patients' suggestibility to cure, etc. Thus the question: When does informed con-

Disclosure of private information from client to professional is one-way, unlike other interpersonal confidentiality contexts.

PAGE 123

In addition to the public's trust of providers, the trust or distrust of medical technology is often a significant factor.

PAGE 676

sent interfere with physicians' effectiveness and with the dynamics of cure?

Little attention has been paid to the fact that the practice of Hippocratic medicine makes patients more incompetent than they need be. Indeed patients' incompetence can become a self-fulfilling prophecy as a consequence of medical practices. That the stress of illness leads to psychological regression, to chronologically earlier modes of functioning, has been recognized for a long time. Precious little, however, is known about the contributions that physicians' attitudes toward and interactions with their patients make to the regressive pull. Also, little is known about the extent to which regression can be avoided by not keeping patients in the dark, by inviting them to participate in decision making, and by addressing and nurturing the intact, mature parts of their functioning. This uncharted territory requires exploration in order to determine what strains will be imposed on physicians and patients alike, if Anna Freud's admonition to students of the Western Reserve Medical School is heeded:

> *. . . you must not be tempted to treat [the patient] as a child. You must be tolerant toward him as you would be toward a child and as respectful as you would be towards a fellow adult because he has only gone back to childhood as far as he's ill. He also has another part of his personality which has remained intact and that part of him will resent it deeply, if you make too much use of your authority.*
>
> *(quoted in Katz, 1972, p. 637)*

PHYSICIANS. Traditionally physicians have asserted that their integrity, training, professional dedication to patients' best medical interests, and commitment to "doing no harm" are sufficient safeguards for patients. The complexities inherent in medical decision making, physicians maintain, require that trust be patients' guiding principle. The idea of informed consent does not question the integrity, training, or dedication of doctors. Without them, informed consent would be of little value. What the idea of informed consent does question is the necessity and appropriateness of physicians' making all decisions for their patients; it calls for a careful scrutiny of which decisions belong to the doctor and which to the patient.

Physicians have preferences about treatment options that may not necessarily be shared by patients. For example, no professional consensus exists about the treatment of breast cancer. The advantages and disadvantages of lumpectomy, simple mastectomy, radical mastectomy, radiation therapy, chemotherapy, and various combinations among these are subject to much controversy. Dr. Bernard Fisher, chairman of the National Surgical Adjuvant Breast Cancer Project, has said that we simply do not know which method is best (Fisher, 1970). Thus the question must be answered: How extensive an opportunity must patients be given to select which alternative? Informed consent challenges the stereotypical notion that physicians should assume the entire burden of deciding what treatment *all* patients, *whatever* their condition, should undergo. Indeed, can the assumption of this burden be defined purely on medical grounds in the first place? Is not the decision in favor of one treatment for breast cancer over another, like many other treatment decisions, a combination of medical, emotional, aesthetic, religious, philosophical, social, interpersonal, and personal judgments? Which of these component judgments belong to the physician and which to the patient?

Much needs to be investigated in order to learn the practical human limits of any new obligations to disclose and to obtain consent:

1. Informing patients for purposes of decision making requires learning new ways of interacting and communicating with patients. Such questions as the following will have to be answered: What background information must patients receive in order to help them formulate their questions? How should physicians respond to "precipitous" consents or refusals? How deeply should doctors probe for understanding? What constitutes irrelevant information that only tends to confuse? What words and explanations facilitate comprehension? Physicians have not been in the habit of posing such questions.
2. Underlying informed consent is the assumption that physicians have considerable knowledge about their particular specialties, keep abreast of new developments, and are aware of what is happening in other fields of medicine that impinge on their area of professional interest. This is not so; indeed, it may be asking too much. Moreover, since physicians have their preferences for particular modes of treatment, can they be expected to present an unbiased picture of alternative treatments?
3. Physicians have consistently asserted that informed consent interferes with compassion (Silk, 1976). Doctors believe that, in order to maintain hope or to avoid the imposition of unnecessary suffering, patients in the throes of a terminal illness, and other patients as well, should not be dealt with honestly. But the evidence for such allegations is lacking. When physicians are asked to support them with clinical data, they are largely unable to do so (Okin, 1961). Indeed, the few studies

that have been conducted suggest that most patients do not seem to yearn for hope based on deception, but for hope based on a reassurance that they will not be abandoned, that everything possible will be done for them, and that physicians will deal truthfully with them. Moreover, evidence is accumulating that informed patients become more cooperative, more capable of dealing with discomfort and pain, and more responsible. Whether the often alleged conflict between "compassionate" silence and "cruel" disclosure is myth or reality remains to be seen. Disclosure may turn out to be a greater burden to those who have to interact with patients than to the patients themselves.

4. Informed consent confronts the role of faith in the cure of disease and the complex problems created by the uncertainties inherent in medical practice. To some extent the two issues are intertwined. The effectiveness of a therapeutic program, it has often been said, depends on three variables: the "feeling of trust or faith the patient has in his doctor and therefore in his therapy . . . the faith or confidence the physician has in himself and in the line of therapy he proposes to use . . . and the therapy [itself]" (Hoffer, 1967, p. 124). Informed consent could interfere with the first two variables and thus undermine the effectiveness of treatment. Precisely because of the uncertainties in medical decision making, the physician, to begin with, defends himself against those uncertainties by being more certain about what he is doing than he realistically can be. There is perhaps some unconscious wisdom in what he has been doing since Hippocrates' days, for the unquestioned faith the doctor has in his own therapy is also therapeutic in its own right. Thus, to be a more effective healer, a physician may need to defend himself against his uncertainties by believing himself to be more powerful than he is. That defense will be threatened by informed consent, for it would now require him to be more aware of what he does not know, and therapeutic effectiveness in turn might suffer. Finally, patients' response to treatment also depends on faith in the physician and his medicines. Knowing of the "ifs" and "buts" may shake patients' faith and undermine the therapeutic impact of suggestibility, which contributes so much to recovery from illness.

Physicians' traditional counterphobic reaction to uncertainty, adopting a sense of conviction that what seems right to them is the only correct thing to do, has other consequences as well. Defensive reactions against uncertainty have led to overenthusiasm for particular treatments that have been applied much more widely than an unbiased evaluation would dic-

See Also

Autonomy: When Dysfunction Limits Sovereignty

INFORMED CONSENT AND THE LIMITS OF SELF-DETERMINATION

Patients' capacity for self-determination has been challenged on the grounds that neither total understanding nor total freedom of choice is possible (Ingelfinger, 1972). This of course is true. Any informed-consent doctrine, to be realistic, must take into account the biological, psychological, intellectual, and social constraints imposed upon thought and action. But those inherent constraints, which affect all human beings, do not necessarily justify treating patients as incompetents. Competence does not imply total understanding or total freedom of choice.

What needs to be explored is the extent to which medicine, like law, should presume competence rather than incompetence, in interactions with patients. Neither presumption comports fully with the psychobiology of human beings; both of them express value judgments on how best to interact with human beings. Once the value judgment is made, one can decide on the additional safeguards needed to avoid the harm that any fiction about human behavior introduces.

The idea of informed consent asks for a presumption in favor of competence. If that is accepted, it may also follow that human beings should be allowed to strike their own bargains, however improvident. The then Circuit Judge Warren E. Burger, in commenting on a judicial decision to order a blood transfusion for a Jehovah's Witness, had this to say: "Nothing in [Justice Brandeis's 'right to be let alone' philosophy, suggests that he] thought an individual possessed these rights only as to *sensible* beliefs, *valid* thought, *reasonable* emotions or *well-founded* sensations. I suggest he intended to include a great many foolish, unreasonable and even absurd ideas which do not conform such as refusing medical treatment even at great risk" (*Application of President of Georgetown College*, 1964). A physician may wish, and even should try, to persuade his patients to agree to what he believes would serve their medical interests best; but ultimately he may have to bow to his patients' decision, however "senseless" or "unreasonable," or withdraw from further participation. The alternatives, deception or coercion, may be worse, for either would victimize not only patients but physicians as well.

— JAY KATZ

Courts in at least eleven states have ordered women against their wishes to give birth by cesarean section rather than vaginal delivery.

PAGE 477

tate. The ubiquitous tonsillectomies performed to the psychological detriment of untold children is a classical example. Moreover, by not acknowledging uncertainty to themselves, doctors cannot acknowledge it to their patients. Thus consciously and unconsciously physicians avoid the terrifying confrontation of uncertainty, particularly when associated with poor prognosis. As a result, communications with patients take the form of an evasive monologue. The dialogue that might reveal these uncertainties is discouraged (Davis, 1960).

While disclosure of information would reduce patients' ignorance, it would also diminish doctors' power within the physician-patient relationship. As Waitzkin and Stoeckle (1972) have observed, the "physician enhances his power to the extent that he can maintain the patient's uncertainty about the course of illness, efficacy of therapy, or specific future actions of the physician himself" (p. 187). Thus new questions arise: What consequences would a diminution of authority have on physicians effectiveness as healers? How would patients react to less powerful doctors? Would they accept them or turn to new faith healers?

Conclusion

The narrow scope that courts have given to the informed-consent doctrine may reflect a deeply held belief that the exercise of self-determination by patients is often against the best interests of otherwise responsible adults and that those interests deserve greater protection than personal freedom. It may also reflect a judicial recognition of law's limited capacity to regulate effectively the physician-patient relationship. Therefore, once having suggested that patients deserve at least a little openness in communication, courts may have concluded that they had gone as far as they could. Judges, at least for the time being, have largely left it up to the medical profession to confront the question of patients' greater participation in medical decision making.

Despite their snail's pace, the courts' approach may have merit. Implementing a right of self-determination has tremendous consequences for medical practice. Many difficult problems, each with vast ethical implications, need to be considered by the medical profession. Thus introspection and education, responsive to the legal and professional problems that new patterns of physician-patient interaction will create, may ultimately provide firmer foundations for new patterns of physician-patient interactions than forced change through outside regulation. The latter, however, may increase if the profession does not rise to the challenge of addressing these long-neglected problems.

— JAY KATZ

The previous article is reprinted from the first edition (1978). It is followed by a Postscript prepared for purposes of updating the original article—Ed.

POSTSCRIPT

General developments

Although case law has not materially changed since 1978, when the *Encyclopedia of Bioethics* was first published, courts have expanded the concept of informed consent to cover more situations and more categories of patients. The duty of disclosure is now seen in new contexts, such as the duty of a physician to inform a patient of the consequences of refusing treatment (e.g., *Truman* v. *Thomas,* 1980; *Battenfield* v. *Gregory,* 1991). The doctrine is no longer centered on the concept of "unwanted touching," so in most (but not all) states, physicians can be liable for failure to explain the possible side effects of drugs they prescribe. On the other hand, some state legislatures have enacted statutes substantially restricting a patient's right to sue a physician for damages for failure to obtain informed consent.

The most profound change in the legal concept of informed consent has come with the expansion of its principles to persons other than the clearly competent, literate adults involved in the pre-1980 cases. Much of the litigation in the 1980s and 1990s involves the rights of minors, psychiatric patients, pregnant women, the elderly, and the incompetent. Issues of the patient's right to information and decision making may now arise at the end of life, including situations in which the patient or family insists on treatment that physicians believe to be futile, and situations in which families wish life-sustaining therapy terminated while physicians want to continue it.

Special situations

PREGNANT PATIENTS. During the 1980s, there was a series of cases in which pregnant women were subjected to court-ordered treatments, such as cesarean sections, that they had wished to refuse. These court orders were granted on the theory that the fetus was "medically neglected" under state child-abuse laws. After Angela Carder, a terminally ill pregnant woman whose husband and mother refused to consent to a cesarean, died along with her very premature infant following court-ordered surgery (*A.C.*, 1990), professional organizations began to issue statements urging that such refusals of treatment be respected.

MINORS. With increasing frequency, young people over the age of fourteen or so are gaining greater autonomy in decision making about health-care matters. This includes decisions about "Do Not Resuscitate" orders when young patients are terminally ill (*Belcher* v. *Charleston,* 1992; *Swan,* 1990) as well as in less serious situations (*Cardwell* v. *Bechtol,* 1987). There

See Also

Persuasion, Coercion, and Manipulation in Health Care

is also an increased awareness among physicians of the need to provide confidential care to adolescents. Of course, if such care is provided, the young person alone must consent, since the parents will not be informed (Council on Scientific Affairs, 1993).

PSYCHIATRIC PATIENTS. Admission, even involuntary commitment, to a mental hospital does not preclude a patient's ability and right to consent to many aspects of his or her care, including agreeing to or refusing medication. In order to lose such a right to consent, the patient must be found by a court to be incompetent as well as mentally ill. Moreover, a psychiatric patient is presumed as capable of giving informed consent to participate in research as he or she is of making decisions about treatment.

Limits on self-determination

Informed consent does not mean that a patient is always entitled to have whatever care he or she wishes. A physician who deems a therapy "nonbeneficial" does not have to provide it. An institution in which a patient is hospitalized, however, may not have the right to discontinue life-prolonging therapy over the patient's or the family's objection even if the physicians see no hope of recovery. Of course, a physician is never obligated to provide treatment he or she believes is worthless (e.g., laetrile for a cancer patient) when other qualified practitioners would agree with that assessment, or treatment he or she believes unnecessary, such as prescription of an antibiotic for a cold. If the treatment is one in which the physician does not believe or is not willing to provide, but one accepted by even a small minority of "mainstream" physicians, the physician may have an obligation to refer the patient to someone who will use the alternative therapy the patient wants.

Economic constraints on self-determination

Could physicians be found liable if they fail to inform a patient about a very expensive therapy they are quite sure the patient cannot afford, even if the physicians cannot offer an alternative? For example, many states do not pay for transplant surgery for adult Medicaid patients. If a Medicaid patient with breast cancer has had a recurrence after conventional chemotherapy, is the physician obligated to tell her about bone marrow transplants with high-dose chemotherapy, which can cost $100,000 or more, if the state will not pay for it? It would seem that the physician would have such an obligation. No court has ever suggested that a patient has the right only to information about the treatment alternatives that the patient's third-party payer is willing to fund.

As an increasing number of patients find their way into health-maintenance organizations or other managed-care programs, where their physicians may be salaried employees of the organization, this problem is likely to become more acute. Presumably the organization, wishing to control costs, will not want patients to know about expensive therapies they are unwilling to provide, and thus will pressure their employee-physicians not to inform patients about those treatments. It is likely that the economic factors in health care will be the leading issue in informed-consent litigation for some time to come.

— ANGELA RODDEY HOLDER

Certain types of psychological dysfunction undermine the autonomous capacities required to meet the threshold for sovereignty.

PAGE 61

JUSTICE

At some time or another, virtually all of us become involved in disputes about justice. Sometimes our involvement in such disputes is rooted in the fact that we believe ourselves to be victims of some form of injustice; sometimes our involvement is rooted in the fact that others believe us to be the perpetrators or at least the beneficiaries of some form of injustice affecting them. Sometimes the injustice at issue seems to require for its elimination a drastic reform, or even a revolutionary change in the political system. Sometimes it seems to require only some electoral pressure or administrative decision, as may be required in ending a war. Whatever the origin and whatever the practical effect, such disputes about justice are difficult to avoid, especially when one is dealing with issues, like the distribution of income or health-care resources, that have widespread social effects.

Reasonable resolutions of such disputes require a critical evaluation of the alternative conceptions of justice available to us. In philosophical debate at the end of the twentieth century, five major conceptions of justice are defended: (1) a libertarian conception, which takes liberty to be the ultimate political ideal; (2) a socialist conception, which takes equality to be the ultimate political ideal; (3) a welfare liberal conception, which takes contractual fairness or maximal utility to be the ultimate political ideal; (4) a communitarian conception, which takes the common good to be the ultimate political ideal; and (5) a feminist conception, which takes a gender-free society to be the ultimate political ideal.

JUSTICE

Five Major Perspectives

1. libertarian
2. socialist
3. welfare liberal
4. communitarian
5. feminist

All these conceptions of justice have certain features in common. Each regards its requirements as belonging to the domain of obligation rather than to the domain of charity; they simply disagree about where to draw the line between these two domains. Each is also concerned with giving people what they deserve or should rightfully possess; they simply disagree about what it is that people deserve or rightfully possess. These common features constitute a generally accepted core definition of justice. What we need to do, however, is examine the aspects of each of these conceptions of justice over which there is serious disagreement in order to determine which conception, if any, is most defensible.

"Justice will not condemn even the devil himself wrongfully."

THOMAS FULLER
GNOMOLOGIA, 1732

Libertarian justice

Libertarians frequently cite the work of Friedrich A. Hayek, particularly *The Constitution of Liberty* (1960), as an intellectual source of their view. Hayek argues that the libertarian ideal of liberty requires "equality before the law" and "reward according to market value" but not "substantial equality" or "reward according to merit." Hayek further argues that the inequalities due to upbringing, inheritance, and education that are permitted by an ideal of liberty actually tend to benefit society as a whole.

In basic accord with Hayek, contemporary libertar-

IN THE BALANCE

perhaps no issue is more complicated for ethicists than the question of what constitutes fair distribution of health-care resources.

ians define "liberty" as "the state of being unconstrained by other persons from doing what one wants." Libertarians go on to characterize their moral and political ideal as requiring that each person have the greatest amount of liberty commensurate with the same liberty for all. From this ideal, libertarians claim that a number of more specific requirements—in particular a right to life; a right to freedom of speech, press, and assembly; and a right to property—can be derived.

"One man's justice is another's injustice."

RALPH WALDO EMERSON
CIRCLES, 1841

The libertarians' right to life is not a right to receive from others the goods and resources necessary for preserving one's life; it is simply a right not to be killed. So understood, the right to life is not a right to receive welfare. In fact, there are no welfare rights in the libertarian view. Accordingly, the libertarian's understanding of the right to property is not a right to receive from others the goods and resources necessary for one's welfare but, rather, a right to acquire goods and resources either by initial acquisition or by voluntary agreement.

By defending rights such as these, libertarians can support only a limited role for government. That role is simply to prevent and punish initial acts of coercion—the only wrongful acts for libertarians.

Libertarians do not deny that it is a good thing for people to have sufficient goods and resources to meet their basic nutritional needs and basic health-care needs, but they do deny that government has a duty to provide for such needs. Some good things, such as the provision of welfare and health care to the needy, are requirements of charity rather than justice, libertarians claim. Accordingly, failure to make such provisions is neither blameworthy nor punishable.

"Fiat justitia ruat coelum *[Let justice be done though heaven should fall].*"

LATIN SAYING

A basic difficulty with the libertarian's conception of justice is the claim that rights to life and property, as the libertarian understands these rights, derive from an ideal of liberty. Why should we think that an ideal of liberty requires a right to life and a right to property that excludes a right to welfare? Surely it would seem that a right to property, as the libertarian understands it, might well justify a rich person's depriving a poor person of the liberty to acquire the goods and resources necessary for meeting basic nutritional needs. How, then, could we appeal to an ideal of liberty to justify such a deprivation of liberty? Surely we couldn't claim that such a deprivation is justified for the sake of preserving a rich person's freedom to use the goods and resources he or she possesses to meet luxury needs. By any neutral assessment, it would seem that the liberty of the deserving poor not to be interfered with when taking from the surplus possessions of the rich what they require to meet their basic needs would have priority over the liberty of the rich not to be interfered with when using their surplus possessions to meet their luxury needs. But if this is the case, a right to welfare—and possibly a right to equal opportunity as well—would be grounded in the libertarian's own ideal of liberty.

Socialist justice

In contrast with libertarians, socialists take equality to be the ultimate political ideal. In the *Communist Manifesto* (1848), Karl Marx and Friedrich Engels maintained that the abolition of bourgeois property and bourgeois family structure is a necessary first requirement for building a society that accords with the political ideal of equality. In the *Critique of the Gotha Programme* (1891), Marx provided a much more positive account of what is required to build a society based on the political ideal of equality. In such a society, Marx claimed, the distribution of social goods must conform, at least initially, to the principle "from each according to his ability to each according to his contribution." But when the highest stage of communist society has been reached, Marx added, distribution will conform to the principle "from each according to his ability to each according to his need."

At first hearing, this conception might sound ridiculous to someone brought up in a capitalist society. The obvious objection is, how can you get people to contribute according to their ability if income is distributed on the basis of their needs and not on the basis of their contributions?

The answer, according to a socialist conception of justice, is to make the work that must be done in a society as enjoyable, in itself, as possible. As a result, people will want to do the work they are capable of doing because they find it intrinsically rewarding. For a start, socialists might try to get people to accept currently existing intrinsically rewarding jobs at lower salaries—top executives, for example, to work for $300,000, rather than $900,000, a year. Yet ultimately, socialists hope to make all jobs as rewarding as possible, so that after people are no longer working primarily for external rewards while making their best contributions to society, distribution can proceed on the basis of need.

Socialists propose to implement their ideal of equality by giving workers democratic control over the workplace. They believe that if workers have more to say about how they do their work, they will find their work intrinsically more rewarding. As a consequence, they will be more motivated to work, because their work itself will be meeting their needs. Socialists believe that extending democracy to the workplace will necessarily lead to socialization of the means of production and the end of private property. Socialists, of course, do not deny that civil disobedience or even revolutionary action may be needed to overcome opposition to extending democracy to the workplace.

However, even with democratic control of the workplace, some jobs, such as collecting garbage or changing bedpans, probably cannot be made intrinsically rewarding. Socialists propose to divide such jobs up in some equitable manner. Some people might, for example, collect garbage one day a week and then work at a more rewarding job for the rest of the week. Others would change bedpans or do some other menial work for one day a week and then work at a more rewarding job the other days of the week. Socialists believe that by making jobs intrinsically as rewarding as possible, in part through democratic control of the workplace and an equitable assignment of unrewarding tasks, people will contribute according to their ability even when distribution proceeds according to need.

Another difficulty raised concerning the socialist conception of justice is in the proclaimed necessity of abolishing private property and socializing the means of production. It seems perfectly possible to give workers more control over their workplace while the means of production remain privately owned. Of course, private ownership would have a somewhat different character in a society with democratic control of the workplace, but it need not cease to be private ownership. After all, private ownership would also have a somewhat different character in a society where private holdings, and hence bargaining power, were distributed more equally than they are in most capitalist societies, yet it would not cease to be private ownership. Accordingly, we could imagine a society where the means of production are privately owned but where—because ownership is so widely dispersed throughout the society and because of the degree of democratic control of the workplace—many of the criticisms socialists make of existing capitalist societies would no longer apply.

Welfare liberal justice: The contractarian perspective

Finding merit in both the libertarian's ideal of liberty and the socialist's ideal of equality, welfare liberals attempt to combine both liberty and equality into one political ideal that can be characterized as contractual fairness or maximal utility.

A classic example of the contractual approach to welfare liberal justice is found in the political works of Immanuel Kant, who claimed that a civil state ought to be founded on an original contract satisfying the requirements of freedom (the freedom to seek happiness in whatever way one sees fit as long as one does not infringe upon the freedom of others to pursue a similar end), equality (the equal right of each person to restrict others from using his or her freedom in ways that deny equal freedom to all), and independence (which is necessarily presupposed for each person by the free agreement of the original contract).

According to Kant (*Theory and Practice*, Part II, 1792), the original contract, which ought to be the foundation of every civil state, does not have to "actually exist as a fact." It suffices that the laws of a civil state are such that people would agree to them under conditions in which the requirements of freedom, equality, and independence obtain. Laws that accord with this original contract would then, Kant claimed, give all members of society the right to reach any degree of rank that they could earn through their labor, industry, and good fortune. Thus, the equality demanded by the original contract would not, in Kant's view, exclude a considerable amount of economic liberty.

The Kantian ideal of a hypothetical contract as the moral foundation for a welfare liberal conception of justice has been further developed by John Rawls in *A Theory of Justice* (1971). Rawls, like Kant, argues that principles of justice are those that free and rational persons who are concerned to advance their own interests would accept in an initial position of equality. Yet Rawls goes beyond Kant by interpreting the conditions of his "original position" to explicitly require a "veil of ignorance." This veil of ignorance, Rawls claims, has the effect of depriving persons in the original position of the knowledge they would need to advance their own interests in ways that are morally arbitrary.

According to Rawls, the principles of justice that would be derived in the original position are the following:

1. Special conception of justice:
   a. a principle of equal political liberty
   b. a principle of equal opportunity
   c. a principle requiring that the distribution of economic goods works to the greatest advantage of the least advantaged
2. General conception of justice:
   a principle requiring that the distribution of all social goods works, to the greatest advantage of the least advantaged

The general conception of justice differs from the special conception of justice by allowing trade-offs between political liberty and other social goods. According to Rawls, persons in the original position would want the special conception of justice to be applied in place of the general conception of justice whenever social conditions allow all representative persons to benefit from the exercise of their political liberties.

Rawls holds that these principles of justice would be chosen in the original position because persons so situated would find it reasonable to follow the conservative dictates of the "maximin strategy" and *maximize*

"It is compassion rather than the principle of justice which can guard us against being unjust to our fellow men."

ERIC HOFFER
THE PASSIONATE STATE OF MIND, 1954

"Ius est ars boni et aequi *[Legal justice is the art of the good and the fair].*"

LATIN SAYING

the *minimum*, thereby securing for themselves the highest minimum payoff.

Rawls's defense of a welfare liberal conception of justice has been challenged in a variety of ways. Some critics have endorsed Rawls's contractual approach while disagreeing with him over what principles of justice would be derived from it. These critics usually attempt to undermine the use of a maximin strategy in the original position. Other critics, however, have found fault with the contractual approach itself. Libertarians, for example, have challenged the moral adequacy of the very ideal of contractual fairness because they claim that it conflicts with their ideal of liberty.

This second challenge to the ideal of contractual fairness is potentially the more damaging because, if valid, it would force its supporters to embrace some other political ideal. This challenge, however, would fail if it were shown that the libertarian's own ideal of liberty, when correctly interpreted, leads to much the same practical requirements as are usually associated with the welfare liberal ideal of contractual fairness.

"He who knows only his own side of the case, knows little of that."

JOHN STUART MILL
ON LIBERTY, 1859

Welfare liberal justice: The utilitarian perspective

One way to avoid the challenges that have been directed at a contractarian defense of welfare liberal justice is to find some alternative way of defending it. Historically, utilitarianism has been thought to provide such an alternative defense. It has been claimed that the requirements of a welfare liberal conception of justice can be derived from considerations of utility in such a way that following these requirements will result in the maximization of total happiness or satisfaction in society. The best-known classical defense of this utilitarian approach is certainly that presented by John Stuart Mill in *Utilitarianism* (1861).

In Chapter 5 of this work, Mill surveyed various types of actions and situations that are ordinarily described as just or unjust and concluded that justice simply denotes a certain class of fundamental rules, the adherence to which is essential for maximizing social utility. Thus Mill rejected the idea that justice and social utility are ultimately distinct ideals, maintaining instead that justice is in fact derivable from the ideal of social utility.

Nevertheless, a serious problem remains for the utilitarian defense of welfare liberal justice. There would appear to be ways of maximizing overall social utility that do injustice to particular individuals. Think of the Roman practice of throwing Christians to the lions for the enjoyment of all those in the Colosseum. Did this unjust practice not maximize overall social utility?

John Rawls (1971) makes the same point somewhat differently. He criticizes utilitarianism for regarding society as a whole as if it were just one person, and thereby treating the desires and satisfactions of separate persons as if they were the desires and satisfactions of just one person. In this way, Rawls claims, utilitarianism fails to preserve the distinction between persons. But is Rawls right? It may well be that a proper assessment of the relative merits of the contractual and utilitarian approaches to welfare liberal justice will turn on this very issue.

Communitarian justice

Another prominent political ideal defended by contemporary philosophers is the communitarian ideal of the common good. Many contemporary defenders of a communitarian conception of justice regard their conception as rooted in Aristotelian moral theory. In the *Nicomachean Ethics* (1962), Aristotle distinguished between different varieties of justice. He first distinguished between justice as the whole of virtue and justice as a particular part of virtue. In the former sense, justice is understood as what is lawful, and the just person is equivalent to the moral person. In the latter sense, justice is understood as what is fair or equal, and the just person is the one who takes only a proper share. Aristotle focused his discussion on justice in the latter sense, which further divides into distributive justice, corrective justice, and justice in exchange. Each of these varieties of justice can be understood to be concerned with achieving equality. For distributive justice, it is equality between equals; for corrective justice, it is equality between punishment and the crime; and for justice in exchange, it is equality between whatever goods are exchanged. Aristotle also claimed that justice has both its natural and conventional aspects: this twofold character of justice seems to be behind his discussion of equity, in which equity, a natural standard, is described as a corrective to legal justice, a conventional standard.

Few of the distinctions Aristotle made seem tied to the acceptance of any particular conception of justice. One could, for example, accept the view that justice requires formal equality, but then specify the equality that is required in different ways. Even the ideal of justice as giving people what they deserve, which has its roots in Aristotle's account of distributive justice, is also subject to various interpretations. An analysis of the concept of desert would show that there is no conceptual difficulty with claiming, for example, that everyone deserves to have his or her needs satisfied or that everyone deserves an equal share of the goods distributed by society. Consequently, Aristotle's account is helpful primarily for clarifying the distinctions belonging to the concept of justice that can be made without committing oneself to any particular conception of justice.

See Also
John Stuart Mill

Yet rather than draw out the particular requirements of their own conception of justice, contemporary communitarians have frequently chosen to defend their conception by attacking other conceptions of justice; by and large, they have focused their attacks on the welfare liberal conception of justice. Alasdair MacIntyre, for example, argues in "The Privatization of the Good" (1990a) that virtually all forms of liberalism attempt to separate rules defining right action from conceptions of the human good. MacIntyre contends that these forms of liberalism not only fail but must fail because the rules defining right action cannot be adequately grounded apart from a conception of the good. For this reason, MacIntyre claims, only a version of a communitarian theory of justice that grounds rules supporting right action in a complete conception of the good can ever hope to be adequate.

But why cannot we view most forms of liberalism as attempting to ground moral rules on part of a conception of the good—specifically, that part of a conception of the good that is more easily recognized, and needs to be publicly recognized, as good? For Rawls, this partial conception of the good is a conception of contractual fairness, according to which no one deserves his or her native abilities or initial starting place in society. If this way of interpreting liberalism is correct, in order to evaluate welfare liberal and communitarian conceptions of justice properly, we would need to do a comparative analysis of their conceptions of the good and their practical requirements. Moreover, there is reason to think that once the practical requirements of both liberal and communitarian conceptions of justice are compared, they will be quite similar.

Feminist justice

Defenders of a feminist conception of justice present a distinctive challenging critique to defenders of other conceptions of justice. In *The Subjection of Women* (1869), John Stuart Mill, one of the earliest male defenders of women's liberation, argued that the subjection of women was never justified but was imposed on women because they were physically weaker than men; later this subjection was confirmed by law. Mill argued that society must remove the legal restrictions that deny women the same opportunities enjoyed by men. However, Mill did not consider whether, because of past discrimination against women, it may be necessary to do more than simply removing legal restrictions: he did not consider whether positive assistance may also be required.

Usually it is not enough simply to remove unequal restrictions to make a competition fair among those who have been participating. Positive assistance to those who have been disadvantaged in the past may also be required, as would be the case in a race where

some were unfairly impeded by having to carry ten-pound weights for part of the race. To render the outcome of such a race fair, we might want to transfer the ten-pound weights to the other runners in the race for an equal period of time. Similarly, positive assistance, such as affirmative-action programs, may be necessary if women who have been disadvantaged in the past are going to be able to compete fairly with men.

In *Justice, Gender and the Family* (1989), Susan Okin argues for the feminist ideal of a gender-free society, that is, one in which basic rights and duties are not assigned on the basis of a person's sex. Being male or female is not the grounds for determining what basic rights and duties a person has in a gender-free society. Since a conception of justice is usually thought to provide the ultimate grounds for the assignment of rights and duties, we can refer to this ideal of a gender-free society as "feminist justice."

Okin goes on to consider whether John Rawls's welfare liberal conception of justice can support the ideal of a gender-free society. Noting Rawls's failure to apply his original position-type thinking to family structures, Okin is skeptical about the possibility of using a welfare liberal ideal to support feminist justice. She contends that in a gender-structured society like that of the United States, male philosophers cannot achieve the sympathetic imagination required to see things from the standpoint of women. In a gender-structured society, Okin claims, male philosophers cannot do the original position-type thinking required by the welfare liberal ideal because they lack the ability to put themselves in the position of women. According to Okin, original position-type thinking can really be achieved only in a gender-free society.

Yet, at the same time that Okin despairs of doing original position-type thinking in a gender-structured society, she purportedly does a considerable amount of

MIND ON JUSTICE

The ideal of justice as "giving people what they deserve" is rooted in Aristotle's thinking on distributive justice in the Nicomachean Ethics.

"It is justice, not charity, that is wanting in the world."

MARY WOLLSTONECRAFT
A VINDICATION OF THE RIGHTS OF WOMAN, 1792

J

JUSTICE

The Provision of Just Health Care

"It is only a man here and there who has any tolerable knowledge of the character even of the women of his own family."

JOHN STUART MILL
THE SUBJECTION OF WOMEN, 1869

"Earthly power doth then show likest God's When mercy seasons justice."

SHAKESPEARE
THE MERCHANT OF VENICE

just that type of thinking. For example, she claims that Rawls's principles of justice "would seem to require a radical rethinking not only of the division of labor within families but also of all the nonfamily institutions that assume it" (Okin, 1989, p. 104). She also claims that "the abolition of gender seems essential for the fulfillment of Rawls's criterion of political justice" (Okin, 1989, p. 104). So Okin's own work would seem to indicate that we can do such thinking and that her reasons for thinking we cannot are not persuasive. To do original position-type thinking, it is not necessary that everyone be able to put themselves imaginatively in the position of everyone else. All that is necessary is that some people be able to do so. Some people may not be able to do original position-type thinking because they have been deprived of a proper moral education. Others may be able to do original position-type thinking only after they have been forced to mend their ways and live morally for a time.

Of course, even among men and women in a gender-structured society who are in a broad sense capable of a sense of justice, some may not be able to do such original position-type thinking with respect to the proper relationships between men and women; these men and women may be able to do so only after the laws and social practices in our society have significantly shifted toward a more gender-free society. But this inability of some to do original position-type thinking does not render it impossible for others who have effectively used the opportunities for moral development available to them to achieve the sympathetic imagination necessary for original position-type thinking with respect to the proper relationships between men and women.

What conclusion should we draw from this discussion of libertarian, socialist, welfare liberal, communitarian, and feminist conceptions of justice? Should we draw the conclusion defended by Alasdair MacIntyre in *After Virtue* (1981) that such conceptions of justice are incommensurable and, hence, there is no rational way of deciding between them? Many philosophers have challenged this view, and even MacIntyre, in *Three Rival Versions of Moral Enquiry* (1990b), has significantly qualified it, now claiming that it is possible to argue across conceptions of justice.

Another conclusion that we might draw from this discussion of conceptions of justice is that if the ideal of liberty of libertarian justice can be shown to require the same rights to welfare and equal opportunity that are required by the welfare liberal conception of justice, and if the communication critique of welfare liberalism can be rebutted, it may be possible to reconcile, at a practical level, the differences between welfare liberal justice, socialist justice, and feminist justice. If this can be done, all that would be necessary to reasonably resolve disputes about justice would be to clarify what the shared practical requirements of these conceptions of justice are and simply to act on them.

The provision of just health care

Assuming that it is possible to show that libertarian, welfare liberal, socialist, communitarian, and feminist conceptions of justice have the same practical requirements as a right to welfare and a right to equal opportunity, then in order to determine the morally appropriate level of health care, it would be necessary to determine what provision of health care would be required by these rights. Since a right to welfare and a right to equal opportunity are usually associated with a welfare liberal conception of justice, it would seem reasonable to use John Rawls's original position decision procedure—a procedure favored by welfare liberals—to determine what level of health care would be required by a right to welfare and a right to equal opportunity.

In *Just Health Care* (1985) and *Am I My Parents' Keeper?* (1988), Norman Daniels develops just such an account of health care. Daniels imagines people behind a veil of ignorance trying to determine how they should allocate health-care services over their lifetimes. Behind this veil of ignorance, people are to imagine themselves ignorant of their actual age so that they could be young or old. Daniels claims that people using this Rawlsian decision procedure would reserve certain life-extending technologies for their younger years and thus maximize their chances of living a normal life span, even if that meant reducing the medical resources that would be available in their old age.

The consequences of using a Rawlsian decision procedure to determine the morally appropriate level of health care required by a right to welfare and a right to equal opportunity are (1) a focus on death-preventing level of health care for the young, (2) a focus on a life-enhancing health care for both young and old, and (3) a willingness to cut back on death-preventing health care for the old to some extent when it conflicts with (1) and possibly when it conflicts with (2) as well.

Yet these consequences remain indeterminate until we can specify the amount of resources that are to be devoted to health care rather than to meeting the various other needs and wants that people have. It will not do simply to have each person choose the level of health care that he or she prefers because we cannot assume that everyone will have sufficient income to purchase whatever level of health care he or she wants or needs. Rather, there seem to be two options.

One option is to specify an optimal and affordable level of health care and then guarantee this level of health care to all legitimate claimants. The other option is to specify a decent minimal level of health care and guarantee that level of health care to all legitimate claimants, but then allow higher levels of health care to be purchased by whoever has the income and desire to do so. Of course, both these options will leave some people dissatisfied. The equal-health-care option will leave dissatisfied people who would have preferred and could have afforded a higher level of health care that would have been available under the multitiered health-care option. The multitiered health-care option will leave dissatisfied people who would receive only the decent minimum level of health care under that option but who want or need more health care than they will be receiving. Is there any just resolution of this conflict?

Assuming again that we are trying to determine the morally appropriate level of health care required by a right to welfare and a right to equal opportunity, it is surely the case that nothing less than a guaranteed decent minimum level of health care to all legitimate claimants would be morally acceptable. But is a multi-tiered option for health care morally permissible, or is the option of an equal level of health care morally required?

To answer this question, we must take into account all the morally legitimate claimants to our available resources. They include not only the members of the particular society to which we happen to belong but also distant peoples and future generations as well. Once we recognize how numerous are the morally legitimate claimants on the available resources, it becomes clear that all that we can hope to do is provide a decent minimal level of health care to all claimants. Given the morally legitimate claims that distant peoples and future generations make on our available resources, it is unlikely that we will have sufficient resources to allow people to purchase higher levels of health care (the multi-tiered option). Morally, we would seem to have no other choice than to favor the same level of health care for everybody (the equal-health-care option).

In preferring the equal-health-care option, we appealed not to the ideal of equality itself but, rather, to the goal of providing all legitimate claimants with a decent minimum level of health care. Given that available resources are limited, to meet the goal of providing a decent minimum of health care to all legitimate claimants, equality of health care for all legitimate claimants is required. In this context, no one can have more than equality if everyone is to have enough. This choice would clearly be favored by people behind a Rawlsian veil of ignorance, assuming that the hypothetical choosers are understood to represent all morally legitimate claimants.

Nor could one reasonably object to the ideal of including distant peoples and future generations within the class of morally legitimate claimants, because each of the five conceptions assumes that each human being has the same basic rights. So if these basic rights that each human being has include a right to welfare and a right to equal opportunity, the requirements to provide each human being with a decent minimum of health care would clearly follow.

Nevertheless, there remains the question of how to specify this minimum level of health care that all legitimate claimants are to receive. The problem here is how to specify how much of the available resources should go to providing everyone with a decent minimum of health care rather than providing for the satisfaction of people's other needs and wants. Yet here, too, the question seems resolvable with the aid of a Rawlsian hypothetical choice procedure. We simply need to introduce behind the veil of ignorance the knowledge of the relevant technology for meeting people's basic needs and the knowledge of available resources to decide how much of the resources should be devoted to providing a decent minimum level of health care and how much should be devoted to meeting the other needs and wants that people have.

In this way, we should be able to determine what specific requirements of just health care are grounded in a right to welfare and a right to equal opportunity. Moreover, these specific requirements of just health care would be further supported if it can be shown that the rights from which these health-care requirements are derived are themselves the shared practical requirements of libertarian, welfare liberal, socialist, communitarian, and feminist conceptions of justice.

— JAMES P. STERBA

"Justice delayed is justice denied."

WILLIAM EWART GLADSTONE
ATTRIBUTED

"Justice delayed is democracy denied."

ROBERT F. KENNEDY
TO SECURE THESE RIGHTS
1964

L

LABORATORY TESTING

Laboratory testing is an essential part of contemporary health care in developed countries and a major contributor to the high costs of that care. Consider, for example, the case of Mrs. K., hospitalized in the intensive-care unit of a New York City hospital for twenty-five days in 1983 until her death after multiple organ failure. Charges for her hospital stay (not including doctor bills) totaled $47,311. Of this total, the second highest category of charges (after $12,000 in intensive-care room charges) was for laboratory services: $11,201 (Hellerstein, 1984). Despite the high volume and costs of laboratory testing, the moral dimensions of this activity did not attract much attention or commentary for many years. Beginning in 1985, however, the development and use of a diagnostic test for human immunodeficiency virus (HIV) focused widespread attention on a number of moral issues in testing, including informed consent, confidentiality, accuracy, access, and safety (Bayer et al., 1986). In the 1990s the U.S. Human Genome Project directed renewed attention to all of these moral issues as they bear on myriad new tests for various genetic conditions (Fost, 1993).

The term "laboratory testing" does not denote a single specific practice but rather a set of similar practices performed in several different settings, by different kinds of professionals, for a number of reasons. Primary-care physicians perform routine tests in small office labs; highly specialized pathologists and technicians carry out more complicated tests in large hospital or independent commercial labs. Not surprisingly, these different settings, actors, and purposes raise different ethical issues. This review will begin with the moral interests of the patient and then broaden its focus to include other relevant interests and perspectives.

COMMON REASONS FOR LABORATORY TESTS

- medical (to diagnose a patient's disease)
- legal (to identify the source of blood or tissue samples in a criminal investigation)
- financial (to qualify for life insurance)
- social (to identify drug abuse in the workplace)

LAB ASSISTANT

Recent ethical questions about how much laboratory testing is really *necessary have risen with the tide of higher health-care costs and the AIDS epidemic.*

See Also
AIDS; Epidemics

L

LABORATORY TESTING

Access to Testing

The Nuremberg Code requires that the subject be told "the nature, duration, and purpose of the experiment."

PAGE 403

Because laboratory testing is an integral part of health care, patients' expectations regarding testing can be understood as applications of their more general health-care interests. Patients have general interests in securing access to effective and affordable health care, avoiding unnecessary care, controlling what is done to or for them, knowing about their condition and its treatment, and limiting others' access to sensitive personal information about themselves. Applying these general patient interests to laboratory testing, we can construct a scenario that approaches the ideal from the patient's point of view. In this scenario, all patients have ready access to accurate and affordable laboratory tests. Patients are not subjected to unnecessary tests, and overreliance on testing does not result in neglect of other diagnostic tools, such as history taking and physician examination (see Eichna, 1980; Griner and Glaser, 1982). All material information about proposed tests and test results is shared with patients, and patients give their implicit or explicit consent, as appropriate, for all tests. Test results are kept strictly confidential and given only to those directly involved in the care of the particular patient.

Others, including health-care professionals, third parties, and society at large, have interests that sometimes conflict with patient interests. Let us now consider how these other interests can conflict with specific patient interests in the context of laboratory testing.

Access to testing

Because laboratory tests can provide information essential for the diagnosis and treatment of disease, they offer obvious benefits for patients. Modern clinical laboratories equipped to perform technologically sophisticated tests are costly enterprises, however, and lack of resources precludes access to most laboratory testing for most of the world's people. Even in affluent nations like the United States, where testing is widely available, its costs contribute to the rapidly escalating overall cost of health care. In one clinical chemistry laboratory in a large university medical center over a ten-year period (1980-1990), the number of billable tests performed increased an average 12.1 percent annually, from some 300,000 tests in 1980 to 650,000 tests in 1990, and gross billings increased a striking 25.8 percent annually, from $5.6 million in 1980 to $19 million in 1990 (Benge et al., 1993). Hospitals like this one may have raised laboratory testing prices artificially high in order to shift the cost of caring for Medicare and uninsured patients on to patients with retrospective, fee-for-service private health insurance (Conn, 1993). Despite such cost shifting by some providers, indigent patients still encounter obstacles to receiving needed health care; broader access to care in the United States awaits basic reforms in the overall distribution and financing of health care (see, e.g., Callahan, 1990; *Clinton Administration*, 1993).

Access to testing can also be limited for nonfinancial reasons. HIV screening of all prospective blood donors, for example, was proposed early in 1985 in order to protect the nation's blood supply. Because gay men and members of other groups at higher risk for AIDS (acquired immunodeficiency syndrome) had been asked, since 1983, to refrain from donating blood, it appeared that these persons would not have access to the newly developing screening tests. To resolve this problem, the federal government eventually agreed to fund alternative testing sites where persons at risk for infection could receive testing (Silverman and Silverman, 1985).

Access to testing is not a benefit unless the tests performed provide generally accurate information about a patient's condition. Quality control is, therefore, an essential part of laboratory testing. Concerns about quality control in laboratory testing led to the passage of the Clinical Laboratory Improvement Act of 1967 (CLIA '67) and the Clinical Laboratory Improvement Amendments of 1988 (CLIA '88) by the U.S. Congress (Centers for Disease Control, 1992). CLIA '88 was designed to extend quality-assurance regulations to all clinical laboratories, including small physician office labs. New quality-control and personnel standards in this area bring with them additional costs, however, and so illustrate a tension between ensuring quality, on the one hand, and promoting easy access to testing and controlling its costs, on the other. In written comments on the first CLIA '88 implementation regulations proposed by the Health Care Financing Administration (HCFA) in 1990, some 60,000 physicians argued that the regulations were unduly burdensome and would force them to close their office labs. In response to those criticisms, HCFA relaxed its requirements significantly in the revised final clinical laboratory regulations issued in February 1992 (Anderson, 1992).

Knowledge and control

Patients want to be treated, to be sure, but they also want to be informed about their condition and its treatment and to have an active role in decisions about their health care. These latter two interests are expressed in the legal doctrine of informed consent to treatment, which requires that competent patients be given the opportunity to consent to or refuse proposed treatment on the basis of information about treatment benefits, risks, and alternatives (U.S. President's Commission, 1982). The amount of information to be communicated and the nature of the consent process vary with the treatment in question. In the case of routine lab tests on blood and urine, for example, where the purpose of the test is simple and obvious and the risks of testing are minimal, little or no additional information about the tests may be

TESTING
Sometimes Unnecessary

In contrast to the lack of access to testing for some patients, other patients are subjected to unnecessary testing, that is, tests that do not make a useful contribution to these patients' care. Patients' interests in avoiding the financial and physical burdens of unnecessary testing may conflict with a variety of interests of their caregivers. An informal list of reasons physicians order laboratory tests compiled by Lundberg (1983) includes peer pressure, public relations, legal requirements, medicolegal need, CYA, personal profit, hospital profit, research, curiosity, insecurity, frustration at nothing else to do, to buy time, "fishing expeditions," personal education, to report to an attending physician, and habit.

Defensive medicine is perhaps the most commonly cited reason for ordering medically unnecessary tests. Physicians may order a laboratory test, despite their belief that it will not make a significant contribution to the care of the patient, in order to protect themselves from the threat of malpractice liability. There are, however, reasons for questioning whether this threat is genuine or serious enough to justify self-interested action by physicians at some financial, and often physical, cost to patients. The standard of care required of physicians is based on what is "reasonable and necessary." Unnecessary medical tests should, therefore, not be part of the standard of care. Paradoxically, if all physicians rush to do unnecessary tests for defensive purposes, such tests may become "standard" in the sense that everyone does them. Increasing emphasis on outcomes research and practice guidelines may help to eliminate such inappropriate standards.

Performing medically unnecessary laboratory tests in order to profit financially from the revenues they generate is a clear violation of the physician's professional responsibility to act in the patient's best interests. Concerns about tests ordered for financial gain are especially pronounced when physicians refer patients to independent clinical laboratories in which they have an ownership interest (called self-referrals). U.S. federal legislation enacted in 1989 prohibits most physician referrals of Medicare patients to clinical laboratories in which they hold an interest (Iglehart, 1990).

— JOHN C. MOSKOP

required, and consent may be implicit in the act of seeking care. Other kinds of lab tests, however, where the purposes of testing are complicated and the physical or psychosocial risks of testing are significant (e.g., HIV testing, tumor biopsies, genetic testing), may require a much more formal information and consent procedure. Informed consent for genetic testing of a couple for cystic fibrosis carrier status, for example, may require extensive counseling regarding the nature of cystic fibrosis, the limitations of current tests, treatment options, procreative options including abortion, and possible psychosocial consequences, such as discrimination in insurance and employment (Fost, 1993). In view of the significant consequences of a diagnosis of HIV infection, many states have specially mandated written informed consent for HIV testing (Gostin, 1989).

Lawmakers have seen fit to limit individual control over testing decisions in the interests of specific third parties and of society at large. In the United States, for example, HIV screening is mandatory for blood donors, military recruits, active-duty military personnel, prospective immigrants, and federal and some state prison inmates. Commentators have praised mandatory HIV screening of blood donors for its success in protecting the blood supply but have criticized other mandatory screening programs for their high cost, limited contribution to public health, and compromise of individual rights (Field, 1990; Gostin, 1989). For example, two U.S. states, Illinois and Louisiana, adopted mandatory premarital HIV screening programs in the 1980s, but both repealed their programs within two years. In its first year of operation (1988), the Illinois program identified only twenty-three HIV-positive persons among 159,000 tested, at a total cost of $5.6 million (Field, 1990).

Some health professionals and hospitals have proposed policies of routine HIV testing of all hospital patients or all patients undergoing elective surgery (see Hagen et al., 1988). Routine HIV screening would clearly benefit those patients who learn from the screening that they are HIV-infected and begin therapy to prevent or postpone its complications (Jewett and Hecht, 1993). Such benefits do not, however, seem great enough to justify the abandonment of informed consent for HIV testing, nor are they usually the primary reason proponents defend these policies. Rather, proponents point out that routine screening would enable caregivers to take appropriate precautions to protect their own safety in caring for HIV-infected patients. Opponents of such policies argue that the universal blood and body fluid precautions for health-care settings first recommended by the Centers for Disease Control in 1985 and mandated by the Occupational Safety and Health Administration in 1991 are the most effective means of protection against disease transmission, and therefore routine hospital screening

From 1985, when the HIV antibody test was first developed, it became the focus of controversy.

PAGE 47

for HIV infection is neither necessary nor desirable (Moskop, 1990).

Confidentiality

Access to the information generated by laboratory testing is necessary for managing patient care and for informing patients about their condition and its treatment. Much, if not most, of the information produced by lab tests is quite technical and is meaningful only to trained professionals, but some information, such as diagnosis of HIV infection, a sexually transmitted or genetic disease, cancer, or pregnancy, is potentially very sensitive. Patients often have an interest in keeping this information confidential and in limiting disclosure of test results to those who have a need to know in order to provide effective care for them.

Despite the obvious moral significance of these confidentiality interests, social policy limits confidentiality in a variety of ways in order to address the needs and interests of others (Dickens, 1988). For example, physicians report information about infectious diseases to state and federal agencies for epidemiological and public-health purposes, such as identifying and notifying the contacts of sexually transmitted disease and HIV patients regarding their risks. Contact tracing of HIV-infected patients, once strenuously resisted by AIDS advocacy organizations in the name of confidentiality, has gained wider acceptance and endorsement by professional organizations for its public-health value and for enabling infected persons to secure early treatment (Bayer, 1991). Similarly, physicians and genetic counselors may feel a duty to disclose information about a patient's serious genetic condition to relatives who are at significant risk of developing the same condition or passing it on to their children, even if the patient is unwilling to permit such disclosure (Fost, 1993). The proper balance between the duty to respect confidentiality and the duty to warn in these cases remains deeply controversial.

This entry has reviewed some of the major issues in laboratory testing but by no means exhausted the field. For example, the increasing use of sophisticated DNA typing in criminal investigations and trials (Annas, 1992) and the use of laboratory testing by employers and insurance companies (U.S. Congress, 1991; Murray, 1993) raise complex moral and legal questions. Laboratory testing has become, and will remain, a topic of lively moral concern.

— JOHN C. MOSKOP

◆ **theoretical bioethics**
The intellectual foundations of bioethics.

LAW AND BIOETHICS

Bioethics began as, and remains, an interdisciplinary field. If developments in biology and medicine have fueled the bioethics train and philosophy has laid down the tracks on which it has run, then law has been the engineer at the controls of the locomotive and statutes and court decisions have thrown the switches that guided the train through the rail yards. Law's influence on bioethics has been so pronounced as to be unmistakable, yet so pervasive as sometimes to be unnoticed.

It might be argued that law's role was pronounced for purely historical reasons: Bioethics began as an American phenomenon and hence was shaped by certain aspects of American culture. Lacking an established church or a single heritage of values, though committed to the rule of law and to the equality of all persons, Americans have a habit of turning to courts to resolve moral conflicts. Moreover, other features of the terrain also indicated a major role for the law. Bioethics frequently presents central civic issues, among them these: When does a human entity first become (or cease being) a legal person? What conduct of health-care professionals treating incurably ill patients would constitute murder? May parents be paid for transferring to other persons the rights of custody and control over their children? Does the prospect of gaining knowledge of potential benefit to the community ever justify using people without their consent or even their knowledge?

Dependence on the legal system to settle many ethical and social issues generated by medicine and the life sciences does more than merely provide a means for resolving disputes. Reliance on the legal system denotes that an issue should be understood as having two opposing sides that will do battle for their respective rights to act in a particular fashion or to restrain the other side from acting in a contrary fashion. Moreover, as a means of discovering and articulating principles, the law favors certain implicit and explicit values.

The relationship of law and bioethics has not, however, been unidirectional: Bioethics has also affected the law. While much of law is concerned with commerce and institutions, both public and private, bioethics is essentially about people and about the fundamental choices that determine and even define their lives. If the law has brought to bioethical cases an attention to rights and procedure, bioethics has enriched legal analysis with life-and-death dramas. It would strain the point to say that medicine saved the law, as Stephen Toulmin observed medicine did for philosophy (Toulmin, 1982). But the ethical dilemmas arising from medicine and its associated scientific disciplines have helped to humanize the law, providing a setting in which the central struggles of our times—of individual rights and the collective good, of liberty as against equity and equality, of justice and fairness, of personal wishes versus expert judgment or the will of

See Also
AIDS and Confidentiality
Bioethics

the majority—are played out with unparalleled urgency and vitality. When the question is whether a life is worth living, for example, the answer is consequential. And when legal institutions falter in answering such questions, then lawyers and others are reminded that perfect legal solutions may not exist for all bioethical dilemmas. Bioethics raises fundamental challenges for theorists as well as practitioners of the law about the harm that society may impose upon a minority in order to uphold values believed to be of fundamental importance to the majority, or the limits of the law as a guide to human conduct. Yet the focus of this essay is not the theoretical connection between morality and law, but rather the law as a practical force in shaping and defining bioethics.

What is the law?

SOURCES OF LAW. The term "law" carries a number of meanings. In ordinary speech, it usually refers to specific criminal or regulatory provisions ("It's against the law to . . ."). This usage also reflects the common equation of law with statutes, denoting not just criminal statutes but also those governing civil or procedural matters, such as the ownership of property or how one is called for jury duty. A fuller understanding of the law would emphasize other important sources. Of particular prominence today are the detailed and voluminous regulations issued by governmental departments and administrative agencies to implement the powers and carry out the duties conferred on them by statutes. Although statutes are sometimes quite detailed, many areas of human activity (especially of an industrial or commercial nature) are so complex that the legislature must almost of necessity confine itself to framing the basic legal structure, while delegating the task of supplying all the details to those with greater time and expertise at the administrative level, subject to various degrees of public, executive, legislative, and judicial oversight.

Especially in countries, including the United States, whose legal systems are derived from the English model, judicial decisions are a source of law at least as important as statutes. In some decisions, judges interpret statutes and hence give meaning and shape to them; while in others, judges decide issues not directly addressed by statutes and effectively make new law. At one time, when statutory rules covered only a small portion of human affairs, most of English law consisted of judicial resolution of individual disputes, collectively known as "the common law." To this day, many areas of law have a strong common-law flavor, which is constantly reinforced and renewed by judges' decisions about novel issues. Even in countries with civil-law systems based on Roman law or the Napoleonic Code, judges participate in the crafting of the law by their interpretation of code provisions.

Finally, in legal systems that follow the model of the United States, in which all activities of the government—including making and interpreting the law—are subject to limits specified in a constitution, no statement of the law would be complete without reference to the text of that supreme law, as well as the authoritative interpretations of its provisions by the courts.

Even these sources—statutes, regulations, judicial decisions, and the constitutions—do not exhaust the meaning of "the law," which also connotes the legal system, the institutions, and the processes through which the law is applied. In this sense, the law encompasses the processes and rules of courts and administrative bodies (for example, on admission of evidence), as well as the more informal standards or practices that are reflected in the action of those law-applying people and institutions (such as public prosecutors or bureaucrats) who have wide discretion in administering statutes and regulations. Within their sphere of authority, the law is what they say it is. Indeed, to the extent they are not expressly forbidden, the customs and practices of people in any field may properly be described as part of the law, though those customs and practices may formally be denominated "law" only when explicitly incorporated into a judicial opinion, statute, or regulation.

Seen in this way, the law is a basic framework for society; it is a system not only for promulgating official policies and procedures and for administrating prosecutorial, judicial, and regulatory affairs but also for providing explicit or implicit sanction for the private arrangements through which activities and relationships are ordered. Of course, many people would not identify the law as the source for the way they conduct their affairs. Instead, they would point to the influence of family and community customs or values, as well as to explicit moral or religious teachings. But as members of society, they must still operate within the law; this means that if their private arrangements run afoul of the expectations of society as embodied in the law, these arrangements may be limited or nullified. For example, in a number of U.S. jurisdictions, legislatures or judges have declared contracts for women to bear children for couples (so-called surrogate motherhood) to be null and void, as against public policy, even though a purported contract is freely and knowingly agreed to by all parties.

The existence of such private ordering as an important but often overlooked source of lawmaking also serves as a reminder that even in a society, such as the United States, with a high proportion of lawyers, lawmaking is not restricted to lawyers. From the local to the national level, many members of the legislative and executive branches of government are not lawyers;

The public believes that lawyers should not violate usual ethical norms for the sake of their clients' interests.

PAGE 676

See Also
Ethics

L

LAW AND BIOETHICS

What Is the Law?

indeed, the federal constitution does not even require that judges be legally trained. Law is one of the three traditional learned professions (along with medicine and the clergy). Its members are licensed by the state and admitted "as officers of the court" to practice "at the bar of justice." Accordingly, like physicians, they are governed by ethical standards articulated by their profession through its associations as well as through the decisions of judges passing on cases of alleged transgression of professional obligations.

Around the world, most legal education occurs in schools affiliated with universities. Characterizing legal education in the early twentieth century as akin to a trade school, Thorstein Veblen opined that "the law school belongs in the modern university no more than a school of fencing or dancing" (Veblen, 1965 [1918], p. 211); but this complaint is no longer justified, if indeed it ever was. Today, schools provide much more than mere vocational training, and scholarship is not limited to exegesis of doctrine; it encompasses empirical, normative, and theoretical work. Nonetheless, the law is a practical field, not simply one of the liberal arts and sciences.

See

"Legal Approaches to Sexuality," page 667

HEALTH LAW. Traditionally, medicine and law intersected in civil or criminal cases in which proof of medical facts was at issue. From the medical side, those involved were usually pathologists, who became specialists in "forensic medicine," as the field was known to prosecutors and criminal-defense attorneys; on the legal side, torts specialists who handled a large proportion of malpractice cases (and some of whom held degrees in both law and medicine) described their expertise as encompassing "medical law." With the tremendous growth in health care and research beginning in the mid-1960s, health-care law—or more simply health law—emerged as a new field that includes these areas and more. It is one of the fastest-growing, most diverse, and most exciting legal specialties.

Health law draws on practically the entire corpus of traditional doctrinal fields—civil, criminal, constitutional, property, and procedural—as well as many other specialized areas, such as labor, insurance, antitrust, and government regulation. Practitioners represent hospitals and other health-care providers; academic research centers; physicians, nurses, and other health-care professionals and nonprofessional employees; insurance carriers and employers that provide health insurance as an employee benefit; manufacturers and distributors of

LAW
Divisions and Layers

Traditionally, for purposes of basic study and classification, law has been divided along such doctrinal lines as tort law, criminal law, contract law, constitutional law, equitable remedies, property law, wills and trusts, and civil and criminal procedure. Each of these areas is characterized by prototypical relationships among parties and a set of analytic and practical devices for structuring those relationships and determining the outcomes of disputes. In recent years, legal scholarship has taken on several additional layers.

One is an enrichment of the tools brought to the law's tasks by combining with another discipline: legal anthropology, law and economics, legal history, law and literature, law and philosophy, law and psychology or psychoanalysis, sociology of law, and law and religion, to mention prominent examples. Each of these combined subdisciplines has not only a methodology but also its own theories and assumptions. Furthermore, additional schools of thought have arisen—such as legal realism, critical legal studies, feminism, and critical race studies—that provide perspectives on the law by combining the tools of several disciplines and a set of attitudes toward legal, social, economic, and personal relationships. Plainly, a person working in an interdisciplinary field may bring one of the analytic perspectives to bear—for instance, a feminist approach to legal history or a legal-realist perspective on law and economics.

A third way of dividing the domain of law is by focusing on its application to specialized types of personal, commercial, institutional, and sociopolitical activities. (The range of specialized areas of the law seems virtually limitless; attorneys now practice antitrust law, art law, bankruptcy law, civil-rights law, commercial law, education law, employment and labor law, entertainment law, family law, insurance law, intellectual-property law, juvenile and dependency law, media and broadcast law, mental-health law, probate law, public and private international law, regulated industries law, sports law, securities law, and even space law, to name a few.) Whether from an academic or a practice vantage point, specialized fields of law usually link traditional doctrinal categories with information and methods derived from the disciplinary and analytic approaches just described. For example, people working in family law will draw not only on legal doctrines from remedies, from property law, from wills and trusts, and from criminal and civil law and procedure, but also on psychological, sociological, or feminist analyses and perspectives; while those pursuing antitrust law will draw not only on various aspects of business law and criminal and civil law but also on law and economics studies and perhaps historical and sociological analysis as well.

— ALEXANDER MORGAN CAPRON

drugs and medical devices; patients and their families; and governmental departments and agencies that finance and regulate the individuals and institutions providing health care. Although cases involving ethic-al dilemmas are the ones that draw public attention, they are the exception for most health lawyers, who are more likely to spend their time drafting contracts for the purchase of goods and services; bargaining about insurance reimbursement; preparing staff bylaws, checking professional peer activities, or handling other issues that arise in accreditation, credentialing, or certification of practitioners or institutions; negotiating with government agents about licensing, taxation, and environmental controls; or litigating a case of professional malpractice (Macdonald et al., 1991).

The impact of law on bioethics

The relationship of law and bioethics is complex and multifaceted. One need not share the view of a leading legal commentator—"American law, not philosophy or medicine, is primarily responsible for the agenda, development, and current state of American bioethics" (Annas, 1993, p. 3)—to conclude that the law has strongly influenced the methodology of bioethics, the central focus of bioethics, and the values of bioethics. "And—to the considerable extent that bioethics is an American invention and export—the influence of American law has been felt even in societies in which legal institutions play a less pronounced role than they do in the United States" (Capron, 1994, p. 43). Law's role in shaping bioethics has at least five facets.

METHODOLOGY. Related to the addressing of bioethical cases through the law is a second facet, the law's largely inductive methodology. This method is especially associated with the common law, the process through which judges render decisions specific to the facts of the individual cases before them that are grounded in, or justified by, the decisions in prior cases whose facts are sufficiently analogous. Not only do judges often apply the same methodology when interpreting statutes, but legislatures, in drafting statutes, usually operate concretely and incrementally, building on court decisions and existing legislation (or borrowing from other jurisdictions) rather than attempting to operationalize grand principles. The law's fact-based, inductive method provides a counterpoint to the "principlism" that characterizes much philosophically oriented analysis in bioethics. Of course, this approach is not unique to the law, but it reinforces other case-based traditions in ethics, such as casuistry and Jewish ethics.

PROCEDURAL EMPHASIS. Third, recognizing that midlevel ethical principles such as autonomy, beneficence, justice, and nonmaleficence cannot solve most bioethical dilemmas (which arise precisely when conflict occurs among these unranked principles), and that pluralistic societies do not necessarily hold enough moral views in common to agree upon the correct resolution of most controversies, many bioethicists have welcomed "a procedural ethic, based on respect of the freedom of the moral agents involved, even without establishing the correctness of any particular moral sense" (Engelhardt, 1986, p. 45). This emphasis on procedure is familiar to lawyers, though the suggestion that bioethics should concentrate on acceptable decision-making processes rather than substantive rules draws objections from some legal scholars who see in proceduralism the risk of a slide into "the arbitrary exercise of power" (Annas, 1988, p. xiii).

Even when they have mandated that procedures be followed, the courts have not insisted that bioethical disagreements outside court employ all the procedural niceties that attach to judicial proceedings. Indeed,

LAW AND BIOETHICS
Famous Cases

Notable cases have played a major role not merely in the development of bioethics but also in making it, by the 1990s, a prominent part of private reflection and public discourse. Difficult ethical issues are nothing new to the health professions. Yet until recently, issues were examined largely behind closed doors by physicians and nurses and an occasional theologian. In democratic societies, legal proceedings are usually open (though sometimes parties are permitted to use fictitious names, to help preserve their privacy). Consequently, the media are able not merely to report about a difficult decision that must be taken but also to put a human face on it by recounting the drama as it unfolds in the hearing room.

And bioethics cases are often very dramatic. A familiar example: As Karen Quinlan's parents argued during 1975-1976 in the New Jersey courts for authority to order her ventilator turned off, her photograph appeared so often in the media that it was probably more familiar to most Americans than the faces of their local members of Congress. Likewise, bioethical breaches—particularly scandalous ones, such as the Nazi physicians' experiments on concentration camp prisoners and the Tuskegee syphilis study—not only generate landmark judicial rulings but also provoke adoption of new statutory or administrative law.

— ALEXANDER MORGAN CAPRON

What kind of medicine and health care do we need for the kind of society we want?

PAGE 72

L

LAW AND BIOETHICS

The Impact of Law on Bioethics

Ethics lies at the heart of the life sciences because facts and values can no longer be clearly separated.

PAGE 72

See Also

Rights Talk: More Harm Than Good?

Bioethics: Do the Ends Justify the Means?

judges, legislators, and administrators alike have not always been very clear about the mandate and membership, much less the process, of institutional committees to make judgments about medical treatment and research. For example, in its landmark *Quinlan* decision, the New Jersey Supreme Court held that the guardians of unconscious patients could order life-sustaining treatment forgone with the agreement of the treating physician, provided a multiprofessional committee at the hospital concurred; yet it said nothing about how that committee should gather, hear, or evaluate evidence or otherwise reach conclusions (*In re Quinlan*, 1976).

RIGHTS ORIENTATION. The issues in bioethics are some of the most sensitive and most divisive confronted by our society, not least because of the rapid development of the life sciences. In both the laboratory and the clinic, novel problems are constantly generated by new capabilities for organ transplantation and mechanical replacement, for genetic diagnosis and therapy, for assisting reproduction, for sustaining life, for modifying human behavior, and for myriad other means of altering nature; such problems also arise out of major changes in the way health services are organized and financed. These developments and changes challenge existing social and professional norms; where those challenges are substantial and intractable, the people involved not infrequently turn to courts, legislatures, or executive agencies to protect their rights. "The concept of rights . . . has its most natural use when a political society is divided, and appeals to cooperation or a common goal are pointless" (Dworkin, 1977, p. 184).

Concern over abuses of patients and research subjects has been a major theme in bioethics, reinforced repeatedly by instances in which health-care professionals and institutions have acted—sometimes from good motives and occasionally not—to the detriment of people in their care. The law has offered bioethics not just a procedural response but also a long tradition of protecting people from harm by assertion of their rights; indeed, a rights orientation seems inherent in the law's perspective on the relationship of the health-care system to patients and research subjects.

Certain risks to patients arise from the imbalance inherent in this relationship—the vulnerability and dependence that illness creates, physicians' superior knowledge and technical mastery, and the way the organization of health care enhances professionals' power and prestige. From ancient times, medical ethics proclaimed the duties of beneficence and fidelity to patients' interests in order to guard against harm to patients. Yet, as bioethicists have pointed out from the first, this traditional view of medical ethics is problematic because physicians not only promised to serve their patients' interests but often took it upon themselves to define those interests. Lawyers aided this assault on medical paternalism with concepts borrowed from civil-rights law, such as political liberty and equality of treatment. From the 1960s onward, bioethicists adopting this stance "had much in common with the new roster of rights agitators" for consumers, racial and sexual minorities, and women (Rothman, 1991, p. 245).

The increase in the rights orientation coincided with the increasing effectiveness of medical interventions. Armed with wonder drugs, high-tech surgery, and new methods of resuscitation and intensive care, physicians saw their power to influence their patients' futures increase dramatically from the middle of the twentieth century; and that power became the subject of disputes concerning how it was to be distributed in the physician-patient relationship. Legal commentators suggested—and most bioethicists embraced—a reformulation of that relationship in terms of patients' rights (Annas and Healy, 1974). The dominance of the rights orientation dismays many health-care professionals, who lament the adversarial tone they feel law has introduced into the practice of medicine. There may be a legitimate complaint here, but physicians have historically denied that they are making anything but medical decisions for patients. It has taken bioethicists to point out that once alternatives become available, the choice between them is usually based on value judgments, not medical judgments, and doctors have no special expertise that justifies their values taking precedence over patients' values. Rights are crucial to dealing with power inequality, even where one might prefer to conceive of relationships in terms of caring and connection. This tension remains a recurring theme in law and bioethics.

Although the incorporation of such central legal doctrines as informed consent into the core of bioethics can hardly be doubted, the transformative effects of law on medical practice are less clear. Commentators such as George Annas, who take a patients' rights approach, find many instances where those rights are still abused (Annas, 1988); whereas scholars such as Jay Katz, who look at physicians' behavior, emphasize that powerful factors in physicians' training and psychology have prevented them from adopting a stance of open discussion and shared decision making (Katz, 1984). At the same time, other critics argue that the authority the law took from physicians is often transferred to lawyers and judges, not to patients; and that moreover, by replacing professional discretion with legal rules, the law has given physicians the unintended message that they need not exercise ethical judgment (Hyman, 1990). Even if physicians do not react in this fashion, the law's inclination to view relationships in terms of rights changes the way bioethical issues are analyzed and potentially displaces other forms of moral discourse traditionally associated with medicine. For example, by emphasizing what one has the right to do without helping to define what is the right thing to do, the law may have undermined the specifically moral aspects of bioethics (Schneider, 1994). "[N]othing but confusion of thought can result," as Justice Oliver Wendell Holmes observed, "from assuming that the rights of man in a moral sense are equally rights in the sense of the Constitution and the law" (Holmes, 1920, p. 172).

SPECIFIC VALUES. Besides leading toward a rights orientation, the reliance upon the legal system imports specific values. These values are not unique to the legal system, though they tend to be associated with it, nor are they controversial, though they are not without consequence. That is, when one of these values is given preference in the resolution of a problem, other values, such as those that may be favored by medicine or by other philosophical systems, are likely to be overridden. The values usually associated with the law include justice, as opposed to progress or efficiency; equality, as opposed to inherent differences or measures of quality; due process, as opposed to scientific proof; and individual self-determination over one's life and body, as opposed to beneficence, psychological interdependence, or communal welfare. The law's values are generally those of liberal society: personal autonomy within a setting of ordered liberty in which individuals have wide but not unlimited freedom. Especially in pluralistic democracies, the law sets boundaries on the enforcement of majoritarian morality, thereby protecting many individual choices from interference.

Not all liberal societies treat the values involved in the same way. For example, although revolutions in France and the United States in the late eighteenth century drew on the same sources in articulating basic rights, the Declaration of the Rights of Man and the Citizen in France in 1789—unlike the Declaration of Independence in the United States in 1776—emphasized that individuals have duties as well as rights (Glendon, 1991). This difference between the American and European views of rights, which persists to this day, has important implications as bioethicists attempt to address such issues as self-risking behavior and limits on the allocation of scarce community resources to health care.

Law and bioethics as a field

As a field of study, law and bioethics can be viewed from several perspectives. First, from the vantage point of a nonlawyer doing bioethics—whether at a policy level or in individual clinical situations—one needs at least some understanding of the law and legal institutions. Moreover, institutional ethics committees usually include at least one lawyer, who can provide analytic abilities as well as expertise on statutory, regulatory, and case law.

Second, "law and bioethics" is a subject of increasing interest to students, scholars, and practitioners of law. In one view, law and bioethics can be seen as a subset of health law that deals with medical decision making, genetic and reproductive technology, human subjects research, and the like. In fact, health-law casebooks today typically include chapters or sections on bioethics. But this view does not fully capture the way in which bioethics is generally conceived. By the early 1960s, long before health law emerged as a separate field, courses dealing with bioethics were being taught at American law schools, although the first casebook with the title *Cases, Materials, and Problems in Bioethics and Law* was not published until 1981 (Shapiro and Spece, 1981). That volume, like other legal books dealing with bioethical issues, not only describes "the new biology" and recounts the dilemmas engendered by modern medicine and bioetechnology; it also discusses ethical theories and concepts, such as proportionality and personhood, that have crept from ethics into legal opinions. Nonetheless, law and bioethics is not just a subset of law and philosophy (or law and religion), since attention is usually focused on philosophical concepts not for their own sake but as they relate to understanding society's appropriate responses to technical developments that deeply affect people's lives and relationships. Most of the text of such books is drawn from reports of medical and scientific developments and from the rich array of relevant cases, statutes, and regulations, as well as commentaries about them (Capron and Michel, 1993).

In addition to academic attention, law and bioethics has been examined through commissions established by national and state governments through statutes and executive orders. These bodies have advanced bioethical analysis and promulgated legislative and administrative proposals (U.S. Congress, 1993).

Although people looking at the topic "law and bioethics" from the perspective of the latter field are likely to view it as a legitimate area of scholarship and practice, it is largely unrecognized among lawyers at large, who treat it neither as one of the distinctive "law and . . ." interdisciplinary fields nor as a distinct special application of law ("bioethics law") akin to employment law, sports law, and the like. The Association of American Law Schools does not categorize courses or teachers under such a heading, nor does the *Index to Legal Periodicals*, despite the existence in law journals of bioethics symposia as far back as the late 1960s (Capron and Michel, 1993). The literature of law and bioethics is not found only in law reviews or, for that

Feminist ethics emphasizes the context of moral decisions.

PAGE 70

See Also
Bioethics: Feminist Perspectives

L

LAW AND MORALITY

Moral Status and Legal Status

"Morality consists in suspecting other people of not being legally married."

GEORGE BERNARD SHAW

matter, in scholarly journals of other disciplines such as philosophy. It also appears in medical and health-policy journals and in bioethics publications, such as the *Hastings Center Report*, the *Kennedy Institute of Ethics Journal*, and the *Journal of Law, Medicine, and Ethics*.

One important aspect of legal scholarship that can legitimately be said to be part of the "law and bioethics" literature is abortion. Recent treatments of this subject have been enriched by feminist legal analysis, which itself is greatly influenced by theorists such as Carol Gilligan and Nel Noddings, whose work concerns moral development and the different ways in which women and men may resolve moral dilemmas. This influence is perceptible not only in subjects dealing directly with women, such as abortion, maternal-fetal issues, and reproductive technology, but also in less obvious places such as analyses of ethics committees. Since feminist analysis emphasizes relationships and nurturance, it is not surprising to see that as the literature of law and bioethics moves beyond the rights orientation, feminist insights become important in developing a better legal understanding of the relationship between patients and health caregivers (Capron and Michel, 1993).

Conclusion

Scholars differ on the precise influence the law has had in shaping the content, methods, and focus of the interdisciplinary field of bioethics, but all would agree that the influence has been significant. Both those who applaud and those who bemoan the law's influence seem to agree that the law has done more than merely allow the enforcement of, or provide redress for breach of, existing moral rights possessed by participants in the health-care system. Rather, the law has—through its orientation toward rights and through the values implicit in the processes it has fostered—established new rights and preferred certain values over others. On the positive side, this has helped promote the autonomy of patients and subjects, the openness of the processes by which decisions are reached, and equality of respect and concern for all participants. On the negative side, it has diminished the sense of community and of duties that attach to rights, while increasing many providers' sense of adversariness in their relationship to patients.

In a society in which ethical standards were sufficiently complete to address even novel technical problems, widely enough shared to be accepted without question by all or nearly all persons, and consistent and coherent enough never to lead to uncertain or contradictory results, bioethics might operate with little reference to the law. As Grant Gilmore observed, "A reasonably just society will reflect its values in a reasonably just law. The better the society, the less law there will be. In Heaven there will be no law and the lion will lie down with the lamb" (Gilmore, 1975, p. 1044). Until that time, the law will continue to play a large role in bioethics—not only providing a relatively neutral means through which troubling issues can be addressed and contended points resolved in a manner that is socially sanctioned, but also shaping bioethics through its concerns for justice and fair procedures, equality, and personal self-determination.

— ALEXANDER MORGAN CAPRON

LAW AND MORALITY

Bioethical problems are often discussed in legal as well as in moral contexts. Lawyers as well as ethicists are involved with such questions as abortion, euthanasia, and experimentation upon human beings. This is not surprising; the law is seriously concerned with protecting such basic rights as life, bodily integrity, and privacy—the rights involved in these ethical questions.

The overlap between law and morality has been a source of the substantial debate about the relation between law and morality, a debate not confined to the bioethical context. It is best divided into two main issues, although the discussion of these issues often overlaps: (1) What, if any, bearing does the moral status of a rule have on its status as a law? (2) To what extent, if any, should the legal system be used to enforce moral perspectives?

Moral status and legal status

Western legal thought has been dominated by a natural-law tradition. There are many variants of this tradition, and the differences among them will be discussed below; what they have in common is a belief in a body of laws governing all people at all times, and in a source for those laws other than the customs and institutions of a given society. Such beliefs are frequently accompanied by the additional beliefs that no society is authorized to create laws that conflict directly with natural laws, and that any such conflicting laws may therefore be invalid. In short, the natural-law tradition asserts the existence of a set of laws whose status as laws is based upon their moral status.

The beginning of this tradition lies in the ancient world. Aristotle (384-322 B.C.E) drew a distinction between the part of justice that is natural and should have the same force everywhere, and the part that is legal and has its force only in those places where it has been adopted by the people who live there. That distinction was developed extensively by the Stoics, who emphasized two further points about natural justice: that it is based upon right reason and that it is in agreement with nature. Cicero (106-43 B.C.E), whose legal writings are based upon the Stoic tradition, emphasized the claim that no legislation can alter the validity of natural laws, which remain binding on all people. Some of these ideas were incorporated into Roman law, and the later Roman lawyers probably identified *jus naturale* (the philosophical notion of natural law) with *jus gentium* (a system of laws that had developed in the Roman world and governed the relations among free men independently of their nationality). This identification strengthened the idea of natural law as universal law.

These classical ideas gave rise to a number of different natural-law traditions, the two most important of which are the religious tradition culminating in the writings of Saint Thomas Aquinas (1224-1274) and the secular tradition, exemplified by Hugo Grotius (1583-1645) and John Locke (1632-1704).

Saint Thomas Aquinas defined a law as an ordinance of reason for the common good, promulgated by the individual who has the care of the community. He then distinguished four types of laws: eternal laws, natural laws, human laws, and divine laws. The eternal laws are laws promulgated by God on the basis of divine reason. The natural laws are the eternal laws implanted by God in human beings, in that human beings are naturally inclined toward their proper acts and ends. In short, Saint Thomas postulated an eternal, unchanging set of laws implanted by God in human beings and knowable by reason. Human laws are valid only insofar as they do not conflict with divinely promulgated, unchanging laws. Valid human laws either are conclusions drawn from the basic natural laws or are determinations of details left undetermined by the natural laws.

The natural-law theories of Grotius and Locke also contain theological references, and Saint Thomas does emphasize the rational basis of natural law. Nevertheless, Grotius and Locke represent a different tradition of natural law, one that puts more emphasis on natural law as rationally derivable than on natural law as divinely ordained. In addition, their tradition, especially in the writings of Locke, puts great emphasis on the natural law's protection of natural rights, rights that all human beings have independently of the state and its laws. Locke explicitly drew the conclusion that a state loses its legitimacy insofar as its laws are in violation of natural rights, such as the right to life or liberty.

These natural-law traditions continue to influence discussions about the relation between the law and bioethics. Writers influenced by the theological version of the natural-law tradition continue to argue that any valid law must be in conformity with the divinely ordained natural law. Thus, many Roman Catholic writers (e.g., Grisez and Boyle, 1979) argue that there must be civil laws prohibiting abortion and euthanasia because those procedures are in conflict with the natural law. To those who would object that this is an illegitimate use of the law to enforce morality, these writers reply that it is the very nature of legitimate law to prohibit such activities. The most important recent reiteration of this view is found in the 1987 statement from the Congregation for the Doctrine of the Faith entitled *Instruction on Respect for Human Life in its Origin and on the Dignity of Procreation*. Having argued that abortion from the moment of conception and various forms of assisted reproduction are immoral, the Congregation goes on to claim that there must be laws prohibiting both because "The task of the civil law is to ensure the common good of people through the recognition of and the defence of fundamental rights and through the promotion of peace and of public morality" (1987, p. 35).

NATURE'S LAW

Stoic philosopher and Roman statesman Marcus Tullius Cicero wrote that no legislation can alter the rule of natural law.

Writers influenced by the ideas of natural-rights thinkers like Locke continue to argue that no purported law is legitimate if it allows the violation of the basic rights of human beings. This type of argumentation is particularly prevalent in countries such as the United States, where the courts possess the ability to declare laws unconstitutional when they infringe upon basic human rights. U.S. Supreme Court decisions from *Griswold* v. *Connecticut* (1965), in which the Supreme Court ruled that a Connecticut law prohibiting the use of contraceptives is unconstitutional, to *Roe* v. *Wade* (1973), in which the Supreme Court ruled that women have a constitutional right to abortions at least in the first two trimesters, have indicated that jurists are prepared to extend those rights to include ones not explicitly mentioned in the Constitution, suggesting to many—but by no means all—commentators that they

"The people's good is the highest law."

CICERO
DE LEGIBUS (ON LAWS)

Views about the moral status of human fetuses are even more far-ranging than views about their legal status.

PAGE 235

See Also

The Legal Status of Human Fetuses

The Moral Status of Human Fetuses

are implicitly invoking some natural-law theory of rights.

The natural-law tradition has not been universally accepted. There has also been a long tradition of thinkers, dating back to antiquity, who have insisted that the only laws that exist are those adopted by a given society, and that there is no necessary connection between the legal status of a law and its moral status. Defenders of this position, the position of legal positivism, are not opposed to the moral criticism of individual laws and of whole legal institutions; positivists often advocate changes in the law on the basis of moral considerations. But the positivists insist that an immoral law, however much it should be changed, remains valid as a law until it is repealed by the society's appropriate social mechanisms.

Jeremy Bentham (1748-1832) and John Austin (1790-1859) were the two most influential proponents of this view, although earlier figures like Jean Bodin (1530-1596) and Thomas Hobbes (1588-1679) should also be mentioned. The basic thesis of positivism has often been conflated with another of Austin's theories, the imperative theory of law, which held that law is the command of the sovereign. Since this latter theory has not survived critical examination, it is crucial to distinguish it from the basic theme of positivism: that what the law is, is a separate question from what the law ought to be. H. L. A. Hart, the most influential contemporary positivist, placed particular emphasis on drawing this distinction.

Some legal positivists have taken their view to mean that laws must be obeyed no matter how immoral they are. But the most important positivists, Bentham and Austin, clearly argued that there are circumstances in which an immoral law should be violated despite its status as a law; this of course weakens the force of the claim that a law retains its status as a law despite its immorality.

In any case, legal positivists insist that questions about the relation between law and morality must be settled independently of questions about what the law is. The legal status of a rule is independent of its moral status. This leads us, therefore, to the second of our questions: When ought the law to be used to enforce certain moral positions?

Use of the legal system to enforce morality

The law is clearly used on some occasions to enforce moral viewpoints. We believe that murder is wrong and that the coercive mechanism of the law should be used to prevent murders. However, even if we believe that euthanasia is wrong or that one should come to the aid of others in distress, should the law be used to enforce these beliefs?

John Stuart Mill (1806-1873), in his classic *On Liberty* (1859), advocated the liberal answer to that question—that society should use the coercive mechanisms of the law only to prevent actions that harm someone other than the performer or another who has consented to the performance of the action. In other words, Mill argued that the social enforcement of morality was inappropriate when only the agent or others who had consented would be harmed. In his elaboration of this position in *The Moral Limits of the Criminal Law* (1984-1988), the most important elaboration of the liberal position in the twentieth century, Joel Feinberg has argued that actions might be criminalized if they were profoundly offensive, even if not harmful, to others.

Mill's followers have therefore opposed the existence of laws creating "victimless crimes," among which they have included laws against suicide and voluntary euthanasia, unless such laws are required to protect against mistake and abuse. They have also approved of court decisions that allow rational adults to refuse medical treatment on religious or on other grounds, even though the refusal would result in their dying.

Adherents of the liberal approach have in recent years expanded upon it and modified it in a number of ways. One question that has received considerable attention is determining whose consent is valid. The current understanding of mental illness makes it very difficult to accept a sharp dichotomy between those competent to consent and those incompetent, since there are many degrees of mental disturbance. Some (including Buchanan and Brock, 1989) have responded that the standard for competency must be more demanding when the decision is more momentous. Others (including Brody, 1988) insist that we must recognize that competent decisions may be overridden when the costs to the individual are great and the person's decision making is impaired, even if he or she is somewhat competent.

Another question that has received considerable attention is the extent to which society can legitimately use the law temporarily to prevent an individual from carrying out certain decisions, to see whether the individual will change his or her mind or whether the choice is truly voluntary. Within the liberal framework, could we legally require, for example, a period between a request for voluntary euthanasia and the implementation of that request? Following Joel Feinberg, many liberal authors have allowed for this form of weak or soft paternalism.

A third question that has received considerable attention is the legitimacy of legally imposing certain positive moral duties. Mill was primarily concerned with challenging the legitimacy of laws prohibiting

LAWS TO PREVENT HARM
About the Liberal View

A number of points must be kept in mind about the liberal position. First, it does not require legislation prohibiting all actions that harm others. Whether there should be legislation will depend upon such factors as the existence of harmful consequences and the possibility of enforcement. All that the liberal position entails is that such actions, because they harm others, are candidates for appropriate legal prohibition.

Second, actions that harm others may be prohibited legally, even when others consent, if their consent is not valid. This point is extremely important in connection with legislation governing medical experimentation. Consider, for example, the problem of experiments on children, where the experiments are not primarily intended to aid in their therapy and where there are potential hazards. Given that the consent of the children may not count if they are young enough, and given that the relevance of parental consent is unclear, Mill's principles could allow for enforcing some socially determined moral standards in this area. In fact, the 1993 U.S. regulations on research involving children enforce a very strict moral standard; the risks must represent only a minor increase over minimal risk, and the information must be of vital importance.

Third, this liberal position is not identical either with the English common-law tradition or with American constitutional law. Both have allowed for legal prohibitions that are unacceptable in the liberal framework. For example, the consent of the person killed in an act of voluntary euthanasia has been, at least until the early 1990s, no defense against a charge of murder in either legal system. Some of the language in the U.S. Supreme Court case *Cruzan* v. *Missouri Department of Health* (1990) suggests that many judges are now prepared to say that the right of a competent adult to refuse life-preserving therapy is a protected constitutional right, a result that liberals would applaud. Nothing in the text of this decision, however, suggests the extension of that view to assisted suicide or voluntary active euthanasia.

— BARUCH A. BRODY

immoral actions; it is unclear how he would have dealt with Good Samaritan laws—laws that would, for example, require trained medical personnel to come to the aid of accident victims. Would such laws that require positive actions, and not mere forbearances, be a legitimate legal enforcement of morality?

A final question that has received considerable attention is whether society can pass laws designed to prevent harm to animals. If it could, this would markedly change the liberal attitude toward laws governing experimentation on animals. Peter Singer (1979) and Tom Regan (1983) are two liberal authors who have advocated the extension of the liberal tradition in this way.

From its very beginning, the liberal tradition has had its critics. Writers in the natural-law tradition objected, of course, to the liberal presupposition that the moral and legal status of rules could be separated. But even some of those who agreed with positivism have argued that there is a wider scope for legislating morality than the scope allowed by Mill.

James Fitzjames Stephen (1829-1894), in his influential *Liberty, Equality, Fraternity* (1873), argued that one of the purposes of both the criminal and the civil law is to promote and encourage virtue while discouraging vice. Stephen conceded that certain areas of morality could not be dealt with by the law because the relevant laws could not be enforced without destroying privacy and individual rights; he claimed, however, that there are many areas of morality that should be treated by the law despite Mill's strictures. This point of view has been extended by Patrick Devlin, a distinguished English jurist. Devlin contends that the continued existence and strength of a society require a common moral code. There is, therefore, a social interest in the preservation of such a code, and it is at least sometimes appropriate to enforce part of the code through the use of the law. Devlin limits his conclusions to cases where this enforcement of morality will not violate human rights. He applied this approach to English abortion legislation in the 1960s. He argued that the severe punishment of the illegal abortionist cannot be justified on the grounds that such a person poses a threat to the health of the mother, since that threat exists primarily because the abortionist's activities are illegal. Instead, such laws can be explained and justified only as an attempt by society to protect its fundamental views on sexuality and on human life.

A number of recent authors (Bellah et al., 1985; MacIntyre, 1981; Sandel, 1982) have emphasized, in different ways, the importance of communities and a sense of community values, and they have seen this as standing in opposition to the liberal account. This new communitarianism no doubt has significant implications for the legislation of morality in areas related to

"Privilegia paucorum non faciunt legem *[The privileges of a few do not make common law].*"

ST. JEROME
EXPOSITION ON JONAH

See Also

Declaring Rights: Moral Claims and Force of Law

Sissela Bok has examined the concern about the trustworthiness of lawyers, not by their clients but by the public.

PAGE 675

"Law is a bottomless pit; it is a cormorant, a harpy that devours everything."

JONATHAN SWIFT

bioethics, but those implications have not yet been studied systematically.

There are, then, a number of differing systematic approaches to the question of which aspects of morality should be enforced legally. In addition to those systematic approaches, various authors and courts have suggested additional considerations that must be weighed in deciding whether legally to enforce moral standards. Among the most prominent of the considerations are the following.

"THERE OUGHT TO BE A LAW . . ."—BUT FIRST, CONSIDER

1. respect for differing views in a pluralistic society
2. respect for privacy
3. consequences of passing such a law
4. difficulty of distinguishing fraudulent from legitimate cases
5. "slippery-slope" arguments

1. ***Respect for differing views in a pluralistic society.*** In the 1973 discussion of abortion statutes in *Roe* v. *Wade*, the U.S. Supreme Court suggested that legislation enforcing a moral viewpoint is inappropriate when those who are experts in the relevant area disagree as to the legitimacy of that viewpoint. This principle is in keeping with a wider movement against legislating disputed moral positions. A number of important considerations support this mode of thought. To begin with, people seem to have a right to follow their own conscience rather than to be compelled to follow the conscience of the rest of society. Moreover, there are tremendous detrimental consequences for a society when many of its citizens feel that the law is being used to coerce them into following the moral views of others. Such considerations are even more important in societies where there are substantial moral disagreements among the citizens. One author who has particularly stressed the importance of respecting differing views in a pluralistic society is H. Tristram Engelhardt, Jr. (1986).

2. ***Respect for privacy.*** There are laws that cannot be enforced without infringing the privacy of the citizens involved. Following a long tradition that appealed to this point, the U.S. Supreme Court suggested (in *Griswold* v. *Connecticut*, 1965), that such laws are illegitimate because of the inability to enforce them in an acceptable fashion. For that reason, the Court declared unconstitutional a Connecticut law prohibiting the use (and not merely the production) of contraceptive devices. It has also been argued that laws regulating the patient-doctor relation are inappropriate because they can be enforced only by the state's entering into and examining a relation that must be private. Many authors have criticized the U.S. "Baby-Doe" law (P.L. 98-457, 1984), which limits on moral grounds the decision-making authority of parents and physicians with regard to severely disabled newborns, because it involves state intrusion into a private relation.

3. ***The consequences of passing such a law.*** It is sometimes argued that certain moral positions ought not to be enforced legally because the laws that codify them will be violated anyway, and their surreptitious violation will lead to many tragic results. Thus, it has been argued that laws prohibiting abortion only result in women's seeking unsafe, illegal, and very dangerous abortions. Again, it has been argued that laws prohibiting voluntary euthanasia or allowing to die only result in surreptitious acts of voluntary euthanasia and in informal decisions to "let the patient die," acts and decisions that can be abused. Many studies of such abuses (by, e.g., Bedell and Delbanco, 1984; Evans and Brody, 1985) led in the 1980s to more formal policies governing such decisions.

Considerations 1-3 are reasons why certain actions should not be illegal, whether or not they are immoral. Most authors would agree that these legitimate considerations must be balanced against others that argue for the criminalization of the acts in question. These include the extent of the harmful consequences of the actions in question and the extent to which they involve infringements of the rights of others.

There are, in addition, considerations for making actions illegal even if they are not immoral. Two deserve special notice:

4. ***The difficulty of distinguishing between fraudulent and legitimate cases.*** Suppose that there are no moral objections to voluntary euthanasia. Some have argued that it would be wise legally to prohibit such killings because it is difficult to distinguish cases of honest requests from cases of consent obtained by subtle fraud or duress. Again, some have argued that despite the moral permissibility of experimenting upon consenting adults, there should be laws prohibiting experiments conducted upon prison inmates, because one cannot tell when the consent of such inmates is truly voluntary.

5. ***Slippery-slope arguments.*** It is often argued that legalizing certain morally acceptable actions would later lead to irresistible pressures for legalizing immoral actions, and that the only way to avoid sliding down this slippery slope is to prohibit even the acceptable actions. Thus, it has been argued that voluntary euthanasia should be illegal, even if morally acceptable, as a way of ensuring against the later legalization of involuntary euthanasia. Naturally, both of these factors must be weighed against the possible desirable results of legalizing the morally acceptable actions.

Conclusion

It is clear, then, that there are no easy answers to questions about the relation between law and morality. There are strong considerations favoring legal positivism, but there are other considerations favoring a natural-law doctrine. And even if one is a legal positivist, there are conflicting considerations that one has to weigh in deciding on the appropriate relation between one's moral code and society's legal code.

— BARUCH A. BRODY

LIFE

Like many of the concepts foundational to the field of bioethics, life is a subject about which there is both long-standing conviction and increasing uncertainty. The beginnings and endings of life, as well as its creation, have become subject to greater technological modification, particularly through the rise of the modern biological sciences and new reproductive and genetic technologies. In the late twentieth century, increasing technological control over the management, regulation, and production of life and lifelike systems, as well as the accelerating commodification of life forms, raise questions about the limits of what can or should be done to life itself. Hence, seemingly timeless and universal human attitudes toward life, such as mourning in the wake of its loss and joy in its creation, are today accompanied by profound ambiguities concerning the meaning, value, and definition of life.

Some commentators have claimed that even a few decades ago life was more often understood as an absolute value—for example, among medical professionals, for whom the protection of life was an unquestioned moral duty (Parsons et al., 1972). Related arguments hold that the technologization of life has produced a shift away from an understanding of life as an absolute value, and toward more relative assessments of the quality of life (Parsons et al., 1972, pp. 405-410). The appearance of an entry entitled "Life" in an encyclopedia of bioethics would support the position that life itself has become the object of increased management in the form of decision making.

In contrast to the urgent call for guidelines concerning the subject of life is the difficulty of defining this term. Neither philosophers, theologians, nor scientists can offer a clear understanding of life. This is in part due to the wide-ranging uses of the term. Not only does life have many meanings as a noun, it is a key term within a wide range of systems of thought from religion to science. In all of the many senses in which the word is used, definitions of it have varied historically in relation to changing social forces and cultural values. Contemporary moral, legal, theological, and scientific uncertainty attends the origins of life, the relative importance of human versus other forms of life,

the beginnings and endings of life, the creation and destruction of life, and the nature of life. These and other concerns follow from the definitional issues, raised by the concept of life itself, that remain subject to dispute and ongoing transformation.

Historical and cultural variations

To be animate or vital is a condition for which cross-culturally and transhistorically there exists a range of modes of recognition. Broadly speaking, notions of life, or of a vital force, are often connected to beliefs about the supernatural, divinity, and sacredness. It is also generally the case that understandings of life are often made most explicit in relation to death (Bloch and Parry, 1982; Huntington and Metcalf, 1979). These features characterize both Judaeo-Christian and classical understandings of life, the two predominant sources of its definition in the Euro-American tradition prior to the rise of modern science.

According to the Judaeo-Christian tradition, life is interpreted and valued as a gift from God. The Old Testament relates that God created man (Adam) in his own likeness, with dominion over all living things. In the Garden of Eden, life was everlasting; and Adam and Eve's expulsion, through which they became mortal, was both a sign of divine displeasure and a partial rescinding of the gift of life. According to the New Testament, the gift of everlasting life was restored through the sacrifice of God's only begotten son, Jesus, and his resurrection to the kingdom of Heaven. Consequently, only those who believe in the resurrection of Christ have "life" in the Christian sense. When Jesus states "I am life" (or "I am the way, the truth, and the life"), it is the resurrection promised to believers in the life, death, and salvation of Christ that is invoked. The historian Barbara Duden notes:

> *In most of the New Testament and in two thousand years of ecclesiastical usage, to "have life" means to par-*

LIFE BEGINS

Now that biotechnicians can manipulate the creation of life, age-old human understandings of "life" are tangled in profound ambiguities.

"It is the preservation of the species, not of individuals, which appears to be the design of Deity througout the whole of nature."

MARY WOLLSTONECRAFT
LETTER, 1796

ticipate as a believing Christian in the life of Christ. . . . Even the dead live in Christ, and only those who live in Christ can have life in this world. Of those who exist outside this relationship, the Church has consistently spoken of those who "live" under conditions of death. (Duden, 1993, p. 102)

Blood is a key symbol of life in the Christian tradition as well as in much secular culture, most notably medicine. To give the "gift of life" is more literally possible today than ever before in the context of organ donation, whereby a body part of a deceased person may "live on" in the body of another person, or a living donor may sacrifice a body part (such as a kidney) on behalf of a relative. The capacity to donate not only blood and vital organs but also egg and sperm cells, and the increasing availability of bodily tissues through a service sector and a marketplace, complicate the understanding of life as a "gift" (Parsons et al., 1972; Titmuss, 1971). The sacrificial importance of the body and the blood of Christ makes the exchange of body tissue a potent symbolic practice, as does the definition of kin ties in terms of "blood relations."

The association between the flow of blood and the flow of life anticipates the notion of germ plasm (the hereditary material of the germ cells) as the basis for heredity; this in turn gives rise to the modern scientific concept of the gene, which is today described as the essence of life. While the gene in some senses represents the triumph of mechanistic explanations of life itself, the most reductionist accounts of genes as "selfishly" reproducing entities defined by the attainment of their own inbuilt "ends" may seem not dissimilar from that of the most influential proponent of vitalism, Aristotle.

Aristotelian definitions of life were predominant for nearly two millennia, in part because Aristotle was among the few philosophers of antiquity to pay significant attention to the problem of defining life. According to Aristotle, life is defined by the possession of a soul, or vital force, through which an entity is rendered animate and given shape. The attainment of a predetermined end point is seen as the purpose of life in Aristotelian terms, a purpose that is contained in itself, independent of any external causal agent. This view is known as entelechy—a telos, an ultimate end that is self-defined as the achievement of a final form.

Although the Aristotelian view was based on close observations of the natural world and eschewed any notion of divine creation, it is strongly criticized by modern scientists for its teleologism (conflation of an endpoint with a cause) and essentialism (predeterminism), which are dismissed as metaphysical and therefore insufficiently empirical. Cartesian accounts of animation, which defined life in terms of the organization instead of the essence of matter, succeeded Aristotelian vitalism in the seventeenth century. From the perspective of mechanism, which explained motion or aliveness purely in terms of the articulation among parts of a whole (as in the ticking of a watch), Aristotelian vitalism came to be seen as mystical, nonobservable, and therefore unscientific.

The history of the concept of life in Western science, from which many of the most authoritative contemporary definitions of it are derived, underscores the importance of change and variation in the meanings of this term (Canguilhem, 1994; Schroedinger, 1956). Eighteenth-century natural historians employed a horizontal ordering strategy to classify diverse life forms into taxonomies of kind or type. A vertical ranking of the value of these life forms (known as the great chain of being, descending from God to humanity and thence to other living entities) was based on their proximity to the divine. According to this conceptual framework, "life" comprised a diverse array of animate entities classified epistemologically and ranked theologically in terms of proximity to God. The sacred act of divine creation that brought life into being was, in this schema, paralleled by the secular production by natural philosophers, such as Carolus Linnaeus (1707-1778), of a classification system through which life forms were named, defined, and ordered according to their perceived nature, which was seen to be immutable.

The stability of these vertical ranking and horizontal classifying axes was irrevocably shaken by the gradual acceptance of the evolutionary model of life, in particular the work of Charles Darwin, which, over the latter half of the nineteenth century, gained acceptance in Europe and America. With the rise of Darwinian theories of evolution came a radical new understanding of life: as an underlying connectedness of all living things. It was the evolutionary view of life as a distinct object of study in its own right that gave rise to the modern notion of "life itself"; not until this time could such a thing have been conceived. Many of the current dilemmas in bioethics demanding our attention came to be understood as a direct result of the emergence of this particular conceptualization of life.

As the historian Michel Foucault points out, life itself did not exist before the end of the nineteenth century; it is a concept indebted to the rise of the modern biological sciences.

Historians want to write histories of biology in the nineteenth century; but they do not realise that biology did not exist then, and that the pattern of knowledge that has been familiar to us for a hundred and fifty years is not valid for a previous period. And that if biology was unknown, there was a very simple reason for it: that life itself did not exist. *All that existed*

L

LIFE

Historical and Cultural Variations

"Although human life is priceless, we always act as if something had an even greater price than life. . . . But what is that something?"

ANTOINE DE SAINT-EXUPÉRY
NIGHT FLIGHT, 1931

was living beings, which were viewed through a grid of knowledge constituted by natural history.
(Foucault, 1970, p. 128; emphasis added)

Life, in the sense of life itself, is thus a concept linked closely to the rise of the modern life sciences, founded on notions of evolutionary change, the underlying connectedness of all living things, and a biogenetic mechanism of heredity through which life reproduces itself. As the foundational object of the modern life sciences, the concept of life itself does not exist as a thing, as something visible or tangible. Only its traces are accessible, through the forms in which life manifests itself. Like Newtonian gravity, Darwinian life is a principle or force subject to an orderliness decipherable by science, such as the process of natural selection by which evolution is understood to proceed.

Problems in defining life

The definition of life is not only contested from within the scientific community; it is also troubled by the proximity of lifelike systems, especially those that are computer-generated, to the requisite features of animate existence. There may well be, as Stephen Levy notes in his account of artificial life, a "particular reluctance to grant anything synthetic or man-made the exalted status of a life-form" (1992, p. 6). Yet insofar as the biogenetic definition of life itself relies on an informational model, of DNA as a message or a code, the distinction between life and nonlife is readily challenged by complex informational systems that are to a degree self-regulating and that have the capacity both to replicate themselves and to evolve. If, as some have claimed (Oyama, 1985), information is the modern equivalent of form, then life is transformed from an absolute property into a receding horizon merging with artificial, synthetic, or virtual "life." (See also Langton, 1989, and Levy, 1992.)

Today, both the border between human and nonhuman life and the distinction between life and death are increasingly blurred. Genetic science offers the possibility of transspecies recombinations effecting a merging of human and animal body parts. Artificial-life scientists using information technology distinguish computer-generated organisms, which live, evolve, reproduce, and die, from the "wet" life forms they imitate (Levy, 1992). Health professionals distinguish degrees of death: dead (in the sense of brain-dead); double dead (respiratory failure); and triple dead (no body parts suitable for donation). Such distinctions indicate the increasing difficulties of establishing the parameters of life and death.

In sum, life itself may be charted along the course of its four-billion-year history to its estimated point of origin, and along this path may be classified and analyzed scientifically according to established principles, such as the operation of natural selection, and specific qualities, such as the possession of DNA. It is from the perspective of the modern life sciences that the most elaborate and definitive accounts of life are constructed, and from these in turn that the concept of life itself emerges. Yet the instability of these definitional parameters, like those of previous eras that they replaced, ensures their continued transformation.

Life as a moral issue

Despite the ubiquity and authority of biological definitions of life, they are also reductionist and materialist, relying upon mechanistic and objective terms that are ultimately most meaningful to professional specialists. Most people, when asked "What is life?" do not appeal to Darwinian principles.

Many of the more everyday definitions of life can be classed as processual or phenomenological, referring to the course of events comprising the life of an individual or other entity (including inanimate objects, as in the expression "shelf life"). Expressions such as *c'est la vie* ("that's life") invoke the fortuitous and inexplicable dimensions of life, very much in contrast to scientific accounts, which emphasize order and predictability even while admitting great uncertainty. Such expressions convey a sense of limits to the capacity for rational understanding, and especially prediction or control, in relation to the vicissitudes of life and living.

The lengthy debate in early modern science concerning mechanism (the presumption that animate and inanimate entities alike are composed of matter, which can be explained through inherent principles of structure and function) versus vitalism (the presumption of an inherently inexplicable vital force differentiating the quick from the dead) opposes the ancient association of lifelike properties with mystery and the sacred to their accessibility through instrumental reason (see Merchant, 1980). In relation to the moral questions concerning life—whether as a process, a possession, or a right—the vitalistic notion of life as something inexplicable and deserving of reverence and protection is far more prevalent than the more mechanistic and instrumental account dominant within science. In both secular and religiously derived accounts, life does not need to be fully explicated or rational to be seen as uniquely deserving of protection, especially human life.

◆ vitalism
A doctrine that the processes of life are not explicable by the laws of physics and chemistry alone and that life is in some part self-determining.

The protection of life

In his discussion of abortion and euthanasia, two of the most controversial areas of debate concerning human life, philosopher Ronald Dworkin emphasizes the importance of recognizing that life is not exclusively or even primarily understood by many people in terms of

See Also

The Moral Status of Human Fetuses

Life, Quality of

scientific explanations, but rather in terms of a value more akin to sacredness. In relation to moral dilemmas, he claims, life does not present itself as a question of objective fact, but rather as a truth, or a "quasi-religious" principle held to be self-evident through "primitive conviction" (Dworkin, 1993).

Dworkin's approach thus differs from the more utilitarian arguments about the beginnings and endings of life propounded by philosophers and other commentators who use rights or interest-based approaches to questions of the meaning and value of life. In demarcating the value of life as a "quasi-religious" one, something essentially felt rather than reasoned, Dworkin returns the question of the value of life to an older, more traditional paradigm linked to notions of divinity or a vital force.

Social scientists have shown the value of life to be a key symbolic resource in struggles of many kinds, including both ways of life (as in the preservation of ethnic traditions or indigenous cultures) and life forms (such as endangered species). Anthropologist Faye Ginsburg's study of the abortion debate in a midwestern American community, for example, demonstrates the symbolic dimensions of life as a subject of dispute extending to notions of citizenship, nationalism, and the sexual division of labor (Ginsburg, 1989). Precisely because the preservation of human life may be seen as an absolute moral value, it proves readily amenable to the social function of grounding other beliefs and practices.

Both the notion of biological viability and the definition of the person to whom rights are ascribed invoke a particular construction of life. Viability, for example, is strictly biologically determined: it is measured by the ability of a fetus to survive biologically. The question of the social viability of a child's life, such as its likelihood of receiving adequate nurture, shelter, protection from disease, or sustenance is not considered part of the criteria valid in determining the morality of a decision to terminate a pregnancy.

Feminists have been prominent in the challenge to the notion of the person often used by antiabortionists on similar grounds. It is undeniably the case that an embryo is human, that it is a being, and that it is a form of life. That it is a living human being is therefore undeniable. Yet it is no more or less a living human being in this sense than an egg or sperm cell, or for that matter a blood cell, none of which is considered a per-

SCIENTIFIC PERSPECTIVES

Life as Defined by Modern Science

From the vantage point of the modern life sciences, life itself has come to be associated with certain qualities, including movement, the ability to reproduce and to evolve, and the capacity for growth and development. Other criteria for defining life as opposed to nonlife include the capacity to metabolize, in particular through the possession of cells. These characteristics of aliveness in turn comprise key areas in the study of life forms, and in the forms of connectedness and interrelatedness among them. Whereas the comparative anatomy or morphology of animals and plants was the definitive technique for the classification of life forms during the classical period of natural history, it is molecular biology that today provides the primary analytic perspective on the essence of life, which is seen to be DNA, or the genetic code. It is DNA, composed of nucleotide chains that guide the manufacture of essential proteins, that all living beings are said to have in common. Thus DNA is the substance and mechanism of heredity intrinsic to the neo-Darwinian notion of life itself. (For an historical account of Darwinian notions of life itself, see Jacob, 1973. For a contemporary view, see Pollack, 1994.)

The most definitive accounts of life itself today rely on evolutionary and genetic models. "The possession of a genetic program provides for an absolute difference between organisms and inorganic matter," claims the biologist Ernst Mayr, one of the great twentieth-century exponents of evolution as a unifying theme in modern biological thought (Mayr, 1982, p. 55). "Life should be defined by the possession of those properties which are needed to ensure evolution by natural selection," states John Maynard Smith, one of the leading evolutionary biologists in Britain (Maynard Smith, 1986, p. 7).

In addition to offering the most definitive accounts of life, the modern life sciences provide the most detailed and substantive information on the subject. In the article "Life" written for the Encyclopaedia Britannica, Carl Sagan notes: "A great deal is known about life. . . . Anatomists and taxonomists have studied the forms and relations of more than a million separate species of plants and animals." A range of biological specialties have together compiled "an enormous fund of information" on the origin, diversity, interaction, and complexity of living organisms and the principles that order their existence (Sagan, 1992, p. 985).

Yet even such definitive accounts of life from established scientific figures are often admittedly provisional. Both within and outside the scientific community there is considerable uncertainty about what is being studied when the subject is life itself. As Sagan notes perfunctorily, "There is no generally accepted definition of life" (Sagan, 1992, p. 985).

— SARAH FRANKLIN

son or seen as entitled to civil rights. Increasingly, antiabortionists have used biologically based arguments to support their position, even when it is derived from religious principles. Hence, it is the potential for an embryo—unlike an egg, a sperm, or a blood cell—to develop into a human being that is often stressed. This argument is based on an embryo's possession of a unique genetic blueprint, which some established theologians claim is evidence of ensoulment (see Ford, 1988).

Hence, arguments against abortion based on fetal viability, or those that stress the genetic potential of the fetus to develop into a person, are based on a particular model of life, according to which its sanctity may be represented in biogenetic terms. Historian Barbara Duden has called this historically recent turn toward biology as an arbiter of moral decision making the "sacralisation of life itself" (Duden, 1993). Life, in this sense, is not a biological fact but a cultural value, an essentialist belief, or even a fetish.

The geneticization of life itself

Similar claims have been made regarding the biogenetic definition of life as possession of a genetic blueprint. Critical biologists have argued against the genetic reductionism or genetic essentialism such definitions risk (see Hubbard, 1990). Social scientists also have warned of the dangers of eugenicism implicit in such a view (Nelkin and Lindee, 1995); other scholars have minimized such risks (Kevles, 1986).

Advocates of a "strong" genetic essentialism argue not only that genes are the essence of life but that life itself is consequently based on the selfish desire to reproduce itself. From this vantage point, humans are mere epiphenomena of a primordial genetic drive to self-replicate, and human moral or ethical systems are a complex admixture of altruism motivated by strategic sacrifice, which benefits one genetic trajectory or another (Dawkins, 1989).

The belief that life processes will one day be subject to much greater control through instrumentalized understandings of their genetic code is the basis for a major expansion in the biotechnology industry, and corresponding scientific research, since the early 1980s. International scientific projects such as the attempt to map the human genome, by sequencing all of the DNA in the twenty-three pairs of human chromosomes, reflect the increasing importance of genes and genetic processes to the understanding of life itself. (For a description of the Human Genome Project, see British Medical Association, 1992, and Cook-Deegan, 1994. For an account of the ethical dimension, see Kevles and Hood, 1992. For a critical account, see Hubbard and Wald, 1993.) In turn, increasing information about the role of genes in heredity will pose new choices and decisions, as well as dilemmas, for many. On the one hand, new diagnostic procedures utilizing genetic screening to detect severe, chronic, degenerative, and often terminal disorders caused by a single gene are claimed to offer greater reproductive choice and control, and the potential to alleviate human suffering and disease. On the other hand, the identification of gene "defects" poses worrisome questions, especially when linked to notions of individual predisposition, genetic selection, and the elimination of "undesirable" traits. Controversies such as that attending the putative discovery of a "gay gene" underscore the dangers of social prejudice wedded to genetic determinism in the name of greater reproductive choice and control.

Altering the genetic code of an individual entity, be it human, plant, or animal, is most controversial when

FIGHTING OVER "LIFE"
Arguments Based on Rights and on Biology

Abortion is one of the best-known arenas of controversy in which both definitions of life and the value of human life are paramount and explicitly formulated. Opponents of abortion argue that life begins at conception and therefore that the deliberate termination of a pregnancy is the taking of a human life, which is seen to be immoral or even comparable to murder. Proponents of a woman's right to control her own fertility, including the choice to terminate an unwanted pregnancy, often argue on the basis of consequentialism, that is, that the moral value of an act should be measured in reference to its outcome. Rights-based claims are used by both sides, antiabortionists stressing the right to life of the fetus, which they argue to be paramount, and pro-choice advocates stressing a woman's right to control her own reproduction, on which they, in turn, place primary importance.

Current legislation on abortion in many industrialized countries, including the United States, invokes a combination of rights-based arguments and biologically based distinctions. Hence, for example, the 1973 U.S. Supreme Court decision in *Roe* v. *Wade*, which currently determines abortion law in the United States, combines protection of the individual right to privacy with a biologically based definition of fetal viability as the determinant of the upper time limit for abortion. The same standard holds in Great Britain.

— SARAH FRANKLIN

The principle of "ownership of one's person," once used in arguments against slavery, now appears in disputes concerning body parts.

PAGE 442

See Also

Infants' Rights: The Baby Doe Case

"Life is far too important a thing ever to talk seriously about."

OSCAR WILDE

the alteration has the potential to be replicated in subsequent generations, therefore resulting in irreversible and cumulative hereditary effects. Although a distinction is currently maintained between somatic cell gene therapy (genetic alteration of nonreproductive bodily tissue) and germ-line gene therapy (genetic modification of the egg or sperm cells, or the early embryo), this boundary is known to be unstable. Considerable ethical concern therefore surrounds the advent of human gene therapy, now practiced in both Great Britain and the United States. (For further discussion, see British Medical Association, 1992.) The release of genetically engineered organisms into the environment, largely in the form of plants and microorganisms, has also attracted controversy, in particular concerning the labeling of foodstuffs and the limits of acceptable risk.

It is the biogenetic definition of life, then, that informs many of the moral debates about the protection of life, whether human, animal, or environmental—the latter category denoting the ecosystem as a complex "living whole." (For a discussion of protecting life as "biodiversity," see Wilson, 1992; also Kellert and Wilson, 1993.) Confusions about when life begins, for example, as in debates about fetal rights, derive from a biogenetic definition of life, which is continuous: each life form has its origin in the lives of those preceding it, and their connectedness underscores the interrelation of life itself. Given such a definition of life, clear demarcations concerning the beginnings and endings of life, of a life, or of life itself are understandably subject to dispute.

Artificial life

New techniques for technologically assisting the creation of life (e.g., assisted conception) and for prolonging life or redesigning life (genetic engineering) add to the difficulties of establishing a clear basis for decision making by health professionals, relatives, policymakers, or legislators. Technology now enables the production, extension, and even redesign of life forms, including humans, animals, plants, and microorganisms. Increasingly sophisticated medical technology has affected both the beginning and the ending of human life. Life-support technologies can artificially sustain human life in the context of severely restricted life functions both at the beginning of life (perinatal support) and toward the end of life, in cases where the individual becomes fully dependent on technology for respiration. Cases of prolonged "vegetative" human existence raise difficult questions as a result of the availability of technologically maintained biological viability. Insofar as a person is more than a biological life, difficult decisions concerning continued treatment for a person who is only minimally alive are the inevitable result of modern technology's capacity to sustain baseline survival functions indefinitely.

Technology also affects the creation of life itself. As medical scientists acquire ever greater command of genetic structure, the question of the ethical acceptability of the creation of life forms such as the Harvard "oncomouse," genetically engineered to develop cancer so it can be used in the design of new drugs for the treatment of human disease, must be addressed. The subject of a major patent dispute in the European Parliament, and removed from the market in 1993 by its manufacturer, DuPont, the oncomouse was among the first higher life forms to be defined as a technology, comparable to other forms of laboratory apparatus. As both a mammal and a scientific instrument, the oncomouse inhabits a domain subject to increasing ethical, commercial, and political controversy (Haraway, 1992).

Most significant, the oncomouse raises the question of ownership of life, which is established as an inviolable right for humans within the liberal democratic tradition and was described by humanist philosopher John Locke as "ownership of one's person." This principle, used in arguments favoring the emancipation of women and the abolition of slavery (both women and slaves being considered chattels), is more recently evident in disputes concerning body parts. In the landmark case of *John Moore* v. *California Regents*, conflict over the use of Moore's body tissue in the design of a drug, through production of an immortal cell line derived from his spleen cells, culminated in a U.S. Supreme Court decision prohibiting the individual ownership of bodily tissue. Ownership of human life in this case was declared not subject to extracorporeal extension.

The question is again different in the case of the "right to life" of the oncomouse, or the "geep," the transspecies hybrid of a goat and a sheep produced through genetic manipulation. Here, the question concerns the deliberate production of a life that brings great suffering to the resultant organism. Only the greater good to humans of such developments can justify their deliberate creation by scientists. But the basis for ethical decision making in such an instance remains indeterminate.

Conclusion

Many of the ethical questions addressed to life itself concern the degree of protection it requires. These questions in turn depend on how life is defined. Whether they concern the beginnings or endings of life, its creation, redesign, or sustenance under technological conditions, the underlying definition of life itself is a fundamental force shaping ethical decision making. Scientifically, life is defined according to the modern life sciences in a biogenetic idiom, which con-

See Also

Reproductive Technologies

Asexual Reproduction: Cloning: 'Hello, Dolly'

structs it as a continuous and connected force unto itself, manifested by the self-replicating properties of DNA. In the liberal humanist tradition, human life is also seen as a possession, and the persistent association of life with sacredness is well established. The rights to life, the protection of life, and the quality of life are extended to some degree to other life forms, on the principle of avoiding cruelty and suffering. In none of these areas are definitive boundaries or limits available upon which to base ethical practice. Instead, as definitions of both life and death are subject to ongoing transformation, so are the ethical frameworks brought to bear on the creation, management, and protection of all life forms.

— SARAH FRANKLIN

LIFE, QUALITY OF

QUALITY OF LIFE IN CLINICAL DECISIONS

Quality of life is one of the most important but controversial issues in clinical ethics. The contemporary development of the concept and its use as a normative criterion in clinical decision making date from the period after World War II, when advances in medical technology increased tremendously. Along with other ethical criteria—for example, a medical indications policy (Meilaender, 1982; Ramsey, 1978; U.S. Department of Health and Human Services, 1985); the ordinary-extraordinary means criterion (Connery, 1986; Johnstone, 1985; Reich, 1978a); or the reasonable person standard (Veatch, 1976)—quality of life is used in conflict situations to help make clinical decisions about whether or not to forgo or to withdraw medical treatment from patients.

Modern medicine has the capacity through the application of technology to save lives that until relatively recently would have been lost to acute disease or accident. As a consequence, some of these lives either are shaped by severe disabilities or chronic illness or continue to exist only at the biological level (for example, infants born with multiple congenital abnormalities; elderly patients who suffer chronic illnesses after recovery from an acute illness; and patients in a persistent vegetative state (PVS). Quality of life is frequently proposed as a criterion in making treatment decisions about these patients, whose lives might be saved only to be lived out in severely impaired conditions.

Quality-of-life considerations arise in several key areas of clinical ethics: termination or shortening of human life, including issues of abortion and euthanasia; limiting human reproduction, such as through contraception, sterilization, or abortion; interventions that alter the genetic and biological nature of humans, such as embryo cloning or eugenic engineering; and public policy areas, including economics, ecology, and cultural development (Reich, 1978a). This article will focus principally on the first issue.

Quality-of-life considerations raise a number of important questions that bear specifically on clinical ethics:

1. Given the tremendous advances in medical technology and the implicit imperative to use it, what are the goals and limits of medicine?
2. What is normatively human, and thus, what is it that we value about life?
3. Are quality-of-life judgments purely subjective, or are there objective criteria that guide them?
4. Can there be a life that is so burdened by pain or disability that it can be judged not worth living?
5. Who should decide to terminate treatment?
6. Is it morally legitimate to include considerations of the patient's prior medical condition in a decision about forgoing future medical interventions? and
7. Is it morally legitimate to include in treatment decisions the potential burdens on affected others who will have to care for a severely handicapped patient?

The following sections will provide some preliminary clarifications and conceptual frameworks for understanding quality of life; define quality of life and identify the spectrum of positions that come under the general heading of this normative criterion; articulate the evaluative status of life that is adopted in the various quality-of-life positions and compare the so-called quality-of-life ethic with the sanctity-of-life ethic; and analyze both the normative dimensions of quality-of-life judgments and the normative theories that justify these judgments.

Preliminary clarifications

Statements or claims about a "quality" or "qualities" of life can be either evaluative or morally normative (Reich, 1978a; Walter, 1988). Evaluative claims or statements indicate that some value or worth is attached either to a characteristic of the person (for example, capacity to choose) or to a type of life that is lived (for example, free of pain and handicap). Thus, evaluative statements assess that the quality, and by implication the life that possesses the quality, is desired, appreciated, or even considered sacred. These

The quality at issue is of the relationship between the patient's medical condition and his ability to pursue human purposes.

PAGE 444

See Also

Infants' Rights: The Baby Doe Case

Cases of prolonged "vegetative" human existence raise difficult questions.

PAGE 442

statements, however, do not establish whether an action to support or to terminate life is morally right or wrong, nor do they specify which action would be morally obligatory. On the other hand, morally normative or prescriptive claims about a quality of life always involve a moral judgment on the valued quality and, by implication, a judgment on the life that possesses the quality. These latter statements, then, not only presume that a quality—for example, cognitive ability—is valued, but they also entail judgments about whether, and under which conditions, one must or ought to protect and preserve a life that possesses the valued quality or qualities. Thus, one could formulate a prescriptive claim that "any life that has cognitive abilities always ought to be given all medical treatment." Evaluative statements about quality of life do bear on clinical decisions, but the more important and controversial issues are concerned with the validity and use of the normative claims about quality of life, especially with regard to patients who lack any ability to participate in the clinical decision.

Many different perspectives could be used in establishing, defending, and assessing evaluative and normative claims in the area of quality of life. A feminist perspective could be used to analyze and critique an evaluative claim that proposes the discursive quality of rationality to be superior to a rationality based on the qualities of affectivity and caring (e.g., Gilligan, 1982; Sichel, 1989). A perspective from the elderly (Kilner, 1988) or the disabled community could be used to assess the normative claim that the qualities of youth, physical beauty, independence, and athletic ability—qualities that are extolled and prized in modern Western culture—are necessary for one to live well. Sociological perspectives could be used to study the cultural patterns of commitment to quality of life (e.g., Gerson, 1976), or legal perspectives to study the jurisprudential implications of these claims on the disabled (e.g., Destro, 1986). Each of these perspectives, and more, would be important to consult in adequately assessing both evaluative and normative claims about quality of life. However, the remainder of this article will use only the philosophical and theological perspectives that have been developed in the literature on quality of life vis-à-vis treatment decisions.

Definitions of quality of life

There is much ambiguity about what "quality of life" means, and consequently there is little agreement about the definition of this criterion. First, there is the word "life." It can refer to two different realities in this context: (1) vital or metabolic processes that could be called "human biological life"; or (2) "human personal life" that includes biological life but goes beyond it to include other distinctively human capacities, for example, the capacity to choose or to think. Anencephalic infants and PVS patients have biological life, but they do not possess human personal life.

◆ **quality**

peculiar and essential character: nature; degree of excellence: grade; a distinguishing attribute: characteristic

Similarly, "quality" can refer to several different realities. Sometimes the word refers to the idea of excellence. So defined, its meaning is bounded only by the horizons of our imaginations and desires. It is difficult to discover any objective criteria to assess quality-of-life judgments under this definition. Consequently, one may fear that patients whose lives cannot achieve the expected level of imagined or desired excellence, such as the handicapped or the dying, will either not be offered any life-sustaining treatment or will be actively killed.

Another possible definition is to understand "quality" as an attribute or property of either biological or personal life. Most proponents of quality of life subscribe to this general definition. Some authors identify quality of life with a single valued property of life, while others identify it with a cluster of valued properties. Thus, this definition represents a spectrum of positions. At one end of the spectrum is the original position of Richard McCormick, who isolated only one quality or attribute to be considered as the minimum for personal life: the potential for human relationships (McCormick, 1974). For McCormick, a Down syndrome baby would possess the potential for human relationships, but an anencephalic infant would not. At the other end of the spectrum, Joseph Fletcher originally defined the indicators of "humanhood" by reference to fifteen positive qualities, among them self-awareness, concern for others, curiosity, and balance of rationality and feeling, and five negative properties, among them, that humans are not essentially parental (Fletcher, 1972). He believed that many, if not all, severely handicapped children would not possess the attributes necessary to live a life of quality. Between these two ends a number of "median" positions exist that identify quality of life with valued properties of life. For example, Earl Shelp has proposed minimal independence as the central property in his quality-of-life position. He includes in this basic property the abilities to relate to others, to communicate, to ambulate, and to perform the basic tasks of hygiene, feeding, and dressing (Shelp, 1986). From this perspective, many, but not all, Down syndrome children would possess the necessary attributes to live a life of quality.

James Walter has suggested that the word "quality" should not primarily refer to a property or attribute of either physical or personal life. Rather, the quality that is at issue is the quality of the relationship that exists between the medical condition of the patient, on the one hand, and the patient's ability to pursue human purposes, on the other. These purposes are understood as the material, social, moral, and spiritual values that transcend physical, biological life. The quality referred to is the quality of a relation and not a property or attribute of life (Walter, 1988). Thus, for patients to judge that they possess a quality of life means that the patients themselves would evaluate that, based on their medical condition, they are able to pursue values important to them at some qualitative or acceptable level.

Evaluative status of life

When quality of life is defined by reference to a property or attribute of physical life, then some basic questions are raised about the value of physical life itself. What is it that we value about our physical lives? Do we value biological existence in and for its own sake, or because of the presence of some property or attribute in that life, for example, cognitive ability? What theological or philosophical justifications can be offered for one's evaluations of life?

Many who define quality of life basically by reference to a property do not attribute intrinsic value to physical life. For example, in some of his writings McCormick has suggested that physical life does not possess inherent value but is a good to be preserved precisely as the condition of other values (McCormick, 1981, 1984). Based on his theological convictions that physical life is a created, limited good and that the ability to relate to others is the mediation of one's love of the divine, McCormick resists attributing to physical life itself the status of an absolute value. Kevin O'Rourke and Dennis Brodeur (1986) have stated that physiological existence as such is not a value if that life lacks any potential for a mental-creative function. Other quality-of-life proponents such as David Thomasma and his colleagues have described physical life as only a conditional value (Thomasma et al., 1986). According to these positions, what is valuable or worthwhile about physical life is either the properties that inhere in life or the values that transcend biological existence but whose pursuit is conditioned on the presence of physical life.

When quality of life is not defined as a property or attribute but rather as a qualitative relation between the patient's medical condition and his or her ability to pursue human values, then a different evaluative status is accorded to physical life. Walter (1988) has argued that physical life, as a created reality, is an ontic value, that is, a true and real value that does not depend on some property to give it value. He has tried to acknowledge that physical life is objectively a value in itself, though it may not always be experienced as such by some patients. Thus, physical life is not simply a useful or negotiable good; on the other hand, neither is it an absolute value that must be preserved in every instance.

Some commentators have attempted to address questions about the evaluative status of life by contrasting the quality-of-life ethic with the sanctity-of-life ethic (e.g., Johnstone, 1985; Reich, 1978b; Weber, 1976). Most proponents of a sanctity-of-life ethic (e.g., Connery, 1986; Johnstone, 1985; Meilaender, 1982; Reich, 1978a) do not argue that physical life itself is an absolute value. In this regard, at least, they agree with all proponents of the quality-of-life ethic. However, these authors frequently claim that when quality of life is understood as a property of life, either no value or only varying degrees of value is accorded to physical life. Possessing no intrinsic worth, physical life must receive its value based on whether it possesses one or more of the valued qualities, for example, neo-cortical function.

The sanctity-of-life position argues that this view is intolerable on several counts. First, quality of life does not acknowledge the equality of physical lives and the equality of persons because it assigns only relative or unequal value to physical lives and persons when certain valued qualities are only partially present or totally absent. Second, quality of life denies that all lives are inherently valuable, and so it leaves open the possibility that some lives can be deemed "not worth living." Finally, it is charged that the quality-of-life position adopts a two-level anthropology committed to protecting physical life only as an instrumental value (Reich, 1978b). Consequently, it is argued that the sanctity-of-life position is far superior because it affirms the equality of life on the basis that physical life is truly a value or good in itself. Life is not merely a useful or negotiable value, dependent on some other intrinsically valuable property.

In conclusion, it is not always clear how useful it may be to contrast sanctity of life with quality of life, as if each position could be represented by an individual and distinct "ethic." Because there are many positions that fit under each one of these "ethics," the terms and results of the comparison really depend on which two positions are selected.

Normative considerations of quality of life

The most important issues related to quality of life in clinical decisions are those concerned with the normative dimensions of the criterion. This level involves several considerations:

1. assessments about what is considered normatively human in making clinical decisions to treat or not to treat;
2. normative moral theory that grounds and justifies moral obligations;

"As a well-spent day brings happy sleep, so life well used brings happy death."

LEONARDO DA VINCI
NOTEBOOKS, 1508–1518

"The time of life is short; To spend that shortness basely were too long."

SHAKESPEARE
KING HENRY IV

L

LIFE, QUALITY OF

Quality of Life in Clinical Decisions

"Death closes all:
but something ere
the end,
Some work of noble
note, may yet be
done,
Not unbecoming
men that strove
with gods."

ALFRED, LORD TENNYSON
ULYSSES, 1842

DECISION POINT
Who Decides When "No One's Home"?

Some authors (e.g., Ramsey, 1978) argue that quality-of-life judgments should never be permitted in treatment decisions for patients who lack decision-making capacity. Only competent patients can make these judgments for themselves; no one may morally substitute his or her quality-of-life judgments for those of someone else. Thus, the moral criterion that applies in treatment decisions for patients who lack decision-making capacity is whatever is medically indicated. However, quality-of-life proponents argue that the medical indications policy could be devastating for these patients. If surrogates do not apply some measure of the quality-of-life criterion, these patients may be condemned to lives of pain, suffering, or burden that no person with decision-making capacity would reasonably choose (Hastings Center, 1987). Most of the following considerations will be concerned with the use of quality-of-life judgments in cases involving patients who lack decision-making capacity.

When some proponents of this criterion define quality of life as a property or attribute that gives value to physical life, they are either implicitly or explicitly defining what is normatively human, that is, how personhood ought to be defined. For example, when Joseph Fletcher originally defined the fifteen positive and five negative indicators of humanhood, he was defining the nature of personhood, and therefore, who is morally entitled to medical care. If a handicapped neonate or adult lacked a number of the indicators of humanhood but needed medical treatment to survive, in Fletcher's view (1972), the patient should not be treated.

— JAMES J. WALTER

3. limits to moral obligations to preserve life, and the moral justifications for these limits.

The first issue is definitional in nature, although it also entails some normative features. The second issue relates to the debate over deontology, which determines the rightness of actions by reference to moral rules or the doing of one's duty, and teleology, which determines moral rightness by reference to the ends or consequences of actions. The third issue involves a discussion of the nature and degree of obligation in moral duties to preserve life.

Before turning to actual positions and their normative implications, it is important to distinguish cases where quality-of-life judgments are made by patients who possess decision-making capacity, and those cases where patients—for example, PVS patients, neonates or severely mentally handicapped adults from birth—lack the capacity to decide. Many issues need to be faced once patients with decision-making capacity are permitted to make treatment choices based on their own assessments of quality of life. However, these problems may pale in comparison to the application of the quality-of-life criterion to situations where a proxy or surrogate must make a decision to terminate treatment.

The moral obligation to treat or not to treat patients is derived from the objective presence or absence of a valued property that gives worth and moral standing to the patient's life. When the properties that define humanhood are absent, the patient is not considered a moral subject who possesses any rights to health care. The moral theory that Fletcher adopts in his quality-of-life position is a form of teleology called consequentialism. In this theory, any moral claim about the value of a patient's life or any moral duty to provide medical treatment is almost entirely based on predictable qualitative consequences for the patient or for others whose interests are involved in the situation.

In a similar position on quality of life, Earl Shelp (1986) has sought to articulate the quality or property that defines the normatively human for handicapped neonates and the extent to which parents and the medical community have moral obligations to these never-competent patients. He adopts a quality-of-life position that corresponds to the main features of a property-based theory of personhood. A property-based theory, as opposed to a genetic-based theory, seeks to designate a desired quality or property that must be present before one can consider a particular human life to be an unqualified member in the moral community.

Shelp has argued that any neonate must possess the possibility of attaining a "minimal independence" before the child can be considered a person in a full sense. If the newborn will never have the capacity of minimal independence, even with the help of modern medicine, then the parents can decide on the basis of quality-of-life considerations that their child, who is in need of medical treatment, should not be treated.

The normative position that underlies Shelp's quality-of-life criterion is a type of a socially weighted calculus. Because he believes that no newborn, whether normal or impaired, is a full member of the moral community (person), he maintains that there is no compelling reason why a severely defective newborn's

See Also
Rights in Bioethics: Is there a "Right to Die"?

interests should take priority over those of the parents or siblings who are already persons in a moral sense. In fact, the interests of the ill newborn can be weighed against the independent interests of those whom the child will affect. Thus, if the burden imposed on others is unreasonable or disproportionate, then a decision to forgo or terminate all treatment for the imperiled child is morally legitimate.

What may be problematic in both Fletcher's and Shelp's versions of quality of life, and certainly what worries all opponents of quality-of-life positions, is that their views appear to define and prescribe the "good life" in terms of the quality or qualities necessary to live a minimal moral existence. Their positions then become entrapped within what William Aiken (1982) has called the "exclusionary" use of quality of life. The lack of certain valued qualities in a patient's life is a way of positively excluding potential patients from the normal standards of medical and moral treatment.

Other versions on the spectrum of quality-of-life positions do not limit the meaning of quality of life merely to a property of life and then establish moral obligations on the basis of the presence or absence of the property. In addition, these positions do not define the normatively human by reference to a valued attribute and then identify it with quality of life. For them, quality of life functions as a way to include what they believe are morally relevant factors in the clinical decision that are often excluded by other criteria. In other words, some proponents of this normative position hold that quality of life is a patient-centered way of discovering the best interests of a patient.

These authors (e.g., Sparks, 1988) argue that in the clinical situation for noncompetent patients, we should be trying to discover what is in their best interests. They recognize that other criteria, such as the ordinary-extraordinary means criterion, have also been used to determine the patient's best interests, and that these criteria have been used to ground moral duties to patients in treatment decisions. However, they argue that these criteria often exclude some morally relevant factors needed to make an adequate and informed moral judgment, for example, the experienced burdens of the patient's prior medical condition in cases of spina bifida.

A comparison of the quality-of-life criterion with the ordinary-extraordinary means criterion might be helpful in illustrating the point that these authors are making. Those who subscribe to the ordinary-extraordinary means criterion argue that all ordinary means of preserving life are morally obligatory, but extraordinary means are morally optional. They do permit surrogates to use what could be called a limited version of the quality-of-life criterion. Surrogates can legitimately include quality-of-life considerations in their treatment decisions, but these considerations are only valid where the treatment itself would cause either excessive harm or leave the patient in a debilitated state (Connery, 1986; Reich, 1978b). For example, a surrogate could morally refuse quadruple amputation because the surgery itself would leave the patient with such an extremely low quality of life that the patient would have no duty to undergo the surgery.

All too often, however, the use of this criterion excludes all quality-of-life considerations that cannot be directly connected to the treatment itself or to its application. For example, the fact that a child who is born with Lesch-Nyhan syndrome will have a very poor quality of life is not considered relevant in the clinical decision to treat the child for a life-threatening condition. Lesch-Nyhan is an incurable genetic disease that causes its victims to suffer uncontrollable spasms and mental retardation. Once the young patients of this disease develop teeth, they gnaw their hands and shoulders, and they often bite off a finger or mutilate other parts of their bodies.

Some proponents of the quality-of-life criterion (e.g., McCormick, 1986; Sparks, 1988) identify this criterion with the category of "patient's best interests." They adopt what they believe is a patient-centered, teleological assessment of the best interests of the patient. If a patient in a life-threatening condition does possess at least a minimal ability to relate to others, then it can be presumed that the patient would want treatment; thus, treatment should be provided. This form of the quality-of-life criterion maintains that physical life itself is the ground of a prima facie duty to preserve it.

However, other factors—for example, the patient's prior medical condition, which might include permanent loss of all sentient and cognitive abilities, or the financial cost to the family and society of caring for these patients—also come to bear in determining the actual moral duty these patients have to preserve their own lives. Proponents of this version of the criterion argue that medical interventions to continue the lives of accurately diagnosed PVS patients and neonates born with anencephaly or hydranencephaly are unwarranted. These patients have reached the limits of their moral obligations to preserve their own lives, based on an assessment of their best interests. Any medical intervention to save their lives would only perpetuate a condition that most people who possess decision-making capacity would judge burdensome and intolerable. These authors do not judge that some patients' lives are not worth living; however, they do argue that the experienced burdens on patients' lives prior to treatment must be considered in determining

Some hold that quality of life is a patient-centered way of discovering the best interests of a patient.

PAGE 447

"Do not go gentle into that good night,
Old age should burn and rave at close of day;
Rage, rage against the dying of the light."

DYLAN THOMAS
DO NOT GO GENTLE INTO THAT GOOD NIGHT, 1952

L

LIFE, QUALITY OF

Quality of Life in Clinical Decisions

"I can resist everything except temptation."

OSCAR WILDE
LADY WINDERMERE'S FAN, 1892

QUALITY OF LIFE
Caring at Any Cost?

One of the more difficult questions involved in the debate over the use of quality-of-life judgments is whether one can include in the assessment of best interests of the patient any of the burdens that accrue to affected others. For example, when a family must face the tragic situation of financially and psychologically caring for a severely handicapped child, many would find such a lifelong commitment quite burdensome. Must one discount in treatment decisions the burdens experienced by the family and society in caring for these children, and focus only on the burdens imposed on the child either by the disease or by the treatments themselves? Or is it morally legitimate to include at least some of the burdens imposed on the family and society in assessing the patient's best interests? In other words, how broadly should one interpret the category of "best interests of the patient"? And finally, should the interests of others be considered in their own right? These are some of the questions that the proponents of quality of life regularly ask in clinical situations.

— JAMES J. WALTER

the patient's best interests, and thus whether the patient himself or herself has a moral obligation to preserve life.

Richard Sparks (1988) is critical of any position that tries to understand the proportionality of benefits and burdens in a way that weighs a severely handicapped child's claims against the interests, claims, and rights of others who are affected, whether within the family or in society. He is also critical of quality-of-life proponents like McCormick, whom he sees as too narrowly defining the range of burdens in these cases. Sparks suggests the phrase "total best interests" as a way not only of including the burden experienced by the patient but also of including the broader social factors, for example, the financial cost, psychic strain, and inconvenience borne by others. He reasons that the patient's social nature must be taken into account, not only in calculating benefits (for example, the benefit to the patient derived from his or her ability to relate to others), but also in calculating burdens (for example, psychic strain to the family or financial cost to society).

Sparks's version of the quality-of-life criterion rejects a socially weighted calculus similar to the one Shelp adopts in determining the best interests of the patient. He judges that such a calculus denies the inherent worth of each individual patient, and that it weighs the benefits and burdens experienced by the patient against those of affected others. Although he argues that the burden to others should be included in assessing the total best interests of the patient, this burden is only one factor among many that must be considered. What is essential is that one not construe the burden to the patient and the burden to affected others as being in competition with one another when making decisions to terminate medical treatment.

By trying to construe the social burdens from the patient's perspective, Sparks believes one can avoid the competitive atmosphere that is part of the socially weighted position. His version of quality of life seems to imply that the child would not, and perhaps should not, want to be treated if it were an excessive social burden because the child's best interests would not be served if these burdens were placed on those who must care for him or her.

The spectrum of definitions and positions representing quality of life makes it difficult to identify any one quality-of-life ethic for analysis or critique. Though there are some shared features among the various positions, in the end it is necessary to assess the validity or invalidity of each position on its own merits.

— JAMES J. WALTER

"If the physician presumes to take into consideration in his work whether a life has value or not, the consequences are boundless and the physician becomes the most dangerous man in the state."

ATTRIBUTED TO CHRISTOPH HUFELAND IN
FREDRIC WERTHAM
A SIGN FOR CAIN 1968

LIFESTYLES AND PUBLIC HEALTH

The people of every nation would be healthier if they adopted healthier lifestyles. Ninety percent of those who die of lung cancer would not have contracted the disease if they had not smoked. Exercise, sensible diet, and compliance with treatment for high blood pressure can, and do, prevent countless episodes of cardiovascular disease. Practicing safe sex reduces the risk of contracting AIDS. Use of seat belts and motorcycle helmets lowers the chance of injury from accidents on the road.

The prospect of improving health and reducing illness through changes in living habits rather than through curative health care is attractive on a number of grounds. Since it is preventive, it avoids the distress of disease; side effects and iatrogenic consequences may be fewer; cost may be lower; and the healthier ways of living may be rewarding in their own right. For these reasons, any government that failed to promote healthy lifestyles could be faulted on ethical grounds.

Nevertheless, the encouragement of healthier

lifestyles has drawn moral criticism in the literatures of bioethics and health policy. The chief concern is that governmental (and even private) attempts to bring about changes in living habits will encroach on personal liberty or privacy. A second complaint is that lifestyle-change programs may have the wrong motives, and may have undesirable social and psychological effects.

Health versus liberty

INTERVENTION: WHAT JUSTIFICATION? Nearly everything we do affects health in some way, if only because the time spent could be devoted to exercise or other health-enhancing behavior. The notion of unhealthy lifestyles, however, is typically associated with a small number of habits. Smoking, the leading killer in the United States, always takes first place, closely followed by alcohol and other drug abuse, lack of exercise, and being overweight. Other risk factors affected by individual choice veer toward the medical, including behavioral change intended to control serum cholesterol and hypertension, perhaps including compliance with doctors' orders. Construed still more broadly, a "healthy lifestyle" would include living in a region not plagued by pollution or recurring natural disasters; avoidance of unsafe jobs; and purchasing the safest cars and appliances.

Attempts to change unhealthy behavior through education and exhortation are relatively unproblematic from the moral point of view. But these measures are less likely to be effective than programs that seek to influence behavior more directly through penalties, taxes, restrictions, or prohibitions. These, however, involve or border on coercion, and in some cases, as with sexual behavior, they necessarily intrude into a person's most private domains.

The fact that good health may be valued by every person does not by itself justify these interventions, since for some people the health risks seem to be less important than the benefits derived from the risk-taking behavior. Few would seriously assert that eating rich ice cream or smoking falls within the category of fundamental human rights, but each encroachment on individual autonomy is commonly regarded as standing in need of justification, especially in the United States, which has a cultural history marked by an ideology of individualism. Three kinds of justification have been offered for programs aiming to change lifestyles: (1) paternalist concern for the person's good; (2) protection of others from burdens involuntarily imposed by the risk-taking behavior; and (3) the public's stake in the nation's health.

PATERNALIST JUSTIFICATIONS. In the United States, paternalist justifications are rarely provided as such. Though exceptions and counterexamples abound, lip service is still paid to the tradition of John Stuart Mill's *On Liberty.* It is easier to argue for motorcycle helmet laws as a means of reducing the costs of medical care than as a means of protecting human life, despite the greater importance of the latter. When paternalism is explicitly defended, however, it is usually on the grounds that the choices the paternalistic policy prohibits are not fully voluntary ones: Bad habits, such as smoking and overeating, may be sustained by addiction or genetic predisposition. This "soft" paternalism avoids the need to argue for the "hard" paternalist view that even fully voluntary choices may be overruled if the state concludes that the individual might benefit.

For many unhealthy habits, the argument that the behavior is not fully voluntary is easy to make. The individual choice may be determined by chemical, psychological, or social causes. Once a person is addicted to nicotine, it is extremely difficult to stop smoking, as millions of unhappy smokers know; the same holds true for alcoholics and those addicted to legal or illegal drugs. The original decision to try cigarettes, alcohol, or drugs is often made during adolescence, when the individual's ability to resist peer pressure is typically weak.

Nevertheless, the soft paternalist argument faces a number of objections. Not all unhealthy choices are obviously involuntary. The decision to engage in unprotected sex, for example, may be the result of partner coercion, or inner compulsion or denial, but it may also stem from the individual's dislike of condoms or not having a condom. Moreover, even the person whose behavior is shaped by an addiction may be capable of deciding to seek professional help in breaking the addiction. The decision to forgo seeking help, a "second-order" choice about choice, is not necessarily rendered involuntary by the "first-order" addiction. In these instances, paternalistic intervention will be of the hard variety, which involves the authorities acting on the principle that their goals for the individual should be imposed on the individual's own goals.

Intervention aimed at altering lifestyle choices on paternalist grounds may overemphasize the goal of health at the expense of other goals. If the paternalist justification is strongest when the unhealthy choices are least voluntary, these may also be the occasions when the choices are most difficult to influence, and the degree of coercion required may be objectionable in itself. Smokers subjected to very high excise taxes, for example, may suffer from the taxes without giving up cigarettes. Finally, the behavior in question may be difficult to change without considerable meddling in the individual's culture and milieu, whether these champion "wine, women, and song," or risk taking and violence, or quiet (and unathletic) contemplation. The life

"I believe every human has a finite number of heartbeats. I don't intend to waste any of mine running around doing exercises."

NEIL ARMSTRONG

"Abstinence is as easy to me as temperance would be difficult."

SAMUEL JOHNSON

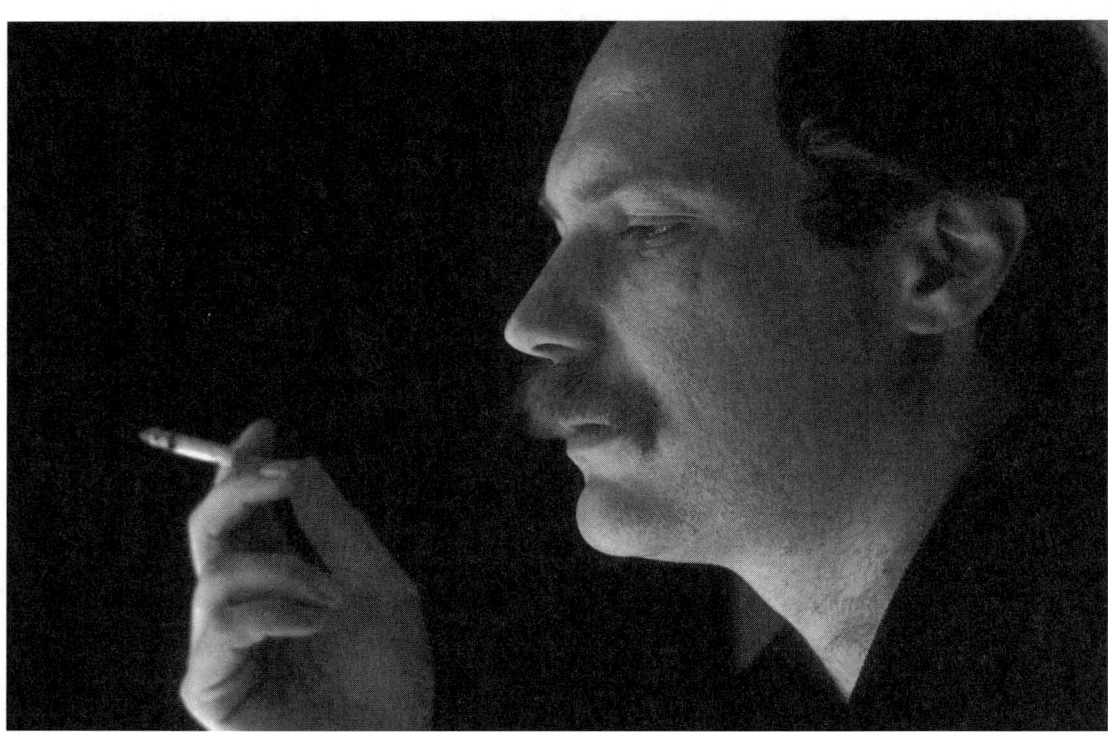

HEALTH vs. LIBERTY

A government would be negligent to not promote healthier lifestyles, but in doing so it risks encroaching on personal freedoms and privacy.

of the fitness-loving moderate is not for everyone, even if it is most conducive to long life and good health.

FAIR DISTRIBUTION OF BURDENS. Mill's principle of liberty sought to limit intervention to the protection of others from the effects of one's own actions; "self-regarding" behavior is thus the domain of the individual, while others have a say in the regulation of "other-regarding" behavior. Critics have long noted that the boundary is indistinct; nearly everything we do has effects on others. Sexual behavior, the most private of acts, is not at all self-regarding in the era of the AIDS epidemic. And since few people pay all their health-care bills out of pocket, any behavior that necessitates care will impose a financial burden on other parties.

If these behavioral choices are to be protected, they will have to find some shelter other than Mill's principle. In the case of AIDS, an argument might be made that intrusive regulation would violate a right of privacy, where "private" does not mean "self-regarding" (AIDS transmission is anything but that) but "intimate" or "personal." This right might not be defensible in light of the seriousness of the AIDS epidemic, however; and in any case, other unhealthy habits and choices—for example, smoking, which incurs risks to others through passive smoke inhalation—fall outside of this personal zone. Since there is no general right of liberty when our choices affect the lives of others, the individual's prerogative to maintain unhealthy practices must be decided on other grounds.

> "To the average cigarette smoker the world is his ashtray."
>
> ALEXANDER CHASE
> PERSPECTIVES, 1966

Paternalist arguments aim at justifying interventions that seek to curb unhealthy behavior. Arguments that point to the burden of unhealthy behavior for other people, however, may or may not share this aim. They may indeed seek to justify curbs on the behavior in order to forestall the imposition of burdens. But this can also be accomplished by requiring the individual to pay his or her own way, perhaps through excise taxes, without any diminution of the unhealthy behavior. Finally, the individual whose choices result in illness may be made to pay for his or her own health care, or to forfeit any claim on the resources of others, or, at the least, to be placed at the end of the line when resources are scarce.

These steps represent a particular understanding of distributive justice. They seek to impose the true costs of choices on the one who chooses, so that these costs will be taken into account at the moment of choice. Those who believe that the welfare state should assist its citizens in meeting their basic needs, in this view, should not regard all needs as equal. Unhealthy lifestyles create avoidable needs, and individuals should be held responsible for these choices. Those who refuse to take care of themselves, in this view, forfeit at least some of the liberties (to individual choice) and the entitlements (to help, on an equal footing, in time of need) that others deserve.

As with the paternalist justification for intervention in lifestyle choices, this argument concerning the fair sharing of burdens faces a number of objections. One might argue that distinguishing between patients with similar health-care needs on the basis of personal responsibility for illness introduces a concept of fault more at home in the legal world than in the system of health care. Treating all patients according to need, without regard to such factors as status, ability to pay, or fault, is a powerful way of affirming the importance of those aspects of people in virtue of which they are equal, relative to those that divide, distinguish, and rank us. This equality is important both to us as patients and to doctors and other health-care providers, whose first instinct should be compassionate response to human suffering.

On more technical grounds, the burden-sharing argument rests the case for intervention into unhealthy lifestyles on the outcome of an economic calculation: that the habit in question incurs a net cost. The problem is that those who die prematurely because of unhealthy habits avoid burdening others with the cost of maintaining them in their old age. Economists have long debated whether smokers burden others or relieve others of a financial burden of care; the answer may vary by country, depending on such variables as the cost of health care and the cost of living. If there are places in which smokers actually save society money, the burden-sharing argument would entail penalties for those who do not smoke.

Care must be taken, moreover, in stating the burden-sharing argument. Insurance, including health insurance, protects against risk, but it also can make risk taking less unwise. Those Americans who play football, for example, can regard America's health-care system as a partial safety net; the sport would be too dangerous for many without it. In this light, the burden-sharing argument might succeed in justifying special and higher insurance premiums for risk takers, but unless the risk takers refused to pay these fees, it would not justify curbs on the actual risk taking. Even the special fees would be unjustified if there were rough equivalence in the degree of risk taken by a large number of coinsureds, one person's motorcycle riding offsetting another's sedentary library dwelling.

PUBLIC HEALTH. The third justification for intervention on behalf of healthier lifestyles points to the collective health of the public as a common good. In material terms, a healthy population enhances economic productivity and the nation's capacity to defend itself. General health also provides some degree of protection from the spread of infectious disease. Theorists of public health have contended, moreover, that the "public health," meaning the sum of each person's health, constitutes a further goal of public policy that can be distinguished from both the paternalist and the burden-sharing arguments.

Another feature of the public-health perspective is the "prevention paradox," the observation that many critical prevention policies affecting lifestyles produce large aggregate savings in lives but little demonstrable benefit to each individual. For example, seat-belt policies may save thousands of lives nationally but only marginally reduce the risk for each individual who drives. Similarly, changes in fat intake will strongly reduce the number who die prematurely from heart disease but affect the chances of each individual only slightly.

The prevention paradox thus arises from the fact that even small changes in the behaviors of tens of millions of individuals involved in low to moderate lifestyle risks avert thousands of deaths. The prevention paradox further underscores the emphasis in public health on rates of disease and deaths averted, and the difficulty of producing mass changes in behaviors through voluntary measures alone.

Far more important than the government's stake in a healthy work force is the centuries-old tradition of governmental responsibility to protect the health and safety of the public, construed as a public or common good. The public-health perspective is rooted in the democratic and constitutional tradition of assigning to elected officials and members of executive agencies responsibilities for protecting the common good, where this has been interpreted by courts as involving the protection of health and safety (and morals as well, which accounts for the long entanglement of public health and moralism). The public-health or regulatory power of government has long been justified on the grounds that reasonable restrictions on liberty and property, as weighed by the legislature, to promote the common good are the very essence of the regulatory power. This tradition is rooted in theories of government and the duties of citizens that antedate the rise of concerns with paternalism and Mill's famous essay.

Motives and effects of intervention programs

The preceding discussion of arguments for intervention in unhealthy lifestyles has taken the arguments at face value. Critics, however, have suggested that the real motivations for these policies are usually unannounced. The actual motivation, in this view, is moral—or, to be more precise, moralistic, proceeding from a rarely examined and rarely defended set of moral premises. Once these are made explicit, according to the critics, both the motive and the policies are rendered less attractive.

One sign that lifestyle intervention has a moralistic motive, according to critics, is the selectivity of targets. Many kinds of behavior have negative health effects that are not equally addressed. Promiscuity, lack of exercise, and overweight are merely the medieval vices of lust, sloth, and gluttony. These habits have negative effects on health, to be sure; but so do other kinds of

"The only way to get rid of a temptation is to yield to it."

OSCAR WILDE
THE PICTURE OF DORIAN GRAY, 1891

"Preserving the health by too severe a rule is a wearisome malady."

LA ROCHEFOUCAULD,
MAXIMS, 1665

behavior not viewed as vices. Childbirth, for example, presents a certain level of risk to every woman and a decided risk for some; but because it is socially approved, there is no thought of penalizing, taxing, or discouraging the behavior. The burden-sharing argument presents itself as a neutral act of accounting; but, in the critics' view, it is actually concerned with the costs of behavior deemed undesirable on moral grounds while it tolerates behavior of which it approves, no matter how costly.

The moral perspective from which lifestyle intervention is urged, moreover, has been criticized as "healthism," a parochial view that elevates health from a self-interested goal to a virtue. In this light, "personal responsibility for health" stems not from the need to avoid burdening others with the costs of one's care but from the conviction that healthy people (at least, those who choose health) are better people, morally speaking. This perspective is also said to be linked to an ideology that emphasizes the degree to which one's state of health is a function of choices one makes, rather than the whims of nature or the safety of one's environment and workplace.

"The trouble about always trying to preserve the health of the body is that it is so difficult to do without destroying the health of the mind."

G. K. CHESTERTON
ON THE CLASSICS, 1930

One of the most frequent complaints about the lifestyle debate is that it is used to "blame the victim" and undercut the justification for collective action. Thus, those who wish to restrict in various ways the availability of alcohol or tobacco, to limit overall use of these risky products, meet counterclaims that these are not problems of regulation but of individual responsibility and education. The advocates for regulation, in effect challenging the motivation of this view, argue that their opponents do not really want to see a well-financed campaign against smoking and drinking but want no official action at all. Instead, they want wider acceptance of the view that these are problems that will be resolved only when people take more responsibility for their own health and safety.

Conclusion

Though this entry has dwelt on the difficulties in making a convincing case for intervening in unhealthy lifestyles, the collective weight of such lifestyles should not be exaggerated. Much of the bioethical literature on lifestyles indicates that the choices posing the greatest problem for public-health authorities are those which involve personal or intimate behavior, are entirely self-regarding, and represent fully voluntary behavior. Little in our behavioral repertoire falls in this narrowly defined category, however, and those who wish to pursue this promising avenue to health can enter the argument on an even footing.

— DANIEL WIKLER
DAN E. BEAUCHAMP

"Love is only a dirty trick played on us to achieve the continuation of the species."

W. SOMERSET MAUGHAM

LOVE

Love is a disposition of the self that manifests in solicitude for the welfare of the other, and usually a delight in his or her presence. It is a curbing of the self-centered tendency and a transfer of interests to another for his or her own sake, on the basis of the other's positive properties or existence per se.

Love is not always distinguished from care, but such a distinction may be argued for. To care is to be neither indifferent nor unconcerned; something does matter and therefore cannot be treated apathetically (Ruddick, 1990; Gilligan, 1982). To love is to champion the other's interests with the anxiety of care deepened and intensified. Love does not necessarily require radical self-denial, but it may. Its controlling motive must always be the good of others, so that unselfishness replaces selfishness.

This article considers the foundational debates about love, and relevant issues in bioethics.

Foundational debates

A first debate distinguishes love based on some perceived positive attribute in the other from love based on value bestowed by the lover. The former love is reason dependent, that is, X can provide property-based reasons for loving Y. The attractive properties of the object account for the presence of love and determine its longevity (Soble, 1990). Critics of a strictly property-based love believe that it leaves love too insecure, since the properties for which X loves Y may disappear, or X may no longer perceive them as attractive. They therefore introduce a love of bestowal, or a nonappraising love. While a wholly nonappraisive love may be foreign to human nature, any love worthy of the word requires a security or commitment that goes beyond strictly appraisive categories (Singer, 1987).

A closely related debate concerns whether love is an acquisitive desire seeking the agent's good or a benevolent one seeking the other's good (Hazo, 1967). Acquisitive tendencies include desires for food, drink, possessions, and merely instrumental relations with others, such as, sexual relations without care or commitment. Some contend that strictly acquisitive love is not really love at all, because it implies indifference to the other's welfare except as a means to self-gratification, that is, as a means of acquiring a good for the self, with benevolence never a controlling motive. For love to be genuinely present, assisting and protecting the other must be the controlling motive. Love and indifference to the other's good are incompatible. Good for the self, while not controlling, can acceptably remain as a motive, for instance, personal satisfaction in caring, moral development, mutuality (as in friendship), gratification, or social recognition. Thus did the eighteenth-century British moralists such as Francis Hutcheson and Joseph Butler insist that benevolence is perfectly coincident with self-love. The property-based love considered above can be benevolent, as in the compassion of friendship.

A third debate concerns the desire for reciprocity. Giving and receiving love is characteristic of friendship, marriage, and other forms of companionate love. Søren Kierkegaard (1962), in order to test the selflessness of love's motivation, rejected these spheres of reciprocity, and stated that the highest form of love is love for the dead, since surely they cannot reciprocate. In contrast with Kierkegaard, mutuality of love, even if asymmetrical, can be viewed as essential for reliable expectations regarding the conduct of the others, as necessary for predictable relationships, and as reinforcing benevolence (Becker, 1986). Insofar as love involves giving as well as receiving, "Love lives not only from the ecstasy of fulfillment, but from a loyalty not yet fulfilled" (Daniel Day Williams, 1968, p. 14). Even love for the stranger, while it should not require a response in kind, should never refuse such response (Toner, 1968). Yet love can exist unrequited.

A fourth debate concerns the order of love (*ordo caritatis*), that is, the balance of love for friends and family (special relations) with love for the stranger. With respect to Christian ethics, for example, while Augustine could easily accept special relations in his order of love, "The agapic normative tradition represented by Outka and exemplified in the extreme by Kierkegaard is very uneasy about special relations" (Purvis, 1991, p. 19). Theological debate juxtaposes two opposing approaches: In the first, particular and special relations "function as a sign of and call toward a love more universal in scope"; In the second, we begin with "universal love—true charity—and justify particular loves, if at all, on the basis of Christian love in the fullest sense" (Meilaender, 1987, p. 22).

Bernard Williams (1973) has argued against the impartiality of utilitarianism, for it creates a rift between moral obligations and heartfelt personal commitments. He thinks this rift violates the "integrity" of the moral agent. In a number of religious and philosophical traditions, particular and exclusive forms of love are haunted by the requirement of radical universal love. But in recent decades, "special relations" and reciprocities have increasingly been recognized in philosophical and religious ethics as having moral value. No moral calculus indicates the proper balance between love for those near and dear, and love for strangers. However, love for humanity should never be eclipsed by proximate ties.

Finally, there is debate about the extent to which love requires self-denial. Clearly love requires the abrogation of selfishness, but it is a mistake to confuse the valid ideal of unselfishness with selflessness, its invalid exaggeration (Saiving, 1979). Selflessness violates the reasonably reciprocal structures of most social existence, and obscures the extent to which self-concern or care for the self is necessary for love of the other to be sustained in commitment. Moreover, selflessness is questionable because it invites exploitation of the moral agent and fails to correct the other's harmful behavior (Outka, 1972). Feminism, psychology, philosophy, and theology increasingly converge on this point. Analysis of intermediate norms between self-preference and radical self-denial, such as parity, other-preference, and self-subordination is imperative.

GOING OUR WAY

Love—as elusive of strict definition as the meaning of life—gives philosophers of ethics no end of varieties and subtleties to explore.

Love and bioethics

LOVE FOR HUMANITY. While some have suggested that love for humanity is an unrealistic ideal, or even a way of obscuring a failure to love those who are near (Camus, 1991), it remains a moral ideal in most traditions. Insofar as the moral idealism of universal love is absent from society, it may be true that love is relegated to the private sphere due to masculine thinking that associates public life with greatness in the form of self-assertion (Bologh, 1990). Love for humanity can be property based if grounded in some universal aspect of persons, such as the Stoic notion of reason or the Judaeo-Christian concept of the self as being in the image of God. It can also be interpreted as a love of bestowal, especially when human capacities dim.

"Love is sweet, but tastes best with bread."

YIDDISH PROVERB

Beginning with the Hellenistic age, Greek antiquity developed the norm of *philanthropia*, referring to a generous hospitality even to the stranger. One Hip-

L

LOVE

Love and Bioethics

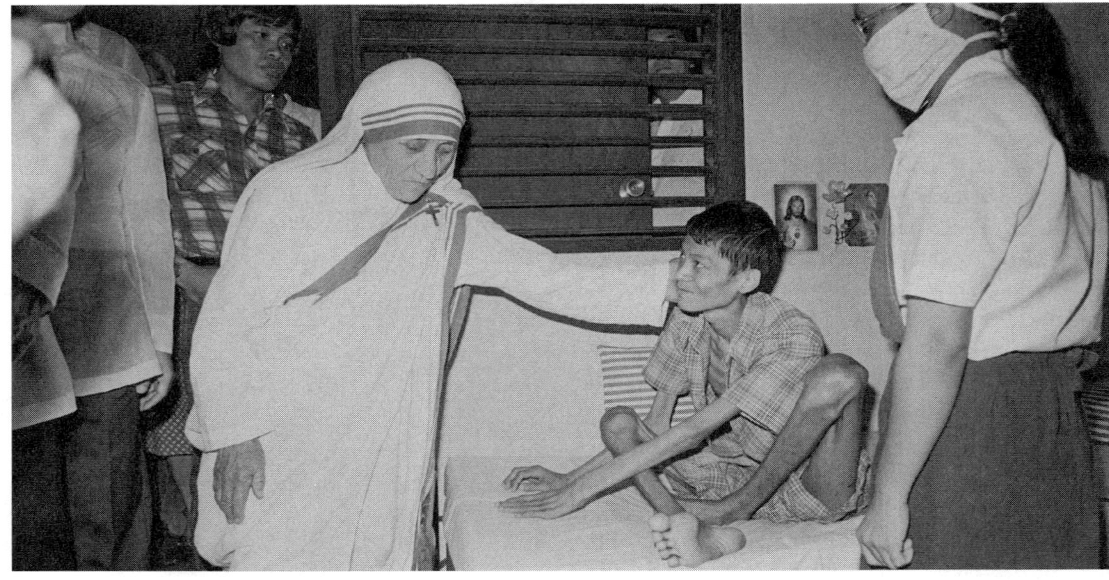

SOUL OF COMPASSION

Around the world, many regard Mother Teresa of Calcutta as the ultimate Good Samaritan—the embodiment of love in action.

pocratic precept is "Where there is love of humanity [*philanthropia*], there is love of medical science." Influenced by the demands of Stoic ethics, the physician is to assist "even aliens who lack resources" (Temkin, 1991, p. 32). The ideal of love for humanity is found among the Stoics, Cynics, Pythagoreans, Hellenized Jews, and early Christian theologians, where *philanthropia* was often used interchangeably with *agape*, the New Testament Greek word for love of humanity (Ferguson, 1959). There is debate over the extent to which the Hippocratic notion of *philanthropia* is indebted to early Eastern Christianity, and vice versa.

"[The poor] don't need pity, they need love and compassion."

MOTHER TERESA

It is not clear whether the commandment in Leviticus to "Love your neighbor as yourself" originally applied to Jews only or to non-Jews as well (Lev. 19:18). However, in medieval Judaism it was certainly applied to the non-Jew, as is clear in the writings of the rabbi-physician Moses Maimonides. "Love thy neighbor as thyself" is central to Jewish medical ethics (Green, 1982). In Christianity, building on Judaism, the practice of medicine was profoundly influenced by the story of the Good Samaritan, who assisted a wounded stranger by the roadside (Luke 10:33-34). After three centuries of persecution, Christians opened hospitals and made care of the sick an expression of love. Christians were unusually heroic in the leprosarium. It is argued that Christianity gave rise to a decisive change in attitude toward the sick, who now even assumed what may be described as a preferential position (Sigerist, 1943). Mother Teresa, awarded the Nobel Peace Prize in 1979, has devoted her exemplary life to love for the homeless and sick strangers on the streets of Calcutta. It has been suggested that a postmodern moral philosophy could gain much through a recovery of the saintly examples of "compassion, generosity, and self-sacrifice" (Wyschogrod, 1990). The story of the Good Samaritan continues to spur voluntary caring in American culture (Wuthnow, 1991).

The story of the Good Samaritan and the requirement that all Christians assist the sick and those in need disinterestedly (Matt. 25:35-46) deeply shaped Western medical culture. A classic expression of love ethics is that of the seventeenth-century physician Sir Thomas Browne, for whom the foundation of all medical virtue "is love for God, for whom we love our neighbor. For this, I think, is charity, to love God for Himself and our neighbor for God" (Browne, 1966, p. 98). Religious women in the United States, from the Sisters of Charity to the Sisters of Mercy, nursed the sick and opened numerous hospitals. During the Civil War and various nineteenth-century epidemics, the actions of these nurses won the respect of American society. Lutheran deaconesses and Episcopalian sisters also engaged in nursing ministry (Stepsis and Liptak, 1989). A contemporary physician writes that the virtue of charity, that is, "benevolent self-effacement," shapes "the whole of medical morals" (Pellegrino, 1989).

An ethics of love for humanity implies that health-care professions in the past were driven by moral idealism at least as much as by self-interest. Universal love generally does not require radical self-denial, nor an abandonment of familial and other proximate forms of love, although on some occasions it may. The health-care professional has a duty to be self-concerned, even as a necessary condition for being able to serve others. Since no exactness is possible in determining the right symmetry among self-love, neighbor love, and love for family and friends, considerable latitude must be allowed for individual conscience. A simple assertion of physician self-effacement without attention to some general symmetry and competing obligations is inadequate.

Universal love may imply justice according to need (Childress, 1985). A summary of the contemporary Protestant literature concludes that love requires "at least a basic provision of medical care" (Bouma et al., 1989, p. 162). Gene Outka (1974) contends that universal love overlaps with theories of justice according to need. Love may require that basic human needs be met, regardless of the recipient's productivity, merit, or contribution to society as measured by a utilitarian calculus. Human beings as such, regardless of their resources and achievements, deserve adequate health care to remove them as much as is possible from suffering.

PREFERENTIAL LOVE. One form of preferential love is romantic love. This includes an intense longing for union with the other, profound physiological arousal, aesthetic attraction, desire for reciprocity, degrees of benevolence, and some idealization of the beloved. There is a general condemnation of romantic love between physicians and patients. Leon Kass, drawing on the notion of purity in the Hippocratic oath and tradition, believes that the role of the physician is antithetical to that of the sensual lover, that "medical and erotic gazing" must be kept separate lest the patient be manipulated and abused in the midst of bodily exposure and vulnerability (1985). The weight of medical tradition supports this view, as does ethical concern with respect for patients. The American Medical Association concurs: "Sexual or romantic interactions between physicians and patients detract from the goals of the physician-patient relationship, may obscure the physician's objective judgment concerning the patient's health care, and ultimately may be detrimental to the patient's well-being" (1992, p. 40).

Kant noted that in romantic love and sexual relations, the "appetite for another human being" can be harmful, for through sexual appetite one human being often plunges another into "the depths of misery," casting him or her aside "as one casts away a lemon which has been sucked dry" (1963, p. 163). Similarly, feminists have long regarded romantic love with moral suspicion. At the end of the eighteenth century, Mary Wollstonecraft wrote that girls are inculcated with the coercive assumption that their happiness and fulfillment depend on romantic love, love that is inevitably fleeting and that diverts women's attention from education and other, more lasting goods. After a man falls out of love, a woman has little to depend on professionally, and no self-reliance (Wollstonecraft, 1975). Wollstonecraft described preoccupation with delicacy and beautification as slavishness. Germaine Greer writes in the tradition of Wollstonecraft: "Love, love, love—all the wretched cant of it, masking egotism, lust, masochism, fantasy under a mythology of sentimental postures . . ." (1971, p. 165). Psychoanalyst Karen Horney (1934) writes of the obsession with romantic love that hinders women's self-realization in work and achievement, resulting in an emptiness that increases with age. Feminist literary critics have condemned fairy tales that present figures, such as Sleeping Beauty, fulfilled through the romantic kiss of a prince.

A more sympathetic interpretation is that romantic love has allowed women to become the objects of devotion, thus providing them with "an inherent value that had not existed in the ancient world," as well as a degree of equality and a freedom to love the man of choice (Singer, 1987, p. 12). Romantic love can be viewed positively as a context for compassion and benevolence, and as a precursor to what psychologists call companionate love. Elaine Hatfield maintains that romantic love often evolves into companionate love, "the affection we feel for those with whom our lives are deeply entwined" (1988, p. 205). Irving Singer holds that the romantic "falling in love" can lead to the more stable "being in love," followed by companionate or marital love. Psychiatrists have interpreted romantic love both negatively, as delusional overvaluation and the result of the self's inadequacies, and positively, as a source of meaning in life (Frankl, 1984). Willard Gaylin (1986) and others who find such meaning are highly critical of any theorists who justify sex without love, or who reduce sex to discussions of technique.

Another form of preferential love is companionate love. It is associated in the psychological literature with enjoyment, acceptance, commitment, trust, respect, mutual assistance, confiding, understanding, and spontaneity. A study of couples married fifteen years or more indicates that the most common explanation of longevity is "My spouse is my best friend" (Davis, 1985). The word "companion" derives from the Latin ("with bread"), referring to the fellowship between those who share a meal. Companionate love can include marital love, friendship, and the affection between those bound together by common experiences. It differs from universal love because it is preferential and directed only toward those who are known. In moral philosophy the importance of friendship has been rediscovered. Friendship has been interpreted as a locus for the expression of sympathy, compassion, and a willingness to sacrifice that goes beyond ordinary expectations (Blum, 1980).

American medical ethics since the 1970s has tended to devalue companionate love as a model for the physician-patient relationship. The more adversarial approach may be partly explained by the beginnings of contemporary medical ethics in concern over abu-

"As blood is to the body, prayer is to the soul."

MOTHER TERESA

"Ours is a humble service. We try to remain right down on the ground."

MOTHER TERESA
INTERVIEW, 1975

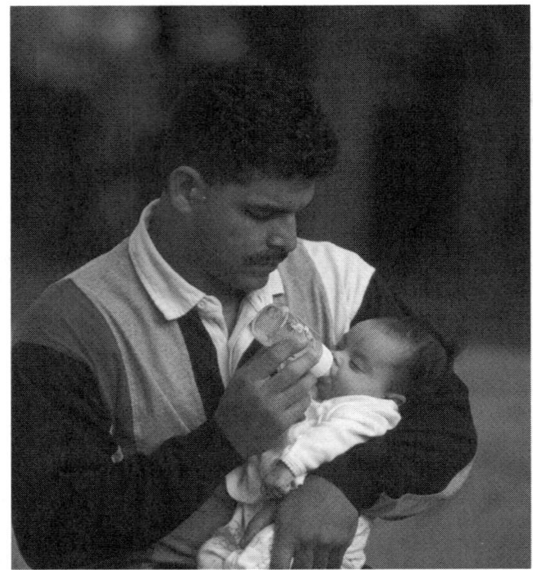

GIVING CARE

Some philosophers see parental love as a primary source of the child's moral behavior later in life.

sive human experimentation (Rothman, 1991). If that is true, American medical ethics has roots in the image of physicians at their worst, which leads directly to the assumption that patients must be protected from their doctors. In many cases patients need protection, especially from those who might want to justify unjustifiable coercion with an appeal to "friendly" motives.

The modern health-care system treats the patient anonymously, and allows little opportunity for the trust of friendships to develop. But more centrally, the friendship model is suspect on the grounds that it inherently threatens patient autonomy, that is, has paternalistic tendencies (Veatch, 1985). The friendship model is judged "psychologically oppressive," and the satisfaction of even authentic patient desire for friendship is wrong because "its satisfaction would diminish autonomy" (Illingworth, 1988).

"The power our loved ones have over us is almost always greater than the power we have over ourselves."

LA ROCHEFOUCAULD
MAXIMS, 1665

In contrast with many American medical ethicists, the Spanish historian of medicine and ethics Pedro Laín Entralgo highlights the central importance of friendship for the physician-patient relationship: "Rather than a provision of technical help, rather than diagnosis and therapy, the relation between doctor and patient is—or ought to be—friendship, *philia*. For the ancient Greeks, this *philia* was the basis of the relationship" (1969, p. 17). Laín Entralgo suggests that philia, which has its roots in benevolence, is distinct from *eros*, with origins in visual pleasure: The art of hearing characterizes friendship, while sight is appropriate for *eros*. His conclusion is that "medical *philia*," characterized by attentive hearing and communication, should continue to define the physician-patient relationship. James F. Drane provides an American model of "medical friendship" as follows: "The affective dimension of the doctor-patient relationship has all the generic notes of an ordinary friendship: There is pleasure in one another's company, confidences are shared, and there is an exchange of benefits" (1988, p. 85). Care, confidentiality, beneficence, honesty, respect, and forgiveness have been traditionally understood as aspects of friendship.

PARENTAL LOVE. The traditional physician-patient relationship has been widely condemned as paternalistic—or, to use a nonsexist word, parentalistic. Parental love is subject to a series of criticisms. As a general rule, physicians have over the centuries assumed an authoritarian parental role over patients, whose submission is akin to filial piety. Much of Enlightenment Anglo-American political thought emerged from John Locke's necessary refutation of Sir Robert Filmer's patriarchalism, that is, of fatherhood writ large so as to justify the absolute power of kings. Daughters and daughters-in-law have been manipulated by some parents into coerced roles as filial caregivers. The broad arguments against parental love include the temptation to play savior, wielding inordinate power to "protect" others, denying initiative and autonomy, and establishing unhealthy dependencies.

Outside of bioethics, the ideal of parental love is undergoing a recovery. Theologian Sally McFague warns against the potential oppression of the parental metaphor but adds, "Nevertheless, in spite of these qualifications, the maternal metaphor is so powerful and so right for our time that we *should* use it" (1989, p. 139). In an age of nuclear and ecological threat, McFague claims that a metaphor emphasizing nurture and "life as a gift" is necessary, for parental love "nurtures what it has brought into existence, and wants it to grow and be fulfilled." She holds that the ethical task is to "universalize parenthood." Paul Ramsey saw in parental love a divine likeness: "We procreate new beings like ourselves in the midst of our love for one another, and in this there is a trace of the original mystery by which God created the world . . ." (1970, p. 38). Nel Noddings views parental affection as the wellspring of all human caring and moral behavior. "The caring attitude that lies at the heart of all ethical behavior is universal," she argues. Noddings does not think that the starting point for ethics should be an analysis of moral judgment and moral reasoning but, rather, "our earliest memories of being cared for" (1984, p. 5). It is a well-established psychological fact that children who are uncared for will themselves never be able to care.

But any ethic of parental love must attend deeply to the respect for freedom and individuality that love requires. Outka includes respect for freedom as one of the three purposes of love (1972). James F. Childress stresses that a love ethic has the tendency to become paternalistic, and that more attention in theological ethics should be given to this problem (1982). Concern with respect for freedom is imperative.

Bioethics needs to reflect systematically on the meaning and value of parental love. In order to further interpret such phenomena as surrogate mothering, reproductive technologies, adoption, infanticide, and the fate of congenitally imperiled newborns, the field of biomedical ethics might gain from an in-depth analysis of parental love with respect to its natural or cultural foundations, and the extent to which such love can be expected to shoulder sometimes onerous burdens. Numerous issues in human reproduction finally must be related to the meaning of parenthood and its relationship to human nature. Raymond M. Herbenick (1975), for example, argues that infertile couples have a right to experience parenthood and parental love, so that abortion should be legally proscribed, in order to procure infants for adoption. Many would find such a suggestion highly oppressive of women.

— STEPHEN G. POST

"Love is the only gold."

ALFRED, LORD TENNYSON
BECKET, 1884

M

MARRIAGE AND OTHER DOMESTIC PARTNERSHIPS

Marriage is the legally recognized union of a man and woman as husband and wife. It endures until terminated by annulment, divorce, or the death of either spouse. As an institution, marriage provides a social structure for sexual relations, procreation, and the sharing of familial property. Marriage creates particular moral rights and duties between partners; some religious groups believe that marriage has spiritual significance. Domestic partnerships are other types of sexual relationships that endure over a period of time, include a shared domestic life, and involve some public acknowledgment by the partners of that shared life. Domestic partnerships may be heterosexual or homosexual.

This entry focuses on the history of moral ideas concerning marriage and domestic partnerships in Western civilization. Throughout much of Western history these influential ideas were articulated primarily by educated males. Thus, most statements concerning the role of wife, concubine, or lesbian partner describe that role from the male perspective. Moreover, this entry concentrates on normative views; the life experience of married couples and domestic partners is a different matter. Finally, these ideas often reflect the perspective of the educated, upper classes; the historical reality for the majority of couples who were poor may have differed from these ideal statements.

"With this ring I thee wed."

SOLEMNIZATION OF MATRIMONY, IN THE BOOK OF COMMON PRAYER

Over time the primary moral meanings of marriage have changed, but ideals whose roots are in earlier periods of history still influence our thinking and

MATRIMONY

Marriage terms and conditions may vary, but ideals rooted in earlier times still influence matrimonial customs today.

"*To have and to hold from this day forward, for better for worse, for richer for poorer, in sickness and in health, to love and to cherish, till death us do part.*"

SOLEMNIZATION OF MATRIMONY, IN THE BOOK OF COMMON PRAYER

"*Wilt thou . . . forsaking all others, keep thee only unto [him; her], so long as ye both shall live?*"

SOLEMNIZATION OF MATRIMONY, IN THE BOOK OF COMMON PRAYER

practice today. Marriage and domestic partnerships are crucial human relationships. Assumptions about and structures surrounding both marriage and domestic partnerships have important bioethical implications for matters such as reproductive issues, domestic violence, proxy decision making, and health-care access.

The moral end in marriage

According to both Plato and Aristotle the main purpose of marriage, in the upper classes, was the begetting of the male children who would become good citizens for the polis, or Greek city-state. Aristotle advised that marriages should be arranged so that a couple's prime reproductive years coincided, because high-quality offspring were the main good of marriage. Thus, in the *Politics* he suggested the marriage of a man about thirty-seven years old to a woman about eighteen years old.

Among the ancient Hebrews, the patriarchal family was the root of communal stability and well-being. Marriage channeled sexuality for the sake of the extended family and the people of Israel. Procreation was a chief good of marriage, especially the birth of male heirs. A wife's sexuality and fertility were family assets belonging exclusively to her husband. Polygyny and concubinage were permitted for wealthy, powerful males.

In rabbinic and later Judaism, men and women were expected to marry and bear children who would perpetuate the covenant. Procreation is a *mitzvah*, or a religious obligation, for the husband. The assumption is that his wife will cooperate, but procreation is not a moral command for her. Marriage also allows Jewish men and women to handle sexual desire in a stable, orderly way.

Augustine (354-430 C.E.) determined the view of Christianity for many centuries when he declared that the ends of Christian marriage were procreation, sexual fidelity, and *sacramentum*, marriage's function as a sign of the enduring love between Christ and the church. A Christian marriage must be indissoluble to function as *sacramentum*.

After the Roman Empire disintegrated, Christian leaders struggled to control marriage and its termination in order to promote marital indissolubility. Converts to Christianity from Germanic tribes were accustomed to concubinage and to divorce initiated by either the husband or the wife. It was centuries before church officials gained social control over the formation and annulment of marriages (Glendon, 1989).

During the Middle Ages, Christian theologians emphasized the voluntary exchange of marriage vows by the partners. The church refused to recognize marriage based on a betrothal promise exchanged by families. Thus, the church protected the free choice of the spouses in a social context in which marriage for the landed classes was a crucial economic and, at times, political decision of the family.

The Protestant theologians who led the Reformation accepted the traditional ends of Christian marriage:

CELIBACY AND THE VALUE OF CHRISTIAN MARRIAGE

Throughout early and medieval Christian history, the value of marriage was relativized by admiration for religiously committed celibacy. The apostle Paul favored celibacy as a means to focus one's entire energies on the impending Kingdom of God. Still, Paul accepted marriage for most Christians as a necessary alternative to sinful sexual behaviors (1 Cor. 7:8-9, 29-35). Paul viewed celibacy as a charism granted by God only to some (Countryman, 1988).

From the second through the fourth centuries C.E., the Mediterranean world turned toward asceticism. Marriage with its sexual passion and its reproduction of corruptible bodies needed religious justification. The Christian church fathers were increasingly attracted by religious virginity, a vow by one not yet sexually experienced to forgo all sexual activity in order to devote herself or himself to God's service. Still, these Christian thinkers affirmed the fundamental goodness of marriage and procreation as aspects of God's good creation.

In Western Christianity by the fourth century, a lengthy ethical controversy arose over the widespread practices of clerical marriage and concubinage. During the eleventh and twelfth centuries, church reformers made a major effort to require clerical celibacy, culminating with the First Lateran Council's decrees in 1123.

The Protestant reformers challenged the view that committed celibacy was superior to marriage. Martin Luther (1483-1546) esteemed marriage as a divinely ordained institution. He emphasized one's duty to God in the midst of worldly activities and, hence, offered a positive evaluation of the demanding household activities of husband and wife. Luther believed that very few persons received the divine grace to remain celibate. The Reformers extolled chaste marriage as the vocation of almost all adult Christians.

— BARBARA HILKERT ANDOLSEN

conception of children and avoidance of sexual sins. However, leaders of the Anglican church articulated explicitly a third purpose for marriage: mutual support, solace, and companionship. The Puritans recognized, as a primary good, the love that developed between spouses within marriage. Some Puritans advised that a child be allowed to refuse a potential partner selected by the parents, if the child felt that it would be impossible to learn to love the spouse *after marriage*.

The development and distribution of reliable means of birth control and a secular birth-control movement challenged the centrality of procreation as a basic good of marriage. In the twentieth century, mainstream Protestant churches decided that it was morally acceptable for spouses to limit procreation for the good of the family while remaining sexually active. Even the Roman Catholic magisterium explicitly acknowledged the moral worth of conjugal relations as a unique expression of love and mutual self-giving between spouses, as well as a means of procreation. By the late twentieth century, loving sexual intimacy was highly valued in its own right, and procreation was no longer viewed by many as the principal moral purpose for marriage. Thus, a serious question arose: "Is the moral distinction between marriage and other committed, sexually intimate relationships still valid, if marriages are no longer understood primarily as unions for the purpose of procreation?"

The ideal relationship between husband and wife

Throughout Western history it has been difficult for male thinkers to imagine women as equal marital partners. One exception is Plato's depiction of the relationships among men and women in the group he called the "guardians," who constituted the ruling strata in his ideal republic. Male and female guardians would have radically equal lives with respect to both procreation and public service. The guardians should practice communal marriage, child rearing, and property holding. Otherwise, Plato feared, the governing class would act to advance the interests of particular households, established by monogamous marriage with particular heirs, instead of promoting the welfare of the entire polis. Plato offered *Republic* as an intellectual ideal. In his more realistic treatment of community life, contained in *Laws*, Plato recommended a traditional, patriarchal family structure.

Aristotle asserted that upper-class males are naturally suited to rule in marriage and the polis. There is a type of friendship between husband and wife, but it is a friendship of unequals in which the husband, as the superior party, should gain superior benefits. For example, it is morally appropriate for the wife to love her husband more than he loves her (*Nicomachean Ethics*, VIII).

Among the Hebrew people, the relationship between Adam and Eve served as the paradigm of human sociality. It is not good for human beings to be alone (Gen. 2:18). Men valued marriage to a faithful wife enough to use it as a metaphor for the community's relationship with God. God is a benevolent husband and Israel ought to be a faithful wife. Similarly, in Ephesians 5:22-32, a loving, but male-dominated, marriage served as a key religious analogy. The husband is to the wife as Christ is to the church. Therefore, the wife ought to be submissive to her husband, and the husband ought to have a self-giving love for his wife.

Actually Jesus, as presented in the gospels, took little interest in the patriarchal family, which was a central social institution in his culture. For Jesus, faithful commitment to the Kingdom of God was crucial, even if it threatened to disturb family bonds (Luke 14:26). Jesus' statements concerning adultery and divorce implicitly undermined key social privileges of the patriarchal husband. When questioned about marriage, Jesus advocated lifelong, reciprocal sexual fidelity (Mark 10:2-12; Matt. 19:3-9).

For the rabbis, loving companionship was a boon experienced in a fortunate marriage. The Talmud proclaims "any man who has no wife lives without joy, without blessing, and without goodness" (Yebamoth 62b). Sexual intercourse ought to be enjoyed by the married couple. Indeed, a husband is bound by *onah*, a duty to provide sexual satisfaction for his wife. Many rabbis have held that the Sabbath, the holiest day of the week, is an especially appropriate time for spouses to make love. Yet, sexuality has its moral limits, even within marriage. Among the most important limits are the laws of *niddah*, the family purity laws that restrict sexual contact with a menstruating wife.

Augustine held that between man and woman there is the possibility of a friendly companionship based on the rule of the husband and the obedience of the wife (*De bono conjugali*, I). According to Thomas Aquinas (1225-1274), men enter into marriage for the sake of procreation, since a man can have a more satisfying partnership with another man in any other endeavor (*Summa Theologiae*, I.92.1). Nevertheless, he acknowledged that a husband and wife may experience a unique friendship as a result of their sexual relationship and joint domestic activity (*Summa Contra Gentiles*, III, II, 123). Yet, Aquinas believed that the more rational husband rightfully served as head of the household.

Luther held that God willed that wives be subject to their husbands. Yet, a virtuous wife was a valued helpmate in all things, and she established a relationship of deep mutual respect with her husband. According to Luther, marital love that desired union with the

"Marriage is popular because it combines the maximum of temptation with the maximum of opportunity."

GEORGE BERNARD SHAW

spouse as a full partner was "the greatest and purest of [human] loves" (*Sermon on the Estate of Marriage*). Despite the greater Puritan appreciation of the value of companionship in marriage, beloved wives were still not full equals of their husbands. Rather, ministers taught that both nature and God had given the husband dominion over the wife; and the good wife accepted the authority of her husband.

John Stuart Mill (1806-1873) acknowledged the injustices done to women in patriarchal marriage. In nineteenth-century England, married women's wages and property were largely controlled by their husbands, and child custody was controlled by the father. Mill said that real friendship in marriage was subverted by social practices that subordinated women to men. He insisted that husband and wife can share familial authority. Unfortunately, Mill undermined his own demands for sexual equality when he declared that a traditional division of labor—husband as breadwinner, wife as housekeeper and nurturer—was best for most families. Nevertheless, Mill recognized: "The moral regeneration of mankind will only really commence, when the most fundamental of the social relations [marriage] is placed under the rule of equal justice . . ." (Mill, 1988, p. 103).

In 1991, 14.6% of people who had ever been married admitted having at least one affair while married; in 1996, 17.8% said they had had extramarital sex.

NATIONAL OPINION RESEARCH CENTER, UNIVERSITY OF CHICAGO, 1996

The later twentieth-century feminist movement forced ethicists to grapple with the unequal power dynamics within heterosexual relationships, particularly within marriage. Ethicists have confronted the high incidence of sexual abuse and domestic violence in marriages and domestic partnerships. As a result, religious ethicists began to articulate a new norm for marriage and domestic partnerships: just love. This norm entails both fair treatment of the spouses/partners and just, institutional patterns that safeguard the equal human dignity of both spouse/partners. When a norm of just love is employed, marriages marred by abuse or domination are judged morally deficient. Domestic partnerships characterized by tenderness, a mutual commitment to the well-being of the partner, reciprocal fairness, and a struggle to achieve social equality are judged morally laudatory.

"In every house of marriage there's room for an interpreter."

STANLEY KUNITZ
ROUTE SIX, 1979

Marriage, community, and individual freedom

Since the Enlightenment, there has been a greater emphasis on personal autonomy and a greater reliance on contracts as a mechanism to structure moral obligations. Both these trends have subtly influenced marriage. In a number of countries, the power to regulate marriage and divorce has been taken away from the churches. In the eyes of the state, marriages have become a matter of civil contract.

Immanuel Kant (1724-1804) taught that a voluntary, juridical marriage contract granting the spouses reciprocal, exclusive sexual access to each other's bodies tempered the inherently exploitative character of sexual passion. He asserted that, outside of marriage, people are apt to treat their sex partners as things to be used and discarded. Marriage alone safeguards the personal dignity of the sexual partner. In marriage, people can preserve the species without debasing their partners (Kant, 1930).

For Georg Wilhelm Friedrich Hegel (1770-1831), marriage was a basic human institution that allowed persons to reconcile their being in community with their freedom as individuals. However, Hegel was able to harmonize individuality and community within marriage partly by assuming that women had a unique nature that was fulfilled precisely by working at home to promote family happiness. According to Hegel, a united family was appropriately represented in the marketplace and the state by its male head (Hegel, 1942).

While for Hegel the complementarity of heterosexual partners was conducive to marital unity, marriage still required that both spouses restrain their individuality for the sake of the relationship. Ironically, marriage began with a contract in which the individual parties agreed to transcend, through marriage, the individuality that was a prerequisite for making any contract. Paradoxically, however, through self-surrender in marriage, both husband and wife deepened their selfhood.

Theorists from Mary Wollstonecraft (1992) to Susan Okin (1989) have criticized the injustices suffered by women within the institution of male-dominated marriage. Simone de Beauvoir (1908-1986), in particular, explored the history of marriage as a social mechanism for the control of women's sexuality, reproductive power, and domestic services. Beauvoir observed the contradictions inherent in marriage as a permanent commitment between radically free moral actors. According to Beauvoir, an erotic relationship should involve a willing surrender to desire with a partner recognized as another free subject of desire; it should not be a marital duty. Ultimately, Beauvoir asserted that women's economic, political, and cultural equality are a necessary precondition for an egalitarian marriage, a freely chosen commitment made by self-sufficient subjects (Beauvoir, 1953).

Contemporary bioethical issues

Today, marriage is esteemed as a unique opportunity to experience emotional intimacy and self-fulfillment, including sexual self-fulfillment. But many persons, particularly committed religious persons, hold an ideal of marriage as a solemn promise to share the life destiny of the spouse until death. There is a potential conflict in marriage and other committed domestic partnerships between a relationship contingent on experiencing self-fulfillment and a promise to remain with the partner during difficult times. For example, does a person have a special obligation to care for a spouse/partner suffering a protracted illness, even if the relationship is no longer "self-fulfilling"? Is the obligation to continue to care weightier for those who exchange marriage vows?

Many persons view marriage as the socially preferred location in which to conceive and rear children. Another potential ethical tension exists between marriage-domestic partnerships, which make a moral claim on each partner only as long as intimacy and self-fulfillment are provided, and long-term, responsible child rearing (see Blustein, 1982). For example, when a child suffers from a severe illness, the consequences for the adult caregivers' marriage/partnership can be devastating.

In addition, the moral preference accorded to child rearing within marriage is disputed. Some unmarried persons, including some gay men and lesbians, request technological assistance with reproduction. Should medical services to facilitate conception be restricted to heterosexual, married couples? Or are other domestic partners capable of equally reliable, loving nurture of children?

In the modern period, love has become the primary

DOMESTIC PARTNERSHIPS

Some Historical Reflections

Heterosexual domestic partnerships outside of marriage have been recognized and sometimes tolerated in Western history. Concubinage was a practice in which the community acknowledged the long-lasting domestic and sexual relationship between a man and a woman, but did not grant the woman and her children the same legal protections afforded through marriage. In the early centuries, the Christian church accepted concubinage, if the partners were monogamous. During the Middle Ages, Christian clerics disparaged sexual relationships outside of marriage and sought to discourage concubinage, particularly clerical concubinage, through social penalties. Finally, in the Roman Catholic church, concubinage for any believer was condemned at the Council of Trent (1545-1563). In some jurisdictions, two people living together as husband and wife, but without a marriage ceremony, created a legally recognized bond—a common-law marriage.

Homosexual activity has been known throughout European-American history. However, it was not until the late nineteenth century that experts theorized that some persons have a permanent erotic orientation toward others of the same sex. Therefore, most of the thinkers discussed here probably could not even have imagined that same-sex couples might create long-lasting relationships in which domestic activity and companionship were shared along with sexual intimacy.

For example, Plato extolled highly the total relationship—sexual, intellectual, and spiritual—between a younger man and his older, more virtuous mentor/lover. Still, Plato expected male citizens to establish households with wives. In contrast, John Chrysostom (d. 407 C.E.) denounced homosexual activity, because, if sexual desire could be satisfied with the same sex, men and women would have less motivation to establish harmonious marriages (*Ad Romanos*, iv).

In rabbinic Judaism, a Talmudic saying advised against two men sleeping together under a shared blanket, for fear of homosexual contact (M. Kiddushin 4:14). Other rabbis considered strict observance of this rule too scrupulous, specifically because they claimed that homosexuality was virtually unknown among Jewish men. Lesbian acts were disparaged, but since these did not involve a "spilling of the [male] seed," they were considered not a serious moral evil. Still, Moses Maimonides (1135-1204) cautioned husbands and fathers to control their wives' and daughters' friendships, lest the women engage in lesbian sexual activity.

There is limited historical material documenting relationships akin to contemporary homosexual domestic partnerships. In 342 C.E., the Theodosian Code of the Byzantine Empire condemned the passive male partners in homosexual marriages, although no punishment was prescribed. However, historians disagree about whether the term "marriage" was used descriptively or facetiously. This ban on homosexual marriage was reiterated when medieval law codes were reformed in conformity with ancient Roman models.

One arena in which intense same-sex relationships—some genital, some not—might have flourished were monasteries and convents. (There are many, often exaggerated, criticisms of perverse monastic homosexual practices.) When monasteries and convents were closed in Protestant territories during the Reformation, a socially approved way to concentrate on same-sex relationships was foreclosed.

In some localities in the United States, couples can register with a designated municipal office as domestic partners. Legal status as domestic partners carries a variety of property and other rights that vary from jurisdiction to jurisdiction. A growing number of public and private employers are providing health-care coverage for dependent domestic partners on a basis comparable to spouses. In some cases, benefits are offered to all domestic partners. In other cases, benefits are restricted to homosexual partners, since heterosexual partners have the option to marry.

— BARBARA HILKERT ANDOLSEN

norm for marriage. A naive expectation that love animates marriage might contribute to social blindness toward domestic violence. In addition, the tradition that viewed the husband as responsible for order in the household has been used to legitimate husbands' use of physical force to control their wives. Thus norms about love and authority in the family have played a part in medicine's overly slow realization that domestic violence is a leading cause of injury to women.

Ethical rhetoric that praised the companionship of husband and wife while simultaneously prescribing wifely subordination showed that love as a moral value was not synonymous with equality. Society has been challenged to forge a new ethic of equality for heterosexual partners. This has become a crucial ethical task for society, because it is in the male-dominant household that children learn that relationships of dominance and subordination are morally acceptable.

"Lord Illingworth: *The Book of Life begins with a man and a woman in a garden.* Mrs. Allonby: *It ends with Revelations.*"

OSCAR WILDE
A WOMAN OF NO IMPORTANCE, 1893

Throughout much of history, marriage has been understood as a social institution essential to the fundamental welfare of society. Moral support from the community contributes to the stability of many marriages. There is dispute about whether society ought to offer moral support for long-term, committed homosexual relationships, for example, through social customs, legal recognition, or religious ceremonial affirmation.

There has been limited ethical attention to marriage and domestic partnerships as economic relationships. Questions of economic justice between spouses-partners, particularly when a relationship is terminated, have not been adequately addressed. It is most often the female partner who suffers serious economic disadvantages when a long-term heterosexual relationship ends. Among the economic harms suffered by such women is diminished access to, or quality of, health care for themselves and their children.

"A rich child often sits in a poor mother's lap."

DANISH PROVERB

In industrialized welfare states, routine provision of medical insurance coverage to the spouses of workers is an important entitlement. With major restructuring of the U.S. health-care system in prospect, it is difficult to discuss how marital status influences access to health care. Still, there are questions of justice that need to be considered. Under health-care reform, will innovative health-insurance benefits for domestic partners be eliminated, retained, or even extended to more people?

Society accords many privileges to marriage partners. Domestic partners do not always receive the same social recognition of their central, shared-life relationship. In medical settings, married people customarily receive such benefits as credit for spouses' blood donation, special visitation opportunities, and routine participation in discharge planning. In health-care matters, there is a legal presumption that one is the proxy decision maker if one's spouse becomes incompetent. Health-care proxy documents, for those who have them, allow domestic partners to make medical decisions for a partner who becomes incompetent. Still, if love, an intimate knowledge of the patient's values, and a paramount concern for the well-being of the patient are what is presumed to qualify marriage partners as proxy decision makers, other domestic partners should qualify morally as substitute decision makers on similar grounds.

Marriage and domestic partnerships are central life relationships with complex, disputed moral meanings. There are many complicated ethical questions about one's responsibilities to self, spouse/partner, children (if any), and society. Our moral assumptions about marriage and domestic partnerships will influence our bioethical judgments in many situations.

— BARBARA HILKERT ANDOLSEN

MATERNAL-FETAL RELATIONSHIP

MEDICAL ASPECTS

During the last decades of the twentieth century, perinatal medicine has made tremendous advances in scientific knowledge and in the successful application of this knowledge toward improving pregnancy outcomes. These advances have also brought a dramatic change in medicine's conceptualization of the fetus. No longer is the fetus defined predominantly as a part of the pregnant woman, but rather as a distinct entity that can be the independent focus of diagnostic tests and individual therapies: "A second patient with many rights and privileges comparable to those previously achieved only after birth." It is the widely shared view of obstetricians that the fetus is a patient to whom they owe ethical duties. The purpose of this article is to delineate the medical advances that have brought about this change in fetal identity and to discuss the impact of these changes on pregnant women and the obstetrical decision-making process.

Pregnancy and fetal therapies

Perinatal technologies have benefited the fetus by increasing the understanding of normal fetal development as well as improving prenatal diagnostic capabilities and therapeutic interventions. The fetus can be visualized with ultrasound, its well-being assessed with fetal heart-rate monitoring, and its diseases diagnosed with chorionic villus sampling, amniocentesis, and fetal blood sampling. Increases in diagnostic capabilities have been accompanied by the development of techniques to treat the fetus directly in utero. Our increasing ability to act on behalf of the fetus has made its claims to our care more compelling.

Prenatal technologies designed to benefit the fetus range from the simple to the complex, with differing risks and benefits for both the pregnant woman and her fetus. The most commonly used technology with the intention of improving fetal outcome is electronic fetal monitoring (EFM). EFM was introduced in the United States in the early 1970s with the promise that it would enable early detection of fetal hypoxia in labor and alert the physician to perform an immediate delivery, preventing the serious consequences of oxygen deprivation, including brain damage and stillbirth. Its use rapidly expanded from high-risk pregnancies to all pregnancies; in 1978, it was estimated that two-thirds of all U.S. pregnancies were monitored. Unfortunately, the wide acceptance of this technology occurred before adequate studies had been done to assess its efficacy and safety. There have now been six prospective randomized trials of EFM that have been unable to demonstrate a decrease in intrapartum fetal death or better newborn health in low-risk pregnancies. However, the use of EFM was shown to double the C-section (cesarean-section) rate for the indication of fetal distress, thus exposing more women to the increased morbidity and mortality risks of C-section without the promised fetal benefit.

A C-section entails a greater risk of maternal morbidity and mortality than does a vaginal delivery. The mortality rate associated with C-section is between two and four times that associated with a vaginal delivery. Maternal morbidity is also more frequent and usually more severe with a C-section. The common causes of morbidity associated with C-sections are infection, injury to the urinary tract, and hemorrhage with the possible risk of transfusion. Even an uncomplicated C-section requires a much longer recovery period for the mother at a time when she is experiencing increased physical and emotional demands.

The simplest fetal therapies are medications given to a pregnant woman for the benefit of her fetus. A well-accepted treatment of a woman who develops mild diabetes during pregnancy is to give her insulin until delivery. This practice benefits the fetus by preventing its excessive growth and associated birth trauma and by avoiding the potential neonatal difficulties of an infant of a diabetic mother. While insulin is not essential for the pregnant woman's health, it may be beneficial by reducing her risk of C-section delivery and the potential harms of a mildly elevated glucose to her own organ systems. Digoxin is a medication administered to pregnant women for the benefit of a fetus with cardiac arrhythmia. Unlike insulin, digoxin offers no benefit to the health of the pregnant woman.

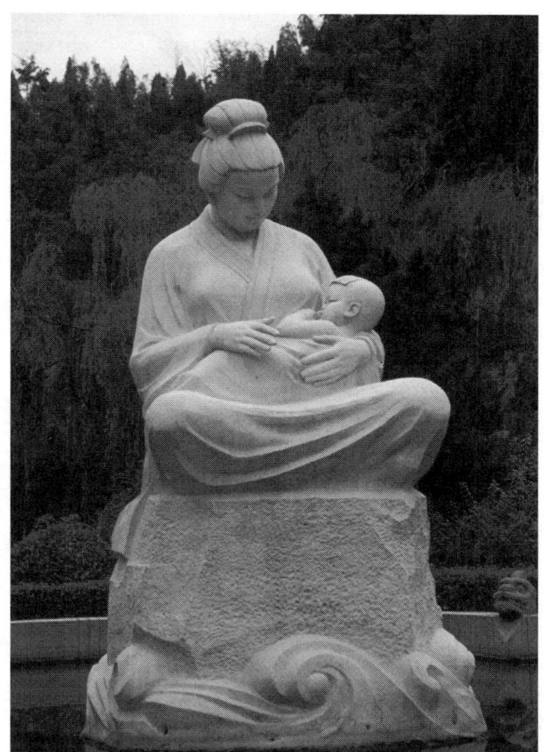

TWO IN ONE

Late 20th-century thinking often regards the fetus not simply as a part of the pregnant woman but as a distinct entity with its own rights and privileges.

The risks to the pregnant woman of ingesting insulin or digoxin are minimal if administered appropriately. In summary, these pharmacologic fetal therapies confer benefit upon the fetus and are minimally invasive; one offers some benefit for the pregnant woman; the other solely benefits the fetus.

An accepted but more invasive therapy of sole benefit to the fetus is a fetal blood transfusion for isoimmunization from Rh disease (a condition in which the immune system of the pregnant woman destroys the blood cells of the fetus resulting in fetal death if severe and untreated). The most common technique is cordocentesis, in which a needle is placed through the maternal abdominal and uterine wall into the umbilical blood vessel for the purpose of transfusing blood into the fetus. This technique is not without its risks for both the fetus and the pregnant woman. This procedure poses a 2 percent chance of fetal death. It also increases the risk of fetal bradycardia (a dangerous lowering of the heart rate), a condition that mandates an emergency C-section for the safety of the fetus. All the maternal risks of C-section delineated above are increased in an emergency C-section, with the addition of the increased risk of death from general anesthesia. Cordocentesis is an example of an accepted fetal therapy that is potentially beneficial for the fetus and invasive for the pregnant woman, with significant risks to her in complicated cases.

"Some are kissing mothers and some are scolding mothers, but it is love just the same."

PEARL S. BUCK
TO MY DAUGHTERS, WITH LOVE, 1967

The most invasive fetal therapy is in utero fetal surgery. Several operations are being investigated. One example is the surgical removal of a lung mass in the fetus. The rationale for the surgery is that without prenatal removal, the fetal lungs will be unable to grow sufficiently to support survival after birth. The pregnant woman must undergo a major abdominal operation and take medications to prevent the preterm labor that might be caused by the surgery. The surgery entails the usual risks associated with a C-section but at a higher rate because of the type of uterine incision, the thickness of the uterine wall, and the need for general anesthesia. Because of the type of uterine incision necessary for this fetal surgery, the woman must have a C-section in this pregnancy, even if her fetus is stillborn, as well as in all future pregnancies. Due to the experimental nature of this procedure, the long-term benefit is yet to be established.

Neonatal advances and obstetrical decision making

Simultaneous advances in neonatology have had a significant impact on obstetrical knowledge and care. The gestational age at which survival is possible in the modern intensive care nursery has been pushed back continuously over the past few decades to the age of twenty-four to twenty-five weeks (fifteen to sixteen weeks premature). Many fetuses/babies who in the past would have been considered nonviable now survive and develop normally. However, the cost of this success is measured in hundreds of thousands of dollars per premature infant and in the potential for severe lifelong impairments.

This improved neonatal survival has had two significant influences on the perspective of obstetrical providers. Most have seen or participated in the care of very premature babies; thus fetuses in utero from twenty-four weeks on possess a very concrete human image for those who care for them. In addition, the possibility of survival beginning at twenty-four gestational weeks creates an argument for aggressive obstetrical management at earlier and earlier stages of pregnancy. The lower the gestational age at birth and the lower the birth weight, the lower the chance of survival and the higher the risk of severe physical and mental impairment. Between twenty-four to twenty-

See Also

Legal Moralism: Smoking and Public Health

PREGNANCY AND MATERNAL HEALTH

Maternal morality in pregnancy fell dramatically in the United States from more than one in 200 in 1935 to less than one in 10,000 in 1994. Most of this reduction was accomplished earlier in this century through improved surgical techniques and increased access to safe blood products, antibiotics, intravenous fluids, and improved prenatal care.

Despite these improvements, pregnancy still poses the risk of serious illness and, in rare cases, death. It has been calculated that the risk of mortality in pregnant women is 179 times that of the risk of death among women using the safest method of birth control. The major causes of maternal death are hypertensive disorders of pregnancy, pulmonary embolism, uterine hemorrhage, and sepsis. The risks of pregnancy are proportional to the age of the pregnant woman and to her underlying state of health. Women with medical illness may note worsening of their disease during pregnancy, sometimes with serious long-term consequences. But even women who begin a pregnancy in excellent health may find themselves suddenly confronting the morbidity and mortality risks associated with cesarean section (23.5% of all U.S. deliveries in 1990), postpartum hemorrhage (4-8% of all deliveries), or pre-eclampsia (a pregnancy-related condition that can lead to seizures, strokes or death in the pregnant woman) (5% of all pregnancies).

Pregnant women may experience preterm labor (U.S. incidence is 10%), the development of premature contractions that if not stopped can result in delivery of the fetus before adequate development has occurred. Preterm delivery poses significant risk of disability and death for the fetus. While preterm labor itself does not pose a health risk to the pregnant woman, many of the treatments recommended for its treatment have significant maternal side effects. The three drugs commonly used to treat (attempt to stop) preterm labor have serious side effects ranging from nausea, vomiting, dizziness, flushing, tremor, and jitteriness to life-threatening risks of pulmonary edema (fluid in the lungs), alterations in blood chemistries (hypokalemia, hyperglycemia), heart rate abnormalities (tachycardia, arrhythmias), hypotension, respiratory depression, and cardiac arrest.

For all women, pregnancy is a complex physiologic process; almost every organ system undergoes adaptation to support the maternal-fetal unit. It is important to appreciate the range of symptoms experienced by many pregnant women due to these physiologic changes. These include nausea, vomiting, fatigue, syncope (fainting), round ligament pelvic pain, backache, heartburn, hemorrhoids, constipation, urinary frequency, carpal tunnel syndrome (numbness and tingling of the hands), pedal edema, and sciatica (hip and leg nerve pain). Thus, while pregnancy is described as a normal physiologic process, it is not without common discomforts and the potential for serious illness. Most pregnant women willingly assume these sacrifices for their developing fetus.

— NANCY MILLIKEN

eight weeks the likelihood of survival increases from 20 percent to 90 percent, with a 20 percent incidence of severe neonatal impairment in the survivors. Complicating this situation is the inaccuracy of techniques to estimate gestational age and fetal weight. The inability to predict with certainty before birth either the survival or the likelihood of impairment creates legitimate divergent perspectives on what to do in individual pregnancies and ensures difficult decision making for obstetricians and pregnant women.

Formerly, a woman who developed preterm labor at twenty-five weeks would have been allowed to deliver vaginally and comforted regarding the certain death of her baby. Today, that pregnant woman will be faced with the option and probable recommendation that the fetus be monitored in labor and delivered by C-section if needed for fetal benefit. A C-section at this gestational age is riskier for her than one at term and because the type of uterine incision required commits her to C-section delivery of future pregnancies. The chance of the infant's survival is between 30 and 50 percent depending on its weight (which is difficult to predict prior to delivery). If the infant does survive, there will be a significant chance of neurologic or physical impairment. Some women will choose to take any risk for a slim possibility of fetal benefit, and accept aggressive obstetrical management. Other women decide that the risk of C-section in this and future pregnancies combined with the potential suffering for their premature infant is not worth the slight chance of being able to take home a normal or mildly impaired child. They choose to let "nature take its course," and hope that their next pregnancy will be free of complications. For the obstetrician faced with this clinical dilemma, the uncertainty of prognosis (this fetus might do well), the availability of technologic intervention (C-section), the desire to do something, and the legal fear of doing nothing may prompt him or her to advocate intervention as the baby's only hope. This is a persuasive argument for most pregnant women, especially if alternatives are not presented as legitimate.

The beneficial effects of fetal therapies and neonatal advances are impressive when successful: Babies previously at high risk of stillbirth, birth trauma, hypoxia, and neonatal death now have a greater chance of being born safely and having a near normal development. However, some babies who would have died now survive but with significant handicaps and at a significant cost to the physical, emotional, and financial well-being of the mother, her child, and her family. Some therapies are recommended with hope of fetal benefit but without good scientific evidence and with known maternal risks of death and morbidity. Pregnant women must be able to choose the best medical option based upon accurate scientific knowledge

PROTECTION?

If a state criminalizes the use of cocaine by pregnant women in order to protect the fetus, should tobacco and alcohol also be forbidden?

and an honest appraisal of the uncertainties involved in medical science.

Pregnancy and fetal development

Increased understanding of fetal development has allowed identification of environmental factors that can promote or impair the development of a healthy fetus. The placenta was once felt to operate as a barrier allowing only those substances beneficial to the fetus to pass. Now it is known that the placenta is an efficient transporter of many substances to the fetus, regardless of their toxicity, including both therapeutic and recreational drugs. Media coverage has focused on the rising incidence of crack cocaine use by pregnant women. It has been estimated that 11 percent of pregnant women use an illegal drug during their pregnancies and that 75 percent of these women use cocaine. While there are methodologic shortcomings in the studies of cocaine's effect on pregnancy, many serious sequelae of using this drug have been suggested, including an increased spontaneous abortion rate; suspected cardiac, genitourinary, facial, and limb abnormalities (though these may be alcohol-related); growth retardation; and in utero strokes. Obstetrical complications include preterm delivery, abruption (placental separation), and fetal distress. Newborns who have been exposed to cocaine in utero experience withdrawal symptoms, making them more irritable and less able to bond with caregivers. Many believe that cocaine-exposed babies will be more likely to experience learning disabilities.

Alcohol is a well-known danger to the developing fetus. Fetal alcohol syndrome has been identified in the

"For thy sake,
Tobacco, I
Would do anything
but die."

CHARLES LAMB
A FAREWELL TO TOBACCO
1805

"It is now proved beyond doubt that smoking is one of the leading causes of statistics."

FLETCHER KNEBEL
READER'S DIGEST, 1961

*"Thou art thy mother's glass, and she in thee
Calls back the lovely April of her prime."*

SHAKESPEARE
SONNET 3

offspring of women who consumed excessive alcohol during their pregnancy; it is defined by a triad of symptoms: gross physical retardation; central nervous system dysfunction, including mental retardation; and characteristic facial abnormalities. Fetal alcohol effects are more common; they include cardiac, genitourinary, skeletal, and muscular anomalies; hypoxia; irritability; and hyperactivity. While excessive alcohol use during pregnancy has clearly been documented to cause significant fetal harm, no minimum safe level of consumption has been established. Many experts have recommended total abstinence from alcohol during pregnancy as the only way to avoid all possible harm.

Smoking has significant effects on pregnancy outcome. Approximately 30 percent of U.S. women of childbearing age smoke. Cigarette smoking results in reductions in birthweight, length, and head circumference. It has been estimated that between 20 and 40 percent of all low birthweight births in the United States can be attributed directly to smoking. Smoking has also been associated with higher rates of spontaneous abortion, preterm birth, perinatal mortality, and deficits in later physical, intellectual, and emotional development. A comparison of the known perinatal dangers of alcohol, smoking, and cocaine consumption illustrates that the legal substances a pregnant women may ingest are no less medically harmful than the illegal ones.

Public policy aimed at improving perinatal outcomes by reducing the use of fetotoxic substances by pregnant women must be grounded in medical knowledge. Recreational drug use by most pregnant women is an addiction; they do not consume the drug to harm the fetus but to satisfy an acute physical or psychological need. To address the problem of addiction, comprehensive and supportive programs designed to enlist the individual in her own recovery are necessary. There have been documented successes in programs that emphasize early identification of women at risk for substance abuse and that utilize comprehensive education, prenatal care, psychological intervention, and social services. However, there are very few substance abuse programs available to pregnant women. In one notable case of criminal prosecution of a woman for drug use during her pregnancy, the accused woman had sought drug treatment during her pregnancy without success.

Punitive approaches to addictive disease are generally ineffective. They have the potential to drive the addicted individual away from the very care that could be beneficial. Because the developing fetus is so vulnerable to uterine exposure to toxins, it is critical that pregnant women not be deterred from care. Prenatal care alone, in the presence of continuing drug use, can improve perinatal outcome for the drug-exposed fetus.

Obstetrical decision making

While a pregnant woman and her fetus may be conceptualized as two independent patients, they are in fact intimately interdependent, and actions taken to benefit one may pose a risk to the other. A pregnant woman may suffer from a serious illness that requires a treatment that will itself pose risk to her fetus; premature delivery to improve maternal health and chemotherapy for maternal cancer are two examples. Alternatively, treatment for the benefit of the fetus (C-section delivery, treatment of preterm labor, fetal surgery) may pose a risk to the pregnant woman. In addition, a medical treatment for presumed fetal benefit may interfere with the nonmedical needs of the pregnant woman.

These situations have been described by many as maternal-fetal conflict when they more accurately might be described as maternal-physician conflict. When an obstetrician agrees with the pregnant woman's choice and underlying values, no conflict ensues, even in the presence of potential fetal risk. The disagreement that does occur often is based on differing views of what is beneficial for the pregnant woman and her fetus and what are acceptable maternal risks to achieve obstetrical goals.

Obstetricians have a predominant focus on the current pregnancy. Appropriately, they emphasize the medical health of their patient and the fetus, give expert advice to improve pregnancy outcome, and urge women to follow this advice as a priority in their lives. However, medical recommendations are at times influenced by the fear of malpractice, research interests, a reluctance to give up, and a provider's own personal values.

A pregnant woman's values may differ from those of her providers and she may place a different value on the physician's medically based goals. Like other adults, a pregnant woman must and does make decisions about her prenatal activity within the broader context of her life. Her obligation to her fetus is sometimes weighed against her obligations to her other children, her parents, her partner, or others with whom she has a special relationship. Her decision may be influenced by religious or other strongly held personal beliefs.

Some have argued that pregnant women should be forced to undergo certain treatments if the benefit to the fetus would be substantial and the risk to the woman would be minimal or low. Medical uncertainty and medical practice make this a difficult policy to administer rationally or fairly. As delineated above, perinatal medicine is limited by diagnostic and prognostic uncertainty. This is best illustrated by a legal case in which a judge ordered a woman to undergo a forced C-section. In seeking the court order, the obstetrician testified that without delivery by C-section, the fetus had a 99 percent chance of dying and the pregnant woman had a 50 percent chance of mortality. However, the pregnant woman fled the court's jurisdiction and had an uneventful vaginal delivery. The ability to predict fetal distress in labor is frequently inaccurate. Because of this uncertainty, a policy of enforcing obstetrical recommendations would allow obstetricians to make the wrong decisions sometimes but would never allow a pregnant woman to be wrong or right about decisions that profoundly affect her life.

The problem of precisely defining fetal risk is matched by the complex task of delineating what constitutes an acceptable risk of harm for the mother. Risks, no matter how small in the medical context, may take on a different meaning within the context of an individual's life. The small risk of maternal death from a C-section may be very significant to a single woman who is the sole supporter of her children. Bed rest for the prevention of preterm labor may mean the loss of work and health insurance for her whole family. A Jehovah's Witness who is forced to receive blood may believe she is condemned to eternal damnation and may undergo significant stress or rejection within her religious community.

If obstetricians are given the authority to force pregnant women to follow their recommendations, this force may be used in a very arbitrary way. Not only is there variation in obstetrical diagnostic and prognostic accuracy, there are obstetrical debates about the appropriate management of various conditions. The medical justifications in the reported cases of requests for court-ordered C-sections have included breech presentation, prior C-section, and rupture of membranes for twenty-four hours without signs of febrile morbidity. Many obstetricians would disagree with each of these indications for C-section. Furthermore, the women who have been subjected to court orders have been shown to be more likely subjects of other forms of discrimination. In one study of forced C-sections, 81 percent of the women belonged to a minority group and 24 percent did not use English as their first language, and all requests for the court orders involved women who received care at a teaching hospital or who were receiving public assistance.

If the use of force by doctors against pregnant women were to be legitimized, it would have negative implications for their therapeutic relationship. The relationship would become less cooperative and supportive and more adversarial; compromise in situations of disagreement would become less and less possible. Under these circumstances of care, some women might lie about their behaviors or symptoms, fearing that their obstetrician would use this information to force upon them unacceptable treatment. Others might avoid prenatal care completely. The adversarial climate created by the use of force would decrease the effectiveness of obstetricians in improving maternal and fetal health.

Conclusion

Perinatal advances have dramatically improved the perinatal survival and well-being of fetuses/babies, fulfilling the obstetrical goals of prenatal providers and the personal goals of pregnant women. Increased understanding of the developing fetus and improved technologies have given the fetus an enhanced human identity and status as a direct patient of the obstetrician. The new therapeutic options with their maternal risks have created difficult ethical decisions for the pregnant woman and her obstetrician. A discussion regarding the legitimate use of force against pregnant women for fetal benefit has begun. The resolution of this debate must take into account the implications of the uncertainty inherent in medicine, the maternal risks associated with fetal therapies, the inevitable influence of an obstetrician's personal values upon his or her medical recommendations, the harmful influence of force in any therapeutic relationship, and the ethical and constitutional rights of all parties, including pregnant women.

— NANCY MILLIKEN

ETHICAL ISSUES

Only since the 1960s has it been recognized that the fetus in utero can be harmed by a range of maternal behaviors. Now that it is known that drinking, smoking, and using drugs during pregnancy can harm the unborn child, the question of what moral obligations a pregnant woman has to the fetus she carries has become a significant issue in biomedical ethics. When conflicts arise between what a pregnant woman wants to do or believes is right to do, on the one hand, and what may be best for the fetus, on the other, how and on what basis should those conflicts be resolved? And who should be involved in resolving them?

This article attempts to provide a conceptual framework for thinking about maternal-fetal conflicts. Whether one believes that women have moral obligations to their fetuses in utero depends largely on one's view of the moral status of the fetus—possibly the central issue in the abortion debate. The debate over whether (and at what developmental stage) fetuses can be harmed is a heated one. Pro-lifers think that fetuses can be harmed, and base their opposition to abortion on the ground that being killed is the ultimate harm. They also oppose behavior on the part of pregnant women that is likely to have less severe effects on the

◆ **obstetrician/gynecologist (ob/gyn)**
A physician specializing in obstetrics (related to childbirth) and the reproductive system of women.

See Also

Informed Consent

Special Situations: Pregnant Patients

Trust

fetus. By contrast, many pro-choicers deny that fetuses (or at least early gestation fetuses) can be harmed. However, even if the pro-choice view of the fetus is the correct one, it does not follow that pregnant women are free to drink, smoke, or use drugs during pregnancy, if they are planning to have the baby. For if the pregnant woman does not abort but goes to term, her behavior during pregnancy can have lasting, destructive effects on the born child. Concern for the born child is a common ground that unites all people, regardless of their stance on abortion. This distinction between the fetus per se and the fetus-who-will-be-born differentiates maternal-fetal conflicts from the issue of abortion. Yet these conflicts are not entirely unrelated to the problem of abortion, because both issues concern justifications for restricting or controlling women's behavior during pregnancy.

Conceptualizing maternal-fetal conflict

People have moral obligations to other people, both those existing today and those who will exist in the future. The mere fact that people do not now exist is no reason to discount the interests they will have when they come into existence. If people today do nothing about the national debt, if they allow the ozone layer to be depleted, if they pollute the air and water, then actual (as opposed to possible or potential) individuals, living in the future, will be harmed by what is done, or is not done, today. There is a responsibility to these actual, though future, people not to destroy the world they will live in. That they do not now exist does not obviate present obligations to them. Similarly, women have moral obligations to their future children, that is, the ones they will bring into the world.

In the United States, as in most societies, the primary responsibility for protecting the interests of children belongs to their parents. Although parents have a great deal of discretion in deciding how to care for and raise their children, they do not have absolute freedom. In industrialized nations, at least, it is widely accepted that parents are not only morally but also legally obligated not to inflict injury on their children, to feed and clothe them, to provide them with necessary medical care. It would seem, then, that pregnant women who intend to complete their pregnancies have comparable moral obligations to avoid harming their not-yet-born children. However, preventing prenatal harm is not the only morally relevant consideration. The woman's own interests count, too. How are conflicts between the interests of the future child and the interests of the pregnant woman to be resolved?

Some object to the very notion of "maternal-fetal *conflict*." They regard this as being misleadingly adver-

FETAL RIGHTS?

The Moral Status of the Unborn

One of the thorniest issues in bioethics is the moral status of the fetus. (Here, the term "fetus" is used to refer to the unborn during all stages of pregnancy.) One view is that fetuses are merely potential children who do not have full-fledged moral rights, or perhaps any rights at all. According to this view, attempts to limit reproductive choices or coerce behavior during pregnancy violate very basic moral rights to bodily self-determination.

A different view is that fetuses are "pre-born children," with all the rights of born children. Someone who regards the fetus in this way will think that a pregnant woman has the same moral obligations to protect her fetus from harm as she has to protect her born children. In keeping with this view of the fetus, some states have adopted "fetal rights" legislation, for example, making behavior during pregnancy that puts the fetus at risk of damage or death a form of child abuse.

Those who differentiate morally between fetuses and children tend vigorously to oppose "fetal rights" legislation, often seeing it as part of a larger political agenda to make abortion illegal. Even apart from the abortion question, many people are concerned that any attempts to control women's behavior during pregnancy violate their rights to privacy and self-determination. At the extreme, the position taken by some feminists and civil libertarians is that whatever a woman does during her pregnancy is her own business. They have opposed even noncoercive measures, such as a bill requiring the posting of signs warning pregnant women of the dangers of alcohol consumption (Sack, 1991).

However, if a woman decides not to abort, but to carry to term, then her behavior during pregnancy may have an adverse effect not only on the fetus but also on the child who is born. Whatever one's position on the moral standing of fetuses, born children clearly have moral status and rights.

The right not to be injured is one of the most basic moral and legal rights. To extend this right to prenatal injury requires only the recognition that a person can be injured by events that occurred before his or her birth—indeed, even before conception. Here is an example of preconception injury: In the 1940s, diethylstilbestrol (DES) was sometimes prescribed to prevent miscarriage. Not only was the drug ineffective, it sometimes resulted in damaged reproductive systems in the female children of women who used it. When these girls grew up, their reproductive abnor-

(continued)

sarial, pitting pregnant women against the children they will bear, when in most cases their interests are inseparably intertwined. A less adversarial framework stresses that what is good for pregnant women, such as better prenatal care, is also good for fetuses. While this is undeniable, some women want to do things, such as smoking or using drugs or alcohol, that risk harming their unborn children. Admittedly, behavior that endangers the fetus often endangers the health of the pregnant woman, but this does not necessarily make their interests identical. What if the woman is willing to risk her own health for the enjoyment the tobacco or alcohol or cocaine brings? She may decide—perhaps irrationally, perhaps not—that use of the substance is in her own interest, all things considered. That does not mean it is in the interest of her as-yet-unborn baby. It is wishful thinking to pretend that the possible harmful effect on the pregnant woman prevents the possibility of conflict.

Others object to characterizing the conflict as one between mother and fetus. In the so-called obstetrical cases (e.g., forced cesareans), the conflict may not be between mother and fetus. Rather, it is between mother and doctor, who disagree about what is best for both mother and child. In one case, doctors sought a court order because the fetus's umbilical cord was wrapped around its neck, a clear indication for an emergency cesarean. The woman, who had nine children, refused surgery out of concern for her own health, a belief in "natural childbirth," and an intuition that the delivery would turn out fine, despite the doctors' dire predictions. She delivered vaginally, and the child was fine (Rhoden, 1986).

Attempts to prevent prenatal harm often impose risks or burdens on pregnant women, particularly when an intervention, such as a cesarean section or blood transfusion, is deemed necessary to protect the unborn child. The moral question then becomes how much risk, burden, or sacrifice a woman must undergo for the sake of her future child.

Moral obligations to the not-yet-born

It is important to distinguish the question of moral obligation and responsibility from legal obligation. Only the most extreme legal moralist would advocate compelling people to do whatever they morally ought to do. Claims that women have moral obligations to their future children should not be construed as advocating legal coercion.

Thinking about moral obligations to future children in the context of general parental obligations to children prevents sentimentalizing pregnancy and the imposing of especially stringent obligations on pregnant women, or thinking that pregnant women are

---

FETAL RIGHTS?

(continued)

malities sometimes led to miscarriages and premature births. Prematurity can cause cerebral palsy. Thus, a child might be born with cerebral palsy due to a premature birth ultimately caused by her grandmother's ingestion of DES years before her own conception (*Enright by Enright* v. *Eli Lilly & Co.*, 568 N.Y.S.2d [Ct. App. 1991]). The legal right to recover for injuries negligently inflicted during pregnancy has been widely recognized in the United States since the landmark case of *Bonbrest* v. *Kotz* (65 F. Supp. 138 [D.D.C. 1946]). Courts have been much more reluctant to accept a right to recover for preconception injuries, primarily out of a concern to confine liability within manageable limits.

The important point for bioethics is that recognition of a moral right to be free from injuries inflicted before birth is not based on recognition of the fetus as having the moral status of a person. The concern is not primarily for the fetus but for the surviving child. At the same time, attempts to protect children from prenatal injury can be accomplished only through the body of the pregnant woman. As a result, some women have been subjected to forced cesareans (Annas, 1982; Rhoden, 1986, 1987; Nelson and Milliken, 1988). With the development of new fetal therapies and surgery, women could be asked, or even required, to undergo possibly painful and risky procedures for the sake of the not-yet-born child (Robertson, 1982). Thus, if the focus is exclusively on the prevention of harm to the future child, there is a risk of forgetting that the pregnant woman is a person in her own right, not merely a "fetal container" (Annas, 1986). The moral question, then, is how to balance the interests and rights of the pregnant woman against those of her not-yet-born child.

Most women who are expecting a child voluntarily adapt at least some of their behavior to protect their babies. But what if the woman is an alcoholic or a crack addict? What if, for religious or other reasons, she refuses a cesarean section her doctor thinks is necessary to prevent serious damage to her nearly born baby? Such cases "pit a woman's right to privacy and bodily integrity . . . against the possibility of a lifetime of devastating disability to a being who is within days or even hours of independent existence" (Rhoden, 1987, p. 118). How should such conflicts be resolved? What moral obligations do women have to prevent harm to the children they intend to bear?

— BONNIE STEINBOCK

During the 1980s, there was a series of cases in which pregnant women were subjected to court-ordered treatments.

PAGE 412

BODY AND BLOOD
Legal, Moral Obligations to Share?

There are compelling arguments against the government's using coercive and punitive measures to regulate women's actions in order to promote healthy births. Most people do not want to live in a society in which they can be compelled to undergo surgery or to sacrifice body parts, even if it would be morally incumbent on them to do so. Placing limits on what can be demanded of citizens, especially where bodily integrity is involved, is essential to a free society. This helps to justify the conviction that people are not legally obligated to donate parts of their bodies, even if others need them for life itself.

The situation is different when we consider people's moral obligations. While an absolute ban on forced donation seems the correct legal response, a balancing approach seems more appropriate from a moral perspective. Whether one has a moral obligation to donate a body part, or undergo invasive surgery, depends on the degree of risk and sacrifice incurred, balanced against the need of the endangered individual. Perhaps people are morally required to donate replenishable body parts, such as blood, to others who need it. Blood donation takes only an hour, has no lasting effects, and causes only slight discomfort to most donors. Where a special relationship exists between the potential donor and the needy person, there may be a moral obligation to incur greater risks and sacrifices. Parents may be thought to have a moral obligation to donate blood and bone marrow, and perhaps even nonreplenishable body parts, such as kidneys, to their children, because of their duty to protect and care for their children, and because parents are supposed to love their children. Certainly a parent who refused to give a kidney to a dying child, saying, "It's my body, and I do not feel like donating," would be rightly regarded as morally deficient.

— BONNIE STEINBOCK

morally required to subordinate all their interests to their fetuses. After all, parents are not morally required to avoid any and all risks to their children's health. The obligation is, rather, to avoid *unreasonable* risks of *substantial* harm.

With a few notable exceptions (King, 1979; Robertson, 1982; Shaw, 1984), most commentators have argued that a pregnant woman should not be forced to undergo medical treatment even when this is judged necessary to preserve the life or health or her fetus (Annas, 1982; Gallagher, 1987; Johnsen, 1986; Nelson and Milliken, 1988; Rhoden, 1986, 1987). Cesarean sections are major surgery and, while generally very safe, are associated with higher rates of maternal mortality, morbidity, and increased pain than occur with vaginal delivery. Requiring a woman to undergo a cesarean requires her to risk her own life and health for the sake of her not-yet-born child. This is contrary to our legal tradition, which forbids the forced use of the body of one person to save another. In one widely cited case, *Shimp* v. *McFall* (10 Pa. D. & C.3d 90 [1978]), a court refused to order David Shimp to donate bone marrow to his cousin, Robert McFall, who was dying of aplastic anemia. The court emphasized that there is no legal duty to rescue others. It would seem to follow that compelling a pregnant woman to undergo medical treatment for the sake of the fetus, when this is not required of other potential rescuers, violates equal protection.

What are the implications for women whose doctors advise a cesarean section for fetal indications? Most women, faced with the possibility of a stillbirth or having a baby born with cerebral palsy, readily consent to the treatment their doctors recommend. Occasionally, however, a woman rejects a physician's recommendation. The moral justifiability of her refusal depends largely on her reasons for refusing. Typically, women who refuse cesareans do so out of religious objections, concern for their own health, or belief that a vaginal birth is best for the baby, and they disagree with the doctors' assessment of the risk. These are not selfish or unimportant reasons. Refusing a cesarean for such reasons is not obviously immoral. By contrast, it would be immoral for a woman to refuse a cesarean, and risk having her nearly born child die or suffer permanent disability, for a trivial reason, such as wanting to avoid a scar in order to be able to wear a bikini. One can morally condemn such a refusal, even if one thinks that she should not be compelled to submit to a cesarean.

"Lifestyle cases," where the risk to the child comes from nonessential behavior, such as drinking alcohol, smoking tobacco, or using drugs, present a different situation. In lifestyle cases, the welfare of the future child appears paramount. If the woman forgoes these substances, the only harm done to her is loss of pleasure and choice—in fact, abstention is likely to benefit her physically—while the potential harm to the child is serious. On the other hand, when the risk to the fetus is slight, the obligation of the pregnant woman is less clear.

See Also

Court-Ordered Cesarean Sections

Public Health and the Law

Consider, for example, drinking during pregnancy. Heavy drinking during pregnancy can cause fetal alcohol syndrome (FAS), which is typically marked by severe facial deformities and mental retardation. One study showed that even moderate drinking—defined as one to three drinks daily—during early pregnancy can result in a lowering of IQ by as much as five points (Streissguth et al., 1989). Perhaps most important, there is no established "safe" level of alcohol consumption. While there is no evidence that a rare single drink during pregnancy does damage, there is no guarantee that it does not. The safest course is therefore total abstention. But is the safest course the morally obligatory one? We do not require this standard of parents regarding their already born children. Having a single drink occasionally in pregnancy is arguably morally permissible, primarily because the risk of causing harm is very low (perhaps nonexistent), but also because the nature of the harm (loss of a few IQ points) is not so serious as to justify moral condemnation. For a child of normal intelligence, the loss of five IQ points is not devastating. (At the same time, five IQ points can mean the difference between a mildly and a severely retarded child.)

If the occasional drink should be considered a matter of individual discretion, binge drinking, which has a 35 percent chance of subjecting a baby to full-blown FAS, clearly qualifies as an unreasonable risk to the health of a baby. So does smoking crack cocaine. Whether women have a moral obligation not to drink heavily or smoke crack during pregnancy is profoundly complicated by the fact that these behaviors are often the product of addictions. They are less than fully voluntary—some would say they are not voluntary at all. If a woman cannot modify her behavior, then she cannot have a moral obligation to do so.

But is it true that someone who is addicted cannot modify his or her behavior? The distinction should be drawn between being able to stop doing something at will, and not being able to stop at all. Although it is difficult to get over addictions, many smokers, alcoholics, and drug users do manage to change their behaviors. We can recognize that it may be very difficult for some women to fulfill their moral obligations to the babies they intend to bear, and acknowledge that they will need help to do so, without denying that they have such obligations.

Should drug or alcohol treatment be imposed on addicted pregnant women? Perhaps—if it could be shown that coerced treatment works, and therefore protects babies from prenatal harm. However, discussion of the justifiability of coerced treatment seems premature when there are not enough treatment programs for pregnant addicts who want to get over their addictions. Many in-patient alcohol rehabilitation programs exclude pregnant women, largely due to a fear of liability. The situation is even worse for pregnant drug addicts (Chavkin, 1990); sudden withdrawal of drugs can be as damaging to the fetus as continued exposure. As a result, a few treatment programs are able or willing to treat pregnant addicts. Even in areas where there are such treatment programs, there are not nearly enough spaces for all who want help. The absence of treatment programs makes it virtually impossible for substance abusers to fulfill their moral obligations to the children they intend to bear, even with the best will in the world.

To summarize, all women who intend to bear children have moral obligations to protect those children from the serious risk of substantial harm. Heavy smoking, binge drinking, and use of drugs such as crack cocaine and heroin constitute such risks. However, the moral wrongness of engaging in such behaviors during pregnancy is affected by the woman's ability to stop. A woman who is not addicted to cocaine, but who goes on using it during her pregnancy (perhaps on the weekends, because she enjoys it), fully aware of the risks she imposes on her future child, acts very wrongly indeed, and is properly blamed. It would be inappropriate similarly to condemn the pregnant woman who wants what's best for her baby and tries to get help with her addiction, only to be turned away because of the dearth of drug programs. Such a woman is trying to do the right thing; blame properly belongs with society for failing to help her. Nevertheless, if her baby is born damaged due to her drug use, she will—and should—feel moral regret at the harm caused by her drug habit, even if she should not be blamed.

The intention to bear a child

Some people object to making the future child, rather than the fetus, the locus of moral obligation, on the grounds that the existence of the future child depends entirely on the pregnant woman's decision. These critics find it unacceptable that a woman can avoid her obligations to her not-yet-born child by ensuring that it not be born (that is, by aborting it). Moreover, a woman may decide to abort, but later change her mind and continue the pregnancy. During the period when she thought she would have an abortion, she may have continued to smoke and drink. As long as she did not intend to bring a child into the world, there was no one for whose sake she should abstain; continuing to smoke or drink seems morally acceptable in this light. Yet if she changes her mind and continues the pregnancy, she may have harmed the child she bears. Is she now morally blameworthy for the harm she causes?

Two responses can be made. The first is to recognize that moral responsibility for outcomes can extend beyond harms knowingly risked, to harms uninten-

At its most expansive, legal moralism is the belief that behavioral codes are foundational to a social order.

PAGE 558

tionally caused. The fact that a woman did not intend to continue a pregnancy at the time she engaged in heavy drinking or used drugs does not entirely absolve her from blame. Even though she does not intend to have a baby at the time of the risky behavior, the failure to consider the possibility that she might change her mind may be negligent, and thus blameworthy. The second response concerns the futility of crying over spilt milk. It says that there is nothing a woman can do about her past behavior, and that if she changes her mind and decides to carry the pregnancy to term, she should focus on what she can do to ensure her baby's health. For example, giving up smoking in the second or third trimester gives the not-yet-born child a better chance than continuing to smoke throughout the pregnancy. If, despite her efforts, the baby is born damaged (a fairly unlikely result), the woman does not completely escape responsibility, but her blameworthiness is mitigated by the fact that she acted rightly once she decided to continue the pregnancy.

Another objection to making "the child she intends to bear" rather than the fetus the object of the pregnant woman's moral obligation is that often women do not "intend" to bear children. Drug addicts, in particular, may regard pregnancy as something that "happens" to them, often as a result of bartering their bodies for drugs, rather than something they intend. Nor do they necessarily choose to give birth: They may not be able to afford an abortion, or it may not be available in a particular geographical area. For some women, abortion is not a morally or culturally acceptable option. Do restrictions on the choice of whether to bear a child affect the woman's moral obligations to the child she bears? It can be argued that these restrictions do not affect how the woman ought to act, but they may affect how much she is to be blamed if she acts wrongly.

Consider a woman who deliberately gets pregnant, intending to have a baby. If she goes on drinking and smoking and using recreational drugs, knowing of the possible effects on her baby's health and making no effort to stop, she acts very wrongly indeed. By contrast, consider a woman who has no responsibility for becoming pregnant (she was raped), in a jurisdiction that prohibits abortion. She is the victim of two grave injustices, first in being raped and second in being denied an abortion. Still, that would not justify behavior likely to inflict severe damage on the child she will perforce bear. Ideally, she should behave as if the pregnancy were chosen, since she is prevented from terminating the pregnancy. That is, she should stop smoking, drink moderately or not at all, and so on. However, her failure to do so is certainly less blameworthy than the failure of a woman who has chosen to conceive and bear a child. Most cases will fall somewhere in between the extremes of deliberate conception and forced childbirth. In general, the fewer options a woman has regarding pregnancy and childbirth, the less she deserves blame for failing to fulfill her obligations to her future child. However, women are not relieved of moral responsibility simply because they do not see pregnancy as a choice.

◆ **Rh disease**
A condition in which the immune system of the pregnant woman destroys the blood cells of the fetus and, if severe and untreated, results in fetal death.

Conclusion

Deciding to have a baby carries with it certain moral responsibilities. Children have a moral right to be protected from harm, whether inflicted post- or prenatally. This right to be free from harm imposes obligations on those in a position to protect children, including their mothers during pregnancy. Yet a single-minded focus on the risk of harm to the future child ignores the impact on the pregnant woman. She is not a "fetal container" but an individual in her own right, one whose interests must be considered in determining morally permissible options.

Another factor in determining the moral obligations of pregnant women to their future children is the degree of risk and the nature of the harm. Just as parents are not morally required to avoid any and all risks to their born children, neither are pregnant women morally obligated to curtail their own interests to avoid even the slightest risk of harm.

Distinct from the question of the obligations women have to their future children is the issue of their blameworthiness for failing to fulfill those obligations. In general, blameworthiness is mitigated by the inability to have done otherwise. Such factors as addiction and the degree of control over reproductive ability must be considered in assessing morally the conduct of pregnant women.

— BONNIE STEINBOCK

LEGAL AND REGULATORY ISSUES

The intimate relationship between a woman and a fetus developing within her body has long given rise to vital questions of morality, religion, science, medicine, law, and public policy. The United States in the early 1980s witnessed a new strand of legal and public policy issues—separate from the issue of abortion—concerning the maternal-fetal relationship when women continue pregnancy and give birth. Courts, legislatures, and state prosecutors increasingly sought to compel women to behave in ways deemed likely to promote the birth of healthy babies. Women faced pregnancy-related restrictions and penalties, including civil suit, criminal prosecution, and court-ordered surgery, aimed at a wide range of conduct: driving an automobile, failing to follow a doctor's advice, drinking alcohol, and taking prescription and illegal drugs, among others. This article describes the status of such efforts and

See Also
Behavior Control

explores the implications for children's well-being and women's liberty.

Law versus morality

In general, women have a strong interest in giving birth to healthy children and go to great lengths to increase the likelihood that they will do so. Widespread consensus exists that a woman who chooses to bear a child has a moral obligation to consider the effects her actions will have on her future child. Current public policy recognizes a role for the government in supporting women's ability to have the healthy pregnancies they desire. Existing programs seek to help women overcome obstacles such as poverty and dangerous addictions by providing prenatal care, food, housing, and drug and alcohol treatment, though the adequacy and appropriate scope of such programs is hotly debated.

Far more controversial are the rare instances when governmental action coerces rather than supports, and seeks to compel women to change their behavior. Should the government use punitive measures to regulate women's actions in an effort to promote healthy births? Should the government thereby transform women's moral obligations into legally required standards of conduct?

The current U.S. legal system generally deems the pregnant woman the proper person to make decisions during pregnancy and does not recognize competing fetal rights that would provide a basis for overriding her decisions. Women retain the freedom to make their own judgments and to balance their obligations to their future children against other responsibilities, such as to family and to work. This approach is consistent with women's constitutional rights to liberty, privacy, and equal protection, guaranteed by the U.S. Constitution as well as by state constitutions.

Beginning in the early 1980s, however, some commentators called for greater regulation of women's actions during pregnancy (Shaw, 1984; Robertson, 1983). Arguing that fetuses, as future children, deserve legal protection from their mothers, they advocate that women be held liable for actions during pregnancy that may be harmful to fetal development. Many more commentators have opposed adversarial approaches, arguing that they not only infringe on women's freedoms but also are ineffective, even counterproductive, in promoting healthy births (Johnsen, 1986, 1992; American Medical Association [AMA], 1990; Annas, 1987; Gallagher, 1987). The remainder of this article examines some particular forms of pregnancy-related restrictions aimed at women, including exclusionary employment policies, civil suits for prenatal injuries, criminal prosecution, loss of child custody, and court-ordered surgery.

MATERNAL-FETAL RELATIONSHIP
Biological Aspects

Beliefs about the independent moral and religious status of the fetus vary widely among Americans. The physical status, however, is clear: A fetus cannot exist apart from a particular woman prior to "viability," which occurs at approximately twenty-four to twenty-eight weeks' gestational age. Only the pregnant woman can sustain a fetus's growth and meet its needs. That a fetus does not and cannot exist wholly apart from a woman makes the maternal-fetal relationship unique.

During pregnancy, a woman and the fetus developing within her body profoundly affect each other. A fetus makes unparalleled physical and psychological demands on a woman, subjecting her body to tremendous physical adjustments and creating significant risks for even the healthiest woman. Concomitantly, with the fetus completely dependent upon and entirely within a particular woman's body, her actions, experiences, and physical health during and even prior to pregnancy substantially affect fetal development and the health of her child at birth. Throughout their reproductive lives, women inevitably confront innumerable decisions, large and small, that create varying probabilities of harm or benefit to fetal development.

The biological realities of the maternal-fetal relationship may not dictate any particular social response, but they highlight the need to scrutinize the impact on women of any law or policy aimed at fetuses. If not formulated with care, governmental policies adopted to promote healthy births can substantially and unnecessarily intrude on women's fundamental liberties and ability to decide how to live their lives, and may in fact decrease the likelihood of healthy births.

— DAWN E. JOHNSEN

Exclusionary employment policies

The U.S. Supreme Court has not directly considered the constitutionality of a governmentally imposed pregnancy-related restriction. The Court, however, has reviewed the legality of a private employer's exclusion of all fertile women from employment viewed as potentially harmful to fetal development (*International Union, United Auto Workers* [*UAW*] v. *Johnson Controls*, 1991). The Supreme Court ruled in

During the 16th and 17th centuries there was a concerted effort to stem the practice of infanticide throughout Europe.

PAGE 372

French historian Phillipe Ariès says the idea of a separate childhood was unknown until the later Middle Ages.

PAGE 375

What is the moral status of infants with mental and physical disabilities?

PAGE 375

March 1991 that a policy prohibiting fertile women from working in positions where they would be exposed to lead discriminated against women on the basis of pregnancy, in violation of a federal antidiscrimination law. Although a private employer's policy was at issue, some of the reasoning of the Supreme Court and the lower appellate court applies equally to governmental attempts to regulate women's decisions and actions for the sake of the health of their future children.

The Supreme Court acknowledged that "[e]mployment late in pregnancy often imposes risks on the unborn child," but found that "Congress made clear that the decision to become pregnant or to work while being either pregnant or capable of becoming pregnant was reserved for each individual woman to make for herself." The Court implied that the individuals most directly affected, rather than a court or employer, are best situated to balance competing factors and make such decisions: "Decisions about the welfare of future children must be left to the parents who conceive, bear, support, and raise them rather than to the employers who hire those parents" (*International Union, UAW* v. *Johnson Controls*, 1991, pp. 205-206).

Two lower court opinions in the case highlight the difficulties and dangers of allowing anyone other than the woman directly affected to make these judgments. Judge Frank Easterbrook noted: "How does the risk attributable to lead compare, say, to . . . driving a taxi? A female bus or taxi driver is exposed to noxious fumes and the risk of accidents, all hazardous to a child she carries. Would it follow that taxi and bus companies can decline to hire women? That an employer could forbid pregnant employees to drive cars because of the risk accidents pose to fetuses?" (*International Union, UAW* v. *Johnson Controls*, 1991, p. 917). Judge Richard Cudahy asked: "What is the situation of the pregnant woman, unemployed or working for the minimum wage and unprotected by health insurance, in relation to her pregnant sister, exposed to an indeterminate lead risk but well-fed, housed, and doctored? Whose fetus is at greater risk? Whose decision is this to make?" (*International Union, UAW* v. *Johnson Controls*, 1991, p. 902).

Criminal prosecutions for actions during pregnancy

The most common form of adversarial governmental action against women for engaging in behavior viewed as harmful to fetal development has been criminal prosecution. State prosecutors have relied on laws that clearly were not intended to create special restrictions on women's actions during pregnancy, including laws prohibiting child abuse, distributing drugs to a minor, or murder.

Several prosecutions have been based on women's otherwise lawful actions. One of the first occurred in 1986, when a California woman was prosecuted for allegedly causing her infant son to be born severely brain damaged, and ultimately to die, as a result of her own excessive loss of blood during delivery. The prosecution claimed that, by waiting a number of hours before obtaining medical care when she went into labor and began bleeding vaginally, the woman had violated a statute that required parents to provide their children with clothing, food, shelter, and medical care. Other prosecutions have involved alcohol use during pregnancy. A Massachusetts woman who suffered serious injuries in a car accident, including a miscarriage, was prosecuted for involuntary manslaughter of the fetus because she allegedly caused the accident by driving while intoxicated. In another reported case, a pregnant woman in Wyoming who notified the police that her husband had physically assaulted her was arrested for child abuse when they detected she had been drinking. The charges were ultimately dismissed in all three of these cases (Johnsen, 1992).

In many more cases, women have been prosecuted for using illegal drugs while pregnant. Of course, a woman's pregnancy does not immunize her from prosecution under generally applicable laws prohibiting the use or possession of drugs. In some cases, however, women were subjected to special prosecutions and greater penalties for the express reason that they were pregnant at the time they used drugs. Although some pleaded guilty in return for reduced sentences, women have prevailed in the overwhelming majority of cases where they challenged the prosecution because the statutes were not intended to apply to prenatal behavior (Johnsen, 1992).

Both of the two high state courts that have considered such a case ruled that the statute had been misapplied. In 1992, the supreme court of Ohio dismissed an indictment for child endangerment against a woman who allegedly used cocaine while pregnant (*Ohio* v. *Gray*, 1992). Also in 1992, the supreme court of Florida reversed a woman's conviction under a statute prohibiting the distribution of a controlled substance to a minor and imposing a penalty of up to thirty years' imprisonment. In holding that the statute was not intended to apply to prenatal behavior, the court rejected the "State's invitation to walk down a path that the law, public policy, reason and common sense forbid it to tread" (*Johnson* v. *State*, 1992, p. 1297).

Loss of child custody for actions during pregnancy

States have attempted to deprive women of custody of their children based solely on women's actions during pregnancy, rather than on the customary determination of the current ability of the woman and other family members to care for the child. While most cases involved a woman's use of illegal drugs during pregnancy, several courts have based custody decisions on activity that was lawful but seen as detrimental to fetal development. For example, in 1987 a Michigan woman temporarily lost custody of her infant and was charged with child abuse because while pregnant she had taken Valium without a prescription to relieve pain from injuries she suffered in a car accident (*In re J. Jeffrey*, 1987).

The first high state court to consider this issue, the supreme court of Connecticut, ruled in 1992 that state law did not allow the termination of parental rights based on a woman's use of cocaine during pregnancy. The court concluded that the legislature had determined that the threat of loss of custody of their children would cause women to avoid prenatal care and substance abuse treatment and "would lead to more, rather than fewer, babies being born either without adequate prenatal care or damaged by prenatal drug abuse, or both" (*In re Valerie D.*, 1992, p. 764).

Although the use of illegal drugs during pregnancy may at first glance seem to be the strongest justification for punitive governmental action such as the imposition of enhanced criminal penalties or deprivation of child custody, these approaches have been widely repudiated. The government clearly has a strong interest in preventing pregnant women from using dangerous drugs. Commentators, however, have with remarkable consistency agreed that this interest is best pursued through programs that help women overcome drug and alcohol dependencies and obtain prenatal care. Entities such as the U.S. General Accounting Office (GAO) and the AMA have argued that fear of prosecution and loss of custody of their children will discourage women from seeking care and increase the number of unhealthy births (GAO, 1990; AMA, 1990). As the Florida Supreme Court noted: "Rather than face the possibility of prosecution, pregnant women who are substance abusers may simply avoid prenatal care or medical care for fear of being detected. Yet the newborns of these women are, as a group, the most fragile and sick, and most in need of hospital neonatal care" (*Johnson* v. *State*, 1992, pp. 1295-1296).

Court-ordered cesarean sections

Courts in at least eleven states have ordered women against their wishes to give birth by cesarean section rather than vaginal delivery (Kilder et al., 1987). The severe bodily intrusion of this court-ordered surgery contrasts sharply with our legal system's general refusal to order invasive medical procedures or to force one person to assume any personal risk to save the life of another. Although judicial opinions are rare in these time-pressured cases, three published appellate court decisions illustrate both the motivations behind and the harm caused by such court orders.

In the first published appellate court decision, the supreme court of Georgia in 1981 declined to lift a court order authorizing the performance of a cesarean section against a woman's religious objections where the examining physician found a "ninety-nine percent certainty" that the child would not survive a vaginal delivery and a 50 percent chance the woman would die (*Jefferson* v. *Griffin Spalding County Hospital Authority*, 1981, p. 459). With no analysis of the constitutional and policy implications, the court granted "temporary custody" of the fetus to the state and gave it full authority to make all surgical decisions concerning the birth. In the end, a court-ordered cesarean section was not performed; despite the physician's predictions, the woman gave birth by vaginal delivery to a healthy baby without adverse effects.

Both appellate courts that have considered the constitutionality of a coerced cesarean section declared it unconstitutional (*In re A.C.*, 1990; *Baby Boy Doe*, 1994). In the first, a District of Columbia court ordered a woman who was twenty-six weeks pregnant and terminally ill with cancer to undergo the surgery. The woman did not consent to the cesarean and her husband, parents, and attending physicians all opposed it on the ground that the woman's health and comfort should be the first priority. The cesarean section was performed nonetheless. The fetus was not viable and did not survive. The woman died two days after the cesarean section. After the woman's death, a three-judge panel of the D.C. Court of Appeals issued an opinion explaining why it had affirmed the order. The Court acknowledged, "... [w]e well know that we may have shortened [her] life span," but found that, because she was likely to die soon of cancer, the value of the woman's life was outweighed by the fetus's admittedly "slim" chance of survival (*In re A.C.*, 1987, pp. 613-614).

The full D.C. Court of Appeals reversed the decision of the three-judge panel, ruling that "in virtually all cases the question of what is to be done is to be decided by the patient—the pregnant woman—on behalf of herself and the fetus" (*In re A.C.*, 1990, p. 1237). The court found that a court order compelling a woman to have a cesarean section violates her rights to bodily integrity and to refuse medical treatment, protected under both common law and the U.S. Constitution. The court graphically described the violent bodily intrusion that would be required to enforce an order against a woman who resisted: "[She] would have to be

◆ **prenatal diagnosis**
Identifying fetal defects.

See Also
Trust
Communication: Shared Decision-Making
Informed Consent

The worldwide epidemic of HIV infection and AIDS provided the context for important fetal research in the 1990s.

PAGE 242

REGULATORY ISSUES

Gender and Racial Disparities

Pregnancy-related restrictions and penalties directed at women raise serious concerns about gender discrimination. As the Supreme Court noted in the 1991 *Johnson Controls* case, the company's justification for excluding women from jobs for the good of their future children echoed the nineteenth-century rationale for restricting women's ability to work outside the home or participate in political or civic affairs. Virtually all attempts to impose special behavioral restrictions in order to improve infant health have been targeted solely at women, even where evidence suggests that the activity at issue can cause damage to sperm, as is the case for exposure to lead, smoking, drinking alcohol, and using certain drugs.

Significant evidence reveals that pregnancy-related restrictions also have been imposed in a racially discriminatory manner. A 1987 survey of court-ordered cesarean sections published in the *New England Journal of Medicine* found that 80 percent of the women against whom orders were sought were African-American or Asian (Kolder et al., 1987). A 1990 study, also published in the *New England Journal of Medicine*, found that African-American women were ten times more likely than white women to be reported to health authorities when they tested positive for illegal drug use during pregnancy (Chasnoff et al., 1990). Another 1990 survey of forty-seven women prosecuted for behavior during pregnancy found that 80 percent of the prosecutions were against women of color (Paltrow, 1992).

— DAWN E. JOHNSEN

fastened with restraints to the operating table, or perhaps involuntarily rendered unconscious by forcibly injecting her with an anesthetic, and then subjected to unwanted major surgery. Such actions would surely give one pause in a civilized society . . ." (*In re A.C.*, 1990, p. 1244, n. 8). Indeed, in another case a court-ordered cesarean section was performed by tying the woman to the operating table and forcibly removing her husband from the room (Gallagher, 1987).

An Illinois appellate court similarly ruled in 1994 that ordering a woman to give birth by cesarean section would violate her constitutional rights. Citing *In re A.C.*, the court held that "a woman's competent choice in refusing medical treatment as invasive as a cesarean section during her pregnancy must be honored, even in circumstances where the choice may be harmful to her fetus" (*Doe*, 1994, p. 330). The woman's physician had testified that the chances that the fetus would survive a natural labor were close to zero. In fact, the woman vaginally delivered a healthy baby three weeks after the state unsuccessfully sought the court order (*Doe*, 1994).

A number of medical and public-health organizations have opposed court orders overriding a pregnant woman's decision concerning medical treatment. The AMA is among the organizations that has endorsed respect for women's constitutional right to bodily integrity: "[D]ecisions that would result in health risks are properly made only by the individual who must bear the risk. Considerable uncertainty can surround medical evaluations of the risks and benefits of obstetrical interventions. Through a court-ordered intervention, a physician deprives a pregnant woman of her right to reject personal risk and replaces it with the physician's evaluation of the amount of risk that is properly acceptable" (AMA, 1990, p. 2665). The practice of seeking court orders not only violates women's right to evaluate the risks and uncertainties involved in their medical care, it is counterproductive to the goal of promoting healthy pregnancies and births because it causes women to distrust physicians. Citing a case in which a woman left the hospital to avoid a court-ordered cesarean section, the AMA expressed concern that "women may withhold information from the physician. . . . Or they may reject medical or prenatal care altogether . . ." (AMA, 1990, pp. 2665-2666).

Conclusion

Attempts to impose special pregnancy-related restrictions or penalties on women have been relatively rare and typically have been invalidated by courts and opposed by interested organizations and most commentators. The threat of criminal prosecution, loss of custody of children, and court-ordered medical interventions would likely deter the women who are most at risk of poor birth outcomes from seeking prenatal care and drug and alcohol treatment.

The government can, however, do a great deal to improve the health of children by helping women to have healthy pregnancies. For example, experts agree that the high rate of infant mortality in the United States can be drastically cut by providing prenatal care to the approximately one-third of American women who receive inadequate or no prenatal care. Drug treatment programs routinely turn away pregnant women, and the few that will treat women during pregnancy have long waiting lists. Government studies have shown that expending the funds necessary to provide these services would actually save taxpayers three to four times as much in reduced infant health-care costs.

While creating legal conflicts between a woman and the fetus within her is ineffective and even counterproductive, laws and policies that respect women's rights can effectively promote the healthy pregnancies and births that are in the interests of all.

Dawn E. Johnsen is Deputy Assistant Attorney General, Office of Legal Counsel, United States Department of Justice. The views expressed here do not necessarily reflect the positions of the Department of Justice of the United States.

— DAWN E. JOHNSEN

NATURAL LAW

Natural law is perhaps the most ancient and historically persistent concept in Western ethics. Philosophers like Aristotle regarded nature as a ground of justice. Theologians like Thomas Aquinas distinguished between natural and supernatural sources of morality and law. By it Thomas Jefferson sanctioned a revolution. With it political reformers like Martin Luther King, Jr., justified civil disobedience. Upon it political philosophers like John Locke have built theories of the origin and limits of the civil state; and international lawyers, such as Hugo Grotius and Samuel Pufendorf, the order of justice between states. Despite disagreements about the theory of natural law, international bodies appeal to unwritten sources of rights to health care.

U.S. constitutional law has used natural law to clarify and sometimes amend the written law. Natural law undergirds the Thirteenth (1865) and Fourteenth Amendments (1868), which outlawed slavery and secured rights of U.S. citizens against state jurisdictions. Natural law also serves as a method of judicial interpretation, from which the judge looks beyond the written text of the Constitution in order to identify and vindicate rights of citizens. Today, constitutional debates have become the most public and controversial forum of natural-law discussion (Dworkin, 1985; Ely, 1980). Inasmuch as natural law is widely regarded as the moral basis for rights of privacy or personal autonomy, it is implicated in some of the most difficult biomedical issues, including abortion, reproductive technologies, and euthanasia.

The question of natural law emerges when we consider human laws and customs (Sokolowski, 1992). None is perfect, and some appear to be wicked. We then ask, What is the norm of reason in matters of morality and justice? Are moral norms merely the artifacts of human reason, devised to serve the circumstances of a particular culture? Or is there a ground that transcends cultures and histories? On what basis can laws be morally criticized and rectified?

Since these questions are fundamental to all ethical inquiry, what makes natural law different from other normative theories? There is no tidy answer. An array of moral theorists, using different theories, agree (1) that there are objective, though unwritten, moral grounds for right reason in the legislation and adjudication of human law, and (2) that moral reason must be guided by, and respect, certain values inherent in human nature (e.g., rationality and the capacity for free choice). If natural law means that moral and legal norms are grounded in reason, and that right exercise of human reason requires respect for goods inherent in human nature, then it would be exceedingly difficult not to hold a natural-law theory of one sort or another.

The health-care professional exploring natural-law

NATURE'S LAW

Sometimes called the father of natural law, Aristotle (384–322 B.C.) said that "what is by nature just" has the same force everywhere.

issues will face a debate often abstract and bewildering. First, what starts as a debate over particular issues in law, politics, or health care often becomes a debate over the concept of natural law itself. Second, what distinguishes one natural-law theory from another is not always clear; there seem to be as many different theories of natural law as there are theorists. In any case, one must remember that the rubric "natural law" often hides important disagreements among its proponents, as well as significant agreements among those who dispute its particular formulations and applications. Third, until recently natural-law thinking for the most part has not directly addressed biomedical issues. A well-developed body of natural-law literature, as found in legal, moral, and political theory, does not yet exist for biomedical issues. Thus, it will be helpful to summarize some of the main historical and philosophical themes of natural law.

Ancient themes

Ancient Greek philosophers asked whether law and morality are due principally to nature or to convention. Aristotle, who is sometimes credited as the father of natural law, contended that "[w]hat is just in the political sense can be subdivided into what is just by nature and what is just by convention. What is by nature just has the same force everywhere and does not depend on what we regard or do not regard as just" (*Nicomachean Ethics*, 1134b18). While Aristotle certainly held that there are standards for judging whether a law is "in accord with nature" (*Rhetoric*, 1373b6), whether he had a doctrine of "natural law" is much debated (Miller, 1991). The proposition that moral judgment is rooted in the soil of nature, and not merely in human artifice, does not necessarily mean that nature is a "law."

The form of natural-law theory that came to influence Western culture arose from the confluence of Stoic, biblical, and Christian Scholastic ideas. Cicero, the ancient authority most often cited by Christians, wrote:

> *True law is right reason in agreement with nature; it is of universal application, unchanging and everlasting; it summons to duty by its commands, and averts from wrongdoing by its prohibitions. . . . It is a sin to try to alter this law, nor is it allowable to attempt to repeal any part of it, and it is impossible to abolish it entirely. . . . [there is] one master and ruler, that is, God, over us all, for he is author of this law, its promulgator, and its enforcing judge.* (De Re Publica, *3.22.33*)

Similarly, Thomas Aquinas said that "the participation in the eternal law by rational creatures is called the law of nature" (*Summa theologica*, 1947, I-II, q. 91, a. 2). Nature *as law* requires the notion that natural standards are promulgated by God. The human intelligence finds itself not merely in a natural order but under a divine commonwealth, which is a rule of law in the exemplary sense.

◆ **natural law**
a body of law or a specific principle held to be derived from nature and binding upon human society, with moral reason guided by certain values inherent in human nature, such as rationality and the capacity for free choice

Aquinas and natural law

Since the theory of natural law as developed by Thomas Aquinas is widely regarded as the epitome of the premodern position, let us summarize his view. In the *Summa theologica*, Aquinas maintains that for something to be called law, it must be (1) reasonable, in the sense of directing action; (2) ordained to the common good; (3) legislated by the proper authority; and (4) duly promulgated (I-II, q. 90). The eternal law, whereby the world is ruled by divine providence, satisfies these criteria in an exemplary way (q. 91, a. 1). Natural law, however, is principally that part of divine reason accessible to the human intelligence. It is not to be confused with the order of the physical or biological world. Law is predicated only by a kind of similitude with the order found in nonrational entities (q. 91, a. 2 ad 3).

The first principle of the natural law is that "Good is to be done and pursued and evil avoided" (q. 94, a. 2). By nature, the human agent is inclined toward certain intelligible goods. Though Aquinas never claimed to provide an exhaustive list, these goods include life, procreation and care of offspring, entering into society, and knowing the truth about God. The first precepts of natural law take the form that something is to be done and pursued with respect to these goods, or resisted if contrary to them. Why call the precepts "natural"? Because the objectives of action are grounded in human nature antecedent to our deliberation and choice. In this sense, nature signifies the (human) essence directed to its specific operation. The term "natural" also indicates that the first precepts stand as the basic axioms of action, and are known naturally (*naturaliter*) rather than learned by study or by inference. Why call the objects of these inclinations "precepts" or "law"? Aquinas maintains that human agents are capable of seeing that certain goods are worthy of pursuit; they also grasp, in an elementary way, that in choices one is morally bound to act in accord with these goods.

The first precepts, however, are not a complete moral code. Aquinas holds that human reason must develop and apply them. First precepts are developed in terms of "secondary precepts," which spell out further implications for human action. For example, from the precept that one must act in accord with the good of life and resist what is contrary to it, we reason that murder is wrong. The first precepts also require "determinations," supplied by custom and positive laws. The

See Also
Sexism as Natural Law

"determinations" are ways that the natural law is made effective in the human community. Thus, while the care and education of offspring are enjoined upon humankind by a first precept of the natural law, how, where, and when the duty is discharged are determined by custom or positive law. Here, the virtue of prudence is paramount.

In the Thomistic scheme, the moral order in human law and politics is a kind of ecosystem, requiring for its proper function not only the universally binding precepts of natural law but also good customs, intelligently framed and emended positive laws, and acquired virtues, by which the laws are obeyed not just externally but also in the interior act of the will. It is therefore not advisable to isolate the doctrine of natural law in Aquinas from the rest of his account of moral agency. First, Aquinas flatly rejects the idea that human beings ever existed in a pure state of nature (I, q. 95, a. 1), unlike the ahistorical "state of nature" models of the modern era. Created in grace and wounded by sin, the concrete human condition, according to Aquinas, is in need of tutoring and, ultimately, of transformation by divine grace. Aquinas insists, for example, that the two great ends of the natural law—the love of God and of neighbor—obscured by sin and evil customs, require repromulgation by divine positive law (q. 100, aa. 5, 11). Second, the greater part of his *Treatise on Law* (I-II, qq. 90-108) puts the natural law in the double context of the divine positive law of the Old Testament (*lex vetus*) and the New Testament Law of Grace (*lex nova*). Biblical history shapes Aquinas's fully considered judgment and exposition of the natural law.

Aquinas can be absolved of the charge that he confuses moral and physical meanings of nature, as well as the charge that his account is ahistorical. Yet his theory of natural law does rely on a teleological conception of providence, and the historical cast of his thought is informed by the biblical narrative. These features are not accidental. To the extent that modern theorists reject the credibility of the teleological science of nature, and aim to provide an account of natural law that is neutral with respect to theological suppositions, the Thomist theory will be of more historical than systematic interest.

Modern theories

In modern times, the concept of natural law has undergone considerable doctrinal and institutional development. Although the theological framework of natural law was maintained as part of public rhetoric well into the nineteenth century, it was no longer the main interest of natural lawyers. As Lloyd Weinreb notes: "The puzzles with which Aquinas and others grappled when they tried to understand the place of humankind in nature appear in [modern] guise as part of the effort to describe the relationship of the individual to the state" (1987, p. 67). This shift of perspective and emphasis, from cosmological and theological themes to the more narrow political and legal issues of natural law, is complicated. Leo Strauss (1953) has argued that the ancient and modern theories are so radically different that they ought not to be confounded. Whether there is continuity or discontinuity between premodern and modern versions of natural law remains a disputed subject in the scholarly literature. While we cannot discuss this in detail, we can cite at least two problems that have shaped the modern approach.

NATURAL LAW AND MODERN SCIENCE. By the seventeenth century, the phrase "natural law" was expropriated by the modern sciences to denote purely

NATURAL LAW AND THE PUBLIC ORDER OF RIGHTS

The humane focus of natural law concerns legal and political problems of the relationship between the individual and the state. In the seventeenth and eighteenth centuries, human nature rather than authority allegedly vested in churches or kings came to represent the legitimate origin of the state and its rule of law. Philosophers and jurists wrested natural law from the controversial settings of religion and custom, and attempted to reduce it to self-evident laws of reason sufficient to ground a public order of law and rights. While the well-known dictum by Hugo Grotius that the natural law would have validity even if God did not exist captures something of the modern temper, even more pertinent is his assertion that "[j]ust as mathematicians treat their figures as abstracted from bodies, so in treating law I have withdrawn my mind from every particular fact" (Grotius, 1925, Prolegomena nos. 11, 58). Modern natural-law theorists emphasize apodictic, nongainsayable propositions, and filter out anything dependent upon the mediation of culture and religion. These theories are expected to cut through religious and political controversy in order to secure that minimum of rational consensus needed for public purposes (Gewirth, 1984). In contrast with the ancients and medievals, the minimalistic bent of modern theories is not designed to mesh with the virtue of prudence.

— RUSSELL HITTINGER

"There is but one law for all, namely, that law which governs all law, the law of our Creator, the law of humanity, justice, equity–the law of nature, and of nations."

EDMUND BURKE
IMPEACHMENT OF WARREN HASTINGS, 1794

N

NATURAL LAW

Natural Social Necessities

"Two things fill the mind with ever-increasing wonder and awe . . . the starry heavens above me and the moral law within me."

IMMANUEL KANT
CRITIQUE OF PRACTICAL REASON, 1788

descriptive or predictive aspects of natural bodies. In optics, astronomy, and physics, the relation between nature and law no longer expressed the *human* participation in divine providence but, rather, the intelligible, measurable, and predictable regularities in physical nature (Ruby, 1986). Teleological understanding was abandoned in favor of mechanistic explanations that relied exclusively upon material and efficient causes. The success and prestige of the physical sciences made it difficult thenceforth to interrelate the moral and physical meanings of natural law without falling into equivocation. How, for example, can law be predicated on nature without conflating physical and moral necessities? In the physical sciences, law denotes the measurable and predictable properties of things that have no freedom. But in the practical or moral sphere, law denotes principles that govern human freedom. These two meanings of natural law—nature as amenable to description and prediction, and nature as a prescriptive norm of freedom—present an ongoing theoretical difficulty in modern thought about the subject.

Natural social necessities

Given the new scientific meanings of nature and law, as well as the practical need to devise principles of justice sufficient to limit the modern state, two approaches to natural law dominate the modern period. One tradition keys natural law to what is needed for survival and societal peace. By nature, human beings are vulnerable, and need a certain minimal protection of their interests. Thomas Hobbes set the pattern of this tradition. Other examples of this approach are David Hume's "circumstances of justice," Oliver Wendell Holmes's "can't helps," and H. L. A. Hart's "minimum natural law." Natural law sets a background for customs and laws prohibiting violations of life, limb, and property. The advantages of this approach are at least threefold. First, the desire to protect one's life and property, insofar as it can be described and predicted, comports with the physicalist model of nature and law favored by the modern sciences. Second, it picks out elementary goods and bads that are apt to win consensus. These basic needs do not seem to depend upon the idiosyncrasies of particular individuals and their private life plans. Third, at least in the Anglo-American world, issues of life, limb, and property are easily recognized and adjudicated within a system of positive law.

However, natural necessities provide little or no reason to recognize absolute moral norms or rights that might resist the utilitarian calculations of a political majority acting for its alleged interests in peace and security. As Oliver Wendell Holmes said in his famous essay on natural law: "The most fundamental of the supposed preexisting rights—the right to life—is sacrificed without a scruple not only in war, but whenever the interest of society, that is, of the predominant power in the community, is thought to demand it" (Holmes, 1918, p. 314). It is one thing to say that any system of positive law must work against the background of natural human necessities; it is quite another to hold that these pervasive natural facts about the human condition carry any prescriptive or moral force.

Natural right of autonomy

Another tradition, typified by Kant's dictum that one "[m]ust act as if the maxim of your action were to become through your will a universal law of nature" (Kant, 1981, no. 421, p. 30), emphasizes the autonomy of moral agents. This natural law can be expressed in the categorical imperative that humanity in one's person and in the person of others must be respected as an end in itself. As developed by many modern theorists, autonomy is a concept variously described as "moral independence" (Dworkin, 1985, p. 353), "the free choice of goals and relations as an essential ingredient of individual well-being" (Raz, 1986, p. 369), and "personal sovereignty" (Reiman, 1990, p. 43). Is autonomy a fact about human nature, or is it a moral ideal? There is disagreement about this (Schneewind, 1986). Reiman, for example, maintains that "Personal sovereignty [indicates] a natural fact about human beings, consideration of which will lead us to the natural ground of equality between human beings" (1990, p. 43). Put thus, autonomy embraces both a natural fact and a moral principle.

Some version of the autonomist theory is the preferred approach in much of contemporary natural-law theory, for the autonomist position emphasizes specifically moral principles of law rather than mere natural necessities. It seeks to tell us not what agents typically want or need, but how and why human beings must be respected. Moreover, it comports with the humanistic premise that human beings have a native dignity based upon a rational capacity to determine their conduct. It is the rational capacity that sets (at least some) human beings apart from other entities of nature, and constitutes the axioms of the moral world.

Despite its wide appeal, three problems routinely crop up in connection with the autonomist position. First, it is not always clear whether we are enjoined to respect the capacity for autonomy or the rightful exercise of that capacity. If we are enjoined to respect the capacity itself, are we thereby duty bound to respect the agent when he or she uses the capacity in a wicked way? In short, do agents have a moral right to do moral wrong? Second, the rights and obligations that flow from this "natural" fact of autonomy are difficult to formulate except in very general terms. What can a right to autonomy mean, except that persons ought not to be treated as mere objects; and what can this mean, except

See Also

Natural Law: Is There a "Right to Autonomy"?

that a person ought to be treated according to sound moral considerations (Raz, 1986)? Hence, while autonomists emphasize a natural right to be treated equally, it is a humanist premise rather than the conclusion of moral reasoning (Raz, 1986). Third, we can ask whether the natural capacity for self-determination is adequate for moral reasoning about the status of other nonhuman species, prehuman entities (genetic material), incipient human life (embryos), and human beings whose autonomy is diminished.

Catholic natural-law theory

The Roman Catholic church is the only international institution to hold a natural-law doctrine in both the premodern and modern phases of the theory. Conciliar decrees, papal encyclicals, and canon law both reaffirm the natural law and have applied it across a range of moral issues (Fuchs, 1965; Finnis, 1980b). The encyclical *Veritatis splendor* (1993) gives considerable attention to natural law. Drawn chiefly from the work of Augustine and Aquinas, the papal formulation of natural law in *Veritatis* is traditional, emphasizing the status of natural law as real law, promulgated by God. Although there is only passing reference to biomedical issues, the encyclical represents perhaps the clearest exposition of the theoretical underpinnings of natural law by a modern pope. The concept of natural law has also recently been applied to natural rights. The new Code of Canon Law (1983) asserts the right of the church to address secular affairs insofar as such affairs pertain to "fundamental rights of the human person" (canon 747/2).

Over the past three decades natural-law debate has focused upon the encyclical *Humanae vitae* (1968), which condemned contraception as a violation of the natural law, not because it is artificial but because it is contrary to nature. The encyclical's premise is that marriage (apart from considerations of sacramental theology) naturally contains both a procreative and a unitive good. The moral question is whether these goods can be deliberately separated in the particular conjugal act. The natural-law reasoning of *Humanae vitae* has been interpreted in quite different, and sometimes contradictory, ways by moral theologians. A 1991 study finds that at least six natural-law positions have emerged in the debate (Smith, 1991). This is because the encyclical is terse, and does not spell out its argument in the fashion of an academic exercise. But it is also due to the fact that the encyclical outlines an argument at three levels, each of which is open to debate: (1) that the conjugal act must preserve the intrinsic order toward the procreative end; (2) that the unitive and procreative goods of marriage must not be separated; (3) that the integrity of marriage cannot be maintained in its totality unless it is maintained in each and every conjugal act. Hence, its analysis of nature concerns not only the natural order of the sexual function but also the natural goods of marriage as well as the nature of the human sexual act itself. Whatever might be said about the document, it does not present a simple natural-law argument.

Critics like Charles Curran (1985) have charged that *Humanae vitae* confuses the physical and moral structures of human acts. Curran also charges the encyclical with adopting a "classicist worldview and methodology" that comports with neither the methods of the sciences nor the relativizing of nature by the history of salvation (1985). Bernard Häring raises objections similar to Curran's. Not only in matters of reproduction, but also more generally in biomedical issues, Häring notes that the physician no longer defines himself as a servant of "ordered potentialities and powers of nature." Rather, he "increasingly considers himself an architect and sculptor of the given stuff of nature" (Häring, 1973). So, too, the moral theologian, he argues, must emphasize the divine mandate to creatively mold and intervene in nature. As so often happens in debates about natural law, the practical issue at hand (in this case, contraception) quickly opens onto the more abstract philosophical and theological questions about the meaning of nature and how it relates to norms of conduct.

In 1987, Joseph Cardinal Ratzinger, prefect of the Congregation for the Doctrine of the Faith, issued *Instruction on Respect for Human Life* (*Donum vitae*). The *Instruction* addressed a number of biomedical issues, including experimentation upon human embryos; methods of prenatal diagnosis; and in vitro fertilization, both homologous (the meeting in vitro of the gametes of married spouses) and heterologous (the use of gametes coming from at least one donor other than the spouses). Whereas *Humanae vitae* contended that the procreative good cannot deliberately be suppressed in favor of the unitive good, Cardinal Ratzinger argued that the natural law also prohibits separating procreation from the unity and love of the spousal act. While the argument is similar to *Humanae vitae*, Cardinal Ratzinger makes it clearer that natural law is a moral law, not to be confused with a "set of norms on the biological level." By nature, the conjugal act is a "personal" act of love between spouses. This guarantees that the transmission of life is an act of procreativity rather than mere reproduction. The *Instruction*, therefore, maintains that in vitro fertilization, whether homologous or heterologous, is contrary to the personal and unitive meaning of the marital act.

With respect to human rights, Cardinal Ratzinger argues that in vitro fertilization violates not only the natural structure of the marital act but also the "inalienable rights" of the child. The child cannot be treated as an object serving the interests of the parents but, rather,

"When exploring the differences between civilizations, their attitude toward nature must be given a prominent place."

ERIC HOFFER

WORKING AND THINKING ON THE WATERFRONT, 1969

CHURCH SPOKESMAN

The Vatican's Joseph Cardinal Ratzinger (right) based some of the central arguments of Instruction on Respect for Human Life *(1987) on the authority of natural law.*

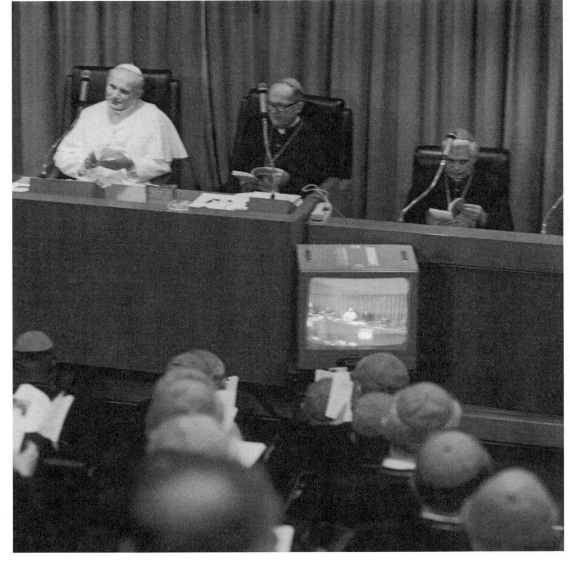

must be treated as an end in itself. Parents have only the right to perform those acts that are per se ordered to procreation. Were parents to have a right to reproduce, by whatever means, then the child would be an object to which one has a right of ownership. At least on matters of bioethics, the *Instruction* represents an important development in the linkage between a traditional natural-law conception of the marital act with distinctively modern arguments concerning natural rights.

Natural-law theory is in a period of transition among Catholic scholars. Some scholars working in the Thomistic tradition now emphasize the role of the virtues rather than the juridical themes of natural law (Bourke, 1974; MacIntyre, 1988). Others, notably John Finnis (1980a) and Germain Grisez (1983), have developed a theory of the relationship between practical reason and "basic human goods" (e.g., life, knowledge, play, aesthetic experience, sociability, practical reasonableness, and religion). The aim of the theory is to identify moral norms governing how basic goods ought to be chosen. It was first undertaken by Germain Grisez (1964; 1983); John Finnis (1980a) has systematically applied Grisez's work to the whole field of jurisprudence. The natural-law component of the theory is much criticized. Some argue that it has no clear connection to the Thomistic doctrine of natural theology (Hittinger, 1987); others, particularly proportionalists, argue that absolute moral norms are not easily generated by such generalized forms of human well-being (McCormick, 1981). Although there is considerable agreement among Catholic philosophers and theologians that natural law is important, there is less agreement about how to deal systematically with the subject.

Natural law in law and bioethics

Constitutional and legal issues have occupied recent

secular debates over natural law. It is noteworthy that the philosophical ground of the debate between natural lawyers and legal positivists continues to be revisited (see essays in George, 1992). At a more concrete level, however, discussion has focused upon civil liberties, particularly the right of privacy. Since this area of the law is the bellwether for many important biomedical questions, we will briefly outline the state of this discussion.

In *Griswold* v. *Connecticut* (1965), the Supreme Court invalidated a Connecticut statute forbidding the sale to and use of contraceptives by married people. The Court held that a zone of privacy protects marriage from intrusive governmental actions. Since the Constitution and its amendments do not mention the right of privacy, the Court was widely regarded as using natural law in constitutional interpretation. Indeed, the use of natural law was more controversial than the result in this particular case. In *Eisenstadt* v. *Baird* (1972), which invalidated a Massachusetts statute prohibiting the sale of contraceptives to unmarried people, Justice William Brennan reasoned that the right of privacy generally covers the decision of individuals, married or single, to make decisions about whether to "bear or beget" children. In *Roe* v. *Wade* (1973), the right to privacy was extended to abortion. Since then, it has been cited by lower courts as precedent for paternal refusal to allow the implantation of embryos. Other biomedical issues have also surfaced in the courts in terms of natural rights: "There is a fundamental natural right expressed in our Constitution as the 'right to liberty,' which permits an individual to refuse or direct the withholding or withdrawal of artificial death-prolonging procedures . . ." (*Cruzan* v. *Harmon*, 760 S.W.2nd 408, 434 [Mo. banc 1988] [Higgins, J., dissenting]).

It is unfortunate that some of the thorniest biomedical questions have been formulated legally in terms of a right to privacy. The moral substance of the right is often moved to the periphery in favor of the controverted issue of natural law as a tool of constitutional interpretation. Setting aside the legal questions, we can ask what are the ground and scope of a right to privacy. It is widely held that the moral basis of the right rests upon the natural autonomy of individuals to make decisions about their bodies, with respect not only to sexual conduct but also to many life-and-death concerns. The notion of the body as property has a long philosophical pedigree in the Anglo-American world (e.g., John Locke); the notion that there exists a field of private or self-regarding actions is traceable to a number of different moral theorists (e.g., John Stuart Mill). Moral and legal theorists generally have attempted to unite these themes under a right of autonomy or moral independence (surveyed in Hittinger, 1990). In *Planned Parenthood* v. *Casey* (1992), the U.S. Supreme Court reaffirmed its holding in *Roe* v. *Wade*. It is significant, however, that the Court discussed the right in the language of autonomy, and

NATURAL LAW
Is There a "Right to Autonomy"?

Two problems attend the formulation of a right to autonomy. First, it is not clear that a natural right to autonomy can be applied with analytic precision. Even if we narrow the scope of autonomous actions to those that relate to use of the body, it would seem that contraception, abortion, and euthanasia are very different kinds of acts—not only materially but also morally. Hence, it can be objected that although autonomy is a necessary element in our consideration of these issues, it is not a sufficient condition for how they ought to be settled. Second, in Western history, the great tradition of natural rights has concerned the limitation of the coercive power of the state. In legislation and in public policy, a natural rights argument can be expected to shed light upon the principles that ought to govern the ends and the means of public force. But the right of autonomy provides only the most inchoate ground for distinguishing between legitimate and wrongful actions on the part of the state. Why, for example, should the state be prevented from intruding upon decisions about reproduction but not those concerning suicide or euthanasia? All these acts concern the body, and are plausible instances of the individual's interest in his or her autonomy. If the difference consists in the moral specifications of the acts (if, for example, abortion is adjudged morally licit or at least indifferent, while suicide and assisted euthanasia are deemed morally wicked), then autonomy needs to be augmented with other principles in order to draw a line between what belongs to the individual and what belongs to the state. If, on the other hand, one has a natural moral right to act autonomously regardless of the moral specifications of the acts, then one would seem to have a natural right to do wrong. While a government might have other reasons to tolerate wicked acts, it is unclear how a government can be bound to respect a right to do a moral wrong.

— RUSSELL HITTINGER

"The Judaic religion has been the first and only one to separate God and man from nature. In all other religions God and nature are identical."

ERIC HOFFER
WORKING AND THINKING ON THE WATERFRONT, 1969

NATURAL LAW

Natural Law in Law and Bioethics

brought this language under the legal rubric of "liberty" (in section one of the Fourteenth Amendment), rather than "privacy." Because privacy has such disputable grounds in the positive law, this move from privacy to liberty in *Casey* can be read as an effort to find more secure grounds in the positive law for the moral right to autonomy.

Since bioethics encompasses matters of physiological well-being, moral choice, and justice, some version of natural law might seem indispensable to how we should frame and resolve the issues. Despite theoretical problems and disagreements, nature stubbornly remains a standard for health (Kass, 1985). Until nature is exorcised, it will continue to invite natural law reflection on norms of medical practice. Modern technology urgently bids us to investigate the moral relevance of the contrast between nature and art. Furthermore, it would be hard to imagine a future in which citizens stop making claims about rights in the area of health care and the allocation of its resources. Natural law has become part of our repertoire of moral discourse about rights. Yet, as one critic of natural law has stated the problem: "Either the allegedly universal ends [of natural law] are too few and abstract to give content to the idea of the good, or they are too numerous and concrete to be truly universal. One has to choose between triviality and implausibility" (Ely, 1980, p. 51). The same can be said of any of the standard normative theories of ethics, whether deontological or utilitarian. With respect to any abstract theory, especially one as prodigious as natural law, one must look carefully at its different versions, and also take the applications of the theories on a case-by-case basis.

— RUSSELL HITTINGER

P

POPULATION ETHICS

DEFINITION OF POPULATION ETHICS

Population studies deal with fertility, mortality, and migration. Fertility refers to human reproduction, mortality to death, and migration to the movement of people from one region to another. The articles on population ethics and population policies in this compendium take up only those aspects of fertility and migration with close links to health care and the life sciences, that is, to bioethics.

Population ethics has two main foundations: moral principles and factual information. Moral principles come from religious traditions, philosophy, declarations of human rights, and other sources. Factual information derives from careful analysis of what is happening or has happened in a given place or situation. Judgments about the ethics of population policies require the application of moral principles to cases based on solid, factual information. Vague principles or a poor understanding of how population programs really operate lead to questionable judgments about population ethics.

The articles on normative approaches and on religious traditions show similarities and differences in the moral principles applied to population policies. One major normative framework, accepted in principle by most countries, includes the universal statements on human rights developed by the United Nations. By endorsing and defining rights such as life, liberty, and welfare, the United Nations has established ethical standards applicable to all social programs, including those dealing with population. The major religious traditions of the world also have their own perspectives on fertility control and migration. Many of these are fully compatible with U.N. statements on human rights, but some are not. The main conflicts over population ethics arise when governments, most of which have officially accepted U.N. standards on human rights, violate those rights in their own population programs.

The articles on population policies apply moral principles to strategies used in fertility control, health standards required in that field, ethical issues in programs involving migration and refugees, and the work

"Our opinions about things we do not know are not likely to be balanced and moderate."

ERIC HOFFER
WORKING AND THINKING ON THE WATERFRONT, 1969

TOO MANY PEOPLE?

Debates about whether rapid population growth threatens human societies show the need for solid factual understanding and clear moral principles.

P

POPULATION ETHICS

Definition of Population Ethics

of donor agencies dealing with fertility control and migration and refugees. Strategies of fertility control can range from the application of force to information campaigns aimed at voluntary changes in attitudes and behavior. They include compulsion, which has been used to force China's one-child-per-couple policy; strong persuasion, such as the application of heavy government and community pressure on potential users of fertility control; financial incentives and disincentives given to users, field workers, and communities; and educational or information campaigns aimed at promoting greater acceptance of fertility control. The ethical issues are most serious with the use of compulsion and least serious, though still significant, with information campaigns.

"Technology made large populations possible; large populations now make technology indispensable."

JOSEPH WOOD KRUTCH
HUMAN NATURE AND THE HUMAN CONDITION, 1959

Debates over whether rapid population growth poses problems for human societies also show the need for clear moral principles and solid factual understanding. Advocates enter those debates with different principles and factual information.

The moral principles guiding discussions about population problems include preventing environmental pollution (Ehrlich and Ehrlich, 1990); keeping population size within the carrying capacity of the world (Hardin, 1993); and promoting economic growth (World Bank, 1984). Each principle leads to a different focus on factual information. Those concerned with pollution analyze data about global warming, acid rain, and depletion of the ozone layer. Those proposing to keep population size within the carrying capacity of the world look, for example, at figures on population density. Students of economic growth consider the many links between birthrate and economic development, including relationships among fertility, education, and health care. Because each concern leads to a different meaning of a population problem and a different selection of information, it is difficult to compare one problem definition with another.

Two research practices have held back the development of an adequate factual base for population ethics. One practice begins with conclusions and then selects only those facts consistent with them. Analysts claiming that rapid population growth has had negative consequences for economic development often cite facts supporting that conclusion and leave out contrary evidence (World Bank, 1984). Those claiming benefits from rapid population growth do the same (Simon, 1990).

The second practice involves assigning more or less weight to population conditions than objective research would support. Some advocates of fertility control claim that rapid population growth has caused starvation and political instability in the developing countries. Such simple interpretations overlook the many other influences leading to those conditions, such as the lack of food in poor countries, corruption among political leaders, and ethnic conflicts.

See Also

Fertility Control; Population Policies; Freedom and Coercion

The strategies countries use to control fertility have provoked the sharpest debates about population ethics. China and India have used outright coercion to promote sterilization or abortion. In China, women found to be pregnant with unauthorized children have been forced to undergo abortions (Aird, 1990). Between 1975 and 1977, police in some parts of India rounded up eligible men and required them to be sterilized (Gwatkin, 1979). Indonesia's use of strong community pressures to increase use of contraceptives has also been controversial. To gain new users the Indonesian government has relied on such methods as repeated visits to eligible women from village heads, family-planning workers, and members of Acceptors Clubs; pressure to accept intrauterine devices during "safaris" attended by prominent public officials; and promoting a positive image of small families. Those defending coercion and heavy social pressures argue that countries such as China, India, and Indonesia require vigorous methods of fertility control to curb swelling populations. Voluntary methods, they say, will work too slowly to prevent damage to the economy and create impossible demands for a nation's schools and other public services. Critics respond that applying force and heavy pressure violates human rights and disregards international agreements on fertility control, such as the 1974 World Population Plan of Action (United Nations, 1975).

Policies on migration and refugees also raise questions of ethics. Under what conditions, if any, do residents of one country have the right to enter another? Are the moral claims of potential migrants stronger when they are facing starvation, persecution, or violence? Do countries have the right to bar or expel immigrants they see as harmful to their national interest, as the United States did with Haitian immigrants in the early 1990s? What obligations, if any, does a government have to undocumented aliens within its borders? Can it deny them health-care services regularly available to its own citizens? What kinds of aid should donor agencies, such as the World Food Program or the International Committee for the Red Cross, provide to migrants, refugees, and displaced persons? And how should that aid be distributed?

Issues of medical risks and proper standards of health care arise in fertility control as well as migration and refugee programs. Family-planning programs sometimes put more emphasis on achieving numerical targets for clients than on safeguarding the freedom and health of users. Field workers may promote medically unsafe methods of fertility control, fail to disclose the risks of a given method, or be unavailable to deal with the side effects that do occur. Or they may insert the subdermal contraceptive Norplant and then refuse to remove it at the client's request (Ubinig, 1991). Fertility-control programs also differ in the health support they provide to users, such as local clinics to deal with minor problems or hospitals to handle serious complications.

Questions about standards for health care also arise in programs for refugees. Program managers often have to decide whether refugees should be sent back to countries from which they fled, where they may be tortured, imprisoned, or killed. If they are kept in camps, what should be done to prevent the high rates of illness sometimes seen in those settings? Possible preventive measures include providing adequate food, safe water, suitable shelter, sanitation, immunization of vulnerable groups, and a primary health-care system.

International donor agencies, such as the World Bank, the United Nations Population Fund, and the U.S. Agency for International Development, also face moral choices in their assistance to fertility-control programs. Among those choices are whether donors should support programs known or thought to involve coercion, such as that in China; whether those organizations funding a variety of projects, such as the World Bank, should put pressure on countries to initiate fertility-control programs as a precondition for other aid; and how far and in what ways they should ensure that recipients of their funds provide honest explanations of methods to clients and adequate health support for complications or side effects.

In migration and refugee programs, ethical principles affect decisions about who receives assistance and who does not. Are those decisions based mainly on the health and welfare needs of those to be served or on other criteria, such as racial or ethnic politics? This question is particularly salient in countries where the government controls donor access to areas in which its political opponents want to be evacuated. Donors must likewise make moral choices in designing programs for migrants or refugees. In interventions for disaster relief, they must often choose between strategies providing rapid action by outsiders, such as building homes, or slower methods of educating residents in how to become more self-sufficient (Parker, 1994). Instead of constructing new homes after an earthquake, donors might show community members how to build their own homes using earthquake-resistant methods of construction. The result could be greater self-sufficiency and better protection against future disasters.

Population ethics thus involves the application of moral principles to what are often complex empirical situations. Its greatest challenges are to select principles that are broadly applicable to population issues, rather than those that advance some specific interest, and to explore their implications with an adequate factual understanding of the circumstances involved.

— DONALD P. WARWICK

IS THERE A POPULATION PROBLEM?

Policy analysts, the popular press, and scholars often speak of "the population problem." This phrase usually means that the existence of too many people on the planet will cause difficulties or even catastrophes for individuals, couples, countries, or the world. It can also mean that a country or region has too few people for its economic, social, or political welfare.

The first definition argues that rapid population growth, large population size, or high population density can bring widespread poverty, famine, air pollution, poor public health, drought, more children than can be educated in national school systems, overcrowded cities, or other serious harms. Under the second definition, too few people can reduce a country's population below the number that the government wants, decrease the size of the labor force, change the size and mix of ethnic groups in ways that can cause conflict, or create a population with few young and many old people. In either case the location of the problem can be the world, geographic regions such as sub-Saharan Africa, single countries, cities, or other regions within a country.

Those stating that there is a population problem base their assertions on three elements: perceived threats to social, moral, or political values; factual evidence; and theories explaining how population creates the conditions that threaten values. Much of the confusion in discussion of population problems arises from ambiguity or disagreement about these three elements.

Every statement of a population problem explicitly or implicitly expresses concern about values such as preventing famine, having an adequate number of workers and jobs, and giving couples the opportunity to determine their family size. Whether the concern is with too many or too few people, those stating that there is a problem always mention or allude to some moral, social, or political value. They also directly cite factual evidence to support their case or imply that this evidence exists. The evidence may be quantitative, such as figures on the relationship between population size and the number of teachers and schools in a country, or qualitative, such as the judgments of political scientists on a country's strength in foreign affairs, or a combination of the two. And every claim that there is a population problem involves a theory or conceptual scheme showing the links between too many or too few people and indi-

In 1997, total world population was 5.85 billion, according to United Nations estimates.

THE NEW YORK TIMES ALMANAC, 1998

Of the 5.85 billion people alive in 1997, fifty-one percent live in six countries: China, India, the U.S., Indonesia, Brazil, and Russia.

THE NEW YORK TIMES ALMANAC, 1998

P

POPULATION ETHICS

Is There a Population Problem?

In 1997, China's population was 1.244 billion, India's was 906.2 million, and the U.S., with 271.6 million people, was the world's third most populated nation.

THE NEW YORK TIMES ALMANAC, 1998

"The projected slowing down of world population growth is based on assumptions of increased use of contraception in developing countries and an aging of the global population."

THE CAMBRIDGE FACTFINDER, 1993

POPULATION INDICATORS BY REGION AND CONTINENT, 1990–97

Region/Continent	population estimate ('000s) 1997	2025
World total	5,848,700	8,039,100
More developed regions	1,178,400	1,220,300
Less developed regions	4,670,300	6,818,900
Africa	758,400	1,453,900
Asia	3,538,500	4,784,800
Europe	729,200	701,100
Latin America and the Caribbean	491,900	689,600
North America	301,700	369,000

Source: United Nations Population Fund, The State of the World Population 1997

cators of the values at stake in the discussion. Economic theories, for example, may try to show how, specifically, rapid population growth has created or will create unemployment.

Confusion about whether there is a population problem arises when analysts are vague about the values advanced or threatened by population size; omit relevant factual evidence; or use theories that have little validity. Advocates are vague about values advanced or threatened when they state that there is a population problem without indicating the social, moral, or political goods affected by population size. Some writers simply take it for granted that the world is now too crowded and go on to say what should be done about it. Omitting relevant factual evidence leads to charges of bias in statements about population problems. So does the use of theories that aim more at making the case for a problem than at objectively weighing the influence of population conditions.

Whether or not there is a population problem is critical to the ethics of population control. If rapid or limited population growth, population size, and population density do indeed cause serious damage, societies and governments will have some ethical justification for trying to change those conditions. If, on the other hand, pronouncements about population problems fail to state the values affected, are selective in their choice of factual evidence, or rely on dubious theories, the ethical justification for policies to deal with those problems will be tenuous.

The following discussion illustrates the complexity of making statements about population problems by comparing four approaches:

- Paul and Anne Ehrlich
- World Bank
- U.S. National Academy of Sciences
- Julian Simon

It reviews the values at stake in each approach, the completeness of the factual evidence cited, and the theories invoked to link population conditions to outcomes reflecting the values of concern.

Approaches to the population problem

In *The Population Bomb* Paul Ehrlich made this statement about population growth:

> *The battle to feed all of humanity is over. In the 1970s and 1980s millions of people will starve to death. . . . Although many lives could be saved through dramatic programs to "stretch" the carrying capacity of the earth by increasing food production and providing for more equitable distribution of whatever food is available . . . these programs will only provide a stay of execution unless they are accompanied by determined and successful efforts at population control.* (1971, p. xi)

During the 1970s and 1980s, high birthrates did not produce the levels of starvation Ehrlich predicted, in part because of the Green Revolution, which led to much higher food production than in the 1960s. Nonetheless, in their 1990 book *The Population Explosion* Paul and Anne Ehrlich continued to argue that the human race would face starvation and widespread disease unless societies immediately controlled their birthrates.

> *Human inaction has already condemned hundreds of millions more people to premature deaths from hunger and disease. The population connection must be made in the public mind. Action to end the population explosion* humanely *and start a gradual population* decline *must become a top item on the human agenda: the human birthrate must be lowered to slightly below the human deathrate as soon as possible.*
> (Ehrlich and Ehrlich, 1990, pp. 22–23)

The authors blame overpopulation for starvation in Africa, homelessness and drug abuse in the United States, global warming, holes in the atmosphere's ozone layer, fires in tropical forests, sewage-blighted beaches, and drought-stricken farm fields.

The World Bank has taken a different approach to the population problem. The *World Development Report 1984* (World Bank, 1984) acknowledges that the evidence on this subject is complex but concludes that "population growth at the rapid rates common in most of the developing world slows development" (p. 105). This statement echoes the remarks of the Bank's president in the foreword: "What governments and their peoples do today to influence our demographic future will set the terms for development strategy well into the next century" (p. iii). In the World Bank's view, high fertility and rapid population growth bring on a problem by creating conditions, such as lower-quality education, that block economic development.

In 1971 the National Academy of Sciences (NAS) claimed that rapid population growth causes serious harm to economic development in sixteen ways. It holds down growth in per capita income; leads to unemployment and underemployment; creates mass poverty; distorts international trade; aggravates political, religious, linguistic, and ethnic conflicts; retards the mental and physical development of children; and has other negative consequences.

Fifteen years later the NAS (National Research Council, 1986) issued a report that backs away from the earlier conclusions. According to that report, slower population growth may benefit developing countries, but there is little evidence for judging whether its impact will be large or small. Furthermore, the results of population growth will depend not only on numbers of people but also on the effectiveness of government administration, social institutions, and the resources of specific countries. Thus, over a decade and a half the NAS shifted from a negative to a more neutral assessment of the impact of demographic growth.

Values, evidence, and theories

The statements just reviewed show the difficulty of having a coherent discussion about "the population problem." The main reason is that the authors are concerned about different values, do not use all available factual evidence, and base their conclusions on different conceptual schemes and theories.

For Paul and Anne Ehrlich, central values include avoiding starvation, protecting the environment, preserving the world's resources, and maintaining public health: "*The Population Explosion* is being written as ominous changes in the life support systems of civilization become more evident daily. It is being written in a world where hunger is rife and the prospects of famine and plague ever more imminent" (Ehrlich and Ehrlich, 1990, p. 10). The World Bank shows greater concern with promoting economic growth, providing the world with adequate food supplies, having public services such as health and education, and protecting the environment. Both reports of the NAS address similar values. The values guiding Julian Simon's work include showing the benefits of population growth for human welfare and economic development; removing or

JULIAN SIMON'S VIEW
Reasons for Optimism

Julian Simon (1990) gives a much more optimistic view of population growth than do the Ehrlichs, the World Bank, and the NAS. He first questions what he calls myths about population and resources. For example, while some say that the food situation in developing countries is worsening, Simon holds that per capita food production has been increasing about 1 percent each year. Responding to arguments that higher population growth means lower per capita economic growth, Simon states: "Empirical studies find no statistical correlation between countries' population growth and their per capita economic growth, either over the long run or in recent decades" (1990, p. 45). Simon also offers evidence challenging statements that the world is running out of natural resources and raw materials and that energy is becoming more scarce.

Simon argues that having additional children improves productivity in the more developed countries and raises the standard of living in less developed countries. Over a period of thirty to seventy years in the more developed countries, each additional person contributes to increased knowledge and technical progress by "inventing, adapting, and diffusing new productive knowledge" (1990, p. 48). Over the same time period in the less developed countries, more children lead to more work done by parents, stimulate agricultural and industrial investment, and bring other benefits. Simon calls people "the ultimate resource" and holds that population growth increases that resource.

The four approaches have different notions of how population growth affects economies and societies. The Ehrlichs are consistently gloomy about the impact of population growth on human societies. The World Bank is seriously concerned about its effects, and generally negative in its conclusions, but willing to consider different points of view and some evidence challenging its position. Like the World Bank, the NAS focuses on population growth and economic development, but comes to very different conclusions in its 1971 and 1986 reports. Simon plays down the harms and underscores the advantages of population growth for economic development and social welfare.

— DONALD P. WARWICK

"Whatever the rate of population growth is, historically it has been that the food supply increases at least as fast, if not faster."

JULIAN L. SIMON
INTERVIEW IN WIRED MAGAZINE, 1997

World population is projected to pass the six billion mark in 1999 and reach 8.04 billion in 2025.

THE NEW YORK TIMES ALMANAC, 1998

reducing popular fears about population growth and the availability of resources; and convincing the public that "life on earth is getting better, not worse" (1990, p. 21).

What evidence do these writers use, and how representative is that evidence of all that was available? In *The Population Bomb*, Paul Ehrlich does not try to be objective. He opens his first chapter with these words:

> *I have understood the population explosion intellectually for a long time. I came to understand it emotionally one stinking hot night in Delhi a few years ago. My wife and daughter and I were returning to our hotel in an ancient taxi. The seats were hopping with fleas. The only functional gear was third. As we crawled through the city we entered a crowded slum area. The temperature was well over 100, and the air was a haze of dust and smoke. The streets seemed alive with people. People eating, people washing, people sleeping. People visiting, arguing, and screaming. . . . People defecating and urinating. People clinging to buses. People herding animals. People, people, people, people. (1971, p. 5)*

Ehrlich goes on to specify the nature of the problem, summarize what is being done to deal with it, state what needs to be done, and tell readers what they can do to help. The book makes its case more by an appeal to the moral and political concerns of its readers than by presenting factual evidence.

The Population Explosion has a more scholarly tone, but still limits the findings presented to those that would be widely interpreted as supporting the authors' claims about overpopulation. It has chapters on shortages of food in developing countries; the difficulties facing agriculture; greenhouse warming, acid rain, and other damages to Earth's ecosystems; and urban air pollution, crowding, and hazards to public health. The Ehrlichs adduce no evidence challenging or qualifying their conclusions. They conclude with a chapter showing what readers can do to stop the population explosion.

Like the Ehrlichs, Simon gives a one-sided presentation of his findings. He contrasts popular views of bad news about population with the "unpublicized, good-news truth" (1990, p. 42) deriving from his own analysis. He summarizes commonly cited statements, such as that the food situation in developing countries is growing worse, and then offers his own view under the heading of *fact*. Instead of presenting a balanced summary of research findings, he tries to attack the popular belief with as many findings as he can assemble that will be widely interpreted as contrary.

The World Bank (1984) admits that judging the evidence about the consequences of population growth is not easy and summarizes some conflicting views on that subject. But it does not mention dozens of cross-national studies that contradict its main conclusion, including work by Simon Kuznets (1974) and Ester Boserup (1965, 1981). This research shows no relationship between the rates of growth of population size and the growth rates of per capita income. Nor does the Bank's report explore the possibility, put forth by Boserup and Simon, that population size, population growth rate, and population density contribute to technological progress. According to one reviewer, "the Report can be evaluated from two different perspectives: as a position paper making the best case for a point of view; or as a summary of current knowledge. It is clearly much more successful as the first than as the second" (Lee, 1985, p. 129).

The two reports by the NAS are also mainly concerned with economic growth, but they differ in their approach to the studies they cite. The 1971 report selects evidence that supports its conclusions about the negative consequences of population growth and neglects research whose findings challenge or contradict those conclusions. The 1986 study is much better balanced in its coverage of the evidence and more cautious in arriving at conclusions. The authors draw a clear distinction, for example, between conditions caused by population growth and those only associated with such growth.

The four approaches also differ in their use of theories and conceptual schemes. In *The Population Bomb*, Paul Ehrlich has no social-scientific theory; he argues almost entirely by assertion. He assumes that the connections between population growth and conditions such as starvation are evident and therefore need no conceptual or theoretical justification. As is the case with their choice of evidence, in *The Population Explosion* Paul and Anne Ehrlich select only those conceptual frameworks showing the negative consequences of population growth. The World Bank recognizes the diversity of theories about the impact of population growth, but chooses a model that eliminates the possibility of any positive effects, such as those mentioned by Julian Simon. The 1971 NAS report also relies heavily on conceptual models showing the harms done by population growth. The 1986 NAS report applies concepts and theories allowing for a fairer evaluation of the relationships between population growth and economic development.

Much of the debate about whether there is a population problem and what it means stems from the different values and concerns behind statements of problems; selective use of evidence; and choosing theories to support preestablished conclusions rather than to arrive at impartial conclusions. Until analysts remove the ideology and biases commonly found in discussions about population problems, the confusion will continue.

The population problem: Where and when?

Most discussions of the population problem focus on the world at large or regions such as developing countries. It is also possible to examine the impact of population growth, size, and density on single countries. This is the focus of the work done by the Population Division of the Department of International Economic and Social Affairs (DIESA) of the United Nations (Chamie, 1994). The Population Division assumes that, whatever the impact of population size, density, and growth across the world, single countries will have different views on what those concepts mean to them. Since the mid-1970s DIESA has maintained the Population Policy Data Bank to assess the perceptions and policies of governments regarding fertility.

At the end of the 1980s, 44 percent of U.N. member countries reported that their fertility levels were too high and 12 percent that they were too low (Chamie, 1994). If one defines a population problem as a government's perception that its fertility is either too high or too low, then 56 percent of U.N. member countries had a problem. The response to that problem depended on whether the governments thought that their fertility was too high or too low.

The first group, usually in countries with low per capita incomes, often set up programs of birth control. Countries reporting that their fertility is too low, such as France, Greece, Hungary, and Switzerland, adopt financial incentives and other policies to encourage more births (McIntosh, 1986). Singapore has been unusual in shifting from the perception that it would have too many people to its current view that it requires higher fertility. These differing perspectives show the importance of asking where and why population is a problem. While many studies focus on the world or on developing countries, the research done by DIESA underscores the importance of opinions and policies in single nations.

The single countries mentioned show agreement on the definition of a population problem. The value of most concern is the government's perception of whether it has too many, too few, or the right number of people. This may be a limited way of defining a population problem, but it does have a consistent point of reference: the views of the government. The evidence used is also the same: the information collected for the Population Policy Data Bank. Conceptual frameworks and theories differ about the reasons for governments' perceptions of a population problem and about why they do or do not take action on population issues. But consistency in the value behind the data and in the evidence used makes it much easier to compare definitions of population problems than in the four approaches outlined earlier.

Another critical question about population growth, size, and density is how they will affect the future. Paul Ehrlich's *The Population Bomb* and William and Paul Paddock's *Famine 1975* (1967) show that confident predictions of disasters are often wrong. But that experience does not mean students of population problems should stop looking to the future. Instead, they should make their predictions but be modest enough to indicate that, because they do not know everything that will happen between the time of writing and the time of the predicted event, they may be mistaken about the predicted events.

A related question concerns the obligations of the present generation to future ones. Do people living now have a duty to preserve the world so that future societies and individuals will have the resources and health conditions currently available? There is no simple answer. Over time, serious problems, such as the pollution of London a century ago, have been resolved and new problems, such as the depletion of water supplies in some regions, have arisen.

Two principles can help reflection on this topic. First, U.N. organizations and governments should pay explicit attention to the long-term consequences of population policies. Rather than taking a passive stance in debates on this topic, they should encourage and, if necessary, subsidize research on how population growth, population size, and population density affect the future. Second, the present generation has no right to adopt or accept population policies likely to damage the health and welfare of future generations. These might include actions leading to widespread environmental pollution, deforestation, and poor conditions of public health.

Recommendations

How can students of population policy reduce the bias now seen in many discussions of population problems and provide a solid basis for comparing different statements of those problems?

POINTERS FOR RATIONAL STUDY AND DISCUSSION OF POPULATION ISSUES

1. Specify the geographic focus of the analysis.
2. Indicate the moral, social, or political values of concern in the analysis.
3. Use all relevant evidence, not just studies supporting the author's point of view.
4. Specify theories guiding the analysis.
5. Base conclusions on careful analysis and the weight of the evidence.
6. Base policy recommendations on evidence rather than on personal preferences.

"First, humanity's condition will improve in just about every material way. Second, humans will continue to sit around complaining about everything getting worse."

JULIAN L. SIMON
THE STATE OF HUMANITY

P

POPULATION ETHICS

History of Population Theories

If present trends continue, the world in 2000 will be more crowded, more polluted, less stable ecologically and more vulnerable to disruption than the world we live in now.

GLOBAL 2000 REPORT TO THE PRESIDENT OF THE UNITED STATES, ENTERING THE TWENTY-FIRST CENTURY, 1980

First, commentators should explicitly state the geographic focus of their analysis. Is it the universe? All the countries in the world? Some region of the world, such as sub-Saharan Africa or South America? A single country? Regions within a single country, such as cities or rural areas? Or some combination of those options, such as a country as a whole and its urban and rural areas? Given the great differences in population, economic, social, and political conditions across nations, specifying the geographic focus would immediately help observers to see similarities and differences across the territory covered. Tables such as those in the World Bank's annual *World Development Report* would be helpful for that purpose.

Second, those discussing population problems should indicate the moral, social, or political values of concern in their analysis. This recommendation should apply whether the observer claims that the region being analyzed has too many, too few, or an adequate number of people. Values often found, explicitly or implicitly, in such analyses include promoting economic growth; preserving the environment; preventing a decline in the region's population; increasing the size of the dominant ethnic group or changing the sizes of ethnic minorities; and maintaining the availability of schools and other social services for the region's inhabitants.

Third, scholarly analyses of population problems should use all relevant evidence rather than just studies that support the author's point of view. Discussions of population growth and economic development should make full use of the numerous cross-national comparisons on that subject. When, as often happens, the sources of evidence lead to different conclusions, that situation should be mentioned.

Fourth, those discussing population problems should specify the theories or conceptual frameworks guiding their analysis. It is particularly important to indicate how population conditions, such as growth rates and size, influence conditions such as economic growth or the availability of schools. Many publications have used conceptual models that attribute more influence to population than it deserves, partly because other relevant influences are not considered. Such is the case with the 1971 NAS study on the consequences of rapid population growth. By using a more thorough conceptual framework and considering a broader range of evidence, the 1986 NAS study in effect retracts many of the conclusions in the 1971 report.

Fifth, conclusions should be based on the results of careful conceptual or theoretical analysis and the weight of the evidence rather than on a priori judgments by the authors. Following this recommendation will often mean reporting contradictory or inconsistent evidence and arriving at qualified judgments. The greatest single source of confusion in present statements on population problems is a strong ideological bias in writing. This bias has led to vagueness about the values at stake, use of incomplete theories and conceptual schemes, citation only of those parts of the evidence consistent with the authors' preconceptions, and conclusions based more on ideology than on a fair assessment of the evidence.

Sixth, policy recommendations in statements about population problems should be based on the evidence presented rather than on the personal preferences of the authors or the donors who have supported them. For example, after a lengthy discussion of the links between population growth and economic development, the 1986 NAS report suggests that governments should establish family-planning programs. This recommendation has little to do with the main lines of the report, which says nothing about family planning. This practice is intellectually misleading, for it suggests that the policy suggestions flow directly from the scholarly analysis, which in this case they do not.

Conclusions

Is there a population problem? When the focus is on single countries, when the source of information is the Population Policy Data Bank maintained by the United Nations, and when the definition of the population problem is the government's opinion on whether it has too many, too few, or the right number of people, it is possible to answer that question. But when the focus is on the world as a whole, and authors are concerned with different values, use different theories and sources of evidence, and become advocates for a particular point of view, there is and can be no answer.

To have more comparable notions of population problems, authors must clearly identify the geographical region they are discussing; indicate the values of concern to them; use all available evidence; apply theories or conceptual schemes that consider all relevant influences; weigh the evidence objectively; and draw only those conclusions supported by their analysis. The ideological discourse seen in current discussions of population problems must give way to scholarly analysis. When these criteria are met, more accurate, less biased, and more comparable discussions of population problems will be available.

DONALD P. WARWICK

HISTORY OF POPULATION THEORIES

Ancient and medieval theories

Like most general theories of Western civilization, those concerning population evolved first in ancient

Greece. Both policies and their conceptual frameworks varied in their details, but there was much consistency from one city-state to another. The typical pronatalist policies were intended not to induce a growth in numbers but to prevent their decline (Stangeland, 1904, chap. 1; Hutchinson, 1967, chap. 2). In the ideal city-state that Plato pictured in *Laws*, the population was to be kept stable at 5,040 (the product of 1 × 2 × 3 × 4 × 5 × 6 × 7) by encouraging or inhibiting fertility or by infanticide. If the population grew much beyond this optimum, the community was to establish colonies. To neglect measures that would keep the population more or less fixed, according to Aristotle, would "bring certain poverty on the citizens, and poverty is the cause of sedition and evil" (*Politics*, 2.9).

Greek thought on population, in sum, was characterized by an overriding concern with policy, and thus a relative indifference to empirical or conceptual analysis. Policy was to be applied, moreover, to aggregates ridiculously small by present-day standards. And whether the meaning of "population" was in accord with the modern sense is often not clear; in most instances the term may have referred only to citizens, thus omitting females, children, slaves, and aliens.

In its far larger arena, Rome's policy was more consistently pronatalist. As imperial hegemony spread from Italy throughout the Mediterranean basin and beyond, the center was troubled by moral decay, the dissolution of the family, and a slower growth of population. Successive pronatalist measures culminated in three enactments under Augustus (63 B.C.E.-14 C.E.), which punished celibacy and adultery and rewarded prolific couples (Stangeland, 1904, pp. 30-38). Since they had little apparent effect, the laws were repeatedly amended and finally repealed under Constantine (ca. 288-337).

As the empire gradually disintegrated, many came to believe that the end of the world was imminent, and various sects offered competing dogmas appropriate to the apocalypse. The early Christian church gradually developed its own doctrine with a compromise between libertine and ascetic, but emphasizing the latter (Noonan, 1965). Catholic thought reached its apogee in the *Summa Theologica* of Thomas Aquinas (ca. 1224-1274). For him, a marriage between Christians is not merely a means of obeying the injunction to replenish the earth but also a spiritual bond, a sacrament. The function of intercourse is procreation (Bourke, 1967).

Early modern theory

The dominant theme of the early modern period was the view that population growth is precarious and has to be fostered. Just as the mercantilist state hoarded gold, so it hoarded people, and for the same reason—to increase its economic, political, and military power. If rapid population growth resulted in what was termed "overcrowding," the mercantilist solution was to ship the surplus to colonies, where the settlers and their progeny could continue to aggrandize the state's power in another quarter of the globe.

Modern demography began with the efforts of mercantilist states to keep track of their populations (Glass, 1973). William Petty (1623-1687) was the first exponent of what he called "political arithmetic." John Graunt (1620-1674) constructed the first crude life table. Gregory King (1648-1712) calculated population estimates based on local enumerations, which he corrected for technical errors. On the Continent, Johann Peter Süssmilch (1707-1767) used Protestant parish records to estimate Prussia's fertility and mortality. Richard Cantillon (ca. 1680-1734) held that internal migration, deaths, and especially marriages (and therefore births) varied according to the prevailing standard of living and the structure of the demand for labor. François Quesnay (1694-1774), who founded what was later called physiocratic thought, analyzed the implicit bounds to population growth.

The philosophes of eighteenth-century France varied greatly on many issues, but most also found reason to favor policies stimulating population growth. Charles-Louis de Secondat, Baron Montesquieu (1689-1755), believed that the entire world had undergone depopulation and recommended pronatalist decrees. According to Voltaire (1694-1778), a nation is fortunate if its population increases by as much as 5 percent per century. Louis de St.-Just (1767-1794) held that one can usually depend on nature "never to have more children than teats," but to keep the balance in the other direction requires the state's assistance. By this notion of an equitable family law, as inspired by Jean-Jacques Rousseau (1712-1778), marriages should be encouraged by state loans, and a couple that remained childless after several years ought to be forcibly separated.

The two utopians that Thomas Robert Malthus opposed in the first edition of his *Essay on the Principle of Population*, William Godwin (1756-1836) and Marie-Jean Caritat, Marquis de Condorcet (1743-1794), focused their attention on the wholly rational age they discerned just over the horizon. According to them, in a world from which diseases had been wholly eliminated, the span of life would have no assignable upper limit. People would devote themselves to more important tasks than, in Condorcet's words, "the puerile idea of filling the earth with useless and unhappy beings."

"Fortunately for this planet, these gloomy assertions [in the Global 2000 Report*] about resources and environment are baseless."*

JULIAN L. SIMON
1980

P

POPULATION ETHICS

History of Population Theories

SOCIAL GOOD

Known for warnings on population growth, Thomas Malthus (1766–1834) opposed contraceptives because they would permit individual sexual gratification without benefiting society.

Malthus

Malthus summarized or contravened earlier ideas so effectively that, for more than a century and a half, subsequent theorists have generally taken him as a benchmark. Unfortunately, many references to "Malthusian" thought are based, at best, on the first edition of *Essay on the Principle of Population* rather than on the much enlarged and thoroughly revised later editions—or, at worst, on a total misunderstanding of what he stood for (Petersen, 1979, chap. 4).

Thomas Robert Malthus (1766-1834) was a professor at the newly founded East India College, occupying Britain's first chair in the new discipline of political economy. He spent much of his life collecting data on the relation between population and its social, economic, and natural environments, bringing his theory into accord with these facts and adjusting it to criticism. There were seven editions of the *Essay* in all.

According to the principle of population as expounded in the *Essay*, population, "when unchecked," doubles once every generation. Among "irrational animals" this potential is realized, and its "superabundant effects are repressed afterwards by want of room or nourishment." But rational human beings can consider the consequences of their reproductive potential and curb their natural drive. With humans, thus, there are two types of control of population growth: "preventive checks," the chaste postponement of marriage, and "positive checks," the deaths resulting from too large a population relative to its subsistence. Tension between numbers and food can have a beneficial effect: A man who postpones marrying until he is able to support a family is goaded by his sex drive to work hard, thus contributing to social progress. For this reason Malthus opposed contraceptives, for their use permits individual sexual gratification with no benefit to society.

Through the successive editions of the *Essay*, Malthus increasingly stressed the negative correlation between station in life and size of family. This, in his view, was the principal clue to solving what later became known as "the population problem." In order to bring the lower classes up to the self-control and social responsibility exercised by those with more money and education, Malthus asserted, the poor should be given more money and education. "The principal circumstances" that induce prospective parents to have fewer children are "liberty, security of property, the diffusion of knowledge, and a taste for the comforts of life." Those that tend to increase procreation are "despotism and ignorance." The thesis that upward mobility into the middle class effects a decline in fertility, though it is far less familiar than that relating population growth to food, is in retrospect Malthus's most important contribution.

For many decades Malthus's reputation was far below that of lesser social analysts. Recently it has become apparent that much of present-day demography was at least partly stimulated by Malthus and that those who denounced him as a false prophet had typically begun by misrepresenting his ideas.

Population optima

Most of the populations that Malthus discussed tended to grow too rapidly relative to the available resources, and he recommended institutional checks to their fertility. But the extraordinarily rapid growth of the American colonies, whose population was doubling every twenty-five years, he held to be of great benefit. In other words, each country has an optimum size and rate of growth, depending on the social and economic conditions. Malthus neither used the term "optimum" nor developed the concept beyond an implicit statement, but he planted the seed of the theory. Malthus's principle that the population tends to increase by a geometrical ratio and food by an arithmetical ratio can be reformulated as a law of diminishing returns. If to a fixed acreage of land more and more labor is added, return per person may first rise but then will decline as the work force increases beyond its most efficient size. The first definition of "the optimum" was based on this schema: It is that population which under given conditions produces the highest per capita economic return.

Soon, however, the optimum came to mean simply "the best population," with each analyst furnishing a particular yardstick of what is "good." By this route the theory of population optimum could be regarded as a

MIGRATION

We are all born and we all die, but only some of us move from one place to another. Unlike fertility and mortality, migration is not a biological process. Indeed, many determinants of migration are political: Movements are subsidized, restricted, or forced, and the status of migrants in their new homeland depends on the state's laws on aliens. If we conceive of migration following the usual definition—as the relatively permanent movement of persons over a significant distance—the specifications "permanent" and "significant" must be set by more or less arbitrary criteria. Partly for this reason, migration statistics are generally imprecise and subject to capricious interpretation.

Migration changes the size of population and the rate of growth in the two areas involved, but usually not in the simple fashion that common sense suggests. Most migrants are young adults, and their movement changes the age structure, and thus the birth and death rates, in both areas. Given a sedentary population and a stimulus to emigrate, typically some leave and some do not. There is self-selection by age, sex, family status, and occupation, as well as possibly by intelligence, mental health, and independence of character. Since migration is not unitary, it cannot be analyzed in supracultural terms but must be differentiated even at the most abstract level with respect to the social conditions obtaining. Generalizations about migration, thus, developed mostly outside of standard population theories.

— WILLIAM PETERSEN

version of social choice theory, with a wide variety of open questions (Dasgupta, 1987). Should the population be related to the present institutional structure or to some supposed future ("socialism," for instance)? Should the criterion of "good" be economic welfare, military strength, the conservation of resources, or some combination of these? This conundrum is aggravated by the fact that optima vary greatly, according to the goal that society sets. And should the standard relate exclusively to the number of people or also to their age structure, rate of growth, level of skill, and other characteristics that affect how efficiently the society can operate?

Obviously, no judgment concerning "the optimum" can be very precise. Whether a country of western Europe, say, is underpopulated or overpopulated is less a demographic-economic measurement than a more or less arbitrary opinion. The norm can be applied meaningfully only at the extremes. The colonies that became the United States were definitely underpopulated, as Malthus pointed out. And in some of today's less developed countries, by the judgment of most demographers, the rapidly growing populations impede a rise in the people's well-being.

Demographic transition

The number of people in the world is increasing at an unprecedented rate to unprecedented totals, and the basic reason is no mystery: Mortality has fallen sharply, and in many areas fertility has not. As originally formulated (e.g., Landry, 1934), this so-called demographic transition was conceived as taking place in three broad stages: (1) preindustrial societies, with high fertility more or less balanced by high mortality and a consequent low natural increase; (2) societies in transition, with continuing high fertility but declining mortality and a consequent rapid natural increase; and (3) modern societies, with both fertility and mortality stabilized at low levels and a consequent more or less static population. In its barest form this theory is one of the best-documented generalizations in the social sciences.

Collapsing the whole of human history into these three demographic types means, of course, that not only details but also important distinctions are passed over. When actual populations are reconstituted, so simplistic a theory often proves to be less a guide to research or policy than an invitation to misunderstanding. And this has been so concerning each of the three stages (Chesnais, 1986).

It is assumed that the mortality of primitive peoples was high relative to that in advanced societies, but estimates of the longevity in ancient times can hardly be very precise. Whether or not preindustrial peoples were warlike, lived in a favorable climate, developed cultural norms promoting cleanliness, and so on certainly influenced their death rates. And the usual formula—that since the mortality of primitive humans was high, their fertility must have been close to the physiological maximum if the group was to survive—is also questionable. From an early survey of contemporary primitive cultures, Alexander Carr-Saunders (1922) concluded that *all* of them included customs intended to restrict the increase of population. There is no reason a priori to postulate that all prehistoric peoples reproduced like unthinking animals, incurring the cost of a subsequent unnecessarily high mortality.

In stage 2, the first steps toward a modern industrial society bring about a decline in mortality—but also often, contrary to the theory, a rise in fertility. Improved health can result in greater physiological ability to reproduce. Whatever means had been used to reduce population growth, such as infanticide in Toku-

"Population, when unchecked, increases in a geometrical ratio. Subsistence increases only in an arithmetical ratio. A slight acquaintance with numbers will show the immensity of the first power in comparison of the second."

THOMAS MALTHUS
AN ESSAY ON THE PRINCIPLE OF POPULATION, 1798

The annual rate of world population growth peaked at about 2% in the early 1960s, and by 1997 had slowed to 1.5%, meaning that worldwide population grew by 81 million in 1997.

THE NEW YORK TIMES ALMANAC, 1998

gawa, Japan, may not survive modernization. If the age at marriage had been set well past puberty, as in early modern western Europe, the institutions bolstering this norm often became less effective. Religious practices or taboos unintentionally inhibiting fertility, such as the one prohibiting the remarriage of widows in Hindu India, may dissipate. Most remarkably, family-planning programs can result in a rise in fertility, for if women are able to depend on controls later in their reproductive life, many begin childbearing at an earlier age. In short, the effect of modernization is partly to increase fertility and partly to decrease it (Heer, 1966).

Moreover, the early analysts of the demographic transition failed to forecast the decline of mortality in less-developed countries. Over the past two centuries or so, as the main advances were applied in medicine, surgery, public sanitation, agriculture, and nutrition, Western populations gradually improved in health and longevity. During the last several decades, however, some of the most recent techniques have been transferred to areas lacking most prior scientific controls; peoples cared for until recently by witch doctors acquired access to antibiotics. In Ceylon (now Sri Lanka), to take one striking example, the estimated expectation of life at birth increased from forty-three years in 1946 to fifty-two in 1947; the gain achieved in this one year had taken half a century in most Western countries.

Efforts to reduce fertility

Because of the continuing high fertility and the sharp decline of mortality in less-developed countries, their populations have grown at rates high enough to stimulate widespread control measures. Some of these programs have been successful, but many have achieved far less than their proponents hoped they would, in part because none has an appropriate theory underlying it.

Is a large and rapidly growing population indeed a problem? Leaders of the independence movements of pre-1940 European colonies held that their countries' poverty derived not from excessive procreation but from imperial misrule, and this view often persisted after independence. The very slow start of India's programs to check its population growth, for instance, was due in part to Jawaharlal Nehru's initial ambivalence. Among those who accept the thesis that too many people can impede modernization, proponents have often advocated *either* birth control *or* industrialization, as though one or the other were the sole relevant factor.

The theories underlying birth-control programs, often implicit rather than spelled out in papers, reports, or books, can be summed up in the following propositions:

THEORIES UNDERLYING BIRTH-CONTROL PROGRAMS

1. *Elements of "traditional" society constitute the principal impediment to the spread of contraception.* But, as we have noted, most traditional cultures include antinatalist tendencies and, on the other hand, modern nationalism is often strongly pronatalist.
2. *The most important variable in any program is the contraceptive means to be used.* But the history of the West suggests that, given the will to reduce fertility, people will make effective use of whatever means are available to them—coitus interruptus and illegal abortion in France, postponed marriage or nonmarriage in Ireland, and so on.
3. *The agency through which contraception can be most effectively disseminated is the state.* But this contradicts, again, the history of the decline of Western fertility, where officialdom typically opposed the private neo-Malthusian leagues and their successors.
4. *Population policy can be equated essentially with family policy: That is, zero population growth can be realized by inducing each pair of parents to have an average of only two children.* But the rate of growth depends also on the proportion of the population that is of childbearing age, and in less-developed countries that is generally very high.
5. *It is so important that the population crisis be solved that policy-oriented action and knowledge-oriented research must be collapsed into a single operation.* This procedure violates the scientific canon that truth can be effectively sought only in a setting made as value-free as possible. As a consequence, field workers and analysts are encouraged to accept spurious results as valid, for it is very difficult to ascertain the actual sentiments and behavior patterns of respondents.

In sum, the many attempts to reduce fertility in less-developed countries have typically been made with little regard to what had been learned from the prior decline in family size in the industrial West. Perhaps the best link between the two is the wealth-flow theory, so designated by John Caldwell. The crucial factor is whether children are productively useful to their parents and care for them in their old age; if so, as in African cultures he studied, the incentive is to procreate to the maximum feasible. If, however, parents incur net costs for the long-term care and education of their children, who generally contribute little to household finances, the inevitable tendency is to reduce the number brought into the world. By concentrating on the family budget, Caldwell (1982) was able to elucidate both the historical decline of fertility in the West and the partial success of family-planning programs in less-developed countries.

Conclusions

Intellectual history includes few population theories in the narrow sense; most theories were developed as usually minor adjuncts to systematic statements about the society or the economy. Even this thin conceptual framework, however, may have profound ethical implications, for long before anything scientific was known about the determinants and consequences of population growth, statesmen, theologians, and scholars proposed—and their societies sometimes adopted as policies—rules of behavior allegedly suitable to their environment.

Until the modern era, the usual policy orientation was pronatalist, for it was generally assumed both that more people were better than fewer and that realizing a faster growth required state aid. Though not the first to take a contrary position, Malthus was by far the most important. Paradoxically, the greatly increased concern with policy in recent decades has not been accompanied by a more precise definition of goals. The judgment of whether a population is too large or too small

THE FATHERLAND AND THE MOTHERLAND
Theories of Population in Totalitarian States

A focus on economic or cultural factors can mean that political influences on fertility are bypassed. More generally, theories developed in the democratic West are in many respects ill suited to analyze such past totalitarian societies as the Soviet Union and Nazi Germany. Though their cultures differed greatly, these two countries had certain features in common, many of which related to population theory and its application.

1. The Nazi party and the Communist party were defined as omnipotent, able to cope with any increase in population. According to the first Soviet delegate to the U.N. Population Commission, "I would consider it barbaric for the Commission to contemplate a limitation of marriages or of legitimate births, and this for any country whatsoever, at any period whatsoever. With an adequate social organization it is possible to face any increase in population" (quoted by Sauvy, 1952, vol. 1, p. 174; cf. Petersen, 1988).
2. Population theory had the same purpose as any other science—to bolster the power of the party in power (Besemeres, 1980). In particular, the need of the totalitarian state for labor was reflected in theories on how to maintain a high rate of population growth and in such applications as family subsidies.
3. Efforts to stimulate the birthrate, however, were hampered by the ruling party's hostility to the family, which by its legal and emotional links between generations helps to maintain a traditional opposition to radically new ideas and practices. Both Nazi Germany and the Soviet Union tried to establish institutions that could replace the family, such as brothels in which SS men could impregnate young women certified as racially pure, or the Soviet children's homes in which the state could convert orphans and the offspring of political dissidents into reliable instruments of the Communist party. But such substitutes never produced a large enough crop, and policy toward the family therefore vacillated in both countries.
4. The need for a high fertility was enhanced by the recklessness with which sectors of the population designated as hostile or inferior were killed off. The terror most closely associated with the Nazis was the mass slaughter of Jews, based on the outpouring of writings on *Rassenkunde* (race science). More often Communists defined their victims as class enemies (though antagonism to ethnic minorities was also a constant element of Soviet life), but the difference was not fundamental: The slaughter began in different sectors of the population and was sometimes concentrated there, but in both cases it spread to the whole society (Hilberg, 1973; Conquest, 1990).
5. Totalitarian ideology was based on what in German is called *Stufenlehre*, a doctrine of stages. All analysis, all planning, began not in the empirical present but in the inevitable perfect future, homogenized into a "classless" (*Judenfrei*, "Jewless") sameness. The road to this paradise could be seen clearly only by the Nazi party and the Communist party, whose function was to move the rest of the population toward its destiny. The ruthless terror that was often needed was warranted, thus, by the glorious community that would ensue.

— WILLIAM PETERSEN

P

POPULATION ETHICS

Normative Approaches

obviously depends on a reasonably precise designation of the optimum, which has remained perhaps the most controversial concept in demography.

In past times, tyrants and conquering armies slaughtered many aliens, variously defined, but the combination of ruthless nationalism with scientific means of disposing of "inferior" sectors of the population is an innovation of the twentieth century. Partly because of a reaction against totalitarian genocide, demographers have given less systematic attention than warranted to such population characteristics as health or skill, though in many contexts these may be more important than mere numbers.

In recent decades the most striking characteristic of demography has been the attempt to dispense with theory in the solution of population problems widely recognized as critical. The substitution of "concern" for competence has not led, however, to many successes. In spite of the proliferation of antinatalist programs in less-developed countries and of the numbers of potential parents who accept the contraceptives made available, the world's population continues to grow at a rapid rate.

— WILLIAM PETERSEN

NORMATIVE APPROACHES

Population policies raise profound questions of ethics. Is China justified in using coercion to enforce its policy of one child per couple? Is it legitimate for government officials and community peers in Indonesia to apply strong pressure to promote birth control? Should U.S. judges be free to require the insertion of Norplant, a long-lasting, subdermal contraceptive, when sentencing women they consider unfit to be mothers (Feringa et al., 1992)? Do the wealthiest nations of the world have a moral obligation to accept refugees from poor countries?

◆ **freedom, negative**
internal: the absence of internal psychological or physiological (such as genetic conditions) obstructions that inhibit the fulfillment of goals, desires, and interests; external: the absence of external pressures and constraints, such as coercion and interference by others, or limits on choices of actions.

Answers to such questions require ethical principles applicable to population policies across all countries and cultures. Principles that reflect the standards of only one country or region, such as the United States or Europe, may not persuade leaders and peoples of other countries.

Three schools of thought have guided debates on these principles. The first argues that government programs of any kind must respect human rights as stated in the Universal Declaration of Human Rights adopted by the United Nations in 1948; the International Covenant on Economic, Social, and Cultural Rights (1976); the International Covenant on Civil and Political Rights (1976); and many related U.N. statements (Nickel, 1987; Claude and Weston, 1989). A second school holds that the morality of population interventions must be determined by the country that carries them out, for it has the problem and best understands how to deal with it. This school accepts no universal standards of human rights. It considers attempts by others to impose such standards to be infringements on national sovereignty. The third school recognizes some or all of the human rights affirmed by the United Nations, but claims that when population growth or density create desperate economic or social problems for a country, its government has the right to limit individual reproductive freedom for the common good.

See Also

Race Science: Bad Science Breeds Social Control

The Idea of Eugenics: Three Strands

This article develops a framework of ethical principles based on the Universal Declaration of Human Rights, later U.N. statements on human rights, and regional declarations on the same subject, particularly the European Convention on Human Rights. It then applies those principles to population policies. It concludes by contrasting this approach with another ethical framework known as "stepladder ethics."

Five key principles

Ethical evaluation of population policies requires five principles to guide decisions as well as criteria for determining when one principle can be sacrificed for another.

ETHICS OF POPULATION POLICIES

Five Principles for Evaluation

1. life
2. freedom
3. welfare
4. fairness
5. truth-telling

Life heads the list, for without it people cannot benefit from the other four principles. Article 3 of the Universal Declaration of Human Rights states: "Everyone has the right to life, liberty and security of person." The International Covenant on Civil and Political Rights is more specific: "Every human being has the inherent right to life. This right shall be protected by law. No one shall be arbitrarily deprived of his life" (Part III, Article 6).

Life means not only being alive, but enjoying good health and having reasonable security against the actions of others that cause death, illness, severe pain, or disability. Policies on fertility control, migration, and refugees threaten this principle when they take no action to assist people facing starvation or slaughter and when they create incentives for female infanticide (Aird, 1990; Brown and Shue, 1981). Policies endanger health when they promote methods of fertility control, such as sterilizations, oral contraceptives, the intrauterine device (IUD), or injections, that can pose grave risks to physical well-being. Among such risks are cardiovascular diseases, tubal infertility, pelvic inflammatory disease, and septic abortion (National Research Council, 1989; Schearer, 1983). Fertility-control programs may also damage the health of users when they overlook sexually transmitted diseases, such as gonorrhea, or other reproductive-tract infections, including genital herpes, chancroid, genital warts, vaginal infections, and infections of the upper reproductive tract (Dixon-Mueller and Wasserheit, 1991).

Freedom is the capacity and opportunity to make reflective choices and to act on those choices. Freedom requires knowledge about the choices available, such as options for fertility control or migration; a chance to make choices without coercion or strong pressure from others; awareness that one is making choices and of the issues at stake in each; and the possibility of taking action to carry out the choices made (Warwick, 1982, 1990; Veatch, 1977). Restrictions on any of these conditions, such as ignorance of options, decisions made while an individual is being tortured, or barriers to acting on choices made, void or limit freedom.

U.N. statements strongly endorse freedom. According to the Universal Declaration, everyone has the right to freedom of thought, conscience, and religion (Article 18); freedom of opinion and expression (Article 19); freedom of peaceful assembly and association (Article 20); freedom from slavery and servitude (Article 4); and freedom from arbitrary interference with privacy, family, home, or correspondence (Article 12). Both the International Covenant on Economic, Social, and Cultural Rights and the International Covenant on Civil and Political Rights open with this statement: "All peoples have the right of self-determination. By virtue of that right they freely determine their political status and freely pursue their economic, social, and cultural development" (Part I, Article 1, in both covenants). In the World Population Plan of Action developed at the World Population Conference in 1974, delegates agreed to the following statement on reproductive freedom: "All couples and individuals have the basic right to decide freely and responsibly the number and spacing of their children and to have the information, education, and means to do so . . ." (World Population Conference, 1975, p. 7).

Welfare means a standard of living adequate to provide food, clothing, housing, health care, and education. Affirmed in Articles 25 and 26 of the Universal Declaration, this standard was both repeated and broadened in the International Covenant on Economic, Social, and Cultural Rights. That statement spoke specifically about the right to continuous improvement in living conditions; the steps needed to protect the right to be free from hunger; the right of everyone to the highest attainable standard of physical and mental health; the widest possible protection and assistance for the family; special protection for mothers before and after childbirth; and protection of children and young persons from social and economic exploitation, including work that threatens their lives or is harmful to their morals and health. The World Population Plan of Action of 1974 also explicitly tied population policies to human welfare: "The principal aim of social, economic, and cultural development, of which population goals and policies are integral parts, is to improve levels of living and the quality of life of the people" (World Population Conference, 1975, p. 7). Population programs, therefore, should not aim only to raise or lower fertility, reduce mortality, or control migration, but to be instruments for promoting human welfare.

Fairness refers to an equitable distribution of the benefits and harms from population policies. It does not require an equal distribution of benefits and harms, but it does demand that one individual or group should not receive disproportionate advantages or disadvantages from a given policy. The Universal Declaration strongly endorses fairness in Article 1: "All human beings are born free and equal in dignity and rights." Article 2 continues: "Everyone is entitled to all the rights and freedoms set forth in this Declaration, without distinction of any kind, such as race, colour, sex, language, religion, political or other opinion, national or social origin, property, birth, or other status." The 1967 U.N. Protocol Relating to the Status of Refugees established principles for determining fairness in refugee and immigration policies.

In 1972, Ugandan President Idi Amin Dada ordered the expulsion of between 40,000 and 50,000 Asians living in Uganda. His action is an extreme example of the unfairness seen when the costs of population policy are borne by a single ethnic group. India's use of coercion to promote sterilization among beggars and other poor people between 1975 and 1977 was another case of unfair policy implementation (Gwatkin, 1979). Other examples include the testing only in low-income areas of contraceptives designed for all women (Holmes et al., 1980), and failing to tell uneducated candidates for sterilization how this operation is carried out, what it means for fertility, and what medical risks and side effects accompany it. In each of these cases the political, economic, social, and medical harms of population interventions fall more heavily on one group than another.

Truth-telling requires accurate information about population policies and avoiding lies, misrepresentations, distortions, and evasions about their content, implementation, and consequences. Though truth-telling is not explicitly stated in U.N. declarations of human rights, it is a prerequisite for the other four principles cited. Lies about policies of fertility control,

A century ago, most people died before the age of 50; by 1996, average life expectancy globally reached 65; in some countries it is approaching 80.

THE NEW YORK TIMES ALMANAC, 1998

Over the next 30 years, almost 98% of population growth is projected to take place in developing countries.

THE NEW YORK TIMES ALMANAC, 1998

migration, and refugees can jeopardize human life when they involve fatal risks, such as death from infections or from being shot in enemy territory. They limit freedom by depriving individuals of the knowledge necessary to make an informed choice, such as information about the side effects of sterilization. Lies harm welfare when they cause risk to one's income, education, or job prospects, and they violate fairness when they are more likely to be told to one group, such as the poor or an ethnic minority, than to others.

Life, freedom, welfare, fairness, and truth-telling can conflict with each other. Faced with what they see as excessive population growth, government officials may claim that the common welfare demands restrictions on reproductive freedom and allows distortions of the truth, such as not disclosing the medical risks of contraceptives, in order to make birth control seem attractive. Also citing the national interest, political leaders may decide to exterminate members of a specific religion, such as Jews in German territory during World War II; expel an entire ethnic group from the country, as happened in Uganda; or put severe limits on the entry of immigrants they define as hostile to the national interest, as happened when the U.S. government used ships to block the entry of Haitian refugees in the early 1990s. All three policies subordinate fairness toward religious and ethnic groups to local definitions of the common welfare. Are such policies justified, or are there some principles that cannot be sacrificed to promote others?

The Universal Declaration puts no relative weights on the many rights it endorses. However, later agreements do set priorities among rights. In Article 15, the European Convention on Human Rights states that even in national emergencies, governments cannot use murder, torture, degrading punishments, slavery, or servitude. These rights thus hold the highest rank. Nothing, including government concerns about the damage due to population growth, can override them. The International Covenant on Civil and Political Rights, drafted after the European Convention, accepts all the rights that the Convention declares immune to being overridden and adds others, particularly freedom of thought, conscience, and religion. Henry Shue (1980) and James Nickel (1987) suggest comparable criteria for weighing human rights while Sissela Bok (1978) discusses the value of truth-telling and the conditions under which it may be suspended.

Application to population interventions

The viability of any framework of population ethics depends on its ability to illuminate right and wrong in specific policies, strategies, and sets of actions. Policies set the directions for population interventions, strategies show the broad plans for following those directions, and actions indicate what happens in the field, whether intended or not. The ethics of the three are not necessarily the same. Policies may be stated in humane terms and yet be accompanied by strategies that are coercive. Strategies can be expressed in benign language but, through deliberate initiatives or neglect, lead to field actions that compromise truth, limit freedom, damage human welfare, and in extreme cases, threaten life. Ethical analysis must pay close attention not only to official statements of policies and strategies, but also to how the programs they generate are carried out.

The five ethical principles will now be applied to three examples of interventions begun by population policies. In each case the aim will be to lay out the key principle or principles involved and to indicate how apparent tensions among principles might be resolved.

THE "POPULATION PROBLEM." Population policies usually begin with some notion of a problem. For strong advocates of fertility control, such as Paul Ehrlich and Anne Ehrlich (1990), the problem is captured in phrases such as "the population bomb" or "the population explosion." According to others, particularly Julian Simon (1981), population growth brings many benefits to society, including the stimulation of human creativity. And for some, fertility, migration, and refugees are complex phenomena that must be carefully studied and that may produce no catchwords that draw public attention.

Any definition of a population problem, or a statement that there is none, must be governed by the principle of truth-telling. Those claiming a problem exists should indicate the good promoted or the evil created by fertility, migration, and refugees. What, precisely, has population done to make it qualify as a problem or a nonproblem?

Statements of a problem should also give a fair summary of the evidence bearing on the subject and its limitations. If the findings are drawn from simulations, or cover a small sample of the countries in the world, those points should be disclosed. Scholars violate truth-telling when they say or imply that simulations done through a hypothetical model of reality are equivalent to data on what people or organizations actually do. Further, when scholars who write on population work for or are funded by organizations promoting or trying to prevent action on population, such as the World Bank or a right-to-life committee, can it be determined whether they have remained objective or have taken on the advocacy role of their sponsors? If scholars have merged research and advocacy, do they indicate where research stops and advocacy begins? Truth-telling requires that all relevant information be presented, even when it may harm one's active endorsement of a policy.

Claims that a problem exists must next show the specific connection between research evidence and the good or evil that makes it a problem. That connection often proves elusive. Data showing that the poorest nations of the world have the highest fertility and the wealthiest nations the lowest fertility may seem to establish a link between population growth and economic development. Indeed, such data are commonly used to support claims of a "population bomb." Yet many studies have failed to show that rapid population growth holds back economic development in the industrialized or developing countries, and a few suggest that it may have advantages (Boserup, 1990; National Research Council, 1986). To meet the standard of truth-telling, scholars should not, as often happens, cite only those studies that support the view of a population problem to which they subscribe and omit contrary evidence.

USING COERCION. China has used coercion to force some of its citizens to limit fertility. "Coercion" means using or threatening to use physical force or severe deprivation in order to make people do things they would not normally do. Governments apply physical force when they order armed police or military officers to take citizens against their will to clinics that perform abortion or sterilization, or when they credibly threaten with torture couples who have more than two children. They use severe deprivation when they require that poor citizens be sterilized before they can obtain a job or receive food supplies necessary for their own and their family's welfare; warn that parents with more than a certain number of children will be put in prison or have their houses demolished; or use other threats that carry serious risks to life, health, and welfare.

China's coercive policies show the severe tensions between limiting population for the common good and life, freedom, and fairness. If, in response to the one-child norm, Chinese couples have used female infanticide to raise their chances of having a son, compulsion clashes with the infant girl's right to life. Government officials may say that they never intended to encourage infanticide, but that statement does not absolve them

COERCIVE POLICIES

China's Missing Girls

China has relied on coercion to carry out its one-child-per-couple policy (Aird, 1990). The Chinese government claims that its policies are voluntary, but its pressure on field workers to meet their targets, particularly in cities, has led to coercive implementation. According to Tyrene White: "Beijing's penetration to the household is awesome. In 1979 mobilization campaigns for 'voluntary' sterilizations, abortions, and adoption of contraceptive measures were widespread, and the fine line between persuasion and coercion was crossed frequently" (1987, p. 315). Two other scholars comment: "During 1979 and in some subsequent years, in some urban areas and provinces, women pregnant with a second or higher order child were required to abort the pregnancies. Instances of mandatory sterilization were also reported" (Hardee-Cleaveland and Banister, 1988, p. 275).

China's use of coercion and heavy pressures to reduce fertility has, from indications, led to female infanticide and adoption (Johansson and Nygren, 1991). In traditional China, men had the basic duty of continuing the descent line of their fathers by having a son. This boy could carry on the family name, support his parents in their old age, and inherit their property. Failure to have a son showed ingratitude to one's ancestors and discredited men in their own communities. This tradition has continued to the present. If a man's only child is a daughter, he and his neighbors may feel that he has not fulfilled one of his most basic duties in life. Yet a successful one-child policy would mean that many males could not have a son. Demographic analysis strongly suggests a clash between a couple's normal desire to keep and raise their daughters and the limits on having sons imposed by the country's policies on fertility control.

Terence Hull (1990) shows that in 1987 the sex ratios in China—the number of males per 100 females—were nearly 111, compared to an earlier reference norm of 106. Using comparable data, Sten Johansson and Ola Nygren (1991) estimate that from 1985 through 1987 the average number of missing girls (those normally expected to be in the population but, in fact, missing from it) was about 500,000 per year or 1,500,000 for those three years alone. These authors and others writing about the many millions of missing girls in China attribute this phenomenon to the one-child-per-couple policy. They offer four possible explanations: infanticide caused by deliberate actions of the parents or neglect leading to fatal illnesses; a higher proportion of abortions for female than male babies; births not properly registered with the authorities, usually because they were beyond the local quota for couples; and the practice of offering female children for adoption. The evidence offered by Johansson and Nygren suggests the presence of excess female infant deaths, whether from infanticide or other reasons; unregistered babies; and female adoption.

— DONALD P. WARWICK

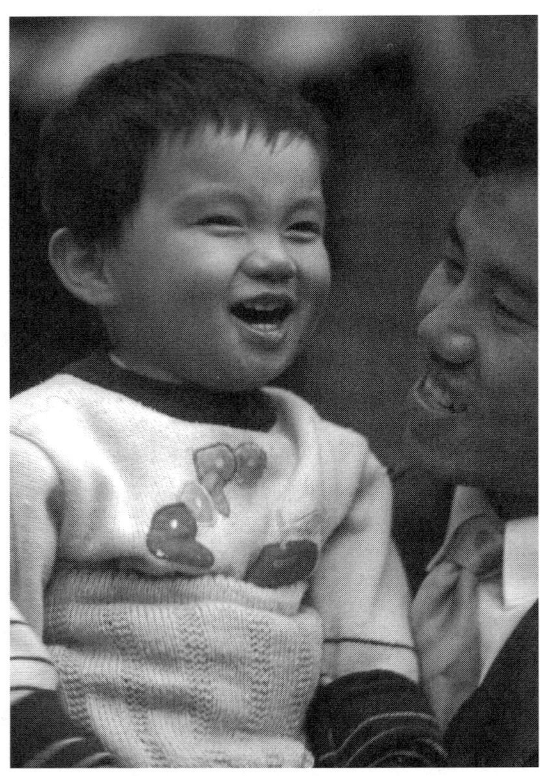

A BOY, PLEASE

Chinese fathers' traditional duty to have a son and the government's one-child rule have caused an unnatural imbalance in male-to-female survival ratios.

of responsibility for the deaths that take place. A full ethical analysis of policies must take account not only of official declarations and intentions, but also of the actions to which they lead. If, as seems to be the case, the policy of one child per couple has led to infanticide, by U.N. standards of human rights this sacrifice of life cannot be justified by the argument that China's overpopulation demands stringent control of fertility. In social policies, life holds such a high value that it cannot be traded off for even the most compelling public claims.

Coercive policies also put unjustifiable limits on human freedom. Unlike life, freedom can be and often is restricted for the common good. Laws, tax regulations, and many other policies indicate what individuals and groups must and must not do. But forcing citizens to undergo sterilizations or abortions that they do not want, as has happened in China, violates the principles of liberty and human dignity endorsed in all U.N. declarations of human rights. The moral question is not whether individuals should be totally free to set their family size—which they are not in any country or culture—but whether some limits on reproductive choice violate human rights. Using force to promote small family sizes does violate those rights.

China's population interventions further raise the question of fairness. Policies leading directly or indirectly to female infanticide, the abortion of female children, or female adoption put a far heavier burden on girls than boys. Abortion and infanticide mean that, through the decisions of their parents, girls stand a lower chance than boys of being born or of surviving to be adults. With adoption, young girls survive but do not have the same opportunity as male children to be raised by their parents. All three outcomes violate fairness by providing more benefits to boys than to girls and more harms to girls than to boys.

INADEQUATE MEDICAL SUPPORT. Fertility control programs in low-income countries sometimes lead to a conflict between efficiency in delivering services and health care for those receiving the services. To raise efficiency, program managers may insist that field workers meet the targets set for them and threaten with severe punishments those who do not comply. During India's birth-control campaign between 1975 and 1977, which relied heavily on forced sterilization, the Chief Secretary of the state of Uttar Pradesh sent this telegraph to his subordinates: ". . . Failure to achieve monthly targets will not only result in the stoppage of salaries but also suspension and severest penalties. Galvanise entire administrative machinery forthwith and continue to report daily progress by . . . wireless to me and secretary to Chief Minister" (Gwatkin, 1979, p. 41).

Managers and staff working under such pressures often provide little or no health support for those receiving their services. In India during the period mentioned, hundreds of men died from infections that developed after hastily performed sterilizations with no medical follow-up (Gwatkin, 1979, p. 47). Other health hazards caused by fertility-control methods include severe, and sometimes fatal, upper reproductive-tract infections among women not properly screened for the intrauterine device; medical complications produced by using the Dalkon shield and high-dose oral contraceptives in developing countries when their risks were well-known in the United States and Europe; reproductive-tract infections among thousands of women in poor countries; and disruptions of the menstrual cycle, heavy bleeding or spotting, weight gain, depression, headaches, dizziness, fatigue, bloating, or loss of libido among women using the injectable contraceptive Depo-Provera (National Research Council, 1989; Schearer, 1983).

Ethical responsibilities of fertility-control programs

Given these risks to life and health, officials responsible for fertility-control programs face three questions of ethics. The first question concerns the amount of information about the hazards of a particular method that should be disclosed by program staff to their clients. With heavy pressure from their superiors to meet their targets, field workers often emphasize the benefits of a method and conceal its risks. This practice violates the principle of freedom, which requires that clients have reasonable information about risks and benefits to make an informed choice about fertility control. Even when clients cannot grasp sophisticated explanations of medical hazards, they can be told what is at stake in language that they understand. When the risks not disclosed are serious, clients may also face threats to their life, their health, or their welfare.

The second ethical question concerns the adequacy of health services to deal with the hazards created by methods of fertility control. Some argue that, given the severity of the population problem, governments are morally justified in operating fertility-control services well ahead of health-support services. Others, particularly groups supporting the rights of women in family-planning programs, claim that this strategy not only violates human rights but produces a backlash against birth control. Clients who have not been told of any possible side effects or complications from the methods offered and who then suffer poor health can retaliate in many ways. They may discontinue the methods they have started, accept a method but not use it, start rumors about the physical dangers of birth control, stay away from family-planning clinics and field workers, enlist religious leaders or political parties to make fertility control a political issue, vote against the government in the next election, or, if they are truly angry, riot against the government in power. Many of these reactions followed India's use of coercion between 1975 and 1977.

The third ethical question is fairness in the distribution of medical harms and benefits among individuals and groups. This issue arises in the testing as well as the distribution of fertility-control methods. Beginning with the contraceptive pill, whose main evaluation was carried out in Puerto Rico, drug companies have often tested new methods of fertility control on poor individuals in developing countries. Government regulations on testing in those countries have been far less strict than in the United States. Moreover, the low-income individuals chosen for the testing asked few questions about what was being done and were unlikely to mount political protests or begin lawsuits to receive compensation for damage to their health. Dur-

NORMATIVE APPROACHES

Stepladder Ethics: A Contrast

Ethical principles based on internationally accepted standards of human rights contrast sharply with the stepladder ethics proposed by Bernard Berelson and Jonathan Lieberson (1979). Berelson was president of the Population Council, a visible center of research, training, and advocacy on population policy, and Lieberson was a philosopher who served as adviser to the Population Council and taught at Columbia University. These two authors commanded attention and respect, and their article was the first and last systematic analysis of ethics to appear in *Population and Development Review*, the leading journal on population policy.

Berelson and Lieberson offered this pivotal statement about population ethics: "Employ less severe measures where possible and only ascend to harsher measures if the problem at hand, as a matter of (established) fact, is clearly grave enough to warrant it" (1979, p. 596). They continued: ". . . The degree of coercive policy brought into play should be proportional to the degree of seriousness of the present problem and should be introduced only after less coercive means have been exhausted. Thus overt violence or other potentially injurious coercion is not to be used before noninjurious coercion has been exhausted" (1979, p. 602). Their moral stepladder involves beginning with voluntary policies and, if they fail, moving up the scale of pressure on people to the point justified by the seriousness of the population problem. They do not mention fertility-control measures involving threats to life, but, by their logic, governments facing exceptionally severe problems from population growth would be allowed to use those methods as well.

The authors state that they are writing out of a Western, individualistic mode, and recognize that other countries draw ethical principles from different philosophical and political traditions. They do not mention U.N. declarations on human rights, or the widely varying views of the world's religions on methods of fertility control. They apply their Western code to the strategies adopted by countries whose local standards are very different from their own. Leaders in countries populated by Catholics, Buddhists, and Muslims, for instance, might vigorously challenge the principle of allowing governments to use any form of coercion in limiting fertility. Stepladder ethics provides no means of developing cross-national ethical principles whose morality derives mainly from religion or from assumptions that differ from those of the authors, including human rights.

Stepladder ethics thus differs greatly from principles based on universally accepted human rights. Norms such as life, freedom, fairness, and welfare provide a basis for developing ethical guidelines for population policies that apply to every society. Like all ethical principles, those norms need clear definition and are often violated in practice, but they open the way for discussion among persons from diverse political systems and religious traditions and beliefs.

— DONALD P. WARWICK

ing the distribution of fertility-control methods, poor individuals in many countries likewise have received less adequate explanations and suffered more health hazards than those with higher incomes. As one example, for many years the U.S. government, citing health risks, banned the domestic use of the injectable contraceptive Depo-Provera. But it saw no problem including Depo-Provera as part of the contraceptive services in poor nations supported by U.S. foreign aid.

Four ethical guidelines help to resolve these conflicts. First, no program should knowingly threaten the life of its clients by using methods that can cause death or by failing to provide health services. If, as happened in India, sterilized males apply animal dung to areas of pain, and if that folk remedy proves fatal, fertility-control programs must take all possible steps to prevent its use.

Second, programs must offer health care for all users of methods with serious medical risks. In its villages, Indonesia has developed a simple system of health care often located in the home of the village head or another resident. Should clients show symptoms that cannot be treated there, they are referred to the nearest health clinic or hospital.

Third, clients must be told, in words they understand, about the risks as well as the benefits of fertility-control methods. To deny potential users information about risks unjustifiably limits their freedom of choice. Explanations need not be elaborate to be accurate, but they must be given.

Fourth, the distribution of risks and benefits from fertility-control programs should be fair, though not necessarily equal. Poor persons should not be the main candidates on whom fertility-control methods are tested, nor should some groups of citizens receive adequate health support while others receive little or none.

To promote user freedom and welfare, program designers and field workers can be trained to adopt the standards of quality suggested by Judith Bruce (1990). Quality care requires technical competence that gives accurate information to users in language they understand; informed consent that shows sensitivity to concerns about modesty among women and girls; pain management; and continuous rather than one-time service to clients. Instead of aiming only to avoid violations of human rights, which might attain that goal but result in mediocre care, staff can be taught to seek high client satisfaction with fertility-control services.

◆ **Depo-Provera, or depot-medroxyprogesterone (DMPA)**
a long-acting hormonal contraceptive that is given as a deep intramuscular injection.

Conclusions

To be applicable to the hundreds of countries and cultures across the world, population ethics must be based on widely shared norms. Principles drawing on the assumptions of a single society or culture will often be rejected by those from other backgrounds. Moreover, to be viable in helping decisions about population policies, the principles chosen should have priorities assigned to them. They must be able to answer one of the most challenging questions in ethics: Is it morally acceptable to sacrifice one principle, such as life, for another, such as the common welfare?

This article proposes four principles based on international declarations of human rights: life, freedom, welfare, and fairness. It adds truth-telling as a fifth principle valuable in itself and necessary in reaching the other four. When these principles clash, life receives first priority. In contrast to stepladder ethics, which grants no human rights, the ethical framework proposed here bans any method of population control with serious risks of death or those relying on torture, slavery, servitude, or other degrading punishments.

If adopted, this ethical framework would have the same advantages and limitations as all universal codes of human rights. The main advantage is that it can be used to educate policymakers and field workers on what is and is not morally acceptable in population programs. When a program violates its standards, U.N. organizations, including the Commission on Human Rights, or private groups, such as Amnesty International, could document the abuses of human rights and demand more humane policies or practices. As has already happened, universal codes can also stimulate geographic regions, such as Europe and Latin America, or major religions to examine human rights from other perspectives. S. M. Haider (1978) and his associates, for example, found many parallels and some differences between Islamic teaching and the Universal Declaration of Human Rights.

The key drawback to this framework is that, like other declarations of human rights, it might be viewed as noble in the abstract but unworkable in practice. Critics could say that it embodies foreign rather than national standards and takes no account of the difficulties with population control that face an overcrowded nation. Even so, it would give local and international advocates of human rights criteria that could be used to develop political and moral pressure to end abuses such as forced sterilization and abortion. And it would avoid the charge, leveled against stepladder ethics, that its ethical standards derive from one country or region, such as the West.

A normative framework based on internationally accepted standards of human rights offers no simple answers to the complex ethical difficulties found in population programs. It does, however, provide a foundation for discussing morality among those who hold widely different views about politics, religion, ethics, and culture. Without that foundation there will never be any serious analysis or lasting agreement about what should and should not be done in population policies and programs.

— DONALD P. WARWICK

RELIGIOUS TRADITIONS

How and to what extent religion influences population policies and the practices of individuals, couples, and larger groups is a very complex question. Although specific religious teachings about marriage, ideal family size, and the permissibility of birth control or abortion would seem to bear on reproductive decision making, the actual effects of these religious beliefs and teachings are not easily traced. Explicitly pronatalist doctrines that espouse the value of having many children and oppose birth limitation sometimes have little effect on reproductive behaviors or policies, while other aspects of religion, seemingly remote from reproductive decision making, can have powerful demographic effects.

Until recently, most major religions stressed marriage as a religiously sanctified state and were pronatalist in outlook; such teachings reflected the perilous demographic circumstances in which these religions were formed. Although Eastern Orthodox Christianity and most Protestant denominations have come to accept the use of contraception for family planning, some other major traditions have concretized traditional religious pronatalism in specific beliefs that discourage the use of birth control. Roman Catholicism continues to prohibit contraception and sterilization; Orthodox Judaism forbids use of the condom or any male methods that prevent insemination. Classical Islam, Hinduism, and Confucianism, while more permissive regarding use of birth control, share the traditional religious bias in favor of marriage and large families. Although abortion has played an important role in societies that have undergone population stabilization, no historical religious tradition favors the use of abortion for purposes of limiting the size of the family.

Other features of religious practice and teaching would seem to have a strong pronatalist effect. Many traditions stress the importance of offspring, especially sons, in carrying out vital religious rituals and in maintaining family continuity. The *Rigveda* (VI.61.1), Hinduism's foundational sacred text, terms a son a *rnachyuta*, one who removes the moral debts of a father and spares him from hell. In Judaism, key rituals emphasize the importance of children, especially male offspring: a son's *bris*, or circumcision ceremony, is a major source of religious joy; children play an important part in the Passover service; and the kaddish rite for the dead is ideally performed by a surviving son.

In African tribal societies, veneration of the ancestors is a central religious activity. Whatever immortality awaits the individual after death depends on survivors' continued performance of family rites. Individuals without progeny are viewed as pitiful figures who may become marauding spirits after death (Molnos, 1968). Since ancestors profoundly affect the circumstances of the living, family prosperity and health require the existence of an ample number of descendants to maintain the family cult. In contrast to Euro-American views, popular opinion in some African societies favors providing a scarce, lifesaving medical therapy to a bachelor over a family man (Kilner, 1990). This reflects the belief that an individual's religious and social significance is not established until he or she founds a family.

Popular religious beliefs, as opposed to formal teaching, must also be factored into thinking about reproductive behavior. Orthodox Islam, for example, does not actively prohibit the use of birth control, and most Muslims live under governments with official family-planning programs (Omran, 1992). But popular attitudes about kismet, or fate, and the idea that Allah appoints each couple the children they are to have contribute to a widespread reluctance to adopt family-planning methods (Fagley, 1967). In Africa and elsewhere, popular beliefs about reincarnation or the existence of "souls in heaven" awaiting birth contribute to a reluctance to employ birth control.

Teachings and practices regarding women are another significant aspect of religion that contributes to high birthrates. Hinduism regards women as of lower karmic status and able to effect spiritual ascent by having children and fulfilling family duties. In different ways, most other traditional religions echo these beliefs, removing women from the central sphere of political and religious life and locating whatever spiritual fulfillment that is available to them in the home (Ruether, 1974; Carmody, 1989).

Multiple demographic consequences follow from this history of marginalization of women and treatment of them as "second-class" religious citizens. Early marriage is associated with larger completed family size. Religious values that encourage child marriage, as in India, or that discourage women's education and career preparation before marriage are therefore major contributors to higher birthrates. The existence of highly differentiated social roles for men and women also may lead to larger completed family size, since sons and daughters are less "interchangeable" in terms of their ability to fulfill parental needs (Johnson and Burton, 1989). When religiously influenced values consign women to the home, their social, economic, and spiritual value comes to depend on their reproductive success. In polygynous African tribal societies, a

◆ **oral contraceptive (OC)**
the most widely used reversible method of birth control, it provides a chemical means to prevent ovulation.

See Also

Abortion: Jewish, Roman Catholic, Protestant, and Islamic Perspectives

FAMILY PLANNING
How Influential Is Religion?

Whatever the influence of religion at the level of national policies, there is considerable evidence that religious teachings about birth control or family size play a relatively insignificant role in couples' reproductive decision making. Decades ago, sociologists noted that socioeconomic modernization is normally accompanied by a "demographic" transition—from the high birthrates of agricultural and traditional societies to the lower birthrates and family-planning practices of urbanized societies (United Nations, 1977). Once economic and social modernization begins, this demographic transition occurs regardless of the religious basis of the society, casting doubt on the importance of the "religious factor" in reproductive behavior.

More recently, demographers and social scientists have tried to determine the precise role played by religious, economic, or social factors in reproductive decision making. While these studies have not settled all questions, some broad conclusions are widely accepted. Social and economic modernization are held to play a powerful role in reproductive behavior, usually eclipsing specific religious teachings about family size. For example, Joseph Chamie's (1981) study of fertility and religion in Lebanon shows that whatever their traditions teach, educated, urban, middle-class Catholic or Muslim couples make similar decisions about family size and reproduction; and lower-income, agricultural families have higher birthrates, regardless of their creed. In both cases, social and economic circumstances are determinative. The impact of purely religious doctrine on fertility appears significant only while a society is going through economic and social transition, when such doctrine may delay acceptance of birth control.

— RONALD M. GREEN

◆ **natural family planning**
intercourse is avoided entirely during the female's fertile period, and contraceptives are not used.

woman's standing among her co-wives depends on the number of her children. Her material well-being also depends on the number of progeny she has to help her with home-based economic tasks and agriculture (Molnos, 1968). Although the consequences of religious teachings and institutional practices about gender have not been measured, they may be among the most important and persistent religious influences on fertility.

These beliefs and practices affect fertility through the behavior of individuals and couples. At the institutional and policy levels, religion affects population through its impact on national and international family-planning programs. During the early 1970s, the Roman Catholic church's opposition to contraception made it difficult for the governments of some Latin American nations to mount family-planning programs (McCoy, 1974). During the 1980s, opposition to abortion by evangelical Christian groups in the United States, among others, led the U.S. government to cease support for international family-planning programs that offered abortion services or counseling. In contrast, some religious pronouncements on behalf of responsible parenthood by religious leaders in Islamic countries may have contributed to the success of family-planning programs. On balance, it is not clear how much difference religious involvement in population policy or programs makes. For example, official Roman Catholic opposition to birth control and abortion has had little or no effect on altering the very low birthrates in Catholic countries such as Austria, Ireland, or Italy.

If a religious group is a minority and holds strong pronatalist views that are heightened by opportunities for group reinforcement, there may be some independent impact of religious teachings on fertility (Kennedy, 1973; Day, 1984; Williams and Zimmer, 1990). Studies of Mormons in the United States, for example, suggest that a pronatalism deeply rooted in Mormon theology and family values, and heightened by intragroup reinforcements, contributes to birthrates among Mormons higher than would be expected among groups of similar social and economic standing (Heaton and Calkins, 1983; Heaton, 1986).

Religious teachings and doctrines, then, may influence reproductive behavior and population growth rates, but probably far less so than the amount of attention given inside and outside religious communities to specific teachings on marriage, birth control, or abortion would suggest. Among religious teachings, those less directly related to reproductive decision making, especially the religiously sanctioned subordination of women, may have the most powerful impact on fertility.

— RONALD M. GREEN

ISLAMIC PERSPECTIVES

Population issues in Islam are the product of the interplay of faith and experience, Muslim belief and local social realities. Like Islam itself, in which unity of faith has been expressed by a diversity of practice, so the application of Islam to population issues has been conditioned by local circumstances and customs as well as personal piety. Understanding the issue of population control in Islam requires an appreciation both of the

See Also

Theological Support for Family Planning

history of Islamic thought and practice and of its implementation in Muslim countries today.

The impact of Islam on population policies reflects the continuous interaction of religious teaching, local cultural traditions, and national politics. The diverse results of that interaction lead to great variation in the population policies of Muslim countries. Thus the government's approach to fertility control in Indonesia and Egypt differs greatly from that in Saudi Arabia and Iran. The first two have long had active fertility-control programs supported by senior Islamic officials. Saudi Arabia has no active family-planning program. Iran, for religious and political reasons, discontinued its family-planning program after the country's revolution in 1979 (Ross, 1991). However, in 1992, responding to severe economic and social conditions, including a rapid population growth, Iran reinstated its program with the approval of the religious leaders (*ulama*).

Muslim attitudes toward population control are influenced by beliefs and values concerning the nature and purpose of society, the family, marriage, procreation, and child rearing; they also reflect responses to several centuries of Western influence and dominance. The locus of Muslim norms and ethical standards is the Shari'a, Islamic law, which constitutes the blueprint for the ideal Islamic society. Shari'a consists of those rules and institutions that God has revealed in the Qur'an. In the early centuries of Islam, pious scholars in various Muslim capitals attempted to delineate God's law for the community. They produced a body of law that combined God's word with human interpretation and application of that word. The difference between the divine component of the law and human interpretations or applications of it has provided the rationale for legal change.

Islamic law is based upon four sources: the Qur'an, which Muslims believe is the literal and perfect word of God; the Sunnah, or example of the Prophet Muhammad; analogical reasoning; and the consensus of the community. Islamic law constitutes a comprehensive ideal that provides guidelines for personal and social life, a Muslim's duties to God (worship), and duties to society (social transactions). Jurists also recognized a number of subsidiary sources. Among the most relevant utilized for social and legal reform is public welfare. Sunni and Shiite Islam, the two major groups or traditions within the Islamic community, have a number of law schools, or schools of legal thought. Their laws, while in general agreement, nevertheless include a diversity of orientations, rules, and methods.

Muslim family law, covering marriage, divorce, and inheritance, has long been considered the heart of the Shari'a, an especially sacrosanct component of Islamic law. Historically, the family has been regarded as the basis of Muslim society. As the nucleus of the Islamic community, it is where the next generation receives its religious, social, and cultural training. In modern times, Muslim families, like those in much of the world, have undergone significant change. This is especially clear in the shift from extended to nuclear families as well as in greater educational and employment opportunities for women. These changes have been the subject of continued debate and legal reform.

Reforms in family or gender issues, from family law to population policies, have been widespread and the subject of controversy. During the latter part of the twentieth century, after Muslim nations had gained their independence from European colonial powers, many continued to look to the West for their models or paradigms of development. Political, economic, legal, and social changes were Western-inspired or -oriented, as were modern Muslim elites. As a result, social change, like political and legal reform, has often been judged both in terms of its relationship to the Islamic tradition and its law and within the context of reactions to Western influence, if not hegemony, in the Muslim world.

Africa is the world's fastest-growing region. By 2050, Africa will contain 23% of the world's people.

THE NEW YORK TIMES ALMANAC, 1998

Marriage and the family

Marriage in Islam is a sacred contract, though not a sacrament, between two individuals and also between their families (Esposito, 1980). Sexuality in Islam is centered on marriage and the family. The married state is the norm—indeed, the ideal—for all Muslims, prescribed by Islamic law and embodied in the life of Muhammad, the exemplar of Muslim life. Celibacy, while permitted if necessary, is not regarded as an ideal. Though procreation and the formation of the family are among the primary purposes of marriage, Muslim jurists from early in Islamic history permitted contraception to limit the size of a family.

Islamic teachings on methods of fertility control depend on the method used. While open to the use of coitus interruptus and methods of contraception such as the pill, many Muslim scholars oppose any form of abortion; others accept it only to save the life of the mother during the first 120 days of pregnancy. Though some Islamic jurists accept sterilization to avoid having more children, most oppose this method unless it is a medical treatment.

Contraception

In contrast to the Christian and Jewish traditions, from earliest times the Islamic tradition showed acceptance of family planning and contraception. From the tenth to the twentieth centuries, the vast majority of legal scholars and all the major schools of law accepted coitus interruptus between a husband and wife. Early acceptance of birth control was built on a combination of sacred texts, biological knowledge, and reason (Musallam, 1978). The Qur'an contains no clear or explicit text regarding birth control. However, the traditions (*hadith*) of the Prophet do. Though some *hadith* forbid birth control, the majority permit it. Muslim jurists were able to construct an argument based on *hadith* and the biological knowledge of the times to declare birth control by means of coitus interruptus as licit. They argued that such means do not limit or counter God's power because they are not foolproof. Thus, if God wanted a woman to become pregnant, his will could and would prevail despite the practice of coitus interruptus.

The prominent religious scholar al-Ghazali (d. 1111) is representative of the majority of Sunni Muslim jurists who accepted the use of contraception through coitus interruptus. For Ghazali, coitus interruptus was not only licit but also permissible, regardless of the need to practice it, because there was no explicit text in the Qur'an or Sunnah against it, nor was there clear judicial precedent based on an explicit text:

> *We have ruled out its [coitus interruptus] . . . prohibition because, to establish prohibition, one has to have a text [from the Qur'an or Sunnah] or resort to analogous reasoning based on a precedence for which a text is available. In this case . . . there is neither a text nor a precedent for analogical reasoning.*
>
> *(Omran, 1992, p. 80)*

The vast majority of Sunni and Shiite jurists believed that birth control through the use of coitus interruptus was permissible. However, because it deprived a woman of her right to children and to sexual satisfaction, her consent was required.

Despite the historical record of jurists regarding the permissibility of contraception, some scholars, such as Ibn Hazm (d. 1064), and local religious leaders viewed contraception as prohibited by Islam because they regarded increase in the number of Muslims as a Prophetic (Muhammad's) command. Though the Qur'an has no text that forbids contraception, critics of contraception interpret it to construct and legitimate their case. Among the major arguments offered are that it (1) constitutes infanticide, which is expressly forbidden by the Qur'an; (2) is contrary to belief in God's power and in divine providence, articulated in the Qur'an's teaching that God is the all-powerful creator and ruler or overseer of the world, and that he determines and controls the destiny of all (81:29 and 11:6); (3) ignores the Qur'anic mandate to trust or rely on God; and (4) ignores the necessary connection between marriage and procreation, the primary purpose of marriage.

◆ **coitus interruptus**
intercourse in which the penis is withdrawn prior to ejaculation to prevent the deposit of sperm in the vagina.

In modern times, many Muslims, reacting to the impact of Western colonialism and imperialism, have argued that by diminishing the number of Muslims, contraception undermines the power of the Muslim community. More specifically, they charge that birth-control campaigns and programs are part of a Western conspiracy to limit development in the Muslim world and thus subdue Islam.

Modern Islamic thought

The adoption of Western-inspired legal systems in many Muslim countries in the nineteenth and twentieth centuries limited the scope of Islamic law and the prestige and authority of religious scholars. However, because of the centrality of the family in Muslim society, in most countries family-law and family-planning issues continued to be strongly influenced by Islamic law and ethics. Consciousness of and concern over the implications of a population explosion in areas with limited and shrinking resources, the battle against poverty and illiteracy, urbanization, education and changing expectations, and the development of modern methods of contraception have made the issues of fertility control more prominent and contentious in Muslim societies. Government-sponsored family-planning programs and policies have become common in Muslim countries such as Indonesia, Egypt, Iran, and Bangladesh. Government intervention and implementation of such programs have met with mixed success. In many Muslim countries, when governments introduced fertility-control programs, they often looked to Islamic religious leaders to legitimate their programs and to mobilize popular support. Even when they did not support fertility control, Islamic scholars, viewing it as subject to Islamic law and as a critical area of social intervention, felt it was necessary for them to give moral guidance to Muslim believers.

Legal scholars have generally provided an Islamic rationale for various modern methods to control population growth. Modern Sunni and Shiite jurists, such as Lebanon's Sheikh Muhammad M. Shamsuddin, employing the legal principle of reasoning by analogy, have argued that since birth control in the form of coitus interruptus has been accepted for so long in Islam, then by analogy other, more modern forms of birth control that achieve the same effect are acceptable (Omran, 1992). Both individual jurists and assemblies of religious scholars have issued *fatwas* (formal legal opinions) that have endorsed contraception and in turn not only have informed the consciences of individual Muslims but also have been employed by governments from Egypt to Indonesia to support their birth-control policies and programs.

On the basis of the clear legal precedent of the acceptance of contraception in the form of coitus interruptus, modern jurists have argued for the permissibil-

See Also

Islamic Views: The Theological Context

Islam: On Reproduction and Islam: On Marriage and Sexuality

ity of modern chemical and mechanical forms of birth control, such as the diaphragm, the contraceptive pill, and IUDs. Egypt's Sheikh M. S. Madkour, for example, citing the opinions of early jurists, wrote:

> *We may say that the first mechanical method known as* coitus interruptus, al-azl *in Arabic, used by our ancestors to prevent pregnancy, corresponds to the device used these days by women and known as the diaphragm or ring to block the uterine aperture, or to another device used by men, the condom. Both are designed to prevent the semen from reaching the ovum and fertilizing it. The second method . . . for temporary contraception [is] . . . the contraceptive pill. Under this heading may also be included the injectables much advertised and supposed to be effective for several months . . . [and] every other beneficial drug which may be discovered by the medical profession for this purpose. The third . . . is the [IUD], . . . which . . . prevents the fertilized egg from attaching itself to the uterine wall, and the uterus expels it instead.*
>
> *(Omran, 1992, p. 81)*

Sheikh Tantawi, the mufti of Egypt, senior official consultant on Islamic law, in his 1988 *fatwa* recognized several reasons for practicing contraception. Couples may wish to postpone or space the birth of children for financial reasons; others may wish to do so in order to provide a separate room for a son and daughter; even those who are well off but already have three children may wish to avoid another birth because they live in an overpopulated country (Omran, 1992).

Jurists have found many licit reasons for couples to practice contraception: to avoid pregnancy due to health risks to the wife or children resulting from repeated pregnancies, transmission of hereditary or infectious diseases, or genetic risks of inbreeding; economic hardship; to better provide for children's education; and even to preserve a wife's beauty (Omran, 1992).

Muslim jurists have addressed infertility within the context of family planning. They have tended to show the same openness and flexibility in their treatment of infertility. Thus, chemical and surgical treatment, as well as artificial insemination between a husband and wife, are permitted. Insemination of a wife with her husband's sperm or in vitro fertilization is allowed. However, procedures that involve someone other than a spouse, such as inseminating a woman with sperm from a man who is not her husband, are forbidden. Children who result from such procedures are regarded as illegitimate.

Religion, government, and population issues

During the post-World War II period, governments in the Muslim world, faced with rapid population growth, cited religious, demographic, and nationalist reasons for instituting family-planning programs. Some utilized the prestige and authority of the religious establishment to legitimate family-planning policies. In Egypt, the government has often looked to the leadership and scholars of Cairo's al-Azhar University, a historic and authoritative international center of Islamic learning, for support. *Fatwas* obtained from experts (muftis) in Islamic law have played a prominent role in legitimating population policies throughout the Muslim world. However, differences often exist between official religious decrees and the more conservative responses of local religious leaders and popular beliefs. Since there is no organized church or hierarchy in Islam, and no clear text from revelation or consensus of scholars exists, local religious leaders and their followers are free to hold a variety of opinions.

Islam has legitimated and reinforced traditional pronatalist beliefs and practices in areas where social conditions have made large families desirable. Agricultural and pastoral societies have regarded large families as providing a source of labor, insurance against the loss of help due to high mortality or marriage, and social security in old age. Poverty, illiteracy, lack of educa-

ISLAMIC PERSPECTIVES
Sterilization and Abortion

As is the case with contraception, there is no clear text of the Qur'an or Sunnah that forbids sterilization. Although some diversity of opinion exists, the majority of jurists have maintained that sterilization for purposes of contraception, as opposed to its use for medical treatment, is forbidden. Whatever the debate among scholars, local Islamic leaders have tended to oppose sterilization. In recent years, a number of Sunni and Shiite jurists have called for a reconsideration of the legality of sterilization (Omran, 1992).

Abortion is a far more complex and contentious matter. There is a consensus among religious authorities that abortion after 120 days, when the fetus becomes "ensouled" and thus is a person, is absolutely prohibited except to save the mother's life. While many if not most jurists allow abortion as a means of contraception within 120 days of conception, this scholarly and theoretical position stands in sharp contrast with actual practice—abortion is condemned by most religious leaders and omitted from public-sector programs.

— JOHN L. ESPOSITO

"If whatever trees are in the earth were pens, and He should after that swell the seas into seven seas of ink, the Words of God would not be exhausted."

KORAN, 31:27

birth rate
the ratio between births and individuals in a specified population and time.

"Man says: 'How is it possible, when I am dead, that I shall then be brought forth alive?' Does he not remember that We have created him once, and that he was nothing then?"

KORAN, 19:66–67

tional and employment opportunities, and high mortality often foster and promote a belief in the necessity of a large family. Thus, many Muslims have been raised in a social context in which a primary emphasis on procreation in marriage and large families has been the traditional ideal and norm, a custom reinforced by the preaching and teaching of local religious leaders.

Local beliefs, attitudes, and values have reinforced high fertility rates. Values such as early marriage for women and emphasis on fertility and large families, in particular the importance of having a male child, pressure a young wife to gain the status of motherhood to "prove herself." Women also want to avoid the stigma of infertility and with it the possibility of divorce or of the husband taking a second wife. The importance of motherhood is reflected in the common practice in many Arab countries, once a woman has given birth to a male child, to call her by the name of that firstborn male child, that is, "mother of. . . ."

CONTRACEPTIVE PREVALENCE RATES IN ISLAMIC COUNTRIES

Moderate to High Prevalence (1994)	
Algeria	36%
Egypt	47
Indonesia	50
Tunisia	50
Turkey	63
Low Prevalence Rates (1990)	
Afghanistan	2%
Saudi Arabia	1
Somalia	0
Yemen	2

Government-sponsored programs have varied considerably in their impact and effectiveness. Moderate-to-high contraceptive prevalence rates were indicated in 1994 for Turkey, Tunisia, Indonesia, Algeria, and Egypt. Muslim countries with low rates reported in 1990 include Somalia, Saudi Arabia, Afghanistan, and Yemen (Ross et al., 1992). Bangladesh's poor performance has been attributed to a "population control battlefield" between contending religious and social forces (Hartmann, 1987); Indonesia, on the other hand, has been identified as a family-planning success story. Since the 1970s, Indonesia has used a carrot-and-stick approach of incentives and state pressure. This policy, combined with socioeconomic changes such as reduced infant mortality, increased educational levels, and rural-to-urban migration, has led to a significant decline in fertility (Hartmann, 1987). Initially, many local religious leaders opposed family-planning programs on moral grounds and because they believed that growth in population was necessary in order to spread Islam. Efforts by the government, early in the program, to consult with religious leaders, and the government's decision to exclude sterilization and abortion from the program, helped counter the opposition.

The role and influence of religious leaders has varied and can often prove significant. The influence of Islam on people's acceptance or rejection of government-sponsored fertility-control programs depends not only on moral teachings of a religious tradition but also on how those teachings are interpreted to local people by religious leaders. If, as in Indonesia, many of those leaders support the program and use occasions such as marriage ceremonies to suggest the value of family planning, acceptance will typically be greater than if those leaders tell believers that using contraceptives to limit birth violates Islamic teaching. Postrevolution Shiite Iran provides a unique example of religious leaders, the *ulama*, functioning as both the executors and the formulators or legislators of new *fatwas* on family planning.

The Egyptian government has addressed the population question since the beginning of the rule of Gamal Abdel Nasser in 1952. Because of religious sensibilities, the government moved slowly, employing only the pill. Religious officials, from the government-appointed mufti of Egypt to the rector of the state-supported al-Azhar University, issued a series of *fatwas* endorsing the use of contraceptives. However, many think the religious establishment has been co-opted by the government. Thus, while Nasser and his successors could marshal the support of the religious establishment, local religious leaders continued to condemn contraception as immoral as well as contrary to Islam, and reinforced traditional emphasis on procreation and acceptance of the will of God, as did other opinion makers, such as midwives.

Like many other countries, Egypt has utilized a centralized, top-down approach, bypassing or ignoring local and regional realities. In 1953, Nasser was concerned that Egypt's population would leap to 44 million (Warwick, 1982). However, little was done about fertility control until the mid-1960s.

In Lebanon, religious sectarianism and communalism have both determined and limited the success of government policy. Lebanon was created as a confessional state whose delicate balance was based upon a system of proportional representation: Maronite Christians were dominant, followed by Sunni and Shiite Muslims and Druze. However, tensions between Christians and Muslims were exacerbated by the socioeconomic dominance and advancement of the

demography
the statistical study of human populations esp. with reference to size and density, distribution, and vital statistics.

Maronites, who had a lower fertility rate than the Muslims. By the mid-1970s, social realities proved explosive, and civil war broke out. The Shiite community, the poorest and most disenfranchised, had grown, and constituted one-third of Lebanon's population.

Given the precarious balance of power and social tensions, the Lebanese government for more than two decades shied away from any official promotion of family planning. However, while contraceptives remained illegal, the government indirectly supported private family-planning projects (Warwick, 1982).

Conclusion

Islam has a well-established body of teaching on fertility control that is closely linked to its views on marriage and the family. The interpretation of these teachings varies from country to country. The openness of individual Muslims to fertility control depends on many variables, including interpretations by local religious leaders of how it should be regarded by Muslims. Countries differ greatly in the extent to which Islamic religious leaders cooperate with government-sponsored fertility-control programs.

Much of the Muslim world faces rapid population growth in a situation of limited resources. Containment or reversal of this trend remains hampered by widespread poverty, illiteracy, and debates about the morality of birth control. In this struggle, the criticisms of local religious leaders combine with voices of many militant Muslims who attack government-sponsored family-planning programs and Western aid as a conspiracy to limit the size of the Muslim community in order to contain and dominate it more effectively.

— JOHN L. ESPOSITO

JEWISH PERSPECTIVES

"Pronatalism" is the contemporary word describing the classic Jewish tradition regarding fertility. To begin with the religious component of the Jewish culture, procreation is counted as a positive *mitzvah* (a commandment or virtue), given pride of place at the top of rabbinic formulations of Bible commandments. *P'ru ur'vu* ("Be fruitful and multiply," or better, "Be fruitful and increase"—more arithmetic than geometric) in the first chapter of Genesis is a general blessing to other creatures; for humans, it is a behavioral imperative to reproduce. Bible commentators explain this difference in terms of the human differential: The command mode is needed because humankind, created in the image of God, might seek to devote itself entirely to the spiritual and intellectual, and might neglect the material and physical. Accordingly, Scripture thus negates the antiprocreative or celibate views of some cultures. Alternatively, the commandment addresses the fact that only humans are aware of the consequences of sexual activity; they might seek to avoid the attendant responsibilities of procreation while indulging the sexual drive.

On another level, a rabbinic Bible commentary observes that, throughout the first chapter of Genesis, the seal of approval—the announcement that "the Lord saw that it was good"—is repeated for each element of creation. But after Adam was created, "the Lord said, 'It is not good that man [Adam] should be alone.'" Only that which can endure is good; if humankind does not procreate, it will not endure.

Nor will God himself endure, according to the Talmud, without us to acknowledge him: "Not to engage in procreation," we are told, "is to diminish the Divine image." That is why the verse "for in the image of God has He created man" (Gen. 9:6) is followed immediately by the reaffirmation of Genesis 9:7, "Be fruitful and increase" (*Yevamot* 63b). More to the point, when the later verse (Gen. 17:7) introduces the Lord who will be "thy God and [that] of thy 'descendants after thee,'" the Talmud asks, "If there are no 'descendants after thee,' upon whom will the Divine Presence rest? Upon sticks and stones?" (*Yevamot* 64a). Without human progeny and continuity, there is no one to worship God. Without the physical body, there is no soul.

The biblical commandment is, as usual, spelled out in its details in *Mishnah* and *Gemara*, the two components of the Talmud, setting forth the halakah, the definitive legal ruling as formulated by the Codes. The halakah of "be fruitful" requires that a couple replace itself, that is, give birth to at least a son and a daughter. Having several sons or several daughters still does not fulfill the commandment. Yet, after the fact, the Talmud counts "grandchildren like children," so that parents with progeny of just one gender can be reassured that their children's children will help them measure up. Actually, even two children of different genders are only the bare minimum; in Maimonides' codification, the effort to procreate must continue. In *Tosafot*, authoritative critical commentaries from medieval France printed on the margin of the Talmud, the fear is expressed that letting the minimum number suffice could result in ethnic extinction (*Bava Batra* 60b). Infant mortality, as well as the possibility that the offspring may not live to adulthood or not reproduce, requires that more than one son and one daughter be conceived and born.

The duty to go far beyond the minimum has its rationale in the rabbinic dimension of the procreative *mitzvah*, where it is called, in brief, *la-shevet* or *la-erev*. (Deriving legal teaching from biblical books other than the Pentateuch is termed "rabbinic"; only the Five Books of Moses are the source of law called "biblical.") The biblical support for the first, *la-shevet*, is Isaiah (45:18): "Not for void did He create the world, but for

◆ **pronatalist**
fertility-raising policy, such as those that deny access to contraception.

See Also
Pronatalism: Be Fruitful and Multiply

"One generation passeth away, and another generation cometh: but the earth abideth for ever. The sun also ariseth."

ECCLESIASTES, 1:4–5

habitation [*la-shevet*] did He form it." The second, *la-erev*, comes from Ecclesiastes (11:6): "In the morning sow thy seed, and in the evening [*la-erev*] do not withhold thy hand [from sowing], for you know not which will succeed, this or that, or whether they shall both alike be good." These verses strongly suggest a moral imperative to continue beyond the minimum.

The broader dimension of the *mitzvah* is very much an operative part thereof. To illustrate its legal implications, a Sefer Torah (scroll) belonging to an individual requires special care and may not ordinarily be sold for its proceeds. There are two exceptions: It may be sold (1) to finance tuition for the study of Torah, and (2) to dower a bride and thus enable her to marry and procreate. What if she already has a son and daughter? The power of the rabbinic extension of the *mitzvah* is now seen in the ruling that a Sefer Torah may be sold to finance the remarriage of that woman, so that she may fulfill *la-shevet* or *la-erev*.

The traditional pronatalist stance is vividly evident in modern-day rabbinic rulings with respect to reproductive technology. Just as illness or pathology are the targets of Judaism's mandate to heal, whereby Sabbath and dietary laws—and the rest of the Torah—are to be set aside to allow healing procedures to do their work, so barrenness and infertility are seen as pathological states to be overcome by aggressive therapies that may also supersede ritual laws. This equation of barrenness with illness means that fertility problems are to be overcome by such exigencies as in vitro or in utero fertilization, even artificial insemination or gestation by a host mother, for cases in which usual (or "natural") conception and birth are not possible. The principle of the primacy of fertility as a desideratum in a pronatalist tradition is given concrete form by the contemporary application of these legal provisions.

Another technical detail of Jewish law places the *mitzvah* (commandment) of procreation on the man rather than on the woman, though of course both are needed for procreation and both share in the *mitzvah* (virtue). This position may have its basis in the theoretical permissibility of polygamy or polygyny, whereby a man could marry more than one wife, but both paternity and maternity would still be known. The husband has to "worry about" the *mitzvah*'s accomplishment. An actual sex-role difference derives from the "Be fruitful and increase" of Genesis, which goes on to say "Fill the earth and conquer it." The male is the conqueror, the aggressive one; the female, as the more passive, should not have to "go seeking in the marketplace" (*Yevamot* 65a). If that observation is rooted in anthropology, an explanation based more on ethics is offered by a Bible commentator of the twentieth century, Rabbi Meir Simcha HaKohen (d. 1921): Both the pain and the risk of childbearing are borne by the woman, not the man. Since the Torah's "ways are ways of pleasantness, and all its paths are peace" (Prov. 3:17), the Torah could not in fairness command a woman to undergo pain and assume risk; this must be her choice and it becomes her virtue. For the man, exposed to neither pain nor risk, there is both the command and the responsibility to heed the command (*Meshekh Hokhmah* to Gen. 1:28).

The discussion of what is and what is not a commandment refers to the formulations of the Sinai Covenant, which did in most cases reaffirm the pre-Sinai imperatives of Genesis, and as such applies only to the covenanted Jewish community. What of the rest of the world? A system called "the Seven Commandments of the Children of Noah" was discerned by the Talmudic sages; it is derived from God's charge to Noah after the flood and applied to his descendants in the world at large. These commandments include basic moral imperatives against murder, incest, cruelty to animals, and a directive to establish general law and order. Hence, the Sinai legislation cannot be imposed on mankind in its specifics. Many Jewish teachers see the thrust of *la-shevet* as generally applicable, for that biblical verse holds forth the *telos*, or ultimate end, of the earth, that it be inhabited and populated.

Contraception and abortion

Sentiments toward procreation go hand in hand with views and practices of contraception and abortion. The halakah of contraception includes both the problem of method—whether or not a particular means completes the sexual union, or is not onanistic—and of motive—whether medical reasons or convenience are determinant. Contraception is clearly permitted where medically indicated, with even the less preferable methods. For nonmedical reasons, only methods such as rhythm or the pill may be used, providing the motive is acceptable. The preferable methods, such as the pill or Norplant, are not occlusive and not onanistic because sperm has an unimpeded trajectory. Coitus interruptus and the use of condoms are the least acceptable methods. But where AIDS, for example, is a threat, the condom's prophylactic properties take precedence, on the Talmudic principle that "[avoiding] danger is more serious than [avoiding] transgression" (*Chulin* 10a). This clear, medical permission means, incidentally, that in marital relations contraception is to be preferred over sexual abstinence.

Medical reasons are essentially what govern resort to abortion. The distinction is made between murder and killing of the fetus: If abortion were murder, it could only be considered if the life of the mother were at stake; as killing, or taking of only a potential human life, it can be considered to save her health or well-being, emotional as well as physical. As with contra-

See Also

Abortion: Jewish Perspectives

ception and pronatalism, Orthodoxy takes a less liberal position on abortion in theory and in practice than do the Conservative and Reform alignments.

The voluminous Responsa (formal replies to queries by rabbinic authorities) on these subjects are addressed to the individual couples and to their queries in deed. Global questions are also addressed, such as population control for ethical reasons as a concern for humanity and for available resources. The counsel of one rabbinic authority invoked the notion of "lifeboat ethics," whereby the lifeboat in which we all find ourselves, like Noah's Ark according to a Talmudic observation, must be kept from sinking as a result of overpopulation. The solicitude in halakic legislation for the welfare of existing children and their mother, before adding to one's family, was also invoked to argue for ecological responsibility.

Birthrate and the state of Israel

Advocacy of world population limitation is not contradicted by efforts to raise the Jewish birthrate. To the extent that growth globally threatens human well-being and Earth's ecology, it is an imperative concern for us all. But the Jewish people, constituting less than 1 percent of the world's population, would not adversely affect that picture even if their numbers doubled. Replacing Jewish losses would not upset the geophysical numerical balance; it would merely keep Judaism alive. Other minorities should similarly be allowed to maintain their existing numbers. Jewish aspirations, as reflected in synagogue liturgy, are not to become predominant in the world, but merely to "preserve the remnant of Israel."

That liturgical phrase refers, of course, to the People of Israel, but the State of Israel reflects similar concerns. At least one reason for the state's establishment in 1948 was demographic. When Palestine was ruled by British mandate, a "white paper" was issued that severely limited immigration by Jews, even hapless Holocaust survivors and internees of Europe's displaced-person camps. Whatever else sovereignty and independence provide, here they were necessary primarily to remove quotas and barriers to Jewish immigration.

After Israel was founded under the sponsorship of the United Nations and Jewish refugees were admitted, interior population growth was encouraged. The Hebrew word for immigration is *aliyah*, or ascendance to the Land of Israel. Now a new term was coined—*aliyah penimit*, or internal immigration—to refer to

JEWISH "PRONATALISM"
Historical Imperatives

Attitudes toward procreation among Jews were not, of course, shaped by the law alone. Pronatalism partakes of the personal and cultural: In the face of all God's promises, Abraham protests to God (Gen. 15:2): "What canst Thou give me, seeing that I go childless?" The anguish of the barren woman is a recurrent theme in the Bible and beyond. On the other hand, fecundity is the most cherished blessing, exemplified idyllically in the Psalmist image (Ps. 128) of one "whose wife is a fruitful vine" and whose "children are as olive plants around the table" and whose ultimate satisfaction is the sight of "children [born] to thy children."

The natural impulse was buttressed by a national one. Historical circumstances of frequent massacres and forced conversions, with their resulting decimation of Jewish communities, added the impulse to compensate for losses to an existing instinct to procreate. The yearning for offspring was deepened, addressing positively the need to replenish depleted ranks. This contrasts to the response of despair reflected in an antiprocreative stance taken by some Christian sects in the face of evil. The Gnostics in the first century, the Manichees in the fifth century, and the Cathars in the twelfth century are among the groups that taught and lived by the belief that procreation is to be avoided in a world of evil unredeemed. Apprehensiveness about the eventual well-being of offspring, the Talmud teaches, should not be a reason for not bearing children. This was King Hezekiah's worry, to which the response of Isaiah (38:1-10) is understood to mean: "The secrets of God are none of your business. You fulfill your duty [of procreation]" (*Berakhot* 10a).

In the post-Holocaust days, both the individual and the Jewish collectivity have been encouraged to make up for the physical losses of that tragic period. Nonetheless, realization of this impulse or teaching has not been evident across the board. In fact, the Jewish birthrate in the United States and other developed nations in recent decades was lower than, or as low as, that of the rest of the population. Upward socioeconomic mobility, and an increased pursuit of secular education and professional opportunity, has kept the birthrate down in assimilated families. Jews have, in fact, been visibly active in the movement for zero population growth, advancing a cause they consider ecologically necessary. Reform and, to a greater extent, Conservative Jews generally answer to the influence of Judaic tradition alongside of social considerations, while Orthodox families register the highest rates of reproduction.

— DAVID M. FELDMAN

new births in Israel, encouraged as a patriotic act to build the nation and its defenses. Also, since the very raison d'etre of the establishment of the state was as a restored homeland and a haven of refuge, the Law of Return was promulgated. It called for the "ingathering of the exiles," inviting Jews to be rehabilitated in their ancestral home, and granting them automatic citizenship upon their arrival.

The politics of population power have been evident not only in control of the disputed territories of Judea and Samaria (West Bank) but also in Israel proper and in the peace efforts begun in 1993. Nationalists express the concern that a disproportionate increase in the Arab birthrate or Arab immigration could effectively dissipate the Jewish character of the world's only Jewish state. On the other hand, during the early 1990s, massive absorption of Jews from the former Soviet Union and from Ethiopia took place; this influx demonstrated the profound demographic and cultural, as well as political, consequences of population factors.

— DAVID M. FELDMAN

Do restrictions on the choice of whether to bear a child affect the woman's moral obligations to the child she bears?

PAGE 474

ROMAN CATHOLIC PERSPECTIVES

Roman Catholic teaching on population is a complex blend of theological beliefs, ethical norms, and empirical judgments. The distinctive characteristic of Roman Catholic doctrine is the sustained and significant place its teaching on contraception has held in its population position. Indeed, the detailed discussion of contraception in Catholic moral theology at times conveys the impression that this one issue constitutes the whole Catholic position on population ethics.

It is necessary, therefore, to distinguish two related but not identical moral questions in Catholic theological ethics: the morality of contraception and the teaching on population policy. John Noonan's classic work on contraception identifies moments in the history of the tradition when demographic trends affected the official teaching of the church, but it points out that these instances do not stand out as major determinants in the development of Catholic doctrine on contraception (Noonan, 1965). Noonan's analysis illustrates the complexity of the Catholic response to falling birthrates in the late Roman Empire, in the medieval period, and again in the nineteenth century. During those periods the Catholic position criticized the idea of restraining population growth but did not assert that procreation of children should be fostered without regard to other values. The balancing factors in the Catholic position are the linking of procreation to education and the high status accorded virginity in Catholic life.

It is possible, therefore, to trace a relationship between contraception and population policy throughout Catholic teaching; yet until the twentieth century, the dominant idea is the prohibition of contraceptive and other birth-limiting practices, with the population issue treated as a minor theme. Even in Pius XI's encyclical *Casti Connubii* (1930), which Noonan describes as "a small summa on Christian marriage" (1965, p. 426), the population issue receives only indirect reference. A systematic treatment of the morality of population policy as a distinct issue in its own right is not evident in Catholic thought until the time of Pius XII (Hollenbach, 1975). Beginning with Pius XII's address to the Italian Association of Catholic Midwives in 1951 and continuing through the teachings of Popes John XXIII and Paul VI, Vatican II, the Synod of Bishops (1971), and John Paul II, one can find an articulated ethical doctrine on population policy. The ethical teaching responds to two dimensions of the contemporary population debate: first, intensification of the debate about the relationship of population and resources; second, the move by governments and international institutions to design policies to affect demographic trends.

It is possible to distinguish in the Catholic teaching two species of moral analysis: One focuses on the context of population policy; the other, on the content of the procreative act. David Hollenbach distinguishes these two dimensions as the public and private aspects of Catholic teaching (Hollenbach, 1975).

Population policy

The public dimension is found generally in the social teaching of the church; the principal documents relating to population policy are *Gaudium et Spes* (1965) (Gremillion, 1976), *Populorum Progressio* (Paul VI, 1967), and the interventions of the Holy See on the occasions of international conferences about population, resources, and the environment. These documents manifest a social, structural analysis of the population issue, seeking to place demographic variables within a broadly defined socioeconomic context. The tenor and style of analysis is exemplified in Paul VI's message for the 1974 U.N. Population Year. The Pope's message argues for a broadly based approach to demographic problems with the category of social justice used as a principal theme (Paul VI, 1974a). This perspective is reaffirmed in the Holy See's intervention at the 1984 U.N. Population Conference (Schotte, 1984).

The main presupposition of all these statements is that the population problem is one strand of a larger fabric involving questions of political, economic, and social structure at the national and international levels. While acknowledging the existence of a population problem, this view asserts that it is morally wrong and practically ineffective to isolate population as a single factor, seeking to reduce population growth without simultaneously making those political and economic changes that will achieve a more equitable distribution of wealth and resources within nations and among nations (Rich, 1973; Paul VI, 1974a, 1974b).

The ethical categories used in analyzing the social aspect of the population problem are drawn from Catholic social teaching developed principally in the papal documents from 1891 to 1991 (Calvez and Perrin, 1961; Gremillion, 1976; Pavan, 1967; O'Brien and Shannon, 1992). The foundation of the argument is that the human person, endowed with the gifts of reason and free will, possesses a unique dignity or status in the world. The person, in Christian thought, is regarded as the pinnacle of God's creative action; the uniqueness of the person is argued in Catholic thought in both philosophical and theological terms. The dignity of the person is the source of a spectrum of rights and duties articulated as claims upon and responsibilities toward other persons and society as a whole. The distinguishing mark of the Catholic theory of rights, setting it apart from a classical, liberal argument, is the assertion of the social nature of the person. Society and state are necessary and natural institutions that are presupposed and required for full human development.

The strong social orientation of Catholic political philosophy holds that the way in which society, state, and subordinate social institutions are designed and structured is a moral question of the first order. Society and state are not self-justifying; they exist for the purpose of achieving the common good, defined as the protection and promotion of the rights and duties of each person in the society (Gremillion, 1976).

The central category used in evaluating the organization of social structures and institutions is social justice. This concept has roots in medieval Catholic teaching, but it has been developed and refined in the social encyclicals *Quadragesimo Anno* (1931) (O'Brien and Shannon, 1992) and *Mater et Magistra* (John XXIII, 1961), as well as in the third synodal document, "Justice in the World" (1971), and in the social teaching of John Paul II (O'Brien and Shannon, 1992). As social justice is used in these documents, it measures the role of key social institutions in procuring a fair distribution of wealth and resources nationally and internationally. In Pacem in Terris, the normative framework for assessing social institutions is expanded beyond justice to include truth, freedom, and charity (John XXIII, 1963).

The articulation of these categories in Catholic social teaching manifests two stages of development, both pertinent to a population ethic. The social teaching of the period from 1891 through the 1930s focuses on the nation as the unit of analysis; social justice principally means justice within the nation.

Beginning with Pius XII and continuing through John Paul II, the scope of analysis is broadened to focus on the international community. This move from assessing justice within the nation to justice among nations can be charted in the emergence of key concepts. John XXIII (1961) is the first to discuss the international common good as a standard for measuring national policies. The implication of this idea is that an adequate assessment of a state's policy must be calculated in terms of its impact on other states and peoples as well as upon its own citizens. For transnational questions like population and food policy, such a category of analysis opens a whole new set of questions. A similar expansion of a traditional category is found in "Justice in the World" in its discussion of international social justice (Gremillion, 1976). The concept explicitly addresses the structures through which states relate to each other in political and economic affairs. John Paul II develops the notion of solidarity as the ethical category that can direct the increasing interdependence of world politics and economics (O'Brien and Shannon, 1992).

At both the national and international levels, the categories of common good, social justice, and freedom of choice for individuals and families in society are used to define the population question. Among social institutions, the family, based on the covenant of marriage, holds a unique place in Catholic thought (Hollenbach, 1975). It is regarded as the basic cell or unit of society and the Catholic church. In the social hierarchy, reaching from the person through the state to the international community, no other association, save the Catholic church itself, is accorded such status. The demands of the common good and the requirements of social justice are articulated in terms of providing the family and its members with those conditions of life that satisfy basic human needs, protect personal dignity, and allow human development through the exercise of rights and responsibilities in society.

High on the list of inviolable rights is that of marrying and having a family (Hollenbach, 1975). To protect this right and other such rights for each person, Catholic social teaching establishes two parameters: positively, it calls upon the society to guarantee a basic minimum of material welfare, and negatively, it prohibits the state from any significant interference in the exercise of these rights. To summarize the public dimension of Catholic teaching, it accords primary attention to the context of the population question, focusing on the requirements of social justice that should be met as the first step in dealing with the relationship of resources and people. These requirements in specific form include questions of international trade, development assistance, agricultural reform, foreign-investment policies, consumption patterns, and the structure of social relationships within nations. In

Population ethics involves applying moral principles to complex situations.

PAGE 491

P

POPULATION ETHICS

Roman Catholic Perspectives

Whether or not there is a population problem is critical to the ethics of population control.

PAGE 492

CATHOLIC TRADITION
The Teaching on Contraception

In contrast to the public teaching that focuses on societal structures, the tradition concerning private matters focuses upon the nature of the conjugal relationship and specifically upon the morality of the conjugal act. The principal issue involves analyzing permissible means of preventing contraception. The private aspect of the tradition is rooted in the extensive Catholic teaching on contraception, which has developed in very complex and detailed fashion since the second century (Noonan, 1965).

The modern expression of the private issues of the tradition is found in Pius XI's *Casti Connubii* (1930), Pius XII's Address to the Italian Catholic Union of Midwives (1954), Paul VI's *Humanae Vitae* (1968), and John Paul II's *Familiaris Consortio* (1982). The principal private issues in the tradition include the morality of abortion, contraception, and sterilization; in the official teaching, all are rejected as means of preventing conception of birth. The only sanctioned means of limiting conception is some form of natural family planning, that is, one that excludes contraceptives. In contrast to the discussion among theologians on the public tradition, there is a very significant division between the official teaching on contraception and an analysis of contraception by theologians (Hoyt, 1968; Curran, 1969). While official teaching forbids all forms of contraception, many prominent theologians hold for the legitimacy of contraceptive techniques and the use of sterilization under specified conditions.

— J. BRYAN HEHIR

addition to these contextual issues in the population debate, Catholic teaching also includes a private dimension as regards the content of the procreative relationship.

Population policy and the teaching on contraception

The private dimension of the tradition on population policy has public implications; it seeks to prevent any public policy that would either constrain or induce individuals to procure an abortion or to use contraceptives or would prevent them from choosing to have children. There are themes of coherence and consistency between the public and private aspects of the Catholic tradition: Both are concerned with the procreative process as a sacred dimension of human relationships; both seek to preserve maximum freedom for the couple to determine when to exercise procreative rights; both stress that society and the state exist to serve their members, and the relationship of the state to citizens is articulated in terms of social justice and personal freedom.

Having acknowledged these elements of continuity, it is equally important to illustrate the tension that prevails between the public and private dimensions of Catholic teaching on population policy. The tension can be analyzed by examining two principal texts: *Populorum Progressio*, representing the public dimension, and *Humanae Vitae*, representing the private one (Paul VI, 1967, 1968). These texts, in turn, must be assessed in light of the teaching of John Paul II on population policy. Paragraph 37 of *Populorum Progressio* is a carefully articulated and expansive statement of Catholic teaching on population policy (Gremillion, 1976). The passage contains the following elements:

1. an acknowledgment that a population problem exists in the world;
2. an affirmation that governments have a right and competency to deal with the problem;
3. a prescription that governmental action must be in accord with the moral law. This specific treatment of population policy is couched in the context of Paul VI's most detailed statement of the need for international reform in the political and economic order. Hence, the paragraph presupposes that the social justice requirements are being addressed, and in that context the paragraph speaks to the question of measures to restrict population growth.

This passage is the clearest statement in Catholic teaching affirming the right of governments to intervene in the population question; left undefined, however, is the permissible scope of governmental intervention. The phrase that renders the policy ambiguous is that public intervention must be "in conformity with the moral law." In this area of public policy, what measures fall within the moral law? One way to clarify and specify the public tradition is to use *Humanae Vitae* as the guide for interpreting the moral law. The principal argument of the encyclical is that the moral law requires each and every act of intercourse to be open to procreation. A supporting reason offered for this position is that any compromise on this point opens the way to unregulated governmental intrusion into the sacred domain of family life (Gremillion, 1976). Presumably, then, the conjunction of *Humanae*

See Also

Abortion: What the Gospels (Don't) Say

Questioning the Church: Three Central Issues

Vitae and *Populorum Progressio* would limit the scope of governmental intervention to supporting and fostering only that means of population restraint approved in *Humanae Vitae.*

This is a restrictive reading of the texts; another view would stress the distinction between public and private dimensions of Catholic moral teaching as the key to interpreting Catholic teaching on population policy. This distinction is crucial in recognizing the different ethical norms used in Catholic thought for personal and social morality. A characteristic feature of Catholic social teaching is its sense of the multiple levels of society (Murray, 1960). The state is distinguished from society, and voluntary associations are distinguished from the state. Each principal part of the societal fabric is regarded as having a specific, limited role to play.

Two corollaries flow from this carefully delineated perspective on society. First, there is the recognition that personal conceptions of morality cannot be directly translated into requirements of social morality or public policy; to attempt to do so ignores the distinct nature of social and institutional relationships in society and thereby "makes wreckage not only of public policy but also of morality itself" (Murray, 1960, p. 286). Second, a recognition of two related but distinct levels of moral discourse—public and private—yields the jurisprudential distinction of moral law and civil law (Murray, 1960). While every human action and all human relationships fall under the moral law, only those that have a demonstrable effect on the public order and are open to state regulation without sacrificing other proportionately significant values are to be included under civil law or public policy. Since Catholic theology recognizes distinctions between public and private morality and between civil and moral law, it is possible for Catholic teaching to oppose an action or policy on moral grounds but not be inevitably committed to seek legal or political means to prevent its implementation.

The use of these distinctions between public and private morality and between civil and moral law could yield a more flexible reading of *Populorum Progressio.* First, such a reading would accent the state's right to intervene in the population question. Second, it would then treat the *Humanae Vitae* argument as being principally applicable in the area of personal morality and not an adequate framework for examining population policy. Third, it would acknowledge the disputed character of *Humanae Vitae* in the Catholic community, even as a norm of personal morality. The purpose of bringing to light the opposing Catholic views on papal teaching regarding contraception (as expressed in *Humanae Vitae*) would simply be to acknowledge that, when such dispute exists within the Catholic community, there is strong reason not to seek to make such a norm a standard of public policy in a pluralistic world. Finally, while not interjecting the specific prescriptions of *Humanae Vitae* into public debate, such a Catholic stance could still speak to the limits of permissible state intervention on population questions. The criteria for setting limits could be drawn from the human-rights standards of the public ethic in the tradition, including a stance against abortion (on human-rights grounds), protection of the person from coercion regarding procreative practice (particularly regarding sterilization), and a respect for religious and moral pluralism as a guide for governmental action.

This broadly designed "public" approach to population policy, one cast in terms of human rights and social justice, is defensible in terms of principles of Catholic moral theology. It is not, however, the direction Pope John Paul II has set for the church's approach to population questions since his election to the papacy in 1978. His approach has been to tie the public and private dimensions of policy more tightly together, thereby raising the visibility and role of the teaching on contraception in the overall direction of policy. The impact of John Paul's leadership can be found in his own teaching and in the positions the Holy See has taken in international conferences on population-related issues.

Teaching of John Paul II

John Paul's influence can be summarized in terms of four contributions. First, in his encyclical on Catholic moral theology *Veritatis Splendor* (1993), the pope reaffirmed the structure of moral argument that sustains traditional Catholic teaching, not only on abortion but also on sterilization and contraception. The encyclical did not break new ground on these issues, but the effect of it has been a call for greater restraint on theological dissent from the teaching on contraception and sterilization. The scope of *Veritatis Splendor* is much broader than specific issues of sexual morality; its influence on population policy lies in its resistance to an interpretation of Catholic teaching that would treat contraception as an internal issue of church discipline but not a position to be espoused in public policy. Prior to the encyclical, the pope's thinking was made clear in the Holy See's intervention at the 1984 U.N. Conference on Population at Mexico City. The Vatican's statement affirmed "that the Catholic Church has always rejected contraception as being morally illicit. That position has not changed but has been reaffirmed with new vigor" (Schotte, 1984, p. 207).

Second, the weight given to the private dimension of Catholic teaching does not, however, mean that John Paul II has forsaken the broader public dimensions of the teaching on population policy. Indeed, the

"When the representatives of the Church have talked about such things as sexual love they may have said the right things, but they said very few of them and they have generally said them in the wrong style."

CHARLES WILLIAMS

AFFIRMING LIFE

Since becoming Pope in 1978, John Paul II has "reaffirmed with new vigor" the Roman Catholic Church's rejection of contraception and abortion.

second dimension of his contribution to population policy in the church has been to expand and develop the social justice theme espoused by Paul VI and the 1971 Synod of Bishops. John Paul's contribution is found in a series of encyclical letters, from *Redemptor Hominis* (1979) through *Centesimus Annus* (1991). In his social teaching, John Paul develops a moral vision rooted in human rights, including both political and economic rights, and shaped by principles of social justice and solidarity. The papal teaching takes the international community as the unit of analysis, and John Paul II argues that a broadly defined notion of human, economic, and social development should be the context for examining population questions. John Paul II substantially extends Paul VI's critique of international institutions and practices in the socioeconomic order. Like his predecessor, John Paul II primarily emphasizes deep and extensive changes in international economic policies as the response to demographic pressures. In *Sollicitudo Rei Socialis,* he argues that "one must denounce the existence of economic, financial and social mechanisms which . . . often function almost automatically, thus accentuating the situation of wealth for some and poverty for the rest" (O'Brien and Shannon, 1992, p. 404). In the same encyclical, John Paul II cites the need "for a solidarity which will take up interdependence and transfer it to the moral plane" (1992, p. 411). In subsequent teaching, he explicates some of the policy demands of solidarity as they affect international distribution, problems of the Third World debt, and protection of human rights within nations and through the work of international institutions.

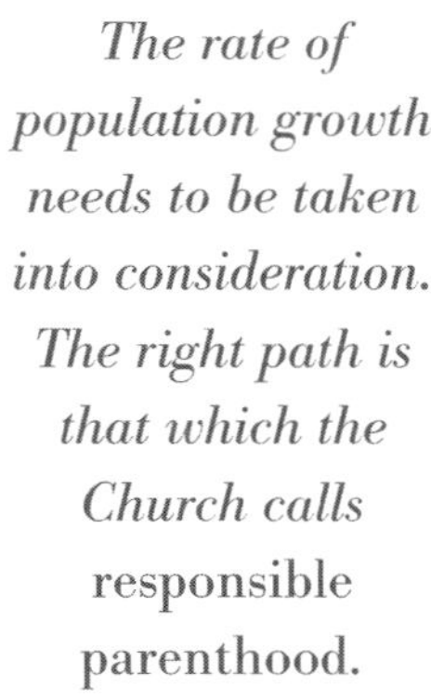

The rate of population growth needs to be taken into consideration. The right path is that which the Church calls responsible parenthood.
POPE JOHN PAUL II
CROSSING THE THRESHOLD OF HOPE, 1995

Third, a dimension of Catholic teaching which holds a prominent place in the pontificate of John Paul II is the relationship of migration and population. The teaching and the practice of the church both testify to a deep concern for the welfare of migrants and refugees. At the level of the Holy See, in the structure of national episcopal conferences, and in the work of dioceses and religious orders, the pastoral care of migrants and refugees holds a substantial place in the ministry of the church.

This ministry is supported by Catholic teaching on migration. The perspective on the right of the person to emigrate and immigrate is based on Catholic teaching on human rights and on the moral structure of the international order. The right of the person to emigrate places upon the international community, and states within it, the responsibility for developing fair policies regarding immigration. Catholic teaching does not assert an unlimited duty to receive migrants and refugees, but it does not specify particular limits either. The emphasis of the teaching falls on a duty of international solidarity that then must find expression in international and national policies regarding migrants and refugees. In John Paul II's teaching, "the state's task is to ensure that immigrant families do not lack what it ordinarily guarantees its own citizens as well as to protect them from any attempt at marginalization, intolerance or racism . . ." (John Paul II, 1994, p. 718).

This expansive conception of the duty of states to be open to the movement of populations when they are driven by war, famine, economic necessity, or human-rights violations provides another social instrumentality, along with the teaching on social justice, to complement the Vatican's restrictive policy regarding the limitation of population.

In summary, there is substantial continuity between Paul VI and John Paul II on the public dimensions of population policy. The public argument about human rights and social justice remains the context in which population policy is addressed. Within that context, however, there is a difference in the way John Paul II relates the public and private dimensions of Catholic teaching.

This is the fourth aspect of his teaching, and it does not point toward more active Catholic engagement concerning population issues. Paul VI had acknowledged the objective dimensions of demographic problems, and the duty of governments to address these; John Paul II places the emphasis in a different direction. He also acknowledges that population growth can create "difficulties for development," but his concern is principally about the abuses public agencies commit in pursuit of population policies (O'Brien and Shannon, 1992). There is undoubtedly a need for the multiple concerns expressed by the pope himself and by the Holy See in its 1984 intervention at Mexico City. The values and principles stressed in the Holy See's intervention at the Mexico City conference and reiterated in 1994 by Pope John Paul II in preparation for the U.N. Population Conference at Cairo—protection of the rights of the person and the family, resistance to conditioning economic assistance on the basis of population targets, restraints on the role of the state—are necessary for an ethically sound population policy. But there is less positive encouragement or guidance for the state or international agencies to take responsibility for population issues. The principal guidance for public authorities is to reject abortion, sterilization, and contraception in the implementation of population policy. These restrictions are matched with a statement of the duty states have to create conditions within which parents can make responsible choices about family size (e.g., John Paul II, 1994).

Clearly, any Catholic policy will oppose abortion because of the deeply held conviction that a human life is at stake, and it will be deeply suspicious of state intervention in any decisions and choices about procreation that are basic to the dignity and freedom of married couples. The question of whether all forms of contraception would have to be explicitly opposed, save that described in Catholic thought as "natural family planning," is what lay implicit in Paul VI's statement of 1967. John Paul's response is decisively in the direction of treating abortion, sterilization, and contraception in similar fashion; although different in nature, all three are to be opposed in population policy.

The basic lines of Catholic policy, in both its public and private dimensions, have been firmly set for centuries. The policy combines a powerful vision of economic justice and human rights with a comprehensive resistance to most specific measures of population limitation. At the level of implementation, does the policy framework allow for or manifest any differentiation? Two possibilities exist: at the level of pastoral care and the level of principles and rules of conduct.

The pastoral level involves the advice, counsel, and direction provided by the ministers of the church to Catholics as guidance for conscience. The pastoral level also involves the degree of activism that marks Catholic life on population issues at national and local levels of the church. The other possibility for differentiation would involve an attempt to change the basic principles of Catholic teaching in its public or private dimensions.

In his history of the teaching on contraception, John Noonan illustrates the fact that some difference has often marked the church's life between what has been prohibited at the level of principle and how distinctions were made to accommodate the specific conditions in the lives of individuals. In the years since *Humanae Vitae* (1968) was issued, substantial differences have existed between the principles of the encyclical and the choices individuals have made, often with advice from theologians or pastors. John Paul II has been vigorous in his attempt to close this gap. While pastoral practice undoubtedly affects the population issue, its primary impact is felt not at the level of church policy or involvement in the public debate on population issues but in the lives of individuals.

In terms of the principles of Catholic population policy, it is useful to compare the universal teaching and the role of the church within nations. It is clear that the church ministers in nations with very different approaches to population policy, some close to Catholic principles and others in direct opposition to either the public or private dimensions of Catholic teaching. It is also clear that in the period since the Second Vatican Council, there has been greater possibility in Catholic polity for national episcopal conferences to take initiatives in applying the church's teaching to specific local circumstances. Examples of this include Latin American hierarchies addressing human rights and economic justice, and the hierarchy of the United States engaging the issues of nuclear deterrence and economic policy.

Population policy, however, is not an area where much latitude exists for national or local voices. The Holy See, through its teaching office and its diplomatic

"Often the woman is the victim of male selfishness, in the sense that the man, who has contributed to the conception of the new life, does not want to be burdened."

POPE JOHN PAUL II
CROSSING THE THRESHOLD OF HOPE, 1995

"The right to life means the right to be born and then continue to live until one's natural end."

POPE JOHN PAUL II
CROSSING THE THRESHOLD OF HOPE, 1995

engagement, is clearly the primary and predominant voice on population issues. National hierarchies may coexist with governmental programs that differ from Catholic teaching, but they seldom seek to challenge or change the principles of Catholic teaching to meet their local situations. Examples of national teaching that do seem to press for some change in the understanding or application of the teaching (particularly in its private dimensions) are recognized as rare exceptions. Such is the case of the Indonesian bishops who issued a statement in 1968 and then were required to provide clarification of their position in 1972 (Indonesian Bishops, 1972). The normal practice for episcopal conferences is to take the Holy See's principles as the premise of their position and then try to relate these principles to the broader policy debate in their own countries; this has been the policy followed by the U.S. bishops in their 1973 and 1994 statements on the population question (National Conference, 1973; U.S. Cardinals, 1994).

In the 1984 U.N. Conference on Population in Mexico City and in the preparatory debate leading to the 1994 Cairo conference, John Paul II has forcefully reasserted the papal role as the decisive voice on population issues. His position of tightly integrating the public and private dimensions of the teaching, and seeking to shape global policy in both areas, sets the standard for any other voice in the Catholic church. No Catholic policy would forsake either the socioeconomic principles of justice or its opposition to abortion as a method of population limitation. The effect of John Paul II's leadership is to reaffirm these dimensions and to diminish the likelihood that any distinction will be made in the policy debate between the public and private dimensions of Catholic teaching (John Paul II, 1994).

— J. BRYAN HEHIR

Can the church credibly defend its antiabortion position while disallowing the most effective forms of birth control?

PAGE 31

EASTERN ORTHODOX CHRISTIAN PERSPECTIVES

Population questions have not received a great deal of treatment in Orthodox theology or ethics. What little has been written comes out of other, related interests. Even in patristic times, population concerns usually appeared within the framework of discussion on Christian marriage and attendant issues, the most important of which was the place of procreation as a purpose, or even as *the* purpose, of marriage. The fourth-century writings of Saint John Chrysostom, for example, suggest that the purpose of marriage is in part determined by population considerations.

Recent literature

The relevant Eastern Orthodox literature on the contemporary situation may be divided into two periods.

FIRST PERIOD: 1933-1969. During this time, Orthodox thinking discounted the threat of overpopulation, which was either ignored or seen as a dubious argument to support birth control. If it was taken seriously, it was perceived to be a false issue, unsupported by the evidence. This position aimed to undercut support for conception control, especially in regard to maintaining the strength of ethnic groups. Many traditionally Orthodox countries (e.g., Greece, Bulgaria, Romania, Serbia) were experiencing a reduced birthrate, which was often perceived as putting them at a political and military disadvantage in relation to neighboring countries. Hence, their interest was in increasing rather than decreasing their populations.

The first important work of this period appeared in 1933: Seraphim G. Papakostas's *To zetema tes teknogonias: To demographihon problema apo Christianikes apopseos* (The Question of the Procreation of Children: The Demographic Problem from a Christian Viewpoint), which places birth control and population concerns within family ethics. The population issue appears under the rubric "The Arguments of the Supporters [of birth control]," where the author holds that arguments drawn from the threat of overpopulation, financial considerations, the improvement of conditions of life for both individual and nation, and other such positions are inadequate to justify the practice of birth control. After discussing the relationship between population and cultivated land, Papakostas concludes that "the means of support are increasing faster than the population" (p. 53). Numerous factors contribute to overpopulation, he argues, and all must be functioning in order for it to occur. His conclusion is that "the danger of overpopulation is non-existent" (p. 57).

In 1937 the Holy Synod of the Church of Greece, its highest governing body, issued an encyclical against the practice of birth control that reflected Papakostas's views. (Papakostas was very likely the author of the encyclical.) Although the document treats birth control almost without reference to the population issue, the encyclical does characterize birth control as an agent of "permanent harm to the Greek Nation because of the reduction of the population."

A similar treatment of the subject, written by the *hegoumenos* (abbot) of one of the monasteries of Athos, Gabriel Dionysiatou, was published in 1957. In this work, *Malthousianismos: To englema tes genoktonias* (Malthusianism: The Crime of Genocide), concern with overpopulation is believed to be unwarranted. The author, however, does not foresee the progress of technology and the resulting increase of agricultural productivity and distribution. The study is based on the view that the primary purpose of marriage is the procreation of children.

SECOND PERIOD: 1970 TO THE PRESENT. The second period of the treatment of the population issue, beginning in 1970, continues to deal with its relationship to birth control. A significant number of writers now feel that birth control is not the unmitigated evil described in the previous period. Most have adopted their view not because of population issues but through a rejection of Augustinian understandings of sin and "concupiscence" and a more Eastern patristic understanding of the purposes of marriage. While the Western patristic approach drew moral teaching primarily from natural law, the Eastern view was based on a Trinitarian approach that emphasized the interpersonal dimensions of marriage.

Of great importance is Alexander Stavropoulos's *He ekklesia tes Hellados enanti tou problematos tes technogonias* (The Church of Greece and the Question of the Procreation of Children), published in 1977. Using textual analysis, Stavropoulos shows that both Papkostas's work and the encyclical of 1937 were based not on patristic sources but on Western prototypes. As a result of Stavropoulos's work, the encyclical ceased to be considered an authoritative text for Orthodox theological and ethical reflection. Efforts were made to include the issue of conception control in the themes of a forthcoming Great and Holy Council of the Orthodox church, but eventually it was dropped.

Some Orthodox writers treat the issue on the basis of theological grounds without reference to population concerns (Meyendorff, 1975; Constantelos, 1975; Zapheiris, 1974, 1991; Harakas, 1982). During this period a revival of patristic thought and method in theology, emphasizing the importance of the interpersonal dimensions of Eastern Orthodox Christianity, has been instrumental in changing the attitude toward ethical issues as well. These theological developments focus on the human dimensions of Orthodox Trinitarian theological perspectives, since the doctrine of the Holy Trinity as "three persons in unity" is seen as paradigmatic for human beings, in that the goal of human life is growth toward Godlikeness.

Several new treatments of birth control in relation to population issues have appeared in this period. The debate now focuses on the actual (or the mistakenly perceived) danger of overpopulation. In *The Sacrament of Love*, Paul Evdokimov (1985) makes explicit reference to the danger of overpopulation as an argument for the use of birth control.

Similarly, Nicon Patrinacos (1975) deals with ethnic demographic implications, placing the population issue in historical perspective. Explaining the traditional emphasis on the procreative dimension of marriage, he notes: "As with all societies and nations of [the Byzantine] era, numbers were extremely important to the survival of the country and nation" (p. 3). He comments that many factors explain Orthodox emphasis on population increase: high infant mortality; population depletion resulting from frequent wars; and lack of adequate sanitary conditions, medical care, and food. Unlike the writers of the pre-1970 period, Patrinacos is convinced of the reality and dangers of the population explosion. Rather than discounting it, he takes it as one of the chief elements of his moral reasoning. He condemns as evasive and morally irresponsible those positions that ignore the issues created by overpopulation. He is convinced that "unlimited reproduction of our own kind has reached the point of impoverishing rather than enriching humanity" (p. 46).

Patrinacos holds that the command God gave to Adam and Eve to multiply and populate the Earth has been realized. The church must now provide new guidance: "Birth control is, in more than half of today's world, as important and as urgent as feeding the millions of starving. More births would mean more hunger, more pain, more deaths" (p. 48).

The revival of the patristic mind-set in Orthodox theology, with its emphasis on both divine and human relationality, makes untenable the older argument that the only or primary purpose of marriage is procreation. The theology of marriage has come to focus on the interpersonal unity and relationship of spouses. Studies by Megas Farantos (1983), Paul Evdokimov (1985), Haralambos Hatzopoulos (1990), Chrysostom Zapheiris (1991), W. Basil Zion (1992), and Stanley Harakas (1992), among others, reject the previous approach as not reflective of authentic Eastern Orthodox perspectives, and approve conception control within marriage. Some of these writers connect conception control to population issues.

Nicholas Bougatsos's 1994 work, *He rhythmise tes teknogonias: Orthodoxos kai Hellenike apopse* (The Regulation of Childbearing: Orthodox and Hellenic View), discounts the issue of overpopulation for Greece and Europe in general (it does not deal with population issues in the Third World). Nevertheless, Bougatsos argues that for theological reasons, different approaches to the issue of conception control are ethically possible. These may include the practice of birth control by spouses for a number of reasons, among them the enhancement of interpersonal relations and growth in the unity of Christian marriage.

A population agenda for Orthodox Christian ethics

The crucial differences between the earlier and later aspects of this discussion are traceable both to theological outlooks and to concern with issues of population. The foundations now exist for the development of an Orthodox population ethic, which might include a number of elements.

THEOLOGICAL APPROPRIATENESS OF POPULATION CONCERNS. It is true that "the Fathers of

Official religious decrees often differ from popular beliefs and local religious leaders' more conservative responses.

PAGE 513

Sunni and Shiite jurists believed that because coitus interruptus deprived a woman of her right to children and to sexual satisfaction, her consent was required.

PAGE 513

the Church were . . . uninterested in the economic implications of population growth . . . and early Christian writers can, indeed, hardly be considered to have had a population policy" (Callahan, 1970, p. 187). However, contemporary Orthodox ethics is concerned with population as both an imperative of present existential realities and a demand of the implications of the faith. Orthodox ethics cannot ignore the implications of the fact that there has been an enormous increase in the rate of world population growth, especially in the Third World. It cannot limit its teachings on conception control to the geographical areas where its members reside. Humanity must "maintain some balance between [its] numbers and the finite dimensions of this planet" (Freedman, 1964, p. 18).

THEOLOGY OF HUMAN DOMINION OVER THE EARTH. Theological anthropology has ecological and population implications. Traditionally, political implications have been discerned in humanity's creation in the image of God by finding parallels between the kingship of God and that of political leaders. The same doctrine requries human responsibility for creation, including ecological and population dimensions. Further, the dominion of humanity over the environment is an appropriate aspect of the Orthodox doctrine of divine providence in conjunction with the doctrine of "synergy," which calls for the cooperation of the human with the divine. Orthodox ethicists (e.g., Demetropoulos, 1970) have expressed some renewed interest in this approach.

ETHICAL DOCTRINE OF PHILANTHROPY. One of the chief theological and ethical categories of Eastern Christianity is *philanthropia*, a concept that transcends mere charity and includes the heartfelt identification of God, the church, and the individual Christian with all of humanity. *Philanthropia*, long a fruitful concept for Eastern Orthodox thought and life (Constantelos, 1968), has implications for population issues.

FERTILITY GUIDELINES. Orthodox personal ethics and the ethics of marriage and family have not adequately elucidated the implications of population realities. Both church leaders and scholars tend to leave such issues to "private conscience" or the "guidance of father confessors," although public teaching on the matter is now more widespread than it was earlier (Harakas 1982; Meyendorff, 1975).

JUSTICE AND DISTRIBUTION POLICIES. The Orthodox churches tend to focus on national cultures and heritages. This is a result of their strong "incarnational" emphasis, based on the theological teaching in regard to the second person of the Holy Trinity, the Son, who took on full human nature and lived on Earth. The divine, as fully present in the created human reality of the one person Jesus Christ, becomes a model for all creation and relationships. Sacraments, icons, and church architecture are religious examples of this modeling in that in and through them the divine is made significant. Relationships, both formal and informal, are also imbued with the divine. Among these, marriage and marital relationships are thus understood incarnationally.

Global perspectives focusing on structural injustices, especially as they relate to population concerns, are equally incarnational concerns. The Orthodox Christian conscience has always had a universal dimension. Orthodox anthropology does not permit the view that equitable food distribution policies are utopian, nor that population concerns are limited to a single nation or region (Patrinacos, 1975).

AN ECUMENICAL APPROACH. Concern for population problems must be a shared endeavor. This may come closest to the original intent of Orthodox involvement in the ecumenical movement, the original justification of which was based on interchurch cooperation toward the solution of social problems. The ecumenical approach, however, must go beyond church cooperation and include collaboration with local and international agencies concerned with hunger and population problems.

POLICY AND PRACTICE. The recent direction in Orthodox thought has been to become more deeply involved in social issues. If this increased social involvement is to be put into practice seriously, Orthodox leaders will seek practical policy changes. For example, if birth control is to be considered by the Orthodox to be "one of the more effective means by which a balancing between eaters and food to be eaten, consumers and goods, and services and labor" can occur (Patrinacos, p. 48), this implies a commitment to a positive emphasis on conception control, coupled with sex education founded on a deeply considered theology of marriage. In addition, the Orthodox church must develop acceptable practices to influence national and international policymaking, legislation, corporate decision making, and public opinion. Serious concern with population issues necessarily requires what has been called "eco-tactics" (De Bell, 1970)—what used to be called in Orthodox history "whispering in the ear of the Emperor in the name of Christ."

In conclusion, both the imperatives and the potentials for involvement by the Orthodox church in population concerns are found within its tradition.

— STANLEY S. HARAKAS

PROTESTANT PERSPECTIVES

Protestantism generally includes all Christian movements, denominations, and sects whose histories can be traced to or related to the sixteenth-century Reformers, especially Martin Luther and John Calvin. Hundreds of such Christian bodies exist worldwide. They represent very diverse theological orientations and forms of church discipline. It is possible to characterize a "mainstream" position on many theological and ethical issues held by major denominational families associated with the World Council of Churches (WCC), including Anglicanism (or Episcopalianism), Lutheranism, Presbyterianism, Methodism, Congregationalism, and various national united churches, such as the United Church of Canada and the Church of North India. Many other Protestant bodies, such as the Assemblies of God, Southern Baptists, and Jehovah's Witnesses are outside such a consensus. Even within the so-called mainline churches sharp differences exist. On many issues, some Protestants take positions completely at odds with others even within their own denominations while finding themselves in agreement with persons in other denominations or even with non-Christians. In recent years, there has been a sharp increase in numbers of Protestants in traditionally Roman Catholic Latin America, in Africa, and in parts of Asia. At the same time, there has been a marked falling off of active participation in the churches in such traditionally Protestant countries as Sweden and the United Kingdom.

It is therefore difficult to generalize about any one Protestant position on population ethics. This article focuses primarily on the mainstream churches and theologians for three reasons. First, these bodies represent the main currents of Protestant Christian history. Second, these bodies have taken the most explicit positions on population issues. Third, theologians representing these bodies present us with the clearest connections between distinctively Protestant theological emphases and ethical applications.

Early Protestant thought on population

The Reformers did not have theories about population as such, although their views on human sexual relations and procreation are relevant to discussions about methods of limiting population growth. Both Luther and Calvin understood sexual relations within marriage as a morally acceptable outlet for sexual drives quite apart from the purpose of procreation. Both, especially Calvin, also viewed sexual relations within marriage as an expression of loving companionship between a husband and wife (Fagley, 1960). Early Protestantism coincided in time with the decimation of Europe's population through the plague and the Hundred Years' War, so discussions of population during that period—which were mostly by secular writers—emphasized the need for population growth, not limitation. In contrast, Robert Malthus, whose demographic theories, published in 1798, first expressed alarm over excessive population growth rates, was a Protestant clergyman. His views derived more from economic thought than from Protestant theology, but the laissez-faire economic theories that exerted primary influence upon him may themselves have been encouraged by individualistic aspects of Protestant thought, especially the heightened importance of the "calling" each person has from God and the demand that each person respond, through faith, to God's grace (Weber, 1950).

Population issues were not intrinsically important to nineteenth-century Protestant thought except at three points. First, Malthus's pessimistic views of population growth were countered by various Protestant divines who considered them an impious reflection on the goodness of God's providence (Hutchinson, 1967). Second, in Anglo-Saxon countries, attitudes toward sexual relations during the Victorian era were often repressive. This gave rise to some rejection of contraceptive methods of birth control early in the twentieth century. Third, the nativist movement in North America, which sought to inhibit immigration from Roman Catholic countries, arose almost exclusively among Protestants. That movement exerted influence on subsequent anti-immigration legislation until the mid-twentieth century.

Theological support for family planning

Protestant support for planned parenthood dates from early in the twentieth century. The early American movement in support of family planning and use of artificial methods of birth control, exemplified especially by Margaret Sanger (1883-1966, founder of Planned Parenthood), was more secular and humanist than Protestant, but it began to attract a serious following among Protestant thinkers and churches. The Lambeth Council of worldwide Anglicanism declared in 1930 that contraceptive methods could be justified when there is "a clearly felt moral obligation to limit or avoid parenthood and where there is a morally sound reason for avoiding complete abstinence." (Noonan, 1986, p. 125). During the thirty years thereafter, a strong consensus developed among mainline denominations and theologians in support of that position.

The preeminent Protestant theologian of that period, Karl Barth, wrote, "There is agreement to-day among all serious Christian moralists . . . that although the choice for or against generation and conception is not a matter for human caprice, it should not be left to chance and therefore lack the character of true decision, but must always be a matter of free obedience and therefore free consideration and decision" (Barth, 1968, p. 273). Artificial means of contraception must not, he wrote, be considered evil "just because they are

"Set me as a seal upon thine heart, as a seal upon thine arm: for love is strong as death; jealousy is cruel as the grave."

SONG OF SOLOMON, 8:6

See Also

Protestant Views: Effects of the Reformation

so manifestly artificial" (Barth, 1968, p. 275). Dietrich Bonhoeffer, another European theologian of the midcentury, wrote, "It would not be right for blind impulse simply to run its course as it pleases and then to go on to claim to be particularly pleasing in the eyes of God; responsible reason must have a share in this decision" (Bonhoeffer, 1955, p. 177). While Bonhoeffer strongly opposed abortion, on the grounds that in the pregnancy "God certainly intended to create a human being" (Bonhoeffer, 1955, p. 176), he explicitly related support for planned parenthood to rapid population growth rates, which concerned him.

Barth's and Bonhoeffer's views are ultimately grounded in their respective views of creation. God's purposes for human life can be supported or obstructed by events in the natural order, including human interventions. When couples have children for which they are not prepared, this falls outside God's life-giving intentions. The same can be said of whole societies or of the world in general: Too rapid population growth can diminish the possibilities for humanity to find its God-intended fulfillment in the created order. Barth, therefore, did not limit his ethical perspective on family planning to decisions by individual couples about what is right for them. There was also the question of what was best for society as a whole. Humankind, in his view, is no longer under the divine command of Genesis 1, "Be fruitful, and multiply."

The Roman Catholic church's detailed discussion of contraception gives the impression that this one issue constitutes the whole Catholic position on population ethics.

PAGE 518

A leading American liberal theologian, Albert C. Knudson, expressed typical American Protestant thought in insisting:

1. that procreation is not the only purpose of sexual intercourse;
2. that "there is nothing in the use of contraceptives that is inconsistent with a sincere faith in Divine Providence," since there is no religious duty to let nature run its own course; and
3. that the general improvement in the standard of living requires lowering the rate of population growth (Knudson, 1943, pp. 209-210).

The first two of these points have been so generally characteristic of mainline Protestant thought and official denominational statements that one is hard pressed to find exceptions. The third has been in some dispute.

The evolution of Protestant views in the twentieth century

We may broadly characterize three main periods in the middle to later twentieth-century Protestant church teaching on population matters.

The first period, roughly from the Lambeth statement of 1930 to the late 1960s, emphasized the companionate, love-enhancing possibilities of sexual intercourse within the bonds of marriage while deemphasizing the moral obligation of married couples to have children. Contraception was generally accepted as a morally legitimate means toward the end of expressing love within marriage for its own sake. Birth control, or "planned parenthood," was, however, considered mainly within the family unit. Couples should be able to have as many children as they wish: no more, no less. Since the real issue was whether people could decide to limit their family size by conscious decision and employing contraceptive means, the net effect of such teaching was to encourage a diminishing birth rate. But during this period comparatively little attention was given to the world population growth rate.

The second period, coinciding with the emergence of the environmental movement in the late 1960s and 1970s and the publication of neo-Malthusian literature on the "population explosion," found Protestant teaching focusing primarily on the dangers of population growth and a corresponding moral responsibility by societies to find ways to limit it. Many of the mainline church declarations date from this period, with revisions added in subsequent years.

The third period, beginning in the late 1970s and corresponding to the growth of the liberation theology movement (the movement that began in the 1960s and that emphasizes freedom from external oppression as a central theme of Christian faith), witnessed greater criticism of neo-Malthusianism as a way to avoid social justice issues in the distribution of the world's resources. There was less inclination to treat population growth rates themselves as the primary problem. During this period, the mainline denominations continued to affirm the importance of family planning and to recognize the morality of the use of contraceptive measures of birth control. But there was a growing tendency to consider population limitation as a by-product of increased social justice and economic prosperity rather than the reverse.

In the United States, this period also witnessed the rise of evangelical Christian movements critical of mainline denominations and of what was taken to be their laxness in sexual morality and family values. Evangelicals often deemphasized the population issue while reemphasizing the restriction of sexual intercourse to marriage and strongly opposing abortion. Evangelicals, as a force in U.S. politics, played a role in the decision by the administration of President Ronald Reagan to oppose the United Nations Fund for Population Activities at the Second World Conference on Population (Mexico City, 1984) and to withdraw funding from the International Planned Parenthood Federation.

Official positions of mainline Protestant churches

Official statements by mainline denominations illustrate the continuing importance of views developed in each of these three periods.

Among the mainline denominations, the United Methodist Church developed what may be the most systematic position on population ethics. The principal outlines of its position were adopted in 1972 as part of a broader declaration of social principles. Subsequent revisions did not substantially modify this position, although various resolutions adopted by the denomination's General Conference show the influence of the third period of Protestant thinking. In its 1992 form the United Methodist statement cites the strains on food, mineral, and water supplies by growing populations and asserts, "People have the duty to consider the impact on the total world community of their decisions regarding childbearing, and should have access to information and appropriate means to limit their fertility, including voluntary sterilization" (United Methodist Church, 1992, p. 40). A 1980 resolution by that denomination adds a theological rationale: "Our goal in history is that everyone may have the conditions of existence necessary for the fulfillment of God's intentions for humanity. Our context in history is the preciousness of life and the love of God and all creation" (United Methodist Church, 1992, p. 345).

The United Methodists have also dealt at length with questions related to the migration of populations. While stopping short of supporting unlimited movement across national borders, the Methodist statement reminds its readers of biblical support for strangers and sojourners, and calls upon the leaders of all nations "to welcome generous numbers of persons and families dislocated by natural disasters, war, political turmoil, repression, persecution, discrimination, or economic hardship" (United Methodist Church, 1992, p. 510). This document also calls upon governments "to alleviate conditions and change internal politics that create a momentum for the migration of people over the world" while seeking "protection of the basic human rights of immigrants . . . for both documented and undocumented, permanent or transient refugees or immigrants" (United Methodist Church, 1992, pp. 509-510).

Another mainline denomination, the Presbyterian Church in the U.S.A. (and its predecessor denominations), advocated voluntary planned parenthood and population limitation as early as 1965. In that year, the General Assembly of the United Presbyterian Church in the United States of America (UPCUSA) (one of the predecessor communions) called upon the United States to "assist countries who request help in the development of programs of voluntary planned parenthood as a practical and humane means of controlling fertility and population growth" (Presbyterian Church in the U.S.A., 1991). In 1971, that body came to "recognize that reliance on individual desires and private decisions to effect voluntary [birth] control, however well supported by information and means, will not be sufficient to provide the necessary limitation of population growth unless there is a radical and rapid change in the attitudes and desires" (Presbyterian Church in the U.S.A., 1991). This document challenged "the assumption that couples have the freedom to have as many children as they can support," asserting that "we can no longer justify bringing into existence as many children as we desire" (Presbyterian Church in the U.S.A., 1991). In 1984, the Presbyterian General Assembly again voiced its awareness "of the increasing size of the world's population and conscious[ness] of the potential consequences of unlimited growth, of resource limitations, of insufficient public responses, and of unmet population needs" (Presbyterian Church in the U.S.A., 1991). It called "upon the U.S. government to participate fully in the International Conference [on population] and to give generous and continuing financial and logistical support to United Nations programs designed to address specific population needs" (Presbyterian Church in the U.S.A., 1991).

The American Baptist Churches adopted a policy statement in 1976 supporting "efforts to develop programs which encourage family planning in an environment of free individual choice" (American Baptist Churches, 1976). Subsequent declarations emphasized social and economic justice without much specific application to population questions. A 1988 resolution indicated the denomination's internal divisions on the abortion question while opposing abortion "as a means of avoiding responsibility for conception" or "as a primary means of birth control" (American Baptist Churches in the U.S.A., 1988, p. 9).

The Friends Committee on National Legislation (FCNL) has long supported family planning, but that position receives comparatively little emphasis in statements adopted during what I have characterized as the third period in the evolution of Protestant views on population. A lengthy 1987 statement on a variety of social-political-economic issues, for instance, merely repeats the FCNL's "support for safe and non-coercive family planning as one element of an effective national population policy" (FCNL, 1988, p. 5).

The same 1987 statement does, however, contain a much lengthier section dealing with immigration and refugees. That section expresses the belief that "the world should evolve toward a global community whose people can choose freely where they wish to live and work" (FCNL, 1988, p. 6). The FCNL's "long-range

A crucial element in Buddhist population ethics is individuals' autonomy to choose their own destiny and to be responsible for their own actions.

PAGE 535

The Eastern view of the purpose of marriage was based on a Trinitarian approach that emphasized marriage's interpersonal dimensions.

PAGE 525

ideal" is, therefore, "a world of open borders that ensures both asylum for refugees escaping oppression and freedom to migrate for those who hope to improve their living conditions" (FCNL, 1988, p. 6). Such a world would require "a more equitable distribution of the world's wealth, more respect for human rights, and greater tolerance of differences than exist at present (FCNL, 1988, p. 6).

The Unitarian Universalist Association continues to support family planning as a response to "the crush of overpopulation" that "is frequently associated with increasing the pollution of the water, air, soil, and ozone shield, and further depleting the earth's finite resources" as well as being a factor in "aggressive and destructive behavior." This denomination, like the other mainline churches, supports full access to contraception while going further than most in its direct support for "the right to choose abortion" (Unitarian Universalist Association, 1990, p. 56).

This sampling of denominational statements on population-related issues in the latter third of the twentieth century suggests no diminution of commitment to planned parenthood and the full rights of access to contraceptive technologies. At the same time, churches devoted less attention to population issues during the 1980s and 1990s and seemed more reluctant to grant full moral legitimation to abortion.

Protestant denominational statements do not generally enjoy the authoritative status of Roman Catholic papal encyclicals, though they do reflect deliberation by official bodies. When the official statements are seriously inconsistent with the deeper convictions of members, mechanisms are usually present to enact changes. That fact itself reflects a deep historic theme in most Protestant theology: God has immediate access to every believer. Consequently, the views of every church member, when expressed in good faith, must be taken seriously. Not surprisingly, therefore, Protestant viewpoints on population policy and other issues can change without threat to the basic body of shared doctrine. It is more difficult to ascertain the extent to which denominational statements on such issues reflect nontheological sociocultural influences. But the deliberative process of decision making in Protestant churches generally affords ample opportunity, over time, for purely secular influences to be criticized on the basis of shared faith traditions.

Protestant positions into the twenty-first century

Projecting the future of Protestant views on population, there seems little prospect that the basic commitments to planned parenthood will change during the period ahead. The amount of emphasis given to the issue may well vary, however, with perceptions of the effects of population growth rates and patterns of migration. Protestant churches worldwide will doubtless continue to reflect a wide variety of views on these and other subjects. Historically, however, Protestant views on such issues have tended to be framed in response to empirical problems and opportunities. Evidence mounts that the churches will increasingly have to respond to global environmental problems, and the continuing growth of world population will remain a significant factor in that (Nash, 1991). The churches' response to population migration may be even more interesting as the world moves into the twenty-first century. Toward the end of the twentieth century, ethnic nationalism was felt as a major political force in some parts of the world, such as the Middle East, the former Yugoslavia, and the former Soviet Union. Nevertheless, the growing integration of global economics, increased facilities for communication and transportation, and the conclusion of the Cold War between the United States and the Soviet Union all point toward greater pressure on the increasing irrelevance of national boundaries. While addressing problems related to population growth, religious bodies may find it equally necessary to respond to archaic restrictions of movement.

J. PHILIP WOGAMAN

HINDU PERSPECTIVES

Hinduism includes a complex array of teachings related directly and indirectly to population dynamics (fertility, mortality, and migration) and to the ethics of population-related behavior. Its rich heritage spans millennia and embraces diverse populations. Hindus are found in many world regions, both within and beyond South Asia, its area of origin. Hinduism is the predominant religious tradition of India (for a general overview, see Hiltebeitel, 1987). It is practiced in one form or another by about 80 percent of the approximately 800 million people living there. Another 20 million Hindus live in nations other than India, including Fiji, Indonesia, Singapore, Guyana, Trinidad, Canada, the United States, and the United Kingdom. Diaspora Hindu communities increased in number and prominence in the United States beginning in the late 1960s, when the law was changed to allow immigration of educated professionals. The construction of major Hindu temples in such cities as Pittsburgh, Chicago, New York, and Washington, D.C., demonstrates the vitality of this international growth.

Basic Hindu teachings on population-related ethics and behavior will have different impacts depending on the context in which Hinduism is practiced. Within a particular locality, socioeconomic class, caste, and ethnicity are associated with differences in awareness of

POPULATION ETHICS
Hindu Teachings

Several key teachings of Hinduism relate to population dynamics and have implications for how governments might formulate policy. A primary value is on *ahimsa* (this word combines the prefix a, non, with *himsa*, harm, thus meaning nonviolence or nonkilling). A well-known source of Hindu teachings on proper behavior, *The Laws of Manu* (Doniger and Smith, 1991), describes the model of four life stages (*ashramas*): student, householder, celibate, forest dweller. Manu's guidelines about marriage stipulate that the best form involves the father giving a virgin daughter, implying that the marriage is arranged by the parents of the bride and groom. Repeated statements in *The Laws of Manu* emphasize the importance for a woman of bearing offspring, especially sons. Other popular classical Hindu myths, such as in the epic *Mahabharata*, contain messages relevant to population. One is that the world is overpopulated, and that renunciation of the world is a valid means for release from personal, familial, and other worldly attachments. Celibacy is honored as reflecting a high level of self-control and spiritual attainment. Teachings about celibacy are linked with a strongly enunciated value on premarital chastity for females.

It is likely that these general teachings are known to Hindus throughout India and across most social divisions. It is also likely that links between people's knowledge of Hinduism and their population practices vary markedly across regions because India's demography differs dramatically by region and class (see Miller, 1981). Fertility is much higher in the northern plains than in the south and east. Mortality is more gender-differentiated in the northern plains, with excess female mortality, and is less severely skewed by gender in the south and east.

Thus we are confronted with a puzzle: Basic Hindu teachings are espoused by India's Hindu population more or less equally, but Hindu demography does not present a smooth pattern. We must therefore assume a loose linkage between Hindu teachings and demographic outcomes such as fertility rates and child survival by gender. In other words, as an explanatory variable affecting population dynamics, Hindu teachings are partial at most.

— BARBARA D. MILLER

and adherence to Hindu religious teachings. Moreover, social resistance to certain aspects of orthodox Hindu religious teachings is being voiced around the world, particularly by ethnic minorities and women's groups.

This article first considers key aspects of Hindu religious teachings. It then focuses on Hindu values in India and how they contribute to demographic practices and outcomes. Last, it offers some observations on how members of Hindu communities in the United States are revising Hindu values related to population.

Population issues in India

FERTILITY. Reproduction should, according to Hindu cultural norms, take place only within marriage. Stigma is attached to a premarital pregnancy, a situation that may bring serious consequences to the persons involved. A high premium is placed on marriage as a universal life stage through which, ideally, everyone should pass. As a householder, one marries, has children, and raises them. Reproduction is the primary goal of marriage. For Hindu women, the key to auspiciousness (a highly desired status for women that implies the opposite of stigma) involves being married, being devoted to one's husband, and bearing sons. All these values are clearly pronatal.

Hindu values support the bearing of children within marriage, and they emphasize the bearing of sons. Sons provide social security for their aged parents. The social security function of sons is especially marked in the northern Indian kinship system, which is followed strictly by Hindus and Jains. North Indian kinship rules stipulate that a daughter must marry a man from outside her natal village while a married son remains with his parents and brings a bride into his family. Another primary value of Hindus is to have a son light one's funeral pyre; a daughter cannot perform this task. The Sanskrit word for "hell" is *put*; the word for son, *putra*, means "the one who saves his ancestors from hell" (May and Heer, 1968, p. 200). Given mortality rates of the mid-1960s, demographers estimated that in order for a man to have a son who would be alive when he was sixty-five years old, his wife would have to bear seven children. Preference for male children operates to promote fertility and also plays a role in excess female mortality and indirect fertility reduction as discussed below. Desire for sons prompts families to keep trying until they have one, and then to have a second or third son as well.

The pervasiveness of the Hindu teachings on the value of having sons may be regionally variable in terms of intensity. Social surveys across the nation reveal that a stated preference for sons is stronger in the northern region than in the south and east (Dyson and Moore, 1983). This difference arises because socioeconomic factors such as the gender division of labor, marriage

Catholic political philosophy holds that society and state are not self-justifying; they exist to serve the common good.

PAGE 519

and kinship patterns, and the costs of marriage operate to affect the level of son preference (Miller, 1981; Dyson and Moore, 1983).

Other important fertility-reducing factors related to Hindu beliefs include ritually determined rules for sexual abstinence that limit the frequency of intercourse. One study found a total of 120 days mentioned for abstention (Nag, 1972). Such rules may be linked to a lower frequency of intercourse among Hindus than among Muslims, since the latter do not have such ritually proscribed days. Also important are the positive value placed on male self-control, including control of sexuality, and male anxiety about semen loss (Bottero, 1991). No one knows how much of an effect these conditions might have on the frequency of intercourse or actual reproductive rates, but one could posit at least some impact on both compared with non-Hindu populations.

Hindu views concerning widowhood may also lower fertility, since widows should not remarry and therefore should not reproduce (Mandelbaum, 1974). Restrictions on widow remarriage most significantly decreases fertility when women are widowed at a young age, as they often are in India.

Direct methods of fertility control, such as condoms, birth-control pills, or sterilization, are not antithetical to Hindu teaching since sexual intercourse is not seen solely as a means to achieve pregnancy. In contrast with this fairly liberal understanding, the famous leader of the independence movement and national hero, Mohandas Gandhi, supported abstinence as the only appropriate contraceptive.

Abortion for sociomedical reasons has long been legally allowed in India, except in the predominantly Muslim state of Kashmir (Chandrasekhar, 1974). In spite of legal provisions for abortion, safe services are lacking (Dixon-Mueller, 1990). This situation reflects the political priorities of the central and state governments more than religious doctrine.

Sex-selective abortion, a practice begun in the 1980s, is done almost exclusively to abort female fetuses. One study of a large number of hospital births in the Ludhiana area of the state of Punjab in northwestern India found that after 1983, when sex-selection became possible through amniocentesis, the sex ratio at birth rose from a normal of 105 boys per 100 girls to 117 boys per 100 girls in 1989 (Sachar et al., 1990). Many feminist activists in India wish to maintain a woman's right to seek an abortion while striving to ban sex-selective abortion. The debate on prenatal sex

HINDU TRADITIONS
Adapting in the U.S.

In the United States, most Hindus are middle or upper class (Helweg and Helweg, 1990), although large populations, especially in New York City and New Jersey, are less well off. Among this employed and generally well-educated population, fertility rates are low, infant and child mortality rates are low, and longevity is high.

The value placed on having a son among the Hindu population of the United States is an important but unresearched question. Undocumented sources indicate numerous cases of demand for prenatal sex determination, in order to keep male fetuses, by South Asian immigrants in the United States and Canada. As of 1994, U.S. law prohibits abortion based on the sex of the fetus, but people circumvent this rule. They may have a test done ostensibly to reveal genetic abnormalities in the fetus and, in the process, find out its sex. If the fetus is female, they go to another doctor and present a story about genetic abnormalities in their family that cannot be proved or disproved because the relatives who are claimed to have the genetic problems are in South Asia. On this basis, the couple requests an abortion.

Within the teachings of Hinduism, nothing specifically argues against sex-selective abortion per se, since traditional teachings do not address the topic of abortion from a gender-specific perspective. This issue will pose a challenge for contemporary theologians and ethicists working within the Hindu tradition.

Another issue being quietly contested in the everyday lives of Hindus and Jains in the United States is premarital chastity. In opposition to the more liberal sexual mores among the general population, many Hindu and Jain parents apply pressures on their children, especially daughters, to maintain their virginity before marriage. Depending on how conservative the family is, more or less intergenerational conflict ensues.

Many Hindu and Jain communities have started Sunday schools (never a tradition in India) and summer camps where religious values are instilled in young children and teenagers. Such values include premarital chastity. At the same time, marked liberalizing changes are being made in some Hindu rituals in the United States, as a response to lowered fertility rates (many Hindu families have only one child) and an interest in treating daughters the same as sons. In the early 1990s, the Hindu-Jain temple of Pittsburgh held its first *upanayana* (sacred thread) ceremony for girls. Several liberal-minded leaders promoted this reform of Hindu tradition, which restricts the *upanayana* ceremony to boys of the upper castes.

— BARBARA D. MILLER

selection in the public media in India has been largely secular.

MORTALITY. India is well known for its gender bias in survival of males and females. Hindu teachings that favor males provide the ideological justification for better treatment of males than females. But it is not possible to explain the scarcity of females relative to males in the Indian population solely on Hinduism. North India and neighboring Pakistan, which is predominantly Muslim, have similar gender patterns in mortality. Recent demographic data on China reveal substantial differences in mortality rates between males and females there as well. Economic, political, and social factors are important in explaining this phenomenon.

In the northern plains of India, son preference is linked with behavior termed "daughter neglect" (Miller 1981, 1987). This neglect, which takes the form of biased allocations of food, medical care, and psychological attention, can be fatal. It skews the sex ratio among children as well as in the general population. In northern India, census data from the first part of the twentieth century indicated that unbalanced juvenile sex ratios favoring boys characterized all major religious groups in the area: Sikhs, Hindus, Muslims, and Jains. Son preference interacts with daughter neglect to create excess female child mortality. The indirect fertility-reducing effect of excess female child mortality is clear: If daughters experience higher mortality than sons, then the number of future childbearers is reduced in comparison with what would be the case without excess female child mortality. In such a demographic regime, the ratio of living sons to daughters is maintained over time, as brides are brought in from other villages and regions to marry sons; thus, no "shortage" of brides to produce future sons is perceived or experienced.

Hindu beliefs seem implicated in the high mortality rates of widows, which are caused by general neglect and nutritional deprivation (Chen and Dréze, 1992). More extremely, the low value placed on a woman once her husband has died relates to the uncommon practice of sati, the suicide of a Hindu widow on the funeral pyre of her husband. In general, the value of female self-sacrifice is long-standing in Hinduism, and it supports socialization patterns of girls that train them in self-denial of food and other resources.

MIGRATION. According to traditional Hindu teaching, migration beyond the boundaries of India was grounds for outcasting. Since the late nineteenth century, however, the rate of migration of Hindus outside of India has increased substantially (Madhavan, 1985), and anxiety about "outcasting" appears to be nonexistent among migrants. With international migration, Hindu traditions are being reshaped in local contexts.

The challenge of change

Neither Hinduism nor population dynamics is static. Contemporary movements in Hinduism range from conservative trends that could be termed fundamentalist to more liberal tendencies among some migrant communities. The greatest challenges to the study of the relationship between Hindu teachings and population lie in the following directions: the links that individuals make in their thinking between Hindu tenets and their own demographic practices; the reactions of Hindu theologians to new questions such as sex-selective abortion; and governments' policies in dealing with such problems as population growth and excess female mortality within a moral framework that would be acceptable to Hindu constituents.

— BARBARA D. MILLER

BUDDHIST PERSPECTIVES

Buddhism is a dominant cultural force in most parts of Asia. Theravada Buddhism, also known under the name of Hinayana or "Small Vehicle," prevails in such Southeast Asian countries as Sri Lanka, Thailand, Burma, Cambodia, and Laos; its sister sect, Mahayana Buddhism, or "Great Vehicle," is currently found in Tibet, Japan, Taiwan, and Korea. This article focuses on Theravada Buddhism, especially as practiced in Thailand.

Though Therevadins have their own sacred literature that distinguishes them from the rest of Buddhism, they do share certain central beliefs with other Buddhists. Among these beliefs are those concerned with *samsara*, *karma*, and *nirvana*, which are the key concepts of all forms of Buddhism. *Samsara* refers to the round of existence, or the cycle of rebirth, in which all beings revolve according to their *karma*. This perpetual cycle comprises three realms of rebirth, namely, the realm of desire (*kamaloka*), the realm of forms (*rupaloka*), and the formless realm (*arupaloka*). These realms have thirty-one subspheres containing different forms of life, such as humans (*manussa*); animals (*tirachan*); ghosts or unhappy departed beings with deformed bodies (*peta*); spirits or wandering ghostly beings (*bhuta*); hell-beings or tortured beings (*niraya*); titans (*asura*); and gods (*deva*). The realm of desire consists of the higher spheres of gods; the middle spheres, of sentient beings, humans, and animals; and the lower spheres, of ghosts, spirits, and hell-beings. The celestial realm of forms and the formless realm are the abodes of the most refined and subtle beings (*brahman*). Despite differences in life span, beings in all realms are subject to death and rebirth.

Karma means intentional, mental, verbal, or physical action and its result (*vipaka*). The sequence of

A 1992 United Methodist Church statement called on leaders of all nations "to welcome generous numbers of persons and families dislocated by natural disasters, war," and other hardships.

PAGE 529

actions, or deeds, and their effects, known as the law of *karma*, act both as the natural law of cause and effect (operating in the physical realm) and as the moral law (governing the moral sphere that regulates the movement of beings between rebirths). Rebirths of all beings are the natural results of their own deeds, good or bad, and not "rewards" or "punishment" imposed by a supernatural, omniscient ruling power. All beings reap what they sowed in the past, and all will be reborn according to the nature of their present deeds—they are "heirs" to their actions. When a being dies, the karmic result, acting as the individual life-force, passes to other lives, endlessly exalting or degrading successive rebirths. This life-force will become completely inactivated only with the cessation of craving (*tanha*), the inherent force of karmic action. Such cessation is referred to as *nirvana* and can be achieved through following the Middle Path (*Majima Patipada*) consisting of wisdom (*panna*), morality (*sila*), and concentration (*samadhi*).

Repeated statements in The Laws of Manu emphasize the importance for a woman of bearing offspring, especially sons.

PAGE 531

Buddhist concepts in population growth and control

There is no fixed number for population in *samsara* existence. It is in a state of flux, with continual migration of beings from one realm to the others regulated by the law of *karma* and continuously readjusted to the nature and the quality of *samsara* dwellers. An increase of population in one realm means a decrease of population in others, and vice versa. Human rebirth is considered incomparably precious because the human realm is the only place where there is enough suffering to motivate humans to seek ways to transcend misery and enough freedom to act on their aspirations. In the higher and lower spheres, by contrast, beings are fully reaping the karmic results, good and bad: The gods are too absorbed in the blissful state to find ways out of *samsara* existence while animals, ghosts, spirits, and hell-beings are in irremediable misery and have little freedom to do either good or evil. These suffering beings will gain the precious human rebirth only when the results of bad *karma* that led to their lower rebirths are exhausted. When this happens, the results of their previous good actions performed when they were human will lead them to better rebirths and, sooner or later, to the human level again.

From this view, an increase in the human population is desirable for it means more beings will have the rare human opportunity to transcend suffering. In theory, then, Buddhists should welcome population growth. But the fact that increasing numbers of Buddhists use contraceptives in countries such as Thailand, where 98 percent of the population is Buddhist, seems to indicate a different position. Family planning has been quite successful in both urban and rural areas of Thailand. Apart from the contributing factors of the economy, social change, and education, there are some Buddhist tenets that may account for the low fertility rate. The most important one is the emphasis on the quality of human life concomitant with the high value it gives to human rebirth.

In the Buddhist perspective, the rare human rebirth is meaningless if there is no quality in it. The value of life does not depend on its duration but on its quality. For life to be worth living, it should be lived with the ultimate purpose of attaining *nirvana*, the final emancipation. This goal, however, like all spiritual progress, cannot be achieved without a certain degree of material and economic security. Below the level of subsistence, human life lacks real meaning because it consists only of hunger, illness, and unrelieved misery. This emphasis on material necessities was made by the Buddha as a necessary condition for a truly enlightened, meaningful life. The Buddha himself once refused to preach to a starving man until his hunger had first been appeased. He also recommended that monks who lead the life of renunciation depend on the lay community for food, shelter, and clothing.

This emphasis on life's material necessities is an important part of the Buddhist perspectives on population control and thus needs to be considered together with the Buddhist endorsement of human rebirth. That is, human rebirth, though desirable, needs adequate supporting conditions (*upatthambhaka*) to enable it to be worthwhile. Since famine is one of the most powerful forces (*upapilaka*) working against spiritual development, Buddhism does not approve of population growth disproportionate to a society's available resources of food. Because of this, Buddhists in Thailand and other countries do not attribute large family size to good *karma*. Unlike the Hindu householder, who believes he must have sons to perform the prescribed rituals for him after his death, Buddhist parents are not anxious to have sons to be ordained as monks. Although ordination is considered a meritorious act that will ensure good rebirth after death, many other means of receiving merit are also available, including offering food to monks, listening to sermons, and building or repairing temples.

The lack of anxiety for sons or large families supports the practice of family planning among Thai Buddhists. Unlike abortion, which is still socially unacceptable in Thailand and not as widely practiced as it is in Japan, birth control is believed by Thai Buddhists to be in line with Buddhist teachings concerning marriage and family life. Though the Buddha considered celibate life superior to married life, he did not advise it for all his followers. Realizing that all humans were at different stages of spiritual evolution, he did not commend the same codes of conduct to all. To his

BUDDHIST VIEWS
Contraception and Karma

For Thai Buddhists birth control, unlike abortion, does not transgress the Buddhist precept of nonkilling, nor does it interfere with the working of the law of *karma*. In Buddhist understanding, conception begins only when three factors merge: the coitus of the parents, the woman's generative capability, and the presence of the *gandhabba*, the karmic life force of one who has died. By preventing pregnancy, birth control makes human rebirth more difficult but it does not interfere with the operation of the law of *karma*.

From the Buddhist viewpoint, the fruition of good or bad *karma* requires the right supporting conditions; without them the karmic life-force cannot express itself. Only beings who are fully qualified for human rebirth can be reborn in the human realm. Under unfavorable physical conditions a being, though possessing the good *karma* to be reborn as a human being, must dwell in his or her sphere waiting until the opportune moment. Buddhism does not oblige parents to open the gate of human rebirth to all beings with good *karma* by having as many children as they can. The Buddhist concept of *karma* assigns to each person sole responsibility for his or her own life. According to the Buddhist analysis of human nature, one's sexual life is the outcome of the urge to satisfy one's sexual craving. Whether sexual activity produces children or not is a matter to be decided by the couples themselves. The autonomy of individuals to choose their own destiny and to be responsible for their own actions is a crucial element in Buddhist population ethics.

— PINIT RATANAKUL

lay followers who could not lead the austere life of monks and nuns, he recommended marriage but stressed spiritual progress, and not procreation, as its main goal. For those with children he devised a code of discipline, emphasizing responsible childbearing and child rearing.

Self-restraint and the control of the senses and passions are recommended as important forms of population control and to prevent the sexual indulgence that widespread use of artificial means of birth control may lead to. Following this teaching, many Buddhists in Thailand, Sri Lanka, and Burma have contributed to population control by practicing sexual continence, leading celibate lives as monks or nuns, and using contraceptives.

— PINIT RATANAKUL

POPULATION POLICIES

STRATEGIES OF FERTILITY CONTROL

Changes in attitude and culture

Demographic transition theory posits that the Western fertility transition (the reduction in family size that began in France in the late eighteenth century and more generally in northwestern and central Europe and the English-speaking countries of overseas European settlement in the second half of the nineteenth century) was the product of changing attitudes, culture, and social structures, as well as of material conditions. It follows that one way of accelerating fertility decline in contemporary Third World countries might be to change attitudes and society by means of educational and motivational campaigns aimed at altering attitudes on family size, or the prime desirability of children, or altering behavior with regard to age at marriage, or the practice of birth control.

Hinduism includes a complex array of teachings related to population dynamics and ethics.

PAGE 530

Such campaigns inevitably raise questions both about whether they constitute an assault on cultures and whether that can be justified, and about whether they are actually presenting proven facts about the advantages to be derived from controlling family size. The justification for the attempt to change cultures is usually either that people will benefit in a range of ways from liberation from restrictive traditions, or that the advantages likely to result from decreasing rates of population growth outweigh any damage done to societies by changing the society or fertility behavior at an earlier time than economic development and social change would have spontaneously brought about. The ethical issues involved are sharpened by the fact that the encouragement for such campaigns usually originates in the West and through international organizations.

At individual level, motivational campaigns are deemed necessary by many advocates of family-planning programs on the grounds that contraception is innovational behavior in the society, requiring support and leadership. Indeed, they argue, the adoption of family planning in a society with low levels of contraceptive use involves substantial psychic costs. Such motivational efforts to change individual behavior, and inevitably the nature of societies that favor large families, constitute only a modest part of contemporary

Third World population programs, probably more because they have proved to be relatively difficult and unrewarding than because of misgivings about attacks on culture. Most national family-planning programs have found it easier to provide plentiful cheap or free contraceptives, to inform potential clients where they are to be obtained, to offer incentives or disincentives, or, in some programs, to employ directly coercive measures.

Justifying changing attitudes and culture

From the time of Thomas Malthus's publication of the first version of *An Essay on the Principle of Population* (1798), his followers were able to claim that the danger presented by population growth outstripping subsistence was so great as to justify quite extreme measures. Those measures included long-delayed marriage and strict abstention from sexual relations while single. Because such behavior was in accordance with middle-class morality of the time, and because he argued that expenditure on assisting the poor in accordance with the Poor Laws was pointless since any resultant reduction in mortality would result in additional population growth and ultimately just as much misery, the English establishment was largely convinced by the analysis.

It was the socialists, especially Karl Marx, who accused Malthus of preaching a political message—less taxation for the rich and less help for the poor—in the guise of a social analysis. This debate led to opposition to organized birth control by many socialists that still continues, with the claim that the advocates of birth control aim to postpone the appearance of capitalism's contradictions. From about the 1870s, the new birth-control movement stressed the situation of women and the range of disabilities they suffered from continuous childbearing. This movement certainly aimed at changing society, but the most accurate historical judgment is that the movement was the outgrowth of the culture itself.

Most sensitivity to induced cultural change arises when the stimuli are external and the debate really centers on international efforts to curb Third World population growth. No social scientists have had more influence on these programs than the group of demographers associated during the 1940s and 1950s with Princeton University's Office of Population Research and its director, Frank Notestein. They focused their interest first on the historic fertility transition in the West, then on European colonies in Asia and Africa, and finally on all developing countries, arguing that social-science knowledge should be employed to accelerate a global transition to low levels of fertility and slow population growth.

Notestein's attitudes and interpretations influenced a generation of demographers and the new Third World family-planning programs. He concluded that the human race had survived only because cultural props, such as the idealization and religious sanctification of high female fertility and the mandating of early female marriage, had kept birth rates "artificially high" in order to overcome the ravages of high levels of mortality. As mortality declined (as evidenced by a widening gap between birth and death rates and accelerating population growth), the props became not only outdated but even dangerous, and efforts to make them wither at a faster rate could hardly be condemned. Notestein believed that fertility decline would be enhanced by the replacement of extended families by nuclear families, which he regarded as freeing individuals from the control of their relatives and, in agreement with Wilbert Moore, as being necessary to produce societies more attuned to the modern economy. He wrote of producing "a population increasingly freed from its old taboos" through "the development of a rational and secular point of view" (Notestein, 1945, 1953). Donald Warwick (1982) identified views of this type in a 1969 report justifying the development of a family-planning program in Kenya. Notestein was not a cultural relativist and certainly believed that people were better off when they were freed from their ancient taboos and had ready access to contraception. In the 1940s he thought that this would come only from evolutionary historical change, but by the 1960s he was happy to see this process hastened by national family-planning programs and their "educational" efforts.

The belief that family-planning programs were ethically justified in attempting to change societies because they liberated individuals and raised living standards can hardly be treated alone, for the programs were just one part of massive post-World War II international efforts to accelerate economic development, efforts that were also characterized by the belief that people would benefit from a loosening of the bonds of traditional society and traditional families, as well as from being richer. Family-planning programs drew attention to more sensitive issues because they dealt with very intimate personal behavior that was often the central concern of traditional culture and religion. Agencies providing international aid claimed that Third World governments represented their people and cultures, and hence that programs those governments requested usually were ethically correct. The problem with this stance was similar to that encountered with building dams or clearing tropical rain forests: Governments tended to represent the educated, modernizing elites with international viewpoints and economic interests, while the resistance came from remoter populations with older traditions still more intact.

Orthodox anthropology does not permit the view that equitable food distribution policies are utopian.

PAGE 526

In the 1950s and 1960s, the international family-planning movement suspected that most people in developing countries did not favor fertility control and that a great deal of persuasion would be needed to change that situation. The moral basis for attempting this change was at first very largely the Malthusian one: that future catastrophe threatened and individuals might be required to make sacrifices or to moderate their behavior for the eventual common good. The threat of exponential population growth was demonstrated by a virtual demographic industry devoted to producing ever more sophisticated projections of population growth and centering on the United Nations Population Division's series beginning in 1951. This apparently threatening growth was contrasted with the likely limited availability of resources, especially food. In a 1968 paper, "The Tragedy of the Commons," Garrett Hardin argued that "the population problem has no technical solution; it requires a fundamental extension in morality" (p. 1243). His conclusion was that "freedom to breed is intolerable," and his direction for population programs was "Mutual coercion mutually agreed upon." His argument has two obvious weaknesses. First, there was no proof that there was no technical solution. Many demographers believed that population growth could be halted within the bounds set by agriculturalists for the ceiling on food production while continuing to allow reproductive free choice. Second, mutual agreement was always improbable; at best it was likely to be majority coercion of the minority. Proponents of views similar to Hardin's were William and Paul Paddock (1967) and Paul Ehrlich (1968).

Fertility control as a concern of women

Different ethical issues had begun to emerge in the West in the nineteenth century, issues associated with names like Marie Stopes and Margaret Sanger. The family-planning associations and clinics were mostly run by women for women, on the grounds that reproduction and its containment was predominantly a female concern because, at the individual level, women had more to lose or gain than did men. In the United States there was persistent legal prosecution of doctors and others who gave contraceptive advice or distributed or mailed information on the subject. Some doctors were sent to jail for years, and in 1917 Sanger spent a month in prison. The opposition to family planning was partly religious, especially among Catholics, on the grounds that contraception was against the divine law, but mostly moral, on the grounds that contraceptive knowledge would encourage premarital sexual relations and that such intimate discussion of the psychology of sex was "obscene, lewd and lascivious." These were the words of the 1873 Comstock Law, which forbade the use of the mail for distributing contraceptive information. The main thrust of the law was against the mailing of erotic postcards, which had become common, but sections were added to curb the propagation of birth-control advice.

Twentieth-century feminist scholars have tended to argue that traditional culture, far from deserving to be hallowed as a social consensus, usually takes the form of a patriarchy dominated by men who exploit women. Sandra Tangri argued in the first volume of *Signs* (1976) that women should have control over their own bodies, and that family-planning programs were commendable if they supported that achievement; however, population control was a secondary issue, and "the concrete needs of individuals should take precedence over some abstract notion of what is good for society" (p. 899). Judith Bruce (1987) argued that everyone needs to feel some unease about the fact that women's bodies are the main vehicle for achieving population control—indeed, family-planning programs appear to blame women for the world's difficulties. Bruce also felt

FERTILITY CONTROL
Limitations Advocated by Environmentalists

About 1966, when Kenneth Boulding coined the phrase "Spaceship Earth," a greater emphasis began to emerge on the limitations imposed on human growth by all resources, the need to save the environment, the fragility of Earth, and the need for a long-term strategy of sustainable growth. These concerns culminated in a debate in the late 1960s, mostly in the pages of *Science*, where Kingsley Davis (1967) argued that it was irresponsible to rely on family-planning programs alone for the containment of population growth and that more positive governmental initiatives would be needed to change the nature of the family. Bernard Berelson (1969) replied that the record of family-planning programs did provide evidence that they could halt population growth in time, that they were acceptable to individuals and morally tolerable to providers, in that coercion or direct attempts to change society's basic units were not required. The issue here, conspicuous since Malthus, was whether all humankind and all cultures would have to concede some independence in order to ensure the survival of the human race on the planet.

— JOHN C. CALDWELL

"Where is she so fair whose uneared womb / Disdains the tillage of thy husbandry? / Or who is he so fond will be the tomb / Of his self-love, to stop posterity?"

SHAKESPEARE
SONNET III

See Also
Fertility Control
Julian Simon's View: Reasons for Optimism

that secrecy might in many circumstances be unethical, yet, given the patriarchal traditions of societies in many developing nations, there might well bea moral good in family-planning programs in such societies providing contraception that was female-controlled and undetectable, thus investing women with reproductive decision-making power. International agencies, while having a commitment to the self-determination of societies, also became at least as dedicated to furthering the rights of women and their children, with little reference to culture or stage of history.

Economics and other issues

The ethical value of the case for employing more forcible family-planning programs depends on the strength of the proof of the cases put forward by those advocating such measures, and also on an estimate of what is lost to the individual and to society in implementing the programs. In spite of very plausible theoretical models, there is surprisingly little empirical evidence that countries with more slowly growing populations have benefited economically in contrast with comparable societies having high rates of population growth (although Ansley Coale [1967] has pointed out that in all countries where fertility is low, over 90 percent of children attend primary school and at least half of the population lives in urban areas). Colin Clark (1967) and Julian Simon (1981) have argued that there is every reason why economic gains have not accrued from slowing population growth. They argue that the real price of most raw materials has been falling persistently and that they are either in virtually limitless supply or easily substitutable. Less convincingly, they argue that past rises in food production were as rapid as population growth and that this would probably continue to be the case even if special efforts were not made to control population growth. Simon (1981, p. 67) becomes more agnostic on the issue: "It is not necessary or useful to discuss whether there is an 'ultimate' limit to the supply of any natural resource including food. . . . We know for sure that the world can produce vastly more food than it now does." Simon also argues that people are the important resource and that large populations have more taxpayers and more geniuses. The latter argument is very different from the conclusion that might be drawn from the experience of Athens in the fifth century B.C.E.: that the right conditions and circumstances, rather than sheer numbers, are more likely to produce geniuses.

◆ **rhythm method**
a form of family planning that prescribes sex only during the woman's infertile period.

Huge international survey programs, including the KAP (knowledge, attitudes, and practices with regard to family planning) surveys of the 1960s-1970s, the World Fertility Surveys of the 1970s-1980s, and the Demographic and Health Surveys of the 1980s-1990s, have been employed to show that there is a KAP gap: Many Third World women have more children than they desire, because they have insufficient access to contraception, are troubled about employing it, or are overruled by husbands and other relatives. The exact size of the gap is difficult to estimate, as Charles Westoff showed in a revision of some of his earlier conclusions (Westoff and Pebley, 1981). Donald Warwick (1982) has argued that the surveys came to these conclusions by employing international questionnaires, little modified for different societies, and addressed themselves only to women of reproductive age.

The Catholic church argues that the ethical case against promoting national family-planning programs offering artificial contraception rests not on a denial that rapid population growth threatens living standards but on the fact that the use of artificial contraception is in conflict with natural law, and that too much concentration on population control denies the high value that should be placed on human life and ignores the cooperation that fecundity displays with the creative activity of God. There are elements of these views in all the major religions. Marxists have argued that each economic system has its own laws and that the creation of national family-planning programs assumes a wrong priority: First, socialist societies should be created that will have very different relations to employment, resource utilization, and even population growth. Some critics, especially in the United States, see problems not in family-planning programs as such but in those that advocate or facilitate abortion, or provide information or services to adolescents. Family-planning programs have been regularly attacked in Africa, by men arguing with politicians or writing to the press, for putting the idea of risk-free, nonmarital sexual activities before unmarried young women or wives, and in both Africa and Asia for using the media or billboards to present messages about delicate matters in a way that is an affront to the cultures.

Family-planning programs in practice

The attempt to increase fertility control by changing attitudes and culture is close to what W. Parker Mauldin and colleagues have called "program effort," the factor that they have determined to be one of the main components in determining family-planning success (Mauldin and Ross, 1991). The organized influences on individual women, families, or communities usually come from three sources: family-planning workers or visitors, usually women, who take their message from door to door; messages in the media; and political leadership in the form of exhortations from national or local leaders. Very little research has been reported on the content of their messages—especially those of the all-important family-planning workers—so the content cannot be assessed. It is clear that these

See Also
Social Issues: The Future of Fertility Control

messages promise a better future if family size is restricted, less commonly offer women better health, and provide reassurance about the safety of contraception and the lack of serious side effects.

Family-planning workers are regarded as successful if they receive more clients and keep them practicing family planning by means of these assurances rather than according to the extent to which they involve themselves in a dialogue with clients, trying to assess whether economic gains are likely or if the side effects make the use of contraception more unpleasant than it is worth. In the better programs, family-planning workers arrange for clients to secure medical advice or to change contraception, and frequently they provide some forms of contraception. Sometimes their jobs, their promotion, or part of their income—and always their self-respect and the esteem in which the program holds them—depend on how persuasive they can be. The program at Matlab, Bangladesh, run by the International Centre for Diarrhoeal Disease Research, recruited as family-planning workers only educated young women, practicing family planning and married into the leading and most powerful families of the district, so that they could provide leadership and change models (Caldwell and Caldwell, 1992).

In rural south India, John Caldwell and his colleagues (Caldwell et al., 1988) found that the decision of women to be sterilized depended to a great degree on the firm conviction of the family-planning worker that this was the proper and moral thing to do, and that economic benefits would flow to the family from this action. They also found that the workers regarded such certainty as evidence of just how professional they were, even though off duty most were much less certain that contraception was safe and that family limitation was certain to bring economic benefits to individuals and families. The greater material success attained by those who had restricted fertility could not be proved by the social-science research. In both Matlab and south India, the success of the workers depended on the frequency of their visits and on a reluctance of women and families continually to disappoint them.

Kim Streatfield (1986) reports that the Indonesian family-planning program in Bali achieved much of its success through meetings of the *banjar*, a subvillage unit. The headman presented the government policy in monthly meetings and stated that subsequent decisions were supposed to be by consensus, with behavior conforming to these decisions. Certainly there was at least moral pressure on individuals: In the case of couples who did not appear to be complying with the family-planning guidelines, the husbands were regularly questioned. There was also pressure on the headman, who had to make quarterly reports to a government official on the use of family planning by each married person in his *banjar*.

In south India, where a woman's parents-in-law have traditionally dominated most of the couple's decision making, family-planning workers, who represent official government policy, approach the wife directly. As a result, parents now tend to regard family planning as the business of the young. More direct efforts to change family structures aim at increasing female autonomy, often by providing women with work or an income, as has occurred in an experimental project in Vellore, south India, and as is planned by the nongovernmental development organization BRAC (Bangladesh Rural Advancement Committee) in Matlab.

Some family-planning programs have, under the leadership of the government, employed group pressures to encourage family planning. For example, successive regimes from the Dutch colonizers onward have remolded Indonesia's community organization to the government's purposes. In a society where few people

SPREADING THE WORD
Media Effectiveness Compared

Research on every Third World continent shows that radio has more impact on family-planning practice than any other segment of the media. It is widely accessible, heard by women even when they are in another room, and understood even by illiterates. The message is of better economic circumstances and health, of the safety of contraception and where it can be obtained. Television has been less successful, although experimental programs, such as one shown in three Nigerian cities, have increased levels of family planning. Newspaper articles have had less impact than might have been anticipated, possibly because more men than women read newspapers. In some societies, women's magazines have been more successful. Firm, moral statements by national leaders have been widely found to be effective. One example is the repeated statement by President Ibrahim Babangida of Nigeria, "Four is enough." Most women in the country know the slogan, which appears to have been successful at least in part because of the legitimation thereby given by the state for women to make reproductive decisions without consulting their husbands or husbands' relatives.

—JOHN C. CALDWELL

P

POPULATION POLICIES

Strategies of Fertility Control

Freedom requires knowledge about the choices available, such as options for fertility control or migration.

PAGE 503

P

POPULATION POLICIES

Strategies of Fertility Control

In the late 1960s and early 1970s, some African-Americans accused family planners of "genocidal" intentions.

PAGE 214

wish to be outsiders, the present government has employed the village structure to propagate the family-planning message powerfully. Annual campaigns, run mostly in rural areas by retired army officers, arouse enthusiasm for practicing family planning. The government has changed the community, and the community has changed the family. In China the government has used workplace and residential groups to argue the case for family planning with all defaulters from the program. This can also happen more spontaneously: In Matlab, Bangladesh, more couples practice contraception in those villages where the leader has been convinced by the program's arguments (Caldwell and Caldwell, 1992). In south India, during the 1975-1977 emergency, the period when Prime Minister Indira Gandhi ruled by decree and forcefully accelerated various development programs, including national family planning, local elites backed the government and insisted to their employees and potential employees that fertility control was in the national economic interest (Caldwell et al., 1988). China has attempted to limit fertility not only by strongly encouraging small families but also by exhorting later marriage.

Asian national family-planning programs from India to Korea have raised levels of contraceptive use and reduced fertility through a kind of moral leadership in which national political leaders and the programs themselves argue that they know what is good for the country and its citizens. This success is understandable in Confucian and Hindu societies, where there is a long history of elite and religious moral leadership, but more surprising in Southeast Asia, although in some countries in that region armies have assumed a not dissimilar role. Opposition in India has come from the Muslim community, who charge that Hindus have always worshiped government, while the Muslims have a book and a prophet. Asian programs may have received their original ideologies from the West and some of their program ideas from international agencies, but their governments have long been indigenous driving forces, with a commitment to changing society and culture in regard to reproduction and many other things.

In Singapore and Malaysia, the governments have changed their messages with regard to family values and marriage in order to attempt to halt or reverse the fertility decline. In sub-Saharan Africa, many politicians and bureaucrats avoid identifying themselves too closely with the family-planning programs or their messages so as not to be accused of deserting African culture.

The ethical issues

Most family-planning workers and media campaigns, with the support and at the direction of programs, provide potential clients with messages about the economic benefits likely to accrue to them from smaller families, and about the safety of contraception and the unimportance of side effects—messages that are more assured, optimistic, and unilateral than the proven facts will sustain. They do this with a feeling that it is their professional duty rather than that they are presenting a dubious case. Neither they nor the programs indicate that these overly optimistic messages are unethical because they identify the overriding good as being on another plane: saving the planet, delaying famine, raising living standards, or freeing women from the burden of large families. It might be argued that research has not demonstrated any certainties in these areas either. But it is probable that it will eventually be shown that slower population growth will bring individual and community benefits, and that policymakers should support what is probably true rather than cause damage by procrastinating until there is certainty. As Ruth Macklin wrote, "In a world of scarce resources, it surely seems immoral to pour money and personnel into ineffective or minimally effective programs in the interest of preserving freedom of contraceptive choice. These funds and workers could contribute to more effective efforts elsewhere, or in some other field" (1981, p. 356). Dennis Hodgson (1983) charged that not only family planners but also demographers have been activists, attempting to promote the programs rather than being social-scientifically objective.

Family-planning programs, like all modernizing and technical-aid-driven programs, have little interest in preserving indigenous cultures from change. They will bow to national governments, which they regard as preserving the national interest, but not to minorities, or even majorities who prefer the old ways. It might be argued, but rarely is, that family-planning programs are different from other aid programs in that they attempt to change sexuality, reproduction, and fertility, as well as the family and marriage—matters that lie at the heart of most cultures. The question could also be raised, as Paul Demeny (1988) has: Since the West achieved small families without external encouragement or help, why should the contemporary Third World be treated differently? Most actors in the programs would argue that it is unethical to hinder development and not to attempt to close the gap between the West and the rest of the world. Interestingly, for a considerable period two of the most aggressive family-planning programs adopted the view that there were cultural minorities who should be shielded from the full force of the national family planning program: in China with regard to the non-Han minorities and in Indonesia in terms of the outer islands.

International programs and national governments have made value-laden decisions in other areas of pop-

See Also

Minorities and "Birth Controllers": A History of Skepticism

ulation behavior with even fewer hesitations about ethical issues than in the family planning field. In the health field, they have mandated compulsory vaccination and a range of other public-health measures; in terms of marriage, they have set minimum ages and sometimes demanded health tests; with regard to migration, they have limited international migration and, more rarely, rural-urban migration. In all these areas they have followed George Bernard Shaw's admonition against governments allowing so much freedom that they refuse to legislate about which side of the road to drive on.

The West and international organizations took the initiative in urging Third World family-planning programs because they increasingly believed that rapid population growth was hampering economic development in poor countries and that too large a global population would eventually impoverish everyone. By the 1980s they also felt that even a population that could still be adequately fed might be too high for the preservation of the world's environment and of its indigenous fauna and flora and their habitats. Some groups also felt that all women of the world had a moral right to gain access to the knowledge and facilities needed to control family size. Many Westerners assumed that the West would provide leadership because of its greater capacity for research and training and the provision of expertise and funds, but perhaps also because postdemographic-transition societies were felt to have a better perspective on the situation. There is little evidence that fear of being swamped by huge Third World populations was a major motivation; rather, there was a fear that these populations might come to inhabit the world's slums because of the deleterious economic effects arising from their inability to control the growth of their numbers.

— JOHN C. CALDWELL

Strong Persuasion

As a category of fertility control measures, "strong persuasion" lies at an intermediate level of severity. Fertility change brought about by manipulation of economic incentives can often be considered ethically innocuous, while change enforced by stringent physical sanction or threat is widely viewed as ethically inadmissible. Strong persuasion, roughly situated between incentives and compulsion, encompasses social and administrative pressures or economic penalties that lessen but do not extinguish a person's perceived freedom to act contrary to the approved behavior. This approach has characterized particular phases of antinatalist (fertility-reducing) strategies in a number of societies, and it characterizes many policies proposed for countries where rapid population growth is seen as harmful and has resisted milder measures. Some pronatalist (fertility-raising) strategies also entail strong persuasion.

THE SCOPE OF REPRODUCTIVE FREEDOM. Ethical assessment of strategies employing persuasion would typically start from the premise that individuals are autonomous actors with well-established preferences concerning fertility. If choice is not constrained by ignorance or extreme poverty, reproductive freedom exists when fertility decisions are based on those preferences. Fertility decisions are of course influenced by the effect that family size has on family economic well-being. Incentive strategies can make use of this effect without seriously curtailing reproductive freedom. Strong persuasion, by definition, does seriously curtail it.

The ethical position that would accord individuals full reproductive freedom in this sense derives from the concept of "negative" liberty or freedom in Western liberal thought. Negative freedom is immunity from interference by others. The scope of a person's activities to which that freedom applies sets the bounds of a private sphere of behavior. Political philosophies differ in views of how extensive the private sphere should be. Its bounds might depend, for example, on the supposed minimum degree of interference needed to ensure social harmony or, more relevant here, on the extent to which particular activities of a person are seen as potentially harming others (Berlin, 1969; Patterson, 1991). If it were not for the possibility of causing harm, reproductive behavior would have a compelling claim to be considered private.

International declarations and conventions bear out this position with respect to the responsibilities of national governments. The Universal Declaration of Human Rights asserts a general protection of privacy, which signatory states have undertaken to recognize. Subsequent international declarations, although carrying less weight, have identified numerous more specific human rights, among them one that confers on individuals the freedom to choose the number of their children (United Nations, 1990).

The ethical problem is not so simply resolved, however. No society countenances complete reproductive freedom. In most contemporary societies, for example, monogamy is enforced, as is a minimum age of marriage; there are rules against incest. By and large, such restrictions do not occasion protest as infringements on individual choice. In some societies, abortion is limited or prohibited—a measure that may "compel" a pregnant woman to give birth. In this case, protest is more common, but the issues extend well beyond those of privacy. Other pressures on fertility are so long-standing that they are barely recognized as such, being built into the society's institutions. American society, Judith Blake has argued, is "pervaded by time-honored pronatalist constraints" (Blake, 1972, p. 105). Thus,

Citing health risks, the U.S. banned domestic use of the contraceptive Depo-Provera, but let it be sent to poor nations receiving U.S. foreign aid.

PAGE 508

In the northern plains of India, son preference is linked with behavior termed "daughter neglect."

PAGE 533

there is some arbitrariness in declaring that numbers of children should be an inviolable object of choice. Bernard Berelson and Jonathan Lieberson make this point when they write, "We see no fundamental ethical or philosophical difference between sanctions on monogamy or vaccination on the one hand, and sanctions on fertility on the other—only sociological and historical differences" (Berelson and Lieberson, 1979, p. 604).

Exclusion of all stringent fertility-control measures from ethical admissibility therefore cannot be drawn from abstract libertarian principle. Support for such a standpoint appears to derive from convention—one that emerged in historical situations where societal welfare was not drastically affected by the aggregate demographic result of individual free choice. As Paul Demeny has remarked, James Madison wrote nothing about fertility, but if the United States in his time had had a population of one billion instead of four million, and could foresee a near-term doubling of that size, "the Federalist Papers would probably have given the question of population growth, and the question of what Americans might do about it, a great deal of attention" (Demeny, 1986, p. 483).

If reproductive freedom is less than absolute, ethical assessment of fertility-control strategies must involve a weighing of individual interests against some broader set of interests—typically, those of a community or larger society of which the individual is a member. This group whose interests are to be considered is often called the "moral community." There is a range of ethically defensible positions on the scope of the moral community. What, for example, should be the significance of national borders in delimiting it? Should moral consideration be extended to nonhuman sentient creatures (a case that is increasingly being argued)? Moreover, if the familiar practice of time-discounting is permitted, reducing the weight of future members of the group in the calculation, can some analogous discounting be applied to geographical distance or to remoteness in kinship or level of sentience (Bayles, 1980; Feinberg, 1980)?

Taking just the case of the "society" (most often identified with nation), the potential existence of a societal interest in decisions bearing on family size or composition is clear: The size no less than the socialization of the next generation has implications for a society's identity and well-being, and thus may properly be a concern of its members as a whole. The case is analogous to that of admitting new members through immigration. How social interests are determined—in particular, the degree of participation and consent entailed and the protection granted to dissent—is a critical issue, but it is no different here than in any other policy domain. There are circumstances in which the societal interest in modifying reproductive behavior may be very strong: for example, where fertility is at a level that causes population size to double in a generation or to fall by one-third. A canvassing of policy preferences in such societies might well endorse vigorous efforts to moderate the pace of change.

CASES OF STRONG PERSUASION. To give empirical content to the discussion of the ethics of such efforts, consider some cases of fertility control where the term "strong persuasion" appears to be applicable.

1. India's family-planning program has long favored sterilization (mainly of men) over reversible contraceptive methods, with financial incentives offered to clients and to the officials and private "motivators" who recruit them. Except during the nineteenth-month period in 1975-1977 when civil liberties were suspended under a declaration of national emergency and press-gang methods of recruitment were reportedly widespread, India has stressed the voluntary nature of its program. Nominal voluntarism, however, has been compatible with active recruitment efforts, encouraged by the incentives offered the recruiters and in some regions—especially during the campaigns associated with the "vasectomy camps" that were an important constituent of the program—by pressures on program officials to achieve target numbers of clients. In a highly stratified society, clients came disproportionately from the most disadvantaged groups, where effects of incentives were strongest, susceptibility to browbeating greatest, and assurance of informed consent weakest (Gwatkin, 1979; Vicziany, 1982).

2. In Indonesia, the government's family-planning program, begun around 1970, has sought to mobilize regional and local government officials from provincial down to village level to generate administrative pressures in support of its efforts to increase use of modern contraception—chiefly, pills and intrauterine devices (IUDs). With reversible methods dominant, initial acceptance is a less serious decision for a couple than in the case of sterilization. However, antinatalist effect then requires long-term contraceptive use: Continuation rates are as important as acceptance rates. As in India, special drives—here, "safaris"—have sometimes been associated with reports of strong-arm recruitment tactics. A distinctive additional feature of the Indonesian program has been its use of program clients as a pressure group within each local community, informally backed by village leaders, in gaining new recruits and monitoring continuation. Especially in rural areas, nonacceptance of program services may have called for some degree of defiance of authority. In Bali, where a person's cultural ties to his or her hamlet were particularly strong, the community pressures invoked by the program were formalized at the hamlet level—for

example, by making the contraceptive use or nonuse of each couple a matter of public record and, more generally, by bringing contraceptive practice into the arena of socially pressured conformity. At such closeness of range, persuasion is necessarily strong (Warwick, 1986; Streatfield, 1986).

3. China experienced a 50 percent decline in fertility during the 1970s. A vigorous antinatalist campaign—"later-longer [birth intervals]-fewer"—instituted in 1971, combined provision of contraception and abortion services with close surveillance of couples' demographic behavior and imposition of political penalties for noncompliance. The campaign worked through the dense network of Communist party-controlled intermediate institutions: production teams and brigades, communes, study groups, and party cells. This political pressure modified the existing parental benefit-cost calculus on the value of children, tipping the balance sharply toward low fertility. Pressure reportedly shaded into compulsion in some regions, depending on local interpretations of central policy dictates—although less commonly than during the initial years of the subsequent "one child per family" campaign begun in 1979 (Banister, 1987; Greenhalgh, 1990).

4. Although not in any sense reflecting an intentional fertility policy, in some European societies before industrialization the leadership of local communities exercised fairly stringent oversight within their boundaries of marriage or establishment of a household—factors then directly if incompletely governing fertility. In English parishes of the seventeenth and eighteenth centuries, for example, there was a community responsibility to support indigent members, creating a collective incentive to limit their numbers. Together, the parish system, property requirements for marriage, and the Poor Laws constituted a devolved institutional framework through which community interests could influence fertility. The framework was later dissolved by the changes in labor relations and mobility wrought by the industrial revolution. Analogous community-level systems of demographic control could be found in many other parts of Europe and in Japan (McNicoll, 1975).

A common feature of these cases is that fertility, or behavior bearing on fertility, is the subject of close-at-hand social or administrative pressure on individuals or couples. Often there is some intimation of political or economic sanctions for noncompliance, but social sanctions such as shaming or ostracism may be perceived to be just as severe. There are ethically relevant differences in the overall degree of pressure imposed, in the justice or fairness of its application across the population, and in the intrusiveness of the methods of fertility control employed.

CRITERIA FOR ETHICAL ACCEPTABILITY. In their review of the ethics of fertility control programs, Berelson and Lieberson (1979) argue that there is a hierarchy of permissible interventions paralleling the degree of gravity of the fertility problem: "The degree of coercive policy brought into play should be proportional to the degree of seriousness of the present problem and should be introduced only after less coercive means have been exhausted" (p. 602). As a practical political proposition, this may be regarded as common sense: use the minimum pressure to attain a given objective, assuming that the objective is legitimately set. Strong persuasion would be defensible for a middle range of fertility predicaments, plausibly including the cases of India, Indonesia, and China cited above. However, as an ethical maxim, what Berelson and Lieberson call "the stepladder approach" is quite vague. It reflects the authors' denial that there can be a set of agreed ethical principles applicable to all demographic situations. Donald Warwick criticizes them for this stance: Their framework, he writes, "is politically expedient, lacking in solid ethical foundations, and easily becomes a rationalization for suppressing civil liberties" (Warwick, 1990, p. 33).

An alternative way of assessing the ethical standing of fertility control measures is to judge each against a set of value criteria. Daniel Callahan (1971) selected three: freedom, justice, and security/survival. Warwick (1990) added two more: truth-telling and welfare. Strategies using strong persuasion would barely pass the test of freedom and, in many cases, would fail one or more of the other criteria. For example, adverse side effects of proffered contraceptive methods may not be explained, violating "truth-telling" and, if damage to health follows, security/survival. This approach identifies a subset of control strategies that pass muster on all counts. However, it does not rank them; more important, it does not distinguish among strategies that fail one or more of the tests. Thus it may be of little help in determining a best course of action in the more serious demographic predicaments in which strong persuasion is likely to be contemplated. In both approaches, assessment of a proposed strategy employing strong persuasion requires combining judgments on factors that are strictly incommensurable—deciding, for example, whether a reduction in freedom can be offset by a gain in welfare. The chief difference between the two approaches lies not so much in the choice of which criteria, beyond freedom, are to be applied as in how serious the fertility problem has to be for some departure from voluntarism to be acceptable.

Gauging how much reproductive freedom has been sacrificed in a particular fertility control strategy is complicated by the fact that fertility preferences may shift. Preferences change in fairly predictable ways over the course of economic and social development. For example, urbanization and industrialization create con-

Whether contraception, sterilization, and abortion should be permitted, prohibited, or coerced by government has generated intense controversy in countries as different as the U.S., Romania, India, Ireland, and China.

PAGE 222

ditions that powerfully favor smaller families. When accompanied or soon followed by rapid economic development, strong antinatalist persuasion, where it is adopted, is thus likely to be operative in influencing behavior only for a limited period: individual demand for fertility control soon takes over as the driving force of demographic change. By the end of the 1980s, this shift had probably occurred in Indonesia and in parts of China. At the same time, economic development brings greater population mobility and freer information flows, making tight political or administrative control of fertility less feasible.

To some extent, preferences can also be manipulated. All governments attempt this in some policy domains. At its worst, the result is an insidious extension of direct pressures on behavior. In relatively open societies, however, such efforts are often better seen as part of the give-and-take of politics—analogous in the public domain to commercial advertising—than as a deliberate undermining of consumer sovereignty. The Indonesian government, for example, has used a barrage of publicity measures to instill in the population the ideal of a small family. The behavioral effect is uncertain but is likely to have been small in comparison to the government's wielding of village-level peer pressures. Subsequently, both efforts would have been dwarfed in their effect by the rapid social and economic changes that have made children much more costly to parents.

POLICY FAIRNESS. The justice or fairness of a strategy of strong persuasion is clearly central to an ethical assessment, but the application of such a criterion is not straightforward. One interpretation of distributional equity might favorably regard China's efforts to limit fertility to one or two children per couple. The policy seeks to impose a radical equality of fertility outcome across the population: "Fairness" is achieved. Equality of outcome would, of course, disguise substantial inequalities in perceptions of pressure: persons with strong preferences for large families suffer greatly, some others with different preferences not at all. This is a familiar problem with any rationing scheme: The half-serious proposal of Kenneth Boulding (1964) to establish a market in childbearing rights was aimed at

FERTILITY POLICY
Seeking Fairness across Genders, Generations, and Nations

The extent to which culturally entrenched gender inequality warrants ethical respect is contentious. Acceptance of universal criteria of gender equality is clearly gaining in the modern world. Most present-day governments give at least nominal recognition to equal rights for women and support international instruments containing strong endorsements of equality, suggesting their recognition of ethical judgments made from that premise. Equalizing responsibility for and risks of fertility control between men and women would be an immediate corollary.

An analogous problem of equity arises between generations. Children have interests in the number of siblings they have. Those interests, however, are often ignored when a couple is deciding on family size. Moreover, any particular couple, even if it did take account of those interests, has no influence over the fertility decisions of other couples and thus over the size and per-capita inheritance of the next generation as a whole. This predicament, in which an outcome recognized to be unfavorable can result from the separate, rational decisions of individuals, is familiar in many social contexts and is known in game theory as "the prisoner's dilemma." In the field of population, it is one of the standard justifications for strong state action to restrain rapid growth (Hardin, 1968). The many philosophical intricacies of intergenerational equity in fertility policy are discussed by Richard Sikora and Brian Barry (1978). Broader custodial claims by government—for example, claims to stewardship of environmental stability or of biodiversity—can be grounds for sterner policy interventions, although the fertility connection in such arguments is often fairly tenuous.

Finally, there are equity-based ethical issues in efforts to persuade another society to adopt measures to alter its demographic behavior, paralleling the situation of families within a society. The persuasion contained in international instruments like the 1984 Mexico City Declaration on Population and Development is vanishingly weak, in deference to national sovereignty. Overt pressure from international agencies like the World Bank to introduce antinatalist measures would probably be resisted by most governments, even though far-reaching policy realignment is frequently demanded and obtained in other spheres. Behind the scenes, however, pressure to adopt or strengthen antinatalist programs is probably fairly common in international dialogues on foreign assistance. Formally, the bargaining situation vis-à-vis population policy is quite similar to other circumstances where effects of activities in one country spill over its frontiers—for example, the case of "greenhouse gas" emissions—although fertility control may evoke sharper national sensibilities. Of course, nominal accession to such pressure, if lacking domestic political support, is unlikely to translate into effective fertility-control measures.

— GEOFFREY MCNICOLL

alleviating that objection. Directing antinatalist persuasive efforts at disfavored minority groups or at those with least political access, such as the groups lowest in socioeconomic status, would be deemed ethically objectionable on equity grounds. It may be objectionable even if their fertility were higher than average. Such groups are often poorly placed to resist strong persuasion by program officials and in consequence, as the Indian case might suggest, would tend to become prime program targets.

Other dimensions of justice or fairness are also raised by persuasion-based fertility policy. Three deserving particular attention are equity between men and women, equity across generations, and equity between societies. The common assumption that the two members of a couple have similar family-size desires is often invalid. The fallback position that whatever differences do exist are private matters to be negotiated between them is undercut where there are institutionalized power differences between husband and wife affecting whose preferences dominate. The traditional patriarchal family, still common in South Asia and Africa, embodies such differences. Another example is the institution of *purdah*, which severely constrains the life choices available to women in some Muslim societies. Persuasion that in effect seeks to modify behavior in the direction of the preferences of the weaker party may contribute to equity.

FERTILITY-CONTROL METHODS. Ethical justification of strong persuasion in a given fertility situation can never be carte blanche, since ethical assessment of the specifics of the control measures proposed is also needed. A given amount of pressure judged in terms of the fertility outcome may entail varying degrees of intrusiveness into individual or family behavior, depending on the details of the measures employed. Protection of privacy, an ethical value bound up with freedom, calls for minimizing that intrusiveness. This principle does not give a simple ranking of fertility-control methods but would, for example, prefer social pressure to adopt safe, reversible contraceptive practice over comparable pressure for sterilization. Browbeating a woman to have an abortion, a practice reported in some studies of China's antinatalist program, would of course be found highly objectionable. Outcome-based persuasion directed at reducing, say, fourth or higher-order births but leaving choice of means open and providing a range of safe and convenient contraceptive options for both men and women might appear less intrusive than persuasion directed at, say, acceptance of IUDs or contraceptive implants.

Cultural acceptability is a consideration in such rankings of specific measures. The more acceptable the measure, the less the perceived pressure submitted to in adopting it. Among the cultural factors that affect whether a measure is deemed objectionable are notions of privacy, shame, and personal autonomy; beliefs about health and therapeutics; and the expected level of communication between sexual partners. Cultural acceptability may also be influenced by the kinds of pressures routinely applied elsewhere in the society in efforts to change other behaviors or those that are exercised in social life generally. If daily life is minutely regulated, whether by an intrusive government or by neighborly meddlesomeness, pressures on fertility may be a comparatively small additional invasion of privacy. Practices such as neighborhood surveillance of pregnancies in urban China or the month-by-month listing of couples' contraceptive status in village registers in Bali should be judged not alone but along with the polities they manifest.

Some religious beliefs and moral codes make distinctions among birth-control methods. Particular methods—abortion most frequently—may be prohibited outright. For believers, the sanctions for violating such a prohibition, possibly extending into afterlife, can clearly warrant the term "strong persuasion." The position of the Roman Catholic church on contraception, as set out in Pope Paul VI's 1968 encyclical *Humanae Vitae*, entails discriminating between "natural" and "artificial" methods. The church opposes all forms of artificial birth control. In this case, however, the perceived strength of the sanctions has been vitiated, at least in the United States and other affluent countries, by shifts in Catholics' attitudes toward church authority in that domain. Contraceptive behavior in these countries has shown an increasing departure from the church's teaching on the subject, and differences between the family size of Catholics and non-Catholics have largely vanished.

PRONATALIST STRATEGIES. Most of the above discussion has been concerned with antinatalist strategies, the principal arena of ethical debate on population policy matters. Looking ahead, it is likely that situations of very low fertility and rapid natural decrease of population will become increasingly common. Immigration is at best a partial substitute for births: with very low fertility, the scale of immigration needed to maintain a nation's population size and limit the rise in its average age may be incompatible with maintenance of its cultural identity. Assuming a compelling social interest in demographic continuity, fertility policy would then reemerge on the public agenda, directed at pronatalist objectives.

Pronatalist strategies based on incentives have a long history but have shown at best modest results for quite large public expenditures. Strong pronatalist persuasion, a more recent phenomenon, has perhaps even less to show (David, 1982). Two contrasting instances

The socialists, especially Marx, accused Malthus of preaching a political message in the guise of a social analysis.

PAGE 536

◆ **antinatalist**
fertility-reducing policy, such as forced sterilizations.

where such policies did have significant demographic effects were in Romania and Iran. In 1966, Romania outlawed abortion, previously widely practiced, resulting in an estimated 40 percent more births over 1966-1976 than would have been expected in the absence of the policy shift, albeit with the excess concentrated in the initial years. In Iran, the enforcement of traditional sex roles and dismantling of the family-planning program after establishment of the Islamic Republic in 1979 were accompanied by a substantial rise in fertility.

In most respects, the ethical issues raised by pronatalist strategies mirror those of antinatalist strategies. Economic incentives can be designed to be ethically inoffensive, but the scale of transfers needed to make them effective may be too large a burden on public revenue. Strong persuasion, as before, is ethically problematic, even well short of Romanian- or Iranian-style restrictions. A nation facing rapid demographic decline might well arrive at a collective decision to try to raise fertility by means formally analogous to the community-level peer pressure discussed earlier and involving the same array of ethical considerations. The Romanian and Iranian measures could call on no such demographic rationale or implied social consensus; in revoking options and opportunities formerly available, both were ethically retrogressive.

The chief objection to complete reproductive freedom is that societies have legitimate interests in their demographic futures. The proposition is readily assented to when the society is a nation-state and the policy issue is the number of immigrants to be admitted. Fertility policy, concerned with the other source of new members, entails balancing the interests of individuals as parents or members of a family against their interests as citizens. Traditions of Western liberalism, taken over and elaborated in international covenants on human rights, emphasize freedom from interference by government as a salient value. Where social interests, properly determined, are seriously threatened by existing levels of fertility, there is an ethically defensible case for abridging that freedom. Ethical assessment of particular fertility-control strategies requires weighing that abridgment against the perceived threat. It also requires testing the strategies against additional standards—especially that of fairness. This procedure, however, does not yield a cut-and-dried ranking or decision on admissibility. A problem of judgment remains, in which cultural features of the society and perhaps the political predilections of the assessor will play a part.

— GEOFFREY MCNICOLL

Marxists have argued that each economic system has its own laws and that the creation of national family-planning programs assumes a wrong priority.

PAGE 538

Compulsion

Compulsion in fertility control goes far beyond persuasion. To compel (or coerce; the terms are often used interchangeably), a fertility-control measure must employ force, the threat of force, or extreme penalties and pressures that leave people no choice but to comply. Compulsion need not be absolute—some people may be able to withstand pressures that overwhelm others—but it must be powerful enough to compel many people to act in ways contrary to their wishes. When individuals use contraception against their will, abort wanted pregnancies, or are forced to undergo sterilization, they are evidently experiencing compulsion, even if the inducements employed to achieve these results are only psychological.

Some family-planning advocates limit the term "coercion" to the use of physical force. For ethical purposes, that definition is too narrow. Incentive and disincentive measures may, in some circumstances, result in compulsion. People who practice family planning out of fear of public humiliation; strong peer pressures; such penalties as loss of food, housing, employment, possessions, or essential services; or simply because of threats and intimidation are acting under compulsion even if no overt force is in evidence.

Incentives for couples who accept contraception or abide by family size limits are usually not coercive unless they involve services essential to life or health (e.g., food or medical care) that are not readily available to those who do not comply. Disincentives are not coercive for those who can disregard them and have the children they want, but they may be coercive for people whose subsistence or general welfare is seriously threatened by them. Threats are not coercive if there is no follow-up and no one takes them seriously. However, when people comply with family-planning demands out of fear, they are clearly acting under compulsion.

NATIONAL FERTILITY POLICIES. National fertility policies may be either pronatalist (fertility-raising) or antinatalist (fertility-reducing). Pronatalist policies are sometimes, as in the case of Germany in the 1930s, prompted by concern that low fertility or negative population growth rates threaten national political or economic well-being, or the belief, as in the People's Republic of China in the early 1950s, that a large population is a source of economic, political, and military power. The leadership of a country whose population is not growing may fear aggression by more populous or faster-growing neighbors or an overwhelming influx of immigrants differing in language, culture, or ethnicity. Pronatalist policies may also reflect religious values that treat procreation as a fulfillment of natural law or divine commandment.

Antinatalist policies are usually inspired by the view that current fertility levels constitute an impossible or undesirable burden on the government because of the costs of providing health care, education, employment, housing, and other essential services, or the belief that population growth threatens prospects for economic development, improved living standards, nutrition, the supply of natural resources, the environment, and the survival of humankind and other species. This view is often taken as received wisdom that requires no further investigation and needs only to be asserted to be proven. For example, since 1974 the government of China has justified its family-planning program on the grounds that population growth threatens economic development and living standards in general, including education, employment, housing, and even food supply.

However, these arguments, like the pronatalist arguments they superseded, consist largely of categorical assertions never put to an empirical test and sometimes contain contradictions. Although the Chinese government claims that population growth prevents it from investing in consumer needs, it has been spending heavily for armaments since the late 1980s. In 1993, the government insisted that China's then modest natural increase rate threatened economic growth at the same time that it worried publicly about "overheating" in an economy growing at about 14 percent per year, faster than any other in the world! Such incongruities suggest that official explanations do not necessarily reveal the actual reasons for national policies. China is not the only country to which this caveat applies.

National fertility policies can be completely voluntary, but some use compulsion and go to great lengths to conceal and deny the fact. Denial helps avoid domestic and international criticism on humanitarian grounds and obviates the necessity of justifying coercion. The Chinese government has consistently maintained, in spite of abundant contrary evidence, that its program is voluntary; foreign supporters of the Chinese program, including the United Nations Population Fund and the International Planned Parenthood Federation, ostensibly accept and reiterate the Chinese claims.

PRONATALIST COMPULSION. The most common forms of pronatalist compulsion are government policies that deny access to contraception or abortion. In the early 1950s the Chinese government denounced birth control as a foreign plot to "kill off the Chinese people without shedding blood," banned imports of contraceptives, and prohibited abortion. Restrictions on abortion are also found throughout Latin America except Cuba. Until the collapse of Communist governments in 1990 and 1991, liberal abortion laws prevailed in eastern Europe except in Romania, but in 1991 and 1992 Poland, Czechoslovakia, and Hungary adopted measures that increasingly restricted the practice. Legislation adopted in Poland tripled the cost of contraceptives, making them less accessible to many people (Boland, 1992). Prohibiting particular contraceptive measures may constitute compulsion in the absence of effective alternatives, but only if the prohibition is enforced. Brazil, for example, has a law against sterilization that is generally ignored; an estimated 40 percent of Brazilian women have been sterilized.

Some people have applied the term "coercive" to traditional pronatalist values emphasizing the need to bear children to ensure family prosperity, provide support in old age, carry on the family line, or demonstrate virility or fecundity—attitudes common in many developing countries, especially among rural people. These values are often reinforced by religious institutions favoring large families or condemning specific birth-control practices. Cultural factors are indeed coercive when they compel couples (or women) to have children against their will, specifically in situations in which the desires of women to limit childbearing are overridden by prevailing norms and institutions in a male-dominated society (but not in cases in which both husband and wife accept the cultural imperatives and comply willingly).

Pronatalist compulsion is usually not as coercive as antinatalist compulsion. Even the most coercive pronatalist policies have been relatively ineffectual except for brief periods (Demeny, 1986b), probably because government strategies for compelling pregnancy are more easily and inconspicuously evaded than are those for preventing or terminating pregnancy. Antinatalist compulsion leaves couples no choice but to have fewer children than they might want. Pronatalist compulsion may narrow the range of contraceptive options but can seldom stop couples from limiting fertility if they are resolved to do so. Voluntary fertility control was practiced quite effectively in several European countries long before modern contraceptive techniques had been devised and without recourse to abortion.

ANTINATALIST COMPULSION. Antinatalist compulsion has been brought to public attention in recent years by the conspicuously coercive family-planning measures employed in India and China. A sterilization program promoted by the Indian government in the mid-1970s generated compulsion because of demands from the top that assigned targets be achieved by whatever means necessary. In April 1976 the government issued a national policy statement authorizing state legislatures to adopt legislation for compulsory sterilization. One state, Maharashtra, did so, but instances of forced sterilization were widely reported in other areas as well. Local officials used control over permits, licenses, employment, and school admissions, and denial of food rations, salary forfeitures, threats, and physical force to compel people to submit. One analyst attributed the coercion to intense central government pressure on local authorities to carry out large numbers of sterilizations immediately, with no excuses accepted and no questions asked

Basic human welfare consists largely in being free in the fullest possible sense.

PAGE 247

See Also

Freedom and Coercion: The Value of Freedom

P

POPULATION POLICIES

Strategies of Fertility Control

PHYSICAL COMPULSION

Pregnant without Government Permission?

Physical compulsion is the most direct and extreme form of compulsion used in fertility control. In includes such measures as rounding up women pregnant without government permission and transporting them to clinics for forced abortions—sometimes in handcuffs, bound with ropes, or in hog cages, practices reported from time to time in China and in Tibet. Physical compulsion is also involved when urban doctors in China, threatened with loss of their jobs if they permit unauthorized newborns to leave the hospital alive, destroy them during delivery by injecting lethal substances into their fontanels or crushing their heads with forceps, as was reported by several sources in the 1980s (Aird, 1990). It is implicit in the mass "mobilizations" for abortion, sterilization, and IUD insertion, from which people reportedly sometimes flee their homes and go into hiding because, once apprehended, they have no choice but to submit.

Physical compulsion occurs without overt force when women in China who ask for removal of IUDs or reversal of sterilizations are refused, and when women in Bangladesh suffering serious side effects from Norplant implants (subcutaneous devices that release fertility-inhibiting hormones for five years or more) are told they cannot be removed (Ubinig, 1991). Fertility-control techniques that are effective for long periods or permanently, such as long-lasting injections or implants, are more susceptible to compulsory applications than are contraceptives that depend upon user initiative and sustained efforts. This is especially true for measures that can be implemented without the consent or knowledge of the recipient while other medical services are being provided, such as injections of chemical abortifacients, abortions, and sterilizations.

— JOHN S. AIRD

◆ **compulsion**
employing force, the threat of force, or extreme penalties and pressures that leave people no choice but to comply with demands.

(Gwatkin, 1979). Between July and December 1976, six million people were sterilized. The Indian experience provoked a public reaction that helped to bring down the government.

The Chinese family-planning program has used compulsion more extensively than has any other national program. The compulsion began early in the 1970s, with an attempt to impose a two-to-four-child limit by requiring women to use intrauterine devices (IUDs) to prevent further pregnancies. Chinese sources do not reveal exactly how this policy was implemented, but the media openly advocated publicizing individual "birth plans," setting target figures for contraceptive use, and conducting "mass mobilizations." Those who resisted were to be declared "class enemies" and subjected to "political struggle" (Aird, 1981).

Pressures for compliance escalated during the rest of the decade, except for a brief remission in 1978, and culminated in the adoption of the one-child policy in 1979. Another remission occurred in 1980, but by 1981 the pressures were resumed and reached a peak in 1983, when Chinese government policy, adopted by the State Family Planning Commission with prior approval of the Communist Party Central Committee and the State Council, demanded IUD insertion for women with one child, sterilization for couples with two or more children, and abortion for pregnancies without official approval. Mobile birth-control surgery teams ranged over the countryside, apprehending those to whom the policy applied and carrying out the operations on the spot; many of these operations had complications because some of the teams were inadequately trained. Nearly twenty-one million sterilizations were performed in 1983 alone, three-quarters of them on women. Most of them were undoubtedly involuntary, as was implied by Chinese sources at the time. One source revealed that the purpose of the sterilization requirement was not just to eliminate third and higher-order births but also to make couples with one child avoid further pregnancies. This explanation implies that sterilization was compulsory and was meant to be intimidating.

Strong adverse public reaction obliged the regime to moderate its policies in 1984. Sterilization quotas were abandoned, family-planning workers were advised to be "fair and reasonable" and avoid coercion, and the categories of special circumstances under which some couples could be allowed a second child were increased; thereupon enforcement of policy requirements promptly lapsed. For a few years most provinces allowed rural couples whose first child was a girl to have a second child, and several provinces allowed all rural couples to have two children. These measures were intended to enlist public support for the elimination of higher-order pregnancies, but they did not work. Alarmed by rising birthrates, the central authorities attempted to tighten up again, and by the end of the decade, policy enforcement had become very strict.

In April 1991, the central authorities ordered a further major escalation, with startling results. For the first time, fertility in China dropped below the replacement level in 1992, and coercion increased sharply. The

See Also
Behavior Control
On Coercion and Manipulation

authorities demanded that the crackdown continue without change to the end of the century. New population targets were established, and efforts to penalize officials who failed to fulfill them were intensified. Provincial family-planning regulations were stiffened, and new laws were adopted to control fertility among migrants, to limit adoptive families to one child, and to eliminate childbearing by those deemed unfit for "eugenic" reasons. The 1983 rules for IUD insertion, sterilization, and abortion were reinstated. The one-child limit is rigidly maintained in most urban areas, and the number of exceptions permitted in rural areas is being reduced. Since the 1950s most ethnic minorities had been subjected to somewhat less stringent rules (e.g., a two-child limit) to avoid charges of "Han chauvinism," but in the early 1990s steps were taken to narrow their options as well (Banister, 1987; Aird, 1990).

FORMS OF COMPULSION. Threats and commands issued by officials are often coercive in societies in which the authorities exercise such power that people dare not defy them. Intimidation is clearly the intent of the "heart-to-heart talks" with family-planning cadres that Chinese women reluctant to practice family planning are obliged to endure until they succumb to the pressure. The same applies to the "study classes" for nonconforming women, who are forced to attend and are not allowed to return home until they promise to comply (Aird, 1990; Mosher, 1983). A threat of legal action against nonconformists is implicit in the provision in the Chinese Constitution making family planning a citizen's "duty" and in provincial regulations mandating family-planning requirements, as well as in the requirement that an official permission slip be obtained from local authorities before starting a pregnancy. In the 1980s, Balinese Hindus who resisted birth-control demands were threatened with expulsion from their villages or with refusal to allow them to cremate deceased relatives in the village graveyards, both awesome threats in the context of their culture (Warwick, 1990). In India, government officials used their status to bully beggars into submitting to sterilization (Warwick, 1990).

Peer pressure can sometimes be made coercive in the service of family-planning programs. In China such pressures are deliberately instigated by imposing collective punishments for individual noncompliance. In several Chinese provinces in the late 1980s, rural couples eligible under official policies to have a second child were refused permission until all unauthorized pregnancies in their village were terminated. In some factories, bonuses and expansion plans were denied to the entire work force if a single employee had an unauthorized child (Aird,1990). Under these circumstances, offending couples in essentially closed communities can be ostracized and subjected to reprisals by local officials and by neighbors or coworkers until the stress reaches unbearable levels.

Incentives that include vital necessities can amount to compulsion for the indigent. In Bangladesh, a destitute woman seeking free food was told she must first be sterilized (Warwick, 1990), and other women were required to undergo sterilization to qualify for health care (Hartmann, 1990). In Egypt in the early 1970s, some women were forced to buy contraceptive pills if they wanted other medical treatment (Warwick, 1990). In general, incentives are more compelling for poor families than for the rest of the community.

Penalties and incentives applied to local officials to make sure they attain their family-planning targets often cause them to resort to compulsory measures. Target numbers of acceptors of IUDs, sterilization, implants, and other contraceptive methods are generally intended to pressure local authorities to obtain compliance from their people. In China, national targets for population size and rate of growth are allocated to the provinces, which are expected to set lower-level targets accordingly. Other targets are

FERTILITY CONTROL
Economic Incentives

Some of the disincentives imposed on violators of family-planning rules in China are so severe that they are obviously meant to be coercive, and often are. Provincial family-planning regulations may require a couple that has an unauthorized child to forfeit 20, 30, or 40 percent of their total income for up to fourteen years (Aird, 1992). One-time penalties may be several times the family's total annual income (Barnett, 1992). Other penalties include cutting off electricity, water, and food allotments; confiscating household possessions, livestock and farm implements; expelling people from their homes; and even tearing down the houses (Aird, 1992). In 1993, for the first time there were reports of family-planning violators being beaten with electric batons. In India some couples were told that their children could not attend school until one of the parents was sterilized. Unemployed workers were required to show sterilization certificates before they could be hired. Some villages were allowed irrigation water at subsidized prices only if they had the requisite number of sterilizations (Warwick, 1982).

— JOHN S. AIRD

◆ **strong persuasion** *between incentives and compulsion, social and administrative pressures or economic penalties that lessen but do not extinguish a person's perceived freedom to act contrary to approved behavior.*

See Also
Nonvoluntary Sterilization

From the 1870s, the new birth-control movement stressed the situation of women and the disabilities they suffered from continuous childbearing.

PAGE 536

POPULATION GROWTH AND ECONOMIC DEVELOPMENT What Correlation?

In the late 1960s, Simon Kuznets and Richard Easterlin warned that the effects of population growth on economic development were not well understood and that there was no correlation between population growth and per capita income in developing countries (Kuznets, 1967; Easterlin, 1967). In 1971, a study by the National Academy of Sciences concluded, on the basis of evidence from India and Mexico, that rapid population growth had serious negative consequences. However, in 1973, Julian Simon and Avery Guest challenged the notion of overpopulation (in Pohlman, 1973), and in 1977, Simon cited evidence that moderate population growth stimulates economic development, rapid and slow growth are slight deterrents, and no growth or a decline in population seems to be a strong deterrent (Simon, 1977).

In 1986, a second National Academy of Sciences study, drawing on extensive international statistical data, found that population growth plays a relatively minor role in economic development, insufficient to justify extreme fertility-control measures. One participant in the study, Samuel Preston, noted that "so much of the [doomsday] rhetoric is simple-minded and incorrect, casually attributing any human problem to there being too many humans" (1985, p. 10). Meanwhile, some of the more sensational doomsday predictions, notably Paul Ehrlich's warning of an inescapable worldwide famine in the 1970s (Ehrlich, 1968), failed to come true. In many heavily populated developing countries, per capita food availability rose instead.

— JOHN S. AIRD

designed to increase the percentages of women using contraception or accepting one-child certificates, and to reduce the percentages of third and higher-order births. Chinese provinces are ranked according to their success in meeting their targets, and laggard provinces are ordered to catch up with the rest.

The pressures are transmitted mainly through a nationwide system of signed contracts called the "responsibility system." Provincial and lower-level leaders in China who fail to meet their targets may lose bonuses, promotions, and even their jobs (Aird, 1990). When such systems are instituted without effective safeguards against coercion, local leaders naturally assume that the higher levels are not deeply concerned about preventing it. Even targets not intended to be compulsory can lead to coercion at the grass-roots level, as has happened in India, Bangladesh, the Philippines, Indonesia, and Vietnam (Warwick, 1982; Cohen, 1991; Hafidz et al., 1992; Banister, 1989, 1991). Organizations such as the World Bank and the U.S. Agency for International Development have sometimes made target attainment a prerequisite for continued assistance to client countries, thus creating conditions in which local authorities may feel obliged to resort to compulsory measures (Hartmann, 1991-1992).

Ethical considerations

Granted that most of the measures described above are either compulsory or tend to lead to compulsion in implementation, are compulsory family-planning measures unethical? Certainly they violate the right of reproductive freedom embraced by the world population conferences at Bucharest in 1974 and at Mexico City in 1984, and in other international declarations on human rights. All international agencies promoting family planning and most professionals in the field at least nominally subscribe to the Mexico City declaration that all individuals and couples have the right to "decide freely and responsibly the number and spacing of their children," and that parents should be allowed to fulfill their responsibilities "freely and without coercion" (International Conference on Population, 1984). The rationale for including reproductive freedom among the basic human rights is that decisions about childbearing are so personal and so important for the happiness of parents that they should be protected against encroachments by state authority.

However, the consensus about the inviolability of reproductive freedom is not as solid as public declarations make it seem. Many family-planning advocates, demographers, economists, and environmentalists have accepted the view that world population growth constitutes a serious threat to human welfare and even to the survival of the planet. In one form or another, this view has become the received wisdom in intellectual circles throughout much of the Western world. Although few of its adherents have openly advocated compulsory family planning, many have privately accepted the idea. In 1978 a survey taken of members of the Population Association of America found that 56 percent of the respondents believed that compulsory measures must be taken in the future to avoid catastrophe, and 34 percent felt that some countries needed to adopt such measures immediately (Population Association of America, 1978). Some people of this persuasion urge consideration of measures that go "beyond family planning" and openly express admiration for the aggressive tactics used in China.

Presumably those who express guarded approval of compulsory family planning consider it a lesser evil from a humanitarian standpoint than the consequences of continued population growth, and hence a legitimate exercise of authority by the state in its role as protector of the public welfare. But is this perception valid? On this question there is sharp disagreement among demographers and economists. The broad consensus about the dangers of population growth that existed through the 1960s has seriously eroded in subsequent years (Menken, 1986; Demeny 1986a; Warwick, 1990). The idea of an imminent "population crisis" has not been sustained either by relevant statistical evidence assembled during the 1970s and 1980s or by actual experience in developing countries.

Obviously the last word has not been written on this issue. The debate among demographers and economists will undoubtedly continue, and the final outcome is uncertain. Still, it seems unlikely that the notion of a "population crisis," in the world as a whole or in particular countries, can be demonstrated beyond reasonable doubt. If the relationship between population growth and human welfare were as direct, preponderant, and negative as the "crisis" view assumes, at least a modest correlation should have appeared by now in international statistics. Instead, as Preston observed, the relation appears "about as random and unstructured as any . . . in the social sciences" (1985, p. 11). Moreover, demographic projections are not meant to be predictions, and in the long term often turn out to be wide of the mark; economic forecasts are generally much more inaccurate and often contradictory. Prognostications that combine both surely compound the probability of error. There is therefore no justification for the certainty with which conclusions about the effects of population growth on human welfare are usually advanced.

In view of the lack of definitive knowledge about the consequences of population growth, there seems to be no empirically sound basis for antinatalist encroachments on reproductive freedom. If the case for compulsion can ever be made, it must be based on evidence that is systematic, substantial, and conclusive. The interpretation of the evidence must not be entrusted to persons and institutions with a vested interest in the outcome, which would exclude most family-planning advocates and agencies, at least some demographic and economic research institutions, the agencies that fund their activities, and other organizations and individuals that have an ax to grind on the questions at issue. Despite much public rhetoric from interested quarters, no such case has yet been made. Until an unequivocal verdict has been reached under circumstances with proper safeguards, compulsory fertility-control measures must be regarded as unethical.

— JOHN S. AIRD

HEALTH EFFECTS OF FERTILITY CONTROL

Concern about possible side effects of contraceptives is the most common reason women in the United States at risk of unintended pregnancy give for not using them (Silverman et al., 1987). Because many people do not consider the beneficial effects of contraceptive use on women's current and future health, there may be unbalanced perceptions of their real health effects.

Sexually transmitted diseases (STDs), including human immunodeficiency virus (HIV) infection, continue to spread in the United States and worldwide. As the incidence of STD rises, so does the incidence of upper genital tract infections and ectopic (tubal) pregnancy, potential consequences of STD infection that can lead to infertility. Also, because more and more women are postponing childbearing until the middle or later years of their reproductive life, preventing infertility has become an important companion goal of postponing pregnancy.

To choose an appropriate method of contraception, individuals need to know whether they have a medical condition (e.g., high blood pressure) that might rule out the use of certain methods; whether their own behavior (e.g., having multiple sexual partners or smoking) contraindicates the use of a method; or whether the method itself could threaten their health.

To assess the health consequences of contraceptive choices among sexually active, fecund women who do not want to become pregnant, investigators compare the risks of pregnancy, infertility, heart disease, cancer, and death faced by women using various methods with those faced by women using no method. Because of the paucity of information from other countries, the assessment that follows is based on data primarily from the United States and the conclusions also pertain to the United States.

Preventing pregnancy

Pregnancy rates among women who use no contraceptive method are at least four times as high as the rate among those using any method (Trussell et al., 1990). Failure rates vary widely. The highest rates occur among typical users of periodic abstinence, withdrawal, or barrier and spermicide methods (10 to 22 percent become pregnant in the first twelve months of use), followed by users of the pill and the intrauterine device (IUD) (3 to 4 percent), and by women who rely on implants, injectables, or sterilization (less than 1 percent) (Harlap et al., 1991).

"So much of the [doomsday] rhetoric is simple-minded and incorrect, casually attributing any human problem to there being too many humans."

SAMUEL PRESTON
NATIONAL ACADEMY OF SCIENCES, 1985

"Those who would sacrifice a generation to realize an ideal are the enemies of mankind."

ERIC HOFFER
THE PASSIONATE STATE OF MIND, 1954

Women who use no method during their entire reproductive life span and who never have an induced abortion have far more births than women who use any of the contraceptive methods and have a birth every time they become accidentally pregnant (eighteen vs. five, respectively, or fewer) (Harlap et al., 1991). Likewise, among women who terminate all their pregnancies by induced abortion, those using no method of contraception have far more abortions than contraceptive users, including women who use the least effective methods (thirty-five vs. six, respectively, or fewer). Among women using the least effective methods—periodic abstinence, withdrawal, condoms, or spermicides—those who have an abortion every time they become pregnant have more pregnancies than those who give birth every time they become pregnant, because they would be exposed to the risk of a subsequent pregnancy much sooner than women who carry every pregnancy to term. However, regardless of how women resolve their pregnancies, use of even the least effective contraceptive results in many fewer pregnancies than use of no method.

Preserving fertility

Most women and men in the United States have more than one sexual partner during their lifetime. Two-thirds of all U.S. women who have ever had intercourse have had more than one partner. Many of them, especially young women, have more than one partner within a short time (Kost and Forrest, 1992). With each new sexual partner, a woman faces the risk of becoming infected with an STD.

Some STDs can cause upper genital tract infections—such as pelvic inflammatory disease (PID) or infections following pregnancy (whether it ends in spontaneous abortion, induced abortion, or birth)—that can damage a woman's reproductive organs and lead to ectopic pregnancy or tubal infertility. The more episodes of upper genital tract infection a woman has, the more likely it is that a subsequent pregnancy will be ectopic. Moreover, once a woman has experienced an ectopic pregnancy, it is more likely that subsequent pregnancies will be ectopic. Women who have had an ectopic pregnancy are likely to become infertile, and the risk of infertility rises quickly with increasing numbers of ectopic pregnancies.

Among women at low risk of STD infection, estimated rates of tubal infertility for those using any contraceptive method are lower than rates for women using no method (who have a high risk of pregnancy-related upper genital tract infections because of their large numbers of pregnancies). Among women at high risk of STDs, the contraceptive method used can have a significant effect on the risk of developing tubal infertility. For these women, rates of tubal infertility are lowest among users of barrier and spermicide methods and highest among those using the IUD, periodic abstinence, or no method (Harlap et al., 1991).

Protecting health

Pregnancy and childbirth, once major causes of mortality among women in the United States, are now much safer; however, they still account for 1 to 2 percent of all deaths each year among women aged fifteen to forty-four (National Center for Health Statistics, 1990). Ectopic pregnancy is the outcome with the greatest risk of death, and induced abortion the one with the least. Other pregnancy-related deaths are from giving birth, upper genital tract infections, and rare cancers associated with abnormal embryonic development (e.g., trophoblastic disease). By preventing pregnancy, contraceptives reduce the risk of such deaths. In many parts of the world where pregnancy and childbirth are still major causes of death, contraceptive use can have an even greater impact on the risk of maternal mortality.

Mortality rates among users of various methods differ according to the failure rate of each method; that is, methods with the highest failure rates have higher risks of death than those with lower failure rates. Women who have a contraceptive failure and choose to have an abortion face a lower risk of death than those who choose to give birth. Using no contraception carries the greatest risk of death, although choosing abortion rather than childbirth greatly reduces the risk.

In the United States, only a few deaths can be directly attributable to the contraceptive method (about one or fewer per 100,000 users; see Kost et al., 1991). Methods that carry such risks are oral contraceptives, long-acting hormonal methods, tubal sterilization, and vasectomy. The risk of death from a sterilization operation is a one-time risk to the person being sterilized (male or female). The method-related deaths for users of oral contraceptives and long-acting hormonal methods result from cardiovascular disease.

CARDIOVASCULAR DISEASE. Researchers have found that women who took oral contraceptives in the 1970s had an increased risk of cardiovascular disease (Sartwell and Stolley, 1982; Stadel, 1981a, 1981b). However, since the discovery of this association, use of the pill has become safer. The doses of estrogen and progestin have been markedly reduced, and available evidence suggests that compared with the earlier formulations, current preparations are associated with a lower risk of cardiovascular disease among users relative to that of earlier preparations (Croft and Hannaford, 1989; Porter et al., 1985; Vessey et al., 1989).

Oral contraceptive use has been shown to affect only certain cardiovascular diseases, such as myocardial infarction (heart attack), venous thrombosis and embolism (blood clots), and two kinds of strokes—those resulting from subarachnoid hemorrhage and those caused by thrombosis or embolism (nonhemorrhagic strokes). The risk of cardiovascular disease increases with age, partly because the prevalence of predisposing risk factors (e.g., high blood pressure, diabetes, and physical inactivity) increases with age. Smoking also increases the risk among all women, whether or not they use oral contraceptives.

The overall added risk of cardiovascular disease for users of oral contraceptives is very low in young women and nonsmokers who are healthy and who have no predisposing factors for the disease. It is now possible to identify many women who are at high risk for cardiovascular disease prior to their using the pill. For example, women older than age thirty-five who smoke and younger women who smoke heavily (25 or more cigarettes a day) are contraindicated for pill use because, for some cardiovascular diseases, oral contraceptive use adds to the already increased risk from smoking. Thus, such women can either choose another method or quit smoking (the latter option is likely to have other health benefits, as well). Women without such contraindications can be reassured that the likelihood of their developing a cardiovascular illness due to oral contraceptive use is extremely small.

Minipills, injectables, and implants contain no estrogen, and their daily doses of progestin are considerably lower than those found in combined oral contraceptives. For this reason, such progestin-only methods may have little effect on a user's risk of cardiovascular disease (Harlap et al., 1991). However, conclusive data on these effects are not yet available.

CANCERS. In the United States, cancers of the reproductive system—those affecting the cervix, ovaries, endometrium, or breasts—make up about 40 percent of all cancers diagnosed in women. Media reports of an association between oral contraceptive use and breast cancer have left millions of women wondering if their past or current use of the pill has endangered their health, or even their lives. Of all women aged fifteen to forty-four who have had intercourse, 79 percent have used oral contraceptives; about 25 percent of those women are current users (Forrest, 1990).

Cervical cancer is thought to be related, at least in part, to infection by certain strains of human papilloma virus, an STD. The risk of this cancer is related to the number of sexual partners a woman, or her partner, has had. Cervical cancer is more likely to be diagnosed among women older than thirty than among those who are younger; and in every age group, women who have never used barrier and spermicide methods are

THE PILL AND CANCER
What Are the Risks?

The full relationship between oral contraceptive use and breast cancer is still unclear. Among all women aged fifteen to fifty-four, the risk of a breast cancer diagnosis is the same among "ever-users" and "never-users." Furthermore, studies have shown that women who first use the pill at age twenty-five or older have the same rate of breast cancer diagnosis as women who never use it (Prentice and Thomas, 1987). Some studies have suggested that women who begin use of the pill in their adolescence or early twenties are more likely than those who begin use later to be diagnosed with breast cancer in their thirties and early forties. However, the evidence also suggests that at older ages, these women have lower rates of breast cancer than women who never used the pill (Paul et al., 1986; United Kingdom National Case-Control Study Group, 1989; Wingo et al., 1990).

Several explanations have been suggested for the apparent increase in the risk of breast cancer diagnosis among oral contraceptive users in the middle reproductive ages (25-34) and for the possible decrease in risk at older ages. Because pill users are screened for breast cancer more frequently than nonusers (Skegg, 1988), their breast cancers may be detected earlier. Another hypothesis is that the hormones in oral contraceptives accelerate the growth of an undiagnosed breast cancer (or of certain types of breast cancer) but do not cause its initial development. This effect would be consistent with the way pregnancy temporarily increases the risk of breast cancer (Bruzzi et al., 1988).

To put into perspective the pill's overall effect on the risk of cancers—ovarian, endometrial, and breast cancers combined—ever-users of the pill in each age group can expect fewer cancer diagnoses than never-users except at ages twenty-five to thirty-four, when women who have ever used oral contraceptives will experience nearly the same overall incidence of cancer as women who have never used the pill.

Overall, any pill-related increases in the risk of breast cancer are more than offset by corresponding decreases in ovarian and endometrial cancers, so women who have used oral contraceptives develop fewer cancers than women who have never used them. The difference between the two groups widens in the middle to late reproductive years as the incidence of ovarian and endometrial cancers rises.

— KATHRYN KOST

almost twice as likely as even occasional users of those methods to develop this cancer.

The risks of ovarian and endometrial cancer rise steadily with age, but the likelihood of being diagnosed with either of these cancers among women who have ever used the pill is about 30 to 80 percent less than the incidence among those who have never used it, depending on length of use; the risk is lowered by longer duration of pill use. In addition, the protective effect continues for many years after pill use ends (Harlap et al., 1991; Booth et al., 1989; La Vecchia et al., 1984; Schlesselman, 1989).

What, if any, bearing does the moral status of a rule have on its status as a law? To what extent, if any, should the legal system be used to enforce moral perspectives?

PAGE 432

Conclusion

As women pass through different stages of their reproductive life, each contraceptive method offers a somewhat different combination of risks and benefits, not only to their current well-being but also to their chances of being able to bear children and remain in good health in the future. As their needs, options, and preferences change over time, women must reevaluate their choice of contraceptive.

Physicians and other medical providers should take a more active role in helping both their female and male patients make contraceptive choices by initiating discussion of their childbearing aspirations, their sexual behavior, their individual and family health history, their health habits, and perhaps most important of all, their willingness and ability to use a particular method consistently and correctly. In addition, medical providers should encourage discussion of ongoing experience with a method in the event that it is no longer meeting the patient's needs. Individuals who have been educated about how current or future behavior might affect their health and influence the effects of a contraceptive method can make better-informed choices about their behavior and select methods that are better tailored to their own concerns and goals.

Three factors—multiple sexual relationships, smoking, and irregular or incorrect method use—have particularly strong effects on whether a woman will be able to reach her reproductive and health goals. A sexually active woman who does not want to become pregnant greatly increases her chances of maintaining good health if she and her partner use contraceptives consistently and follow some general guidelines for the selection of a method. Couples should use barrier and spermicide methods when their relationship is not mutually monogamous or when one of them has an STD (for protection against infection, infertility, and cervical cancer); use oral contraceptives at some time during the woman's reproductive years (for protection against ovarian and endometrial cancer); stay informed and aware of health conditions (such as high blood pressure) and behavior (such as smoking) that may contraindicate their use of particular methods; and rely on an extremely effective method once childbearing is completed.

Because pregnancy can affect women's health in numerous ways, the prevention of pregnancy has a significantly beneficial effect on women's health. Yet the virtual elimination of pregnancy-related complications by the most effective contraceptive methods—the pill, the IUD, long-acting hormonal methods, and sterilization—is a benefit often overlooked when the health effects of methods are considered.

— KATHRYN KOST

TOUCH NOT?

In the age of AIDS, ethicists ask what steps the state is morally obligated or allowed to take toward HIV-positive prostitutes and customers.

PROSTITUTION

While the term "prostitution" has been applied to various human activities, in contemporary industrialized societies it commonly refers to a practice in which a woman makes herself sexually available to a man for a fee or some form of material compensation. Since indiscriminate, nonamorous sexual activity is considered in many societies to be debasing to women, when women act in this way for material gain their sexual and economic behavior is regarded as a form of prostitution. Commercialized sexual transactions typically are highly stigmatizing for the women, and sometimes the men, who participate in them; the existence of such activities is often treated as a sign of personal, spiritual, and social corruption and decay. As a potent symbol of moral disorder, prostitution is commonly viewed as a threat to social cohesion and individual well-being. In other words, prostitution is seen to corrupt and defile both the social body and the physical human body. This association between prostitution and degeneration or disease informs many legal, political, and intellectual responses to prostitution.

Moral Questions

Some moral questions that prostitution poses can be raised, in general, about nonmarital and nonamorous sex. Does sexual activity outside marital and romantic social relationships degrade or harm the participants? Does it create harms for innocent third parties—for example, by contributing to the spread of sexually transmitted diseases, by weakening marital bonds or marriage as an institution, or by demeaning sexual activity? And does extramarital casual sexual activity inevitably conflict either with moral duties to loved ones or with some moral principle or ideal—such as universal human respect, faithfulness, honesty, or fairness?

Prostitution also raises moral questions pertaining to its social origins and consequences. Does prostitution reflect and reinforce the social subordination of women? Is prostitution produced and reproduced, in part, by social privileges based on race, ethnicity, class, and age? If prostitution is a function of the social dynamics of power and privilege, then is the prostitute's behavior determined by pernicious social forces rather than informed choice? Finally, the economic aspects of prostitution pose further ethical issues. Are prostitutes economically coerced and exploited by others? Does an organized practice that commercializes sex create a public danger or nuisance? And is the performance of a sexual act for money, without any other purpose or motive, morally base or reprehensible? Does it represent the encroachment of market forces into inappropriate areas of people's lives, leading to the domination of materialistic values over other values?

The existence of prostitution involving children or adolescents, both male and female, raises some different moral concerns. Since children and adolescents are

PROSTITUTION
Historical Perspectives

Women have engaged in materially compensated sexual activities with men with whom they had no ongoing social relationship (unlike mistresses or concubines) in a variety of social, cultural, and historical contexts. In ancient Babylon, for example, women offered sexual services to male temple patrons, and even to the gods, as part of a religious ritual aimed at promoting the fertility of nature (Lerner, 1986; Goldman, 1983). In ancient India, female children were recruited for temple prostitution, and were trained in dancing and music (Bullough and Bullough, 1987). In ancient Greece and China, women prostitutes, or courtesans, provided extramarital companionship, entertainment, and sexual services to men from the highest social classes. Chinese Taoists apparently believed that certain forms of sex could promote a man's health and longevity, and that these personal benefits could be derived from prostitutional sex (Bullough and Bullough, 1987).

Brothel prostitution, publicly sanctioned and regulated, was popular in many medieval European cities. The Christian church condemned prostitution but saw its existence as a necessary evil. Prostitution provided an outlet for sexual desires that, if left unfulfilled, could lead to more sinful sexual behaviors. While celebrating virginity and celibacy and condemning all nonmarital sexual acts, the church fathers nevertheless were sympathetic to the social and economic plight of prostitutes. They were viewed as capable of repentance and potentially worthy of salvation (Rossiaud, 1988; Otis, 1985).

In the contemporary industrialized world, prostitutes are active predominantly in urban centers and ply their trade in a variety of ways. In some Asian cities where tourism is promoted, prostitutes are typically associated with bars and hotels, which offer the prostitute's services to their customers (Truong, 1990). In the contemporary United States and parts of Europe, prostitutes solicit customers on city streets (streetwalkers), through houses of prostitution and massage parlors (brothel workers), and through escort services and private networks (call girls). In colonial Nairobi, Kenya, during the first part of the twentieth century, prostitutes predominantly served an indigenous colonial work force; they typically took customers to their own rooms, where they could sell other domestic comforts such as food and baths (White, 1990).

The existence of labor forms similar to contemporary prostitution in a variety of historical and cultural settings has led many theorists to view prostitution as an inevitable component of human civilization. Some theorists attribute prostitution to a natural male (or human) desire for unlimited sexual gratification in an economy where opportunities for sex are in scarce supply (Ericsson, 1980). Other theorists see prostitution not as an inevitable human practice but as one that is contingent upon forms of social stratification that arose historically in capitalist and patriarchal societies (Overall, 1992; Pateman, 1983). For these theorists, prostitution is an extreme form of the dehumanized social relations that exist in capitalist and patriarchal social orders. However, given the variety of human sexual activities, both religious and economic, to which "prostitution" refers, it is unlikely that a single causal account will explain its existence.

— LAURIE SHRAGE

P

PROSTITUTION

Legal Aspects

presumably incapable of fully understanding the significance and consequences of sexual activity, especially paid sexual activity, their participation in prostitution is likely to involve a substantially higher degree of coercion and exploitation than prostitution involving only adults. Sexual activity with preadult prostitutes may involve a nonconsenting partner or the lack of a partner's informed consent. Depending upon the age of the minor prostitute, it may endanger the prostitute's physical and mental health. In addition, child prostitution promotes the moral corruption of children.

Approximately 17% of men interviewed admitted to having paid for sex, though less than 1% said they had done so in the past 12 months.

NATIONAL OPINION RESEARCH CENTER, NORC, GENERAL SOCIAL SURVEY, 1996

A relatively small portion of prostitution involves male prostitutes (adults, children, and adolescents) with female and male customers. Since indiscriminate, nonamorous heterosexual sexual behavior by men typically receives less social disapproval, male prostitutes with female clients—like the male clients of female prostitutes—have received little attention from moralists, social theorists, and the criminal justice system. Male prostitutes who serve a predominantly gay male clientele are more frequently subjects of moral and social analysis. Theorists and social reformers who have considered this latter group typically raise the same moral questions about their behavior as those above concerning the activities of female and child prostitutes. In short, the gender biases that condition the commercial sex industry also condition intellectual and social responses to it.

Prostitution sometimes involves sexual behaviors that are socially stigmatizing even in noncommercial contexts: same-sex sex, interracial sex, sadistic and masochistic sex, group sex, and child-adult sex. Prostitution involving such behaviors raises moral questions that pertain to the origins, consequences, and acceptability of these behaviors. This entry will focus on the most common form of prostitution: heterosexual prostitution involving adult female prostitutes.

Legal aspects

In many countries across Europe, Asia, and America, prostitution is legally prohibited or heavily regulated. In the contemporary United States, prostitution is illegal everywhere except in certain counties of Nevada. Prostitution in these counties is limited to licensed brothels, and prostitutes are subject to mandatory health exams, curfews, and residence restrictions. In England, following the Wolfenden Report (1957), private acts of prostitution are legal, whereas any public manifestation of prostitution, such as the open solicitation of customers or advertising through public media, is illegal. In some countries, like Germany, prostitution has been decriminalized and, in certain cities, deregulated to some extent. Many groups, ranging from feminist organizations like the National Organization for Women to prostitute collectives like COYOTE (Call Off Your Old Tired Ethics), support removing criminal sanctions from the prostitute's work (Cooper, 1989; Matthews, 1986; Delacoste and Alexander, 1987).

Laws prohibiting prostitution usually aim to protect society against the spread of venereal disease, to prevent the erosion of a shared public moral order, to protect women both from exploitation by others and from self-inflicted harm, and to prevent the creation of a public nuisance. Yet antiprostitution laws may be ineffective in achieving these aims.

Many legal scholars have argued that the criminalization of prostitution neither eliminates nor reduces prostitution, but only increases the difficulty of imposing health safeguards and of monitoring and curtailing the spread of disease through commercial sex. Legalized prostitution would allow the state to introduce measures that might better protect the health of the prostitute and her customer, and thus the health of all citizens.

Others have argued that criminalizing prostitution to preserve a shared public moral order falsely presupposes the existence of homogeneous moral beliefs and attitudes regarding prostitution. For it may not be the case that all social groups or religions regard the sale of sexual services as inherently immoral. At least, it is incumbent upon those who justify the criminalization of prostitution in this way to demonstrate the existence of a shared moral perspective regarding prostitution. If this presupposition is false, then criminalizing prostitution may preserve values that are not widely held. Moreover, even if there were a public consensus regarding the moral status of prostitution, some theorists question whether it is the proper role of the state to attempt either to influence moral values or to inhibit private sexual conduct between consenting adults.

Some feminist theorists have argued that laws prohibiting prostitution do not protect women but, rather, render them more vulnerable to abuse from others. Laws against prostitution often lead to the harassment of poor women, who are frequently subject to the arbitrary and abusive application of such laws by local officials (Walkowitz, 1980; Cooper, 1989; Symanski, 1981). Moreover, such laws diminish the prostitute's ability to seek legal redress for harms she may suffer from clients or her associates. In addition, laws that aim to protect adult women from self-harm and exploitation by others may be overly paternalistic, since they assume that women are incapable of determining what is in their own best interest. Perhaps the only sort of laws that might protect women are those that criminalize the coercive and exploitative behaviors of the prostitute's customers and managers.

Finally, while the prevention of a potential public nuisance may provide a good reason for regulating prostitution, it does not support imposing laws to prohibit it. The nuisance to others that an organized commercial sex industry might pose can be contained by denying it access to noncommercial districts and by imposing normal standards for business operations on the industry.

In sum, unless there are better reasons than those considered here for applying criminal sanctions to people who participate voluntarily in acts of prostitution, outlawing prostitution may be neither feasible nor justifiable. Yet, like other labor forms and commercial operations that create risks for workers, customers, and society at large, prostitution could be regulated by the state. The regulations imposed could seek to protect the prostitute, as well as the customer and society. These regulations could especially seek to prevent large-scale commercial interests from drawing profits in ways that dehumanize or degrade workers (Matthews, 1986).

Prostitution, AIDS, and drugs

The current AIDS epidemic raises both new and old moral questions regarding prostitution. Is prostitution partly responsible for the spread of AIDS? What steps is the state morally obligated or allowed to take toward HIV-positive prostitutes and customers? Are HIV-positive prostitutes and customers who practice safe sex entitled to as much privacy as HIV-positive dentists or surgeons, for example? Do the moral rights of innocent third parties (such as the spouses, partners, and children of prostitutes and customers) outweigh the privacy rights of prostitutes and customers? What steps is the state morally obligated or permitted to take to protect prostitutes from being coerced into performing, or to prevent prostitutes and customers from consensually performing, sexual acts where the risk of HIV exposure is high?

While many prostitutes are HIV-positive, some researchers have argued that prostitutes are more likely to be exposed to HIV through intravenous drug use than through commercial sexual activities, in which they are more likely to take precautions (Delacoste and Alexander, 1987; Decker, 1987). Some have argued that since profits in prostitution depend upon the commercial sex industry's ability to offer services that are relatively safe, tolerating prostitution will promote safer sexual practices, especially those involving condom use. However, the profit motive may encourage some "safe" sexual practices that are highly problematic, such as the use of presumably virginal child prostitutes, or voyeuristic sex in which the voyeur pays to watch a couple engage in unsafe sex, and so on. In these cases, prostitution is safe only for the customer. In order to prevent commercial interests from overriding the rights of prostitutes and children, the state should regulate commercial sexual interactions, and stringently enforce criminal laws pertaining to the sexual violation and commercial exploitation of children.

Many researchers have observed and confirmed a significant correlation between women who work as prostitutes and women who are drug addicts or substance abusers (Goldstein, 1979). Does prostitution lead to drug use, or does drug use lead women to prostitution? What are the moral implications of these possible causal relationships? If prostitution characteristically leads women to substance abuse or drug dependency, then there may be some features of the work that encourage drug use. Theorists have identified a number of possible features of prostitution that may contribute to the prostitute's evolution into a substance abuser: Prostitutes operate in a social milieu where drug abuse is common; the work of a prostitute, or the social stigma it creates, requires mood alteration or mental escape; the commission of the criminal act of prostitution lowers one's inhibitions toward committing other criminal acts; and prostitutes are encouraged to become drug addicts by pimps who wish to control them. The features of prostitution that lead to substance abuse may be alterable, and thus social policies regarding prostitution should be designed to minimize these features.

Where substance abuse leads women to prostitution, the causes appear to be primarily economic. Women who are drug addicts may find prostitution sufficient or necessary to support an expensive drug habit. However, the fact that drug addiction can lead to prostitution does not seem to illuminate any morally relevant aspect of prostitution.

Prostitution as the subordination of women

Some feminist theorists have argued that prostitution involves not just the exploitation of female bodies or sexuality, but of female persons, because the product purchased or consumed in prostitution cannot be separated from the person who exchanges it—a separation that may be made in other kinds of trade (Pateman, 1983; Barry, 1979). Other feminists have argued that prostitution inevitably involves illegitimate forms of human subordination. On this view, prostitution has a value or purpose only when it is performed for someone socially privileged by gender, race, class, or age, and by someone socially disadvantaged by the same factors; thus when these illegitimate forms of social privilege disappear, so will prostitution (Overall, 1992). Yet there are cases where prostitution is performed by men for women (Karch and Dann, 1981), by working-class people for each other (White, 1990), and by white North Americans and Europeans for Asians (e.g., the "blond geishas" in Japan). Thus, in some cases the customer may be socially privileged by some factors while the prostitute is socially privileged by others. In short,

Veterans (37.1%) were three times as likely to have paid for sex as those who did not serve in the military.

NATIONAL OPINION RESEARCH CENTER, NORC, GENERAL SOCIAL SURVEY, 1996

See Also

Sexual Surrogates: Simply Technical Training?

"Prisons are built with stones of law, brothels with bricks of religion."

WILLIAM BLAKE
PROVERBS OF HELL, 1790

"Habit, n., a shackle for the free."

AMBROSE BIERCE
THE DEVIL'S DICTIONARY, 1906

prostitution appears desirable to some participants even when the social power and status of the prostitute and customer are, on balance, seemingly comparable.

In the United States, the commercial sex industry does appear to be organized by, and may ultimately serve to reproduce, cultural ideologies that place women in subordinate social roles (Shrage, 1989). Prostitution in this context reflects the cultural ideology that men have sexual needs that can be met by impersonal sexual encounters, and that while men benefit from heterosexual intercourse in these contexts, women are harmed and defiled. The composition of the prostitute work force also reflects racist and pernicious social myths about the sexuality of women of color (Shrage, 1992). While prostitution may not involve the subordination of women in all societies, in the contemporary United States and many similar industrialized parts of the world, it reflects beliefs that continue to promote the subordination of women.

Yet the commercialization of sex is neither a universal cause nor a symptom of the subordination of women. Rather, the degraded social position of women and the cultural myths that sustain it in a particular society can shape sex commerce into a practice that reflects and reinforces women's subordinate social status (Dominelli, 1986). Therefore, those who oppose the subordination of women should challenge not sex commerce but the cultural ideologies and customs that give it its historically specific form. This should involve devising social policies regarding trafficking in sex that challenge cultural myths regarding proper sexual and social roles for women and men. Moreover, social policies that economically empower women—especially single mothers—and reduce their level of financial dependence on others would also serve more directly to challenge the subordination of women than would the repression of sex commerce.

Some feminist prostitutes have argued that prostitution itself challenges the subordination of women. Since prostitution affirms a woman's right to control her own body, including the right to exploit it for economic gain, it challenges the notion that women are economically dependent on men (Pheterson, 1989). Yet, just as it is unlikely that prostitution inherently supports and reflects the subordination of women, so it is unlikely that prostitution inherently supports and reflects the social empowerment of women. In the United States, for example, prostitution may challenge deeply instilled stereotypes of women as nonproviders, but it reinforces the pernicious notion that it is a woman's primary function to satisfy men sexually.

Conclusion

Most of the moral questions about prostitution, and some of the medical and empirical concerns upon which they rest, can be answered only by studying particular cases of sex commerce. It is possible, then, that the moral status of prostitution in colonial Nairobi or ancient Babylon, for example, may be different from the moral status of an outwardly similar phenomenon in contemporary Asia. Moral theorists need to examine the cultural factors that shape sex into work, that form the provision of sex into an occupation, and that place the sex worker under the moral category of prostitute—a person who alienates from herself a basic human good for material gain. In some cases prostitution may involve illegitimate forms of human subordination and exploitation (for example, where child prostitutes or impoverished women are involved), and thus may approach something akin to rape—that is, coerced sex. In other cases, prostitution may occur between persons of comparable social status and means, as part of a voluntary and mutually satisfying arrangement. Moral theorists need to pay close attention to the social and cultural contexts in which prostitution occurs in order to isolate features that morally distinguish different cases. In this way we can explore and question the conceptualization of sex commerce in terms of the powerful metaphors of disease and degeneration.

— LAURIE SHRAGE

PUBLIC HEALTH AND THE LAW

LEGAL MORALISM AND PUBLIC HEALTH

Modern public health, which uses organized community effort, law, and regulation to save lives and prevent disease, has long been entangled with legal moralism, which uses the same measures to protect society against behavior that is viewed in some quarters as "offensive, degrading, vicious, sinful, corrupt, or otherwise immoral" (Schur and Bedau, 1974, p. 1). "Morals offenses" have "included mainly sex offenses, such as adultery, fornication, sodomy, incest and prostitution, but also a miscellany of nonsexual offenses" (Feinberg, 1973). Legal moralism has cultural and religious origins, but its deepest roots are in purity rituals codified in religious and secular codes (Douglas, 1966). Purity rituals are avoidance rituals designed to make the environment and the community safe from the threat of uncleanness and contamination and to promote social order. These codes governed diet, sexual conduct, bodily cleanliness, and avoidance of contamination.

In its most expansive expression legal moralism is

the belief that these behavioral codes, regulations, and legal proscriptions are foundational to a social order. To the moralist, drug taking, vice, crime, and sexual promiscuity not only harm the self and others but also threaten, through contagion and example, to loosen the bonds that hold society together. It is the connection between the proscribed conduct or practice and the theories about how the spread of this conduct threatens social order that so often results in the confusion of public health and moralism. Because moralism is often expressed in terms of public-health theories of contagion, it has proved difficult to separate the two modes of thought.

The belief that immorality is contagious also often includes the belief that immorality causes disease. Barbara Gutmann Rosenkrantz's authoritative history of public health in Massachusetts cites a review of Lemuel Shattuck's 1850 report on the health of the state, noting that the "sanitary movement does not merely relate to the lives and health of the community; it is also a means of moral reform. . . . The ultimate connection between filth and vice has been noted by all writers upon this subject" (Rosenkrantz, 1972, p. 2).

Moralism in public health arises when society or groups in society respond to a health crisis more by voicing objections to a social practice or to a group engaged in that practice than by rationally assessing the dangers of disease and the best ways to prevent its spread. The parallels between theories of disease causation found in public health and legal moralism are often challenged and overturned by scientific theories of disease causation. While public-health campaigns and officials have often addressed problems moralistically in the past, the long-term trend indicates a separation of the two ways of thinking. Moralism has also suffered attacks from religious groups that emphasize social justice or inwardness more than adherence to religious rules. Finally, moralism is challenged by the modern and postmodern tolerance of a wider range of sexual expression and by the spreading support for political liberties and rights of privacy for all citizens, even those accused of immoral practices.

Moralism's most potent threat to public health comes from the ways in which epidemics and moral dissolution are believed to be inextricably tied together. This entanglement makes the victims of new outbreaks of certain diseases seem a threat to society itself. It also leads to powerful drives to stigmatize and shame the epidemic's victims, in the use of legislation and regulation to invoke shame and public denunciation for a category of persons or in what have been called "status degradation ceremonies" (Garfinkel, 1956). The current struggle in the fight against acquired immunodeficiency syndrome (AIDS) is the best-known contemporary example of the confusion between moralism and public health.

Thus, the purpose of the policies of the United States in incarcerating prostitutes during World War I was not just to prevent the spread of syphilis and venereal disease but also to shame and punish a class of individuals and to close and solidify the ranks of a nation going to war (Brandt, 1987). This moral campaign of imprisonment took priority over the use of new medical treatments for syphilis and gonorrhea, which, while still primitive, were surely more effective.

Modern public-health problems, especially those of a contagious or epidemic nature, provide a constant temptation for legislators, health officials, and the public to confuse the ends of preventing harm to individuals and communities and of proscribing immorality. Yet it would be wrong to conclude that all proscriptions of a practice or behavior are tantamount to moralism. Moralism and social disapproval are not the same thing, even though the latter may be an echo of the former. Social disapproval or even indignation about a practice remains a potent ally of many public-health campaigns.

Public health and alcohol policy

Legal moralism has played a prominent role in alcohol policy, particularly in movements to prohibit all drinking in the United States, in England, and in the Nordic countries. The history of alcohol policy, more than that of most public-health problems, reveals the difficulty in separating health issues from moralizing claims. It also reveals how some of the ways we seek to avoid moralism can be counter to science and to the health and safety of the public.

In the United States, Prohibition, or the outlaw of the manufacture and sale of alcoholic beverages, was enforced from 1917 until 1933. The Prohibition movement is a fascinating intermingling of progressive and scientific thinking, moralism, and religious fundamentalism. For example, the Progressive period in U.S. history (roughly 1890 to 1920) was not just a period when the states began to expand their powers over child labor, over the working conditions of adults, or of assuring safe food and water by strengthening the regulatory power of the states over private property; it was also a period that witnessed the rise of movements to protect the decency and purity of the public through antipornography legislation, crackdowns on prostitution (especially during World War I), and American Prohibition (Brandt, 1987).

There is little doubt that the various reform movements that culminated in the passage of the Prohibition amendment brought to the nation's attention a social problem (drunkenness, the saloon, and an overly powerful liquor interest) that demanded state and fed-

"The manufacture, sale or transportation of intoxicating liquors . . . for beverage purposes is hereby prohibited."

FROM AMENDMENT XVIII TO THE CONSTITUTION OF THE UNITED STATES, 1919

"Drinking makes such fools of people, and people are such fools to begin with that it's compounding a felony."

ROBERT BENCHLEY

LIQUOR LAWS

"Legal moralism" has been a strong force in public policies on alcohol, as during Prohibition in the U.S. from 1919 to 1933.

"The eighteenth article of amendment to the Constitution of the United States is hereby repealed."

FROM AMENDMENT XXI TO THE CONSTITUTION OF THE UNITED STATES, 1933

eral legislation. Also, the record shows clearly that the results of Prohibition, measured solely in public-health terms, were sharply reduced overall consumption of alcohol and related steep declines in serious public-health problems like cirrhosis, admittance to public hospitals for alcohol-related disorders, and the like (Moore and Gerstein, 1981; Beauchamp, 1980).

The strong secular and progressive side to the movement for Prohibition saw the saloon as a great social problem, one that undermined the public health and safety and promoted domestic violence and crimes against women. Both the movements for women's suffrage and the movement against slavery frequently were headed by leaders who also advocated Prohibition. Yet this began to change in the last decade of the nineteenth century. The women's movement had focused its energies on winning suffrage, and the movement against slavery had long since been replaced by Reconstruction. During the concluding decades of the agitation for Prohibition, the first two decades of the twentieth century, support for Prohibition came primarily from Protestant churches; national Prohibition's justification shifted more and more toward the moralistic claim that drink was the root of most of society's evil. (Moralism is often characterized by inflated claims of the evils or dangers from a substance or a practice, even in very small quantities or isolated and scattered acts.) The intertwining of moralism and public policy, especially for alcohol and drug taking, seems more common in nations where fundamentalist forms of Protestantism that stress adherence to religiously sanctioned behaviors are widespread, or in Muslim nations, where similar fundamentalism obtains; Catholic societies have never had successful Prohibition movements (although temperance movements are found in Ireland).

The backlash to Prohibition produced theories of alcoholism that sought both to deny its moralistic forebears and to establish a new and scientific theory of causation, called the disease concept of alcoholism. This was the belief that alcoholism was caused by an inability to control drinking. In parallel fashion, and also to separate itself from a discredited past, the new alcoholism movement denied the public-health benefits of Prohibition, and as late as the 1960s leading national experts claimed that Prohibition caused people to drink more. The links between what a society drinks generally and the level of alcohol problems were viewed as part of a neoprohibitionist agenda.

The attempt to purge society of moralistic remnants of Prohibition has often been met with surprises. For example, there were strong drives to prohibit alco-

LEGAL MORALISM
Smoking and Public Health

At the turn of the twentieth century, smoking was treated as morally offensive. Churches proscribed cigarette smoking and urged public action. But the long-term popularity of smoking spread too quickly, and the campaign was eventually abandoned. Soon smoking was regarded as cosmopolitan and modern. Cigarette smoking rates grew and became widely and culturally approved (Warner, 1986). In the 1950s epidemiological studies appeared in the United States and England noting the link between smoking and lung cancer and the possible links with heart disease. The U.S. Surgeon General issued a widely discussed report compiling very strong and extensive research suggesting that smoking was one of the most lethal hazards of our times.

The social climate against smoking began to turn in the late 1960s and 1970s. Antismoking sentiment rose, and cigarette advertising on television was banned. The risks of smoking for third parties was noted. Communities and entire states began to legislate against smoking in public places. Higher taxes on cigarette smoking were advocated. Smoking rates in most industrial societies fell, but most impressively in the United States. This sharp decline is not only due to the extensive public discussion devoted to the hazards of smoking but also to the growing sense of social and even moral disapproval of smoking by the larger society. This social disapproval was sometimes seen as a resurgence of moralism. But there is scant evidence that the strong current of disapproval against smoking adds up to moralism.

— DAN E. BEAUCHAMP

hol in Norway, Sweden, and Finland during the 1920s and 1930s. Only Sweden avoided Prohibition, in a narrow national referendum vote. In Finland, during the late 1960s and 1970s, the drive to eliminate the rural remnants of their national prohibition legislation of the 1930s led to a sharp relaxation of drinking laws throughout society and the elimination of prohibition in rural areas. The experts believed that restrictions actually encouraged drinking of distilled beverages in unsocialized ways and that by eliminating prohibition, drinking would actually decrease. Yet the measures to liberalize drinking were followed by steep increases in drinking rates and associated problems such as public drunkenness (Beauchamp, 1980). Subsequently, state authorities and their advisers retreated from a too-uncritical relaxation of drinking legislation, shifting the justification for alcohol policy more toward a public-health model that accepted limits on all drinking as a necessary part of a sound policy and as not necessarily moralistic.

Western democracies during the 1970s and 1980s witnessed declines in drinking rates, attributed by experts to a growing cultural conservatism and a widening awareness of the public-health consequences of heavy drinking and high levels of per capita consumption. This new period was likely also solidified by the fact that heavy drinking became socially and even morally undesirable, just as smoking became morally undesirable. While drunkenness and addiction were still viewed less punitively, the public began to register its strong disapproval of heavy drinking, especially when it posed risks to others, such as in drinking and driving, or any drinking at all by teenagers. More broadly, the era when drinking itself was not seen as the problem was replaced with a period in which all drinking remains somewhat under a public-health cloud. The evidence that some forms of drinking might promote a healthier heart has caused that cloud to lift only a little.

Moralism and the AIDS epidemic

As Allan Brandt notes, the battle against venereal diseases in the first decades of the twentieth century and the rise of AIDS more recently give evidence that moralism remains a powerful element in the social construction of society's definition of these diseases (Brandt, 1987). Early in the twentieth century, syphilis was a symbol of a "society characterized by a corrupt sexuality. Venereal disease has typically been used as a symbol of pollution and contamination, [and of] . . . a decaying social order. Venereal disease makes clear the persistent association of disease with dirt and uncleanness as well" (Brandt, 1987, p. 5).

The most serious challenge to modern public health by legal moralism entered with the AIDS epidemic and HIV-related diseases. Because anal sex and frequent sex with multiple partners heightens the risk of transmission of the HIV virus and because intravenous drug use also seriously elevates the risk of infection from contaminated needles, legislation that seeks to regulate these behaviors—which are widely proscribed in many states—is always open to the charge of moralism.

Early in the epidemic in the United States, bathhouses frequented by homosexual patrons became targets of public-health regulations. Many in the gay community charged that the measures were aimed less

"If the headache would only precede the intoxication, alcoholism would be a virtue."

SAMUEL BUTLER

See Also
AIDS

PUBLIC HEALTH AND THE LAW

Legal Moralism and Public Health

"I have taken more out of alcohol than alcohol has taken out of me."

WINSTON CHURCHILL

at fighting the epidemic than at proscribing homosexuality. These advocates argued, quite plausibly, that the regulations would have little impact on the course of the epidemic in San Francisco or New York, the two cities where conflicts primarily arose. This was because the bathhouses were the site of only a fraction of the proscribed behaviors. Advocates also argued that city officials and state public-health authorities had caved in to political pressures (Bayer, 1991b).

The same charge of moralism and discrimination was also brought when public-health officials attempted to introduce methods of identifying the sexual partners of those who were AIDS victims, or when state medical societies sought legislation to make AIDS and HIV diseases reportable to state health authorities (Bayer, 1991b). (All states require private physicians to report certain communicable diseases to state health officials.) Ronald Bayer, in his book Private Acts, Social Consequences (1991b), has provided the best chronicle of the clash between public-health legislation and the civil libertarians defending AIDS victims. As Bayer says, "These two abstractions, liberty and communal welfare, are always in a state of tension in public health policy" (1991b, p. 16).

It is likely, however, that the AIDS epidemic has permanently altered the landscape of public-health policy, and not just in the United States. No longer will it be possible to easily equate public health only with the use of powers to restrict power and liberty to promote the public health or to see the realms of public health and individual liberty as radically distinct. The growing awareness is that a sound public-health policy requires more than restrictions on liberty and property to promote the communal welfare. It also may require the expansion of private liberties and rights for groups suffering social discrimination based on moralism.

— DAN E. BEAUCHAMP

See Also

The Idea of Eugenics: Three Strands and Genetic Studies: Under the Shadow of Eugenics

R

RACE AND RACISM

In the biomedical sciences of the United States and in their wider cultural context, ideas about race and gender play a prominent but unacknowledged role. Despite their apparent universality, concepts of race and gender vary over time and place. Different beliefs about race and gender, and their social results, are found in other cultures past and present. Both are, in fact, cultural constructions, one culture's folk theories of human biological variation. The great variability to be found in racial and gender notions is indicative of their local cultural construction.

Biological and behavioral assertions concerning race are without empirical validity. After decades of research, largely in anthropology, the social and cultural bases of racial conceptions have become clear. Because "race" is a folk-culture concept, it is here used in its ethnographic connotation. While many, perhaps most, cultures of the world do not hold racial theories, such theories are important to consider in discussions of biomedical ethics, especially in the United States. Given the demonstrably negative social, psychological, and health results of the perpetuation of the invidious distinctions represented by racial (and gender) identities and the antipathy generated by their stereotypes, the continued use of racial identities in biomedical work may be said to represent a serious ethical, as well as a biomedical research, problem.

Historical constructions of race

Race is one of a number of popular cultural conceptions about human variability. The Western concept was developed in its present scientific and related lay versions largely in the nineteenth century (Barkan, 1992; Gossett, 1965; Naroll and Naroll, 1973; Stocking, 1968). At its most abstract level, race is an explanation for observed human variation; people differ in appearance because they belong to different races. Behavior is also implicated; people behave differently because they belong to different races. Racism is a set of negative beliefs held by individuals or groups with respect to a population thought to be biologically distinct. Such beliefs about fundamental biological differences came late to the Western world, but not as a result of scientific progress.

The ancients—whether the civilizations of Nubia and Egypt or the later Minoan, Mesopotamian, Greek, and Roman civilizations—held no beliefs about essential human biological or racial differences. There was recognition that people differed in appearance, language, custom, and even ethics (MacIntyre, 1966), but such differences were not considered reflections of immutable, biological differences among humans. Nor could there have existed assertions that biology determined behavior, for most of these civilizations were composed of a variety of physical and cultural types in various stages of assimilation to a tit-

"The so-called white races are really pinko-grey."

E. M. FORSTER
A PASSAGE TO INDIA, 1924

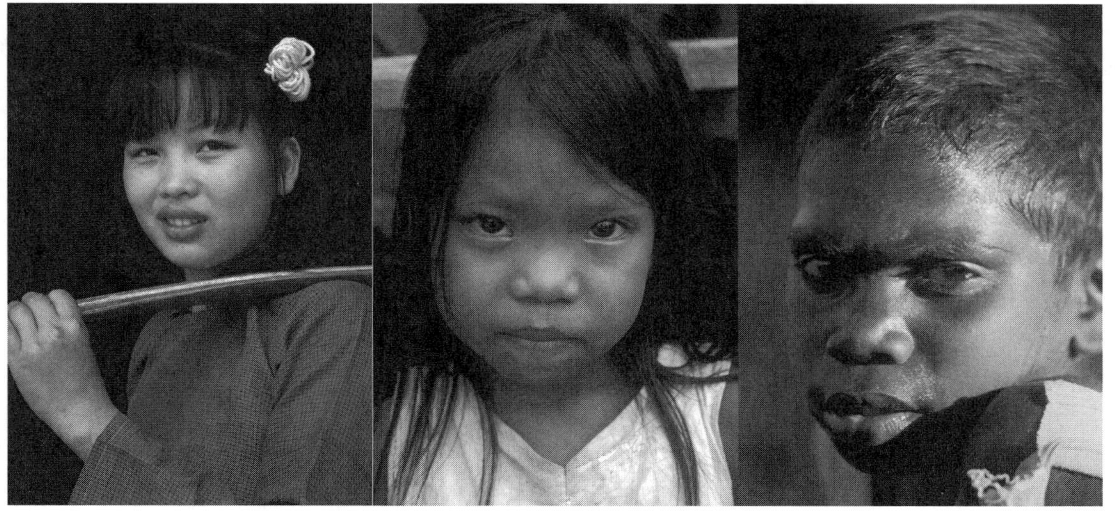

VARIATIONS

The concept of race (like that of gender) is largely a social construction; "race" as we know it today did not exist until the mid-1700s.

RACE AND RACISM

Historical Constructions of Race

"If we cannot end now our differences, at least we can help make the world safe for diversity."

JOHN F. KENNEDY
ADDRESS AT AMERICAN UNIVERSITY, WASHINGTON, D.C., 1963

◆ **race**
a family, tribe, people, or nation belonging to the same stock; an actually or potentially interbreeding group within a species; a division of mankind possessing traits that are transmissible by descent and sufficient to characterize it as a distinct human type.

ular ethnic identity (e.g., Sherwin-White, 1967). Were this not the case, the ancient empires could not have expanded their numbers through the recruitment of physically and culturally different peoples, for they would have thought them fundamentally different and nonassimilable.

An important step in the development of the notion of race is to be found in the work of the Swedish botanist and taxonomist Carolus Linnaeus (1707-1778). Linnaeus built upon earlier notions of "species," distinct groups of living things that cannot interbreed. Linnaeus proposed a classification comprising six human "groups"; he did not use the term "race." These human groups were understood as neither pure nor (biologically) stable; they were not represented as distinct species. Such an assertion would have been contradicted at the time by considerable evidence of interbreeding of Europeans and other groups. Such empirical evidence was later ignored in the West.

The French naturalist and founder of invertebrate paleontology George Louis Buffon (1707-1788) introduced the term "race" into the biological literature in 1749. The term then did not refer to distinct human groups with separate origins or biologies (Montagu, 1964). Buffon's and Linnaeus's early reflections on human difference regarded such differences, correctly, as representing variations of a single species.

In the eighteenth and nineteenth centuries, English and German philosophy and science began the construction of ideas of fundamental, incommensurate biological differences dividing human groups (Barkan, 1992; Boas, 1940; Gould, 1981). While evolutionist views of monogenesis (a theory of a single origin of all humans) replaced polygenesis (a theory of multiple, separate origins) and creationist views (those based on religious beliefs and not on investigations of the natural world) in Europe, nineteenth-century theories were largely alike in expressing "racist" sentiments, though the sentiments were not recognized as such. Triumphant nineteenth-century evolutionism fitted well in racist science.

Monogenecists assigned to non-Europeans fates of early separation from a "main" line of Europeans. Jean-Baptiste Lamarck (1744-1829) suggested that differences among human groups around the world were to be attributed to the inheritance of acquired characteristics. He implicated the role of the environment in evolutionary change, although he misconstrued the mechanism of biological change.

Non-Europeans, and many eastern and southern Europeans, were believed to have a common origin by many western European scholars, but were seen as less evolved. Some were said to be little different from non-human primates (Barkan, 1992; Stocking, 1968). And some ethnic groups of western Europe created "racial" alliances. English historians of the nineteenth century repeatedly referred to the "rational and freedom-loving" character of the English as racial traits of the Anglo-Saxon, believed to be a branch of the "German race" (Gossett, 1965). As with the Nazi "race science" of the next century, the notion of the German race excluded most people commonly regarded in the United States as belonging to a "white race" (e.g., the French and other circum-Mediterranean people, Celtic ethnics, the Slavic people) as well as people from what are commonly regarded as other "races" in U.S. ideology—Asians, Africans, and Native Americans.

In England, Sir Francis Galton (1822-1911), the father of statistical manipulation, lent both ideas and methods to racial theories. He coined the term "eugenics," and conceived of this new "science" as a program of "racial" improvement. The idea of group biological improvement was carried to horrendous extremes by Nazi "hygienists." Galton's work on head size and intelligence lent credence to later racist work in the United States as well, such as that of physician Robert Bean of Virginia. His work, in 1906, purportedly showed that parts of the brain were of different sizes in "Whites and Negroes" (in Gould, 1981). He also claimed to have found measurable differences in males and females and between higher and lower classes. His interpretations and biased readings, soon disproved (Gould, 1981), showed the affinity of the ideas of racism, sexism, and elitism in the United States that are also apparent in English science.

Sir Cyril Burt, dean of twentieth-century educational psychology in England, studied twins during the first half of the twentieth century. He purported to show that twins raised apart had the same IQ. It appears he sought scientific proof for the English folk notion that nature determined human abilities such as intelligence. As a consequence, his views were widely received for decades and influenced the establishment of national examinations. The examinations were used to limit the educational opportunities of millions of young people in Britain. In the 1970s, it was discovered that the late scientist had, in fact, fabricated most of his data. He had also fabricated his long-time research assistants, who supposedly collected most of the data, as well as his coauthors (Gould, 1981). The advocates of nature over nurture suffered a heavy blow when this key body of literature was discredited.

In the United States, a multicultural society usually referred to as "multiracial," Burt's elitist arguments were converted to racist (and sexist) theories by his students, psychologists such as Hans Jurgen Eysenck and Jensen (Gould, 1981), as well as others (Fausto-Sterling, 1992). Research aimed at showing that African-Americans and other "minorities" were intrinsically less intelligent than the generic "White race." Within

"RACE SCIENCE" Bad Science Breeds Social Control

The Nazi "race science" of the 1930s reverted to nineteenth-century polygenesis to explain differences among racial groups and to assert its group's alleged superiority (Montagu, 1964). Some Germans were likewise seen as unfit; they were the disabled, the mentally ill, and the homosexual. In contemporary German society, popular and medical beliefs still express the model of mental illness that considers the mentally ill to be biologically different from "normal" people (Townsend, 1978).

As is evident, both English and German cultures exhibit biological theories of human difference. A brief historical look suggests that the ideas of these two cultures are related. In both systems, differences are held to be intrinsic and groups are hierarchically ranked, allegedly in terms of abilities. In the relatively isolated society of England, the Germanic notion of inherent differences and similarities based upon shared "blood" was doubtless introduced by invading Germanic tribes in the fifth century. The idea remained but was applied to internal social differences within England. This focus transformed the theory of difference based upon blood into the English notion of "breeding" that was and is applied to members of the British (which includes the Celtic peoples) social system. It produced Britain's rigid class systems wherein abilities are said to be differentially inherited by those differing in breeding. This conception of inborn qualities then serves to justify the respective social positions of society's members.

— ATWOOD D. GAINES

each group, moreover, women were said to be less capable than men. Many flaws appear in this sort of research. One of the major problems is the fact that social labels, such as White and Black, were used to make genetic arguments; the arguments were flimsy because they regularly excluded from consideration profound differences in the social and educational experience of the members of the various social categories. This was done in order to arrive at (prejudged) conclusions of inborn racial differences.

A similar idea concerning mental illness was developed in German psychiatry in the mid-1800s. The leader of nineteenth-century German psychiatry, Wilhelm Griesinger, adopted a biological definition of mental disorders. His dictum was that "mind diseases are brain diseases" (Gilman, 1985). The idea that mental illness was based in biology and not social environment was actually borrowed from German philosophy, which in turn had taken the idea from popular German culture. Griesinger passed on this popular prejudice in his psychiatric science to a follower, Emile Kraepelin. Kraepelin became the twentieth century's father of biological psychiatry and the creator of a racially based "comparative psychiatry" (Gaines, 1992a; Gilman, 1985). This influential figure made the case for the biological basis of major mental diseases such as schizophrenia. His ideas were greatly influential on Nazi and contemporary U.S. biological psychiatry (Barkan, 1992; Gaines, 1992c; Gilman, 1985).

The critique of scientific racism

Evolutionists explained the increasing knowledge of human diversity in biological terms (Barkan, 1992; Gossett, 1965). The allegedly different developmental levels of various societies were said to indicate inferior inborn abilities in the societies' people compared with the usual apex of evolution found in (western) Europe. Eastern Europe, not a direct heir to the Renaissance, has been considered marginal in much of western European thought and totally alien and inferior in Germanic thought. History tells us, however, that Europe was the last of the world's areas to develop the hallmarks of civilization, hallmarks largely borrowed from others who were later alleged to be less evolved than (western) Europeans.

ANTHROPOLOGICAL ARGUMENTS. Racist evolutionist ideas, and many not evolutionist, permeated much of medicine, psychology, biology, and other sciences in Europe and the United States at the beginning of the twentieth century. Among the first to lead a concentrated and protracted attack on scientific racism was Franz Boas (1858-1942). A German immigrant, Boas was the foremost anthropologist of his time and the founder of U.S. anthropology. Among many other things, Boas's research demonstrated the plasticity of the human form and the overlap in measurements (anthropometry) of anatomical features previously asserted to be unique to specific racial groups. These findings flatly contradicted the conceptions of races as stable, unchanging, and distinct physical types. Time has continued to enhance our understanding of the enormous plasticity of human biology, a biology so changeable that it has produced all the variations in the human form found in the world in less than 180,000 years.

Boas himself demonstrated how rapidly biology can change, as well as the nonempirical basis of racial differences, by showing that very different anthropomet-

"I have a dream that my four little children will one day live in a nation where they will not be judged by the color of their skin, but by the content of their character."

MARTIN LUTHER KING, JR.
SPEECH AT CIVIL RIGHTS MARCH ON WASHINGTON
1963

◆ **racism**
a set of negative beliefs held by groups with respect to a population thought to be biologically distinct.

See Also
Genetics and Racial Minorities

ric readings could be obtained from the children of immigrants to the United States when compared with their parents. The cause was the change in environmental factors, especially nutrition. These measurements indicated, according to the current, specific racial measurement norms, that people in the same family appeared to belong to completely different racial groups (Boas, 1940).

Boas also advanced fatal arguments against notions of the relatedness of race to behavior. He showed that so-called races did not exhibit distinct religious, linguistic, or general cultural patterns. People of a variety of races spoke the same language and practiced the same religion. And members of the same race spoke different languages, held different religious beliefs, and otherwise exhibited distinct cultures. Race could not be shown to determine even major forms of human behavior (Boas, 1940; Stocking, 1968). Many of the positions advanced by Boas remain the most powerful antiracist arguments. It is remarkable that he began his assault on scientific racism before 1910, a time when blatantly racist statements were common in science and in the White House (see Brandt, 1985).

Eugenics, a political, economic, and social policy that espouses the reproduction of the "fit" over the "unfit" and discourages the birth of the "unfit."

PAGE 301

Evolutionary schemes were soon generally recognized as based on biased conjecture. There were no empirical bases for the evolutionary stages of Karl Marx, Herbert Spencer, Edward Tylor, or any of the other evolutionary theorists. Boas replaced evolutionist theorizing with the study of the historical diffusion of cultural traits. Historical diffusionism based its arguments on empirical evidence from all the branches of anthropology, physical anthropology, linguistics, archaeology, and sociocultural anthropology as well as from history. Such evidence was used to demonstrate that the current cultural (or physical) features or organization of any group were a result of contact and borrowing from other groups it had encountered. Of less influence in cultural change were innovation and creativity. Cultural arrangements, then, had more to do with a particular history of contact than with innate abilities related to alleged evolutionary stages. This understanding replaced a notion of the evolution of a single human general culture with an understanding of particular cultures' histories.

Evolutionists rank people and cultures from low to high, worst to best. Implicit in evolutionist thinking is the idea of progress, the idea that things are changing for the better. Evolution and progress are unrelated in fact and must be kept separate. Evolutionary change is simply descent with modification; there is no implication of improvement or superiority of later social or biological forms over earlier ones.

But evolutionists depicted some groups, such as Africans, as being near the apes because the groups were perceived as different. They were said to resemble nonhuman primates, such as chimpanzees and apes, who were described as having thick lips, curly hair, and dark skin. This representation has persisted despite the fact that nonhuman primates actually have straight hair covering their rather white skin and are totally lacking lips. That is, nonhuman primates exhibit precisely the characteristics claimed by Europeans as indicative of their own racial superiority.

While racism is still common, though less so than earlier in the twentieth century in the United States, evolutionist notions containing the idea of progress persist. A counter to these ideas is one of Boas's most enduring contributions: his articulation of the notion of "cultural relativism," which is not a theory but a descriptive reaction to wide experience with other cultures. While evolutionists ranked people and cultures, anthropologists after Boas came to see them in relative terms; cultures were not better or worse than one another, they were simply different. One could not judge a culture using values from another; cultures must be evaluated using internal, not external, criteria. Relativism has become a central tenet of anthropology, the science of culture.

Biomedical sciences often evidence not the relativism of Boas but the hierarchical evaluative thinking indicative of evolutionism. An implicit ranking system appeared in medicine and persists in notions of defects afflicting groups of people. Historians of medicine show that this idea was disseminated by medicine's association of specific illness states with specific ethnic groups (called races) and/or genders (Chesler, 1972; Gilman, 1985; Pernick, 1985). This was but one of many techniques for the pathologization of often fictitious differences.

Difference from an implicit standard, that is, Anglo, male, adult (Gaines, 1992a; Gilman, 1985), in medical and psychiatric thought has been represented as problematic, dangerous, exceptional, pathological, defective, weak, vulnerable, and/or requiring "special" treatment (Gaines, 1992a; Osborne and Feit, 1992). Ultimately, the idea communicated is that culturally defined "others"—in the United States, non-European ethnics, women, and children—are simply, and inherently, "not normal" (Ehrenreich and English, 1973; Gilman, 1985).

One significant problem with the theories about natural racial groups is the fact that the precise number of them has never been agreed upon. Throughout the last century and a half, enumerations of groups said to constitute races fluctuated from author to author. Indeed, the number of racial groups is still changing. A recent example is the creation, starting in the early 1980s, of a Hispanic race.

The dynamics of the numbers of races should not be surprising given that the boundaries created to distinguish among the various groups have no empirical bases. Such discriminations are everywhere the arbitrary choice of an author (Gould, 1981; UNESCO, 1969; Stocking, 1968). The lack of fixed criteria for differentiation is reflected in the changes over time in racial labels of individuals in modern health statistical records (Hahn, 1992), in local and personal history (Domínguez, 1986), and in the ever-changing number of races, a number that varies somewhere between one race and three hundred. The correct number is one.

THE HETEROGENEITY OF RACE. Analyses of biogenetic differences of human groups lead to the recognition of a great variety of characteristics, most of which are shared in various proportions. Local configurations of traits (height, color, etc.) produce a huge number of distinguishable groups. On the African continent, there are about one thousand biologically distinguishable groups, as opposed to races (Hiernaux, 1970). Human groups are not divisible into groups that exhibit unique, nonoverlapping physiological characteristics. Differences in biology are always local differences that are characteristic of a local inbreeding population. What is seen as normal human biology also changes from culture to culture (see Kuriyama, in

"MELTING POT"

Racial Theories in the United States

Most observers in the United States, whether lay or scientific, believe that observation of racial differences and racial antipathy has existed since time immemorial, being an understandable outcome of the encounter of dissimilar social groups. However, this is understandable only in a specific cultural context and is not an accurate rendering of the history of cultural contact.

The deleterious effect of "racism" on perception and cognition is obvious if the ancestry of U.S. racial groups is examined. Misrepresentations appear in scientific research as well as the popular media. The two—research and media—engage in a kind of cultural conversation that confirms the reality of race. An objective look at the ancestry of members of the major groups in the United States reveals race as a fatal conceptual problem in public health and medical research.

In the United States, most people labeled by self and others as Native Americans are biologically part European; in many cases, they are largely so. Many such individuals also have West African ancestry. Virtually all American "blacks," or African-Americans, are biologically part European. In many if not most cases, more of their ancestors came from Europe than from West Africa. Quite commonly, African-Americans also have Native American ancestry (Blu, 1980; Domínguez, 1986; Gaines, "Medical/Psychiatric Knowledge," in Gaines, 1992a; Hallowell 1976; Naroll and Naroll, 1973; Watts, 1981).

All classificatory whites claiming multigenerational descent in the South can be shown to have West African ancestry and, very likely, Native American ancestry (Domínguez, 1986; Hallowell, 1976; Naroll and Naroll, 1973). This is not surprising since most of the colonists who settled in the U.S. South were single males. The relatively few unmarried females were generally of lower status and in long-term bond service. Without Native American and African women, European males in the South could not have had offspring. In the move westward into what was northern Mexico, where the Spanish had settled with Native Americans a century before the English came to the East Coast, one finds again that those "Americans" who went were primarily males from the South and the East. For this reason, the descendants of these early settlers in the West (settlers who were themselves illegal immigrants because this was northern Mexico) are today of mixed ancestry, although this is not publicly known.

Another distortion relates directly to Latinos, Mexicans, and other groups of "Hispanics." Latinos are descendants of western European, Native American, and West African peoples. This mixture is what the term "la raza" means: a "race" born of a mixture of elements. Because many Mexicans are actually Indians or partly so, the difference between Native Americans (many of whom are Spanish-speaking) and Hispanics is often only nationality, a matter of sociolegal definition and not biology. In other instances, Hispanics have no Native American ancestry but do have West African along with their western European ancestry. In many Latino groups (such as those of Venezuela and Puerto Rico), West African ancestry is virtually universal.

Despite the very definition of Latino as people of mixed cultural and biological ancestry, this language group has been homogenized in the scientific literature and, in the 1980s, became a discrete biological group, a "race" (Gaines, "Medical/Psychiatric Knowledge," in Gaines, 1992a; Hahn, 1992). In reality, the groups seen as discrete in the United States—white, African-American, Native American, and Latino—are not at all biologically distinct. Indeed, individuals in any of the categories may embody the same mixture of ancestors as do individuals in the others. The difference in the group to which one is assigned depends not on biology but on local context and social history. These groups represent social categories that are unstable and without common biogenetic content.

— ATWOOD D. GAINES

R

RACE AND RACISM

Cultural Systems of Racial Classification beyond the United States

> *"Racism is the dogma that one ethnic group is condemned by nature to congenital inferiority and another group is destined to congenital superiority."*
>
> RUTH FULTON BENEDICT
> RACE: SCIENCE AND POLITICS, 1940

Leslie and Young, 1993). Just as the cultural elements exhibited by individuals of ethnic groups vary, so does the biology of members of so-called races.

The central problem for racial classifications is that there exist no intrinsically significant human features. Cultures have selected specific features as worthy of concern and hence as criteria of inclusion or exclusion. The selection of any one trait—such as skin, hair, or eye color; body hair; height; weight; religion; or place of birth—as a criterion of group exclusion or inclusion is, by definition, arbitrary. The selected characteristics represent historical attributions of meaning in local cultural contexts, not the expression of universal human nature or physical characteristics.

VARIABLE RACIAL CRITERIA. In considering the referents of the term "race," no fixed criterion exists even within the United States. Many nonbiological criteria are used to identify races. The term is applied, for example, to people from a region or geographical direction, one usually designated from the perspective of Europe (e.g., Asians/Orientals). Another referent of this cultural term "race" is a specific continental location (e.g., African, [Native] American). A new basis for a racial group has also emerged quite recently—language. Hispanic, a new racial identity in the United States, may be attributed on the basis only of a surname; here language is biologized.

Putative skin color is commonly used as a marker of race, for example, white, red, black, brown, yellow. This use of color-as-race continues despite the fact that Asians run the gamut in complexion from white to black, as in southern India. The same range of skin color is found among people labeled black or white in the United States. The lack of real color "lines" produces cases of people who are black but look white or the reverse, as well as many other oddities. In such instances, it is social history (i.e., knowledge of ancestry) that produces assignment to an allegedly biological category.

A final criterion of race in the United States is religion. Judaism is employed to demarcate an allegedly biologically distinct group. But it is clear that Jews conform to the local physiological characteristics of the communities in which they reside (e.g., Germany, Poland, Russia, England, Scandinavia, Spain, France). The Jews in the United States represent a (fictional) biological group created by religious intolerance.

If a cultural approach has some predictive value, one can anticipate that the antipathy of U.S. people toward Arabs in the 1980s and 1990s will likely result in the social construction of yet another historically unknown race—Muslims. (The British have used the term "Wogs.") Some indication of this process may be seen in the descriptions of the 1990s conflict in the former Yugoslavia. The U.S. media described the conflict as between "Muslims, Serbs, and Croats," although the Muslims were themselves either Serbs or Croats whose ancestors converted to Islam.

Because racism clearly influences cognition, perception, and affect (emotion), it could well appear in psychiatric classifications as a specific disorder. Rather than a condition of professional psychiatric concern, racism and its twin, sexism, instead appear as significant implicit elements in psychiatric (mis)diagnosis and (mis)treatment (Adebimpe, 1981; Chesler, 1972; Good, 1993).

The erroneous views of race found in the United States encode several distinct ideas: (1) a fixed number of distinct biological populations, or races, exist in nature; (2) races have distinctive physical, mental, and/or behavioral characteristics; (3) racial characteristics (physical and behavioral) are naturally reproduced over time; and (4) specific group characteristics—physical, mental, and often moral—are hierarchically ranked, that is, some groups are superior to others (Boas, 1940; Gould, 1981; Stocking, 1968; Montagu, 1964). These assumptions, however, are not the only extant racial views of human difference.

Cultural systems of racial classification beyond the United States

Some writers have argued that capitalism, with a need for cheap labor and for justifying expropriation of land and resources, provided the political context and motivation that drove science to create a defensible basis in biology for immoral acts such as slavery and genocide (Rex and Mason, 1988). Certainly, Europeans' encounters with Native Americans and imported West Africans affected their constructions of human difference (Gossett, 1965). However, it appears more likely that racial views are a form of "ethnobiology," a cultural classificatory theory about the nature of human variability (Gaines, 1992a), because some racial ideologies predate capitalism. As well, various capitalist countries exhibit distinctive notions of race. Their differing views have resulted in very different treatment of those designated as belonging to different races.

RACE IN JAPAN AND SOUTH AFRICA. In Japan, a modern, industrial, and scientific society, a conception of human races exists that differs from that of the United States. Japanese sciences hold, and offer evidence to support, that the Japanese are a race distinct from Koreans, Chinese, the indigenous Ainu people, and the outcast Eta group (DeVos and Wagatsuma, 1966). In contrast, U.S. science and society hold that all these people from the East constitute a single biological race, along with South Asians, Indonesians, Filipinos, and others. These people do not evidence a common language, culture, or physical appearance, so the U.S. cultural system converts a geo-

RACE

European Concepts

Both English and German science and society produced biological constructions of affinity and difference (Gaines, 1992a). Those who are alike share a common "blood" in Germany and "breeding" in England. Those of the same blood constitute a "race." This German belief is a kind of biological essentialism. It is a much more exclusive notion of race than that found in the United States. It is in reality a kind of ancient kinship theory, a theory of a coherent, related descent group (Gaines, 1992a) that later merged with evolutionist ideas. As such, it is much narrower than U.S. notions. In contemporary Germany, the cultural system of group membership based upon descent from a common ancestor continues. It determines social identity as well as citizenship and suitability to hold political office, for non-Germans cannot hold office or become citizens.

The same system of social classification is found in Alsace, the culturally Germanic northeastern province of France. The biological German system exists alongside a very different, French cultural system that determines ethnic identity by other means. It accords in-group identity to those sharing French civilization and culture. Membership is primarily based on language, not appearance or place of birth (Gaines, 1992a). The term "race" in France thus refers to people who share a particular language and civilization. Both can be acquired, but the latter only by means of the former. Anyone can become French; being French is a linguistic-existential state, not a biological one as in the case of the German system.

The so-called racist groups of France may be seen as "culturalists"; their targets are not races but culturally distinct groups, such as unassimilated Muslims. French-speaking sub-Saharan Africans are not targets of the French racism. North Africans have been historically white even though their complexions run the gamut from black to pale. The conflicts in France thus cannot be based upon race, though they are reported as such in the U.S. media where cultural differences are always interpreted as "racial differences."

— ATWOOD D. GAINES

graphical designation of people, borrowed from Europe, into an "Asian race."

In South Africa, there exists yet another system that classifies "racial groups." There, before the official collapse of apartheid, a sociolegal system was in place that distinguished four groups: Black, White, Asian, and Coloured. All people with ancestry in more than one of the first three groups were categorized as Coloured. Chinese were Asian, but Japanese were White. Each group historically has had different rights and privileges (see Schwartz, in Gaines, 1992a). All have equal status, at least legally, in the new South Africa.

In the United States, unlike South Africa, science and society ignore mixed ancestry and label individuals as wholly belonging to the least prestigious group of his or her parents, that is, to one exclusive category or another. In medical research, epidemiological studies, and clinical practice, people of mixed ancestry—that is, most Americans—are treated as if they had no ancestry except (West) African, Native American, Asian, or European. Designations are assumed to refer to homogeneous, distinct biological groups. If "admixture" is noted, researchers tend to ignore European ancestry and focus on genetic "vulnerabilities" deriving only from the subject's putative "minority" ancestry (Duster, 1990; Gaines, 1985; Wailoo, 1991).

In the United States, virtually all people called black or African-American, a term coined by anthropologist Melville Herskovits, would be classified in South Africa as Coloured because of their mixed ancestry (West African, western European, Native American). Indeed, all U.S. residents who claim long lines of U.S. antecedents would be likewise classified because they too have mixed ancestry. The same would hold true for most Native Americans and Latinos. Ironically then, the major U.S. "racial" groups, those with major antipathies and conflicts enduring over centuries based on their "racial differences," all would be classified in South Africa as belonging to the same racial group—Coloured.

Race as a key variable in biomedical research and practice

The ideas of race enumerated above underlie almost all medical and psychiatric research in the United States that pertains to group differences other than age or sex (Gaines, 1992a; Hahn, 1992; Robbins and Regier, 1991; Osborne and Feit, 1992). Remarkably, these beliefs concerning the existence or homogeneity of human populations called "races" have not the slightest scientific (or logical) basis; no empirical evidence has ever existed for the differentiation of humanity into broad racial groups (Gould, 1981; Montagu, 1964; UNESCO, 1969). In reality, thousands of biologically distinct human groups exist

"The great masses of the people . . . will more easily fall victims to a big lie than to a small one."

ADOLF HITLER
MEIN KAMPF
(MY STRUGGLE), 1933

See Also

Genetics and the Power of the State

R

RACE AND RACISM

Race as a Key Variable in Biomedical Research and Practice

"I started with this idea in my head, 'There's two things I've got a right to . . . death or liberty.' "

HARRIET TUBMAN
C. 1868

(Hiernaux, 1970; Montagu, 1964; Naroll and Naroll, 1973; Watts, 1981).

Assertions of the biological bases of differences among races are used to justify caste systems; that is, the results of oppression, discrimination, and poverty are commonly used to justify further discrimination and prejudice (Boas, 1940; DeVos and Wagatsuma, 1966; Naroll and Naroll, 1973; Thomas and Sillen, 1972). As is shown below, medical research, theory, and practice often play this same role in U.S. society and thereby serve as "scientific" justification for the persistence of popular conceptions of racial difference and of racism (Brandt, 1985; Gilman, 1985; Duster 1990).

Racial groups are mental constructs. As mental constructs they cannot evidence medical conditions. Yet "one of the most common methodological blunders in scientific studies of the significance of racial differences in the United States is the tacit acceptance of this phantasmic notion of race as the basis for establishing research samples" (Harris, 1968,p. 264). Given this, it can be noted that a folk medicine, or "ethnomedicine," is largely a creation of cultural beliefs. Its practices serve to reinforce and even justify those beliefs. Such is precisely the nature of medical research on group differences in the United States. This supportive role may be seen in research on afflictions said to appear only in certain populations.

THE MYTH OF RACE-SPECIFIC DISEASES. In biology or psychology, research science is used to reach conclusions that are in fact a priori assumptions; "prejudice not . . . documentation dictates conclusions" (Gould, 1981 p. 80). In today's medical and scientific community, expressed ideas concerning ethnic and gender inferiority are largely implicit. They are replaced in the medical literature by vague assertions such as vulnerability, susceptibility, tendency, increased risk, and difference. One aspect of this discourse that constructs and maintains racial difference concerns "race-specific diseases." Since it is believed that races are distinct groups with their own biologies, it stands to reason that they would exhibit particular diseases. Sickle-cell anemia is a case in point.

At the beginning of the twentieth century, sickle-cell anemia was found originally through laboratory analysis of the blood of five patients—two European-Americans, two "mulattos" (in the parlance of the time, persons of mixed European and West African ancestry, but very largely the former), and one "Negro" (who doubtless was also part European). The findings were reported in the medical literature, however, as a condition found only in Negroes (Wailoo, 1991). In fact, this condition has existed in most world populations including the Mediterranean, Middle Eastern, Indian, Filipino, and South American. Instructively, the condition is not found among people in eastern, southern, or central Africa. Rather, it is found largely in West Africa, the ancestral area of most people in the Americas with African ancestry. Clearly, the condition is not a "racial disease" but rather a characteristic of some local populations.

Tay-Sachs disease is said to be a Jewish disease. In fact, it is a disorder found in a specific local population of the eastern Mediterranean from which some Jews, as well as Arabs, came. Jews not from this area, and not descended from people who were, have no risk of developing the disorder. The same is true of the so-called Portuguese disease, a degenerative, fatal neurological disease said to afflict Portuguese people. The afflicted are in reality descended from a single person (one Joseph) who carried the gene causing the disease. It is purely by chance that the antecedent person was Portuguese. Unrelated Portuguese are not at risk for developing the disease. In Tay-Sachs and the Portuguese diseases, specific sites of affliction are generalized to all in the racial category of the afflicted. "Local biologies" (Gaines, 1992a) are ignored in favor of "racial" ones.

The medical assertion that certain diseases are peculiar to specific races is without merit. The fiction is maintained through a number of techniques. Findings in a single person of a racial group are regularly generalized to all members of that putative group (Brandt, 1978; Wailoo, 1991); a part is made to stand for a whole. For example, a clinical finding that Indians in Britain required lower therapeutic levels of certain psychotropic medications became the basis for research comparing "Asians" and "Caucasians" (Lin et al., 1990; Lin et al., 1986; Mendoza et al., 1992).

Tendencies discerned in research are commonly reinterpreted to suggest significant differences in research on hypertensive medications; "diuretics are best for 'blacks' and beta-blockers for 'whites.'" Since members in neither group have common ancestry in the United States, such stereotypes can limit diagnosis of problems to groups "known" to be afflicted; others are then overlooked, misdiagnosed, or considered to be exceptions. As such, they do not challenge the stereotype, though logically such exceptions should call into question the very notion of racial distinctiveness.

Despite the absence of any scientific basis, the idea of race represents the basic population variable, aside from age and sex, on which inquiries focus and in terms of which results are interpreted and recommendations made. The huge body of literature on race-specific problems and racial comparisons are actually of unknown scientific value, though they represent a rich corpus for cultural study.

As long as medical science continues in its archaic racial folk beliefs, its claims to objective, acultural, and disinterested status in the health field are seriously

See Also

Maternal–Fetal Relationship: Regulatory Issues: Gender and Racial Disparities compromised. Because these and gender beliefs are purely popular, modern medical sciences appear as cultural medicines, ethnomedicines, albeit professional ones (Gaines, 1992c; Hahn and Gaines, 1985). The validity of racial conceptions has been challenged and its use compromised. The continued use of racial conceptions in biomedical research and practice looms as a central conceptual and methodological problem in the biomedical sciences.

CONSEQUENCES OF RACIAL BELIEFS. Common to intentional and unintentional discriminatory motivations is the unstated theory that ancestry in nonwhite groups "taints" the individual, not only determining identity but also causing disease. This is the implicit pathologization of perceived "difference" typical in research on high blood pressure and diabetes as well as a variety of other conditions (Cowie et al., 1989; Harris, 1991; Jones and Rice, 1987). Affliction is attributed to the fact that the individuals are "minority," by which is meant biologically different and therefore "defective."

Considering the study of diabetes in African-Americans more closely, it is found that while no risk factors and very few cases of diabetes exist in West Africa, individuals classified as African-Americans are still commonly said to be at "high risk" for developing the disease because of their "racial or ethnic ancestry." The presence of diabetes in these populations has other probable causes that are normally overlooked in research. They are (1) the European genetic background of the African-Americans; (2) poverty and related poor nutrition caused by discrimination; and (3) the high animal-fat content of the dominant northern European diet.

Racial thinking leads researchers to ignore oppression, racism, and discrimination—all of which can implicate the researchers themselves—as well as other cultural and biological factors. Research is confined to allegedly biological problems existing as defects within the afflicted. The real biogenetic makeup of individuals goes unanalyzed while their social identity is blamed for their illness.

Research on the treatments of choice and treatment recommendations in U.S. biomedicine demonstrates that medical and psychiatric diagnoses and therapeutic choices are often made on the basis of patients' social identity, be it race, class, or gender rather than objective need (Brandt, 1985; Ehrenreich and English, 1973; Gilman, 1985; Good, 1993; Lindenbaum and Lock, 1993; Osborne and Feit, 1992). Historically, this includes the differential use of anesthesia; the poor didn't need it but the wealthy did, as they were more delicate! (Pernick, 1985).

The form of intervention in psychiatry, pharmacotherapy, and psychotherapy is today heavily dependent on racial and/or sexual stereotypes rather than on empirical psychiatric signs or symptoms (Katz, 1985; Gaines, 1982, 1992a, 1992c; Littlewood, 1982). Blacks and Hispanics are often seen as belonging to that group of patients termed "psychologically unsophisticated" or "not psychologically minded" (e.g., Leff, 1981; MacKinnon and Michels, 1971; Sudack, 1985). Psychopharmacotherapy is seen as more "appropriate" for such patients than forms of "talk" therapy.

It should be recalled that U.S. psychiatry in the nineteenth century "found" that psychiatric disorders afflicted black slaves who otherwise "unaccountably" ran away from their masters. This is a historical version of a biological psychiatry and posits that all conditions are biological and will ultimately yield to somatic interventions. Environment, in this view, can be discounted or its consideration delayed until suspected "biological components" can be studied.

In medical research, behavior is also related to race. Medical researchers often choose research topics that implicate behaviors judged as immoral or incautious when dealing with minority populations, for example, number of sex partners, unwed mothers, and drug addiction (Gaines, 1985; Osborne and Feit, 1992). In this way, medical research also becomes moral research and supports blame-the-victim thinking.

In the psychiatric literature, neo-evolutionist racial theories lurk behind some assertions. Certain groups, such as the English, are said to be more evolved and psychologically normal (see Leff, 1981). In this view, somatization is allegedly less evolved and is characteristic of less developed "traditional" or "primitive" societies. The position inserts a cultural view of emotion and thought into a not-too-implicit neo-evolutionist scheme.

In the West, emotions are believed to be natural, universal, and distinct from cognition. But anthropological research has shown that specific emotions are not universal nor are they naturally distinct from cognitive or bodily states and functions (see Good et al., Lutz, Obeyesekere, Schieffelin, in Kleinman and Good, 1985). While highly valued in a very few cultures, psychologization of distress is not "natural," but rather a learned, shared, and transmitted cultural approach (Kleinman, 1988). Psychologization is not found in many areas of Europe itself, for example, the Mediterranean and eastern Europe (Gaines, 1992c; Gaines and Farmer, 1986; see Good et al. in Kleinman and Good, 1985), or in China, Japan, or India (Kleinman and Good, 1985; Leslie and Young, 1993).

Research on racial differences provides the scientific bases for the maintenance of popular and scientific racial ideology in the United States. This ideology clearly leads to differential evaluation of social actors in medical and nonmedical contexts. As such, biomedical

"No race has a monopoly on vice or virtue, and the worth of an individual is not related to the color of his skin."

WHITNEY MOORE YOUNG, JR.
BEYOND RACISM, 1969

R

RACE AND RACISM

Race as a Key Variable in Biomedical Research and Practice

practices can be said to contribute to the social problems caused by racism. These problems include unequal access and poor medical outcomes (Good, 1993). The use of racial categories in biomedical research and practice, then, may be seen to breach the medical profession's own primary ethical injunction "to do no harm."

RACE AND CLINICAL STUDIES. That racial groups are considered unequally in U.S. biomedical science and society is clearly demonstrated by the infamous and tragic Tuskegee syphilis study. In 1932, the U.S. Public Health Service (PHS) began a prospective study of syphilis infection among four hundred rural Alabamans who were black male sharecroppers. The researchers asserted that the study could be a "natural experiment" because it was assumed (for racist reasons) that "such people" were all infected and would not seek treatment for their condition (Brandt, 1978). For these reasons, the PHS argued that it could observe the natural history of syphilis infection in these black men. As it happened, the subjects, who had been unknowingly selected, began to seek treatment almost immediately.

Rather than provide health care, the PHS initiated a vast conspiracy to prevent the subjects from receiving care from any source. It conspired with local and state health officials, clinics and hospitals, and the U.S. Army, in which some of the men had enlisted, to prevent disclosure to the subjects of their diagnosis and to prevent treatment of their affliction.

Despite the fact that the natural experimental premise was invalidated in short order, this horrendous project continued over four decades until 1972, when public outcries finally stopped it. Until that time, however, the study was often reported in the medical literature without raising ethical concerns about informed consent, the sometimes fatal use of these human subjects, or the conspiracy to prevent them from receiving efficacious treatments (Brandt, 1978, 1985).

Aside from specific research projects that indicate differential concern for specific groups in the United States, "minorities" in day-to-day medical settings are

"PREDISPOSITIONS"

Genes, Race, and Violence

Biomedicine conceives of its domain as the discovery and manipulation of nature (see Gordon, in Lock and Gordon, 1988). Its wider culture perceives nature as something to be dominated and controlled (Pike, 1992). Ideas of nature, as well as those of difference and inferiority that are encoded in racial and gender identities, greatly affect practice and research in U.S. biomedical sciences. Classes of people believed to be closer to nature are seen as requiring control and guidance, even domination. Such people—among them women, children, non-Anglo or non-Germanic European ethnics (e.g., French, Italian, Spanish, Celtic, and Slavic people), Africans and their descendants, Native Americans, Hispanics, Pacific Islanders—are, in the United States, rather widely believed to be emotional, and therefore dangerous, unpredictable, and wild. Comments about "natural abilities" (intuitive, musical, irrational, fierce, shrewd) or characteristics of particular groups indicate their closeness to nature; they, like animals, are thought to be dominated by instinct and irrationality, not by "reason," a European cultural and masculine virtue (Chesler, 1972; Fausto-Sterling, 1992; Kleinman and Good, 1985; Pike, 1992).

The imputation of wildness, impulsiveness, and irrationality is doubtless a culturally constituted defensive projection of aggression that actually exists in the dominant group (Gilman, 1985; Pike, 1992). It is used to justify control, domination, and even extermination, as with Africans and Native Americans in the United States and non-German ethnics and the disabled in World War II Germany.

A similar logic appears in contemporary U.S. society. Urban violence, born of repression, discrimination, violence, and poverty, is recast as "genetic predispositions to violence or criminality" in individuals and the groups to which they are ascribed, especially after periods of civil unrest. However, rather obvious examples of genetic predispositions toward criminality and violence in the dominant group are regularly ignored as are centuries of clear provocations of African-Americans.

If researchers were indeed interested in a dispassionate evaluation of genetic components of violence and criminality, it would be appropriate to study people descended from generations of individuals all of whom have committed crimes of a serious nature. In the United States, such a population would be the many immigrants from Russia or Germany, as well as their offspring. Another group of subjects would be the descendants of slave traders and owners. Mass murderers and serial killers in the United States and Europe are virtually always white; their relatives would be suitable subjects of biological research on white criminality. These data might suggest some genetic basis for the inheritance of violent tendencies, if one were to think in "racial" terms. But researchers on violence and its causes regularly ignore such evidence. It appears that violence and criminality are possible genetic predispositions only when they appear in individuals belonging to specific low-status racial groups.

— ATWOOD D. GAINES

often underdiagnosed for problems that could be treated (e.g., heart disease) and overdiagnosed for others. For example, blacks are regularly misdiagnosed with schizophrenia. These misdiagnoses lead to confinement and inappropriate pharmacological regimens. Loss of freedom and improper use of powerful psychotropic medications may themselves lead to chronicity in the illnesses that are left untreated, illnesses that led the patient to the attention of health professionals in the first place (see Adebimpe, 1981; Mukherjee et al., 1983; Bell and Mehta, 1980; Good, 1993). This is one means by which medicine creates chronicity of particular disorders as well as increases in the reported incidence of these disorders in a specific population. The circular logic is completed by the subsequent tendency to diagnose in an individual a disorder that is reported as "common" in members of his or her racial or ethnic group.

It is important for a full understanding of the role of racial classifications in the biomedical field to see it as part of a cultural system. This allows for the recognition of both the clearly concerned altruistic practitioners and researchers and the profoundly troubling aspects of racial thought in biomedical practices. In this view, the problems of racial thinking may be seen to arise frequently from the use of popular racial notions by force of tradition—tradition in the Weberian sense, wherein it is one source of authority for human action (Weber, 1978). The use of racial categories is thus not necessarily racist.

Conclusions

The U.S. version of human biology is a folk biology that assumes that social categories—"races"—are reflections of nature rather than culture. As a result, biomedical work, as well as public health care, is conducted and interpreted in these terms. In clinical practice in U.S. medicine, every patient record begins with three basic bits of information thought to be of critical importance: age, race, and gender (e.g., "A thirty-seven-year-old black female presented with . . ."). This is a significant part of the discourse of medicine that reconfirms the cultural conceptions that race, age, and sex are natural and empirical realities that make a difference.

Specific forms of communalism, such as racism and sexism, are intrinsic to U.S. society. As a result, they are fundamentally part of its medical institutions, because U.S. medicine is a reflection of the culture that created it. Culturally specific prejudice makes U.S. biomedicine an expression of a particular culture and its history. That culture has held and still expresses empirically problematic and ultimately unethical conceptualizations of human variation. However, neither contemporary medicine nor society remains monocultural; different ethnic and gender voices are being heard advocating what may be seen as more cultural and therefore humane and equal medical-research concerns and treatment. In many scientific fields, the lessons learned from the Nazi atrocities—as well as the inclusion of Jews, African-Americans, and women in collegial relations—has helped to reduce scientific racism and sexism since the 1950s (Barkan, 1992). Trends of pluralism begun then continue and expand.

Modern biomedical thought in the United States appears to lag in its understanding of the bases of human differences. The basis is culture, not biology. Even though racial terms are now often exchanged for ethnic ones, the problems persist in biomedicine and related sciences. Ethnicity has a cultural referent, and race has a putatively biological one. The two terms are incommensurate and cannot be used interchangeably.

Intentionally or unintentionally, biomedicine conserves, employs, and disseminates racial and gender-biased conceptions in its theory and practice. Such actions may be seen to derive both from habit and from nefarious intent. Comparisons are at the heart of science. U.S. science, along with U.S. popular society, has always thought that comparisons of black versus white or other races are the more or less "natural" ones to make in a "multiracial" society. Some others yet seek to show one group's superiority over others.

Biomedical enterprises will surely be subject to increasing ethical and practical criticism in the future "both from without and within its cultural tradition by those it fails to serve and those it serves to fail" (Gaines, 1992c). The growing understanding of the cultural biases of the professional medicines (and sciences) of the world suggests that medicines, like their particular medical ethics, reflect local cultural realities. A pluralistic medicine is needed in a multicultural country such as the United States. In such a country, a single medical voice may easily lead to, if not generate, bioethical conflicts. A medicine without cultural understandings, unreflective of its own cultural foundations, is inadequate, and an inadequate medicine cannot be of great help in a multicultural society.

— ATWOOD D. GAINES

"After all there is but one race–humanity."

GEORGE MOORE
THE BENDING OF THE BOUGH, 1900

REPRODUCTIVE TECHNOLOGIES

INTRODUCTION

The development of effective and imaginative approaches to the management of human infertility has focused public attention on the techniques themselves and on their ethical and legal implications.

Most requests for sex selection in developed nations are probably covert, with women requesting prenatal diagnosis on the basis of anxiety about the health of the fetus.

PAGE 580

Although differing widely in their complexity, these methods have one characteristic in common: the separation of human reproduction from the act of coitus. An understanding of these reproductive technologies is essential to an overall consideration of ethical issues surrounding them.

Artificial insemination

Artificial insemination involves the mechanical placement of spermatozoa into the female reproductive tract. Inseminations are separated into two broad categories: those utilizing the semen of the husband or designated partner (AIH) and those employing semen of a third party, or donor insemination (DI). Since the ethical and moral issues surrounding AIH and DI take on different dimensions, each will be considered separately.

AIH constitutes effective treatment when, for whatever reason, the male partner is unable to ejaculate within the vagina. Some males are unable to ejaculate during coitus but can ejaculate through masturbation or the use of vibratory stimuli. Certain anatomical abnormalities result in faulty semen placement. Hypospadias, a penile abnormality in which the opening of the urethra is located a distance from the tip of the glans penis, causes the ejaculate to be deposited at the periphery of the vagina even when the penis is well within. Retrograde ejaculation is a condition usually caused by a complication of prostatic surgery resulting in the formation of a channel that causes the ejaculate to be directed away from the penis and retrograded into the bladder. After ejaculation, semen for artificial insemination can be recovered from the bladder by catheterization.

Normal vaginal intercourse may be precluded by congenital or acquired vaginal abnormalities. In rare cases, the vagina is constricted as the result of in utero exposure to the hormone diethylstilbestrol (DES) or possibly by past trauma. Psychological problems in the male or female or both may interfere with normal coital exchange.

In recent years, AIH has been recommended when the semen displays deficiencies in numbers of sperm or their ability to move. Laboratory techniques have been developed to separate and concentrate the most active spermatozoa. These are then introduced into the uterine cavity, closer to the site of fertilization. Intrauterine insemination has been used with variable results in cases of male infertility and in couples with unexplained infertility (Blasco and Mastroianni, 1991).

TECHNIQUES OF OBTAINING SEMEN. Semen for use in artificial insemination is usually obtained by masturbation. An alternate possibility is intercourse using a plastic condom. Coitus interruptus is not recommended, as the first portion of the ejaculate, which contains the majority of active, motile spermatozoa, is sometimes lost. In cases of obstruction of the vas deferens, which serves as the conduit for spermatozoa, spermatozoa have been obtained surgically from the epididymis, the storage depot for spermatozoa. Specimens so obtained have been used successfully for both the gamete intrafallopian tube transfer (GIFT) procedure and in vitro fertilization (IVF).

TIMING OF THE INSEMINATION. Placement of spermatozoa should be timed to coincide with the twelve hours immediately preceding ovulation. Approximately twenty-four hours before ovulation, increased levels of luteinizing hormone (LH) can be detected in the urine, using a color indicator to predict ovulation. The day-to-day development of the egg-containing ovarian follicle can be monitored with pelvic ultrasound. To enhance the accuracy of ovulation timing still further while causing the release of additional eggs for fertilization, the use of human gonadotropins to induce ovulation has become increasingly popular.

INSEMINATION AND SEX SELECTION. Insemination has also been used in an effort at sex selection. Various treatments have been recommended to separate the X-chromosome-bearing (female-producing) from the Y-chromosome-bearing (male-producing) spermatozoa. Success rates in the production of male offspring in the 80 percent range are claimed (van Kooij and van Oost, 1992). Such techniques are useful in animal husbandry but do not yield a consistently satisfactory success rate in humans. Sex selection would be useful to avoid a sex-linked genetic disease. Sex preselection based solely on preference for a boy or a girl has much wider social implications.

DONOR INSEMINATION. Donor insemination was mentioned as a method of treating infertility in the nineteenth century. As DI has become more widely used, the legal climate has become more favorable and the status of the offspring much less uncertain. With this has come awareness of the importance of careful counseling and the use of appropriate permission forms. There has not yet been a case in U.S. law in which the anonymous sperm donor has been assigned parental responsibility.

The clinical indications for donor insemination are related mainly to deficiencies in the semen. The most clear-cut cases are those in which the male partner suffers from azoospermia (no spermatozoa). Indications have been extended to include those in whom some spermatozoa are present but the quality of the specimen is poor. Known hereditary disorders in the male partner, such as Huntington's disease, Tay-Sachs, or hemophilia, are also indications for DI.

In vitro fertilization (IVF) has widened the possibility of conception with severely deficient semen. Donor insemination is sometimes used in IVF when

SELECTION AND SCREENING
Donor and Recipient

A couple considering donor insemination should be thoroughly counseled. If either partner has reservations, it is wise to accept these at face value and encourage consideration of other options, including adoption. The man's fertility should be thoroughly evaluated, and efforts made to correct any abnormalities. The woman also should be thoroughly evaluated for factors that might contribute to infertility. Both partners are usually required to review and sign a detailed informed-consent form.

SELECTION AND SCREENING OF DONORS. In most circumstances, the donor is anonymous. Occasionally there is a request that a close relative (usually a brother or even a father) be used. In such cases, the couple should be encouraged to consider carefully the potential for future familial conflicts. Analysis of donor semen should meet the normal standards for fertility (American Fertility Society, 1986). The donor should be in excellent health and be screened for any family history of genetic disorders. Serologic tests for syphilis and serum hepatitis B antigen are obtained initially and after six months. The genitalia are cultured for gonorrhea and chlamydia. An initial screening for the AIDS virus antibodies is performed and repeated after six months because the antibody test for AIDS may not turn positive until several months after infection. Most centers now use frozen semen exclusively. If a donor is providing repeated specimens, periodic reevaluation of his health status is essential. Clinics should maintain records of pregnancies and set a limit on the number of pregnancies any one donor may produce. To decrease the possibility of consanguinity in a given population, an arbitrary limit of ten or fewer pregnancies is recommended.

It is important to maintain confidential donor records, including all of the information on the screening procedures, so that it is available on an anonymous basis if it is needed for medical reasons in the future.

— LUIGI MASTRONIANNI, JR.

there is failure of fertilization using the male partner's specimen.

TECHNIQUE OF INSEMINATION. The standard insemination involves placing the specimen, thawed if it has been frozen, into the cervical canal by means of a small, flexible cannula. As the vaginal speculum is removed, the remainder of the specimen is placed in the vagina, at the outer cervical canal. The patient remains supine for twenty minutes or so. The specimen may be held in place with a cervical cap, which is removed four to six hours after insemination. For intrauterine insemination, a plastic cannula is passed through the opening of the cervix into the uterine cavity, where the concentrated, pretreated (i.e., washed) spermatozoa are deposited.

CRYOPRESERVATION OF SEMEN. Since the first successful insemination with freeze-stored semen in 1953, this technique has had a significant impact on clinical practice. In the 1970s, formal semen banks were established, largely to address the needs for long-term preservation of the specimens of men who had undergone vasectomy. Semen also is preserved prior to chemotherapy or radiation, which might result in sterility. Although there is no formal reporting system, information accumulated over the years has failed to uncover an increased incidence of genetic defects among the offspring resulting from insemination with cryopreserved semen.

The response of spermatozoa to cryopreservation is unpredictable and varies on an individual basis. Some specimens freeze well and others do not. The pregnancy rate is lower overall with frozen semen. The only reliable way to determine whether a specimen is suitable for cryopreservation is to cryopreserve it, thaw it, and evaluate the impact of the procedure on the quality of sperm motility. Specimens are usually stored in individual straws or small vials so that fractions may be thawed while the remainder is preserved for future use. The Ethics Committee of the American Fertility Society has determined that cryopreservation of human semen is ethically and medically acceptable, but does speak of the lack of uniformity in standards among sperm banks and of the importance of establishing certification standards (American Fertility Society, 1986). Most large university centers use only cryopreserved semen for donor insemination.

In vitro fertilization

In vitro fertilization and embryo transfer (IVF-ET) is increasingly common in infertility practice (Society for Assisted Reproductive Technology, 1993). Initially used exclusively in women with damaged fallopian tubes, the indications for IVF-ET have been extended to include male factor infertility and cases in which no cause for the infertility can be uncovered. Much as artificial insemination separates procreation from the coital act, in vitro fertilization separates fertilization from the normal maternal environment, allowing the initial phases of development to occur outside the

Arguments against sex selection are based on the premise that it helps to perpetuate gender stereotyping and sexism.

PAGE 581

Sex selection violates the principle of equality between the sexes.

PAGE 581

It is important to seek solutions to the problem of sex selection now, because it has the potential to change entire societies.

PAGE 582

reproductive tract, followed by transfer of the embryo into the uterus. The first successful in vitro fertilization was carried out in a normally ovulating woman whose tubes had been surgically removed. A single egg (ovum, oocyte) was obtained by aspiration at the time of laparoscopy. The oocyte was fertilized in vitro and transferred to the uterus after two days.

In later developments, the ovaries were stimulated with human urinary gonadotropins to induce development of several follicles, each containing an ovum, in a given cycle. This approach is now standard. Follicular development is followed by means of blood estrogen levels, and the size of the growing follicles is measured by ultrasound. When the follicles are judged ready for ovulation, a second hormone, human chorionic gonadotropin (hCG), is administered to induce ovulation. This causes further development of the follicles and the maturing of oocytes within them. The oocytes complete their first division in a process referred to as meiosis, releasing half their complement of chromosomes in a small, round structure, the first polar body. The maternal chromosomes are now ready for the second meiotic division, which occurs after the ovum has been penetrated by the spermatozoa. Within two to three hours of the expected time of ovulation, the oocytes are aspirated from their follicles.

In the early phases of IVF development, this was carried out with the aid of the laparoscope. The procedure required general anesthesia and involved placing a telescope through the umbilicus for visualization of the pelvic structures. The oocytes were obtained by needle aspiration. Today, ova are obtained by ultrasound-guided transvaginal aspiration. This procedure can be done without general anesthesia, and the overall approach to in vitro fertilization is greatly simplified.

Another major clinical problem in the early phases of IVF development was that occasionally a patient would ovulate before the oocytes could be obtained, and the cycle would have to be canceled. Analogues of the gonadotropin-releasing hormone (GnRH) are now used to prevent this. These analogues are capable of blocking the release of the patient's pituitary gonadotropins, and the ovaries can be brought under the complete control of exogenously administered hormones. The number of follicles that develop varies from patient to patient, and even in the same patient from one cycle to the next. By and large, the aim is to obtain as many oocytes as possible in a given treatment cycle, especially if the couple has selected cryopreservation as a possible option.

IVF treatment is both physically and emotionally demanding. Several visits for hormone determinations and ultrasound are required. Ovum recovery, although relatively safe, is not without complications. Rarely ovarian infection occurs, which can further compromise the fertility status of the patient. This point is particularly pertinent when oocytes are being obtained for donation.

A freshly ejaculated semen specimen is obtained for insemination. The ova are placed in individual containers and mixed with spermatozoa that have been prepared by separating them from the semen and incubating them in a solution designed to enhance their fertilizability. It is useful to have a cryopreserved semen specimen on hand in the event that a fresh specimen cannot be obtained when needed. The inseminated ova are cultured for approximately twenty-four hours and then inspected for evidence of fertilization.

Much has been learned about human fertilization through in vitro fertilization. When it is removed from the woman's body, the ovum is surrounded by layers of small, loosely packed cells, the cumulus oophorus. An inner layer of more densely arranged cells, the corona radiata, immediately surrounds the oocyte. These cells interface with the zona pellucida, a translucent protein shell that immediately surrounds the egg. Penetration past these barriers is accomplished through a sequence of interactions between spermatozoa and the ovum and its layers (Kopf and Gerton, 1990). When the spermatozoon reaches the zona pellucida, a series of chemical communications occurs. These condition the spermatozoon so that it can penetrate through the zona pellucida. Once past the zona, the spermatozoon attaches to the egg membrane and is then incorporated into the egg cytoplasm, the tail along with the head. The head is then transformed into a pronucleus. The second polar body is released and the nucleus of the egg is transformed into a pronucleus. The pronuclei then join and the chromosomes are intermingled in preparation for the first cell division. Twenty-four hours after insemination, there are two pronuclei and two polar bodies. This constitutes evidence that the penetration has been successful and fertilization is in process. After two days, the embryo has developed to the four-to-eight-cell stage and is ready for transfer into the uterus.

EMBRYO TRANSFER. The dividing embryos are incorporated into the end of a catheter that is then passed through the cervical opening into the uterine cavity, where they are discharged. The pregnancy rate is progressively improved if more than one embryo is transferred. If more than four are transferred, there is a greatly increased possibility of multiple pregnancy. Twins are not a problem, but triplets or more greatly increase the possibility of fetal loss. Therefore, in many IVF programs no more than four fertilized oocytes are transferred. The availability of cryopreservation has made such decisions easier.

The issue of when meaningful human life begins is pivotal in any discussion of IVF. The fertilization process is a complex series of events. The spermatozoon must be exposed to the environment of the female reproductive tract for a period of time before it acquires the ability to penetrate the layers surrounding the recently ovulated oocyte. This process, referred to as "capacitation," takes between one and two hours in the human. It is reproduced in vitro in the fluids utilized for sperm preparation. The series of events involving penetration through the zona pellucida requires complex chemical communication between sperm and egg. After the spermatozoon has penetrated into the cytoplasm, completion of fertilization, although increasingly probable, is not assured.

The events that follow, including the formation and subsequent fusion of the pronuclei, occupy more than twenty-four hours. In the natural sequence of events, the conceptus remains in the fallopian tube for approximately three days. At the eight-to-sixteen-cell stage, it is transported into the uterus. There it develops into a fluid-filled structure, the blastocyst, that attaches to the uterine lining, or endometrium, on the sixth to seventh day after fertilization. The blastocyst is incorporated into the endometrium and invades blood vessels. Development occurs rapidly thereafter, but it is not until the fourteenth day that it develops unique characteristics. This coincides with the formation of the primitive streak, a linear region that can be identified on the early embryonic disk; it signals the beginning of the development of a distinct category of cells. Until this point, there is the potential for division into identical twins. Each of the individual cells in the early conceptus has the potential to develop into a complete adult. On or about day five or six, specialized cells, the trophoblasts, are formed. They provide the point of attachment for the placenta and are essential to the nourishment of the growing embryo. The Ethics Committee of the American Fertility Society applies the term "pre-embryo" to the conceptus through the first two weeks of gestation (Ethics Committee, American Fertility Society, 1986). It takes the position that the moral status of the pre-embryo is different from that of either the unfertilized eggs and spermatozoa or the later stages in embryonic development.

CRYOPRESERVATION OF PRE-EMBRYOS. Techniques for freeze-preserving pre-embryos have contributed to the success of human in vitro fertilization and embryo transfer. The incidence of multiple pregnancy, which increases dramatically if more than four pre-embryos are transferred, can be reduced with the availability of cryopreservation. Pre-embryos not transferred during the treatment cycle can be utilized in subsequent spontaneous ovulation cycles. When pregnancy occurs in the initial treatment cycle and pre-embryos have been cryopreserved, a number of future options must be considered. These issues should be reviewed and decisions made before the pre-embryos are frozen. Patients whose response to stimulation clearly indicates that more than four oocytes will be recovered should consider their options well in advance of ovum recovery. Those who for whatever reason, including deeply felt moral reservations, choose not to cryopreserve may wish to have sperm added to no more than four oocytes and have all of the fertilized specimens transferred. Remaining ova can be disposed of in their unfertilized state. Another alternative short of cryopreservation is to fertilize all available ova and select only the best of the resulting pre-embryos, as determined by their appearance and rate of cell division, for replacement, discarding the remainder.

The standard consent form should contain a detailed description of the possibilities to consider if a decision is made to cryopreserve human pre-embryos. As far as is known, cryopreservation of human pre-embryos is not associated with adverse fetal effects. Generally it is agreed that the pre-embryos will be frozen and stored for use in subsequent cycles. Unforeseen situations can occur, such as failure of equipment, although backup freezer systems and liquid-nitrogen holding facilities are usually available in the event of such an occurrence.

In most major centers, the disposition of unused frozen pre-embryos is reviewed in advance of cryopreservation. Handling of these pre-embryos is subject to the couple's joint disposition. They agree that if one partner is unwilling or unable to assume responsibility for the fertilized eggs, the responsibility reverts to the other partner. If that person is not willing or able to assume ownership, the hospital or clinic usually reserves the right to dispose of the pre-embryos in accordance with policies in existence at the time.

Micromanipulation of oocytes and embryos in vitro

Instruments have been developed to allow manipulation of gametes and pre-embryos under magnification. These techniques of micromanipulation have been used extensively in laboratory mammals. More recently they have been applied to human eggs, spermatozoa, and pre-embryos. When the oocyte is not penetrated by spermatozoa that are otherwise apparently normal, micromanipulation can be used to insert a spermatozoon mechanically through the zona pellucida into the space between the zona and the oocyte (subzonal insertion or SUZI) or directly into the oocyte itself (intracytoplasmic sperm insertion or ICSI). Pregnancies that would otherwise be impossible can occur as a result of this procedure.

Micromanipulation has been extended to pre-embryos. It has been suggested that the second polar body, the cell that is released from the ovum at the time it is penetrated by the spermatozoon, be removed for

Testing is best carried out in the context of reproduction, but preferably before marriage or pregnancy.

PAGE 314

chromosome analysis in an effort to determine whether the embryo is genetically normal. This approach could be used in couples at risk of genetic abnormalities and would avoid the onus of a decision to terminate the pregnancy later on. Individual cells have been removed from the embryo for analysis without apparent harm (Tarin and Handyside, 1993). Other possibilities may eventually emerge, including the removal and storage of individual cells as clones of the embryo that is transferred. Many of these approaches have not yet attained clinical practicality, but they raise moral, ethical, and legal issues that it would be wise to address now.

Gamete intrafallopian tube transfer

The procedure referred to as gamete intrafallopian tube transfer (GIFT) involves the transfer of freshly recovered ova and conditioned spermatozoa into the fallopian tubes. Thus, fertilization actually occurs in vivo. GIFT is not applicable to all infertility patients. Those with damaged or absent fallopian tubes are obviously not candidates. GIFT has been recommended for couples with unexplained infertility and women with extratubal disease, such as pelvic adhesions or endometriosis. The success rate following GIFT, 30-35 percent, is roughly twice that of in vitro fertilization (Society for Assisted Reproductive Technology, 1993). Although fertilization occurs within the fallopian tube, GIFT is certainly assisted reproductive technology and is clearly separated from the coital act. When more than four ova are recovered at the time of a GIFT procedure, one or more are usually fertilized in vitro and cryopreserved for transfer in subsequent cycles. Transfer of the ova and spermatozoa into the fallopian tubes is usually carried out by means of laparoscopy. Techniques employing ultrasound-guided transuterine transfer are being developed to obviate laparoscopy.

Oocyte donation

The clinical indications for the use of donor ova usually are rather straightforward. They include premature menopause and the inability of the wife to produce genetically normal oocytes. On the surface, the ethical issues surrounding the use of donor oocytes should be no different from those involved in the use of donor semen. They are compounded, however, by the risks involved in obtaining oocytes compared with

HUMAN FERTILITY

Surrogate Gestational Mothers/Womb Mothers

Human in vitro fertilization has opened the possibility that the resulting pre-embryos can be transferred to a woman other than the woman providing the oocytes. The second woman, referred to variously as a surrogate carrier, a womb mother, a placental mother, or a surrogate gestational mother, provides the gestational but not the genetic component of that pregnancy. Usually arrangements are made for the couple whose egg and sperm produced the embryo to adopt the newborn.

In another type of surrogacy, a husband's spermatozoa are used to inseminate a woman other than his wife. This surrogate mother carries the gestation to term. Agreement is reached before the procedure is carried out that the contracting couple will have custody of the resulting child.

In everyday infertility practice, there are circumstances that seem to justify these procedures. Consider a woman who was born without a uterus but with normal, functioning ovaries. Her husband is normally fertile. The patient's sister had a tubal sterilization after three pregnancies and is healthy in every way. The patient's sister's husband is entirely in agreement with the patient's sister's desire to act as a gestational surrogate mother. Oocytes are obtained from the patient, they are fertilized with her husband's spermatozoa, and the pre-embryos are transferred to her sister's uterus. In this situation we are virtually 100 percent confident that the pregnancy resulted from the procedure and is not an accidental result of coitus between the surrogate and her husband. The offspring is the genetic product of the husband and wife and has no direct genetic relationship to the patient's sister.

Other cases involve the use of a surrogate mother who contributes 50 percent of the chromosomal makeup of the offspring; this represents a more complex situation. The birth mother who clearly is genetically related to the offspring will be giving up her newborn child (hers in terms of both birth process and genetics). Indications for the use of a surrogate gestational mother include any condition in which there are functioning ovaries but an absent or nonfunctioning uterus. The uterus may be congenitally absent or may have been removed because of disease; it may be nonfunctional as a result of in utero DES exposure. A surrogate carrier may also be considered if pregnancy is ill-advised for reasons of maternal health. Another issue concerns responsibility for the child in the event that it is abnormal or damaged as a result of premature birth or birth trauma. There are also issues of the health status and behavior of the surrogate gestational mother during pregnancy. One must consider the impact of drugs or alcohol and the possibility of transmission of diseases. Finally, there is the issue of payment to the surrogate gestational mother. The possibility for exploitation certainly exists.

— LUIGI MASTROIANNI, JR.

obtaining a semen specimen. For example, ovarian infection could occur following ovum retrieval, which could result in permanent sterility (Tureck et al., 1993). In addition to the cost of the procedures, which is usually borne by the couple requiring the oocytes, there is also the question of payment to the donor for her time, pain, and suffering.

In contrast to spermatozoa, oocytes are difficult to cryopreserve; hence, menstrual cycle coordination between the recipient and the donor is required. Alternatively, donor oocytes may be fertilized with the husband's sperm, and the pre-embryos cryopreserved for future transfer. Sources of donor oocytes include the excess eggs from patients undergoing in vitro fertilization, oocytes obtained incidental to an operative procedure such as a sterilization, or a specific donation by a relative or close friend. Increasingly, the source of the eggs is a paid "volunteer." The availability of this technology allows pregnancy in women who are well past the ordinary childbearing age (Sauer et al., 1990, 1993).

Conclusion

The techniques employed in what is known as the "new assisted reproductive technologies" are varied and challenging. They range in complexity from seemingly straightforward artificial insemination to micromanipulation of ova, spermatozoa, and pre-embryos—and perhaps, in the future, to treatment of genetic disease by gene insertion in vitro. Just as the techniques vary, so do the ethical issues surrounding them. In no other field is there a greater opportunity for interaction among the physician-scientist, ethicist, moral theologian, social scientist, and legal scholar.

— LUIGI MASTROIANNI, JR.

SEX SELECTION

Sex selection may be performed at three stages before birth: (1) before conception, by separation of X- (female) and Y- (male) bearing sperm; (2) before implantation of an embryo in the womb, by use of in vitro fertilization and embryo selection; and (3) after a pregnancy is established, by prenatal diagnosis and selective abortion of fetuses of the sex not desired. Preconception methods of sex selection have not proved reliable. Most of these depend on separation of X- and Y-bearing sperm, which may somewhat increase the odds of conceiving a child of the desired sex but does not guarantee a particular result. Preimplantation embryo selection could offer an alternative to parents who would find abortion for sex selection morally objectionable. Embryos not implanted could be frozen and stored rather than being destroyed. Although technically possible, this method will likely appeal to few, because of its high cost and the low success rate of in vitro fertilization (Robertson, 1992). Thus, around the world, most sex selection before birth occurs through prenatal diagnosis, including amniocentesis, chorionic villus sampling, or ultrasound, followed by selective abortion. Ultrasound, although not definitive, may show the male genitals; its major use is for parents who desire a son and who are willing to abort a fetus that is not clearly male.

Sex selection may be morally justifiable in some cases to give parents the option of avoiding the births of males with serious genetic disorders, usually called X-linked disorders, that a healthy mother can transmit to her sons but not to her daughters. These include hemophilia and some forms of muscular dystrophy. A male fetus whose mother carries a gene for an X-linked disorder has a 50 percent chance of having the disorder. Some X-linked disorders cannot be diagnosed before birth. Identification of fetal sex gives parents the option of selective abortion of male fetuses who are at 50 percent risk of having severe medical problems. This use of prenatal diagnosis falls within medically accepted uses of prenatal diagnosis to provide parents with information on which to make decisions about fetuses with serious genetic disorders.

Most sex selection has no relationship to genetic disorders. It is solely for the sex desired by the parents. Two ethical issues are involved. The first is whether families should be able to choose the sex of their children, and if so, under what conditions. The second is whether abortion is justified as a means to this end. Although about one-third of the U.S. public favors use of preconception methods of sex selection (Dixon and Levy, 1985), relatively few (5 percent) approve of prenatal testing and abortion for this purpose (Singer, 1991). A substantial minority (38 percent), however, would approve the use of abortion for sex selection if a couple already had three children of the same sex, regardless of whether these were boys or girls (Singer, 1991).

Direct requests for prenatal diagnosis for sex selection have been few in Western nations, in view of (1) the absence of a strong cultural preference for children of a particular sex, and (2) personal and cultural objections to the use of abortion for this purpose. Although the majority of Americans believe that abortion should be available to others in a wide variety of situations, including sex selection, few would use it themselves (Wertz et al., 1991). In any case, the numbers of requests for prenatal diagnosis for sex selection cannot be documented in Western nations, because few parents make open requests.

Medical professionals in the United States appear increasingly willing to perform prenatal diagnosis for those making requests for sex selection, however. According to a 1975 survey of 149 clinically oriented

Some statutes explicitly make newborn screening voluntary, but it often is done without informed consent.

PAGE 315

The patient's consent is a prerequisite to genetic testing.

PAGE 316

Currently, few explicit legal safeguards exist to ensure that genetic data will not fall into the wrong hands.

PAGE 318

geneticists and counselors, 15 percent would recommend amniocentesis for sex selection in general and 28 percent would do so for a couple with one girl who wanted to have only two children and who wanted to be sure that their final child would be a son who could carry on the family name (Fraser and Pressor, 1977).

SEX SELECTION AROUND THE WORLD

Percentage*	Nation
30	Brazil
47	Canada
29	Greece
60	Hungary
52	India
33	Israel
38	Sweden
24	United Kingdom
62	United States

*Percentage of doctoral-level geneticists who would perform a prenatal diagnosis for a couple with four daughters who desired a son and would abort a femuale fetus (Wertz and Fletcher , 1989b, 1989c, 1990)

In giving reasons for acceding to parents' requests, many geneticists in the 1985 survey said that sex selection was a logical extension of parents' acknowledged rights to choose the number, timing, spacing, and genetic health of their children. These geneticists regarded withholding any service, including sex selection, as medical paternalism and an infringement on patient autonomy. Those who would refuse prenatal diagnosis said that it was a misuse of scarce medical resources designed to look for serious genetic abnormalities, that sex was not a disease, or that they disapproved of the abortion of a normal fetus. Most regarded sex selection as a private procedure involving only the interests of doctor and patient, rather than as a procedure that could affect the wider society or the status of women. Few, except for geneticists in India, mentioned the societal implications of sex selection. Women, who comprised 35 percent of doctoral-level geneticists in the United States, were twice as likely as men to say that they would actually perform prenatal diagnosis for the couple with four daughters in the case above (Wertz and Fletcher, 1989b, 1989c, 1990).

Most requests for sex selection in developed nations are probably covert, with women requesting prenatal diagnosis on the basis of anxiety about the health of the fetus. Most geneticists in the United States (89 percent) and around the world (73 percent) would perform prenatal diagnosis for an anxious woman aged twenty-five with no medical or genetic indications for its use (Wertz and Fletcher, 1989b, 1990). Parents are usually asked if they wish to know the fetal sex, though some clinics do not provide the information unless specifically requested (Wertz and Fletcher, 1989c). In effect, sex selection as facilitated by prenatal diagnosis is therefore available to most families.

For some women having prenatal diagnosis for medically indicated reasons, such as maternal age over thirty-five, knowledge of fetal sex may present a troubling or even unwelcome possibility for choice. For example, a woman aged forty with three sons, whose pregnancy is unexpected and who has always wanted a daughter, could decide to have prenatal diagnosis, which is medically indicated by her age and genetic risk, and to find out the fetus's sex before deciding whether to continue the pregnancy. Knowledge about fetal sex affects abortion decisions among some women (about 16 percent) having prenatal diagnosis on the basis of advanced maternal age, especially if the pregnancy was not intended (Sjögren, 1988).

The major use of prenatal diagnosis for sex selection occurs in those developing nations where there is a strong preference for sons. In some nations, such as India, the majority of prenatal diagnostic procedures are performed for sex selection rather than detection of fetal abnormalities. Ultrasound, although not always accurate, is affordable even to villagers and poses no risk to the mother. In many nations of Asia, sex selection contributes to an already unbalanced sex ratio occasioned by neglect of female children. An estimated sixty to one hundred million women are "missing" from the world's population (Sen, 1990), including twenty-nine million in China and twenty-three million in India. Whereas in the United States, the United Kingdom, and France, there are 105 women to every 100 men, and in Africa and Latin America the proportions of women and men are roughly equal, in much of Asia, including Pakistan, Afghanistan, Turkey, Bangladesh, India, and China, there are fewer than 95 women for every 100 men (United Nations, 1991). Families desire sons for economic reasons. In these nations, where most people have no social security or retirement pensions, sons are responsible for caring for parents in their old age. Daughters usually leave the parental family to live with their husbands and help care for their parents-in-law. Even if a daughter stays in the parental home, she seldom has the earning power to support her parents. In some nations, a daughter represents a considerable economic burden because her family must pay a dowry to her husband's family in order to arrange a marriage. A son's religious duties at his parents' funerals, though often cited as a reason for son preference in India, are of less importance than economic factors. These religious duties can be performed by other male relatives. As elsewhere in the world, cultural sex stereotypes and sexism also play a role in the desire for sons.

ETHICAL ARGUMENTS IN FAVOR OF SEX SELECTION

1. would enhance quality of life for a child of the preferred sex
2. would enhance quality of life for the family
3. would enhance quality of life for the mother
4. would help limit the population

According to these arguments, families that have the sex "balance" that they desire would be happier. Children of the "unwanted" sex, usually female, would be spared the abuse, neglect, and early death that is their documented fate in some developing nations (Verma and Singh, 1989) and that may occur to a less obvious extent elsewhere. Women would not be abused by their husbands for not bearing children of the desired sex. Women would not suffer repeated pregnancies and births in order to produce at least one child of the desired sex, usually a son. Families would not have more children than they could afford in order to have a child of the desired sex. Many families in developing nations would prefer to have at most two children. These couples could limit their family size and still have a son to support them in their old age, instead of continuing to have children until they have a son. The threat of world overpopulation might recede.

Each of the arguments above can be effectively countered. Arguments that sex selection will lead to a better quality of life for families, children, or women are comprehensible only in the context of a sexist society that gives preferential treatment to one sex, usually the male. Instead of selecting sex, it should be possible to improve quality of life by making society less sexist. Although sex selection could prevent some abuse of unwanted female children and their mothers in the short run, it does not correct the underlying abuses, namely the social devaluation of women in many parts of Asia and the gender stereotyping of children of both sexes in the rest of the world.

There is no good evidence that sex selection will reduce population growth in developing nations. Most families try to have the number of children that is most economically advantageous. If they could select sex, and if one sex presented an economic advantage over the other, some families might have more children—all of the advantaged sex—than they would have had in the absence of sex selection. Education of women in developing nations and increased opportunities for their employment outside the home are probably more effective means of reducing population growth than sex selection. In developed nations, sex selection will likely have no effect on population size, because most families do not have more children than they wish in order to have a child of a particular sex (Dixon and Levy, 1985).

Arguments against all types of sex selection are based on the premise that all sex selection, including selection for the "balanced family" desired in most Western nations, helps to perpetuate gender stereotyping and sexism (Overall, 1987; Warren, 1985). Sex selection violates the principle of equality between the sexes (U.S. President's Commission, 1983). In a nonsexist society, there should be no reason to select one sex over the other. Michael Bayles has examined concerns that might be put forward for sex preference, including replacing oneself biologically, carrying on the family name, rights of inheritance, or jobs requiring either men or women. He points out that none of these reasons are valid (Bayles, 1984). A child's sex does not make that child biologically any more "my" child than a child of the other sex. In modern societies, women as well as men can carry on the family name, inherit estates, and carry out most jobs. Conversely, men can care for children, elderly parents, or relatives with disabilities, tasks that usually fall on women in developed nations and that could in the future lead to a preference for daughters. Mary Anne Warren points out that even in a nonsexist society, however, there would remain a natural desire for the companionship of a child of one's own sex (Warren, 1985). This is not a strong argument in favor of sex selection. Any activity that a parent can enjoy with a child of one sex, such as sports, vacations, or hobbies, can be enjoyed with a child of the other sex.

Another argument against sex selection is that it could increase gender inequalities, even in developed nations where parents usually prefer sons and daughters equally. Although these preferences are slight, there is evidence that in the United States families would prefer that the firstborn be a boy or that they have two sons and a daughter if they are to have three children (Pebley and Westhoff, 1982). Firstborns tend to receive more economic advantages than laterborns. A society in which firstborns tended to be sons would tend to give more power to males.

There are additional arguments against sex selection if it takes place after conception. Prenatal diagnosis for this purpose is a misuse of a costly, and in some nations scarce, medical resource. If use of prenatal diagnosis for sex selection becomes widespread, this could discredit all uses of prenatal diagnosis, including use to detect serious disorders in the fetus. Sex selection undermines the major moral reason that justifies prenatal diagnosis—giving parents information on which to make deci-

In 1990 the Danish Parliament adopted a resolution advocating a ban on the use of genetic data in employment decisions.

PAGE 318

Genetic testing's ethical issues include education and counseling, confidentiality, and justice.

PAGE 319

sions about fetuses with serious and untreatable genetic disorders. Using prenatal diagnosis to select sex could lead toward selection on cosmetic grounds, such as height, or weight, or eye, hair, or skin color, if analysis for such characteristics in the fetus ever becomes technically possible. Some parents would select for such purposes, especially for weight (Wertz et al., 1991).

Laws prohibiting sex selection could do more harm than good in most nations, because such laws could lead to further interference with reproductive freedom. Some would argue that instead of focusing on sex selection, societies should work toward equality of the sexes and against gender stereotyping, including the stereotyping of fetuses (Rothman, 1986), and should establish a moral climate against sex selection of any kind. Sex selection is not a medical service; doctors are not forced to accede to patient requests or offer referrals. Doctors could also consider withholding information about fetal sex, although this would put control into the hands of doctors and could lead to a resurgence of medical paternalism.

In nations where sex selection has become a social problem, however, laws may be useful as interim measures to prevent widespread abuses of prenatal diagnosis, at least until women achieve equality. Even if laws cannot be adequately enforced, they may be symbolically important in establishing the equality of women (Verma and Singh, 1989; Wertz and Fletcher, 1989c). Long-range solutions are education for women and equality in the work force. Societies generally place higher value on women if their work is recognized as productive (which usually means work outside the home), if they have some economic rights, and if there is an awareness of the social changes necessary to overcome inqualities. In developing nations, women's longevity and the ratio of women to men are in direct parallel with women's participation in the work force (Sen, 1990). Thus in sub-Saharan Africa, where many women work outside the home, women outnumber men, while in Pakistan, India, and Bangladesh, where relatively few women work outside the home, there are fewer women than men. The solution to sex selection in these nations seems to lie in women's entry into the paid work force.

It is important to seek solutions to the problem of sex selection now, because it has the potential power to change entire societies. If preconception methods become available, societies and individuals may act on their preferences with little possibility of legal or moral restraint. Sex selection could further unbalance the already unbalanced sex ratio in many parts of the world and could lead to greater numbers of "missing women." Professionals need to reconsider a trend toward honoring all patient requests, including sex selection. Prospective parents need to reconsider the consequences of unlimited choice.

— DOROTHY C. WERTZ

ARTIFICIAL INSEMINATION

There are two distinct approaches to artificial insemination (AI). Homologous artificial insemination, known by the acronym AIH (artificial insemination, husband), uses a husband's sperm to inseminate his wife. Heterologous artificial insemination (AID, for artificial insemination, donor) uses sperm from a man other than the woman's husband. Traditionally, AID has been used by married couples so that the wife can bear a child in cases of the husband's infertility or genetic incompatibility between the couple. AID is now also used by single woman who desires to have a child but does not have a marital or other stable heterosexual partner, or by a woman in a life partnership with another woman. AID also is used in implementing a surrogacy agreement under which a woman will bear a child to be relinquished to the semen donor or a third party after birth.

Selecting and testing donors

Many problems and concerns associated with AI have stemmed from broad physician discretion to select patients and donors and to determine whether and how to screen them. Until recently there were no clearly accepted guidelines, and individual attitudes and values of practitioners still can control whether a person will be accepted for AI. Similarly, a practitioner may choose potential donors on the basis of individual views about appropriate "matching." Because of the secrecy long characterizing AID practice, established medical standards based on custom that might be used in tort actions are lacking.

The 1978 study mentioned earlier revealed that screening for genetic anomalies and even communicable disease was surprisingly lax among many practitioners. There was also disparity in the numbers of women inseminated by the sperm of one donor, with some responses raising concern about the potential for accidental incest. The later OTA study (U.S. Congress, OTA, 1988) revealed improvement in these practices, with a major testing change in response to concern about transmission of AIDS to impregnated women through semen from seropositive donors. This has since led to increased testing of donors as well as recordkeeping on the parties; with the aura of secrecy lifting, expanded donor screening to deal with more than concern about AIDS seems inevitable.

Attempts to "medicalize" AID

Despite the lack of clear standards for physicians, some states have attempted to "medicalize" AID through statutes providing that it can be performed only by licensed physicians. This type of regulation is considered futile by many because of the ease with which the process can be effected without medical assistance as well as understandable reluctance to prosecute a woman for performing the insemination herself. More problematic are some state statutes that provide for terminating a sperm donor's parental rights only if AID is performed by a physician, making it possible for a donor to assert paternity in other circumstances. The ethical objection to this form of law is that the penalty is borne as much or more by the child as by a parent.

Designating the physician as gatekeeper without established guidelines or standards has led to legal and practical problems. A Virginia physician who performed AID using his own semen without his patients' knowledge or agreement was convicted of criminal fraud. But such a scenario leaves many unanswered questions, including whether it is ethical for a physician who satisfies basic health and genetic requirements to use his semen if nothing is done to mislead the patient and there is disclosure and consent.

Further difficulties have been raised by physician failure to adhere to statutory requirements that can enable parental status to be fixed clearly. For example, most state laws on artificial insemination address only the circumstance of AID for a married woman with her husband's consent; some of these require that consent be in writing, and some instruct the physician to file a copy of it with a specified legal agency. Courts have confronted cases in which a physician failed to obtain written consent and situations in which a husband questioned the continued nature of his consent when conception occurred only after a lengthy period.

Reflecting long-standing legal concern for upholding the legitimacy of children, some courts have found that oral consent can provide adequate compliance even in the face of a statutory provision for written consent, and others have determined that a physician's failure to file the consent agreement with a designated state agency according to the statutory mandate does not affect a child's legitimate status if consent has in fact been obtained.

Establishing paternity

Until several decades ago, results of blood tests could serve only to rule out paternity except in highly unusual cases, and even then they were usable only in a limited number of situations. There was a strong legal presumption that a child born to a married woman cohabiting with her husband was his legitimate offspring, and in many jurisdictions neither spouse could give testimony that would render a child illegitimate. Fathers of illegitimate children were considered to have little constitu-

ARTIFICIAL INSEMINATION
Background

A relatively simple process, until some two decades ago AID in the United States was practiced largely in an aura of secrecy and with little regulation despite complex legal questions that could stem from it. This situation reflected prevailing attitudes that discouraged public discussion of private sexual practices. Legislators shied from regulation because of aversion to controversy, the perception that the practice was limited, and a sense of futility because the legal problems seemed insoluble without broad reform of legitimacy and paternity laws at a time when family-law reform was not a pressing issue.

Social, legal, and scientific developments since the 1970s have led to more critical focus on AI and the legal and ethical issues it raises. Effective birth-control methods and legal abortion, along with social and economic changes enabling more single mothers to keep their children rather than relinquish them for adoption, sharply reduced the number of healthy neonates available for adoptive placement. At the same time, vastly expanded scientific knowledge about genetics and wider popular awareness of the impact of hereditary disease increased demand for artificial insemination from couples seeking to avoid genetic conditions or diseases. AI usage and acceptance increased significantly as a result, though past secrecy practices and their vestiges make it difficult to quantify the extent of the increase. A 1978 study based on practitioner responses to a questionnaire estimated between 6,000 and 10,000 births annually through AID in the United States. A broader study by the Office of Technology Assessment (OTA) of the U.S. Congress in 1986-1987 indicated that there were 30,000 births through AID and 35,000 through AIH during a comparable period one decade later (U.S. Congress, OTA, 1988).

AI was once the only alternative for effecting conception other than through coitus. Practices such as in vitro fertilization and surrogate embryo transfer now represent other choices, though they are far more technology-dependent. Among new terms introduced to reflect the expanded options (and avoid confusion with AIDS), "assisted conception" is currently the most widely accepted; it was chosen by the National Conference of Commissioners on Uniform State Laws for its 1988 Uniform Act on Status of Children of Assisted Conception, a model statute that has generated little legislative response. AID remains the most popular procedure and the one for which physician involvement or significant technical assistance is least needed.

— WALTER WADLINGTON

If it were not for the possibility of causing harm, reproductive behavior would have a compelling claim to be considered private.

PAGE 541

Political philosophies differ in views of how extensive the private sphere should be.

PAGE 541

tional protection regarding assertion of parental rights, particularly if the mother was married to someone else. Not surprisingly, it was then widely believed that under almost any predictable scenario a successful challenge of the husband's being the father would be extremely unlikely if an AID practitioner kept no records and carefully matched the blood types of all the parties. Some physicians sought further to lessen the odds of successful legal challenge by mixing a sterile husband's sperm with that of an anonymous donor. Dubbed "confused" or "combined" artificial insemination (CAI), the practice was a form of medical/legal gamesmanship undertaken on the questionable premise that it would overcome the presumption of paternity of a husband in courts of a state with no statute legitimizing offspring of consensual AID by married couples. CAI is largely discredited today. However, a woman may be inseminated with the sperm of different donors during a particular AID cycle.

Earlier assumptions that paternity would not be challenged or could not be established affirmatively have proved to be unrealistic. Tissue typing now permits affirmative proof of paternity to a high degree of probability. The presumption of legitimacy is far easier to challenge, and legal limitations on the testimony of husbands and wives have eroded substantially. Concurrent with these developments, fathers of illegitimate children have been accorded greater constitutional protection of their parental rights. With the recent shift to recordkeeping because of concern about HIV transmission, information about donors should be more accessible to courts unless statutes are enacted to preclude this.

Risk awareness

Given the uncertainty still prevalent in many situations and the differing state laws, questions are now being raised about whether physicians should tell their patients about potential legal problems. Laws determining what information a physician must disclose to a patient generally come from tort law governing informed consent. Criteria may vary between states, but a patient ordinarily should be informed about the risks of serious harm that a procedure poses, as well as feasible alternative strategies.

However, it must be recognized that informed-consent law developed in the context of disclosure of health risks and medical alternatives. The risks most likely to deter a patient from choosing AID, in contrast, are largely legal, including questions about kinship status, whether a sperm donor might assert parentage, and confidentiality in the event of legal actions such as divorce. Another legal hazard is that siblings related by half blood through a common sperm donor might marry without awareness of their kinship. If the relationship were discovered, such a marriage would automatically be void under most state laws without the need for an annulment.

Adoption, one of the most feasible alternatives to AID, is a legal rather than a medical procedure. Judicial expansion of the doctrine of informed consent or specific legislation thus might be necessary to legally require communication of such nonmedical information. However, the medical need for disclosure might be based on potential psychological harm to the child, the mother, or the husband. Even so, although a physician seemingly has an ethical obligation to advise that there may be serious legal risks as well as a legal alternative, it is unclear and probably doubtful that there is a legally enforceable duty to make such disclosure.

The special case of AIH

Paternity concerns associated with AID are obviated by AIH. At one time questions of legitimacy were raised in the courts in the context of marriages annulled for impotence (inability to copulate) after birth of an AIH child. Today most jurisdictions have laws providing that a biological child of the parties to a void or voidable marriage is deemed their legitimate offspring.

The Ethics Committee of the American Fertility Society has concluded that AID is acceptable for demonstrated medical indications such as male infertility, husband's genetic disorder, or ejaculatory dysfunction. However, in its 1986 and 1990 reports, it noted that questions remain about the efficacy of AIH in a number of instances, including manipulation for the purpose of sex selection, and that use of AIH for such uncertain purposes should be regarded as a clinical trial.

Further ethical and religious objections and concerns

An early and long-standing objection to artificial insemination is its "unnaturalness," whether accomplished through AIH or AID. A further concern is that it separates procreation from sexual expression, and thus a child born as a result of the procedure does not stem from a true conjugal relationship. An opposing view is that rational human control over nature is a major human achievement and that the new technology and understanding can benefit mankind. Variations between these arguments present differing views about determining the circumstances under which assisted conception can be deemed morally justifiable.

Some opponents regard AID as ethically tantamount to adultery. Others who would not categorize it as adultery nevertheless object because of concern that it could lead to adultery by a married woman wishing to have a child and using third-party sperm without medical intervention. Trial courts in Canada (1921)

SPERM BANKING

Until recently sperm banking received little regulatory attention. The American Fertility Society now provides specific guidelines dealing with donor screening, and though they have no statutory authority, they should become increasingly important in establishing standards of practice that may be used in legal actions.

A widely recommended current practice to avoid HIV transmission is to test a donor at the time semen is taken and to retest six months later. This provides an illustration of the newly expanded recordkeeping.

Cryopreservation, used in sperm banks, offers prospect of posthumous use of a donor's sperm. With AIH, this could continue family lineage; it also could create genealogical nightmares and raise complex testamentary issues in both AIH and AID because of the pervasive emphasis on biological parentage in estate law. Model language in the Uniform Act on Status of Children of Assisted Conception would assure that a sperm donor is not the father of a child conceived after his death.

Today some men have sperm cryopreserved before undergoing chemotherapy or entering an occupation with radiation hazards, making questions about posthumous use of donor sperm likely to increase. Surprisingly little attention has been paid to this potential issue by donors and sperm banks at the time deposits are made.

— WALTER WADLINGTON

and the United States (1954) suggested that AID might even constitute legal adultery, though subsequent cases have followed the opposing tack of a Scottish judge who opined that insemination could be performed by the woman herself, and there is no legal concept of self-adultery.

Another objection has been based on the reliance on masturbation for collecting donor semen. For the Roman Catholic Church, this is particularly objectionable; because the procedure replaces rather than facilitates the conjugal act, it is a sign of the dissociation of the sexual union and procreation. The Roman Catholic Church has further condemned AID as contrary to the unity of marriage and conjugal fidelity, which demand that a child be conceived in marriage (Catholic Church, 1987).

There has been disagreement within Judaism over the ethical implications of AI. Many commentators express the view that AIH is permissible in limited circumstances if certain halakic guidelines are respected, but some rabbis have objected on the theory that it is a sin to emit sperm other than in its permitted place. AID is more widely opposed, particularly among Orthodox rabbinical authorities, both because it might be regarded as adultery and because the practice could lead to intermarriage between half siblings (see, e.g., Lasker, 1988).

Objections to use of AID by unmarried heterosexual couples, same-sex couples, or single women center on the question of whether it is morally justifiable to utilize assisted conception for others than a family who otherwise would be unable to procreate safely if at all. This objection is complicated by ethical and legal debate about what constitutes a family. The most widespread legislative approach has been to facilitate AID for married couples by providing a method for them to proceed with some guarantee that they will have exclusive parental rights. By omitting reference to nonmarried couples, other parties are relegated to the use of basic rules on paternity and legitimacy that were not designed to deal with AID.

In addition to uncertainty about parent-child status, fear of identifying AID with selective breeding caused the practice to be wrapped in a shroud of secrecy. Selective breeding became an especially objectionable popular concern after revelations about the goal of a "master race" under the National Socialist regime in Germany. Even so, at least one sperm bank in the United States has been established to accept donations from persons of superior intellect, such as Nobel laureates. According to newspaper accounts, the mother of one of the first offspring born through AID with such sperm previously had lost custody of children for abusing them by trying to drive them to intellectual success.

PAYMENT FOR SEMEN. The term "sperm donor" is a misnomer because compensation of persons supplying semen has been a long-standing practice, whether the intermediary is an AID practitioner or a commercial sperm bank. Views about the morality of selling body parts and recent statutes banning some such sales raise the question of whether payments for semen should be continued. Statutes prohibiting organ sales usually exempt regenerative tissue or semen. But the 1986 report by the Ethics Committee of the American Fertility Society recommends that semen should not be purchased. Similarly, the 1979 draft recommendations of the Council of Europe with regard to artificial insemination would forbid payment to semen donors except for reimbursement of expenses.

Aside from the ethical objection to making a commodity of human tissue (and particularly semen), there is the health concern of avoiding encouragement of per-

Men in Africa have argued against family-planning programs for putting the idea of risk-free, nonmarital sexual activities in the minds of unmarried young women or wives.

PAGE 539

Strong persuasion encompasses social and administrative pressures or economic penalties that lessen but do not extinguish the freedom to act contrary to approved behavior.

PAGE 541

ARTIFICIAL INSEMINATION
What Effect on Children?

The fact that AID produces an offspring that is genetically linked to one person in a couple makes this alternative more attractive than adoption to many couples, even though the same ethical problems do not exist for those who adopt because they are dealing with a child already in being. While it is accepted practice to tell adopted children about their special status at an early time and in a manner designed to make them feel wanted rather than rejected, parents may choose not to tell their children about conception through AID. Today's more extensive recordkeeping and major strides in establishing paternity significantly increase the chances that a child will learn about AID parentage. This might result from medical testing, but there also is evidence that many couples utilizing AID discuss this with third parties, increasing the likelihood that a child may learn of it even if the parents remain silent.

Given the pattern of increasing willingness to depart from a long accepted pattern of confidentiality for adoptions (at least for those effected through state or private agencies), it seems inevitable that demands for similar treatment will be raised for children of AID now that paternity is more readily determinable through records and testing.

— WALTER WADLINGTON

sons with infectious or hereditary diseases to sell their semen, a situation analogous to that of blood donors. The state of Oregon provides that a man who is aware that he has a transmissible disease or defect should not donate semen. However, the only means for enforcing the prohibition seemingly would be through a damage action against a donor by one acquiring the disease or defect through the donor's knowing violation.

ACCESS TO AI: HOW MUCH PERSONAL AUTONOMY IN A LEGAL CONTEXT? Though existence of a broad right to procreate—an especially strong recognition of personal autonomy—has been asserted by persons seeking to enforce surrogacy contracts in which a third party's womb is utilized, it also might be raised by someone denied access to AID for use outside surrogacy. The paucity of judicial attention to the latter may reflect both the wide access to medical assistance for AID and the fact that it can be accomplished without such access. A federal appeals court in 1990 denied a male prisoner's request to facilitate procreation with his wife through AIH. However, because prisoners sustain some recognized diminution of their legal rights during imprisonment, this particular limitation on use of AIH does not serve to define the parameters of any right to procreate through AIH or AID in other contexts.

A few states have sought to assure greater access to AI by requiring that issuers of health insurance with obstetrical coverage provide coverage at least for basic procedures in reproductive assistance that could include AI.

Ethical and political divisions

Popular attention has been captured by surrogacy and more exotic assisted-conception techniques, but AI remains the most widely used. And it still presents serious issues in need of resolution. The key problem in AI from a legal standpoint is that under many current state laws, parentage and legitimacy remain unclear because even statutes that seek to clarify such issues are often narrow in scope. To no small extent this situation results from objections to use of AI by unmarried persons, including same-sex couples. Ultimately these issues may be resolved only in the context of a broader review of rights based on nonbiological relationship in matters such as child custody and adoption. However, failure to deal with serious status problems because of religious or ethical disagreement seems inconsistent with family-law approaches in areas such as divorce, where it is recognized that the civil law provides basic guidelines that should not obstruct the tenets of individual religious groups who are free to follow their own beliefs.

— WALTER WADLINGTON

IN VITRO FERTILIZATION AND EMBRYO TRANSFER

In in vitro fertilization (IVF), a woman's ovaries are stimulated with fertility drugs to produce multiple eggs. The physician monitors the woman's response by examining urine samples, blood samples, and ultrasound imaging. After giving her an injection to control the timing of the egg release, the physician retrieves the eggs in one of two ways. In a laparoscopy, done under general anesthesia, the surgeon aspirates the woman's eggs through a hollow needle inserted into the abdomen, guided by a narrow optical instrument called a laparoscope. In the more recently developed transvaginal aspiration, done with local anesthesia, the physician inserts the needle through the woman's vagina, guided by ultrasound.

After they are retrieved, the eggs are placed in separate glass dishes and combined with prepared spermatozoa from the woman's partner or a donor. The dishes are placed for twelve to eighteen hours in an incubator designed to mimic the temperature and conditions of

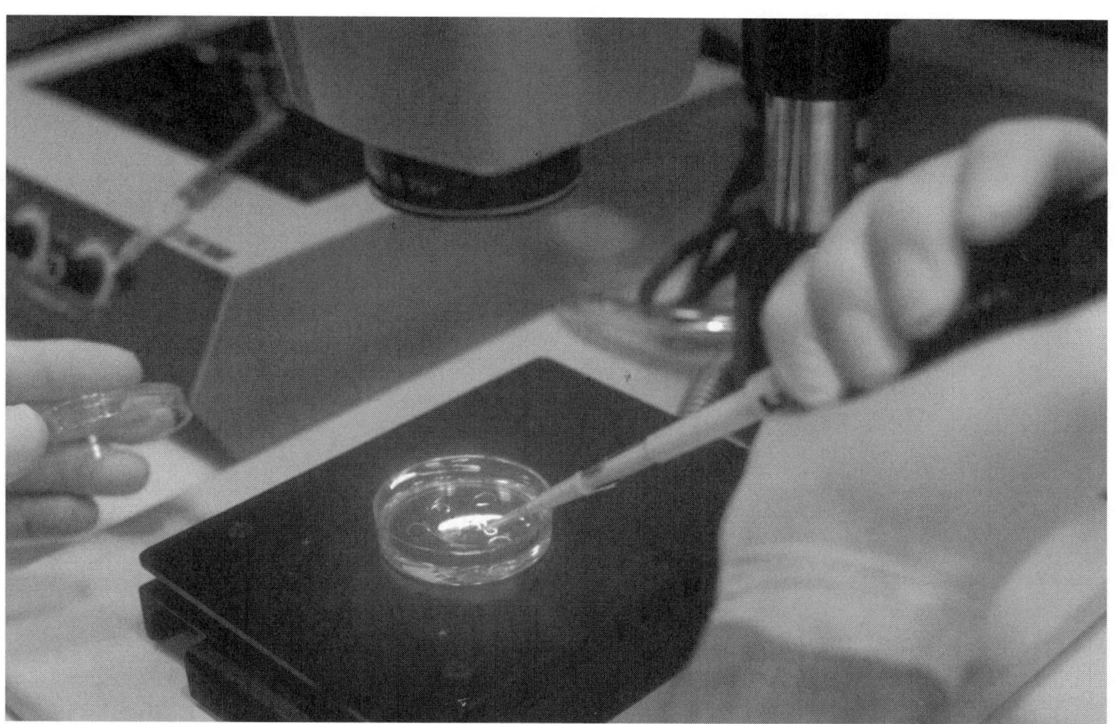

SPERM + EGG

In vitro fertilization was originally designed to help women with blocked fallopian tubes to become pregnant. The first birth from IVF was in England in 1978.

the body. If a single spermatozoon penetrates an egg, IVF has occurred.

A fertilized egg subdivides into cells over a period of forty-eight to seventy-two hours. Microscopic in size, it is generally called a pre-embryo or an embryo after it has divided into two or more cells. When the embryos have divided into four to sixteen cells, they are placed in a hollow needle (catheter) that is inserted into the woman's vagina. The embryo or embryos are released into the woman's uterus in the procedure known as embryo transfer. Implantation in the uterine wall, if it takes place, will occur within days after transfer; a pregnancy is detectable about two weeks after the transfer.

In established IVF clinics, the odds that a continuing pregnancy and birth will occur after embryo transfer are 20-30 percent. Because problems can arise at all stages of IVF, such as the inability to retrieve eggs or secure fertilization, the odds are less if they are calculated from the time fertility drugs are first given. Data from several national registries indicate a delivery rate of 9-13 percent if calculated from the starting point of hormonal stimulation (Cohen, 1991). The birthrates tend to cluster among clinics, so that some clinics account for a large percentage of the total births while others have few or no deliveries (Medical Research International, 1992). Tens of thousands of embryo transfers are carried out each year internationally, and thousands of babies have been born. Clinicians reported over 12,000 deliveries following IVF in one five-year period (1985-1990), and in one country (the United States) alone (Medical Research International, 1992).

Present and future variations

The first birth following IVF occurred in England in 1978 (Steptoe and Edwards, 1978). The technique was originally designed to circumvent blocked or damaged fallopian tubes in women trying to become pregnant. During the late 1970s and early 1980s, physicians combined the male partner's sperm and the female partner's eggs and transferred the embryos shortly after fertilization. If the couple had a large number of embryos, physicians either transferred all at once, creating the risk of a multiple pregnancy, or disposed of extra embryos, wasting the embryos and being morally problematic.

The start of embryo freezing in the early 1980s has given physicians greater control over the number of embryos transferred at once. Two to four embryos are transferred in the first IVF cycle, and the remaining embryos, if any, are frozen for later thawing and transfer. Embryo freezing saves the woman from the hormonal stimulation of repeated start-up IVF cycles, and it allows embryo transfer when the woman's body has returned to a more natural state. By enabling the transfer of a small number of embryos at once, it reduces the odds of a multiple pregnancy and the subsequent risk this poses to the woman and the fetuses. Controlled transfer of embryos is arguably less morally problematic than the selective abortion of fetuses in a large multiple pregnancy. The birth of the first infant to have been frozen as an embryo took place in Australia in 1984. Embryo freezing is now a routine option in IVF.

Another variation that has increased the flexibility of IVF is the use of donated sperm, eggs, and embryos

REPRODUCTIVE TECHNOLOGIES

In Vitro Fertilization and Embryo Transfer

When embryos have developed and have been preserved in vitro, disputes about their fate have involved potential heirs, gamete providers, and institutions.

PAGE 237

to circumvent fertility problems such as low sperm count in the male partner, lack of ovulation in the female partner, or lack of fertilization with the couple's own eggs and sperm, or to help couples at high risk avoid passing on a serious genetic disorder to their children. Sperm and embryo donation are more straightforward than egg donation, which is complicated by the need to synchronize the menstrual cycles of the donor and recipient. Women are either paid for their services in donating eggs or they donate in the course of their own medical treatment. In addition, some women donate eggs for their sisters or other close relatives. Donation of eggs or sperm raises questions about, among other things, confidentiality of medical records, the child's sense of identity, and the psychological well-being of the donor.

The embryos in IVF can be transferred to a surrogate if the genetic mother does not have a uterus or cannot carry a child to term for other reasons. Although the surrogate is usually unrelated, there have been instances of embryo transfer to the sister or even the mother of a woman who cannot carry a fetus to term. In the latter case, the surrogate is the child's gestational mother and genetic grandmother.

Sperm microinjection is another technique used in connection with IVF. If the male partner has low sperm count or poor sperm quality, a healthy spermatozoon can be manually inserted into the egg with special microinstruments. This alternative to sperm donation allows the transfer of embryos genetically related to the couple. This and other microsurgical procedures remain experimental and infrequent.

Another procedure for IVF is the examination of sperm, eggs, and embryos for chromosomal and genetic abnormalities. Preimplantation diagnosis has been conducted on an experimental basis in the United States, Britain, and other European countries. It is being developed for couples at high risk for passing to their children a genetic disorder such as cystic fibrosis or Tay-Sachs disease but who will not terminate a pregnancy and are therefore not candidates for prenatal screening.

Preimplantation diagnosis includes polar-body analysis (analyzing the DNA of the first polar body of the human egg), trophectoderm biopsy (examining extra-embryonic cells surrounding the inner cell mass), and embryo biopsy (removing a single cell from a four- or eight-cell embryo). It also includes chromosomal analysis to select only female embryos for transfer to couples who are at high risk for passing on a sex-linked disease, such as hemophilia, to male children. Pregnancies and births have been reported following embryo biopsy and sex preselection. Many variables remain to be worked out in preimplantation diagnosis, and physicians urge caution before expanding it in the IVF setting (Trounson, 1992). Correcting genetic flaws after they have been diagnosed is a distant, though foreseeable, possibility (Verlinksy et al., 1990).

Ethical issues in IVF

A recurring and unresolved issue in IVF involves the status of the embryo (McCormick, 1991). The Ethics Advisory Board, set up by the U.S. Department of Health, Education and Welfare, and later disbanded without its recommendations' being acted on, issued a report in 1979 stating that "The human embryo is entitled to profound respect, but this respect does not necessarily encompass the full legal and moral rights attributed to persons" (U.S. Department of Health, Education and Welfare, 1979, p. 107). The Warnock Commission issued a report in Britain in 1984 that also accorded the embryo a "special status," though not the same status "as a living child or adult" (Warnock, 1985).

The notion that the embryo is an entity with a special status deserving special respect is contested by those who regard the embryo as fully a human being from the moment of conception. An instruction issued by the Vatican concluded that the "human being must be respected—as a person—from the very first instant of his existence" (Catholic Church, 1987; Shannon and Cahill, 1988). The unique genetic makeup of the embryo, among other things, is given as evidence of its individuality.

Beliefs about the embryo's status are central to conclusions about what in IVF is permissible and what is not. Some observers who regard the embryo as a human being believe IVF is ethically acceptable provided all embryos are transferred and given a chance to survive. Others believe external fertilization is always immoral. If the embryo is regarded as a human being, it has "full human rights," including the right not to be experimented upon without its consent (Ramsey, 1972a, 1972b). Even if one regards IVF as no longer experimental, the conclusion of immorality still extends to IVF's variations, which begin as experimental procedures posing the risk of higher-than-normal embryo loss.

If, on the other hand, the embryo is regarded as only potentially a human, fewer ethical strictures on IVF techniques apply. The Ethics Advisory Board concluded that IVF was ethically acceptable for married couples and that research on human embryos was acceptable provided the research was designed to establish IVF safety, would yield "important scientific information," complied with federal laws protecting research subjects, and proceeded only with the consent of tissue donors. No research was to take place beyond the fourteenth day after fertilization. After fourteen days, the embryo begins to develop an embryonic disk

See Also

Embryo Custody Disputes: Tangled Claims

or "primitive streak" and is no longer capable of spontaneous twinning, which means it is on the way to becoming a single individual.

IVF is highly selective in the people it can help. An expensive procedure covered by few insurance companies, it is available primarily to affluent couples. Critics question the wisdom of directing scarce resources to an elective and costly procedure with low odds of success (Callahan, 1990). Others advise paying more attention to preventing infertility in the first place (Blank, 1988). Aggressive marketing of IVF, including marketing that distorts success rates to make them seem greater than they actually are, arguably creates needs by making couples feel they ought to try IVF because it is there to try and by interfering with alternatives such as adoption or stopping efforts to conceive.

Concerns about the support of IVF and embryo research have been integrated into formal policy in a number of countries (Knoppers and LeBris, 1991). For example, the British Human Embryology and Fertilisation Act of 1990 created a licensing authority to conduct on-site visits to clinics in which human embryos are manipulated, review research proposals, and ensure that quality control is maintained in the laboratories (Morgan and Lee, 1991). A restrictive law in Germany, by contrast, makes criminal a range of techniques not therapeutic for the embryo, including sex preselection for nonmedical reasons ("German Embryo Protection Act," 1991). Among the international documents relating to embryo manipulations are a recommendation from the Parliamentary Assembly of the Council of Europe that the Council of Ministers provide a "framework of principles" governing embryo and fetal research ("Parliamentary Assembly," 1989) and a set of principles relating to IVF and its variations ("Council of Europe," 1989).

Fifteen states in the United States mention embryos in their statutes, but legislators passed most laws with abortion and fetuses in mind rather than IVF and embryos. Some of these laws would presumably make embryo research illegal, but their constitutionality has not been tested (Robertson, 1992). In 1989 the

IN VITRO FERTILIZATION
Social and Moral Objections

In vitro fertilization has been criticized as a fundamentally dehumanizing technique that takes place in a laboratory, involves the scientist as a third party, is geared to the production of human beings, and is aimed at conquering nature and producing a "quality" child (Kass, 1985). The language of IVF and its business and marketing overtones contribute to a situation in which tissues and children are treated as commodities to be produced and in which intimacy is devalued (Lauritzen, 1990). The Vatican instruction concluded that IVF is unnatural because the sperm are secured by masturbation and the union takes place outside the body. Tissue donation is especially illicit, as it is "contrary to the unity of marriage, [and] to the dignity of the spouses" (Catholic Church, 1987).

Some feminists have expanded on this theme by criticizing laboratory conception as an intervention that divides reproduction—once a continuous process taking place naturally within the woman's body—into discrete and impersonal parts subject to a male-dominated medical profession (Arditti et al., 1984). They argue that in IVF, women are perennial research subjects in an unending set of techniques that have significant emotional costs (Williams, 1989); that IVF benefits men and compromises women; and that it curtails women's autonomy and magnifies gender-based power differences in society (Wikler, 1986). Other feminists support IVF if it is bounded by feminist ethics and if it builds women's control over reproduction rather than taking it away (Sherwin, 1989).

IVF's variations challenge notions of the family, the interests of the potential child, the distribution of societal resources, and the rights of prospective parents. Tissue donation from relatives creates new biological if not legal relationships—for example, when a sister donates an egg to a sister for IVF or a brother donates sperm for his brother's IVF attempt. Embryo freezing creates the prospect of some embryos being stored indefinitely or transferred in a later generation, possibly endangering the resulting child's sense of identity. It also sets the stage for custody disputes and conflicts over the disposition of unwanted embryos (*Davis* v. *Davis*, 1992).

Embryo diagnosis for genetic defects raises safety questions for the embryo and potential child. Conceivably, it will lead to screening for many genetic problems and not just the life-threatening disorders envisioned now. On the one hand, discarding embryos after tests reveal a genetic abnormality might be less morally contentious than aborting pregnancies, at least for those who believe the embryo has a lesser status than a fetus. On the other hand, discarding "defective" embryos may blunt societal sensibilities and invite fertile couples into the costly and uncertain IVF procedure. The ability to preselect embryos according to sex raises concerns that the technique will be used for nonmedical reasons to give couples a child of their preferred gender, which may be male (Wertz and Fletcher, 1989).

— ANDREA L. BONNICKSEN

A National Academy of Sciences study found that population growth's minor role in economic development did not warrant extreme fertility-control measures.

PAGE 550

U.S. Supreme Court reviewed Missouri's abortion statute but declined to address the constitutionality of the statute's preamble that "the life of each human being begins at conception" (*Webster* v. *Reproductive Health Services*, 1989). This definition of personhood appears to contradict the Court's abortion rulings, but by leaving it untouched, the Court left the embryo's legal status unclear.

Several states have passed laws mandating insurance coverage for IVF under certain conditions (U.S. Congress, Office of Technology Assessment, 1988). The federal government does not fund proposals involving human embryos; by law, research must be reviewed by an ethics board ("Protection of Human Subjects," 1975), but no board has replaced the Ethics Advisory Board, which was disbanded in 1979. This has led to a de facto funding moratorium.

Conclusion

Prior to and in the years following the first successful use of IVF, critics argued that it challenged the sanctity of marriage and family, posed the threat of psychological and physical harm to unborn children, involved the immoral destruction of human embryos, made women experimental pawns in research in which men asserted control over reproduction, and introduced the senseless creation of people in an era of overpopulation. It was also said to admit no clear stopping point, use scarce medical resources, and amount to an elective technique that did not cure infertility.

Supporters argued that IVF would spare couples the psychological trauma of infertility, meet the needs of tens of thousands of women with blocked fallopian tubes, lead to knowledge that would help ensure healthy children, and preserve the family by bringing children to couples who truly want them. They responded to criticism by saying IVF was no more unnatural than cesarean births, should not be diminished merely because it did not cure infertility, posed no apparent risks to children, and was not immoral, in that embryos were only potential human beings.

Today, basic IVF has shifted from experimental to standard medical practice. It is widely available, is regarded as safe, and is the only viable way women with blocked fallopian tubes can conceive a baby genetically related to them. New technical additions ensure, however, that external fertilization will remain at center stage in the ongoing bioethics debate over reproductive technologies.

The lasting unanswered questions relate to the high value placed on genetic parenthood, equitable access to techniques across race and class, the impact of laboratory conception on women's control over reproduction, and whether priority ought to be placed on conception in a time when discussions are directed to ways of reducing the gap in medical services available to richer and poorer citizens.

Perhaps most significant, however, is the matter of the limits to be placed on reproductive technologies. It appears that the scope of refinements is nearly endless. Should substantive and procedural limits be placed by government on any of IVF's variations? If so, which, and why? Understanding the reasons for placing limits is as important as understanding the reasons laboratory conception is pursued with such intensity in the first place.

— ANDREA L. BONNICKSEN

SURROGACY

Surrogacy, a reproductive arrangement involving three or more persons, typically comes into play for several reasons: when the female member of a married couple is unable to conceive a child, or unable to gestate a child for physical and/or psychological reasons; or, though able to conceive and gestate a child, unwilling to do so for some medical reason—for example, a genetic disease that she does not wish the child to inherit—or even for some strictly personal reason—for example, a schedule interruption that would interfere with her career. If she and her husband desire to rear a child to whom they are at least 50 percent genetically related, they may decide to seek a woman who is willing to carry a pregnancy to term for them. Less typically, unmarried couples may seek the services of a surrogate mother for reasons similar to those of married couples. So, too, may single women and single men, with the specific aim of single-parenting a child genetically related to them.

There are two types of surrogate mothers: those who gestate an embryo genetically related to them (partial surrogacy) and those who gestate an embryo genetically unrelated to them (full surrogacy) (Singer and Wells, 1985, p. 96). In cases of partial surrogacy, a woman agrees (1) to be artificially inseminated with the sperm of a man who is not her husband; (2) to carry the subsequent pregnancy to term for a fee (commercial surrogacy) or out of generosity (noncommercial surrogacy); and (3) to relinquish the child at birth to the couple or single person. Although the contractual arrangements are the same in cases of full surrogacy, the medical ones are not since the woman gestates an embryo that is not genetically hers.

Although it is tempting to substitute the term "gestational mother" for the term "surrogate mother," so as not to prejudge which of two or more women is indeed the moral and/or legal mother of a child, such relabeling is conceptually confusing. Not all gestational mothers are surrogate mothers. For example, although a woman to whom an embryo is donated is her child's gestational mother, she is not her child's surrogate mother. What makes a gestational mother a surrogate mother is that she both begins and ends her pregnancy with the intention of relinquishing the baby to someone else.

Moral arguments for and against surrogacy

In addition to traditional arguments for and against surrogacy, there are several feminist ones. Relying largely on Kantian perspectives and/or natural-law perspectives, often related to official Roman Catholic teachings (Shannon and Cahill, 1988), traditional opponents of surrogacy object to it for five reasons. First, they claim that surrogacy is unnatural since it involves techniques like artificial insemination by donor (AID) and/or in vitro fertilization (IVF), both of which are "artificial" means to the "natural" end of procreation. Second, they note that the surrogate mother offers not simply her gestational services but herself as a human person. Thus, only someone who is morally prepared to endorse slavery should morally endorse surrogacy. Third, they argue that just as a prostitute degrades herself when she offers herself as a sex object, a surrogate mother degrades herself when she offers herself as a reproductive container. Fourth, they maintain that introducing a third party into the process of procreation weakens the marital relationship. A woman might fantasize about the "potency" of the man who artificially inseminated her, and a man might marvel at the "fecundity" of the surrogate mother, regarding her as somehow better than his infertile wife. Fifth,

SURROGACY
Feminist Arguments Pro and Con

Feminist arguments for and against surrogacy seek to correct the male biases that often limit traditional pro and con arguments. These biases may be manifest in any number of ways, but they often appear "in rationalizations of women's subordination, or in disregard for, or disparagement of, women's moral experiences" (Jaggar, 1992, p. 361). Although there are various diverging feminist positions on surrogacy, three lines of thought are particularly prominent.

Liberal feminists, who believe that women's liberation depends on women having the same educational, political, and economic opportunities and rights as men, argue that women, provided they do not harm anyone in the process, should be permitted to use whatever reproduction-controlling and/or reproductive-aiding technologies they need to live as men's equals. Preventing a woman from working as a surrogate mother, or from hiring a surrogate mother, violates her reproductive freedom just as much as preventing a woman from using birth control or having an abortion.

In contrast to liberal feminists, *Marxist feminists*, who believe that women's liberation depends on the destruction of a capitalist system that makes some people the economic pawns of other people, argue that when a woman offers her reproductive services not as a gift but as a commodity, her action is most likely coerced. For the most part, surrogate mothers who sell their reproductive services are considerably poorer than the men and/or women who buy them. Unable to support herself and/or her family, a woman will sometimes sell the only thing she has of value: her body. To say that a woman "chooses" to do this, says the Marxist feminist, is simply to say that when a woman is forced to choose between poverty and exploitation, she sometimes chooses exploitation as the lesser of two evils. Although most surrogate mothers should not be blamed for their choice, it is an unfree one that results in their degradation, and no decent society can sit idly by as some women are reduced to "baby-making" machines.

Radical feminists, who believe that women's liberation ultimately depends not only on a political and economic revolution but also on a sexual revolution capable of radically transforming male and female gender roles, deepen the Marxist feminist analysis of exploitation to include noneconomic exploitation. Whereas Marxist feminists emphasize that under capitalism there is always a price high enough to entice even the most resistant person to sell what is most precious, radical feminists emphasize that, frequently, women agree to serve as surrogate mothers simply because they wish to be recognized as "good"—that is, generous, loving, altruistic—women. Traditionally, the more sacrificial a woman is, the more society praises her. It matters not how much she hurts herself in the process.

Radical feminists also urge that far from being "collaborative," surrogacy is a reproductive arrangement that creates divisions among persons, but especially among women. Relatively rich persons hire relatively poor women to meet their reproductive needs, adding childbearing services to the child-rearing services that economically disadvantaged women have traditionally provided to economically privileged persons. Worse, reproductive technologists sort women into three classes: genetic mothers, gestational mothers, and social mothers. In the future, no one woman will beget, bear, and rear a child. Rather, genetically superior women will beget embryos in vitro; strong-bodied surrogate mothers will carry these "test-tube babies" to term; and sweet-tempered women will rear these newborns from infancy to adulthood (Corea, 1985).

— ROSEMARIE TONG

Artificial insemination involves the mechanical placement of spermatozoa into the female reproductive tract.

PAGE 574

they insist that surrogacy erodes the mother-child relationship, since the surrogate mother deliberately becomes pregnant with the intention of giving up the child (Krimmel, 1983). When she does this for a fee, her act becomes indistinguishable from "baby-selling," a practice that most moralists condemn as a form of slavery.

Traditional proponents of surrogacy maintain that their opponents base their case on faulty reasoning. First, they note that if the line between the "natural" and the "artificial" separates moral from immoral practices, then society ought to forbid intravenous feeding—an "unnatural" way of eating—as well as in vitro fertilization—an "unnatural" way of procreating. Second, they observe that since someone cannot buy something that already belongs to him, a genetic father cannot buy his genetic child from the woman who gestated it. Third, they claim that it is no more degrading to offer one's sexual or reproductive services to others than it is to offer one's "brain power" or "muscle power" to them. Fourth, they object that a surrogate mother does not necessarily jeopardize the marital relationship of the couple who hire her. She intrudes on them only as much as they permit her to do so. Fifth, they argue that there is nothing inherently wrong with intentionally and voluntarily procreating a child that one does not plan to parent, provided that those who do plan to parent the child have the child's best interests at heart.

Invoking both utilitarian reasoning, according to which an action is right if it maximizes the utility (pleasure or happiness) of those affected by the action, and contractarian reasoning, according to which contracts freely entered into ought to be honored, traditional proponents of surrogacy make one final observation on its behalf. They note that surrogacy is simply a new form of "collaborative reproduction"—that is, a mode of reproduction that requires more or other than the energies, efforts, and endowments of a couple (Robertson, 1983). Since society has not morally condemned genetic parents for soliciting and/or accepting other people's help in rearing their children (for example, through such social arrangements as adoption, step-parenting, foster-parenting, wet-nursing, and babysitting), they argue that society ought not to morally condemn genetic parents who require other people's assistance in bearing their children.

Public-policy approaches to surrogacy

Several public-policy approaches to surrogacy have been articulated, ranging from its criminalization to its strict enforcement as a matter of contract. In 1985 the United Kingdom passed the Surrogacy Arrangements Act, which make serving as a surrogacy broker a criminal offense. Lawyers, physicians, and social workers—as well as certain newspaper and media personnel—are subject to fines and/or imprisonment if they initiate or participate in commercial surrogacy arrangements (Surrogacy Arrangements Act, 1985). Those who favor the criminalization of commercial surrogacy concede that even noncommercial surrogacy involves the possibility that some people will use other people as means to their own ends. However, they insist that such exploitation becomes significantly probable and not simply possible whenever financial interests are involved. The main problem with criminalizing surrogacy arrangements, be they commercial or noncommercial, is that such a stratagem may constitute an unjustified restriction on procreative freedom. If an individual or couple cannot have a genetically related child without the assistance of a surrogate mother, then, arguably, the state must show that there is no less restrictive way to prevent the harms that surrogacy allegedly causes.

Less restrictive ways to regulate surrogacy include its assimilation into adoption law and its enforcement as a matter of contract. Those who recommend that surrogacy be assimilated into adoption law argue that there is little difference between making arrangements to adopt a woman's baby as soon as she knows she is pregnant and making arrangements to adopt a woman's baby shortly before she becomes pregnant. Therefore, the same rules that govern adoption should govern surrogacy arrangements. Adoption rules permit payment, but only for the woman's reasonable medical expenses. Moreover, the adopting couple may pull out of the negotiations at any time before the adoption papers are signed; and the woman who plans to relinquish her child is given an opportunity after its birth to change her mind. Perhaps the strongest argument in favor of the adoption approach is that it harmonizes with the long-standing legal view that the woman who gives birth to a child is that child's mother. Thus, lawyer George Annas insists that whether or not the surrogate mother is genetically related to the child, the state should recognize her as the child's legal mother because "she will definitely be present at the birth, easily and certainly identifiable, and available" to care for the child (Annas, 1988, p. 24).

Nevertheless, despite all of surrogacy's similarities to adoption, it remains fundamentally different. As feminist Phyllis Chesler sees it, adoption is a child-centered practice whereby adults, willing to give children the kind of love they need to thrive, take into their homes and hearts children who are already conceived or born. In contrast, surrogacy is an adult-centered practice whereby children are deliberately conceived and brought into existence so that adults can have someone to love (Chesler, 1988). Worse, by insisting on a 50 percent genetic link, the child becomes genetically prearranged rather than unconditionally accepted (as adopted children are).

In contrast with those who seek to regulate surrogacy through adoption law, those who seek to regulate it through contract law regard surrogacy as a business transaction between consenting adults for reproductive services. Supporters of the contract approach claim that all disputes between surrogate mothers and contracting persons should be regarded as breaches of contract to be remedied either by a specific performance or a damages approach. Under the specific performance approach, for example, the state would take the child away from a balking surrogate mother, remanding the child's custody to its legal parent or parents (that is, the contracting person or persons). In contrast, under the damages approach, the state would require a balking surrogate mother to pay monetary damages to the contracting person or persons in lieu of relinquishing the child.

Whatever its theoretical merits, the damages approach suffers from practical disadvantages. For example, since most surrogate mothers are poor compared with those who contract for their services, they may not be able to pay the damages assessed against them; and, even if they are able to pay the assessed damages, the money will not adequately compensate the relatively rich but childless contracting person or persons. However, the greatest objection to any contract approach to surrogacy, whether it favors specific performance or damages, is that if the law enforces surrogacy arrangements as it enforces any contract, it may contribute to the view that children are just another consumer good to be bought and sold at will.

Social perspectives on surrogacy

When one looks at surrogacy arrangements worldwide, one is led to conclude that such arrangements are ordinarily negotiated by relatively privileged infertile persons who have the $25,000 or more to pay both the surrogate broker's and the surrogate mother's fees. Although one hears about relatively poor people reproducing a child "collaboratively" and "altruistically," for the most part the people who participate in such arrangements are family members and/or friends. In any event, some commentators have observed that the issue is not whether surrogacy is commercial or noncommercial. Rather, the issue is why, given a burgeoning world population, infertile people are frantically seeking ways to add to its numbers. After all, there is something ironic about infertile people seeking to augment their reproductive powers through artificial insemination, in vitro fertilization, and surrogacy arrangements even as fertile people seek to control their reproductive powers through contraception, abortion, and sterilization.

But even if people have a right to procreate or not procreate children who are genetically related to them, society needs to ask itself why, with very rare exceptions, genetic connection is viewed as the ultimate determinant of parenthood. Because (full) surrogacy permits a split between begetting and bearing a child, it forces society to reconsider the role that genes should play in assigning parental rights and responsibilities. It can, in fact, be claimed that what makes one a parent is not so much a genetic contribution to a child as it is a gestational connection or parental relationship to him or her.

In addition to inviting society to focus on the necessary and sufficient conditions for parenthood, surrogacy invites society to ask itself some profoundly disturbing questions about procreative freedom. Is it "liberating" for infertile persons to believe that unless they can produce a child genetically related to them, their lives will be without real joy? Similarly, is it "liberating" for a woman to sell her reproductive services to anyone who wishes to pay for them, even if she must regard herself as an incubator? Finally, is it "liberating" for children to be "sold" by surrogate mothers who do not want a relationship with them and/or to be "bought" by persons who do want a relationship with them, provided, as many surrogacy contracts stipulate, they are born without disease or defect?

As attractive as is the ideal of collaborative parenting—a state of affairs in which two or more people, able fully to share all parental blessings and burdens, together beget, bear, *and* rear a child—it is an ideal that is particularly difficult to achieve in a racist, sexist, and classist society. Until society comes to terms with the full implications of procreative freedom, it must use its powers of moral persuasion and legal coercion to eliminate any exploitative aspects of surrogacy. Certainly, society must pay particular attention to the interests of women and children as it seeks to formulate good public policies for the regulation of an arrangement that transforms a number of our most fundamental relationships, including parenthood.

— ROSEMARIE TONG

CRYOPRESERVATION OF SPERM, OVA, AND EMBRYOS

The technical ability to freeze sperm, embryos, and eventually ova for long periods and then thaw them without destroying their biologic potential offers several new reproductive options for both fertile and infertile individuals. It makes the donation of eggs, sperm, or embryos to treat infertility a more efficient and safe procedure. It also allows individuals and couples to preserve sperm, eggs, and embryos to protect against future reductions in gametic viability due to age, dis-

Cryopreservation has had a significant impact on clinical practice since the first successful insemination with freeze-stored semen in 1953.

PAGE 574

As far as is known, cryopreservation of human pre-embryos is not associated with adverse fetal effects.

PAGE 577

R

REPRODUCTIVE TECHNOLOGIES

Cryopreservation of Sperm, Ova, and Embryos

ease, or occupational exposure, and permits posthumous reproduction to occur.

As with any technological deviation from the natural mode of conception, these techniques raise both medical questions of safety and efficacy and ethical, legal, and social questions about prohibition, restriction, or regulation of these practices. Once cryopreservation is medically established as safe and effective, its ethical, legal, and social acceptability depends on a general acceptance of noncoital and assisted means of reproduction, with specific issues relating to the particular technique in question.

Sperm

Cryopreservation of sperm is now well established medically and socially as a commercial enterprise. Sperm banking occurs as an aspect of infertility practice, or as an option for men who foresee damage to their gametes as a result of disease or occupational exposure. In the former case, a commercial sperm bank recruits sperm providers, screens them medically and socially, and usually pays them a fee for their sperm (technically they are vendors rather than donors of sperm though the latter word is commonly used to describe their role). The sperm is then distributed to doctors or others who practice artificial insemination with donor sperm, who in turn resell or distribute it to recipients.

A main legal and ethical issue with regard to this practice is the duty of the sperm bank to screen sperm donors and their sperm for infectious diseases, including the human immunodeficiency virus (HIV). Guidelines of the American Fertility Society, the main professional organization of physicians treating infertility, now recommend that donated sperm be screened for HIV diseases. Because there may be a six-month gap before HIV transmission shows up on antibody screening tests, screening requires that the donated sperm be quarantined for six months so that a second test can be performed on a sample to ensure that it is not HIV-infected. Failure to screen in this way is unethical and could make the sperm bank legally liable for transmission of HIV to recipients and offspring.

There are no laws that restrict to whom sperm banks may sell their sperm, and in the United States, the buying and selling of sperm is not generally covered by federal or state laws against selling organs, though several European countries prohibit the prac-

ASEXUAL REPRODUCTION

Cloning: "Hello Dolly"

Ioning, as defined in the Bioethics Thesaurus, is asexual single-parent reproduction resulting in offspring with the same genetic blueprint as the parent. The term is derived from the Greek word for propagating plant life from a cut twig, or 'cloning.'

On February 24, 1997, researchers from the Roslin Institute in Edinburgh, Scotland, under the direction of Dr. Ian Wilmut, reported the birth of a sheep clone. The clone was produced by "somatic cell nuclear transfer cloning" where DNA-containing nuclei from unfertilized sheep eggs were replaced with a different ewe's mammary gland cells that had been rendered inactive in a test tube. The modified eggs were reactivated electrically and then implanted into the wombs of 13 other sheep. The one resulting lamb, Dolly, born July 5, 1996, is the genetic twin of the mammary gland DNA donor. Dr. Wilmut and his team speculate that "by inducing donor cells to become quiescent it will be possible to obtain normal development from a wide variety of differentiated cells" which in turn may be used for applications such as drug development and tissue transplantation.

On the same day that Dr. Wilmut revealed the success of their cloning experiment to the public, President Bill Clinton requested that the U. S. National Bioethics Advisory Commission (NBAC) study the "profound ethical issues" raised by Dolly's creation. The commission concluded that it would be unethical at this time to use cloning for human reproduction because of the potential for physical harm to the resulting child, and recommended federal legislation prohibiting such an act. NBAC noted that such legislation should not affect animal cloning research or experiments with cloning sequences of human DNA, and cautioned that any cloning laws should contain sunset clauses to ensure ongoing review of related research. On March 4, 1997, President Clinton issued a memorandum banning the use of federal funds for human cloning experiments.

During 1997, reports of successful cloning of both sheep and cows were reported in the United States. Now that cloning has gone beyond the realm of science fiction, the nature vs. nurture debate is highlighted: does "individuality" result from our genetic makeup, our environment, or a combination of the two? If the physical safety of cloning can be guaranteed, what would make it different from the other forms of in vitro reproductive technologies that are currently accepted? Ultimately, the possibility of cloning asks us to reexamine what it means to be human in a world where all forms of life may be capable of redefinition.

— NATIONAL REFERENCE CENTER FOR BIOETHICS LITERATURE

SHOCK OF THE LAMB

In 1997, Scottish embryologist Ian Wilmut stunned scientists by cloning from adult cells, a procedure long believed impossible. The lamb was named after Dolly Parton.

tice. Thus a bank could sell sperm to a single woman or representative organizations for use in inseminating single women. Despite fears that a bank or physician who provides sperm to an unmarried woman could be held liable for financial support of a child born as a result, no such legal liability has yet been imposed. While some persons find artificial insemination of single women to be unethical, and the practice is prohibited in some countries, it can allow women who otherwise could not bear children to reproduce, and unmarried women who are committed to reproduction in this way have been shown to be able childrearers.

Commercial sperm banks also provide service to individuals or couples who wish to store sperm for later use because of treatment of disease, occupational exposure, or fear of later impotence. Because no legislation specifically applies to this practice, its legal status would depend upon basic contract law. The depositor would be entitled to keep the sperm in the bank and retrieve it under conditions specified in the contract of deposit. Thus sperm could be released to the depositor or to his designee posthumously, if that is envisaged, and the bank would perhaps have no obligation to maintain the sperm past a specified time if failure to pay storage charges should occur. Clear specification of rights and duties in the original contract is essential. While posthumous release of stored sperm to the appropriate designee could lead to the birth of a child without a rearing father, this situation is similar to the insemination of an unmarried woman and should be treated similarly. Whether a child born posthumously will be able to share in a deceased's estate is a matter of state inheritance law that does not affect the ethical, legal, or social acceptability of the practice.

The bank would, of course, have a legal duty to return the correct sperm to the depositor. At least one case has arisen in which the bank returned the wrong sperm, which led to the birth of a child who was not of the same race as the depositor. In such instances, suits for damages are likely to be successful. An important issue will concern damages, because there is no way to establish that in fact the lost gametes would have implanted and produced a child. In addition, some states regulate the operation of sperm banks as medical or clinical laboratories to protect the health and safety of consumers of their services.

Many of the issues that arise with commercial sperm banks would also apply to physicians who recruit sperm donors directly. They too would have ethical and legal duties of reasonable care to assure that donors have been tested for genetic and infectious disease. They would also be free to inseminate single

IVF treatment is both physically and emotionally demanding.

PAGE 576

The first successful in vitro fertilization was carried out in a normally ovulating woman whose tubes had been surgically removed.

PAGE 576

women and use sperm posthumously, if that is the clear intention of the parties.

Ova

The ability to freeze and then successfully thaw ova has not yet been developed, due to the larger size of the ovum and the great amount of fluid in it. Once this ability is developed, egg banking will occur.

Frozen ova have less ethical significance than frozen embryos. Once the technical ability to freeze and thaw ova safely is developed, they will play an important role in enabling women to initiate pregnancies through in vitro fertilization (IVF), which involves hormonal stimulation of the ovaries to produce ova, often many more than are needed for fertilization at that time; freezing the extra ova will minimize the need for additional cycles of egg retrieval. Rather than inseminate all eggs retrieved in a cycle of IVF treatment, many couples will prefer to freeze extra eggs, which can then be thawed and inseminated for later attempts at pregnancy. Cryopreservation of ova, rather than embryos, may thus become the preferred method of storage.

Once ova freezing and banking begins, the same issues that currently arise with cryopreservation of sperm will occur. Commercial ova banks, which may be associated with sperm and embryo banks or exist independently, will be established. No doubt such banks will both buy or procure eggs from women and then resell them to doctors and couples in need of an egg donation. The main issues will then concern what the precise arrangement is between the donor and the bank concerning subsequent use, whether the bank will be responsible for genetic and infectious disease screening, and whether the bank will be responsible for any rearing costs of offspring.

With eggs that have been frozen for subsequent use in initiating pregnancy in an infertile couple, the agreement between the woman or couple and the storage facility will be of paramount importance. The depositor of the eggs will be the owner and will control release or discard of cryopreserved ova within the limits of the storage facility's policies. Thus the contract between the depositor and the facility would largely control deposits of eggs prior to disease treatment or occupational exposure or to use then or at a later time. As long as the depositor has paid storage charges, she would be entitled to have the eggs stored; to expect reasonable care to be taken in their maintenance; and to have the eggs released, transferred, or discarded as directed. Posthumous release and use of stored eggs should be as acceptable as posthumous release and use of stored sperm. As with sperm banking, failure of payment could lead to the bank taking the eggs out of storage, but it would not be entitled to transfer them to other persons in lieu of payment unless there were a specific agreement to that effect. Professional or even legislative regulation of ova banking to ensure standards of health and safety can also be expected.

Embryos

Cryopreservation of embryos (sometimes referred to as preimplantation embryos or "pre-embryos") is now a well-established adjunct to IVF programs. Standard IVF treatment often produces more eggs than can be safely fertilized and placed in the uterus at one time. Rather than fertilize only the number of eggs that could be safely transferred or fertilize all retrieved eggs and discard the surplus, cryopreservation allows all eggs to be fertilized, a safe number such as two or three placed in the uterus, and the rest frozen for later use. At a later time, the frozen embryos can be thawed and placed in the uterus, donated to others, or discarded. Although the success rate is not as great as with fresh embryos, the pregnancy rate of both fresh and frozen embryos from a single egg-retrieval cycle is 15 to 20 percent greater than the rate from use of fresh embryos alone. Until the ability to freeze and thaw ova is developed, the excess eggs retrieved in a cycle of IVF treatment are likely to be inseminated and then cryopreserved for use during a later cycle.

The main issues that arise with cryopreservation of embryos concern the ethical and legal status of embryos and the locus of dispositional authority over frozen embryos. While some persons have argued that embryos are persons or moral subjects with all the rights of persons, and others claim that embryos are merely tissue with no special status or rights, a wide ethical and legal consensus in the United States, Europe, and Australia views embryos as "deserving of special respect, though not the respect due persons." As a result, embryos may be created, frozen, donated, and even discarded or used in research when there is a valid need to treat infertility or pursue a legitimate scientific goal and rules concerning consent of the gamete providers and institutional review board approval have been followed.

With regard to dispositional authority over frozen embryos, it is now well established that the couple providing the gametes has dispositional authority within the limits of state law and the conditions of storage set by the IVF program or storage facility. If they agree to have embryos created from their gametes cryopreserved, they are "owners" of the embryos and may decide on any disposition of frozen embryos that their agreement with the storage facility and applicable statutes permit.

Since the frozen gametes are the joint property of the persons providing the gametes, their joint consent is needed for disposition until they relinquish or transfer their dispositional authority to others. To maximize their control over embryos and to introduce administrative efficiency into the operation of embryo banking, they should also give written directions at the time of storage for disposition of frozen embryos in the future if the providers have died, divorced, are unavailable for decision, or are unable to agree between themselves on disposition.

In such cases, the IVF program or embryo bank should be able to rely on this prior agreement in decisions concerning stored embryos. This will give advance control to the parties and clear directions to the bank, and will minimize costly disputes about what to do with stored embryos. Although no court has yet been faced with a case directly involving a disputed contract, there have been cases recognizing the right of the depositing couple to remove their frozen embryo from a bank against the bank's wishes. There is also legal authority recognizing the validity of such advance contracts for disposition in case disputes arise.

The *Davis* v. *Davis* case (1992) illustrates the wisdom of giving effect to the prior agreement. A couple had frozen seven embryos pursuant to their efforts to have children via IVF. They subsequently decided to divorce but could not agree on disposition of the frozen embryos. The husband opposed thawing them and using them to start pregnancy, while the wife insisted that she or another person have them placed in her. The Tennessee Supreme Court finally resolved this issue by ruling that an agreement between the parties for disposition in the case of divorce would have been binding, and that in the absence of such an agreement, the relative burdens and benefits of a particular solution must be examined. In that case if the party wishing to retain the embryos had other means of obtaining embryos, such as by going through IVF again with a new partner, that party's wish to have children could still be satisfied without foisting unwanted parenthood on the party who wished that the embryos not be used. On the other hand, if there was no other way for that party to be reasonably able to produce embryos, so that the existing embryos were the last resort or chance to have offspring, then they should be entitled to use them. In that case, fairness would require that the objecting party not have to provide child support. In the facts presented to it, the court ruled in favor of the husband, who did not want frozen embryos implanted after divorce, because the wife had alternative ways to reproduce.

Ethical and legal codes for assisted reproduction in other countries have not yet addressed the problem that arose in the Davis case. A country could take the position that all embryos must be preserved, or that provision of gametes for IVF is a commitment to have all resulting embryos placed in the uterus. However, the American preference to have the parties control disposition in the case of divorce or disposition by prior agreement might also be recognized, for it maximizes the procreative liberty of the parties directly involved.

The authority of the gamete providers over the disposition of frozen embryos can be limited by law or the policies of the banks or facilities where frozen embryos are stored. For example, some European countries (Spain and Germany) prohibit embryo discard and research, while others (Great Britain, for example) limit the period of storage to a maximum of ten years or the reproductive life of the woman, whichever is longer. While U.S. legislation on these issues is largely absent, the Ethics Committee of the American Fertility Society (1986) has recommended a similar maximum period of storage, and individual embryo banks and programs for religious or administrative reasons have imposed limitations on dispositions that involve discard, donation, or release of frozen embryos to other programs. As long as the storage facility makes clear its restrictions on disposition of frozen embryos, it may impose these restrictions on couples who request storage of embryos at that facility.

Conclusion

Cryopreservation of sperm, ova, and embryos offers individuals options to extend or enhance their reproductive ability and should presumptively be recognized as adjuncts of their procreative liberty. If this view is accepted, principles of informed consent and contract will inform and regulate most of the transactions and activities that occur with cryopreserved gametes and embryos. In some cases legislation to protect the parties' wishes and ensure the health and viability of stored gametes and embryos may also be desirable.

— JOHN A. ROBERTSON

ETHICAL ISSUES

The introduction of in vitro fertilization (IVF) in 1978 sparked anew an intense ethical debate about the use of innovative reproductive technologies that had raged a decade earlier (McCormick, 1978). Questions were raised about whether these technologies would harm children and parents and alter people's understanding of the meaning of procreation, family, and parenthood. Gradually the controversy subsided as healthy children were born from these procedures; committees in at least eight countries issued statements indicating that they considered the use of IVF ethically acceptable in principle (Walters, 1987). Arguably, one reason for this readiness to embrace IVF and other new reproductive techniques was that they enabled couples to create offspring in a way that seemed an extension of the natural way of procreating. Although IVF involved joining

Conflicts are also possible between ova providers and gestational parents.

PAGE 238

R

REPRODUCTIVE TECHNOLOGIES

Ethical Issues

"Where there is the necessary technical skill to move mountains, there is no need for the faith that moves mountains."

ERIC HOFFER
THE PASSIONATE STATE OF MIND, 1954

sperm and ovum in a glass dish, the resulting embryo, once implanted, went through a natural period of gestation that culminated in the birth of a child. A second reason was that these technologies, with the exception of artificial insemination by donor, allowed people to have children who were genetically their own. Louise Brown, the first child created through IVF, resulted from the union of the gametes of her biological parents. Third, the children born of these new means of reproduction were born into traditionally structured families. These techniques were assumed to have been developed for use by married couples who, with the new baby, would form what was ordinarily defined as a nuclear family.

In the 1990s, these rationales for accepting novel reproductive technologies are being challenged by medical advances and a changing social environment. Human intervention in the procreative process has become more frequent, more complex, and more highly technological. Oocytes can be removed surgically from one woman and, after fertilization, transferred to another in the procedure of oocyte donation. Women can lend their wombs to others for the incubation of children who have no genetic connection to such "surrogates." Embryos created in vitro can be cryopreserved and stored for use in future years by their genetic parents or by others. Consequently, it is difficult to argue that such innovative measures are mere extensions of the natural way of reproducing. Parthenogenesis (stimulating an unfertilized egg to develop and produce offspring by mechanical or chemical means), cloning (deriving genetically identical organisms from a single cell or very early embryo), and ectogenesis (maintaining the fetus completely outside the body) are on the horizon. Furthermore, third, fourth, and fifth parties, such as oocyte donors, surrogate mothers, and (some suggest) even fetuses and cadavers, are joining sperm donors to assist those who are childless to have offspring. New forms of assisted reproduction are increasingly being used to create children who are not tied to those who will raise them by biological or hereditary links. Finally, these technologies are no longer used almost exclusively to create traditional nuclear families. Unmarried heterosexual and homosexual couples and single women and men now have greater access to them. Such scientific and social changes give new emphasis to the older unresolved ethical questions about the uses of these technologies and raise new questions.

Ethical questions raised by the use of the new reproductive technologies

The initial ethical question created by these technologies is whether they ought to be used at all. Different religious traditions vary tremendously in their judgments about the licitness of the use of these novel techniques. The Roman Catholic church declared the use of new reproductive technologies morally unacceptable (Catholic Church, 1987) because they separate the procreative, life-giving aspects of human intercourse from the unitive, lovemaking aspects, and these, according to Catholic teachings, are morally inseparable in every sexual act. The creation of a child should involve the convergence of the spiritual and physical love of the parents; fertilization outside the body is "deprived of the meanings and the values which are

REPRODUCTIVE TECHNOLOGIES

Feminist Ethical Concerns

Feminists, too, are split about the use of the new reproductive technologies. Some argue that these novel methods define and limit women in ways that demean them, for example, as "fetal containers." They maintain that the desire of many women, both fertile and infertile, for children is, in large part, socially constructed (Bartholet, 1992; Williams, 1992). The cultural imperative to have children drives infertile women to undergo physically, emotionally, and financially costly treatment. They are thrust into the hands of a predominantly male medical establishment that uses women as "living laboratories" whose body parts they manipulate without regard to the consequences (Rowland, 1992). Male experts sever what was once a continuous process of gestation and childbirth for women into discrete parts, thereby fragmenting motherhood (Corea, 1985).

In contrast, other feminists argue that the new reproductive technologies enhance the status of women by providing them with an increased range of options. By circumventing infertility and providing women with alternative means of reproducing, these technologies extend reproductive choices and freedoms (Jaggar, 1983; Andrews, 1984; Macklin, 1994). In their view, the charge that surrogacy exploits women is paternalistic because it questions women's ability to know their own interests and to make informed, voluntary, and competent decisions (Macklin, 1990); women have the ability and right to control their bodies and to make autonomous choices about their participation in such practices, these feminists argue.

— CYNTHIA B. COHEN

See Also

Questioning the Ethics of Preimplantation Embryo Research

expressed in the language of the body and in the union of human persons" (Catholic Church, 1987, p. 28).

Certain other religious groups, such as the Lutheran, Anglican, Jewish, Eastern Orthodox, and Islamic, view some of these methods as ethically acceptable because God has encouraged human procreation (Lutheran Church, 1981; Episcopal Church, 1982; Feldman, 1986; Harakas, 1990; Rahman, 1987). According to these bodies, it is sufficient that love and procreation are held together within the whole marital relationship; each act of sexual intercourse need not be open to the possibility of conception. Still other religious groups hold that there is no necessary moral connection between conjugal sexual intercourse and openness to procreation, and consequently they accept the use of the new reproductive technologies with few qualifications (Smith, 1970; Simmons, 1983; General Conference, 1985). In Hindu thought, for instance, although there is no authoritative teaching on this subject, the mythologies of ancestors appear to allow IVF, oocyte donation, embryo implantation, and surrogacy (Desai, 1989).

Some people recommend adoption over the use of the new reproductive technologies because they view the latter as physically and emotionally debilitating and unlikely to succeed, whereas adoption, while not easy, provides a home and family for children in need (Bartholet, 1993). Yet adoption is a second choice for many infertile couples because of its perceived drawbacks. These include the declining number of healthy children available for adoption, the long and emotionally draining wait, the expense, and the difficult and often frustrating system with which adoptive parents must deal (Lauritzen, 1993). Although the use of assisted reproduction presents some of the same problems as adoption, it offers what some infertile couples consider distinct advantages: It allows them to have children who are genetically related to at least one of them and (except in the case of surrogacy) makes the experience of pregnancy and birth available to the woman. The desire to reproduce through lines of kinship and to connect to future generations exerts a powerful influence, as does the hope of experiencing the range of fulfilling events associated with pregnancy and childbirth (Overall, 1987).

Individual choice, substantial harm, and community values

A central issue in the debate about the use of reproductive technologies concerns the scope that should be given to individual discretion over their use. Some philosophical commentators, emphasizing personal autonomy, enunciate a broad moral right to reproduce by means of these technologies (Bayles, 1984; Brock, 1994). They borrow from legal discussions of the right to reproduce, which some legal theorists take to include the liberty to use methods of assisted reproduction (Robertson, 1986; Elias and Annas, 1987). To limit individual choice about noncoital means of reproduction, the state must show that the use of specific reproductive technologies threatens substantial harm to participants and the children born to them (Robertson, 1988). The philosophers influenced by such legal positions maintain that individuals have great leeway in their choice of whether to procreate, with whom, and by what means. They have a right to enter into contractual arrangements giving them access to these technologies and to utilize third parties in their reproductive efforts. Those who take this approach concede that substantial adverse effects on others, particularly the children, would justify restricting individual use of assisted reproduction.

Since the primary reason for accepting these innovative methods is to bring children into the world, a major consideration in assessing them is whether or not they harm these children. Critics contend that these techniques may cause social and psychological problems to the resulting children because of confusion they engender over divided biological parentage and the social stigmatization to which they may be subjected (Callahan, 1988). John Robertson responds that this criticism is logically incoherent. When the alternative is nonexistence, he argues, it is better for the children to have been born—even though they may experience some harm from the means used to bring them into the world—than never to have existed at all (Robertson, 1986). In most cases, the difficulties they face are not so great as to render life a complete loss.

There are several problems with this influential response. One is that it justifies allowing almost any harm to occur to children born as a result of the use of these techniques in that it can almost always be said they are better off alive. Moreover, this argument presupposes that these children are waiting in a world of nonexistence to be summoned into existence and that they would be harmed by not being born. Since children do not exist at all prior to their arrival in this world, there are no children who could be harmed by not being born. When we say that it is better for a child to have been born, we do not compare that child's current existence with a previous one. Instead, we make an after-the-fact judgment that life is a good for an already existing child, even though that child may have suffered some harm from the technology used to bring him or her into the world. Critics of the use of the new reproductive technologies, however, make a before-the-fact judgment about children who do not exist, but who might. They maintain that it would be wrong to bring children into the world if they would suffer certain substantial harms as a result of the methods by

Much of the debate about the moral status of the fetus focuses on the relevance of its potential for full or unquestionable personhood.

PAGE 235

See Also

Fetal Rights? The Moral Status of the Unborn

which they are created. This is a logically coherent claim that justifies considering whether the new reproductive technologies severely damage children born as a result of their use.

The criterion of avoiding substantial harm, while valid, may provide inadequate ethical constraints on various ways of employing the new reproductive arrangements. The criterion is derived from a position that especially prizes individuality, liberty, and autonomy—quite possibly at the cost of values that are served by the building of families and communities, and by accounting for the common good (Cahill, 1990). Taking respect for individual freedom as the primary value, according to Allen Verhey, runs the danger of reducing the value of persons to their capacities for rational choice and denying the significance of the communities that shape them. People are not just autonomous individuals, they are also members of communities, some of which are not of their own choosing. Freedom is insufficient for an account of the good life in the family. Thus, it may be morally legitimate to recommend limits to individual choice about assisted reproductive techniques, not only to protect the children born of these methods but also to uphold basic community values. What is at issue, he suggests, is what kind of society we are and want to become (Verhey, 1989).

Ethical issues related to the introduction of third parties

The introduction of third parties into procreative acts, according to some critics, imperils the very character of society by threatening the nuclear family, the basic building block of U.S. society (Ethics Committee, 1986; Callahan, 1988). Religious commentators and groups, in particular, have expressed concern about the effect of the use of gamete donors and surrogates on the relation between married couples within the nuclear family. Richard McCormick, a Roman Catholic theologian, argues that when procreation takes place in a context other than marriage (as when single women use artificial insemination by donor, for example) and another's body is used to achieve conception (as in the case of surrogacy, for example), total dedication to one's spouse is made more difficult; in Roman Catholic terminology, it also violates "the marriage covenant wherein exclusive, nontransferable, inalienable rights to each other's person and generative acts are exchanged" (Ethics Committee, 1986, p. 82).

In Islamic law, artificial insemination by donor is rejected on grounds that the use of the sperm of a man other than the marriage partner confuses lineage and might also constitute a form of adultery because a third party enters into the procreative aspect of the marital relation. The practice is highly controversial in the Jewish religion because (1) some consider it a form of adultery; (2) some take the resulting child to be illegitimate; and (3) if the donor is unknown, the practice might eventually result in incestuous marriage between siblings. Most other religious groups that have commented on surrogacy also reject it because it depersonalizes motherhood and risks subjecting surrogates and procreation itself to commercial exploitation. Such practices will lead people to regard children as products who, in Oliver O'Donovan's terms, are "made" rather than "begotten" (O'Donovan, 1984).

Those who wish to counter concerns about adultery distinguish between adultery and the use of a gamete or womb contributed by a third party to assist a married couple to have a child. A necessary element of adultery, they contend, is sexual intercourse; neither gamete donation nor surrogacy involves sexual contact between the recipient and the donor. Moreover, unlike adultery, no element of unfaithfulness need inhere in participation in gamete donation. Indeed, a couple may participate in gamete donation just because they have a strong commitment to their marriage, rather than out of disdain for it (Lauritzen, 1993). When only one parent can contribute genetically to the procreation of a child, but both can nourish and nurture a child, this argument runs, it is ethically acceptable for them to have a child by means of third-party collaboration.

The use of third parties in the provision of the new reproductive technologies leads to confused notions of parentage, critics note, since it severs the connection between the conceptive, gestational, and rearing components of parenthood. It can be difficult to predict who will be declared the rearing parent in different reproductive scenarios, despite the fact that they embrace the same set of facts. For instance, in IVF followed by embryo transfer, the woman who gestates an embryo provided by someone else is considered the mother of the resulting child, but in artificial insemination by donor she is not. Those who respond to this criticism, in attempting to develop a consistent ethical basis for awarding the accolade of parenthood, give priority either to the interests of the children born of these technologies or to those of their adult progenitors.

Those who view the interests of the children as of prime importance argue that genetic connections should constrain the freedom to choose parental status in that biological kinship relations are important to children's development and self-identity (Callahan, 1988). Purposefully to break the link between procreation and rearing, these commentators maintain, harms children born of these procedures because it obscures their identity within a family lineage. Indeed, it has been argued that the biological relationship between gamete donors and the children who result from their contributions carries an obligation for donors to support and nurture those children (Callahan, 1992). Respondents observe that it is not considered wrong to separate the genetic and rearing components of parenthood in such well-established arrangements as adoption, stepparenting, blended families, and extended kin relationships. This precedent suggests that, although the genetic relation may be important, it is not essential to parenthood. Caring for and raising a child are of greater significance for parenthood than providing the genetic material or gestational environment, according to this view. Consequently, the rearing parent should have moral priority over the genetic parent in the interests of the child (Lauritzen, 1993). Others focus on the interests of the parents when the choice is between the genetic and the gestational mother, and they contend that the gestational mother should prevail because of her greater physical and emotional contribution and the risks of childbearing (Elias and Annas, 1986).

Parents who are not the biological progenitors of the children they raise and those who provide them with gametes often fear social stigmatization. This raises the question of whether anonymity and secrecy should be used to envelop all who participate in the use of the new reproductive technologies for their own protection. Anonymity has to do with concealing the identity of the donor; secrecy has to do with concealing the fact that recipients have participated in gamete donation. The practice of artificial insemination by donor has historically been carried out in secrecy with anonymous donors to protect family and donor privacy; oocyte donation, which began with openness about the identity of donors, is moving in that direction as well. The major argument against this development takes the interests of the children as primary and contends that since the personal and social identity of children is dependent on their biological origins, they ought to know about their genetic parents (National Bioethics Consultative Committee, 1989). Several countries that accept this argument have adopted regulations allowing children, when they reach maturity, to gain access to whatever information is available about donors who contributed to their birth.

Technologies of assisted reproduction, especially those involving third parties, facilitate the creation of models of family that depart significantly from the traditional nuclear family. As single persons, homosexual couples, and unmarried heterosexual couples increasingly gain access to these technologies, both religious and secular bodies express concern about weakening mutual commitment within the family and about the welfare of the resulting children. Sherman Elias and George Annas observe that "it seems disingenuous to argue on the one hand that the primary justification for noncoital reproduction is the anguish an infertile mar-

ASSISTED REPRODUCTION

Psychology of Nontraditional Families

Some psychologists claim that children who grow up in these nontraditional families will suffer psychological and social damage because they will lack role models of both genders and may consequently develop an impaired view of sexuality and procreation (McGuire and Alexander, 1985). Moreover, they argue, two parents are better able than one to cope with the demands of childrearing. Other studies have been used to vindicate the opposite conclusions (McGuire and Alexander, 1985). Since few studies have been carried out on the consequences for children of atypical family arrangements that emerge when the new reproductive technologies are employed, it is difficult to provide any clear evidence to support or undermine these opposing contentions. A further concern voiced is that using new reproductive technologies to assist single people and homosexual couples to have children involves a misuse of medical capabilities because these methods are not being employed to overcome a medical problem but to circumvent biological limits to parenthood.

To others, however, the use of new methods of assisted reproduction by single people and homosexual couples mirrors the reality that U.S. society has begun to move away from the nuclear family (Glover, 1989). They see the inclusion of homosexual parents within the meaning of family as a move toward greater equality in a society in which those who are homosexual suffer from prejudice and discrimination. If single people and homosexual couples can offer to a child an environment that is compatible with a good start in life, the *Glover Report to the European Commission* maintains, they ought to have access to these techniques, but it is appropriate for those providing them to make some inquiries before proceeding (Glover, 1989). The Royal Commission on New Reproductive Technologies of Canada approved of allowing infertility clinics to provide single heterosexual and lesbian women access to donor insemination on grounds that no reliable evidence could be found that the environment in families formed by these gamete recipients is any better or any worse for the children than in families formed by heterosexual couples (Canada, Royal Commission on New Reproductive Technologies, 1993).

— CYNTHIA B. COHEN

ried couple suffers because of the inability to have a 'traditional family,' and then use the breakup of the traditional family unit itself as the primary justification for unmarried individuals to have access to these techniques" (Elias and Annas, 1986, p. 67). The Warnock Report, developed by a commission of inquiry into the use of artificial means of reproduction in Great Britain in 1984, concluded that "the interests of the child dictate that it should be born into a home where there is a loving, stable, heterosexual relationship and that, therefore, the deliberate creation of a child for a woman who is not a partner in such a relationship is morally wrong" (Warnock, 1985, p. 11).

Increasing information about the role of genes in heredity will pose new choices and decisions, as well as new dilemmas.

PAGE 441

Ethical issues related to commodification

A concern of special ethical significance is that the introduction of third parties into some of the new reproductive techniques carries with it the danger of commodification of human beings, their bodies, and their bodily products. Giving payment of any sort to surrogates and gamete donors, some argue, risks making them and the children produced with their assistance fungible objects of market exchange, alienating them from their personhood in a way that diminishes the value of human beings (Radin, 1992). Third parties who assist others to reproduce should be viewed as donors of a priceless gift for which they ought to be repaid in gratitude, but not in money.

Others argue that persons have a right to do what they choose with their bodies and that when they choose to be paid, their reimbursement should be commensurate with their services (Robertson, 1988). The value of respect for persons is not diminished by using surrogates and gamete donors for the reproductive purposes of others if those third parties are fully informed about the procedure in which they participate and are not coerced into participating—even when they are paid (Harris, 1992). There is a presumption on all sides that third parties should not be specifically compensated for their gametes, wombs, or babies. Several groups that have considered the matter, though, such as the Warnock Committee in Great Britain (Warnock, 1985) and the Waller Committee in Australia (Victoria, 1984), allow third-party payment for out-of-pocket and medical expenses. The American Fertility Society goes further when it maintains that gamete donors should be paid for their direct and indirect expenses, inconvenience, time, risk, and discomfort (Ethics Committee, 1990). It would be unfair and exploitive not to pay donors for their time and effort, John Robertson argues (Robertson, 1988).

Offering large amounts of money to third parties incommensurate with the degree of effort and service that these persons provide may diminish the voluntariness of their choice to participate in assisted reproduction, particularly when they have limited financial means. There is concern that a new economic underclass might develop that would earn its living by providing body parts and products for the reproductive purposes of those who are better off economically. This would violate the principle of distributive justice, which requires that society's benefits and burdens be parceled out equitably among different groups (Macklin, 1994). However, if poor women and men have voluntarily and knowingly accepted their role in these reproductive projects, it could be seen as unjustifiably paternalistic to deny them the opportunity to earn money. The possibility of exploitation of the poor must be weighed "against a possible step toward their liberation through economic gain" from a new source of income connected to innovative methods of reproduction (Radin, 1987).

Ethical issues related to the uses of embryos, fetuses, and cadavers

When the process of fertilization is external, the embryo becomes accessible to many forms of intervention. During the brief extracorporeal, in vitro period, embryos can be frozen, treated, implanted, experimented on, discarded, or donated. Theoretically, embryos that result from IVF could be cryopreserved for generations, so that a woman could give birth to her genetic uncle, siblings could be born to different sets of parents, or one sibling could be born to another. A 1993 experiment in which human embryos were split reawakened concerns about these sorts of possibilities, which had remained dormant since a mid-1970s controversy about cloning human beings (National Advisory Board, 1994). (Cloning, either by transplanting the nucleus from a differentiated cell into an unfertilized egg from which the nucleus has been removed or by splitting an embryo at an early stage when its cells are still undifferentiated, results in individuals who are genetically identical to the original from which they are cloned.)

Advocates of embryo splitting view it as a way of obtaining greater numbers of embryos for implantation in order to enhance the chances of pregnancy for those who are infertile (Robertson, 1994). Critics claim that cloning in any form negates what we view as valuable about human beings, their individuality and uniqueness. It risks treating children as fungible products to be manipulated at will, rather than as unique, self-determining individuals. These critics maintain that twinning that occurs in nature is an unavoidable accident that does not involve manipulation of one child-to-be to produce a duplicate (McCormick, 1994). Defenders of cloning respond that the similarity of identical twins does not diminish their uniqueness or

See Also
Artificial Life

their sense of selfhood. In any case, cloned individuals would not be identical in that the genome does not fully determine a person's identity. Environmental factors, such as family upbringing and the historical context, weigh heavily in influencing the expression of genes (National Advisory Board, 1994).

In 1993 scientists in the United Kingdom announced the possibility of using for infertility treatment eggs and ovaries taken from aborted fetuses (Carroll and Gosden, 1993). The eggs could be fertilized in vitro and then transferred into infertile women who lack viable eggs; the ovaries could be transplanted directly into women to mature and produce eggs. This would help meet the shortage of oocytes for those who lack their own. Such uses of aborted fetuses, however, are highly contentious and strike some as grotesque. Many who object to abortion on ethical grounds maintain that this procedure, like other forms of fetal tissue use, would encourage the practice. Moreover, it seems self-contradictory for a woman to consent to abortion and at the same time consent to become a grandmother. Children created by this procedure, it could be argued, would know little about their genetic heritage or about their mother, other than that she was a dead fetus, and would therefore be at risk of both psychological and social harm.

Female cadavers provide another potential source of oocytes for those who are infertile. It has been proposed that women consider donating their ovaries for use by others after their death, much as individuals donate organs such as kidneys and livers (Seibel, 1994). It may soon be possible to collect immature eggs from cadavers, mature and fertilize them in vitro, and then transfer them into infertile women. This procedure would have an advantage over the use of eggs from aborted fetuses in that the recipient would be able to learn the medical and genetic history of the adult donor. An argument for this practice is that it would allow the continuation of the family's biological heritage and serve to console the grieving family because some aspect of their deceased relative will have been preserved. Postmortem recovery of eggs would be done with the consent of the donor and would therefore respect individual rights and allow freedom of choice for individuals and their close relatives.

This proposal is grounded in an analogy between organ and gamete donation. Yet gamete donation is different in that it involves the provision of an essential factor for bringing a child into existence; it is not life-saving but life-giving. The interests of the resulting children, consequently, provide a major consideration to be taken into account in determining whether such procedures ought to be pursued. The difficulty noted earlier in connection with the introduction of third parties arises in this instance as well. Children develop their identity and self-understanding, in part, through their relationships with their biological parents. Consequently, they might face serious psychological and social harm if one of their biological parents were a cadaver. Indeed, this concern amounts to a central social concern as well, in that the prospect of using gametes derived from the newly dead in order to create children endangers our perception of the respect due to the dead human body and our view of procreation as ideally grounded in an interpersonal relationship between living persons.

CLONING
Fears of Abuse

It is the potential for abuse of cloning that disturbs most critics. The possibility of cryopreserving cloned embryos suggests the option of implanting cloned embryos and bringing them to term should their already-born twin need a tissue or organ transplant. In another scenario, embryos derived from parents who are likely to produce "ideal specimens" would be cloned and sold on a "black market." Critics condemn such potential applications of cloning because they diminish the value of embryos and of human beings by treating them as objects available for any use by others (National Advisory Board, 1994). They are concerned that the deep desire of the infertile for children, in combination with scientific zeal and market forces, will create strong pressure to clone embryos without a view to the ethical considerations involved.

— CYNTHIA B. COHEN

Ethical issues related to access and justice

Although those able to procreate naturally can decide whether and when to do so, the choice to reproduce among those who need medical assistance to do so is more limited. In part, this is because they enter a health-care system in which providers have responsibilities both to candidates for infertility treatment and to the resulting child, because they are assisting in the creation of a new human being. Although physicians have a special obligation to respect the autonomy and freedom of those who are candidates for treatment, they are not obligated to provide them with all treatments that they request (Chervenak and McCullough, 1991). As one of several groups of gatekeepers of the new reproductive technologies, some physicians use a medicalindications criterion to bar access to these

Genetics grew out of theoretical and experimental work that observed how traits were inherited from generation to generation.

PAGE 325

See Also
Asexual Reproduction: Cloning: "Hello, Dolly"

technologies to some patients, as when, for example, the physical risk of pregnancy is too great. Yet many physicians find that they cannot easily separate medical indications from indications that are psychological, social, and ethical. Questions requiring judgments that go beyond those that are strictly medical arise in many situations. These questions include possible treatment for candidates who wish to create "designer babies" of a certain sex, intelligence, and/or race; couples who want to use a surrogate mother for frivolous reasons related to personal convenience; infertile single women who request access to both oocyte and sperm donation in lieu of adoption; women of advanced reproductive age who want to have children despite the risk to their own health; and couples who appear severely dysfunctional and prone to violence and child abuse. Physicians are not usually trained to address ethical questions that arise in such situations. Because physicians have personal and professional biases and are part of a largely unregulated and profitable infertility industry, it might be appropriate to assign the gatekeeper role to a specially trained group of professionals who are not physicians. Another possibility is to utilize guidelines for the use of the new reproductive technologies prepared by physician professional associations, institutional ethics committees, private-sector ethics boards, public ethics commissions, and state and national regulatory agencies; such guidelines should address not only medical but social, psychological, and ethical issues (Cohen, 1994; Fletcher, 1994).

As long as IVF services and gametes are in short supply, questions will arise about how to select candidates from among those who seek access to the new methods of assisted reproduction. Those persons who are infertile or who carry a serious genetic disease may have a greater first claim than those who are not infertile but who wish to use these methods to select the features of their children or as a matter of personal convenience. This is because the need of the former is a more basic need, directly related to the goal of remedying a difficulty in normal species functioning. A more refined set of rationing priorities would take account of such factors as the number of children an individual or a couple already has; whether they have a support system in place to assist them to care for a child adequately; and the greater medical risk to certain recipients of treatment, such as women of advanced reproductive age. These considerations would be grounded in the interests of the potential children and of their would-be parents, as well as in

ETHICS OF ACCESS
Is Infertility a Disease?

Public-policymakers and private health-care insurance regulators also affect who gains access to the new reproductive technologies. If they define infertility treatment as a response to a disease rather than to a social need, a case for financial support of the new reproductive technologies can be made. Because infertility is a physical condition that impairs normal function, many commentators regard it as something like a disease, the victims of which are in need of help from medical science (Overall, 1987). However, it can also be argued that since reproductive technologies do not correct the condition causing infertility, they do not constitute medical treatment for a disease. Yet many well-accepted treatments do not correct the underlying condition but only its symptoms or disabilities. Given the importance to many people of having a biological child and the fact that normal functioning allows this, the claim has been made that infertility should be treated as a disease on a par with other physical impairments. Historically, the "barren" woman or man has not been accorded sympathy; the availability of infertility treatment might disarm similar current discriminatory attitudes toward those who are infertile.

Even if infertility were defined as a disease, however, this would not indicate that its treatment would be ethically mandatory. The U.S. health-care system does not have infinite resources and cannot provide everyone with every desired or desirable health service. Should the new reproductive technologies be subject to more severe criteria for funding than are set for other medical techniques? Because infertility is a physical dysfunction with significant effects on the life plans of those it affects, it can be contended that a just society should include reproductive technologies among the range of treatments covered. The opposing argument is that the costs of such treatment and its relatively low likelihood of success do not justify its inclusion.

A related issue arises from the fact that only a limited range of people—those with greater financial resources—benefit from the new reproductive technologies. Access depends on economic factors, culture, race, and social class. Those in the United States who are poor have little access to specialty services such as infertility clinics because public and private insurers provide limited coverage. If poor people participate at all in the use of these technologies, they do so as surrogates or occasionally as oocyte donors. Thus, the use of new reproductive technologies has potential for creating further unjust schisms in our society between rich and poor and between one subculture and another.

— CYNTHIA B. COHEN

the need to distribute the number of children among couples in an equitable way.

Conclusion

Behind many of the ethical issues raised by the new reproductive technologies lie difficult questions about the importance of genetic parenthood, the nuclear family, and the welfare of children, as well as the role that society should play in overseeing the creation of its citizens. Perplexity about how to resolve these questions is due, in part, to the speed with which these technologies are being developed. There is a growing concern that they are being created too rapidly, before the old technologies, such as artificial insemination, have been integrated into the ethical and social fabric. As the rate of reproductive change accelerates, the ability to provide ethical safeguards for the creation and use of the new reproductive technologies diminishes. This may be the most persuasive reason to provide some form of direction and regulation of the new reproductive technologies that incorporates defensible ethical limits to their use.

— CYNTHIA B. COHEN

LEGAL AND REGULATORY ISSUES

Reproductive freedom is not a simple concept. Encompassing far more than abortion, it also includes the choice of whether and with whom to procreate, how many times to procreate, and by what means. It includes the choice of the social context (e.g., marital, communal, or solitary) in which the reproduction takes place and, to some extent, the characteristics of the children people will have (gender, presence or absence of certain diseases). It is grounded, for some moral philosophers, in self-determination, individual welfare, and equality of expectation and opportunity (Brock, 1992).

Noncoital reproduction, that is, reproduction achieved despite the absence of sexual intercourse, allows single, homosexual, and infertile people to start and rear families. Often, it entails such controversial techniques as extracorporeal maintenance of an embryo, screening and storage of gametes, or the reproductive assistance of men and women who do not plan to maintain a relationship with the child they help to conceive or gestate.

Thus, new reproductive technologies enable individuals to exercise more reproductive choices. This, in turn, invites exploration of the depths of cultural relativism and the meaning of genetic linkage; the preference for the heterosexual couple as the paradigm for family life; the role of the state as the regulator versus facilitator of individual aspirations; and the role of the state and the professional as the gatekeeper to the technologies that permit people to circumvent infertility or conventional forms of procreation.

Under U.S. law, states can outlaw or regulate certain aspects of reproductive technologies. Areas for possible state intervention include protection of the extracorporeal embryo; protection of patients (and their resulting children) who seek to use reproductive technologies; regulation of contract (i.e., "surrogate") motherhood; definition of family forms and familial relationships in light of gamete transfers and use of contract birth mothers; and limitation on commercialization of the techniques. But the extent to which states can ban or regulate noncoital reproduction depends on the extent to which procreation is protected by state and federal constitutions, and the extent to which ancillary practices, such as payment for gametes or services of a contract mother, are viewed as part of the act of procreation or as independent acts of commercial negotiation.

In the United States, the more zealously procreation is guarded by constitutional guarantees and the more broadly the definition of procreation is drawn, the more compelling and narrowly drawn must be state efforts to restrict use of noncoital procreation. Those restrictions, when they exist, will be manifested in both common law and statutory law, usually with regard to the fields of contracts, property, or family law. Because the details of such law vary tremendously from state to state, this article focuses primarily on the overarching constitutional issues that limit state policymaking and lawmaking in this field, and compares national responses.

What can states do to regulate reproductive technologies?

Even assuming that constitutional protection for procreation remains grounded in a fundamental rights analysis, possibilities remain for areas of state regulation of who may use noncoital reproduction and how they may proceed. First, many aspects of noncoital reproduction arguably do not amount to "procreation," and therefore are more amenable to state control. Donor gametes and surrogacy do not permit an infertile person to procreate; rather, they allow fertile persons to reproduce without partners or to bypass the infertility of their partners.

Artificial insemination by donor (AID), for example, can be used by single or lesbian women who want to become pregnant but who find the thought of sexual intercourse with a man distasteful. Almost half the states in the United States have statutory language governing AID that appears to ignore the possibility of such a use, leaving the legal status of the donor-father unclear (U.S. Congress, Office of Technology Assessment [OTA], 1988b). Canada and France have also

It is the biogenetic definition of life that informs many of the moral debates about the protection of life, whether human, animal, or environmental.

PAGE 442

See Also

Rights Talk: More Harm Than Good?

had national commissions recommend that single and lesbian women be barred from using donor insemination in order to conceive (Liu, 1991; McLean, 1992). Because such women could physically procreate without donor insemination, albeit with great discomfort, it can be argued that such restrictions do not impinge upon a fundamental right to procreate and are therefore potentially tolerable.

Of course, the restrictions would still be subject to challenges based on the unequal treatment of single or lesbian women as compared with the married, heterosexual population. AID for a married couple in which the husband is infertile is also nothing more than a medical alternative to the social solution of adultery; the AID itself does not enable the infertile man to procreate. Nevertheless, in Canada, France, and much of the United States, this form of AID is viewed as therapeutic, seemingly because the "unit" of infertility (i.e., the "patient") is seen as a monogamous, married, heterosexual couple, not as an unmarried individual.

In typical surrogacy arrangements, in which the husband is fertile and the wife infertile, the surrogacy arrangement, like AID, does not permit the infertile wife to procreate, nor is the fertile husband unable to procreate without resorting to surrogacy. Rather, surrogacy allows the husband to procreate without commit-

LEGAL ISSUES

Is There an Affirmative Right to Procreate?

The right to procreate, that is, the right to bear or beget a child, appears to be one of the rights implied by the U.S. Constitution. It is grounded in both individual liberty (*Skinner* v. *Oklahoma*, 1942) and the integrity of the family unit (*Meyer* v. *Nebraska*, 1923), and is viewed as a "fundamental right" (*Griswold* v. *Connecticut*, 1965), one that is essential to notions of liberty and justice (*Eisenstadt* v. *Baird*, 1972).

The U.S. Supreme court has not explicitly considered whether there is a positive right to procreate—that is, whether every individual has a right to actually bear or beget a child and thereby has a claim on the community for necessary assistance in this endeavor. It has, however, considered a wide range of related issues, including the right of a state to interfere with procreative ability by forcible sterilization (*Skinner* v. *Oklahoma*, 1942), the right of individuals to prevent conception or to terminate a pregnancy (*Roe* v. *Wade*, 1973; *Webster* v. *Reproductive Services*, 1989; *Planned Parenthood* v. *Casey*, 1992), and the right of individuals to rear children in nontraditional family groups (*Moore* v. *City of East Cleveland, Ohio* 1977).

Since the 1942 *Skinner* decision, lower courts have accepted the notion that states may not forcibly sterilize selected individuals unless such a policy can withstand strict constitutional scrutiny. The basis for requiring this level of scrutiny is the assertion that the "right to have offspring," like the right to marry, is a "fundamental," "basic liberty." Further, the *Skinner* and *Eisenstadt* decisions arguably hold that the right to use contraception or to be free of unwarranted sterilization is an aspect of individual, rather than marital, privacy. As stated in *Eisenstadt*: "If the right to privacy means anything, it is the right of the individual, married or single, to be free of unwarranted government intrusion into matters so fundamentally affecting a person as the decision to bear or beget a child" (*Eisenstadt* v. *Baird*, 1972).

But the right to privacy is no longer the primary justification for abortion rights, or, by extension, reproductive rights. The 1992 *Planned Parenthood* v. *Casey* decision specifically based its opinion on "liberty" (rather than privacy) rights, and concluded that abortion remains protected from state efforts to prohibit abortion. The emphasis on "liberty" language changes the focus of abortion rights from one of limitations on governmental power (as discussed in "privacy"-based decisions) to one of individual control of one's person. The opinion attempts to explain why abortion is an essential "liberty" for women because it permits control of one's body and one's personal destiny.

Justice Antonin Scalia's dissent mocks this attempt. After reciting the list of phrases used elsewhere by his colleagues, such as "a person's most basic decision," "a most personal and intimate choice," "originat[ing] within the zone of conscience and belief," "too intimate and personal for state interference," Scalia complains that "the same adjectives can be applied to many forms of conduct that this Court . . . has held are not entitled to constitutional protection—because, like abortion, they are forms of conduct that have long been criminalized in American society. Those adjectives might be applied, for example, to homosexual sodomy, polygamy, adult incest, and suicide" (p. 785).

Scalia's dissent highlights the potentially far-reaching implications of what the plurality has written regarding the fundamental importance of controlling one's fertility. The *Casey* plurality opinion lays out an argument for reexamining the 1879 *Reynolds* v. *U.S.* decision (upholding the power of the state to outlaw polygamous marriage) and the 1986 *Bowers* v. *Hardwick* decision (upholding the power of the state to criminalize homosexual behavior), a task critical to determining whether states can restrict noncoital reproduction to married couples. It also lays the groundwork for cases sure to arise concerning prenatal diagnosis, sex selection, cloning, and (ultimately) parthenogenesis.

— R. ALTA CHARO

ting adultery and with some assurance, as in the AID scenario, that the couple will be able to retain exclusive custody of the resulting child. As with AID, such a use of contract motherhood is viewed as therapeutic by many. While even this use of surrogacy has engendered opposition ranging from criminalization to mere unenforceability in countries such as Australia, Canada, England, and France, and in some portions of the United States, it has never encountered the same degree of approbation as the so-called surrogacy of convenience, in which a rearing mother finds it useful to hire someone else to carry the child (Liu, 1991; McLean, 1992).

Indeed, much of the debate surrounding the most famous surrogacy case in the United States, *Baby M (1988)*, focused on whether the rearing mother had declined to become pregnant due to career concerns and undue worry about her health, or rather due to legitimate concern that pregnancy would seriously worsen her multiple sclerosis. This debate exemplifies the increased willingness of the American public to regulate or ban surrogacy when it is not perceived as a cure for a medical problem such as infertility, a sentiment reflected in the constitutional analysis that permits greater state regulation where the right to procreate is not directly implicated.

Egg donation to a woman who cannot ovulate but who can carry to term does not technically allow the recipient to procreate, as she will not "reproduce" in the genetic sense. But it does allow her to experience pregnancy and childbirth, which for women are intimately associated with genetic procreation. In terms of both biological significance (gestation is, of course, a biological activity) and emotional impact, this would seem to be close to procreation, even in its more narrow definition. Thus, it is difficult to categorize this activity in terms of whether it allows an infertile person to "procreate."

Despite this fact, there is considerable hesitation about permitting egg donation. Whereas sperm donation is widely accepted, egg donation entails significantly more medical discomfort and even risk on the part of the donor. This in turn raises the specter, at least in the United States, of increased payments for the donation. For some, such payments represent an undue incentive to undergo medical risks, as well as an unacceptable commercialization of human gametes. Nevertheless, at least in California, there is a thriving egg donation practice.

Even those aspects of noncoital reproduction that clearly involve procreation can be regulated or banned, if there is a sufficiently compelling state interest. It is true that artificial insemination by husband (AIH), and in vitro fertilization (IVF) using a couple's own gametes (whether or not a contract mother is hired to carry the child to term), permit an otherwise infertile man or woman to procreate genetically. By bypassing the fallopian tube defect or permitting intrauterine insemination of the husband's concentrated semen, these techniques actually help infertile individuals to participate in the act of reproduction. But a compelling state interest in the protection of embryos and fetuses, for example, could justify significant restraints on even AIH and IVF.

Is there a compelling state "interest" in embryos and fetuses?

The most likely claim for a compelling state purpose to outlaw or regulate IVF is that of protection for the extracorporeal embryo, whether or not accompanied by a contract with a gestational surrogate.

The *Webster* v. *Reproductive Services* (1989) and *Planned Parenthood* v. *Casey* (1992) decisions indicate that the U.S. Supreme Court is now quite tolerant of symbolic legislative statements concerning the sanctity of embryonic life and of significant restrictions on the exercise of constitutionally protected rights, such as abortion, in the name of protecting these early life forms. It seems likely that the court would uphold state statutes, such as the one in Louisiana, that regulates management of extracorporeal embryos. Such restrictions may include prohibiting nontherapeutic experimentation on the embryo, embryo discard, and unnecessary creation of "surplus" embryos for the purpose of experimentation. It might also attempt to regulate transfer of embryos. By declaring that life begins at conception, as was done in the Missouri statute upheld in *Webster*, and by equating the rights of embryos to the rights of children, states could demand that embryo transfers be viewed as adoptions.

This was the approach taken by the trial court in the case of *Davis* v. *Davis* (1992), a Tennessee divorce case that struggled with determining the legal status of several frozen embryos that were left over from unsuccessful IVF treatments and became the subject of a divorce dispute. Characterizing the question as one of child custody, and viewing the embryos as children, the trial court then awarded custody to the parent whose actions would be in the best interests of the embryos. By assuming that embryos have "interests," and then defining one of those interests as an interest in being born, the trial court awarded the embryos to the wife, who intended to have them implanted in her womb in the hope of bringing them to term.

By contrast, the appellate court backed away from the characterization of the embryos as "children" and the resulting "best interests" analysis. Without ever explicitly calling the embryos property, the court pro-

◆ **ectogenesis**
the development of a fetus completely outside the body.

See Also

The Legal Status of Human Fetuses and The Moral Status of Human Fetuses

Personhood: Central Yet Irresolvable

Research involving pregnant women must have a therapeutic goal for the woman, or risks to the fetus must be minimal.

PAGE 234

Research with fetuses must be intended to provide significant knowledge inaccessible by other means.

PAGE 234

ceeded to treat them as property held jointly by the couple, and thereby concluded that disposition of the embryos must be by agreement because each party had an equal property interest in them.

The Tennessee Supreme Court reviewed available models for disposition of the embryos when unanticipated contingencies arise. Those models range from a rule requiring, at one extreme, that all embryos be used by the gamete-providers or be donated for uterine transfer (such as is required under an as yet unchallenged Louisiana statute), and, at the other extreme, that any unused embryos be automatically discarded. The Tennessee Supreme Court, when it considered the *Davis* case, was aware of the *Planned Parenthood* v. *Casey* (1992) decision, which reiterated the *Roe* (1973) holding that a state may express an "interest" in a fetus. Unfortunately, like *Roe*, *Planned Parenthood* v. *Casey* fails to identify *what* this interest might be or *why* it arises, leaving the *Davis* court with little guidance on how to extend the state interest argument to nonabortion settings.

Numerous commentators have struggled to identify this state interest (Joyce, 1988; Tooley, 1984). Many begin with the premise that a sufficiently detailed biological understanding of embryo potential will yield an answer:

> *[E]very living individual being with the natural potential, as a whole, for knowing, willing, desiring, and relating to others in a self-reflective way is a person. But the human zygote is a living individual (or more than one such individual) with the natural potential, as a whole, to act in these ways. Therefore the human zygote is an actual person with great potential. . . .* (Joyce, 1988, p. 169)

But others argue that the genetic blueprint of a person cannot be entitled to the same moral standing as that of the person himself or herself, because any inherent "right" to live is premised on the idea that it is in the "interest" of the entity to continue existing (Tooley, 1984). Where, as with a zygote, there is no self-concept, there can be no "interest" in continuing to exist, no "desire" to continue to exist, and therefore no "right" to continue to exist.

Such an argument refutes the *Davis* trial court's treatment of the frozen embryos as children with an interest in being brought to term. But the appellate court's assumption that they must therefore be treated as property is equally unjustified. Society may choose nonetheless to grant rights to the zygote or fetus, for any number of reasons, if such steps do not unduly impinge on another liberty recognized by society, such as the liberty of men and women to control their reproductive futures.

In fact, Justice John Paul Stevens takes on this issue in his concurring opinion in *Planned Parenthood* v. *Casey*:

> *Identifying the State's interests—which the States rarely articulate with any precision—makes clear that the interest in protecting potential life is not grounded in the Constitution. It is, instead, an indirect interest supported by both humanitarian and pragmatic concerns. Many of our citizens believe that any abortion reflects an unacceptable disrespect for potential human life and that the performance of more than a million abortions each year is intolerable; many find third-trimester abortions performed when the fetus is approaching personhood particularly offensive. The State has a legitimate interest in minimizing such offense. . . . These are the kinds of concerns that comprise the State's interest in potential human life.*
> *(*Planned Parenthood v. Casey, *1992, 120 L. Ed. 2d 674 at p. 739)*

Struggling with the task of expressing a state interest in embryonic life without unduly impinging upon the reproductive rights of adult men and women, the Tennessee Supreme Court in the *Davis* case concluded that embryos are neither children nor property, but occupy an intermediate status based on their potential for development. This, in turn, would not convey a right to be born under either state or federal constitutional law but would demand some protections. These include implantation where possible, freedom from unnecessary creation or destruction, and dignified management.

The Tennessee court's characterization of an intermediate status for embryos is the most intriguing part of the opinion, as it did not present a coherent theory of that status and its implications. There are, of course, models of intermediate property status. Animals, for example, are treated as property with no "right to life," but at the same time are protected from cruel and painful treatment by their owners. Works of art may be owned, but "moral rights" possessed by the artist in some jurisdictions prohibit defacing or destroying the art. Land may be owned subject to numerous restrictions on use that would permanently destroy some publicly valued attribute. Which, if any, of these models describes the intermediate status held by the embryos? And on what basis? This is indeed the key question left totally unanswered by the Tennessee court. As it stands, though the opinion gives some narrow, nearly regulatory guidance to IVF clinics, it offers little to those wondering in general whether other restraints on embryo creation and management are in order.

Other countries have struggled with the same

dilemma. Most often, as in England and Australia, the compromise solution is chosen, in which limited experimentation is permitted on unavoidably abandoned embryos. Deliberate creation of embryos for the purpose of experimentation is frowned upon. Occasionally a stricter view is adopted, as in Germany, where embryo experimentation is simply banned. Generally, however, where embryos are to be created in order to permit implantation and gestation, even extracorporeal maintenance or embryo freezing is tolerated (U.S. Congress, OTA, 1988b; Liu, 1991; McLean, 1992).

What is the state interest in the children conceived noncoitally?

Related to state interest in the protection of extracorporeal embryos is its interest in protecting the children born following noncoital conception. This takes its most frequent form in suggestions for limiting use of these technologies to married couples, on the theory that being born into a single-parent home is harmful to a child. On this basis, almost two-thirds of physicians surveyed in 1987 and a number of states either explicitly or implicitly deny artificial insemination services to unmarried women (U.S. Congress, OTA, 1988a, 1988b).

While some may deplore this practice, the fact that unmarried persons are not considered a "suspect" class in constitutional jurisprudence (i.e., they are not considered a class in need of special protection from discriminatory legislation because they are fully able to use the political system to protect their interests), means that such discriminatory practices are largely immune to constitutional challenge as an abridgment of their right to equal protection of the laws. Unless procreation, and specifically the use of artificial insemination, is viewed as a fundamental right, such persons will be limited to challenges under state and federal civil rights statutes in their pursuit of equal access to these technologies.

To the extent that the right to procreate implies a right to create a family, constitutional law from the nineteenth century remains unchallenged in its support for criminalization of family forms, such as polygamy, that fly in the face of Western European tradition. While there have been twentieth-century cases in support of broadening the definition of "family," there has not yet been any case in which the right to marry is extended beyond a heterosexual couple. Thus, whatever the right to privacy entails, it does not appear to guarantee the right to form familial relationships that achieve the same legal recognition as that bestowed by marriage.

Generally, current interpretations of constitutional law appear to support the assertion that for married couples there is a right to privacy embedded in the wording and history of the constitution and that such privacy extends to reproductive decision making free from unwarranted governmental intrusion. While case law suggests that individuals are entitled to this privacy in equal measure, judicial hostility to claims of a right by homosexuals to marry or engage in sexual activity (*Bowers* v. *Hardwick*, 1986), by minors to have unrestricted access to abortion (*Hodgeson* v. *Minnesota*, 1990), and by physicians to give full information concerning abortion (*Rust* v. *Sullivan*, 1991) suggest limitations on Supreme Court extension of this right.

Indeed, much of the state activity concerning contract motherhood has been directed at protecting the children conceived through these arrangements. In the event a surrogate changes her mind, a custody dispute can break out between the birth mother and the genetic father. Reluctant to extend parental status to the adopting mother without terminating the parental status of the birth mother, but also determined to see the child placed in the safest home, courts have been in a quandary. Most often the solution has been to refuse to use the contract as the basis for a custody decision, and instead to rely on traditional family notions of child welfare. Next, courts have generally refused to terminate the birth mother's status as a presumptive legal parent. But despite these findings, most courts also award custody to the genetic father and his wife, as it is this couple who is usually better able financially and socially to convince the court that they can provide a secure home for the baby (U.S. Congress, OTA, 1988b; McLean, 1992).

Other concerns regarding contract motherhood

Another state interest in surrogacy stems from the fact that the contracts typically entail promises by the contract mother to refrain from certain behaviors such as drinking, smoking, or the use of illicit drugs, as well as affirmative promises to follow prescribed prenatal care regimes and to undergo prenatal testing for fetal health. Enforcing such contract promises raises constitutional issues, requiring a relinquishment of significant autonomy on the part of the contract mother. This is particularly true with regard to promises to follow prescribed medical care, which may entail submission to invasive tests and even surgery, in the case of cesarean sections.

Surrogacy also raises the specter that the hiring couple might gain what amounts to a property interest in the body of the contract mother. This is particularly true where gestational surrogacy is employed, and the child the contract mother is carrying is genetically related to the hiring parents but not to her. At least one court has been known to issue a "prenatal adoption"

◆ **commercial surrogacy**
when a woman agrees to carry to term an embryo genetically related to her for a fee. In noncommercial surrogacy a woman does so out of generosity.

See Also

Pregnancy and Maternal Health

Fetal Rights? The Moral Status of the Unborn

In the early 1980s, some commentators called for greater regulation of women's actions during pregnancy.

PAGE 475

order, in which the hiring husband and wife were declared the legal parents of the fetus still within the gestational mother's body (*Smith* v. *Jones*, 1988). In such a case, the hiring parents would have a legally recognized interest in the development of the fetus. Indeed, as parents they might have a legal duty to protect the fetus from harm, as has been confirmed by cases that hold pregnant women criminally liable for behaviors that threaten fetal health. How to protect fetuses while not compromising the physical integrity and legal autonomy of the gestational mother poses a significant constitutional challenge.

Gestational surrogacy also raises fundamental questions about the definition of parenthood, particularly of motherhood. While the law has consistently given preference to biological parents over nonbiological parents, with specific exceptions carved out for adoption and AID, it has never before been forced to consider the definition of "biological." As of the mid-1990s, only one state has considered the problem. In California, a dispute developed between a couple (the Calverts) whose gametes had been used to conceive a child who was subsequently brought to term by a hired gestational contract mother named Anna Johnson. The trial and appellate courts both concluded that the genetic relationship, which defines "natural" parent for men, would define the "natural" parent for women. The two lower courts specifically rejected the notion that gestation is a biological relationship formed by the indisputable fusing of maternal and fetal well-being during the nine months of pregnancy that could equally well form the basis for defining the "natural" mother.

California's lower court decisions in *Johnson* v. *Calvert* (1991), stating that a gestational mother is no more than a foster parent to her own child, are almost without precedent worldwide. Only Israel, bound by unique aspects of religious identity law, has adopted a genetic definition of motherhood. Every other country that has examined the problem—including the United Kingdom, Germany, Switzerland, Bulgaria, and even South Africa with its race-conscious legal structure—has concluded that the woman who gives birth is the child's mother.

The California Supreme Court's 1993 opinion on *Johnson* v. *Calvert* declined to find either the genetic or the gestational mother to be the definitive "natural" parent. Instead, it chose to view either relationship as a presumptive form of natural parenthood. Then it specifically declined the invitation to have the law reflect what had actually happened, that is, the birth of a child with two biological mothers, one gestational and the other genetic. Agreeing that acknowledging more than one natural mother would be, as the trial court stated, a "recipe for crazymaking," the California Supreme Court said that whichever of the two biologically related women had been the intended mother would then be declared the "natural" mother. It continued by stating that in the event that the gestational and genetic mothers are not the same person, and that the intended mother is neither the genetic nor gestational parent, she would nonetheless be considered the "natural" mother. Thus the court avoided what is at base the most interesting question raised by the use of reproductive technologies: the possibility of declaring more than one woman to be a "natural" parent of a child. To do so, of course, would require escaping the confines of the heterosexual couple as the paradigm for a family and acknowledging that some people become parents by virtue of genetic connection, others by gestational connection, and still others by contract—whether a marital contract with a genetic or gestational parent, or a reproductive technology contract that creates relationships with children conceived with donor gametes or carried to term by contract mothers.

What is the state interest in access to quality services?

A final and overarching area of state interest lies in consumer access and protection. Only a handful of states have legislation mandating insurance coverage for the most expensive of these technologies, IVF. Those states, including Arkansas, Hawaii, Maryland, Massachusetts, Texas, and Wisconsin, have responded to political pressure from organized medicine as well as from infertility support groups. But no state has yet asserted that insurance coverage is required by virtue of the fact that procreation is a fundamental right that may, for some people, be exercised only when using an expensive technology. Indeed, in the context of abortion services, the Supreme Court has made clear that states may forbid Medicaid or other public funding of such services, although they are clearly linked to the exercise of a fundamental right. In fact, the *Webster* decision upheld a state prohibition on the use of public facilities for abortion services, even when no public funds are used.

Where IVF and other reproductive technology services are being provided, however, the state may well choose to regulate them for the sake of protecting patients from unscrupulous practices. These may include misleading advertising, inadequate facilities, insufficiently trained personnel, and negligent screening of gamete donors for genetic and infectious diseases that might be transmitted to recipients. Even in the exercise of a fundamental right, the state may enforce regulations designed to protect the patient.

Another consumer issue involves the regulation of commercialization of reproductive technologies. Although sperm donation has continued apace in countries where no payment is permitted, most commentators agree that the availability of donor gametes and contract mothers in the United States would be severely reduced if commercialization were prohibited. Nonetheless, even when viewing access to reproductive technologies as an exercise of freedom to procreate, several state courts have concluded that there is ample state authority to prohibit commercialization (*Doe* v. *Kelley*, 1981; *Baby M*, 1988). The basis for this conclusion can vary. One line of argument, focusing on surrogacy, characterizes it either as baby-selling or as the sale of parental rights, both of which traditionally have been forbidden despite significant libertarian arguments in favor of free markets for both. These prohibitions on selling children or parental rights would easily extend to prohibitions on the sale of embryos, if embryos are characterized as children. Prohibitions on the sale of semen and ova probably could be justified on the same basis as the current prohibitions on organ sales, despite the same line of libertarian arguments.

Other arguments in favor of prohibiting commercialization focus on the effect such activities have on public morals, on the creation of property interests in the bodies of others, and on the fear that the creation of an industry surrounding the sale of gametes, embryos, and reproductive services will create a class of professional breeders. A 1987 survey of surrogacy brokers by the OTA revealed significant discrepancies in economic and educational backgrounds of those who hire contract mothers and those who work as contract mothers (U.S. Congress, OTA, 1988a), leading to the conclusion that the two groups would be unlikely to wield equal bargaining power during the preconception contract negotiations or during postbirth custody disputes.

All of these arguments would probably fail if subjected to the strict scrutiny brought to bear on state interference with a fundamental right. But the reluctance of U.S. courts to view commercialization of reproductive services as an expression of procreative freedom reduces the degree of scrutiny to which state restrictions are subjected. Any rational state purpose will suffice if the restriction interferes with a privilege rather than a fundamental right.

Conclusion

The legal and regulatory issues surrounding reproductive technologies concern the ability of a government to ban or restrict noncoital reproduction because it may harm embryos, children, consumers, or public morals. Where governments choose not to ban the practice, they may wish to regulate it, for example, by limiting what types of prospective parents may use it, which adults will be related to the resulting children, and what kinds of ancillary practices—such as research or commercialization—will be permitted. In the United States, the details of such regulation are a function of state legislation and the resolution of novel cases by the courts. But the federal Constitution places significant limits on how far such legislation or judicial lawmaking may interfere with the opportunity of individuals to exercise procreative choice.

— R. ALTA CHARO

RIGHTS

SYSTEMATIC ANALYSIS

Rights are of practical importance primarily, although not exclusively, because of the duties they imply. Thus, many jurists and moral philosophers have maintained the logical correlativity of rights and duties. The strong form of this doctrine asserts that every right implies a correlative duty and every duty implies a correlative right. For example, the creditor's right to be paid logically implies the debtor's duty to pay, and the debtor's duty to pay logically presupposes the creditor's right to be paid. But the duties of charity seem to invalidate this strong thesis. Although a wealthy person has a moral duty to contribute to those in need, no poor individual or charitable organization has a correlative right to receive a contribution, because the donor has the right to choose how to distribute his or her charitable donations.

This instance suggests a weaker form of the doctrine of the correlativity of rights and duties. Although every right implies some correlative duty, not every duty implies a correlative right. Even this thesis may be too strong. Physicians licensed in Missouri have a right to practice in any community in that state. But this implies neither that the residents of Missouri have a duty to enable them to practice medicine by becoming their patients nor that the state has a duty not to interfere with their practice by drafting them to serve in the Missouri National Guard. Presumably, the physicians' right to practice implies that they should not be arbitrarily prevented from exercising this right, but the content of any implied duty need not be correlative with or as extensive as the physicians' liberty to practice medicine in Missouri. In short, although rights do imply duties, the exact logical relations between rights and duties remain controversial.

The nature of rights

The essential connection between rights and duties suggests that rights might be equivalent to duties. John Austin (1885) defined a legal right as a relative legal duty. Thus, the creditor's right to be paid is the debtor's duty of payment to the creditor and nothing more. The

The more broadly the definition of procreation is drawn, the more compelling must be state efforts to restrict use of noncoital procreation.

PAGE 605

See Also
Infants' Rights: The Baby Doe Case
Rights Talk: More Harm Than Good

concept of a right is that of a duty thought of from the perspective of the party to whom that duty is owed. John Stuart Mill (1861) similarly conceived of a moral right as a relative moral duty, a moral duty owed to the person who would be harmed by its nonperformance.

Joel Feinberg (1980) has argued that any reduction of rights to duties omits what is most distinctive of and valuable in rights, namely, claiming, to have a right is to be in a position to demand that to which one is entitled, much as one can claim one's coat by presenting a claim check to the attendant at a cloakroom. He defines a right as a valid claim. A legal right is a claim, the recognition of which is justified by some system of legal rules; a moral right is a claim justified by the principles of an enlightened conscience.

H. L. A. Hart (1982) maintains that what is distinctive about rights is that they determine the proper distribution of freedom. My right to paint my house purple is my liberty to paint my house purple or not to do so as I choose, together with a protective perimeter of duties of others not to interfere with my choice, for example, by stealing the purple paint I have purchased or trespassing upon my property and battering me. Thus, Hart defines a right as a protected choice.

Neil MacCormick (1977) objects that many of our most fundamental rights allow no room for free choice. Under U.S. law, one's constitutional right not to be enslaved cannot be waived by one who might choose to escape from abject poverty by becoming the slave of some benevolent master. He defines a right as a protected interest. The content of any right is something that is presumed to be in one's interest, and the function of rights is to secure the possession of these goods to each and every individual right-holder.

A rather different interest theory of rights has been proposed by Joseph Raz (1986). He defines a right as an interest-based reason sufficient for the imposition of some duty or duties upon others. Thus, he conceives of rights in terms of their role in practical reasoning; they function as intermediate conclusions between the individual interests upon which they are grounded and the duties they imply.

Ronald Dworkin (1977) also conceives of rights in terms of their role in practical reasoning, especially in the justification of political decisions. Although every action of the government requires some justification, an appeal to the public welfare is usually sufficient. But when some law or state action infringes upon a right of some individual, this justification is no longer adequate. He therefore defines a right as an individual trump over social utility. Accordingly, the function of rights is to provide special protection to the individual against any government action aimed at maximizing some social goal or set of social goals.

If there is any consensus in these very different conceptions of rights, it is that the concept of a right is essentially distributive, that is, rights are ascribed to and possessed by each individual or entity in a group separately rather than collectively. Whereas the many benefits and harms to various affected parties of any action are summed together in the act's total utility, each individual person has his or her own right that demands respect independently of the rights or welfare of any other individuals.

Possessors of rights

Any theory about the nature of rights implies something about the kinds of beings that could possess a right. If a right really is a protected choice, then any ascription of rights to a being incapable of free choice would be, as Hart (1955) points out, empty. One of the reasons that MacCormick (1977) adopts a protected-interest theory of rights is to explain how newborn infants, who are incapable of choice but do have interests, can possess moral and legal rights. Still, his theory implies that only beings with interests could possibly be right-holders.

The immediate implications of some conception of rights are often unacceptable to a moral philosopher or a morally sensitive person. For example, Feinberg defines a right as a valid claim and explains what it is to have a claim in terms of the activity of claiming. This seems to imply that only a being capable of claiming could possess a right. Although Feinberg (1980) recognizes that infants are incapable of claiming anything as their due, he believes that they clearly do have legal and moral rights. How is this possible? Adults, normally parents or guardians, can claim their rights for them. Thus, he extends the range of possible right-holders by maintaining that a right-holder can be represented by someone else. But what kind of a being can be represented? His answer is that only when a being has interests can another act on his or her behalf. On the basis of this principle he ascribes rights to children and even some nonhuman animals, but denies that plants or mere physical objects could possess rights.

What of human fetuses? Fetuses are surely incapable of free choice or of claiming and probably do not yet possess any interests. Therefore, most theories of the nature of rights seem to imply that they could not be right-holders. One way to extend the possession of rights to fetuses, however, is to appeal to their potentiality for claiming or interests or personhood or whatever is required by one's conception of a right. Because the human fetus already possesses the qualification for being a right-holder in potentiality, it already has at least some capacity to possess rights. At the other end of life, some argue that the dead can have rights because, while alive, they had interests that survive their

See Also
Rights of Patients/Clients

death, for example, interests in their reputations or in having their wills respected.

Tom Regan (1983) uses two lines of reasoning to extend the ascription of rights from human beings to nonhuman animals. One argument begins with our ascriptions of rights to humans. He points out that the usual hypotheses about what qualifies one to possess rights, such as rationality or personhood, fail to explain our firm judgments that, for example, brain-damaged children or very senile patients have rights. Regan argues that any criterion broad enough to be consistent with our moral convictions about the rights of humans will imply that some animals can also possess rights. Another argument begins with our recognition that some of our duties concerning animals are direct duties, duties owed to animals. For example, we have a duty not to cause animals to suffer unnecessarily, not in order to prevent ourselves from becoming callous to human suffering, as Immanuel Kant (1959) suggested, but for the sake of the animals themselves. Regan then argues that the best explanation of our direct duties to animals is the hypothesis that they are grounded on the rights of animals. What gives animals as well as humans the inherent value that confers rights is not merely being alive, but having a life that fares well or ill for them. No consensus about the kinds of beings that could possess rights has yet emerged.

The grounds of rights

The grounds of anyone's right are the reasons why he or she has that right, the qualifications of the right-holder together with the norms that confer the right. Everyone agrees that the law grounds legal rights, that it is the rules and regulations of any legal system that confer legal rights upon those subject to that system. There is, however, room for disagreement about the precise nature of those laws.

Hart (1955) maintains that the law consists of a set of social rules practiced in some society and applied in its courts. He maintains that a legal right arises from the application of some legal rule to a particular case. Dworkin (1977) argues that the adjudication of hard cases, cases where no valid legal rule implies any clear decision, requires an appeal to legal principles. Unlike a legal rule that either decides a case or is completely inapplicable, a legal principle can have more or less weight and may conflict with other legal principles that also apply to any hard case. He concludes that our fundamental legal rights are grounded on principles rather than rules.

There is also debate about whether every posited rule or principle is legally valid. Suppose that a legislature enacts a statute purporting to legitimize slavery. Would this statute confer on anyone a genuine legal right to own another human being? Thomas Aquinas would have argued that it does not because an unjust law is no law at all. Law can impose duties and confer rights only by virtue of being a dictate of reason, and no command that conflicts with the natural law, the moral law evident to reason, can be rational. Austin (1885) rejected any such natural-law theory. What the law is, is one thing; what it ought to be, another. Hence, any law posited by legislation that commands a relative duty thereby confers a valid legal right.

There is considerably more disagreement about the grounds of moral rights. The view first enunciated by William of Ockham (1285-1349) and most familiar in the political theory of John Locke (1960) is that natural law, the moral rules commanded by God and self-evident to human reason, grounds moral rights much as the law posited by human legislators and judges confers legal rights. Skepticism about the existence of any divine legislator and doubts about the self-evidence of any moral rules have gradually made this traditional theory less credible than heretofore.

Mill (1861) defined a moral right in terms of a relative moral duty and argued that utility is the ground of our duties. Because our fundamental moral obligations are actions that tend to promote the happiness or mitigate the unhappiness of all those affected by them, those individuals who would be harmed by our failure or refusal to so act have moral rights to the performance of those duties owed to them.

Dworkin (1977) and others object that to ground moral rights upon social utility is to deprive rights of their primary function of protecting the individual against mistreatment inflicted to maximize social goals. MacCormick (1977) and Raz (1986), in somewhat different ways, preserve the essentially distributive nature of rights, without severing their connection with human well-being, by holding that individual interests ground moral rights. Not all of one's interests confer rights, of course, only those interests of sufficient importance to impose upon others some duty or duties to promote, or at least not damage, those interests.

Kant (1959) denied that goals, whether they be social utility or individual interests, can impose the categorical imperative of duty. Our fundamental moral obligation is to treat all persons, all rational agents, as ends in themselves and not merely as means to some ulterior end. Accordingly, most contemporary Kantians ground moral rights upon respect for persons, that is, upon the dignity of each individual moral agent.

Moral rights have traditionally been correlated with the duties of justice, in contrast with the duties of charity that are not owed to any particular individual. John Rawls (1971) has argued that the principles of justice are those principles concerning the basic structure of

See Also

Fetal Rights? The Moral Status of the Unborn

Fighting over "Life": Arguments Based on Rights and on Biology the political and economic institutions of their society that would be chosen by rational individuals in the "original position," roughly a position in which no person can impose his or her will upon another or predict what place he or she will have in the society to be regulated by those principles. Thus, the basic moral rights of the individual are grounded, not on any actual agreement, but on a hypothetical contract to which the members of any society would agree unanimously, were they fully rational and choosing under ideal conditions. Each of these theories of the grounds of rights needs further development, and none of them has yet achieved general acceptance.

Rights in political theory

Conceptions of the ideal society and of the authority of government are determined to a considerable degree by the place of rights in one's social and political philosophy. Libertarians regard individual liberty as inviolable and advocate a minimal government and a laissez-faire economic system. They tend to make rights, whether thought of as natural rights along Lockean lines or as utilitarian social institutions, central to their theory. They give primacy to the individual rights to life, liberty, and property, and conceive of these as negative rights, rights that others not deprive one of life, interfere with one's liberty of thought or action, or take away one's property or the free use thereof.

Liberals also regard individual liberty as central to their political theory, although they conceive of liberty and assess its value in various ways. They typically advocate democratic political institutions, including a set of basic civil rights, to set constitutional limits on the powers of government. Many regard these civil rights as legal protections of more fundamental human rights. They tend to affirm a wider range of rights than libertarians and to recognize that individual rights impose positive as well as negative duties upon others. Thus, one's right to due process might impose a duty upon the state to provide an impoverished person with legal counsel as well as a duty not to prejudice a jury. Some, but not all, liberals supplement the traditional civil and political rights with a set of social and economic rights, such as the right to social security or to an adequate standard of medical care.

Communitarians insist that the cultural traditions and social practices of a community are necessary for the full development of our human capacities and the realization of our well-being. Therefore, they reject the "atomism" of traditional natural-rights theory. Because

RIGHTS
Basic Categories

The basic categories are institutional rights that are conferred by some sort of organization or social convention, and moral rights that are conferred by moral grounds independent of human beliefs or practices. (To be sure, some philosophers deny that there are any noninstitutional rights, but moral rights figure prominently in many ethical and political theories.) The most important species of institutional rights are legal rights conferred by the rules or principles of some legal system; the most fundamental species of moral rights are human rights (traditionally called natural rights) that one possesses simply by virtue of being human and whether or not they are recognized by the institutions of one's society. (In a secondary sense, human rights are those rights conferred upon all human beings by some legal system, most notably in those nations that have ratified the European Convention on Human Rights [Council of Europe, 1990].) Human rights are contrasted with every species of special moral rights that one possesses by virtue of some special status, for example as a citizen, or as a doctor, or as a subject of biomedical research.

Many jurists and moral philosophers adopt conceptual distinctions introduced by Wesley Newcomb Hohfeld (1919) to distinguish between claim rights, liberty rights, power rights, and immunity rights. The creditor has a claim against the debtor to payment if and only if the debtor has a duty to the creditor to pay the amount owed. A man has a liberty to grow a beard simply because he has no duty not to do so. A patient has a power to render surgery permissible because the patient has the ability, by consenting to be operated on, to confer upon the surgeon the liberty to operate. An owner has an immunity against having his or her property given away by another because no unilateral act of another would constitute a donation of one's property.

Another important distinction, applying primarily to claim rights, is that between positive and negative rights. A positive right is one that implies a positive duty of some second party, a duty to do some sort of action; a negative right imposes a negative duty, a duty not to act in some specific manner. Thus, one who has medical insurance typically has a positive right to be reimbursed for medical expenses, and every patient has a negative right not to be operated upon without consent. Our labels for rights are often misleading in this respect. For example, the patient's right "not to be abandoned" is probably a positive right that imposes upon one's physician the duty either to provide necessary medical care or to arrange for someone else to provide such care.

— CARL WELLMAN

individuals are not born autonomous moral agents and could not become fully human in a state of nature, they cannot possess any absolute human rights independent of and holding against society. Because human motivation is not exclusively egoistic and rationality is not confined to maximizing one's own self-interest, the authority of government is not derived from any social contract between completely independent individuals. Communitarians believe that their criticisms undermine, not only libertarian theories of rights like Robert Nozick's (1974), derived from Locke's (1960) natural law philosophy, but also liberal theories of rights like those of Dworkin (1977), who conceives of rights as trumps against social goals, and Rawls (1971), who grounds basic rights in a hypothetical contract entered into by individuals in an original (presocial) position.

Although their philosophies may vary in fundamental ways, all feminists oppose the oppression of women and believe that the previously neglected experiences and contributions of women will enrich moral, social, and political theory. In their struggle for social and political equality, most early feminists campaigned for equal civil rights and appealed to women's equal human rights. Without renouncing these rights, some recent feminists have become more critical of traditional theories of rights and more dubious of the appeal to rights as an instrument to eradicate the oppression of women. Elizabeth Wolgast (1987) has argued that the social atomism of natural-rights theory is contrary to the experience of women, who find the substance of their lives, for better or worse, to consist primarily in their interpersonal relations with those close to them. The equality of civil and human rights presupposes an abstract justice of universal moral rules inconsistent with the ethics of very particular responsibilities in concrete contexts that better fits the experience of caregivers such as wives and mothers. Although equal rights are supposed to protect the weak, women often find themselves unable to claim their moral rights against husbands or physicians upon whom they are economically or medically dependent.

Where are we now in our systematic analysis of rights? We have several coherently developed conceptions of the nature of a right and enough discussion to identify the strengths and weaknesses of each. Available theories of the kinds of beings that could possess rights are more scarce and less satisfactory; only Joel Feinberg's (1980) appeal to interests and a few responses to it are very rigorous. Although pronouncements about the grounds of rights, especially moral rights, are common enough, plausible theories that are clearly explained and systematically defended are almost totally lacking. Finally, criticisms of theories of rights by communitarians and feminists have revealed, not so much defects in rights themselves, as important aspects of our legal, political, and moral life neglected by traditional and even much recent jurisprudence and ethical theory.

— CARL WELLMAN

RIGHTS TALK
More Harm Than Good?

Carol Smart (1989) points out that it is often hazardous for a woman to appeal to her rights in a legal system dominated by males. This is partly because rights oversimplify complex power relations; for example, a battered wife is usually physically weaker than her husband and may lack the skills to enable her to leave "his" home and support herself. Again, the appeal to any right can often be met by an appeal to some counterright; although a wife has a right not to be molested, her husband has a right to live in "his" home and to see "his" children. Because each individual right-holder must prove that her right has been violated, even a number of court cases will fail to remedy a widespread social harm affecting large numbers of women.

Mary Ann Glendon (1991) adds that the U.S. dialect of rights talk impoverishes political discourse. Because rights are asserted as absolutes with an unqualified peremptory content, our rights talk heightens social conflict and inhibits dialogue that might resolve our social problems. Its emphasis upon individual demands and silence about our responsibilities to others renders it deficient in dealing with the distress of the poor, the homeless, the unemployed, and the marginalized members of our society. Its presupposition of the lone rights-bearer neglects the dimension of sociability so important for human character, competence, and civic virtue. For example, formulating problems of family rights in terms of the rights of the individual members of the family ignores the social and economic conditions that families require in order to flourish.

— CARL WELLMAN

RIGHTS IN BIOETHICS

Rights in bioethics are a subclass of the broader notion of moral and legal rights described in the preceding article. Some rights in bioethics are both moral and legal, such as the right of patients to be informed about and grant permission for recommended medical treat-

See Also

Reproductive Technologies: Legal Issues: Is There an Affirmative Right to Procreate?

ments. This and other rights of patients have been recognized in judicial rulings or statutes enacted by legislatures, and in philosophical ethics applied to medical practice and research. Some rights in bioethics have the status of *moral rights merely*, for example, the claim that there exists a right to health care. That claim asserts a moral right, implying that a corresponding legal right ought to exist. As of early 1993, the U.S. federal government had not enacted legislation that would legally establish the claim to a right to health care. Many other nations legally guarantee a right to health care for all citizens.

There is a middle ground between legally established rights and moral rights merely.

PAGE 619

Rights as claims

Even when claims asserting moral rights in bioethics are backed up by laws, those laws can be overturned or restricted and new laws enacted, thus altering the legal rights while leaving the claims about moral rights intact. One prominent example is the claim in support of a woman's right to terminate a pregnancy. Moral claims asserting a woman's right to control her own body were made before the 1973 ruling in *Roe* v. *Wade*. In that case the U.S. Supreme Court declared that the constitutional "right of privacy . . . is broad enough to encompass a woman's decision whether or not to terminate her pregnancy." However, in its 1989 decision in *Webster* v. *Reproductive Health Services*, the Supreme Court restricted that constitutional right by indicating that it would allow states to place additional conditions on the circumstances in which a woman may exercise her right.

Alterations in legal rights also occur in statutes. An example is that of laws pertaining to HIV infection. At the beginning of the AIDS epidemic, claims about the rights of people with HIV infection were asserted but not legally supported. By the late 1980s, however, many states had passed legislation granting people the right not to have their blood tested for HIV infection without their knowledge and consent, laws ensuring a right to confidentiality of people with HIV infection, as well as the right not to be discriminated against because of their HIV-positive status.

The area of *moral rights merely* tends to be more problematic than the sphere of legal rights. It is generally easier to put forward relevant and cogent reasons or evidence in support of the claim that a legal right exists than it is to justify a claim about the existence of a disputed moral right. That is because legal rights are written down in statutes, found in the Constitution and interpreted by the courts, and appear in judicial opinions that declare the common law, while moral rights asserted as mere claims may lack widespread support or other objective evidence of their existence.

In both the legal and moral domains, rights may be surrounded by inescapable vagueness, even when the existence of a right is not in dispute. For example, patients are normally held to have a right to confidentiality in the physician-patient relationship. Yet even legal requirements concerning confidentiality are rarely stated in the form of absolutes. If a patient confides to a psychiatrist an intention to harm another person and the therapist has some grounds for believing that the patient will carry out the stated intention, must the therapist maintain confidentiality or can a breach be justified? A well-known precedent was set in 1974 in the case of *Tarasoff* v. *The Regents of the University of California*, which established a psychotherapist's "duty to warn" or to take other preventive steps if the therapist knows or should know that a patient poses a danger to others.

Another difficulty lies in the correct ordering of rights in situations when more than one right can be claimed. For example, the patient's right to confidentiality normally prevents a physician from disclosing a patient's diagnosis without the consent of the patient. But suppose the patient's blood has been tested for HIV antibodies and the result is positive. The patient requests that the physician not disclose this fact to his wife. One claim asserts that a person at risk of acquiring a lethal infection has a right to that information, so the wife should be told; the competing claim asserts the patient's right to confidentiality, prohibiting the physician from disclosing to the wife. Laws in some states permit but do not require a physician to disclose HIV information to a spouse or other known sex partner. These examples illustrate the problems that can surround legal as well as moral rights.

The language of rights can also generate confusion. A deeply cherished right in free societies is the right to life, which prohibits innocent people from being killed by the state and promises state protection against other threats to the lives of citizens. However, "the right to life" has taken on a new meaning since being adopted by groups with a political agenda. In the sphere of bioethics, those beliefs include a nearly absolute prohibition of abortion, as well as opposition to practices such as termination of life support and honoring living wills. Most "right to life" groups do not include opposition to the death penalty as part of their political agenda. This can be explained by their concern for "innocent" life, thereby excluding from those deserving protection people who have been convicted of crimes. By casting their moral position in terms of a "right to life," these groups make it appear that anyone who favors a woman's right to an abortion or a patient's right to have life support withdrawn must therefore reject the proposition that people have a right to life. The confusion stems from applying a general moral claim asserting the "right to life" to a highly controversial area like abortion, and

See Also

Declaring Rights: Moral Claims and Force of Law

to honoring living wills, which is a widely accepted practice.

The growth of the field of bioethics has been accompanied by a multitude of claims about rights. However, as long ago as 1914 Justice Benjamin Cardozo established an important judicial precedent when he articulated the right of patients to consent to treatment: "Every human being of adult years and sound mind has a right to determine what shall be done with his own body; and a surgeon who performs an operation without his patient's consent commits an assault, for which he is liable in damages" (*Schloendorff* v. *New York Hospital*). Yet even that extension into the medical sphere of the fundamental human right to be free from bodily assault established only the patient's right to consent to invasive medical procedures. Not until 1957, in the landmark decision in *Salgo* v. *Leland Stanford Jr. University Board of Trustees*, did a court rule that patients have a right to *informed* consent, thereby obligating physicians to disclose certain information about the procedures to be carried out before seeking the patient's consent.

A different historical current following World War II culminated in the right of research subjects (including patients enrolled in clinical studies) to voluntary, informed consent to serve as a subject of human experimentation. The atrocities committed by the Nazis in the name of biological and medical research led to the promulgation in 1948 of the Nuremberg Code, which mandated that subjects of experimentation must grant their fully voluntary and informed consent to any request from a researcher to participate in a medical experiment. Exposés of unethical research carried out by respected phsyician-researchers in the United States heightened the awareness of the medical community, the federal government, and members of the public, eventually leading to the drafting of regulations governing federally funded research involving human subjects (Rothman, 1991). Although the wording of these regulations is not always framed in the language of rights, the clear intent is to ensconce the moral rights of research subjects in law. In addition to informed consent regarding the purpose, procedures, risks, benefits, and alternatives to participation, these rights include the right to refuse to participate in research, the right to withdraw at any time without prejudice to ongoing or future medical care, and the right to confidentiality.

Rights claims in bioethics have been made on behalf of patients generally (Annas, 1989), as well on behalf of special populations or classes of patients: children, people who are mentally ill or mentally retarded, the elderly, prisoners, and certain classes of patients such as people with AIDS. Since it is only women who can become pregnant, the right of women throughout the world to obtain safe, legal abortions has been a major concern. As a moral right, the right to an abortion is claimed under the broader right of a woman to "control her own body," or under the right to self-determination.

Recently in the United States, rights have been claimed on behalf of women and minorities in the realm of biomedical research. Stemming from observations that women and minorities have been underrepresented in a large number of clinical investigations, this claim asserts their right to equitable access to medical treatments still in the experimental stage. More generally, claims have been made for the inclusion of much larger numbers of women in biomedical research, since past studies have yielded information that can reliably be used to benefit only men with health problems. Underlying these claims asserting the rights of special populations is a demand for equitable treatment and for recognition of basic human attributes.

Should the law be used to enforce moral beliefs?

PAGE 434

In an earlier era, when physicians maintained greater authority in their relationship with patients and fewer rights of patients had been explicitly recognized, there was little need for doctors to issue claims about their own rights. As the right of patients to have their autonomy respected has become widely acknowledged, rights claimed by physicians have begun to increase. A small number of physicians has claimed the right to refuse to perform invasive procedures on patients known or suspected to be HIV-infected, on the grounds that physicians should not be required to undergo unreasonable risks to their life or health. A somewhat larger number of doctors has asserted their "right to know" a patient's HIV status, in order that they may take proper precautions to avoid becoming infected. Dr. Neal Rzepkowski, an HIV-infected physician who was forced to resign his position as an emergency room physician when his infection became known, claimed his "right to work" in denying that patients have the right to know about his HIV status. Some physicians now claim the right to decline to provide treatments they deem "futile," arguing that respect for patients' autonomy does not require doctors to comply with whatever patients may demand.

Prominent examples of rights

The previous article describes two basic categories of rights: institutional rights conferred by some sort of organization or social convention, and moral rights, of which human rights are the most fundamental species. The following are among the most prominent examples of rights in bioethics falling under both of these basic categories.

THE RIGHT TO LIBERTY. The category of liberty rights includes a number of prominent examples in

RIGHTS IN BIOETHICS
Is There a "Right to Die"?

The "right to die" has been presented to courts as part of the right of privacy and as an expression of patients' right to refuse treatment (Rhoden, 1988). Yet the phrase "the right to die" illustrates how confusing the language of rights can become. What may be referred to in the moral language of rights as "the right to die" must, in the legal domain, be placed into a different category, since no legally established right to die exists. Moreover, since most of the circumstances in which this right is claimed involve patients' or their families' request to withhold or withdraw life-sustaining treatment, the most accurate expression of this right is "the right to refuse medical treatment." To go beyond that well-established moral and legal right is to assert the right to assisted suicide or to have active euthanasia performed. Although claims to these latter rights have been asserted and the initiatives appeared on election ballots in the state of Washington in 1991 and in California in 1992, as of early 1993 there were no statutes in the United States that grant individuals the right to assisted suicide or to active euthanasia.

Recent years have witnessed the expansion of a patient's right to refuse medical treatment to cover a future time when they have lost their mental capacity. The first legislative enactment in this area was the Natural Death Act, passed by the California legislature in 1976. The right to decide about future medical treatment falls into the larger category known as "advance directives," which can be executed in the form of a living will or by appointing a health-care agent whose authority goes into effect when the patient loses decisional capacity. All fifty states now have legislation recognizing patients' rights in the form of a living will, appointment of a health-care agent, or both. The legal right of relatives to refuse life-sustaining treatment for a patient who has not executed a living will or health-care proxy remains unclear, although a moral right has been claimed by many who argue that an incapacitated patient's relatives are best situated to decide about the appropriateness of continued medical treatment (Rhoden, 1988).

— RUTH MACKLIN

bioethics. Several court decisions in the 1970s established a number of rights for individuals involuntarily confined on grounds of "dangerousness to self or others." The chief moral reason for challenging involuntary commitment to a mental institution is that the practice constitutes an infringement of individual liberty. Such challenges are based on the claim that the right to liberty has priority over other rights in cases where rights conflict (Szasz, 1963). In the case of *Wyatt* v. *Stickney* (1972), the court listed many subsidiary rights of individuals confined in mental institutions. These included a right to the least restrictive conditions necessary for treatment, the right to be free from isolation, the right not to be subjected to experimental research without consent, the right to a comfortable bed and privacy, the right to adequate meals, and the right to an individualized treatment plan with a projected timetable for meeting specific goals.

A second prominent appeal to a liberty right is found in the U.S. Supreme Court's ruling in 1990 in *Cruzan* v. *Director, Missouri Department of Health*, the first "right to die" case to come before the Court. Nancy Cruzan was a young woman who had remained in a persistent vegetative state for several years following an automobile accident. Her parents eventually requested that artificially administered nutrition and hydration be withdrawn, a request that was denied by the Missouri Supreme Court on grounds that "clear and convincing" evidence of the patient's wishes was lacking. Although the U.S. Supreme Court held that the Constitution does not preclude a state from requiring clear and convincing evidence of an incompetent patient's wishes to forgo life-sustaining treatment, the Court's opinion nevertheless assumed that autonomous patients have a constitutionally protected "liberty interest" in refusing unwanted medical treatment.

The U.S. Supreme Court again invoked liberty rights in its ruling in a 1992 abortion case, *Casey* v. *Planned Parenthood Association of Southeastern Pennsylvania.* Although the Court did allow states to impose some restrictions on a woman's right to an abortion, it upheld the constitutional right to an abortion established in *Roe* v. *Wade.* However, in *Casey* the Court did not refer to the right to privacy but, instead, to basic rights of liberty found in the liberty clause of the Fourteenth Amendment, as well as in past cases that recognized rights to bodily integrity and "a person's most basic decisions about family and parenthood."

Problems in assessing rights claims in bioethics

Problems in assessing rights claims fall into different categories, of which two leading types are discussed here: (1) the status of entities to which rights are attributed and (2) conflicts of rights.

See Also

Law and Morality

Bioethics: The General Questions

BEARERS OF RIGHTS. This class of problems concerning the evaluation of rights claims arises out of the need to determine what properties are essential in order to qualify as a bearer of rights. Disagreements abound concerning the status of entities to which rights are attributed: Is the fetus a creature to whom rights can properly be ascribed? Can rights be ascribed only to humans, or are nonhuman animals appropriate bearers of rights? Are nonexistent entities, such as future generations or an individual's not yet conceived children, ones to which rights can correctly be attributed? In this last example, different actions or policies might rest on the answers to questions about the bearers of rights. Some claims about the rights of future generations address environmental concerns, as in assertions that future generations have a right to clean air and water. If such a right does exist, then present generations have certain obligations to refrain from acts of pollution that might not harm existing populations but would pose a hazard long in the future. Another claim holds that an individual's (or a couple's) future progeny has a right not to be afflicted with an inherited genetic disorder. If that right exists, then the individual or couple with a heritable disorder could have an obligation to refrain from procreating.

The debate over the fetus as a bearer of rights has several layers. At the most fundamental level, the question is whether an entity resulting from fertilization of a human egg by human sperm at any point during the nine-month gestational period properly can be said to have rights. Although different kinds of rights might be claimed on behalf of the fetus, the one that has received the most attention is the right to life. The debate on this issue is closed on one side by those who

DECLARING RIGHTS
Moral Claims and Force of Law

There is a middle ground between legally established rights and *moral rights merely.* It consists of rights claims issued by trade or professional associations, such as the American Hospital Association, and national or international organizations like the World Health Organization and the United Nations. Also in this middle ground are statements that assert the rights of special populations, such as children, the handicapped, or the mentally retarded. These declarations and bills lack the force of law, but they can nonetheless establish a strong societal presumption in favor of recognizing the moral rights asserted in them.

The American Hospital Association first proclaimed a set of patients' rights in its 1973 statement "A Patient's Bill of Rights," which listed twelve specific rights (the statements comprising these rights have undergone periodic revisions since the 1973 version). Some patients' rights are cast in a general form, such as the first right affirmed: "The patient has the right to considerate and respectful care." What remains unclear about the "Patients' Bill of Rights" is the recourse that patients have if their stated rights are violated. Unlike legally established rights, there is typically no clear procedure or publicly known method by which a patient can bring grievances against the hospital or its staff, or obtain remedies when rights have been violated.

The principles stated in the Constitution of the World Health Organization include a central claim about rights: "The enjoyment of the highest attainable standard of health is one of the fundamental rights of every human being without distinction of race, religion, political belief, economic or social condition." The WHO Constitution also includes a statement about the responsibility of governments for the health of their people. If there is a correlativity of rights and duties, this governmental responsibility can be viewed as embodying a correlative duty implied by the stated fundamental right of every human being to the highest attainable standard of health.

An example of a declaration of rights aimed at a special population is the Declaration of General and Special Rights of the Mentally Handicapped, which was adopted by the International League of Societies for the Mentally Handicapped in 1968 and in modified form by the General Assembly of the United Nations in 1971. The main precept of this and related documents is that mentally retarded persons are held to have all the fundamental rights of anyone else of their age and nationality. Among these are the right to education and training appropriate to developmental status, the right to guardianship or other form of protective advocacy, and the right to marry and to procreate. This last clause gives rise to a potential conflict of rights in places where laws permit involuntary sterilization of mentally retarded persons, including the provision that parents may consent to sterilization on behalf of their mentally retarded offspring.

Another international statement claiming the existence of rights was agreed upon by the representatives of 136 governments in the World Population Plan of Action in Bucharest in 1974: "All couples and individuals have the basic right to decide freely and responsibly the number and spacing of their children and to have the information, education and means to do so." As is true of other examples, the rights enumerated in this statement of reproductive rights imply the existence of correlative duties on the part of some agency, most probably a government, to guarantee their fulfillment.

— RUTH MACKLIN

contend that rights begin at the moment of birth but not before. For others, who argue that at some stage of its development a fetus acquires rights, the problem shifts into the next category—conflicts of rights.

Disputes over the proper bearers of rights are not limited to embryos and fetuses, but also include animals. One side argues that only human entities can properly be said to have rights, while opponents contend that nonhuman beings qualify. Animal rightists claim that the lives of animals are as valuable as those of humans, and that animals have inherent rights that give rise to correlative duties on the part of humans. An intermediate view is held by animal welfarists, who deny that animals have rights yet maintain that animals deserve humane treatment when they are raised and slaughtered for food or used in laboratory experiments. In this view, humans have duties to animals grounded on their welfare, or their capacity to suffer.

Rights-based claims are used by both sides—abortion opponents and proponents of a woman's right to choose.

PAGE 441

CONFLICTS OF RIGHTS. Problems arise in both the moral and the legal domains when rights come into conflict. A well-known conflict appears in the context of abortion, pitting the alleged right to life of the fetus against the right of the pregnant woman to self-determination, or the right to control her own body. But there are other conflicts in the maternal-fetal domain as well. If an obstetrician recommends a cesarean section in the hope of obtaining a better outcome for the infant-to-be, the pregnant woman may decide not to undergo the increased risk to herself of a surgical delivery. She may then seek to exercise her right to refuse treatment, a right embodied in the broader right to informed consent to treatment. The woman's right would then conflict with the alleged right of the fetus—its "right to life" or its "right to be born healthy," depending on whether its life or health was in jeopardy. It is sometimes held that it is not the rights of the fetus that pose this conflict but, rather, those of the child-to-be. That is still problematic, since it is open to question whether entities that do not yet exist (such as the "child-to-be") can properly be said to have rights.

The problem of defining fetal risk is matched by the complexity of delineating what constitutes an unacceptable risk of harm for the mother.

PAGE 469

Two situations noted earlier illustrate the potential for conflicts of rights. The first is that of people who are involuntarily committed to mental institutions on grounds that they are likely to commit acts of violence. The right of a person who has committed no crime to remain free is pitted against society's right to protection when the individual is judged "dangerous to others." The second situation is an HIV-positive individual's right to confidentiality, which may clash with the right of a sex partner or needle-sharing partner to information that might prevent acquisition of a fatal condition.

Advances in medical technology have created conflicts of rights that are unprecedented or rarely encountered. An example is the range of new reproductive technologies and practices: in vitro fertilization, freezing of embryos, and surrogacy. The practice of surrogacy can result in disputes over who has a right to the infant when a woman who has served as a surrogate is unwilling to give up the child after birth. The biological father can claim a right to the child on grounds of his paternity and also on the basis of the contractual agreement in which the surrogate promised to give up the child at birth. The surrogate can claim a right to the child on the same genetic basis when she has been artificially inseminated. Even when she serves only as a "gestational surrogate," she might claim a right to the infant because of her contribution through nine months of gestation and during labor and childbirth. Reasonable people disagree about which claims about rights in disputed surrogacy arrangements have greater validity, and state statutes and court cases have yielded contradictory answers to this question (Gostin, 1990).

Another advance in medical technology, the capability to freeze and store embryos for future use, can create a conflict of rights between the gamete contributors. In one case, a couple who had created and frozen seven embryos for possible future implantation into the woman decided to divorce. A legal battle ensued (*Davis* v. *Davis*, 1992), with each member of the couple claiming a right with respect to the embryos. The wife sought control of the embryos, contending that it might be her only chance to have her own biological children, while the husband sought veto power over her decision on the grounds that it would impose on him the burdens of unwanted parenthood. Although a lower court awarded the embryos to the woman, who sought to implant them, that decision was later reversed. The Tennessee Supreme Court said that the "issue centers on the two aspects of procreational autonomy—the right to procreate and the right to avoid procreation." The court ruled that "the party wishing to avoid procreation should prevail, assuming that the other party has a reasonable possibility of achieving parenthood by means other than the use of the pre-embryos in question."

Another case involved a dispute between an in vitro fertilization (IVF) program and a couple over custody of a frozen embryo. In the case of *York* v. *Jones* (1989), a couple who had been using the services of the IVF program at the Jones Institute in Norfolk, Virginia, moved to California and wanted to transport their remaining frozen embryo to a Los Angeles program. The Virginia program refused to grant permission. The court denied the clinic's efforts to dismiss the couple's lawsuit, thus resolving the question in favor of the couple's right to remove the embryo for transfer to another IVF program. The case did not address the question of whether control over frozen embryos should be construed as a custody or a property right.

In all these examples of conflicts, debates rage over which rights ought to take precedence. Regardless of the evidence or reasons put forward relevantly and cogently in support of such claims, decisions concerning the priority of one person's rights over those of another are likely to remain controversial when the rights in conflict appear to be legitimate. To resolve any conflict of rights, a judgment must be made about which rights weigh more heavily or under precisely what conditions the rights of one person take precedence over the rights of another. When conflicts are brought to court, a judge may resolve the issue, but judicial decisions at one level are sometimes overturned by a higher court, and courts at the same level have been known to reverse themselves at a later time.

Conclusion

In addition to the bioethics rights discussed in this article, numerous others have been claimed on behalf of all people as well as particular groups. It is evident that some of the rights claimed in bioethics are difficult if not impossible to fulfill, since it is not within the power of any single individual or even a government to take all the necessary steps to satisfy them. But as with any moral ideal, rights claims in bioethics serve an important function in setting forth the human needs and conditions requisite for attaining a just society.

— RUTH MACKLIN

S

SEXISM

Sexism is both the belief that one sex is superior to the other and the many consequences of this belief. The term "sexism" almost always refers to men's claimed or perceived superiority over women; the occasionally expressed belief that women are superior to men is referred to as female chauvinism and does not affect men's economic or social status in the way that male sexism affects women's status. Feminists coined the term "sexism" in the mid-1960s as a way to characterize the condition they sought to remedy (hooks, 1984). Given its origin as a political term, sexism has been more a rhetorical device than an analytic tool, and the term often conflates discrimination against women and the oppression of women. By distinguishing between discrimination and oppression, we can fully appreciate the scope, nature, origins, and effects of sexism, and its importance as a category in ethical thought and in bioethics.

Discrimination and oppression are analytically distinct (Young, 1990). To discriminate means to distinguish. Hence, not all discrimination is a concern for ethicists, but only those discriminations that raise ethical issues, such as those based on prejudices and considered unjust or unfair or disrespectful. To oppress means to thwart, to use force or other means to control and to hold down. Oppression is necessarily wrong from the standpoint of fairness, justice, and equality. Not all forms of discrimination, then, are oppressive, and not all forms of oppression are discriminatory: Oppression can be indiscriminate, directed at everyone. By distinguishing between discrimination and oppression, we can clarify four different senses of sexism. Depending on which definition is used, the nature, origins, effects, and remedies for sexism are different.

Classic sexism

This most common account of sexism posits that discrimination between men and women leads to women's oppression. Classic sexism presumes that when the biological distinction of sex, between male and female, becomes the cultural distinction of gender, which marks men and women, then biological differences are changed into a cultural category that oppresses women.

"We hold these truths to be self-evident, that all men and women are created equal."

FIRST WOMAN'S RIGHTS CONVENTION, SENECA FALLS, N.Y., 1848

WOMEN VOTE

Not until 1920 did American women have a right to vote—two years after British women (over 30) gained suffrage.

S

SEXISM

Classic Sexism

"The right of citizens of the United States to vote shall not be denied or abridged by the United States or by any State on account of sex."

FROM AMENDMENT XIX TO THE CONSTITUTION OF THE UNITED STATES, 1920

See Also

Natural Law

Feminists thus point to the existence of prejudices or practices that constrict women's opportunities and restrict their lives, and conclude that discriminations affecting women are wrong.

Most feminists believe that sexism is ubiquitous. Feminist historians argue that all known cultures engage in gender distinctions, and in virtually all historical societies, men have dominated in spiritual, public, economic, and cultural life. Archaeologists and anthropologists argue that some prehistoric and nonindustrial societies were and are more egalitarian than most societies recorded in Western history (Sanday, 1981; Anderson and Zinsser, 1988).

In Western societies, feminist scholars can point to many instances of sexism directed against women, from the story of the creation of humans in the Old Testament (where God created Adam first) to current social conditions of women. Aristotle doubted women's rationality; Roman law made the father the head of the household. Contemporary institutions continue to reflect the exclusion of women from some spheres of life: Women hold relatively few public offices, are excluded from the ranks of the clergy in many religions, remain largely excluded from the military, are less educated and hold fewer academic appointments than men, are rarely included among the highest ranks of corporation officers, and are generally more marginal members of the working force. Few women are economically independent, and women remain largely responsible for family life and domestic work, even in societies that boast of greater equality in these realms (United Nations, 1991). Violence against women is at epidemic levels (Radford and Russell, 1992). Culturally, women have been excluded throughout most of Western history from central roles in the cultural production, and are often treated as inferiors in cultural work.

Feminists have argued against sexism throughout the world in the nineteenth and twentieth centuries (Jayawardena, 1986). Many cultures have practiced ways of controlling women and their sexuality. The dislocations caused by changing patterns of employment and consumption in an increasingly globalized economy seem to have particularly harmful effects on women (Joekes, 1987). Amartya K. Sen, a development economist, has argued that at present the numbers of women and men in the world are unbalanced: As he describes it, this fact means that millions of women are "missing" from the world's population. To Sen, this demographic imbalance points to systematic devaluation of women's lives: Women receive less food, education, and medical attention (Sen, 1990).

Within this account of classic sexism, different views exist of the origin and nature of the oppression embodied in sexism. Some liberal feminists see this oppression as a sum total of individual discriminatory acts. They view sexism as a result of continued prejudice; because the distinctions between men and women played a larger role in earlier human societies, they persist. The continuation of sexism is the result of the inability of societies to discard some of their outmoded traditional habits. Hence, the fact that sexism has deep historical roots does not mean that it cannot be eliminated through careful reconstruction of social institutions (Okin, 1989).

Another strand of liberal feminism posits that sexism originates primarily from Western practices of childrearing. Children's psychological development, including their senses of gender and of identity, depend on how they interact with caregivers in the first years of life. Because women do most of the caregiving to infants, boys and girls have different patterns of psychological relationship to these primary caregivers; boys learn to separate from others while girls learn to remain connected. These gender differences in "object relations" continue to inform the differing psychology of men and women. By this theory, eliminating the gendered division of parenting that predominates in Western society would eliminate sexism (see Chodorow, 1978).

Other feminists view the discrimination against women and the resulting oppression of women as

SEXISM AS NATURAL LAW

Opponents of feminism view sexism as an ideological construction put forth by misguided feminists. According to this approach, discrimination by sex is a result of the natural differences between men and women, especially in reproduction and physical strength. Hence, while discrimination exists between women and men, the sex-based distinctions that exist in societies are not discriminatory in any pejorative sense but necessary for the proper functioning of human society. Hence, "sexism" is ideological, in the sense of being a false belief, because it is an attempt by women to change the natural order. Those who view sex differences as natural can agree with feminists that women and men have different roles, and that women have largely been excluded from some spheres of life, but believe that these differences do not constitute oppression. To try to remedy such discriminations, such thinkers argue, will cause more harm than good (Goldberg, 1973; Schlafly, 1977).

— JOAN C. TRONTO

deeply embedded in social institutions, so that merely changing individuals' prejudiced attitudes and practices will not alleviate sexism. Some of these feminists are influenced by Marxist ideas and view sexism as a concomitant of private property. As long as it is necessary to ensure the proper inheritance of private property, men must regulate women's sexual activities (Engels, 1972). Friedrich Engels argued that since the systematic exploitation of women began with property, women's oppression would end with the Communist revolution. A number of socialists have challenged the simplicity of this argument, and the treatment of women under so-called socialist regimes has not been encouraging (Hansen and Philipson, 1990).

Thus, a point of contention about the nature of classic sexism is whether it is a matter of prejudice and discriminatory attitudes, beliefs, and practices that are expressed by individuals or groups; or whether sexism is a systemic form of discrimination that permeates social, political, and economic institutions. A parallel exists with the study of racism, where racism often appears to be only a matter of individual attitudes rather than a quality inherent in social institutions. Those who believe racism is a more intractable problem often refer to this phenomenon as "institutional racism"; there is a parallel understanding of institutional sexism (see, e.g., Hall and Sandler 1982; Rothenberg, 1992).

This split within the understanding of classic sexism matters greatly for the study of ethics on two levels. First, the tasks involved in solving an attitudinal and a behavioral problem are different from those involved in changing institutions fundamentally. Second, responsibility for sexism is quite different depending upon whether it is simply a matter of prejudice or a more deeply rooted social phenomenon. If sexism is simply a matter of prejudice, then those who believe that they no longer harbor prejudiced attitudes are no longer sexist. On the other hand, if sexism is a part of the social structure, then simply changing one's attitudes does not equal a solution to the problem. In recent years in the United States, some attitudes expressed toward women have become more favorable, but no equal transformation in women's economic, political, and social standing has occurred (see Faludi, 1991). This fact suggests that seeing sexism as institutionalized is more plausible.

Androcentrism

Androcentrism argues that sexism does not begin from a conscious act of discriminating between men and women; it begins from the assumption that men's experiences are universal, and that women's experiences are essentially similar to men's. Androcentrism is the view that men's lives and experiences, their bodies, behaviors, activities, and beliefs, should serve as the normal starting point when thinking about humans (MacKinnon, 1987). Those who argue that androcentrism describes sexism contend that in defining the male experience as normal, women's experiences, lives, bodies, and so forth are necessarily viewed as lacking, as a departure from the normal. Androcentrism grows from the recognition that while discriminations may not even be stated as such, they may still have oppressive consequences (MacKinnon, 1987).

An example of androcentrism is the medical practice of considering male bodies as normal, and excluding women from clinical trials because female hormones make medical observations more complicated. As a result, women may receive less medical attention, and less may be known about how diseases such as heart disease affect women. Another example of androcentrism is the sexism implicit in language, where linguistic practices shape conceptions—for example, that an unmarked reference to "doctor" is not the same as the marked category "woman doctor" (Miller and Swift, 1988; Tannen, 1990). Hence, androcentrism does not highlight overt discrimination as connected to oppression but explores how the assumption of the male as normal gives rise to women's oppression.

Masculinism

Masculinism raises the possibility of oppression arising without any prior discrimination—indeed, of oppression arising out of categories presumed to be universal and nondiscriminatory. Critics of masculinism argue that many categories that seem not to distinguish gender have the effect of discriminating among men and women and leading to women's oppression because they contain hidden assumptions about the superiority of men and an implicit preference for masculinity over femininity. For example, Susan Bordo has argued that Descartes's mind-body distinction, while ostensibly not about men and women at all, results in the denigration of women because it implicitly associates mind with masculinity and body with femininity and posits the superiority of mind over body (Bordo, 1987).

Conclusion

These different accounts of the nature of sexism obviously have a profound effect on how bioethicists might address the problem of sexism. Adopting the first understanding, sexism is not even a problem. Among the other three definitions, which are not necessarily mutually exclusive, the depth to which investigators must go to try to understand and to remove the effects of sexism vary. If one adopts a classic, liberal view, then removing one's own prejudice is enough. If sexism is also deeply rooted in social institutions, then one must

"Woman's degradation is in man's idea of his sexual rights. Our religion, laws, customs, are all founded on the belief that woman was made for man."

ELIZABETH CADY STANTON
LETTER TO SUSAN B. ANTHONY, 1860

"No written law has ever been more binding than unwritten custom supported by popular opinion."

CARRIE CHAPMAN CATT
SPEECH AT SENATE HEARING ON WOMAN SUFFRAGE, 1900

be cognizant of its effects throughout those institutions: For example, economic oppression may affect access to medical services. If sexism is androcentrism, then thinkers and practitioners must constantly be on their guard to make certain that categories, practices, and experiments do not presume the male as normal even though they are not overtly discriminatory. If sexism is understood as masculinism, then all of the categories and practices used by bioethicists must be explored to determine whether they contain a hidden gendered dimension.

The existence of sexism raises problems of social justice and challenges notions of basic equality (see, e.g., Okin, 1989). It also raises questions about related forms of discrimination and oppression, and about whether the elimination of sexism requires the recognition of multiple oppressions. To admit, for example, that discrimination on the basis of gender roles is wrong raises the question of whether it is proper to discriminate against gay men and lesbians on the basis of their sexual orientation, a form of discrimination called heterosexism. To admit that sexism is wrong because discrimination leads to oppression raises questions among feminists about how to cope with racism among women. Those feminists who see sexism as a form of androcentrism or masculinism will argue that eliminating sexism will result in much more broad-reaching social changes. For example, some feminists argue that because women are less warlike than men, eliminating sexism requires a commitment to pacifism (Ruddick, 1989). Others suggest that sexism is a discrete phenomenon and that to broaden it to include other forms of discrimination or undesirable social practices weakens the focus on gender.

"Sexism" is a term of disapprobation; it raises fundamental ethical questions because if sexism exists, it challenges our ability to treat everyone fairly and equally, and with respect. By pointing to the existence of sexism, feminists have raised the centrality of asking about gender in all areas of ethical inquiry.

— JOAN C. TRONTO

75% of all married women interviewed had had premarital intercourse; 12% waited until marriage to have sex for the first time.

NATIONAL SURVEY OF FAMILY GROWTH, 1997

SEX THERAPY AND SEX RESEARCH

SCIENTIFIC AND CLINICAL PERSPECTIVES

Sex has many varied functions—allowing procreation, providing reassurance of desirability and worth, and forging bonds between individuals. Human beings have not been content to view sex as a natural physical experience. Instead, they invest it with additional significance, seeing it as a special gift conveying the message of love and affection, a means to dominate and control, or even an evil requiring punishment. Beliefs and attitudes about what is normal, about what is right and ideal, establish the boundaries of sexual expression within a given culture. Beliefs and behaviors vary widely among different times and places. It is not surprising, then, that the fields of sex therapy and sex research are laden with paradox and with issues of value and ethics. This article describes the current status of sex therapy and research, highlighting those aspects that give rise to these issues.

Sex research

Scientific and clinical interest in human sexuality is ancient. One of the earliest records of medical thinking, the Hunan Papyrus, demonstrates a clear awareness of the sexual transmission of certain diseases. Writings from China, India, Persia, and other ancient cultures reflect an avid interest in descriptive research, categorizing and classifying both sexual behavior and techniques designed to increase erotic pleasure and to overcome certain conditions which we now refer to as sexual dysfunctions. Several therapeutic techniques that were developed in the United States in the 1980s for the treatment of sexual dysfunctions have been described, with minor differences, in Taoist manuals attributed to Master Tung-hsuan, who is believed to have been a physician living in seventh-century China.

Henry Havelock Ellis is generally considered the "father" of modern sex therapy and research. His multi-volume *Studies in the Psychology of Sex* (1896-1928) established an enduring framework for the conceptualization of sexuality. His work challenged the nineteenth-century pseudoscientific theories that linked nonreproductive sexual activity with insanity and disease. Unlike Ellis, whose work focused exclusively on sexuality, Sigmund Freud (1856-1939) included sexuality as a central aspect of a comprehensive theory of personality. Overcoming the barriers of intolerance and prudery that had silenced public and scientific discussion, Ellis and Freud ensured the subject would remain a legitimate focus for scientific inquiry.

Until the 1930s, however, knowledge about sex had been based largely on the systematic observation of what Donn Byrne (1977) referred to as "animal sex, native sex, or crazy sex," that is, studies of the behavior of other species, other (nonindustrialized, non-Western, "primitive") cultures, or people seeking psychotherapy for emotional disturbances. In 1938, Alfred Kinsey and his colleagues (Pomeroy, 1972) began a series of studies that lasted two decades, using questionnaires and conducting interviews with thousands

S

SEX THERAPY AND SEX RESEARCH

Scientific and Clinical Perspectives

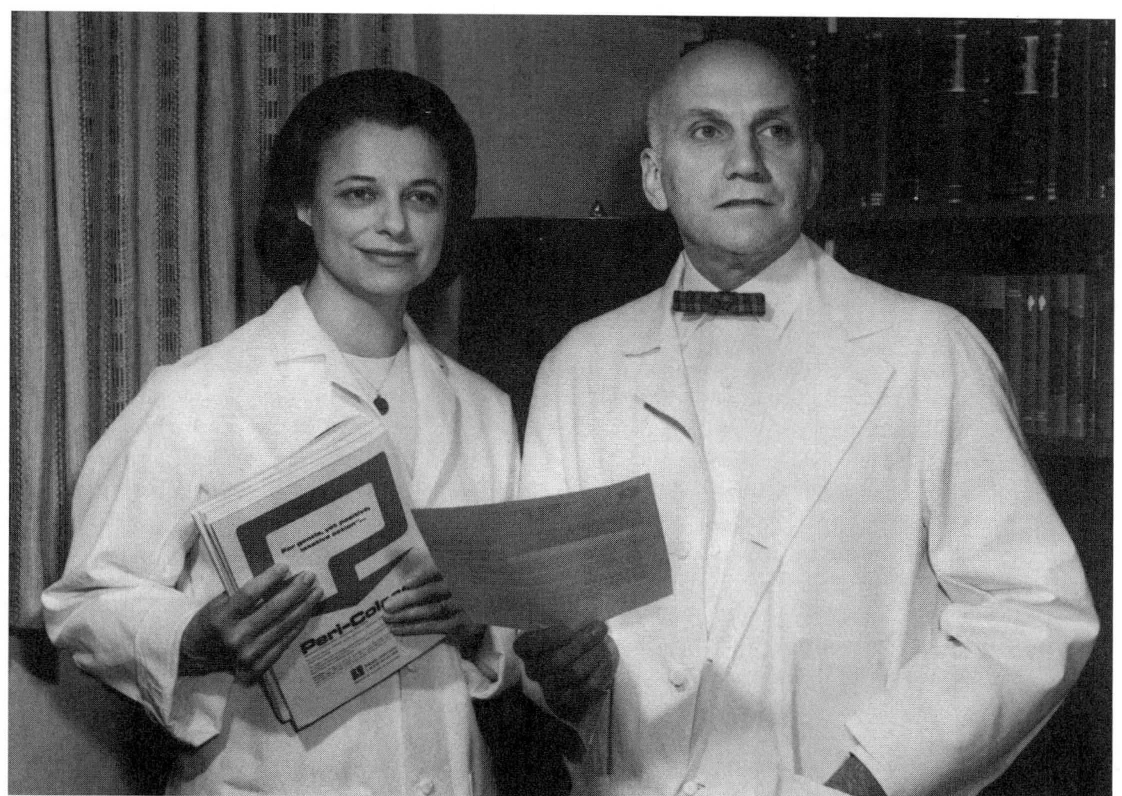

SEX PIONEERS

William Masters and Virginia Johnson (later married) sparked an outcry over science's invasion of privacy. Their work led to sex therapy as a profession.

of Americans about their sexual experience and behaviors, providing a rich description of the behavior of "normal" Americans. Kinsey's work provided the foundation for the first studies of human sexual response based on direct observation and physiological measurements. Beginning in the 1950s, studies by William Masters and Virginia Johnson (1966, 1970, 1976, 1977) dispelled many prevalent myths about normal sexual response and provided valuable information about the mechanisms and treatment of various sexual problems.

The public outcry against the landmark research of Masters and Johnson (1966) on the anatomy and physiology of human sexual function spoke volumes about society's acute discomfort that sex, heretofore shrouded in privacy, should enter the public domain of scientific inquiry. Although the study's contribution to the creation of a social climate more conducive to the scientific study of sexual behavior was profound, it was Masters and Johnson's publication of *Human Sexual Inadequacy* (1970) that led to the emergence of sex therapy as a distinct professional entity.

Just as earlier sex researchers had faced loss of membership in their professional organizations and even excommunication from their churches, twentieth-century scientists have faced social, personal, and political resistance. Vern Bullough (cited in Allgeier and Allgeier, 1988) suggested that, given "this kind of mindset," contemporary researchers are implicitly encouraged to limit their attention to those aspects of sexuality that are relevant to the solution of social problems such as divorce, teen pregnancy, venereal disease, prostitution, homosexuality, and "other forms of stigmatized activity" (p. 39). Although the concerns raised by the AIDS epidemic heighten the need for understanding, many governments and foundations remain reticent about supporting basic research on sexual behavior ("Ethics and Research," 1990).

Notwithstanding these handicaps and its infant status, contemporary sex research is a broad and active field that ranges from theological analyses of the sexuality of Jesus to the bioengineering of devices to measure the intensity of uterine contractions during orgasm. Generally, the domain of research topics can be classified as studies of sexual attitudes, knowledge, and beliefs; sexual orientation and gender identity; sexual function (anatomy and physiology); sexual fantasies and feelings, such as attraction and bonding; and sexual behaviors, ranging from courtship behavior to the paraphilias (sexual deviations, characterized by preference for nonhuman objects in achieving arousal, imposition of humiliation or suffering, or coercion of nonconsenting partners).

Research methods include psychological testing, surveys, interviews, case histories, direct observation, and biochemical and physiological measurement. Maneuvering in an area shrouded by considerable sensitivity and secrecy, the inherent necessity to draw sam-

> *"As we make sex less secretive, we may rob it of its power to hold men and women together."*
>
> THOMAS SZASZ
> THE SECOND SIN, 1973

S

SEX THERAPY AND SEX RESEARCH

Scientific and Clinical Perspectives

Nearly 14% of women aged 20–24 had sex before age 15; for these women, the median age at first intercourse was 16.6 years old.

NATIONAL SURVEY OF FAMILY GROWTH, 1997

ples from volunteer and/or patient populations often limits the generalizability of research results. Such constraints highlight the need to replicate studies with a variety of samples, situations, and cultures.

Sex counseling and therapy

Sex counseling is primarily educative. It tends to focus entirely on the presenting sexual concern, and usually requires only a few (one to three) visits. Many sexual problems, however, are complex and require a more extensive approach to diagnosis and management. Sex therapy is distinguished by its effort to place the sexual problem within the broader context of personality and relationship. While education is part of the therapy process, a variety of treatment approaches are used.

The goal of sex therapy is to resolve sexual problems. Most often the term "sex therapy" is used to refer to the treatment of the psychosexual dysfunctions characterized by interference with normal physiological sexual response (desire, excitement, orgasm) or function. For the purpose of this article it will also include the treatment of those disorders that involve sexual expression in manners that do not have social approval, such as exhibitionism and coercive sex. Problems of gender identity and sexual orientation are discussed elsewhere. Many different dissatisfactions and worries bring people to seek the services of sex therapists. Consequently, the practice of sex therapy is characterized by its diversity.

SEX COUNSELING. Some clients need only information—or more frequently, the correction of misinformation. Some need only reassurance, perhaps an expert's permission to abandon unrealistic "standards" for beauty and behavior promulgated by the media, for example. Others come as part of a couple, seeking an intermediary who will help them communicate their desires and expectations when they are without an adequate vocabulary, or burdened by embarrassment or fear of wounding the partner. Many seek encouragement and practical advice in sorting out the day-to-day problems of a stressful life that leaves little time or energy for sex. Some need help in adapting to physical limitations imposed by arthritis or a recent heart attack. Still others want to learn new positions and techniques to enrich sex that has become predictable and stale.

The sex education component may attempt to modify emotional and attitudinal factors that elicit the patient's anxiety about sex. The most common model (Bjorkstein, 1976) is the Sexual Attitude Restructuring Process (SAR), a workshop developed by the National Sex Forum, which involves exposure to sexually explicit media accompanied by group discussions in which reactions are explored.

SEX THERAPY: CONCEPTUAL FOUNDATIONS. The techniques and formats used in sex therapy are largely derived from three intellectual traditions: the psychotherapeutic approach, the behavioral, and the medical. Some sex therapy programs offer an eclectic approach, making use of all three.

Psychotherapeutic approaches are based on the assumption that sexual difficulties arise from psychological factors. Adherents of psychoanalytic theory, especially that based on the work of Freud, trace the origin of dysfunction to unresolved conflicts that arise in childhood. Treatment is directed toward the search for, and resolution of, these conflicts, focusing on the integration of the total personality rather than the immediate sexual symptom. Treatment tends to be lengthy and expensive, and its effectiveness in alleviating sexual symptoms is largely subjective and hence unmeasurable. Other psychotherapeutic approaches, derived from a variety of conceptual frameworks, place greater emphasis on sexual experiences occurring later in life, including communication difficulties, injurious relationships, and the incorporation of faulty attitudes and beliefs into the personality structure.

Behavioral approaches are characterized by the assumption that sexual responses, including behavior, are learned, and can therefore be unlearned and/or replaced by more desirable responses. Anxiety is seen as the predominant mechanism that mediates sexual problems, whether the problem is largely cognitive (e.g., concern over strength of erection) or emotional (e.g., a phobia that blocks arousal). Without extensive probing into the client's past, personality, or relationships, behavioral approaches deal directly with the sexual problem by using conditioning techniques designed to overcome anxiety or to lessen sensitivity to stimuli that provoke anxiety. The most commonly used techniques are based on systematic desensitization, but others, ranging from aversive conditioning to sexual fantasy alteration, supplement the therapists' arsenal of useful behavioral techniques.

Cognitive-behavioral approaches, which combine elements of both behavioral and cognitive psychologies, have also proved useful in treating many disorders. An excellent overview of these approaches is found in an article describing their use in treating victims of sexual abuse for their psychological distress and the sexual problems that have occurred as a result of their victimization (Talmadge and Wallace, 1991).

Medical approaches focus on the contribution of organic factors to the development of sexual dysfunction. Helen Singer Kaplan (1974) describes five major categories that affect sexual functioning: neurological, vascular, and endocrine disorders; debilitating diseases; and drugs (illicit, prescription, and over-the-counter). Systematic inquiry into the physiological mechanisms that govern the sexual system is a recent phenomenon and has focused mostly on male populations. This gender bias can be attributed to several factors, one being the preponderance of male researchers in the field. Others include the female's ability to hide sexual dysfunction by "faking" satisfaction, the reluctance of many women to discuss sexual matters, and a lack of concern by some women about the loss of sexual function as long as their affectional needs are being met. Much remains to be learned, especially about the effects of various medications and illnesses on female sexual functioning.

ADVANCES IN SEX THERAPY. The field of sex therapy has witnessed dramatic shifts in its base of knowledge and theory that have affected profoundly the ways in which care should be provided. Following the pioneering research of Masters and Johnson in the 1960s, behavioral therapies derived from those developed by Joseph Wolpe and his associates formed the central element in sex therapy (Wolpe, 1958; Lazarus and Rosen, 1976; Masters and Johnson, 1976). Prior to this time sexual problems had been viewed largely as the result of emotional conflict, and sex therapy was primarily the domain of the psychotherapist. While anxiety—seen either as a learned response or as the result of intrapsychic or intrapersonal forces—was previously viewed as the predominant factor in virtually all cases of sexual dysfunction, it became clear in the 1970s that illnesses and drugs caused a substantial proportion of sexual disorders. Consequently, an evaluation by a physician with sufficient expertise in sexual medicine is often necessary before therapy is undertaken.

Two conceptual advances resulting from research and extensive clinical experience over the past three decades have revolutionized the field of sex therapy. The first was the recognition of separate, but interlocking, phases of the sexual response cycle (excitement, plateau, orgasm, and resolution, as originally conceptualized by Masters and Johnson, 1966). The second was the understanding that a multiplicity of psychological and physical factors act in very specific ways to "produce a variety of disorders that are responsive to specific and rational treatment strategies" (Kaplan, 1979, p. 4). These advances led to clinical developments that address the immediate and specific determinants, greatly improving treatment outcomes.

To a considerable extent, the effectiveness of any therapeutic approach depends on two factors. The nature of the problem heavily influences outcome; for example, successful treatment of the inability to expe-

SEX THERAPY
Professional Practice

The specific approaches used in the process of sex therapy vary considerably, depending on the nature of the sexual complaints and, of course, the theoretical bent of the therapist. The classic approach, originally developed by Masters and Johnson for use with heterosexual couples, involves a two-week program of daily therapy with the couple removed from their usual family and work environment. The couple is assigned two therapists (one male, one female), so that each will have a "friend in court," and the couple is treated as a unit. Since this approach is impractical for many patients, other therapists use modifications including the use of one therapist, willingness to treat those with homosexual and bisexual orientations, provision of treatment to individuals as well as couples, use of group therapy (Barbach, 1980), and the inclusion of traditional psychotherapy, especially when behavioral therapies are not working (Kaplan, 1979).

However, certain components are shared by most treatment programs. A first step is an assessment of the sexual problem, which may include a consultation visit to identify the problem and discuss approaches to treatment; a detailed sexual history, which may be accompanied by an assigned autobiography describing sexual attitudes, experiences, and feelings; paper and pencil tests of sexual knowledge, attitudes, and beliefs; and a medical history and physical examination, including a guided sexological exam designed to educate patients about their sexual organs.

Specific behavioral exercises appropriate to the diagnosed disorder are then assigned for practice. Sex education is provided, and the therapist(s) and patient(s) meet to share feedback from the assignments, discuss concerns and plans, and facilitate the couple's communication. Joseph LoPiccolo and his colleagues, for example, offer a treatment program for women with inhibited orgasm, which includes masturbation training, role-playing exaggerated orgasmic responses to reduce her anxiety about the sensation of loss of control that may occur with orgasm, and the practice of orgasmic behaviors such as breath-holding during arousal. In addition the woman and her partner undertake skill training, using sensate focus homework exercises that include exploration, touching, and caressing the partner's body while genital touching and intercourse are initially prohibited, thereby learning to give and receive pleasure while freed from the pressure to "perform" (LoPiccolo, 1978).

— SHARON K. TURNBULL

rience orgasm is much more likely than alleviating low sexual desire (libido). Effectiveness also varies with the precision in the selection of treatment strategies and the extent to which they are based on accurate and complete diagnoses. Brief behavioral approaches, for example, are replaced by or supplemented with psychotherapy when a history of incest or childhood sexual abuse emerges during the course of treatment. Brief sex therapy methods have proved remarkably effective when used with appropriately selected patients. Treatment failures rise considerably in the presence of substantial medical and psychological problems or serious marital conflict.

In addition to being questionable ethically, therapies used to change sexual orientation have not been very effective, and their use has declined in recent years. Instead, most therapists now focus on helping their homosexual patients adapt to the stress of living in a disapproving society (Diamant, 1977).

The escalation of sexual aggression over the past several decades has been accompanied by the development of numerous treatment programs for sex offenders, generally for those who are incarcerated. "Conspicuous by its absence from the vast literature on offender typologies and treatment approaches is any general claim of treatment efficacy" (Dvoskin, 1991, p. 229). The few programs whose outcomes have been carefully evaluated yielded only modest results, discouraging research and program development in an area of acute need.

At any one time, only 4 or 5% of adults are cohabiting, but 25% of adults in 1996 reported having lived together at one time in their lives.

NATIONAL SURVEY OF FAMILY GROWTH, 1997

QUALIFICATIONS FOR PROFESSIONAL PRACTICE OF SEX THERAPY. One of the crucial issues facing any emerging discipline is that of professionalization. Who should be allowed to practice the specialty? What knowledge, skills, and attitudes should they possess, and who should certify their competency to practice? How does the discipline police itself to prevent exploitation of the public by the unscrupulous and the incompetent? These questions have been widely debated since the emergence of sex therapy as a profession in the 1970s, but they remain unresolved. Without doubt, the area is susceptible to charlatans seeking profit or outright sexual exploitation. Referral by physicians who are aware of the credentials and practices of therapists provides some protection from the unscrupulous. Many professional sex therapy organizations also provide patient referrals to practitioners. Most have developed codes of ethical behavior that prohibit sexual contact between therapists and clients, and establish procedures to discipline or terminate membership of those who violate them.

Sex therapy treatment ranges from hypnosis and biofeedback to implants and microsurgical procedures to increase penile blood flow, and depends on a variety of practitioners. Especially problematic are health professionals who, protected by the licensing of their primary professions, may undertake to do therapy with insufficient training in the specialized evaluation and treatment of sexual disorders. Attention given to sexuality and sex therapy in the professional training of physicians, nurses, psychologists, and social workers has increased considerably since the 1960s. But complete answers to the question of which disciplines can ethically practice sex therapy, and how much and what sort of specialized training should be required, await the maturing of the profession.

— SHARON K. TURNBULL

ETHICAL ISSUES

Simply defined, sex is a physical act, a biological drive. Sexuality is a broader term, encompassing sexual orientation, beliefs and attitudes, morality, and personal identity with its attendant concepts of femininity and masculinity.

Sexual expression, and consequently sex therapy and research, are heavily dependent upon the culture within which they occur. Beliefs and attitudes about what is normal, what is desirable, and what is moral vary widely across time and place. For example, the JudaeoChristian belief, influential for many centuries, that procreation is the primary or even sole legitimate purpose of sex leads to a view in which nonreproductive activities such as masturbation and homosexuality are seen as a threat to health and morality.

The concept of romantic love, with its origins in the harems of early Arabic culture, was not adopted by Western cultures until the sixteenth century, when romantic love and intimacy (as opposed to economic and political interests) became accepted as the basis for an enduring sexual bond such as marriage (Tannahill, 1992). This linkage of sex and such personal, intrinsic factors as romantic love introduces numerous ethical issues and concerns about relationship, alienation, and commitment (Allgeier and Allgeier, 1988).

Sexuality is central to one's personal identity, and its expression is inextricably intertwined with the experiences of a given culture and its history, religion, and politics. The way sexuality is defined by that culture greatly influences the goals and the means of therapy and research. The possibility of a truly unbiased, value-free endeavor is greatly strained. While sex research and therapy share the same ethical precepts as other disciplines, the special factors surrounding the subject of sex make this domain somewhat different.

The further sex therapy and research move from a purely biological model to embrace the richer concerns of sexual psychology, sociology, and politics, the greater the risk of introducing moral conflict and bias.

This is the basis of many of the dilemmas facing the widening field.

The nature of sex

The ethical therapist or researcher must be sensitive to the special vulnerabilites created by the nature of sex itself. Sex concerns are often cloaked in privacy and occasionally even in secrecy. The experience of fusion, a transitory dissolution of interpersonal boundaries, obtained in sexual union satisfies a great libidinal hunger for attachment, for merger with an other. The intimate connection between sex, attachment, and identity magnifies the obligation of the therapist toward the patient, particularly to do no harm.

Given that sexual expression is often one of the deepest and most personal experiences, what unknown dangers await the client who enters therapy for a sexual problem? Since sex may be merely one troubled area of an overall relational system, tinkering with just the genital system often causes underlying emotional and relational problems to surface. Should therapists, like the maps of old, warn clients of possible consequences before assigning exercises that quite commonly evoke unexpected feelings that themselves demand therapeutic attention?

The social construction of sex

What unquestioned values and presuppositions are embedded in sex therapy and research because their development occurred largely within the context of the predominantly white, middle-class North American scientific establishment? How appropriate are therapeutic modalities designed originally for the treatment of heterosexual married couples, for example, in treating the sexual problems of a gay couple or a bisexual individual? Do members of ethnic minority groups encounter barriers to therapy because they are likely to be judged by standards which are not their own?

Cultural expectations, shared beliefs, and definitions about what is normal can influence the professional as well as public labeling of sexual behaviors, thoughts, and feelings (Szasz, 1980). It was not until 1973 that the American Psychiatric Association, in recognition of the absence of any direct correspondence between sexual preference and mental disorder, acted to remove homosexuality from its list of recognized mental disorders.

A sizable literature speaks to the inherent risks that attend the social construction of sexuality, suggesting that the power politics of sexuality have profoundly influenced the way in which it has been defined. Culturally influenced beliefs about female sexuality, for example, have both reflected and determined the treatment of women throughout history (Laqueur, 1990). In the absence of reliable data to the contrary, various societies (and the scientific communities of their times) have felt free to speculate widely about the very nature of female sexuality. At times societies have believed women to be insatiable or, at other times, incapable of desire; insisted that a woman could conceive only if she experienced orgasm; and judged her as less psychologically mature if she experienced clitoral orgasms to be as satisfying as vaginal ones, which presumably were produced by intercourse with a male partner. The work of Phyllis Chesler (1972) and others suggests that women, especially those who deviate from the predominant cultural expectations regarding sexuality and gender role, are particularly vulnerable to being described by the medical establishment as neurotic, or at best, as incompliant with care.

The controversy surrounding infibulation provides a dramatic example of the collision of cultures. Infibulation, also called "female circumcision," is widely practiced in large parts of Africa and the Middle East. The practice entails amputation of the clitoris and sometimes, as well, sewing the vaginal lips together or excising them. Feminists and health officials plead for the enforcement of laws prohibiting the practice, which mutilates large numbers of young girls, rendering intercourse an unsatisfying if not painful experience and resulting in the deaths of many. Governments have been slow to respond, defending their inaction by noting that intervention would be tantamount to criminalizing ethnicity, restricting the individual's right to practice the usual behaviors of the culture. They point to the reluctance of the women themselves to abandon this ancient rite of passage designed to confer femininity, while critics argue that this is yet another example of the conditioning of women to allow a male-dominated culture to define the nature of woman's sexuality.

A growing rift in the women's movement that accompanies the emergence of "sexual agency" feminism brings additional challenges to the issue of who defines a woman's sexuality. Confronting the notion that sex is fraught with male dominance and female submission, the "sexual agency" movement challenges the predominant assumption of female victimhood (Brownmiller, 1975; Dworkin, 1991; Faludi, 1991) and calls for an assertion of an aggressive sexual liberation and equality—demanding a return of sex from the political realm to the personal (Roiphe, 1993; Wolf, 1993).

Values of the therapist

What of the therapists themselves? What attitudes, values, and longings do they bring to the therapeutic relationship? Whether they practice sex therapy as specialists or as other health-care professionals who address patients' sexual problems, therapists themselves often experience powerful emotional reactions that affect their ethical decisions. The therapist's automatic

"We may eventually come to realize that chastity is no more a virtue than malnutrition."

ALEX COMFORT

While we have sex in the mind, we truly have none in the body.

D. H. LAWRENCE
LEAVE SEX ALONE, 1929

investment in keeping marriages together, abhorrence of abuse (physical, emotional, or financial), or strong preference for egalitarian relationships can profoundly influence therapy. It is assumed that the therapist must have a positive attitude about sexuality as a creative, life-enhancing force, and be conflict-free and tolerant. Recognizing that these virtues may be rare, therapists have an obligation to disclose any personal values or preferences that might hinder their ability to respond to the needs of the patient. The first and least controversial duty of patient care is to provide care. Ironically, it is the most frequently violated. Physicians, who are in an ideal position to detect and treat sexual problems, often neglect to inquire about the development of sexual problems known to be related to various medical illnesses and the medications they prescribe. The obligation to evaluate and treat reversible sexual dysfunction is not diminished by the professional's own personal level of discomfort with the subject.

Surrogacy's defenders argue that if "natural" is moral and "artificial" is immoral, then society may as well prohibit intravenous feeding.

PAGE 592

Many of the ethical dilemmas therapists face place them squarely in a double-bind situation, where any action taken can evoke guilt or a sense of helplessness in the therapist. Take, for example, the principle of confidentiality. Patients and research subjects must be assured that the information they provide will be kept private. Any breach of confidentiality raises the specter that the patient's relationship with others could be harmed. Without the guarantee of confidentiality, many persons would be reluctant to disclose sensitive information, even if it meant forgoing a solution to their sexual problems. Knowing this, what would constitute the most ethical action by a couple's therapist following a patient's disclosure of a homosexual affair of which his partner is unaware? Balanced against the obligation for truth-telling to the spouse, a bind is inevitable. Ultimately, every therapist has an obligation to analyze carefully the principles that must guide care, explore his or her own moral boundaries, and respectfully consider the impact of choices on the patient as an individual and in relationship to family and the broader community.

Despite all of surrogacy's similarities to adoption, it remains fundamentally different.

PAGE 592

Little is known of the psychological mechanisms that those who do sex therapy use to manage their own feelings in these difficult situations. Undoubtedly, many health professionals and sex therapists wrestle with the difficult issues, while others cling rigidly to the rules of professional conduct embodied in the various codes of ethics endorsed by their professional organizations, blind to and poorly defended against the ordinary human needs and passions that may draw them and their colleagues into liaisons that prove dangerous to both themselves and their patients.

Special issues in therapy

SEXUAL CONTACT BETWEEN THERAPIST AND PATIENT. Although there are a very few therapists who openly advocate sexual therapist-patient intimacy as a part of sex therapy, it is generally considered unethical, destructive to the therapeutic relationship, and charged with the potential for doing great psychological harm to the patient (Charlton, 1993; Lebacqz and Barton, 1991; Rutter, 1991).

Even though the discussions with the therapist, reading and viewing materials, and homework assignments are explicitly sexual, overt sexual activities do not occur in the therapist's presence. With the exception of the conduct of a complete physical exam by a physician or nurse practitioner, the patient will not be asked to disrobe.

By virtue of role and expertise, therapists hold a position of greater power, not only with power over the patient's emotional state but with the authority to define the nature of the relationship. The factors of power, trust, and dependency raise the possibility that the patient cannot freely give consent to sexual contact, that is, that the dynamics of the relationship render the

SEXUAL SURROGATES
Simply Technical Training?

In North America, the use of sexual surrogates has been extremely contentious and is not widely practiced. Sexual surrogates are, however, often utilized in other countries. In Japan, for example, people without partners can attend "sex school" (Allgeier and Allgeier, p. 258), trying various positions and techniques with clothed models under an instructor's supervision.

Most sexual therapies involve exercises that require a partner. Some therapists, attempting to help clients who do not have a partner, provide sexual surrogates (paraprofessionals working under the supervision of the therapist) to engage in private sexual activity with the patient. Critics contend that the use of surrogates differs little from prostitution, and that the use of surrogates provides only "technical" training, failing to evoke and address the interpersonal and emotional issues often involved in sexual dysfunction. Defenders of the practice cite the screening, training, and supervision that surrogates undergo and argue that it is not ethical to deprive those without cooperative partners of the care they need. It seems unlikely that the controversy surrounding this issue will end until the effectiveness of this approach is clarified.

— SHARON K. TURNBULL

patient unable to withhold consent. Consequently, external controls on the sexual exploitation of trust have been encoded in the standards of professional conduct of virtually all licensing bodies and professional associations in the United States that represent specialists in sex therapy or others who practice sex therapy as one component of their helping professions. Although these codes may vary in detail (e.g., as to whether they proscribe sexual contact with *former* clients and patients), they generally hold that no matter how provocative or consenting the patient, the therapist, by virtue of the unequal power in the relationship, always bears the burden of blame and liability.

There is no evidence to suggest that sex therapists are any more likely than those in other disciplines to violate the boundaries that prohibit sexual contact within professional relationships of trust. Indeed, the considerable attention devoted to this issue by the young discipline (and the inclusion of prohibitions in the codes of ethics of most professional organizations) may have afforded some level of protection against the risk and has encouraged some training programs to devote significantly more attention to the issue of the attraction that can arise in the course of therapy, helping clinicians to develop appropriate mechanisms for managing their reactions and feelings.

Professionalization

The sheer magnitude of the need for services suggests that efforts to limit the practice of sex counseling and therapy to those with specialized training may be doomed from the outset. Masters and Johnson (1970) estimate that approximately 50 percent of all married couples will develop a sexual dysfunction that would benefit from therapy. Does the pressure to create a speciality with elevated standards of training and care risk raising the public's expectations of care while placing it beyond their reach?

Prior to the professionalization of sex therapy, the work fell to others—beauticians and bartenders, priests and courtesans. More recently, these resources have been augmented by a flood of self-help manuals, articles in the popular press, and "family life" classes in schools and churches. Assuming that nonprofessionals will continue to play a role for some time to come, how should professional sex therapists work with them to ensure that appropriate information and care is provided, helping them to provide accurate information and advice and to make referrals for professional treatment of sexual dysfunction in cases where it is needed?

With little forethought a system comprising various levels of care is emerging. School programs, community agencies, and the popular press have increased the knowledge of the general population. Many health-care providers have accepted a larger role in basic counseling and brief therapy, and there has been a tremendous increase in the availability of multidisciplinary programs that specialize in the treatment of complex or difficult cases. Professional ethics requires that coordination of the various components of the system become a priority in an effort to conserve scarce resources and to see to it that patients find the appropriate level of care. In addition, there is a twofold implication of the exclusion of coverage for sex therapy in most health insurance programs: those without sufficient wealth seldom receive treatment, and, consequently, our ability to generalize about the effectiveness of therapy may be limited.

The research endeavor

Numerous ethical issues emerge from research into sexual response, dysfunction, and behavior. As in other fields, most research projects are scrutinized in advance by review boards to safeguard subjects by protecting them from physical or psychological harm, securing their informed consent, and ensuring their freedom from coercion.

Subjects are usually guaranteed anonymity and confidentiality. Beyond these concerns, research procedures must minimize the risk that the study might negatively affect the subject's emotional state, sexual adjustment, or relationships. A study might involve exposure to erotic material some prefer to avoid or require that the subject divulge highly personal information. Another study might involve the observation

SEX RESEARCH
Leave Children Alone?

A troublesome research issue is the use of children as research subjects. Answers to many fundamental questions about human sexuality reside in childhood, among them the emergence of sexual orientation, the formation of beliefs and attitudes, and the development of paraphilias (sexual deviations, characterized by preference for nonhuman objects in achieving arousal, imposition of humiliation or suffering, or coercion of nonconsenting partners). In the interest of protecting children from sexual stimulation, or from the emotional distress that would presumably follow, research about sexual attitudes and behaviors has generally depended on retrospective reports by adult subjects, or where children have been involved, limited to rather innocuous topics.

— SHARON K. TURNBULL

"Sexual intercourse began
In nineteen sixty-three
(Which was rather late for me)–
Between the end of the Chatterley ban
And the Beatles' first LP."

PHILIP LARKIN
ANNUS MIRABILIS, 1974

or measurement of physiological responses during sexual activity. The principle of informed consent requires that subjects be informed of all the procedures they will undergo, including any aspects that might be embarrassing or damaging to them, before they consent to participate.

Several ethical issues surround research into strategies designed to treat the paraphilias that may result in incarceration (e.g., rape or pedophilia). First is the ethical obligation to avoid coercion of the subject's participation in the research—for example, by raising the hope of early release. Another issue relates to the type of treatment approaches that have been used. Allgeier and Allgeier (1988) note that although other techniques, for example, cognitive behavioral approaches and heterosexual skills training, have been increasingly used, the previous reliance on painful approaches, such as castration and aversion therapies that pair arousing stimuli for deviant behavior with unpleasant events such as electric shocks or chemicals that induce nausea or vomiting, seen aimed more at punishing than curing. Questions regarding the efficacy of treatment programs abound (Schwartz and Cellini, 1988)—suggesting that ineffective programs that accelerate the release of unsuccessfully treated inmates could actually increase the incidence of sexual offenses by providing a false sense of security. Unfortunately, few resources are available to those who are not incarcerated. Treatment programs are unavailable to the "many . . . on parole [who] request treatment" (Dvoskin, 1991). The growing public concern about the incidence of crime, short sentences, and the early return of offenders to the community heightens the need for increasing both the effectiveness and availability of these programs.

"Sexuality throws no light upon love, but only through love can we learn to understand sexuality."

EUGEN ROSENSTOCK-HUESSY

Setting the priorities for research in a field where much awaits exploration is an ethical dilemma in itself. What choices should be made about the allocation of scarce resources? What role should researchers play in informing public policy? For example, should the paucity of research concerning the sexual functioning of women in response to various medical disorders and treatments be rapidly redressed? What of the special needs of those in populations long neglected—those with physical or emotional disabilities? What priority should be given to the investigation of pedophilia, incest, and the realms of the psyche where sex and violence merge? If we neglect these areas, we do so at great social cost.

Alternatively, should the fundamental questions have priority? What causes a person to be heterosexual? Or homosexual? What are the connections between sex and eating, sex and pain, danger, or profound grief? What is the biochemistry of sexual attraction and arousal? And ultimately, what does sex have to do with love?

— SHARON K. TURNBULL

SEXUAL DEVELOPMENT

Anatomy is not destiny. Even biology in its broadest sense does not strictly determine psychosexual identity. Sexual development, like other facets of human development, does have biological foundations that help in

STAR-CROSS'D

A statue of Romeo and Juliet in New York's Central Park depicts the joyous intoxication of first love.

S

SEXUAL DEVELOPMENT

The stages of sexual development

NO HURRY

In young adulthood, lovers learn to savor the moments, and, in the words of poet William Matthews, "get it over with as slowly as possible."

orienting the growing and enculturating individual. A genetically encoded "blueprint" is provided that normally orchestrates sexual developmental events according to a more or less predictable timetable. This biological impetus is not, however, sufficiently determinative to account for the end product. Children are taught along the way how to be (or not to be) sexual beings in their sociocultural time and place in history. Nature and nurture interweave in sexual development; we sometimes refer to the "nature" part of growing up as "maturation," to differentiate its stages and processes from those that are more directly the result of "nurture"—socioenvironmental influences, especially learning and behavioral shaping. "Biopsychosocial" is the term used in medicine and psychiatry for an integrative model of human development, health, and disease.

Social and moral issues arise around the events encountered at each stage of the development of human sexuality—and follow from them, as well. Sexual attitudes, customs, and practices, all historically and culturally variable, interact in complex ways with chromosomal, hormonal, and anatomical influences. An analysis of the ethics of sexual development must therefore include issues of individual, embodied sexuality and also of sexual relationships, understood using concepts of biology, psychology, and culture.

Ethical analysis is complicated by the varying answer to the question, "Whose ethics?" Sometimes ethical questions confront the growing child, but infants have little if any capacity for moral reasoning, and children after the age of five are just developing their moral and ethical sense. More often, therefore, the issues of sexual development perplex the child's caregivers and teachers, who seem to young people to be overburdened with exhortations. And always there are crucial social issues. Fundamental concepts—the nature of bodies, of pleasure and its limitations or dangers, of sin and shame, and of the human identities of men and of women—shape social values on gender and sexuality; these in turn shape individual ethics and practices, and what we teach our children. Religion and government have always concerned themselves with human sexuality, including gender roles and reproductive practices; and family values centrally define positions on sex roles, sexual choices and behaviors, and reproduction. At issue when others influence children is the tension between respecting and caring for their individual development of desires and choices, versus attempting to "socialize" them—that is, to protect them from the dangers of impulsive and ignorant choices, and to teach them the values of their culture's adult society.

The result is a fully developed and personalized sexuality, reflecting an amalgamated complex of idiosyncratic and sociocultural meanings, symbols, and associations. Sexual fantasy and behaviors, or quiet reflection about one's sexuality and its interpersonal impact, are ethical and spiritual matters, with a heavier freight of ethics and aesthetics than of logic. Still, specific sexuality is experienced as an unscripted commu-

"Therefore love moderately; long love doth so; Too swift arrives as tardy as too slow." [Friar Laurence to Romeo]

SHAKESPEARE
ROMEO AND JULIET
1597

nion and dyadic meditation in a rare, precious zone of interpersonal ecstasy, spontaneity, and enthusiasm that becomes increasingly important in postindustrial bureaucratized societies.

The stages of sexual development

PRENATAL SEXUALITY. By the time we are born we have (in most cases) come to have a distinct biological sex under the absent or present influence of the Y-chromosome on the bipotential gonad of the fetus. If Y is present, testes differentiate and produce androgens so that a male develops; if not, a female develops. Thus, the basic template of the embryo (the "default" that will develop unless hormones intervene) is female—a relatively late scientific discovery, contradicting the metaphor of woman as created from Adam's rib. Other intrauterine factors, notably maternal hormones, may complement or interfere with chromosomally destined gender development.

There are ethical issues even at this stage. Individuals and cultures frequently value male babies over females, a gender preference that has been expressed after birth by female infanticide. This is a contemporary as well as a historical practice, documented in large numbers in (for one example) China under the pressure of government-mandated limits on family size (Tannahill, 1992). Technologies of prenatal testing now make it possible to select the desired sex before birth via abortion. Available statistics, like those showing a preponderance of abortions of female fetuses in certain cultures, suggest that where the choice is available, social and individual values of caring for gender equality are tested against the pervasive legacy of discrimination against females.

We may soon be able to manipulate the hormonal environment of the developing fetus to "fine-tune" its sexuality—to ensure, let us say, that a boy will be more aggressive, or a girl less so. Although the origins of sexual orientation are not yet clear and are probably complex, many researchers believe that there is a genetic component. If so, it may become possible to detect and "correct" or abort homosexually destined infants prena-

DEFINING TERMS
Sex and Gender

We use the adjective "sexual" in describing many things: maleness or femaleness, behaviors surrounding intercourse, fantasies that excite. Confusing simple efforts at definition, "sexual" may point to biological aspects of being male or female, to social roles and behaviors, or to psychological phenomena.

BIOLOGICAL SEX. This seemingly simple concept becomes complicated under the close inspection of sex researchers, who distinguish six categories of biological maleness or femaleness (Reinisch, 1990): chromosomal sex (the XX-female or XY-male chromosome pattern); gonadal sex (ovaries or testicles); hormonal sex (having more androgenic hormones than estrogens and progestins yields male characteristics); anatomical sex, internal (uterus or prostate gland); anatomical sex, external (clitoris and labia, or penis and scrotum); and brain sex (female and male brains show some differences in structure and levels of chemicals; their significance is not yet clear).

GENDER. "Biology" ("sex") refers to male and female, "gender" to masculinity and femininity.

Core gender identity. "I am a girl" or "I am a boy": This vital part of identity begins with the sex assignment made at birth, usually by an authority (doctor or midwife) based on the appearance of the external genitals. "It's a girl!" or "It's a boy!" answers the question often asked even before "Is it healthy?" (The rare doubtful assignment of "I'm not sure, it isn't exactly a boy *or* a girl" reflects those accidents of nature in which hermaphroditism or some other sexual abnormality has occurred.) Everyone in the infant's environment confirms the assigned sex in the name given, the way it is held or played with, the color and kind of clothing provided, and innumerable other ways, deliberate and otherwise. As the child grows, messages become more explicit; for example, certain ways of acting or dressing are forbidden or encouraged for little girls, others for little boys. All of this is absorbed into the deepest levels of the child's sense of who he or she "is." Between the ages of eighteen months and three years, the child will normally have acquired an abiding core gender identity. Even in cases where the biological sex was not apparent at birth, core gender identity has been established in accordance with the gender assignment if it was unambiguously made by the parents; it has been found to be virtually immutable after 30 months of age (Money and Ehrhardt, 1972; Stoller, 1979).

Gender role. Usually congruent with gender identity, gender role refers to the way a person enacts femininity or masculinity—what one does to suggest to others that one is a boy or girl, a man or woman. This evolves and is refined throughout life but is largely built through learning acquired (consciously and unconsciously) in childhood.

Sexual orientation. This is based on one's attraction to and falling in love with partners of either the same or the opposite sex, or both.

Reproductive role. This refers to one's becoming or not becoming (choosing not to be, or being unable to be) a parent.

—JOAN A. LANG
PAUL L. ADAMS

tally. When there is no actual abnormality (excessive maternal hormones, or drug-generated chromosomal defects, for example), such interventions would reveal a value for personal or cultural preferences more than for human diversity.

STAGES OF SEXUAL DEVELOPMENT

- prenatal sexuality
- infantile sexuality
- sexuality of small children
- childhood sexuality
- preadolescent sexuality
- adolescent sexuality
- young adult sexuality
- mid-life sexuality
- late life sexuality

INFANTILE SEXUALITY. When Sigmund Freud made infantile sexuality a cornerstone of his psychoanalytic theory of psychosexual development, he caused great and continuing controversy. Yet it is observably true that by the time of birth the baby girl is capable of physiological sexual readiness, showing clitoral turgor and vaginal lubrication cyclically in the initial neonatal hours; the baby boy shows penile erections that may have been observed prenatally by ultrasound imaging, and sometimes at the moment of birth (Rutter, 1980). Such readiness seems to be species-specific and phylogenetically programmed. It is perhaps the first indication of a way in which humans are unique from other mammals: We have sexual desires, urges, and acts that know no oestrus, no season.

We vaunt our kinship with mammals, however, by our mouthy behavior, particularly sucking. Freud believed that this "oral activity" was the first manifestation of the sexual instinct (libido), defining the oral stage as that when pleasurable excitation of the mucosal membranes of the mouth and lips is at center stage for the infant.

Mothers with suckling babies hold creatures of great dependency in their arms. As the mother initiates and responds in her attachment to the baby, the baby senses times of maternal tension and relaxation, and learns a human style in reciprocal interaction. Homilies are delivered while caregiving: "Be nice, don't be so lazy, can you really be hungry already? Don't you dare fall asleep on me and wake me up in half an hour," and so on. The baby is nourished on values along with milk.

Until about two years old the infant functions cognitively in a sensorimotor way (Piaget, 1956) that is regained for many, even when old, at times of sexual delight.

The enormous vulnerability and dependency of human babies confer ethical responsibilities on their caregivers. Powerful messages about bodies, sensual pleasures, gender, and desire are conveyed in these early, mostly nonverbal communications; these will contribute to the foundations of the child's developing sexuality. Early attachments are not meant to be delibidinized or intellectualized, for that risks minimizing their earthy and sexy qualities; life itself for the infant is derived from, and made pleasurable by, the body of another. Infantile attachment is a good groundwork for developing tenderness, trust, and sexuality. The later capacity for skin eroticism, so invaluable to sensual and sexual pleasure, probably depends on the infant's having enjoyed skin-to-skin contact with the body of another who enjoys this contact too.

Infants are avid social learners in many more ways than previously thought. They smile, gaze, recognize; they live within relatedness to others. Sensorimotor infants thrive in durable and reliable relationships of great dependency. Later, they can grow up to be not independent but interdependent and reliable. The dilemmas of infancy—trust versus mistrust, autonomy versus shame and doubt (Erikson, 1963), merger versus separation-individuation (Rank, 1936; Mahler and Furer, 1968)—are existential issues in being human that recur in all stages of the life cycle and do not disappear after one phase-specific hassle. During the first years of life, security must be consumed by an infant, and the more adults who can dispense parental security and sensual holding, the better.

TODDLERS AND SMALL CHILDREN. By 30 months of age a host of establishments of selfhood have emerged—the body image, the core gender identity, the nuclear self concept—as confluences of nature and nurture. Girls and boys both are made mainly under the care of women. Both sexes thus form their primary identifications originally with the mother. Freud hypothesized that this gave boys a surer path to adult (hetero) sexuality, as girls had to switch to men for their objects of sexual desire. Later theorists pointed to a different complication for boys, who must differentiate their gender identity from that of the mother (Greenson, 1978). Yet again, girls' sense of separateness may suffer from the lack of such a contrapuntal sounding board (Chodorow, 1978).

The extent to which body image includes an accurate knowledge and a valuing of clitoris and labia or penis and scrotum depends on the willingness of caregivers to name and value these parts. Often, vague or coy nicknames or the ominous "down there" substitutes

"Sexual enlightenment is justified insofar as girls cannot learn too soon how children do not come into the world."

KARL KRAUS
1874–1936

*"Amoebas at the start
Were not complex;
They tore themselves apart
And started Sex."*

ARTHUR GUITERMAN
FROM SEX

for accuracy. The body ego can then remain hazy or, worse, become devalued; this blurring of self-knowledge may threaten an individual's trust in bodily sensations and perceptions as important sources of information about either self or external reality. Gender role may then depend more upon generic self-labeling based on messages about gender assignment from others (Fast, 1984). Worse, the child may associate his or her genitals (girls are more vulnerable because their anatomy is less available for their own inspection) with the "dirty" and embarrassing experiences that too often mar toilet training.

After age two and up to about seven years, the typical child functions cognitively on a "preoperational" level (Piaget, 1956), preparing for "concrete" operations that usually occur from ages seven to eleven. Selfhood and attitudes of self-regard, as well as sexual self-definition, develop on these early cognitive levels. Children will candidly express curiosity about sex, as about everything around them, if they are not inhibited from doing so. "Where did I come from?" demands an accurate yet uncomplicated answer, suitable for the nonabstract cognitions of the curious child, and uncontaminated by the mist of anxiety and shame that can confuse and frighten.

Only toward the end of this age range do sex-role differentiation and strong structuring of masculine or feminine gender roles, and other sociocultural aspects of sex development, take root. A child's capacity to learn societal preferences in sexual matters depends on cognitive level; hence, bright children may more easily be both enculturated and made skeptical (Kohlberg, 1966). Studies in the United States of children three and four years old show 80 percent of them to have marriage as a goal, although they seldom emphasize the sexual aspects of marriage at their age; interestingly, by the time they are thirty, 80 percent are married. Sociocultural construction of heterosexism (thinking and acting as though only heterosexuality were normal, often leading to unfair treatment of bisexual or homosexual individuals) is pervasive.

Consistently boyish or girlish behavior is not well established and distributed to the socially appropriate gender group until kindergarten; and even then, and

EARLY STIRRINGS
Also Known as "Latency"

Children (7 to 11 years). Long called "latency," these years for most children are not devoid of sexual desire and experience. Masturbation may be the most common sexual activity, but the highest rate of sex play among children occurs between the ages of six and ten years; boys often masturbate in groups. Children often shift from generalized sex play to deliberate pursuit of erotic arousal by the age of eight or nine. An increasing percentage of children under thirteen have had coitus, some of them homosexual anal intercourse, or oral-genital sexual experiences (Reinisch, 1990).

These sexual experiences are not always with age-mates, which may be harmless, but sometimes with much older persons, which is harmful and exploitative. As a clinical rule of thumb, child sexual abuse is assumed when there is an age discrepancy of more than five years between the older perpetrator and the younger victim. Moralists and social reformers have returned to Freud's original "seduction theory," focusing on actual adult molestation of children, rather than attributing such reports to fantasies or the unconscious desires of children. The women's movement has had a vital role to play in this rediscovery of childhood sexual abuse.

Curiously, masturbation has historically received more public attention as a moral issue. In the United States as recently as the nineteenth century, common devices to discourage and punish children's masturbation included straitjackets, or metal mittens, "genital cages," and special spike-lined tubes to prevent erections. Doctors actually advised parents to wrap cold, wet sheets around persistent masturbators, or to tie their hands to bedposts; more drastic prescriptions included applying leeches, electric current, or hot irons to genitals, or even castration and clitoridectomy (surgical removal of the clitoris) (Reinisch, 1990). Children appear not to be naturally ashamed when they discover the pleasure of genital self-stimulation, but they are easily made to feel shame and guilt, thus producing anguished questions: "Should I masturbate at all? Only when no suitable sexual partner is available? How often? How?"

For parents and educators, the parallel issues involve reacting to the child's sex play (with self or others), and teaching her or him about privacy, modesty, and what is good or bad, permitted or forbidden. Contrast the typical advice of twentieth-century counselors in the West—that when children reach the ages of two or three years, parents can begin to teach them that self-touching is appropriate in private—with the reaffirmation in the Roman Catholic catechism that sex for any purpose other than procreation is wrong. Clearly this is not a settled question, despite advances since the days when medical texts solemnly declared that idiocy could result from "self-abuse."

—JOAN A. LANG
PAUL L. ADAMS

thereafter, rigid stereotyping may not occur if it is not enforced. Conversely, "tomboyishness" (girls) and "sissiness" (boys) need not predict adult sexual orientation or preference. Even cross-dressing in childhood does not foretell homosexuality later, since over half of heterosexual adults recall such dressing in childhood and many homosexuals do not. Homosexual adults seldom have any uncertainty about their core gender identity, even when males are effeminate or females are "butch."

Feminist theorists have undertaken considerable reassessment of historically taken-for-granted social arrangements and gender-restricted roles and have raised serious questions about the price paid in pain and gender- and sexual-identity disturbances or constrictions. Humanity can ill afford to force individuals to suppress parts of their potential talents and human qualities as the "ticket of admission" to social affirmation of their sexual or gender identity.

Caregivers and educators often face the dilemma of how to transcend their own life experience. How can one accurately satisfy the innocent curiosity of children if one's own upbringing transformed simple questions into something different, fascinating but forbidden, embarrassing, even "nasty"?

Even young children can reflect on how they treat others who are "different"; in this as in many things, they take cues from grown-ups. Cruelty toward "sissies" has emotionally scarred many boys whose temperament and play preferences did not fit the "macho" mold. Girls have it easier, for a change, in that so-called tomboys are generally better tolerated—at least before puberty. But the question of "gender nonconformity" troubles many caregivers. Should a child whose behavior does not meet societal gender rules be taken to a doctor or religious leader to be "fixed"? Are marriage and parenting the only sexual roles to which children should aspire? Unfortunately, experts do not agree on how to distinguish children whose gender identity is seriously troubled, and who may benefit from professional help, from those whose unconventionally unfolding selves need only loving support and acceptance. For parents, caregivers, and counselors, the ethical imperatives are competence, respect, and care (Young, 1966).

PREADOLESCENCE. In late latency, even before the pubertal onslaught has appeared, many preadolescents become sexually active. Many of these youngsters engage in what some have called a normal homosexual phase. A first love experience outside the family with someone who is so much like oneself may provide validation of one's worth naturally and gracefully in a loving homoerotic interchange (Sullivan, 1953). That loving crush dispels loneliness for many a preadolescent, confirms his or her value, and may sometimes (but not always) give some opportunity for homosexual involvement.

Whether or not one is ethically troubled by these activities will depend on one's views about premarital sex in general, and about homosexuality in particular. "Compulsory heterosexuality" (Rich, 1982) has been held by many, but not all, cultures to be the only acceptable goal of childhood sexual socialization. Many families hold religious beliefs that characterize homosexuality as sinful and unacceptable. Even parents who tolerate in principle the concept of normal homosexuality may fear that their child will be unhappy, subject to discrimination and danger, and unable to enjoy family and parenting if he or she shows signs of same-sex love.

ADOLESCENCE. By age fourteen a conscience is established, so all sexuality thenceforth is expressed with some degree of ethical sensitivity and illumination. Also, by age eleven to fifteen years, the reasoning powers of the youth with normal IQ have matured to the adult level of formal operations (Piaget, 1956). Pubarche occurs mainly in the same years, so body and brain are ready to handle mature tasks and pleasures. Readiness for adult sexuality is present. In the United States, about two-thirds of boys and almost half of girls will have had sexual intercourse by the age of eighteen (Rutter, 1980).

Adolescent sexuality is always recognized as a potent force, but it often faces a societal moratorium of sorts, especially in societies that prize virginity and chastity. This is the age for moralistic questions about sexuality and sexual ethics, which have never been more keenly debated than they are today. In epochs with a high incidence of sexually transmitted diseases, a backlash routinely emerges to curb sexual freedom for adolescents. HIV infection and AIDS certainly impede the sexual freedom of today's adolescents; indeed, they erect a prospect of safe sexuality only with multiple barriers in place, diminishing intimacy and shared moistures. Public-health warnings and education appear to be ineffective among many adolescents, who are generally depicted as feeling invulnerable and immortal.

Still, from ages twelve to eighteen years, the sexual repertoire enlarges: For a large percentage of adolescents, coitus occurs before age eighteen; for many, oro-genital experimentation occurs; for many, pregnancy has occurred; for some, offspring have been born. But age alone is not the only telling marker of sexuality, for we are sexually programmed to be like all other human beings in only a few traits. Gender, class, and race also have an impact; we tend to resemble our ethnic, economic, and cultural subgroupings, sexually speaking. Hence, by adolescence one's sexual activities and choices are quite similar to others with whom we feel identi-

◆ **adolescent**

a person between thirteen and eighteen years old.

See Also

Gender Identity and Gender-Identity Disorders and Homosexuality

Adolescents

"Love between the sexes is a sin in theology, a forbidden intercourse in jurisprudence, a mechanical insult in medicine, and a subject philosophy has no time for."

KARL KRAUS
1874–1936

fied. Lower-class males, for example, show earlier coitus than do their middle-class counterparts. Poor adolescents seem to use sexuality as a property substitute, as a medium of exchange, and as a source of prestige, entertainment, and selfhood consolidation (Rutter, 1980).

Then again, there are some ways in which each of us is like no others on the planet; we feel "first" or "unique" proudly, and that our individuality is laden with enormous value. Our developing sexual behavior, usually held private and secret, during all the phases of our lifetime provides for the psychologist a shorthand notation on our emerging personality. Most believe today that character, or personality, determines sexuality: We are as we use our genitals with and without others. (That consensus did not reign in periods when some experts held that sexuality determined character rather than being determined by it [Fromm, 1948].)

Adult sexuality

Although development need not and should not stop after adolescence, and psychological theory has increasingly explicated the various stages of adult development, most of the ethical debates surrounding adult sexuality have been elaborated under such topics of scholarship as sexuality and homosexuality per se. The following sections will therefore touch more briefly on some specifically developmental aspects of the ethics of adult sexuality.

YOUNG ADULTHOOD. From eighteen to twenty-five years, sexuality becomes more patterned, heterosexism and machismo more rigidly established, and marriage and childbearing much more common. Gays come out. Sexual careers are carved out, typecast, settled into, and sometimes show ossification during young adulthood. One's own way of being sexual gets settled for many. Some embrace the option of chastity during this age period; some embrace a homosexual orientation; others choose the bisexual option.

Most adults remember their first sexual encounter with another person, or at least remember their first orgasm when awake. It is not always a delightful milestone. But if it was not strictly an exercise in power or exploitation, every sexual interaction is usually remembered and cherished. Many who are heterosexual virtuosi turn in their dreams mainly to the face-to-face missionary position, which, though occasionally denigrated, is also characterized (Comfort, 1972) as providing supremely close, intimate, and egalitarian loving. Often we harbor fantasies of new sexual possibilities still unattained. Human sexuality, not bound to times of oestrus, thrives on fantasy. The human neural organization of hand-eye-mouth and the integrating cerebral cortex enable us to live symbolically, to "play brain" and to attain arousal simply by imagining a desired partner or other sufficiently stimulating images, thus sliding us from everyday into erotic reality (Davis, 1983). Sexual arousal brings us joyful interludes from the tedium of the workaday world.

MID-LIFE. Parenthood has become a central focus of daily life and personal identity for many between the ages of twenty-five and forty-five years. Libidinized caregiving to mate and children can create a more fulfilled sexual being. If previous developmental issues have not been resolved, however, becoming a parent may activate old conflicts and inhibitions, to the detriment of sexual pleasure. The struggle to redeem sexuality from what has been called the "wet-blanket" pattern may produce a push toward extramarital affairs, raising ethical issues about monogamy and fidelity versus "self-actualization" and passion as a need or even a right. Jealousy forces reexamination of the ethics of commitment: When is the promise of exclusivity mature, when is it the product of a childish and illusory sense of ownership? Tempted, some may question whether to deny lustful yearnings for the sake of the partner who would be hurt, or to shun such self-denial as a form of bondage. To talk about such issues as a couple or to decide them privately is also an issue in many marriages. As children pass through the lively stages of sexual development, their parents can hardly avoid being touched by resonances of unfinished business in their own psychosexual history.

Some eschew pairing and childbearing with a measure of cynicism in their decision; others may be fully generative without reproducing biologically and devote their lives to altruistic caring for the young of the species.

LATE LIFE. Sexual desire and activity continue throughout life for most people. They are intimate aspects of one's moral career and are not readily disclaimed, even when health is failing. Widowhood or single status after age 50, when women in particular are sometimes judged "old" even today, can crimp sexuality. If confidence in sexual attractiveness is not undermined, however, this life stage often brings an opportunity for new bonding and a new lease on life and love. The empty nest may facilitate the sexuality of a man and woman, or may unhinge them radically. The old person who has lived with one mate for forty years or more (Young, 1966) may well ask, if our sexuality when young was to be called love, what superlative word do we have in English for a fidelity of love and sex that has weathered a long span, in sickness and health and with a delight in sexuality, the nurturing of offspring, and growing old together?

—JOAN A. LANG
PAUL L. ADAMS

SEXUAL ETHICS

Insofar as bioethics is concerned with human bodily health, it has an interest in the way health is influenced by and contributes to sexual functioning. There is a sense, then, in which bioethics includes sexual ethics, or at least some of the key questions of sexual ethics, such as the meaning of human sexuality and the causes and effects of sexual attitudes, orientations, and activities. Concepts of the human person—of desire and obligation, disease and dysfunction, even of justice and purity—can be found overlapping in various bioethical and sexual ethical theories. Like bioethics generally, sexual ethics considers standards for intervention in physical processes, rights of individuals to self-determination, ideals for human flourishing, and the importance of social context for the interpretation and regulation of sexual behavior. Bioethics specifically incorporates issues surrounding contraception and abortion, artificial reproduction, sexually transmitted diseases, sexual paraphilias, gendered roles and sexual conduct of the medical professionals, and sex research, counseling, and therapy. All of these issues are importantly shaped by moral traditions, so that health professionals frequently find themselves called upon to deal with questions of sexual ethics.

Historically, medicine has interacted with philosophy and religion in shaping and rationalizing the sexual ethical norms of a given culture. Medical opinion often simply reflects and conserves the accepted beliefs and mores of a society, but sometimes it is also a force for change. In either case, its influence can be powerful. For example, from the Hippocratic corpus in ancient Greece to the writings of the physician Galen in the second century C.E., medical recommendations regarding sexual discipline echoed and reinforced the ambivalence of Greek and Roman philosophers regarding human sexual activity. Galen's theories retained considerable power all the way into the European Renaissance. The interpretation of syphilis as a disease rather than a divine punishment came in the fifteenth century as the result of medical writings in response to a high incidence of the disease among the socially powerful. In nineteenth-century western Europe and North America, medical writers were enormously influential in shaping norms regarding such matters as masturbation (physicians believed it would lead to insanity), homosexuality (newly identified with perversions that medicine must diagnose and treat), contraception (considered unhealthy because it fostered sexual excess and loss of physical power), and gender roles (promoted on the basis of medical assessments of women's capacity for sexual desire). Today sex counseling and therapy communicate, however implicitly, normative ethical assumptions. Indeed, so great has been the influence of the medical profession on moral attitudes toward sexual options that critics warn of the "tyranny of experts," referring not to moral philosophers or religious teachers but to scientists and physicians.

The history of sexual ethics provides a helpful perspective for understanding current ethical questions regarding human sexuality. This article focuses on Western philosophical, scientific-medical, and religious traditions of sexual ethics and on the contemporary issues that trouble the heirs of these traditions. A historical overview of sexual ethics is not without its difficulties, however, as critical studies have shown (Brown, 1988; Foucault, 1978; Fout, 1992; Plaskow, 1990).

First of all, while it is possible to find a recorded history of laws, codes, and other guides to moral action regarding sexual behavior, it is almost impossible to determine what real people actually believed and did in the distant past. Or at least the historical research has barely begun. Second, ethical theory regarding sex (e.g., what is to be valued, what goals are worth pursuing, what reasons justify certain sexual attitudes, activities, and relationships) is predominantly theory formulated by an elite group of men. Women's experiences, beliefs, and values are largely unrecorded and, until recently, have been almost wholly inaccessible. The same is true of men who do not belong to a dominant class. Third, what we do find through historical research is necessarily subject to interpretation. It makes a difference, for example, whether one is looking for historical evaluations of human sexual desire or historical silences about sexual abuse of women. Finally, if one takes seriously the social construction of gender and sexuality, it is not clear that any kind of coherent historical narrative is possible. All of these difficulties notwithstanding, it is possible to survey (with appropriate caution) a Western normative and theoretical history regarding sex and to gain from the richness of varying contemporary interpretations. Central strands of this history can be traced to classical Greek and Roman antiquity, Judaism, and early and later developments in Christianity.

Ancient Greece and Rome

GENERAL ATTITUDES AND PRACTICE. Ancient Greece and Rome shared a general acceptance of sex as a natural part of life. Both were permissive regarding the sexual behavior of men. In Athens, for example, the only clear proscriptions applicable to citizen-class men were in incest, bigamy, and adultery (insofar as it violated the property of another man). The focus of sexual concern in the two cultures was significantly different, however. For the Greeks, adult male love of adolescent boys occupied a great deal of public atten-

Family-planning programs have been criticized in Africa and Asia for affronting sensibilities by using billboards to present messages about delicate matters

PAGE 539

For believers, the sanctions for violating a prohibition, possibly extending into the afterlife, can warrant the term "strong persuasion."

PAGE 545

SEX IN ANTIQUITY
Same-Sex Relationships

Homosexuality was accepted in both Greek and Roman antiquity. Especially for the Greeks, however, it was less a matter of some men being sexually attracted only to men (or, more likely, boys) than a matter of men generally being attracted to beautiful individuals, whether male or female. Desire was of greater interest, as both possibility and problem, than its object; and desire was not essentially differentiated according to the gender of its object. Greek men were expected to marry, in order to produce an heir. Yet love and friendship, and sometimes sex, between men could be of a higher order than anything possible within marriage (for gender equality obtained between men, despite differences in age). Same-sex relations were not thereby wholly unproblematic, however, as cultural cautions against male passivity attested. Moreover, the ethos tended not to support a positive evaluation of sexual relationships between women. Lesbian relations were often judged negatively because they counted as adultery (since women belonged to their husbands) or because a cultural preoccupation with male sexual desire made sex between women appear unnatural.

— MARGARET A. FARLEY

tion, whereas the Romans focused public concern on heterosexual marriage as the foundation of social life.

Marriage for both Greeks and Romans was monogamous. In Greece, however, no sexual ethic confined sex to marriage. Marriage as the expected pattern for citizen-class individuals was based not on the affective bond between husband and wife but on what were considered natural gender roles regarding procreation and service to the city. Male human nature was generally assumed to be bisexual, and the polyerotic needs of men were taken for granted. Concubinage, male and female prostitution, and the sexual use of slaves were commonly accepted. In practice, much of this was true in ancient Rome as well, even though ideals of marital fidelity became much more important. The development of marriage as a social institution was, however, considered a central achievement of Roman civilization. This included a growing appreciation of the importance of affective ties between wives and husbands.

Greece and Rome were male-dominated societies, and for citizens a gendered double standard prevailed in regard to sexual morality. Both Greek and Roman brides, but not bridegrooms, were expected to be virgins. In Greece, the only women who were given some equal status with men were a special class of artistically and educationally sophisticated prostitutes, the *hetaerae.* Generally women were considered intellectually inferior to men. In addition, Greek husbands and wives were unequal in age (wives were much younger) and in education. Wives had no public life, though they were given the power and responsibility of managing the home. In the Roman household, on the contrary, the husband retained power and could rule with an entirely free hand. Here the ideal of the *patria potestas* reached fulfillment. Mutual fidelity was much praised, but in fact absolute fidelity was required of wives while husbands could consort freely with slaves or prostitutes. Although by the first century C.E., women in Rome had achieved considerable economic and political freedom, they could not practice the sexual freedom traditionally granted to men.

In both Greece and Rome, abortion and infanticide were common. Concern about the need to limit population influenced Greek sexual practices at various times, whereas efforts to improve a low birthrate in imperial Rome led to legal incentives to marry and to procreate. Divorce was more readily available in ancient Greece than in Rome, but eventually both cultures provided for it and for the resulting economic needs of divorced women; in Greece, husbands continued to administer their former wives' dowries, while in Rome a woman took her dowry with her.

Scholars today tend to dispute the belief that the last years of the Roman Empire saw a great weakening of sexual norms, a sexual dissipation at the heart of a general moral decline. The favored historical reading is now the opposite: that general suspicion of sexuality grew, and normative restrictions of sexual activity increased. In part, this was the result of the gradual influence of philosophical theories that questioned the value of sexual activity and emphasized the dangers in its consequences.

GREEK AND ROMAN PHILOSOPHICAL APPRAISALS. Michel Foucault's influential history of Graeco-Roman theory regarding sex identifies two problems that preoccupied philosophers: the natural force of sexual desire, with its consequent tendency to excess, and the power relations involved in the seemingly necessary active/passive roles in sexual activity (Foucault, 1986, 1988). The first problem contributed to the formulation of an ideal of self-mastery within an aesthetics of existence. Self-mastery could be achieved through a regimen that included diet, exercise, and various practices of self-discipline. The second problem yielded criteria for love and sex between men and boys. Active and passive roles were not a problem in adult

male relations with women or with slaves, for the inferior passive role was considered natural to women, including wives, and to servants or slaves. This was a problem, however, for citizen-class boys, who must come to be equal with men. The solution, according to some philosophers (e.g., Demosthenes), was to regulate the age of boy lovers and the circumstances and goals of their liaisons with men. Others (e.g., Plato) preferred transcending and eliminating physical sex in erotic relations between men and boys.

The aspects of Greek and Roman thought about sex that were to have the most influence on subsequent Western theory included a distrust of sexual desire and a judgment of the inferior status of sexual pleasure, along with the inferior status of the body in relation to the soul. While sex was not considered evil, it was considered dangerous—not only in its excess but also in its natural violence (orgasm was sometimes described as a form of epileptic seizure); in its expenditure of virile energy (it was thought to have a weakening effect); and in its association with death (nature's provision for immortality through procreation made sex a reminder of mortality) (Foucault, 1986).

The Pythagoreans in the sixth century B.C.E advocated purity of the body for the sake of cultivating the soul. The force of their position was felt in the later thinking of Socrates and Plato. Although Plato moved away from a general hostility to bodily pleasure, he made a careful distinction between lower and higher pleasures (in, for example, the *Republic, Phaedo, Symposium,* and *Philebus)*: Sexual pleasure was a lower form of pleasure, and self-mastery required domination over its demands. Plato advocated unleashing, not restraining, the power of eros for the sake of uniting the human spirit with the highest truth, goodness, and beauty. Insofar as bodily pleasures could be taken into this pursuit, there was no objection to them. But Plato thought that sexual intercourse diminished the power of eros for the contemplation and love of higher realities and that it even compromised the possibility of tenderness and respect in individual relationships of love (*Phaedrus*).

Aristotle, too, distinguished lower and higher pleasures, placing pleasures of touch at the bottom of the scale, characteristic as they are of the animal part of human nature (*Nicomachean Ethics*). Aristotle, more this-worldly than Plato, advocated moderation rather than transcendence. However, for Aristotle the highest forms of friendship and love, and of happiness in the contemplation of the life of one's friend, seemed to have no room for the incorporation of sexual activity or even for Platonic eros. Aristotle never conceived of the possibility of equality or mutuality in relationships between women and men, and he opposed the design for this that Plato had offered in the *Republic* and *Laws.*

Of all Graeco-Roman philosophies, Stoicism probably had the greatest impact on later developments in Western thought about sex. Musonius Rufus, Epictetus, Seneca, and Marcus Aurelius, for example, taught strong doctrines of the power of the human will to regulate emotion and of the desirability of such regulation for the sake of inner peace. Sexual desire, like the passions of fear and anger, was in itself irrational, disruptive, liable to excess. It needed to be moderated if not eliminated. It ought never to be indulged in for its own sake but only insofar as it served a rational purpose. Procreation was that purpose. Hence, even in marriage sexual intercourse was considered morally good only when engaged in for the sake of procreation.

With the later Stoics came what Foucault calls the "conjugalization" of sexual relations (1988, p. 166). That is, the norm governing sexual activity was now "no sex outside of marriage," derived from what others have called the "procreative" norm. Marriage was considered a natural duty, excused only in special circumstances such as when an individual undertook the responsibilities of life as a philosopher. The good effects of marriage included progeny and the companionship of husband and wife. It became the context for self-control and the fashioning of the virtuous life. Plutarch (in *Dialogue on Love*) took the position that marriage, not homosexual relationships, was the primary locus for erotic love and for friendship.

Overall, the Graeco-Roman legacy to Western sexual ethics holds little of the sexual permissiveness that characterized ancient Greece. The dominant themes carried through to later traditions were skepticism and control. This may have been due to the failure of almost all Greek and Roman thinkers to integrate sexuality into their best insights into human relationships. Whether such an integration is possible in principle has been at least a tacit question for other traditions.

The Jewish tradition

Earliest Jewish moral codes were simple and without systematic theological underpinnings. Like other ancient Near Eastern legislation, they prescribed marriage laws and prohibited rape, adultery, and certain forms of prostitution. In contrast with neighboring religions, the Jews believed in a God who is beyond sexuality but whose plan for creation makes marriage and fertility holy and the subject of a religious duty (Gen. 2:24). At the heart of Judaism's tradition of sexual morality is a religious injunction to marry. The command to marry holds within it a command to procreate, and it assumes a patriarchal model for marriage and family. These two aspects of the tradition—the duty to procreate and its patriarchal context—account for many of its specific sexual regulations.

While the core of the imperative to marry is the

The chief objection to complete reproductive freedom is that societies have legitimate interests in their demographic futures.

PAGE 546

Until society comes to terms with the full implications of procreative freedom, it must use moral persuasion and legal coercion to eliminate any exploitative aspects of surrogacy.

PAGE 593

command to procreate, marriage was considered a duty also because it conduced to the holiness of the partners. Holiness referred to more than the channeling of sexual desire, though it meant that also; it included the companionship and mutual fulfillment of spouses. In fact, monogamous lifelong marriage was considered the ideal context for sexuality, and in time it became the custom and not only an ideal. Yet the command to procreate historically stood in tension with the value given to the marriage relationship. Thus while the laws of *onah*, of marital rights and duties, aimed to make sex a nurturant of love (Lamm, 1980), polygamy, concubinage, and divorce and remarriage were long accepted as solutions to a childless marriage. Only in the eleventh century C.E. was polygamy finally banned (much later in the East), and it was only in the twelfth century that Maimonides explicitly condemned concubinage (Novak, 1992).

Judaism has traditionally shown a concern for the "improper emission of seed" (appealing to interpretations of Gen. 38:9). Included in this concern have been proscriptions of masturbation and homosexual acts. The latter in particular have been considered unnatural (Lev. 18:22, 20:13), failing in responsibility for procreation, beneath the dignity of humanly meaningful sexual intercourse, indicative of uncontrolled (and hence morally evil) sexual desire, and a threat to the stability of heterosexual marriage and the patriarchal family. Lesbian relations were not regulated by biblical law, and in rabbinic literature were treated far less seriously than male homosexuality.

Throughout the Jewish tradition there has been a marked difference in the treatment of women's and men's sexuality (Plaskow, 1990). In part, this was because of women's subordinate role in the family and in society. The regulation and control of women's sexuality was considered necessary to the stability and the continuity of the family. Premarital sex, extramarital sex, and even rape were legally different for women than for men. In the biblical period, husbands but not wives could initiate divorce (Deut. 24:1-4), although later rabbinic law made it possible for either to do so. Adultery was understood as violating the property rights of a husband and could be punished by the death of both parties. Women's actions and dress were regulated in order to restrict their potential for luring men into illicit sex. The laws of *onah* required men to respect the sexual needs of their wives; but the laws of *niddah* (menstrual purity) had the symbolic consequence, however unintended, of associating women with defilement.

The perspective on sex, in all the branches of Judaism, has been an enduringly positive one, yet not without ambivalence. The sexual instinct was considered a gift from God, but it could still be called by the rabbis the "evil impulse" (*yetzer hara*) (Plaskow, 1990). The tradition was not immune from the suspicion regarding sex that, with the rise of Stoic philosophies and the advent of certain religious movements from the East, permeated all Middle Eastern cultures. Interpretations of the relation between sexuality and the sacred have not been univocal, as evidenced in differences between mainstream Jewish thinking and kabbalistic mysticism. Hence, some issues of sexual ethics have not been resolved once and for all. Contemporary developments in the Jewish tradition include growing pluralism regarding questions of premarital sex, contraception, abortion, gender equality, and homosexuality (Borowitz, 1969; Feldman, 1974; Plaskow, 1990; Biale, 1992; Posner, 1992). Current conflicts involve the interpretation of traditional values, the analysis of contemporary situations, and the incorporation of hitherto unrepresented perspectives, in particular those of heterosexual women and of gays and lesbians.

Christian traditions

Like other religious and cultural traditions, the teachings of Christianity regarding sex are complex and subject to multiple influences, and they have changed and developed through succeeding generations. Christianity does not begin with a systematic code of ethics. The teachings of Jesus and his followers, as recorded in the New Testament, provide a central focus for the moral life of Christians in the command to love God and neighbor. Beyond that, the New Testament offers grounds for a sexual ethic that (1) values marriage and procreation on the one hand, and singleness and celibacy on the other; (2) gives as much or more importance to internal attitudes and thoughts as to external actions; and (3) affirms a sacred symbolic meaning for sexual intercourse, yet both subordinates it to other human values and finds in it a possibility for evil. As for unanimity on more specific sexual rules, this is difficult to find in the beginnings of a religion whose founder taught as an itinerant prophet and whose sacred texts were formulated in "the more tense world" of particular disciples, a group of wandering preachers (Brown, 1988, pp. 42-43).

EARLY INFLUENCES ON CHRISTIAN UNDERSTANDINGS OF SEX. Christianity emerged in the late Hellenistic age, when even Judaism was influenced by the dualistic anthropologies of Stoic philosophy and Gnostic religions. Unlike the Greek and Roman philosophies of the time, Christianity's main concern was not the art of self-mastery and not the preservation of the city or the empire. Unlike major strands of Judaism at the time, its focus was less on the solidarity and continuity of life in this world than on the continuity between this world and a life to come. Yet early Christian writers were profoundly influenced both by

Judaism and by GraecoRoman philosophy. With Judaism they shared a theistic approach to morality, an affirmation of creation as the context of marriage and procreation, and an ideal of single-hearted love. With the Stoics they shared a suspicion of bodily passion and a respect for reason as a guide to the moral life. With the Greeks, Romans, and Jews, Christian thinkers assumed and reinforced views of women as inferior to men (despite some signs of commitment to gender equality in the beginnings of Christianity as a movement). As Christianity struggled for its own identity, issues of sexual conduct were important, but there was no immediate agreement on how they should be resolved.

THE SEXUAL ETHICS OF SAINT AUGUSTINE AND ITS LEGACY. Against the Manichaeans Augustine argued in favor of the goodness of marriage and procreation, though he shared with them a negative view of sexual desire as in itself an evil passion. Because evil was for Augustine, however, a privation of right order (something missing in what was otherwise basically good), he thought at first that it was possible to reorder sexual desire according to right reason, to integrate its meaning into a right and whole love of God and neighbor. This reordering could be done only when sexual intercourse was within heterosexual marriage and for the purpose of procreation (*On the Good of Marriage*, 6). Intercourse within marriage but without a procreative purpose was, according to Augustine, sinful, though not necessarily mortally so. Marriage, on the other hand, had a threefold purpose: not only the good of children but also the goods of fidelity between spouses (as opposed to adultery) and the indissolubility of the union (as opposed to divorce).

In his later writings against the Pelagians (*Marriage and Concupiscence*), Augustine tried to clarify the place of disordered sexual desire in a theology of original sin. Although for Augustine the original sin of Adam and Eve was a sin of the spirit (a sin of prideful disobedience), its effects were most acutely present in the conflict between sexual desire and reasoned love of higher goods. Moreover, this loss of integrity in affectivity was passed from one generation to another through the mode of procreation—sexual intercourse. In this debate Augustine argued that there is some evil in all sexual intercourse, even when it is within marriage and for the sake of procreation. Most of those who followed Augustine disagreed with this, but his basic formulation of a procreative ethic held sway in Christian moral teaching for centuries.

Some early Christian writers (e.g., John Chrysostom) emphasized the Pauline purpose for marriage—marriage as a remedy for incontinence. Such a position hardly served to foster a more optimistic view of sex, but it did offer a possibility for moral goodness in sex-

STOICS AND GNOSTICS
No Joy of Sex

Gnosticism was a series of religious movements that deeply affected formulations of Christian sexual ethics for the first three centuries C.E. (Noonan, 1986). For example, some Gnostics taught that marriage was evil or at least useless, primarily because the procreation of children was a vehicle for forces of evil. This belief led to two extreme positions—one in opposition to all sexual intercourse, and hence in favor of celibacy, and the other in favor of any form of sexual intercourse so long as it was not procreative. Neither of these positions prevailed in what became orthodox Christianity.

What did prevail in Christian moral teaching was a doctrine that incorporated an affirmation of sex as good (because part of creation) but seriously flawed (because the force of sexual passion as such cannot be controlled by reason). The Stoic position that sexual intercourse can be brought under the rule of reason not by subduing it but by giving it a rational purpose (procreation) made great sense to early Christian thinkers. The connection made between sexual intercourse and procreation was not the same as the Jewish affirmation of the importance of fecundity, but it was in harmony with it. Christian teaching could thus both affirm procreation as the central rationale for sexual union and advocate celibacy as a praiseworthy option (indeed, the ideal) for Christians who could choose it.

With the adoption of the Stoic norm for sexual intercourse, the direction of Christian sexual ethics was set for centuries to come. A sexual ethic that concerned itself primarily with affirming the good of procreation, and thereby the good of otherwise evil tendencies, was reinforced by the continued appearance of antagonists who played the same role the Gnostics had played. No sooner had Gnosticism begun to wane than, in the third century, Manichaeanism emerged. It was largely in response to Manichaeanism that Saint Augustine formulated his sexual ethic, an ethic that continued and went beyond the Stoic elements incorporated by Clement of Alexandria, Origen, Ambrose, and Jerome.

— MARGARET A. FARLEY

There seems little prospect that the basic Protestant commitments to planned parenthood will change during the period ahead.

PAGE 530

It is difficult to generalize about any one Protestant position on population ethics.

PAGE 528

ual intercourse without a direct relation to procreation. However, from the sixth to the eleventh century, it was Augustine's rationale that was codified in penitentials (manuals for confessors, providing lists of sins and their prescribed penances) with detailed prohibitions against adultery, fornication, oral and anal sex, contraception, and even certain positions for sexual intercourse if they were thought to be departures from the procreative norm. Gratian's great collection of canon law in the twelfth century contained rigorous regulations based on the principle that all sexual activity is evil unless it is between husband and wife and for the sake of procreation. A few voices (e.g., Abelard and John Damascene) maintained that concupiscence (sexual passionate desire) does not make sexual pleasure evil in itself, and that intercourse in marriage can be justified by the simple intention to avoid fornication.

Overall, the Christian tradition in the first half of its history developed a consistently negative view of sex, despite the fact that Augustine and most of those who followed him were neither anti-body nor anti-marriage. The statement that this tradition was negative must be a qualified claim, of course, for it was silent or vacillating on many questions of sexuality (e.g., on the question of homosexuality); and there is little evidence that Christians in general were influenced by the more severe sexual attitudes of their leaders (Boswell, 1980). The direction and tone that the early centuries gave to the tradition's future, however, were unmistakable. What these leaders were concerned about was freedom from bondage to desires that seemingly could not in themselves lead to God. In a quest for transformation of the body along with the spirit, even procreation did not appear very important. Hence, regulation of sexual activity and even the importance of the family were often overshadowed by the ideal of celibacy. As Peter Brown's massive study has shown, sexual renunciation served both eros and unselfish love, and it suited a worldview that broke boundaries with this world without rejecting it as evil (Brown, 1988).

THE TEACHING OF AQUINAS. Thomas Aquinas wrote in the thirteenth century, when rigorism already prevailed in Christian teaching and church discipline. His remarkable synthesis of Christian theology did not offer much that was innovative in the area of sexual ethics. Yet the clarity of what he brought forward made his contribution significant for the generations that followed. He taught that sexual desire is not intrinsically evil, since no spontaneous bodily or emotional inclination is evil in itself; only when there is an evil moral choice is an action morally evil. Consequent upon original sin, however, there is in human nature a certain loss of order among natural human inclinations. Sexual passion is marked by this disorder, but it is not morally evil except insofar as its disorder is freely chosen.

Aquinas offered two rationales for the procreative norm the tradition had so far affirmed. One was the Augustinian argument that sexual pleasure, in the fallen human person, hinders the best working of the mind. It must be brought into some accord with reason by having an overriding value as its goal. No less an end than procreation can justify it (*Summa theologiae*, I-II.34.1, ad 1). But second, reason does not merely provide a good purpose for sexual pleasure. It discovers this purpose through the anatomy and biological function of sexual organs (*Summa theologiae* II-II.154.11; *Summa contra Gentiles* III.122.4, 5). Hence, the norm of reason in sexual behavior requires not only the conscious intention to procreate but also the accurate and unimpeded (i.e., noncontraceptive) physical process whereby procreation is possible.

From the procreative norm there followed other specific moral rules. Many of them were aimed at the well-being of offspring that could result from sexual intercourse. For example, Aquinas argued against fornication, adultery, and divorce on the grounds that children would be deprived of a good context for their rearing. He considered sexual acts other than heterosexual intercourse to be immoral because they could not be procreative. Aquinas's treatment of marriage contained only hints of new insight regarding the relation of sexual intercourse to marital love. He offered a theory of love that had room for a positive incorporation of sexual union (*Summa theologiae* II-II.26.11), and he suggested that marriage might be the basis of a maximum form of friendship (*Summa contra Gentiles* III.123).

Though what had crystallized in the Middle Ages canonically and theologically would continue to influence Christian moral teaching into the indefinite future, the fifteenth century marked the beginning of significant change. Finding some grounds for opposing the prevailing Augustinian sexual ethic in both Albert the Great and in the general (if not the specifically sexual) ethics of Aquinas, writers (e.g., Denis the Carthusian and Martin LeMaistre) began to talk of the integration of spiritual love and sexual pleasure, and the intrinsic good of sexual pleasure as the opposite of the pain of its lack. This did not reverse the Augustinian tradition, but it weakened it. The effects of these new theories were felt in the controversies of the Reformation.

PROTESTANT TEACHINGS ON SEX. Questions of sexual behavior played an important role in the Protestant Reformation beginning in the sixteenth century. Clerical celibacy, for example, was challenged not just in its scandalous nonobservance but also as a Christian ideal. Marriage and family replaced it among the reformers as the center of sexual gravity in the Christian life. Martin Luther and John Calvin were both deeply influenced by the Augustinian tradition regarding original sin and its consequences for human sexuality. Yet both developed a position on marriage that was not dependent on a procreative ethic. Like most of the Christian tradition, they affirmed marriage and human sexuality as part of the divine plan for creation, and therefore good. But they shared Augustine's pessimistic view of fallen human nature and its disordered sex drive. Luther was convinced, however, that the necessary remedy for disordered desire was marriage (*On the Estate of Marriage*). And so the issue was joined over a key element in Christian sexual ethics. Luther, of course, was not the first to advocate marriage as the cure for unruly sexual desire, but he took on the whole of the tradition in a way that no one else had. He challenged theory and practice, offering not only an alternative justification for marriage but also a view of the human person that demanded marriage for almost all Christians.

According to Luther, sexual pleasure itself in one sense needed no justification. The desire for it was simply a fact of life. It remained, like all the givens in creation, a good so long as it was channeled through marriage into the meaningful whole of life, which included the good of offspring. What there was in sex that detracted from the knowledge and worship of God was sinful, but it had simply to be forgiven, as did the inevitable sinful elements in all human activity. After 1523, Luther shifted his emphasis from marriage as a "hospital for the incurables" to marriage as a school for character. It was within the secular, nonsacramental institution of marriage and family that individuals learned obedience to God and developed the important human virtues. The structure of the family was hierarchical, husband having authority over wife, parents over children.

Calvin, too, saw marriage as a corrective to otherwise disordered desires. He expanded the notion of marriage as the context for human flourishing by maintaining that the greatest good of marriage and sex was the society that is formed between husband and wife (*Commentary on Genesis*). Calvin was more optimistic than Luther about the possibility of controlling sexual desire, though he, too, believed that whatever fault remained in it was "covered over" by marriage and forgiven by God (*Institutes of the Christian Religion*, 2.8.44). Like earlier writers, he worried that marriage as a remedy for incontinence could nonetheless in itself offer provocation to uncontrolled passion.

As part of their teaching on marriage, Luther and Calvin opposed premarital and extramarital sex and homosexual relations. So concerned was Luther to provide some institutionally tempering form to sexual desire that he once voiced an opinion favoring bigamy over adultery. Both Luther and Calvin were opposed to divorce, though its possibility was admitted in a situation of adultery or impotence.

MODERN ROMAN CATHOLIC DEVELOPMENTS. During and after the Roman Catholic Counterreformation, from the late sixteenth century on, new developments alternated with the reassertion of the Augustinian ethic. The Council of Trent (1545-1563) was the first ecumenical council to address the role of love in marriage, but it also reaffirmed the primacy of procreation and reemphasized the superiority of celibacy. In the seventeenth century, Jansenism, a morally austere and ultimately heretical movement, reacted against what it considered a dangerous lowering of sexual standards and brought back the Augustinian connection between sex, concupiscence, and original sin. Alphonsus Liguori in the eighteenth century gave impetus to a manualist tradition (the development and proliferation of moral manuals designed primarily to assist confessors) that attempted to integrate the Pauline purpose of marriage (as a remedy for incontinence) with the procreative purpose. Nineteenth-century moral manuals focused on "sins of impurity," choices of any sexual pleasure apart from procreative marital intercourse. Then came the twentieth century, with the rise of Catholic theological interest in personalism and the move by the Protestant churches to accept birth control.

In 1930, Pope Pius XI responded to the Anglican approval of contraception by reaffirming the procreative ethic (*Casti connubii*). But he also gave approval to the use of the rhythm method for restricting procreation. Moral theologians began to move cautiously in the direction of allowing sexual intercourse in marriage without a procreative intent and for the purpose of fostering marital union. The change in Roman Catholic moral theology from the 1950s to the 1970s was dramatic. The wedge introduced between procreation and sexual intercourse by the acceptance of the rhythm method joined with new understandings of the totality of the human person to support a radically new concern for sex as an expression and a cause of married love. The effects of this theological reflection were striking in the 1965 Second Vatican Council teaching that the love essential to marriage is uniquely expressed and perfected in the act of sexual intercourse (*Gaudium et spes*, 49). Although the Council still held that marriage is by its very nature ordered to the procreation of children, it no longer ranked what the tradition considered the basic ends of marriage, offspring and spousal union, as primary and secondary.

In 1968, Pope Paul VI insisted that contraception is immoral (*Humanae vitae*). Rather than settling the issue for Roman Catholics, however, this occasioned

"Masturbation: the primary sexual activity of mankind. In the nineteenth century, it was a disease; in the twentieth, it's a cure."

THOMAS SZASZ
THE SECOND SIN, 1973

See Also

Population Ethics: Teaching of John Paul II

intense conflict. The majority of moral theologians disagreed with the papal teaching, even though a distinction between nonprocreative and antiprocreative behavior mediated the dispute for some. Since then, many of the specific moral rules governing sexuality in the Catholic tradition have come under serious question. Official teachings have sustained past injunctions, though some modifications have been made in order to accommodate pastoral responses to second marriages, homosexual orientation (but not sexual activity), and individual conscience decisions regarding contraception. Among moral theologians there has been serious debate (and by the 1990s, marked pluralism) regarding premarital sex, homosexual acts, remarriage after divorce, infertility therapies, gender roles, and clerical celibacy (Curran and McCormick, 1993).

POST-REFORMATION PROTESTANTISM. Twentieth-century Protestant sexual ethics developed even more dramatically than Roman Catholic sexual ethics. After the Reformation, Protestant theologians and church leaders continued to affirm heterosexual marriage as the only acceptable context for sexual activity. Except for the differences regarding celibacy and divorce, sexual norms in Protestantism looked much the same as those in the Catholic tradition. Nineteenth-century Protestantism shared and contributed to the cultural pressures of Victorianism. But in the twentieth century, Protestant thinking was deeply affected by biblical and historical studies that questioned the foundations of Christian sexual ethics, by psychological theories that challenged traditional views, and by the voiced experience of church members.

It is difficult to trace one clear line of development in twentieth-century Protestant sexual ethics, or even as clear a dialectic as may be found in Roman Catholicism. The fact that Protestantism in general was from the beginning less dependent on a procreative ethic allowed it almost unanimously to accept contraception as a means to responsible parenting. Overall, Protestant sexual ethics has moved to integrate an understanding of the human person, male and female, into a theology of marriage that no longer deprecates sexual desire as self-centered and dangerous. It continues to struggle with issues of gendered hierarchy in the family, and with what are often called "alternative lifestyles," such as the cohabitation of unmarried heterosexuals and the sexual partnerships of gays and lesbians. For the most part, the ideal context for sexual intercourse is still seen to be heterosexual marriage, but many Protestant theologians accept premarital sex and homosexual partnerships with general norms of noncoercion, basic equality, and so on. Every mainline Protestant church in the 1990s has task forces working particularly on questions of homosexuality, professional (including clergy) sexual ethics, and sex education. Traditional positions have either changed or are open and conflicted.

◆ **legal moralism**
a principle using community effort, law, and regulation to protect society against behavior that some regard as immoral, such as sex offenses, and holding that these proscriptions are foundations of social order.

Modern sexology: Philosophical, medical, social scientific

The contemporary shaking of the foundations of Western sexual ethics, religious and secular, is traceable to many factors. These quite obviously include the rapid development of reproductive technologies, none more important than the many forms of contraception. But there have been other factors as well, such as changes in economic structures under capitalism and in social structures following major shifts of population to urban centers. Of important influence, too, has been the rise of the modern women's movement and of movements for gay and lesbian civil rights. Along with these developments, as both cause and effect, there have been significant contributions from disciplines such as history, psychology, anthropology, sociology, and medicine. Philosophy has generally followed these changes, though in the late twentieth century it, too, has contributed to cultural alterations in perspectives on sex.

PHILOSOPHICAL DEVELOPMENTS. As surveyors of the history of philosophy note, philosophers have not paid much attention to sex. They have written a great deal on love but have left sexual behavior largely to religion, poetry, medicine, or the law (Baker and Elliston, 1975; Soble, 1991). After the Greeks and Romans, and medieval thinkers such as Thomas Aquinas whose work is philosophical as well as theological, there is not much to be found in the field regarding sexuality until the twentieth century. Some exceptions to this are the sparse eighteenth-century writings on sex and gender by David Hume, Jean-Jacques Rousseau, Immanuel Kant, Mary Wollstonecraft, and Johann Gottlieb Fichte, and the nineteenth-century writings of Arthur Schopenhauer, Karl Marx, Friedrich Engels, John Stuart Mill, and Friedrich Nietzsche. Most of these writers reinforced the norm of heterosexual procreative sex within marriage. Hume, for example, in his "Of Polygamy and Divorce" (1742), insisted that all arguments finally lead to a recommendation of "our present European practices with regard to marriage." Rousseau's *La Nouvelle Héloïse* (1761) deplored the faults of conventional marriage but strongly opposed divorce and marital infidelity. Kant defended traditional sexual mores, although in his *Lectures on Ethics* (1781) he introduced a justification for marriage not in terms of procreation but of altruistic love, arguing that only a mutual commitment in marriage can save sexual desire from making a sexual partner into a mere means to one's own pleasure. Schopenhauer viewed sexual love as subjectively for

See Also
Family Planning: How Influential Is Religion?

pleasure, though objectively for procreation; his strong naturalism paved the way for a more radical theory of sex as an instinct without ethical norms (*The Metaphysics of Sexual Love*, 1844).

Philosophers in these centuries came down on both sides of the question of gender equality. Fichte, for example, asserted an essentially passive nature for women, who, if they were to be equal with men, would have to renounce their femininity (*The Science of Rights*, 1796). But Mary Wollstonecraft in her *A Vindication of the Rights of Women* (1792), and Mill in his "The Subjection of Women" (1869), offered strong challenges to the traditional inequality of gender roles in society. Marx and Engels critiqued bourgeois marriage as a relationship of economic domination (e.g., in their *The Origin of the Family, Private Property and the State*, first published by Engels in 1884). Schopenhauer, reacting to feminist agendas, advocated polygamy on the basis of a theory of male needs and female instrumental response (*On Women*, 1848). Nietzsche, like Schopenhauer, moved away from traditional ethical norms but also reinforced a view of the solely procreative value of women (*Thus Spake Zarathustra*, 1892).

Twentieth-century European philosophers attempted to construct new meanings for human sexuality in the light of new philosophical theories of freedom and interpersonal love. Jean-Paul Sartre analyzed sexuality as an ontological paradigm for human conflict (*Being and Nothingness*, 1943); Maurice Merleau-Ponty tried to challenge this and to go beyond it (*The Phenomenology of Perception*, 1945); Simone de Beauvoir fueled a feminist movement with a stark and revealing analysis of sexism and its influence on the meaning of both gender and sex (*The Second Sex*, 1949). With the exception of Bertrand Russell (*Marriage and Morals*, 1929), it was not until the late 1960s that British and American philosophers began to turn their attention to sexual ethics. Then, however, key essays by analytic philosophers began to appear on issues such as sexual desire, gender, marriage, adultery, homosexuality, abortion, sexual perversion, rape, pornography, and sexual abuse (Baker and Elliston, 1975; Shelp, 1987; Soble, 1991). All of these efforts were profoundly influenced by nineteenth- and twentieth-century contributions from other disciplines.

FREUD AND PSYCHOANALYSIS. The emergence of psychoanalytic theory brought with it new perceptions of the meaning and role of sexuality in the life of individuals. Whatever the final validity of Sigmund Freud's insights, they burst upon the world with a force that all but swept away the foundations of traditional sexual morality. Augustine's and Luther's assertions about the indomitability of sexual desire found support in Freud's theory, but now the power of sexual need was not the result of sin but a natural drive, centrally constitutive of the human personality (*Three Essays on the Theory of Sexuality*, 1905). Past efforts to order sexuality according to rational purposes could now be understood as repression. After Freud, when sex went awry, it was a matter of psychological illness, not moral evil. Taboos needed demythologizing, and freedom might be attained not through forgiveness but through medical treatment.

Yet psychoanalytic theory raised as many questions as it answered. Freud argued for liberation from sexual taboos and from the hypocrisy and sickness they caused, but he nonetheless maintained the need for sexual restraint. His theory of sublimation called for a discipline and channeling of the sexual instinct if the individual and society were to progress (*Civilization and Its Discontents*, 1930). The concern for sexual norms therefore remained, and Freud's own recommendations were in many ways quite traditional. But new work had clearly been cut out for thinkers in both secular and religious traditions.

SCIENCE, SOCIAL SCIENCE, AND MEDICINE. Freud was not the only force in nineteenth- and twentieth-century scientific and social thought that shaped changes in Western sexual mores. Biological studies of the human reproductive process offered new perspectives on male and female roles in sex and procreation. Animal research showed that higher forms of animals masturbate, perform sexual acts with members of the same sex, and generally engage in many sexual behaviors that were previously assumed to be unnatur-

CIGAR = CIGAR

Sigmund Freud (1856–1939) urged liberation from sexual taboos and from the ills of repression, but also saw the need for sexual restraint.

"Freud is the father of psychoanalysis. It has no mother."

GERMAINE GREER
IN THE PORTABLE CURMUDGEON, 1987

S

SEXUAL ETHICS

Interpretive Theories: Sex, Morality, and History

"The poets and philosophers before me discovered the unconscious; what I discovered was the scientific method by which the unconscious can be studied."

FREUD
ON HIS SEVENTIETH BIRTHDAY, 1926

al for humans because they were unnatural for animals. Anthropologists found significant variations in the sexual behavior of human cultural groups, so that traditional notions of human nature seemed even more questionable. Surveys of sexual activities in Western society revealed massive discrepancies between accepted sexual norms and actual behavior, undercutting consequential arguments for some of the norms (e.g., the fact that 95% of the male population in the United States engaged in autoerotic acts made it difficult to support a prohibition against masturbation on grounds that it leads to insanity).

Modern sexology, then, has incorporated the work not only of sexual psychology but also of biology, anthropology, ethnology, and sociology—the research and the theories of individuals like Richard von KrafftEbing, Havelock Ellis, Magnus Hirschfield, Alfred Kinsey, Margaret Mead, William Masters, and Virginia Johnson. The results have not all been toward greater liberty in sexual behavior, but they have shared a tendency to secularize and medicalize human sexuality. In theory, sex has become less an ethical or even an aesthetic problem than a health problem. In practice, experts of all kinds—physicians, counselors, psychiatrists, social workers, teachers—provide guidance; and the guidance can at least appear to carry moral weight. An example of the intertwining of science, the medical professions, and morality is clear in the long efforts to define and identify sexual deviance or perversion—from Krafft-Ebing in the nineteenth century to the debates in the American Psychiatric Association in the 1970s and 1980s over the classification of homosexuality as a disease.

LESSONS OF HISTORY. Historians, too, have played an important role in the weakening of traditional sexual ethical norms. The very disclosure that sexual prescriptions have a history has revealed the contingency of their sources and foundations. To see, for example, that a procreative ethic rose as much from Stoic philosophies as from the Bible has allowed many Christians to question its validity. Feminist retrievals of elements in the Western tradition have led to critiques of taboo moralities and a consequent need for reconstruction. In an effort to make sense of present beliefs, historians have searched for the roots and developments of these beliefs, and the result has seldom been a reinforcement of the original rationales (Foucault, 1978; Boswell, 1980).

But it is not only the history of ideas that has had an impact on contemporary sexual ethics. It is also the historical excavation of the moral attitudes and actual practices of peoples of the past, and an identification of the shifting centers of influence on the sexual mores of different times and places (D'Emilio and Freedman, 1988; Peiss and Simmons, 1989; Fout, 1992). Sometimes referred to as a history of sexuality rather than a history of theories about sexuality or of institutionalized norms for sexuality, this is a task that is barely under way, and it has strong critics. Yet it has already had an impact on, for example, understandings of homosexuality and what can be called the politics of sex. This kind of history also attempts to provide narratives, describing shifts like the one in the United States from family-centered procreative sexual mores to romantic notions of emotional intimacy to a commercialization of sex and its idealization as the central source of human happiness (D'Emilio and Freedman, 1988). The history of sexuality and of sexual ethics, no less than the analysis of contemporary sexual norms, thus becomes subject to interpretation.

Interpretive theories: Sex, morality, and history

No one may have been more influential in determining current questions about the history of sexuality and sexual ethics than the French philosopher Michel Foucault. His ideas permeate much of the work of other sexual historians as well as philosophers and theologians. Yet his is not the only formative study in the history of sexual ethics, and his conclusions have provoked both positive and negative responses.

MICHEL FOUCAULT: A HISTORY OF DESIRE. Foucault originally planned to write a history of what he called "the experience of sexuality" in modern Western culture. In the course of his work, he became convinced that what was needed was a history of desire, or of the desiring subject. At the heart of this conviction was the premise that sexuality is not an ahistorical constant. Neither is sex a natural given, a biological referent that simply expresses itself in different experiences of sexuality shaped historically by changing moral norms. Sexuality is, rather, a transfer point for relations of power—between women and men, parents and children, teachers and students, clergy and laity, and so forth. Power in this sense is diffused through a field of multiple "force relations immanent in the sphere in which they operate" (Foucault, 1978, p. 92). In other words, sex is not a "stubborn drive" that requires the control of power. Power produces and constitutes sexual desire much more than it ever represses it. Power determines, shapes, and deploys sexuality, and sexuality determines the meaning of sex (Foucault, 1978).

Foucault denied, then, the "repressive hypothesis" as an explanation of the eighteenth- and nineteenth-century Western experience of sexuality. That is, he denied that the Victorian era had been an era of sexual repression and socially enforced silence about sex. He argued, rather, that it had been a time of an expanding deployment of sexuality and a veritable explosion of discourse about sexuality. The questions that interested

him were not "Why are we repressed?" but "Why do we say that we are repressed?" and within this, not "Why was sex associated with sin for such a long time?" but "Why do we burden ourselves today with so much guilt for having made sex a sin?" (Foucault, 1978, pp. 8-9). Since the key to these questions was, Foucault thought, to be found in a study of discourse, he began with an examination of what he considered a Western impulse to discover the "truth" about sex. This, in his view, included a striking Western compulsion to self-examination and self-reporting regarding sexual experience, whether in the discourses of religion, medicine, psychiatry, or criminal justice.

To make sense of the connections between power, sexuality, and truth in the modern period, Foucault revised his project to include a study of the variations on sexual themes in other historical periods. His move to the past began with his thesis that a forerunner of modern discourse on sex was the seventeenth-century Christian ecclesiastical emphasis on confession. To put this in perspective, he undertook studies of pagan antiquity and of Christianity prior to the seventeenth century. Thus, volumes 2 and 3 of his *History of Sexuality* address the sexual mores of the fourth-century B.C.E. Greeks and the first- and second-century C.E. Romans (1990 and 1988, respectively). His unpublished fourth volume (*The Confessions of the Flesh*) examines developments within Christianity. The contrasts (and, as it turned out, the continuities) between the different historical periods shed some light on each period and on the overall Western pursuit of the kind of knowledge that promised power in relation to sex, what Foucault called the *scientia sexualis*.

Foucault came to the conclusion that the sexual morality of the Greeks and Romans did not differ essentially from Christian sexual morality in terms of specific prescriptions. He rejected the commonly held view that the essential contrast between sexual ethics in antiquity and in early Christianity lies in the permissiveness of Graeco-Roman societies as distinguished from the strict sexual rules of the Christians, or in an ancient positive attitude toward sex as distinguished from a negative Christian assessment. Both traditions, he argued, contained prohibitions against incest, a preference for marital fidelity, a model of male superiority, caution regarding same-sex relations, respect for austerity, a positive regard for sexual abstinence, fears of male loss of strength through sexual activity, and hopes of access to special truths through sexual discipline. Nor were these basic prescriptions very different from what could be found in post-seventeenth-century Western society.

Yet there were clear discontinuities, even ruptures, between these historical periods. The reasons for moral solicitude regarding sexuality were different. In Foucault's reading, the ancients were concerned with health, beauty, and freedom, while Christians sought purity of heart before God, and bourgeois moderns aimed at their own self-idealization. The Greeks valued self-mastery; Christians struggled for self-understanding; and modern Western individuals scrutinized their feelings in order to secure compliance with standards of normality. Eroticism was channeled toward boys for the Greeks, abd toward women for the Christians, and was a centrifugal movement in many directions for the Victorian and post-Victorian middle class. The Greeks feared the enslavement of the mind by the body; Christians dreaded the chaotic power of corrupted passion; post-nineteenth-century persons feared deviance and its consequent shame. Sexual morality was an aesthetic ideal, a personal choice, for an elite in antiquity; it became a universal ethical obligation under Christianity; and it was exacted as a social requirement under the power of the family and the management of the modern professional.

Foucault's study of the history of sexuality left open a question with which he had become preoccupied: How did contemporary Western culture come to believe that sexuality was the key to individual identity? How did sex become more important than love, and almost more important than life? He exposed the lack of freedom in past constructs of sexuality, and he critiqued past formulations of sexual prescriptions. But his presentation of current strategies for sexual liberation yielded no less skeptical a judgment. It suggested, rather, that however historically relative sexual ethics may be, moral solicitude regarding sexuality is not entirely a mistake.

CATHARINE MACKINNON: A HISTORY OF GENDERED VIOLENCE. Many Western feminists have shared Foucault's convictions that sexuality is socially constructed and the body is a site of power. Like Foucault, they have exposed continuing roles of medicine, education, and psychology in determining post-eighteenth-century sexual mores. With Foucault, they have emphasized discourse as a key to identifying underlying forces that link power, sexuality, and identity. But feminists fault Foucault for not extending his analytics of power to gender. Legal scholar Catharine MacKinnon, for example, opposes a Foucaultian history of desire on the grounds that the unacknowledged desiring subject is male. A history of sexuality that emphasizes sexual desire and change misses the enduring aspects of history—the unrelenting sexual abuse of women. History, then, remains silent regarding sexual exploitation, harassment, battery, and rape. Without attention to these unchanging experiences of women, MacKinnon argues, there can be no accurate analysis of sex and power.

A feminist theory of sexuality, according to MacKinnon, "locates sexuality within a theory of gender inequal-

See Also

Sexism and Women

ABUSE OF POWER

Some feminist scholars contend that studies of sex and power relations cannot ignore the abuse and exploitation women have endured through history.

ity" (1989, p. 127). It is a mistake, therefore, to adopt the stance that what sex needs is socially constructed freedom, that all sex can be good—healthy, appropriate, pleasurable, to be approved and expressed—if only it is liberated from ideologies of allowed/not allowed. Since sexuality is socially constructed not by a diffuse multiplicity of powers (in Foucault's sense) but by hegemonic male power, it is culturally determined as violent toward women. Pornography is a means through which this social construction is achieved.

"We are effectively destroying ourselves by violence masquerading as love."

R. D. LAING
POLITICS OF EXPERIENCE, 1967

Although not all feminists share MacKinnon's radical critique of historical and contemporary sexual understandings and practices, there is significant agreement that sexuality needs norms, and that past and present norms require gender analysis and critique. From this standpoint, a Foucaultian treatment of male discourse regarding sexuality perpetuates a view of sexuality as eroticized dominance and submission; it fails to expose this conflict as gendered.

EVOLUTIONARY INTERPRETATIONS. Foucault and MacKinnon represent interpretations of the history of sexuality and sexual ethics that deny any progress. They refuse to applaud advances in understandings of sexuality or to sanctify the present as enlightened and free. To some extent, they even reject notions of change in history—Foucault arguing for different, but not causally connected, historical perspectives; and MacKinnon focusing on similarities across time and cultures—indeed, a failure to change. Others, however, have charted an evolutionary process across the Western history of ideas about sex and the moral norms that should govern it. Those who believe that contemporary sexual revolutions have liberated persons and their sexual possibilities belong in this category. So do those who acknowledge the significance of advances in biology and psychology and call for appropriate adjustments in philosophical and theological ethics. Thoughtful commentators do not necessarily conclude that there has been real progress, though they identify evolutionary changes (Green, 1992; Shelp, 1987; Soble, 1991).

Richard Posner belongs to this latter group, offering what he calls an "economic theory of sexuality" (Posner, 1992). That is, he relies heavily on economic analysis both to describe the practice of sex and to evaluate legal and ethical norms in its regard. There are, he argues, three stages in the evolution of sexual morality. These stages correlate with the status of women in a given society (Posner, 1992). In the first stage, women's occupation is that of "simple breeder." When this is the case, companionate marriage is an unlikely possibility, and practices that are considered "immoral" are likely to flourish (e.g., prostitution, adultery, homosexual liaisons).

The second stage begins when women's occupations expand to include "child rearer and husband's companion." Here, companionate marriage is a possibility, and because of this, "immoral" practices that endanger it are vehemently condemned. When companionate marriage is idealized as the only possibility for everyone, societies become puritanical in their efforts to promote and protect it. In the third stage, women's roles are enlarged to include "market employment." Marriages will be fewer, but where they exist, they will be companionate. Other forms of sexual relationship, previously considered immoral, no longer appear to be either immoral or abnormal. This stage characterizes some Western societies more than others—notably, according to Posner, contemporary Sweden.

A very different kind of evolutionary theory can be found in the philosopher Paul Ricoeur's analysis of the symbolism of evil in Western history (Ricoeur, 1967). In this analysis, the Greco-Hebraic history of the consciousness of evil has three moments or stages: defilement, sin, and guilt. The sense of defilement is a pre-ethical, irrational, quasi-material sense of something that infects by contact. Sin is a sense of betrayal, of rupture in a relationship. And guilt is the subjective side of sin, a consciousness that the breakdown of a relationship is the result of an evil use of freedom. According to Ricoeur, sexual morality has appeared historically paradigmatic of the experience of defilement. This association has not been left behind; there remains in the implicit consciousness of the West an inarticulable but persistent connection between sexuality and evil. The result is that ethical wisdom regarding sexuality has remained far behind other developments in Western ethics, even though there has been a significant demythologizing of sex.

Contemporary ethical reconstruction

The turn to history may have relativized much of traditional sexual ethics, but the motivation for the turn is more complicated. Given all the factors that have helped to weaken traditional sexual norms, ethical reflection has been left with very little anchorage. Science and medicine help, but they sometimes add to human suffering experienced in relation to sex. Philosophy and religion find their traditions struggling for relevance, for clarity, for reasonable guidance and more than reasoned inspiration. The turn to history has been an effort to find a truth that continues to be elusive. And history, like other disciplinary efforts, has probably both helped and heightened the need for the quest.

Contemporary efforts in sexual ethics recognize multiple meanings for human sexuality—pleasure, reproduction, communication, love, conflict, social stability, and so on. Most of those who labor at sexual ethics recognize the need to guide sexual behavior in ways that preserve its potential for good and restrict its potential for evil. Safety, nonviolence, equality, autonomy, mutuality, and truthfulness are generally acknowledged as required for minimal human justice in sexual relationships. Many think that care, responsibility, commitment, love, and fidelity are also required, or at least included as goals. With social construction no longer ignored, the politics of sex has become an ethical matter for persons and societies, institutions and professions. New questions press regarding the ways in which humanity is to reproduce itself and the responsibilities it has for its offspring. In all of this, sexual ethics asks, How is it appropriate—helpful and not harmful, creative and not destructive—to live and to relate to one another as sexual beings?

— MARGARET A. FARLEY

SEXUAL ETHICS AND PROFESSIONAL STANDARDS

The Hippocratic oath gives early expression to a general prohibition against professionals taking advantage of the vulnerability of clients or patients and their families to enter into sexual relations: "Whatever house I may visit, I will come for the benefit of the sick, remaining free of all intentional injustice, of all mischief and in particular of sexual relations with both female and male persons, be they free or slaves" (Verhey, 1987, p. 72). The prohibition was reiterated for mental-health professionals by Sigmund Freud (Schoener et al., 1989). From these roots grows a general prohibition against professional-client sexual relations, including relations between teacher and student, supervisor and supervised, clergy and parishioner, therapist and client, and physician and patient. In some professions, the taboo has been so strong that sexuality is the problem professionals "don't talk about" (Rassieur, 1976) or "the problem with no name" (Davidson, 1977).

Yet some famous therapists (e.g., Carl Jung) have been notorious for having sexual relations with their clients (Schoener et al., 1989). Studies of various professions indicate a rate of sexual contact between professionals and clients or patients of between 5 and 11 percent (Schoener et al., 1989; Bonavoglia, 1992). The phenomenon has become sufficiently widespread to be called a "national disgrace" (Pope and Bouhoutsos, 1986) and an "epidemic" (Rutter, 1989).

In the ten years following the publication of *Betrayal* (Freeman and Roy, 1976), which described one woman's successful lawsuit over sexual misconduct by a psychiatrist, over $7 million was paid out in legal claims. In the face of revelations of misconduct, professional societies began to insert clear prohibitions into their codes: "sexual intimacies with clients are unethical" (American Psychological Association, 1981); "the social worker should under no circumstances engage in sexual activities with clients" (National Association of Social Workers, 1980); "sexual relations between analyst and patient are antithetic to treatment and unacceptable under any circumstance" (American Psychoanalytic Association, 1983). Even in the controversial field of sex therapy, direct sexual contact between therapist and client is discouraged; sexual surrogates are used instead (Masters et al., 1977).

Several jurisdictions have enacted laws making it a felony for a psychotherapist (including clergy) to have sexual contact with a client, and at least one holds the therapist's employer liable if the employer knew or should have known of a history of sexual abuse (Bonavoglia, 1992; for statutes, see Schoener et al., 1989). Sexual contact is variously defined, but generally includes not only sexual intercourse but also intimate touching and other sexualizing of the relationship.

The vulnerability of clients and the power of professionals mean that professionals can take advantage of clients. Sexual relations between professional and client are therefore an abuse of professional power—an illegitimate use of that power for the professional's own ends instead of for the ends of healing the client (Lebacqz and Barton, 1991; Schoener et al., 1989; Rutter, 1989; Fortune, 1989).

Moreover, the vulnerability of patients or clients and the power gap between client and professional may compromise the freedom needed to give truly informed consent for sexual intimacies (Pope and Bouhoutsos, 1986; Lebacqz and Barton, 1991). The psychotherapeutic notion of transference (redirecting childhood feelings toward a new object) suggests a special vulnerability that may literally paralyze

Until society comes to terms with the full implications of procreative freedom, it must use moral persuasion and legal coercion to eliminate any exploitative aspects of surrogacy.

PAGE 593

patients, making them unable to resist a therapist's advances (Freeman and Roy, 1976). Noting special vulnerabilities in the sexual arena, Karen Lebacqz and Ronald Barton (1991) propose that *sexual* intimacies differ from other acts to which patients, clients, and parishioners might continue to consent.

Some argue that vulnerability does not end when therapy ends and that there should be a prohibition on posttherapy sexual contact (Schoener et al., 1989; Rutter, 1989). John C. Gonsiorek and Laura S. Brown proposed that sexual relations posttherapy should never be permitted where there was significant transference or where the client was severely disturbed, but might be permitted after two years with former clients who were not disturbed and showed little transference (Gonsiorek and Brown, 1989). Such a proposal raises difficult issues regarding who would make this judgment, but it reflects a clear principle that the base for determining whether sexual relations are permissible is the relative power and vulnerability of professional and client. Sexual contact might not be wrong where the power gap is minimized. Although few codes of professional ethics address the posttherapy issue, in 1993, the American Psychiatric Association explicitly addressed it: "Sexual activity with a current or former patient is unethical" (APA, 1993).

In a similar vein, Lebacqz and Barton (1991) argue that romantic or sexual relations might be acceptable under circumstances where the power of professional and client is relatively equal and the relationship is under public scrutiny—for example, when clergy date parishioners with whom they are not involved in a pastoral counseling relationship and members of the church are informed.

All commentators agree, however, that "sexualizing . . . therapy is a betrayal of a trusting relationship" (Pope and Bouhoutsos, 1986, p. 54) and that no sexual relationship should be permitted where there is a counseling or therapeutic relationship involved (Pope and Bouhoutsos, 1986; Fortune, 1989; Rutter, 1989). The professional-client relationship that involves psychotherapy or particular vulnerability on the part of the client is a "forbidden zone" for sexuality (Rutter, 1989).

Professional-client sexual contact must be addressed on institutional, not just personal, levels.

PROFESSIONAL ETHICS

Clients Are Vulnerable

The prohibition against professional-client sexual contact rests on three foundations: the likelihood of great harm from the sexual contact, the responsibility of the professional to work for the good of the client, and the vulnerability of the client and the power gap between client and professional, which raises questions even in the absence of demonstrable harm.

There is growing consensus that significant harm is done to patients or clients who enter sexual relations with professionals in whom they have vested trust: "[T]he balance of the empirical findings is heavily weighted in the direction of serious harm resulting to almost all patients sexually involved with their therapists" (Pope and Bouhoutsos, 1986, p. 63). A few therapists have argued for the beneficial effects of sexual relations between therapist and client (Shepard, 1971; Schoener et al., 1989), but their data have been challenged (Pope and Bouhoutsos, 1986; Schoener et al., 1989). Studies of women who have had sexual relations with their gynecologists, psychotherapists, and clergy all point to deleterious consequences including loss of trust, poor self-concept, loss of confidence in one's judgment, and difficulty establishing subsequent relationships (Pope and Bouhoutsos, 1986). Several commentators have noted the similarities to incest because of the power of the professional and have argued that the consequences are as deleterious as those of incest (e.g., Fortune, 1989). Others note that women who enter relations with therapists often have a history of sexual abuse, and thus are being revictimized (Rutter, 1989; Pope and Bouhoutsos, 1986).

Sexual contact between professional and client thus subverts the legitimate goal of the profession—the healing or making whole of one who is wounded and vulnerable (Verhey, 1987). There is both exploitation of the client for benefit of the professional and a failure to provide the services implied by the professional role.

However, harm and failure to help are not the only ethical issues at stake. Several commentators argue that the power of the professional is morally relevant (Lebacqz, 1985; Lebacqz and Barton, 1991). Professionals may hold several types of power: Asclepian power—the power of professional training; charismatic power—the power of personal magnetism and authority; social power—the power of the role and its authority (Brody, 1992). By contrast, the client lacks the power of the role and of its associated training. In addition, female clients facing male professionals generally lack the social power that men have in a sexist context (Lebacqz, 1985; Lebacqz and Barton, 1991). Clients are vulnerable.

— KAREN LEBACQZ

Professional societies and supporting organizations such as churches are complicit when they fail to punish offenders, try to cover up the problem, blame the victim, and otherwise minimize the issue (Fortune, 1989; Bonavoglia, 1992). Underreporting is a significant issue: 65 percent of therapists in one study had seen clients who were sexually abused by a previous therapist; they judged that abuse harmful in 87 percent of cases but reported it in only 8 percent (Schoener et al., 1989). Peter Rutter acknowledges the reluctance of men to blow the whistle on each other (Rutter, 1989). Gary Richard Schoener notes that the professional literature "documents more in the way of inaction than of active and creative study leading toward solutions" (Schoener et al., 1989). Professional misconduct damages the profession and institutions as well as individuals (Fortune, 1989). Lack of internal regulation within the professions has led some U.S. state legislatures (e.g., Minnesota) to pass laws that hold institutions as well as individuals responsible for sexual misconduct of professionals (Lebacqz and Barton, 1991).

Underlying social and cultural patterns—sexism, the eroticization of domination, and the maldistribution of power in society—are causal factors (Lebacqz and Barton, 1991; Rutter, 1989). Since Phyllis Chesler's early feminist exposé of therapy in *Women and Madness* (1972), feminists have paid attention to the ways in which traditional therapy often reinforces passive and self-destructive behaviors for women, including behaviors that would make women likely victims of sexual abuse. Dynamics of sexual contact cannot be understood without recognizing sex-role patterning and power imbalances in the general culture (Schoener et al., 1989; Lebacqz and Barton, 1991; Brown and Bohn, 1989). Evidence indicates, for example, that male clients may not experience the sexualizing of relationships to be as harmful as female clients do (Pope and Bouhoutsos, 1986). Such gender differences may reflect social patterning of male and female sexuality, in which men gain and women lose power when entering a sexual relationship. There is also evidence that women therapists do not engage in sexual contact with clients as frequently as male therapists do, and that they judge it more harmful (Schoener et al., 1989).

The traditional prohibition against sexual contact between professionals and their clients continues to be reaffirmed in spite of arguments and practices to the contrary. An adequate ethical framework requires attention not only to professional responsibility, harm, and power imbalances but also to institutional structures and to cultural dynamics of sexuality and power.

— KAREN LEBACQZ

SEXUAL IDENTITY

Because some terms are deeply embroiled in controversial debates, the task of defining them itself becomes controversial. So it is with the term "sexual identity." Providing any definition immediately situates the definer within a particular perspective. One important perspective, which has served as the backdrop of much contemporary discussion, claims that the term refers to the distinct biological types of "male" and "female." This "traditionalist" definition of "sexual identity" has sometimes been associated with one or more of the following additional positions: that certain specific and "complementary" psychological attributes and social roles, specifically those of "masculinity" and "femininity," correspond to each of these distinct biological types; that a "natural" sexual attraction exists between these two biological types; that this attraction is most naturally satisfied through the act of intercourse; and that the act of intercourse, while naturally motivated by attraction, should also be motivated by other concerns, most importantly love and the desire to have children within the context of marriage.

> *"The identity crisis . . . occurs in that period of the life cycle when each youth must forge for himself some central perspective and direction."*
>
> ERIK ERIKSON
> YOUNG MAN LUTHER, 1958

One or all of these claims have been challenged over the last few decades by feminists; by those advocating various forms of sexual liberation; by gays and lesbians; and by scholars influenced (or not) by these movements. All of these challenges raise questions about what we mean by "sexual identity." Some of the positions developed in response to the above set of views have themselves been challenged. For the sake of clarity, we can group the challenges and counterchallenges around the following set of questions:

1. The sex question: Are there really two distinct biological types, "male" and "female"?
2. The gender question: How should we think about the relationship between biology and psychological attributes and forms of behavior?
3. The question of sexuality: What constitutes sexual desire? What are the various ways in which it can be characterized?
4. The question of sexual ethics: How ought we to think about sexual practices? Which, if any, should be condoned, which prohibited, and why?

Sex

Over the past few decades, many have come to disbelieve the claim that there exist two sexes without gradations. Some feminists have argued that, biologically, it is more useful to think of many of the physical characteristics associated with sexual difference as mani-

See Also

Gender Identity and Gender Identity Disorders

fested across the human species in a range of degrees, rather than as being associated exclusively with either sex. They claim that only a social desire to emphasize difference has caused us to think of such variations in stark, bipolar ways. Thus, for example, though we often think of men as "bigger" than women, many individual women are taller, heavier, longer limbed, and so forth, than many men. Similarly, while we tend to think of women and men as possessing very distinctive hormones, in actuality the situation is more complex. For example, the hormones estrogen and androgen are often thought of as the "female" and "male" hormones, respectively, suggesting that men have one and women the other. In reality, both hormones are found in both women and men, and after menopause, women often exhibit a lower ratio of estrogen to androgen than do men of a comparable age (Spanier, 1993). These feminists argue that many of the striking differences we see are at least partially the consequence of social pressures exerted on women and men to manifest such differences. Thus women are encouraged to remove body hair and to buy shoes that make their feet look as small as possible.

"'After all,' as a pretty girl once said to me, 'women are a sex by themselves, so to speak.'"

SIR MAX BEERBOHM
YELLOW BOOK, 1894

Some cultural historians claim that the view of men and women as possessing sharply differentiated bodies has developed only within the last few centuries. Thomas Laqueur (1990), for example, points out that prior to the eighteenth century, women's bodies were thought of as less developed versions of men's bodies. In this "one-sex" view, the vagina was not thought of as different from the male penis but, rather, as an inverted form of it. But during the eighteenth century, there emerged a view of "the two-sex body," that is, of female and male bodies being fundamentally different. With this new development, organs that had previously been referred to by the same name were given separate names. Thus, what had previously been "the testicles" now became differentiated into "the testicles" and "the ovaries." Others that previously had no name were given names, for example, the vagina. Even parts of the body remote from reproductive functions, such as the skeleton and the nervous system, began to be depicted as distinctive for women and men.

Gender is not merely a function of chromosomal, hormonal, or anatomical traits.

PAGE 252

Recent research in biology suggests that differentiating the male from the female is no simple task. Various indicators of "maleness" and "femaleness" are individually sometimes ambiguous. Even when all of the indicators are clear, they do not necessarily cohere. For example, within contemporary science the standard distinguishing criterion has been taken to be the presence or absence of the Y chromosome. Most people possess two sets of chromosomes, one from each parent; females are understood to be those with two X chromosomes and males those with one X chromosome and one Y chromosome. However, there are problems with any neat application of this criterion. Some individuals inherit only one X chromosome but no Y chromosome. Or a piece of a Y chromosome may become attached to an X chromosome, producing an individual with an XXY pattern.

Even those individuals who possess a standard XX or XY pattern may exhibit characteristics that would incline many not to identify them by their chromosomal pattern. An XY individual may have testes that do not secrete the male hormone testosterone, or may have cells that are not sensitive to testosterone. That person will end up looking more like a female than a male (Lowenstein, 1987). There are also XY individuals who look female at birth and are raised as girls, but who develop masculine bodily features at adolescence. There are XX people whose adrenal glands secrete large amounts of male hormones. One consequence is clitoral enlargement, causing them to be taken for boys at birth. As adults they may also possess increased muscle mass and hairiness (Lowenstein, 1987). In short, recent scientific research has supported the point that even the biological distinction between male and female is not always clear-cut.

Gender

Until the emergence of the second wave of feminism in the 1960s, the term "gender" was used primarily to indicate differences between female and male forms within language. Differences between women and men were commonly indicated by the term "sex," as in the phrase "the battle of the sexes." Feminists, however, began to use the term "gender" to refer to what they argued were socially constructed differences between women and men. It was felt that the term "sex," when applied to differences between women and men, suggested that such differences were biological in origin. A new term was needed to refer to differences that were a product of society.

Studies done within the social sciences pointed to the great differences among societies in expectations of what was appropriate behavior for men and women. For example, the anthropologist Michelle Zimbalist Rosaldo noted that there are some societies where women trade or garden, and others where men do; some where men are prudish and flirtatious, and others where women are (Rosaldo and Lamphere, 1974). Psychologists and other social scientists stressed the importance of socialization in structuring an individual's sense of self. Thus, John Money and Anke Ehrhardt (1972) reported that when children were assigned a gender at birth that did not match their chromosomal sex, it was most likely that their adult sense of self would conform to their assigned gender rather than to their chromosomal sex.

The term "gender" has been very useful in making possible a greater recognition of the social construction of differences between women and men. Recently, however, some scholars have been raising questions about how "gender" should be understood, and particularly how its relationship to "sex" should be interpreted. Using the term "sex" to describe biological differences, and "gender" to describe socially constructed ones, ignores the fact that biological distinctions are themselves social constructions. That modern biology, for example, interprets the penis as an organ distinct from the vagina is a social construction, more a consequence of changing cultural metaphors than of new scientific evidence (Laqueur, 1990).

Another problem is that the relationship between psychological traits and biological phenomena is still often understood to be that the former "follows" from the latter. While "gender" emphasizes that many psychological traits are social constructions, it does not necessarily undermine the view that such traits follow from biological differences. All it adds is that the path from biology to psychology proceeds by way of social construction.

Any model that claims that psychology follows from biology has problems accounting for those individuals whose socialization deviates from the norm. In other words, to the extent that "gender" is still viewed as tied to "sex," we have problems explaining the phenomena of girls who grow up exhibiting "masculine" psychological traits and boys who grow up with a "feminine" sense of self. The most striking examples of such cases are transsexuals, people who experience a dramatic misalignment between their physical features and their internalized sense of self. Such people frequently desire physical restructuring of their bodies to bring the physical and the psychic into alignment.

The term "gender" may still suggest, as did the term "sex," that people's psychic lives and behavior are necessarily unified, that it is appropriate to talk about a male or a female "identity." One suggestion has been that we talk about "gender" not as describing individual identity but as describing acts or performances we all play out (Butler, 1990). Such a model allows us to move the focus of "gender" from the individual to the activity. This type of shift is consistent with an overall tendency on the part of many contemporary scholars to think of "gender" as a type of social coding that is applied not only to behavior but also to psychic stances and to bodies. The recognition that bodies, like behavior, are socially coded in turn undermines the distinction between "sex" and "gender" insofar as the former had been understood as naturally "given" and the latter as the consequence of social construction (Scott, 1988).

Sexuality

At least since the 1890s in industrialized Western countries, one paradigm of sexuality has been dominant: that which describes as "normal," genital-genital intercourse between one male and one female, and as "abnormal" or "perverse," sexual practices that fall outside that paradigm. "Perverse" practices include but are not limited to the following: voyeurism; exhibitionism; incest (sex between close relatives); oral sex; anal sex; sex with children (pedophilia); sex involving more than two persons; sex between humans and animals (zoophilia); sex with oneself (masturbation); sex involving the use of visual images (pornography); sex with a corpse (necrophilia); transvestism (an individual heightens his or her sexual pleasure by dressing in garments associated with the opposite sex); sex associated with the giving or experiencing of pain or humiliation (sadomasochism); sex strongly associated with a particular object or part of the body (fetishism); and sex between members of the same sex (homosexuality).

Homosexuality has, in particular, been the subject of much attention and debate over the last decades. The stigmatizing label "homosexuality" has been used to negatively characterize certain individuals since the late nineteenth century (Weeks, 1989); laws have been enacted against it and people have been jailed for practicing it (e.g., the English playwright Oscar Wilde). During the twentieth century, medical doctors and other scientific specialists have depicted it as a pathology and, as with other pathologies (but not accepted practices), have searched for causes (Bayer, 1987).

Much debate has centered on the question of whether homosexuality is a product of genetic inheritance or other biology, or is a consequence of socialization. During the 1960s and 1970s, homosexual men (who increasingly adopted the label "gay") and homosexual women (lesbians) began to form political organizations to resist the laws, practices, and beliefs that stigmatized them. They argued that homosexuality was not a perversion or a pathology, to be outlawed or cured, but a difference in preference that should be tolerated within a free and open society. The American psychiatric community has moved away from a description of homosexuality as pathology. In December 1973 the board of trustees of the American Psychiatric Association moved to delete the category "homosexuality" as necessarily a pathology from the second edition of the *Diagnostic and Statistical Manual of Psychiatric Disorders*, retaining "ego dystonic homosexuality" to cover those not comfortable with their sexual orientation. In yet another revision, any specific reference to homosexuality was removed altogether, but the term "sexual orientation distress" was retained

"Psychoanalysis is confession without absolution."

G. K. CHESTERTON
IN THE PORTABLE CURMUDGEON, 1987

◆ **fetishism**
sex strongly associated with a particular object or part of the body.

See Also

Gender Assignment: Sometimes Not So Simple

Homosexuality

The APA abandoned its view of homosexuality as a pathology, yet maintains the diagnostic category "sexual orientation distress."

PAGE 255

to permit treatment of those disturbed about their sexuality (Bayer, 1987).

Other questions have been added to the debate, among them whether homosexuality describes a particular kind of person or, more appropriate, a specific type of activity. Social historians have pointed out that the category "the homosexual" was constructed in the latter part of the nineteenth century to depict a specific type of person, followed shortly by the construction of "the heterosexual" (Katz, 1983; Halperin, 1990). Prior to the creation of "the homosexual," people who engaged in acts we would label as homosexual were not necessarily seen to require a special label. This is at least partially a consequence of the fact that the sex of one's partner has not always been viewed as an overriding feature of the sex act. For example, within many Native American societies, certain men, "the berdache," took on many of the tasks and characteristics associated with women. These men would have sex with other men. However, what was seen as distinguishing the sexual practices of the berdache was not that they had sex with other men but that they took the passive role in sex. Their male partners were not distinguished from men who had sex only with women (Williams, 1986). For such reasons, Eve Sedgwick has observed that given the many dimensions along which genital activity can be described, it is quite amazing that the sex of object choice has emerged as central during the twentieth century, and has come to define what we mean by "sexual orientation" (Sedgwick, 1990).

How we conceive of sexual practices defines much of our thinking about sexuality. The emphasis on the "normal" practice of heterosexual intercourse implies that sex between persons of the same gender and any sexual activity that does not lead to intercourse will be abnormal or "perverse" (or what Freud called "inverse"). These are not only clinical categories; they often function as strong moral terms of condemnation as well. Thus homosexuality is attacked both as pathology and as voluntary wrongdoing, by those who see it not only as deviant but also as perverse behavior. The idea that homosexuality is normal sex, and neither pathology nor wrongdoing—an idea that has been widely accepted by many cultures throughout history—is discouraged by the heterosexual paradigm.

Sexual paradigms

Just as matters of individual sexual identity have been oversimplified into a single male-female dichotomy, the many varieties of sexual behavior have often been reduced to a simple distinction between normality and perversion.

The condemnation of homosexuality and other deviant sexual activities and "perversions" brings us into the realm of sexual ethics and to the question of alternative sexual paradigms. A paradigm is an exemplary instance that serves as a standard. A sexual paradigm is an example of sexual activity that is taken as a standard for "normal" sexual behavior. The most obvious sexual paradigm is heterosexual genital-genital intercourse, but in order to employ this paradigm as a norm, we need to specify not only the overt activity but the aims and desires of the participants as well. Is the purpose of sexual intercourse, for example, to produce children? Or is it just "for fun"? Or an expression of love? Or a "conquest"? We can further distinguish between "minimalist" and "murky" paradigms of sexuality. Minimalist accounts tend to define sexuality as a simple, straightforward desire, while murky accounts dig deeper in order to find hidden or unconscious desires. Thomas Nagel (1969), for example, introduces the minimalist notion of "unadorned sexual intercourse," although he adds that such behavior, "unadorned," may well be perverse, and that a typical sexual encounter involves a complex of communicative gestures. Janice Moulton (1976) defines sexuality simply as the desire for physical contact, although she then provides a rich discussion of its many associated meanings. Alan Goldman (1977) isolates what he calls "plain sex," which he defines as "a desire for contact with another's body," and rejects accounts that try to define sexuality in terms of any further goal or purpose.

On the "murky" side, there is the lasting legacy of Plato's *Symposium* and its various discussions of eros. In particular, there is Aristophanes' famous tale about the divine fission of individual human beings out of complete wholes, according to which sexual desire is nothing less than the impossible desire to join together with "one's other half" and become "complete once again," and Socrates' much more effete conception of eros as the love of Beauty as such. Two thousand years of Christian theology have attempted both to chastise and to spiritualize sexuality, and the Tantric traditions of India and Tibet have refined sexuality into a spiritual road to enlightenment. More recently, Sigmund Freud and Carl Jung profoundly deepened our conceptions of sexuality, which is, in their accounts, no mere desire but a focus for the darkest and most explosive secrets of the psyche.

THE REPRODUCTIVE PARADIGM. Biologically, sexuality can be defined in terms of a very specific genetic process, although even that has its ambiguities and confusions. This biological definition and its implied reproductive paradigm play an enormous role in our conceptions of sexuality. Whatever embellishments, variations, and alternatives we and some of our fellow vertebrates have evolved or invented, heterosexual intercourse remains something of an "original text" in our sexual hermeneutics. It can be rejected,

See Also

Treating' Homosexuality: Social Attitudes in the Looking Glass refuted, even reviled, but it must, first of all, be taken account of.

One might distinguish here, in line with a three-thousand-year-old moral tradition, between an individual's purpose and what we might call "nature's purpose." Until the end of the nineteenth century, when teleology or the purposiveness of nature was taken seriously, this phrase could be interpreted literally. Today, in the wake of increasingly antiteleological conceptions of evolution, the phrase "nature's purpose" must be taken as, at best, shorthand for a complex set of causal processes that are themselves the result of chance and natural selection. Even so, one might distinguish between the various drives and desires favored by natural selection because they increase the likelihood of a more adaptive genotype (what Richard Dawkins [1976] calls "the selfish gene"), and the more or less conscious and sometimes articulate desires of an adult human being. But we are not, like most creatures, mere sexual pawns of cunning nature. Some teenagers may not know of the various consequences and the significance of sexual activity, but for most adults this knowledge is profound, if not extensive, and sexuality may never be free of those associations. But whether or not this is the hidden purpose of *all* sexual desire and activity, it is clearly the conscious and conscientious choice of *some* sexual activity. Building a family is not, for most people, the only purpose of sexual activity; but by having sexual intercourse, it is possible to have children. Whatever creative alternatives may be dreamed up by medicine, one undeniable aspect of sexuality is, and will be, its traditional role in procreation.

The view that sexuality and sexual desire are really aimed at reproduction, even if the sexual participants desire only to perform a particular activity without thinking of the consequences, tends to move us from the minimalist view of sexuality to various murky views. The self-evident desires are no longer taken at face value, and a deeper biological (or theological) narrative, which may not be self-evident to the participants, comes into play. Thus the psychological consequences of thousands or millions of years of evolution manifest themselves in desires that may seem straightforward. Or, behind seemingly simple sexual desire lurks the secret of God's creation and the biblical injunction to be fruitful and multiply. But what links all the murky views is that sexuality does have a purpose or purposes, however they are to be explained, and these purposes are typically not self-evident. According to the minimalist views, sex is best understood as "plain" or "unembellished"; the murky views, on the other hand, insist that sex so understood is not understood at all.

THE PLEASURE PARADIGM. The target of many, if not most, of the minimalist accounts is the restricted reproduction of the "procreative" paradigm of sexual activity. For two thousand years, the harsher side of the Bible and the Christian theological tradition has insisted that sex is primarily, if not solely, procreative. The pleasures and desires associated with sexual activity not only are inessential but also are to be minimized. Emphasizing pleasure to the exclusion of the possibility of reproduction—for example, using contraception or engaging in activity that cannot result in impregnation—is forbidden. Essential to sexuality, in the reproductive paradigm, are male ejaculation, female receptivity, fertility, and conception.

In opposition to the reproductive model, with all of its strict prohibitions and limitations, and its suggestions of deep biological drives and purposes, the attractiveness of what we can call the pleasure paradigm is unmistakable. The availability of improved birth control methods since the 1960s has contributed greatly to its appeal. Sex is for pleasure, and what is desired is pleasure. There is nothing murky about this. Indeed, to many people it is self-evident. Accordingly, the restrictions on sexuality that limit and direct it toward heterosexual intercourse drop away, and in effect, anything that feels good is acceptable. Of course, one might well object that pleasure is not in itself sexual, and so one might want to circumscribe pleasures that are sexual from those that are not. But, for the defender of the pleasure paradigm, this requirement comes later. First comes the liberation from the restrictions of the reproductive model. Homosexuality, autosexuality, even bestiality seem to be normal on the pleasure paradigm. Heterosexual intercourse is but one of many activities serving the paradigm, and however many couples may continue to prefer it, it does not have any special claim to normality. According to this paradigm, good sex is that which provides maximum mutual pleasure; bad or mediocre sex is that which fails to satisfy either or both partners.

Once the reproduction model has been rejected, there are no longer the restrictions on either the objects or the obvious aims of sexual activity, but neither is it the case that "anything goes." Homosexuality is no longer a perversion of sex, but rape certainly will be. Almost any sexual activity between consenting adults is acceptable, but forcing sex on a person is not. Sexual activities that will not result in conception are no longer secondary, and sex that is conscientiously prevented from resulting in undesired conception becomes the norm. Masturbation becomes part of the paradigm of acceptable sexuality, even though its lacks the dimension of shared sexual enjoyment. The appeal of the paradigm and the cornerstone of most contemporary sexual ethics is the idea that sex ought to be pleasurable and, within moral but not particularly sexual bounds, unrestricted.

◆ **pleasure paradigm**
physiological and those that arise from ego complexes, satisfying hidden and forbidden desires.

See Also
Fertility Control

The Graeco-Roman legacy to Western sexual ethics holds little of the permissiveness that characterized ancient Greece.

PAGE 643

We might call the pleasure paradigm the "Freudian" model of sexuality, in order to pay homage to the person most responsible for its contemporary dominance. Sigmund Freud, in his *Three Contributions to the Theory of Sex* (1962), argued that sexuality should be conceived as enjoyable for its own sake, not as a means to further ends, whether natural or divine. But the centrality of Freud here also suggests that the pleasure paradigm may not be so simple and self-evident as we originally suggested. Freud is one of the great contemporary architects of "deep," if not labyrinthine, accounts of the psyche and of sexuality in particular. And so, for him and for us, pleasure and satisfaction are not to be construed so straightforwardly. Pleasure, as Aristotle noted more than two millennia ago, is not just a sensation. It is the "bloom" on successful activity. It accompanies but does not constitute satisfaction. But the difficult question is, Satisfaction of what? And here Freud's theory moves from an apparently minimalist physiological model to an extremely murky deep psychology.

In Freud's early theories, the pleasure paradigm rested on a male-dominated biological foundation, a "discharge" model in which sexual pleasure has its origins in the release of tension (catharsis). But the tensions released in sexual behavior are not merely physiological; they also arise from complexes of ego needs and identifications with various sexual "objects," usually (but not always) other people. Thus Freud distinguished, as we still distinguish, between mere physical gratification and "physical satisfaction."

The pleasure paradigm, for all of its seeming simplicity, invites murky interpretations. What is it that is enjoyed? What is it that is satisfied? A sensation is not pleasant in itself but in terms of its context, as a love bite on the shoulder by one's lover or a nasty passerby, respectively, makes evident. Indeed, even orgasm is not pleasant in itself, however often that might be fallaciously supposed; an orgasm in an inappropriate context is typically an extremely unpleasant experience. And so the pleasure Freud postulates is no simple release of tension but the satisfaction, often symbolic and indirect, of some of the murkiest of hidden and forbidden desires.

THE METAPHYSICAL PARADIGM. Some of these motives are so profound that they deserve to be called "metaphysical." Freud's discussion of the Oedipus complex sometimes takes on these ontological overtones, and Jung's various archetype theories surely do. But perhaps the most basic of all metaphysical paradigms of sexuality goes back (at least) to the fable told by Aristophanes in Plato's *Symposium*, and the idea that the gods split what we now call human beings out of complete wholes (with sexual desire being the desire to reunify the divided halves). One need not literally accept the more consciously absurd aspects of the story to appreciate the deep insight captured in the idea of "two out of one" or "merged selves" that Plato's Aristophanes is suggesting.

Sexual activity is an expression of a profound desire that has very little to do with merely physiological need or satisfaction, and the metaphysical paradigm is, accordingly, very much a part of the contemporary conceptions of romantic love and the idea that two people were "made for each other."

Indeed, despite the prevalence of the pleasure model in much of the current literature, there can be little doubt that much more is usually demanded of sexuality than mere pleasure, even mutual pleasure. People demand "meaningful" relationships. The metaphysical model provides this sense of "meaning." Pleasure, according to the metaphysical model, is no longer the purpose of sex, although it will surely appear as its accompaniment. But sex without love, no matter how enjoyable, is to be rejected on this paradigm. Even if it is not "perverse" or "immoral," "plain sex" will be meaningless, and the meaning of a relationship is primary for the metaphysical model.

THE COMMUNICATION PARADIGM. Sex is often "meaningful" without love, however, although sometimes those "meanings" are demeaning, as in a sadomasochistic relationship. What is one to say of the many varieties of sexual activity that are aimed neither at reproduction, nor at pure pleasure, nor at expressions of romantic love and togetherness? What of those relationships that seem to thrive on domination and pain? What does it say about our current paradigms of love that sadomasochistic relationships are now celebrated and preferred by some of our more avant-garde social visionaries? And what of those many tender encounters that, nonetheless, make no pretenses of love?

To explain such aspects of sexuality, a fourth paradigm is in order: sex as communication, as a physical form of expression of one's emotions and attitudes toward other people. It is a language, for the most part a body language, whose vocabulary consists of touches, gestures, and physical positions. It may be an expression of domination and submission; it may be an expression of respect, fear, tenderness, anger, admiration, worship, concern, or (of course) love. In the 1940s Jean-Paul Sartre defended a truncated version of this model in his classic *Being and Nothingness*. He interpreted all sexuality as the expression of conflict, a war for domination and freedom. But what is communicated in sex is rarely this alone, nor is sex plausibly always an expression of conflict. Nevertheless, Sartre forces us to see something that the defenders of the pleasure and metaphysical paradigms of sex prefer not to see: that sexual relationships, even normal, fully consensual sexual relationships, are not always innocent or loving. Sex is a medium for all sorts of emotions, some of them manipulative and even malicious.

The communication paradigm shifts the emphasis in sexuality from the more physical and sensual aspects of reproduction and pleasure to interpersonal roles and attitudes, and from expressions of love alone to expressions of all emotions and attitudes. Thus Sartre's model is clearly a communication model, but it is, like Sartre's view of emotions in general, too narrow, emphasizing only the more conflict-ridden and competitive interpersonal attitudes—one of which, he thinks, is love. In this view, certain sexual positions and activities are visibly more expressive of domination and submission, or equality and respect, or resentment and fear, or shyness and timidity. According to the communication model, these nonverbal expressions are essential to sexuality, its very purpose and content. This does not mean, however, that other sexual aspects need be excluded. The intention to impregnate a woman, for example, may be an expression of male domination and conquest, as in several of Normal Mailer's novels. Pleasure is quite obviously an important aspect of the communication model, but pleasure for its own sake is not. Pleasure—both the giving and the receiving of it, as well as the sharing of it—is vital to the communication of many emotions. But pain may be important as well, and inflicting small amounts of pain, as well as enduring moderate discomfort, is familiar as a means of expression in sex. What distinguishes the communication paradigm from the three more traditional ones is its emphasis on expression of interpersonal emotions and attitudes. These expressions are recognized by the other paradigms, but not as essential and primary.

Now it is evident that the answers to such questions as "What is normal sex?" and "What is perverse?" become immensely complicated. On a strict reproduction paradigm of sexuality, normal sex is whatever minimal genital activity is necessary to promote conception. All else is either irrelevant or immoral. In fact, of course, the reproduction paradigm is usually defended within the moral institution of marriage, and rarely defended without some reference to both love and mutual pleasure. On the pleasure paradigm, by contrast, whatever gives pleasure (to consenting adults) is normal and acceptable. Perversions of this paradigm provide pain instead of pleasure, ignore the pleasure of the other person, or produce pleasure in a manner that is, in the longer run, harmful. On the metaphysical paradigm, normality is sex as an expression of mutual meaningfulness such as mutual love. On the communication paradigm, what is normal becomes extremely complex, for one must view the emotions being expressed and the entire psyches of the people involved to make any intelligent judgment.

Human sexuality seems particularly appropriate for expressing the tender feelings of love and affection, but there are circumstances under which this is absolutely inappropriate (for example, with children); and all too often sexual activity that claims the expression of love as its aim may actually be an avoidance of intimacy. Indeed, the very context of sexual activity—two people alone, attending only to one another—is particularly conducive to intimate communication. What would be a perversion on this paradigm? Perhaps any form of deceit would be, just as lying is a "perversion" of verbal communication. And masturbation, while not exactly perverse, would surely be less than wholly sexual, just as talking to oneself is less than a whole conversation.

Conclusion: The problem of normality

So long as biological specification and sexual intercourse alone define sexuality, "normality," as opposed to "perversion," seems to be easily defined. Males are equipped with certain obvious features, and females are differently equipped with equally obvious sexual features; and "normal" sex is intercourse between male and female. But as more is learned about the complexities of chromosome configuration and the biology of sex, the distinction between male and female—although usually still clear enough—becomes increasingly difficult. And as soon as one adds the essential concerns of psychology and the many worlds of cultural norms, practices, and paradigms to the unfolding medical complications, the traditional view of "normality" becomes a Pandora's box of problems.

This confusion extends to the task of defining a "normal" model of sexuality. Of the various cases and models we have considered, not a single one would be accepted as "normal" in every society and by everyone. Moreover, a pure instance of an ideal type or paradigm is probably nowhere to be found; not even the most pious proponent of a religiously oriented reproductive view would deny the desirability of love, pleasure, and emotional expression in sex, nor would the most enthusiastic hedonist deny the desirability of reproduction on at least some occasions, and perhaps of love and communication as well. And when these four models of sexuality are integrated with the matrix of possibilities that are to be found in the various combinations of gender identity and sexual orientation (and, in the most extreme cases, transsexual biological operations), the result is an enormous number of sexual lifestyles, desires, and activities, every one of which would be insisted upon as "normal," at least according to some people.

How does one decide what is normal and what is not? In one sense, "normal" simply means "statistically predominant," and there are still many people who would insist that this is a proper definition. But it is clear that, in ethical contexts, "normal" also means

Protestant sexual ethics continues to struggle with issues of gendered hierarchy in the family and with "alternative lifestyles."

PAGE 648

Social theories of the body examine the interrelationships between social orders and the bodies within their jurisdiction.

PAGE 85

morally "correct." But in an area where most behavior is private, and involves only consenting adults and a great many individual differences, the relevance of statistics is easily challenged. Furthermore, what is statistically predominant in one portion of a population may be relatively rare and considered "perverted" in another. If sexual normality includes subjective preferences and psychological as well as biological considerations, then any definition of sexual normality will give priority to certain preferences and paradigms over others. But which ones? The traditional religious standards? The more modern "anything goes between consenting adults" attitude? The current "local standards" criterion of the courts, which assumes that it can be made clear how large or small a domain—a home, a town, or a state—is "local"?

The problem of normality thus becomes a dilemma. It begins with a built-in ambiguity between the statistically dominant and what ethically ought to be. The first is ascertained easily enough, assuming either truthful informants or extremely intrusive investigators; but the second, the quest for a sexual ethics, arises from within diverse psychological, cultural, and personal settings that presuppose many of the norms and attitudes that are to be investigated.

The result of these complexities should not be the abandonment of a search for ethical norms or the rejection of the concepts of normality and perversion. What emerges instead is an extremely complex matrix of considerations to be taken into account, in which tolerance is a wise approach and mutual understanding is the desirable outcome. In other words, what is needed in the examination of sexual identity is not just a good deal of medicine, biology, social psychology, and anthropology. It is also a good deal of appreciation for diversity and complexity. It is with this appreciation for diversity and complexity that the contemporary quest can proceed.

— ROBERT C. SOLOMON
LINDA J. NICHOLSON

SEXUALITY IN SOCIETY

SOCIAL CONTROL OF SEXUAL BEHAVIOR

The twentieth century has witnessed an explosion of knowledge about the physiology, psychology, and sociology of human sexuality, thanks to the revolution in public acceptability of discourse about sexual conduct and the freeing of scholarly interest that followed the pathbreaking works published in the late Victorian era by Richard von Krafft-Ebing (1886), Havelock Ellis (1901), and Sigmund Freud (1955a, 1955b). However, controversy still rages over the basic issue of how sexual behavior is molded, encouraged, and discouraged by social customs and practices. Are males naturally more aggressive in seeking sexual contact than females, or is this a product of social patriarchy? Is homosexuality caused primarily by biological factors, or is it largely caused by social experiences during formative stages of the child's development? Is cultural permissiveness responsible for the dramatic increase in reports of sexual harassment and abuse, or are changing mores encouraging victims to name parents, doctors, and priests who were in the past able to hide their misconduct under a cloak of respectability?

The answers to these questions are not only empirical, they are also ethical and political. Our allegedly scientific beliefs about the "naturalness" of certain sexual acts often reflect unacknowledged cultural biases, and our thoughts and theories affect the behavior they label, characterize, and implicitly valorize or demean. As feminists, and historians such as Michel Foucault (1990), have pointed out, the neutral scientific language of medicine is no guarantor of the moral innocuousness of theories about gender and sexual behavior; to the contrary, claims of scientific objectivity about these topics are apt to be all the more dangerous morally for pretending to be value-free.

Theories of sexual behavior cannot avoid assumptions about power and domination that too frequently perpetuate injustices. Thus, Alfred Kinsey's claim that males are naturally more aggressive in initiating sex (Kinsey et al., 1948) is not merely the objective scientific statement it purports to be, but a statement that supports the power of men over women in society. Anyone who is concerned about power and justice needs continually to scrutinize and critique so-called scientific claims about human sexuality by attending to how they perpetuate social stereotypes that are not universal and, by assigning more value to the experiences of certain people (e.g., white heterosexual males), help to empower some and disempower others. One would expect social ethicists to be sensitized to these issues, but the most influential recent theorists of justice (e.g., John Rawls, Ronald Dworkin, Robert Nozick, Michael Walzer) scarcely even mention gender justice, much less consider sexual roles a central matter for ethical scrutiny (see Okin, 1989). One reason for this neglect is the traditional public/private dichotomy that assigns sexual behavior to a private arena outside the concerns of the social theorist. Employment of this dichotomy in the past to keep cases of domestic rape and child abuse out of American courts, on the grounds that they occur within a zone of privacy protected from public scrutiny, shows that it is scarcely an ethically neutral matter for a social scientist to point out how our sexual

See Also

Bodies and the Social Order: Thou Shalt/Thou Shalt Not

SOCIAL CONSTRUCTIONISTS
"Phallic" Fallacies?

According to social constructionists, sexual behavior and gender roles are products of a specific history, culture, and set of social institutions. Emile Durkheim succinctly expressed the constructionist emphasis on the primacy of culture over biology when he argued, at the end of the nineteenth century, that if an adolescent did not have cultural concepts to identify sexual desires, he or she might feel a vague urge but not know what it was, much less how to act on it (Durkheim, 1933; Wallwork, 1972, 1984). A second main feature of the social constructionist approach involves situating sexual role behavior within the prevailing economic and political system, with its male-dominated hierarchies of status and power. The constructionist perspective encourages exploration of the ways in which widespread cultural beliefs about sexual behavior (and the research projects they inspire) serve to perpetuate a patriarchal vision of human nature, social institutions, gender, and sex roles. Constructionists note with concern that the focus in research has more often than not been on the male sexual experience; Masters and Johnson's research, for example, limits sexuality to genitally oriented orgasm (Masters and Johnson, 1966). Feminist critics Alice Rossi (1973) and Leonore Tiefer (1978) complain that research focusing on genital physiology as the standard of sexual involvement evidences a "phallic fallacy" that implicitly devalues the pregenital or nongenital sexual experiences of women, such as the emotionally intense erotic feelings associated with looking at the beloved or anticipating a reunion with him or her.

— ERNEST WALLWORK

lives are influenced by a social ethos that makes such distinctions.

Essentialism and constructionism

Theories about human sexual behavior in its social context range along a continuum stretching from essentialism (or naturalism), on the one hand, to social construction theory, on the other. Essentialism attributes certain sexual and gender behaviors to the unchanging nature of the human species. What is "natural" is "good"; what is social is "artificial" and tends to be "bad" insofar as it inhibits realization of the "proper" natural end of sexual conduct, be it erotic pleasure or procreation. Thomistic natural-law theory is explicitly essentialist in identifying procreation as the "natural" end of human sexuality, but modern sexologists assume essentialism in contending that a wide variety of pleasurable erotic acts are no less "natural" than heterosexual intercourse. Alfred Kinsey, for example, uses an essentialist argument when he draws on the sexual behavior of other mammals, "primitive" cultures, and human physiological capacities to contend that masturbation and homosexual acts are "natural" expressions of sexuality and, hence, irrationally condemned and punished by society. Kinsey also employs essentialist arguments, citing mammalian data, in support of such dubious contentions as that male extramartial coitus is more natural than female extramarital coitus (Kinsey et al., 1953; Irvine, 1990). William Masters and Virginia Johnson (1966) assume essentialism in viewing sex exclusively in terms of physiological responses, unencumbered by social and psychological factors. It is not an issue for Masters and Johnson that the socialization of Western women has discouraged female sexuality; rather the woman's naturally superior sexual responsiveness to the male, as evidenced by her capacity for multiple orgasms, is what counts for them (Irvine, 1990). What is missing in the sexologist's essentialist view of culture as an impediment is any acknowledgement of the multiple ways cultures give meaning to sexual behaviors and structure sexual and gender relationships beyond physiological responses.

The obvious strength of social constructionist theory is that it is able to account for the considerable diversity of sexual behavior and the meanings associated with such behavior cross-culturally, and to link these meanings to other role relationships. The power of society to mold human sexuality is evident in how nonerotic body parts—for example, crushed feet among the Chinese of a former era, the naked foot and even shoes in medieval Europe, and hair—have been eroticized by different peoples at different times (Stoller, 1991). The power of social custom is also obvious when one contrasts the negative conception of homosexuality in the Judaeo-Christian West with its positive evaluation among Melanesian societies and certain African tribes. Among the Sambia in the New Guinea highlands, boys from prepuberty to their midteens are expected to engage in oral-genital sexuality with the older teenage males with whom they live as a prerequisite to becoming heterosexual adult males (Herdt and Stoller, 1990). Because Sambians believe semen is essential for males to grow and mature physically, the ingestion of semen is deemed essential to becoming an adult heterosexual male and to fathering children.

Even within the same society, there are fads and

"The sexual revolution went too far, informationwise. When you find phrases like 'suck face' as a euphemism for 'kiss' it sort of takes the zing out of intimate personal contact."

IAN SHOALES
IN THE PORTABLE CURMUDGEON, 1987

In some professions, the taboo against sexual relations with clients is not talked about, "the problem with no name."

PAGE 653

fashions of sexual behavior. For instance, since the 1960s there has been a dramatic increase in oral-genital behavior in the United States (Janus and Janus, 1993; Walsh, 1989). Among contemporary males in the West, premature ejaculation is defined as a dysfunction for which medical treatment is often sought; but in many developing countries males are expected to reach orgasms quickly (in fifteen to twenty seconds in the East Bay society in Melanesia) and those who take a "long time" are ridiculed (Reiss, 1989).

But it would be a mistake to assume, from the considerable evidence for the importance of the elaborate cultural ideas, stimulants, and norms that surround the biologically limited range of sexual behaviors of which the human body is capable, that social constructionists are winning the battle with essentialists. In fact, the nature-nurture pendulum, which has swung back and forth several times already in the twentieth century, has been swinging back again toward the nature pole as the century ends. During the 1980s and 1990s, biological explanations have been on the ascendancy in many scientific circles. Sociobiologists challenge the constructionist assumption that most sexual behavior is determined by culture, arguing instead that certain basic mammalian and primate traits that lie beneath the social surface determine the configuration of human sexual behavior (Wilson, 1975). At the same time, the biologizing of psychology is well under way, as physiological models and research strategies are held to offer the best route to understanding traditional subjects of psychological inquiry such as mental illness and sexual preference.

Interactionist model

The most plausible position on the essentialism-constructionism debate would appear to be that the biological factors in sexual desire, such as genes and hormones, do not act alone but instead interact with environmental factors, such as visual or auditory erotic stimuli, the significance of which depends in turn upon the individual's subjective erotic sensitivities, identities, fantasies, cognitive schemata, and behavioral patterns. These subjective factors, which lead some people to be excited by depictions of sadomasochistic acts and others not, are themselves influenced by the way a unique individual with certain inherited strengths and vulnerabilities interacts with significant others and specific sociocultural environments during the various psychosexual, ego-social, and cognitive stages of development. Biological factors certainly play a role; for example, testosterone appears to influence the intensity of sexual desire. But biological factors do not invariably cause sexual motives or behavior, for testosterone is itself highly responsive to environmental stimuli. Nurture, psychological development, subjective fantasies and beliefs, erotic stimuli, moral and aesthetic standards, social roles and expectations, and ego strengths and weaknesses all mold the range of the individual's sexual potentialities in certain directions rather than others. This molding is clear from the inability of biologists and sociobiologists, who study determinants that have operated within the species for thousands of years, to explain changes in sexual customs within a single generation or variations in sexual customs that occur in the same gender cross-culturally. Unfortunately, we do not yet possess a theoretical model sufficiently complex and nuanced to integrate and assign proper weight to all the multiple factors, including the individual's self-control, that influence human sexual behavior. The sociological point of view adopted here, which falls at the constructivist end of the essentialism-constructionism continuum, remains one among several plausible selective perspectives on social control of sexual behavior. Others are history, anthropology, ethnography, psychoanalysis, and social psychology.

Social control requirements

Sexual behavior, defined broadly as any action or reaction involving erotic arousal or genital responses, is viewed by most sociologists as sufficiently problematic to require some degree of social control. One explanation often proffered for this social-control requirement, whether as controlled permission or regulated prohibition, is that at some point in the distant past human beings lost the preformed automatic sexual instincts of the lower animals—that is, the sexual control that is in nature—and came to depend upon culture and social institutions to guide the varied reproductive and nonreproductive behaviors that are considered sexual. The loss of preformed instinctual patterns of sexual behavior, by freeing human beings from the comparatively rigid behavior patterns of other animals, helped to create the great adaptability of the human species to its changing environment. It is also meant, with the human female's loss of the periodic estrus of other mammals, that the human female and male were potentially capable of sex at any time. Sexual motives came to pervade virtually all aspects of human life in a way that is uniquely characteristic of the species. At the same time, because the sexual drive differs from instinctual needs like respiration, thirst, and hunger, which must be gratified for the individual organism's survival, sexual desire was modified by subtle psychological and social influences.

The transmission of family and communal property, prestige, and power is another crucial consequence of sexual liaisons that societies attempt to handle by means of legalized sexual union in marriage and the begetting of "legitimate children." Any dramatic increase in the number of illegitimate children and

SOCIAL CONTROL
Sex as "Powder-Keg"

Social control of sexual behavior has been necessitated in all social units—from the family to the clan, tribe, local community, and state—in part by the serious threats to social stability and maintenance of group life over time created by the potential for sex on demand all the year round. One such threat is incest, which is inimical to the group's evolutionary survival as well as to the psychological well-being and functioning of those who might be victimized by it. Another serious social consequence of sex on demand is the likelihood of children, which every society has a stake in limiting; assigning to families peacefully; and raising, educating, and training to be law-abiding, productive contributors. Still another consequence of sexual behavior that has required its social control is its potential for either reinforcing or disrupting existing roles and status hierarchies by creating strong new social bonds. Any rape or seduction of young girls or boys, or any adulterous relation, is liable to spark violence or some other disruption of the existing social order.

— ERNEST WALLWORK

abandoned wives strains the system of distributing limited economic resources, shifting some of the burden from the family onto the rest of the community. The perpetuation of a society's religious ideals, moral norms, and laws is also intertwined with the monitoring of sexual conduct, since the way sexual conduct is controlled is often paradigmatic of the way the society expects individuals to pursue other moral and spiritual goals (Stone, 1985). The well-known sexual asceticism of the Puritan, for instance, was only one part of a lifestyle that affected every aspect of the Puritan's life, just as the idealization of female virginity affects every aspect of the life of the traditional Southern Italian villager (Parsons, 1969).

IDEALS AND TABOOS. Social control of sexual behavior is exercised most obviously by widely shared, explicit ideals of sexual behavior that form the basis for taboos against inappropriate conduct. Taboos are backed by social punishments ranging from mild disapproval and loss of status to ostracism, imprisonment, and death. Within Judaism and Christianity, the standard-of-standards has been heterosexual intercourse in the context of marriage. Accordingly, masturbation, homosexuality, and extramarital sexuality have been condemned and often severely punished. Among the Greeks during the classical period, pederasty was idealized as the purest form of love, but it was also hedged about by rigid taboos. The relationship was limited to an older free man and a pubescent free boy. Oral and anal intercourse were unacceptable, and if a boy allowed himself to be penetrated anally, he lost his rights to citizenship. For the Greek male, what was important was not whether one's partner was male or female, but whether one was dominant or submissive.

SOCIAL ROLES. In addition to the values and norms shared throughout a culture, social control is also maintained by the basic institutions of society, especially the family, religion, schools, medicine, and law. An institution is defined sociologically as a stable cluster of values, norms, statuses, and roles that develop around a basic need of society. An important function of an institution is to socialize developing individuals through inculcation of social roles, which are social actions that take account of social expectations. A person's role is not simply what he or she habitually does (for this may not be socially significant), nor even what he or she is expected to do, if an expectation is only what one might predict from past actions. The role is what is expected of him or her, in the sense of what is approved or required, by, say, fashion, tradition, charismatic authority, or standards of rationality.

Gender roles, which indicate how males and females are expected to behave, significantly influence sexual behavior. In Western culture, the expectation has been that the woman is more passive and receptive, and more attuned to emotional connections, than the male, who is expected to be more aggressive, autonomous, and focused on power. Such gender roles have an effect on sexual conduct, independent of explicit sexual standards. For example, rape is strongly disapproved of in contemporary culture, yet date rape is disturbingly frequent, in part because males are socialized to dominate women in most social situations involving power. Hence, if a male's charm and powers of psychological persuasion fail in a sexual situation, coercion remains as a last resort. Here, as in most sexual acts, erotic desire is only one of several motivations that enter into the behavior. In addition, the need to maintain the male-dominant role identity and the propensity for males in Western societies to turn anger at frustration into aggression and violence are equally powerful motives.

Recently, sociologists have applied "script theory" to sexual behavior in order to account for the more specific patterns that enable participants to make reasonably good guesses about the sequence of events probable in an otherwise loosely structured social situation (Gagnon and Simon, 1973; McKinney and Sprecher, 1989). Scripts are mental schemas that enable partici-

Laws have been enacted making it a felony for therapists or clergy to have sexual contact with a client.

PAGE 653

See Also

Rape: Too Often, the First in a Series of Offenses

pants to jointly structure the interaction so that uncertainty is systematically reduced and cooperation enhanced. Sexual scripts enable participants to decode novel situations by reading the meaning of certain actions and to organize the situation into sequences of specifically sexual interactions (e.g., nonverbal courtship behaviors signaling availability like smiling, gazing, hair flipping, the "opening line," leaning close, and the proverbial invitation to see one's etchings). However, research on conflicts between the sexes in dating and marriage also shows that scripting is far from perfect, that the sexes often miscue each other or are dissatisfied in predictable ways—say, with the male's excessive sexual demands or emotional constriction, or the woman's unresponsiveness or moodiness.

Empirical beliefs—especially medically sanctioned ones—about the consequences for the individual's health of various sexual practices also play a significant role in the social control of sexual behavior. In classical Greece, for example, physicians recommended sexual moderation to prevent the excessive loss of life force in the too-frequent ejaculation of semen. In ancient China, somewhat similar beliefs about the consequences of excessive semen loss led to the cultivation of special techniques of intercourse without ejaculation in order to conserve the *yang* (the positive, light masculine principle whose interaction with *yin*—the negative, dark feminine principle—was believed to influence the destiny of creatures and things). And, of course, doctors within the Judaeo-Christian milieu have for millenia warned that masturbation would bring about some dreaded disease, disfigurement, or insanity. In our own time, fear of AIDS has dramatically changed sexual behavior, primarily by altering beliefs about the risks of unprotected sexual intercourse. It is one of Foucault's main contentions that medical beliefs, precisely because they are so important to patients, provide physicians with power that historically has often been used to dominate and control unjustly (Foucault, 1990).

◆ **social control**
controlled permission or regulated prohibition of behaviors, with desire, for example, modified by psychological and social influences.

It is easy to be impressed by the ideals, moral rules, and prudential teachings that are set forth so impressively in explicit doctrine by leading social authorities. But these action guides are not always reinforced by other cultures or even by other institutions in the same cultural context. Complex societies are not systematic cultural ensembles, despite the beliefs of sociological functionalists like Emile Durkheim and Talcott Parsons. Illicit sexual cultures—like red-light districts or the houses of prostitution that flourished in medieval Europe (Ariès and Bejin, 1985)—exist side by side with licit sexual cultures, counterbalancing and correcting excessive asceticism, and on some points canceling out the influence of the licit culture. A complex interrelationship often exists between these cultures, so there is often plenty of room for compromises and loopholes. Moreover, the different social-status groups and classes of the same society usually have different sexual cultures. For example, libertine elites, concentrated around courts (as in ancient Egypt, classical Greece and Rome, imperial China, India, and Japan) have surrounded themselves with a rich panoply of erotic art, pornographic literature, artificial physical stimuli, toys, and partners not encouraged among lower social ranks (Stone, 1985).

Control and permissiveness

The so-called sexual revolution that occurred in the post-World War II epoch is sometimes viewed—erroneously—as releasing the individual from the constraining pressures of social control. But the new permissiveness is more accurately perceived as substituting new and, in some instances, somewhat different social standards, controls, and permissions for older ones. The most important contemporary cultural standards focus less on the legitimation of sex by marriage and more on the goods of sensual pleasure, intimacy, the autonomy of the parties (violated in the case of rape and harassment), and the basic equality of partners. Some salient features of the sexual revolution are the greater explicit public acknowledgment of sexuality (for example, in films, "soap operas," talk shows, and advice columns); the availability of cheap and reliable contraception, particularly birth control pills, which have for the first time in history released women from the fear of unwanted pregnancies; the increased availability of erotic stimulants (e.g., adult magazines, pornographic videos, computer networks); the rise of feminism and correlative decline in social inequality between the sexes; the increased acceptance or tolerance of sexual behaviors that were formerly disapproved, like masturbation, homosexuality, extramarital sexual affairs, and oral-genital sex; and the dramatic increase in teenage sexual conduct and at younger ages. There has also emerged in recent years a "recreational ideology," which holds that the purpose of sexual activity is not procreation or even mutual affection, but physical pleasure.

Although these changes reflect a certain permissiveness, there is evidence that men and women today have higher expectations, demands, and worries about their sexual performance (McKinney and Sprecher, 1989; Janus and Janus, 1993). The liberating views of sexologists have brought in their train new demands for mutual orgasm and standards of erotic performance that not all couples are capable of realizing at all times. Rising concern about date rape on university campuses in the United States is giving rise to explicit policies, sometimes accompanied by detailed lists of "do's" and "don'ts," designed to make sure there is willing and ver-

See Also

A Contemporary Critique: Social Theories of the Body

bal consent to each individual sexual act, for example, kissing, fondling of breasts, touching of genitals, intercourse. New policies, grievance procedures, and punishments are proliferating to prevent and punish sexual harassment and rape (Gross, 1993).

The permissiveness associated with the sexual revolution also coexists with the continuation of strong cultural constraints on frank interpersonal communication about sexual behavior that has disturbing implications for preventing unwanted pregnancies and venereal diseases and for containment of the AIDS epidemic. Western society has a long history of prudishness about sexual topics that stretches back several millennia into the biblical period, when writers of the Hebrew Bible and Christian New Testament used euphemisms like "flesh," "loin," "thigh," "side," and "feet" (for penis), "lewdness" (for female genitals), and "one flesh" (for intercourse) in lieu of explicit sexual terms (Baab, 1962). Despite the new sexual permissiveness, and research showing that, for example, 20 percent of the American female population have had coitus by age 15 (Hayes, 1987) and that 59 percent of secondary school students have had sexual intercourse (Kann et al., 1991), parents continue to find it difficult to talk with their children in a knowledgeable way about sexual behavior. In a 1987 national survey, 69 percent of adult Americans viewed premarital coitus as "always wrong" for fourteen- to sixteen-year-olds (Davis and Smith, 1987). Research suggests that many adolescents perceive their parents as not very well informed about sex and as negative, rigid, and conservative in their attitudes toward sexuality (Metts and Cupach, 1989). Although adolescents tell researchers they would like to learn more about sex from their parents, their perceptions as well as the reported attitudes of many parents discourage open communication.

The difficulty parents have communicating information about sex is also found among many professionals charged with conveying information about sex to children, such as schoolteachers, clergy, and physicians. Research shows that adolescents learn most of their information about sexuality, such as petting and sexual intercourse, from same-sex peers, who are often ill-informed about contraception or the prevention of sexually transmitted diseases. However, some studies indicate that some sexuality education programs are able to convey factual information about anatomical and physiological aspects of sexuality, and to influence understanding of the risks of sexual behaviors (Orbuch, 1989; Metts and Cupach, 1989). Unfortunately, most teenagers remain unprepared for their first sexual encounters. Much remains to be done in communicating information about how to avoid unwanted pregnancies and infection by the human immunodeficiency virus (HIV) that causes AIDS.

Constraints on open discussion of sexual desires and practices is one factor in the high rape rates. Research shows that young men remain reluctant to declare their desire for sexual intercourse to a new date, while young women are less than open about their reluctance. Discussion of contraceptive measures is apparently still difficult for couples who have not had coitus, despite the threat of AIDS (Reiss, 1989). The culture of sexual permissiveness is thus riddled with constraints on forthright discussion of choosing among alternative sexual options. To help counter these constraints, health-care professions need improved educational programs on human sexuality, more training in public health, and opportunities to cultivate skills of communicating with patients as knowledgeable allies and responsible agents, not as passive recipients of authoritative information and advice.

A peculiar problem with many attempts to control sexual behavior is that the constraints and repressions designed to foster licit or safe sex often themselves contribute to the flourishing of illicit or unsafe sexual behavior, which becomes all the more alluring, exciting, and frequent precisely because it is prohibited. The firmest social controls of sexual behavior appear to be those that acknowledge the unique value of sexual desires, fantasies, and actions in human life in a spirit of tolerance toward nonharmful illicit wishes and behaviors, even as actual conduct is directed toward goals that are compatible with the best interests of the individuals involved and the groups of which they are a part.

— ERNEST WALLWORK

LEGAL APPROACHES TO SEXUALITY

This article discusses law's relationship to sexuality from an explicitly American perspective, although the framework suggested here may lend itself to application in other cultural contexts.

Sexual status and sexual conduct

From the point of view of American law, sexuality has two dimensions: status and conduct. Sexuality as status, in law as in the culture at large, contains two primary alternatives—heterosexuality and homosexuality—although recent efforts on the part of those claiming bisexual status to make political alliance with gay and lesbian activists may presage increased legal recognition of this third alternative. Law's affirmative involvement with issues of sexual status consists chiefly of the grant of the marriage license to heterosexual unions aspiring to some permanence, and the denial of that license to

◆ **repression**
a defense mechanism, operating unconsciously, that banishes unacceptable ideas, affects, or impulses from consciousness or that keeps out of consciousness what has never been conscious.

See Also
Law and Morality

same-sex unions with the same aspiration. Less actively, but with greater impact on the lives of homosexual people, law has largely declined to recognize differential treatment on the basis of sexual orientation as a form of prohibited discrimination (Mohr, 1988).

Sexuality as conduct also has two principle aspects. The first encompasses explicitly sexual acts, of which intercourse is perhaps the paradigmatic example. Law prohibits intercourse, and sometimes other sexual activity, in a wide variety of situations, either where one of the parties has not consented or is deemed unable to consent, or where the intercourse or other activity, although consensual, is deemed to offend norms of public decency or order. Child sexual abuse, sexual assault and rape, statutory rape (intercourse with a woman, or in a few states with an individual, who is considered too young to provide meaningful assent), and incest are uniformly prohibited. Traditionally, a woman in the marriage relationship was, by law, sexually available at all times to her spouse. Since the 1970s, however, these laws have changed in many states and wives have legally charged husbands with rape. Prostitution—the buying and selling of sex—is authorized only in Nevada. Sodomy, both homosexual and heterosexual, is unlawful in a large minority of states. Sex before marriage and outside of marriage is still prohibited in some states, although enforcement of these prohibitions is virtually nonexistent because of the mismatch between the law and prevailing cultural practices and attitudes.

Another way in which law regulates sexual intercourse is by controlling or limiting the choices available to men and women before and after intercourse. The extent to which a state can limit access to abortion consistent with the mandates of federal and state constitutions has been a hotly contested issue, as the Supreme Court's decision in *Planned Parenthood of Southeastern Pennsylvania* v. *Casey* (1992) amply illustrates. The use of contraception by adults remains constitutionally protected, yet access to particular contraceptive techniques remains subject to regulation on health grounds, in a cultural context in which health concerns have frequently provided a pretext for political intervention. President Bill Clinton's reversal in 1993 of the Bush administration's opposition to the introduction of RU-486, a "morning-after pill" and early abortifacient, provides a dramatic example of this interplay between policies and medicine. Unsuccessful battles to introduce contraceptives into the nation's high schools are reminders that contraceptive freedom does not generally extend to minors, despite everything known about their active sexuality and their exposure to sexually transmitted diseases (Miller et al., 1990).

◆ **paraphilias**
sexual deviations in which unusual or bizarre imagery or acts are necessary for sexual excitement.

In other contexts, law precludes procreation as a consequence of intercourse. The eugenics movement in the United States in the 1920s and 1930s produced laws compelling the sterilization of certain classes of criminals and those with mental disabilities or illness. These laws remain on the books in several states, and have never been deemed flatly unconstitutional, although they are no longer enforced. In the contemporary context, most if not all states provide a mechanism by which those legally responsible for sexually active people determined to be mentally incompetent can petition the state to authorize sterilization or contraception.

The second aspect of sexuality as conduct encompasses sexual displays the law views as expressing or arousing sexual receptivity or interest, and thereby offending norms of public decency or order. The sexual displays regulated by law are varied in character; they include solicitation, public nudity, and provocative dressing (toplessness for women) and cross-dressing (transvestism for men), as well as all forms of pornography. In this arena, too, enforcement is by no means uniform, and constitutional freedoms of speech and expression have created uncertainty even about the legitimacy of regulation.

Law's multiple relationships to legal status and conduct

Law's relationship to sexuality is in part constituted by law's account of what in the sexual arena is permissible and what is prohibited, which behaviors are to be encouraged and which are to be discouraged. Statutes passed by legislatures establish guidelines for behavior and award privileges to those who comply or assess penalties against those who do not. Under the auspices of statutes, regulators promulgate implementing regulations. Judges determine the constitutionality of statutory law and the validity of regulation; they apply the language of statutes and regulations to particular individuals and circumstances, and they preside over the development and application of specific bodies of judge-made law. Thus, state criminal statutes have frequently made sodomy a crime, and the U.S. Supreme Court determined, in 1986, that these statutes violated no constitutional mandate (*Bowers* v. *Hardwick*, 1986).

States have traditionally controlled the provision of abortion through both statute and regulation, and the Supreme Court continues to decide, in a high-profile series of cases, which restrictions violate women's privacy or liberty interests (Dworkin, 1993). In the absence of statutes permitting the marriage of same-sex partners, the judge-made law of contract is occasionally invoked to regulate the distribution of assets upon dissolution of a gay or lesbian union. Judges may decline to make this body of law available to a nontraditional union in the same way that they routinely decline to enforce contracts of prostitution.

See Also

Law Abortion: The Implications of Abortion Law

This relationship between law and sexuality is importantly shaped, however, by the fact that law's authority is actually invoked in sexual matters by public agencies or private parties in only a small fraction of the cases in which it might be. The gap between the law as announced and as invoked has a variety of origins.

Sometimes those who might initiate action against a violator do not know that the law offers them protection. For example, when Justice Clarence Thomas's nomination to the Supreme Court was threatened by the charge that he had harassed Professor Anita Hill while she was a young employee working under his supervision, the legal norms governing sexual conduct in the workplace received massive publicity. Sexual-harassment claims by female employees increased sharply in the months that followed.

Sometimes the enforcement of legal norms governing behavior that tends to be very private is simply impractical; sodomy, unlike public nudity, seldom comes to the attention of law-enforcement personnel. The norm serves, therefore, not as a general prohibition but as a tool in the arsenal of law-enforcement authorities wishing to target a particular individual or couple for enforcement action, a troublesome use of prosecutorial discretion. Sometimes police and prosecutors make conscious decisions not to investigate or prosecute certain offenses. This decision may be because investigation will be difficult or costly and the success of prosecution uncertain. It may be because the offenses in question constitute low priorities or particular victims belong to groups whose protection is a low priority. For example, prostitutes have not often been successful rape claimants, while "virtuous" white women raped by black strangers are the most favored rape complainants (Estrich, 1987). It may be because crimes have been left on the statute books long after public sentiment has changed. (Laws against adultery and premarital sexual contact have this character.) Or it may be because those charged with enforcement are dubious of the wisdom of the regulation or of its application to a particular situation. Many rape prosecutions, especially those involving parties who are not strangers, founder for one or more of these reasons. Those who have argued that specific victims of pornography should be allowed to bring civil actions against pornographers and distributors of pornography base their argument, in part, on the reluctance of public authorities to take appropriate action (MacKinnon, 1987).

Those who urge giving private parties greater responsibility for or authority to initiate legal action must also confront the reality that individuals are often unwilling or unable to invoke the law even when they understand that a legal norm has been violated. For

THOMAS VS. HILL
A Public Wake-up Call

If law's relationship to sexuality is influenced by the limited nature of actual legal interventions in sexual matters, it is just as crucially influenced by limited public understanding of the legal norms governing sexuality. How social actors perceive law's application to their own or others' sexual status or conduct may derive from actual individual or institutional knowledge of the law or of enforcement practices; but it may equally derive from impressions gleaned from a limited number of personal experiences or from stories emphasized by the media. Generalizations, often derived from limited information, then guide an individual's interaction with the legal system around sexual matters—setting standards for personal conduct, governing expectations about how the system will respond to legal violations, and providing the initiative for involvement in political efforts to change the law or replace its agents.

The national experience surrounding the charges that Clarence Thomas had sexually harassed Anita Hill illustrates this dynamic. The many interviews and polls conducted by the press demonstrated that public understanding of the law of sexual harassment was extremely limited prior to the publicity surrounding Thomas's confirmation hearings. In particular, many men expressed great surprise that behavior they had considered normal, playful, flattering, or flirtatious might be considered unlawful if addressed to a woman co-worker. In reaction, they interpreted the law as more draconian and restrictive than the history of its application warranted. This response led them to articulate a new code of conduct for themselves going well beyond any legal requirement, and at the same time to express the conviction that the law was unrealistic if not ridiculous.

Given this multilayered relationship between law and sexuality, it is as important to appreciate what law does not do as what it does, as important to know how laws are implemented as to know what they say, and as important to know what people think the law is as to know how it might be interpreted by some authoritative source.

— CLARE DALTON

Abelard and John Damascene maintained that concupiscence does not make sexual pleasure evil in itself.

PAGE 646

In ancient Greece, male human nature was generally assumed to be bisexual, and the polyerotic needs of men were taken for granted.

PAGE 642

The Pythagoreans advocated purity of the body for the sake of cultivating the soul.

PAGE 643

example, the trauma of childhood sexual abuse often results in the repression of memory (Ernsdorff and Loftus, 1993). If the memory ever surfaces, it may be long after the time for bringing legal action has passed. Potential claimants may be fearful of retribution on the part of the one they accuse; this is often true for sexual-harassment claimants and battered women who charge their abusers with physical and sexual violence. They may be anxious about the costs, both financial and emotional, involved in being a complaining witness or a plaintiff. They may fear having their credibility challenged or their character impugned, and may see participation in the legal system as just another opportunity to be victimized; many sexual-harassment and rape victims articulate this concern. Finally, claimants in some circumstances may be able to resolve the situation without recourse to the formal mechanisms offered by the legal system.

Victorian and modern visions of sexuality

In addressing issues of sexual status and performance, the contemporary legal system incorporates and reflects two very different visions of social and family life. Still influential is the vision we associate with the Victorian era. This vision incorporates an explicitly patriarchal family and social structure in which the interests of women and children are subordinated in culture and law to those of men, while women's value in the domestic sphere is emphasized and their opportunities outside that sphere are narrowly circumscribed. It also incorporates a sexually repressive culture in which sexual expression and practice is tightly controlled in law and in public while deviancy flourishes in private. The contrasting "modern" vision aspires to an egalitarian family and social structure that radically augments the rights of women and children both inside and outside the home, and to a culture of sexual tolerance and openness (Grossberg, 1985; Okin, 1989; Thorne and Yalom, 1992).

While there is no question that the law has gradually incorporated elements of the modern vision, an open struggle between the two visions continues within the legal system, as it does in the culture at large. For example, until the last quarter of the nineteenth century most states permitted a husband to use physical discipline to "chastise" his wife, and guaranteed him sexual access to her at all times. By the end of the century, wife abuse was no longer tolerated by the criminal law, and yet most states continued to grant husbands immunity from civil suit by their injured wives in the interests of domestic "harmony" and the privacy of family life. The right of sexual access, however, remained unimpaired, and the criminal justice system largely ignored wife abuse, refusing to arrest or prosecute batterers. Only in the 1970s, in the wake of the battered-women's movement, did the enforcement picture begin to change and marital rape immunities begin to erode. Many men and women, however, continue to believe that a marriage license takes away a woman's right to say no to sexual intercourse.

For many people the struggle between the two visions of social and family life is an attempt to find an appropriate balance. In the area of abortion, spousal and parental notification rules provide an example. In *Planned Parenthood* v. *Casey*, the one state regulation struck down as imposing an undue burden on women's exercise of their abortion rights was that requiring not spousal consent, but spousal notification (*Planned Parenthood*, 1992). The justices were explicit that the specter of an abusive and controlling husband doing violence to his pregnant wife drove this decision. On the other hand, parental notification and consent rules have been routinely upheld for minors, with only very narrow judicial bypass provisions for cases in which a young woman can justify to a judge both her capacity to make a mature decision and the need to withhold information from a parent. As a culture, we continue to support significant parental control over children, while we are much less tolerant of the idea that a husband should wield authority over his wife.

For some, particularly those conservatives influenced by religious fundamentalism, the struggle is largely to restore a Victorian vision of family and social life. Those who oppose abortion on this basis also frequently oppose contraception, believe that intercourse should be linked to procreation, and endorse a traditional division of family labor in which the woman attends to the home and the children, while the man is the principal breadwinner. While this constituency may be heartened by the erosion of women's freedom with respect to abortion since *Roe* v. *Wade* (1973), and by the Supreme Court's willingness to condemn consensual homosexual intercourse as a deviant social practice in *Bowers* v. *Hardwick* (1986), the legal system otherwise provides diminishing support for conservative family ideology.

The tools of regulation

In situating itself with respect to sexuality, and in generating the specifics of regulation, the legal system draws on a variety of sources of cultural authority and deploys a variety of principles and policies. Sometimes the shift from the Victorian to the modern vision has involved reliance on new or different principles and policies, or the invocation of new sources of cultural authority and a frontal attack on the old. On other occasions, the very same principles and policies invoked to support the Victorian vision have proved adaptable enough to support the modern vision, when applied in new and different contexts. On many occasions, the same sources of cultural authority invoked by law in support of the Victorian vision have themselves abandoned or modified that support and now offer the law new support for the modern vision.

The two principal external sources of authority guiding legal regulation of sexuality have been morality and medical science. Morals derive either from secular ethical precepts or from religion, but the role of religion is complicated by the religious diversity within U.S. society and by the fact that its constitutional order insists on the separation of church and state. However, when moral precepts, even those rooted historically in specific religious traditions, are broadly accepted within society and thus secularized, they become a legitimate basis for legal intervention. When law steps in to regulate, it justifies its intervention by appeals to the secularized form of the moral mandate: to public decency or public order; to the value of life or the state's practical interest in heterosexual unions; to the "degeneracy" of certain sexual practices. When social consensus around a moral issue begins to erode, the link between particular moral notions and their specific religious underpinnings becomes exposed again, and law's endorsement of one side of the debate can be challenged as an improper conflation of church and state. In the United States of the 1980s and 1990s, this form of challenge to the moral basis of law can be seen most dramatically in the abortion debate and in the debate over the legitimacy of homosexual unions.

The issues involved in law's reliance on medical science have a different valence, since the concerns here are perceived to be those of knowledge rather than faith, of description rather than prescription. In areas involving sexuality, medical science has provided law with an understanding of what is necessary to protect public health and welfare and with guidelines about sexual status and conduct. In addressing the fundamental issue of sexual identity, medical science has drawn and redrawn the lines between aspects of sexuality that depend upon genetic programming, aspects that are the product of physical or mental disease or malfunction, and aspects that are the product of willed or chosen conduct. Changes in the medical understanding of homosexuality, for example, have in turn been central to legal debates about the appropriateness of regulating homosexual relationships and practices. In the abortion arena, law has turned to medicine in search of a scientific and secular ruling about when life begins, hoping to be able to adopt a definition free of religious bias.

The problems inherent in the relationship between law and medical science have two interrelated sources. First, medical science does not stand still, and law often lags behind the newest understanding. Compul-

LIMITS TO SEXUAL REGULATION
The Role of Privacy and Autonomy

What of the legal principles governing the regulation of sexuality? Several of those legitimizing intervention have already been spelled out: maintaining public order, decency, health, and welfare. These laws fall within the traditional "police power" of the state. Another traditional basis for governmental intervention has been to encourage forms of association and sexuality that promote the state's conception of its interests. Matrimony and childbearing and rearing within matrimonial relationships are the clearest historical examples. However, the concepts of public order, decency, health, and welfare, and indeed of the state's interests, are malleable enough to serve the modern vision of social and family life.

The legal principles limiting regulation of sexuality have traditionally been those of privacy and autonomy, especially those forms of autonomy protected by First Amendment freedoms of thought and speech. Both these principles reflect a constitutional order that sees government as a threat to liberty; both are prepared to accord some cultural space to sexual activity and expression that deviate from widely held cultural norms, to guard against the erosion of liberty.

In the shift from the Victorian vision to the modern vision, the principles of privacy and autonomy have been pressed into service in new contexts while their hold over other arenas has been challenged. The privacy accorded family life was an important bulwark to the patriarchal authority of the male head of household, but it no longer serves to shield family members from charges of sexual abuse. Instead, privacy provides the foundation for the constitutional protection accorded both abortion and contraception, whose availability serves to bolster women's claims to sexual freedom and egalitarian participation in both private and public spheres. Efforts to have sodomy statutes declared unconstitutional, however, have demonstrated the limits of the privacy principle. In *Bowers* (1986), the Supreme Court declined to rule that private, consensual, homosexual conduct between adults was constitutionally protected.

— CLARE DALTON

Would "Good Samaritan" laws that require positive action, and not mere forbearance, be a legitimate legal enforcement of morality?

PAGE 435

sory sterilization laws provide a dramatic example; the genetic "science" on which these laws were based has been entirely discredited, and yet not all such laws have been repealed. Second, medical science is not as value-free as the deferential legal community often assumes; many shifts in the medical understanding of sexuality reflect shifts in values more than they do real advances in knowledge. Law's deference thus renders it susceptible to influence by medical science on matters about which medicine has no particular expertise or authority.

Since the 1970s, the legal principle of equality has been invoked increasingly by champions of the modern vision of social and family life. Equality has provided a basis for the abolition of old intrafamilial immunities and has supported the exposure of family abuses. Equality has translated the private pain of sexual harassment in the workplace into a public claim of discrimination when the job itself or other workplace privileges are conditioned on consent to sexual activity, or when the harassment creates a hostile working environment (MacKinnon, 1979; *Meritor Savings Bank* v. *Vinson*, 1986).

Equality has also offered a new analysis of pornography. Where previous regulation of pornography depended on the "obscenity" that made it offensive to norms of public decency, the new analysis emphasizes the role pornography plays in endorsing and promoting the sexual objectification of women and thereby denying women equal status in society (MacKinnon, 1987, 1993). This characterization more properly represents what is at stake in the regulation of pornography. By the mid-1990s, however, none of the municipal ordinances based on it had survived constitutional scrutiny. The violation of women's right to be free of discrimination must still be weighed against the First Amendment freedoms of pornographers, distributors, and users; in this balance, the opponents of pornography have not prevailed. Importantly, women themselves are divided on this issue; many see the proliferation of pornography as enabling a liberating sexuality for women and support the First Amendment arguments made on pornography's behalf (Strossen, 1993).

Finally, equality is frequently offered by advocates as a basis for outlawing differential treatment on the basis of sexual identity and for providing a protected sphere in which gay and lesbian people can enjoy both privacy and autonomy in their experience of their sexuality (Mohr, 1988; "Sexual Orientation and the Law," 1993). As with pornography, this argument has made little headway within the legal system.

Conclusion

In matters relating to sexuality, the balance law strikes between the impetus to regulate and the impetus to stay government's hand is an uncertain one, informed always by shifting cultural values. Issues resolved in the direction of regulation in one era may be revisited and resolved in the direction of abstention in the next. In the decades to come, it seems likely that the most contested territory is going to involve, first, the extent to which regulation of sexuality will be directed toward achieving the egalitarian vision of social and family life, freeing women and children from sexual exploitation and abuse, and second, the extent to which law will be persuaded to lift the burden of regulation currently imposed on homosexual conduct, and to give protection in the name of equality to those who claim homosexual status.

— CLARE DALTON

T

TRUST

Trust between patients and providers

Trust between patients and providers is a central topic for bioethics. Consider the trust (or distrust) involved when someone contemplates major surgery: First of all, there is the relation between the surgeon and patient. The patient needs from the physician both a high level of competence (both judgment and skill) and a concern for the patient's well-being. For health-care professionals to behave in a responsible or trustworthy way requires both technical competence and moral concern—specifically, a concern to achieve a good outcome in the matter covered, which is sometimes called "fiduciary responsibility," the responsibility of a person who has been entrusted in some way. The moral and technical components of professional responsibility have led sociologist Bernard Barber to speak of these as two "senses" of trust (Barber, 1983). However, if the patient trusts the surgeon, it is not in two senses; the patient trusts the surgeon simply to provide a good, or perhaps the best, outcome for the patient. To fulfill that trust, the surgeon needs to be both morally concerned for the patient's well-being (or at least health outcome) and technically competent.

Because the exercise of professional responsibility characteristically draws on a body of specialized knowledge that is brought to bear on the promotion or preservation of another's welfare, to trust someone to fulfill a professional responsibility is to trust that person to perform in a way that someone outside that profession cannot entirely specify, predict, or often even recognize. In drawing attention to this point, Trudy Govier says that trust is "open-ended" (Govier, 1992). The point is not captured in the frequent suggestion

WORKS BOTH WAYS

As trust bonds a tried-and-true couple, patients need confidence in their physicians' care, and doctors in patients' truthfulness.

that trust is necessary because the trusting party cannot control or monitor the trusted party's performance. It would do the patient little good to have full prescience of all the events in the operation, or even the ability to guide the surgeon's hand, unless the patient also happened to be a surgeon. Although a typical patient might be able to recognize some acts of gross malpractice, such as being stitched up with foreign bodies left inside, the patient would not know the implications of most of what he or she saw and would have no idea of how to improve the surgeon's performance. For this reason, from the point of view of the patient, there are no good alternatives to having trustworthy professionals. There are no good alternatives in these circumstances because the patient must rely on the discretion of the practitioner.

Philosophers like John Ladd (1979) and legal theorists like Joel Handler (1990) have drawn attention to the role of discretion in many areas of professional practice. They have argued that because of the role of discretion, the criteria for morally responsible practice cannot be specified in terms of rules or rights alone. The centrality of discretion makes it all the more difficult to separate competence (having adequate knowledge and skill) and moral elements (exercising sufficient concern for the client's well-being) in the professional's behavior.

The provider—in this case the surgeon—also must trust the patient. At a minimum, the surgeon depends on the patient to disclose all information relevant to the case so as to minimize the risks of unexpected events in the operating room. If the patient disappoints the surgeon and does not disclose all relevant information, the negative consequence for the surgeon is, at most, to impair the surgeon's professional performance. The disappointment does not carry a risk of death or disability for the surgeon. The difference in the severity of risk is one of the many aspects of a trust relationship that is counted as a difference of power in that relationship. The lesser severity of consequence for the provider—in this case the surgeon—can obscure the mutuality of trust in the patient-provider relationship.

When the provider is a nurse or physical therapist rather than a surgeon, the provider's central tasks often require an understanding of the patient's experiences, hopes, and fears. Although some nursing, such as the work of the surgical nurse who assists in the operating room, does not depend on an understanding of the patient's experience, most nursing does. Postsurgical nursing care is a good example. This care typically includes motivating the patient to do things such as coughing and breathing deeply in order to reduce the risk of postoperative lung infection. These acts are often quite uncomfortable. Such nursing requires an understanding of the individual patient's state of mind and the ability to motivate the patient—the ability to inspire confidence and hope in patients.

CHANGING THE STANDARDS OF THE PATIENT-PROVIDER RELATIONSHIP. When sociologist Talcott Parsons put forward his influential theory that professionals function as trustees, or in a "fiduciary" capacity (Parsons, 1951), the standard for the so-called fiduciary aspects of the relationship between patients and physicians was that the provider furthered the patient's well-being by being entrusted to make medical decisions in the best interests of that patient.

The doctrine of informed consent for medical procedures was adopted only gradually over the next two decades as a check on provider discretion. This doctrine has been implemented to require informed consent only for a very circumscribed set of procedures. To treat competent persons against their will is considered battery, in legal terms. Therefore, there is a foundation in law for the prohibition of forced or nonconsensual treatment of all types. In practice, however, information is often given only for major procedures, and practitioners tend to assume consent for lesser interventions, including most medical tests. Although patient-oriented practitioners will offer an explanation of why they are ordering a particular test, others will explain only when explicitly asked. For procedures other than surgery, formal requests for consent are rare unless there is a significant risk of death or severe disability from the procedure.

Furthermore, most patients are well informed only about the risk of death or significant permanent injury in circumstances in which informed consent is legally or institutionally mandated. Significant risk—such as becoming temporarily psychotic as a result of the trauma of open-heart surgery, as a result of intensive-care procedures, or from the sleep deprivation that often results from those procedures—is rarely disclosed to patients. The rationale for not telling a patient about to have bypass surgery or enter intensive care is that the risk will seem so shocking that the patient will refuse needed care.

IMPLEMENTING THE FIDUCIARY STANDARD. Ironically, although the fiduciary responsibility in health care has often been viewed primarily as the responsibility of physicians, as was noted above, it is other classes of providers, especially nurses, who are educated in a way that prepares them to understand patients' experience. Although there is much to recommend the new fiduciary standard in health care, its realization requires either a major change in medical education or a change in the relations among members of the health-care team, so that those who are prepared to oversee and foster shared decision making have the authority to do so. Without such changes, the trust

◆ **trust** *n.*

assured reliance on the character, ability, strength, or truth of someone or something.

◆ **trust** *v.*

to rely on the truthfulness or accuracy of; to place confidence in: rely on.

COMMUNICATION
Shared Decision-Making

Although the standard of informed consent is enforced by law and institutional practice only for certain risks of major procedures, the U.S. President's Commission for the Study of Ethical Problems in Medicine and Biomedical and Behavioral Research (President's Commission) has urged that the informed-consent standard be replaced by another, more comprehensive standard, the standard of "shared decision making."

The President's Commission's 1982 report, *Making Health Care Decisions*, advocated such a shift, which would presumably apply to most significant health-care decisions. The rule of informed consent requires only the recognition of the patient's right of veto over the alternatives that the provider has presented to the patient. In contrast, shared decision making requires participation of the patient in setting the goals and methods of care and, therefore, in formulating the alternatives to be considered. This participation requires that patients and practitioners engage in complex communication, which the practitioners have a fiduciary responsibility to foster. This new standard is particularly appropriate for a pluralistic society, in which the responsible provider may have an idea of the patient's good that is significantly different from the patient's own idea.

The responsibility to foster shared decision making requires significant skill on the part of medical professionals in understanding patients of diverse backgrounds and in fostering communication with them in difficult circumstances—circumstances in which their communication may be compromised by fear and pain as well as by a lack of medical knowledge. Although some physicians, notably primary-care providers, have sought the skills to fulfill the responsibility to foster such communication, this responsibility is not one that medical education prepares physicians to accept.

— CAROLINE WHITBECK

that one's health care will be shaped by one's own priorities and concerns is not well founded.

In many cases, distrust of either individual providers or medical institutions has been warranted, especially for women, people of color, and the poor, whose experience has often been discounted or who have been viewed as less rational or less competent than white males. Annette Dula argues that historical events, from the Tuskegee syphilis study to the experience with screening for sickle-cell carrier trait, confirm that trust of the health-care system on the part of African-Americans is often not warranted (Dula, 1992). The problem is one of the need not only for assurance but also for evidence that the former conditions no longer prevail.

Many poor or uninsured people have not even had a significant patient-provider relationship; when they are able to obtain health care, it is often with a provider whom they see in only a single clinical encounter. It is therefore impossible to establish a trusting relationship that would serve the patient's health interest. If society is obliged to provide decent health care for its citizens, this failure of the health-care system is a betrayal of trust not by individual providers but by society and its health-care institutions.

Trust and family members

Trust among family members is at least as important an issue for health care as is trust in the provider-patient relationship. The trustworthiness of parents and guardians to decide the care of children and other dependent family members is widely discussed, and trust among family members is beginning to receive more attention in connection with the writing of living wills and health proxy statements. The issues of the competence of family members to give various forms of care or to make technical decisions, and the sufficiency of their concern for the patient's well-being, parallel those issues for providers. The matter is further complicated by the phenomenon of psychological denial that interferes with decision making about the health care of a person who is important in one's own life. Denial, as well as incompetence or lack of commitment to the patient's welfare, may compromise a person's decisions or care when the health or life of a close friend or relative is gravely threatened. Therefore, warranted trust in family members to provide or decide one's care requires confidence not only in their competence and in their concern for one's well-being but also in their psychological ability to come to terms with the situation.

Other areas of trust in health care

There is also the question of the public's trust in a class of professionals, which is distinct from the question of the public's concern that, should they become clients of these professionals, their interests will be well served. For example, Sissela Bok (1978) has examined the concern about the trustworthiness of lawyers, not by their clients but by the public. Of par-

If obstetricians are given the authority to force pregnant women to follow their recommendations, this force may be used in a very arbitrary way.

PAGE 469

A priest sees people at their best, a lawyer at their worst, but a doctor sees them as they really are.

PROVERB

ticular concern is lawyers' commitment to keep the crimes of their clients confidential, even certain ongoing or planned crimes. The public believes that lawyers should not violate usual ethical norms for the sake of their clients' interests. The corresponding issue in health care is the fear that providers will, in protecting patient confidentiality, put the public health or the safety of individuals at undue risk. The question of ethical criteria for breaking confidentiality is regularly discussed, especially in the case of a sexually transmitted disease or a patient intent on harming another person. However, there is no widespread public concern that health-care providers may be going so far in protecting patient confidentiality that they are derelict in protecting the public.

In addition to the public's trust of providers, the trust or distrust of medical technology is often a significant factor. The risk is particularly salient in the case of artificial organs, joints, and other body parts. In place of the components of competence and concern of a trusted provider, the qualities required of a technology to warrant trust are its performance (it performs the function it was designed to perform) and its relative safety (it is relatively unlikely to cause accidents or to have other injurious side effects). Of course, with such life-critical technologies as artificial organs, the performance issue is itself a safety issue.

There are many aspects of the health-care system on which patients rely but which most rarely consider. Many people become fully aware of their trust only when that trust is disappointed. A case in point is the discovery that research misconduct occurred in a major breast cancer study. The belated revelation of misconduct made patients aware of their trust in medical research.

The morality of trust

Although Sissela Bok has discussed trust as a moral resource since the 1970s, the question of the morality of trust relationships—the question of the circumstances under which, from a moral point of view, one ought to trust—was not explicitly discussed until Annette Baier's 1986 essay, "Trust and Anti-Trust." Two earlier essays were important in laying the foundation for this major turn in the discussion. In 1984, Ian Hacking provided a devastating assessment of the use of game theory to understand moral questions, such as the Prisoner's Dilemma, which will be discussed below. Baier herself argued in 1985 for broadening the focus in ethics from obligations and moral rules to the subject of who ought, as a moral matter, to be trusted and when. As Kathryn Addelson points out, Baier's change of focus establishes a general perspective on ethical legitimacy that is shared by all—both the powerful and those whom society labels "deviant"—rather than privileging the perspective of those who make, instill, and enforce moral rules (Addelson, 1994).

Baier's general account of the morality of trust illuminates the strong relation between the trustworthy and the true. A trust relationship, according to Baier, is decent to the extent that it stands the test of disclosure of the premises of each party's trust (Baier, 1986). For example, if one party trusts the other to perform as needed only because the truster believes the trusted is too timid or unimaginative to do otherwise, disclosure of these premises will tend to insult the trusted party and give him or her an incentive to prove the truster wrong. Similarly, if the trusted party fulfills the truster's expectations only through fear of detection and punishment, disclosure of these premises may lead the truster to suspect that the trusted would betray the trust, given an anonymous opportunity to do so.

Although explicit discussion of moral trustworthiness is relatively recent, both professional ethics and the philosophy of technology have given considerable attention to the concept of responsibility. Since being trustworthy is key to acting responsibly in a professional capacity, or to being a responsible person if one considers responsibility a virtue, the literature on responsibility provides at least an implicit discussion of many aspects of the morality of trust, much of which is relevant to the subject of trust in health care.

Conceptual relationships

Trust involves both confidence and reliance. Annette Baier argues that if we lack other options, we may continue to rely on something even when we no longer trust it (Baier, 1986). Similarly, we may have confidence in something, or confidence in our expectations concerning it, without relying on it. To rely only on what we can trust is a fortunate circumstance.

Niklas Luhmann (1988) urges a different distinction between confidence and trust, suggesting that "trust" be used only when the truster has considered the alternatives to trusting. Such use is incompatible with unconscious trust, a phenomenon to which Baier draws attention. Luhmann's discussion of the distinction between trust and confidence highlights the element of risk in trusting. Risk or vulnerability does characterize situations in which trust is necessary, in contrast to situations in which one's control of the outcome makes trust unnecessary. However, the element of risk taking in trust is captured in the notion of reliance when trust is understood as confident reliance. Being vulnerable in one's reliance does not require that one have considered the alternatives, if any, to such reliance.

Although one often trusts people, their intentions and goodwill, there is also trust in mere circumstances

See Also

AIDS and Confidentiality and Protective Privilege and Public Peril: The *Tarasoff* Case or events: One may trust that a taxi will come along shortly, even if no taxi has been ordered, without believing anything about another person's reliability in providing a taxi.

The risk taken in trusting does leave the truster liable to disappointment (or worse), whether that trust is of persons or events. But only when trust is in other people, and not merely in the events involving them, can one be let down by them. Suppose that a person is awakened every weekday by another person's calling for a neighbor. If the first person has come to rely on being awakened, but one day the other person does not come for the neighbor or does so quietly, the first person's expectations will be disappointed. But the person will not have been disappointed or let down by the one who usually picks up the neighbor. To be disappointed by another person, that person must at least be aware of doing or not doing the act in question. Here the person doing the calling for the neighbor is not aware of waking up the first party, much less of being trusted to do it. As Baier mentions (1986), it is possible for there to be trust of which the trusted person is unaware, and so one might let down another without being aware of letting that person down.

Niklas Luhmann (1979) has shown how trust simplifies human life by endowing some expectations with assurance. To consider all possible disappointments, defections, and betrayals by those on whom we rely, the possible consequences of those disappointments, and any actions that one might take to prevent those disappointments or change their effect is prohibitively costly in terms of time and energy. Trust reduces that burden.

The literature on trust

Sociologists like Bernard Barber (1983) and Luhmann (1979, 1988) have written on many facets of the notion of trust, and legal theorists have reflected on the distinct, though related, notion of a legal trust. Until the 1980s, however, the explicit attention given to the common notion of trust, or confident reliance, in Anglo-American philosophy was largely in relation to such questions as how the "prisoners" in the so-called Prisoner's Dilemma might solve their problem of assurance with regard to one another's behavior so as to cooperate in achieving a mutually beneficial outcome.

Recent literature on trust has examined trust in a variety of different social circumstances, involving a wide range of objects and systems, persons in a wide variety of roles, and matters in which they might be trusted or distrusted. For example, some writers focus on cases of the breakdown of trust in war, under the influence of the Mafia, or in some other extreme situation. Differences in the domain of application of the notion of trust lead to an unusually wide range of estimates of its character and importance. They also lead to disparate distinctions between trust and such notions as reliance, faith, vulnerability, and confidence, as well as to different conclusions about the moral value and the moral risks associated with trust.

TRUST AND "THE PRISONER'S DILEMMA"

In the Prisoner's Dilemma, each of two prisoners will receive a light sentence if neither confesses to a crime, and a more severe sentence if both confess; but if one confesses and the other does not, the latter will be freed, but the former will receive the most severe sentence of all. Without assurance about each other's behavior, and in spite of knowing that both would be better off if neither confesses, both are likely to confess and be less well off.

— CAROLINE WHITBECK

Those who write about trust in a market context often take economic rationality—according to which each person simply seeks to maximize his or her goals by the most efficient means—as their model. They then often regard trust as a way of coping with "imperfect rationality," understood as uncertainty about the facts or about one another's behavior, and how to estimate the consequences for the achievement of one's goals. The economic model of rationality is not readily applicable in considerations of ethics because it was designed to avoid consideration of values other than efficiency, and it treats moral considerations as nonobjective "personal preferences." Where a market context is assumed, the relatively minor risk of being a "sucker" is likely to be mentioned as a barrier to trust. (See, for example, Dasgupta, 1988.) In discussions of trust among family members or between nations (Bok, 1990a), much more is recognized to be at stake.

Feminists like Trudy Govier argue that attention to trust relationships will bring attention to other relationships, such as those between parents and children, that have been neglected when contracts are the focus of attention. Such relationships, however, together with the features of trust that are prominent in them, continue to be ignored in much of the literature on trust. For example, Geoffrey Hawthorn mentions a parent's nonegotistic motives toward his or her child, only to turn immediately to "more ordinary" instances of nonegoistic motives (Hawthorn, 1988).

Bernard Williams (1988), who begins his own essay with a discussion of the Prisoner's Dilemma, argues that the problem of how nonegoistic motivation is to

"The art of medicine consists in amusing the patient while nature cures the disease."

VOLTAIRE

"Truth does not do as much good in the world as the semblance of truth does evil."

LA ROCHEFOUCAULD
MAXIMS, 1665

be encouraged and legitimated does not have a general solution. He argues that the problem of trust or cooperation is not one that can be solved in a general way at the level of decision theory, social psychology, or the general theory of social institutions. To ensure cooperation in a given situation requires an understanding of the ways in which the people in that situation are motivated. Williams believes that solutions to the problem of cooperation are found only for particular historically shaped societies, rather than for society in general. He argues that investigating the sorts of combinations of motivations that make sense in that society might lead to a general perspective on the problems of cooperation in such a society. However, as he says, "there is no one problem of cooperation: the problem is always how a given set of people cooperate" (1988, p. 13). Those whose cooperation is of the greatest interest in bioethics are patients, their families, the health-care providers, and the policymakers who shape the health-care system.

—CAROLINE WHITBECK

VALUE AND VALUATION

Though values are integral to human experience, it is only in modern societies that they have gained an explicit place in ethics. In traditional societies, values generally operate as components of the common culture that are taken for granted. Their moral discourse focuses on the rules that define primary human obligations and on notions of moral excellence. Values first acquire ethical importance where individuals have wide choices about how they are to live their lives. These choices lead to a plurality of value perspectives whose competing claims may appear to express little more than subjective preferences. The challenge to ethics, then, is to devise ways of assessing values critically in relation to normative moral discourse.

In European civilizations, wide value choices were first opened up by the rise of capitalism and of liberal democratic states. In this context, value considerations are never far removed from market dynamics or from basic principles of human liberty. Although class and status factors bar many from the benefits of these modern social formations, their impact on human life remains pervasive, compelling us for the sake of social order to accommodate various value orientations.

The concept of values

We take note of the realities in our world that matter to us. Values are concepts we use to explain how and why various realities matter. Values are not to be confused with concrete goods. They are ideas, images, notions. Values attract us. We aspire after the good they articulate. We expect to find our own good in relation to what they offer.

Because values are linked to realities we experience, they have an objective reference. They disclose features in our everyday world to which we attach special importance. Positive values are balanced by disvalues. Disvalues express what we consider undesirable, harmful, or unworthy about particular phenomena. They identify realities that we resist or strive to avoid. Virtually everything we experience has valuative significance: objects, states of affairs, activities, processes, performances, relational networks, and so on.

Values are linked to acts of valuation (Scheler, 1973). For every value that appears, there is a corresponding valuative orientation (Husserl, 1970). This orientation may not be fully self-conscious; still less is it an expression of critical judgment. It is, nonetheless, the subjective basis for the appearance of values. Without valuing subjects, there can be no such thing as values.

In an elemental sense, values are disclosed by feelings (Ricoeur, 1966). Explicit value language comes later, if at all. How do I know that health is good? I know because I feel good when I am healthy. The positive feeling signals the presence of value. How do I know that a performance of Shakespeare's *Hamlet* is good? Even an informed aesthetic judgment has an affective basis: I was moved by it. In being moved, I apprehend value. My primal awareness of value becomes explicit as I identify the features in a phenomenon that draw me to it. Human languages furnish a rich vocabulary for conversations about values.

The correlation between values and valuative acts does not imply that values are purely subjective or that they are merely secondary embellishments of empirical fact. On the contrary, the notion of an empirical reality devoid of all valuative meaning is itself an abstraction. As our perceptions disclose an object's reality, so our affections disclose its worth (Ricoeur, 1966). By means of perceptions and affections, we apprehend facets of the realities we encounter. Apart from corresponding acts of consciousness, however, nothing whatever can appear.

VIRTUE = STRENGTH

Virtue denotes moral excellence and right behavior. In the Middle Ages, virtues—powers from above—were the seventh order of angels in the celestial hierarchy.

See Also

Priorities Among Values

VALUE AND VALUATION

Values and Human Needs

Unlike the American Declaration of Independence, the French Declaration of the Rights of Man (1789) emphasized that individuals have duties as well as rights.

PAGE 429

Values and human needs

Values are intimately related to human needs and desires (Niebuhr, 1960; Ogletree, 1985; Ricoeur, 1966). We value realities that satisfy basic needs and fulfill deeply felt aspirations. We associate disvalues with realities that threaten or diminish human well-being. Human well-being is only part of the story. With a growing environmental consciousness, value discussions embrace nonhuman life forms as well, perhaps creaturely well-being as a whole. Human life then gains its value within a natural world that has intrinsic worth. Religious communities honor a world-transcending center of values from which all lesser values derive their significance.

There are as many kinds of values as there are regions of experience where we distinguish good or bad, better or worse, beneficial or harmful: sensory values, organic values, personal values, interpersonal values, social values, cultural values, and spiritual values (Scheler, 1973). Social values can be differentiated into economic, political, legal, associational, and familial subsets. Cultural values embrace religious, moral, cognitive, and aesthetic interests (Parsons, 1969). The formal value types all contain values and disvalues. Notions of creaturely well-being are implied if not stated.

Value issues in biomedical practice

Virtually all kinds of values figure in biomedical practice. Organic values are basic: life, health, vigor, bodily integrity. The purpose of medicine is to save lives and to promote healing. Yet the ill and injured are never merely "patients," organisms suffering treatable maladies; they are persons with dignity who have their own life plans (May, 1991; Ramsey, 1970). Personal values, therefore, qualify organic values. Patients as persons may in no case be subjected to medical procedures without informed consent. Ideally, they participate actively in their own healing.

Organic values are inherently problematic. Our impulses press us to strive for life, strength, and agility. Yet these strivings are limited by our vulnerability to illness, injury, disability, and, finally, certain death. Modern medicine inclines us to define the limits of organic life not as natural features of finitude but as problems to be solved. This tendency requires us to make value judgments about the boundaries of medical intervention. Medical practices inattentive to these boundaries can deprive the dying of the personal space they need to achieve closure in their life pilgrimages.

At this point, organic values are qualified by more encompassing value commitments. Such commitments can help us to accept life's limits, acknowledge goods more noble than our own survival, and endure sufferings and disappointments with grace and wisdom. Life, death, health, and illness are never purely physiological; they are moral and spiritual as well. Health care must also have moral and spiritual as well as physiological dimensions (Cousins, 1979; May, 1991; Nelson and Rohricht, 1984).

Professional and economic values intersect medical practice in similar ways. Physicians have specialized knowledge that equips them to provide socially valued services. They enjoy social status as professionals who maintain standards for medical practice. In this role, they are public guarantors of prized social values (May, 1983). Physicians in the United States offer services for fees, primarily through third-party payments. Accordingly, medical practice is also a market transaction, and physicians are businesspeople with economic interests. The stake in economic values qualifies professional devotion to patient well-being.

The organization of health care profoundly conditions its operative values. Modern medicine requires sophisticated technologies affordable only to large medical centers. These institutions, usually constituted as corporations, dominate medical practice in the United States. The technologies they use are typically produced and supplied by global corporations. The income they receive derives largely from corporate employee-benefit plans and from insurance firms that service them. Health-related industries have become a major component of the economy, perhaps inappropriately overriding the legitimate claims of other social goods. Powerful economic and political interests support the continued growth of medical enterprises with little regard for wider social ramifications.

Because the desire for quality medical services is urgent, intense public debate surrounds federal policies that bear upon the organization, regulation, and funding of health care. The struggle is to determine appropriate government roles for the oversight and financing of biomedical activities. In this struggle, conflicting political values intersect health-care practices as public actors respond to constituent interests.

Similar sociocultural analyses could be directed to the roles played in the health-care system by values resident in families, religious communities, research institutes, medical colleges, the legal system, the media, and the arts. Ethical studies of the intersection between biomedical practices and social processes uncover a volatile mix of conflict-laden value issues.

Fluidity of values

Values are not only pervasive but also fluid. Any concrete experience harbors many values and disvalues, none of which is definitive or self-contained. Illness can be a physical malady, a ruthless disruption of personal plans, an economic disaster, an opportunity for self-discovery, a moment of human bonding, an occasion for medical virtuosity, or a case study in biomedical research (May, 1991). Each of these meanings captures some of the values that belong to a particular experience. As attention shifts, one set of values continually flows into another.

Our terminology for values is similarly fluid. The word "health" can be used descriptively; it also identifies an important value. "Justice" can designate a basic moral principle; it can refer equally to a value worthy of promotion in social arrangements. The term "objective" may characterize "value-free" inquiry, but it also designates a cognitive value.

Because of their fluidity, values resist schematic classification. Attempts to construct comprehensive value schemes do, however, have heuristic significance. They heighten awareness of the range of our valuative connections with our world, and they stimulate reflections on what belongs to human well-being (Hartmann, 1932; Perry, 1926; Scheler, 1973).

Moral values

Within the value field, we can isolate a subset of moral values. Moral values cluster around personal identity, interpersonal relationships, and the makeup of groups, associations, social institutions, whole societies, and even the global community (Scheler, 1973). Numerous values—dignity, integrity, mutual respect, loyalty, friendship, social cohesion, fairness, stability, effectiveness, inclusiveness—are moral in import. Anthropocentric values are supplemented and corrected by the moral claims of animals and, more broadly, by the moral claims of the environment, a self-sustaining ecosystem. Even religious devotion to the divine life has moral dimensions, for the faithful are obliged to honor God as the final bearer of value.

Moral values enjoy precedence within the value field because they identify the basic loci of all valuing experience—that is, valuing subjects in relationship. Where moral values are secure, we can cultivate a wide array of values. Where moral values are in danger, all values are at risk.

Even so, in our responses to concrete cases we regularly rank some nonmoral values above specifically moral ones. Faced with a health emergency, our regard for life itself, an organic value, surpasses normal preoccupations with human dignity, a moral value. We do what we can to save a life! At the same time, we know that life as such is but one value among many. Prolonging human life can never, therefore, be the primary goal.

Similarly, human beings can often best advance their own good through value commitments that transcend specifically moral considerations. Cognitive, aesthetic, and especially spiritual values finally stand "higher" than moral values in most value schemes because they bestow significance on existence in its travail and woe. Yet these values still require for their realization valuing subjects who are bearers of moral value.

We normally discuss moral values in terms of rights and duties. Rights identify claims that others properly make on us. These claims intersect our value-oriented projects and disclose our duties. A physician's professional judgment about a course of therapy is subject to the patient's informed consent. The abortion debate hinges on differing assessments of fetal rights against a pregnant woman's right to choose.

VALUES IN SOCIETY AND CULTURE

In traditional societies, the most crucial value issues are largely settled. To be viable, a society requires a shared set of reasonably cohesive values. This shared value cluster composes the society's moral identity. It is expressed in many ways within the common culture: public rituals, speeches, novels, paintings, school textbooks, standard histories, and scholarly investigations.

Modern societies with market economies and liberal democracies are not able to sustain comprehensive value syntheses. At best, they promote what John Rawls calls a "thin" theory of the good—that is, elemental goods that all are presumed to need and want whatever else they might also desire (Rawls, 1971). Within the framework of basic goods, such societies host a multiplicity of concrete value orientations, reflecting the diverse priorities of individuals and groups within the society.

Some question whether we can sustain even a "thin" theory of the good without a widely shared, substantive value synthesis fostered in basic social institutions (MacIntyre, 1984). The disintegration of traditional cultural values tends to undermine interest in the common good. Private preoccupations with individual advantage and "interest group" politics then displace public discourse about the good of the society as a whole. Likewise, political battles are fought without the restraints of civility necessary to social order. Value theory becomes urgent when basic values are in dispute. Its task is not only to advance critical investigations of persistent value disputes but also to show how various value streams within a pluralistic society can contribute to the good of all.

— THOMAS W. OGLETREE

◆ **principlism**
the value of particular moral principles, including respect for persons and their autonomy, that help in the actual making of decisions.

See Also
Law and Morality

"What we obtain too cheap, we esteem too lightly; it is dearness only that gives everything its value."

THOMAS PAINE
THE AMERICAN CRISIS, NO. 1, 1776

Duties consist of obligations and prohibitions. Obligations specify what we must do no matter what else we might also hope to accomplish. Hospital emergency rooms must treat seriously injured persons regardless of whether they can pay, offering such care as a part of normal operations. Prohibitions specify what we must not do regardless of larger objectives. We must not use human beings as research subjects without their consent no matter how important the research may be.

It is for the sake of moral values that basic rights and duties are binding. We may set such mandates aside only when extraordinary measures are required to safeguard the values they protect. For the sake of human dignity, physicians are normally obliged to do all they reasonably can to sustain the lives of their patients. Precisely for the sake of human dignity, however, this obligation loses its force when further medical interventions would only prolong the dying process.

Values and human action

Value awareness gains practical importance in terms of action (Ricoeur, 1966). We adopt courses of action that promise results favoring our prized values; we act to inhibit developments that endanger our values. Values guide decision making, disposing us to choose one course of action over another. We justify our decisions in terms of the values they are designed to promote.

Matters do not always turn out as we expect. We may lack the skill, the power, the influence, or the knowledge to achieve our objectives. In medical practice, few surprises follow the skilled application of routine therapies proven to be effective for treating particular ills. Physicians do not stay within safe territory, however. They regularly confront medical problems that they cannot diagnose with confidence and for which there are no known clinical responses with assured results. Medical outcomes frequently fall short of human hopes. They include side effects whose disvalues outweigh desired values. "Side effects" belong to action consequences even when they do not reflect our intentions.

When our actions affect the actions of others, uncertainty increases. Other people may not react as we expect. They may misunderstand our intentions or respond carelessly. We may misread their value commitments. Perhaps the relevant network of human interactions is so vast and complex that it surpasses what we can grasp. Here, too, the outcomes may not fit our values. Prediction is most reliable for highly routine actions with widely understood purposes. It is least reliable for novel initiatives, such as new directions in policy.

Because we cannot fully control or predict the consequences of our actions, the fit between actions and values is inexact. This inexactness carries over into value assessments. We may readily name the values that attach to desired outcomes. Before we can evaluate a course of action, however, we have to consider the uncertainties. We have to weigh the disvalues that could accompany significant miscalculations.

Considerations of value differ from discussions of duty by virtue of the inexact fit between values and action. Duty refers not to the likely outcomes of actions but to actions as such, which are largely in our power. It specifies ground rules that order human activity. In general, we may pursue a larger vision of the good only within constraints set by these ground rules. In its early stages, biomedical ethics properly gave precedence to the delineation of basic moral duties.

The fit between values, action, and action consequences remains close enough, however, that values must figure in the ethical examination of action. I am accountable to myself and others not simply for the conformity of my actions to rules that define my duties but also for values and disvalues that reside in the results of my actions. In decision making, I project the likely outcomes of actions I am considering and I weigh probabilities that qualify my projections. I also bring into view risks of unpleasant surprises. Practical reflection on values depends on substantial knowledge of the social dynamics that structure action.

Critical reflection on values

The scrutiny of values has four crucial layers: (1) the reflective identification of our operative values; (2) assessments of the fit between these operative values and considered judgments about creaturely well-being; (3) analyses of value relations in order to identify compatible and incompatible values sets; and (4) imaginative constructions of value syntheses capable of ordering life priorities in personal, communal, and social contexts.

The investigation of values begins with description. We seek to become self-conscious about the values we prize, taking note of value commitments ingrained in stable life patterns and ongoing institutional involvements. The descriptive task is informed by historical studies of normative traditions and of social developments leading to current practices. As we make our operative values explicit, we are often stimulated to reorder our priorities. We recognize that existing arrangements do not reflect our convictions about what matters most in life.

The relation that values have to basic human needs suggests a second step in value studies. British utilitarians and American pragmatists sought to test our presumptive values by empirical investigations (Bentham, 1948; Dewey, 1931). Their aim was to discover life practices and value attachments that truly accord with primary human needs. Much human-science research functions as value inquiry of this sort, shedding light on value patterns that tend to promote human well-being in contrast to those that finally prove dysfunctional. Historical, philosophical, and theological reflections can also inform such inquiry. For ethics, the challenge is to clarify the contributions empirical studies can make to the critical assessment of values and to incorporate those contributions into constructive philosophical and religious thought.

The third step is an analysis of value relations. Not all values are compatible with one another, at least not in practical terms. We cannot both affirm free speech and shield people from all offensive public expressions. We cannot protect the environment without constraining market freedoms. Likewise, we cannot guarantee everyone health care that fully utilizes the most advanced medical technologies while also controlling aggregate health-care costs. Critical thought examines values in terms of their fit with one another. It dramatizes the necessity of choices among different sets of values. We bypass some values and endure relative disvalues for the sake of value combinations that reflect considered priorities.

The crucial step in the critical study of values is the imaginative construction of coherent value syntheses capable of guiding action. Because modern societies harbor a multiplicity of value perspectives, attempts to determine value priorities take place in several contexts.

Individuals develop a mature moral identity by clarifying the connections and priorities that order personally cherished values. Value syntheses are no less vital for families, special-interest associations, and religious bodies. These collectives gain moral, and perhaps religious, identity through shared value commitments. Organizations that give concrete form to economic, legal, political, and cultural institutions are themselves more effective when they make their defining values explicit.

Coherent sets of values are not easily achieved or sustained. They enjoy the greatest authority when they emerge as critical appropriations and transformations of normative value traditions within contemporary life settings. Because of the complexity of experience, value syntheses can never fully overcome areas of ambivalence or wholly resolve internal strains. Within limits, we can accommodate value conflicts that we acknowledge and honor. Such conflicts may even stimulate creativity.

Within comprehensive value syntheses, value priorities normally run in two contrary directions. Elemental sensory, organic, and economic values enjoy priority over higher political, cultural, and spiritual values in the sense that they furnish the conditions necessary to the appearance of the higher values. Political, cultural, and spiritual values enjoy priority over more basic sensory, organic, and economic values in the sense that they bestow meaning and significance on the more elemental values. Moral values play the mediating role because they identify the loci of value experience. These contrasting modes of priority can shed light on concrete values conflicts.

Public value syntheses

A basic value of modern societies is the protection of private spaces for people to pursue diverse visions of the good. Social cohesion rests, then, on minimal agreements that allow individuals and groups to live together in their diversity. In the United States, the prevailing value synthesis combines liberal democratic principles and principles of free-market capitalism. Enduring controversies concern the nature and extent of appropriate government intervention in market processes. Less clearly articulated are images of a greater national community embracing many races, cultures, and religions. The latter images are countered by persisting patterns of racism, ethnocentrism, and religious intolerance.

In biomedical ethics, the most urgent challenge is to form a public value synthesis that can guide health-care reform. Though difficult disputes remain, there is considerable agreement that a good system will guarantee basic care for all, maintain acceptable standards of quality, foster an active partnership between patients and physicians, take account of the defining values of those who give and receive care, sustain advanced biomedical research, hold total costs to manageable levels, and protect contexts for personal preferences and individual initiatives in delivering and receiving care. These values—especially the contention that all people must have access to basic medical services—all have important moral dimensions.

Any workable system will include value trade-offs. It will require a reexamination of standards of quality care, a balance between health-care needs and other social goods, and a workable mix of economic incentives and government regulations that maintains discipline within the system while allowing space for individual initiatives. Any system will also confront limits. Moral creativity requires imaginative responses to limits in the promotion of creaturely well-being.

Because of the subtleties involved, bioethics cannot easily incorporate notions of value and valuation into deliberations about basic human duties. Yet values pervade human experience. They even shape our perceptions of the obligations and prohibitions that set constraints on our actions. As we examine more comprehensively the moral issues that reside in biomedical practice, the more we will discover the necessity of systematic value assessments. Critical value studies will

The U.S. version of biology is a folk biology that assumes that social categories—"races"—are reflections of nature rather than culture.

PAGE 573

"All virtue is summed up in dealing justly."

ARISTOTLE
NICOMACHEAN ETHICS, 4TH C. B.C.

tend as well to force a shift in the dominant structure of moral reasoning, from the linear logic of the syllogism to the more nuanced process of weaving multiple value considerations together into an illuminating pattern of moral understanding. While the resulting judgments may appear less precise and decisive, they will probably be more true to life.

— THOMAS W. OGLETREE

VIRTUE AND CHARACTER

"Virtue" is the translation of the ancient Greek *arete*, which meant any kind of excellence. Inanimate objects could have *arete*, since they were assumed to have a *telos*, that is, a purpose. Thus, the *arete* of a knife would be its sharpness. Animals could also have *arete*; for example, the strength of an ox was seen as its virtue. Though an animal could possess *arete*, the Greeks assumed natural potentialities in men and women to be virtues requiring enhancement through habits of skill. Therefore, Aristotle defined virtue as "a kind of second nature" that disposes us not only to do the right thing rightly but also to gain pleasure from what we do" (Aristotle, 1962, 1105b25-30).

Since there are many things that "our nature" as humans inclines us to do, Aristotle argues, there can be many human virtues. How particular virtues are constituted can vary with different understandings of "human nature" and the different social roles and their correlative skills. Yet the virtues, according to Aristotle, are distinguished from the arts, since in the latter excellence lies in results. In contrast, for the virtues it matters not only that an act itself is of a certain kind, but also that the agent "has certain characteristics as he performs it; first of all, he must know what he is doing; secondly, he must choose to act the way he does, and he must choose it for its own sake; and in the third place, the act must spring from a firm and unchangeable character" (Aristotle, 1962, 1105a25-30).

The word *hexis*, which Aristotle uses for "character," is the same word that denotes the habitual dispositions constitutive of the virtues. Character, therefore, indicates the stability that is necessary so that the various virtues are acquired in a lasting way. Character is not simply the sum of the individual virtues; rather, it names the pattern of thought and action that provides a continuity sufficient for humans to claim their lives as their own (Kupperman, 1991). However, the material form associated with character may vary from one society to another. Therefore any definition of virtue, the virtues, and character can be misleading because it can conceal the differences between various accounts of the nature and kinds of virtues as well as character.

The role of virtue in recent moral philosophy

Ancient philosophers as well as Christian theologians, though offering quite different accounts of the virtues, assumed that any account of the well-lived life had to take virtue into consideration. Modern moral philosophy, in contrast, treats virtues—if it treats them at all—as secondary to an ethics based on principles and rules. The attempt to secure an account of morality that is not as subject to variations as an ethics of virtue certainly contributed to this displacement of virtues. The first edition of the *Encyclopedia of Bioethics*, for example, had no entry on virtue or character.

In his widely used and influential introduction to philosophical ethics, William Frankena manifests the approach to ethics that simply assumed that considerations of virtue were secondary. According to Frankena, ethical theory should be concerned primarily with justifying moral terms and clarifying the differences between appeals to duty and consequences. The virtues, to the extent they were discussed by theorists such as Frankena, were understood as supplements to the determination of right and wrong action. The virtues in such a theory were seen more as the motivational component in more basic principles, such as benevolence and justice. As Frankena put it,

> *We know that we should cultivate two virtues, a disposition to be beneficial (i.e., benevolence) and a disposition to treat people equally (justice as a trait). But the point of acquiring these virtues is not further guidance or instructions; the function of the virtues in an ethics of duty is not to tell us what to do, but to insure that we will do it willingly in whatever situation we may face.* (Frankena, 1973, p. 67)

Frankena's understanding of the nature and role of the virtues drew on the commonsense view that in order to know what kind of person one ought to be, one needs to know what kind of behavior is good or bad. Unless one knows what constitutes acts of truth-telling or lying, one has no way to specify what the virtue of truthfulness or honesty might entail. Ethical theories were assumed to be aids to help people make good decisions on the basis of well-justified principles or rules. Virtues were secondary for that endeavor.

This account of ethics seemed particularly well suited to the emerging field of bioethics. It was assumed that the task of medical ethics was to help physicians and other health-care providers make decisions about difficult cases created by the technological power of modern medicine. Whether a patient could

See Also
Conscience

DETERMINING GOODNESS
Not by Motivation Alone

Both philosophers (Pincoffs, 1986) and theologians (Hauerwas, 1985) have challenged the assumption that ethics in general and biomedical ethics in particular should be focused primarily on decisions and principles. It is a mistake, they argue, to separate questions of the rightness or goodness of an action from the character of the agent. To relegate the virtues to the motivation for action mistakenly assumes that the description of an action can be abstracted from the character of the agent. To abstract actions from the agent's perspective fails to account for why the agent should confront this or that situation and under what description. Those who defended the importance of virtue for ethics argued, following Aristotle, that *how* one does *what* one does is as important as what one does.

— STANLEY HAUERWAS

be disconnected from a respirator was analyzed in terms of the difference between such basic rules as "do no harm" and "always act that the greatest good for the greatest number be done." The case orientation of medical decision making seemed ideally suited to the case orientation of ethical theory exemplified by Frankena.

In their influential book, *Principles of Biomedical Ethics*, Tom L. Beauchamp and James F. Childress retain the structure of ethics articulated by Frankena. Their account of biomedical ethics revolves around the normative alternatives of utilitarian and deontological theories and the principles of autonomy, nonmaleficence, beneficence, and justice. Each of these fundamental principles has correlative primary virtues—that is, respect for autonomy, nonmalevolence, benevolence, and justice—but these "virtues" play no central role. Beauchamp and Childress justify leaving an account of virtue to the last chapter by saying that there are no good arguments for "making judgments about persons independent of judgments about acts or . . . making virtue primary or sufficient for the moral life" (Beauchamp and Childress, 1983, p. 265).

The renewed interest in the nature and significance of virtue ethics has been stimulated by the work of Alasdair MacIntyre, in particular his book *After Virtue* (1984). MacIntyre's defense of an Aristotelian virtue theory was but a part of his challenge to the presuppositions of modern moral theory. MacIntyre attacked what he called "the Enlightenment project," the attempt to ground universal ethical principles in rationality qua rationality—for example, Kant's categorical imperative (Kant, 1959). MacIntyre agrees that principles and rules are important for ethics, but he rejects any attempt to justify those principles or rules that abstracts them from their rootedness in the historical particularities of concrete communities. The narratives that make such communities morally coherent focuses attention on the virtues correlative to those narratives. For the Greeks, for example, the *Odyssey* acted as the central moral text for the display of the heroic virtues. To separate ethics from its dependence on such narratives is to lose the corresponding significance of the virtues.

MacIntyre's defense of an ethics of virtue is part of his challenge to the attempt to secure agreement among people who share nothing besides the necessity to cooperate in the interest of survival. Enlightenment theories of ethics, MacIntyre argues, falsely assume that an ahistorical ethics is possible; a historical approach tries to justify ethical principles from anyone's (that is, any rational individual's) point of view.

Renewed interest in the ethics of virtue has accompanied a renewed appreciation of the importance of community in ethics. Those commentators who emphasize the importance of community presume that morally worthy political societies are constituted by goods that shape the participants in those societies to want the right things rightly. Therefore ethics, particularly an ethics of virtue, cannot be separated from accounts of politics. Such a politics cannot be reduced to the struggle for power but, rather, is about the constitution of a community's habits for the production of a certain kind of people—that is, people who have the requisite virtues to sustain such a community.

"Chance reveals virtues and vices as light reveals objects."

LA ROCHEFOUCAULD
MAXIMS, 1665

Bioethics and the ethics of virtue

In the past the practice of medicine was thought to be part of the tradition of the virtues. As Gary Ferngren and Darrel Amundsen observe, "If health was, for most Greeks, the greatest of the virtues, it is not surprising that they devoted a great deal of attention to preserving it. As an essential component of *arete*, physical culture was an important part of the life of what the Greeks called *kalos kagathos*, the cultivated gentleman, who represented in classical times the ideal of the human personality" (Ferngren and Amundsen, 1985, p. 7). It should not be surprising, therefore, that not only was health seen as an analogue of virtue but medicine was understood as an activity that by its very nature was virtuous.

In medical ethics, the "ethics of virtue" approach tends to focus on the doctor-patient relationship. The trust, care, and compassion that seem so essential to a

See Also

Virtue Ethics: Ego and the Common Good

Virtue would not go so far without vanity to bear it company.

LA ROCHEFOUCAULD
MAXIMS, 1665

therapeutic relationship are virtues intrinsic to medical care. Medicine requires attention to technical knowledge and skill, which are virtues in themselves; however, the physician must also have a capacity—compassion—to feel something of patients' experience of their illness and their perception of what is worthwhile (Pellegrino, 1985). Not only compassion but also honesty, fidelity, courage, justice, temperance, magnanimity, prudence, and wisdom are required of the physician.

> *Not every one of these virtues is required in every decision. What we expect of the virtuous physician is that he will exhibit them when they are required and that he will be so habitually disposed to do so that we can depend upon it. He will place the good of the patient above his own and seek that good unless its pursuit imposes an injustice upon him, or his family, or requires a violation of his own conscience.*
>
> *(Pellegrino, 1985, p. 246)*

The importance of virtue for medical ethics has been challenged most forcefully by Robert Veatch. According to Veatch, there is no uncontested virtue ethic. The Greeks had one set of virtues, the Christians another, the Stoics another; and there is no rational way to resolve the differences among them. This is a particularly acute problem because modern medicine must be practiced as "stranger medicine," that is,

> *medicine that is practiced among people who are essentially strangers. It would include medicine that is practiced on an emergency basis in emergency rooms in large cities. It would also include care delivered in a clinic setting or in an HMO that does not have physician continuity, most medicine in student health services, VA Hospitals, care from consulting specialists, and the medicine in the military as well as care that is delivered by private practice general practitioners to patients who are mobile enough not to establish long-term relationships with their physicians. (Veatch, 1985, p. 338)*

Virtue theory is not suited to such medicine, Veatch argues, because "there is no reasonable basis for assuming that the stranger with whom one is randomly paired in the emergency room will hold the same theory of virtue as one's self" (Veatch, 1985, p. 339). The ethics of "stranger medicine" is best construed, Veatch contends, on the presumption that the relationship between doctor and patient is contractual. Such a relationship is best characterized by impersonal principles rather than in terms of virtue. The virtues make sense only within and to particular communities, and therefore only within a "sectarian" form of medicine.

Veatch's argument exemplifies what Alasdair MacIntyre calls the Enlightenment project. Yet MacIntyre would not dispute the descriptive power of Veatch's characterization of modern medicine. He thinks medicine is increasingly becoming a form of technological competence, bureaucratically institutionalized and governed by impersonal ethical norms. MacIntyre simply wishes to challenge the presumption that this is a moral advance. Put more strongly, MacIntyre challenges the presumption that such a medicine and the morality that underlies it can be justified in the terms Veatch offers. In particular, he asks, how can one account for the trust that seems a necessary component of the doctor-patient relationship without relying on an ethic of virtue?

Contrary to Veatch, James Drane (1988) and others argue that medicine does not exist within a relationship between strangers, but in fact depends on trust and confidence, if not friendship, between doctor and patient. Ethics, they hold, is not based on principles external to medical care and then applied to medicine; rather, medicine is itself one of the essential practices characteristic of good societies. Medicine thus understood does not need so much to be supplemented by ethical considerations based on a lawlike paradigm of principles and rules; on the contrary, medical care becomes one of the last examples left in liberal cultures of what the practice of virtue actually looks like. Those who work from an ethics of virtue do not come to medicine with general principles justified in other contexts, to be applied now to "medical quandaries"; rather, they see medicine itself as an exemplification of virtuous practices.

Here medicine is understood in the Aristotelian sense, as an activity—that is, as a form of behavior that produces a result intrinsic to the behavior itself (Aristotle, 1962). In MacIntyre's language, medicine is a practice in which the goods internal to the practice extend our powers in a manner that we are habituated in excellence (MacIntyre, 1984). Put simply, the practice of medicine is a form of cooperative human activity that makes us more than we otherwise could be.

MacIntyre's account of practice and Aristotle's account of activity remind us that the kinds of behavior that produce virtue are those done in and for themselves. Thus virtue is not acquired by a series of acts—even if such acts would be characterized as courageous, just, or patient—if they are done in a manner that does not render the person performing the actions just. As Aristotle says, "Acts are called just and self-controlled when they are the kinds of acts which a just and self-controlled man would perform; but the just and self-controlled man is not he who performs these acts, but he who also performs them in the way that the just and self-controlled men do" (Aristotle, 1962, 1105B5-9).

There is an inherently circular character to this account of the virtues that cannot be avoided. We can

become just only by imitating just people, but such "imitation" cannot be simply the copying of their external actions. Becoming virtuous requires apprenticeship to a master; in this way the virtues are acquired through the kind of training necessary to ensure that they will not easily be lost. How such masters are located depends on a social order that is morally coherent, so that such people exhibit what everyone knows to be good. Medicine, because it remains a craft that requires apprenticeship, exemplifies how virtue can and should be taught.

William F. May (1992) suggests that the very meaning of a profession implies that one who practices it is the kind of person who can be held accountable for the goods, and corresponding virtues, of that profession. Medicine as a profession functions well to the extent that medical training forms the character of those who are being initiated into that practice. This does not imply that those who have gone through medical training will be virtuous in other aspects of their lives; it does imply, however, that as physicians they will exhibit the virtues necessary to practice medicine.

In *Becoming a Good Doctor: The Place of Virtue and Character in Medical Ethics*, James Drane (1988) suggests that the character of the doctor is part of the therapeutic relationship, and that there is a structure to the doctor-patient relationship that is based on the patient's trust that the physician will do what is necessary to help the patient heal. The physician's task, Drane argues, is not to cure illness but to care for patients, and such care depends on the character of the physician. Drane, in contrast to Robert Veatch, argues that medicine must remain a virtuous practice if it is to be sustained in modern societies.

Paul Ramsey's (1970) insistence that the focus of medicine is not the curing of illness but the care of patients "as persons" can be interpreted as an account of medicine commensurate with an emphasis on the virtues. The particular character of the judgments clinicians must make about each patient is not unlike Aristotle's description of practical wisdom, or *phronesis*. According to Aristotle, ethics deals with those matters that can be other; a virtuous person not only must act rightly but also must do so "at the right time, toward the right objects, toward the right people, for the right reasons, and in the right manner" (1962, 1106B20-23). Similarly, physicians must know when to qualify what is usually done in light of the differences a particular patient presents. From this perspective, medicine is the training of virtuous people so they are able to make skilled but fallible judgments under conditions of uncertainty.

The increasing recognition of the narrative character of medical knowledge (Hunter, 1991) reinforces this emphasis on virtue and character. That the disease entities used for diagnosis are implicit narratives means medicine is an intrinsically interpretative practice that must always be practiced under conditions of uncertainty. Accordingly, patient and physician alike bring virtues (and vices) to their interaction that are necessary for sustaining therapeutic relationships.

Continuing problems for an ethics of virtue

To construe medicine as a virtue tradition establishes an agenda of issues for investigation in medical ethics. How are the virtues differentiated? Are there some virtues peculiar to medicine? How are different virtues related to one another? How is the difference between being a person of virtue and character, and the possession of the individual virtues, to be understood? Can a person possess virtues necessary for the practice of medicine without being virtuous? Can a person be courageous without being just?

"Virtue is more clearly shown in the performance of fine actions than in the nonperformance of base ones."

ARISTOTLE
NICHOMACHEAN ETHICS

Such questions have been central to the discussion of the virtues in classical ethical theory. For example, Aristotle maintained that none of the individual virtues could be rightly acquired unless they were acquired in the way that the person of practical wisdom would acquire them. Yet one could not be a person of practical wisdom unless one possessed individual virtues such as courage and temperance. Aristotle did not think the circular character of his account was problematic because he assumed that the kind of habituation commensurate with being "well brought up" is the way we were initiated into the "circle."

Yet in what sense the virtues are habits remains a complex question that involves the question of how the virtues are individuated. For Aristotle some of the virtues are "qualities" that qualify the emotions, but not all the virtues are like courage and temperance in that respect. Aristotle's resort to the artificial device of the "mean" for locating the various virtues has caused more problems than it has resolved. These matters are made even more complex by the importance Aristotle gives to friendship in the *Nicomachean Ethics*, where it is treated as a virtue even though it is not a quality but a relation.

The Christian appropriation of the virtues did little to resolve these complex issues. For Saint Augustine the virtues of the pagans were only "splendid vices" insofar as they were divorced from the worship of God. In "Of the Morals of the Catholic Church," Augustine redescribed the fourfold division of the virtues as four forms of love:

> *that temperance is love giving itself entirely to that which is loved; fortitude is love readily bearing all things for the loved object; justice is love serving only*

"Rudeness is the weak man's imitation of strength."

ERIC HOFFER
THE PASSIONATE STATE OF MIND, 1954

"The art of medicine consists in amusing the patient while nature cures the disease."

VOLTAIRE

> *the loved object, and therefore ruling rightly; prudence is love distinguishing with sagacity between what hinders it and what helps it. The object of this love is not anything, but only God, the chief good, the highest wisdom, the perfect harmony. So we may express the definition thus, that temperance is love keeping itself entire and uncorrupt for God; fortitude is love bearing everything readily for the sake of God; justice is love serving God only, and therefore ruling well all else, as subject to man; prudence is love making a right distinction between what helps it toward God and what might hinder it.* (1955, p. 115)

Thomas Aquinas, influenced profoundly by Augustine and Aristotle, provided an extraordinary account of the virtues that in many ways remains unsurpassed. According to Aquinas, charity, understood as friendship with God, is the form of all the virtues. Therefore, like Augustine, he maintained that there can be no true virtue without charity (Aquinas, 1952). Unlike Augustine, however, Aquinas grounded the virtues in an Aristotelian account of human activity, habits, and passions. For Aquinas, therefore, the virtues are dispositions or skills necessary for human flourishing.

Aquinas's account of the virtues does present some difficulties, however. Even though he followed Augustine's (and Plato's) account of the four "cardinal" virtues—prudence, courage, temperance, and justice—neither he nor Augustine successfully argued why these four should be primary. (Aristotle does not single out these four as primary.) Indeed, it is clear from Aquinas's account that he thought of the cardinal virtues as general descriptions that required more specification through other virtues, such as truthfulness, gentleness, friendship, and magnanimity (Aquinas, 1952).

These issues obviously bear on medicine considered as part of the virtue tradition. Are there virtues peculiar to the practice of medicine that require particular cultivation by those who would be doctors? If the virtues are interdependent, can a bad person be a good doctor? Or, put more positively, do the virtues required to be a good doctor at least set one on the way to being a good person? If the Christian claim that the "natural virtues" must be formed by the theological virtues of faith, hope, and charity is correct, does that mean that medicine as a virtue requires theological warrant?

Some of these questions have not been explored with the kind of systematic rigor they deserve. MacIntyre, however, suggests some promising directions. For example, he has argued that practices are not sufficient in themselves to sustain a full account of the individual virtues, their interrelations, or their role in areas such as medicine. Practices must be understood within the context of those goods necessary for the display of a whole human life and within a tradition that makes the goods that shape that life intelligible (MacIntyre, 1984). Those initiated into the practice of medicine, for example, might well have their moral life distorted if medicine as a virtue was not located within a tradition that placed the goods that medicine serves within an overriding hierarchy of goods and corresponding virtues. Yet what such a hierarchy would actually consist of remains to be spelled out.

These matters are made more complex to the extent that those who stand in virtue traditions cannot draw on the distinction between the moral realm and the nonmoral realm so characteristic of Kantian inspired moral theory. Once distinctions between the moral and the nonmoral are questioned, strong distinctions between deontological ethics, consequential ethics, and the "ethics of virtue" are equally questionable. L. Gregory Jones and Richard Vance (1993) argue, for example, that to assume that the virtues are an alternative to an ethics of principles and rules simply reproduces the assumption that there is a distinct realm called "ethics" that can be separated from the practices of particular communities. It was this assumption that led to the disappearance of virtue from modern moral theory.

For example, Aristotle thought that how a person laughed said much about his or her character. Therefore, what we consider matters of personal style and/or etiquette were considered morally significant by the ancients. For the virtues to encompass such matters as part of human character makes problematic the distinction so crucial to modernity—that is, the distinction between public and private morality. Thus, from such a perspective, what physicians do in their "private time" may well prove important for how they conduct themselves morally as physicians.

Equally troubling is the role "luck" plays in an ethics of virtue. For example, Aristotle thought that a lack of physical beauty made it difficult for a person to be happy: "For a man is scarcely happy if he is very ugly to look at, or of low-birth, or solitary and childless" (1962, 1099A35-37). Modern egalitarian sensibilities find it offensive to think that luck might play a role in our being virtuous (Card, 1990), yet the Greeks thought it unavoidable for any account of the virtuous and happy life. Indeed, as Martha Nussbaum (1986) has argued, the very strength the virtues provide create a "fragility" that cannot be avoided. Illness may well be considered part of a person's "luck" that limits the ability to live virtuously. Medicine may thus be understood as the practice that can help restore a person to virtue.

How medicine and an ethics of virtue are understood differs greatly from one historical period to another as well as from one community to another. To

the extent that medicine can no longer be sustained as a guild, perhaps it should no longer be construed in the language of the virtues. As Mark Wartofsky asks, "How is benevolence, as a distinctively *medical* virtue, to be interpreted in those forms of the practice where the individual patient is literally seen not as a person but only through the mediation of the records, laboratory reports, or a monitoring of data in a computer network?" (Wartofsky, 1985, p. 194).

Yet many continue to argue that any treatment of medicine that makes the virtues of both physician and patient secondary cannot be a medicine anyone should desire or morally support. Truthfulness, for example, is a virtue intrinsic to the care of patients; without it, whatever care is given, even if it is effective in the short run, cannot sustain a morally healthy relationship between patient and physician. Good medicine requires communication and participation by the patient that can be secured only by the physician's telling the patient the truth as well as the patient's demanding truthful speech. Without such truthful communication, the patient, as Plato argued, is reduced to the status of a slave (Drane, 1988). Ironically, in the name of freedom, the kind of medicine Veatch (1985) envisioned looks like a medicine fit for slaves—admittedly an odd conclusion since Veatch assumes that a contractual relation between physician and patient is the condition for a free exchange. Moreover, even Veatch continues to assume that truth-telling is a virtue necessary for medicine to survive as a practice between strangers.

For his part, Drane raises issues at the heart of any account of the virtues as well as of medicine as a virtue tradition. If it is true that truthfulness is a virtue intrinsic to the practice of medicine, can that virtue conflict with, for example, the virtue of benevolence? Plato and Aristotle assumed the unity of the virtues. Accordingly, the virtues would not conflict with one another if they were rightly oriented to a life of happiness. Aquinas held that the virtues might conflict during the time we are "wayfarers," but not in heaven. Drane resolves the possibility of such conflict by suggesting that medicine requires the truth to be spoken, but benevolently. One may doubt, however, whether this attractive suggestion resolves all questions about the conflict among the virtues, particularly in medical care.

Questions of virtue also relate to issues of justice in the distribution of health care. For if the patient can ask medicine to supply any need abstracted from a community of virtue, then there seems no way to limit in a moral way the demands for medical care. In such a situation, those who have more economic and social power can command more than is due medically, since medicine seems committed to meeting needs irrespective of the habits that created those needs. Liberal political theory has often tried to show how a just society is possible without just people; a "medicine of strangers" may result in a maldistributed medicine.

UNSOUGHT VIRTUE
Patients and Patience

If medicine is to be construed in the tradition of the virtues, the virtues and character of patients must be considered. The very term "patient" suggests a necessary virtue that is closely associated with Christian accounts of the virtues. If we must learn to live our lives patiently, then illness may appear in quite a different light than it does in those accounts of the moral life that have no patience with patience. For example, if suffering is thought to be an occasion to learn better how to be patient, then a medicine of care may be sustainable even when cure cannot be accomplished.

Karen Lebacqz (1985) suggests that the circumstances in which patients find themselves, especially the circumstance of pain and helplessness, can invite them to become accepting and obedient. These traits, which may appear virtuous, may just as likely be vices if they are not shaped by fortitude, prudence, and hope. Lebacqz suggests that these virtues are particularly relevant to the condition of being a "patient," because they provide the skills necessary to respond to illness in a "fitting" manner. No *one* way of expressing these virtues suits all patients; yet they do provide the conditions for our learning the tasks required in health and illness.

— STANLEY HAUERWAS

"Certain flaws of character, if displayed to advantage, shine brighter than virtue itself."

LA ROCHEFOUCAULD
MAXIMS, 1665

Conclusion

There is no consensus about the nature of virtue and/or the virtues that a good person should possess. That should not be surprising: the attempt to introduce the virtues into bioethics has gone hand in hand with an emphasis on the inevitable historical character of ethical reflection. If, as MacIntyre (1984) has argued, the virtues can be described only in relation to a particular tradition and narrative, then the very assumption that a universal account of ethics—and in particular, of medical ethics—is problematic. Yet the very character of medicine as a practice whose purpose is care for the ill remains one of the richest resources for those committed to an account of the moral life in the language of the virtues.

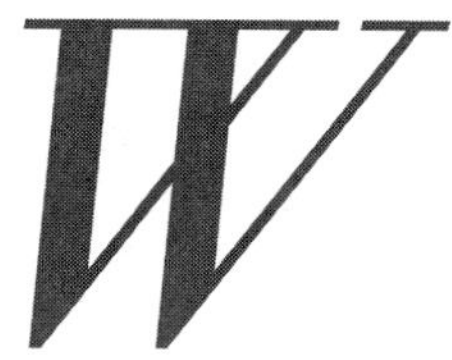

WOMEN

HISTORICAL AND CROSS-CULTURAL PERSPECTIVES

A central problem of women's history is that women have been defined by men using concepts and terms based on men's experiences. Such androcentric thought pervades all domains of knowledge. Scholarship in women's studies, developed largely since the late 1960s across a broad range of disciplines, shows that attitudes, customs, laws, and institutions affecting women are grounded in religious and functionalist perspectives according to which "woman" is said to have been created from and after man; has been identified with her sexuality and defined by her sexual function; and has been confined to roles and relationships that are extensions of her reproductive capacity. Alongside this history stands a centuries-old feminist critique that challenges as self-serving and often misogynist the assumptions and intentions of the religions, philosophies, sciences, and familial and political institutions that have shaped the experiences of women in most eras and cultures. Moreover, both the definition of women and its critique reflect a Eurocentric bias that today is the subject of much criticism. This article summarizes the scholarship produced since the mid-1970s by historians of women, reflecting their collective efforts to compensate for ahistorical assumptions and to constitute a written record both more inclusive of the experiences of women and more open to differences of perspective. It assumes that the history of women requires consideration of moral and ethical as well as social, economic, and political issues.

Women defined

From ancient times it has been customary to define "woman," in relationship to man, as a limited and contingent part of a dimorphic species. Western cultures have placed heavy constraints on female lives, sometimes justifying these constraints by attributing to women, such as Pandora and Eve, responsibility for human misfortunes resulting from their allegedly weaker self-control or greater lasciviousness. Despite the existence of exceptional women in myth and history, most women in most historical societies have been confined to positions of dependency. Ultimately, whether on the basis of their capacity for pregnancy and resulting physical vulnerability or the use of women's fertility in forging relationships of social and economic value, women, like children, have been denied an independent voice. Seen as "lesser men" by the fathers of Western philosophy, women have been viewed as "Other," as not-man, through a discourse in which human being was embodied in the male sex (Beauvoir, 1952).

"Women have served all these centuries as looking-glasses possessing the magic and delicious power of reflecting the figure of a man at twice its natural size."

VIRGINIA WOOLF
A ROOM OF ONE'S OWN
1929

Deprived of political power and identified with sexual temptation, women have been subject to myriad laws and customs that have at once prescribed and enforced their secondary status. Men have termed women "the sex"; defined them primarily in terms of their sexuality; and, as masters of family and public power, created and staffed the institutions that control female sexuality. In the early fifteenth century, the Italian-born French author Christine de Pizan (1364-ca. 1430) challenged the prevailing androcentric definition of her sex, declaring that the evil attributed to women by learned men existed in men's minds and that, if permitted education, women would become as virtuous and capable as men.

Resistance and rebellion by individual women have a long history; and organized protest, termed "feminism" only since the 1890s, is traceable through a history that is continuous for at least two centuries. However, the condition of women has only occasional-

GLOBAL SISTERHOOD

Communications and air travel have drawn the first and third worlds closer, and international conferences have brought attention to women's issues around the world.

WOMEN

Historical and Cross-Cultural Perspectives

"The great question . . . which I have not been able to answer, despite my thirty years of research into the feminine soul, is 'What does a woman want?'"

ERNEST JONES
LIFE AND WORK OF SIGMUND FREUD, 1955

ly been viewed as a general problem of social justice. The "woman question," as it was phrased in the nineteenth century, was debated as a political, social, and economic, but rarely as a moral issue; women's rights and responsibilities were discussed as matters of expediency. In the great democratic revolutions of the late eighteenth century, the "inalienable rights of man" were not extended to women. Men, as heads of traditional patriarchal families, continued to speak for their dependents, women as well as children. While some Enlightenment philosophers, most notably Theodore von Hippel (1741-1796), had admitted the abstract equality of all human beings, and others, such as the Marquis de Condorcet (1743-1794), advocated women's accession to equal education and to full civic rights, social arrangements nevertheless made it expedient to ignore their claims. Ultimately, most efforts to improve women's status and condition have been justified on grounds of expediency: if women voted, said the suffragists of 1915, war would be less likely; if mothers earned fathers' wages, said the feminists of 1985, fewer children would live in poverty.

Most matters related to women, then, whether intellectual constructs or social institutions, whether constraining or enlarging women's options, whether produced by misogynists or feminists, have rested on utilitarian grounds. Woman, first of all as an individual human being, was rarely the subject of thought or decision; woman as wife and mother or potential mother has been the ideal type. Even for suffragist leaders of the nineteenth and twentieth centuries, the resort to arguments of expediency over considerations of justice or ethics has itself been an expedient (Kraditor, 1965). By the 1990s, however, following two decades of reexamination of all domains of knowledge by scholars in women's studies, feminist theorists began to challenge arguments based on expediency (while sometimes using them as well) and to demand a voice in the discourse through which both knowledge and social institutions are established. Noting injustice in the treatment of women, and the absence of concern about women at the center of most modern and contemporary philosophical systems, they criticize ethical theory itself as a hegemonic expression of the values of a dominant class or gender (Walker, 1992).

It is simpler, and historically has been more effective, to argue the needs of women in terms of their differences from men—their needs as wives and mothers, their concerns with nurturant values, their familial and social responsibilities. Women often do speak "in a different voice," reflecting different moral concerns and material circumstances (Gilligan, 1982). Women have been and remain deeply divided over their own definition of self: as individuals entitled to, and now demanding, equality of treatment with men; or as persons with gender-specific differences and resulting relationships with families, friends, and communities to whom they bear responsibilities that limit individual autonomy and rights. "Equal rights feminists" have been challenged for basing their claims on an abstract concept of personhood that denies female specificity. Rather than buttressing the claims of individualism based in nineteenth-century liberal philosophy (Fox-Genovese, 1991; Pateman, 1987), they should, according to this view, emphasize the need for men as well as women to acknowledge their dependence on and debts to the communities that are essential to their existence.

"WOMAN"

No Simple Definitions

Scholars today recognize that neither "man" nor "woman" has a single, fixed meaning; cross-cultural and international differences defy simple definition. The concept of separate spheres of human activity labeled public and private, political and personal, society and family, however, has a long history; the reality of women's lives was obscured by these universalizing categories of analysis often used by philosophers, politicians, and professors. As the twenty-first century approaches, historians of women have firmly established the historicity of women, a critical first task. Women's lives, as well as their consciousness, vary, not only by era but also by class, race, age, marital status, region, religion, education, and a host of factors peculiar to individual circumstances. Implicit in this work is a political message: that changes over time past make future change conceivable. Also implicit is an accusation of injustice against a system of societal arrangements that has suppressed women, for the questions raised in this scholarship deal often with omissions, silences, and double standards. This form of scholarship elicits new knowledge and conjectures about human possibilities.

— MARILYN J. BOXER

Furthermore, through failure to emphasize female differences, women may continue to be measured through a single, male-constructed lens that ignores or denigrates female-specific experiences. Yet woman along with man should be the measure of all things—and the universalizing of human experience based only on consideration of dominant cultures should be avoided. Awareness of the dimensions of this "equality vs. difference" question is critical to understanding a wide range of historical and contemporary issues regarding the status of women. Can gender-specific needs of individuals such as pregnant women be acknowledged in law that also supports equality of treatment for all individuals? Can employment preferences be granted to men if, historically, most women have not pursued a given occupation? How should a history grounded in gender distinctions be interpreted (Scott, 1988)?

Women in traditional Western societies

As the story has been reconstructed, women in history have become increasingly visible (Bridenthal et al., 1987). New anthropological studies suggest that women may have enjoyed greater equity with men in prehistorical times (Sanday, 1981). Agrarian economies with relatively little differentiation of tasks allowed for more egalitarian relationships within families; families themselves constituted societies, and participation was not dichotomized by gender, or sex roles. The classical world, with its more advanced economies, and greater wealth and militarism, vested both property rights and citizenship only in men, as heads of households. Separated into family and polity, society became a male world of civic virtue. Relegated to the household, women became men's property, and a double standard of sexuality was constructed to assure female subjection to patriarchal family interests. A woman's honor, and that of her family, was identified with her chastity. The virtue of a woman, said Aristotle, was to obey. Differentiation by class allowed some variation of roles for women; but Plato's philosopher queens aside, no women could claim equal treatment in regard to property, citizenship, marriage, criminal law, or access to social institutions. Women existed to reproduce and to serve men's needs; rights in their progeny were assigned to men.

INFLUENCE OF CHRISTIANITY. The spread of Christianity brought new possibilities for women: for some, a role in spreading the new religion; for all, a promise of spiritual equality. Christianity created new opportunities for women's voices to be heard, especially by instituting marriage laws requiring consent and by establishing, in some instances, inheritance and property rights for women. Monasteries and convents, while providing shelter for the destitute, also offered education and alternative careers for a small, often highborn, minority. The high Middle Ages saw the foundation of the first universities in the Western world, beginning in 1088 with Bologna, whose famous twelfth-century legal scholar, Gratian, incorporated into his influential study Aristotle's dualistic view of women as passive and men as active, in law as well as reproductive physiology.

This Aristotelian dualism was also advanced by the work of Thomas Aquinas in the thirteenth century; he combined his reading of Aristotle with the Christian view of creation to assert that woman was a "defective and misbegotten" man, assigned by nature to the work of procreation. The rebirth of learning thus gave new life to the hoary tradition of defining women as not-men and for men, in terms of qualities they lacked and services they provided. Renaissance thinkers transmitted across the ages classical Greece's sharp distinction between polity and household. The literature of courtly love notwithstanding, as dynastic power was reconstituted in bureaucratic and political structures, the separation of public and private arenas of human activity increased; and relative to aristocratic men, upper-class women faced new restrictions. Growth of the market economy, however, probably had a more liberating effect on rural and urban women of other classes.

Neither the Renaissance nor the Reformation, both considered watersheds in European history, brought reformed ideas about women to the fore. The advent of Protestantism meant the closing of nunneries that had allowed some women, notably those who could offer a dowry to the church, agency outside marriage. It also deprived all classes of women of the succor of the Virgin Mary and female saints. However, Protestantism did provide some literate women as well as men direct access to the word of God in the Bible. By ending clerical celibacy, it opened opportunities to ministers' wives, and ultimately, especially in the dissenting sects, it allowed women wider participation in church affairs. In the Counterreformation, some Catholic laywomen formed communities through which they provided social services for the poor, ill, and orphaned. Nuns continued to serve as teachers, nurses, and social workers. But Catholics and Protestants alike, following the biblical injunction of Paul, taught women silence in public and subjection to men in private.

URBAN VS. RURAL EXPERIENCE. Controversy over the effects of the Renaissance and Reformation on women's lives continues to fuel debate among historians of women. In an increasingly complex society, generalizations fail to satisfy: some women prospered, enjoyed education by leading humanist scholars such as Erasmus, and wielded power on behalf of dynastic lines. Urban craftsmen's wives shared in domestic production and local marketing of goods, and helped to manage artisanal workshops. City women developed professions of their own, largely in the healing arts, midwifery, and retail establishments, especially those purveying food. But most wage-earning women worked as domestic servants, frequently for a decade before marriage and sometimes for their entire lives; "maid" had become synonymous with "female servant."

However, most women, like most men, lived in

"One is not born a woman: one becomes a woman. No biological, psychological or economic destiny can determine how the human female will appear in society."

SIMONE DE BEAUVOIR
THE SECOND SEX, 1949

"The history of men's opposition to women's emancipation is more interesting perhaps than the story of that emancipation itself."

VIRGINIA WOOLF
A ROOM OF ONE'S OWN
1929

rural settings, where all members of the household pooled their labor in a family economy organized to produce the goods and services essential to supporting and reproducing themselves. They lived within households and made essential contributions to the economic survival of their families. Labor needs over the family's life cycle determined the status, residence, and welfare of most people (Tilly and Scott, 1978). Only after centuries-long structural changes in agriculture and industry, in company with a demographic shift that reduced both mortality and fertility, did the employment of female productive capacity generate public debate over a "woman question." Ultimately it was a shift in the location of women's traditional work—especially making cloth and garments—from the household into the factory, and the ensuring restructuring of (especially married) women's economic contribution to the family, that created the conditions for feminist debate. Only then did the question "Should a woman work?" or "Should she have a 'right to work'?" make sense.

EFFECTS OF POLITICAL AND SCIENTIFIC DEVELOPMENTS. In addition to religious reformation and the expansion of commerce and trade, other major trends in the early modern period led to new institutions and novel ideas that affected women's lives and challenged traditional views of women's "nature." Political centralization and the rise of science also meant change in women's lives. According to one recent interpretation, the great witchcraft persecution of the sixteenth and seventeenth centuries reflected not only religious and gender conflict but also efforts to legitimize political authority by exercising new forms of social control over individual behavior (Larner, 1981). Because women's relative physical and economic weaknesses made their recourse to magic power seem plausible, and because their alleged sexual insatiability predisposed them to temptation by the devil, 80 percent of the victims of witch-hunts were female—often older, single, eccentric women lacking male protection.

Ultimately science disproved many misogynist notions about the female body. However, despite studies in embryology challenging the Aristotelian view of women's passivity in reproduction that also buttressed attitudes and customs denying them agency in society, only in the late nineteenth and early twentieth centuries were such classical and false assumptions finally displaced by scientific knowledge.

Although by the eighteenth century the economic, political, and intellectual structures that maintained traditional attitudes and institutionalized age-old practices toward women were subject to a multitude of challenges, time-honored patterns persisted. Just as in the thirteenth century Thomas Aquinas had recapitulated Aristotle, so the influential eighteenth-century philosopher Jean-Jacques Rousseau reinforced belief in woman's role as the helpmate of man. Like Adam's Eve, Rousseau's Sophie, the ideal wife of his ideal citizen, Émile, was created to serve, support, and console the chief actor on the human stage, the man to whom she was legally subject. The Napoleonic Code of 1804, and similar codes of law subsequently promulgated across Europe, required married women to obey their husbands. Voices that demanded inclusion of civil rights for women along with the "Rights of Man"—Condorcet in France, von Hippel in Germany, Mary Wollstonecraft in England—were silenced as the Age of Reason gave way to an Age of Steel. Men alone wrote and signed the new "social contract"; as "natural" dependents, women could not aspire to citizenship.

And yet women increasingly did claim civil rights. Despite the negative examples of Wollstonecraft (dead after childbirth and infamous more for her unconventional lifestyle than for her contributions to radical philosophy), Marie Antoinette, Olympe de Gouges (author of *The Declaration of the Rights of Woman and the Female Citizen*, 1791), and Jeanne Manon Roland (dead on the Jacobins' guillotine, ostensibly for having violated the boundaries of conventional femininity), and despite increasingly restrictive legal codes and an ideology of domesticity that won widespread support across class lines, new philosophic currents, based in the Enlightenment concept of human perfectibility, generated the first organized movements for women's rights.

Women in transforming societies

Inspired by the French Revolution, women in the nineteenth century began to form groups through which collectively to advocate improved treatment of their sex. By the mid-nineteenth century, organized groups we now call "feminist" were formed in France, England, the United States, Prussia, and even Russia, to challenge women's subject status. The new protest took place in the context of economic as well as political transformation in western and central Europe and the United States. Revolutionary changes in methods of agriculture and transportation, and the rise of an enlarged market economy, industrialization, and urbanization brought profound alteration to family structures and relationships. More young people, including women, could claim and find opportunities for social and geographic mobility and economic independence.

Especially for women, however, escape from the confines of the patriarchal family brought new vulnerabilities (Tilly and Scott, 1978). With female wages far below subsistence levels, a woman alone required assistance, and might trade sex for survival, risking dismissal from employment for her "loose morals" or extreme deprivation if deserted by her male partner.

Social reformers responded, purportedly in women's defense. Not all protesters and reformers called for "equality" for women; few, if any, entertained ideas of identical rights and responsibilities for both sexes. Utopian schemes for the total reconstruction of society aside, debate over the status of women most often focused on ways to "protect" them: to shelter traditional women's work from the intrusion of men; to safeguard women (along with children) from unsafe conditions and/or excessive hours of labor; to secure for women rights to inherited property, their own earnings, and custody of their persons as well as some share in legal authority over their children in cases of divorce. Divorce itself, largely illegal or difficult to obtain before the twentieth century, was one of many reform issues about which women themselves differed, often on the basis of class, religion, or ethnicity.

EQUAL BUT DIFFERENT. Differentiation between "individualistic" and "relational" forms of feminism heightens current debate over the definition of feminism. It also parallels a major controversy among feminist theorists that cuts to the heart of moral issues regarding women. Must arguments undergirding a political movement on behalf of women—the various forms of feminism—be grounded in the assumption that human beings are identical? If so, equal-rights law can be used to deny pregnant women special insurance and employment benefits. Equality so defined may demand identity of treatment.

Alternatively, to emphasize women's particularity, to focus on sexual differences, may invite legislation (and buttress attitudes) restricting women's options in the guise of acknowledging their special needs. Precisely this argument was long used to justify labor laws that denied many excellent employment opportunities to all women because they required occasional work during evening hours or involved physically demanding tasks. More recently, women workers in potentially hazardous industries have faced coerced sterilization or loss of employment on grounds of their capacity for reproduction. But to deny that women on the basis of their sex constitute a special class can also deprive them of support they may need—for example, in pregnancy. It can even, some argue, destroy the very basis for a political movement in their name and interest.

This "difference versus equality" debate, often in inchoate form, has led to extended conflict over definitions of feminism and feminist demands. It also raises fundamental issues regarding individual rights, family responsibilities, and the prerogatives of government. In the nineteenth century, reformers called for legislative action to ameliorate the worst abuses of industrialization and urbanization. Reformers ranged from British industrialists who wanted to improve the quality of the labor force to French Social Catholics who sought to base solutions to societal problems on Christian principles to Prussia's "Iron Chancellor" Otto von Bismarck, who schemed to reduce the threat of socialist revolution. Whether impelled by religious, philanthropic, political, or economic motives, they shared the recog-

DEFINING FEMINISM
Early Varieties

Emphasis by historians on the woman-suffrage movement, which began as a minority concern within women's groups in the mid-nineteenth century and peaked near the beginning of the twentieth, has obscured not only the larger concerns of women activists but also deep differences within feminist movements. Campaigns for "equal rights," grounded in the assumptions of liberal individualism, became dominant to a greater extent in England and the United States than elsewhere. Contemporary English-language dictionaries tend to define feminism as a movement toward political, social, educational, economic, and legal rights for women equal to those of men. This has been termed "individualistic" feminism (Offen, 1988).

The feminisms of continental Europe in that earlier era, as well as later women's movements in Third World countries, reflected a closer association with the social question—that is, with issues of class and nation—and with family relationships and community ties. This constitutes a "relational" form of feminism. Socialist feminists, while cognizant of women's needs for education and encouragement to participate fully in political struggles in support of class goals, declined to envision as their purpose access to equal—and equally exploitative—conditions with working-class men. Others, including Catholic feminists in large numbers, insisted on improvement of women's status in order to enhance their performance in traditional women's roles and relationships. In some countries, notably the United States, a "century of struggle" for women's rights grew out of religious ferment and the recognition that no subjected person, woman or slave, could be fully responsible to God as a moral being. Nineteenth-century equal-rights feminism and the concurrent movement for "protective legislation" offered contrasting answers to the "woman question."

— MARILYN J. BOXER

"Feminism is the most revolutionary idea there has ever been. Equality for women demands a change in the human psyche more profound than anything Marx dreamed of."

POLLY TOYNBEE
IN THE GUARDIAN, 1987

nition that such innovations increased governmental powers over persons' lives. They also found that they could succeed, against strongly held liberal tenets favoring laissez-faire practice, by exposing the physical, and allegedly moral, dangers to female (and young) persons posed by the new working and living conditions. Working women rarely spoke for themselves in these debates, and even feminist voices, largely from the middle class, were little heeded.

Beginning in the 1840s with the first laws limiting women's night work, every policy of the interventionist states, acting in lieu of a patriarchal family to regulate female behavior, extended the premise that women needed special consideration and that men must provide them with protection, even against themselves. The nineteenth-century debate over short hours and the twentieth-century controversy over state regulation of reproduction share the assumption that adult women, as individual citizens, cannot or should not be empowered to make decisions affecting their own persons. Whether arguing against a woman's working outside the home at night, on behalf of keeping her husband home from the cabaret, or championing limits on abortion, advocates of restrictive legislation link women's rights with those of others: husband, child, family, state.

Similar arguments may be employed on occasion in support of male-specific measures such as military conscription, which subordinates individual freedom to national security. Such denial of personal autonomy, however, remains the exception for men and, moreover, often brings with it rights of citizenship. Women, on the other hand, are assumed to serve the interests of others at all times, and rarely gain comparable advantage. Historically, legislation concerning women has not distinguished among them by race, ethnicity, or class, by marital status, age, preference, or capacity, assuming marriage and motherhood to be the overriding obligation and destiny of all women, and conflating childbearing with child rearing. As historians have highlighted in recent books, the interests of women and their calls for "freedom" may even be seen as at odds with those of the family. This, of course, is true especially of the type of family associated primarily

20TH-CENTURY ADVANCES

Holding Steady This Time

The history of women in the twentieth century reveals the centrality of the "woman question" to the social, economic, and political concerns of many nations. During wars and revolutions, traditional notions of "women's place" and struggles over woman suffrage have been eclipsed by calls for female labor and patriotic support. Apparent feminist advances, however, have frequently led to the reinstitution of traditional norms. Following both world wars, women were summarily discharged from good-paying jobs or offered less skilled and less rewarding employment. However, structural changes in commerce and industry have escalated demand for female workers, especially in clerical, teaching, and other service occupations dominated by women; expansion of educational opportunities has augmented female literacy and professional expertise; advances in public health, nutrition, and medicine have continued to increase female life expectancy and decrease infant mortality; and new technologies have reduced the need for labor-intensive household chores. All of these changes tend to free many women for long periods of productive activity outside the family. As more and more countries have been swept into the global economy and information network, women's movements, often linked (and sometimes subordinated) to nationalism, have appeared around the world. Along with efforts to improve women's health and education, Third World feminists are challenging double standards in law and culture as well as such practices as clitoridectomy, marriage by capture, and sati (Johnson-Odim and Strobel, 1992).

Unlike earlier waves of feminist protest, the mid-twentieth-century rebirth of feminism called into action sufficient numbers of educated and strategically placed women and their male supporters to successfully challenge many social priorities and institutional structures. Though feminists are sometimes wrongly perceived as a "special interest" group reflecting only the needs and desires of middle-class white women in developed nations, their pressure, especially since the 1970s, has achieved significant change in legal status, medical treatment, and workplace conditions of benefit to all women. It has opened to women professions long monopolized by men, including medicine, law, the ministry, and the professoriate, whose collective powers of definition long buttressed gender biases. In some cases, most notably medicine, this represents a restoration to women of roles they held prior to the institution of professional schools and licensure, from which they were excluded. As health-care providers, women today often challenge the gender distinction between male doctors who "cure" and female nurses who "care." Women's health centers tend to stress women's need to question conventional medical procedures and to encourage women to assume an active role in determining their own treatment (Jaggar, 1983).

— MARILYN J. BOXER

with the white, Western world (Bell and Offen, 1983; Degler, 1980); studies of the African-American family in the United States, and of extended families in other cultures, stress their function as sources of strength as well (Jones, 1985).

Women challenging epistemology

Modeled on the "self-help" agencies for women's health that first developed in the late 1960s and influenced medical practice, this new women's liberation movement has flourished in the academy, especially in the United States but increasingly in Europe and in some instances in Africa, Asia, and Latin America. The field of women's studies, which began as a search for feminist foremothers and a female past lost to history, has expanded across the disciplines to question old methodologies, ask new questions, identify new sources, reinterpret received wisdom, develop new female perspectives, and challenge the very construction of knowledge—not only about the "nature" of women but also about all the constructs in the natural and social sciences based on androcentric experience. Grounded in advocacy for the rights of women to equality in education, culture, and society, it is a form of moral as well as scientific inquiry.

Among the earliest paradigms developed from the new scholarship in women's studies was the "social construction of feminity." Whether psychologists rereading Sigmund Freud, sociologists reinterpreting Erik Erikson, or historians rediscovering Heinrich Kramer and James Sprenger's notorious late-fifteenth-century handbook on witchcraft, these scholars found in the sciences as well as the humanities a pervasive confusion of description with prescription. Proceeding from male-imposed definitions of female nature and proscriptions limiting female behavior as old as written records of humankind, men as philosophers, preachers, physicians, politicians, patriarchs, and professors had labeled unconventional women abnormal, criminal, ill, even pathological—or, alternatively, not "real women." The "eternal feminine" of Western mythology falsely universalized descriptions of an idealized (implicitly) white woman (Spelman, 1988; Chaudhuri and Strobel, 1992).

Historical and cross-cultural studies that belie many such interpretations have now been done. The new women's history, increasingly inclusive of women of color and international perspectives (Offen et al., 1991; Johnson-Odim and Strobel, 1992), lays bare the many consequences of the absence of female voices and agency, and the fundamental ways in which justice has been denied to half the human species. Women's history tells a tale of misconceptions, biases, and injustices that have oppressed women and limited their freedom of choice—and, hence, their moral responsibility. It also reveals the many and differing contributions, perceptions, and struggles that constitute the female past. Although this historical perspective faces challenges, sometimes by groups of women who remain dependent on traditional sex roles for economic support and social recognition, it nevertheless offers the potential for transformation of benefit to all (Jaggar, 1983). It rests, moreover, on the principles of justice.

To the extent that ethical considerations require attribution of personhood and personal agency to every human being, ethical behavior toward women calls for disclosure and discussion of the full record of women in history. It demands that women be defined by their particular positions within specific and changing contexts and allowed choices reflecting the full range of their human attributes. It calls for major societal change. Inspired by new knowledge and the new feminisms, women have begun as never before to speak in their own voices and to claim equality despite their differences—envisioning difference without hierarchy. The "woman question," as posed by women today, can no longer be answered in terms of expediency. The ground has shifted: in the new world, women stand along with men as individuals endowed equally, if perhaps differently, with moral rights and moral responsibilities.

— MARILYN J. BOXER

HEALTH-CARE ISSUES

Most ethical issues in patient care and biomedical research affect men and women in the same ways, but there are some important differences related to biological factors, psychosocial experiences, and cultural background, as well as to differences in life experiences. These are exemplified in emerging health-care areas, such as the new reproductive technologies; in medical research; and in the data indicating that different treatment options are often made available to women and men (National Institutes of Health, 1990). This article will explore some of the ethical issues that arise in the health care of women. It will examine situations that characterize North American and European health-care settings, which therefore may not be relevant to other cultures or even to all segments of Western cultures. Areas of focus will be (1) aspects of the relationship between physicians, the health-care system, and female patients; and (2) specific aspects of the health care of women, including mental-health care.

General aspects of the therapeutic relationship

The relationship between health-care providers and their patients has been described as paternalistic (Notman and Nadelson, 1978). Women have generally been subordinate in the relationship between the sexes in

WOMEN

Health-Care Issues

health care as well as in other areas of their lives (Baker Miller and Mothner, 1971; West, 1984). A large body of literature documents that norms of behavior and social roles for women have supported stereotypic expectations of greater compliance, dependence, and passivity, especially in relationships with men. Although many of these stereotyped roles of men and women have changed, aspects persist and are still reflected in the expectations and responses of women as patients (Nadelson and Notman, 1991). These stereotypes also influence the expectations of physicians and other health-care providers in caring for women.

Although research, consumerism, and the erosion of the authoritarian role of the physician have influenced understandings of and attitudes about men's and women's characteristics and social roles, vestiges of these old stereotypes persist. Women patients continue to be approached with advice, commands, directions, or decisions about their illness or treatment more often than they are included as partners or collaborators in plans for their care (Nadelson and Notman, 1977). The relationship between physician or researcher and patient can assume the quality of a parent-child interaction rather than a partnership.

Men also experience a kind of paternalism in their relationships with physicians and the health-care system, but there are differences in the ways that men and women are treated, based on beliefs about men's and women's capabilities and roles. Women's complaints, for example, are often pejoratively labeled "psychogenic," implying that they are not to be taken seriously (Lennane and Lennane, 1973). This labeling may, in part, explain some of the gender differences in the treatment of certain diseases, such as cardiac disease, which is often not recognized in women. As a result, when women have procedures like a coronary bypass, they are typically sicker and require emergency surgery. Women are also referred later for revascularization procedures, and fewer women are referred for exercise rehabilitation (Wenger et al., 1993).

◆ **feminine ethics**
the description of moral experiences and intuitions of women and the exploration of how traditional approaches have neglected to include women's perspectives.

Women also often perceive themselves in ways that are consistent with the view that they are passive or compliant. This parent-child model, in which the patient accepts that she will relinquish an active role in her treatment, can result in diminished communication and compromised care. At times of crisis and in gratitude for being helped, the patient may overlook the depreciation implicit in the paternalistic model. The dependent, compliant response of the woman patient can interfere with active efforts to recuperate, an important part of the process of recovery from trauma and illness (Notman and Nadelson, 1978). All people can regress, to some extent, in the face of illness and pain. The tension between active participation and the wish to be taken care of is a particular problem for women because of their socialization to be more passive, and because of the authority and power dynamics that have characterized their relationships with men.

See Also

Trust Between Patients and Providers

PROFESSIONAL-PATIENT SEXUAL RELATIONSHIPS. Another problem in the relationship between the female patient and the male physician is the potential for sexualization of the relationship. The danger is reinforced in this relationship by the intimate nature of the interaction, which exposes private information as well as body parts.

Sexual relationships between patient and physician have received a great deal of attention, from the public as well as from the profession. Although the incidence of sexual contact between physicians and patients is difficult to document accurately, reports suggest that it is a significant problem (Council, 1990). In the past, sexual activity with patients was defended by some physicians as not necessarily harmful, and possibly therapeutic, but the profession has judged it to be categorically exploitative and unethical, and studies have determined that it is damaging (Bouhoutsos et al., 1983; Burgess, 1981; Feldman-Summers and Jones, 1984; Gabbard, 1989; Herman et al., 1987; Kluft, 1989; Pope and Bouhoutsos, 1986).

Efforts to enforce ethical guidelines forbidding sexual activity between doctor and patient have been hampered by concerns about confidentiality and public exposure that have made it difficult for patients to register formal complaints (Marmor, 1970). Substantial progress, however, has been made since the mid-1980s. Civil actions have been brought in the courts, and several states have adopted criminal, civil, and licensing regulations that specifically proscribe sexual behavior on the part of psychotherapists, physicians, other health-care providers, and others in positions of authority, such as teachers and employers (Jorgenson et al., 1991).

Many factors can lead to exploitative behavior by physicians and other health-care providers. Some behave unethically because of character flaws; others are vulnerable to sexual involvement because they are depressed, lonely, disappointed, or stressed. Their personal problems may lead them to respond sexually to a patient who enhances their feelings of importance and effectiveness, or who is physically appealing. Other physicians who become involved in exploitative behavior are compromised by alcoholism or substance abuse. Some women patients behave in ways that they do not consciously intend to be seductive, but can be interpreted to be, in response to the anxiety induced by their feelings about their illness. The physician can misinterpret this behavior and take advantage of the situation.

TRANSFERENCE. Understanding the concept of transference can clarify aspects of the doctor-patient relationship that may otherwise be difficult to comprehend. It refers to the attitudes and feelings brought to a relationship from past experiences with important figures, such as parents. Thus the need to please, or to gain love—through acquiescence or seductive behavior—can be brought into the doctor-patient relationship as if it were a response by the patient to the physician. Because of the transference that is inevitable in the doctor-patient relationship, questions have been raised about whether the patient is able to give truly informed consent to a sexual relationship (Herman et al., 1987; Kluft, 1989). Sexual interaction with a patient or client has been considered analogous to rape or incest because of the exploitative nature of the act and the problem of consent in the context of a relationship where the power and influence of the physician is so disproportionate (Gabbard, 1989; Nadelson, 1989a; Council, 1990).

Almost any doctor-patient relationship can become sexual, regardless of the age of the patient and of the doctor, or of the appropriateness of the sexual activity. It is always incumbent on the doctor to maintain appropriate therapeutic boundaries.

Specific problems in the health care of women

REPRODUCTIVE DECISIONS. An important sphere of ethical consideration arises from the characteristics of women's bodies and their reproductive roles. Decisions about childbearing, the availability of contraception or sterilization, the performance of surgery involving reproductive organs, and the use of in utero fetal surgery to cure a fetal defect have profound consequences because they affect the family, the society, and future generations. Thus, how much autonomy a woman does or should have in deciding these questions has been a matter of intense debate.

> *Social response to women's reproductive abilities typically has made their bodies part of the public domain in a way that men's are not. . . . And as wombs have become increasingly public spaces medically, they have also become increasingly public politically; women's choices, not only about how they manage their pregnancies, but also about how they will manage their work, their leisure, their use of both legal and illegal drugs, and their sexuality, are further subject to society's scrutiny and to the law's constraints.*
>
> (Nelson, 1992, p. 13)

Historically and economically, women generally have not been in a position to set or achieve their own reproductive goals; such goals have not been considered by families or by society to be distinct from their goals and values. Decisions about medical or surgical procedures that have an impact on female sexuality and childbearing have often been made by the members of a family or community rather than by the woman affected. Such decisions have often been based on uninformed assumptions about the patient's best interest, or without consideration of the patient's desires. They have been based on societal or family considerations, such as the desire for more or fewer children.

These decisions also may reflect the views or values of the physician, although they may be presented as medically indicated. For example, a gynecologist may assume, without discussing the options with a woman, that she would not want additional children after she reaches the age of forty, because she would not want to run the potential risk of having a defective child. A hysterectomy may be recommended even though other options are available in her situation. Thus, the choice has been made for her, without her informed consent.

Decisions about abortion, the rights of the fetus as opposed to those of the pregnant woman, and other reproductive issues, such as surrogate motherhood and the prohibition of contraception in some countries, have brought attention to the role of the woman as an individual who is expected to fulfill societal responsibilities via her fertility, rather than making autonomous decisions.

Hysterectomy. Hysterectomy remains the most frequently performed major surgery in the United States, and its incidence in younger women is increasing (Muller, 1990). There has been considerable debate, among gynecologists and others, about the appropriate indications for this procedure, often in disregard of the meaning of the uterus and bodily intactness for the self-image of many women. The uterus has been considered a "useless" and potentially disease-causing organ after the childbearing years.

The difficulty of establishing uniform indications for performing hysterectomies has been a longstanding problem. That the decision can be made arbitrarily and without specifically agreed-on criteria is suggested by the variation in the numbers of procedures performed in different communities with similar population bases, as well as by the differences in rates of hysterectomies performed by male and female gynecologists (Roos, 1984; Domenighetti et al., 1985).

Hysterectomies have been performed on women who are ambivalent about contraception or for whom contraception presents a problem because of religious beliefs or cultural practices. Thus a medical procedure, with its inherent risks, may be performed when there are safer alternatives available, in order to achieve contraception. Among the ethical questions raised by this practice are the use of medical procedures for nonmedical indications, especially when the risks may be

"Now, we are becoming the men we wanted to marry."

GLORIA STEINEM
MS., 1982

See Also

Reproductive Technologies: Legal Issues: Is There an Affirmative Right to Procreate?"

greater, and the problem of whether a woman can make an informed choice in these circumstances.

Sterilization. In some situations, laws have permitted sterilization of women considered to be socially undesirable, psychologically deviant, or retarded. This practice has been justified in two ways: (1) the protection of the individual (e.g., a mentally retarded woman who is sexually active and may be exploited); and (2) the protection of society against reproduction by "unfit" individuals. Sterilization statutes may, however, be punitive and discriminatory rather than based on science. In many instances, the conditions considered to be indications for sterilization, such as psychosis, criminality, and retardation, have not been clearly evaluated or linked to genetic determinants. The children of psychotic or retarded people were expected to create social problems; society, then, was seen as justified in preventing the conception of such children. Permission for sterilization procedures has often not been obtained, or was obtained from parents or guardians under pressure and without the patient's full awareness of the implications of the procedure. For minors, the decisions have been made by social agencies or physicians. Many patients have been black, poor, and uneducated, and thus especially vulnerable (*Relf* v. *Weinberger*, 1974).

Sterilization raises another ethical issue that is not unique to the procedure, but serves to exemplify the problem of informed and autonomous consent in making irrevocable decisions, when there is a possibility that the procedure might be regretted in the future. A woman may not be informed that sterilization procedures such as tubal ligation are generally irreversible. But even if she is, it has been common practice for health professionals to raise questions about a woman's motivation for sterilization, and even to require psychiatric consultation. Thus, the right of an adult woman to make this choice, when she is appropriately

CONTRACEPTION

Reproductive Control—with Risks

The development of new contraceptive methods over the past few decades has had a profound impact on women's lives by providing effective control of reproduction. Most research on contraceptives has been on techniques for women, and most widely available new contraceptives have been for women. Although this potentially offers reproductive control to women, who are most vulnerable to the hazards of pregnancy, women are also exposed to the risks and side effects of drugs and other potential long-term consequences of contraception that will not be determined for many years. The development of effective contraceptives for women has proceeded more quickly than for men, possibly reflecting the attitude that women should bear responsibility for contraception. It also may result from the pressure brought by women to gain more control of reproduction (Bremmer and de Kretzer, 1976).

The history of contraceptive research has been marred by ethical violations. In an early study, conducted on Mexican-American women, of the side effects of contraceptive pills, one group of women was given active contraceptive pills; another group was given placebos and a vaginal cream known to be a less effective contraceptive (Katz, 1972). The women were not clearly informed that some of them were not protected against pregnancy, and some became pregnant. Abortion was not made available to them, and even if it had been, many would have had moral and religious objections to it. The investigators deceived the women and misused the trust of their subjects by failing to obtain informed consent from those who participated in the study.

The case of the Dalkon Shield, an intrauterine device that was marketed for several years, also exemplifies problems in obtaining informed consent and not adequately testing contraceptive devices. After it had been used extensively, evidence was compiled indicating that uterine infections and deaths could result. The device was then withdrawn from the market (Mintz, 1985).

One consequence of the extensive litigation involving contraception has been a decrease in the development of new techniques and products. Many companies are unwilling to risk this litigation, or to assume the cost of more ethically and clinically responsible research. This outcome illustrates the problems arising when research is dependent on an industry that is also at risk of litigation.

For many years, diethylstilbestrol (DES) was given to pregnant women to prevent spontaneous abortions, without adequate investigation of the other potential consequences of its use. Daughters of women who took DES were later found to be at risk for precancerous changes of the vaginal lining, and in some cases for carcinoma and infertility as well (Apfel and Fisher, 1984). Here, too, the greater vulnerability of women to unpredictable long-term hazards of medication arises from their reproductive roles; too little attention had been paid to the rigorous investigations necessary to establish the safety of medications (Chalmers, 1974).

— CAROL C. NADELSON
MALKAH T. NOTMAN

The American Medical Association and other medical groups hold that a woman cannot be coerced to accept a treatment to benefit her fetus.

informed, is questioned and this may even result in refusal of the procedure. A restriction based on suppositions about her motivation can be viewed as excessively paternalistic.

A small study of women in their early twenties who were seeking voluntary tubal ligation, and who had never been pregnant, found that they based their wish for childlessness on their own negative feelings toward children, on their judgment that they had limited capacity to be mothers, and on their desires to be independent. They had made reasoned decisions based on their beliefs and experiences. The researcher suggested that it is important to assess the character of the decision-making process, in order to determine that there has been no outside pressure and there are no major internal psychological conflicts (Lindenmayer, 1976).

Another study, of women under age thirty who had decided never to have children, reported a strong psychological motivation in these women to make their own decision to elect a tubal ligation (Kaltreider and Margolis, 1977). A history of family disruption, fear of motherhood, and dislike of children characterized this group. The authors suggested that for these women "the choice to be barren was multidetermined, persistent over time," and in agreement with other aspects of their psychological functioning. While there is clearly a need for longitudinal data about the long-term outcome of sterilization and subsequent requests for reversal of the procedure, the ethical consideration remains: that the competent woman be able to make her own informed decision, regardless of whether others believe that it is wrong or that she may change her mind.

Another ethical—as well as social, economic, and political—question involves the need to obtain the agreement of both marital partners for a married woman seeking sterilization or for any procedure that affects reproduction, since presumably both have an interest. For a woman this need has an immediate effect, since it directly affects her body; for a man it involves control of the woman as well as of his reproductive possibilities.

New reproductive technologies. For couples who are infertile due to organ or functional problems, new reproductive technologies have extended the possibility of pregnancy in ways that had previously been only the subject of science fiction. In addition to expanding reproductive options, potentially redirecting the use of health-care expertise and resources, and creating new clinical problems for women who may, for example, be using drugs or techniques that can result in complications or side effects, these techniques have created unusual ethical dilemmas.

Surrogate pregnancy, for example, involves the insemination of a woman who agrees to carry a pregnancy and surrender the baby after delivery. This arrangement has raised many legal and ethical questions, including who the "real" parents are, whether it is justified to offer financial incentives or rewards in such a case, who is responsible if the outcome is "undesirable," and what is the nature of the surrogate mother's consent. There has been controversy about whether a contract made with a surrogate can or should be binding, since the woman may have been under duress or not able to know how she would feel after becoming pregnant and after the baby is born.

The issues were dramatically brought to public attention by the Baby M case, in which the birth mother changed her mind and refused to surrender the baby to the biological father and his wife (Harrison, 1990). Among the many problems raised are visitation rights, the nature of the relationship between the birth mother and the adoptive parents, and the rights of grandparents and siblings. These dilemmas acknowledge the special experience of pregnancy and the tie between the birth mother and the baby.

New reproductive techniques also include early prenatal diagnosis to detect fetal abnormalities. Since these techniques can also be used for sex selection, ethical dilemmas attendant on decisions about abortion, whether for fetal abnormality or for characteristics such as fetal sex, also arise.

Artificial insemination of a woman with sperm from her husband or from another man has been performed for centuries. It has been widely used in cases of male infertility and genetic abnormalities carried by the male, and to enable single women to conceive.

In recent years it has become technically possible to use donor ova as well as sperm, raising ethical questions about who the "real" parent is, and about ownership and responsibility for the fetus and baby. The technique of in vitro fertilization involves retrieving multiple ripe oocytes from a woman whose ovaries have been hormonally primed, mixing ova and sperm in the laboratory, and transferring fertilized ova or gametes into the uterus or fallopian tubes. The least complex situation involves retrieving oocytes from the same woman into whom the fertilized ova are implanted, and fertilization by sperm from a known donor, usually her husband. Ova and sperm can come from other donors, however, resulting in complicated legal and emotional issues of parenthood. Freezing techniques make it possible to keep the fertilized ovum or embryo alive almost indefinitely, thus creating a problem about future ownership and use, particularly if the genetic parents are divorced or if one, or both, dies.

Multiple ova are usually stimulated by the initial hormonal treatment of the woman, and multiple fertil-

◆ **feminist ethics**
various theories, which reveal gender-specific patterns of harm and women's oppression, and a diverse political movement all devoted to making political changes and eliminating oppressive balances of power.

See Also

Reproductive Technologies: Feminist Ethical Concerns

Assisted Reproduction: Psychology of Nontraditional Families

ized ova are usually implanted to ensure a greater likelihood of successful pregnancy. In most instances when there are multiple gametes, not all are allowed to continue to term because of the greater risks in multiple pregnancy. The parents and doctors then must select which to maintain and which to terminate.

In all of these situations, the woman bears the greater burden of the procedure and its outcome because of her physical connection to the pregnancy and delivery. Along with the risks of the pregnancy, the emotional consequences of potentially bearing a defective child are also greater for her, since in all societies women assume the major responsibilities for child rearing.

Pregnancy. Technological advances such as fetal monitoring have brought new ethical issues in the care of women during pregnancy and childbirth. These issues have focused on the responsibilities of a woman for the well-being of her fetus and the treatment of women without their consent when they are pregnant. In the past, because of the high morbidity and mortality rates during pregnancy and childbirth, physicians and parents viewed the fetus as a potential threat to the mother's life and health. As pregnancy and childbirth have become safer, attention has shifted to the well-being of the fetus, and prenatal diagnosis and treatment have become possible. This has caused a shift in perspective, so that women who do not agree to diagnostic and therapeutic procedures on their fetuses can be seen as not acting in the best interests of their unborn offspring (Nadelson, 1991).

Legal action and even prison sentences have resulted for women who are considered to be endangering their fetuses, such as pregnant alcoholics and drug addicts. The argument made in this situation is that the social costs of the effects of substance abuse on the fetus justify intervention. The autonomy of the woman, and the fact that she may not have willingly chosen to be pregnant, complicate the problem. Thus, in these situations the interests of the mother are pitted against those of the fetus to the degree that the fetus is considered to be a separate and equal person (Nadelson, 1993). These examples only begin to touch on the complexity of the issues raised by the changes in morbidity and mortality rates and the development of reproductive technologies. They do not, for example, address whether the stage of fetal development is an important consideration.

◆ **female chauvinism**
the belief that women are superior to men.

Discrimination because of socioeconomic or ethnic factors also appears to be an issue in some situations, for example, where cesarean section or other medical treatment is recommended in the interests of the fetus, and the mother refuses. One British author noted that the issue of forced cesarean section most often had arisen in cases involving poor or foreign women, or those with religious beliefs different from the physician's. This finding suggests that the cultural or socioeconomic dissimilarity between doctor and patient may have been a factor in the recommendation. In most cases, courts had ruled that the cesarean section be performed, but this position began to shift in the early 1990s. Arguments have supported the rights of the mother to the integrity and control of her body, even where refusing intervention may result in the death of the fetus. The reasoning, in one case, stemmed from a decision that a man did not have to take the risk required to donate a kidney to his child, who would otherwise die without the transplant (Shenkin, 1991).

A related issue involves consent for treatment of a fetus in utero, and whether failure to consent constitutes fetal abuse. Conceptualizing the problem in this way implies that the fetus and mother are separate individuals, and that the mother who refuses treatment has committed a crime against another person, a fetus. Thus the court can intervene. However, "Coercing the mother to protect the not-yet-born child poses serious threats to women's privacy and bodily autonomy" (Steinbock, 1992, p. 19). The American Medical Association and other medical groups have made a distinction between mother and fetus, holding that a pregnant woman cannot be coerced to accept a treatment to benefit her fetus. They also emphasize that it is the physician's ethical duty to be noncoercive and to accept the informed decision of the patient (Council, 1990).

The dilemma of whether the fetus and pregnant woman can be considered as a single or a dual unit can be further elucidated. "When the maternal-fetal dyad is regarded as an organic whole, what matters is that combined maternal-fetal benefits outweigh combined maternal-fetal burdens," but when "fetus and pregnant woman are conceptualized as two individual patients . . . it is no longer appropriate to consider effects of treatment on the two combined" (Mattingly, 1992, p. 14). Thus, in the latter view, the benefit and burden to each are separate. When fetal abnormalities pose no threat to maternal health, the risk of treatment is greater for the maternal patient, and she should not be obliged to undergo it. Physicians should not benefit one patient by forcing another to take unwarranted risks.

The arguments regarding endangerment of another person could mean that almost every act of a pregnant woman, even failing to follow a doctor's orders, could affect her fetus and make her vulnerable to legal action (Steinbock, 1992). Here we approach a logically and pragmatically impossible slippery slope.

MENSTRUATION. Many myths persist about menstruation. The existence of behavioral and mood fluctuations with phases of the menstrual cycle and their possible physiological basis have been debated for

See Also

Embryo Custody Disputes: Tangled Claims

Sexuality in Society: Social Roles

years. On the grounds that they are too strongly affected by cyclic changes, women have been considered unsuitable for important positions. Although many women experience no changes premenstrually, for others the days before each menstrual period are characterized by irritability, mood lability, and other symptoms that disappear with the onset of the menstrual period.

Premenstrual syndrome (PMS), a nonspecific term, was said to be responsible for various types of social behavior and psychological phenomena. Crimes committed (Morton et al., 1953; Dalton, 1964), suicide attempts, misbehavior of schoolgirls, psychiatric admissions to emergency rooms, and visits to clinics (Sommer, 1973; Koeske, 1976) have been related to the premenstrual period. A number of studies of suicide attempts (Mandell and Mandell, 1967; MacKinnon et al., 1959) have indicated that a majority occurred in the bleeding phase of the cycle. Most of the early data on PMS consist of self-reports of functioning during the menstrual cycle; they indicate that a small percentage of women feel that their judgment and mental faculties are impaired to some extent, particularly in the premenstrual phase of the cycle.

Reviews of studies of cognitive and perceptual-motor behavior in relation to menstruation have pointed out methodological problems in much of the research (Sommer, 1973). The problem of determining the hormonal status of the subjects, the selection bias toward women with regular cycles, the use of self-reports, and the combination of objective with subjective data complicate evaluation of results. Many studies were not replicated, and correlational studies did not determine causality. A majority of studies using objective performance measures have failed to demonstrate significant cyclic fluctuation in performance.

Barbara Sommer concluded that cyclic effects are seen where the demands of the social milieu and the woman's own expectations predict them, and she suggested that altering these social-psychological expectations of menstrual debility results in the disappearance of the effect (1973). Menstrual variations may reflect responses of the individual to personal and social expectations, identification with important women in her life, or somatic expressions of a wide variety of feelings about herself, her femininity, and her body.

Although there are data suggesting cyclic effects in some women, the use of diagnoses like PMS and the assumption that menstrual fluctuations are pathologic are inappropriate bases for stereotyping women's behavior. The term PMS has been replaced in the *DSM-IV* (American Psychiatric Association, 1994) by

AFTER *ROE* V. *WADE*

New Choices, New Dilemmas

In 1973 the U.S. Supreme Court made abortion a legal procedure in the United States within limits of time and specific circumstances (*Roe* v. *Wade*, 1973). The decision then became the responsibility of the pregnant woman and her physician. Physicians and hospitals, however, may refuse to perform abortions on the grounds of moral convictions and limitation of funds (Nadelson and Notman, 1977). Although it may not be the intent, this policy effectively discriminates against women with limited mobility and finances, since they may have no way of obtaining abortion services if they are not available in their community. They may then be faced with the choice of illegal abortion or continuing an unwanted pregnancy, while women with more financial resources will be able to seek abortion elsewhere. Extralegal procedures increase in frequency in the face of restrictive laws (Callahan, 1970). In addition, illegal abortion is more hazardous to a woman's health, so that the risks for poorer women, who may perceive no alternative, are greater.

In the abortion issue there are differing ethical philosophies, perhaps in unresolvable conflict. Although some argue that, from the moment of conception, the right to life is absolute, others disagree and emphasize that the right to life is the right not to be killed unjustly (Thomson, 1971). Attempts to resolve these conflicting points of view have sometimes medicalized the decision, using physical- and mental-health criteria to justify terminating a pregnancy. Early abortion currently involves less risk than continuing a pregnancy to term. Since physical problems rarely make pregnancy hazardous, emotional indications, including the development of a "post-abortion syndrome" and threats of suicide, have been sought to justify restrictions on the availability of abortion. Emotional repercussions of abortion are rare. In order to emphasize that abortion could have deleterious consequences and therefore should be denied, some abortion opponents have proposed that a post-abortion syndrome exists, and that it has serious emotional sequelae. There are no data supporting the existence of such a syndrome. Invoking a post-abortion syndrome also pathologizes normal reactions to life experiences.

Legal and policy issues focus on the right to privacy, including control of one's body, the freedom of individual choice, and equality. It is clear that women, because they can become pregnant, face a risk and burden that men do not.

— CAROL C. NADELSON
MALKAH T. NOTMA

the term Premenstrual Dysphoric Disorder (PMDD), which specifically delineates psychiatric symptoms. Including this term in any form in the official psychiatric nomenclature (*DSM-IV*) evoked considerable controversy about the stigmatizing effects of its use and the tendency to pathologize reactions to normal fluctuations of mood with variations in life experiences.

Although more research is continuing in this area, many studies still suffer from methodological problems, including the use of nonuniform criteria for the diagnosis, the lack of daily records of mood fluctuations, the failure to accurately correlate menstrual cycle phase with biological data, and the inaccuracies of data based on short periods of observation. Current research using the narrower and more specific criteria to define PMDD suggests that prevalence rates may be much lower than had been estimated for PMS. Using the criteria for Late Luteal Phase Dysphoric Disorder (LLPDD), from the *DSM-III-R* (American Psychiatric Association, 1987), the rates are as low as 4.6 percent in one study (Rivera-Tovar and Frank, 1990) and 6.8 percent in another (Stout and Steege, 1990). The problem of differentiating other disorders from PMDD remains.

The reappraisal undertaken for the *DSM-IV* was based on careful reviews of emerging research, so that the syndrome could validly apply to a very small percentage of women who are seriously incapacitated. The proponents of the PMDD diagnosis feel that it would be unethical to deny those women appropriate treatment, based on solid scientific evidence.

The stigmatizing effect of the diagnosis, however, as is true for many diagnoses, must be considered in the context of the cultural meaning of a body experience. In this case, menstruation and the taboos, beliefs, and expectations associated with it bring a complex set of responses. The diagnosis, even if legitimate, supports and is supported by popular expectations of menstrually related responses and pathology. This attribution can color research and confuse the results. The persistence of the use of the diagnosis of PMS illustrates the problems of addressing a behavior that is embedded in a complex context by questioning only one component of the behavior, raising questions about the diagnosis without considering cultural attitudes toward menstruation.

MENOPAUSE. Endocrinological and social-psychological data (McKinlay, 1989; Parlee, 1990) indicate that many misconceptions have existed about the nature and extent of the symptoms that can be directly ascribed to menopause. Multiple disorders said to be caused by the changing hormonal balance and equated with menopause may, in fact, not be due to these imbalances (Notman, 1990).

Research on menopause also suffers from serious methodological problems, such as relying on case histories, clinical impressions, or analyses of data from selected samples of women under the care of gynecologists or psychiatrists. More reliable studies show that psychological symptoms were not reported more frequently by so-called menopausal women than by younger women (McKinlay and Jeffreys, 1974).

Vasomotor instability, manifested as hot flashes, flushes, and excess perspiration, has been one of the consistent symptoms accompanying menopause. Such phenomena are present in a large number of menopausal women; up to 75 percent report some symptoms (Kronenberg, 1990). The other symptoms investigated—headaches, dizzy spells, palpitations, sleeplessness, depression, and weight increase—do not appear to show a direct relationship to menopause (McKinlay and Jeffreys, 1974).

Not only are many symptoms attributed to menopause not necessarily biological, but menopause itself may not be as central to the midlife crisis for women as had previously been thought (Neugarten et al., 1968; Parlee, 1990; Notman, 1990). The cessation of menses and the accompanying endocrine changes may be less critical than the reaction to menopause as a signal of aging and the awareness that a phase of life has ended. For many women there are concomitant changes in their social role at that time, including the loss of their status as mothers and the disruption of a network of important social relationships.

The stereotyping of menopause as the determining diagnostic entity for midlife depression or midlife stress has led to inappropriate treatment decisions, with insufficient attention paid to social, family, or psychiatric conditions. A wide variety of treatments have been used, as for PMS, with insufficient investigation of the causes of the symptoms.

MASTECTOMY. The increase in incidence of breast cancer in the 1980s, and the sparse resources devoted to research on and treatment of it at that time, suggest either that it was not taken seriously enough, or that it is difficult to stimulate areas of research that do not have special meaning to investigators. Among the questions that need be addressed is the optimal treatment for an individual patient, including indications for a particular type and extent of surgery, for chemotherapy, or for radiation. Understanding of the risks and alternatives is critical. For some women, the knowledge that a disfiguring operation is not inevitable has made it easier for them to seek medical attention for a breast mass.

The controversy about the safety of silicone implants for postmastectomy patients complicates the problem enormously. If evidence regarding complications was indeed withheld from those making the decisions about the safety of silicone implants ("Patients

RAPE
Too Often, the First in a Series of Offenses

Women who have been raped are often blamed, disbelieved, and criticized. As a result, they may be reluctant to seek medical care or to report the rape. This often results in their receiving poor medical care, creating a disparity between them and victims of other aggressions or disasters (Notman and Nadelson, 1976).

Rape is a violent crime that is often misperceived as a sexual experience. The possibility of serious harm or death exists, and the victim's prime concern is to protect herself from injury. Since the absence of consent is crucial to the definition of rape, the victim often has had to demonstrate signs of struggle or to provide witnesses, in order to prove the absence of consent—a requirement that does not occur with other violent crimes.

Health-care personnel may be in dual and conflicting roles with rape victims. Those who first see the victim have to collect evidence for possible prosecution of the rapist, yet they are also obligated to attend to the best interests of their patient, who may not wish to report the crime. Sensitivity to the patient's condition may be in conflict with the need for complete information. The victim's need to gain control can conflict with the requirements for thoroughness in the evaluation.

— CAROL C. NADELSON
MALKAH T. NOTMAN

and Surgeons," 1992), then patients were deceived into believing they were taking less risk than they actually did. This case raises questions similar to those regarding contraceptives.

It also raises important questions about patient autonomy. To what extent does the patient have the right to choose to accept a risk, and at what level of safety should a procedure be forbidden? Unavailability of silicone breast implants can have profound consequences for women who risk losing a breast with no recourse to a reconstructive procedure. The threat of disfiguring surgery causes many women to delay treatment. Not only is the possibility of reconstruction important in helping a woman confront and deal with her illness, but it also has implications for her self-image and relationships.

Mental health

Although women have generally been considered more vulnerable than men to a variety of emotional symptoms and mental illnesses, the actual incidence of mental illness is difficult to determine because descriptions of symptoms and definitions of mental illness vary widely. In an early study documenting variations in the way that men and women were evaluated and in recommendations for treatment, the researchers reported that clinicians' concepts of a mentally healthy, mature man were similar to their concepts of a mentally healthy adult; their concepts of a mentally healthy, mature woman were more like those for a child (Broverman et al., 1970). For instance, healthy women were seen as being more submissive, less independent, less adventurous, more sensitive to being hurt, less aggressive, and less competitive than were healthy men.

Although some controversy surrounds the data analysis from the original study and its current validity, there is still evidence that social stereotypes operate and influence patient care (Widiger and Settle, 1987; Hansen and Reekie, 1990). The differentiation between psychopathology and deviance from culturally accepted norms is particularly relevant for women, who often feel that the help they are offered, especially when they are suffering from psychological distress, supports traditional views about women's roles and behavior, rather than being responsive to their individual needs (Nadelson and Notman, 1991).

Since 1980 specific criteria have been formulated for the diagnosis of psychiatric disorders, enabling researchers to collect epidemiologic data to permit estimates of the incidence and prevalence of various mental disorders. There is increasing evidence that although there are no differences in the overall incidence of mental illness in the population at large, there are gender-related differences in the incidence, diagnosis, treatment, and outcome for mental illnesses (Regier et al., 1984; Weissman, 1991). Woman have been reported to have higher rates of depression, as well as somatization, anxiety, and eating and panic disorders (using *DSM-III-R* [American Psychiatric Association, 1987] criteria). Men are more likely to be diagnosed with alcoholism, substance abuse, early-onset schizophrenia, and impulse and antisocial personality disorders.

There are also gender differences in symptom expression, such as suicide. Although more men commit suicide, more women attempt it (Farberow and Schneidman, 1965). Norman Farberow and Edwin Schneidman found that 69 percent of attempted suicides in the United States were women and 70 percent of completed suicides were men.

One difference in rates of mental illness between

"It is fatal for anyone who writes to think of their sex. It is fatal to be a man or woman pure and simple; one must be woman-manly or man-womanly."

VIRGINIA WOOLF
A ROOM OF ONE'S OWN
1929

See Also

Sexuality in Society: Social Roles

men and women involves marital status. Married men and single women have been reported to have the lowest rates of mental illness (Weissman and Klerman, 1985; Gove and Tudor, 1973). Contrary to popular expectations, marriage would seem to offer men some protection against mental illness and to make women more vulnerable. One hypothesis to explain these data suggests that wives provide care for their husbands, and that the marital relationship often imposes more constraints on women and provides less care for them. Additional data indicate that the women most vulnerable to symptoms are young married women with small children (Brown and Harris, 1978).

"If I have to, I can do anything. I am strong, I am invincible, I am woman."

HELEN REDDY
I AM WOMAN, 1972

Another hypothesis suggests that women are labeled mentally ill when they cannot perform the service and maintenance functions of wife and mother, or other socially accepted roles for women (Chesler, 1972). An alternative explanation of the differences is that women are responding to the stresses of social isolation, particularly from other adults; the physical and emotional fatigue of dealing with small children (and often elderly relatives); and the tensions of confronting the impulses and feelings stirred up in parents by their young children. It has been suggested that women experience greater life stress because of their multiple roles, and because of the greater likelihood that they will live in poverty and be alone as they age (McBride, 1990; Belle, 1990; Rodeheaver and Datan, 1988).

Women experience more sexual and physical abuse than men, and this may be an important factor in the greater incidence of disorders such as depression, posttraumatic stress disorder, and anxiety (Koss, 1990). Depression, for example, has been linked with socialization toward compliance in women. The reasons for most gender differences in mental illness, however, remain unclear, although it appears that complex interactions between biological and psychosocial factors are responsible.

Differences between men and women in the incidence of mental illness are most apparent when they are related to biological and, in particular, reproductive functions. Women, not men, may suffer from reproductively and menstrually related disorders such as postpartum syndromes or symptoms related to menopause, hysterectomy, infertility, abortion, and miscarriage. With the exception of some forms of postpartum disorders and symptoms related to physiologic concomitants during the menstrual cycle and menopause, the psychological specificity of these other syndromes has not been demonstrated.

The readiness with which symptoms and behaviors are attributed to physical events experienced by women, such as menopause, a hysterectomy, or an abortion, attests to the power of societal expectations of women's weakness and vulnerability. These beliefs and values can affect investigators' care in examining data or researching these areas. It is also possible to objectify symptoms and impart causality without looking carefully at individual experience and variability.

Alcoholism and substance abuse are generally grouped with mental disorders. The data indicate that there is a substantial preponderance of men with these disorders. This discrepancy has resulted in a minimization of the incidence or impact of these disorders in women. There has been little research, and thus data on women's specific treatment needs and responses are sparse. Resources for the treatment of women are scarce. An Institute of Medicine report suggested that public concern about male behavior, especially violence, related to alcohol abuse may lead to the development of treatment methods that are less effective for women. Thus, differential access to care is a substantial ethical problem. It is also not clear what percentage of women actually receive treatment, in part because definitions of severe alcohol use vary and also because other variables related to differential access to treatment are not taken into account—such as the availability of child care, so that mothers with dependent children can seek treatment. There is a general tendency to deny the seriousness of alcoholism and substance abuse in women, and this leads to delays in treatment (Reed, 1991; Weisner, 1991).

Conclusion

Social, economic, and technological changes have brought about alterations in relationships between men and women and patients and providers and in the delivery of health care. Although the paternalism that has existed in the health-care system has gradually changed, in part as a result of the changes that have taken place in women's roles since the 1970s, there continue to be inequities in research and clinical care between men and women. Some of this, as we have suggested, derives from the special aspects of women's reproductive roles and the potential consequences for society of allowing women to be autonomous in decisions about their care.

— CAROL C. NADELSON
MALKAH T. NOTMA

Appendixes

Directives on Health-Related Rights and Patient Responsibilities

Ethical Directives for the Practice of Medicine

1. Fourth century B.C.E.–Early twentieth century C.E.

2. Mid-twentieth century–1994

The use of rights language has emerged in recent decades as a strong feature of contemporary bioethics documents. Although the language of rights cannot embrace all that must be said in bioethics, this collection of directives on health-related rights and patient responsibilities heads the Appendix both because it reinforces the common doctrine that all health care is patient-centered and because rights language has become typical of the period on which this edition is reporting.

Most of the documents in this section outline the health-related rights of specific groups of individuals, such as children, mentally retarded persons, and patients. Two documents, however, address topics that are designed to implement these rights. The World Medical Association's Declaration on Physician Independence and Professional Freedom addresses the importance of physicians' professional freedom to support patient rights. The American Medical Association (AMA) perceives patient rights and the corresponding patient responsibilities to be two elements of a mutually respectful alliance between patients and physicians. The AMA's directive on patient responsibilities elaborates upon the view expressed in the AMA's patient rights document, Fundamental Elements of the Patient-Physician Relationship, that "patients share with physicians the responsibility for their own health care."

Directives on Health-Related Rights and Patient Responsibilities

CONSTITUTION OF THE WORLD HEALTH ORGANIZATION

1948

Originally adopted by the International Health Conference held in New York in June–July 1946 and signed by the representatives of sixty-one nations, the following statement is found in the Preamble to the Constitution of the World Health Organization, established in 1948. Especially significant elements are the controversial definition of health as "a state of complete physical, mental and social well-being and not merely the absence of disease or infirmity" and the recognition of health as a fundamental human right.

The States Parties to this Constitution declare, in conformity with the Charter of the United Nations, that the following principles are basic to the happiness, harmonious relations and security of all peoples:

Health is a state of complete physical, mental and social well-being and not merely the absence of disease or infirmity.

The enjoyment of the highest attainable standard of health is one of the fundamental rights of every human being without distinction of race, religion, political belief, economic or social condition.

The health of all peoples is fundamental to the attainment of peace and security and is dependent upon the fullest co-operation of individuals and States.

The achievement of any State in the promotion and protection of health is of value to all. Unequal development in different countries in the promotion of health and control of disease, especially communicable disease, is a common danger.

Healthy development of the child is of basic importance; the ability to live harmoniously in a changing total environment is essential to such development.

The extension to all peoples of the benefits of medical, psychological and related knowledge is essential to the fullest attainment of health.

Informed opinion and active co-operation on the part of the public are of the utmost importance in the improvement of the health of the people.

Governments have a responsibility for the health of their peoples which can be fulfilled only by the provision of adequate health and social measures.

Accepting these principles, and for the purpose of co-operation among themselves and with others to promote and protect the health of all peoples, the Contracting parties agree to the present Constitution and hereby establish the World Health Organization as a specialized agency within the terms of Article 57 of the Charter of the United Nations.

UNIVERSAL DECLARATION OF HUMAN RIGHTS

General Assembly of the United Nations

1948

Adopted in 1948 by the General Assembly of the United Nations, the Universal Declaration of Human Rights is, as stated in its preamble, "a common standard of achievement for all peoples in all nations, to the end that every individual and every organ of society . . . shall strive by teaching and education to promote respect for these rights and freedoms and by progressive measures, national and international, to secure their universal and effective recognition and observance. . . ."

Article five should be compared to article seven of the International Covenant on Civil and Political Rights (Section IV). Article 25 directly pertains to health and health care.

Article 1

All human beings are born free and equal in dignity and rights. They are endowed with reason and conscience and should act towards one another in a spirit of brotherhood.

* * *

Article 3

Everyone has the right to life, liberty and the security of person.

* * *

Article 5

No one shall be subjected to torture or to cruel, inhuman or degrading treatment or punishment.

* * *

Article 16

1. Men and women of full age, without any limitation due to race, nationality or religion, have the right to marry and to found a family. They are entitled to equal rights as to marriage, during marriage and at its dissolution.

2. Marriage shall be entered into only with the free and full consent of the intending spouses.

3. The family is the natural and fundamental group unit of society and is entitled to protection by society and the State.

* * *

Article 25

1. Everyone has the right to a standard of living adequate for the health and well-being of himself and of his family, including food, clothing, housing and medical care and necessary social services, and the right to security in the event of unemployment, sickness, disability, widowhood, old age or other lack of livelihood in circumstances beyond his control.

2. Motherhood and childhood are entitled to special care and assistance. All children, whether born in or out of wedlock, shall enjoy the same social protection.

DECLARATION OF THE RIGHTS OF THE CHILD

General Assembly of the United Nations

1959

Adopted unanimously by the General Assembly of the United Nations on November 20, 1959, the Declaration of the Rights of the Child emphasizes the physical, mental, and moral health and development of children.

* * *

"*Whereas* the child by reason of his physical and mental immaturity, needs special safeguards and care, including appropriate legal protection, before as well as after birth,

* * *

"*The General Assembly*

"*Proclaims* this Declaration of the Rights of the Child to the end that he may have a happy childhood and enjoy for his own good and for the good of society the rights and freedoms herein set forth, and calls upon parents, upon men and women as individuals, and upon voluntary organizations, local authorities and national Governments to recognize these rights and strive for their observance by legislative and other measures progressively taken in accordance with the following principles:

PRINCIPLE 1

"The child shall enjoy all the rights set forth in this Declaration. Every child, without any exception whatsoever, shall be entitled to these rights, without distinction or discrimination on account of race, colour, sex, language, religion, political or other opinion, national or social origin, property, birth or other status, whether of himself or of his family.

PRINCIPLE 2

"The child shall enjoy special protection, and shall be given opportunities and facilities, by law and by other means, to enable him to develop physically, mentally, morally, spiritually and socially in a healthy and normal manner and in conditions of freedom and dignity. In the enactment of laws for this purpose, the best interests of the child shall be the paramount considerations.

PRINCIPLE 3

"The child shall be entitled from his birth to a name and a nationality.

PRINCIPLE 4

"The child shall enjoy the benefits of social security. He shall be entitled to grow and develop in health; to this end, special care and protection shall be provided both to him and to his mother, including adequate pre-natal and post-natal care. The child shall have the right to adequate nutrition, housing, recreation and medical services.

PRINCIPLE 5

"The child who is physically, mentally or socially handicapped shall be given the special treatment, education and care required by his particular condition.

PRINCIPLE 6

"The child, for the full and harmonious development of his personality, needs love and understanding. He shall, wherever possible, grow up in the care and under the responsibility of his parents, and, in any case, in an atmosphere of affection and of moral and material security; a child of tender years shall not, save in exceptional circumstances, be separated from his mother. Society and the public authorities shall have the duty to extend particular care to children without a family and to those without adequate means of support. Payment of State and other assistance towards the maintenance of children of large families is desirable.

PRINCIPLE 7

"The child is entitled to receive education, which shall be free and compulsory, at least in the elementary stages. He shall be given an education which will promote his general culture, and enable him, on a basis of equal opportunity, to develop his abilities, his individual judgement, and his sense of moral and social responsibility, and to become a useful member of society.

"The best interests of the child shall be the guiding principle of those responsible for his education and guidance; that responsibility lies in the first place with his parents.

"The child shall have full opportunity for play and recreation, which should be directed to the same purposes as education; society and the public authorities shall endeavour to promote the enjoyment of this right.

PRINCIPLE 8

"The child shall in all circumstances be among the first to receive protection and relief.

PRINCIPLE 9

"The child shall be protected against all forms of neglect, cruelty and exploitation. He shall not be the subject of traffic, in any form.

"The child shall not be admitted to employment before an appropriate minimum age; he shall in no case be caused or permitted to engage in any occupation or employment which would prejudice his health or education, or interfere with his physical, mental or moral development.

PRINCIPLE 10

"The child shall be protected from practices which may foster racial, religious and any other form of discrimination. He shall be brought up in a spirit of understanding, tolerance, friendship among peoples, peace and universal brotherhood, and in full consciousness that his energy and talents should be devoted to the service of his fellow men."

DECLARATION ON THE RIGHTS OF MENTALLY RETARDED PERSONS

General Assembly of the United Nations 1971

The following Declaration on the Rights of Mentally Retarded Persons was adopted by the General Assembly of the United Nations on December 20, 1971. It is a revised and amended version of the Declaration of General and Special Rights of the Mentally Retarded that was adopted in 1968 by the International League of Societies for the Mentally Handicapped.

* * *

1. The mentally retarded person has, to the maximum degree of feasibility, the same rights as other human beings.

2. The mentally retarded person has a right to proper medical care and physical therapy and to such education, training, rehabilitation and guidance as will enable him to develop his ability and maximum potential.

3. The mentally retarded person has a right to economic security and to a decent standard of living. He has a right to perform productive work or to engage in any other meaningful occupation to the fullest possible extent of his capabilities.

4. Whenever possible, the mentally retarded person should live with his own family or with foster parents and participate in different forms of community life. The family with which he lives should receive assistance. If care in an institution becomes necessary, it should be provided in surroundings and other circumstances as close as possible to those of normal life.

5. The mentally retarded person has a right to a qualified guardian when this is required to protect his personal well-being and interests.

6. The mentally retarded person has a right to protection from exploitation, abuse and degrading treatment. If prosecuted for any offence, he shall have a right to due process of law with full recognition being given to his degree of mental responsibility.

7. Whenever mentally retarded persons are unable, because of the severity of their handicap, to exercise all their rights in a meaningful way or it should become necessary to restrict or deny some or all of these rights, the procedure used for that restriction or denial of rights must contain proper legal safeguards against every form of abuse. This procedure must be based on an evaluation of the social capability of the mentally retarded person by qualified experts and must be subject to periodic review and to the right of appeal to higher authorities.

A PATIENT'S BILL OF RIGHTS

American Hospital Association

1973, revised 1992

In 1973, the American Hospital Association's House of Delegates adopted A Patient's Bill of Rights, which was influential in the development of similar documents in other parts of the world. The first revision of the document, and the only one to date, was approved in 1992. Some of the most notable changes from the 1973 document include: (1) deletion of the "therapeutic privilege" clause that permitted information regarding a patient's condition to be disclosed to family, rather than to the patient, when it was "not medically advisable to give such information to the patient"; (2) addition of the right to execute advance directives; (3) addition of a clause indicating that otherwise confidential information may be released when permitted or required by law for the benefit of third parties; (4) addition of the patients' right to review their medical records; (5) addition of the clarification that a patient's right to expect a hospital to reasonably respond to requests for care and services is limited to those that are "appropriate and medically indicated"; and (6) addition of a list of patient responsibilities.

Introduction

Effective health care requires collaboration between patients and physicians and other health care professionals. Open and honest communication, respect for personal and professional values, and sensitivity to differences are integral to optimal patient care. As the setting for the provision of health services, hospitals must provide a foundation for understanding and respecting the rights and responsibilities of patients, their families, physicians, and other caregivers. Hospitals must ensure a health care ethic that respects the role of patients in decision making about treatment choices and other aspects of their care. Hospitals must be sensitive to cultural, racial, linguistic, religious, age, gender, and other differences as well as the needs of persons with disabilities.

The American Hospital Association presents A Patient's Bill of Rights with the expectation that it will contribute to more effective patient care and be supported by the hospital on behalf of the institution, its medical staff, employees, and patients. The American Hospital Association encourages health care institutions to tailor this bill of rights to their patient community by translating and/or simplifying the language of this bill of rights as may be necessary to ensure that patients and their families understand their rights and responsibilities.

Bill of Rights*

1. The patient has the right to considerate and respectful care.

* These rights can be exercised on the patient's behalf by a designated surrogate or proxy decision maker if the patient lacks decision-making capacity, is legally incompetent, or is a minor.

2. The patient has the right to and is encouraged to obtain from physicians and other direct caregivers relevant, current, and understandable information concerning diagnosis, treatment, and prognosis.

Except in emergencies when the patient lacks decision-making capacity and the need for treatment is urgent, the patient is entitled to the opportunity to discuss and request information related to the specific procedures and/or treatments, the risks involved, the possible length of recuperation, and the medically reasonable alternatives and their accompanying risks and benefits.

Patients have the right to know the identity of physicians, nurses, and others involved in their care, as well as when those involved are students, residents, or other trainees. The patient also has the right to know the immediate and long-term financial implications of treatment choices, insofar as they are known.

3. The patient has the right to make decisions about the plan of care prior to and during the course of treatment and to refuse a recommended treatment or plan of care to the extent permitted by law and hospital policy and to be informed of the medical consequences of this action. In case of such refusal, the patient is entitled to other appropriate care and services that the hospital provides or transfer to another hospital. The hospital should notify patients of any policy that might affect patient choice within the institution.

4. The patient has the right to have an advance directive (such as a living will, health care proxy, or durable power of attorney for health care) concerning treatment or designating a surrogate decision maker with the expectation that the hospital will honor the intent of that directive to the extent permitted by law and hospital policy.

Health care institutions must advise patients of their rights under state law and hospital policy to make informed medical choices, ask if the patient has an advance directive, and include that information in patient records. The patient has the right to timely information about hospital policy that may limit its ability to implement fully a legally valid advance directive.

5. The patient has the right to every consideration of privacy. Case discussion, consultation, examination, and treatment should be conducted so as to protect each patient's privacy.

6. The patient has the right to expect that all communications and records pertaining to his/her care will be treated as confidential by the hospital, except in cases such as suspected abuse and public health hazards when reporting is permitted or required by law. The patient has the right to expect that the hospital will emphasize the confidentiality of this information when it releases it to any other parties entitled to review information in these records.

7. The patient has the right to review the records pertaining to his/her medical care and to have the information explained or interpreted as necessary, except when restricted by law.

8. The patient has the right to expect that, within its capacity and policies, a hospital will make reasonable response to the request of a patient for appropriate and medically indicated care and services. The hospital must provide evaluation, service, and/or referral as indicated by the urgency of the case. When medically appropriate and legally permissible, or when a patient has so requested, a patient may be transferred to another facility. The institution to which the patient is to be transferred must first have accepted the patient for transfer. The patient must also have the benefit of complete information and explanation concerning the need for, risks, benefits, and alternatives to such a transfer.

9. The patient has the right to ask and to be informed of the existence of business relationships among the hospital, educational institutions, other health care providers, or payers that may influence the patient's treatment and care.

10. The patient has the right to consent to or decline to participate in proposed research studies or human experimentation affecting care and treatment or requiring direct patient involvement, and to have those studies fully explained prior to consent. A patient who declines to participate in research or experimentation is entitled to the most effective care that the hospital can otherwise provide.

11. The patient has the right to expect reasonable continuity of care when appropriate and to be informed by physicians and other caregivers of available and realistic patient care options when hospital care is no longer appropriate.

12. The patient has the right to be informed of hospital policies and practices that relate to patient care, treatment, and responsibilities. The patient has the right to be informed of available resources for resolving disputes, grievances, and conflicts, such as ethics committees, patient representatives, or other mechanisms available in the institution. The patient has the right to be informed of the hospital's charges for services and available payment methods.

The collaborative nature of health care requires that patients, or their families/surrogates, participate in their care. The effectiveness of care and patient satisfaction with the course of treatment depend, in part, on the patient fulfilling certain responsibilities. Patients are responsible for providing information about past illnesses, hospitalizations, medications, and other matters related to health status. To participate effectively in decision making, patients must be encouraged to take responsibility for requesting additional information or clarification about their health status or treatment when they do not fully understand information and instructions. Patients are also responsible for ensuring that the health care institution has a copy of their written advance directive if they have one. Patients are responsible for informing their physicians and other caregivers if they anticipate problems in following prescribed treatment.

Patients should also be aware of the hospital's obligation to be reasonably efficient and equitable in providing care to other patients and the community. The hospital's rules and regulations are designed to help the hospital meet this obligation. Patients and their families are responsible for making reasonable accommodations to the needs of the hospital, other patients, medical staff, and hospital employees. Patients are responsible for providing necessary information for insurance claims and for working with the hospital to make payment arrangements, when necessary.

A person's health depends on much more than health care services. Patients are responsible for recognizing the impact of their life-style on their personal health.

Conclusion

Hospitals have many functions to perform, including the enhancement of health status, health promotion, and the prevention and treatment of injury and disease; the immediate and ongoing care and rehabilitation of patients; the education of health professionals, patients, and the community; and research. All these activities must be conducted with an overriding concern for the values and dignity of patients.

DECLARATION OF LISBON ON THE RIGHTS OF THE PATIENT

World Medical Association

1981

Whereas most of the early documents on patients' rights, such as the American Hospital Association's A Patient's Bill of Rights, focus on the rights of individuals within health care facilities (hospitals, nursing homes), the Declaration of Lisbon, adopted in 1981 by the 34th World Medical Assembly at Lisbon, is an international statement of the rights of patients in general. In conjunction with the International Code of Medical Ethics (Section II), it illustrates the relatively recent emphasis placed on "the rights of patients" in addition to the traditional "duties of physicians." Physicians not only "ought" to behave in certain ways, but patients also are entitled to have them do so.

Recognizing that there may be practical, ethical or legal difficulties, a physician should always act according to his/her conscience and always in the best interest of the patient. The following Declaration represents some of the principal rights which the medical profession seeks to provide to patients. Whenever legislation or government action denies these rights of the patient, physicians should seek by appropriate means to assure or to restore them.

a) The patient has the right to choose his physician freely.

b) The patient has the right to be cared for by a physician who is free to make clinical and ethical judgements without any outside interference.

c) The patient has the right to accept or to refuse treatment after receiving adequate information.

d) The patient has the right to expect that his physician will respect the confidential nature of all his medical and personal details.

e) The patient has the right to die in dignity.

f) The patient has the right to receive or to decline spiritual and moral comfort including the help of a minister of an appropriate religion.

DECLARATION ON PHYSICIAN INDEPENDENCE AND PROFESSIONAL FREEDOM

World Medical Association

1986

Adopted in 1986 by the 38th World Medical Assembly at Rancho Mirage, California, this declaration elaborates on section (b) of the 1981 Declaration of Lisbon. Of interest is the declaration's assertion of the need for professional independence in order to ensure the rights of patients and to fulfill professional obligations to them. The document emphasizes concern over conflicts of interest in the area of cost containment and asserts that physicians must advocate for their individual patients.

The World Medical Association, Inc., recognizing the importance of the physician's independence and professional freedom, hereby adopts the following declaration of principles:

Physicians must recognize and support the rights of their patients, particularly as set forth in the World Medical Association Declaration of Lisbon (1981).

Physicians must have the professional freedom to care for their patients without interference. The exercise of the physician's professional judgement and discretion in making clinical and ethical decisions in the care and treatment of patients must be preserved and protected.

Physicians must have the professional independence to represent and defend the health needs of patients against all who would deny or restrict needed care for those who are sick or injured.

Within the context of their medical practice and the care of their patients, physicians should not be expected to administer governmental or social priorities in the allocation of scarce health resources. To do so would be to create a conflict of interest with the physician's obligation to his patients, and would effectively destroy the physician's professional independence, upon which the patient relies.

While physicians must be conscious of the cost of medical treatment and actively participate in cost containment efforts within medicine, it is the physician's primary obligation to represent the interests of the sick and injured against demands by society for cost containment that would endanger patients' health and perhaps patients' life.

By providing independence and professional freedom for physicians to practice medicine, a community assures the best possible health care for its citizens which in turn contributes to a strong and secure society.

FUNDAMENTAL ELEMENTS OF THE PATIENT-PHYSICIAN RELATIONSHIP

American Medical Association

1990, updated 1993

This document, which constitutes one part of the American Medical Association's complete code of ethics, extends the rights language introduced in the 1980 Principles of Medical Ethics (Section II) to a separate statement listing the specific rights of patients. The opening paragraph of the Fundamental Elements also mentions the responsibilities of patients. Points of particular interest include: (1) Right #4 on confidentiality, which contains the therapeutic privilege exception dropped from the Principles of Medical Ethics in 1980 and still not restored to the principles themselves; (2) Right #5 on continuity of care, which implies that treatment may be discontinued, without making alternative arrangements for care, when further treatment is not "medically indicated"; and (3) Right #6, which establishes a basic right to adequate health care, but explicitly does not guarantee the fulfillment of such a right.

From ancient times, physicians have recognized that the health and well-being of patients depends upon a collaborative effort between physician and patient. Patients share with physicians the responsibility for their own health care. The patient-physician relationship is of greatest benefit to patients when they bring medical problems to the attention of their physicians in a timely fashion, provide information about their medical condition to the best of their ability, and work with their physicians in a mutually respectful alliance. Physicians can best contribute to this alliance by serving as their patients' advocate and by fostering these rights:

1. The patient has the right to receive information from physicians and to discuss the benefits, risks, and costs of appropriate treatment alternatives. Patients should receive guidance from their physicians as to the optimal course of action. Patients are also entitled to obtain copies or summaries of their medical records, to have their questions answered, to be advised of potential conflicts of interest that their physicians might have, and to receive independent professional opinions.
2. The patient has the right to make decisions regarding the health care that is recommended by his or her physician. Accordingly, patients may accept or refuse any recommended medical treatment.
3. The patient has the right to courtesy, respect, dignity, responsiveness, and timely attention to his or her needs.
4. The patient has the right to confidentiality. The physician should not reveal confidential communications or information without the consent of the patient, unless provided for by law or by the need to protect the welfare of the individual or the public interest.
5. The patient has the right to continuity of health care. The physician has an obligation to cooperate in the coordination of medically indicated care with other health care providers treating the patient. The physician may not discontinue treatment of a patient as long as further treatment is medically indicated, without giving the patient reasonable assistance and sufficient opportunity to make alternative arrangements for care.
6. The patient has a basic right to have available adequate health care. Physicians, along with the rest of society, should continue to work toward this goal. Fulfillment of this right is dependent on society providing resources so that no patient is deprived of necessary care because of an inability to pay for the care. Physicians should continue their traditional assumption of a part of the responsibility for the medical care of those who cannot afford essential health care. Physicians should advocate for patients in dealing with third parties when appropriate.

PATIENT RESPONSIBILITIES

American Medical Association

1993

The American Medical Association's (AMA) Patient Responsibilities draws upon the recognition, articulated in the preceding Fundamental Elements of the Patient-Physician Relationship, that successful medical care depends upon a collaborative effort between physicians and patients. Originally published in July 1993 as Report 52 in the AMA Code of Medical Ethics: Reports of the Council on Ethical and Judicial Affairs, Patient Responsibilities expands upon the Fundamental Elements document by specifying the responsibilities of patients for their own health care.

The background section of the original report states: "Like patients' rights, patients' responsibilities are derived from the principle of autonomy. . . . With that exercise of self-governance and free choice comes a number of responsibilities." The list of those patient responsibilities, which also appears in the 1994 AMA Current Opinions, follows.

1. Good communication is essential to a successful physician-patient relationship. To the extent possible, patients have a responsibility to be truthful and to express their concerns clearly to their physicians.

2. Patients have a responsibility to provide a complete medical history, to the extent possible, including information about past illnesses, medications, hospitalizations, family history of illness and other matters relating to present health.

3. Patients have a responsibility to request information or clarification about their health status or treatment when they do not fully understand what has been described.

4. Once patients and physicians agree upon the goals of therapy, patients have a responsibility to cooperate with the treatment plan. Compliance with physician instructions is often essential to public and individual safety. Patients also have a responsibility to disclose whether previously agreed upon treatments are being followed and to indicate when they would like to reconsider the treatment plan.

5. Patients generally have a responsibility to meet their financial obligations with regard to medical care or to discuss financial hardships with their physicians. Patients should be cognizant of the costs associated with using a limited resource like health care and try to use medical resources judiciously.

6. Patients should discuss end of life decisions with their physicians and make their wishes known. Such a discussion might also include writing an advance directive.

7. Patients should be committed to health maintenance through health-enhancing behavior. Illness can often be prevented by a healthy lifestyle, and patients must take personal responsibility when they are able to avert the development of disease.

8. Patients should also have an active interest in the effects of their conduct on others and refrain from behavior that unreasonably places the health of others at risk. Patients should inquire as to the means and likelihood of infectious disease transmission and act upon that information which can best prevent further transmission.

9. Patients should discuss organ donation with their physicians and make applicable provisions. Patients who are part of an organ allocation system and await needed treatment or transplant should not try to go outside of or manipulate the system. A fair system of allocation should be answered with public trust and an awareness of limited resources.

10. Patients should not initiate or participate in fraudulent health care and should report illegal or unethical behavior by providers to the appropriate medical societies, licensing boards, or law enforcement authorities.

PATIENT RIGHTS

Joint Commission on Accreditation of Healthcare Organizations

1994

Patient Rights is a section of the Joint Commission on Accreditation of Healthcare Organizations' (JCAHO) Accreditation Manual for Hospitals, 1994. Although many health-care organizations demonstrate their recognition and support of patient/client rights by issuing lists of those rights, no list can assure that the rights are respected. The standards on patient rights included in JCAHO's Accreditation Manual are designed to reflect the implementation, as well as the existence, of institutional policies and procedures for the exercise and protection of a specified set of patient rights.

The scoring of the standards in this chapter will reflect evidence of the implementation of policies and procedures as well as the existence of such policies and procedures.

RI.1 The organization supports the rights of each patient.

RI.1.1 Organizational policies and procedures describe the mechanisms by which the following rights are protected and exercised:

Intent of RI.1 and RI.1.1

The policies and procedures that guide the organization's interaction with and care of the patient demonstrate its recognition and support of patient rights.

No listing of patient rights can assure the respect of those rights. It is the intent of these standards that the organization's interaction with and care of the patient reflect concern and respect for the rights of the patient.

The organization's policies and procedures describe the mechanisms or processes established to support the following patient rights:

- Reasonable access to care;
- Considerate (and respectful) care that respects the patient's personal value and belief systems;
- Informed participation in decisions regarding his/her care;
- Participation in the consideration of ethical issues that arise in the provision of his/ her care;
- Personal privacy and confidentiality of information; and
- Designation of a representative decision maker in the event that the patient is incapable of understanding a proposed treatment or procedure or is unable to communicate his/her wishes regarding care.

* * *

RI.1.1.1 [Organizational policies and procedures describe the mechanisms by which the following rights are protected and exercised:] The right of the patient to the hospital's reasonable response to his/her requests and needs for treatment or service, within the hospital's capacity, its stated mission, and applicable law and regulation;

Intent of RI.1.1.1

In response to the patient's request and need, the organization provides care that is within its capacity, its stated mission and philosophy, and applicable law and regulation. When the organization cannot meet the request or need for care because of a conflict with its mission or philosophy or incapacity to meet the patient's needs or requests, the patient may be transferred to another facility when medically permissible. Such a transfer is made only after the patient has received complete information and explanation concerning the need for and alternatives to such a transfer. The transfer must be acceptable to the receiving organization.

* * *

RI.1.1.2 [Organizational policies and procedures describe the mechanisms by which the following rights are protected and exercised:] The right of the patient to considerate and respectful care;

RI.1.1.2.1 The care of the patient includes consideration of the psychosocial, spiritual, and cultural variables that influence the perceptions of illness.

Intent of RI.1.1.2 and RI.1.1.2.1

The provision of patient care reflects consideration of the patient as an individual with personal values and a belief system that impact his/her attitude toward and response to the care provided by the organization. The organizational policies and procedures that guide patient care include recognition of the psychosocial, spiritual, and cultural values that affect the patient's response to the care given. Organizational policies and procedures allow the patient to express spiritual beliefs and cultural practices that do not harm others or interfere with the planned course of medical therapy for the patient.

* * *

RI.1.1.2.2 The care of the dying patient optimizes the comfort and dignity of the patient through

RI.1.1.2.2.1 treating primary and secondary symptoms that respond to treatment as desired by the patient or surrogate decision maker;

RI.1.1.2.2.2 effectively managing pain; and

RI.1.1.2.2.3 acknowledging the psychosocial and spiritual concerns of the patient and the family regarding dying and the expression of grief by the patient and family.

Note: The term dying is used to refer to an incurable and irreversible condition such that death is imminent. Imminent is seen as impending or about to happen.

Intent of RI.1.1.2.2 Through RI.1.1.2.2.3

All hospital staff are sensitized to the needs of the dying patient in an acute care hospital. Support for the psychological, social, emotional, and spiritual needs of the patient and family demonstrates respect for the patient's values, religion, and philosophy. The goal of respectful, responsive care of the dying patient is to optimize the patient's comfort and dignity by providing appropriate treatment for primary and secondary symptoms as desired by the patient or surrogate decision maker, responding to the psychosocial, emotional, and spiritual concerns of the patient and family, and managing pain aggressively. (The management of pain is appropriate for all patients, not just dying patients. Guidelines such as those published by the Agency for Health Care Policy and Research for Acute Pain Management reflect the state of knowledge on effective and appropriate care for all patients experiencing acute pain.)

* * *

RI.1.1.3 [Organizational policies and procedures describe the mechanisms by which the following rights are protected and exercised:] The right of the patient, in collaboration with his/her physician, to make decisions involving his/her health care, including

RI.1.1.3.1 the right of the patient to accept medical care or to refuse treatment to the extent permitted by law and to be informed of the medical consequences of such refusal, and

RI.1.1.3.2 the right of the patient to formulate advance directives and appoint a surrogate to make health care decisions on his/her behalf to the extent permitted by law.

RI.1.1.3.2.1 The organization has in place a mechanism to ascertain the existence of and assist in the development of advance directives at the time of the patient's admission.

RI.1.1.3.2.2 The provision of care is not conditioned on the existence of an advance directive.

RI.1.1.3.2.3 Any advance directive(s) is in the patient's medical record and is reviewed periodically with the patient or surrogate decision maker.

Intent of RI.1.1.3 Through RI.1.1.3.2.3

The quality of patient care is enhanced when the patient's preferences are incorporated into plans for care. The process by which care and treatment decisions are made elicit respect and incorporate the patient's preferences. Sound medical judgment is provided to the patient or the patient's surrogate decision maker for informed decision making.

In hospitals providing services to neonate, child, and adolescent patients, a mechanisms exists that is designed to coordinate and facilitate the family's and/or guardian's involvement in decision making throughout the course of treatment. The patient is responsible for providing, to the best of his/her knowledge, accurate and complete information about present complaints, past illnesses, hospitalizations, medications, advance directives, and other matters relevant to his/her health or care. The patient is also responsible for reporting whether he/she clearly comprehends a contemplated course of action and what is expected of him/her.

The hospital ascertains the existence of advance directives, and health care professionals and surrogate decision makers honor them within the limits of the law and the organization's mission and philosophy. An advance directive is a document a person uses to give directions about future medical care or to designate another person to give directions about medical care should he/she lose decision-making capacity. Advance directives may include living wills, durable powers of attorney, or similar documents and contain the patient's preferences.

* * *

RI.1.1.4 [Organizational policies and procedures describe the mechanisms by which the following rights are protected and exercised:] The right of the patient to the information necessary to enable him/her to make treatment decisions that reflect his/her wishes;

RI.1.1.4.1 A policy on informed decision making is developed by the medical staff and governing body and is consistent with any legal requirements.

Intent of RI.1.1.4 and RI.1.1.4.1

The patient is given clear, concise explanation of his/her condition and of any proposed treatment(s) or procedure(s), the potential benefit(s) and the potential drawback(s) of the proposed treatment(s) or procedure(s), problems related to recuperation, and the likelihood of success. Information is also provided regarding any significant alternative treatment(s) or procedure(s).

This information includes the identity of the physician or other practitioner who has primary responsibility for the patient's care and the identity and professional status of individuals responsible for authorizing and performing procedures or treatments. The information also includes the existence of any professional relationship among individuals treating the patient, as well as the relationship to any other health care or educational institutions involved in his/her care.

* * *

RI.1.1.5 [Organizational policies and procedures describe the mechanisms by which the following rights are protected and exercised:] The right of the patient to information, at the time of admission, about the hospital's

RI.1.1.5.1 patient rights policy(ies), and

RI.1.1.5.2 mechanism designed for the initiation, review, and, when possible, resolution of patient complaints concerning the quality of care;

Intent of RI.1.1.5 Through RI.1.1.5.2

The organization assists the patient in exercising his/her rights by informing the patient of those rights during the admission process. The information is given to the patient or his/her representative in a form that is understandable to the patient (for example, in a language that is understood by the patient).

The patient has the right, without recrimination, to voice complaints regarding the care received, and to have those complaints reviewed and, when possible, resolved. This right, and the mechanism(s) established by the organization to assist the patient in exercising this right, are explained to the patient during the admission process.

* * *

RI.1.1.6 [Organizational policies and procedures describe the mechanisms by which the following rights are protected and exercised:] The right of the patient or the patient's designated representative to participate in the consideration of ethical issues that arise in the care of the patient;

RI.1.1.6.1 The organization has in place a mechanism(s) for the consideration of ethical issues arising in the care of patients and to provide education to caregivers and patients on ethical issues in health care.

Intent of RI.1.1.6 and RI.1.1.6.1

Health care professionals provide patient care within an ethical framework established by their profession, the hospital, and the law. The health care professional has an obligation to respect the views of the patient or the patient's designated representative when ethical issues arise during the patient's care. Moreover, the hospital has an obligation to involve the patient or the patient's representative in the organizational mechanism for considering such issues. Such mechanisms may include community programs, education programs for patients or their representatives, and education programs for staff members. The hospital also has an obligation to provide education on important ethical issues in health care to caregivers, care recipients, and the community.

* * *

RI.1.1.7 [Organizational policies and procedures describe the mechanisms by which the following rights are protected and exercised:] The right of the patient to be informed of any human experimentation or other research/educational projects affecting his/her care or treatment;

Intent of RI.1.1.7

The patient has the right to know of any experimental, research, or educational activities involved in his/her treatment: the patient also has the right to refuse to participate in any such activity.

* * *

RI.1.1.8 [Organizational policies and procedures describe the mechanisms by which the following rights are protected and exercised:] The right of the patient, within the limits of law, to personal privacy and confidentiality of information; and

RI.1.1.8.1 The patient and/or the patient's legally designated representative has access to the information contained in the patient's medical record, within the limits of the law.

Intent of RI.1.1.8 and RI.1.1.8.1

The patient has the following rights:

•To be interviewed, examined, and treated in surroundings designed to give reasonable visual and auditory privacy;

•To have access to his/her medical record and to have his/her medical record read only by individuals directly involved in his/her care, or by individuals monitoring the quality of the patient's care, or by individuals authorized by law or regulation (other individuals may read the medical record only with the patient's written consent or that of a legally authorized or designated representative); and

•To request a transfer to a different room if another patient or a visitor in the room is unreasonably disturbing him/her and if another room equally suitable for his/her care needs is available.

* * *

RI.1.1.9 [Organizational policies and procedures describe the mechanisms by which the following rights are protected and exercised:] The right of the patient's guardian, next of kin, or a legally authorized responsible person to exercise, to the extent permitted by law, the rights delineated on behalf of the patient if the patient has been adjudicated incompetent in accordance with the law, is found by his/her physician to be medically incapable of understanding the proposed treatment or procedure, is unable to communicate his/her wishes regarding treatment, or is a minor.

Intent of RI.1.1.9

Although the patient is recognized as having the right to participate in his/her care and treatment to the fullest extent possible, there are circumstances under which the patient may be unable to do so. In these situations, the patient's rights are to be exercised by the patient's designated representative or other legally authorized person.

* * *

RI.2 There are hospitalwide policies on the withholding of resuscitative services from patients and the forgoing or withdrawing of life-sustaining treatment.

Intent of RI.2

No single set of policies can anticipate the varied situations in which the difficult decisions about withholding resuscitative services or forgoing or withdrawing life-sustaining treatment will need to be made. However, organizations can develop the framework for a decision-making process. Such a framework would include policies designed to assist the organization in identifying its position on the initiation of resuscitative services and the use and removal of life-sustaining treatment. Policies of this nature need to conform to the legal requirements of the organization's jurisdiction.

* * *

RI.2.1 The policies are developed in consultation with the medical staff, nursing staff, and other appropriate bodies and are adopted by the medical staff and approved by the governing body.

Intent of RI.2.1

Organizational policies that provide a framework for the decision-making process for withholding resuscitative services or forgoing or withdrawing life-sustaining treatment offer guidance to health professionals on the ethical and legal issues involved in such decisions and decrease the uncertainty about the practices permitted by the organization. It is vital that the policies guiding such decisions be formally adopted by the organization's medical staff and approved by the governing body in order to assure that the process is consistent and that there is accountability for the decisions made.

* * *

RI.2.2 The policies describe

RI.2.2.1 the mechanism(s) for reaching decisions about the withholding of resuscitative services from individual patients or forgoing or withdrawing of life-sustaining treatment;

RI.2.2.2 the mechanism(s) for resolving conflicts in decision making, should they arise; and

RI.2.2.3 the roles of physicians and, when applicable, of nursing personnel, other appropriate staff, and family members in decisions to withhold resuscitative services or forgo or withdraw life-sustaining treatment.

Intent of RI.2.2 Through RI.2.2.3

Organizational policies regarding the withholding of resuscitative services or the forgoing or withdrawing of life-sustaining treatment outline a process for reaching such decisions. This process protects the decision-making rights of the patient or his/her designated representative; decreases staff uncertainty about practices permitted by the organization; clarifies the roles and duties, and therefore the accountability, of health professionals; and reduces arbitrary decision-making procedures.

* * *

RI.2.3 The policies include provisions designed to assure that the rights of patients are respected.

Intent of RI.2.3

Organizational policies regarding the withholding of resuscitative services or the forgoing or withdrawing of life-sustaining treatment empower the patient or designated representative to make such decisions and assure that such decisions made by a patient or designated representative explicitly affirm the patient's responsibility for such decision making.

* * *

RI.2.4 The policies include the requirement that appropriate orders be written by the physician primarily responsible for the patient and that documentation be made in the patient's medical record if life-sustaining treatment is to be withdrawn or resuscitative services are to be withheld.

Intent of RI.2.4

Decisions regarding the withholding of resuscitative services or the withdrawal of life-sustaining treatment are communicated to all health professionals involved in the patient's treatment to assure that the decision is implemented.

Note: *This does not mean that for all deaths in which resuscitative services were not utilized there must be an order to withhold resuscitative services.*

* * *

RI.2.5 The policies address the use of advance directives in patient care to the extent permitted by law.

Intent of RI.2.5

The organization is expected to use any advance directives prepared by the patient and known to the organization in the decision-making process surrounding the consideration of the withholding of resuscitative services or the initiation or withdrawal of life-sustaining treatment, to the extent permitted by law and supported by the organization's mission and philosophy.

* * *

Ethical Directives for the Practice of Medicine

1. Fourth Century B.C.E. – Early Twentieth Century

The ethical directives for the practice of medicine included in this section are organized in two primary groups: (1) codes, oaths, prayers, and other directives from the fourth century B.C.E. through the early twentieth century; and (2) directives from the mid-twentieth century through 1994. Documents in the first group are arranged in chronological order; those in the second group are arranged chronologically within thematic clusters, for example, by issuing body, area of the world, and philosophical or religious tradition.

Some of the documents in this section address not only physicians but also health-care institutions and the health professions in general; they are included in this section because many medical ethics codes historically have applied not only to physicians but also to the practice of health care more generally. Ethical directives for medical specialties generally have not been included in this Appendix, due to space constraints; references for a selection of specialty documents appear in the bibliography to the Appendix.

OATH OF HIPPOCRATES

Fourth Century B.C.E.

Attributed to Hippocrates, the oath, which exemplifies the Pythagorean school rather than Greek thought in general, differs from other, more scientific, writings in the Hippocratic corpus. Written later than some of the other treatises in the corpus, the Oath of Hippocrates is one of the earliest and most important statements on medical ethics. Not only has the oath provided the foundation for many succeeding medical oaths, such as the Declaration of Geneva, but it is still administered to the graduating students of many medical schools, either in its original form or in an altered version.

I swear by Apollo Physician and Asclepius and Hygieia and Panaceia and all the gods and goddesses, making them my witnesses, that I will fulfil according to my ability and judgment this oath and this covenant:

To hold him who has taught me this art as equal to my parents and to live my life in partnership with him, and if he is in need of money to give him a share of mine, and to regard his offspring as equal to my brothers in male lineage and to teach them this art—if they desire to learn it—without fee and covenant; to give a share of precepts and oral instruction and all the other learning to my sons and to the sons of him who has instructed me and to pupils who have signed the covenant and have taken an oath according to the medical law, but to no one else.

I will apply dietetic measures for the benefit of the sick according to my ability and judgment; I will keep them from harm and injustice.

I will neither give a deadly drug to anybody if asked for it, nor will I make a suggestion to this effect. Similarly I will not give to a woman an abortive remedy. In purity and holiness I will guard my life and my art.

I will not use the knife, not even on sufferers from stone, but will withdraw in favor of such men as are engaged in this work.

Whatever houses I may visit, I will come for the benefit of the sick, remaining free of all intentional injustice, of all mischief and in particular of sexual relations with both female and male persons, be they free or slaves.

What I may see or hear in the course of the treatment or even outside of the treatment in regard to the life of men, which on no account one must spread abroad, I will keep to myself holding such things shameful to be spoken about.

If I fulfil this oath and do not violate it, may it be granted to me to enjoy life and art, being honored with fame among all men for all time to come; if I transgress it and swear falsely, may the opposite of all this be my lot.

OATH OF INITIATION (CARAKA SAMHITA)

First Century C.E.?

This ancient Indian oath for medical students appears in the Caraka Samhita (or, Charaka Samhita), a medical text written around the first century C.E. by the Indian physician Caraka. Unlike the Hippocratic Oath, which exemplifies only one, minority, school of ancient Greek thought, the Oath of the Caraka Samhita reflects concepts and beliefs found throughout ancient nonmedical Indian literature. The oath contains several uniquely Hindu elements, including the requirements to lead the life of a celibate, eat no meat, and carry no arms.

1. The teacher then should instruct the disciple in the presence of the sacred fire, Brähmanas [Brahmins] and physicians.

2. [saying] "Thou shalt lead the life of a celibate, grow thy hair and beard, speak only the truth, eat no meat, eat only pure articles of food, be free from envy and carry no arms.

3. There shall be nothing that thou should not do at my behest except hating the king, causing another's death, or committing an act of great unrighteousness or acts leading to calamity.

4. Thou shalt dedicate thyself to me and regard me as thy chief. Thou shalt be subject to me and conduct thyself for ever for my welfare and pleasure. Thou shalt serve and dwell with me like a son or a slave or a supplicant. Thou shalt behave and act without arrogance, with care and attention and with undistracted mind, humility, constant reflection and ungrudging obedience. Acting either at my behest or otherwise, thou shalt conduct thyself for the achievement of thy teacher's purposes alone, to the best of thy abilities.

5. If thou desirest success, wealth and fame as a physician and heaven after death, thou shalt pray for the welfare of all creatures beginning with the cows and Brähmanas.

6. Day and night, however thou mayest be engaged, thou shalt endeavour for the relief of patients with all thy heart and soul. Thou shalt not desert or injure thy patient for the sake of thy life or thy living. Thou shalt not commit adultery even in thought. Even so, thou shalt not covet others' possessions. Thou shalt be modest in thy attire and appearance. Thou shouldst not be a drunkard or a sinful man nor shouldst thou associate with the abettors of crimes. Thou shouldst speak words that are gentle, pure and righteous, pleasing, worthy, true, wholesome, and moderate. Thy behaviour must be in consideration of time and place and heedful of past experience. Thou shalt act always with a view to the acquisition of knowledge and fullness of equipment.

7. No persons, who are hated by the king or who are haters of the king or who are hated by the public or who are haters of the public, shall receive treatment. Similarly, those who are extremely abnormal, wicked, and of miserable character and conduct, those who have not vindicated their honour, those who are on the point of death, and similarly women who are unattended by their husbands or guardians shall not receive treatment.

8. No offering of presents by a woman without the behest of her husband or guardian shall be accepted by thee. While entering the patient's house, thou shalt be accompanied by a man who is known to the patient and who has his permission to enter; and thou shalt be well-clad, bent of head, self-possessed, and conduct thyself only after repeated consideration. Thou shalt thus properly make thy entry. Having entered, thy speech,

mind, intellect and senses shall be entirely devoted to no other thought than that of being helpful to the patient and of things concerning only him. The peculiar customs of the patient's household shall not be made public. Even knowing that the patient's span of life has come to its close, it shall not be mentioned by thee there, where if so done, it would cause shock to the patient or to others.

Though possessed of knowledge one should not boast very much of one's knowledge. Most people are offended by the boastfulness of even those who are otherwise good and authoritative.

9. There is no limit at all to the Science of Life, Medicine. So thou shouldst apply thyself to it with diligence. This is how thou shouldst act. Also thou shouldst learn the skill of practice from another without carping. The entire world is the teacher to the intelligent and the foe to the unintelligent. Hence, knowing this well, thou shouldst listen and act according to the words of instruction of even an unfriendly person, when his words are worthy and of a kind as to bring to you fame, long life, strength and prosperity."

10. Thereafter the teacher should say this—"Thou shouldst conduct thyself properly with the gods, sacred fire, Brähmanas, the guru, the aged, the scholars and the preceptors. If thou has conducted thyself well with them, the precious stones, the grains and the gods become well disposed towards thee. If thou shouldst conduct thyself otherwise, they become unfavorable to thee." To the teacher that has spoken thus, the disciple should say, "Amen."

OATH OF ASAPH

Third Century-Seventh Century C.E.?

The Oath of Asaph appears at the end of the Book of Asaph the Physician (*Sefer Asaph haRofe*)*, which is the oldest Hebrew medical text. It was written by Asaph Judaeus, also known as Asaph ben Berachyahu, a Hebrew physician from Syria or Mesopotamia, who lived sometime between the third and seventh centuries* C.E.*, probably in the sixth century. The oath, which in pan resembles the Oath of Hippocrates, was taken by medical students when they received their diplomas.*

And this is the oath adminstered by Asaph, the son of Berachyahu, and by Jochanan, the son of Zabda, to their disciples; and they adjured them in these words: Take heed that ye kill not any man with the sap of a root; and ye shall not dispense a potion to a woman with child by adultery to cause her to miscarry; and ye shall not lust after beautiful women to commit adultery with them; and ye shall not disclose secrets confided unto you; and ye shall take no bribes to cause injury and to kill; and ye shall not harden your hearts against the poor and the needy, but heal them; and ye shall not call good evil or evil good; and ye shall not walk in the way of sorcerers to cast spells, to enchant and to bewitch with intent to separate a man from the wife of his bosom or woman from the husband of her youth.

And ye shall not covet wealth or bribes to abet depraved sexual commerce.

And ye shall not make use of any manner of idol-worship to heal thereby, nor trust in the healing powers of any form of their worship. But rather must ye abhor and detest and hate all their worshippers and those that trust in them and cause others to trust in them, for all of them are but vanity and of no avail, for they are naught; and they are demons. Their own carcasses they cannot save; how, then, shall they save the living?

And now, put your trust in the Lord your God, the God of truth, the living God, for He doth kill and make alive, smite and heal. He doth teach man understanding and also to do good. He smiteth in righteousness and justice and healeth in mercy and loving-kindness. No crafty device can be concealed from Him, for naught is hidden from His sight.

He causeth healing plants to grow and doth implant in the hearts of sages skill to heal by His manifold mercies and to declare marvels to the multitude, that all that live may know that He made them, and that beside Him there is none to save. For the peoples trust in their idols to succour them from their afflictions, but they will not save them in their distress, for their hope and their trust are in the Dead. Therefore it is fitting that ye keep apart from them and hold aloof from all the abominations of their idols and cleave unto the name of the Lord God of all flesh. And every living creature is in His hand to kill and to make alive; and there is none to deliver from His hand.

Be ye mindful of Him at all times and seek Him in truth uprightness and rectitude that ye may prosper in all that ye do; then He will cause you to prosper and ye shall be praised by all men. And the peoples will leave their gods and their idols and will yearn to serve the Lord even as ye do, for they will perceive that they have put their trust in a thing of naught and that their labour is in vain; (otherwise) when they cry unto the Lord, He will not save them.

As for you, be strong and let not your hands slacken, for there is a reward for your labours. God is with you when ye are with Him. If ye will keep His covenant and walk in His statutes to cleave unto them, ye shall be as saints in the sight of all men, and they shall say: "Happy is the people that is in such a case; happy is that people whose God is the Lord."

And their disciples answered them and said: All that ye have instructed us and commanded us, that will we do, for it is a commandment of the Torah, and it behooves us to perform it with all our heart and all our soul and all our might: to do and to obey and to turn neither to the right nor to the left. And they blessed them in the name of the Highest God, the Lord of Heaven and earth.

And they admonished them yet again and said unto them: Behold, the Lord God and His saints and His Torah be witness unto you that ye shall fear Him, turning not aside from His commandments, but walking uprightly in His statutes. Incline not to covetousness and aid not the evildoers to shed innocent blood. Neither shall ye mix poisons for a man or a woman to slay his friend therewith; nor shall ye reveal which roots be poisonous or give them into the hand of any man, or be persuaded to do evil. Ye shall not cause the shedding of blood by any manner of medical treatment. Take heed that ye do not cause a malady to any man; and ye shall not cause any man injury by hastening to cut through flesh and blood with an iron instrument or by branding, but shall first observe twice and thrice and only then shall ye give your counsel.

Let not a spirit of haughtiness cause you to lift up your eyes and your hearts in pride. Wreak not the vengeance of hatred on a sick man; and alter not your prescriptions for them that do hate the Lord our God, but keep his ordinances and commandments and walk in all His ways that ye may find favour in His sight. Be ye pure and faithful and upright.

Thus did Asaph and Jochanan instruct and adjure their disciples.

ADVICE TO A PHYSICIAN

Advice of Haly Abbas (Ahwazi)

Tenth Century C.E.

A leading Persian figure in medicine and medical ethics, Haly Abbas (Ahwazi), who died in 994 C.E.*, devoted the first chapter of his work* Liber Regius (Kamel Al Sanaah al Tibbia) *to the ethics of medicine. An excerpt of his ethical admonition follows.*

The first advice is to worship God and obey his commands; then be humble toward your teacher and endeavor to hold him in esteem, to serve and show gratitude to him, to hold him equally dear as you do your parents, and to share your possessions with him as with your parents.

Be kind to the children of your teachers and if one of them wants to study medicine you are to teach him without any remuneration.

You are to prohibit the unsuited and undeserving from studying medicine.

A physician is to prudently treat his patients with food and medicine out of good and spiritual motives, not for the sake of gain. He should never prescribe or use a harmful drug or abortifacient.

A physician should be chaste, pious, religious, well-spoken, and graceful, and must avoid any kind of sinfulness or impurity. He should not look upon women with lust and never go to their home except to visit a patient.

A physician should respect confidences and protect the patient's secrets. In protecting a patient's secrets, he must be more insistent than the patient himself. A physician should follow the Hippocratic counsels. He must be kind, compassionate, merciful and benevolent, and give himself unstintingly to the treatment of patients, especially the poor. He must never expect remuneration from the poor but rather provide them free medicine. If it is not impossible, he must visit them graciously whenever it is necessary, day or night, especially when they suffer from an acute disease, because the patient's condition changes very quickly with this kind of disease.

It is not proper for a physician to live luxuriously and become involved in pleasure-seeking. He must not drink alcohol because it injures the brain. He must study medical books constantly and never grow tired of research. He has to learn what he is studying and repeat and memorize what is necessary. He has to study in his youth because it is easier to memorize the subject at this age than in old age, which is the mother of oblivion.

A medical student should be constantly present in the hospital so as to study disease processes and complications under the learned professor and proficient physicians.

To be a learned and skillful physician, he has to follow this advice, develop an upright character and never hesitate to put this advice into practice so as to make his work effective, to win the patient's trust, and to receive the benefit of the patient's friendship and gratitude.

The Almighty God knows better than all. . . .

THE 17 RULES OF ENJUIN (FOR DISCIPLES OF OUR SCHOOL)

Sixteenth Century C.E.

The 17 Rules of Enjuin were developed for students by practitioners of the Ri-shu school, an approach to disease that was practiced in sixteenth-century Japan. The text reflects the priestly role of the physician and emphasizes the idea, also found in the Hippocratic Oath, that medical knowledge should not be disclosed outside of the school.

1. Each person should follow the path designated by Heaven (Buddha, the Gods).

2. You should always be kind to people. You should always be devoted to loving people.

3. The teaching of Medicine should be restricted to selected persons.

4. You should not tell others what you are taught, regarding treatments without permission.

5. You should not establish association with doctors who do not belong to this school.

6. All the successors and descendants of the disciples of this school shall follow the teachers' ways.

7. If any disciples cease the practice of Medicine, or, if successors are not found at the death of the disciple, all the medical books of this school should be returned to the SCHOOL OF ENJUIN.

8. You should not kill living creatures, nor should you admire hunting or fishing.

9. In our school, teaching about poisons is prohibited, nor should you receive instructions about poisons from other physicians. Moreover, you should not give abortives to the people.

10. You should rescue even such patients as you dislike or hate. You should do virtuous acts, but in such a way that they do not become known to people. To do good deeds secretly is a mark of virtue.

11. You should not exhibit avarice and you must not strain to become famous. You should not rebuke or reprove a patient, even if he does not present you with money or goods in gratitude.

12. You should be delighted if, after treating a patient without success, the patient receives medicine from another physician, and is cured.

13. You should not speak ill of other physicians.

14. You should not tell what you have learned from the time you enter a woman's room, and, moreover, you should not have obscene or immoral feelings when examining a woman.

15. Proper or not, you should not tell others what you have learned in lectures, or what you have learned about prescribing medicine.

16. You should not like undue extravagance. If you like such living, your avarice will increase, and you will lose the ability to be kind to others.

17. If you do not keep the rules and regulations of this school, then you will be cancelled as a disciple. In more severe cases, the punishment will be greater.

FIVE COMMANDMENTS AND TEN REQUIREMENTS

1617

The Five Commandments and Ten Requirements of physicians constitute the most comprehensive statement on medical ethics in China. They were written by Chen Shih-kung, an early-seventeenth-century Chinese physician, and appear in his work An Orthodox Manual of Surgery.

Five Commandments

1. Physicians should be ever ready to respond to any calls of patients, high or low, rich or poor. They should treat them equally and care not for financial reward. Thus their profession will become prosperous naturally day by day and conscience will remain intact.

2. Physicians may visit a lady, widow or nun only in the presence of an attendant but not alone. The secret diseases of female patients should be examined with a right attitude, and should not be revealed to anybody, not even to the physician's own wife.

3. Physicians should not ask patients to send pearl, amber or other valuable substances to their home for preparing medicament. If necessary, patients should be instructed how to mix the prescriptions themselves in order to avoid suspicion. It is also not proper to admire things which patients possess.

4. Physicians should not leave the office for excursion and drinking. Patients should be examined punctually and personally. Prescriptions should be made according to the medical formulary, otherwise a dispute may arise.

5. Prostitutes should be treated just like patients from a good family and gratuitous services should not be given to the poor ones. Mocking should not be indulged for this brings loss of dignity. After examination physicians should leave the house immediately. If the case improves, drugs may be sent but physicians should not visit them again for lewd reward.

Ten Requirements

1. A physician or surgeon must first know the principles of the learned. He must study all the ancient standard medical books ceaselessly day and night, and understand them thoroughly so that the principles enlighten his eyes and are impressed on his heart. Then he will not make any mistake in the clinic.

2. Drugs must be carefully selected and prepared according to the refining process of Lei Kung. Remedies should be prepared according to the pharmaceutical formulae but may be altered to suit the patient's condition. Decoctions and powders should be freely made. Pills and distilled medicine should be prepared in advance. The older the plaster is the more effective it will be. Tampons become more effective on standing. Don't spare valuable drugs; their use is eventually advantageous.

3. A physician should not be arrogant and insult other physicians in the same district. He should be modest and careful towards his colleagues; respect his seniors, help his juniors, learn from his superiors and yield to the arrogant. Thus there will be no slander and hatred. Harmony will be esteemed by all.

4. The managing of a family is just like the curing of a disease. If the constitution of a man is not well cared for and becomes over-exhausted, diseases will attack him. Mild ones will weaken his physique, while serious ones may result in death. Similarly, if the foundation of the family is not firmly established and extravagance be indulged in, reserves will gradually drain away and poverty will come.

5. Man receives his fate from Heaven. He should not be ungrateful to the Heavenly decree. Professional gains should be approved by the conscience and conform to the Heavenly will. If the gain is made according to the Heavenly will, natural affinity takes place. If not, offspring will be condemned. Is it not better to make light of professional gain in order to avoid the evil retribution?

6. Gifts, except in the case of weddings, funerals and for the consolation of the sick, should be simple. One dish of fish and one of vegetable will suffice for a meal. This is not only to reduce expenses but also to save provisions. The virtue of a man lies not in grasping but rather in economy.

7. Medicine should be given free to the poor. Extra financial help should be extended to the destitute patients, if possible. Without food, medicine alone can not relieve the distress of a patient.

8. Savings should be invested in real estate but not in curios and unnecessary luxuries. The physician should also not join the drinking club and the gambling house which would hinder his practice. Hatred and slander can thus be avoided.

9. Office and dispensary should be fully equipped with necessary apparatus. The physician should improve his knowledge by studying medical books, old and new, and reading current publications. This really is the fundamental duty of a physician.

10. A physician should be ready to respond to the call of government officials with respect and sincerity. He should inform them of the cause of the disease and prescribe accordingly. After healing he should not seek for a complimentary tablet [a wooden board inscribed with complimentary words, hung in the physician's office for propaganda] or plead excuse for another's difficulty. A person who respects the law should not associate with officials.

A PHYSICIAN'S ETHICAL DUTIES

From Kholasah al Hekmah

1770

In 1770 C.E., *during Persia's Islamic era, Mohamad Hosin Aghili of Shiraz wrote the work* Kholasah al Hekmah. *The first chapter of that work contains a list of ethical duties for the physician, which are printed here in condensed form.*

1. A physician must not be conceited; he should know that the actual healer is God.

2. He should praise his teachers and professor and return thanks to them for their kindnesses.

3. He should never slander another physician. The fault of others should occasion the recognition of his own fault, not be the occasion for pride and conceit.

4. He must speak to patients with civility and good humor and never get angry at the misbehavior and insults of patients.

5. He must protect the patients' secrets and not betray them, especially to those the patients do not want to know.

6. In the case of the transmission of disease, the physician must not turn the second patient against the first.

7. He must be energetic in studying diseases and drugs and earnest in the diagnosis and treatment of a patient or disease.

8. He must never be tenacious in his opinion, and continue in his fault or mistake but, if it is possible, he is to consult with proficient physicians and ascertain the facts.

9. If someone mentions a useless or wrong idea, he must not turn it down definitely but say politely, "Maybe it is true in some cases but, in my opinion, in this case it is more probably such and such."

10. If a prior physician has a better knowledge of a patient or disease, he has to encourage the patient to return to the first physician.

11. If he is not successful in the treatment of a case or if he has found the patient did not have confidence in his work or that the patient would like to refer to another physician, it is better to offer an excuse and ask him to consult another physician.

12. He must not be prejudiced against any method of treatment and never continue any wrong practice.

13. In the treatment of disease, he must begin with simple medicine and not recommend any drug as long as the nature of the disease is resistant to it and it would not be effective.

14. If a patient has several diseases, first of all he has to cure the main disease which may be the cause of complications.

15. He should never recommend any kind of fatal, harmful or enfeebling drugs; he has to know that as a physician he has to do what is conducive to the patient's temperament, and temperament itself is an efficient corrector and protector of the body, not fatal or destructive.

16. He must not be proud of his class or his family and must not regard others with contempt.

17. He must not withhold medical knowledge; he should teach it to everyone in medicine without any discrimination between poor or rich, noble or slave.

18. He must not hold his students or his patients under his obligation.

19. He must be content, grateful, generous and magnanimous, and never be covetous, greedy, ravenous or jealous.

20. He must never covet another's property. If someone offers him a present while he himself is in need of it, he must not accept it.

21. He must never claim that he can cure an impoverished patient who has gone to many physicians, and should not jeopardize his own reputation.

22. He should never be gluttonous and become involved in pleasure-seeking, buffoonery, drinking, and other sins.

23. He must not look upon women with lust but must look at them as he looks at his daughter, sister, or mother.

DAILY PRAYER OF A PHYSICIAN ("PRAYER OF MOSES MAIMONIDES")

1793?

Although there is considerable debate about this prayer's true authorship, it was first attributed to Moses Maimonides, a twelfth-century Jewish physician in Egypt. Many now believe it was in fact authored by Marcus Herz, a German physician, pupil of Immanuel Kant, and physician to Moses Mendelssohn. The prayer first appeared in print in 1793 as "Tägliches Gebet eines Arztes bevor er seine Kranken besucht—Aus der hebräischen Handschrift eines berühmten jüdischen Arztes in Egypten aus dem zwölften Jahrhundert" ("Daily prayer of a physician before he visits his patients—From the Hebrew manuscript of a renowned Jewish physician in Egypt from the twelfth century"). The Prayer of Moses Maimonides and the Oath of Hippocrates are probably the best known of the older statements on medical ethics.

Almighty God, Thou has created the human body with infinite wisdom. Ten thousand times ten thousand organs hast Thou combined in it that act unceasingly and harmoniously to preserve the whole in all its beauty—the body which is the envelope of the immortal soul. They are ever acting in perfect order, agreement and accord. Yet, when the frailty of matter or the unbridling of passions deranges this order or interrupts this accord, then forces clash and the body crumbles into the primal dust from which it came. Thou sendest to man diseases as beneficent messengers to foretell approaching danger and to urge him to avert it.

Thou has blest Thine earth, Thy rivers and Thy mountains with healing substances; they enable Thy creatures to alleviate their sufferings and to heal their illnesses. Thou hast endowed man with the wisdom to relieve the suffering of his brother, to recognize his disorders, to extract the healing substances, to discover their powers and to prepare and to apply them to suit every ill. In Thine Eternal Providence Thou hast chosen me to watch over the life and health of Thy creatures. I am now about to apply myself to the duties of my profession. Support me, Almighty God, in these great labors that they may benefit mankind, for without Thy help not even the least thing will succeed.

Inspire me with love for my art and for Thy creatures. Do not allow thirst for profit, ambition for renown and admiration, to interfere with my profession, for these are the enemies of truth and of love for mankind and they can lead astray in the great task of attending to the welfare of Thy creatures. Preserve the strength of my body and of my soul that they ever be ready to cheerfully help and support rich and poor, good and bad, enemy as well as friend. In the sufferer let me see only the human being. Illumine my mind that it recognize what presents itself and that it may comprehend what is absent or hidden. Let it not fail to see what is visible, but do not permit it to arrogate to itself the power to see what cannot be seen, for delicate and indefinite are the bounds of the great art of caring for the lives and health of Thy creatures. Let me never be absent-minded. May no strange thoughts divert my attention at the bedside of the sick, or disturb my mind in its silent labors, for great and sacred are the thoughtful deliberations required to preserve the lives and health of Thy creatures.

Grant that my patients have confidence in me and my art and follow my directions and my counsel. Remove from their midst all charlatans and the whole host of officious relatives and know-all nurses, cruel people who arrogantly frustrate the wisest purposes of our art and often lead Thy creatures to their death.

Should those who are wiser than I wish to improve and instruct me, let my soul gratefully follow their guidance; for vast is the extent of our art. Should conceited fools, however, censure me, then let love for my profession steel me against them, so that I remain steadfast without regard for age, for reputation, or for honor, because surrender would bring to Thy creatures sickness and death.

Imbue my soul with gentleness and calmness when older colleagues, proud of their age, wish to displace me or to scorn me or disdainfully to teach me. May even this be of advantage to me, for they know many things of which I am ignorant, but let not their arrogance give me pain. For they are old and old age is not master of the passions. I also hope to attain old age upon this earth, before Thee, Almighty God!

Let me be contented in everything except in the great science of my profession. Never allow the thought to arise in me that I have attained to sufficient knowledge, but vouch-safe to me the strength, the leisure and the ambition ever to extend my knowledge. For art is great, but the mind of man is ever expanding.

Almighty God! Thou has chosen me in Thy mercy to watch over the life and death of Thy creatures. I now apply myself to my profession. Support me in this great task so that it may benefit mankind, for without Thy help not even the least thing will succeed.

CODE OF ETHICS

American Medical Association

1847

The American Medical Association's (AMA) first code of ethics can be understood only in light of the work in medical ethics done by Thomas Percival, an eighteenth-century English physician. Percival wrote the first comprehensive modern statement of medical ethics in response to a request from the trustees of the Manchester Infirmary to draw up a "scheme of professional conduct relative to hospitals and other medical charities" that would resolve conflicts among infirmary physicians and prevent future conflicts. In 1794, after three years of writing and revising, Percival privately distributed a book titled *Medical Ethics.* Finally published in 1803, Percival's *Medical Ethics* served for many years as a model for the ethics codes of medical societies in both England and the United States.

When the AMA was founded in 1847, its first tasks were to establish standards for medical education and to formulate a code of ethics. Because most of the existing American codes of medical ethics relied heavily on Thomas Percival's work, the AMA followed suit, frequently preserving Percival's wording. The code of 1847, adopted by both the AMA and the New York Academy of Medicine, is excerpted below.

Chapter I. OF THE DUTIES OF PHYSICIANS TO THEIR PATIENTS, AND OF THE OBLIGATIONS OF PATIENTS TO THEIR PHYSICIANS

ART. I—*Duties of Physicians to their Patients*

1. A physician should not only be ever ready to obey the calls of the sick, but his mind ought also to be imbued with the greatness of his mission, and of the responsibility he habitually incurs in its discharge. Those obligations are the more deep and enduring, because there is no tribunal other than his own conscience, to adjudge penalties for carelessness or neglect. Physicians should, therefore, minister to the sick with due impressions of the importance of their office; reflecting that the ease, the health, and the lives of those committed to their charge, depend on their skill, attention and fidelity. They should study, also, in their deportment, so to unite *tenderness* with *firmness*, and *condescension* with *authority*, as to inspire the minds of their patients with gratitude, respect and confidence.

2. Every case committed to the charge of a physician should be treated with attention, steadiness and humanity. Reasonable indulgence should be granted to the mental imbecility and caprices of the sick. Secrecy and delicacy, when required by peculiar circumstances, should be strictly observed; and the familiar and confidential intercourse to which physicians are admitted in their professional visits, should be used with discretion, and with the most scrupulous regard to fidelity and honor. The obligation of secrecy extends beyond the period of professional services;—none of the privacies of personal and domestic life, no infirmity of disposition or flaw of character observed during professional attendance, should ever be divulged by him except when he is imperatively required to do so. The force and necessity of this obligation are indeed so great, that professional men have, under certain circumstances, been protected in their observance of secrecy by courts of justice.

3. Frequent visits to the sick are in general requisite, since they enable the physician to arrive at a more perfect knowledge of the disease,—to meet promptly every change which may occur, and also tend to preserve the confidence of the patient. But unnecessary visits are to be avoided, as they give useless anxiety to the patient, tend to diminish the authority of the physician, and render him liable to be suspected of interested motives.

4. A physician should not be forward to make gloomy prognostications, because they savor of empiricism, by magnifying the importance of his services in the treatment or cure of the disease. But he should not fail, on proper occasions, to give to the friends of the patient timely notice of danger, when it really occurs; and even to the patient himself, if absolutely necessary. This office, however, is so peculiarly alarming when executed by him, that it ought to be declined whenever it can be assigned to any other person of sufficient judgment and delicacy. For, the physician should be the minister of hope and comfort to the sick; that, by such cordials to the drooping spirit, he may smooth the bed of death, revive expiring life, and counteract the depressing influence of those maladies which often disturb the tranquility of the most resigned, in their last moments. The life of a sick person can be shortened not only by the acts, but also by the words or the manner of a physician. It is, therefore, a sacred duty to guard himself carefully in this respect, and to avoid all things which have a tendency to discourage the patient and to depress his spirits.

5. A physician ought not to abandon a patient because the case is deemed incurable; for his attendance may continue to be highly useful to the patient,

and comforting to the relatives around him, even to the last period of a fatal malady, by alleviating pain and other symptoms, and by soothing mental anguish. To decline attendance, under such circumstances, would be sacrificing to fanciful delicacy and mistaken liberality, that moral duty, which is independent of, and far superior to all pecuniary consideration.

6. Consultations should be promoted in difficult or protracted cases, as they give rise to confidence, energy, and more enlarged views in practice.

7. The opportunity which a physician not unfrequently enjoys of promoting and strengthening the good resolutions of his patients, suffering under the consequences of vicious conduct, ought never to be neglected. His counsels, or even remonstrances, will give satisfaction, not offence, if they be proffered with politeness, and evince a genuine love of virtue, accompanied by a sincere interest in the welfare of the person to whom they are addressed.

ART. II—*Obligations of Patients to their Physicians*

1. The members of the medical profession, upon whom are enjoined the performance of so many important and arduous duties towards the community, and who are required to make so many sacrifices of comfort, ease, and health, for the welfare of those who avail themselves of their services, certainly have a right to expect and require, that their patients should entertain a just sense of the duties which they owe to their medical attendants.

2. The first duty of a patient is, to select as his medical adviser one who has received a regular professional education. In no trade or occupation do mankind rely on the skill of an untaught artist; and in medicine, confessedly the most difficult and intricate of the sciences, the world ought not to suppose that knowledge is intuitive.

3. Patients should prefer a physician whose habits of life are regular, and who is not devoted to company, pleasure, or to any pursuit incompatible with his professional obligations. A patient should also confide the care of himself and family, as much as possible, to one physician, for a medical man who has become acquainted with the peculiarities of constitution, habits, and predispositions, of those he attends, is more likely to be successful in his treatment than one who does not possess that knowledge.

A patient who has thus selected his physician, should always apply for advice in whatever may appear to him trivial cases, for the most fatal results often supervene on the slightest accidents. It is of still more importance that he should apply for assistance in the forming stage of violent diseases; it is to a neglect of this precept that medicine owes much of the uncertainty and imperfection with which it has been reproached.

4. Patients should faithfully and unreservedly communicate to their physician the supposed cause of their disease. This is the more important, as many diseases of a mental origin simulate those depending on external causes, and yet are only to be cured by ministering to the mind diseased. A patient should never be afraid of thus making his physician his friend and adviser; he should always bear in mind that a medical man is under the strongest obligations of secrecy. Even the female sex should never allow feelings of shame and delicacy to prevent their disclosing the seat, symptoms and causes of complaints peculiar to them. However commendable a modest reserve may be in the common occurrences of life, its strict observance in medicine is often attended with the most serious consequences, and a patient may sink under a painful and loathsome disease, which might have been readily prevented had timely intimation been given to the physician.

5. A patient should never weary his physician with a tedious detail of events or matters not appertaining to his disease. Even as relates to his actual symptoms, he will convey much more real information by giving clear answers to interrogatories, than by the most minute account of his own framing. Neither should he obtrude the details of his business nor the history of his family concerns.

6. The obedience of a patient to the prescriptions of his physician should be prompt and implicit. He should never permit his own crude opinions as to their fitness, to influence his attention to them. A failure in one particular may render an otherwise judicious treatment dangerous, and even fatal. This remark is equally applicable to diet, drink, and exercise. As patients become convalescent, they are very apt to suppose that the rules prescribed for them may be disregarded, and the consequence, but too often, is a relapse. Patients should never allow themselves to be persuaded to take any medicine whatever, that may be recommended to them by the self-constituted doctors and doctoresses, who are so frequently met with, and who pretend to possess infallible remedies for the cure of every disease. However simple some of their prescriptions may appear to be, it often happens that they are productive of much mischief, and in all cases they are injurious, by contravening the plan of treatment adopted by the physician.

7. A patient should, if possible, avoid even the *friendly visits of a physician* who is not attending him—and when he does receive them, he should never converse on the subject of his disease, as an observation may be made, without any intention of interference, which may destroy his confidence in the course he is pursuing, and induce him to neglect the directions prescribed to him. A patient should never send for a consulting physician without the express consent of his own medical attendant. It is of great importance that physicians should act in concert; for, although their modes of treatment may be attended with equal success when employed singly, yet conjointly they are very likely to be productive of disastrous results.

8. When a patient wishes to dismiss his physician, justice and common courtesy require that he should declare his reasons for so doing.

9. Patients should always, when practicable, send for their physician in the morning, before his usual hour of going out; for, by being early aware of the visits he has to pay during the day, the physician is able to apportion his time in such a manner as to prevent an interference of engagements. Patients should also avoid calling on their medical adviser unnecessarily during the hours devoted to meals or sleep. They should always be in readiness to receive the visits of their physician, as the detention of a few minutes is often of serious inconvenience to him.

10. A patient should, after his recovery, entertain a just and enduring sense of the value of the services rendered him by his physician; for these are of such a character, that no mere pecuniary acknowledgment can repay or cancel them.

Chapter II. OF THE DUTIES OF PHYSICIANS TO EACH OTHER AND TO THE PROFESSION AT LARGE

ART. I—*Duties for the support of professional character*

1. Every individual, on entering the profession, as he becomes thereby entitled to all its privileges and immunities, incurs an obligation to exert his best abilities to maintain its dignity and honor, to exalt its standing, and to extend the bounds of its usefulness. He should therefore observe strictly, such laws as are instituted for the government of its members;—should avoid all contumelious and sarcastic remarks relative to the faculty, as a body; and while, by unwearied diligence, he resorts to every honorable means of enriching the science, he should entertain a due respect for his seniors, who have, by their labors, brought it to the elevated condition in which he finds it.

2. There is no profession, from the members of which greater purity of character and a higher standard of moral excellence are required, than the medical; and to attain such eminence, is a duty every physician owes alike to his profession, and to his patients. It is due to the latter, as without it he cannot command their respect and confidence; and to both, because no scientific attainments can compensate for the want of correct moral principles. It is also incumbent upon the faculty to be temperate in all things, for the practice of physic requires the unremitting exercise of a clear and vigorous understanding; and, on emergencies for which no professional man should be unprepared, a steady hand, an acute eye, and an unclouded head, may be essential to the well-being, and even life, of a fellow creature.

3. It is derogatory to the dignity of the profession, to resort to public advertisements or private cards or handbills, inviting the attention of individuals affected with particular diseases—publicly offering advice and medicine to the poor gratis, or promising radical cures; or to publish cases and operations in the daily prints, or suffer such publications to be made;—to invite laymen to be present at operations—to boast of cures and remedies—to adduce certificates of skill and success, or to perform any other similar acts. These are the ordinary practices of empirics, and are highly reprehensible in a regular physician.

4. Equally derogatory to professional character is it, for a physician to

hold a patient for any surgical instrument, or medicine; or to dispense a secret *nostrum*, whether it be the composition or exclusive property of himself or of others. For, if such nostrum be of real efficacy, any concealment regarding it is inconsistent with beneficence and professional liberality; and, if mystery alone give it value and importance, such craft implies either disgraceful ignorance, or fraudulent avarice. It is also reprehensible for physicians to give certificates attesting the efficacy of patent or secret medicines, or in any way to promote the use of them.

ART. II—*Professional services of Physicians to each other*

1. All practitioners of medicine, their wives, and their children while under the paternal care, are entitled to the gratuitous services of any one or more of the faculty residing near them, whose assistance may be desired. A physician afflicted with disease is usually an incompetent judge of his own case; and the natural anxiety and solicitude which he experiences at the sickness of a wife, a child, or any one who by the ties of consanguinity is rendered peculiarly dear to him, tend to obscure his judgment, and produce timidity and irresolution in his practice. Under such circumstances, medical men are peculiarly dependent upon each other, and kind offices and professional aid should always be cheerfully and gratuitously afforded. Visits ought not, however, to be obtruded officiously; as such unasked civility may give rise to embarrassment, or interfere with that choice on which confidence depends. But, if a distant member of the faculty, whose circumstances are affluent, request attendance, and an honorarium be offered, it should not be declined; for no pecuniary obligation ought to be imposed, which the party receiving it would wish not to incur.

* * *

ART. IV—*Of the duties of Physicians in regard to consultations*

1. A regular medical education furnishes the only presumptive evidence of professional abilities and acquirements, and ought to be the only acknowledged right of an individual to the exercise and honors of his profession. Nevertheless, as in consultations, the good of the patient is the sole object in view, and this is often dependent on personal confidence, no intelligent regular practitioner, who has a license to practise from some medical board of known and acknowledged respectability, recognised by this association, and who is in good moral and professional standing in the place in which he resides, should be fastidiously excluded from fellowship, or his aid refused in consultation when it is requested by the patient. But no one can be considered as a regular practitioner, or fit associate in consultation, whose practice is based on an exclusive dogma, to the rejection of the accumulated experience of the profession, and of the aids actually furnished by anatomy, physiology, pathology, and organic chemistry.

2. In consultations, no rivalship or jealousy should be indulged; candor, probity, and all due respect, should be exercised towards the physician having charge of the case.

3. In consultations, the attending physician should be the first to propose the necessary questions to the sick; after which the consulting physician should have the opportunity to make such farther inquiries of the patient as may be necessary to satisfy him of the true character of the case. Both physicians should then retire to a private place for deliberation; and the one first in attendance should communicate the directions agreed upon to the patient or his friends, as well as any opinions which it may be thought proper to express. But no statement or discussion of it should take place before the patient or his friends, except in the presence of all the faculty attending, and by their common consent; and no *opinions* or *prognostications* should be delivered, which are not the result of previous deliberation and concurrence.

4. In consultations, the physician in attendance should deliver his opinion first; and when there are several consulting, they should deliver their opinions in the order in which they have been called in. No decision, however, should restrain the attending physician from making such variations in the mode of treatment, as any subsequent unexpected change in the character of the case may demand. But such variation and the reasons for it ought to be carefully detailed at the next meeting in consultation. The same privilege belongs also to the consulting physician if he is sent for in an emergency, when the regular attendant is out of the way, and similar explanations must be made by him, at the next consultation.

* * *

7. All discussions in consultation should be held as secret and confidential. Neither by words nor manner should any of the parties to a consultation assert or insinuate, that any part of the treatment pursued did not receive his assent. The responsibility must be equally divided between the medical attendants—they must equally share the credit of success as well as the blame of failure.

8. Should an irreconcilable diversity of opinion occur when several physicians are called upon to consult together, the opinion of the majority should be considered as decisive; but if the numbers be equal on each side, then the decision should rest with the attending physician. It may, moreover, sometimes happen, that two physicians cannot agree in their views of the nature of a case, and the treatment to be pursued. This is a circumstance much to be deplored, and should always be avoided, if possible, by mutual concessions, as far as they can be justified by a conscientious regard for the dictates of judgment. But in the event of its occurrence, a third physician should, if practicable, be called to act as umpire; and if circumstances prevent the adoption of this course, it must be left to the patient to select the physician in whom he is most willing to confide. But as every physician relies upon the rectitude of his judgment, he should, when left in the minority, politely and consistently retire from any further deliberation in the consultation, or participation in the management of the case.

* * *

10. A physician who is called upon to consult, should observe the most honorable and scrupulous regard for the character and standing of the practitioner in attendance: the practice of the latter, if necessary, should be justified as far as it can be, consistently with a conscientious regard for truth, and no hint or insinuation should be thrown out, which could impair the confidence reposed in him, or affect his reputation. The consulting physician should also carefully refrain from any of those extraordinary attentions or assiduities, which are too often practiced by the dishonest for the base purpose of gaining applause, or ingratiating themselves into the favor of families and individuals.

ART. V—*Duties of Physicians in cases of interference*

1. Medicine is a liberal profession, and those admitted into its ranks should found their expectations of practice upon the extent of their qualifications, not on intrigue or artifice.

2. A physician in his intercourse with a patient under the care of another practitioner, should observe the strictest caution and reserve. No meddling inquiries should be made; no disingenuous hints given relative to the nature and treatment of his disorder; nor any course of conduct pursued that may directly or indirectly tend to diminish the trust reposed in the physician employed.

3. The same circumspection and reserve should be observed, when, from motives of business or friendship, a physician is prompted to visit an individual who is under the direction of another practitioner. Indeed, such visits should be avoided, except under peculiar circumstances; and when they are made, no particular inquiries should be instituted relative to the nature of the disease, or the remedies employed, but the topics of conversation should be as foreign to the case as circumstances will admit.

* * *

ART. VI—*Of differences between Physicians*

1. Diversity of opinion, and opposition of interest, may, in the medical, as in other professions, sometimes occasion controversy and even contention. Whenever such cases unfortunately occur, and cannot be immediately terminated, they should be referred to the arbitration of a sufficient number of physicians, or a *court-medical.*

As peculiar reserve must be maintained by physicians towards the public, in regard to professional matters, and as there exist numerous points in medical ethics and etiquette through which the feelings of medical men may be painfully assailed in their intercourse with each other, and which cannot be understood or appreciated by general society, neither the subject-matter of such differences nor the adjudication of the arbitrators should be made public, as publicity in a case of this nature may be personally injurious to the individuals concerned, and can hardly fail to bring discredit on the faculty.

* * *

Chapter III. OF THE DUTIES OF THE PROFESSION TO THE PUBLIC, AND OF THE OBLIGATIONS OF THE PUBLIC TO THE PROFESSION

ART. I—*Duties of the profession to the public*

1. As good citizens, it is the duty of physicians to be ever vigilant for the welfare of the community, and to bear their part in sustaining its institutions and burdens: they should also be ever ready to give counsel to the public in relation to matters especially appertaining to their profession, as on subjects of medical police, public hygiene, and legal medicine. It is their province to enlighten the public in regard to quarantine regulations,—the location, arrangement, and dietaries of hospitals, asylums, schools, prisons, and similar institutions,—in relation to the medical police of towns, as drainage, ventilation, &c.,—and in regard to measures for the prevention of epidemic and contagious diseases; and when pestilence prevails, it is their duty to face the danger, and to continue their labors for the alleviation of the suffering, even at the jeopardy of their own lives.

2. Medical men should also be always ready, when called on by the legally constituted authorities, to enlighten coroners' inquests and courts of justice, on subjects strictly medical,—such as involve questions relating to sanity, legitimacy, murder by poisons or other violent means, and in regard to the various other subjects embraced in the science of Medical Jurisprudence. But in these cases, and especially where they are required to make a post-mortem examination, it is just, in consequence of the time, labor and skill required, and the responsibility and risk they incur, that the public should award them a proper honorarium.

3. There is no profession, by the members of which, eleemosynary services are more liberally dispensed, than the medical; but justice requires that some limits should be placed to the performance of such good offices. Poverty, professional brotherhood, and certain public duties referred to in section 1 of this chapter, should always be recognised as presenting valid claims for gratuitous services; but neither institutions endowed by the public or by rich individuals, societies for mutual benefit, for the insurance of lives or for analogous purposes, nor any profession or occupation, can be admitted to possess such privilege. Nor can it be justly expected of physicians to furnish certificates of inability to serve on juries, to perform militia duty, or to testify to the state of health of persons wishing to insure their lives, obtain pensions, or the like, without a pecuniary acknowledgment. But to individuals in indigent circumstances, such professional services should always be cheerfully and freely accorded.

4. It is the duty of physicians, who are frequent witnesses of the enormities committed by quackery, and the injury to health and even destruction of life caused by the use of quack medicines, to enlighten the public on these subjects, to expose the injuries sustained by the unwary from the devices and pretensions of artful empirics and impostors. Physicians ought to use all the influence which they may possess, as professors in Colleges of Pharmacy, and by exercising their option in regard to the shops to which their prescriptions shall be sent, to discourage druggists and apothecaries from vending quack or secret medicines, or from being in any way engaged in their manufacture and sale.

ART. II—*Obligations of the public to Physicians*

1. The benefits accruing to the public directly and indirectly from the active and unwearied beneficence of the profession, are so numerous and important, that physicians are justly entitled to the utmost consideration and respect from the community. The public ought likewise to entertain a just appreciation of medical qualifications;—to make a proper discrimination between true science and the assumption of ignorance and empiricism,—to afford every encouragement and facility for the acquisition of medical education,—and no longer to allow the statute books to exhibit the anomaly of exacting knowledge from physicians, under liability to heavy penalties, and of making them obnoxious to punishment for resorting to the only means of obtaining it.

VENEZUELAN CODE OF MEDICAL ETHICS

National Academy of Medicine

1918

The Venezuelan Code, first promulgated by the National Academy of Medicine of Venezuela in 1918, was largely the work of Dr. Luis Razetti and for this reason is sometimes called the "Razetti Code." It served as a model for other Latin American codes of medical ethics (Colombia, 1919; Peru, 1922). The Sixth Latin American Medical Congress, meeting in Havana in 1922, recommended that the Venezuelan Code (slightly revised in 1922) serve to unify medical ethical concerns in Latin America. The First Brazilian Medical Congress, held in Rio de Janeiro in 1931, was similarly influenced by the Venezuelan Code.

The Venezuelan Code of 1918 includes many elements characteristic of the codes of its day, with heavy emphasis on the protection of the dignity of the profession, the maintenance of high standards of competence and training, duties toward patients (even regarding their health habits), the rendering of professional services to other doctors, obligations regarding substitute physicians and consultants, professional discipline, fees, and the like.

There are several interesting features in the Venezuelan Code that deserve comparison with other codes:

1. The code insists that there are "rules of medical deontology" that apply to the entire "medical guild"—physicians, surgeons, pharmacists, dentists, obstetricians, interns, and nurses.

2. It places emphasis on physicians' virtues and qualities of character—circumspection, honesty, honor, good faith, respect, and so forth—that serve as a basis for those practices of etiquette that support the honorable practice of medicine.

3. The code prohibits abortion and premature childbirth (morally and legally), except "for a therapeutic purpose in cases indicated by medical science"; but it permits embryotomy if the mother's life is in danger and no alternative medical skills are available.

4. The excerpt below contains an interesting and detailed set of instructions on "medical confidentiality." It combines a strong affirmation of the moral obligation of health professionals to observe confidentiality with many attenuations of that obligation in the interests of the public welfare.

Chapter IX. On Medical Confidentiality

Article 68. Medical confidentiality is a duty inherent in the very nature of the medical profession; the public interest, the personal security of the ill, the honor of families, respect for the physician, and the dignity of the art require confidentiality. Doctors, surgeons, dentists, pharmacists, and midwives as well as interns and nurses are morally obligated to safeguard privacy of information in everything they see, hear, or discover in the practice of their profession or outside of their services and which should not be divulged.

Article 69. Confidential information may be of two forms: that which is explicitly confidential—formal, documentary information confided by the client—and that which is implicitly confidential, which is private due to the nature of things, which nobody imposes, and which governs the relations of clients with medical professionals. Both forms are inviolable, except for legally specified cases.

Article 70. Medical professionals are prohibited from revealing professionally privileged information except in those cases established by medical ethics. A revelation is an act which causes the disclosed fact to change from a private to a publicly known fact. It is not necessary to publish such a fact to make it a revealed one: it suffices to confide it to a single person.

Article 71. Professionally confidential information belongs to the client. Professionals do not incur any responsibility if they reveal the private information received by them when they are authorized to do so by the patient in complete freedom and with a knowledge of the consequences by the person or persons who have confided in them, provided always that such revelation causes no harm to a third party.

Article 72. A medical person incurs no responsibility when he reveals private information in the following cases:

1. When in his capacity as a medical expert he acts as a physician for an insurance company giving it information concerning the health of the applicant sent to him for examination; or when he is commissioned by a proper authority to identify the physical or mental health of a person; or when he has been designated to perform autopsies or give medico-legal expert knowledge of any kind, as in civil or criminal cases; or when he acts as a doctor of public health or for the city; and in general when he performs the functions of a medical expert.

2. When the treating physician declares certain diseases infectious and contagious before a health authority; and when he issues death certificates.

In any of the cases included in (1), the medical professional may be exempt from the charge of ignoring the right of privacy of a person who is the object of his examination if said person is his client at the time or if the declaration has to do with previous conditions for which the same doctor was privately consulted.

Article 73. The physician shall preserve utmost secrecy if he happens to detect a venereal disease in a married woman. Not only should he refrain from informing her of the nature of the disease but he should be very careful not to let suspicion fall on the husband as responsible for the contagion. Consequently, he shall not issue any certification or make any disclosure even if the husband gives his consent.

Article 74. If a physician knows that one of his patients in a contagious period of a venereal disease plans to be married, he shall take pains to dissuade his patient from doing so, availing himself of all possible means. If the patient ignroes his advice and insists on going ahead with his plan to marry, the physician is authorized without incurring repsonsiblity not only to give the information the bride's family asks for, but also to prevent the marriage without the brtidegroom's prior consultation or authorization.

Article 75. The doctor who knows that a healthy wet-nurse is nursing a shyphilitic child should warn the child's parents they they are obligated to inform the nurse. If they refuse to do so, the doctor without naming the disease will impose on the nurse the necessity of immediately ceasing to nurse the child, and he should arrange to have her remain in the house for the time needed to make sure that she has not caught the disease. If the parents do not give their consent and insist that the wet-nurse continue to nurse the child, the doctor shall offer the necessary arguments, and if they nevertheless persist he shall inform the nurse of the risk she runs of contracting a contagious disease if she continues to nurse the child.

Article 76. The doctor can without failing in his duty denounce crimes of which he may have knowledge in the exercise of his profession, in accord with article 470 of the [Venezuelan] Penal Code.

Article 77. When it is a matter of making an accusation in court in order to avoid a legal violation the doctor is permitted to disclose private information.

Article 78. When a doctor is brought before a court as a witness to testify to certain facts known to him, he may refuse to disclose professionally private facts about which he is being interrogated, but which he considers privileged.

Article 79. When a doctor finds himself obliged to claim his fees legally, he should limit himself to stating the number of visits and consultations, specifying the days and nights, the number of operations he has performed, specifying the major and minor ones, the number of trips made outside the city to attend the patient, indicating the distance and time involved in travel in each visit, etc., but in no case should he reveal the nature of the operations performed, nor the details of the care that was given to the patient. The explanation of these circumstances, if necessary, shall be referred by the doctor to the medical experts so designated by the court.

Article 80. The doctor should not answer questions concerning the nature of his patient's disease; however, he is authorized not only to tell the prognosis of the case to those closest to the patient but also the diagnosis if on occasion he considers it necessary, in view of his professional responsibility or the best treatment of his patient. . . .

2. Mid-Twentieth Century–1994

DECLARATION OF GENEVA

World Medical Association

1948, amended 1968, 1983

The Declaration of Geneva was adopted by the second General Assembly of the World Medical Association (WMA) at Geneva in 1948, and subsequently amended by the twenty-second World Medical Assembly at Sydney in 1968 and the thirty-fifth World Medical Assembly at Venice in 1983. The declaration, which was one of the first and most important actions of the WMA, is a declaration of physicians' dedication to the humanitarian goals of medicine, a pledge that was especially important in view of the medical crimes that had just been committed in Nazi Germany. The Declaration of Geneva was intended to update the Oath of Hippocrates, which was no longer suited to modern conditions. Of interest is the fact that the WMA considered this short declaration to be a more significant statement of medical ethics than the succeeding International Code of Medical Ethics.

Only two changes have been made in the declaration since 1948. In 1968, the phrase "even after the patient has died" was added to the confidentiality clause. In the 1983 version, which follows, the sentence regarding respect for human life was modified. Prior to 1983, it read, "I will maintain the utmost respect for human life from the time of conception. . . ."

At the time of being admitted as a member of the medical profession:

I solemnly pledge myself to consecrate my life to the service of humanity;

I will give to my teachers the respect and gratitude which is their due;

I will practice my profession with conscience and dignity;

The health of my patient will be my first consideration;

I will respect the secrets which are confided in me, even after the patient has died;

I will maintain by all the means in my power, the honor and the noble traditions of the medical profession;

My colleagues will be my brothers;

I will not permit considerations of religion, nationality, race, party politics or social standing to intervene between my duty and my patient;

I will maintain the utmost respect for human life from its beginning even under threat and I will not use my medical knowledge contrary to the laws of humanity;

I make these promises solemnly, freely and upon my honor.

INTERNATIONAL CODE OF MEDICAL ETHICS

World Medical Association

1949, amended 1968, 1983

The International Code of Medical Ethics was adopted by the third General Assembly of the World Medical Association (WMA) at London in 1949, and amended in 1968 by the twenty-second World Medical Assembly at Sydney and in 1983 by the thirty-fifth World Medical Assembly at Venice. The code, which was modeled after the Declaration of Geneva and the medical ethics codes of most modern countries, states the most general principles of ethical medical practice.

The original draft of the code included the statement, "Therapeutic abortion may only be performed if the conscience of the doctors and the national laws permit," which was deleted from the adopted version because of its controversial nature. In addition, the words "from conception" were deleted from the statement regarding the doctor's obligation to preserve human life.

The 1983 version of the code, which is still current, reflects several changes from the version originally adopted. There are numerous changes in language, for example, the phrase "A physician shall . . ." replaces "A doctor must. . . ." Substantive changes include the addition of the paragraphs on providing competent medical service; on honesty and exposing physicians deficient in character; and on respecting rights and safeguarding confidences. Also, as in the Declaration of Geneva, the duty of confidentiality is extended to "even after the patient has died." Under practices deemed unethical, collaboration "in any form of medical service in which the doctor does not have professional independence" has been deleted, but the importance of professional independence is emphasized elsewhere in the text.

Duties of Physicians in General

A physician shall always maintain the highest standards of professional conduct.

A physician shall not permit motives of profit to influence the free and independent exercise of professional judgement on behalf of patients.

A physician shall, in all types of medical practice, be dedicated to providing competent medical service in full technical and moral independence, with compassion and respect for human dignity.

A physician shall deal honestly with patients and colleagues, and strive to expose those physicians deficient in character or competence, or who engage in fraud or deception.

The following practices are deemed to be unethical conduct:

a) Self-advertising by physicians, unless permitted by the laws of the country and the Code of Ethics of the National Medical Association.

b) Paying or receiving any fee or any other consideration solely to procure the referral of a patient or for prescribing or referring a patient to any source.

A physician shall respect the rights of patients, of colleagues, and of other health professionals, and shall safeguard patient confidences.

A physician shall act only in the patient's interest when providing medical care which might have the effect of weakening the physical and mental condition of the patient.

A physician shall use great caution in divulging discoveries or new techniques or treatment through non-professional channels.

A physician shall certify only that which he has personally verified.

Duties of Physicians to the Sick

A physician shall always bear in mind the obligation of preserving human life.

A physician shall owe his patients complete loyalty and all the resources of his science.

Whenever an examination or treatment is beyond the physician's capacity he should summon another physician who has the necessary ability.

A physician shall preserve absolute confidentiality on all he knows about his patient even after the patient has died.

A physician shall give emergency care as a humanitarian duty unless he is assured that others are willing and able to give such care.

Duties of Physicians to Each Other

A physician shall behave towards his colleagues as he would have them behave towards him.

A physician shall not entice patients from his colleagues.

A physician shall observe the principles of the "Declaration of Geneva" approved by the World Medical Association.

PRINCIPLES OF MEDICAL ETHICS (1957)

American Medical Association

1957

Until 1957. the American Medical Asssociation.s (AMA) Code of Ethics was basically that adopted in 1847, although there were revisions in 1903, 1912, and 1947. A major change in the code's format occurred in 1957 when the Principles of Medical Ethics printed here were adopted. The ten principles, which replaced the forty-eight sections of the older code, were intended as expressions of the fundamental concepts and requirements of the older code, unencumbered by easily outdated practical codifications. Of note are the therapeutic-privilege exception to the confidentiality clause in Section 9—confidences may be disclosed if "necessary in order to protect the welfare of the individual"—and Section 10, which highlights the tension between physicians' duties to patients and those to society.

Preamble. These principles are intended to aid physicians individually and collectively in maintaining a high level of ethical conduct. They are not laws but standards by which a physician may determine the propriety of his conduct in his relationship with patients, with colleagues, with members of allied professions, and with the public.

Section 1. The principal objective of the medical profession is to render service to humanity with full respect for the dignity of man. Physicians should merit the confidence of patients entrusted to their care, rendering to each a full measure of service and devotion.

Section 2. Physicians should strive continually to improve medical knowledge and skill, and should make available to their patients and colleagues the benefits of their professional attainments.

Section 3. A physician should practice a method of healing founded on a scientific basis; and he should not voluntarily associate professionally with anyone who violates this principle.

Section 4. The medical profession should safeguard the public and itself against physicians deficient in moral character or professional competence. Physicians should observe all laws, uphold the dignity and honor of the profession and accept its self-imposed disciplines. They should expose, without hesitation, illegal or unethical conduct of fellow members of the profession.

Section 5. A physician may choose whom he will serve. In an emergency, however, he should render service to the best of his ability. Having undertaken the care of a patient, he may not neglect him; and unless he has been discharged he may discontinue his services only after giving adequate notice. He should not solicit patients.

Section 6. A physician should not dispose of his services under terms or conditions which tend to interfere with or impair the free and complete exercise of his medical judgment and skill or tend to cause a deterioration of the quality of medical care.

Section 7. In the practice of medicine a physician should limit the source of his professional income to medical services actually rendered by him, or under his supervision, to his patients. His fee should be commensurate with the services rendered and the patient's ability to pay. He should neither pay nor receive a commission for referral of patients. Drugs, remedies or appliances may be dispensed or supplied by the physician provided it is in the best interests of the patient.

Section 8. A physician should seek consultation upon request; in doubtful or difficult cases; or whenever it appears that the quality of medical service may be enhanced thereby.

Section 9. A physician may not reveal the confidences entrusted to him in the course of medical attendance, or the deficiencies he may observe in the character of patients, unless he is required to do so by law or unless it becomes necessary in order to protect the welfare of the individual or of the community.

Section 10. The honored ideals of the medical professional imply that the responsibilities of the physician extend not only to the individual, but also to society where these responsibilities deserve his interest and participation in activities which have the purpose of improving both the health and the well-being of the individual and the community.

PRINCIPLES OF MEDICAL ETHICS (1980)

American Medical Association

1980

The American Medical Association's (AMA) complete code of ethics currently consists of four parts: (1) the Principles of Medical

Ethics, which "broadly define the parameters of ethical conduct for physicians" and are the primary component of the Code; (2) the Current Opinions with Annotations of the Council on Ethical and Judicial Affairs, which is "a comprehensive set of concise statements addressing specific ethical issues in the practice of medicine" and includes extensive annotations of court opinions and pertinent medical, ethical, and legal literature; (3) the Fundamental Elements of the Patient-Physician Relationship, which "enunciates the basic rights to which patients are entitled from their physicians"; and (4) the Reports of the Council on Ethical and Judicial Affairs, which "discuss the rationale behind many of the Council's opinions, providing a detailed analysis of the relevant ethical considerations." The Principles of Medical Ethics are printed below, and selections from Current Opinions comprise the next entry in this section of the Appendix. The Fundamental Elements of the Patient—Physician Relationship appears above, in Section I.

The current Principles of Medical Ethics were adopted in 1980, when the earlier, 1957 principles were revised "to clarify and update the language, to eliminate reference to gender, and to seek a proper and reasonable balance between professional standards and contemporary legal standards. . . ." Among the changes, the 1980 principles, which were shortened to seven principles, introduced the language of rights to replace the traditional language of benefits and burdens and dispensed with the therapeutic-privilege exception to maintaining confidentiality.

Preamble

The medical profession has long subscribed to a body of ethical statements developed primarily for the benefit of the patient. As a member of this profession, a physician must recognize responsibility not only to patients, but also to society, to other health professionals, and to self. The following Principles adopted by the American Medical Association are not laws, but standards of conduct which define the essentials of honorable behavior for the physician.

I. A physician shall be dedicated to providing competent medical service with compassion and respect for human dignity.

II. A physician shall deal honestly with patients and colleagues, and strive to expose those physicians deficient in character or competence, or who engage in fraud or deception.

III. A physician shall respect the law and also recognize a responsibility to seek changes in those requirements which are contrary to the best interests of the patient.

IV. A physician shall respect the rights of patients, of colleagues, and of other health professionals, and shall safeguard patient confidences within the constraints of the law.

V. A physician shall continue to study, apply and advance scientific knowledge, make relevant information available to patients, colleagues, and the public, obtain consultation, and use the talents of other health professionals when indicated.

VI. A physician shall, in the provision of appropriate patient care, except in emergencies, be free to choose whom to serve, with whom to associate, and the environment in which to provide medical services.

VII. A physician shall recognize a responsibility to participate in activities contributing to an improved community.

CURRENT OPINIONS OF THE COUNCIL ON ETHICAL AND JUDICIAL AFFAIRS

American Medical Association

1994

The 1994 revision of the Current Opinions of the Council on Ethical and Judicial Affairs, which replaces the 1992 version, "reflects the application of the Principles of Medical Ethics to more than 125 specific ethical issues in medicine, including health care rationing, genetic testing, withdrawal of life-sustaining treatment, and family violence." A complete list of topics of the Current Opinions and the text of selected opinions follow; the annotations of court opinions and pertinent medical, ethical, and legal literature that follow many of the opinions are not included.

1.00 Introduction
1.01 Terminology
1.02 The Relation of Law and Ethics
2.00 Opinions on Social Policy Issues
2.01 Abortion
2.015 Mandatory Parental Consent to Abortion
2.02 Abuse of Children, Elderly Persons, and Others At Risk
2.03 Allocation of Limited Medical Resources
2.035 Futile Care
2.04 Artificial Insemination by Known Donor
2.05 Artificial Insemination by Anonymous Donor
2.06 Capital Punishment
2.07 Clinical Investigation
2.08 Commercial Use of Human Tissue
2.09 Costs
2.095 Provision of Adequate Health Care
2.10 Fetal Research Guidelines
2.11 Gene Therapy
2.12 Genetic Counseling
2.13 Genetic Engineering
2.132 Genetic Testing by Employers
2.135 Genetic Testing by Health Insurance Companies
2.137 Ethical Issues in Carrier Screening of Genetic Disorders
2.14 In Vitro Fertilization
2.141 Frozen Pre-Embryos
2.145 Pre-Embryo Splitting
2.15 Financial Incentives for Organ Donation
2.155 Mandated Choice and Presumed Consent for Cadaveric Organ Donation
2.16 Organ Transplantation Guidelines
2.161 Medical Applications of Fetal Tissue Transplantation
2.162 Anencephalic Infants as Organ Donors
2.165 Fetal Umbilical Cord Blood
2.167 The Use of Minors as Organ and Tissue Donors
2.17 Quality of Life
2.18 Surrogate Mothers
2.19 Unnecessary Services
2.20 Withholding or Withdrawing Life-Sustaining Medical Treatment
2.21 Euthanasia
2.211 Physician Assisted Suicide
2.215 Treatment Decisions for Seriously Ill Newborns
2.22 Do-Not-Resuscitate Orders
2.23 HIV Testing
3.00 Opinions on Interprofessional Relations
3.01 Nonscientific Practitioners
3.02 Nurses
3.03 Optometry [deleted]
3.04 Referral of Patients
3.041 Chiropractic
3.05 Specialists [deleted]
3.06 Sports Medicine
3.07 Teaching [deleted]
3.08 Sexual Harassment and Exploitation Between Medical Supervisors and Trainees
4.00 Opinions on Hospital Relations
4.01 Admission Fee
4.02 Assessments, Compulsory
4.03 Billing for Housestaff Services and Student Services
4.04 Economic Incentives and Levels of Care
4.05 Organized Medical Staff
4.06 Physician-Hospital Contractual Relations
4.07 Staff Privileges

* * *

2.00 Opinions on Social Policy Issues

2.01 Abortion. The Principles of Medical Ethics of the AMA do not prohibit a physician from performing an abortion in accordance with good medical practice and under circumstances that do not violate the law. (III, IV)

2.015 Mandatory Parental Consent to Abortion. Physicians should ascertain the law in their state on parental involvement to ensure that their procedures are consistent with their legal obligations.

Physicians should strongly encourage minors to discuss their pregnancy with their parents. Physicians should explain how parental involvement can be helpful and that parents are generally very understanding and supportive. If a minor expresses concerns about parental involvement, the physician should ensure that the minor's reluctance is not based on any misperceptions about the likely consequences of parental involvement.

Physicians should not feel or be compelled to require minors to involve their parents before deciding whether to undergo an abortion. The patient—even an adolescent—generally must decide whether, on balance, parental involvement is advisable. Accordingly, minors should ultimately be allowed to decide whether parental involvement is appropriate. Physicians should explain under what circumstances (e.g., life-threatening, emergency) the minor's confidentiality will need to be abrogated.

Physicians should try to ensure that minor patients have made an informed decision after giving careful consideration to the issues involved. They should encourage their minor patients to consult alternative sources if parents are not going to be involved in the abortion decision. Minors should be urged to seek the advice and counsel of those adults in whom they have confidence, including professional counselors, relatives, friends, teachers, or the clergy. (III, IV)

Issued June 1994 based on the report "Mandatory Parental Consent to Abortion," issued June 1992. (*JAMA.* 1993; 269: 82–86)

2.02 Abuse of Children, Elderly Persons, and Others at Risk. The following are guidelines for detecting and treating family violence:

Due to the prevalence and medical consequences of family violence, physicians should routinely inquire about abuse as part of the medical history. Physicians must also consider battering in the differential diagnosis for a number of medical complaints, particularly when treating women.

Physicians who are likely to have the opportunity to detect abuse in the course of their work have an obligation to familiarize themselves with protocols for diagnosing and treating abuse and with community resources for battered women, children and elderly persons.

Physicians also have a duty to be aware of societal misconceptions about abuse and prevent these from affecting the diagnosis and management of abuse. Such misconceptions include the belief that abuse is a rare occurrence; that abuse does not occur in "normal" families; that abuse is a private problem best resolved without outside interference; and that victims are responsible for the abuse.

In order to improve physician knowledge of family violence, physicians must be better trained to identify signs of abuse and to work cooperatively with the range of community services currently involved. Hospitals should require additional training for those physicians who are likely to see victims of abuse. Comprehensive training on family violence should be required in medical school curricula and in residency programs for specialties in which family violence is likely to be encountered.

The following are guidelines for the reporting of abuse:

Laws that require the reporting of cases of suspected abuse of children and elderly persons often create a difficult dilemma for the physician. The parties involved, both the suspected offenders and the victims, will often plead with the physician that the matter be kept confidential and not be disclosed or reported for investigation by public authorities.

Children who have been seriously injured, apparently by their parents, may nevertheless try to protect their parents by saying that the injuries were caused by an accident, such as a fall. The reason may stem from the natural parent-child relationship or fear of further punishment. Even institutionalized elderly patients who have been physically maltreated may be concerned that disclosure of what has occurred might lead to further and more drastic maltreatment by those responsible.

The physician who fails to comply with the laws requiring reporting of suspected cases of abuse to children and elderly persons and others at risk can expect that the victims could receive more severe abuse that may result in permanent bodily injury, emotional or psychological injury or even death.

Public officials concerned with the welfare of children and elderly persons have expressed the opinion that the incidence of physical violence to these persons is rapidly increasing and that a very substantial percentage of such cases is unreported by hospital personnel and physicians. A child or elderly person brought to a physician with a suspicious injury is the patient whose interests require the protection of law in a particular situation, even though the physician may also provide services from time to time to parents or other members of the family.

The obligation to comply with statutory requirements is clearly stated in the Principles of Medical Ethics. In addition, physicians have an ethical obligation to report abuse even when the law does not require it. However, for mentally competent adult victims of abuse, physicians must not disclose an abuse diagnosis to spouses or any other third party without the consent of the patient. Physicians must discuss the problem of family violence with adult patients in privacy and safety. (I, III)

Issued December 1982.

Updated June 1994 based on the report "Physicians and Family Violence: Ethical Considerations," issued December 1991. (*JAMA*. 1992; 267: 3190–3193)

2.03 Allocation of Limited Medical Resources. A physician has a duty to do all that he or she can for the benefit of the individual patient. Policies for allocating limited resources have the potential to limit the ability of physicians to fulfill this obligation to patients. Physicians have a responsibility to participate and to contribute their professional expertise in order to safeguard the interests of patients in decisions made at the societal level regarding the allocation or rationing of health resources.

Decisions regarding the allocation of limited medical resources among patients should consider only ethically appropriate criteria relating to medical need. These criteria include likelihood of benefit, urgency of need, change in quality of life, duration of benefit, and, in some cases, the amount of resources required for successful treatment. In general, only very substantial differences among patients are ethically relevant; the greater the disparities, the more justified the use of these criteria becomes. In making quality of life judgments, patients should first be prioritized so that death or extremely poor outcomes are avoided; then, patients should be prioritized according to change in quality of life, but only when there are very substantial differences among patients. Nonmedical criteria, such as ability to pay, age, social worth, perceived obstacles to treatment, patient contribution to illness, or past use of resources should not be considered.

Allocation decisions should respect the individuality of patients and the particulars of individual cases as much as possible. When very substantial differences do not exist among potential recipients of treatment on the basis of the appropriate criteria defined above, a "first-come-first-served" approach or some other equal opportunity mechanism should be employed to make final allocation decisions. Though there are several ethically acceptable strategies for implementing these criteria, no single strategy is ethically mandated. Acceptable approaches include a three-tiered system, a minimal threshold approach, and a weighted formula. Decision-making mechanisms should be objective, flexible, and consistent to ensure that all patients are treated equally.

The treating physician must remain a patient advocate and therefore should not make allocation decisions. Patients denied access to resources have the right to be informed of the reasoning behind the decision. The allocation procedures of institutions controlling scarce resources should be disclosed to the public as well as subject to regular peer review from the medical profession. (I, VII)

Issued March 1981.

Updated June 1994 based on the report "Ethical Considerations in the Allocation of Organs and Other Scarce Medical Resources Among Patients," issued June 1993.

2.035 Futile Care. Physicians are not ethically obligated to deliver care that, in their best professional judgment, will not have a reasonable chance of benefitting their patients. Patients should not be given treatments simply because they demand them. Denial of treatment should be justified by reliance on openly stated ethical principles and acceptable standards of care, as defined in opinions 2.03 and 2.095, not on the concept of "futility," which cannot be meaningfully defined. (I, IV)

Issued June 1994.

* * *

2.06 Capital Punishment. An individual's opinion on capital punishment is the personal moral decision of the individual. A physician, as a member of a profession dedicated to preserving life when there is hope of doing so, should not be a participant in a legally authorized execution. Physician participation in execution is defined generally as actions which would fall into one or more of the following categories: (1) an action which would directly cause the death of the condemned; (2) an action which would assist, supervise, or contribute to the ability of another individual to directly cause the death of the condemned; (3) an action which could automatically cause an execution to be carried out on a condemned prisoner.

Physician participation in an execution includes, but is not limited to, the following actions: prescribing or administering tranquilizers and other psychotropic agents and medications that are part of the execution procedure; monitoring vital signs on site or remotely (including monitoring electrocardiograms); attending or observing an execution as a physician; and rendering of technical advice regarding execution.

In the case where the method of execution is lethal injection, the following actions by the physician would also constitute physician participation in execution: selecting injection sites; starting intravenous lines as a port for a lethal injection device; prescribing, preparing, administering, or supervising injection drugs or their doses or types; inspecting, testing, or maintaining lethal injection devices; and consulting with or supervising lethal injection personnel.

The following actions do not constitute physician participation in execution: (1) testifying as to competence to stand trial, testifying as to relevant medical evidence during trial, or testifying as to medical aspects of aggravating or mitigating circumstances during the penalty phase of a capital case; (2) certifying death, provided that the condemned has been declared dead by another person; (3) witnessing an execution in a totally nonprofessional capacity; (4) witnessing an execution at the specific voluntary request of the condemned person, provided that the physician observes the execution in a nonprofessional capacity; and (5) relieving the acute suffering of a condemned person while awaiting execution, including providing tranquilizers at the specific voluntary request of the condemned person to help relieve pain or anxiety in anticipation of the execution.

Organ donation by condemned prisoners is permissible only if (1) the decision to donate was made before the prisoner's conviction, (2) the donated tissue is harvested after the prisoner has been pronounced dead and the body removed from the death chamber, and (3) physicians do not provide advice on modifying the method of execution for any individual to facilitate donation. (I)

Issued July 1980.

Updated June 1994 based on report "Physican Participation in Capital Punishment," issued December 1992. (JAMA. 1993; 270: 365–368)

* * *

2.09 Costs. While physicains should be conscious of of costs and not provide or prescribe unnecessary services, concern for the quality of care the patient receives should be the physician's first consideration. This does not preclude the physician, individually, or through medical organizations, from participating in policy-making with respect to social issues affecting health care. (I, VII)

Issued March 1981.

Updated June 1994.

2.095 The Provision of Adequate Health Care. Because society has an obligation to make access to an adequate level of health care available to all of its members regardless of ability to pay, physicians should contribute their expertise at a policy-making level to help achieve this goal. In determining whether particular procedures or treatments should be included in the adequate level of health care, the following ethical principles should be considered: (1) degree of benefit (the difference in outcome between treatment and no treatment), (2) likelihood of benefit, (3) duration of benefit, (4) cost, and (5) number of people who will benefit (referring to the fact that a treatment may benefit the patient and others who come into contact with the patient, as with a vaccination or antimicrobial drug).

Ethical principles require that the ethical criteria be combined with a fair process to determine the adequate level of health care. Among the many possible alternative processes, the Council recommends the following two:

(1) Democratic decisionmaking with broad public input at both the developmental and final approval stages can be used to develop the package of benefits. With this approach, enforcement of anti-discrimination laws will be necessary to ensure that the interests of minorities and historically disadvantaged groups are protected.

(2) Equal opportunity mechanisms can also be used to determine the package of health care benefits. After applying the five ethical criteria listed above, it will be possible to designate some kinds of care as either clearly basic or clearly discretionary. However, for care that is not clearly basic or discretionary, a random selection or other equal consideration mechanism may be used to determine which kinds of care will be included in the basic benefits package.

The mechanism for providing an adequate level of health care should ensure that the health care benefits for the poor and disadvantaged will not be eroded over time. There should also be ongoing monitoring for variations in care that cannot be explained on medical grounds with special attention to evidence of discriminatory impact on historically disadvantaged groups. Finally, adjustment of the adequate level over time should be made to ensure continued and broad public acceptance.

Issued June 1994 based on the report "Ethical Issues in Health System Reform: The Provision of Adequate Health Care," issued December 1993. (*JAMA*. 1994; 272)

2.10 Fetal Research Guidelines. The following guidelines are offered as aids to physicians when they are engaged in fetal research:

(1) Physicians may participate in fetal research when their activities are part of a competently designed program, under accepted standards of scientific research, to produce data which are scientifically valid and significant.

(2) If appropriate, properly performed clinical studies on animals and nongravid humans should precede any particular fetal research project.

(3) In fetal research projects, the investigator should demonstrate the same care and concern for the fetus as a physician providing fetal care or treatment in a non-research setting.

(4) All valid federal or state legal requirements should be followed.

(5) There should be no monetary payment to obtain any fetal material for fetal research projects.

(6) Competent peer review committees, review boards, or advisory boards should be available, when appropriate, to protect against the possible abuses that could arise in such research.

(7) Research on the so called "dead fetus," macerated fetal material, fetal cells, fetal tissue, or fetal organs should be in accord with state laws on autopsy and state laws on organ transplantation or anatomical gifts.

(8) In fetal research primarily for treatment of the fetus:

A. Voluntary and informed consent, in writing, should be given by the gravid woman, acting in the best interest of the fetus.

B. Alternative treatment or methods of care, if any, should be carefully evaluated and fully explained. If simpler and safer treatment is available, it should be pursued.

(9) In research primarily for treatment of the gravid female:

A. Voluntary and informed consent, in writing, should be given by the patient.

B. Alternative treatment or methods of care should be carefully evaluated and fully explained to the patient. If simpler and safer treatment is available, it should be pursued.

C. If possible, the risk to the fetus should be the least possible, consistent with the gravid female's need for treatment.

(10) In fetal research involving a fetus in utero, primarily for the accumulation of scientific knowledge:

A. Voluntary and informed consent, in writing, should be given by the gravid woman under circumstances in which a prudent and informed adult would reasonably be expected to give such consent.

B. The risk to the fetus imposed by the research should be the least possible.

C. The purpose of research is the production of data and knowledge which are scientifically significant and which cannot otherwise be obtained.

D. In this area of research, it is especially important to emphasize that care and concern for the fetus should be demonstrated. (I, III, V)

Issued March 1980.

Updated June 1994.

2.11 Gene Therapy. Gene therapy involves the replacement or modification of a genetic variant to restore or enhance cellular function.

Two types of gene therapy have been identified: (1) somatic cell therapy, in which human cells other than germ cells are genetically altered, and (2) germ line therapy, in which a replacement gene is integrated into the genome of human gametes or their precursors, resulting in expression of the new gene in the patient's offspring and subsequent generations. The fundamental difference between germ line therapy and somatic cell therapy is that germ line therapy affects the welfare of subsequent generations and may be associated with increased risk and the potential for unpredictable and irreversible results. Because of the far-reaching implications of germ line therapy, it is appropriate to limit genetic intervention to somatic cells only until all the short and long-term effects of germ line therapy are certain.

The goal of both somatic and germ line therapy is to alleviate human suffering and disease by remedying disorders for which available therapies are not satisfactory. This goal should be pursued only within the ethical tradition of medicine, which gives primacy to the welfare of the patient whose safety and well-being must be vigorously protected. To the extent possible, experience with animal studies must be sufficient to assure the effectiveness and safety of the techniques used, and the predictability of the results.

Moreover, genetic manipulation generally should be utilized only for therapeutic purposes. Efforts to enhance "desirable" characteristics through the insertion of a modified or additional gene, or efforts to "improve" complex human traits—the eugenic development of offspring—are contrary not only to the ethical tradition of medicine, but also to the egalitarian values of our society. Because of the potential for abuse, genetic manipulation to affect non-disease traits may never be acceptable and perhaps should never be pursued. If it is ever allowed, however, at least three conditions would have to be met before it could be deemed ethically acceptable: (1) there would have to be a clear and meaningful benefit to the child, (2) there would have to be no trade-off with other characteristics or traits, and (3) all citizens would have to have equal access to the genetic technology, irrespective of income or other socioeconomic characteristics. These criteria should be viewed as a minimal, not an exhaustive, test of the ethical propriety of non-disease-related genetic intervention. As genetic technology and knowledge of the human genome develop further, additional guidelines may be required.

All gene therapy should conform to the Council on Ethical and Judicial Affairs' guidelines on clinical investigation and genetic engineering and should adhere to stringent safety considerations. (I,V)

Issued December 1988

Updated June 1994 based on the report "Prenatal Genetic Screening," issued December 1992. (*Arch. Fam. Med.* 1994; 3)

* * *

2.162 Anencephalics Infants as Organ Donors. Anencephaly is a congenital absence of a major portion of the brain, skull, and scalp. Infants born with this condition are born without a forebrain and without a cerebrum. While anencephalics are born with a rudimentary functional brain stem, their lack of functioning cerebrum permanently forecloses the possibility of consciousness.

It is ethically permissible to consider the anencephalic as a potential organ donor, although still alive under the current definition of death only if: (1) the diagnosis of anencephaly is certain and is confirmed by two physicians who are not part of the organ transplant team; (2) the parents of the infant desire to have the infant serve as an organ donor and indicate such in writing; and (3) there is compliance with the Council's Guidelines for the Transplantation of Organs (see Opinion 2.16: Organ Transplantation Guidelines).

In the alternative, a family wishing to donate the organs of their anencephalic infant may choose to provide the infant with ventilator assistance and other medical therapies that would sustain organ perfusion and viability until such time as a determination of death can be made in accordance with current medical standards and relevant law. In this situation, the family must be informed of the possibility that the organs might deteriorate in the process, rendering them unsuitable for transplantation.

It is normally required that the donor be legally dead before permitting the harvesting of the organs ("Dead Donor Rule"). The use of the anencephalic infant as a live donor is a limited exception to the general standard because of the fact that the infant has never experienced, and will never experience, consciousness. (I, III, V)

Issued March 1992 based on the report "Anencephalic Infants as Organ Donors," issued December 1988.

Updated June 1994.

* * *

2.17 Quality of Life. In the making of decisions for the treatment of seriously disabled newborns or of other persons who are severely disabled by injury or illness, the primary consideration should be what is best for the individual patient and not the avoidance of a burden to the family or to society. Quality of life, as defined by the patient's interests and values, is a factor to be considered in determining what is best for the individual. It is permissible to consider quality of life when deciding about life-sustaining treatment in accordance with opinions 2.20, 2.215, and 2.22. (I, III, IV)

Issued March 1981.

Updated June 1994.

* * *

2.19 Unnecessary Services. Physicians should not provide, prescribe, or seek compensation for services that are known to be unnecessary. (II, VII)

Updated June 1994.

2.20 Withholding or Withdrawing Life-Sustaining Medical Treatment. The social commitment of the physician is to sustain life and relieve suffering. Where the performance of one duty conflicts with the other, the preferences of the patient should prevail. The principle of patient autonomy requires that physicians respect the decision to forego life-sustaining treatment of a patient who possesses decisionmaking capacity. Life-sustaining treatment is any treatment that serves to prolong life without reversing the underlying medical condition. Life-sustaining treatment may include, but is not limited to, mechanical ventilation, renal dialysis, chemotherapy, antibiotics, and artificial nutrition and hydration.

There is no ethical distinction between withdrawing and withholding life-sustaining treatment.

A competent, adult patient may, in advance, formulate and provide a valid consent to the withholding or withdrawal of life-support systems in the event that injury or illness renders that individual incompetent to make such a decision.

If the patient receiving life-sustaining treatment is incompetent, a surrogate decisionmaker should be identified. Without an advance directive that designates a proxy, the patient's family should become the surrogate decisionmaker. Family includes persons with whom the patient is closely associated. In the case when there is no person closely associated with the patient, but there are persons who both care about the patient and have sufficient relevant knowledge of the patient, such persons may be appropriate surrogates. Physicians should provide all relevant medical information and explain to surrogate decisionmakers that decisions regarding withholding or withdrawing life-sustaining treatment should be based on substituted judgment (what the patient would have decided) when there is evidence of the patient's preferences and values. In making a substituted judgment, decisionmakers may consider the patient's advance directive (if any); the patient's values about life and the way it should be lived; and the patient's attitudes towards sickness, suffering, medical procedures, and death. If there is not adequate evidence of the incompetent patient's preferences and values, the decision should be based on the best interests of the patient (what outcome would most likely promote the patient's well-being).

Though the surrogate's decision for the incompetent patient should almost always be accepted by the physician, there are four situations that may require either institutional or judicial review and/or intervention in the decisionmaking process: (1) there is no available family member willing to be the patient's surrogate decisionmaker, (2) there is a dispute among family members and there is no decisionmaker designated in an advance directive, (3) a health care provider believes that the family's decision is clearly not what the patient would have decided if competent, and (4) a health care provider believes that the decision is not a decision that could reasonably be judged to be in the patient's best interests. When there are disputes among family members or between family and health care providers, the use of ethics committees specifically designed to facilitate sound decisionmaking is recommended before resorting to the courts.

When a permanently unconscious patient was never competent or had not left any evidence of previous preferences or values, since there is no objective way to ascertain the best interests of the patient, the surrogate's decision should not be challenged as long as the decision is based on the decisionmaker's true concern for what would be best for the patient.

Physicians have an obligation to relieve pain and suffering and to promote the dignity and autonomy of dying patients in their care. This includes providing effective palliative treatment even though it may foreseeably hasten death.

Even if the patient is not terminally ill or permanently unconscious, it is not unethical to discontinue all means of life-sustaining medical treatment in accordance with a proper substituted judgment or best interests analysis. (I, III, IV, V)

Issued March 1981 (Opinion 2.11: Terminal Illness) and December 1984 (Opinion 2.19: Withholding or Withdrawing Life-Prolonging Medical Treatment: Patient's Preferences, renumbered as Opinion 2.21 in August 1989).

In March 1986, the Council on Ethical and Judicial Affairs updated Opinion 2.11 by adopting its policy statement, "Withholding or Withdrawing Life-Prolonging Medical Treatment." This statement was identified as Opinion 2.18 (July 1986) [in August 1989, the opinion number was changed to Opinion 2.20]. Numerous cases cited below simply note the March 1986 statement, without specific reference to the Opinions.

Updated June 1994 based on the reports "Decisions Near the End of Life" and "Decisions to Forgo Life-Sustaining Treatment for Incompetent Patients," both issued June 1991. ("Decisions Near the End of Life." JAMA. 1992; 267: 2229–2233)

2.21 Euthanasia. Euthanasia is the administration of a lethal agent by another person to a patient for the purpose of relieving the patient's intolerable and incurable suffering.

It is understandable, though tragic, that some patients in extreme duress—such as those suffering from a terminal, painful, debilitating illness—may come to decide that death is preferable to life. However, permitting physicians to engage in euthanasia would ultimately cause more harm than good. Euthanasia is fundamentally incompatible with the physician's role as healer, would be difficult or impossible to control, and would pose serious societal risks.

Instead of engaging in euthanasia, physicians must aggressively respond to the needs of patients at the end of life. Patients should not be abandoned once it is determined that cure is impossible. Patients near the end of life must continue to receive emotional support, comfort care, adequate pain control, respect for patient autonomy, and good communication. (I, IV)

Issued June 1994 based on the report "Decisions Near the End of Life," issued June 1991. (Jama. 1992; 267: 2229–2233)

2.211 Physican Assisted Suicide. Physican assisted suicide occurs when a physician facilitates a patient's death by providing the necessary means and/or information to enable the patient to perform the life-ending act (e.g., the physician provides sleeping pills and information about the lethal dose, while aware that the patient may commit suicide).

It is understandable, though tragic, that some patients in extreme duress—such as those suffering from a terminal, painful, debilitating illness—may come to decide that death is preferable to life. However, allowing physicians to participate in assisted suicide would cause more harm than good. Physician assisted suicide is fundamentally incompatible with the physician's role as healer, would be difficult or impossible to control, and would pose serious societal risks.

Instead of participating in assisted suicide, physicians must aggressively respond to the needs of patients at the end of life. Patients should not be abandoned once it is determined that cure is impossible. Patients near the end of life must continue to receive emotional support, comfort care, adequate pain control, respect for patient autonomy, and good communication. (I, IV)

Issued 1994 based on the reports "Decisions Near the End of Life," issued June 1991, and "Physician-Assisted Suicide," issued December 1993. (JAMA. 1992; 267: 2229–2233)

2.215 Treatment Decisions for Seriously Ill Newborns. The primary consideration for decisions regarding life-sustaining treatment for seriously ill newborns should be what is best for the newborn. Factors that should be weighed are (1) the chance that therapy will succeed, (2) the risks involved with treatment and nontreatment, (3) the degree to which the therapy, if successful, will extend life, (4) the pain and discomfort associated with the therapy, and (5) the anticipated quality of life for the newborn with and without treatment.

Care must be taken to evaluate the newborn's expected quality of life from the child's perspective. Life-sustaining treatment may be withheld or withdrawn from a newborn when the pain and suffering expected to be endured by the child will overwhelm any potential for joy during his or her life. When an infant suffers extreme neurological damage, and is consequently not capable of experiencing either suffering or joy a decision may be made to withhold or withdraw life-sustaining treatment. When life-sustaining treatment is withheld or withdrawn, comfort care must not be discontinued.

When an infant's prognosis is largely uncertain, as is often the case with extremely premature newborns, all life-sustaining and life-enhancing treatment should be initiated. Decisions about life-sustaining treatment should be made once the prognosis becomes more certain. It is not necessary to attain absolute or near absolute prognostic certainty before life-sustaining treatment is withdrawn, since this goal is often unattainable and risks unnecessarily prolonging the infant's suffering.

Physicians must provide full information to parents of seriously ill newborns regarding the nature of treatments, therapeutic options and expected prognosis with and without therapy, so that parents can make informed decisions for their children about life-sustaining treatment. Counseling services and an opportunity to talk with persons who have had to make similar decisions should be available to parents. Ethics committees or infant review committees should also be utilized to facilitate parental decisionmaking. These committees should help mediate resolutions of conflicts that may arise among parents, physicians and others involved in the care of the infant. These committees should also be responsible for referring cases to the appropriate public agencies when it is concluded that the parents' decision is not a decision that could reasonably be judged to be in the best interests of the infant. (I, III, IV, V)

Issued June 1994 based on the report "Treatment Decisions for Seriously Ill Newborns," issued June 1992.

2.22 Do-Not-Resuscitate Orders. Efforts should be made to resuscitate patients who suffer cardiac or respiratory arrest except when circumstances indicate that cardiopulmonary resuscitation (CPR) would be inappropriate or not in accord with the desires or best interests of the patient.

Patients at risk of cardiac or respiratory failure should be encouraged to express in advance their preferences regarding the use of CPR and this should be documented in the patient's medical record. These discussions should include a description of the procedures encompassed by CPR and, when possible, should occur in an outpatient setting when general treatment preferences are discussed, or as early as possible during hospitalization. The physician has an ethical obligation to honor the resuscitation preferences expressed by the patient. Physicians should not permit their personal value judgments about qualify of life to obstruct the implementation of a patient's preferences regarding the use of CPR.

If a patient is incapable of rendering a decision regarding the use of CPR, a decision may be made by a surrogate decisionmaker, based upon the previously expressed preferences of the patient or, if such preferences are unknown, in accordance with the patient's best interests.

If, in the judgment of the attending physician, it would be inappropriate to pursue CPR, the attending physician may enter a do-not-resuscitate order into the patient's record. Resuscitative efforts should be considered inappropriate by the attending physician only if they cannot be expected either to restore cardiac or respiratory function to the patient or to meet established ethical criteria, as defined in the Principles of Medical Ethics and Opinions 2.03 and 2.095. When there is adequate time to do so, the physician must first inform the patient, or the incompetent patient's surrogate, of the content of the DNR order, as well as the basis for its implementation. The physician also should be prepared to discuss appropriate alternatives, such as obtaining a second opinion (e.g., consulting a bioethics committee) or arranging for transfer of care to another physician.

Do-Not-Resuscitate orders, as well as the basis for their implementation, should be entered by the attending physician in the patient's medical record.

DNR orders only preclude resuscitative efforts in the event of cardiopulmonary arrest and should not influence other therapeutic interventions that may be appropriate for the patient. (I, IV)

Issued March 1992 based on the report "Guidelines for the Appropriate Use of Do-Not-Resuscitate Orders," issued December 1990. (JAMA. 1991; 265: 1868–1871)

Updated June 1994.

2.23 HIV Testing. HIV testing is appropriate and should be encouraged for diagnosis and treatment of HIV infection or of medical conditions that may be affected by HIV. Treatment may prolong the lives of those with AIDS and prolong the symptom-free period in those with an asymptomatic HIV infection. Wider testing is imperative to ensure that individuals in need of treatment are identified and treated.

Physicians should ensure that HIV testing is conducted in a way that respects patient autonomy and assures patient confidentiality as much as possible.

The physician should secure the patient's informed consent specific for HIV testing before testing is performed. Because of the need for pretest counseling and the potential consequences of an HIV test on an individual's job, housing, insurability, and social relationships, the consent should be specific for HIV testing. Consent for HIV testing cannot be inferred from a general consent to treatment.

When a health care provider is at risk for HIV infection because of the occurrence of puncture injury or mucosal contact with potentially infected bodily fluids, it is acceptable to test the patient for HIV infection even if the patient refuses consent. When testing without consent is performed in accordance with the law, the patient should be given the customary pretest counseling.

The confidentiality of the results of HIV testing must be maintained as much as possible and the limits of a patient's confidentiality should be known to the patient before consent is given.

Exceptions to confidentiality are appropriate when necessary to protect the public health or when necessary to protect individuals, including health care workers, who are endangered by persons infected with HIV. If a physician knows that a seropositive individual is endangering a third party, the physician should, within the constraints of the law, (1) attempt to persuade the infected patient to cease endangering the third party; (2) if persuasion fails, notify authorities; and (3) if the authorities take no action, notify the endangered third party.

In order to limit the public spread of HIV infection, physicians should encourage voluntary testing of patients at risk for infection.

It is unethical to deny treatment to HIV-infected individuals because they are HIV seropositive or because they are unwilling to undergo HIV testing, except in the instance where knowledge of the patient's HIV status is vital to the appropriate treatment of the patient. When a patient refuses to be tested after being informed of the physician's medical opinion, the physician may transfer the patient to a second physician who is willing to manage the patient's care in accordance with the patient's preferences about testing. (I, IV)

Issued March 1992 based on the report "Ethical Issues Involved in the Growing AIDS Crisis," issued December 1987. (JAMA. 1988; 259: 1360–1361)

Updated June 1994.

3.00 Opinions on Interprofessional Relations

* * *

3.02 Nurses. The primary bond between the practices of medicine and nursing is mutual ethical concern for patients. One of the duties in providing reasonable care is fulfilled by a nurse who carries out the orders of the attending physician. Where orders appear to the nurse to be in error or contrary to customary medical and nursing practice, the physician has an ethical obligation to hear the nurse's concern and explain those orders to the nurse involved. The ethical physician should neither expect nor insist that nurses follow orders contrary to standards of good medical and nursing practice. In emergencies, when prompt action is necessary and the physician is not immediately available, a nurse may be justified in acting contrary to the physician's standing orders for the safety of the patient. Such occurrences should not be considered to be a breakdown in professional relations. (IV, V)

Issued June 1983.

Updated June 1994.

* * *

3.08 Sexual Harassment and Exploitation Between Medical Supervisors and Trainees. Sexual harassment may be defined as sexual advances, requests for sexual favors, and other verbal or physical conduct of a sexual nature when (1) such conduct interferes with an individual's work or academic performance or creates an intimidating, hostile, or offensive work or academic environment or (2) accepting or rejecting such conduct affects or may be perceived to affect employment decisions or academic evaluations concerning the individual. Sexual harassment is unethical.

Sexual relationships between medical supervisors and their medical trainees raise concerns because of inherent inequalities in the status and power that medical supervisors wield in relation to medical trainees and may adversely affect patient care. Sexual relationships between a medical trainee and a supervisor even when consensual are not acceptable regardless of the degree of supervision in any given situation. The supervisory role should be eliminated if the parties involved wish to pursue their relationship. (II, IV, VII)

Issued March 1992 based on the report "Sexual Harassment and Exploitation Between Medical Supervisors and Trainees," issued June 1989.

Updated June 1994.

* * *

5.00 Opinions on Confidentiality, Advertising, and Communications Media Relations

* * *

5.05 Confidentiality. The information disclosed to a physician during the course of the relationship between physician and patient is confidential to the greatest possible degree. The patient should feel free to make a full disclosure of information to the physician in order that the physician may most effectively provide needed services. The patient should be able to make this disclosure with the knowledge that the patient will respect the confidential nature of the communication. The physician should not reveal confidential communications or information without the express consent of the patient, unless required to do so by law.

The obligation to safeguard patient confidences is subject to certain exceptions which are ethically and legally justified because of overriding social considerations. Where a patient threatens to inflict serious bodily harm to another person or to him or herself and there is a reasonable probability that the patient may carry out the threat, the physician should take reasonable precautions for the protection of the intended victim, including notification of law enforcement authorities. Also, communicable diseases, gun shot and knife wounds should be reported as required by applicable statutes or ordinances. (IV)

Issued December 1983.

Updated June 1994.

5.055 Confidential Care for Minors. Physicians who treat minors have an ethical duty to promote the autonomy of minor patients by involving them in the medical decisionmaking process to a degree commensurate with their abilities.

When minors request confidential services, physicians should encourage them to involve their parents. This includes making efforts to obtain the minor's reasons for not involving their parents and correcting misconceptions that may be motivating their objections.

Where the law does not require otherwise, physicians should permit a competent minor to consent to medical care and should not notify parents without the patient's consent. Depending on the seriousness of the decision, competence may be evaluated by physicians for most minors. When necessary, experts in adolescent medicine or child psychological development should be consulted. Use of the courts for competence determinations should be made only as a last resort.

When an immature minor requests contraceptive services, pregnancy-related care (including pregnancy testing, prenatal and postnatal care, and delivery services), or treatment for sexually transmitted disease, drug and alcohol abuse, or mental illness, physicians must recognize that requiring parental involvement may be counterproductive to the health of the patient. Physicians should encourage parental involvement in these situations. However, if the minor continues to object, his or her wishes ordinarily should be respected. If the physician is uncomfortable with providing services without parental involvement, and alternative confidential services are available, the minor may be referred to those services. In cases when the physician believes that without parental involvement and guidance, the minor will face a serious health threat, and there is reason to believe that the parents will be helpful and understanding, disclosing the problem to the parents is ethically justified. When the physician does breach confidentiality to the parents, he or she must discuss the reasons for the breach with the minor prior to the disclosure.

For minors who are mature enough to be unaccompanied by their parents for their examination, confidentiality of information disclosed during an exam, interview, or in counseling should be maintained. Such information may be disclosed to parents when the patient consents to disclosure. Confidentiality may be justifiably breached in situations for which confidentiality for adults may be breached. In addition, confidentiality for immature minors may be ethically breached when necessary to enable the parent to make an informed decision about treatment for the minor or when such a breach is necessary to avert serious harm to the minor. (IV)

Issued June 1994 based on the report "Confidential Care for Minors," issued June 1992.

* * *

5.07 Confidentiality: Computers. The utmost effort and care must be taken to protect the confidentiality of all medical records, including computerized medical records.

The guidelines below are offered to assist physicians and computer service organizations in maintaining the confidentiality of information in medical records when that information is stored in computerized data bases:

(1) Confidential medical information should be entered into the computer-based patient record only by authorized personnel. Additions to the record should be time and date stamped, and the person making the additions should be identified in the record.

(2) The patient and physician should be advised about the existence of computerized data bases in which medical information concerning the patient is stored. Such information should be communicated to the physician and patient prior to the physician's release of the medical information to the entity or entities maintaining the computer data bases. All individuals and organizations with some form of access to the computerized data bases, and the level of access permitted, should be specifically identified in advance. Full disclosure of this information to the patient is necessary in obtaining informed consent to treatment. Patient data should be assigned a security level appropriate for the data's degree of sensitivity, which should be used to control who has access to the information.

(3) The physician and patient should be notified of the distribution of all reports reflecting identifiable patient data prior to distribution of the reports by the computer facility. There should be approval by the patient and notification of the physician prior to the release of patient-identifiable clinical and administrative data to individuals or organizations external to the medical care environment. Such information should not be released without the express permission of the patient.

(4) The dissemination of confidential medical data should be limited to only those individuals or agencies with a bona fide use for the data. Only the data necessary for the bona fide use should be released. Patient identifiers should be omitted when appropriate. Release of confidential medical information from the data base should be confined to the specific purpose for which the information is requested and limited to the specific time frame requested. All such organizations or individuals should be advised that authorized release of data to them does not authorize their further release of the data to additional individuals or organizations, or subsequent use of the data for other purposes.

(5) Procedures for adding to or changing data on the computerized data base should indicate individuals authorized to make changes, time periods in which changes take place, and those individuals who will be informed about changes in the data from the medical records.

(6) Procedures for purging the computerized data base of archaic or inaccurate data should be established and the patient and physician should be notified before and after the data has been purged. There should be no commingling of a physician's computerized patient records with those of other computer service bureau clients. In addition, procedures should be developed to protect against inadvertent mixing of individual reports or segments thereof:

(7) The computerized medical data base should be on-line to the computer terminal only when authorized computer programs requiring the medical data are being used. Individuals and organizations external to the clinical facility should not be provided on-line access to a computerized data base containing identifiable data from medical records concerning patients. Access to the computerized data base should be controlled through security measures such as passwords, encryption (encoding) of information, and scannable badges or other user identification.

(8) Back-up systems and other mechanisms should be in place to prevent data loss and downtime as a result of hardware or software failure.

(9) Security:

A. Stringent security procedures should be in place to prevent unauthorized access to computer-based patient records. Personnel audit procedures should be developed to establish a record in the event of unauthorized disclosure of medical data. Terminated or former employees in the data processing environment should have no access to data from the medical records concerning patients.

B. Upon termination of computer services for a physician, those computer files maintained for the physician should be physically turned over to the physician. They may be destroyed (erased) only if it is established that the physician has another copy (in some form). In the event of file erasure, the computer service bureau should verify in writing to the physician that the erasure has taken place. (IV)

Issued prior to April 1977.

Updated June 1994.

* * *

6.00 Opinions on Fees and Charges

* * *

6.11 Competition. Competition between and among physicians and other health care practitioners on the basis of competitive factors such as quality of services, skill, experience, miscellaneous conveniences offered to patients, credit terms, fees charged, etc., is not only ethical but is encouraged. Ethical medical practice thrives best under free market conditions when prospective patients have adequate information and opportunity to choose freely between and among competing physicians and alternate systems of medical care. (VII)

Issued July 1983.

* * *

8.00 Opinions on Practice Matters

* * *

8.08 Informed Consent. The patient's right of self-decision can be effectively exercised only if the patient possesses enough information to enable an intelligent choice. The patient should make his or her own determination on treatment. The physician's obligation is to present the medical facts accurately to the patient or to the individual responsible for the patient's care and to make recommendations for management in accordance with good medical practice. The physician has an ethical obligation to help the patient make choices from among the therapeutic alternatives consistent with good medical practice. Informed consent is a basic social policy for which exceptions are permitted: (1) where the patient is unconscious or otherwise incapable of consenting and harm from failure to treat is imminent; or (2) when risk-disclosure poses such a serious psychological threat of detriment to the patient as to be medically contraindicated. Social policy does not accept the paternalistic view that the physician may remain silent because divulgence might prompt the patient to forego needed therapy. Rational, informed patients should not be expected to act uniformly, even under similar circumstances, in agreeing to or refusing treatment. (I, II, III, IV, V)

Issued March 1981.

* * *

8.11 Neglect of Patient. Physicians are free to choose whom they will serve. The physician should, however, respond to the best of his or her ability in cases of emergency where first aid treatment is essential. Once having undertaken a case, the physician should not neglect the patient, nor withdraw from the case without giving notice to the patient, the relatives, or responsible friends sufficiently long in advance of withdrawal to permit another medical attendant to be secured. (I, VI)

Issued prior to April 1977.

8.12 Patient Information. It is a fundamental ethical requirement that a physician should at all times deal honestly and openly with patients. Patients have a right to know their past and present medical status and to be free of any mistaken beliefs concerning their conditions. Situations occasionally occur in which a patient suffers significant medical complications that may have resulted from the physician's mistake or judgment. In these situations, the physician is ethically required to inform the patient of all the facts necessary to ensure understanding of what has occurred. Only through full disclosure is a patient able to make informed decisions regarding future medical care.

Ethical responsibility includes informing patients of changes in their diagnoses resulting from retrospective review of test results or any other information. This obligation holds even though the patient's medical treatment or therapeutic options may not be altered by the new information.

Concern regarding legal liability which might result following truthful disclosure should not affect the physician's honesty with a patient. (I, II, III, IV)

Issued March 1981.

Updated June 1994.

* * *

8.14 Sexual Misconduct in the Practice of Medicine. Sexual contact that occurs concurrent with the physician-patient relationship constitutes sexual misconduct. Sexual or romantic interactions between physicians and patients detract from the goals of the physician-patient relationship, may exploit the vulnerability of the patient, may obscure the physician's objective judgment concerning the patient's health care, and ultimately may be detrimental to the patient's well-being.

If a physician has reason to believe that non-sexual contact with a patient may be perceived as or may lead to sexual conduct, then he or she should avoid the non-sexual contact. At a minimum, a physician's ethical duties include terminating the physician-patient relationship before initiating a dating, romantic, or sexual relationship with a patient.

Sexual or romantic relationships between a physician and a former patient may be unduly influenced by the previous physician-patient relationship. Sexual or romantic relationships with former patients are unethical if the physician uses or exploits trust, knowledge, emotions, or influence derived from the previous professional relationship. (I, II, IV)

Issued December 1986.

Updated March 1992 based on the report "Sexual Misconduct in the Practice of Medicine," issued December 1990. (JAMA. 1991; 266: 2741–2745)

8.15 Substance Abuse. It is unethical for a physician to practice medicine while under the influence of a controlled substance, alcohol, or other chemical agents which impair the ability to practice medicine. (I)

Issued December 1986.

* * *

9.00 Opinions on Professional Rights and Responsibilities

* * *

9.031 Reporting Impaired, Incompetent, or Unethical Colleagues. Physicians have an ethical obligation to report impaired, incompetent, and unethical colleagues in accordance with the legal requirements in each state and assisted by the following guidelines:

Impairment. Impairment should be reported to the hospital's in-house impairment program, if available. Otherwise, either the chief of an appropriate clinical service or the chief of the hospital staff should be alerted. Reports may also be made directly to an external impaired physician program. Practicing physicians who do not have hospital privileges should be reported directly to an impaired physician program. If none of these steps would facilitate the entrance of the impaired physician into an impairment program, then the impaired physician should be reported directly to the state licensing board.

Incompetence. Initial reports of incompetence should be made to the appropriate clinical authority who would be empowered to assess the potential impact on patient welfare and to facilitate remedial action. The hospital peer review body should be notified where appropriate. Incompetence which poses an immediate threat to the health of patients should be reported directly to the state licensing board. Incompetence by physicians without a hospital affiliation should be reported to the local or state medical society and/or the state licensing or disciplinary board.

Unethical conduct. With the exception of incompetence or impairment, unethical behavior should be reported in accordance with the following guidelines:

Unethical conduct that threatens patient care or welfare should be reported to the appropriate authority for a particular clinical service. Unethical behavior which violates state licensing provisions should be reported to the state licensing board. Unethical conduct which violates criminal statutes must be reported to the appropriate law enforcement authorities. All other unethical conduct should be reported to the local or state medical society.

Where the inappropriate behavior of a physician continues despite the initial report(s), the reporting physician should report to a higher or additional authority. The person or body receiving the initial report should notify the reporting physician when appropriate action has been taken. Physicians who receive reports of inappropriate behavior have an ethical duty to critically and objectively evaluate the reported information and to assure that identified deficiencies are either remedied or further reported to a higher or additional authority. Anonymous reports should receive appropriate review and confidential investigation. Physicians who are under scrutiny or charge should be protected by the rules of confidentiality until such charges are proven or until the physician is exonerated. (II)

Issued March 1992 based on the report "Reporting Impaired, Incompetent, or Unethical Colleagues," issued January 1992.

Updated June 1994.

* * *

9.035 Gender Discrimination in the Medical Profession. Physician leaders in medical schools and other medical institutions should take immediate steps to increase the number of women in leadership positions as such positions become open. There is already a large enough pool of female physicians to provide strong candidates for such positions. Also, adjustments should be made to ensure that all physicians are equitably compensated for their work. Women and men in the same specialty with the same experience and doing the same work should be paid the same compensation.

Physicians in the workplace should actively develop the following: (1) Retraining or other programs which facilitate the reentry of physicians who take time away from their careers to have a family; (2) On-site child care services for dependent children; (3) Policies providing job security for physicians who are temporarily not in practice due to pregnancy or family obligations.

Physicians in the academic medical setting should strive to promote the following: (1) Extension of tenure decisions through "stop the clock" programs, relaxation of the seven year rule, or part-time appointments that would give faculty members longer to achieve standards for promotion and tenure; (2) More reasonable guidelines regarding the appropriate quantity and timing of published material needed for promotion or tenure that would emphasize quality over quantity and that would encourage the pursuit of careers based on individual talent rather than tenure standards that undervalue teaching ability and overvalue research; (3) Fair distribution of teaching, clinical, research, administrative responsibilities, and access to tenure tracks between men and women. Also, physicians in academic institutions should consider formally structuring the mentoring process, possibly matching students or faculty with advisors through a fair and visible system.

Where such policies do not exist or have not been followed, all medical workplaces and institutions should create strict policies to deal with sexual harassment. Grievance committees should have broad representation of both sexes and other groups. Such committees should have the power to enforce harassment policies and be accessible to those persons they are meant to serve.

Grantors of research funds and editors of scientific or medical journals should consider blind peer review of grant proposals and articles for publication to help prevent bias. However, grantors and editors will be able to consider the author's identity and give it appropriate weight. (II, VII)

Issued June 1994 based on the report "Gender Discrimination in the Medical Profession," issued June 1993. (*Women's Health Issues.* 1994; 4:1–11)

* * *

9.065 Caring for the Poor. Each physician has an obligation to share in providing care to the indigent. The measure of what constitutes an appropriate contribution may vary with circumstances such as community characteristics, geographic location, the nature of the physician's practice and specialty, and other conditions. All physicians should work to ensure that the needs of the poor in their communities are met. Caring for the poor should be a regular part of the physician's practice schedule.

In the poorest communities, it may not be possible to meet the needs of the indigent for physicians' services by relying solely on local physicians. The local physicians should be able to turn for assistance to their colleagues in prosperous communities, particularly those in close proximity.

Physicians are meeting their obligation, and are encouraged to continue to do so, in a number of ways such as seeing indigent patients in their offices at no cost or at reduced cost, serving at freestanding or hospital clinics that treat the poor, and participating in government programs that provide health care to the poor. Physicians can also volunteer their services at weekend clinics for the poor and at shelters for battered women or the homeless.

In addition to meeting their obligations to care for the indigent, physicians can devote their energy, knowledge, and prestige to designing and lobbying at all levels for better programs to provide care for the poor. (I, VII)

Issued June 1994 based on the report "Caring for the Poor," issued December 1992. (JAMA. 1993; 269: 2533–2537)

* * *

9.121 Racial Disparities in Health Care. Disparities in medical care based on immutable characteristics such as race must be avoided. Whether such disparities in health care are caused by treatment decisions, differences in income and education, sociocultural factors, or failures by the medical profession, they are unjustifiable and must be eliminated. Physicians should examine their own practices to ensure that racial prejudice does not affect clinical judgment in medical care. (I, IV)

Issued March 1992 based on the report "Black-White Disparities in Health Care," issued December 1989. (JAMA. 1990; 263: 2344–2346)

Updated June 1994.

9.122 Gender Disparities in Health Care. A patient's gender plays an appropriate role in medical decisionmaking when biological differences between the sexes are considered. However, some data suggest that gender bias may be playing a role in medical decisionmaking. Social attitudes, including stereotypes, prejudices and other evaluations based on gender role expectations may play themselves out in a variety of subtle ways. Physicians must ensure that gender is not used inappropriately as a consideration in clinical decisionmaking. Physicians should examine their practices and attitudes for influence of social or cultural biases which could be inadvertently affecting the delivery of medical care.

Research on health problems that affect both genders should include male and female subjects, and results of medical research done solely on males should not be generalized to females without evidence that results apply to both sexes. Medicine and society in general should ensure that resources for medical research should be distributed in a manner which promotes the health of both sexes to the greatest extent possible. (I, IV)

Issued March 1992 based on the report "Gender Disparities in Clinical Decisionmaking," issued December 1990. (JAMA. 1991; 266: 559–562)

Updated June 1994.

9.13 Physicians and Infectious Diseases. A physician who knows that he or she has an infectious disease, which if contracted by the patient would pose a significant risk to the patient, should not engage in any activity that creates a risk of transmission of that disease to the patient. The precautions taken to prevent the transmission of a contagious disease to a patient should be appropriate to the seriousness of the disease and must be particularly stringent in the case of a disease that is potentially fatal. (I, IV)

Issued August 1989.

9.131 HIV-Infected Patients and Physicians. A physician may not ethically refuse to treat a patient whose condition is within the physician's current realm of competence solely because the patient is seropositive for HIV. Persons who are seropositive should not be subjected to discrimination based on fear or prejudice.

When physicians are unable to provide the services required by an HIV-infected patient, they should make appropriate referrals to those physicians or facilities equipped to provide such services.

A physician who knows that he or she is seropositive should not engage in any activity that creates a risk of transmission of the disease to others. A physician who has HIV disease or who is seropositive should consult colleagues as to which activities the physician can pursue without creating a risk to patients. (I, II, IV)

Issued March 1992 based on the report "Ethical Issues in the Growing AIDS Crisis," issued December 1987. (JAMA. 1988; 259: 1360–1361)

Moral Competence

Moral competence follows from understanding the purpose of medical care and calls upon the physician to practice moral discernment, moral agency, and caring in relationships.

Moral discernment is the ability to confront, discuss, and resolve the ethical considerations in a clinical encounter. In particular, it is the ability to:

—use the vocabulary and concepts of ethical and moral reasoning to place a moral dilemma in perspective;

—respect the cultural, social, personal beliefs, expectations, and values that the patient brings to the therapeutic setting;

—respect the patient's chosen lifestyle and acknowledge the conditions and events that have helped to shape that lifestyle;

—confront one's own beliefs, expectations, and values when faced with different perspectives; and

—reflect on the causes and consequences of one's ethical decisions.

Moral Agency is the ability to act on behalf of the patient; to act with respect for social, religious, and cultural differences which may exist between physician and patient. It is the ability to:

—consider the possible consequences of one's actions and to act to affect consequences that are in accord with one's values and those of the patient;

—resolve differences on the basis of principle, rather than power;

—provide medical care that is both professionally appropriate and socially responsible;

—genuinely engage the patient as a fellow human being; and

—keep the confidences of the patient.

A caring and healing relationship between physician and patient is the foundation of medical care. Such a relationship is characterized by an ability to:

—acknowledge the patient's right to self-determination in the process of participating in his or her own care;

—avoid conflicts of interests in one's own personal, professional, and financial relationships with patients, colleagues, and other members of the health care community;

—provide the patient complete, accurate, and timely information about treatment options in the best spirit of informed consent;

—share one's weaknesses and limits as well as one's strengths and virtues; and

—strive for the experience of compassion through progressively deeper understandings of others' behavior.

Technical Competence

Technical competence consists of the knowledge and skills necessary to diagnose and treat disease and disability according to the precepts of medical science and especially of ophthalmology, and to assist in the maintenance of health.

* * *

We acknowledge the importance of these moral commitments and technical capacities to the education, practice and credentialing of ophthalmologists. Further, the curriculum of ophthalmology should specifically address each of these two competencies and the two paths to developing them and should be defined further for purposes of assessment and accountability.

Glossary

abortifacient An agent (as a drug) that induces abortion.

abortion Any termination of a pregnancy by medical, surgical, or natural means.

abruption Placental separation.

abstinence A limited period of time in which intercourse is avoided.

acquired immunodeficiency syndrome (AIDS) A disease at once viral and behavioral that attacks the immune system, resulting in a series of ultimately fatal opportunistic disorders.

actinomycosis Infection or disease caused by actinomycetes, rod-shaped bacteria, especially a chronic disease characterized by hard granulomatous masses in the mouth and jaw.

action tendencies Modes of readiness to act or discharge impulses, such as emotions.

acute salpingitis *See* pelvic inflammatory disease (PID).

adaptations Adjustments or modifications of an organism that makes it more fit for existence in its environment.

adolescents Persons between thirteen and eighteen years old.

adultery Voluntary sexual intercourse between a married person and someone other than the spouse.

advance directive A patient's express wish, considered morally binding and executed in a living will or by appointing a health-care agent or proxy to represent the patient, to refuse medical treatment in the future when he loses his mental capacity.

advocacy The act or process of supporting a cause or proposal.

albumin Used in the treatment of shock and trauma, simple heat-coagulable, water-soluble proteins that occur in blood plasma or serum, muscle, egg whites, milk, and other animal substances and in many plant tissues and fluids.

allele An alternative form of a gene that can be located at a particular site on the chromosome.

allocation, intergenerational With respect to goods and services, how to determine children's fair share of health-care funding in relation to adults. *Intragenerational allocation* determines priorities for funding health-care programs when not all can be funded.

alpha$_1$-antitrypsin deficiency An inherited disease that results in low or no production of the protein alpha$_1$-antitrypsin and leads to damage of many organs, but mainly the lungs and the liver.

alpha-fetoprotein (AFP) A fetal enzyme, present in the amniotic fluid and detected in the mother's blood, with high and low elevations associated with certain birth defects.

altruism Unselfish regard for or devotion to the welfare of others.

Alzheimer's disease A degenerative disease of the central nervous system characterized by premature senile mental deterioration.

amenorrhea No menses.

amniocentesis Commonly performed with ultrasonographic guidance, an invasive technique—needle puncture of the uterus—to study cells in the amniotic fluid and the fluid itself for fetal abnormalities.

anatomo-politics The process in which social institutions seek to normalize, discipline, and regulate the bodies of individuals.

anemia A condition in which the blood is deficient in red blood cells, in hemoglobin, or in total volume.

anencephaly A congenital neural tube defect in which all or part of the brain is missing.

annulment A judicial pronouncement declaring a marriage invalid.

anorexia nervosa A serious eating disorder primarily of young women that is characterized by a pathological fear of weight gain.

anthropometry The study of human body measurements on a comparative basis.

antibiotic A substance produced by or derived from a microorganism and able to inhibit or kill another microorganism.

antinatalist Fertility-reducing policy, such as forced sterilizations.

anti-political politics Using politics as one way to seek and achieve meaningful lives and to serve and protect people.

antiprogestin A drug that blocks progesterone production by the ovaries and prevents implantation of a fertilized egg, or embryo.

antireductionism The belief that the term *life force* is only a metaphor for the structure and mechanisms of organisms and not for their substance.

antiviral agent Destroys viruses or suppresses their replication.

applied ethics The approach to ethics through moral principles, philosophical ethics, theories, and the criticisms each makes of the others for enlightenment.

artificial insemination The mechanical placement of sperm into the female reproductive tract either with a third party's sperm (*heterologous, or donor* [*AID*]) or the husband's or a designated partner's sperm (*homologous, or husband* [*AIH*]) to fertilize the egg.

asceticism The practice of strict self-denial as a measure of personal and spiritual discipline.

assisted suicide Going beyond the right to die and the right to refuse medical treatment, the process of enlisting caregivers to hasten one's death.

atheistic secular humanism A philosophy that rejects the influence of a deity or religion and stresses an individual's dignity, worth, and capacity for self-realization through reason.

autologous transfusion The process in which individuals donate their own blood for storage and future use to ensure their own safety.

autonomous virtues Those virtues derived from the concept of a person as self-governing: self-reflection, direction, reliance, control, independence, and responsibility.

autonomy A right to self-determination within a sphere of personal sovereignty, or freedom from external control.

autosomal Chromosomes common to both sexes.

autosomal recessive disorders Defects that arise when recessive genes, which are harmless to a single carrier, are paired in offspring.

aversive conditioning Therapy intended to change habits or antisocial behavior by inducing dislike for them through pairing arousing stimuli for the deviant behavior with unpleasant events (as electric shock).

azoospermia Lacking spermatozoa.

AZT (azidothymidine) An antiviral drug administered to HIV-infected individuals.

Baby Doe guidelines Rules (1984) that forbid withholding or withdrawing lifesaving care, even those that are deemed inhumane, from a sick infant unless the care can be deemed virtually futile.

balanitis An infection of the head of the penis.

band-shifting The different rates at which DNA fragments of equal length may migrate down an electronically charged gel.

barrier methods Mechanical (condoms, diaphragm, cervical cap) and chemical (spermicidal products) forms of birth control.

behaviorism The study of the relation between publicly observable behavior and the environment in which specific unconditioned reflexes have evolved, because they have survival value, and in which susceptibility to conditioning allows the organism to adapt to environmental changes.

behavior modification Any treatment approach designed to modify the patient's behavior directly, rather than correct the dynamic causation.

beneficence The active promotion of a patient's well-being and the duty to respond to a patient's needs.

best-interests standard A standard applied to those who do not have the ability or authority to make health-care decisions for themselves so that caregivers will identify the patient's immediate and long-term interests and then choose a care option in which the benefits of an intervention or procedure outweigh the burdens.

beta-thalassemia An incurable blood disease of childhood that causes anemia and early death.

bigamy Entering into a marriage with one person while still legally married to another.

Billings method A form of family planning that uses the rhythm method based on observed changes in the vaginal mucus.

bioethics A field of human inquiry into the broad terrain of moral problems in life sciences, encompassing medicine, biology, and important aspects of environmental, population, and social sciences, and is devoted to human survival and an improved quality of life.

biofeedback The technique of making unconscious or involuntary bodily processes (as heartbeats) perceptible to the senses in order to manipulate them by conscious mental control.

biogram A code or program genetically wired into the brain that produces forms of social behavior.

biological determinism The argument that individuals are controlled biologically because of natural selection.

biological psychiatry A racially based comparative psychology that established a biological basis for major mental diseases.

biological sex Six categories of biological maleness or femaleness: chromosomal (XX, female; XY, male); gonadal (ovaries or testicles); hormonal; anatomical, internal (uterus or prostate gland); anatomical, external (clitoris and labia or penis and scrotum); and brain.

biology The science of organisms.

biopolitics or biopower The process in which social institutions seek to regulate the bodies of its total population or subgroups.

birth control Contraception, or the control of the number of children born by preventing or lessening the frequency of conception.

bisexual A person who responds erotically to qualities in a partner regardless of biological sex.

blastocyst The modified blastula (early embryo) of a placental mammal.

block grant An unrestricted federal grant.

blood poisoning Invasion of the bloodstream by virulent microorganisms from a local infection accompanied by chills, fever, and complete exhaustion.

body language A physical form of expression of one's emotions and attitudes toward other people.

brain death Final cessation of activity in the central nervous system, as indicated by a flat electroencephalogram for a predetermined length of time.

break-through bleeding Bleeding between menstrual periods.

breech presentation A fetus presents itself for birth hind end first.

Buddhism Sees worldly life as secondary, with attainment of release from suffering in this or subsequent existences as its central concern.

burnout The phenomenon in which caregivers become utterly exhausted by the physical and emotional demands associated with providing care.

cadaver A dead body intended for dissection.

cannula A thin plastic tube for insertion into a body cavity or into a duct or vessel.

carcinoma A malignant tumor of epithelial (from the membranous cellular tissue that covers a free surface or lines a tube or cavity) origin.

care perspective To perceive moral dilemmas in terms of personal attachment and to avoid hurting persons and instead act in a manner that strengthens and protects attachments between persons.

carrier screening Methods to identify an otherwise healthy person who may be at high risk for having children with a severe genetic disorder.

castration To remove the testes or ovaries and to render impotent.

casuistry A resolving of specific cases of conscience, duty, or conduct through interpretation of ethical principles or religious doctrine.

celibacy A lifestyle decision in which an individual chooses to avoid intercourse for a long time; also the state of not being married.

cervical cap A thimble-shaped latex device that fits over the cervix and stays in place by mild suction.

cervical dysplasia Abnormal cells of the cervix that may progress to cancer.

cervicitis Inflammation of the uterine cervix.

cervix The narrow outer end of the uterus.

cesarean section A surgical incision of the walls of the abdomen and uterus for delivery of offspring.

character The detectable expression of the action of a gene or group of genes; also moral excellence or firmness.

Charismatic Defines the tripartite person as a composite of body, mind, and spirit; also a member of a religious group or movement built around the belief that the Holy Spirit gives the Christian an extraordinary power for the good of the church.

checks on population, positive Deaths resulting from too large a population relative to its subsistence. *Preventive checks* come from the chaste postponement of marriage, thus leading to fewer offspring.

child abuse Distress suffered from repeated injuries at the hands of a parent or surrogate that has been broadened to include withholding medically indicated treatment.

chimera When two embryos fuse into a single new embryo.

chlamydia A bacteria that causes diseases of the eye and urogenital tract.

cholera A disease found in humans and animals that is marked by severe gastrointestinal symptoms.

cholesterol A steroid alcohol present in animal cells and body fluids that regulates membrane fluidity and may cause arteriosclerosis.

chorionic villus sampling (CVS) Commonly performed with ultrasound guidance, an invasive procedure—transcervical or transabdominal—to obtain chorion villi (forerunners of the placenta) and test for fetal abnormalities.

Christian Scientist Practices spiritual healing based on the teaching that cause and effect are mental and that sin, sickness, and death will be destroyed by a full understanding of the divine principle of Jesus's teaching and healing, per the Scriptures.

chromosomal analysis Preimplantation diagnosis for *anomalies*—having too many or too few copies of the many genes that occur together on the abnormal piece of chromosome and can cause severe general learning disabilities—and selecting only healthy embryos for implantation.

circumcision, male The surgical removal of the foreskin that covers the glans of the penis.

cirrhosis Widespread disruption of normal liver structure by fibrosis and the formation of regenerative nodules that is caused by various chronic progressive conditions affecting the liver (alcoholism or hepatitis).

civic republicanism Stresses the need for social order and shared values, emphasizes civic education, and presses the importance of having a propertied stake in society with citizenship as a robust privilege rather than a legalistic, universalistic standing.

civil disobedience Refusing to obey government demands or commands, especially as a nonviolent and usually collective means of forcing concessions from the government.

civil liberty Freedom from arbitrary governmental interference as guaranteed by the Bill of Rights.

classism Prejudice or discrimination based on social rank.

cleavage A series of cell divisions that occur without significant intervening cellular growth.

clinical bioethics Refers to the day-to-day moral decision making of those caring for patients.

clinical psychology Frequently in medical settings, the science of evaluating and psychologically ameliorating mental disorders.

clinical test A procedure to obtain data about an individual's health in response to a specific complaint.

clinical trials Clinical research to determine the safety and effectiveness of new drugs.

clitoridectomy, or sunna The removal of the prepuce of the clitoris and the clitoris itself.

clitoris A small erectile organ at the anterior or ventral part of the vulva (homologous to the penis).

cloning Asexual single-parent reproduction resulting in offspring with the same genetic blueprint as the parent, or DNA donor, either by transplanting the nucleus from a differentiated cell into an unfertilized egg from which the nucleus has been removed or by splitting an embryo at an early stage when its cells are still undifferentiated.

coercion Controlling a patient and restricting the patient's freedom of action by intentionally using credible and severe threats of harm or force or by pressuring a patient to comply, thus making his action costly to pursue and undermining his informed consent.

cognitive functioning Refers to the mental processes of comprehension, judgment, memory, and reasoning.

coitus interruptus Intercourse in which the penis is withdrawn prior to ejaculation to prevent the deposit of sperm in the vagina.

commercial surrogacy When a woman agrees to carry to term an embryo genetically related to her for a fee. In *noncommercial surrogacy* a woman does so out of generosity.

common law A body of judicial resolutions based on custom and precedent and constitutes the basis of the English legal system.

common-law marriage Two people live together and treat each other as husband and wife, but without benefit of a marriage ceremony.

communicable disease A transmittable illness or infection.

communism A theory advocating elimination of private property for a system in which goods are owned in common and are available to all as needed, thus negating the state's control.

communitarian theorist Identifies a community standard of the common good and promotes relationships expected to conform to and promote that common good.

component therapy The practice of giving patients only the particular blood component most desirable for their required therapy, allowing for more efficient use of the blood supply and minimizing the patients' risks of exposure to unneeded substances.

compulsion Employing force, the threat of force, or extreme penalties and pressures that leave people no choice but to comply with demands.

Comstock Act (1873) Made it a federal offense to use the postal service to transport or import obscene materials, including contraceptive and abortion information and equipment.

conceptus Used to describe any stage of development from fertilization to birth.

concubine A woman, as either a mistress or a wife, with whom a man cohabits without being married.

condom A sheath commonly of rubber worn over the penis (a similar device is inserted into the vagina) to prevent conception or venereal infection during intercourse.

confidentiality The communication of, and thus relinquishing personal privacy of, personal and sensitive information to a recipient who is then entrusted not to disclose the information and cause harm.

congenital hypothyroidism An endocrine disorder that results form aberrant development or function of the thyroid gland.

consanguinity A close relation or connection, such as having the same blood or origin.

conscience The morally self-critical part of the self-encompassing standards of behavior, performance, and value judgments.

conscientious refusal To avoid betrayal of deep personal convictions about life or the nature of medicine, a caregiver or patient may seek exemptions from procedures or care plans that threaten their sense of integrity.

consequentialism All moral obligations and virtues can be understood in terms of their outcomes, and all moral obligations are grounded in considerations of pleasure or pain.

constructionists Hold that diagnostic categories of human behavior are relative to social rules and function to maintain conformity and to prevent and control nonconformist sexual behavior.

contact tracing Evoking the duty to warn in programs to treat and control sexually transmitted diseases, it calls for affected patients to reveal the names of their partners so they may be examined and, if necessary, treated interrupting the chain of transmission.

contraception Devices that prevent conception, including sterilization.

contractarianism Holds that distributions of social goods are fair when impartial people agree upon the procedures used for distribution and that each person should have equal right to the most extensive basic liberties compatible with a similar system compatible for all.

contract pregnancy *See* commercial surrogacy.

contragestion A contraction of "contra-gestation" used to describe a medical procedure that falls between contraceptive and abortion.

cordocentesis The treatment for Rh disease in which a needle is placed through the maternal abdominal and uterine walls and into the umbilical blood vessel for transfusing blood into the fetus.

corona radiata The zone of small follicular cells immediately surrounding the ovum in the graafian follicle and accompanying ovum on its discharge from the follicle.

coronary disease Disease of the coronary arteries or veins of the heart.

corporeality A physical, material (not spiritual) existence.

courtesan A prostitute with a courtly, wealthy, or upper-class clientele.

craniotomy Surgical opening of the skull.

creationism The literal acceptance of the early chapters of the Bible and its description of God's creation of matter out of nothing.

critical theory An analysis of the sources of human power that questions whether increases in such power over nature will produce human progress.

cultural bioethics The effort systematically to relate bioethics to the historical, ideological, cultural, and social context in which it is expressed.

cultural relativism A descriptive reaction, based on evaluations using internal (not external) criteria, to wide experience with other cultures.

cybernetics The science of communication and control theory that is concerned with the comparative study of automatic control (nervous, brain, and mechanical-electrical communication) systems.

cyborg ethics and politics A view of the body as a cybernetic body that requires radical pluralism, multiple meanings and imperfect communication, and physical groundedness in a particular location.

cyropreservation Frozen storage.

cystic fibrosis A common hereditary disease, with onset in early childhood, that involves functional disorder of the exocrine glands and is marked by faulty digestion, difficulty in breathing, and excessive loss of salt in the sweat.

cytomegalovirus retinitis An opportunistic infection that usually causes blindness.

cytoplasm The organized complex of inorganic and organic substances external to the nuclear membrane of a cell.

Darwinism Evolutionary biology, a theory of the origin and perpetuation of new species of animals and plants that offspring of a given organism may vary, that natural selection favors the survival of some of these variations over others and gives rise to new species, and that all species have arisen from the same ancestors.

death, degrees of *Death*—brain dead; *double dead*—respiratory failure; *triple dead*—no body parts suitable for donation.

defensive medicine Techniques, such as ordering medically unnecessary tests, physicians employ to protect themselves from the threat of malpractice liability.

deferred consent In an emergency, the postponement of getting the subject's consent or the next-of-kin's permission for up to several days after the subject has been enrolled in a research protocol.

demography The statistical study of human populations with reference to size, density, distribution, and vital statistics.

denial A psychological defense mechanism in which confrontation with a personal problem or reality is avoided by denying its existence and interferes with rational decision making.

deontology Also called *Kantian ethics,* stresses the rights of persons and the duties of others to respect persons as ends in themselves, and focuses on determining which choices most respect an individual's worth and value. Without using or mistreating other people as a means to one's own ends, one is morally obligated to act independent of the effects of one's actions on the well-being of others or oneself.

Depo-Provera, or depot-medroxyprogesterone (DMPA) A long-acting hormonal contraceptive that is given as a deep intramuscular injection.

DES (diethylstilbestrol) A drug prescribed to pregnant women to prevent miscarriage that was ineffective and caused damaged reproductive systems in female offspring.

desensitization Exposing oneself to what is painful to become inured.

diabetes Any various abnormal conditions characterized by the secretion and excretion of excessive amounts of urine.

dialysis When the kidneys are unable to filter blood, the blood is cleansed by passing it through a special machine.

diaphragm A dome-shaped latex device that serves as a mechanical barrier against the cervix.

difference principle A principle of justice that mandates that social and economic institutions should be arranged to benefit maximally the worst off.

DiGeorge's syndrome A chromosomal disorder characterized by low blood calcium levels, underdevelopment of the thymus (organ behind the breastbone in which lymphocytes mature and multiply), and defects involving the outflow tracts of the heart.

digoxin A medication administered to pregnant women for the benefit of a fetus with irregular heartbeats.

dilation and curettage (D&C) A procedure in which the cervix is expanded enough (*dilation*) to permit the cervical canal and uterine lining to be scraped with a *curette* (a sharp, spoon-edged surgical instrument).

dilation and evacuation (D&E) The most common abortion procedure, which uses specially designed forceps, dilation, and vacuum aspiration to remove the uterine contents.

directed donation A blood transfusion in which patients receive blood donated by family and friends.

discretion The ability to make responsible decisions or to show good judgment in conduct and in speech (preserving prudent silence).

discrimination The act, practice, or instance of differentiating categorically rather than individually; also prejudiced action or treatment.

dissociation The separation of whole segments of the personality or of discrete mental processes from the mainstream of consciousness or of behavior.

disvalues Express undesirable, harmful, or unworthy characteristics of particular phenomena that identify realities that people resist or attempt to avoid.

DNA, or double helix The ultimate threads of heredity containing one's genetic code, determined by molecular and physiochemical means.

DNA data-banking Collection and storage of DNA samples from large populations for future identification purposes and to promote the scientific study and clinical use of genetic information.

DNA typing or fingerprinting A technique for identifying people through their genetic constitution, using small regions of DNA found in blood, semen, saliva, or tissue.

do-not-resuscitate (DNR) orders At the patient's and family's previous express request, heroic or life-sustaining measures to prolong the patient's life are withheld or withdrawn.

domestic partnerships Types of sexual relationships, apart from marriage, that last over a period of time, include a shared domestic life, and involve some public acknowledgment by the partners of that shared life.

dominant gene Its effect is seen when only one copy is present and never skips a generation.

double-bind A psychological predicament in therapy in which a person receives from a single source conflicting messages that allow no appropriate response to be made.

double-recessive state Both parents pass on the same gene.

Down syndrome A congenital condition characterized by moderate to severe mental retardation, slanting eyes, a broad short skull, broad hands with short fingers, and trisomy of the human chromosome numbered 21.

***dys*appearance** The vivid but unwanted consciousness of one's body in disease, distress, or dysfunction, leading to the body's self-concealment in the mistaken notion of the immateriality of mind and thought.

dysfunction Impaired or abnormal functioning.

dysgenic policy One that embraces the aims of either positive or negative eugenics.

dysmenorrhea Difficult menstruation that is not related to a disease.

eclampsia A pregnancy-related condition that can lead to seizures, strokes, or death for the woman.

ecology The science of living organisms, especially looking at their behaviors in natural surroundings.

ectogenesis The development of a fetus completely outside the body.

ectopic pregnancy Gestation occurring other than in the uterus.

egalitarianism A theory of justice that, by acknowledging the value of each person, attempts to provide equal access to the same benefits, goods, and services for everyone on the same basis in the hopes of making all people's objective net well-being as equal as possible.

egoism The doctrine that individual self-interest is the actual motive—and valid end—of all conscious action.

ejaculate The semen released by one ejaculation, or sudden discharge.

electroencephalographic activity Brain-wave activity.

emancipated minor Self-supporting minors who are married, who are in military service, or who are not living with and/or financially dependent on their parents/guardians, who, in turn, are not obliged to provide any further care to them.

embryo The fertilized egg after fourteen days of development and the first sign of organ development.

embryo biopsy Preimplantation diagnosis for abnormalities by removing a single cell from a four- or eight-cell embryo.

empiricism A theory that all knowledge originates in experience (without the aid of science).

endogamy Marriage within a specific group as required by custom or law.

endometrium The lining of the uterus.

endoscopy The technique of using an instrument for visualizing the interior of a hollow organ (uterus).

Enlightenment A philosophic movement of the eighteenth century marked by a rejection of traditional social, religious, and political ideas and an emphasis on *rationalism* (reason as the basis for religious truth).

ensoulment An ancient criterion referring to the time at which the embryo or fetus becomes infused with a soul, at about three months.

environmental ethics The belief that humans should protect and respect the environment on the grounds that humans are interconnected with elements of the environment.

Epicureans An ancient school of thought that virtue consisted in seeking one's own greatest pleasure and absence of pain by minimizing one's desires and simplifying one's life.

epidemic A concentrated outburst of disease, often with unusually high mortality, affecting relatively large numbers of people within fairly small areas and in a short time.

epidemiology A branch of medical science that deals with the incidence, distribution, and control of disease in a population; also the sum of the factors controlling the presence or absence of a disease or pathogen.

epididymis The coiled tubular structure where sperm cells mature.

epilepsy Any various disorders marked by disturbed electrical rhythms of the central nervous system and typically manifested by convulsive attacks that usually cloud consciousness.

equal-liberty principle A principle of justice that mandates that each person is to have an equal right to the most extensive system of equal basic liberties compatible with a similar system for all.

equitable access The widest possible distribution of information about the existence and nature of health services and their use that is not based on an ability to pay for them.

essentialism Holds that the objective validity of human understanding across historical periods and cultures can be established scientifically.

estrogen A hormone tending to promote sexual excitement and stimulate the development of female secondary sex characteristics.

estrus Time of fertility.

ethic of care A type of virtue ethic that involves the affective orientation (feelings) and moral commitment (concern) of the caregiver.

ethic of secular pluralism and social peace An ethic for the community as a whole that allows great play to the values and choices of different religious and value subcommunities.

ethic of virtue A focus on personal character and the shaping of those values and goals necessary to be a good and decent person.

ethics The principles of conduct governing an individual or group; also a theory or system of moral values, or notions having to do with morality, virtue, rationality, and ideals of conduct and motivation.

ethnicity A cultural referent for understanding human differences.

ethnobiology A cultural classification theory about the nature of human variability.

ethos The distinguishing character, sentiment, moral nature, or guiding beliefs of a person, group, or institution.

etiology A branch of medicine concerned with the causes and origins of diseases or abnormal conditions.

eudaimonism The view that one's first concern in ethics is with the nature and conditions of human happiness and well-being, especially one's own.

eugenics A science that deals with the improvement (as by control of human mating) of hereditary qualities of a breed or ethnic group. *Negative eugenics* seeks to limit the socially unworthy's breeding and eliminate their deleterious genes from the gene pool whereas *positive eugenics* aims to foster greater representation in society of socially acceptable people by increasing the frequency of their desirable genes.

eunuchoid A sexually deficient individual, especially one lacking in sexual differentiation and tending toward the intersex state.

euthanasia The act or practice of killing or permitting the death of hopelessly sick or injured individuals in a relatively painless way for reasons of mercy.

evolution The long, slow process of development that produced all organisms from the original primitive beginnings. *See also* Darwinism.

excision, or reduction A form of female circumcision in which the prepuce, the clitoris, and the labia minora are removed.

exegete One who practices the exposition, explanation, or critical interpretation of a text.

existentialism Religion-inspired critique of ethics that defends a more emotional and individualistic approach to life and thought and that claims we are all radically free in our choice of actions and values.

faith, or ritual, healing A method of treating diseases by prayer and exercise of faith in God.

fallopian tube Either of the pair of tubes conducting the egg from the ovary to the uterus.

familial The tendency of conditions to run in families.

family planning Planning intended to determine the number and spacing of one's children through birth control.

fecundity Being fruitful in offspring.

female chauvinism The belief that women are superior to men.

female condom, or vaginal pouch The only barrier method controlled by women, a polyurethane sheath secured inside the vagina with a small metal ring and outside by a large metal ring.

female genital mutilation, or female circumcision The practice of surgically removing healthy, normal female genitalia.

feminine ethics The description of moral experiences and intuitions of women and the exploration of how traditional approaches have neglected to include women's perspectives.

feminism The theory of the political, economic, and social equality of the sexes with organized activity on behalf of women's rights and interests.

feminist ethics Various theories, which reveal gender-specific patterns of harm and women's oppression, and a diverse political movement all devoted to making political changes and eliminating oppressive balances of power.

fertilization The union of two specialized cells—egg and sperm—produced by two individuals of one species but opposite gender.

fetal alcohol syndrome (FAS) A condition found in the offspring of women who consumed excessive alcohol during their pregnancy that results in gross physical retardation; central nervous dysfunction, including mental retardation; and facial abnormalities.

fetal reduction Also called *selective termination, abortion, birth,* or *feticide,* surgery performed to remove fetuses from the womb and to facilitate the birth of one or more healthy infants when multiple gestations appear.

fetal tissue research The use of abortion tissues and fetuses in research into the treatment of such diseases as diabetes, leukemia, Alzheimer's disease, and Parkinson's disease.

feticide The act of causing the death of a fetus.

fetishism Sex strongly associated with a particular object or part of the body.

fetoscopy Examination of the pregnant uterus by means of a fiber-optic tube.

fetus The label given to a human embryo after eight weeks' gestation.

fetus ex utero An (electively or spontaneously) aborted fetus.

fibroadenoma A breast condition involving a benign tumor of a glandular structure or of glandular origin.

fibrocystic change Breast condition characterized by the presence or development of fibrous tissue and cysts.

fistula An abnormal passage, or hole (opening), between the posterior urinary bladder wall and the vagina or a hole between the anterior rectal wall and the vagina.

follicle A vesicle in the mammalian ovary that contains a developing egg surrounded by a covering of cells.

fragile X syndrome Due to a trinucleotide repeat (a recurring motif of three bases) in the DNA at that spot on the X chromosome and is associated with a frequent form of mental retardation, usually more severe in males.

fraternal, or dizygotic, twins Twins created when two separate eggs are each fertilized by different sperm, thus sharing only half their genes.

freedom, negative *Internal*—the absence of internal psychological or physiological (such as genetic conditions) obstructions that inhibit the fulfillment of goals, desires, and interests; *external*—the absence of external pressures and constraints, such as coercion and interference by others, or limits on choices of actions.

freedom, positive *External*—having the external means to achieve one's ends and to fulfill one's desires and interests; *internal*—having the free will to fulfill one's goals, be self-reliant, and control one's life.

frigidity Marked sexual indifference, especially in women, or the inability to achieve orgasm during sexual intercourse.

***Frye* hearing** A proceeding by which a judge decides whether the evidence in question is based on theories and practices that have reached general acceptance in the relevant scientific community.

full surrogacy An arrangement whereby a woman is hired to carry to term an embryo formed in vitro by the contracting couple's egg and sperm.

fundamentalism A movement in twentieth-century Protestantism emphasizing the literally interpreted Bible as fundamental to Christian life and teaching, stressing strict and literal adherence to its basic principles.

fundamental rights A claim that something is an entitlement, not a privilege, and that withholding it would be wrong and unjust.

fusion An ancient fable in which the gods split human beings out of complete wholes, and consequent sexual desire is the desire to reunite the divided halves.

gag rule An administrative guideline that forbade employees in federally funded family-planning clinics to provide information or counseling about abortion services.

gamete intrafallopian tube transfer (GIFT) Involves the transfer of freshly recovered ova and conditioned sperm into the fallopian tubes, thus resulting in *in vivo fertilization.*

gamete A mature male or female germ cell (sperm or egg) possessing a haploid chromosome set and capable of initiating formation of a new diploid individual by fusion with a gamete of the opposite sex.

gay Homosexual, usually referring to a man.

gender Generally signifies the male or female nature or identity of a person, based on chromosomal, hormonal, anatomical, psychic, and social components.

gender assignment The decision made to designate a newborn as either male or female based on biomedical knowledge and cultural and moral standards.

gender-identity disorder Also called gender *dysphoria,* discordances between one's felt gender and one's assigned gender.

gene carrier An individual with one copy of a recessive allele that causes a particular trait.

gene therapy The insertion of normal or genetically altered genes into cells to replace defective genes in the treatment of genetic disorders.

genetic counseling With pretest education and counseling, the interaction between a health-care provider and a patient or family member on concerns about the risks of bearing a child with a genetic disorder, reproductive testing options, or the diagnosis of an inherited condition (more than four thousand exist).

genetic linkage The inheritance of one trait along with another that helps establish the relative position of genetic markers along the chromosomes.

genetics A branch of biology that deals with the heredity, or genetic makeup, and variation of organisms.

genetic screening Programs designed to canvass populations of healthy individuals to identify those with genotypes that place them or their offspring at high risk for disease or defect.

genetic testing Diagnostic procedures offered to individuals or families who are at increased risk for developing special disorders or for bearing affected children.

genitor The person who contributes the egg to be fertilized.

genome Unique to each person, the entire genetic sequence.

genotype The genetic makeup of the developing individual.

germ-line therapy The manipulation of the genome in cells that are the progenitors of egg or sperm cells, thus affecting descendants.

gestation Pregnancy, or the carrying of young in the uterus.

gestational contract pregnancy *See* full surrogacy.

gestator The person who contributes the womb and goes through the labor of birth.

globulin Any of a class of simple proteins that are insoluble in pure water but are soluble in dilute salt solutions and occur widely in plant and animal tissues.

Gnosticism The thought and practice distinguished by the conviction that matter is evil, that emancipation comes through esoteric knowledge of spiritual truth held to be essential to salvation, and that the material body is a prison or garment.

gonadotropin A gonadotropic (acting on or stimulating the gonads) hormone (as to induce ovulation).

gonads A reproductive gland (ovary or testis) that produces gametes.

gonorrhea A contagious inflammation of the genital mucous membrane.

Good Samaritan law Requires trained medical personnel to come to the aid of accident victims.

Griswold* v. *Connecticut The U.S. Supreme Court decision (1965) that states may not outlaw a married woman's right to use birth control.

harm to others principle A justification for using coercion against those who would harm others, but not themselves, as long as they are competent adults.

health-care option, equal The option of specifying an optimal and affordable level of health care and then guarantee this level of health care to all legitimate claimants. The *multitiered option* specifies a decent minimal level of health care and guarantees that level of health care to all legitimate claimants but then allows higher levels of health care to be purchased by whomever has the income and desire to do so.

health screening Tests to detect potential diseases in asymptomatic people.

Helsinki solution Found in the World Medical Association's (1991) Declaration of Helsinki, the view that persons who lack the capacity to give informed consent may be enrolled only in therapeutic studies.

hemoglobin An iron-containing respiratory pigment of vertebrate red blood cells that functions in oxygen transport to the tissues after conversion to oxygenated form in the lungs and then assists in carbon dioxide transport back to the lungs after surrender of its oxygen.

hemophilia A sex-linked hereditary blood defect that occurs almost exclusively in males and is characterized by delayed clotting of the blood and consequent difficulty in controlling hemorrhage even in minor injuries.

hemorrhage Heavy or uncontrolled bleeding.

hepatic adenomas Noncancerous liver tumors that may hemorrhage.

hepatitis An inflammation of the liver.

hepatitis A An acute and usually benign hepatitis caused by an RNA virus that does not persist in the blood serum and is transmitted in food and water contaminated with infected fecal matter.

hepatitis B A sometimes fatal hepatitis caused by a double-stranded DNA virus that tends to persist in the blood serum and is transmitted by contact with infected blood or blood products.

hepatitis C Hepatitis due to the hepatitis C virus (HCV), which is usually spread by blood transfusion, hemodialysis, and needle sticks.

heredity The sum of the qualities and potentialities genetically derived from one's ancestors.

heritability A technical concept designating a ratio of the contribution of heredity to the environment within a given population.

hermaphrodite An animal or plant having both male and female reproductive organs, or something that is a combination of diverse elements.

hermeneutics The study of the methodological principles of interpretation of sacred texts.

heterosexual A person who is erotically attracted to members of the opposite sex.

Hinduism A legalistic religion that regulates life in the world through ritual and social observances, mystical contemplation, and ascetic practices.

Hippocratic oath An oath embodying a code of medical ethics usually taken by those about to begin medical practice.

histocompatibility The mutual tolerance of tissues or organs to be grafted.

historical diffusionism Using empirical evidence from science and history to demonstrate that one population's cultural traits are a result of contact and borrowing from other groups it has encountered.

homosexual A person who is erotically attracted to members of the same sex.

homozygous Having the two genes at corresponding loci on homologous chromosomes identical for one or more loci.

hospice A facility or program designed to provide a caring environment for supplying the physical and emotional needs of the terminally ill.

hubris The prideful belief that humans could radically transcend their natural condition.

human chorion gonadotropin (hCG) A human hormone made by chorionic cells in the fetal part of the placenta and detectable within days of fertilization, hCG is directed at and stimulates the gonads.

human genetic intervention To cure or prevent disease, enhance human capabilities with therapies directed at a patient's somatic (nonreproductive) or germ-line (reproductive) cells.

Human Genome Organization (HUGO) Established in 1988 to mediate international cooperation and to harness various national programs into a coherent team for the Human Genome Project.

Human Genome Project (HGP) A multinational effort to catalog all possible human genetic characteristics by obtaining the sequence of all the DNA in the human genome.

human immunodeficiency virus (HIV) A viral agent that infects the patient with a chronic illness that progresses from asymptomatic infection to AIDS.

Huntington's disease A dominant genetic disease (meaning the person who inherits it will manifest the disease) whose onset during middle age degenerates the nervous system and kills the individual.

hybrid An offspring of two animals or plants of different ethnic backgrounds, breeds, varieties, species, or genera.

hylomorphic theory The ancient Greek (Aristotle) view that the matter and form of any being must be mutually appropriate and thus that the embryo or fetus could not have a soul until the body was sufficiently developed.

hyperglycemia Excess of sugar in the blood.

hyperlipidemia Elevated fatty substances in the blood.

hyperplasia An abnormal or unusual increase in the elements composing a part (as cells composing a tissue).

hypertension Abnormally high blood pressure and arterial blood pressure.

hypnosis A state that resembles sleep but is induced by a person whose suggestions are readily accepted by the subject.

hypokalemia A deficiency of potassium in the blood.

hypospadias A penile abnormality in which the opening of the urethra is located away from the tip of the glans penis, causing the ejaculate to be deposited at the periphery of the vagina.

hypothalamus The part of the brain that controls hormone production by the pituitary gland.

hysterectomy Surgical removal of the uterus.

iatrogenic Induced inadvertently by a physician, a surgeon, a medical treatment, or diagnostic procedures (such as a rash).

identical, or monozygotic, twins Genetically identical twins derived from one egg fertilized by one sperm that divides into two separate embryos.

idolatry The immoderate attachment or devotion to something, or the worship of a physical object as a god.

immunology A science that deals with the immune system and the cell-mediated and humoral aspects of immunity and immune responses.

implantation A process by which the pre-embryo attaches to the endometrial surface.

impotence The inability to have sex.

incest Sexual intercourse between persons so closely related that they are forbidden by law to marry.

incompetent Lacking the capacities to develop autonomy or to pursue one's interests effectively; also inadequate or unsuitable for a particular purpose.

incontinence A failure to restrain the sexual appetite; also an inability of the body to control the evacuative functions (urination).

individualists Liberals who start with the free-standing individual as their point of reference and the "good" of that individual as their normative ideal in social theory.

individualized prognostic strategy of treatment Engaging in time-limited trials to give various treatments a chance to work, even when the patient is likely to have ongoing disabilities.

individuation The process of forming a separate, distinct existence.

inductive methodology The process through which judges render decisions specific to the facts of individual cases that are grounded in, or justified by, the decisions in prior analogous cases and in existing legislation.

infanticide The deliberate killing of infants.

infertility Not fertile or productive.

infibulation, or pharaonic circumcision The removal of the prepuce, the clitoris, the labia minora and majora, and the suturing of the two sides of the vulva, leaving a very small opening for the passage of urine and menstrual blood.

informed consent Requires that physicians must disclose to patients information that reasonable persons need to decide on a course of treatment, thus ensuring the patients' autonomy, and letting the patients' own judgments prevail.

instillation abortion A second-trimester abortion procedure that involves amniocentesis and instilling a solution into the amniotic cavity to terminate the pregnancy.

institutional review boards (IRBs) Local boards that approve research needs based on findings that subjects have been selected fairly and that the risks to subjects are minimal.

insulin A protein pancreatic hormone that is essential for the metabolism of carbohydrates and is used in the treatment and control of diabetes.

intensive care unit A specific place within a hospital with special medical equipment and services for taking care of seriously ill patients.

interdisciplinary A methodology that is open to different perspectives and different methodologies of different disciplines.

interest group politics A group of persons, having a common identifying interest that often provides a basis for action, that lobbies government to protect their interests.

interoperative blood salvage A technique used to recycle a patient's own blood during surgery, thus avoiding transfusion.

intracytoplasmic sperm insertion (ICSI) Micromanipulation to insert the sperm mechanically through the zona pellucida and into the egg itself.

intrauterine devices (IUDs) A device inserted and left in the uterus to prevent conception.

intrinsic values Things desired for their own sake.

in vitro fertilization (IVF) Fertilization that takes place outside the body.

in vitro fertilization–embryo transfer (IVF-ET) Allows the initial phases of development to occur outside the reproductive tract, followed by transfer of the embryo into the uterus.

Islam The religious faith of Muslims, including belief in Allah as the sole deity and in Muhammad as his prophet.

Jainism A religion of north India teaching liberation of the soul by right knowledge, right faith, and right conduct.

Jansenism A morally austere and heretical movement based on moral determinism.

Jehovah's Witness A member of a group that witness by distributing literature and by personal evangelism to beliefs in the theocratic rule of God, the sinfulness of organized religions and governments, and in imminent millennium.

judicial bypass procedure The policy of permitting a minor seeking an abortion to ask a judge to waive parental notification requirements if she is mature or notification is not in her best interests.

judicial conscience Makes judgments about past conduct.

justice perspective To perceive moral dilemmas in terms of hierarchical values and impersonal conflicts of claims related to inequality versus equality of individuals, emphasizing fairness, rights, and impartial principles of justice, autonomy, reciprocity, and respect.

karyotyping To determine the chromosomal characteristics of a cell, their representation, or the chromosomes themselves.

kith Long-standing committed relationships resembling kinship that might give a member moral authority to speak on behalf of a patient who is too ill to make treatment decisions.

labor theory of value The idea that an individual invests labor in raw material to produce a product—one's body or offspring—and thus receives ownership and rights over that product, enabling the body to be treated under the paradigm of property rights.

lactation To secrete milk, as in a nursing mother.

laissez-faire economics A doctrine opposing governmental interference in economic affairs beyond the minimum necessary for the maintenance of peace and property rights.

laparoscopy A visual examination of the abdomen by means of a *laparoscope* (narrow, lighted optical instrument), or an operation, such as sterilization of the female or for removal of ova, that involves use of the laparoscope to guide surgical procedures in the abdomen.

law of battery Makes it wrong to touch, treat, or do research upon a person without the person's consent, which could become invalid if any information considered material to the decision is withheld from the patient.

layperson A member of the laity, or the mass of the people, as distinguished from professionals or those specially skilled.

legal moralism A principle using community effort, law, and regulation to protect society against behavior that some regard as immoral, such as sex offenses, and holding that these proscriptions are foundations of social order.

legal positivism The tradition that a law exists because it has been adopted by society, that the law's legal status is independent of its moral status, and that an immoral law remains valid until it is repealed by society.

legislative conscience Anticipates whether a prospective action is at odds with one's basic ethical convictions.

lesbian A female homosexual.

Lesch-Nyhan syndrome An incurable genetic disease that causes its victims to suffer uncontrollable spasms and mental retardation.

liberalism Stresses the individual and his or her rights, downplaying duty or obligations to a wider social whole.

liberationists Contemporary Protestant minority position that calls for the reformulation of moral and religious judgments with special concern for women's well-being and advocates broad-based social change.

libertarianism Holds that competent adults should not be forced to do anything by the state unless it prevents harm to third parties, that people's right to their fairly obtained property is fundamental, and that people do not have a responsibility to be charitable.

libido Sexual drive.

life sciences The study that shapes the way people think about their lives and provides key ingredients in society's vision of itself and the lives of its citizens.

living will A document in which the signer requests to be allowed to die rather than be kept alive by artificial means if disabled beyond a reasonable expectation of recovery.

logical positivism Holds experimentally verifiable science as the paradigm of intellectually meaningful discourse and that any statement that is not empirically or mathematically demonstrable (true) lacks content.

love *Companionate*—includes marital love, friendship, and the affection between those bound together by common experiences; *just*—fair treatment of spouses/partners and just institutional patterns that safeguard the equal human dignity of both spouses/partners; *Platonic*—a close relationship between two persons in which sexual desire is nonexistent; *romantic*—preferential intense longing for union with another, physiological arousal, aesthetic attraction, desire for reciprocity, and some idealization; *unrequited*—feelings that are not returned in kind.

macro eugenics Policies, such as ethnic cleansing, used with whole populations or groups over several generations.

malaria Disease caused by parasites in the red blood cells, transmitted by the bite of anopheline mosquitoes, and characterized by periodic attacks of chills and fever.

malpractice A dereliction from professional duty or a failure to exercise an accepted degree of professional skill or learning by a caregiver rendering services that result in injury, loss, negligence, or damage.

managed competition in care A policy option that aims to foster competition among health-care providers, thus allowing the market to control delivery of services and ostensibly increase quality and lower costs.

mandatory waiting period A statute stipulating that in a specific time period before a surgical procedure, a patient must undergo counseling and give informed consent.

manic depression, or bipolar disorder A major affective disorder characterized by severe mood swings—between mania (excitement manifested by mental and physical hyperactivity, elevated mood, disorganized behavior) and depression—and by a tendency to remission and recurrence.

Manichaeanism A belief in religious or philosophical dualism.

Marxism Holds that extant philosophy and ethics are expressions of underlying economic forces and struggles, class interests, and ideological tools of class warfare that hinder enlightenment.

Marxist feminists Believe that women's liberation depends on the destruction of the capitalist system that makes some people the economic pawns of others.

mastectomy Excision of the breast.

matriarchy A system of social organization in which descent and inheritance are traced through the female line.

mature minor rule A physician may treat a child of fifteen or older without the parents' consent when the patient is mature enough to understand the medical information and to give the same sort of informed consent that would be accepted from an adult patient.

Medicaid Federally funded health care for the poor.

Medicare Federally funded health care for the elderly.

Mendelian gene A single gene of major effect.

Mendel's law, or law of dominance A principle in genetics that has proved to be subject to many limitations: because one of each pair of hereditary units dominates the other in expression, characters are inherited alternatively on an all-or-nothing basis.

menopause The period of natural cessation of menstruation occurring usually between the ages of forty-five and fifty.

micro eugenics Policies used only with families or kinship groups.

micromanipulation Manipulation of gametes and pre-embryos under magnification.

midwife A person who assists women in childbirth.

mimicry The process by which an animal or plant camouflages itself by pretending to be another organism or thing.

mind/body dualism Developed by René Descartes, the assertion that the mind is both entirely distinct from and morally superior to the body.

minimal risk According to U.S. federal rules, the probability and magnitude of harm or discomfort anticipated in research or treatment can not be greater than those encountered in daily life or during routine physical and psychological exams or tests.

minorities Subset populations of a state that have relatively little power and are discriminated against.

miscegenation A mixture of races; also the marriage or cohabitation of persons from different ethnic backgrounds.

molecular biology A branch of biology dealing with the ultimate physicochemical organization of living matter and with the molecular basis of inheritance and protein synthesis.

molecular genetics Based on molecular biological study of nonhuman organisms and the study of human genetic disease, the search for causal chains and physiological mechanisms of molecular phenomena.

monogamy The state or custom of being married to one person at a time.

monogenesis Evolutionary theory of a single origin of all humans.

monotheism The doctrine or belief that there is but one God.

morality A compromise between two inherently conflictual sides of nature, a code of conduct, for the sake of a semblance of decency in the social order.

moral principles Derived from actual practices, refined by reflection and experience, and always open to further revision and reinterpretation in new cases.

moral rights merely A claim that asserts a moral right, implying that a corresponding legal right ought to exist, such as the right to health care.

morbidity The relative incidence of disease.

morning-after, or postcontraception, pill Two treatments of oral contraceptives within seventy-two hours of intercourse to prevent pregnancy.

morphology A branch of biology that deals with the form and structure of animals and plants.

mortality Death; also the proportion of deaths to the population.

muscular dystrophy Any group of hereditary diseases characterized by the progressive wasting of muscles.

mutations A relatively permanent change in hereditary material involving either a physical change in chromosome relations or a biochemical change in the codons that make up genes.

myocardial infarction Heart attack.

nationalism Loyalty and devotion to a nation, or a sense of national consciousness exalting one nation above all others and placing primary emphasis on promotion of its culture and interests as opposed to those of other nations or groups.

natural family planning Intercourse is avoided entirely during the female's fertile period, and contraceptives are not used.

natural law A body of law or a specific principle held to be derived from nature and binding upon human society, with moral reason guided by certain values inherent in human nature, such as rationality and the capacity for free choice.

natural lottery Refers to the inequalities caused by nature, such as health status.

natural selection The major force driving evolution, per Charles Darwin (1859), a natural process that results in the survival and reproductive success of individuals or groups best adjusted to their environment and that leads to the perpetuation of genetic qualities best suited to that environment.

nature v. nurture The controversy over whether genetic inheritance (our innate nature) or environment (upbringing) determines behavior.

naturopathy A system of treatment of disease that avoids drugs and surgery and emphasizes the use of natural agents and physical means.

necrophilia Sex with the dead.

negligence doctrine Concludes that a patient/subject must prove that the physician had a duty to the patient that was breached and consequently damaged or harmed the patient.

neo-Aristotelianism Its precept is moral reason consisting of a set of moral principles found in the human capacities of a moral subject who knows that those capacities constitute a desirable life.

neonate A newborn child or one who is less than a month old.

neoplasia Abnormal tissue formation.

neurosis A mental and emotional disorder that affects only part of the personality, is accompanied by a less distorted perception of reality than in a psychosis, does not result in disturbance of language use, and is accompanied by various physical, physiological, and mental disturbances (anxieties, phobias).

nonmaleficence The ethical principle that physicians should avoid harming their patients and act in their best interests.

no-risk, or minimal-risk, rule Research must be judged to pose either no risk at all or only minimal risk to the potential subject.

Norplant A sustained-release hormonal contraceptive system (levonorgestrel) of six silicone rubber capsules, which are surgically implanted under the skin of the upper arm and act continuously for five years.

nosocomial infection An infection acquired during hospitalization.

noumenal world An aspect in which individuals recognize and respect each other as free, equal, and autonomous.

nulliparous Of or relating to a woman who has not had offspring.

Nuremberg Code Written in (1947) in reaction to the Nazis' eugenics policies, it prohibits research unless the subjects can give informed, mature, voluntary consent.

nymphomania Excessive sexual desire by a female.

obstetrician/gynecologist (ob/gyn) A physician specializing in obstetrics (related to childbirth) and the reproductive system of women.

Oedipus complex Positive libidinal feelings of a child toward the parent of the opposite sex and hostile or jealous feelings toward the parent of the same sex that may be a source of adult personality disorder if left unresolved.

offense principle Authorizes caregivers to limit a patient's liberty to prevent serious offenses to others.

omphaloceles A birth defect with the intestine protruding outside the abdomen at the umbilicus.

oncology The study of tumors.

ontic Of, relating to, or having real being.

opportunity for selection The likelihood that any given trait can be augmented through controlled mating.

option rights The heart of classic liberal theory: the idea that there is a sphere of sovereignty within which the individual cannot be intruded upon by the government, even for the greater good.

oral contraceptive (OC) The most widely used reversible method of birth control, it provides a chemical means to prevent ovulation.

organ donation When body parts or tissues are transplanted to the body of another living person.

organ donor Someone who provides an organ or tissues for transplant purposes either after death or while living (a kidney).

outpatient care Health care that does not require hospitalization and is given in a hospital, clinic, or associated facility for diagnostic treatment.

ovulation The discharge of a mature ovum (egg) from the ovary.

ovum, or oocyte A single egg.

paradigm An exemplary instance that serves as a standard.

paraphilias Sexual deviations in which unusual or bizarre imagery or acts are necessary for sexual excitement.

Parkinson's disease A chronic progressive nervous disease chiefly of later life that is linked to decreased dopamine production and is marked by tremor and weakness of resting muscles and a shuffling gate.

parochialism The quality or state of being limited in range or scope; also narrow.

parthenogenesis Stimulating an unfertilized egg to develop and produce offspring by mechanical or chemical means.

partial surrogacy When a woman carries to term an embryo genetically related to her.

partner notification program *See* contact tracing.

passive eugenics The societal acceptance of deaths by preventable social and economic inequities, such as infant mortality rates.

paternalism The belief that one knows what is best for others and coerces others for their own good, even when those coerced are capable of exercising rational choice.

paternity The state of being a father.

paternity test A test of DNA or genetic traits to determine whether a given man could be the biological father of a given child.

pathology The study of the essential nature of diseases and of the structural and functional changes produced by them.

patient-centered approach A process of shared decision making in which competent patients retain authority over their treatment, with providers recommending and explaining alternatives and allowing patients informed consent and the right to refuse treatment.

patriarchy Social organization marked by the supremacy of the father in the clan or family, with descent and inheritance along the male line.

pederasty Intergenerational sex, usually involving anal intercourse.

pelvic inflammatory disease (PID) Inflammation of the female reproductive tract and especially the fallopian tubes that is caused by sexually transmitted disease, occurs more often in women using IUDs, and is a leading cause of female sterility.

Pentecostal Christianity Any of various Christian religious bodies that emphasize individual experiences of grace, spiritual gifts, expressive worship, and evangelism.

perinatal Occurring in, concerned with, or being in the period around the time of birth.

persistent vegetative state (PVS) Existence only at the biological level with little quality of life.

phenomenology A philosophical movement that describes the formal structure of the objects of awareness and of awareness itself in abstraction from any claims concerning existence.

phenotype The external appearance of the developing individual.

philanthropia A chief theological and ethical category in Eastern Christianity that transcends charity and includes the identification of God, the church, and the individual Christian with all humanity.

phimosis A narrowing of the foreskin that prevents its retraction.

phobia An exaggerated, usually inexplicable and illogical, fear of a particular object, class of objects, or situation.

physical mapping A critical element in the direct analysis of DNA from a chromosome region, with the most useful being a set of ordered clones that contain DNA spanning an entire region of the chromosome.

physiology The study of organisms in the laboratory, often dividing them in an attempt to understand how they work.

pituitary gland A small oval endocrine organ that is attached to the brain and produces various internal secretions directly or indirectly impinging on most bodily functions.

PKU, or phenylketonuria, disease A recessive single-gene inherited condition that prevents the normal metabolism of a substance commonly found in food and that leads to severe nervous system damage and mental impairments but can be prevented or minimized with diet.

placebo An inert or innocuous substance used in controlled experiments testing the efficacy of another substance (as in a drug).

placenta A vascular organ that unites the fetus to the uterus and mediates its metabolic exchanges, regardless of their toxicity.

plasma The fluid part of blood, lymph, or milk as distinguished from suspended material.

plasma fractionation Dividing plasma.

pleasure paradigm Sexual pleasure results in the release of tension, both physiological and those that arise from ego complexes, satisfying hidden and forbidden desires.

pluralism A state of society in which members of diverse ethnic, racial, religious, or social groups maintain an autonomous participation in and development of their traditional culture or special interest within the confines of a common civilization.

polar-body analysis Preimplantation diagnosis for abnormalities by analyzing the DNA of the first polar body of the human egg.

polygamy A marriage in which a spouse of either sex may have more than one mate at the same time.

polygenesis Evolutionary theory of multiple, separate origins of all humans.

polygenic trait A trait, such as intelligence or height, that is influenced by many genes.

polygyny The state or practice of having more than one wife or female mate at one time.

positivism The theory that theology and metaphysics are earlier imperfect modes of knowledge and that positive knowledge is based on natural phenomena and their properties and relations as verified by the empirical sciences.

postabortion syndrome The unproven, so-called psychological distress a woman suffers after an abortion.

postpartum syndrome Depression that occurs after childbirth.

post-traumatic stress disorder A psychological reaction occurring after a highly stressful event that is usually characterized by depression, anxiety, flashbacks, recurrent nightmares, and avoidance of reminders of the event.

potentiality principle Conferring the moral status of a full-fledged adult with specific rights and responsibilities on a fertilized ovum since it has the potential of developing into an adult human.

power of professionals *Asclepian*—the power of professional training; *charismatic*—the power of personal magnetism and authority; and *social*—the power of the role and its authority.

pragmatists Doctrine that the meaning of conceptions is to be sought in their practical bearings, that the function of thought is to guide action, and that truth is preeminently to be tested by the practical consequences of belief.

predestination A theological doctrine that holds people are all creatures of an omnipotent creator who guides those who, with divine grace and forgiveness, are destined for salvation.

pre-embryo What the one-cell fertilized egg becomes after its first cell division and before it implants in the uterus.

preimplantation diagnosis The detection of genetic defects, which cause inherited disease, in human embryos before implantation.

premature Born after a gestation period of less than thirty-seven weeks.

premenstrual syndrome (PMS) Listed as Premenstrual Dysphoric Disorder (PMDD) by the American Psychiatric Association, a varying group of symptoms manifested by some women prior to menstruation that may include emotional instability, irritability, insomnia, fatigue, anxiety, depression, headache, edema, and abdominal pain.

prenatal diagnosis Identifying fetal defects.

presymptomatic testing Procedure to uncover incipient genetic disease before any symptoms appear.

preterm delivery Loss of a pregnancy after viability.

preterm labor The development of premature contractions that if not stopped can result in delivery of the fetus before adequate development has occurred.

prevention paradox The observation that any critical prevention policies affecting lifestyles (i.e., wearing seatbelts, quitting smoking) produce large, aggregate savings in lives but little demonstrable benefit to each individual.

prezygote The one-cell fertilizing egg.

primary tubal infertility Scar tissue blocks the fallopian tubes, resulting in sterility.

primitive streak In the human embryo, a longitudinal axis that forms the template for the spinal column and appears after fourteen days.

primordial The idea that what living things do is an extension of what they are and that people who are similar or related to each other share a common substance (blood).

principle of double effect This principle pertains to acts that have both good and evil effects, allowing moral distinctions. For instance, the Catholic church prohibits direct abortions, but indirect abortions—such as the removal of a fallopian tube in the case of an ectopic pregnancy—are permitted to save the life of the mother.

principlism The value of particular moral principles, including respect for persons and their autonomy, that help in the actual making of decisions.

privileged communications Confidential communications protected by law against disclosure in legal settings.

probity Adherence to the highest principles and ideals.

pro-choice A label for supporters of a woman's right to have an abortion and to use contraceptives.

procreation The act of conceiving offspring.

progestin A progestational hormone, especially progesterone (a female steroid sex hormone).

prolapse The falling down or slipping of a body part from its usual position or relations.

pro-life A label for opponents of abortion and sometimes contraceptives.

promiscuity Sexual behavior not limited to one partner.

pronatalist Fertility-raising policy, such as those that deny access to contraception.

pronucleus The haploid nucleus of a male or female gamete (egg or sperm) up to the time of fusion with that of another gamete in fertilization.

prophylactic A device for preventing a venereal infection or conception.

prostaglandin A hormone that produces uterine contractions.

prostitution Commercialized sexual transactions.

Protestantism All Christian movements, denominations, and sects whose histories can be traced to or related to the *Reformation* and represent diverse theological orientations and church discipline.

provincialism Exclusionary preferences and partialities, or restricted interests and outlook.

proxy consent Parents, guardians, or other responsible relatives may give permission for the use of nonconsenting subjects in research (only when it includes therapeutic interventions related to the subject's own recovery).

psyche The soul, the self, the mind.

psychoanalysis A movement and style of thought in psychology that treats conscience and guilt as forms of aggression directed by the individual against himself.

psychopharmacology The study of the effect of drugs on the mind and behavior.

psychosis Fundamental mental derangement characterized by defective or lost contact with reality.

psychosocial issues Involving both psychological and social aspects and relating to social conditions to mental health.

psychotherapy Treatment of mental or emotional disorders or of related bodily ills by psychological means.

psychotropic Acting on the mind, as in medication.

pubarche When pubic hair begins to appear.

public health The sum of each person's health in the population; the process of using organized community effort, law, and regulation to save lives and prevent disease; and the expansion of private liberties and rights for groups suffering social discrimination based on moralism.

pulmonary edema Fluid in the lungs.

pulmonary thromboembolism The blocking of a blood vessel by a particle that has broken away from a blood clot at its site of formation in the lungs.

purity rituals Avoidance rituals—codes that govern diet, cleanliness, sexual contact—designed to make the environment and community safe from contamination and to promote the social order.

quality assessment of care Detecting problems with quality and finding examples of good performance and outcomes, or end results, of care.

quality assurance of care A complete cycle of assessment (detecting a problem, verifying its existence, and identifying how to correct it) and intervention and studying further to ensure that the problem is corrected and that the intervention posed no additional problems.

quality-of-life judgment *Comparative*—based on considerations of social worth, these judgments try to decide the interests or value of a person's life in relation to the interests or value of other people's lives. Such judgments are *noncomparative* when they ignore a person's social value, contemplate only the quality of a person's life when compared to having no life at all, and are often used with the *best-interests standard.*

quarantine Used in epidemic control, preventive detention or enforced isolation.

quickening The detection of fetal movement, which occurs around sixteen weeks' growth.

Qur'an The book composed of sacred writings accepted by Muslims as revelations made to Muhammad by Allah through the angel Gabriel.

race A putative cultural-based explanation for observed human variation in appearance, origin, language, religion, and behavior, but such observation of differences depends not on biology but on local context and social history.

racism A set of negative beliefs held by groups with respect to a population thought to be biologically distinct.

radical feminists Believe that women's liberation depends on a political, economic, and sexual revolution to transform male and female gender roles and eliminate gender exploitation.

randomized clinical trials (RCTs) Drug trials in which participants are randomly assigned to treatment and control groups, thus allowing a greater inference that any difference in effects is due to the treatment being tested.

rational persuasion Explaining the probable benefits and costs of available treatment alternatives, facilitating patients' exercise of informed consent and enhancing their well-being.

reasonable protection rule In balancing public safety and confidentiality, the law stipulates that protective privilege of confidential information "ends where public peril begins," necessitating disclosure to protect threatened victims from harm.

recessive gene Its effect is seen only when in the *homozygous* condition and can skip generations.

recidivism A tendency to relapse into a previous condition or mode of behavior, especially criminal.

recombinant DNA (r-DNA) techniques The investigation of the nature and composition of the basic molecular building blocks of organisms to gain more insight into the functioning of the cell and how to fabricate new organic forms. Includes gene-tagging and gene-transfer techniques.

reduction The term for the special nature of organisms that claims biology cannot be "reduced" to physics and chemistry.

Reformation A sixteenth-century religious movement marked by rejection or modification of some Roman Catholic doctrine and practice and by establishment of the Protestant churches.

regulatory and policy ethics To fashion legal or clinical rules and procedures designed to apply to types of cases or general practices.

remission A state or period during which a disease's symptoms abate.

Renaissance A movement marked by a humanistic revival of classical influence expressed in vigorous artistic and intellectual activity and the beginnings of modern science.

repression A defense mechanism, operating unconsciously, that banishes unacceptable ideas, affects, or impulses from consciousness or that keeps out of consciousness what has never been conscious.

reproductive freedom The choice of whether and with whom to procreate, how many times, and by what means.

required reporting Legally required disclosures of otherwise confidential information.

research ethics committees (RECs) Local boards that approve research needs based on findings that subjects have been selected fairly and that the risks to subjects are minimal.

research protocols The detailed plan of a scientific or medical experiment, treatment, or procedure.

retrograde ejaculation A condition in which a channel is formed that causes the ejaculate to be directed away from the penis and retrograded into the man's bladder.

Rh disease A condition in which the immune system of the pregnant woman destroys the blood cells of the fetus and, if severe and untreated, results in fetal death.

rheumatoid arthritis A chronic disease of unknown cause that is characterized especially by pain, stiffness, inflammation, swelling, and sometimes destruction of joints.

rhythm method A form of family planning that prescribes sex only during the woman's infertile period.

right to liberty Individuals have a right to freedom of decision and action as long as their actions do not interfere with others' rights.

rights Variously held to be valid claims (legal or moral), protected choice, protected interests (to secure possessions), an interest-based reason sufficient for the imposition of duties upon others, and special protection to the individual against any government action aimed at maximizing some social goal.

risk-benefit assessment Using data appropriate for the locale in which a new technology will be used, tries to determine whether the risks of proposed research or care alternatives are proportional to the benefits for each individual, and uses risk assessment to try to balance the social utility of encouraging studies that maintain respect for and protection of patients' rights and welfare.

risk factor Something that increases a person's chances of developing a disease.

Roe* v. *Wade The U.S. Supreme Court decision (1973) that permitted medically supervised abortions.

RU-486 An antiprogestin drug that, when used with prostaglandin, produces a chemical abortion.

rules ethics Moral judgments based on what one ought to do according to divine command philosophies or independent of the effects of one's actions on the well-being of others or oneself.

sadomasochism The derivation of pleasure from the infliction of physical or mental pain on others or on oneself.

salpingectomy The surgical removal of one or both fallopian tubes.

Samaritan principle The duty to care for the needy sick, even at a cost to oneself, that underlies a physician's broader duty to care for indigent persons. A broader ethic mandates equitable access to all forms of basic health care.

schizophrenia A psychological disorder characterized by loss of contact with the environment, by noticeable deterioration in the level of functioning in everyday life, and by personality disintegration expressed as disorder of feeling, thought (delusions), and conduct.

sciatica Pain along the course of a sciatic nerve, especially in the back of the thigh.

scientific (experimental) method Developed by Francis Bacon, the process of dissecting and manipulating raw material through empirical investigation in order to gain knowledge of its universal laws and regularities.

script theory Mental schemes that enable individuals to structure interactions so that uncertainty is reduced and cooperation enhanced.

secularism Maintains religion and its morality are private considerations, subject to regulation for the public good but not considered in the formation of policy.

self-actualization Realizing fully one's potential.

self-deferral The process of asking individuals who are members of high-risk groups not to donate blood.

self-determination A standard that applies primarily to competent and informed adults, who should be generally free to make their own choices about their well-being as long as they do not harm or violate the rights of others, when making decisions about health care.

self-referrals When physicians refer patients to independent clinical laboratories in which the physicians have an ownership interest.

sentience The ability to feel pain or pleasure.

sepsis A toxic condition resulting from the spread of bacteria or their products from a focus of infection.

septicemia *See* blood poisoning.

seropositive Having or being a positive serum reaction, especially in a test for the presence of an antibody.

severe combined immunodeficiency A disease in children that inactivates the immune system with one malfunctioning gene, which fails to produce an essential enzyme (adenosine diaminase [ADA]).

sexism The belief that one sex is superior to the other and the many consequences of this belief. Some expressions of sexism are *androcentrism*—the view that only men's experiences are normal; *classic*—biological differences become a cultural category to oppress women; *heterosexism*—discrimination against people based on their homosexual orientation; *masculinism*—oppression arises out of categories presumed to be universal but contain hidden assumptions and preferences for masculinity.

sex selection The process of aborting unwanted offspring because of its sex.

sex therapy Treatment to resolve psychosexual dysfunctions characterized by abnormal physiological sexual response or function and disorders that involve sexual expression in manners that do not have social approval.

sexually transmitted disease (STD) Any of various diseases transmitted by direct sexual contact that include venereal diseases and other various diseases (such as AIDS) that can be contracted by other than sexual means.

sexual-orientation distress A diagnostic category, usually limited to homosexuality, that covers those who suffer from an unwanted sexual orientation.

sexual-orientation therapy Techniques to redirect sexual orientation from homosexuality to heterosexuality.

sexual response cycle Phases of excitement, plateau, orgasm, and resolution.

sexual surrogacy Paraprofessionals, working under the supervision of sex therapists, who engage in private sexual activity with the patient.

shared decision making *See* patient-centered approach.

sickle-cell anemia or disease A genetic abnormality in hemoglobin that can cause serious crises and death even before one year of age.

side constraints Things necessary for living together peacefully in a pluralistic society in which many people honestly disagree about values.

situation ethics Moral judgments that are left up to individuals to judge what is best under the circumstances.

slippery-slope arguments Maintains that legalizing or condoning certain morally acceptable actions (voluntary euthanasia) would lead to irresistible pressures for legalizing or condoning immoral actions (involuntary euthanasia).

smallpox An acute contagious febrile disease caused by a poxvirus and characterized by skin eruption with pustules, sloughing, and scar formation.

social cohesion Rests on minimal agreements that allow individuals and groups to live together in their diversity and pursue different visions.

social-compact, or social-covenant, model Does not recognize the primacy of rights and individual choice, instead focusing on social ties and relations of the self as a historical being with debts, obligations, and expectations.

social constructionism The belief that all human understanding develops and has meaning only within particular historical constellations of power.

social-contract theory Incorporates a view of society constituted by individuals for the fulfillment of individual ends, with social goods as aggregates of private goods.

social control Controlled permission or regulated prohibition of behaviors, with desire, for example, modified by psychological and social influences.

social justice Measures the role of key social institutions in procuring a fair distribution of wealth and resources nationally and internationally and requires that all persons in a given society deserve equal access to goods and services that fulfill basic human needs.

social lottery Refers to the inequalities caused by such social factors as wealth, schooling, or family.

social theories of the body Examine the interrelationships between social orders and the bodies within their jurisdiction and hold that the body is the medium through which social institutions derive power, authority, reality, and meaning as the site upon which power and social control are maintained.

socialism Any various economic and political theories advocating collective or governmental ownership and administration of the means of production and distribution of goods.

sociobiology The systematic study of the biological basis of all social behavior.

sodomy Copulation with a member of the same sex or with an animal, usually noncoital and especially anal or oral copulation.

somatic-cell therapy The manipulation of the genome in which the impact of intervention is limited to the individual patient, his tissues, organs, and parts not associated with reproduction.

sonography *See* ultrasound.

speculum An instrument inserted into a body passage for inspection or medication.

spermicides Contraceptives that kill sperm and provide some protection against STDs.

sperm, or semen, banks Provides long-term preservation of sperm for men prior to vasectomy, chemotherapy, or radiation treatment, and affords options for infertility by recruiting sperm donors for use in artificial insemination.

spina bifida A congenital cleft, or bony defect, of the vertebral column with hernial protusion of the meninges (membranes that envelop the brain and spinal cord) and sometimes the spinal cord.

spirit possession The belief that spirits inhabit people and may be regarded as either malevolent, in which case they must be expelled or exorcised, or benevolent, in which case becoming possessed is an act of worship and devotion.

spontaneous abortion A miscarriage, or the spontaneous loss of a pregnancy before viability.

spontaneous mutation Genes that develop without apparent external influence, force, cause, or treatment.

statistical prognostic strategy of treatment Seeks to minimize the number of patients (especially infants) whose deaths would come slowly as well as those who would be profoundly disabled, using statistical data to make selective nontreatment decisions.

statutory rape Intercourse with an individual who is considered too young to provide meaningful consent.

stepladder ethics Ignoring human rights, proposes moving from voluntary policies up the scale of pressure on people to the point justified by the seriousness of the problem being addressed.

sterilization Surgical procedures known by the following labels: *contraceptive*—to make procreation impossible through vasectomy, hysterectomy, or tubal ligation; *punitive*—to deprive of the power to procreate as a punishment (but does not inhibit sex crimes); and *therapeutic*—to terminate one's fertility, usually done to protect the individual's health.

stillbirth The delivery of a fetus who has already died.

Stoicism Emphasizing the brotherhood of man, the belief that every individual has a divine spark and that virtue is rooted in reason alone, for reason is most appropriate to our nature and our true dominion, and attachments to external objects or emotions must be severed since they have no intrinsic value in morality or happiness.

strong persuasion Between incentives and compulsion, social and administrative pressures or economic penalties that lessen but do not extinguish a person's perceived freedom to act contrary to approved behavior.

subjective irresistibility Determining whether a patient can resist pressure or influence.

sublimation A defense mechanism, operating unconsciously, by which instinctual drives, consciously unacceptable, are diverted into personally and socially acceptable channels.

substantive, or normative, ethics Making real value judgments rather than simply analyzing such judgments.

substituted judgment For a patient who was once competent enough to express preferences for health care, caregivers ask families to select the treatment option they believe the patient would have chosen.

subzonal insertion (SUZI) Micromanipulation to insert the sperm mechanically through the zona pellucida into the space between the zona and egg.

superovulation A process that increases the number of eggs that reach maturity in a single reproductive cycle.

surrogacy An adult-centered practice whereby children are deliberately conceived and brought into existence so that adults can have someone to love.

surrogate mother The gestational mother who both begins and ends her pregnancy with the intention of relinquishing the baby to someone else.

syphilis A chronic contagious, usually venereal and often congenital, disease caused by a spirochete and if left untreated produces chancres, rashes, and systemic lesions in a clinical course with three stages continued over many years.

systematic desensitization A widely used form of methodical behavior therapy involving training in deep muscle relaxation, the construction of anxiety hierarchies, and the counterposing of relaxation with the anxiety-evoking stimuli from the hierarchies.

Talmud The repository of rabbinic exposition of biblical law and teaching, spanning more than five centuries.

taxonomy The study of the general principles of scientific classification.

Tay-Sachs disease A hereditary disorder of lipid metabolism typically affecting individuals of eastern European Jewish ancestry that is characterized by the accumulation of lipids (principal structural components of living cells), especially in nervous tissue due to a deficiency of hexosaminidase, and causes death in early childhood.

tdf gene A gene on the Y chromosome called the *testes determining factor.*

teleology A doctrine that explains phenomena with forward-looking questions and explanations, thinking in terms of ends or final causes rather than of prior causes.

testes Paired male reproductive gland that produces sperm and that is contained within the scrotum at sexual maturity.

test-tube baby A child created by artificial insemination.

tetanus An acute infectious disease characterized by tonic spasm of voluntary muscles, especially of the jaw, and caused by the specific toxin of a bacterium that is usually introduced through a wound.

thalassemia Any of a group of inherited disorders of hemoglobin synthesis affecting the globin chain that are characterized usually by mild to severe hemolytic anemia and are caused by a series of allelic genes.

theoretical bioethics The intellectual foundations of bioethics.

theoretical, or philosophical, ethics Questioning what kind of life is best for the individual and how one ought to behave in regard to other individuals and society as a whole.

therapeutic privilege exception to informed consent Permits a doctor to withhold information when, in the doctor's opinion, disclosure would be detrimental to the patient's interests or well-being.

therapy A way of taking charge of oneself and a form of deep self-knowledge about emotions and their roles in one's life that leads to character change.

thrombophlebitis Inflammation of a vein with formation of a thrombus, or blood clot.

thrombosis The formation or presence of a blood clot within a blood vessel.

Torah The body of wisdom and law contained in Jewish Scripture and other sacred literature and oral tradition.

totalitarianism Requires that people identify only with absolute state authority rather than specific others, including family and friends.

total quality management A statistical quality-control method that entails a cycle of system design, examination, action, and redesign that continuously collects and analyzes data on processes and outcomes of care to improve performance.

toxic shock syndrome An acute disease that is characterized by fever, diarrhea, nausea, diffuse erythema, and shock and occurs especially in menstruating females using tampons.

tracheotomy The surgical operation of cutting into the trachea, the main trunk of the system of tubes by which air passes to and from the lungs.

transference Redirecting childhood feelings toward a new object, which usually becomes the therapist in a clinical setting.

transfusion A process that involves removing blood from one individual (a donor) and giving it to another (a recipient) to sustain the latter's life and to replace the red cells or whole blood (red cells, plasma, platelets, and other components).

transgender therapy A range of surgical, hormonal, and psychological therapies to conform anatomy, secondary sex characteristics, and behavior to those of the desired gender without imposing a particular sexual orientation on the patient.

translocations Inherited chromosomal structural rearrangements.

transsexualism The process by which adults verbally and behaviorally identify themselves as male or female in contradiction to their anatomical sex and the behavior expected.

transvaginal aspiration Done with local anesthesia, the insertion of a needle through a woman's vagina, guided by ultrasound, to withdraw eggs from the fallopian tube.

triage The sorting of and allocation of treatment to patients according to a system of priorities designed to maximize the number of survivors.

trochar A sharp-pointed surgical instrument fitted with a cannula and used to insert the cannula into a body cavity as a drainage outlet.

trophectoderm biopsy Preimplantation diagnosis for abnormalities by examining extra-embryonic cells surrounding the inner cell mass.

trophoblasts A thin layer of ectoderm that forms the wall of many mammalian blastulas and functions in the nutrition and implantation of the embryo.

tubal ligation Permanent sterilization procedure for women in which their fallopian tubes are either cut or tied.

tuberculosis A highly variable communicable disease characterized by toxic symptoms or allergic manifestations that primarily affect the lungs.

Turner's syndrome A condition in which the absence of an X chromosome leads to short stature, webbed neck, and subtle neurological deficits in girls.

twinning When an embryo splits into two separate embryos, before fourteen days' growth and implantation.

typhoid fever A communicable bacteriological disease marked by fever, diarrhea, prostration, headache, and intestinal inflammation.

typhus A severe febrile disease that is caused by rickettsias, transmitted by body lice, and is marked by high fever, stupor alternating with delirium, intense headache, and a dark red rash.

ultrasound The diagnostic or therapeutic technique involving the formation of a two-dimensional image, using high-resolution, real-time scanners, to examine and measure internal body structures, to detect bodily abnormalities, and to visualize any part of the fetal anatomy in detail.

umbilicus Naval or any of several morphological depressions.

Unitarian/Universalist A member of a denomination that stresses individual freedom of belief, the free use of reason in religion, a united world community, and liberal social action.

uterus Also called the *womb,* an organ of the female mammal for containing and nourishing the young during development until birth.

utilitarianism In accordance with just rule and conceived and used a reformist moral and political doctrine, seeks to focus resources where they will have the greatest impact for the most people.

utilitarian theorist Endorses relationships and decision making expected to maximize happiness and justifies acts as moral on the bases of the consequences of those acts, promoting those actions with the best possible outcome.

vaginitis Inflammation of the vagina or of a sheath (as a tendon sheath).

valid consent The principle that a physician must only impart that information that the patient/subject needs to make a responsible and voluntary decision and not all the information available.

value synthesis Shared value commitments that are appropriate and transform traditions while accommodating conflicts with imaginative responses all to promote well-being.

value theory Shows how various values contribute to the good of all in a pluralistic society and explores critical investigations of value disputes.

vas deferens The tube or duct that carries sperm.

vasectomy The surgical excision of the vas deferens carrying sperm from the testicles.

venereal disease *See* sexually transmitted disease (STD).

vertical transmission An infection that is passed from mother to infant.

viability The capability of a fetus to survive outside the womb with or without artificial support, variously fixed between twenty to twenty-eight weeks' gestation.

virtues Charity grounded in human activity, habits, and passions; also dispositions or skills necessary for human flourishing.

virtue theorist Advances an account of the virtuous person, endorsing relationships that exemplify and promote the desired virtues.

vitalism A doctrine that the processes of life are not explicable by the laws of physics and chemistry alone and that life is in some part self-determining.

vivisection The cutting of or operation on a living animal usually for physiological or pathological investigation.

voyeurism Habitually seeking sexual stimulation by visual means.

"wait until certainty" approach to treatment The practice of initiating aggressive life-sustaining treatments and waiting until a grim prognosis (death or profound impairment) is clear before discussing alternative treatments.

wealth-flow theory Using a family's budget to predict its procreation rate: greater if children are productively useful and will care for parents in their old age and lesser if parents incur net costs for the long-term care for children who will generally (culturally) contribute little to the household.

welfare conservatives Pro-family movement that focuses on economic issues, such as the rising welfare costs of teenage and illegitimate pregnancies, to support reproductive policy intervention.

welfare rights Those rights to direct provision of services that meet a basic need.

wet nurse A woman who cares for and suckles children not her own.

wide reflective equilibrium The espousal of constant movement back and forth between principles and human experience, letting each other correct and teach the other.

X chromosome A large sex-linked chromosome, containing many genes, of which normally women have two and men have one.

Y chromosome One of the smallest chromosomes, containing relatively few genes, for which normally women have no copies and men have one.

yellow fever An acute destructive infectious disease of warm regions marked by sudden onset, prostration, fever, albuminuria, jaundice, and hemorrhage and caused by a virus transmitted by the yellow-fever mosquito.

zona pellucida A translucent protein shell that immediately surrounds the egg.

zoophilia Sex between humans and animals.

zygote A fusion cell of egg and sperm that combines the genetic information of the two parents, or a fertilized egg.

Index

INDEX

B

C

F

G

I

J

K

L

N

O

P

S

U

W

GREYSCALE

BIN TRAVELER FORM

Cut By Cesar Rosa. Qty 12. Date ____________

Scanned By ______________________ Qty __________ Date ____________

Scanned Batch IDs

________________ ________________ ________________

Notes / Exception

____

____

____

____

____